standard catalog of
PONTIAC
1926-1995

John Gunnell and Ron Kowalke

Published by

krause
publications

700 E. State Street • Iola, WI 54990-0001
Telephone: 715/445-2214

Please call or write for our free catalog of automotive publications. Our toll-free number to
place an order or obtain a free catalog is 800-258-0929 or please use our regular business telephone
715-445-2214 for editorial comment and further information.

Library of Congress Catalog Number: 95-79461
ISBN: 0-87341-369-5
Printed in the United States of America

CONTENTS

FOREWORD

The concept behind Krause Publications' "standard catalogs" is to compile massive amounts of information about motor vehicles and present it in a standard format that the hobbyist, collector, or professional dealer can use to answer some commonly asked questions.

Those questions include: What year, make, and model is the vehicle? What did it sell for new? How rare is it? What is special about it? In our general automotive catalogs, some answers are provided by photos and others by the fact-filled text. In one-marque catalogs such as this one, additional information such as identification number charts, prototype/concept identification, and interesting Pontiac facts is included throughout the book.

Chester L. Krause of Krause Publications is responsible for the basic concept of creating the standard catalogs covering American cars. David V. Brownell, of *Special-Interest Autos*, undertook preliminary work on the concept while editing *Old Cars Weekly* in the 1970s. John A. Gunnell continued the standard catalog project after 1978. *The Standard Catalog of American Cars 1946-1975* was first published in 1982. Meanwhile, Beverly Rae-Kimes and the late Henry Austin Clark, Jr., continued writing and researching *The Standard Catalog of American Cars 1805-1942*, which was published in 1985. In 1987, *The Standard Catalog of Light-Duty American Trucks 1900-1986*, was compiled by John Gunnell and a second edition of the 1946-1975 volume was printed. In 1988, the 1805-1942 volume by Kimes and Clark appeared in its second edition. Also in 1988, James M. Flammang authored *The Standard Catalog of American Cars 1976-1986*, which went into its second edition in 1990. More recently, the 1946-1975 book was re-edited during 1992.

While the four-volume set of standard catalogs enjoyed high popularity as all-inclusive guides for car and light-duty truck collectors, there seemed to be many auto enthusiasts who focused their energies on only one make of car or multiple makes made by closely related manufacturers. This led to creation of standard catalogs about Chrysler Corp., FoMoCo, GM makes, and American Motors. This, *The Standard Catalog of Pontiac 1926-1995,* is a continuation of our examination of the offerings of General Motors, following our successful standard catalogs detailing the histories of Chevrolet, Buick, and Cadillac.

The Standard Catalog of Pontiac was compiled by an experienced editorial team consisting of the automotive staff of Krause Publications and numerous experts within specific areas of Pontiac history. A major benefit of this "teamwork" has been the gathering of more significant facts about each model than a single author might find.

No claims are made that these catalogs are infallible history texts or encyclopedias. Nor are they repair manuals or "bibles" for motor vehicle enthusiasts. They are meant as a contribution to the pursuit of greater knowledge about many wonderful vehicles. They are also much larger in size, broader in scope, and more deluxe in format than most other collector guides, buyer guides, or price guides.

The long-range goal of Krause Publications is to make all of the catalogs as nearly perfect as possible. At the same time, we expect they will always raise new questions and bring forth new facts that were not previously unearthed. All our contributors maintain an ongoing file of new research, corrections, and additional photos that are used, regularly, to refine and expand future editions.

Should you have knowledge you wish to see in future editions, please don't hesitate to contact the editors at *Standard Catalog of Pontiac*, editorial department, 700 East State Street, Iola, WI 54990.

ABBREVIATIONS

ABS - anti-lock braking system
bhp - brake horsepower
Bonn - Bonneville
Brgm - Brougham
BSW - black sidewall tires
bus cpe - business coupe
cabr - cabriolet
Cat - Catalina
cid - cubic inch displacement
Cl Cpl - Close Coupled
conv - convertible
conv cpe - convertible coupe
conv sed - convertible sedan
cpe - coupe
cu. in. - cubic inch
Cus Conv - Custom Convertible
Cus Sed - Custom Sedan
cyl - cylinder
Del Conv - Deluxe Convertible
Del Cpe - Deluxe Coupe
Del Lan Sed - Deluxe Landau Sedan
Del Sta Wag - Deluxe Station Wagon
dr - door(s)
EFI - electronic fuel injection
Eight - eight-cylinder model
ft. - foot/feet
gal - gallon(s)
GM - General Motors Corp.
hatch - hatchback
HEI - high energy ignition
hp - horsepower
HO - high output
HT - hardtop
in. - inch(es)
lan cpe - landau coupe

lan sed - Landau Sedan
lb.-ft. - pound-feet
LE - Luxury Edition
LeM - LeMans
limo - limousine
MFI/MPFI - multi-port fuel injection
mm - millimeters
mpg - miles per gallon
mph - miles per hour
OHC - overhead cam
OHV - overhead valve
phae - phaeton
rds - roadster
rds cpe - roadster coupe
rpm - revolutions per minute
RPO - regular production option
SAE - Society of Automotive Engineers
SE - Special Edition
sed - sedan
SFI/SPFI - sequential fuel injection
Six - six-cylinder model
SOHC - single overhead cam
Spl Sed - Special Sedan
Spl Sta Wag - Special Station Wagon
Spt Cabr - Sport Cabriolet
Spt Cpe - Sport Coupe
Spt Phae - Sport Phaeton
Spt Rds - Sport Roadster
Spt Sed - Sport Sedan
sq. in. - square inch(es)
sta wag - station wagon
TBI - throttle body fuel injection
tr sed - touring sedan
VIN - Vehicle Identification Number
w/ - with
w/o - without

CATALOG STAFF

Manager of Books Division: Pat Klug
Old Cars Division Publisher: Greg Smith
Old Cars Editorial Director: John Gunnell
Old Cars Books Editor: Ron Kowalke
Old Cars Weekly News & Marketplace Editors: Chad Elmore, James T. Lenzke
Pricing: Ken Buttolph

Book Production Team: Bonnie Tetzlaff, Ethel Thulien, Kathy Hines, Tom Nelsen, Tom Payette
Photo Graphics: Ross Hubbard, Wayne Conner
Camera Room: Julie Mattson, Gerald Smith
OCR Scanning: Marge Larson
Cover Design: Phil LaFranka

PHOTO CREDITS

AA - Applegate & Applegate
CG - Catherine Gunnell
CP - Crestline Publishing
HAC - Henry Austin Clark, Jr.
IMSC - Indianapolis Motor Speedway Corp.
JAC - John A. Conde

JAG - John A. Gunnell Collection
JG - Jesse Gunnell
OCW - Old Cars Weekly
PMD - Pontiac Motor Division
RK - Ron Kowalke

HOW TO USE THIS CATALOG

APPEARANCE AND EQUIPMENT: Word descriptions help identify trucks down to details such as styling features, trim and interior appointments. Standard equipment lists usually begin with low-priced base models. Then, subsequent data blocks cover higher-priced lines of the same year.

VEHICLE I.D. NUMBERS: This edition features expanded data explaining the basic serial numbering system used by each postwar vehicle manufacturer. This data reveals where, when and in what order your vehicle was built. There is much more information on assembly plant, body style and original engine codes.

SPECIFICATIONS CHART: The first chart column gives series or model numbers for trucks. The second column gives body type. The third column tells factory price. The fourth column gives GVW. The fifth column gives the vehicle's original shipping weight. The sixth column provides model year production totals (if available) or makes reference to additional notes found below the specifications chart. When the same vehicle came with different engines or trim levels at different prices and weights, slashes (/) are used to separate the low price or weight from the high one. In some cases, model numbers are also presented this way. In rare cases where data is non-applicable or not available the abbreviation "N.A." appears.

BASE ENGINE DATA: According to make of vehicle, engine data will be found either below the data block for each series or immediately following the specifications chart for the last vehicle-line. Displacement, bore and stroke and horsepower ratings are listed, plus a lot more data where available. This edition has more complete engine listings for many models. In other cases, extra-cost engines are listed in the "options" section.

VEHICLE DIMENSIONS: The main data compiled here consists of wheelbase, overall length and tire size. Front and rear tread widths are given for most trucks through the early 1960s and some later models. Overall width and height appears in some cases, too.

OPTIONAL EQUIPMENT LISTS: This section includes data blocks listing all types of options and accessories. A great deal of attention has been focused on cataloging both the availability and the original factory retail prices of optional equipment. Because of size and space limitations, a degree of selectivity has been applied by concentrating on those optional features of greatest interest to collectors. Important option packages have been covered and detailed as accurately as possible in the given amount of space. When available, options prices are listed.

HISTORICAL FOOTNOTES: Trucks are already recognized as an important part of America's automotive heritage. Revealing statistics; important dates and places; personality profiles; performance milestones; and other historical facts are highlighted in this "automotive trivia" section.

SEE PRICING SECTION IN BACK OF BOOK.

DELUXE - SERIES 8BA - EIGHT: The Pontiac Deluxe Eight had the company's longest wheelbase. The extra length was taken up in the hood and runningboards. Fenders varied slightly in the manner in which they overlapped the cowl, but were actually the same with the attachment holes drilled differently. The words "Pontiac 8" appeared on the grille and the hood ornament was a distinctive, circular design instead of the oblong loop style used on sixes. Standard sedan equipment included front and rear arm rests, twin assist straps, oriental grain interior moldings and a dash mounted clock. The eight had "Knee-Action" front suspension, a pressurized cooling system, automatic choke and a new type of clutch.

I.D. DATA: [Series 6BB] Serial numbers were located on top of frame just ahead of steering gear. Starting: 6BB-1001. Ending: 6BB-91362. Pacific Coast numbers were C-1001 to C-1400. Bench seat cars had an "AB" prefix instead of "BB". Engine numbers located on left side of crankcase and on front left corner of cylinder block. Starting: 6-84001. Ending: 6-219182. [Series 6BA] Serial numbers were in the same location. Starting: 6BA-1001. Ending: 6BA-41352. Pacific Coast numbers were C-1001 to C-1300. Engine numbers were in the same location. Starting: 6-84001. Ending: 6-219182. [Series 8BA] Serial numbers were in the same location. Starting: 8BA-1001. Ending: 8BA-38371. Pacific Coast numbers were C-1001 to C-1260. Engine numbers were in the same locations. Starting: 8-44001. Ending: 8-82040.

Model No.	Body Type & Seating	Price	Weight	Prod. Total
8BA	2-dr. Cpe.-2P	730	3250	Note 1
8BA	2-dr. Spt. Cpe.-2/4P	785	3285	Note 1
8BA	2-dr. Cabr.-2/4P	855	3335	Note 1
8BA	2-dr. Sed.-5P	770	3390	Note 1
8BA	2-dr. Tr. Sed.-5P	795	3390	Note 1
8BA	4-dr. Sed.-5P	815	3415	Note 1
8BA	4-dr. Tr. Sed.-5P	840	3420	Note 1

Note 1: Total series production was 38,755.

ENGINE: [Series 6BB] Inline. L-head. Six. Cast iron block. Bore & Stroke: 3-3/8 in. x 3-7/8 in. Displacement: 208 cu. in. Compression Ratio: 6.2:1. Brake hp: 81 @ 3600 rpm. Net hp: 27.34. Main bearings: Four. Valve lifters: Solid. Carb.: Carter one-barrel model 340S. [Series 6BA] Inline. L-head. Six. Cast iron block. Bore & Stroke: 3-3/8 in. x 3-7/8 in. Displacement: 208 cu. in. Compression Ratio: 6.2: 1. Brake hp: 81 @ 3600 rpm. Net hp: 27.34. Main bearings: Four. Valve lifters: Solid. Carb.: Carter one-barrel model 342S. [Series 8BA] Inline. L-head. Eight. Cast iron block. Bore & Stroke: 3-1/4 in. x 3-1/2 in. Displacement: 232.3 cu. in. Compression Ratio: 6.5:1. Brake hp: 87 @ 3800 rpm. Net hp: 33.8. Main bearings: Five. Valve lifters: Solid. Carb.: Carter one-barrel model 322S.

CHASSIS: [Series 6BB] Wheelbase: 112 in. Overall Length: 189-3/4 in. Height: 67-9/16 in. Tires: 16 x 6.00. [Series 6AB] Wheelbase: 112 in. Overall Length: 189-3/4 in. Height: 67-9/16 in. Tires: 16 x 6.00. [Series 8AB] Wheelbase: 116-5/8 in. Overall Length: 194-5/16 in. Height: 67-9/16 in. Tires: 16 x 6.50.

TECHNICAL: Manual synchromesh transmission. Speeds: 3F/IR. Floor mounted controls. Ventilated dry disc clutch. Semi-floating rear axle. Overall Ratio: (std.) 4.55:1; (mountain) 4.85:1; (plains) 4.11:1. Four-wheel hydraulic brakes. Steel spoke wheels.

OPTIONS: Front bumper. Rear bumper. Dual sidemount. Sidemount cover(s). Fender skirts. Set of four bumper guards (3.95). Air Chief Radio (62.50). Air Mate Radio (47.95). Outdraft heater (7.50). Deluxe heater (12.25). Clock (10.00). Cigar lighter (1.50). Radio antenna package (3.00). Seat covers (Santoy). Spotlight(s). R.H. taillight (3.45). Dual horn kit (12.50). Triplex air cleaner (6.50). Set of five wire wheel discs (11.25). Set of five wheel trim rings (8.50). Glove compartment smoker set and clock (13.50). Pull-wind clock (3.95). Safety light (15.95). License frame set (2.45). Luggage set (19.75). R.H. inside visor (2.00).

HISTORICAL: Introduced: September 25, 1935. Innovations: Larger bore eight. Improved clutch. Improved cooling system on eight. New front suspension with King pins mounted in floating bronze bearings. Automatic choke on deluxe models. Model year production: 176,270. The president of Pontiac was Harry Klingler. Pontiac held sixth rank in U.S. auto sales for 1936. The new models were called "The Most Beautiful Thing on Wheels."

BODY STYLES

Body style designations describe the shape and character of an automobile. In the early days, automakers exhibited great imagination in coining words to name their products. This led to descriptions that were not totally accurate. Many of the car words were taken from other fields: mythology, carriage building, architecture, railroading, and so on. Therefore, they have no "correct" automotive meanings; only those brought about through actual use. Some seeming inconsistencies have persisted to recent years, while other imaginative terms of past eras have faded away. One manufacturer's sedan might resemble another's coupe. Some automakers have persisted in describing a model by a word different from common usage, such as Ford calling the Mustang a sedan. Following the demise of the pillarless hardtop in the mid-1970s, various manufacturers continued using the term hardtop to describe their sedans. Some used the descriptions pillared hardtop or thin-pillared hardtop to label what most call a sedan. Descriptions in this catalog generally follow the manufacturers' terms, unless they conflict strongly with accepted usage.

TWO-DOOR (CLUB) COUPE: The Club Coupe designation seems to come from club car, describing the lounge or parlor car in a railroad train. The early postwar Club Coupe combined a shorter-than-sedan body structure with the convenience of a full back seat, unlike the single-seat business coupe. Club Coupe has been used less frequently after World War II, as most two-door models have been referred to simply as coupes. The distinction between two-door coupes and two-door sedans has grown fuzzy, too. Hudson used the term Club Coupe until 1954, the year the company merged with Nash to form AMC.

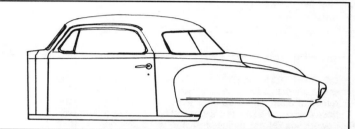

TWO-DOOR SEDAN: The term sedan originally described a conveyance seen only in movies today: a wheel-less vehicle for one person, borne on poles by two men...one ahead and one behind. Automakers pirated the word and applied it to cars with a permanent top that seated four to seven people (including driver) in a single compartment. The two-door sedan of recent times has sometimes been called a pillared coupe or just plain coupe, depending on the manufacturer's whims. On the other hand, some cars commonly referred to as coupes carry the sedan designation on factory literature. One of AMC's most unusual two-door sedans was the Pacer.

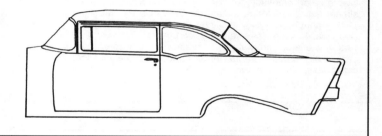

TWO-DOOR (THREE-DOOR) LIFTBACK COUPE: Originally a small opening in the deck of a sailing ship, the term hatch was later applied to airplane doors and to passenger cars with rear liftgates. Most automakers called these cars hatchbacks, but AMC used the term liftback. Various models appeared in the early 1950s, but weather tightness was a problem. The concept emerged again in the early 1970s, when fuel economy factors began to signal the trend toward compact cars. Technology had remedied the sealing difficulties. By the 1980s, most manufacturers produced one or more hatchback models, though the question of whether to call them two-doors or three-doors never was resolved. Their main common feature was the lack of a separate trunk. Liftback coupes may have had a different rear end shape, but the two terms often described essentially the same vehicle. The Gremlin was an interesting hatchback coupe that AMC created.

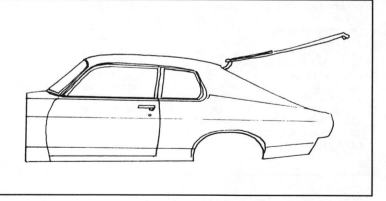

TWO-DOOR FASTBACK: By definition, a fastback is any automobile with a long, moderately curving, downward slope to the rear of the roof. This body style relates to an interest in streamlining and aerodynamics and has gone in and out of fashion at various times. Some fastbacks (Mustangs for one) have grown quite popular. Others have tended to turn customers off. Certain fastbacks are really two-door sedans or pillared coupes. Four-door fastbacks have also been produced. Many of these (such as Buick's late 1970s four-door Century sedan) lacked sales appeal. Fastbacks may or may not have a rear-opening hatch. The Hudson Hornet's fastback styling helped it in stock car racing and the AMX's aerodynamic lines helped its dragstrip and road racing performance.

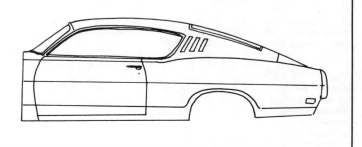

TWO-DOOR HARDTOP: The term hardtop, as used for postwar cars up to the mid-1970s, describes an automobile styled to resemble a convertible, but with a rigid metal or fiberglass top. In a production sense, this body style evolved after World War II. It was first called hardtop convertible. Other generic names have included sports coupe, hardtop coupe or pillarless coupe. In the face of proposed federal government rollover standards, nearly all automakers turned away from pillarless cars by 1976 or 1977. **FORMAL HARD-TOP:** The hardtop roofline was a long-lasting fashion hit of the postwar era. The word formal can be applied to things that are stiffly conservative and follow the established rule. The limousine, being the popular choice of conservative buyers who belonged to the establishment, was looked upon as a formal motor car. When designers combined the lines of these two body styles, the result was the Formal Hardtop. This style has been marketed with two- or four-doors, canopy or vinyl roofs (full or partial) and conventional or opera-type windows, under various trade names. The distinction between a formal hardtop and plain pillared-hardtop coupe (see above) hasn't always followed strict rules. AMC did not offer this body style.

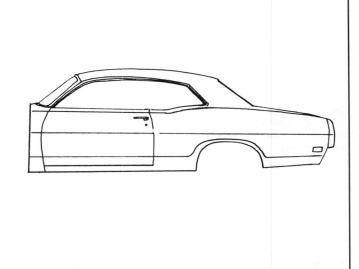

CONVERTIBLE: To depression-era buyers, a convertible was a car with a fixed-position windshield and folding. When raised, the top displayed the lines of a coupe. Buyers in the postwar period expected a convertible to have roll-up windows, too. Yet the definition of the word includes no such qualifications. It states only that such a car should have a lowerable or removable top. American convertibles became almost extinct by 1976, except for Cadillac's Eldorado. In 1982, though, Chrysler brought out a LeBaron ragtop; Dodge a 400; and several other companies followed it a year or two later. Today, many other cars are available in the convertible format. The last AMC ragtop was the Alliance convertible, offered in 1985 and 1986.

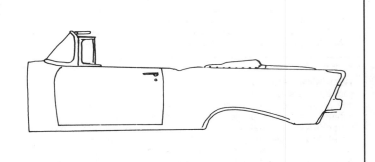

ROADSTER: This term derives from equestrian vocabulary, where it was applied to a horse used for riding on the roads. Old dictionaries define the roadster as an open-type car designed for use on ordinary roads, with a single seat for two persons and, often, a rumbleseat as well. Hobbyists associate folding windshields and side curtains (rather than roll-up windows) with roadsters, although such qualifications stem from usage, not definition of term. Most recent roadsters are either sports cars, small alternative-type vehicles or replicas of early models. Hudson built its last roadster in 1931. Nash ended production of true roadsters in 1930, although a "convertible-roadster" (with roll-up windows) was cataloged through 1932.

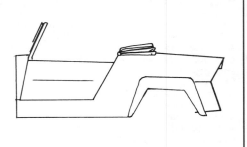

RUNABOUT: By definition, a runabout is the equivalent of a roadster. The term was used by carriage makers and has been applied in the past to light, open cars on which a top is unavailable or totally an add-on option. None of this explains its use by Ford on certain Pintos. Other than this usage, recent runabouts are found mainly in the alternative vehicle field, including certain electric-powered models. The most famous runabout in the AMC family of cars is the first Rambler.

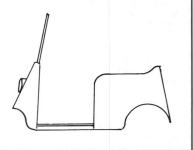

FOUR-DOOR SEDAN: If you took the wheels off a car, mounted it on poles and hired two weight lifters (one in front and one in back) to carry you around in it, you'd have a true sedan. Since this idea isn't very practical, it's better to use the term for an automobile with a permanent top (affixed by solid pillars) that seats four or more persons, including the driver, on two full-width seats.

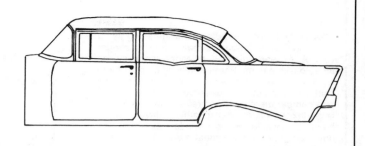

FOUR-DOOR HARDTOP: This is a four-door car styled to resemble a convertible, but having a rigid top of metal or fiberglass. Buick introduced a totally pillarless design in 1955. A year later most automakers offered equivalent bodies. Four-door hardtops have also been labeled sports sedans and hardtop sedans. By 1976, proposed federal rollover standards and waning popularity had taken their toll of four-door hardtop output. Only a few makes still produced a four-door hardtop. They disappeared soon thereafter. AMC's 1957 Rambler Rebel is probably the company's most famous four-door hardtop.

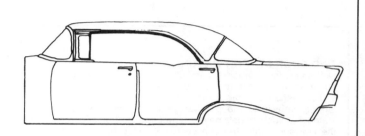

FOUR-DOOR PILLARED HARDTOP: Once the true four-door hardtop began to fade away, manufacturers needed another name for their luxury four-doors. Many were styled to look almost like the former pillarless models, with thin or unobtrusive pillars between the doors. Some, in fact, were called "thin-pillar hardtops." The distinction between certain pillared hardtops and ordinary (presumably humdrum) sedans occasionally grew hazy.

FOUR-DOOR (FIVE-DOOR) LIFTBACK: Essentially unknown among domestic models in the mid-1970s, the four-door liftback or hatchback became a popular model as cars grew smaller and front-wheel drive caught on. Styling was similar to the original two-door hatchback, except for the extra doors. Luggage was carried in the back of the car. It was loaded through the hatch opening, not in a separate trunk. AMC's first hatchback sedan, a five-door model, appeared in the 1984 Encore line.

LIMOUSINE: This word's literal meaning is 'a cloak.' In France, limousine means any passenger vehicle. An early dictionary defined limousine as an auto with a permanently enclosed compartment for 3-5, with a roof projecting over a front driver's seat. However, modern dictionaries drop the separate compartment idea and refer to limousines as large luxury autos, often chauffeur-driven. Some have a movable division window between the driver and passenger compartments, but that isn't a requirement.

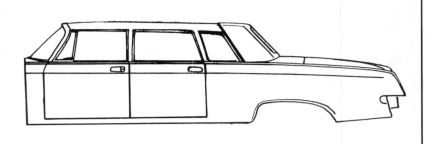

TWO-DOOR STATION WAGON: Originally defined as a car with an enclosed wooden body of paneled design (with several rows of folding or removable seats behind the driver), the station wagon became a different and much more popular type of vehicle in the postwar years. A recent dictionary states that such models have a larger interior than sedans of the line and seats that can be readily lifted out, or folded down, to facilitate light trucking. In addition, there's usually a tailgate, but no separate luggage compartment. The two-door wagon often has sliding or flip-out rear side windows.

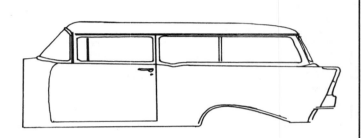

FOUR-DOOR STATION WAGON: Since functionality and adaptability are advantages of station wagons, four-door versions have traditionally been sales leaders. At least they were until cars began to grow smaller. This style usually has lowerable windows in all four doors and fixed rear side glass. The term "suburban" was almost synonymous with station wagon at one time, but is now more commonly applied to light trucks with similar styling. Station wagons have had many trade names, such as Country Squire (Ford) and Sport Suburban (Plymouth). Quite a few have retained simulated wood paneling, keeping alive the wagon's origin as a wood-bodied vehicle. AMC was famous for introducing the four-door hardtop (pillarless) station wagon in the mid-1950s.

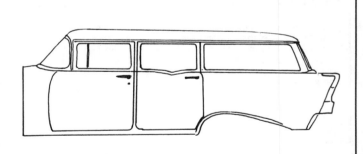

LIFTBACK STATION WAGON: Small cars came in station wagon form too. The idea was the same as bigger versions, but the conventional tailgate was replaced by a single lift-up hatch. For obvious reasons, compact and subcompact wagons had only two seats, instead of the three that had been available in many full-sized models. The Hornet Sportabout station wagon should become a collectible example of this body style, along with early American Eagle station wagons.

DIMENSIONS

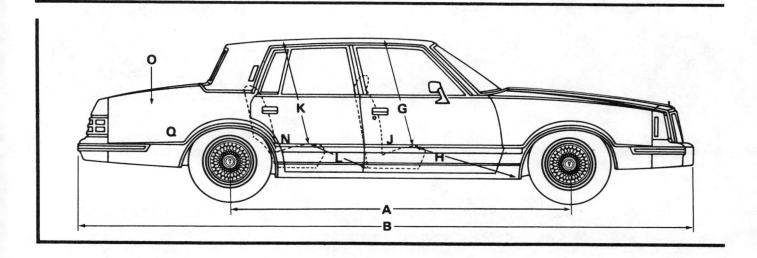

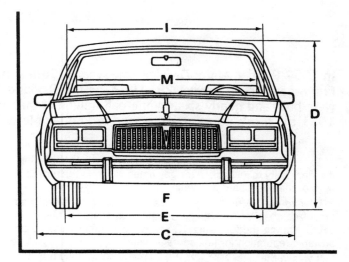

DIMENSIONS
Exterior:
A Wheelbase
B Overall length
C Width
D Overall height
E Tread, front
F Tread, rear
Interior—front:
G Headroom
H Legroom
I Shoulder room
J Hip room
Interior—rear:
K Headroom
L Legroom
M Shoulder room
N Hip room
O Trunk capacity (liters/cu. ft.)
P Cargo index volume (liters/cu. ft.)
Q Fuel tank capacity (liters/gallons)

THE HISTORY OF THE PONTIAC MOTOR DIVISION

First Oakland—1907

First Pontiac—1926

1957 Pontiac

In 1957 Pontiac Motor Division observed its 50th anniversary of automobile production since the company was first organized on August 28, 1907, as the Oakland Motor Car Company. During that time seven million cars were built and nearly six and one-half million of that number were Pontiacs, which were introduced in 1926. In 1931 the firm's name was changed to Pontiac Motor Division when the Oakland car was discontinued.

To trace the history of Pontiac Motor Division to its beginning, it is necessary to go back to the gay nineties and to the nostalgic days of the dashboard and whip socket.

Edward M. Murphy, a successful young businessman organized the Pontiac Buggy Company in Pontiac, Mich., in 1893. During the following 10 years, his company gained an enviable reputation for fine carriage work.

It was in the early 1900s that the far-sighted Murphy began to look with interest at the smoking, sputtering horseless carriages that appeared occasionally on the streets. Sensing the potential of the automobile, which still was branded as an impractical and temporary novelty, he acquired the rights to a two-cylinder engine designed by A.P. Brush, a famous motor pioneer who already had established his reputation in the field of engineering by designing a successful one-cylinder Cadillac and Brush car.

Murphy equipped a section of his buggy works for car production and on August 28, 1907, he founded the Oakland Motor Car Company.

The initial investment of $200,000 in the new automobile manufacturing concern is less than the cost of some of the machines that now equip sprawling plants at Pontiac.

Murphy produced the two-cylinder Oakland for a year. However, it did not sell, so in 1908 he introduced the Oakland Model K, a four-cylinder car that was powerful for its time and competitively priced. A total of 278 four-cylinder Oaklands were produced in 1908 and 491 in 1909.

The growing young Oakland Motor Car Company attracted the attention of William Crapo Durant, one of the organizing geniuses behind the then-forming business that was to become General Motors.

Durant, through his agents, entered into negotiations with the Oakland stockholders and on April 9,1909, Oakland joined General Motors taking its place beside Buick and Oldsmobile. Cadillac joined GM later that year and Chevrolet was added in 1918.

In September, 1909, E.M. Murphy died at age 45. L.L. (Lee) Dunlap, a long-time friend and business associate of Murphy's succeeded Murphy and Oakland continued its growth.

In 1910, production of the Model K Oakland boomed to 4,639, mainly on the basis of its hill-climbing ability. Three years later, Oakland introduced its first "six" along with a fast "four" that was equipped with a self-starter.

After World War I, Oakland pioneered closed bodies in the light car field and skeptics shook their heads. In 1923, Oakland introduced long-lasting, fast-drying Duco lacquer to the auto industry.

In 1925, rumors spread of a new companion car to the Oakland line. Ben H. Anibal, who had been chief engineer for Cadillac, was engaged by General Manager A.R. (Al) Glancy to design a completely new light, six-cylinder car.

Pontiac, the "Chief of the Sixes", made its bow at the New York Auto Show in January 1926. Little did Oakland executives dream at the time that the Pontiac would one day supersede the parent.

The new automobile became as aggressive and powerful in its field as did the colorful Indian chief who 200 years ago banded together the Ottawas, Chippewas, Pottawatomis and Miamis into a powerful confederation.

Embodying many features of high-priced automobiles, yet, costing little more than the least-expensive lines, Pontiac immediately captured public favor and in 1926 a total of 76,742 units were built.

Popularity of Pontiac became so great that Oakland was discontinued in 1932. Pontiac is one of the few companion cars to survive the rigors of competition and today holds the distinction of being the only line introduced by General Motors after formation of the corporation.

Soon after the introduction of Pontiac, it was evident that the original factory site near the center of the city of Pontiac was too small, so 246 acres were acquired on the northern edge of the city for a new plant.

The new facility was to be known as the "daylight plant" because the extensive use of glass skylights provided natural illumination. It was considered a miracle in the construction industry that within 90 days after ground was broken cars were being produced in the new plant.

A new Fisher Body Division plant was built nearby, connected by an overhead closed bridge … a convenience not available to many manufacturers who had to truck-in their bodies.

In 1933, Harry J. Klingler was named general manager of Pontiac, and it was decided to put a "six" back in the line, retaining the "eight" as well. The 1935 models were the first to bear the Silver Streak identification; and sales doubled calling for further factory expansion.

Pontiac produced 330,061 units of its 1941 model, thus becoming the largest producer in its price class and, the fifth largest in the nation. After an outstanding war production record, Pontiac returned to passenger car production in 1945.

To satisfy growing demands, a vast expansion program was launched in 1945 to increase productivity capacity by 50 percent. Pontiac's iron foundry was greatly enlarged. Layout of the engine plant was altered to provide for more machines and heavier production. A new building was erected for increased production of rear axles, and for heat-treating of steel forgings to make them tougher and more durable. Pontiac's electroplating system, one of the largest automatic setups in the new warehouse for handling past-model parts, was put into service.

In 1951, Klingler became vice-president in charge of vehicle production for GM and Arnold Lenz was appointed general manager of Pontiac. Lenz served as general manager until his tragic death in 1952.

R.M. Critchfield succeeded Lenz as general manager and under his guidance Pontiac embarked on the most extensive enlargement and modernization program since 1927. A new car finish building was completed and the engine plant was completely modernized to produce V-8 engines in record volumes. Production for 1955 established a new high of 581,860 cars.

A new era started for Pontiac in 1956 when Semon E. (Bunkie) Knudsen took over the reins as general manager. Knudsen, son of William S. Knudsen, a former GM president, at the time was the youngest GM general manager at age 43. He proceeded without fanfare to make over the Pontiac image.

With a new engineering group headed by E.M. (Pete) Estes,

the new Pontiacs were methodically developed. Starting with the 1959 models, an image of a youthful car with appeal across the spectrum of new car buyers emerged.

In the fall of 1960, following intensive research, development and testing, Pontiac introduced the completely new Tempest series. Unique in conception and fresh in styling, the Tempest became an immediate success and was recognized as the outstanding engineering achievement of the year.

When Knudsen moved to Chevrolet as general manager in 1961, Estes headed Pontiac. Under his direction the division continued to grow in sales volume and facilities.

With the addition of the Tempest, the division moved into third place in sales in 1961. Long regarded as the hot-spot in automobile sales, third place has a reputation of being hard to keep. Several car manufacturers have occupied the position over the years only to lose out to another make.

Pontiac continued its dominance of third place during the 1960s as sales records were shattered.

The division also moved ahead in plant construction and in 1964 three new projects were announced. All were completed the following year and added some 1-1/2 million square feet to Pontiac's home production facilities.

These include a 180,000 square-foot addition to the foundry for new core-making machines, water-cooled cupolas and a new finishing room to make Pontiac's foundry the most modern in the industry.

Also added was a service parts warehouse containing 1,070,000 square feet under one roof to consolidate storage of service parts. A one-story storage and shipping building, 800 feet long and 330 feet wide, to expedite shipments to other Pontiac assembly plants was completed in 1964.

Estes followed Knudsen's footsteps to Chevrolet as general manager in 1965 and John Z. DeLorean was named to Pontiac's top position, moving up from chief engineer of the division.

Before the introduction of its 1966 models, Pontiac announced a completely new overhead camshaft engine as standard equipment on all 1966 Tempest models. This was the first time such an engine had been used in an American passenger car.

In January 1967, Pontiac unveiled the Firebird. Aimed at the youthful sports car market, it was offered with the OHC-6 and with a 400 cubic inch V-8 engine.

1968 was another milestone year for Pontiac. Production and sales records were shattered as 943,253 cars were produced for an all-time high. Pontiac's GTO was chosen Car of the Year by *Motor Trend* magazine for "… being so successful in confirming the correlations between safety, styling and performance."

The presentation of the Golden Calipers trophy marked the fourth time Pontiac had won the trophy, more than any other manufacturer.

Contributing to the GTO success was the innovative energy-absorbing Endura front bumper developed by Pontiac engineering. Hailed as an industry first and projected as a pacesetter for others to copy, the car and bumper attracted nationwide publicity.

Sales boomed in 1968. For the first time, the specialty cars: Tempest, Grand Prix and Firebird, exceeded those of the traditional line. When the final tallies were in, 910,977 Pontiacs had been sold.

The 1969 Grand Prix was a phenomenal success as its sales more than tripled over the previous model year to 105,000. *Car Life* magazine awarded the Grand Prix its "Car of the Year" award.

In February 1969, F. James McDonald returned to Pontiac as general manager, replacing DeLorean who moved up to Chevrolet in the same capacity.

McDonald (who had served as Pontiac's works manager from 1965-'68) returned after spending one year to the day at Chevrolet as director of manufacturing operations.

The division's new 300,000 square-foot ultra-modern administration building opened in early 1970. The five-level

structure, headquarters the general manager and the sales, accounting, data processing, purchasing and public relations departments.

In March 1971, Pontiac entered the compact car market with the low-priced, stylish Ventura II. Built on a 111-inch wheelbase, the Ventura II was offered in two-door and four-door models.

In April 1971, Pontiac dedicated a new multi-million dollar vehicle emissions control and carburetor testing facility. The two-story, 43,000-square-foot building was being used by Pontiac engineers working on the development of vehicle emissions controls of components in the powertrain and the fuel system.

The 1971 calendar year saw Pontiac take firm hold on third place in the auto industry's sales race. Pontiac dealers sold 710,352 cars to capture the hotly-contested third spot in sales for the 10th time in the last 11 years.

In 1972, Pontiac featured a new energy-absorbing bumper on all full-size cars. The system consisted of two telescoping steel boxes that contained urethane positioned between the bumper and the frame of the car. Since the urethane blocks were not damaged by an impact, the bumper could be struck numerous times during the life of the car and continue to absorb energy.

On October 1, 1972, Martin J. Caserio became general manager of Pontiac replacing McDonald who was named Chevrolet general manager. Caserio had been general manager of the GMC Truck & Coach Division since 1966.

The 1973 Pontiac lineup was highlighted by a totally redesigned intermediate series, topped by the stunning Grand Am. This fine road touring car featured a "soft nose" front end made of flexible rubber-like urethane for protection. Pontiac sales of 854,343 for the 1973 model year were the second-best in history.

The 1974 Pontiac lineup featured significant engineering improvements in energy absorbing bumpers and a new Radial Tuned Suspension package.

By 1974 the major construction was completed on a multi-million dollar program to clean up smoke emissions from the Pontiac Casting Plant. Five modern arc-melt furnaces and four electric induction holding furnaces with the latest dust collecting units were installed. Two remaining coke-fired cupolas had modern emission control equipment installed making them as clean as the electric furnaces.

Introduction of the sub-compact Astre, bold restyling of the compact Ventura and extensive use of Radial Tuned Suspension with steel-belted radial tires highlighted introduction of the 1975 Pontiacs. Rectangular headlamps were utilized on the Bonneville and Grand Ville Brougham for the first time.

Pontiac's Golden Anniversary model lineup for 1976 included a new sporty subcompact, the Sunbird, and a new top-of-the-line entry, the Bonneville Brougham. Use of rectangular headlamps was expanded to include the intermediate LeMans, the Grand Prix, and the new Sunbird. The new Pontiacs showed the positive results of Pontiac engineers' continuing efforts to improve fuel economy.

On October 1, 1975, Alex C. Mair was appointed general manager of Pontiac, succeeding Caserio, who became General Motors vice-president and group executive in charge of the automotive components - electrical group. Mr. Mair had been general manager of the GMC Truck & Coach Division since 1972, and previously had been director of engineering for the Chevrolet Motor Division.

Pontiac's 1977 model lineup was headlined by the introduction of the completely redesigned full-size cars, plus Pontiac's two new engines. Catalina, Bonneville, Bonneville Brougham, Catalina Safari, and Grand Safari models all were redesigned--shorter and lighter than their predecessors, they continued to offer as much or more interior and luggage compartment space as earlier models. The new engines--a 2.5-liter (151 cid) cast-iron L-4 and a 4.9-liter (301 cid) V-8--were designed from the outset to provide improved durability and reliability as well as outstanding fuel economy.

Pontiac introduced a new car mid-year in 1977. The Phoenix was added to the Pontiac lineup as the top-of-the-line compact car. It joined the Pontiac Ventura as the only American compact cars to offer a four-cylinder engine. Among other features, the Phoenix offered the first U.S. headlamps completely designed under the metric measurement system.

Complete redesign of the mid-size LeMans and Grand LeMans and of the personal luxury Grand Prix, the return of the Grand Am and continuing engineering and fuel economy improvements were the highlights of Pontiac's 1978 model lineup. The LeMans, Grand LeMans, and Grand Prix were all shorter and lighter than their predecessors, providing significant increases in fuel economy while retaining traditional levels of roominess and comfort. New front and rear design treatments and several new interior trims were offered in the 1978 full-size Pontiacs. The Grand Am was reintroduced with distinctive features that included a soft, flexible rubber front end panel. The Phoenix replaced the Ventura and the Sunbird replaced the Astre as Pontiac's compact and subcompact cars, respectively, for the 1978 model year.

In April 1978, the completely modernized manufacturing office building was dedicated. Occupying the new building were Industrial Engineering, Manufacturing Staff, Reliability Staff, Plant Engineering and Production Engineering.

Pontiac Motor Division sold more new cars--871,391--during the 1978 model year than in any previous model year in its history. Firebirds, led by the performance-oriented Trans Am, continued to be among the most popular cars in the auto industry, setting an all-time model year sales record of 175,607. Pontiac's sporty little Sunbird also set a sales record.

The 1979 model lineup for Pontiac was highlighted by Firebird's new front and rear styling and a new "crossflow" cylinder head designed four-cylinder engine for the Sunbird for improved performance. The 1979 model year marked the first full year since the 1930s that Pontiac offered genuine wire wheels on certain models. Four wheel power disc brakes were introduced as an option on Firebird Formula and Trans Am models. The Grand Safari wagon was renamed the Bonneville Safari to more closely identify it with the Pontiac family of cars. The 400 cubic inch V-8 was discontinued for all Catalina and Bonneville models in the division's efforts to increase its fuel economy average and help General Motors meet stringent federal fuel economy standards.

On November 6, 1978, Robert C. Stempel became Pontiac general manager, succeeding Mair who was named vice-president and group executive in charge of the Technical Staffs Group at the GM Technical Center in Warren, Mich. Stempel was formerly Director of Engineering for Chevrolet Motor Division.

Pontiac introduced its first front-wheel-drive car in April 1979, with a totally redesigned "efficiency-sized" Phoenix. Available in a two-door coupe and five-door hatchback sedan, the Phoenix lineup included the base car, a luxury LJ or a new sporty SJ option. A transverse mounted 2.5-liter (151 cid) four-cylinder L-4 "crossflow" engine was standard in Phoenix with an optional 2.8-liter (173 cid) 60-degree transverse V-6 two-barrel engine available. The 1980 Phoenix was smaller and tightly packaged on the outside, but larger in many respects on the inside, compared to the 1979 Phoenix.

The remainder of Pontiac's 1980 model lineup, introduced in October 1979, included major styling changes to full-size Pontiacs and a revised engine lineup for more fuel efficiency while maintaining good performance. A GM 4.9-liter (301 cid) four-barrel turbocharged engine, produced by Pontiac Motor Division, was introduced as an option federally for Firebird Trans Am and Formula models and a GM 4.3-liter (265 cid) V-8 engine, also produced by Pontiac, was introduced as a down-sized version of the Pontiac produced 4.9-liter (301 cid) V-8. A white Limited Edition Pontiac Turbo Trans Am was chosen as the official pace car for the 64th running of the Indianapolis 500 race, May 25, 1980.

In August 1980, William E. Hoglund, who had been comptroller of General Motors, returned to Pontiac as general manager, replacing Stempel who was appointed managing director for Adam Opel AG in Germany.

A major design change for Grand Prix and a new General Motors Computer Command Control system for all Pontiac carlines (except with diesel) to meet stricter 1981 emission standards highlighted Pontiac's 1981 product lineup. The 1980 Sunbird was carried over through the end of the 1980 calendar year.

The 1981-1/2 Pontiac T1000 made its debut at the Chicago Auto Show in February. Targeted at the price-conscious family buyer in need of inexpensive entry level transportation, Pontiac T1000 models were available as a three-door or five-door hatchback.

Introduced in May 1981, Pontiac's 1982 J2000 models were totally new, efficiently functional front-wheel-drive subcompact cars. Built on a 101.2-inch wheelbase, the J2000 was available as a two-door coupe, four-door sedan, three-door hatchback, or four-door station wagon. Standard powertrain for all J2000 models was a 1.8-liter (1 12 cid) L-4 two-barrel with a four-speed manual transaxle. Pontiac J2000 models were promoted as appealing to both traditional and the important "new values" buyers as a car that was functional but yet offered a blend of flair and excitement in the best Pontiac tradition.

Pontiac Motor Division produced over 700,000 four-cylinder engines during the 1981 model year. During the summer of 1981, the division opened a new engine facility, Plant 55, where it produced additional GM 2.5-liter four-cylinder engines. Pontiac was one of the first in the industry to use microwave measurement for accurately timing these engines built in the new plant. Other technological innovations used in the 712,000-square-foot, 200 million dollar plant, included a functional check that performed several tests, a signature analysis torque rate system and a computer Management Information System.

The world-famous Bonneville nameplate adorned a more fuel efficient luxury car in Pontiac's 1982 fall product introductions. The Pontiac-produced 1982 GM 2.5-liter four-cylinder engine underwent major technological improvements, including elimination of the conventional carburetor, and offered improved driveability and fuel economy through advanced technology of electronic fuel injection (EFI).

All-new ultra-aerodynamic Firebirds and contemporary five-passenger front-wheel-drive Pontiac 6000 models joined the 1982 Pontiac lineup in January

Available in three distinct models--the sporty Firebird coupe, the performance-oriented Trans Am, and the new sophisticated luxury S/E--each had its own specific identity. Firebird featured a 2.5-liter EFI engine, S/E had a 2.8-liter V-6, and the Trans Am was powered by a 5.0-liter four-barrel V-8 engine; all models had a standard four-speed manual transmission. Extensive wind tunnel testing on the Firebird resulted in an excellent drag coefficient that made the car one of the most aerodynamic cars ever produced.

Although the Pontiac 6000 was based on the General Motors X-car platform and powertrain, it was a completely different car inside, outside and underneath with ride and handling characteristics that made it internationally competitive. Available in first level and LE series as a spacious four-door sedan or contemporary two-door coupe, the Pontiac 6000 was powered by a fuel-injected 2.5-liter four-cylinder engine with three-speed automatic transmission as standard equipment. The dramatic wedge shape of the 6000 was the result of many hours of aerodynamic tuning the surface, contour and detail, making the 6000 one of the most aerodynamic sedans available in America.

In April 1982, Pontiac offered a new overhead cam (OHC), fuel-injected four-cylinder engine for its subcompact J2000 models with an automatic transmission. The OHC-fuel injection engine provided exceptional smoothness with a responsive, fuel efficient performance.

The 1983 model lineup saw the introduction of the new Pontiac STE as a high-styled world class performance sedan. The STE was designed to compete head-on with the best import sedans in the special touring market. Standard powertrain was the 130-horsepower high-output 2.8-liter two-barrel V-6 engine.

Also in 1983, Pontiac re-introduced the full-sized Parisienne to its model lineup after a two year absence.

1984 was a banner year for Pontiac as the division took a major step as the expressive performance division of General Motors with the introduction of the revolutionary two-seat sports car, the Fiero. The Fiero was the first production car in the world to utilize a "space frame/chassis" with separate reinforced plastic body panels which Pontiac named "Enduraflex." Pontiac's first two-seater was built on a 93.4 inch wheelbase and powered by a 92 horsepower 2.5-liter four-cylinder engine.

The Fiero was a tremendous success during its first year in the market with sales of nearly 100,000 units--nearly doubling the sales of the previous best selling two-seater in the U.S.

Also in 1984 Pontiac announced it was adding an exciting turbocharged 1.8 liter-engine to its 2000 Sunbird lineup. The impressive turbo churned out 150 horsepower at 5600 rpm.

In January of 1984 GM announced the formation of two new car groups: the C-P-C Group (Chevrolet, Pontiac, GM Canada), and B-O-C Group (Buick, Oldsmobile, Cadillac).

As a part of the C-P-C group, Pontiac was charged with developing a product line for the 1980s that would appeal to the entry-level younger market with exciting, fun-to-drive, performance-oriented sporty vehicles.

In July of 1984 GM announced that the idle Pontiac Motor Home Plant 8, which had built Pontiacs since the 1920s, would be re-activated to build several models of GM rear-wheel-drive midsize passenger cars.

In July 1984 Pontiac General Manager William E. Hoglund was promoted to group executive in charge of the GM Operating Staffs Group. He was later named president of the GM Saturn Corporation.

J. Michael Losh became the 14th general manager of Pontiac replacing Hoglund. Losh had been managing director of General Motors de Mexico.

Calendar year 1984 was Pontiac's best sales year in the previous five as dealers sold 704,684 new cars. The number one nameplate in the Pontiac lineup for 1984 was the Sunbird with sales of 126,916.

In 1985, hot in the tracks of the successful Fiero, STE and Sunbird Turbo, Pontiac introduced the newest in a series of bold image cars, the driver-oriented Grand Am. Available as a two door coupe, the Grand Am was designed to compete head-to-head with the upscale imports and to appeal to the "new values" consumer of the 1980s. Powertrains were the new electronic fuel-injected 2.5-liter four-cylinder or the performance-oriented 125-horsepower multi-port fuel-injected 3.0 liter-V-6.

The 1985 model year saw Pontiac dealers sell 785,617 cars, the best model year sales record since 1979. The Pontiac 6000 was the division's top seller with deliveries of 156,995 units.

The 1986 Pontiac product lineup was highlighted by the addition of several new expressive "Drivers Cars" such as the Grand Am SE, the Sunbird GT, and in early 1986, the bold new Fiero GT. These new models helped Pontiac to achieve the biggest market share gain of any GM division in 1986. Sales reached 840,137, with the Grand Am almost doubling its sales to 190,994 from 98,567 the previous year.

Early in the model year for Pontiac's 1987 lineup the Bonneville was converted to the front-wheel drive H-body platform at the Willow Run, Mich., plant. Also, with the arrival, in the spring of 1987, of the new South Korean import LeMans, an '88 model, Pontiac was able to both offer a much needed for its division entry level subcompact and revive a proven salable name not used since 1981. Sales totaled 715,536 in 1987, led by the Grand Am with 216,065 units sold.

In October 1987 production began on the 1988 Grand Prix, which was built at the new GM assembly plant in Fairfax, Kan. The new front-drive Grand Prix, based on the W-platform, reached sales of 76,723 helping Pontiac to record 740,928 units sold in 1988. The Grand Am was again Pontiac's top seller at 221,438 cars sold. Bonneville's new SSE model came with the new 3.8-liter V-6 as standard powerplant. Fiero had a new Formula version that featured fully independent suspension, which was offered on all Fieros for 1988, the final year the car was produced.

In calendar year 1989 Pontiac offered GM's first all-wheel drive car, the 6000 STE, which had its production delayed from the previous year. Also new were limited editions of the Trans Am 20th Anniversary model and the McLaren Turbo Grand Prix. Only 1,500 of the 20th Anniversary Trans Ams were built, powered by the 3.8-liter turbocharged engine rated at 250 horsepower, while 2,000 McLaren Turbo Grand Prix were assembled. Domestic sales hit 675,422, again led by the Grand Am. John G. Middlebrook replaced Losh and became the 15th general manager of Pontiac.

Pontiac launched the 1990s with its foray into the minivan market via the Trans Sport. This APV (all purpose van), constructed of composite materials on a space frame substructure, could be ordered with seating for five, six, or seven passengers. The popular Firebird also took on a new look for 1991--offered in the spring of 1990--receiving an exterior overhaul to improve aerodynamics and also getting more muscle under the hood.

Through mid-decade the Pontiac lineup consists of familiar names with the exception of the new-for-1995 Sunfire, which replaced the Sunbird. Firebird/Grand Prix/Bonneville/Grand Am/ Trans Sport comprise the rest of the current lineup, and with Pontiac's reputation for "building excitement" car and minivan buyers should have plenty to get excited about well into the next century.

THE ROAD TO THE 30 MILLIONTH PONTIAC... began in January 1926 with the Series 6-27 Coupe (right) and reached the historic mark with the 1992 Pontiac SSEi (left) produced at the Wentzville, Missouri, Assembly Center on Tuesday, October 29, 1991. Pontiac General Manager John G. Middlebrook is shown with these two historic Pontiacs in front of the Pontiac Administration Building.

Following is a list of general managers for Oakland Motor Car Company and Pontiac Motor Division:

OAKLAND MOTOR CAR COMPANY:

1907-08	Edward M. Murphy	1951-52	Arnold Lenz
1909-10	Lee Dunlap	1952-56	Robert M. Critchfield
1911-14	George P. Daniels	1956-61	Semon E. Knudsen
1915	Charles W. Nash	1961-65	Elliott M. Estes
1916-20	Fred W. Warner	1965-69	John Z. DeLorean
1921-23	George H. Hannum	1969-72	F. James McDonald
1924-30	Alfred R. Glancy	1972-75	Martin J. Caserio
1931	Irving J. Reuter	1975-78	Alex C. Hair
		1978-80	Robert C. Stempel

PONTIAC MOTOR DIVISION:

		1980-84	William E. Hoglund
1932-33	William S. Knudsen/P. O. Tanner	1984-89	J. Michael Losh
1933-51	Harry J. Klingler	1989-present	John G. Middlebrook

1926-1942

PONTIAC

PONTIAC 1926-1942

PONTIAC - Pontiac, Michigan - (1926-1942 et. seq.) - In January 1926 the new car was given its official debut at the New York Automobile Show, followed by a sales meeting at the Commodore. The hotel was renamed the "Wigwam" for the day, the conference designated the "Pow Wow" and "Heap Big Eats" being served for lunch. The car named for an Indian chief, the salesmen of the Oakland Motor Car Company believed, was sure to bring plenty of "wampum" into their dealerships. The Pontiac had arrived. It would become a unique car in General Motors history: the only one ever to establish a maiden year sales record (bettering the Chrysler mark of 1924, though overtaken in 1927 by the new Graham-Paige), and it was the only companion car in the GM lineup ever to eclipse its parent. The Pontiac's genesis dated back to the early 1920s when George Hannum was Oakland's general manager and toyed with a low-priced idea car code named "Relot." Alfred P. Sloan liked the concept and set experimental engineers Ormond E. Hunt and Henry M. Crane onto it. Ultimately the idea--Chevrolet chassis with six-cylinder engine--was transferred to Chevrolet for final development. By the mid-1920s, Hannum had been booted out of Oakland, but the car came back to be produced there in order to give a shot in the arm to flagging Oakland sales. Alfred Glancy, a congenially feisty Irishman who for about a dozen years had been what he called "a sort of business doctor for General Motors and the DuPonts," was Oakland's general manager now. As chief engineer, Glancy hired Ben Anibal, who brought with him Fenn Holden, Hermann Schwarze, and Roy Milner. These Four Horsemen, as they were known, had been together for fifteen years already, a decade with Cadillac, a shorter tenure at Peerless—and they readied the production Pontiac. Its name was a natural, the Pontiac Buggy Company had been genesis of the Oakland automobile, and naming this new car from Oakland after the Indian chief made selection of a mascot *fait accompli.* When the pilot model was completed, Glancy invited Oakland executives and area dealers to an official christening during which he broke what he called "the only bottle of champagne in Oakland County"--this was Prohibition, of course—over the Indian head hood ornament, and the Pontiac was on its way, first to New York for the automobile show, then to sales of 76,696 cars its first year. All of them were closed models, incidentally, this directive from Alfred Sloan himself, and probably because he had been embarrassed a few years earlier when Hudson scooped GM in introducing the low-priced Essex coach. There was nothing really remarkable about the new Pontiac; its chassis was completely conventional; its L-head six-cylinder engine had a biggish bore (3.25 inches), the shortest stroke (3.75) thus far in a standard American production car; its displacement was a quite large 185 cubic inches, with 40 hp developed at a rather lazy 2400 rpm. Only "moderate speed operation" was claimed for the Pontiac, which, the Oakland company said, had been "designed specifically to dominate the field of low-priced sixes." And so it did, with a price of $825 for coach or coupe; only the Essex Six was cheaper, and that car at the time boasted only 145 cubic inches and was suffering reliability problems. A sprightly sport roadster and cabriolet were added to the Pontiac line for 1927, and the 100,000th car was produced in March of that year. Four wheel brakes were a 1928 addition, followed in '29 by a new and bigger L-head six-cylinder engine (200 cubic inches developing 57 hp at 3000 rpm), self-energizing brakes, Hotchkiss drive, and a brand-new styling look courtesy of W. Everett Miller, former designer for Murphy, which was a pleasing combination of Oakland, LaSalle, and Oldsmobile. The 500,000th Pontiac was built in June 1929, the stock market crashed that October. Probably of all members of the GM family, it was the people behind the Pontiac who were the most overwhelmed by the Great Depression. From meteoric success, Pontiac fortunes plunged toward despair. Glancy left in 1930 to serve the government in a number of Depression-created public positions, and former Olds president Irving J. Reuter took over the Oakland company. Although there was some corporate level discussion about discontinuing both the Oakland and the Pontiac, the decision was quickly made to kill only the more expensive car. There was no new Oakland at the automobile show in January 1932, and that summer official word came that the name was now Pontiac Motor Company. Joining the Pontiac line of sixes for '32 had been a new V-8 developed from the unit that had previously powered the Oakland. An expensive engine to produce, it was destined for only a single year's run by Pontiac. In January 1933 Pontiac went straight-eight across the board, offering 223.4 cubic inches, 77 hp, an actual 78 mph—and at price tags beginning at $635. "The Big Straight Eight in the Low Price Field," Pontiac advertised; "overbuilt to preserve traditional Pontiac stamina," *Automobile Topics* said, *Automobile Trade Journal* commented on the "striking new streamlined bodies," courtesy

this time of another former Murphy designer, Frank Q. Hershey. In 1934 Pontiacs were provided Knee-Action, and the Pontiac company was given the services of Harry Klingler, the super salesman who had helped to make Chevrolet number one in the industry and who now took over as Pontiac's general manager. During 1935, from the nadir of 42,633 cars in '32, Pontiac production rose to more than 175,000. Reintroduced to the line that year was a six, announced during automobile show week in a deluxe version only slightly less expensive than the eight, with a standard model following a month later, which brought Pontiac closer to the lowest-priced field than ever it had been before. Now there were Pontiacs for just about anybody who could afford any car at all. No-draft ventilation and Turret Top bodies also arrived for '35, as did the Silver Streak styling motif (Frank Hershey's idea) that would distinguish Pontiacs from other cars on the road for years thereafter. Arguing with success seldom being a particularly good idea, Klingler didn't in '36, with Pontiacs merely refined in detail and sales rising above 178,000. But for '37 he decided to splurge with heftier engines (the six now 223 cubic inches for 85 hp, the eight 249 for an even 100) installed in chassis five inches longer (117 for

the six, 122 for the eight). Pontiac had its best year thus far in '37: 235,322 cars. Together with the rest of the industry, company production ebbed appreciably during the 1938 recession year, but by 1940 had risen to a new high of 249,303. The Torpedo was introduced that year, followed in '41 by Harry Klingler's decision to go Torpedo all the way, with eleven different body styles (designed by Bob Lauer and Joe Schemansky under the direction of Vincent Kaptur) and including fastback Streamliners that caught the public fancy immediately. Nineteen forty-one brought another Pontiac production high— 282,087 cars—and fifth place in the industry. What Harry Klingler had accomplished at Pontiac was nothing short of phenomenal. But then Klingler was a phenomenon. During 1941 he began production in Pontiac of Oerlikon anti-aircraft cannon. One month after Pearl Harbor, the Pontiac Motor Car Company became the first in the industry to receive a Navy "E." Conversion to total war production followed on February 10, 1942. For the six years preceding, Pontiac motorcars had been advertised as "built to last 100,000 miles." Many of them on the road in '42 would do far more than that during the car-starved war and early postwar years.

Pontiac Data Compilation
by John A. Gunnell

1926

1926 Pontiac Landau sedan. CG

PONTIAC - SERIES 6-27 - SIX: Fisher bodies with double beading, plate glass windows, V.V. windshield and automatic windshield wipers. Coupe has landau bars on roof and safety lock on right-hand door. Coach has foot rest, carpeting and dome lamp. Triple-steppe front fenders on both models. Drum style headlamps and wraparound type sun visors. Honeycomb radiator with Indian head mascot. Cowl lamps standard. Coupe finished in light Sage Green with Faerie Red striping. Coach finished in Arizona Gray. Black fenders on both.

I.D. DATA: Car number stamped on brass plate on rear frame crossmember. Starting: P-1. Ending: 84262-27. Engine number on block above water pump. All cars built in Pontiac, Mich.

1926 Pontiac roadster. OCW

Model No.	Body Type & Seating	Price	Weight	Prod. Total
6650	2-dr. Coach-5P	825	2335	Note 1

Note 1: Body style breakouts not available. About 42,000 early 1926 models believed built.

6640	2-dr. Cpe.-2P	825	2270	Note 2

Note 2: 204,553 of these cars built between 12/28/25 and 10/31/27.

ENGINE: L-head. Inline. (split-head). Six. Cast iron block. Bore & Stroke: 3-1/4 x 3-3/4 in. Displacement: 186.5 cu. in. Compression Ratio: 4.8:1. Brake hp: 40 @ 2400 rpm. N.A.C.C. hp: 25.35. Main bearings: Three. Valve lifters: Solid. Carb.: Carter one-barrel.

CHASSIS: Wheelbase: 110 in. Overall Length: 151-1/4 in. Front./Rear tread: 56/56 in. Tires: 29 x 4.75.

TECHNICAL: Manual transmission. Speeds: 3F/1R. Floor shift controls. Ventilated single dry disc clutch. Shaft drive. Semi-floating rear axle. Overall ratio: 4.18:1. Mechanical brakes on two (rear) wheels. Wood-spoke wheels. Rim size: 20 in.

OPTIONS: Front bumper. Rear fender guards. Heater. Special colors. Rear mount spare tire (spare rim standard).

HISTORICAL: Introduced January 3, 1926. First Pontiac built by Oakland as a small "companion" car. First series 6-27 models were built December 28, 1925, through February 1, 1927. A total of 76,742 cars were sold in the nameplate's first 12 months.

1926 Pontiac Landau coupe. CP

1926 Pontiac coach. JAG

1926-1/2

PONTIAC - SERIES 6-27 - SIX: The 1926-1/2 Pontiacs, built after August 1926, were sold as early 1927 models. They had some small changes from the original 1926 models. A Landau Sedan was introduced at this time. It had a leather covered top with dummy landau bars. The coupe and coach could now be had in other colors and with different color striping. In October 1926 a 3/4 ton Pontiac Deluxe Delivery truck was added. In November 1926, Deluxe versions of the coupe and Landau Sedan were introduced. They had nickel plated bumpers and fender guards, mohair upholstery and a foot operated headlight dimmer switch. A new type of sun visor with exposed brackets was first seen on these Deluxe cars.

I.D. DATA: Car number stamped on brass plate on rear frame crossmember. Starting: 41716-25. Engine numbers on block above water pump. All cars built in Pontiac, Mich.

Model No.	Body Type & Seating	Price	Weight	Prod. Total
6650	2-dr. Coach-5P	825	2335	Note 1
6640	2-dr. Cpe.-2P	825	2270	Note 1
7160	4-dr. Lan. Sed.-5P	895	2455	Note 1
7160D	4-dr. Del. Lan. Sed.-5P	975	2565	Note 1
6640D	2-dr. Del. Cpe. 2/4P	895	2380	Note 1

Note 1: Body style breakouts are not available. Approximately 34,700 cars were built.

ENGINE: L-head. Inline (split-head). Six. Cast iron block. Bore & Stroke: 3-1/4 x 3-3/4 in. Displacement: 186.5 cu. in. Compression Ratio: 4.8:1. Brake hp: 40 @ 2400 rpm. N.A.C.C. hp: 25.35. Main bearings: Three. Valve lifters: Solid. Carb.: Carter one-barrel.

CHASSIS: Wheelbase: 110 in. Overall Length: 151-1/4 in. Front/RearTread: 56/56 in. Tires: 29 x 4.75.

TECHNICAL: Manual transmission. Speeds: 3F/1R. Floor shift controls. Ventilated single dry disc clutch. Shaft drive. Semi-floating rear axle. Overall ratio: 4.18:1. Mechanical brakes on two (rear) wheels. Wood-spoke wheels. Rim size: 20 in.

OPTIONS: Front bumper (std. on Deluxe). Rear fender guards (std. on Deluxe). Heater. Rear mounted spare tire (spare rim standard).

HISTORICAL: Introduced August 1926. New colors: coupe in blue with red stripe; coach in blue or gray with orange stripe; Landau Sedan in green with red stripe. Deluxe models finished in Peter Pan Blue with matching fenders. Company president is A.R. Glancy. For more information on Deluxe delivery truck see Krause Publications' *Standard Catalog of Light-Duty Trucks.*

1927

1927 Pontiac Landau sedan. OCW

NEW-FINER - SERIES 6-27 - SIX: These were Pontiac's true 1927 models, which were built and sold from January 1927 to July 1927. Smooth, full-crown front fenders were introduced. Flat sun visors with exposed sides were used on all models. A Sport Roadster with a Stewart body was introduced. The Deluxe Coupe was replaced by a Sport Cabriolet (closed coupe) with rumbleseat.

I.D. DATA: Car number stamped on a brass plate on rear frame cross-member. Starting numbers continued from 1926-1/2 series. Ending: 144999 (approximate). Engine number on block above water pump. All cars built in Pontiac, Mich.

1927 Pontiac Deluxe delivery truck . JAG

Model No.	Body Type & Seating	Price	Weight	Prod. Total
Road	2-dr. Spt. Rds.-2/4P	775	2160	Note 1
7430	2-dr. Cpe.-2P	775	2270	Note 1
7460	2-dr. Spt. Cabr.-2/4P	835	2401	Note 1
7440	2-dr. Coach-5P	775	2335	Note 1
7450	2-dr. Lan. Sed.-5P	895	2455	Note 1
7450D	4-dr. Del. Lan. Sed.-5P	975	2565	Note 1

Note 1: Body style breakouts not available. Approximately 68,300 cars were built.

1927 Pontiac Deluxe delivery truck . JAG

ENGINE: L-head. Inline (split-head) Six. Cast iron block. Bore & Stroke: 3-1/4 x 3-3/4 in. Displacement: 186.5 cu. in. Compression Ratio: 4.8:1. Brake hp: 40 @ 2400 rpm. N.A.C.C. hp: 25.35. Main bearings: Three. Valve lifters: Solid. Carb.: Carter one-barrel.

CHASSIS: Wheelbase: 110 in. Overall Length: 151-1/4 in. Front/Rear Tread: 56/56 in. Tires: 29 x 4.75.

TECHNICAL: Manual transmission. Speeds: 3F/1R. Floor shift controls. Improved type ventilated single dry disc clutch. Shaft drive. Semi-floating rear axle. Overall ratio: 4.18:1. Mechanical brakes on two (rear) wheels. Wood-spoked wheels. Rim size: 20 in.

OPTIONS: Front bumper (std. on Deluxe). Rear fender guards (std. on Deluxe). Single sidemount tires on Sport models only. Heater.

HISTORICAL: Introduced January 1927. New body styles include first open Pontiac. Improved clutch. Larger cooling system capacity. Foot operated tilt-beam headlights standard. President of Pontiac is A.R. Glancy.

1927-1/2

PONTIAC - NEW-FINER SERIES 6-27 - SIX: The 1927-1/2 Pontiacs were virtually identical to the true 1927 models, but were sold as 1928 models. The only changes in these cars was the use of a smaller (11-gallon) gas tank plus a few new exterior paint colors. They had lower prices and slight adjustments in shipping weight.

I.D. DATA: Serial numbers were on the right side of the rear frame cross-member or on the frame under the left front fender. Starting: 145000-27. Ending: 204000-27. Motor numbers were on the left side of the crankcase or near the left front corner of the block. Starting: P56250. Ending: P220000 (approximate). All cars built in Pontiac, Mich.

Model No.	Body Type & Seating	Price	Weight	Prod. Total
ROAD	2-dr. R/S Rds.-2/4P	745	2160	Note 1
7430	2-dr. Cpe.-2P	745	2275	Note 1
7460	2-dr. R/S Cabr.-2/4P	795	2345	Note 1
7440	2-dr. Sed.-5P	745	2275	Note 1
7450D	4-dr. Del. Sed.-5P	925	2510	Note 1
7450	4-dr. Lan. Sed.-5P	845	2460	Note 1

Note 1: Body style breakouts not available. Approximately 59,000 cars were built from July-October 1927.

ENGINE: L-head. Inline (split-head) Six. Cast iron block. Bore & Stroke: 3-1/4 x 3-3/4 in. Displacement: 186.5 cu. in. Compression Ratio: 4.8:1. Brake hp: 40 @ 2400 rpm. N.A.C.C. hp: 25.35. Main bearings: Three. Valve lifters: Solid. Carb.: Carter one-barrel.

CHASSIS: Wheelbase: 110 in. Overall Length: 151-1/4 inches. Front/Rear Tread: 56/56 in. Tires: 29 x 4.75.

TECHNICAL: Manual transmission. Speeds: 3F/1R. Floor shift controls. Improved type ventilated dry disc clutch. Shaft drive. Semi-floating rear axle. Overall ratio: 4.18:1. Mechanical brakes on two (rear) wheels. Wood-spoked wheels. Rim size: 20 in.

OPTIONS: Front bumper (std. on Deluxe). Rear fender guards (std. on Deluxe). Single sidemounts on Sport models only. Heater.

HISTORICAL: Introduced July 1927. Interchangeable bronze backed bearings. Automatic spark control. Indirectly lighted dashboard. Last Pontiacs to use vacuum tank. A.R. Glancy was president of Oakland.

1928

1928 Pontiac two-door sedan. OCW

1928 Pontiac coupe. OCW

PONTIAC - NEW SERIES 6-28 - SIX: The true 1928 Pontiacs had a higher, deeper, narrower radiator shell and lower, more sweeping body lines. A cross-flow radiator was introduced. There was a new, raised panel along the top of the hood. Deep crowned front fenders with beaded edges were used. The Deluxe Landau Sedan was renamed the Sport Sedan. A four-door Sport Phaeton with a Stewart body was introduced. Many technical changes were seen in the engine, drivetrain, and running gear. The Indian chief on the hood became an Indian brave. New headlights were used. The Sport Cabriolet was now called Sport Coupe.

1928 Pontiac 6-28 Sport phaeton with Stewart body. JAG

I.D. DATA: Serial numbers were on the right side of the rear frame cross-member or on the frame under the left front fender. Starting: 204001-28. Ending: 334005-28. Motor numbers were on the left side of the crankcase or near the left front corner of the block. Starting: P220001. Ending: P376340 (approximate). All cars built in Pontiac, Mich.

1928 Pontiac rumbleseat roadster. JAC

1928 Pontiac Deluxe delivery truck. JAG

1928 Pontiac 6-28 Sport sedan. JAG

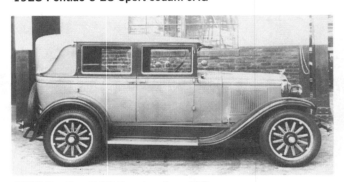

1928 Pontiac 6-28 Sport sedan. JAG

1928 Pontiac four-door sedan. JAG

Model No.	Body Type & Seating	Price	Weight	Prod. Total
ROAD	2-dr. R/S Rds.-2/4P	745	2270	Note 1
PHAE	4-dr. Spt. Phae.-5P	775	2390	Note 1
8250	2-dr. Cpe.-2P	745	2435	Note 1
8260	2-dr. Spt. Cpe.-4P	795	2455	Note 1
8240	2-dr. Sed.-5P	745	2520	Note 1
8820	4-dr. Sed.-5P	825	2595	Note 1
8230	4-dr. Spt. Sed.-5P	875	2640	Note 1

Note 1: Body style breakouts not available. Approximately 130,000 cars were built.

ENGINE: L-head. Inline. (GMR cylinder head) Six. Cast iron block. Bore & Stroke: 3-1/4 x 3-3/4. Displacement: 186.5 cu. in. Compression Ratio: 4.9:1. N.A.C.C. hp: 25.3. Main bearings: Three. Valve lifters: Solid. Carb.: Carter one-barrel.

CHASSIS: Wheelbase: 110 in. Tires: 29 x 5.00.

TECHNICAL: Manual transmission. Speeds: 3F/1R. Floor shift controls. New dry disc clutch. Shaft drive (torque tube). Semi-floating rear axle. Overall ratio: 4.18:1. Four-wheel mechanical brakes. 12-spoke wood artillery wheels.

OPTIONS: Front bumper (std. on Deluxe). Rear bumper (std. on Deluxe). Single sidemount. Heater. Disc wheels. Wind wings (open cars).

HISTORICAL: Introduced January 1928. New Carter updraft carburetor. Larger intake manifold. New Oakland type muffler. Improved steering gear. New frame and front axle. Blossom coincidental ignition lock. New thermostat, steering wheel and dash-mounted gas gauge. New "Daylight" factory opens in Pontiac, Mich. Higher compression GMR cylinder head. Internal front wheel brakes. AC fuel filter and fuel pump. A.R. Glancy remained as president of Oakland.

1928-1/2

PONTIAC - NEW SERIES 6-28 - SIX: New Series 6-28 Pontiacs built after June 1928 were sold as 1929 models. They were identical to the true 1928 models except for minor technical alterations. A Marvel carburetor, heavier 10-spoke Jaxon wood-spoke artillery wheels and a new rear axle ratio were the major changes. An increase in horsepower was noted on specifications sheets.

I.D. DATA: Serial numbers were on the rear frame cross-member or under the left front fender. Starting: 334006. Ending: 410100. Engine numbers were on left side of crankcase or near left front corner of block. Starting: P376341. Ending: P461000 (approximate). All cars built at Pontiac, Mich.

1928-1/2 Pontiac coupe. CP

Model No.	Body Type & Seating	Price	Weight	Prod. Total
ROAD	2-dr. R/S Rds.-2/4P	745	2270	Note 1
PHAE	4-dr. Phae.-5P	775	2390	Note 1
8250	2-dr. Cpe.-2P	745	2435	Note 1
8260	2-dr. Spt. Cpe.-2/4P	795	2455	Note 1
Model No.	Body Type & Seating	Price	Weight	Prod. Total
8240	2-dr. Sed.-5P	745	2520	Note 1
8820	4-dr. Sed.-5P	825	2595	Note 1
8230	4-dr. Spt. Sed.-5P	875	2640	Note 1

Note 1: Body style breakouts not available. Approximately 80,000 series 6-28 Pontiacs were sold as 1929 models.

ENGINE: L-head. Inline. Six. Cast iron block. Bore & Stroke: 3-1/4 x 3-3/4 in. Displacement: 186.5 cu. in. Compression Ratio: 4.9:1. Brake hp: 48 @ 2850 rpm. N.A.C.C. hp: 25.35. Main bearings: Three. Valve lifters: Solid. Carb.: Marvel one-barrel.

CHASSIS: Wheelbase: 110 in. Tires: 29 x 5.00.

TECHNICAL: Manual transmission. Speeds: 3F/1R. Floor shift controls. Dry disc clutch. Shaft drive (Torque tube). Semi-floating rear axle. Overall ratio: 4.36:1. Four-wheel mechanical brakes. Jaxon 10-spoke wood artillery wheels.

OPTIONS: Front bumper (std. on Deluxe). Rear bumper (std. on Deluxe). Single sidemount. Heater. Disc wheels. Wind wings (open cars).

HISTORICAL: Introduced June 1928. First year with Marvel carburetor. New, heavier wheels. Instruments grouped in metal case in center. A.R. Glancy president of Oakland.

1929

1929 Pontiac sedan (with Richard Dix). JAC

PONTIAC - NEW-BIG SIX - SERIES 6-29 - SIX: The true 1929 Pontiacs had new styling derived from the British Vauxhall. The radiator grille had a vertical center divider. A corrugated apron covered the gas tank in the rear. Larger, bullet-shaped headlights were seen. Wider hood sills and more deeply crowned fenders were used. The bodies gained a handsome, concave belt molding. From January to April, a handsome hood with horizontal louvers was employed. Because of heat warpage problems, a vertically louvered hood was used thereafter. Interiors were upgraded. Closed cars had oval rear windows. The new Landaulet featured a collapsible rear roof section. A bigger, more powerful engine was one of many technical changes. Pontiac introduced its first Convertible Cabriolet this year. (Earlier models called Cabriolets were really Sports Coupes). Standard equipment on all models included an automatic windshield wiper, rear view mirror, dash gasoline gauge and combination transmission and ignition lock.

1929 Pontiac coupe. CP

I.D. DATA: Serial numbers were on the right side of rear cross-member or under left front fender. Starting: 410101. Ending: 530874. Engine numbers were on the left side of crankcase or near left front corner of block. Starting: P376341. Ending: P461000 (approximate). All cars built in Pontiac, Mich.

1929 Pontiac roadster. OCW

1929 Pontiac roadster. JAG

1929 Pontiac phaeton. JAG

1929 Pontiac convertible cabriolet. JAG

Model No.	Body Type & Seating	Price	Weight	Prod. Total
ROAD	2-dr. R/S Rds.-2/4P	775	2342	Note 1
PHAE	4-dr. Phae.-5P	825	2407	Note 1
8950	2-dr. Cpe.-2P	745	2532	Note 1
8960	2-dr. Cabr. Conv.-2/4P	845	2537	Note 1
8940	2-dr. Sed.-5P	745	2595	Note 1
8920	4-dr. Sed.-5P	845	2717	Note 1
8930	4-dr. Lan.'et-5P	895	2702	Note 1

Note 1: Body style breakouts are not available. Approximately 120,000 "New Big Sixes" were made as 1929 models.

1929 Pontiac sedan. CP

1929 Pontiac 6-29 coach. JAG

1929 Pontiac Landaulette. JAG

1929 Pontiac four-door sedan. OCW

1929 Pontiac 6-29 four-door sedan. JAG

ENGINE: L-head. Inline Six. Cast iron block. Bore & Stroke: 3-5/16 x 3-7/8. Displacement: 200 cu. in. Compression Ratio: 4.9:1. Brake hp: 60 @ 3000 rpm. N.A.C.C. hp: 26.3. Main bearings: Three. Valve lifters: Solid. Carb.: Marvel one-barrel.

CHASSIS: Wheelbase: 110 in. Overall Length: 169 in. Tires: 29 x 5.00.

TECHNICAL: Improved manual transmission. Speeds: 3F/1R. Floor shift controls. Dry disc clutch. Hotchkiss drive. Semi-floating axle. Four-wheel mechanical brakes. Wood-spoke wheels.

OPTIONS: Front bumper. Rear bumper. Single sidemount. Dual sidemount. Leather sidemount cover(s). Heater. Spotlight. Pedestal mirrors. Wind wings (open cars). Running lamps. Spare tire cover. Lovejoy shock absorbers.

HISTORICAL: Introduced January 1929. Twenty percent more powerful engine. Counterweighted crankshaft. Self-energizing brakes. Adjustable front seats. Improved transmission. Larger carburetor. Wider intake manifold. Larger valves with increased lift. First true Pontiac convertible. A.R. Glancy president of the company.

1929-1/2

PONTIAC - BIG SIX - 6-29A - SIX: This would be the last season for carrying over a mid-year series into the next model year. Pontiacs with serial numbers above 530875-29 were considered 1930 automobiles. There were no specifications changes in these cars, but several models were dropped. Cut from the line were the Convertible Cabriolet and Landaulette Sedan.

I.D. DATA: Serial numbers were on the right side of rear cross-member or under left front fender. Starting: 530875. Ending: 591500. Engine numbers were on the left side of crankcase or near left front corner of block. Starting: 608157. Ending: 673500. All cars built at Pontiac, Mich.

Model No.	Body Type & Seating	Price	Weight	Prod. Total
ROAD	2-dr. R/S Rds.-2/4P	775	2342	Note 1
PHAE	4-dr. Phae.-5P	825	2407	Note 1
8950	2-dr. Cpe.-2P	745	2532	Note 1
8940	2-dr. Sed.-5P	745	2595	Note 1
8920	4-dr. Sed.-5P	845	2717	Note 1

Note 1: Body style breakouts are not available. Approximately 60,625 cars were built in the 6-29A series (August 1929-October 31, 1929).

ENGINE: L-head. Inline. Six. Cast iron block. Bore & Stroke: 3-5/16 x 3-7/8 in. Displacement: 200 cu. in. Compression Ratio: 4.9:1. Brake hp: 60 @ 3000 rpm. N.A.C.C. hp: 26.3. Main bearings: Three. Valve lifters: Solid. Carb.: Marvel one-barrel.

CHASSIS: Wheelbase: 110 in. Overall Length: 169 in. Tires: 29 x 5.00.

TECHNICAL: Improved manual transmission. Speeds: 3F/1R. Floor shift controls. Dry disc clutch. Hotchkiss drive. Semi-floating rear axle. Overall ratio: 4.42:1. Four-wheel mechanical brakes. Wood-spoke wheels.

OPTIONS: Front bumper. Rear bumper. Single sidemount. Leather sidemount cover(s). Heater. Spotlight. Pedestal mirrors. Wind wings (open cars). Running lamps. Spare tire cover. Lovejoy shock absorbers.

HISTORICAL: Introduced August 1929. A.R. Glancy continued as president of Oakland.

1930

1930 Pontiac Sport roadster. HAC

1930 Pontiac four-door sedan. OCW

PONTIAC - BIG SIX - 6-30B - SIX: A sloping windshield characterized the "real" 1930 Pontiac's new looks. Horizontal lines were emphasized by a half-oval belt molding that extended entirely around the car and over the hood to the radiator. The hood had 31 thin, vertical louvers. The vertical cowl feature line was straightened. A host of technical advances were led by improvements to the engine mounting and suspension systems. A Custom Sedan and Sport Coupe were new body styles. Closed cars had oval rear windows again. Plated headlamp buckets were used on Sport and Custom models. Closed models had cadet style sun visors.

I.D. DATA: Serial numbers on right side of rear cross-member or under left front fender. Starting: 591501. Ending: 649000. Engine numbers on left side of crankcase or left front corner of block. Starting: 673501. Ending: 744000 (approximate). All cars built at Pontiac, Mich.

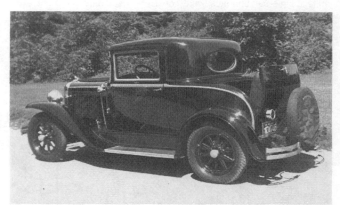
1930 Pontiac 6-30B Big Six Sport coupe. JAG

Model No.	Body Type & Seating	Price	Weight	Prod. Total
ROAD	2-dr. Spt. Rds.-2/4P	765	2345	Note 1
PHAE	4-dr. Phae.-5P	795	2410	Note 1
30307	2-dr. Cpe.-2P	745	2518	Note 1
30308	2-dr. Spt. Cpe.-2/4P	825	2590	Note 1
30301	2-dr. Sed.-5P	775	2630	Note 1
30302	4-dr. Sed.-5P	825	2680	Note 1
30309	4-dr. Cust. Sed.-5P	875	2720	Note 1

Note 1: Body style breakouts not available. Series production total was 62,888 cars in 1930 model year.

ENGINE: Inline. L-head. Six. Cast iron block. Bore & Stroke: 3-5/16 x 3-7/8 in. Displacement: 200 cu. in. Compression Ratio: 4.9:1. Brake hp: 60 @ 3000 rpm. N.A.C.C. hp: 26.3. Main bearings: Three. Valve lifters: Solid. Carb.: Marvel one-barrel.

CHASSIS: Wheelbase: 110 in. Overall Length: 167 in. Tires: 29 x 5.00.

TECHNICAL: Manual transmission. Speeds: 3F/1R. Floor shift controls. Dry disc clutch. Hotchkiss drive. Overall ratio: 4.42:1. Four-wheel mechanical brakes. Wood-spoke wheels. Rim size: 19 inches.

OPTIONS: Front bumper. Rear bumper. Single sidemount. Dual sidemount. Sidemount cover(s). Radio. Heater. Spotlight. Wind wings (open cars). Wire-spoke wheels.

HISTORICAL: Introduced January 1930. Brake drums increased to 12 inches. Metric spark plugs. Four-point, rubber-cushioned engine mounting. Coil lock ignition. Manual gear starter. Ribbing added to base of engine block. Four-wheel hand-brake. Lovejoy shock absorbers standard. Model year production: 62,888. A.R. Glancy company president.

25

1931

1931 Pontiac coupe. AA

PONTIAC - FINE SIX - SERIES 401 - SIX: For 1931 Pontiac featured a longer wheelbase and new bodies. A V-shaped chrome plated radiator with a wire grille was used. Headlamps were chrome plated on all models and mounted on a curved tie bar. One-piece full crown fenders carried parking lights on top. Hoods were secured by a single handle lock on each side. The splash apron on the rear extended from fender to fender. Aluminum moldings decorated the molded runningboard mats. Single-bar bumpers were considered "standard" at slight extra cost. Wire wheels became standard equipment in mid-year. Technical refinements to the engine and chassis and running gear changes were among technical improvements. A new convertible coupe replaced the roadster and phaeton.

I.D. DATA: Serial numbers on right side of rear cross-member or under left front fender. Starting: 649001. Ending: 729000. Engine numbers on left side of crankcase or left front corner of block. Starting: 744001. Ending: 835000. All cars built at Pontiac, Mich.

1931 Pontiac four-door sedan. JAC

Model No.	Body Type & Seating	Price	Weight	Prod. Total
31307	2-dr. Cpe.-2P	675	2558	Note 1
31308	2-dr. Spt. Cpe.-2/4P	715	2618	Note 1
31318	2 dr. Conv. Cpe.-2/4P	745	2598	Note 1
31301	2-dr. Sed.-5P	675	2653	Note 1
31309	4-dr. Sed.-5P	745	2733	Note 1
31319	4-dr. Cus. Sed.-5P	785	2743	Note 1

Note 1: Body style breakouts not available. Model year production total of Series 401 Pontiacs was 84,708 cars.

ENGINE: L-head. Inline. Six. Cast iron block. Bore & Stroke: 3-5/16 x 3-7/8 in. Displacement: 200 cu. in. Brake hp: 60 @ 3000 rpm. N.A.C.C. hp: 26.3. Main bearings: Three. Valve lifters: Solid. Carb.: Marvel one-barrel.

CHASSIS: Wheelbase: 112 in. Tires: 29 x 5.00.

TECHNICAL: Manual transmission. Speeds: 3F/1R. Floor shift controls. Dry disc clutch. Hotchkiss drive. Semi-floating rear axle. Overall ratio: 4.55:1. Four-wheel mechanical brakes. Wire-spoke wheels (Kelsey-Hayes). Rim size: 19 inches.

OPTIONS: Front bumper. Rear bumper. Dual sidemount. Sidemount cover(s). Radio. Heater. Clock. Spotlight. Pedestal mirrors. Trunk rack. Touring trunk. Wood-spoke wheels. Dual windshield wipers. Trippe lights.

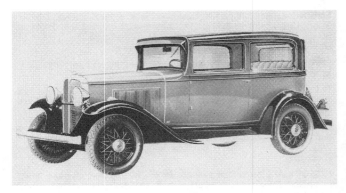

1931 Pontiac two-door sedan. OCW

HISTORICAL: Introduced January 1931. Steeldraulic brakes. Full-pressure lubrication. New AC intake silencer. Improved engine mounting. Heavier, sturdier frame. Inlox spring bushings. Stronger rear axle with Hyatt roller pinion bearings. Redesigned brake toggles. Last year for Oakland.

1932

1932 Pontiac Six two-door sedan. CP

PONTIAC - SERIES 402 - SIX: The Oakland became the Pontiac V-8 in 1932. Pontiac also offered a separate six-cylinder line. The new sixes had a longer wheelbase and longer, roomier bodies. They featured a slanted windshield without an outside sun visor. A new V-shaped radiator with vertical grille bars was used. The sides of the hood had four ventilator doors. Dual horns and front fender lights were standard on Custom models. The six-cylinder hood ornament had an Indian head within a circle.

I.D. DATA: Serial numbers were on the right side of rear cross-member or under left front fender. Starting: 729001. Ending: 763983. Engine numbers on left side of crankcase or near left front corner of block. Starting: 835001. Ending: 879565 (approximate). All cars built in Pontiac, Mich.

1932 Pontiac V-8 Sport coupe. OCW

1932 Pontiac Sport coupe . OCW

Model No.	Body Type & Seating	Price	Weight	Prod. Total
32317	2-dr. Cpe.-2P	635	2689	Note 1
32308	2-dr. Spt. Cpe.-2/4P	715	2734	Note 1
32318	2-dr. Conv. Cpe.-2/4P	765	2694	Note 1
32301	2-dr. Sed.-5P	645	2794	Note 1
32309	4-dr. Sed.-5P	725	2884	Note 1
32319	4-dr. Cus. Sed.-5P	795	2889	Note 1

Note 1: Body style breakouts not available. Total series production was 35,059 units.

1932 Pontiac V-8 four-door Custom sedan. JAG

ENGINE: L-head. Inline. Six. Cast iron block. Bore & Stroke: 3-5/16 x 3-7/8 in. Displacement: 200 cu. in. Compression Ratio: 5.1:1. Brake hp: 65 @ 3200 rpm. N.A.C.C. hp: 26.3. Main bearings: Three. Valve lifters: Solid. Carb.: Marvel one-barrel.

CHASSIS: Wheelbase 114 in. Tires: 18 x 5.25.

TECHNICAL: Synchromesh transmission (Muncie). Speeds: 3F/1R. Floor shift controls. Dry disc clutch. Hotchkiss drive. Semi-floating rear axle. Overall ratio: 4.55:1. Four-wheel mechanical brakes. Kelsey-Hayes wire spoke wheels. Freewheeling standard.

1932 Pontiac Six Sport coupe. JAG

1932 Pontiac Six four-door Custom sedan. JAG

1932 Pontiac Six four-door Standard sedan. JAG

1932 Pontiac Six Sport coupe. JAG

1932 Pontiac Six Sport coupe. JAG

PONTIAC V-8 - SERIES 302 - EIGHT: The 1932 Pontiac V-8s were a continuation of the 1931 Oakland with a new name and updated styling. They used a V-type radiator shell with built-in grille. A slanting windshield was seen. Sun visors were moved from outside to inside. Door-type hood ventilators appeared. All models had new radiator emblems, dual horns, and front fender lights. A bird with raised wings was the V-8 hood ornament.

I.D. DATA: Serial numbers on right side of rear cross-member or under left front fender. Starting: 310001. Ending: 316282. Engine number on left side of crankcase or near left front corner of block. All cars built in Pontiac, Mich.

Model No.	Body Type & Seating	Price	Weight	Prod. Total
32367	2-dr. Cpe.-2P	845	3069	Note 1
32358	2-dr. Spt. Cpe.-2/4P	925	3129	Note 1
32368	2-dr. Conv. Cpe.-2/4P	945	3089	Note 1
32351	2-dr. Sed.-5P	845	3149	Note 1
32359	4-dr. Sed.-5P	945	3224	Note 1
32369	4-dr. Cus. Sed.-5P	1025	3259	Note 1

Note 1: Body style breakouts not available. Total series production was 6,281 units.

1932 Pontiac V-8 Sport coupe. JAG

1932 Pontiac V-8 convertible coupe. JAG

ENGINE: L-head. V-block. Eight. Cast iron block. Bore & Stroke: 3-7/16 x 3-3/8 in. Displacement: 251 cu. in. Compression Ratio: 5.2:1. Brake hp: 85 @ 3200 rpm. N.A.C.C. hp: 37.8. Main bearings: Three. Valve lifters: Solid. Carb.: Marvel one-barrel.

CHASSIS: Wheelbase 117 in. Tires: 17 x 6.00.

TECHNICAL: Synchromesh transmission (Muncie). Speeds: 3F/1R. Floor shift controls. Dry disc clutch. Hotchkiss drive. Semi-floating rear axle. Overall ratio: 4.22:1. Four-wheel mechanical brakes. Wire spoke wheels.

OPTIONS: Front bumper. Rear bumper. Dual sidemount. Sidemount cover(s) (fabric or metal). Radio. Heater. Clock. Cigar lighter. Radio antenna (under runningboard). Spotlight. Trippe lights. Tandem windshield wipers. Dual horns (std. on Custom). Dual taillights (std. on Custom). Pedestal mirrors. Trunk rack. Touring trunk. Rear view mirror.

HISTORICAL: Production of six began December 8, 1931. Production of V-8 began December 22, 1931. Interchangeable steel-backed bearings. Floorboard mounted handbrake. Valve guides with tapered holes. First Pontiac eight and first V-8. Manually operated "Ride Control." Synchromesh transmission with silent second gear. Free wheeling. Smaller tires. Improved cooling. Calendar year registrations: 47,926 cars. Model year production: 41,340 cars. Irving J. Reuter and F.O. Tanner shared general managership of Oakland Motor Co. in early 1932. Pontiac became part of General Motors Corps.' new B-O-P (Buick-Olds-Pontiac) division. The name Pontiac Motors was adopted around June 1932.

1933

1933 Pontiac two-door sedan. JAC

PONTIAC - ECONOMY EIGHT - SERIES 601: The 1933 Pontiacs had a new straight eight plus many styling and technical changes. A new Fisher body with beaver tail rear styling was used. There was a slanting, V-type radiator with vertical bars. The hood had four wide, slanting louvers back towards the cowl. Valanced front tenders gave a streamlined look. There was an airplane type instrument panel on the left and glove compartment on the right of the dash. Pontiacs were made in five different assembly plants. The hood ornament was a brave's head in a circle with a round base.

I.D. DATA: Serial numbers were in the previous locations. Pontiac, Mich., numbers: 770001 to 838455. Oakland, Calif., numbers: C3001 to C5678. Atlanta, Ga., numbers: A1001 to A3195. Tarrytown, N.Y., numbers: T1001 to T10,600. St. Louis, Mo., numbers S1001 to S4996. Engine numbers were in the same location. Pontiac, Mich., numbers: 885001 to 987400. (Numbers for other factories not available).

1933 Pontiac four-door sedan. JAC

Model No.	Body Type & Seating	Price	Weight	Prod. Total
ROAD	2-dr. Rds.-2/4P	585	2675	Note 1
33317	2-dr. Cpe.-2P	635	2865	Note 1
33328	2-dr. Spt. Cpe.-2/4P	670	2930	Note 1
33318	2-dr. Conv. Cpe.-2/4P	695	2905	Note 1
33301	2-dr. Sed.-5P	635	2945	Note 1
33331	2-dr. Tr. Sed-5P	675	2995	Note 1
33309	4-dr. Sed.-5P	695	3020	Note 1

Note 1: Body style breakouts not available. Series production total: 90,198 units.

1933 Pontiac roadster. OCW

ENGINE: Inline. L-head. Eight. Cast iron block. Bore & Stroke: 3-3/16 x 3-1/2 in. Displacement: 223.4 cu. in. Compression Ratio: 5.7:1. Brake hp: 77 @ 3600 rpm. N.A.C.C. hp: 32.52. Main bearings: Five. Valve lifters: Solid. Carb.: Carter one-barrel.

CHASSIS: Wheelbase: 115 in. Overall Length: 181.5 in. Height: 67-3/4 in. Tires: 17 x 5.50.

TECHNICAL: Muncie Synchromesh transmission. Speeds: 3F/1R. Floor shift. Single plate clutch. Torque tube drive. Semi-floating rear axle. Overall ratio: 4.44 1. Four-wheel mechanical brakes. K-H 40-spoke wire wheels. Rim Size: 17 x 3.62 in. Freewheeling standard.

OPTIONS: Front bumper. Rear bumper. Dual sidemounts. Sidemount cover(s). Bumper guards. Radio. Heater. Clock. Cigar lighter. Radio antenna (under runningboard). Spotlight. Disc wheels. Jumbo tires. Trunk rack. Touring trunk. Rear tire cover. Mud guards. Rear view mirror.

HISTORICAL: Entered production December 7, 1932. Closed production October 6, 1933. Individually controlled No-Draft ventilation system. Safety glass in windshield and vent windows. New, stronger frame. Twelve Flxible-Pontiac funeral cars built this year. Roadster reintroduced for one, final season. Model year production: 90,198 units. Late in the year the B-O-P program was dissolved and Harry J. Klinger was appointed Pontiac general manager.

1934

1934 Pontiac four-door touring sedan. AA

PONTIAC - SERIES 603 - EIGHT: Larger Fisher bodies were used for 1934. Deep skirted fenders were seen. Longer, bullet-shaped headlamp buckets appeared. The cowl ventilator opened towards the rear. Horizontal grille type hood louvers were new. Hoods were seven inches longer. Cars with standard equipment had hood ornaments with a brave's head in a circle on a teardrop base. Cars with Deluxe equipment had an Indian maiden hood ornament.

I.D. DATA: Serial numbers were in the previous locations. Pontiac, Mich., numbers were 83850 and up. Engine numbers were in the previous locations. Numbers were 987401 and up.

1934 Pontiac Sport coupe. JAC

Model No.	Body Type & Seating	Price	Weight	Prod. Total
34317	2-dr. Cpe.-2P	675	3185	Note 1
34328	2-dr. Spt. Cpe.-2/4P	725	3260	Note 1
34318	2-dr. Cabr.-2/4P	765	3225	Note 1
34301	2-dr. Sed.-5P	705	3280	Note 1
34331	2-dr. Tr. Sed.-5P	745	3300	Note 1
34309	4-dr. Sed.-5P	765	3350	Note 1
34319	4-dr- Tr. Sed.-5P	805	3405	Note 1

1934 Pontiac convertible cabriolet "Official Speedway" car. IMSC

1934 Pontiac cabriolet. OCW

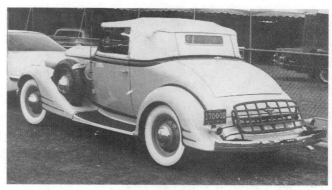

1934 Pontiac cabriolet. OCW

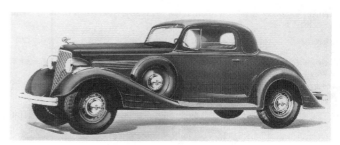

1934 Pontiac coupe. OCW

1934 Pontiac two-door sedan with trunk. OCW

1934 Pontiac Sport coupe. JAG

1934 Pontiac two-door sedan. OCW

1934 Miller-Meteor-Pontiac funeral car. JAG

Note 1: Body style breakouts not available. Series production was 78,859 units.

ENGINE: L-head. Inline. Eight. Cast iron block. Bore & Stroke: 3-3/16 x 3-1/2 in. Displacement: 223.4 cu. in. Compression Ratio: 6.2:1. Brake hp: 84 @ 3800 rpm. N.A.C.C. hp: 32.51. Main bearings: Five. Valve lifters: Solid. Carb.: Carter one-barrel.

CHASSIS: Wheelbase: 117-1/4 in. Overall Length: 187-1/4 in. Height: 68-7/16 in. Tires: 17 x 6.00.

TECHNICAL: Synchromesh transmission. Speeds: 3F/1R. Floor shift controls. Single plate clutch. Torque tube drive. Semi-floating rear axle. Overall ratio: 4.55: 1. Four-wheel mechanical brakes. Wire-spoke wheels.

OPTIONS: Front bumper. Dual sidemount. Sidemount cover(s). Bumper guards. Radio (Air Chief). Heater. Clock. Cigar lighter. Radio antenna. Seat covers. Spotlight. Touring trunk. Spare tire cover. Trunk rack. Standup sedan trunk. Trippe lights. Supertone horn. Right-hand sun visor. Ash receiver set. Right-hand taillamp. Luggage sets. Twin windshield wipers. License plate frame.

HISTORICAL: Production began January 1, 1934. 1934 Pontiac convertible was Indy 500 "Official Speedway" car. Stock Pontiac hit 93 mph at Muroc Dry Lake speed trial. Improved intake manifolding. "Knee-Action" front suspension introduced. Multi-beam headlights. Roomier bodies. New G.M.R. high-compression head. Gaselector added to distributor. Harry J. Klingler general manager. Gas mileage (in tests): 19-24 rnpg.

1935

1935 Pontiac two-door sedan. OCW

1935 Pontiac Eight Sport coupe. JAG

PONTIAC - STANDARD - SERIES 701-8 - SIX: Pontiacs came in Standard and Deluxe six and Improved eight car-lines this year. The Standard six models had transmissions with non-Synchromesh first gears, solid Ibeam front axles and headlamp beam indicators on the instrument dial. They did not have parking lamps on the front fenders. A single taillamp was standard and fenders only came with black finish. The year's new styling featured a waterfall grille and "Silver Streak" trim moldings on the hood. More rounded grille shells and fenders were seen. The hood ornament on sixes was a brave's head in a circle. The headlamps were mounted on pedestals between fenders and grilles.

I.D. DATA: Serial numbers on a plate or right side of frame center of right front wheel. Starting: P6AB-1001. Ending: P6AB-46752. Engine numbers in previous location. Starting Engine No.: 6-1001 and up.

1935 Pontiac Eight two-door sedan (top view). OCW

Model No.	Body Type & Seating	Price	Weight	Prod. Total
2107AB	2-dr. Cpe.-2P	615	3065	Note 1
2111AB	2-dr. Tr. Sed.-5P	695	3195	Note 1
2101AB	2-dr. Sed.-5P	665	3195	Note 1
2119AB	4-dr. Tr. Sed.-5P	745	3245	Note 1
2109AB	4-dr. Sed.-5P	715	3245	Note 1

Note 1: Body style breakouts not available. Series production: 49,302 units.

ENGINE: L-head. Inline. Six. Cast iron block. Bore & Stroke: 3-3.8 x 3-7/8 in. Displacement: 208 cu. in. Compression Ratio: Brake hp: 80 @ 3600 rpm. N.A.C.C. hp: 27.34. Main bearings: Four. Valve lifters: Solid. Carb.: Carter one-barrel (manual choke).

CHASSIS: Wheelbase: 112 in. Overall Length: 189 in. Tires: 16 x 6.00.

TECHNICAL: Manual transmission (non-synchromesh first). Speeds: 3F/1R. Floor shift controls. Single plate clutch. Torque tube drive. Semi-floating rear axle. Overall ratio: 4.44:1. Hydraulic brakes. Steel spoke wheels.

1935 Pontiac Six four-door sedan. JAC

PONTIAC - DELUXE - SERIES 701-A - SIX: The Deluxe sixes had the same wheelbase and engine as standard models. They had "Knee-Action" front suspension and all-Synchromesh transmissions. Multi-beam headlights were used. Streamlined parking lights sat atop front fenders. Single taillamps were regular equipment but dual taillamps were a common option. Styling changes were the same as standard models had.

I.D. DATA: Serial and engine number locations were the same as on the Standard six models. Starting serial no.: 6AA-100. Ending serial no.: 6AA-32,187. Engine nos.: 6-1001 and up.

1935 Pontiac Six cabriolet. OCW

Model No.	Body Type & Seating	Price	Weight	Prod. Total
2107AA	2-dr. Cpe.-2P	675	3125	Note 1
2157AA	2-dr. Spt. Cpe.-2/4P	725	3150	Note 1
2167AA	2-dr. Cabr.-2/4P	775	3180	Note 1
2111AA	2-dr. Tr. Sed.-5P	745	3245	Note 1
2101AA	2-dr. Sed.-5P	715	3245	Note 1
2119AA	4-dr. Tr. Sed.-5P	795	3300	Note 1
2109AA	4-dr. Sed.-5P	765	3300	Note 1

Note 1: Body style breakouts not available. Series production: 36,032 units.

1935 Pontiac Six cabriolet. JAG

ENGINE: L-head. Inline. Six. Cast iron block. Bore & Stroke: 3-3/8 x 3-7/8 in. Displacement: 208 cu. in. Compression Ratio: 6.2:1. Brake hp: 80 @ 3600 rpm. N.A.C.C. hp: 27.34. Main bearings: Four. Valve lifters: Solid. Carb.: Carter one-barrel (manual choke).

CHASSIS: Wheelbase: 112 in. Overall Length: 189 in. Tires: 16 x 6.00.

TECHNICAL: All-Synchromesh. Speeds: 3F/1R. Floor shift controls. Single plate clutch. Torque tube drive. Semi floating rear axle. Overall ratio: 4.44: 1. Hydraulic brakes. Wire-spoke wheels.

1935 Pontiac Six four-door touring sedan. OCW

1935 Pontiac Deluxe Six two-door sedan. JAG

PONTIAC - IMPROVED - SERIES 605 - EIGHT: The eight-cylinder Pontiac chassis had a 4-5/8 inch longer wheelbase. While the main body was identical to that used by sixes, the front end sheet metal was longer. Styling changes were the same as on other car-lines. An Indian maiden hood ornament was used. Dual taillights were standard equipment, along with twin windshield wipers and fender safety lamps. "Pontiac Eight" grille badges were used. The rear windows on four-door sedans and two-door touring sedans featured ventipanes.

I.D. DATA: Serial and engine number locations were as on Standard Six. Starting serial no.: 8AA-1001. Ending serial no.: 8AA-42561. Engine nos.: 8-1001 and up.

Model No.	Body Type & Seating	Price	Weight	Prod. Total
2007	2-dr. Cpe.-2P	730	3260	Note 1
2057	2-dr. Spt. Cpe.-2/4P	780	3290	Note 1
2067	2-dr. Cabr.-2/4P	840	3305	Note 1
2011	2-dr. Tr. Sed.-5P	805	3400	Note 1
2001	2-dr. Sed.-5P	775	3400	Note 1
2019	4-dr. Tr. Sed.-5P	860	3450	Note 1
2009	4-dr. Sed.-5P	830	3450	Note 1

Note 1: Body style breakouts not available. Series production: 44,134 units.

1935 Pontiac Eight Flxible funeral car. JAG

ENGINE: L-head. Inline. Eight. Cast iron block. Bore & Stroke: 3-3/16 x 3-1/2 in. Displacement: 223.4 cu. in. Compression Ratio: 6.2:1. Brake hp: 84 @ 3800 rpm. N.A.C.C. hp: 32.51. Main bearings: Five. Valve lifters: Solid. Carb.: Carter one-barrel.

CHASSIS: Wheelbase: 116-5/8 in. Overall Length: 193-5/8 in. Tires: 16 x 6.50.

TECHNICAL: All-Synchromesh. Speeds: 3F/1R. Floor shift controls. Dry plate clutch. Torque tube drive. Semi-floating rear axle. Overall ratio: 4.55: 1. Hydraulic brakes. Wire-spoke wheels.

OPTIONS: Antifreeze (3.15). Right-hand taillamp (3.45). Dual horn kit (12.50). Triplex air cleaner (6.50). Wheel disc (2.30). Five wheel discs (1.25). Five wheel trim rings (8.50). Four bumper guards (3.95). Outdraft heater (7.50). Deluxe heater (12.25). Heater ports pkg. (4.00). Air Chief radio (62.50). Air Mate radio (47.95). Radio antenna

pkg. (3.00). Glove box smoker set & watch (13.50). Dash watch (10.00). 30-hour mirror watch (3.95). Safety light (15.95). License frame (2.45). Luggage set (19.75). Rear mat (1.75). Visor vanity mirror (1.00). Right-hand inside visor (2.00). Dual sidemounts (not available on standard six).

HISTORICAL: Date of Introduction: December 29, 1934. Innovations: "Suicide" front door hinging. Hydraulic brakes. Micro polished engine bearings. Improved double-drop "KY" frame. Model year production: 129,463 units. Company president: Harry J. Klinger.

1936

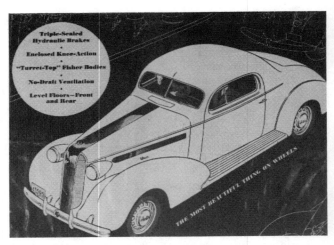

1936 Pontiac Deluxe Eight coupe. JAG

1936 Pontiac Eight four-door touring sedan. AA

MASTER - SERIES 6BB - SIX: The 1936 Pontiac had a new, waterfall grille with a thinner shell, fewer "silver streaks" and the outer sections finished in body color. The horizontal hood louvers came to a point at the front this year. Longer, slimmer headlamps were mounted on the sides of the hood. The fenders no longer had "speedlines" sculpted into them. The Master Six could most easily be identified by its solid front axle. It also had a non-locking glove box, taupe mohair or brown pattern broadcloth upholstery and black bakelite door handle and instrument panel hardware. Two-door sedans at first came only with bucket front seats, with a bench seat option introduced at mid-year, Standard equipment included Delco-Remy ignition, hydraulic brakes, cross-flow cooling and foot-operated starter buttons. Flush mounted taillights were used on some Master Sixes built early in the model year.

1936 Pontiac Deluxe Eight four-door sedan. JAG

I.D. DATA: [Series 6BB] Serial numbers were located on top of frame just ahead of steering gear. Starting: 6BB-1001. Ending: 6BB-91362. Pacific Coast numbers were C-1001 to C-1400. Bench seat cars had an "AB" prefix instead of "BB". Engine numbers located on left side of crankcase and on front left corner of cylinder block. Starting: 6-84001. Ending: 6-219182. [Series 6BA] Serial numbers were in the same location. Starting: 6BA-1001. Ending: 6BA-41352. Pacific Coast numbers were C-1001 to C-1300. Engine numbers were in the same location. Starting: 6-84001. Ending: 6-219182. [Series 8BA] Serial numbers were in the same location. Starting: 8BA-1001. Ending: 8BA-38371. Pacific Coast numbers were C-1001 to C-1260. Engine numbers were in the same locations. Starting: 8-44001. Ending: 8-82040.

1936 Pontiac Deluxe Eight cabriolet. JAG

DELUXE - SERIES 6BA - SIX: The Deluxe Six was virtually identical to the Master Six, except that it had "Knee Action" independent front suspension. Upholstery in closed cars was taupe mohair or modified tweed pattern taupe woolen cloth. Deluxe sixes also had translucent dash knobs and door handle knobs. Additional standard equipment in this series included a larger gas tank, higher capacity six-volt battery and automatic choke.

DELUXE - SERIES 8BA - EIGHT: The Pontiac Deluxe Eight had the company's longest wheelbase. The extra length was taken up in the hood and runningboards. Fenders varied slightly in the manner in which they overlapped the cowl, but were actually the same with the attachment holes drilled differently. The words "Pontiac 8" appeared on the grille and the hood ornament was a distinctive, circular design instead of the oblong loop style used on sixes. Standard sedan equipment included front and rear arm rests, twin assist straps, oriental grain interior moldings and a dash mounted clock. The eight had "Knee-Action" front suspension, a pressurized cooling system, automatic choke and a new type of clutch.

1936 Pontiac Six cabriolet. OCW

1936 Pontiac Master Six coupe. JAG

Model No.	Body Type & Seating	Price	Weight	Prod. Total
6BB	2-dr. Cpe.-2P	615	3085	Note 1
6BB	2-dr. Spt. Cpe.-2/4P	675	3120	Note 1
6BB	2-dr. Cabr.-2/4P	760	3125	Note 1
6BB	2-dr. Sed.-5P	675	3195	Note 1
6BB	2-dr. Tr. Sed.-5P	700	3195	Note 1
6BB	4-dr. Sed.-5P	720	3235	Note 1
6BB	4-dr. Tr. Sed.-5P	745	3245	Note 1

Note 1: Series production was 93,475.

6BA	2-dr. Cpe.-2P	665	3130	Note 1
6BA	2-dr. Spt. Cpe.-2/4P	720	3165	Note 1
6BA	2-dr. Cabr.-2/4P	810	3200	Note 1
6BA	2-dr. Sed.-5P	720	3265	Note 1
6BA	2-dr. Tr. Sed.-5P	745	3270	Note 1
6BA	4-dr. Sed.-5P	770	3300	Note 1
6BA	4-dr. Tr. Sed.-5P	795	3300	Note 1

Note 1: Total series production was 44,040.

8BA	2-dr. Cpe.-2P	730	3250	Note 1
8BA	2-dr. Spt. Cpe.-2/4P	785	3285	Note 1
8BA	2-dr. Cabr.-2/4P	855	3335	Note 1
8BA	2-dr. Sed.-5P	770	3390	Note 1
8BA	2-dr. Tr. Sed.-5P	795	3390	Note 1
8BA	4-dr. Sed.-5P	815	3415	Note 1
8BA	4-dr. Tr. Sed.-5P	840	3420	Note 1

Note 1: Total series production was 38,755.

1936 Pontiac Eight two-door sedan. HAC

ENGINE: [Series 6BB] Inline. L-head. Six. Cast iron block. Bore & Stroke: 3-3/8 in. x 3-7/8 in. Displacement: 208 cu. in. Compression Ratio: 6.2:1. Brake hp: 81 @ 3600 rpm. Net hp: 27.34. Main bearings: Four. Valve litters: Solid. Carb.: Carter one-barrel model 340S. [Series 6BA] Inline. L-head. Six. Cast iron block. Bore & Stroke: 3-3/8 in. x 3-7/8 in. Displacement: 208 cu. in. Compression Ratio: 6.2: 1. Brake hp: 81 @ 3600 rpm. Net hp: 27.34. Main bearings: Four. Valve lifters: Solid. Carb.: Carter one-barrel model 342S. [Series 8BA] Inline. L-head. Eight. Cast iron block. Bore & Stroke: 3-1/4 in. x 3-1/2 in. Displacement: 232.3 cu. in. Compression Ratio: 6.5:1. Brake hp: 87 @ 3800 rpm. Net hp: 33.8. Main bearings: Five. Valve lifters: Solid. Carb.: Carter one-barrel model 322S.

CHASSIS: [Series 6BB] Wheelbase: 112 in. Overall Length: 189-3/4 in. Height: 67-9/16 in. Tires: 16 x 6.00. [Series 6AB] Wheelbase: 112 in. Overall Length: 189-3/4 in. Height: 67-9/16 in. Tires: 16 x 6.00. [Series 8AB] Wheelbase: 116-5/8 in. Overall Length: 194-5/16 in. Height: 67-9/16 in. Tires: 16 x 6.50.

TECHNICAL: Manual synchromesh transmission. Speeds: 3F/1R. Floor mounted controls. Ventilated dry disc clutch. Semi-floating rear axle. Overall Ratio: (std.) 4.55:1; (mountain) 4.85:1; (plains) 4.11:1. Four-wheel hydraulic brakes. Steel spoke wheels.

OPTIONS: Front bumper. Rear bumper. Dual sidemount. Sidemount cover(s). Fender skirts. Set of four bumper guards (3.95). Air Chief Radio (62.50). Air Mate Radio (47.95). Outdraft heater (7.50). Deluxe heater (12.25). Clock (10.00). Cigar lighter (1.50). Radio antenna package (3.00). Seat covers (Santoy). Spotlight(s). R.H. taillight (3.45). Dual horn kit (12.50). Triplex air cleaner (6.50). Set of five wire wheel discs (11.25). Set of five wheel trim rings (8.50). Glove compartment smoker set and clock (13.50). Pull-wind clock (3.95). Safety light (15.95). License frame set (2.45). Luggage set (19.75). R.H. inside visor (2.00).

1936 Superior-Pontiac six-cylinder funeral car. JAG

HISTORICAL: Introduced: September 25, 1935. Innovations: Larger bore eight. Improved clutch. Improved cooling system on eight. New front suspension with King pins mounted in floating bronze bearings. Automatic choke on deluxe models. Model year production: 176,270. The president of Pontiac was Harry Klingler. Pontiac held sixth rank in U.S. auto sales for 1936. The new models were called "The Most Beautiful Thing on Wheels."

1937

1937 Pontiac convertible sedan. OCW

PONTIAC - DELUXE - SERIES 26 - SIX: The 1937 Pontiacs had longer, one-piece solid bodies with Turret tops. The hoodline was higher and the radiator grille was narrower. Silver Streak moldings ran down the center of the hood and over the grille in waterfall fashion. The side grilles had chrome horizontal bars grouped into four lower segments and a narrower upper segment that continued down the sides of the hood. New, one-piece front fenders with a split-pear shape were used. Longer headlamp buckets were mounted on pedestals attached to the fender catwalks. A wider windshield with a rakish 39-degree slant gave a more modern appearance. The six-cylinder hood ornament was a flat, solid Indian head.

I.D. DATA: Serial numbers on top of frame ahead of steering gear (visible upon raising hood). Starting: 6CA-1001. Ending: 6CA-154827 (Pontiac, Mich.). Cars built at Southgate, Calif., had serial number prefix "C". Cars built at Linden, N.J., had prefix "L". Engine numbers on front left corner of block. Starting: 6-220001. Ending: 6-399286.

1937 Pontiac convertible sedan (top up, rear view). OCW

1937 Pontiac convertible sedan (top down, rear view). OCW

Model No.	Body Type & Seating	Price	Weight	Prod. Total
2627B	2-dr. Cpe.-2P	781	3165	Note 1
2627	2-dr. Spt. Cpe.2/4P	853	3165	Note 1
2667	2-dr. Cabr.-2/4P	945	3250	Note 1
2601	2-dr. Sed.-5P	830	3240	Note 1
2611	2-dr. Tr. Sed.-5P	855	3240	Note 1
2609	4-dr. Sed.-5P	881	3265	Note 1
2619	4-dr. Tr. Sed.-5P	906	3275	Note 1
2649	4-dr. Conv. Sed.-5P	1197	3375	Note 1
STAWAG	4-dr. Sta. Wag.-7P	992	3340	Note 1

Note 1: Body style breakouts not available. Series production total was 179,244 cars.

ENGINE: L-head. Inline. Six. Cast iron block. Bore & Stroke: 3-7/16 x 4. Displacement: 222.7 cu. in. Compression Ratio: 6.2:1. Brake hp: 85 @ 3520 rpm. N.A.C.C. hp: 28.3. Main bearings: Four. Valve lifters: Solid. Carb.: Carter one-barrel.

CHASSIS: Wheelbase: 117 in. Overall Length: 193.06 in. Height: 67 in. Tires: 16 x 6.00.

TECHNICAL: Synchromesh transmission. Speeds: 3F/1R. Floor shift controls. Dry disc clutch. Hotchkiss drive. Semi-floating axle. Overall ratio: 4.37:1. Four-wheel hydraulic brakes. Steel disc wheels.

1937 Pontiac four-door touring sedan. HAC

PONTIAC - DELUXE - SERIES 28 - EIGHT: Pontiac Eights were longer cars. They had longer hoods and fenders. Styling was similar to the Pontiac Sixes. The winged nose badge and trunk emblem said Pontiac Eight. The hood ornament was a flat brave's head that projected above the hood moldings and served as a hood latch handle.

I.D. DATA: Serial numbers on top of frame ahead of steering gear. Starting: 8CA-1001. Ending: 8CA-49442. California cars had a "C" prefix. New Jersey cars had an "L" prefix. Engine numbers on front left corner of block. Starting: 8-830001. Ending: 8-139968.

Model No.	Body Type & Seating	Price	Weight	Prod. Total
2827B	2-dr. Cpe.-2P	857	3305	Note 1
2827	2-dr. Spt. Cpe.-2/4P	913	3305	Note 1
2867	2-dr. Cabr.-2/4P	985	3360	Note 1
2801	2-dr. Sed.-5P	893	3385	Note 1
2811	2-dr. Tr. Sed.-5P	919	3380	Note 1
2809	4-dr. Sed.-5P	939	3410	Note 1
2819	4-dr. Tr. Sed.-5P	965	3400	Note 1
2849	4-dr. Conv. Sed.-5P	1235	3505	Note 1

Note 1: Body style breakouts not available. Series production total was 56,945 cars.

1937 Pontiac coupe. OCW

1937 Pontiac Deluxe Six cabriolet. OCW

1937 Pontiac four-door touring sedan. JAG

1937 Miller-Pontiac limousine funeral car. JAG

ENGINE: L-head. Inline. Eight. Cast iron block. Bore & Stroke: 3-1/4 x 3-3/4. Displacement: 248.9 cu. in. Compression Ratio: 6.2:1. Brake hp: 100 @ 3800 rpm. N.A.C.C. hp: 33.8. Main bearings: Five. Valve lifters: Solid. Carb.: Carter one-barrel.

CHASSIS: Wheelbase: 122 in. Overall Length 198.06 in. Height: 67 in. Tires: 16 x 6.50.

TECHNICAL: Drivetrain: Same as Pontiac Six.

OPTIONS: Deluxe radio. Master radio. Deluxe heater. Master heater. Runningboard antennas (dual). Antifreeze. Tenite shift ball. Commercial pickup box (coupes). Locking gas cap. Tour top luggage carrier. Santoy seat covers. Electric dash clock. Pull wind headboard clock. Battery charger. Wheel discs. Dual safety defroster. Electric fan defroster. Electric windshield defroster. Tailpipe extension. License frames. Master guard. License jewel unit. Fog lamp. R.H. taillamp. Safety light. Cigar lighter. Fender marker. Luggage mat. Wheel moldings. Rain deflector. Peep mirror. OSRV. Visor mirror. Fuel pump vacuum booster. Ash receiver. Rear luggage compartment strap. Insect screen. Frost shields. R.H. sun visor. Flexible steering wheel. Sidemount tires. Metal sidemount tire covers. Three-passenger gearshift lever. Oil bath air cleaner.

HISTORICAL: Introduced: November 1936. All-steel bodies. First Pontiac station wagon. New 19:1 steering gear ratio. Larger GM B-bodies. Stronger X-member frames. Two-piece propellor shaft. Hotchkiss drive reintroduced. Calendar year production: 235,322. Model year production: 236,189. Company manager: Harry J. Klingler. Advertised as "America's finest low-priced car." Pontiac claimed its products cost only 15 cents more per day to own than low-priced models. Best sales year in Pontiac history to date.

1937 Superior-Pontiac Guardian ambulance, Deluxe Six chassis. JAG

1937 Superior-Pontiac Rosehill service car, Deluxe Six chassis. JAG

1937 Superior-Pontiac Deluxe Eight Graceland funeral car. JAG

1937 Superior-Pontiac Oakridge funeral car, Deluxe Six chassis. JAG

1938

1938 Pontiac Six station wagon. AA

DELUXE - SERIES 26 - SIX: The 1938 Pontiac used the same body as previous models. Wide, horizontal bars characterized the new grille design, On sixes there was a "6" emblem at bottom center. Chrome ribs ran along the top of the hood and down the center of the radiator grille. There were vertical hood louvers with the Pontiac name between chrome bars near the radiator on the Six. The six-cylinder hood ornament was a long, low Indian head.

I.D. DATA: Serial numbers on top of frame ahead of steering gear (visible upon raising hood), Starting: 6DA-1616 or C-60A-1001. Ending: 6DA60416 or C-6DA-1615 (Pontiac, Mich.) Cars built at Southgate, Calif., were numbered C6DA-2001 to C6DA-8155. Cars built at Linden, N.J., had an "L" prefix. Engine numbers on front left corner of block. Starting: 6-399501. Ending: 6-486022.

1938 Pontiac Deluxe Six station wagon . JAG

Model No.	Body Type & Seating	Price	Weight	Prod. Total
2627B	2-dr. Cpe.-2P	835	3190	Note 1
2627	2-dr. Spt. Cpe.-2/4P	891	3200	Note 1
2667	2-dr. Cabr.-2/4P	993	3285	Note 1
2601	2-dr. Sed.-5P	865	3265	Note 1
2611	2-dr. Tr. Sed.-5P	891	3265	Note 1
2609	4-dr. Sed.-5P	916	3295	Note 1
2619	4-dr. Tr. Sed.-5P	942	3280	Note 1
2649	4-dr. Conv. Sed.-5P	1310	3410	Note 1
STA WAG	4-dr. Sta. Wag.-7P	1110	3420	Note 1

Note 1: No body style breakouts. Series production total was 77,713 cars.

ENGINE: L-head. Inline. Six. Cast iron block. Bore & Stroke: 3-7/16 x 4. Displacement: 222.7 cu. in. Compression Ratio: 6.2:1. Brake hp: 85 @ 3520 rpm. N.A.C.C. hp: 28.3. Main bearings: Four. Valve lifters: Solid. Carb.: Carter one-barrel.

CHASSIS: Wheelbase: 117 in. Overall Length: 192 in. Height: 67 in. Tires: 16 x 6.00.

TECHNICAL: Synchromesh transmission. Speeds: 3F/IR. Floor shift controls (standard). Dry disc clutch. Hotchkiss Drive. Semi-floating rear axle. Overall ratio: 4.37:1. Four wheel hydraulic brakes. Steel disc wheels. Column gearshift $10 extra.

35

1938 Pontiac two-door sedan. JAG

PONTIAC - DELUXE - SERIES 28 - EIGHT: Pontiac Eight again had slightly longer front end sheet metal. Styling was similar to the Pontiac Six. Emblem at bottom center of grille bore "8" designation. Trunk emblem read Pontiac Eight. Louvers on the side of the hood had an extra chrome bar in middle and no Pontiac name. Eight-cylinder hood ornament was a short Indian head with fin-like feathers.

1938 Pontiac two-door sedan. JAG

I.D. DATA: Serial numbers on top of frame ahead of steering gear. Starting: 8DA-1001. Ending: 8DA-15729. California cars had a "C" prefix. New Jersey cars had an "L" prefix. Engine numbers on front left corner of block. Starting: 8-140001. Ending: 8-159441.

1938 Pontiac Eight four-door touring sedan. JAC

Model No.	Body Type & Seating	Price	Weight	Prod. Total
2827B	2-dr. Cpe.-2P	898	3320	Note 1
2827	2-dr. Spt. Cpe.-2/4P	955	3325	Note 1
2867	2-dr. Cabr.-2/4P	1057	3390	Note 1
2801	2-dr. Sed.-5P	934	3395	Note 1
2811	2-dr. Tr. Sed.-5P	960	3385	Note 1
2809	4-dr. Sed.-5P	980	3415	Note 1
2819	4-dr. Tr. Sed.-5P	1006	3410	Note 1
2849	4-dr. Conv. Sed.-5P	1353	3530	Note 1

Note 1: No body style breakouts. Total series production was 97,139 cars.

1938 Pontiac Deluxe Eight four-door touring sedan. JAG

1938 Pontiac cabriolet. JAG

1938 Pontiac four-door convertible sedan: Deluxe Six (top) and Deluxe Eight (bottom). JAG

1938 Pontiac Deluxe Six coupe. JAG

1938 Superior-Pontiac funeral car with carved sides. JAG

ENGINE- :L-head. Inline. Eight. Cast iron block. Bore & Stroke: 3-1/4 x 3-3/4. Displacement: 248.9 cu. in. Compression Ratio: 6.2:1. Brake hp: 100 @ 3700 rpm. N.A.C.C. hp: 33.8. Main bearings: Five. Valve lifters: Solid. Carb.: Carter: one-barrel.

CHASSIS: Wheelbase: 122 in. Overall Length: 196.63 in. Height: 67 in. Tires: 16 x 6.50.

TECHNICAL: Drivetrain: Same as Pontiac Six.

OPTIONS: Deluxe radio (58.25). Master radio (44.70). Dual runningboard antenna (5.25). Overhead antenna (5.25). Deluxe heater (17.95). Master heater (12.75). Defroster (7.90). Tenite shift ball (.50). Commercial pickup box (25.00). Seat covers (set): front (5.95); front & rear (10.95). Battery charger (8.50). Dash electric clock (11.65). Header board windup clock (4.00). Single wheel disc (2.30). Electric windshield defroster (3.00). Tailpipe extension (1.00). Pair, license frames (2.45). Front master guard (2.25). Rear master guard (3.90). Dual horns (10.95). Jewel license unit (4.68). Fog lamp (5.00). R.H. taillamp (4.95). Cigar lighter (2.25). Fender marker (1.25). Rear mats in sedan (2.25); in coupes (3.75). Peep mirror (1.50). Visor mirror (1.00). Rear view mirror (2.95). Wheel molding (1.58). Fuel pump vacuum booster (12.00). Ash receiver (1.25). Single sun visor (2.40). Flexible steering wheel (1.50). Sidemounts (price n.a.).

HISTORICAL: Introduced: October 1937. Improved transmission synchronizers. Quieter gear shift yoke design. Toggle action helper spring added to clutch. Larger generator. Larger water pump with ball bearings. Battery moved under hood. Improved front suspension. Calendar year production: 95,128. Model year production: 97,139. The president of Pontiac was Harry J. Klingler. Advertised as a "better looking, better built, better buy." Factory delivery program.

1939

1939 Pontiac Six four-door touring sedan. AA

PONTIAC - QUALITY 115 - SERIES 25 - SIX: The 1939 Pontiac Quality Six was a new type of economy class model. It employed the Chevrolet A-body shell with Pontiac front end sheet metal, making it a small car with a big car look. All 1939 Pontiacs had a new, streamlined appearance. The thin, rounded nose was brightened by Silver Streak moldings running to the bumper line. There were four groups of four horizontal, louver type grille bars on either side of the Silver Streaks. Each lower group of louvers were shorter. Separate, twin side grilles had multiple vertical bars over high front fender splash aprons. The headlights rested directly on the front fender catwalks. Horizontal louvers were placed on the hood sides near the cowl. The Quality Six came only with conventional runningboards.

1939 Pontiac Deluxe Six convertible. OCW

1939 Pontiac Deluxe Six coupe. OCW

I.D. DATA: Serial numbers on front cross-member behind radiator. Starting: P6EA-1001. Ending: P6EA-43679 (Pontiac, Mich.) Cars built at Southgate, Calif., had a "C" prefix. Cars built in Linden, N.J., had an "L" prefix. Engine numbers on front left corner of block. Starting: 6-486201. Ending: 6-595763.

Model No.	Body Type & Seating	Price	Weight	Prod. Total
2527B	2-dr. Cpe.-3P	758	2875	Note 1
2527	2-dr. Spt. Cpe.-5P	809	2920	Note 1
2511	2-dr. Tr. Sed.-5P	820	2965	Note 1
2519	4-dr. Tr. Sed.-6P	866	3000	Note 1
STA WAG	4-dr. Sta. Wag.-8P	990	3175	Note 1

Note 1: No body style breakouts. Total series production was 55,736 cars.

1939 Pontiac station wagon. OCW

1939 Pontiac Deluxe Eight two-door sedan touring (prototype). OCW

ENGINE: L-head. Inline. Six. Cast iron block. Bore & Stroke: 3-7/16 x 4. Displacement: 222.7 cu. in. Compression Ratio: 6.2:1. Brake hp: 85 @ 3520 rpm. N.A.C.C. hp: 28.3. Main bearings: Four. Valve lifters: Solid. Carb.: Carter one-barrel.

CHASSIS: Wheelbase: 115 in. Overall Length: 190 in. Tires: 16 x 6.00.

TECHNICAL: Synchromesh transmission. Speeds: 3F/IR. Column gear shift controls. Dry disc clutch. Hotchkiss drive. Semi-floating rear axle. Overall ratio: 4.1:1. Four-wheel hydraulic brakes. Steel disc wheels.

1939 Pontiac coupe. OCW

PONTIAC - DELUXE 120 - SERIES 26 - SIX: The 1939 Pontiac Deluxe Six models used the larger GM A-body. They were longer and wider, but lower than Quality Six models. Front end styling changes were similar for both lines. The Deluxe bodies had larger windshields, wider back windows, V-shaped window openings and bright metal beltline trim. They could be ordered with conventional runningboards or streamlined "body skirts."

I.D. DATA: Serial numbers on front cross-member behind radiator. Starting: P6EB-1001. Ending: P6EB-41263 (Pontiac, Mich.) California cars had a "C" prefix. New Jersey cars had an "L" prefix. Engine numbers on front left corner of block. Starting: 6-486201. Ending: 6-595763.

Model No.	Body Type & Seating	Price	Weight	Prod. Total
2627B	2-dr. Cpe.-3P	814	3020	Note 1
2627	2-dr. Spt. Cpe.-5P	865	3055	Note 1
2667	2-dr. Conv. Cpe.-5P	993	3155	Note 1
2611	2-dr. Tr. Sed.-6P	871	3115	Note 1
2619	4-dr. Tr. Sed.-6P	922	3165	Note 1

Note 1: No body style breakouts. Total series production was 53,830 cars.

ENGINE: Same as Quality Six engine.

CHASSIS: Wheelbase: 120 in. Overall Length: 196.25 in. Tires: 16 x 6.00.

TECHNICAL: Drivetrain same as Quality Six except overall gear ratio is 4.3:1.

1939 Pontiac Deluxe Eight Sport coupe. JAC

PONTIAC - SERIES 28 - EIGHT - The 1939 Pontiac Deluxe Eight models used the same body as the Deluxe "120" six models. The Indian head hood ornaments on eight-cylinder cars had a fin-like feather design, compared to the straight-back feather design used on six-cylinder models. A "Pontiac Eight" emblem was affixed to the cars' rear decks. There was also a fancier trim plate around the circular badge on the front bumper.

I.D. DATA: Serial numbers on front cross-member behind radiator. Starting: P8EA-1001. Ending: P8EA-27627 (Pontiac, Mich.). California cars had a "C" prefix. New Jersey cars had an "L" prefix. Engine numbers on front left corner of block. Starting: 8-159601. Ending: 8-194380.

1939 Pontiac Sport coupe. JAG

Model No.	Body Type & Seating	Price	Weight	Prod. Total
2827B	2-dr. Cpe.-3P	862	3115	Note 1
2827	2-dr. Spt. Cpe.-5P	912	3165	Note 1
2867	2-dr. Conv. Cpe.-5P	1046	3250	Note 1
2811	2-dr. Tr. Sed.-5P	919	3225	Note 1
2819	4-dr. Tr. Sed.-5P	970	3265	Note 1

Note 1: No body style breakouts. Total series production was 34,774 cars.

1939 Pontiac Sport coupe. JAG

ENGINE: L-head. Inline. Eight. Cast iron block. Bore & Stroke: 3-1/4 x 3-3/4. Displacement: 248.9 cu. in. Compression Ratio: 6.2:1. Brake hp: 100 @ 3700 rpm. N.A.C.C. hp: 33.8. Main bearings: Five. Valve lifters: Solid. Carb.: Carter one-barrel.

CHASSIS: Wheelbase: 120 in. Overall Length: 196.25 in. Tires: 16 x 6.50.

TECHNICAL: Drivetrain same as Deluxe Six.

OPTIONS: Master radio (Quality Six only). Deluxe radio. Dual horns. R.H. taillight. Fender skirts. Bumper guards. Constant-action wiper pump. Deluxe heater. Electric clock. Wind-up clock. Cigar lighter. Master cowl antenna. Runningboard antenna. Seat covers. Whitewall tires. Spotlight. Exhaust deflector. License plate frame. Weather Chief heater and defroster. Special runningboard. Flexible steering wheel. Ash receiver. Wheel covers. Wheel trim moldings. Oil bath air cleaner. Oil filter. Fog lamps. Sunshine roof.

HISTORICAL: Introduced October 1938. Redesigned clutch. Variable rate Duflex springs. Revised transmission. Improved long-life muffler. Column-mounted Safety Gearshift standardized. Three-passenger front seating. No-Rol device optional. Calendar year registrations: 212,403, Calendar year production: 170,726. Model year production: 144,340. The president of Pontiac was Harry J. Klingler. Advertised as "America's Finest Low-Priced Car." A "see through" 1939 Pontiac Deluxe Six four-door touring sedan with plexiglass body panels was built for exhibition at the 1939 New York World's Fair.

1940

1940 Pontiac four-door touring sedan. OCW

PONTIAC - SPECIAL - SERIES 25 - SIX: Characteristics of 1940 Pontiacs included larger and more streamlined bodies; more massive front fenders with built-in headlight fairings; lower floors and "alligator" type hoods trimmed with three sets of slanting louvers. The 1940 grilles had horizontal bars, arranged in top point formation. The grilles were placed on either side of the "Silver Streak" center rail that carried a Pontiac nameplate and chevron emblem below. The Special Six models employed the small GM A-body. Distinguishing styling characteristics of the series included six-window four-door sedans; exposed lower front door hinges; Key hole-type door handles and gas filler caps on the right rear fenders. They came only with conventional runningboards. The six-cylinder hood ornament was a chrome plated, solid Indian head that also served as a hood latch mechanism. The Special Six had a more rounded rear deck. The Special Six station wagon came standard with a single, side-mounted spare tire.

I.D. DATA: Serial numbers on front cross-member behind radiator. Starting: P6HA-1001. Ending: P6HA-84545 (Pontiac, Mich.) Cars built in Southgate, Calif., had a "C" prefix. Cars built in Linden, N.J., had an "L" prefix. Engine numbers on front left corner of block. Starting: 6-595801. Ending: 6-761162.

Model No.	Body Type & Seating	Price	Weight	Prod. Total
2527B	2-dr. Cpe.-3P	783	3060	Note 1
2527	2-dr. Spt. Cpe.-4P	819	3045	Note 1
2511	2-dr. Tr. Sed.-5P	830	3095	Note 1
2519	4-dr. Tr. Sed.-5P	876	3125	Note 1
STA WAG	4-dr. Sta. Wag.-8P	1015	3295	Note 1

Note 1: No body style breakouts. Total series production was 106,892 cars.

1940 Pontiac cabriolet. JAC

ENGINE: L-head. Inline. Six. Cast iron block. Bore & Stroke: 3-7/16 x 4. Displacement: 222.7 cu. in. Compression Ratio: 6.5:1. Brake hp: 100 @ 3700 rpm. N.A.C.C. hp: 28.3. Main bearings: Four. Valve lifters: Solid. Carb.: Carter one-barrel.

CHASSIS: Wheelbase: 116.5 in. Overall Length: 198.75 in. Height: 66.75 in. Front tread: 58 in. Rear tread: 59 in. Tires: 16 x 6.00.

ENGINE: Synchromesh transmission. Speeds: 3F/IR. Steering column gearshift. Inland single disc clutch. Hotchkiss drive. Semi-floating rear axle. Overall ratio: 4.3:1. Duo-servo hydraulic. Duo-servo four-wheel hydraulic brakes. Steel disc wheels. Rim size: 4.5 in. Drivetrain options: Hill-Holder.

PONTIAC - DELUXE - SERIES 26 - SIX: Deluxe Six models used the larger GM B-body. Front sheet metal styling was the same as for the Special Six models. Concealed hinges were used in all places except lower front doors. The door handles had weather sealed keyholes. Gas filler doors were on the left rear fenders. Buyers could order optional body skirts in place of conventional runningboards. The hood ornament was the same used on Special Six models. Deluxe Sixes had a squared-off rear deck.

I.D. DATA: Serial numbers on front cross-member behind radiator. Starting: P6HB-1001. Ending: P6HB-44296 (Pontiac, Mich.) California cars had a "C" prefix. New Jersey cars had an "L" prefix. Engine numbers on front left corner of block. Starting: 6-595801. Ending: 6-761162.

1940 Pontiac two-door touring sedan. OCW

Model No.	Body Type & Seating	Price	Weight	Prod. Total
2627B	2-dr. Cpe.-3P	835	3115	Note 1
2627	2-dr. Spt. Cpe.-4P	876	3105	Note 1
2667	2-dr. Cabr.-4P	1003	3190	Note 1
2611	2-dr. Tr. Sed.-5P	881	3170	Note 1
2619	4-dr. Tr. Sed.-5P	932	3210	Note 1

Note 1: No body style breakouts. Total series production was 58,452 cars.

ENGINE: Same as Special Six engine.

CHASSIS: Wheelbase: 120.25 in. Overall Length: 199.75 in. Height: 66 in. Front tread: 58 in. Rear tread: 59 in. Tires: 6.00 x 16.

TECHNICAL: Drivetrain same as Special Six.

1940 Pontiac Torpedo four-door sedan. AA

1940 Pontiac Torpedo four-door sedan. OCW

1940 Pontiac station wagon. OCW

PONTIAC - DELUXE - SERIES 28 - EIGHT: The Deluxe Eight models used the same bodies as Deluxe Six models. An "8" emblem was affixed to the front chevron-shaped trim plate. A Pontiac Eight nameplate was on the rear deck. The eight-cylinder hood ornament had a plastic Indian head mounted in a metal base.

I.D. DATA: Serial numbers on front cross-member behind radiator. Starting: P8HA-1001. Ending: P8HA-16817 (Pontiac, Mich.). California cars had a "C" prefix. New Jersey cars had an "L" prefix. Engine numbers on front left corner of block. Starting: 8-194401. Ending: 8-246073.

1940 Pontiac coupe (prototype). OCW

1940 Pontiac Deluxe Six coupe (prototype). JAG

Model No.	Body Type & Seating	Price	Weight	Prod. Total
2827B	2-dr. Cpe.-3P	875	3180	Note 1
2827	2-dr. Spt. Cpe.-4P	913	3195	Note 1
2867	2-dr. Cabr.-4P	1046	3280	Note 1
2811	2-dr. Tr. Sed.-5P	919	3250	Note 1
2819	4-dr. Tr. Sed.-5P	970	3300	Note 1

Note 1: No body style breakouts. Total series production was 20,433 cars.

ENGINE: L-head. Inline. Eight. Cast iron block. Bore & Stroke: 3-1/4 in. x 3-3/4 in. Displacement: 248.9 cu. in. Compression Ratio: 6.5:1. Brake hp: 100 @ 3700 rpm. N.A.C.C. hp: 33.8. Main bearings: Five. Valve lifters: Solid. Carb.: Carter one-barrel. Torque: 175 lb.-ft. @ 1600 rpm.

CHASSIS: Wheelbase: 120.25 in. Overall Length: 200 in. Height: 66-3/8 in. Front tread: 58 in. Rear tread: 59 in. Tires: 16 x 6.50.

TECHNICAL: Drivetrain same as Deluxe Six specifications.

PONTIAC - TORPEDO - SERIES 29 - EIGHT: New this year was the Torpedo Eight using the extra-large GM C-body. These cars had larger windows, wider seats, front and rear ventipanes on four-door sedans and long, gracefully streamlined rear decks. Concealed hinges were used on all doors. The doors were extra-wide. The hood ornament was the same as on Deluxe eights. Front end sheet metal looked like that on other Pontiacs. Eight-cylinder badges were used front and rear. The door locks had weather sealed keyholes. Gas filler tubes were enclosed under "flip-up" lids on the left rear fenders. The window openings were trimmed with bright metal moldings.

I.D. DATA: Serial numbers on front cross-member behind radiator. Starting: P8HB-1001. Ending: P8HB-24376. (Pontiac, Mich.), California cars had a "C" prefix. New Jersey cars had an "L" prefix. Engine numbers on front left corner of block. Starting: 8-194401. Ending: 8-246073.

1940 Pontiac Special four-door touring sedan. JAG

Model No.	Body Type & Seating	Price	Weight	Prod. Total
2927C	2-dr. Spt. Cpe.-4P	1016	3390	Note 1
2919	4-dr. Tr. Sed.-5P	1072	3475	Note 1

Note 1: No body style breakouts. Total series production was 31,224 cars.

ENGINE: L-head. Inline. Eight. Cast iron block. Bore & Stroke: 3-1/4 in. x 3-3/4 in. Displacement: 248.9 cu. in. Compression Ratio: 6.5:1. Brake hp: 103 @ 3700 rpm. N.A.C.C. hp: 33.8. Main bearings: Five. Valve lifters: Solid. Carb.: Carter two-barrel. Torque: 175 lb.-ft. @ 1600 rpm.

CHASSIS: Wheelbase: 121-1/2 in. Overall Length: 207-1/2 in. Height: 65 in. Front tread: 58 in. Rear tread: 59 in. Tires: 16 x 6.50.

TECHNICAL: Drivetrain same as Deluxe Six.

OPTIONS: Vacuum booster fuel pump. Cigar lighter. Electric clock. Deluxe six-tube electric tuning radio. Automatic tuning six-tube radio. Automatic tuning five-tube radio. Portable radio. Master dash heater. Weather Chief dash heater. Auto furnace. Defroster. Fresh air intake. Deluxe steering wheel. White sidewall tire. Glove box light. Trunk light. Directional signals. Vacuum radio antenna. Master grille guards. Fender skirts. Body skirts (except Special Sixes). Wheel discs. Wheel trim rings. Rear view mirror. Cowl antenna.

1940 Pontiac Sport coupe. JAG

1940 Superior-Pontiac limousine coach. JAG

HISTORICAL: Introduced: August 1939. Center armrest in Torpedo sedan. Sealed beam headlights. Safety roll front seat backs. New anti-skid tires. Improved Safety Shift gear control. Tilting and adjustable front seats. New, high-compression cylinder head. New gasoline filter. Calendar year production: 249,303. Calendar year registrations: 235,815. Model year production: 217,001. The president of Pontiac was H.J. Klingler. A plexiglass bodied "see through" Pontiac appeared at the New York World's Fair again. This may have been a new show car, or the 1939 model with a new front end. The "see through" Pontiac survives today in the collection of an Indiana hobbyist.

1941

1941 Pontiac Torpedo four-door sedan. AA

PONTIAC - DELUXE TORPEDO - JA LINE - SIX/EIGHT: A wide grille with horizontal bars was used on 1941 Pontiacs. The parking lights were built into the grille. Headlamps were fully recessed into the new, wider fenders. Speed-line ribbing was molded into the sides of both front and rear fenders. Deluxe Sixes were in Series 25. Deluxe Eights were in Series 27. The sixes had shorter hood ornaments, a "6" badge on the hood and Pontiac lettering on the side. The eights had larger hood ornaments, an "8" badge on the hood and Pontiac Eight lettering on the side. All 1941 Pontiacs were nicknamed "Torpedos." Deluxe Torpedos used the small GM A-body shell with notchback styling. Streamlined body skirts replaced conventional runningboards on all models. The Metropolitan Sedan had four-window styling and was added to the line at mid-year.

I.D. DATA: Serial numbers on left side of dash. Starting: [Six] P6JA-1001/[Eight] P8JA-1001. Ending: [Six] P6JA-80460/[Eight] P8JA-27219. These codes apply to cars built at Pontiac, Mich. Cars built at Southgate, Calif., had a "C" prefix. Cars built at Linden, N.J., had an "L" prefix. Engine numbers on front left corner of block. Starting: [Six] 6-761501/[Eight] 8-246501. Ending: [Six] 6-971768/[Eight] 8-368240.

1941 Pontiac Custom Eight Torpedo station wagon . OCW

1941 Pontiac Custom Eight Torpedo station wagon. OCW

Model No.	Body Type & Seating	Price	Weight	Prod. Total
SERIES 25 (Deluxe Six)				
2527B	2-dr. Bus. Cpe.-3P	828	3145	Note 1
2527	2-dr. Sed. Cpe.-5P	864	3180	Note 1
2567	2-dr. Conv. Cpe.-5P	1023	3335	Note 1
2511	2-dr. Sed.-5P	874	3190	Note 1
2519	4-dr. Sed.-5P	921	3235	Note 1
2569	4-dr. Metro. Sed.-5P	921	3230	Note 1

Note 1: No body style breakouts. Total series production was 117,976 cars.

Model No.	Body Type & Seating	Price	Weight	Prod. Total
SERIES 27 (Deluxe Eight)				
2727B	2-dr. Bus. Cpe.-3P	853	3220	Note 2
2727	2-dr. Sed. Cpe.-5P	889	3250	Note 2
2767	2-dr. Conv. Cpe.-5P	1048	3390	Note 2
2711	2-dr. Sed.-5P	899	3250	Note 2
2719	4-dr. Sed.-5P	946	3285	Note 2
2769	4-dr. Metro Sed.-5P	946	3295	Note 2

Note 2: No body style breakouts. Total series production was 37,823 cars.

1941 Pontiac convertible. OCW

1941 Pontiac Streamliner Torpedo sedan coupe. OCW

ENGINE: [Six-cylinder] L head. Inline. Six. Cast iron block. Bore & Stroke: 3-9/16 in. x 4 in. Displacement: 239.2 cu. in. Compression Ratio: 6.5:1 (7.2:1 optional). Brake hp: 90 @ 3200 rpm. N.A.C.C. hp: 30.4. Main bearings: Four. Valve lifters: Solid. Carb.: Carter one-barrel. Torque: 175 lb.-ft. @ 1400 rpm. [Eight-cylinder] L-head. Inline. Eight. Cast iron block. Bore & Stroke: 3-1/4 in. x 3-3/4 in. Displacement: 248.9 cu. in. Compression Ratio: 6.5:1 (7.2:1 optional). Brake hp: 103 @ 3500 rpm. N.A.C.C. hp: 33.8. Main bearings: Five. Valve lifters: Solid. Carb.: Carter two-barrel. Torque: 190 lb.-ft. @ 2200 rpm.

CHASSIS: Wheelbase: 191 in. Overall Length: 201-1/2 in. Height: 66 in. Front tread: 58 in. Rear tread: 61-1/2 in. Tires: 16 x 6.00.

TECHNICAL: Synchromesh transmission. Speeds: 3F/1R. Column shift control. Inland single disc clutch. Hotchkiss drive. Semi-floating rear axle. Overall ratio: 4.1:1. Duo servo hydraulic brakes on four wheels. Steel disc wheels. Rim size: 4-1/2 in. Drivetrain options: No Rol device to keep car from rolling backwards on hill.

1941 Pontiac Custom Eight Torpedo sedan coupe. OCW

PONTIAC - STREAMLINER TORPEDO - JB LINE - SIX/EIGHT: Sleek, fastback styling characterized Pontiac's 1941 Streamliner Torpedo models. Their rooflines swept from the windshield to the rear bumper in one, smooth curve. The front end sheet metal was of the same design used on Deluxe Torpedos and trim differences between Sixes and Eights were also the same. Beige corded wool cloth upholstery was featured. Streamliners utilized GM's larger B-body. There was also a Super Streamliner sub-series. Supers had the same body styling and trim, but featured two-tone worsted wool cloth upholstery with pin stripes. They also added sponge rubber seat cushions, electric clocks, deluxe flexible steering wheels and divan type seats with folding center armrests. Streamliners (and Customs) had concealed interior steps.

I.D. DATA: Serial numbers on left side of dash. Starting: (six) P6JB-1001/(eight) P8JB-1001. Ending: (six) P6JB-62545/(eight) P8JB-52428. These codes apply to cars built at Pontiac, Mich. California cars had a "C" prefix. New Jersey cars had an "L" prefix. Engine numbers on front left corner of block. Numbers were the same given for Deluxe Torpedo engines.

1941 Pontiac two-door sedan. OCW

Model No.	Body Type & Seating	Price	Weight	Prod. Total
SERIES 26 (Streamliner Six)				
2627	2-dr. Sed. Cpe.-5P	923	3305	Note 1
2609	4-dr. Sed.-5P	980	3365	Note 1
SERIES 26 (Super Streamliner Six)				
2627D	2-dr. Sed. Cpe.-5P	969	3320	Note 1
2609D	4-dr. Sed.-5P	1026	3400	Note 1

Note 1: No body style breakouts. Total production of Streamliner and Super Streamliner Sixes was 82,527 cars.

Model No.	Body Type & Seating	Price	Weight	Prod. Total
SERIES 28 (Streamliner Eight)				
2827	2-dr. Sed. Cpe.-5P	948	3370	Note 2
2809	4-dr. Sed.-5P	1005	3425	Note 2
SERIES 28 (Super Streamliner Eight)				
2827D	2-dr. Sed. Cpe.-5P	994	3385	Note 2
2809D	4-dr. Sed.-5P	1051	3460	Note 2

Note 2: No body style breakouts. Total production of Streamliner and Super Streamliner Eights was 66,287 cars.

ENGINE: The Streamliner Torpedo engines had the same specifications as Deluxe Torpedo engines.

CHASSIS: Wheelbase: 122 in. Overall Length: 207-1/2 in. Height: 65-3/4 in. Front tread: 58 in. Rear tread: 61-1/2 in. Tires: 16 x 6.50.

TECHNICAL: Drivetrain same as Deluxe Torpedo drivetrain.

PONTIAC - CUSTOM TORPEDO - JC LINE - SIX/EIGHT: The extra-large GM C-body was used for 1941 Pontiac Custom Torpedos. This line included a notchback sedan and coupe, plus the standard and Deluxe wood-bodied station wagons. Annual styling changes were the same seen for other lines, as were trim variations between Sixes and Eights. Station wagon bodies were built by Hercules and Ionia. The Ionia bodies had a more rounded rear end treatment. Standard station wagons had imitation leather upholstery while Deluxe types had genuine leather cushions.

I.D. DATA: Serial numbers on left side of dash. Starting: (six) P6JC-1001/(eight) P8JC-1001. Ending: (six) P6JC-6345/(eight) P8JC-12576. These codes apply to cars built at Pontiac, Mich. California cars had a "C" prefix. New Jersey cars had an "L" prefix. Engine numbers on front left corner of block. Numbers were the same given for Deluxe Torpedo engines.

1941 Pontiac Deluxe Torpedo four-door sedan. JAG

Model No.	Body Type & Seating	Price	Weight	Prod. Total
SERIES 24 (Custom Torpedo Six)				
2427	2-dr. Sed. Cpe.-5P	995	3260	Note 1
2419	4-dr. Sed.-5P	1052	3355	Note 1
STA WAG	4-dr. Sta. Wag.-8P	1175	3650	Note 1
STA WAG	4-dr. Del. Sta. Wag.-8P	1225	3665	Note 1

Note 1: No body style breakouts. Total series production (six) was 8,257 cars.

Model No.	Body Type & Seating	Price	Weight	Prod. Total
SERIES 29 (Custom Torpedo Eight)				
2927	2-dr. Sed. Cpe.-5P	1020	3325	Note 2
2919	4-dr. Sed.-5P	1077	3430	Note 2
STA WAG	4-dr. Sta. Wag.-8P	1200	3715	Note 2
STA WAG	4-dr. Del. Sta. Wag.-8P	1250	3730	Note 2

Note 2: No body style breakouts. Total series production (eight) was 17,191 cars.

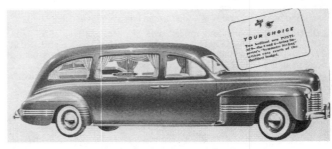

1941 Superior-Pontiac funeral coach. JAG

ENGINE: The Custom Torpedo engines had the same specifications as Deluxe Torpedo engines.

CHASSIS: Wheelbase: 122 in. Overall Length: 201 in. Height: 65 in. Front tread: 58 in. Rear tread: 61-1/2 in. Tires: 16 x 6.50.

TECHNICAL: Drivetrain same as Deluxe Torpedo drivetrain.

OPTIONS: Exhaust deflector. Wheel trim rings. Bumper wing tips. White sidewall tires. Fender skirts. Master grille guards. Deluxe seven-tube radio. Weather Chief heater. Electric clock (std. in Super and Custom). Cigar lighter. Mast radio antenna (std. with radio). Spotlight. Wide runningboards (Custom Torpedo only). Vacuum radio antenna. Master five-tube radio. Safety-flex steering wheel (std. in Super and

Custom). Safe sight airight defroster control. Electric visor vanity mirror. Back window sun baffle. Non-glare rear view mirror. Directional signals. Constant action wiper pump. Glove box light. Luggage compartment light. Chrome fog lamp. Deluxe safety light. Rear bumper hinge guard.

HISTORICAL: Introduced September 1940. New clutch pedal booster. Adjustable sun visors. Power operated convertible top. New bridge type frames. Improved multi-seal brakes. New, built-in, permanent oil cleaner. Dual rear lamps had automatic stop signal feature. New semi-automatic safety shift. Calendar year registrations: 286,123. Calendar year production: 282,087. Model year production: 330,061. The president of Pontiac was H.J. Klingler. Pontiac became the best-selling car in the middle-price class in 1941.

1942

1942 Pontiac Streamliner station wagon. AA

PONTIAC - TORPEDO - KA LINE - SIX/EIGHT: All 1942 Pontiacs looked lower, heavier, and wider. Extension caps on the front doors lengthened the forward fender lines. The hood extended back to the front doors, eliminating the cowl. The grille, bumper and hood were widened and headlamps were farther apart. Long, horizontal parking lamps sat just above the verticle side grilles. The horseshoe shaped center grille had horizontal bars and a circular emblem in the middle of the upper main surround molding. Torpedos used the GM A-body and featured notch back styling. After December 15, 1941, wartime "blackout" trim was used. All parts previously chrome plated were finished in Duco Gun-Metal Gray. The word Pontiac appeared on the hood side molding of six-cylinder models, while the moldings on eight-cylinder cars said Pontiac Eight.

I.D. DATA: Serial numbers on left side of dash. Starting: (six) P6KA-1001/(eight) P8KA-1001. Ending: (six) P6KA-25802/(eight) P8KA-13146. Above numbers for cars built in Pontiac, Mich. Cars built in Southgate, Calif., had a "C" prefix. Cars built in Linden, N.J., had an "L" prefix. Engine numbers on front left corner of block. Starting: same as serial numbers. Ending: same as serial numbers.

1942 Pontiac Torpedo metro sedan. OCW

Model No.	Body Type & Seating	Price	Weight	Prod. Total
SERIES 25 (Torpedo Six)				
2527B	2-dr. Cpe.-3P	895	3210	Note 1
2507	2-dr. Sed. Cpe.-5P	950	3255	Note 1
2527	2-dr. Spt. Cpe.-5P	935	3260	Note 1
2567	2-dr. Conv. Cpe.-5P	1165	3535	Note 1
2511	2-dr. Sed.-5P	940	3265	Note 1
2519	4-dr. Sed.-5P	985	3305	Note 1
2569	4-dr. Metro Sed.-5P	985	3295	Note 1

Note 1: No body style breakouts. Total series production (six) was 29,886 cars.

1942 Pontiac Torpedo business coupe. JAG

Model No.	Body Type & Seating	Price	Weight	Prod. Total
SERIES 27 (Torpedo Eight)				
2727B	2-dr. Cpe.-3P	920	3270	Note 2
2707	2-dr. Sed. Cpe.-5P	975	3320	Note 2
2727	2-dr. Spt. Cpe.-5P	960	3320	Note 2
2767	2 dr. Conv. Cpe.-5P	1190	3605	Note 2
2711	2-dr. Sed.-5P	965	3325	Note 2
2719	4-dr. Sed.-5P	1010	3360	Note 2
2569	4-dr. Metro Sed.-5P	1010	3355	Note 2

Note 2: No body style breakouts. Total series production (eight) was 14,421 cars.

1942 Pontiac Torpedo two-door sedan. OCW

ENGINES: [Six]: L-head. Inline. Six. Cast iron block. Bore & Stroke: 3-9/16 in. x 4 in. Displacement: 239.2 cu. in. Compression Ratio: 6.5:1 (7.5:1 optional). Brake hp: 90 @ 3200 rpm. N.A.C.C hp: 30.4. Main bearings: Four. Valve lifters: Solid. Carb.: Carter one-barrel. Torque: 175 lb.-ft. @ 1400 rpm. [Eight] L-head. Inline. Cast iron block. Bore & Stroke: 3-1/4 in. x 3-3/4 in. Displacement: 248.9 cu. in. Compression Ratio: 6.5:1 (7.5:1 optional). Brake hp: 103 @ 3500 rpm. N.A.C.C. hp: 33.8. Main bearings: Five. Valve lifters: Solid. Carb.: Carter two-barrel. Torque: 190 lb.-ft. @ 2200 rpm.

CHASSIS: Wheelbase: 119 in. Overall Length: 204-1/2 in. Height: 66 in. Front tread: 58 in. Rear tread: 61-1/2 in. Tires: 16 x 6.00.

TECHNICAL: Synchromesh transmission. Speeds: 3F/1R. Column gear shift controls. Single disc clutch. Hotchkiss drive. Semi-floating rear axle. Overall ratio: 4.1: 1. Duo-servo hydraulic brakes on four wheels. Steel disc wheels. Rim size: 4-1/2 in. Drivetrain options: No-Rol Economy (3.9) or Mountain (4.55) axles.

1942 Pontiac Streamliner two-door sedan coupe. OCW

1942 Pontiac Torpedo four-door sedan. JAG

PONTIAC - STREAMLINER - KB LINE - SIX/EIGHT: Streamliner styling changes were the same as Torpedo changes. Streamliners used the larger GM B-body and had fastback rooflines (except station wagons). The 1941 Super models with folding rear seat center armrests were called Chieftains in 1942. The hood side moldings on Sixes and Eights carried different wording.

I.D. DATA: Serial numbers on left side of dash. Starting: (six) P6KB-1001/(eight) P8KB-1001. Ending: (six) P6KB-11115/(eight) P8KB-22928. (Pontiac, Mich.). California cars had a "C" prefix. New Jersey cars had an "L" prefix. Engine numbers on front left corner of block. Starting: same as serial numbers. Ending: same as serial numbers.

Model No.	Body Type & Seating	Price	Weight	Prod. Total
SERIES 26 (Streamliner Six)				
2607	2-dr. Sed. Cpe.-5P	980	3355	Note 1
2609	4-dr. Sed.-5P	1035	3415	Note 1
STA WAG	4-dr. Sta. Wag.-8P	1265	3810	Note 1
SERIES 26 (Chieftain Six)				
2607D	2-dr. Sed. Cpe.-5P	1030	3400	Note 1
2609D	4-dr. Sed.-5P	1085	3460	Note 1
STA WAG	4-dr. Sta. Wag.-8P	1315	3785	Note 1

Note 1: No body style breakouts. Total series production (six) was 12,742 cars (includes 2,458 Chieftains).

Model No.	Body Type & Seating	Price	Weight	Prod. Total
SERIES 28 (Streamliner Eight)				
2807	2-dr. Sed. Cpe.-5P	1005	3430	Note 2
2809	4-dr. Sed.-5P	1060	3485	Note 2
STA WAG	4-dr. Sta. Wag.-8P	1290	3885	Note 2
SERIES 28 (Chieftain Eight)				
2807D	2-dr. Sed. Cpe.-5P	1055	3460	Note 2
2809D	2-dr. Sed.-5P	1110	3515	Note 2
STA WAG	4-dr. Sta. Wag.-8P	1340	3865	Note 2

Note 2: No body style breakouts. Total series production (eight) was 26,506 cars. (Includes 11,041 Chieftains).

ENGINE: Same specifications as Torpedo engines.

CHASSIS: Wheelbase: 122 in. Overall Length: 210-1/4 in. Height: 65-1/4 in. Front tread: 58 in. Rear tread: 61-1/2 in. Tires: 16 x 6.50.

TECHNICAL: Drivetrain same specifications as Torpedos, except overall drive ratio is 4.3: 1.

OPTIONS: Master grille guard. Bumper wing tip guards. Wheel trim rings. Oil bath air cleaner. Electric clock (std. in Chieftains). Safety-flex steering wheel (std. in Chieftains). Five-tube radio. Seven-tube radio. Mast antenna (std. with radio pkg.). Vacuum antenna. Rear view mirror. Weather chief header. Fender skirts. Seat covers.

HISTORICAL: Introduced: September 1941. Steering wheel with center horn button. Bigger front brakes. Oil cleaner redesigned and improved. Triple-sealed brakes. Duplex rear springs improved to eliminate squeaks. Rheostat dash panel lighting. Calendar year production: 15,404. Model year production: 85,555. Company president: H.J. Klingler. Production halted February 10, 1942, because of U.S. entry into World War II. In January 1942, Pontiac became first U.S. automaker to win U.S. Navy "E" pennant for production excellence.

1946-1975

PONTIAC

PONTIAC 1946-1975

1955 Pontiac Custom Star Chief two-door Catalina hardtop, V-8.

The 1946-1948 Pontiacs were reincarnations of the 1942 models in terms of both styling, and engineering. They were as reliable, and value-packed as the cars offered before World War II, but just as predictable, too. These flathead sixes, and eights slowly, but surely gained a reputation as middle-of-the-road cars best-suited for middle class, middle-age buyers in the middle price bracket. In its struggle to market a reliable product at the lowest possible price, Pontiac found itself stuck on a plateau that was out of step with the sporty car boom of the postwar period.

Reaction to the growing youth market came slowly at Pontiac. There was a reluctance to upset the apple cart in quest of modernization. Although old-fashioned, Pontiacs were still selling better than ever through the end of 1953. Hydra-Matic transmission was introduced in 1948, and gained immediate popularity. Newly redesigned bodies with lower lines, and integral rear fenders were the hit of 1949. An attractive Catalina two-door hardtop made the scene in 1950, and rear fender humps, somewhat resembling Cadillac tailfins, were adopted for 1953. The following year, the top Pontiac line featured updated bodies with an extended deck that emphasized the extra luxury buyers associated with the nameplate. But there was still an inline flathead eight below the hood. Unfortunately, this type of powerplant was too much of a throwback to earlier days. Sales took a tumble, and a need for change seemed more than crystal clear.

Work on a V-8 engine for Pontiac had begun as early as 1949 under longtime general manager Harry J. Klingler. Development proceeded slowly at first. In 1951, the conservative Klingler became vice-president of vehicle production for General Motors. Arnold Lenz took over Pontiac, hoping to institute rapid change. When Lenz died in a car/train crash the following year, the V-8 program was set back. R.M. Critchfield succeeded Lenz, and he slowly got the modernization program rolling again. It was 1955 before the new Pontiac engine hit the market, and when it did, sales took an immediate jump to 554,000 units in the model-year.

manager. Knudsen, son of former GM president William S. Knudsen, was the youngest GM general manager at age 43. He proceeded, without fanfare, to make over the Pontiac image.

With a new engineering group headed by E.M. (Pete) Estes, and John Z. DeLorean, a line of new cars with true performance potential was methodically developed. To highlight a move into a competition and factory racing program, an "extra horsepower" engine option with dual four-barrel carburetors, and a full-race camshaft was crafted by staff motor engineer Malcolm R. 'Mac' McKellar. It was released in mid-1956, and became the first in a series of so-called NASCAR, and Super-Duty Pontiac V-8s.

Starting with 1959 models, the image of a sporty, youthful car with appeal across the spectrum of new car buyers emerged at Pontiac. The result was six straight years of low-slung, "Wide-Track," full-size performance machines that outran the majority of competitors in both sales and racing. In the fall of 1960, following intensive research, development, and testing, Pontiac expanded the bottom of its line with a completely innovative compact model called the Tempest.

When Knudsen moved to Chevrolet in 1961, Estes took over at Pontiac. Under his able direction the division continued to grow in sales volume and facilities. The Tempest moved the company into third place in U.S. sales in 1961. Traditionally the "hot spot" of the auto market, Pontiac was able to dominate the third rung during the 1960s.

Pontiac performance reached a peak in 1963 and racing activities were officially curtailed shortly afterwards due to a corporate ban. To maintain its edge in the youth car market, the company skirted another GM policy by dropping its most popular big-car engine (the 389-cid V-8) into medium-sized Tempest bodies in true hot rod fashion. The result was the first Pontiac GTO. A year later, John Z. DeLorean was made manager.

With the introduction of 1966 models, Pontiac announced a completely new overhead cam six-cylinder engine as standard equipment in Tempests. In the middle of the 1967 model-year, the Firebird sports/personal car was unveiled. It was offered in a range of model-options from the ohc six to a new 400 cid V-8. Ram Air induction was optional. A milestone was achieved in 1968 when an all-time high of 940,000 cars left the factory. It was also the first time that sales of Pontiac specialty models such as

Tempests, Grand Prix, and Firebirds, exceeded the sales of traditional lines.

The hit of 1969 was a restyled Grand Prix with a neo-classic appearance. A few months later, the most exciting of all Firebirds was introduced as the semi-race-ready Trans Am. Conceived as a factory sedan-racer, the Trans Am had an engine that was too big to qualify for track competition, but just right for stoplight performance. By this time the government was starting to crack down on factory hot rods of the late 1960s, but the Trans Am passed as a sports car and thereby kept the performance image alive for a few more years.

In February 1969, F. James McDonald became Pontiac general manager. He replaced DeLorean who moved to Chevrolet in the same capacity. The division's new 300,000-square foot, ultra-modern administration building opened early the next year. This was a critical stage for car development programs, due to pressures from the government and insurance companies alike. High-performance was continually de-emphasized in favor of safety and fuel economy gains combined with engine emissions reductions.

During the 1971 calendar-year, Pontiac captured third place in U.S. auto sales for the 10th time in 11 years, but the division's image was losing impact at the same time. The low-priced Ventura II compact hit the market; a new, less powerful 1972 Trans Am appeared; and the nearest thing to a full-sized performance car available was the luxurious Bonneville with a massive 455-cid V-8.

On October 1, 1972, Martin J. Caserio became general manager of Pontiac Motor Division. Under him a new regular fuel Super-Duty V-8 evolved. It became an instant collector's item when ultimately released in late-1973 Trans Ams and Formula Firebirds. Under Caserio the GTO disappeared, and the Firebird came close to meeting a similar fate.

The 1973 Pontiac lineup was highlighted by a totally redesigned intermediate series, topped by the stunning Grand Am. This car was rendered in the image of a European road tourer with a slotted, slanting "soft" nose fashioned of flexible urethane rubber. Calendar-year sales of 854,343 cars were the second best in company history, but similar to 20 years earlier, future trends did not favor Pontiac. The 1974 models featured new engineering, and radial-tuned suspension, while 1975 brought the sub-compact Astre, a more luxurious Grandville Brougham line, and the demise—at least temporarily—of convertibles with Pontiac nameplates.

1946 PONTIAC

1946 Pontiac Torpedo two-door sedan.

TORPEDO SERIES - (SIX) SERIES 25/(EIGHT) SERIES 27 - Torpedos comprised Pontiac's short wheelbase (A-Body) line. Buyers could order any Torpedo on either the six or eight-cylinder chassis ($27-$30 extra for Eights). There was no difference in Series 25 or Series 27 features, except for engine identifying trim. Styling highlights of all Pontiacs were: wraparound bumpers, a massive 14-blade grille, new name-plates and concealed safe-light parking lamps. An Indianhead mascot with upward curved feathers, short moldings atop front fenders, absence of belt moldings and painted pin stripes on the fender "speed-line" ribs distinguished Torpedos. Lettering on hood emblems and badges placed forward of the "speedlines" identified eights. Closed-body Torpedos came with gray tan cloth trims and convertibles were done in cloth combined with black, tan, green, blue, or red leather.

PONTIAC I.D. NUMBERS: VIN located on left side of firewall under hood. First symbol indicated the assembly plant: P=Pontiac, Mich.; C=California (Southgate); L=Linden, N.J.; K=Kansas City, Kan. Second symbol indicated engine type: 6=six-cylinder; 8=eight-cylinder. Next two symbols were series code appearing as last two characters in first column of charts below. Following this came the sequential production number, which began with 1001 at each assembly plant. Engine serial number on raised pad on front left side of block. VINs matched the engine serial number. The 1946 numbers for each series were: [TORPEDO SIXES]: (Mich.) P6LA-1001 to P6LA-17381; (Calif.) C6LA-1001 to C6LA-3314; (Kan.) K6LA-1001 to K6LA-2520; (N.J.) L6LA-1001 to L6LA4721. [TORPEDO EIGHTS] (Mich.) P8LA-1001 to P8LA-13652; (Calif.) C8LA-1001 to C8LA-2786; (Kan.) K8LA-1001 to K8LA-2520; (N.J.) L8LA-1001 to L8LA-3738. [STREAMLINER SIXES]: (Mich.) P6LB-1001 to P6LB35238; (Calif.) C6LB-1001 to C6 LB3696; (Kan.) K6LB-1001 to K6LB-2299; (N.J.) L6LB-1001 to L6LB-5357. [STREAMLINER EIGHTS]: (Mich.) P8LB-1001 to P8LB-39764; (Calif.) C8LB-1001 to C8LB-4257; (Kans.) K8LB-1001 to K8LB-2590; (N.J.) L8LB-1001 to L8LB-6618. Another code located on the firewall tag on Pontiacs is the Fisher Body/style number. It consists of a prefix indicating model year (46=1946) and suffix indicating series number and body type. These numbers appear in the second column of the charts below. Pontiac parts suppliers use these numbers to aid proper parts applications so they are important.

1946 Pontiac Streamliner station wagon. OCW

TORPEDO SIXES

Model Number	Body/Style Number	Body Type & Seating	Factory Price	Shipping Weight	Prod. Total
25LA	46-2527B	2-dr Cpe-3P	1307	3261	NA
25LA	46-2507	2-dr Sed Cpe-5P	1399	3326	NA
25LA	46-2527	2-dr Spt Cpe-5P	1353	3311	NA
5LA	46-2567	2-dr Conv-5P	1631	3591	NA
25LA	46-2511	2-dr Sed-5P	1368	3326	NA
25LA	46-2519	4-dr Sed-5P	1427	3361	NA

NOTE 1: 26,636 Torpedo sixes built; no body style breakouts available.

TORPEDO EIGHTS

Model Number	Body/Style Number	Body Type & Seating	Factory Price	Shipping Weight	Prod. Total
27LA	46-2727B	2-dr Cpe-3P	1335	3331	NA
27LA	46-2707	2-dr Sed Cpe-5P	1428	3391	NA
27LA	46-2727	2-dr Spt Cpe-5P	1381	3376	NA
27LA	46-2767	2-dr Conv-5P	1658	3651	NA
27LA	46-2711	2-dr Sed-5P	1395	3396	NA
27LA	46-2719	4-dr Sed-5P	1455	3436	NA

NOTE 1: 18,273 Torpedo eights built; no body style breakouts available.

1946 Pontiac Streamliner sedan coupe. OCW

STREAMLINER SERIES - (SIX) SERIES 26 (EIGHT) SERIES 28 - Streamliners represented Pontiac's B-Body line. The first postwar Pontiac available (September 13, 1945) was the Streamliner sedan-coupe, which remained the sole product for a time. Streamliners could be identified by straight-back Indian head hood ornaments, chrome beltline moldings and bright moldings on the "speedline" fender ribs. They also had longer front fender crown moldings and were generally larger in size. Interior trims on passenger cars were in gray striped cloth. Station wagons had three seats in standard trim; two seats in Deluxe trim and used imitation leather upholstery and passenger car style interior hardware.

1946 Pontiac Torpedo convertible. OCW

STREAMLINER SIXES

Model Number	Body/Style Number	Body Type & Seating	Factory Price	Shipping Weight	Prod. Total
26LB	46-2607	2-dr Sed Cpe-5P	1438	3435	NA
26LB	46-2609	4-dr Sed-5P	1510	3490	NA
26LB	46-Sta Wag	4-dr Std Sta Wag-8P	1942	3790	NA
26LB	46-Sta Wag	4-dr Del Sta Wag-6P	2019	3735	NA

NOTE 1: 43,430 Streamliner sixes built; no body style breakouts available.

1946 Pontiac Torpedo sedan coupe. OCW

STREAMLINER EIGHTS

Model Number	Body/Style Number	Body Type & Seating	Factory Price	Shipping Weight	Prod. Total
28LB	46-2807	2-dr Sed Cpe-5P	1468	3495	NA
28LB	46-2809	4-dr Sed-5P	1538	3550	NA
28LB	46-Sta Wag	4-dr Std St Wag-8P	1970	3870	NA
28LB	46-Sta Wag	4-dr Del St Wag-6P	2047	3805	NA

NOTE 1: 49,301 Streamliner eights built; no body style breakouts.

1946 Pontiac Streamliner four-door sedan, eight-cylinder.

ENGINES

(SIX) Six-cylinder: L-head. Cast iron block. Displacement: 239.2 cu. in. Bore & Stroke: 3-9/16 x 4 in. Compression Ratio: (standard) 6.5:1, (optional) 7.5:1. Brake hp: 90 @ 3200 rpm. Four main bearings. Solid valve lifters. Carburetor: Carter WAI-537-S one-barrel.

(EIGHT) Eight-cylinder: L-head. Cast iron block. Displacement: 248.9 cu. in. Bore & Stroke: 3-1/4 x 3-3/4 in. Compression Ratio: See Torpedo six. Brake hp: 103 @ 3500 rpm. Five main bearings. Solid valve lifters. Carburetor: Carter WDO548-S two-barrel.

1946 Pontiac Superior-Pontiac funeral coach, Streamliner Eight chassis. JAG

1946 Pontiac Superior-Pontiac ambulance, Streamliner Eight chassis. JAG

CHASSIS FEATURES: [TORPEDO] Wheelbase: 119 in. Overall length: 204.5 in. Front tread: 58 in. Rear tread: 61-1/2 in. Tire size: 6.00 x 16. [STREAMLINER] Wheelbase: 122 in. Overall length: (passenger cars) 210-1/4 in., (wagons) 215-5/8 in. Front tread: 58 in. Rear tread: 61-1/2 in. Tires: 6.50 x 16.

OPTIONS: Rear windshield wiper. Windshield washer. White sidewall discs. Fog lights. Safety light. Weather Chief heater (dash type). Defroster (dash type). Venti-Heat underseat heater and defroster. Five-tube Master radio. Seven-tube Air Mate radio. Eight-tube Air King radio. Mast antenna. Rear fender panels (Torpedo). Rear fender panels with moldings (Streamliner). Sponge rubber cushions (per body style). Kool Kushin. Luggage compartment light. Lock package. Electric visor vanity mirror. E-Z-I non-glare rearview mirror. Non-electric visor vanity mirror. Handbrake lamp. Umbrella holder. Santoy seat covers (per body style). Bumper guards, wheel rim rings, electric clock, exhaust deflector and various lights available in standard accessory packages. All 1946 Pontiacs had three-speed manual transmission with column shifting. Performance options were limited to 3.9:1 (economy) and 4.55:1 (mountain) rear axle gear ratios, a 7.5:1 "high-compression" cylinder head and automatic No-Rol device.

HISTORICAL FOOTNOTES: The first postwar Pontiac was built September 13, 1945. The full model line was back in production by June 10, 1946. Calendar year production was 131,538 cars. Model year production was 137,640 cars. Harry J. Klingler was general manager of Pontiac Motor Division (PMD). George Delaney became the company's chief engineer this season, replacing Ben Anibal, who worked on the development of the first 1926 Pontiacs. The three-passenger coupe was called a business coupe. The convertible was called a convertible sedan-coupe. General Motors two-door fastbacks were also referred to as "Sport Dynamic" coupes.

1947 PONTIAC

1947 Pontiac convertible. OCW

TORPEDO SERIES - (SIX) SERIES 25 - (EIGHT) SERIES 27 - The Torpedos comprised the same line as in 1946. A "Silver Streak" styling theme was continued, now with five bands of chrome on hoods. All Pontiacs had new grilles with four broad, gently bowed horizontal bars. Hoods and fenders were protected by an inverted steer's horn-shaped bar incorporating a die cast plate with Indianhead relief. Torpedos carried no beltline or speedline moldings and had short strips of chrome on the front fender crowns. All 1947 Pontiacs had identical hood ornaments. Interiors were similar to 1946, but due to material shortages some convertibles were built with red, blue or black imitation leather upholstery in combination with tan Bedford cloth. Only the Torpedo sedan-coupe had fastback styling with individual-loop chrome moldings on the side windows.

PONTIAC I.D. NUMBERS: VIN located on left side of firewall under hood. First symbol indicated the assembly plant. P=Pontiac, Mich.; C=California (South Gate); L=Linden, N.J.; W=Wilmington, Del.; K=Kansas City, Kan.; A=Atlanta, Ga. Second symbol indicated engine type: 6=six-cylinder; 8=eight-cylinder. Next two symbols were series code appearing as last two characters in first column of charts below. Following this came the sequential production number, which began with 1001 at each assembly plant. Engine serial number on raised pad on front left side of block. VINs matched the engine serial number. The 1947 numbers for each series were: [TORPEDO SIXES]: (Mich.) P6MA-1001 to P6MA-37322; (N.J.) L6MA-1001 to L6MA-13895; (Kan.) K6MA-1001 to K6MA-8096; (Del.) W6MA-1001 to W6MA-1850; (Calif.) C6MA-1001 to C6MA-7794. [TORPEDO EIGHTS] (Mich.) P8MA-1001 to P8MA-22682; (N.J.) L8MA-1001 to L8MA-

7387; (Kan.) K8MA-1001 to K8MA-4165; (Del.) W8MA-1001 to W8MA-1431; (Calif.) C8MA-1001 to C8MA-4150. [STREAMLINER SIXES] (Mich.) P6MB-1001 to P6MB-27844; (N.J.) L6MB-1001 to L6MB-7877; (Kan.) K6MB-1001 to K6MB-4569; (Del.) W6MB-1001 to W6MB-3976; (Calif.) C6MB-1001 to C6-MB-3976; (Ga.) A6MB-1001 to A6MB-1080. [STREAMLINER EIGHTS] (Mich.) P8MB-1001 to P8MB-56382; (N.J.) L8MB-1001 to L8MB-15246; (Kan.) K8MB-1001 to K8MB-9184; (Del.) W8MB-1001 to W8MB-1954; (Calif.) C8MB-1001 to C8MB-8197; (Ga.) A8MB-1001 to A8MB-1145. Another code located on the firewall tag on Pontiacs is the Fisher Body/style number. It consists of a prefix indicating model year (47=1947) and suffix indicating series number and body type. These numbers appear in the second column of the charts below. Pontiac parts suppliers use these numbers to aid proper parts applications so they are important.

1947 Pontiac Streamliner two-door sedan. OCW

TORPEDO SIXES

Model Number	Body/Style Number	Body Type & Seating	Factory Price	Shipping Weight	Prod. Total
25MA	47-2527B	2-dr Cpe-3P	1217	3245	NA
25MA	47-2507	2-dr Sed Cpe-5P	1305	3300	NA
25MA	47-2527	2-dr Spt Cpe-5P	1261	3295	NA
25MA	47-2567	2-dr Conv-5P	1595	3560	NA
25MA	47-2511	2-dr Sed-5P	1275	3295	NA
25MA	47-2519	4-dr Sed-5P	1331	3320	NA

NOTE 1: 67,125 Torpedo sixes built; no body style breakouts available.

TORPEDO EIGHTS

Model Number	Body/Style Number	Body Type & Seating	Factory Price	Shipping Weight	Prod. Total
27MA	47-2727B	2-dr Cpe-3P	1262	3310	NA
27MA	47-2707	2-dr Sed Cpe-5P	1350	3370	NA
27MA	47-2727	2-dr Spt Cpe-5P	1306	3360	NA
27MA	47-2767	2-dr Conv-5P	1640	3635	NA
27MA	47-2711	2-dr Sed-5P	1320	3370	NA
27MA	47-2719	4-dr Sed-5P	1376	3405	NA

NOTE 1: 34,815 Torpedo eights built; no breakouts per body style.

1947 Pontiac Streamliner four-door sedan. OCW

STREAMLINER SERIES - (SIX) SERIES 26 - (EIGHT) SERIES 28 - Streamliners also stayed basically the same as 1946, except for grille and trim variations. Interiors for coupes and sedans were redesigned with Berwick beige panels for dashboard and windows. Windshield, door and garnish moldings were finished in Autumn Brown with dado-stripe border moldings. All coupes and sedans in this series were fastbacks with full-loop-around window moldings.

STREAMLINER SIXES

Model Number	Body/Style Number	Body Type & Seating	Factory Price	Shipping Weight	Prod. Total
26MB	47-2607	2-dr Sed Cpe-5P	1359	3400	NA
26MB	47-2609	4-dr Sed-5P	1407	3405	NA
26MB	47-Sta Wag	4-dr Std Sta Wag-8P	1992	3775	NA
26MB	47-Sta Wag	4-dr DeL Sta Wag-6P	2066	3715	NA

NOTE 1: 42,336 Streamliner sixes built; no body style breakouts available.

STREAMLINER EIGHTS

Model Number	Body/Style Number	Body Type & Seating	Factory Price	Shipping Weight	Prod. Total
28MB	47-2807	2-dr Sed Cpe-5P	1404	3455	NA
28MB	47-2809	4-dr Sed-5p	1452	3515	NA
28MB	47-Sta Wag	4-dr Std Sta Wag-8P	2037	3845	NA
28MB	47-Sta Wag	4-dr DeL Sta Wag-6P	2111	3790	NA

NOTE 1: 86,324 Streamliner eights built; no body style breakouts available.

1947 Pontiac Streamliner Eight station wagon.

ENGINES

(SIX) Six-cylinder: L-head. Cast iron block. Displacement: 239.2 cu. in. Bore & Stroke: 3-9/16 x 4 in. Compression Ratio: (standard) 6.5:1, (optional) 7.5:1. Brake hp: 90 @ 3200 rpm. Four main bearings. Solid valve lifters. Carburetor: Carter WAI-537-S one-barrel.

(EIGHT) Eight-cylinder: L-head. Cast iron block. Displacement: 248.9 cu. in. Bore & Stroke: 3-1/4 x 3-3/4 in. Compression Ratio: See Torpedo six. Brake hp: 103 @ 3500 rpm. Five main bearings. Solid valve lifters. Carburetor: Carter WCD two-barrel models 630S or 630SB.

CHASSIS FEATURES: [TORPEDO] Wheelbase: 119 in. Overall length: 204.5 in. Front tread: 58 in. Rear tread: 61-1/2 in. Tire size: 6.00 x 16. [STREAMLINER] Wheelbase: 122 inches. Overall length: (passenger cars) 210-1/4 in., (wagons) 215-5/8 in. Front tread: 58 in. Rear tread: 61-1/2 in. Tires: 6.50 x 16.

OPTIONS: Rear windshield wiper. Windshield washer. White sidewall discs. Fog lights. Safety light. Weather Chief heater (dash type). Defroster (dash type). Venti-Heat underseat heater and defroster. Five-tube Master radio. Seven-tube Air Mate radio. Eight-tube Air King radio. Mast antenna. Rear fender panels (Torpedo). Rear fender panels with moldings (Streamliner). Sponge rubber cushions (per body style). Kool Kushin. Luggage compartment light. Lock package. Electric visor vanity mirror. E-Z-I non-glare rearview mirror. Non-electric visor vanity mirror. Hand brake lamp. Umbrella holder. Santoy seat covers (per body style). Bumper guards, wheel rim rings, electric clock, exhaust deflector and various lights available in standard accessory packages. All 1946 Pontiacs had three-speed manual transmission with column shifting. Performance options were limited to 3.9:1 (economy) and 4.55:1 (mountain) rear axle gear ratios, a 7.5:1 "high-compression" cylinder head and automatic No-Rol device.

1947 Pontiac Torpedo four-door sedan. OCW

HISTORICAL FOOTNOTES: Production of 1947 Pontiacs began December 19, 1946. Calendar year output came to 223,015 units. Model year assemblies totaled 230,600 cars. A Pontiac prototype with a rear-mounted straight eight-cylinder engine was constructed in 1947. Aluminum replacement fenders for 1942-1948 models were made available later and at least one modern collector has discovered such fenders on his car. Body styles 47-2567 and 47-2767 were now called convertible coupes. Body styles 47-2507, 47-2707, 47-2607, and 47-2807 were Sport Dynamic coupes and are commonly known as fastbacks today. Body styles 47-2609 and 47-2809 were Sport Dynamic four-door sedans, also with fastback styling.

1948 PONTIAC

1948 Pontiac Torpedo Deluxe four-door sedan, six-cylinder.

TORPEDO SERIES - (SIX) SERIES 25 - (EIGHT) SERIES 27 - There were no radical appearance changes in Torpedos, except for adoption of new Pontiac styling including triple "Silver Streaks," a horizontal grille theme with vertical shafts, and round taillights. The word "Silver Streak" was carried on the sides of the hood with eights having an "8" placed between the two words. The model lineup was expanded by offering several body styles with Deluxe trims. Characterizing standard models were plain fenders and rubber gravel guards. Deluxes had fender moldings, bright metal gravel guards and chrome-plated wheel discs. Gray tan cloth continued as trim on standard Torpedos, but Deluxe types with closed bodies used tan and dark blue pattern cloth combinations. Convertibles came with genuine colonial grain leather or imitation leather upholstery and had instrument boards lacquered in body color.

1948 Pontiac Streamliner two-door sedan coupe. OCW

PONTIAC I.D. NUMBERS: VIN located on left side of firewall under hood. Serial numbers took the form ( )[ ]P{ }-1001 to ( )[ ]P{ }-ending number. First symbol ( ) indicated the assembly plant: P=Pontiac, Mich.; C=California (South Gate); L=Linden, N.J.; W=Wilmington, Del.; K=Kansas City, Kan.; A=Atlanta, Ga.; F=Framingham, Mass. Second symbol [ ] indicated engine type: 6=inline six-cylinder; 8=inline eight-cylinder. Third symbol indicated model year: P=1948. Fourth symbol { } contains a letter indicating series: A=Torpedo; B=Streamliner. Remaining symbols are the sequential unit production number for each car line at each assembly plant. Beginning number at each plant is 1001. Ending numbers for 1948 were: [TORPEDO SIX] (Mich.) 25366; (Calif.) 5150; (N.J.) 5301; (Del.) 4375; (Kan.) 5303; (Ga.) 3429 and (Mass.) 3454. [TORPEDO EIGHT] (Mich.) 18933; (Calif.) 4368; (N.J.) 5471; (Del.) 3854; (Kan.) 4134; (Ga.) 2820; (Mass.) 2720. [STREAMLINER SIX] (Mich.) 18146; (Calif.) 4765; (N.J.) 4350; (Del.) 3772; (Kan.) 5556; (Ga.) 2926 and (Mass.) 2951. [STREAMLINER EIGHT] (Mich.) 61682; (Calif.) 13302; (N.J.) 12359; (Del.) 10616; (Kan.) 16561; (Ga.) 7603) and (Mass.) 7776. Engine serial number on raised pad on front left side of block. VINs matched the engine serial number. Fisher Body/style number on plate under hood on left of firewall can be very helpful for identifi-

cation of model and ordering parts. A prefix to the main number indicates model year, 48=1948. The first two symbols in the main number indicate series 25, 26, 27, or 28. The next two symbols indicate the body style. Some numbers have an alphabetical suffix indicating trim level, such as D=Deluxe. These numbers appear in body/style number column of charts below adjacent to corresponding body style listing.

TORPEDO SIXES

Model Number	Body/Style Number	Body Type & Seating	Factory Price	Shipping Weight	Prod. Total
6PA	48-2527B	2-dr Bus Cpe-3P	1500	3230	NA
6PA	48-2527(D)	2-dr Spt Cpe-5P	1552/1641	3220/3230	NA
6PA	48-2507(D)	2-dr Sed Cpe-5P	1614/1704	3275/3275	NA
6PA	48-2567(D)	2-dr Conv-5P	1935/2025	3525/3530	NA
6PA	48-2511	2-dr Sed-5P	1583	3280	NA
6PA	48-2519(D)	4-dr Sed-5P	1641/1731	3320/3340	NA

NOTE 1: 25,325 Torpedo sixes with Hydra-Matic built

NOTE 2: 13,937 Torpedo sixes with Synchromesh built

NOTE 3: 49,262 total Torpedo sixes built; no body style breakouts available.

TORPEDO EIGHTS

Model Number	Body/Style Number	Body Type & Seating	Factory Price	Shipping Weight	Prod. Total
8PA	48-2727B	2-dr Bus Cpe-3P	1548	3296	NA
8PA	48-2727(D)	2-dr Spt Cpe-5P	1599/1689	3295/3305	NA
8PA	48-2707(D)	2-dr Sed Cpe-5P	1661/1751	3340/3340	NA
8PA	48-2767(D)	2-dr Conv-5P	1982/2072	3595/3600	NA
8PA	48-2711	2-dr Sed-5P	1630	3360	NA
8PA	48-2719(D)	4-dr Sed-5P	1689/1778	3395/3395	NA

NOTE 1: 24,294 Torpedo eights with Hydra-Matic built.

NOTE 2: 11,006 Torpedo eights with Synchromesh built.

NOTE 3: 35,360 total Torpedo eights built; no body style breakouts available.

NOTE 4: "D" suffix indicates car came as both standard and Deluxe.

NOTE 5: Data above slash for standard/below slash for Deluxe.

NOTE 6: Factory info conflicts (i.e. standard convertible probably not made.)

STREAMLINER SERIES - (SIX) SERIES 36 - (EIGHT) SERIES 28 - Streamliners were again larger and more expensive. All Streamliners, two-door and four-door fastbacks (B-Body) and the station wagon, now came standard or Deluxe. As on Torpedos, Deluxe models were distinguished by spear moldings on front fenders, bright gravel guards and chrome plated wheel discs on all cars except wagons. Deluxe interiors had two-tone trims with pillow-and-tuft seatbacks, quarter-sawed mahogany dash and window trim, electric glovebox door clocks, Deluxe steering wheels and other rich appointments. Standard wagons had tan imitation leather seats and Deluxe wagons had red upholstery of the same type.

1948 Pontiac Torpedo Deluxe two-door convertible, eight-cylinder.

STREAMLINER SIXES

Model Number	Body/Style Number	Body Type & Seating	Factory Price	Shipping Weight	Prod. Total
6PB	48-2607(D)	2-dr Sed Cpe-5P	1677/1766	3365/3370	NA
6PB	48-2609(D)	4-dr Sed-5P	1727/1817	3450/3455	NA
6PB	Sta Wag(D)	4-dr Sta Wag-6/8P	2364/2442	3755/3695	NA

NOTE 1: 23,858 Streamliner sixes with Hydra-Matic built.

NOTE 2: 13,834 Streamliner sixes with Synchromesh built.

NOTE 3: 37,742 total Streamliner sixes built; no body style breakouts.

1948 Pontiac Streamliner station wagon. OCW

STREAMLINER EIGHTS

Model Number	Body/Style Number	Body Type & Seating	Factory Price	Shipping Weight	Prod. Total
8PB	48-2807(D)	2-dr Sed Cpe-5P	1724/1814	3425/3455	NA
8PB	48-2809(D)	4-dr Sed-5P	1755/1864	3525/3530	NA
8PB	Sta Wag(D)	4-dr Sta Wag-6/8P	2412/2490	3820/3765	NA

NOTE 1: 98,469 Streamliner eights built with Hydra-Matic.

NOTE 2: 24,646 Streamliner eights built with Synchromesh.

NOTE 3: 123,115 total Streamliner eights built; no breakouts per body style.

NOTE 4: "D" suffix indicates car came as both standard and Deluxe sub-series.

NOTE 5: Data above slash for standard/below slash for Deluxe.

NOTE 6: Station wagon seating: Deluxe=6-passenger; Standard=8-passenger.

1948 Pontiac Streamliner four-door sedan. JAG

ENGINES

(SIX) Six-cylinder: L-head. Cast iron block. Displacement: 239.2 cu. in. Bore & Stroke: 3-9/16 x 4 in. Compression Ratio: (standard) 6.5:1, (optional) 7.5:1. Brake hp: (standard) 90 @ 3400 rpm, (optional) 93 @ 3400 rpm. Four main bearings. Solid valve lifters. Carburetor: Carter WA1-537-S one-barrel.

(EIGHT) Eight-cylinder: L-head. Cast iron block. Displacement: 248.9 cu. in. Bore & Stroke: 3-1/4 x 3-3/4 in. Compression Ratio: Same as on six-cylinder. Brake hp: (standard head) 104 @ 3800 rpm, (optional "high head") 106 @ 3800 rpm. Five main bearings. Solid valve lifters. Carburetor: Carter WCD-630-S two-barrel.

CHASSIS FEATURES: [TORPEDO] Wheelbase: 119 in. Overall length: 204.5 in. Front tread: 58 in. Rear tread: 61-1/2 in. Tire size: 6.00 x 16 tube type. [STREAMLINER] Wheelbase: 122 in. Overall length: (cars) 204.5 in., (wagons) 215-5/8 in. Front tread: 58 in. Rear tread: 61-1/2 in. Tire size: 6.50 x 16 tube type.

OPTIONS: Rear windshield wiper. Windshield washer. White sidewall discs. Fog lights. Safety light. Weather Chief heater (dash type). Defroster (dash type). Venti-Heat underseat heater and defroster. Five-tube Master radio. Seven-tube Air Mate radio. Eight-tube Air King radio. Mast antenna. Rear fender panels (Torpedo). Rear fender panels with moldings (Streamliner). Sponge rubber cushions (per body style). Kool Kushin. Luggage compartment light. Lock package. Electric visor vanity mirror. E-Z-I non-glare rearview mirror. Non-electric visor vanity mirror. Handbrake lamp.

Umbrella holder. Santoy seat covers (per body style). Bumper guards, wheel rim rings, electric clock, exhaust deflector and various lights available in standard accessory packages. All 1948 Pontiacs had three-speed manual transmission with column shifting as standard equipment. A new option was Hydra-Matic Drive ($185). Performance options were limited to 3.9:1 (economy) and 4.55:1 (mountain) rear axle gear ratios, a 7.5:1 "high-compression" cylinder head and automatic No-Rol device.

HISTORICAL FOOTNOTES: The 1948 Pontiacs entered production on December 29, 1947. Model year output came to 245,419 cars, which gave Pontiac a 6.56 percent share of the domestic automobile marketplace. Calendar year production peaked at 253,469 cars, making Pontiac America's fifth ranked automaker.

1949 PONTIAC

1949 Pontiac Chieftain Eight four-door sedan. OCW

STREAMLINER LINE - (SIX) SERIES 25 - (EIGHT) SERIES 27 - The 1949 Pontiacs featured low, sleek envelope bodies. Streamliner coupes and sedans utilized the fastback B-body shell. Station wagons were also incorporated in this line. All these cars came as standards or Deluxes. All station wagons and other standard models had small hubcaps. Standard coupes, sedans and wagons were characterized by an absence of beltline trim along with use of rubber gravel guards and painted headlight rims. Deluxes had belt moldings, chrome gravel guards and bright plated headlight doors. Silver Streak styling was seen again. Silver Streak lettering was placed above front fender spears on Deluxes and high on the fenders of standards. Eights had the number '8' between the two words. Most standard models had gray striped pattern cloth upholstery. Most Deluxes used dark gray broadcloth trims. Convertibles and wagons were trimmed as before, except imitation leather was used only on standard wagons.

1949 Pontiac Streamliner Deluxe four-door sedan. OCW

PONTIAC I.D. NUMBERS: VIN located on tag on left front door post. Matching engine serial number located on raised pad on front left side of cylinder block. Serial numbers took the form ( )-[ ]R{ }-1001 to ( )-[ ]P{ }-ending number. First symbol ( ) indicated the assembly plant. P=Pontiac, Mich.; C=California (South Gate); L=Linden, N.J.; W=Wilmington, Del.; K=Kansas City, Kan.; A=Atlanta, Ga.; F=Framingham, Mass. Second symbol [ ] indicated engine type: 6=inline six-cylinder; 8=inline eight-cylinder. Third symbol indicated model year: R=1949. Fourth symbol { } changed to a letter indicating type of transmission: S=synchromesh; H=Hydra-Matic. Remaining symbols are the sequential unit production number for each car line at each assembly plant. Beginning number at each plant is 1001. Ending numbers for 1949 were: [SERIES 25 SIX with synchromesh] (Mich.) 17919; (Calif.) 4767; (N.J.) 4657; (Del.) 4077; (Kan.) 7406; (Ga.) 3404 and (Mass.) 3613. [SERIES 25 SIX with/Hydra-Matic] (Mich.) 12,320; (Calif.) 4142; (N.J.) 3998;

(Del.) 3425; (Kan.) 5887; (Ga.) 2903; (Mass.) 3012. [SERIES 27 EIGHT with synchromesh] (Mich.) 26,054; (Calif.) 7209; (N.J.) 7398; (Del.) 6200; (Kan.) 10608; (Ga.) 4975 and (Mass.) 5188. [SERIES 27 EIGHT with Hydra-Matic] (Mich.) 68,436; (Calif.) 19,959; (N.J.) 19,989; (Del.) 16,062; (Kan.) 30,890; (Ga.) 12,657 and (Mass.) 13,336. Fisher Body/style number on plate under hood on left of firewall can be helpful for identification of model and ordering parts. A prefix to the main number indicates model year, 49=1949. The first two symbols in the main number indicate series 25 or 27. The next two symbols indicate the body style. Some numbers have an alphabetical suffix indicating trim level, such as D=Deluxe. These numbers appear in body/style number column of charts below adjacent to corresponding body style listing.

1949 Pontiac Chieftain Deluxe four-door sedan. OCW

STREAMLINER SIXES

Model Number	Body/Style Number	Body Type & Seating	Factory Price	Shipping Weight	Prod. Total
6R	2508(D)	4-dr Sed-5P	1740/1835	3385/3415	NA
6R	2507(D)	2-dr Sed Cpe-5P	1689/1784	3360/3375	NA
6R	2561(D)	4-dr Wood Wag-8/6P	2543/2622	3745/3730	NA
6R	2562(D)	4-dr Metal Wag-8/6P	2543/2622	3650/3580	NA

NOTE 1: See Historical Footnotes for series production total.

NOTE 2: Data above slash for standard/below slash for Deluxe.

STREAMLINER EIGHTS

Model Number	Body/Style Number	Body Type & Seating	Factory Price	Shipping Weight	Prod. Total
8R	2508(D)	4-dr Sed-5P	1808/1903	3470/3500	NA
8R	2507(D)	2-dr Sed Cpe-5P	1758/1853	3435/3445	NA
8R	2561(D)	4-dr Wood Wag-8/6P	2611/2690	3835/3800	NA
8R	2562(D)	4-dr Metal Wag-8/6P	2611/2690	3690/3640	NA

NOTE 1: See Historical Footnotes for series production total.

NOTE 2: Data above slash for standard/below slash for Deluxe.

NOTE 3: See *Standard Catalog of American Light-Duty Trucks* for sedan delivery.

1949 Pontiac Chieftain Deluxe two-door convertible, eight-cylinder.

CHIEFTAIN LINE - (SIX) SERIES 25 - (EIGHT) SERIES 27 - Chieftains were characterized by notchback body styling and all models in the line used the General Motors A-body shell. The only dimensional difference between the new Streamliners and Chieftains was that the latter were approximately 3/4-inch higher than comparable B-body styles. Lengths and widths were identical for all models in both lines, except station wagons. Trim variations between sixes and eights or standards and Deluxes were the same as on Streamliners.

CHIEFTAIN SIXES

Model Number	Body/Style Number	Body Type & Seating	Factory Price	Shipping Weight	Prod. Total
6R	2569(D)	4-dr Sed-5P	1761/1856	3385/3415	NA
6R	2511(D)	2-dr Sed-5P	1710/1805	3355/3360	NA
6R	2527(D)	2-dr Sed Cpe-5P	1710/1805	3330/3345	NA
6R	2527B	2-dr Bus Cpe-3P	1587	3280	NA
6R	2567DTX	2-dr Del Conv-5P	2183	3600	NA

NOTE 1: See Historical Footnotes for series production total.

NOTE 2: Data above slash for standard/below slash for Deluxe.

CHIEFTAIN EIGHTS

Model Number	Body/Style Number	Body Type & Seating	Factory Price	Shipping Weight	Prod. Total
8R	2569(D)	4-dr Sed-5P	1829/1924	3475/3480	NA
8R	2511(D)	2-dr Sed-5P	1779/1874	3430/3430	NA
8R	2527(D)	2-dr Sed Cpe-5P	1779/1874	3390/3415	NA
8R	2427B	2-dr Bus Cpe-3P	1656	3355	NA
8R	2567DTX	2-dr Del Conv-5P	2206	3670	NA

NOTE 1: See Historical Footnotes for series production total.

NOTE 2: Data above slash for standard/below slash for Deluxe.

1949 Pontiac Catalina Eight coupe. OCW

1949 Pontiac Catalina Eight coupe (rear view). OCW

ENGINES

(SIX) Six-cylinder. L-head. Cast iron block. Displacement: 239.2 cu. in. Bore & Stroke: 3-9/16 x 4 in. Compression Ratio: (standard) 6.5:1 (optional) 7.5:1. Brake hp: (standard) 90 @ 3400 rpm, (optional) 93 @ 3400 rpm. Four main bearings. Solid valve lifters. Carburetor: Carter WA1-537-S one-barrel.

(EIGHT) Eight-cylinder. L-head. Cast iron block. Displacement: 248.9 cu. in. Bore & Stroke: 4-1/4 x 4-3/4 in. Compression Ratio: Same as sixes. Brake hp: (standard) 103 @ 3800 rpm, (optional) 106 @ 3800 rpm. Five main bearings. Solid valve lifters. Carburetor: Carter WCD two-barrel model 6305B.

CHASSIS FEATURES: Wheelbase: 120 in. all lines. Overall Length: (all cars) 202-1/2 in.; (wagons) 203.8 in. Front tread: 58 in. Rear tread: 59 in. Tires: (standard) 7.10 x 15 (special equipment) 7.60 x 15. Tube type.

OPTIONS: Seven-tube Chieftain radio. Mast antenna. No-Blo wind deflectors. Car cushions. Venti-Seat underseat heater. Venti-Shades. Windshield Sun Visor. Traffic light viewer. Polaroid visor. Rear fender panels (skirts). License frames. Illuminated hood ornament. Wheel trim rings. Steel wheel discs. White sidewall discs. Deluxe steering wheel. Remington Auto-Home shaver. Visor vanity mirror. Tissue dispenser. Direction signals. Compass. Rear window wiper. Windshield

washers. Deluxe electric clock. Glove compartment light. Leather utility pocket. Luggage compartment light. Seat covers. Safti-Jack. Outside rearview mirror. Back-up lights. Safety spotlight. Fog lights. No-Rol. Bumper guards. Grille guard. Exhaust deflector. Venetian blinds. No-Mar gas filler trim. Fuel door lock. Scuff pads. Multi-purpose lamp. Underhood trouble lamp. Jack bag. Tool kit. A three-speed Synchromesh gearbox with column shift was standard on all models. Hydra-Matic four-speed automatic transmission was available at $159 extra. Rear axle ratios: (standard) 4.1:1, (economy) 3.9:1, (mountain) 4.3:1, (Hydra-Matic) 3.63:1.

1949 Pontiac sedan delivery and Pontiac General Manager Harry J. Klingler. OCW

HISTORICAL FOOTNOTES: Calendar year production was 333,957 cars. Model year production was 304,819 cars. The latter included a total of 69,654 Streamliner and Chieftain sixes (29,515 with Hydra-Matic and 40,139 with synchromesh) and 235,165 Streamliner and Chieftain eights (174,449 with Hydra-Matic and 60,716 with synchromesh). Pontiac sold 21.2 percent of the U.S. cars in its price class. Hydra-Matic Drive was installed in 78 percent of all Pontiacs made for the year. During 1949, the company built the three millionth Pontiac made since the marque was introduced in 1926. Prototypes of a new "Catalina" two-door hardtop Sports Coupe were seen this year. Note that Pontiac Motor Division now kept production records by chassis series (six or eight), without regard to car-line (Streamliner or Chieftain). This practice was followed through 1954 and there are no breakouts by car-line of body style available until model year 1955. Standard station wagons continued to feature eight-passenger seating, while Deluxe wagons came with six-passenger seating. Body styles 2527 and 2527D are often called Club Coupes and feature direct-action (noncranking) rear quarter window operation. These styles resemble the two-door sedan, but have shorter roofs and longer rear decks.

1950 PONTIAC

1950 Pontiac Chieftain Deluxe Eight convertible. OCW

STREAMLINER - (SIX) SERIES 25 - (EIGHT) SERIES 27 - The 1950 Pontiacs utilized the popular 1949 envelope bodies with revisions to trim and appointments. The horizontal center grille bar now wrapped around the corners of the body. Deluxes had a chrome body strip, chrome wheel rings, chrome headlight rings and stainless steel gravel guards. Eights had an "8" between the words Silver Streak on the fenders. Streamliners (except Station Wagons and Sedan Delivery trucks) had sloping fastback styling.

1950 Pontiac Streamliner Eight four-door metal wagon. OCW

PONTIAC I.D. NUMBERS: VIN located on tag on left front door post. Matching engine serial number located on raised pad on front left side of cylinder block. Serial numbers took the form ( )-[ ]T{ }-1001 to ( )-[ ]T{ }-ending number. First symbol ( ) indicated the assembly plant: P=Pontiac, Mich.; C=California (South Gate); L=Linden, N.J.; W=Wilmington, Del.; K=Kansas City, Kan.; A=Atlanta, Ga.; F=Framingham, Mass. Second symbol [ ] indicated engine type: 6=inline six-cylinder; 8=inline eight-cylinder. Third symbol indicated model year: T=1950. Fourth symbol { } changed to a letter indicating type of transmission: S=synchromesh; H=Hydra-Matic. Remaining symbols are the sequential unit production number for each car-line at each assembly plant. Beginning number at each plant is 1001. Ending numbers for 1950 were: [Series 25 six with synchromesh] (Mich.) 47948; (Calif.) 5571; (N.J.) 8011; (Del.) 74745; (Kan.) 14626; (Ga.) 4925 and (Mass.) 8048. [Series 25 six with/Hydra-Matic] (Mich.) 15001; (Calif.) 2553; (N.J.) 2999; (Del.) 2534; (Kan.) 3696; (Ga.) 1960; (Mass.) 2575. [Series 27 eight with synchromesh] (Mich.) 3815; (Calif.) 4746; (N.J.) 4619; (Del.) 5558; (Kan.) 11497; (Ga.) 5257 and (Mass.) 4070. [Series 27 eight with Hydra-Matic] (Mich.) 128647; (Calif.) 29630; (N.J.) 19508; (Del.) 17360; (Kan.) 42698; (Ga.) 14851 and (Mass.) 117242. Fisher Body style number on plate under hood on left of firewall can be helpful for identification of model and ordering parts. A prefix to the main number indicates model-year, 50=1950. The first two symbols in the main number indicate series 25 or 27. The next two symbols indicate the body style. Some numbers have an alphabetical suffix indicating trim level, such as B=Business and D=Deluxe. These numbers appear in Body/Style Number column of charts below adjacent to corresponding body style listing.

1950 Pontiac Chieftain Deluxe Eight four-door sedan. OCW

STREAMLINER SIX

Model Number	Body/Style Number	Body Type & Seating	Factory Price	Shipping Weight	Prod. Total
6T	2508(D)	4-dr Sed-6P	1724/1745	3414/3499	NA
6T	2507(D)	2-dr Sed Cpe-6P	1673/1768	3379/3399	NA
6T	2562(D)	4-dr Metal Wag-8/6P	2264/2343	3714/3649	NA

1950 Pontiac Streamliner Six two-door sedan coupe. OCW

1950 Pontiac Chieftain Deluxe Eight two-door sedan. OCW

STREAMLINER EIGHT

Model Number	Body/Style Number	Body Type & Seating	Factory Price	Shipping Weight	Prod. Total
8T	2508(D)	4-dr Sed-6P	1792/1887	3499/3509	NA
8T	2507(D)	2-dr Sed Cpe-6P	1742/1837	3464/3469	NA
8T	2562(D)	4-dr Metal Wag-8/6P	2332/2411	3799/3739	NA

NOTE 1: See Historical Footnotes for series production total.

NOTE 2: Data above slash for standard/below slash for Deluxe.

1950 Pontiac Chieftain Super Deluxe Catalina, eight-cylinder.

CHIEFTAIN LINE - (SIX) SERIES 25 - (EIGHT) SERIES 27 - Chieftains were built off the A-body shell with trim distinctions for Deluxes and eights the same as on Streamliners. A new Chieftain body style was the Catalina two-door Hardtop. It was classified as a Super Deluxe model within the Deluxe sub-series. It came finished only in San Pedro Ivory, Sierra Rust or two-tone combinations of these colors. The interior was done in Rust and Ivory leather combinations.

1950 Pontiac Streamliner Deluxe Eight two-door sedan coupe. OCW

CHIEFTAIN SIX

Model Number	Body/Style Number	Body Type & Seating	Factory Price	Shipping Weight	Prod. Total
6T	2569(D)	4-dr Sed-6P	1745/1840	3409/3414	NA
6T	2511(D)	2-dr Sed-6P	1694/1789	3384/3389	NA
6T	2527(D)	2-dr Sed Cpe-6P	1694/1789	3359/3364	NA
6T	2537SD	2-dr Cat HT-6P	2000	3469	NA
6T	2567DTX	2-dr Conv-6P	2122	3624	NA
6T	2527B	2-dr Bus Cpe-3P	1571	3319	NA

CHIEFTAIN EIGHT

Model Number	Body/Style Number	Body Type & Seating	Factory Price	Shipping Weight	Prod. Total
8T	2569(D)	4-dr Sed-6P	1813/1908	3494/3499	NA
8T	2511(D)	2-dr Sed-6P	1763/1858	3454/3464	NA
8T	2527(D)	2-dr Sed Cpe-6P	1763/1858	3444/3454	NA
8T	2537SD	2-dr Cat HT-6P	2069	3549	NA
8T	2567DTX	2-dr Conv-6P	2190	3704	NA

NOTE 1: See Historical Footnotes for series production total.

NOTE 2: Data above slash for standard/below slash for Deluxe.

1950 Pontiac Streamliner Deluxe Eight four-door sedan coupe. OCW

ENGINES

[SIX] Six-cylinder. L-head. Cast iron block. Displacement: 239.2 cu. in. Bore & Stroke: 3-9/16 x 4 in. Compression Ratio: (standard) 6.5:1; (optional) 7.5:1. Brake hp: (standard) 90 @ 3400 rpm; (optional) 93 @ 3400 rpm. Four main bearings. Solid valve lifters. Carburetor: Carter WA1-719-S one-barrel.

[EIGHT] Eight-cylinder: L-head. Cast iron block. Displacement: 268.2 cu. in. Bore & Stroke: 3-3/8 x 3-3/4 in. Compression Ratio: (standard); 6.5:1 (optional) 7.5:1. Brake hp: (standard) 108 @ 3600 rpm; (optional) 113 @ 3600 rpm. Five main bearings. Solid valve lifters. Carburetor: Carter WCD-719-S two-barrel.

1950 Pontiac Chieftain Deluxe Eight convertible. OCW

CHASSIS FEATURES: Wheelbase: 120 in. all lines. Overall length: (all cars) 202-1/2 in.; (wagons) 203.8 in. Front tread: 58 in. Rear tread: 59 in. Tires: (standard) 7.10 x 15 (special equipment) 7.60 x 15. Tube type.

1950 Pontiac Six sedan delivery. JAG

OPTIONS: Seven-tube Chieftain radio. Mast antenna. No-Blo wind deflectors. Car cushions. Venti-Seat underseat heater. Venti-Shades. Windshield sun visor. Traffic light viewer. Poloroid visor. Rear fender panels (skirts). License frames. Illuminated hood ornament. Wheel trim rings. Steel wheel discs. White sidewall discs. Deluxe steering wheel. Remington Auto-Home shaver. Visor vanity mirror. Tissue dispenser. Direction signals. Compass. Rear window wiper. Windshield washers. Deluxe electric clock. Glove compartment light. Leather utility pocket. Luggage compartment light. Seat covers. Safti-Jack. Outside rearview mirror. Back-up lights. Safety spotlight. Fog lights. No-Rol. Bumper guards. Grille guard. Exhaust deflector. Venetian blinds. No-Mar gas filler trim. Fuel door lock. Scuff pads. Multi-purpose lamp. Underhood trouble lamp. Jack bag. Tool kit. A three-speed synchromesh gearbox with column shift was standard on all models. Hydra-Matic four-speed automatic transmission was available at $159 extra. Rear axle ratios: (standard) 4.1:1, (economy) 3.9:1, (mountain) 4.3:1, (Hydra-Matic) 3.63:1.

HISTORICAL FOOTNOTES: Production of 1950 Pontiacs began November 10, 1949. Calendar year assemblies were a strong 467,655 units. Model year output was also strong at 446,426 cars. The latter included a total of 115,542 Streamliner and Chieftain sixes (24,930 with Hydra-Matic and 90,612 with synchromesh) and a total of 330,887 Streamliner and Chieftain eights (263,188 with Hydra-Matic and 67,699 with synchromesh).

1951 PONTIAC

1951 Pontiac Chieftain Six two-door sedan. OCW

1951 Pontiac Chieftain Deluxe Eight four-door sedan. OCW

STREAMLINER LINE - (SIX) SERIES 25 - (EIGHT) - SERIES 27 - The 1951 "Silver Anniversary" Pontiacs reflected 25 years of advanced engineering. A wing-shaped grille was seen and a Silver Streak theme continued. Streamliners again used the B-body shell with sloping fastbacks on coupes. Deluxes had chrome body strips, bright gravel guards and headlight rings. Belt line moldings on all Deluxe passenger cars (not station wagons), had a dip behind the doors. Standard belt moldings were straight. A script plate reading Pontiac was used on series 25 sixes and on series 27 eights a different script read Pontiac eight.

PONTIAC I.D. NUMBERS: VIN located on tag on left front door post. Matching engine serial number located on raised pad on front left side of cylinder block. Serial numbers took the form ( )-[ ]U{ }-1001 to ( )-[ ]U{ }-ending number. First symbol ( ) indicated the assembly plant: P=Pontiac, Mich.; C=California (South Gate); L=Linden, N.J.; W=Wilmington, Del.; K=Kansas City, Kan.; A=Atlanta, Ga.; F=Framingham, Mass. Second symbol [ ] indicated engine type: 6=inline six-cylinder; 8=inline eight-cylinder. Third symbol indicated model year: U=1951. Fourth symbol { } changed to a letter indicating type of transmission: S=synchromesh; H=Hydra-Matic. Remaining symbols are the sequential unit production number for each car line at each assembly plant. Beginning number at each plant is 1001. Ending numbers for 1951 were: [Series 25 six with synchromesh] (Mich.) 24,016; (Calif.) 3519; (N.J.) 4133; (Del.) 4175; (Kan.) 6567; (Ga.) 3282 and (Mass.) 3181. [Series 25 six with/Hydra-Matic] (Mich.) 6543; (Calif.) 1473; (N.J.) 1592; (Del.) 1562; (Kan.) 1954; (Ga.) 1416; (Mass.) 1323. [Series 27 eight with synchromesh] (Mich.) 31,777; (Calif.) 6224; (N.J.) 5984; (Del.) 6068; (Kan.) 11,644; (Ga.) 5406 and (Mass.) 4177. [Series 27 eight with Hydra-Matic] (Mich.) 119,780; (Calif.) 20,125; (N.J.) 22,197; (Del.) 23,140; (Kan.) 40,060; (Ga.) 18,117 and (Mass.) 14,080. Fisher Body style number on plate under hood on left of firewall can be helpful for identification of model and ordering parts. A prefix to the main number indicates model year, 51=1951. The first two symbols in the main number indicate series 25 or 27. The next two symbols indicate the body style. Some numbers have an alphabetical suffix indicating trim level, such as B=Business; D=Deluxe; and SD=Super Deluxe. These numbers appear in body/style number column of charts below adjacent to corresponding body style listings.

STREAMLINER SIX

Model Number	Body/Style Number	Body Type & Seating	Factory Price	Shipping Weight	Prod. Total
6U	2507(D)	2-dr Sed Cpe-6P	1824/1927	3248/3263	NA
6U	2562(D)	4-dr Sta Wag-8/6P	2470/2556	3603/3523	NA

STREAMLINER EIGHT

Model Number	Body/Style Number	Body Type & Seating	Factory Price	Shipping Weight	Prod. Total
8U	2507(D)	2-dr Sed Cpe-6P	1900/2003	3343/3348	NA
8U	2562(D)	4-dr Sta Wag-8/6P	2544/2629	3698/3628	NA

NOTE 1: See Historical Footnotes for series production total.

NOTE 2: Data above slash for standard/below slash for Deluxe.

CHIEFTAIN LINE - (SIX) SERIES 25 - (EIGHT) SERIES 27 - Chieftains had notchback A-body styling. Trim variations distinguishing standards and Deluxes or sixes and eights were the same as on Streamliners. Convertibles came as Deluxes only. Catalina Coupes came only as Deluxes or Super Deluxes, the latter forming a separate Super sub-series. Deluxe Catalinas (style 2537D) had interiors similar to other Deluxes, but the interior trim on Super Deluxe Catalinas (style 2537SD) came in a Blue and Ivory leather/cloth combination or optional all-leather (in the same colors). Super Deluxe Catalinas can be distinguished externally by horizontally grooved trim plates on their rear roof pillars. The three-passenger Business Coupe was available only in standard trim.

1951 Pontiac Chieftain two-door coupe sedan, six-cylinder.

56

1951 Pontiac Chieftain Deluxe Catalina Eight two-door hardtop. OCW

CHIEFTAIN SIX

Model Number	Body/Style Number	Body Type & Seating	Factory Price	Shipping Weight	Prod. Total
6U	2569(D)	4-dr Sed-6P	1903/2006	3073	NA
6U	2511(D)	2-dr Sed-6P	848/1951	3043	NA
6U	2527(D)	2-dr Sed Cpe-6P	1848/1951	3128	NA
6U	2527B	2-dr Bus Cpe-3P	1713	3193	NA

CHIEFTAIN DELUXE SIX

6U	2537D	2-dr Cat HT-6P	2182	3343	NA
6U	2567DTX	2-dr Conv-6P	2314	3488	NA

CHIEFTAIN SUPER DELUXE SIX

6U	2537SD	2-dr Cat HT-6P	2244	3353	NA

CHIEFTAIN EIGHT

Model Number	Body/Style Number	Body Type & Seating	Factory Price	Shipping Weight	Prod. Total
8U	2569(D)	4-dr Sed-6P	1977/2081	3363/3373	NA
8U	2511(D)	2-dr Sed-6P	1922/2026	3328/3333	NA
8U	2527(D)	2-dr Sed Cpe-6p	1922/2026	3303/3318	NA
8U	2527B	2-dr Bus Cpe-3P	1787	3273	NA

CHIEFTAIN DELUXE EIGHT

8U	2537D	2-dr Cat HT-6P	2257	3428	NA
8U	2567DTX	2-dr Conv-6P	2388	3568	NA

CHIEFTAIN SUPER DELUXE EIGHT

8U	2537SD	2d Cat HT-6P	2320	3433	NA

NOTE 1: See Historical Footnotes for series production total.

NOTE 2: Data above slash for standard/below slash for Deluxe.

1951 Pontiac Chieftain Deluxe four-door station wagon, eight-cylinder.

ENGINES

[SIX] Six-cylinder. L-head. Cast iron block. Displacement: 239.2 cu. in. Bore & Stroke: 3-9/16 x 4 in. Compression Ratio: (standard) 6.5:1; (optional) 7.5:1. Brake hp: (standard) 96 @ 3400 rpm; (optional) 100 @ 3400 rpm. Four main bearings. Solid valve lifters. Carburetor: Rochester BC one-barrel.

[EIGHT] Eight cylinder. L-head. Cast iron block. Displacement: 268.4 cu. in. Bore & Stroke: 3-3/8 x 3-3/4 in. Compression Ratio: (standard) 6.5:1; (optional) 7.5:1. Brake hp: (standard) 116 @ 3600 rpm; (optional) 120 @ 3600 rpm. Five main bearings. Solid valve lifters. Carburetor: (synchromesh) Carter WCD 719S or WCD 719SA; (Hydra-Matic) Carter WCD 720S or WCD 720SA.

CHASSIS FEATURES: Wheelbase: 120 in. all lines. Overall length: (all cars) 202-1/2 in.; (wagons) 203.8 in. Front tread: 58 in. Rear tread: 59 in. Tires: (standard) 7.10 x 15 (special equipment) 7.60 x 15. Tube type.

OPTIONS: Seven-tube Chieftain radio. Mast antenna. No-Blo wind deflectors. Car cushions. Venti-Seat underseat heater. Venti-Shades. Windshield sun visor. Traffic light viewer. Poloroid visor. Rear fender panels (skirts). License frames. Illuminated hood ornament. Wheel trim rings. Steel wheel discs. White sidewall discs. Deluxe steering wheel. Remington Auto-Home shaver. Visor vanity mirror. Tissue dispenser. Direction signals. Compass. Rear window wiper. Windshield washers. Deluxe electric clock. Glove compartment light. Leather utility pocket. Luggage compartment light. Seat covers. Safti-Jack. Outside rearview mirror. Back-up lights. Safety spotlight. Fog lights. No-Rol. Bumper guards. Grille guard. Exhaust deflector. Venetian blinds. No-Mar gas filler trim. Fuel door lock. Scuff pads. Multi-purpose lamp. Underhood trouble lamp. Jack bag. Tool kit. A three-speed Synchromesh gearbox with column shift was standard on all models. Hydra-Matic four-speed automatic transmission was available at $159 extra. Rear axle ratios: (standard) 4.1:1, (economy) 3.9:1, (mountain) 4.3:1, (Hydra-Matic) 3.63:1.

1951 Pontiac Eight sedan delivery. OCW

1951 Pontiac Eight sedan delivery. JAG

1951 Pontiac-Acme limousine-hearse. JAG

1951 Pontiac-Barnette hearse. JAG

1951 Pontiac Chieftain Deluxe Eight two-door sedan. OCW

HISTORICAL FOOTNOTES: Production start-up took place November 27, 1950. The 1951 models were introduced December 11, 1950, and commemorated the company's 25th anniversary year. Arnold Lenz became the general manager of Pontiac Motor Division, but his tenure would be cut short by a tragic accident in 1952. Pontiac made 343,795 cars during the calendar-year. Model-year production came to 343,795 units. This included a total of 53,748 Streamliner and Chieftain sixes (10,195 with Hydra-Matic and 43,553 with synchromesh) and a total of 316,411 Streamliner and Chieftain eights (251,987 with Hydra-Matic and 64,424 with synchromesh). On an industry-wide basis, for the calendar-year, Pontiac built 6.7 percent of America's convertibles; 9.6 percent of domestic hardtops; and 4.7 percent of domestic station wagons. In the final count, car output was down 26 percent from 1950, but still second-best in Pontiac history. Body styles 2507 and 2507D Streamliner sedan-coupes were discontinued in April 1951. Pontiac's dropping of the fastback Streamliner series marked one of the closing chapters in a styling trend for a while. However, the Pontiac fastback would return in the mid-1960s. In 1951, Pontiac's headquarters operations in Pontiac, Mich., sourced 169,087 of 343,795 Pontiacs built or 49.2 percent of production. The Pontiac factory facilities included 5,800,000 square feet of floor area, of which 1,743,443 square feet were added since World War II. Main operations headquartered in Pontiac included car assembly, sheet metal works, an axle plant, a foundry, and an engine factory. Engine blocks made in Pontiac were also furnished to other General Motors divisions. The company also produced the amphibious Otter, a continuous-track military vehicle used in the Korean War. Despite the defense operations, employment at Pontiac, Mich., was reduced from 16,000 workers at the end of 1950 to 12,500 in December 1951.

1952 PONTIAC

1952 Pontiac Chieftain Deluxe four-door station wagon, eight-cylinder.

1952 CHIEFTAIN LINE - (SIX) SERIES 25 - (EIGHT) SERIES 27 - The fastback Streamliner line was discontinued and station wagons joined the A-body notchback styles in the Chieftain line. Grilles were similar to 1951, but all models had four black oblong indentations in the upper grille blade, under a new Pontiac nameplate. Dual sweep spear body moldings, stainless steel gravel guards, and chrome wheel rings and headlight rings characterized Deluxe models. Standard models had Dark Gray check pattern cloth door trim and solid Gray wool cloth seats. Deluxe models were trimmed in rich wool diamond-pattern cloth with a button-back look. Convertibles and Deluxe Catalina Hardtop Coupes had leather and cloth trims. Super Deluxe Catalinas had

two-tone green top grain cowhide seats with leather and cloth trim optional. The Super Deluxe Catalina Hardtop Coupe also carried special horizontally grooved trim plates on the rear roof pillar for outward identification. Standard station wagons featured seats in rust imitation leather. Deluxe station wagons offered a choice of Gray Bedford cord cloth with genuine leather in tan, red, green, blue, or black.

PONTIAC I.D. NUMBERS: VIN located on tag on left front door post. Matching engine serial number located on raised pad on front left side of cylinder block. Serial numbers took the form ( )-[ ]W{ }-1001 to ( )-[ ]W{ }-ending number. First symbol ( ) indicated the assembly plant: P=Pontiac, Mich.; C=California (South Gate); L=Linden, N.J.; W=Wilmington, Del.; K=Kansas City, Kan.; A=Atlanta, Ga.; F=Framingham, Mass. Second symbol [ ] indicated engine type: 6=inline six-cylinder; 8=inline eight-cylinder. Third symbol indicated model year: W=1952. Fourth symbol { } is a letter indicating type of transmission: S=synchromesh; H=Hydra-Matic. Remaining symbols are the sequential unit production number for each car line at each assembly plant. Beginning number at each plant is 1001. Ending numbers for 1952 were: [Series 25 six with synchromesh] (Mich.) 10,041; (Calif.) 1723; (N.J.) 1986; (Del.) 1967; (Kan.) 2745; (Ga.) 1669 and (Mass.) 1551. [Series 25 six with/Hydra-Matic] (Mich.) 3457; (Calif.) 1883; (N.J.) 1210; (Del.) 1223; (Kan.) 1406; (Ga.) 1165; (Mass.) 1103. [Series 27 eight with synchromesh] (Mich.) 16,833; (Calif.) 3440; (N.J.) 3920; (Del.) 3736; (Kan.) 6109; (Ga.) 3444 and (Mass.) 2312. [Series 27 eight with Hydra-Matic] (Mich.) 89,530; (Calif.) 20,083; (N.J.) 23,732; (Del.) 22,776; (Kan.) 39,194; (Ga.) 18,358 and (Mass.) 10,897. Fisher Body/style number on plate under hood on left of firewall can be helpful for identification of model and ordering parts. A prefix to the main number indicates model-year, 52=1952. The first two symbols in the main number indicate series 25 or 27. The next two symbols indicate the body style. Some numbers have an alphabetical suffix indicating trim level, such as D=Deluxe and SD=Super Deluxe. These numbers appear in body/style number column of charts below adjacent to corresponding body style listings.

1952 Pontiac Chieftain Deluxe convertible. OCW

CHIEFTAIN SIX

Model Number	Body/Style Number	Body Type & Seating	Factory Price	Shipping Weight	Prod. Total
6W	2569(D)	4-dr Sed-6P	2014/2119	3278/3278	NA
6W	2511(D)	2-dr Sed-6P	1956/2060	3253/3253	NA
6W	2563(D)	4-dr Sta Wag-8/6P	2615/2699	3593/3528	NA

CHIEFTAIN DELUXE SIX

6W	2537D	2-dr Cat HT-6P	2304	3358	NA
6W	2567DTX	2-dr Conv-6P	2444	3478	NA

CHIEFTAIN SUPER DELUXE SIX

6W	2537SD	2-dr Cat HT-6P	2370	3368	NA

CHIEFTAIN EIGHT

Model Number	Body/Style Number	Body Type & Seating	Factory Price	Shipping Weight	Prod. Total
8W	2569(D)	4-dr Sed-6P	2090/2194	3378/3378	NA
8W	2511(D)	2-dr Sed-6P	2031/2136	3333/3333	NA
8W	2562(D)	4-dr Sta Wag-8/6P	2689/2772	2688/3633	NA

CHIEFTAIN DELUXE EIGHT

8W	2537D	2-dr Cat HT-6P	2380	3443	NA
8W	2567DTX	2-dr Conv-6P	2518	3558	NA

CHIEFTAIN SUPER EIGHT

8W	2537SD	2-dr Cat HT-6P	2446	3448	NA

NOTE 1: See Historical Footnotes for series production total.

NOTE 2: Data above slash for standard/below slash for Deluxe.

NOTE 3: When (D) appears model came in both standard and Deluxe.

1952 Pontiac Chieftain Deluxe two-door sedan. OCW

1952 Pontiac Chieftain Deluxe Catalina two-door hardtop. JAG

1952 Pontiac Chieftain four-door station wagon. OCW

ENGINES

[SIX] Six-cylinder: L-head. Cast iron block. Displacement: 239.2 cu. in. Bore & Stroke: 3-9/16 x 4 in. Compression Ratio: (synchromesh) 6.8:1; (Hydra-Matic) 7.7:1. Brake hp: (synchromesh) 100 @ 3400 rpm; (Hydra-Matic) 102 @ 3400 rpm. Four main bearings. Solid valve lifters. Carburetor: Rochester BC one-barrel.

[EIGHT] Eight-cylinder: L-head. Cast iron block. Displacement: 268.4 cu. in. Bore & Stroke: 3-3/8 x 3-3/4 in. Compression Ratios: (synchromesh) 6.8:1; (Hydra-Matic) 7.7:1. Brake hp: (synchromesh) 118 @ 3600 rpm; (Hydra-Matic) 122 @ 3600 rpm. Five main bearings. Solid valve lifters. Carburetor: Carter WCD 720S or WCD 720SA two-barrel.

1952 Pontiac sedan delivery. OCW

CHASSIS FEATURES: Wheelbase: 120 in. Overall Length: (Cars) 202.5 in. (Station Wagons) 203.9 in. Front tread: 58 in. Rear tread: 59 in. Tires: (standard) 7.10 x 15 (special equipment) 7.60 x 15. Tube type.

OPTIONS: Seven-tube Chieftain radio. Mast antenna. No-Blo wind deflectors. Car cushions. Venti-Seat underseat heater. Venti-Shades. Windshield sun visor. Traffic light viewer. Polaroid visor. Rear fender panels (skirts). License frames. Illuminated hood ornament. Wheel trim rings. Steel wheel discs. White sidewall discs. Deluxe steering wheel. Remington Auto-Home shaver. Visor vanity mirror. Tissue dispenser. Direction signals. Compass. Rear window wiper. Windshield washers. Deluxe electric clock. Glove compartment light. Leather utility pocket. Luggage compartment light. Seat covers. Safti-Jack. Outside rearview mirror. Back-up lights. Safety spotlight. Fog lights. No-Rol. Bumper guards. Grille guard. Exhaust deflector. Venetian blinds. No-Mar gas filler trim. Fuel door lock. Scuff pads. Multi-purpose lamp. Underhood trouble lamp. Jack bag. Tool kit. A three-speed synchromesh gearbox with column shift was standard on all models. Hydra-Matic four-speed automatic transmission was available at $159 extra. Rear axle ratios: (standard) 4.1:1, (economy) 3.9:1, (mountain) 4.3:1, (Hydra-Matic) 3.08:1.

1952 Pontiac Chieftain Deluxe four-door sedan. OCW

HISTORICAL FOOTNOTES: Production of 1952 Pontiacs began in November 1951. The new cars were introduced December 3, 1951. Production was 277,156 cars for the calendar-year giving Pontiac fifth rank in the American auto industry. This was, however, a 19.4 percent decrease from 1951, which followed the general industry trend. Sedan Delivery truck production was held down under NPA Korean War guidelines that favored production of heavy-duty trucks. Only 984 Pontiac Sedan Deliveries were manufactured. Pontiac escaped a complete shutdown during a steel shortage in 1952, although production hit rock bottom in July. The division quickly got up steam after the strike ended, and achieved full utilization of resources in October when 32,843 cars were built. Model-year production included a total of 19,809 Series 25 Chieftain sixes (15,582 with Hydra-Matic and 4227 with synchromesh) and a total of 251,564 Series 27 Chieftain eights (218,602 with Hydra-Matic and 32,962 with synchromesh). Combined model-year assemblies were 271,373. Registration gains in five states--Arizona, Arkansas, Louisiana, Minnesota, and South Carolina--helped Pontiac capture 6.4 percent of 1952 U.S. new-car sales. Seven other states retained their same percentage. Michigan, Pontiac's home state, reported the highest state percentage (7.4), but New York claimed the highest number sold (23,156). In total 1952 car output, Pontiac accounted for 6.39 percent of industry production, against 6.44 percent in 1951. This gave it a secure hold on fifth place. Catalina Hardtops accounted for 19 percent of 1952 volume, edging up from 13 percent in 1951. Hydra-Matic Drive was used in 84 percent of all Pontiacs. Defense work went into high gear in 1952, with strong production on major contracts for all-aluminum amphibious cargo carriers (Otters), 4.5-in. rockets, and twin Bofors-type dual 40-mm cannon--plus a secret project launched late in the fall. With the defense work, Pontiac employment rose from 1951's low of 12,500 workers to more than 17,500. At year's end, Pontiac dealers had practically no new-cars in inventory and many orders for 1953 models. Also at the close of 1952, Pontiac entered its 60th year as a vehicle builder and its 45th in the automotive field--first under the Oakland designation and since 1926 with the Pontiac name. Arnold Lenz was general manager of Pontiac Motor Division. E.R. Pettengill was the administrative assistant to the general manager. L.W. Ward was general sales manager. George A. Delaney was chief engineer. Pontiac general manager Arnold Lenz was killed in a car-train crash at a Lapeer, Mich., railroad crossing. *Motor Trend* road tested the 1952 Pontiac Chieftain Deluxe sedan recording a 21-second quarter-mile run and top speed of 95.24 mph. Fuel economy was 16.4 mpg in overall driving.

1953 PONTIAC

1953 Pontiac Chieftain Deluxe four-door sedan, eight-cylinder.

1953 Pontiac sedan delivery. OCW

CHIEFTAIN LINE - (SIX) SERIES 25 - (EIGHT) SERIES 27 - The 1953 Pontiacs were new from bumper to bumper. Changes included one-piece windshields; wraparound rear windows; new hood ornaments; ignition key starting; stepped-up rear fenders; more massive chrome headlight doors on all models; new grille styling that encircled parking lamps; and "panorama view" instrument panels. Standard models were now called Specials and came with small hubcaps, rubber gravel guards, straight upper beltline trim and short arrow-shaped side trim. Deluxe Chieftains had long "dual streak" body moldings, stainless steel gravel guards with rear fender extensions, dipping belt moldings and chrome full wheel discs. Eights had an '8' emblem between twin "Silver Streaks" on deck lids. Cars finished in Caravan Blue, Spruce Green, Marathon Gray and Black had red Pontiac nameplates in front, while those done in other colors had black nameplates. The Custom Catalina Coupe, was outwardly distinguished by horizontally grooved decorative trim plates at the rear roof pillar edge. This car was available only in Laurel Green, Milano Ivory or two-tone combinations of these hues. A nylon and leather interior of harmonizing tones was featured and an all-leather option was available and frequently ordered.

1953 Pontiac Custom Catalina coupe. JAG

1953 Pontiac Chieftain Deluxe convertible. OCW

PONTIAC I.D. NUMBERS: VIN located on tag on left front door post. Matching engine serial number located on raised pad on front left side of cylinder block. Serial numbers took the form ( )-[ ]X{ }-1001 to ( )-[ ]X{ }-ending number. First symbol ( ) indicated the assembly plant: P=Pontiac, Mich.; C=California (South Gate); L=Linden, N.J.; W=Wilmington, Del.; K=Kansas City, Kan.; A=Atlanta, Ga.; F=Framingham, Mass. Second symbol [ ] indicated engine type: 6=inline six-cylinder; 8=inline eight-cylinder. Third symbol indicated model year: X=1953. Fourth symbol { } is a letter indicating type of transmission: S=synchromesh; H=Hydra-Matic; P=Powerglide. Remaining symbols are the sequential unit production number for each car line at each assembly plant. Beginning number at each plant is 1001. Ending numbers for 1953 were: [SERIES 25 SIX with synchromesh] (Mich.) 18,925; (Calif.) 3115; (N.J.) 3799; (Del.) 3496; (Kan.) 4543; (Ga.) 2888 and (Mass.) 2691. [SERIES 25 SIX with/Hydra-Matic] (Mich.) 3872; (Calif.) 1227; (N.J.) 1163; (Del.) 1180; (Kan.) 1305; (Ga.) 1138; (Mass.) 1058. [SERIES 25 SIX with Powerglide] (Mich.) 1384. [SERIES 27 EIGHT with synchromesh] (Mich.) 35,914; (Calif.) 4469; (N.J.) 8264; (Del.) 6368; (Kan.) 9013; (Ga.) 6391 and (Mass.) 5041. [SERIES 27 EIGHT with Hydra-Matic] (Mich.) 117,860; (Calif.) 28,700; (N.J.) 30,873; (Del.) 28,720; (Kan.) 48,580; (Ga.) 25,799 and (Mass.) 19,391. [SERIES 27 EIGHT with Powerglide] (Mich.) 9950. Fisher Body/style number on plate on left of firewall can be helpful for identification of model and ordering parts. A prefix to the main number indicates model year, 53=1953. The first two symbols in the main number indicate series 25 or 27. The next two symbols indicate the body style. Some numbers have an alphabetical suffix indicating trim level, such as D=Deluxe and SD=Super Deluxe. These numbers appear in body/style number column of charts below adjacent to corresponding body style listings.

CHIEFTAIN SIX

Model Number	Body/Style Number	Body Type & Seating	Factory Price	Shipping Weight	Prod. Total
CHIEFTAIN SPECIAL/CHIEFTAIN DELUXE SIX					
6X	2569W(D)	4-dr Sed-6P	2015/2119	3391/3396	NA
6X	2511W(D)	2-dr Sed-6P	1956/2060	3341/3356	NA
6X	2537D	2-dr Del Cat HT-6P	2304	3416	NA
6X	2567DTX	2-dr Del Conv-6P	2444	3546	NA
6X	2563DF	4-dr Del Sta Wag-6P	2590	3636	NA
6X	2562(F)	4-dr Spl Sta Wag-8/6P	2450/2505	3633/3606	NA
CHIEFTAIN CUSTOM SIX					
6X	2537SD	2-dr Cus Cat HT-6P	2370	3416	NA

NOTE 1: See Historical Footnotes for series production total.

NOTE 2: Data above slash for standard/below slash for Deluxe.

CHIEFTAIN EIGHT

Model Number	Body/Style Number	Body Type & Seating	Factory Price	Shipping Weight	Prod. Total
CHIEFTAIN SPECIAL/CHIEFTAIN DELUXE EIGHT					
8X	2569W(D)	4-dr Sed-6P	2090/2194	3456/3471	NA
8X	2511W(D)	2-dr Sed-6P	2031/2136	3421/3436	NA
8X	2537D	2-dr Del Cat HT-6P	2380	3496	NA
8X	2567DTX	2-dr Del Conv-6P	2515	3626	NA
8X	2562DF	4-Del Sta Wag-6P	2664	3716	NA
8X	2562(F)	4-dr Spl Sta Wag-8/6P	2525/2580	3713/3686	NA
CHIEFTAIN CUSTOM EIGHT					
8X	2537SD	2-dr Cus Cat HT-6P	2446	3496	NA

NOTE 1: See Historical Footnotes for series production total.

NOTE 2: Data above slash for standard/below slash for Deluxe.

NOTE 3: (D) indicates available in both Special and Deluxe sub-series.

1953 Pontiac four-door station wagon. OCW

ENGINES

(SIX) Six-cylinder. L-head. Cast iron block. Displacement: 239.2 cu. in. Bore & Stroke: 3-9/16 x 4 in. Compression Ratio: (synchromesh) 7.0:1; (Hydra-Matic) 7.7:1. Brake hp: (synchromesh) 115 @ 3800 rpm; (Hydra-Matic) 118 @ 3800 rpm. Four main bearings. Solid valve lifters. Carburetor: Carter WCD-2010-S two-barrel.

(EIGHT) Eight-cylinder. L-head. Cast iron block. Displacement: 268.4 cu. in. Bore & Stroke: 3-3/8 x 3-3/4 in. Compression Ratios: (synchromesh) 6.8:1; (Hydra-Matic) 7.7:1. Brake hp: (synchromesh) 118 @ 3600 rpm; (Hydra-Matic) 122 @ 3600 rpm. Five main bearings. Solid valve lifters. Carburetors: (synchromesh) Carter WCD 719S or 719SA; (Hydra-Matic) Carter WCD 720S or 720SA two-barrel.

1953 Pontiac Chieftain Deluxe convertible with continental kit and wire wheel hubcaps . OCW

CHASSIS FEATURES: Wheelbase: 122 in. Overall Length: (passenger cars) 202-11/16 in.; (station wagons) 205.3 in. Front tread: 58.5 in. Rear tread: 59.05 in. Tires: (passenger cars) 7.10 x 15 four-ply; (regular equipment station wagons and sedan deliveries/optional passenger cars) 7.10 x 15 six-ply; (optional passenger cars only) 7.60 x 15 four-ply. Pontiac promoted new "Tru-Arc" safety steering and "Curve Control" front suspension in 1953.

OPTIONS: Power steering ($134). Wood grain Di-Noc exterior trim ($80 all station wagons). Venti-heat underseat heater and defroster. Chieftain seven-tube radio. Directional signals. Autronic Eye. Back-up lamps. Non-glare rearview mirror. Rear fender panels (skirts came with steel underscore on Deluxes). Exhaust deflector. No-Mar fuel guard door trim. Deluxe steering wheel (standard on Deluxes). Illuminated hood ornament. Windshield sun visor. Traffic light viewer. Latex foam seat cushions. Windshield washers. Outside rearview mirror. Visor vanity mirror. Glovebox lamp. Trunk lamp. Underhood lamp. Lighted ashtray. Hand brake signal. Grille guard. Wing guards. E-Z-Eye glass. Dual fog lamps. Rear seat speaker. Electric antenna. Safety spot lamp. Chrome trim rings. Safti-jack. Oil bath air cleaner. (Dealer installed options): Seat covers. Hand spot lamp. Venti-shades. Fold-away umbrella. Draft deflectors; Rear window wiper. Tissue dispenser. Magna Tray. Fuel door lock. Illuminated compass. Color tipon. Road reflector flares. Thermaster refrigerator. Thermaster bottle. Auto-Home Remington electric shaver. Continental tire extension. Simulated wire wheel discs. A three-speed synchromesh gearbox with column-mounted gearshift was standard on all models. Dual-Range four-speed Hydra-Matic drive was available at $178 extra. Two-speed Powerglide automatic transmission (by Chevrolet) was installed in Pontiacs built at Pontiac, Mich., from September 8, 1953, to November 19, 1953, after an August 12 fire at GM's Livonia, Mich., Hydra-Matic factory. Rear axle ratios: (six) 4.1:1; (Eight) 3.9:1; (six/mountain) 4.3:1, (eight/mountain) 4.1:1; (Hydra-Matic) 3.08:1. The high-compression Hydra-Matic cylinder head was available, as an option, on cars with synchromesh.

HISTORICAL FOOTNOTES: A total of 38,914 Chieftain sixes were built. Of these, 33,705 had synchromesh; 4507 had Hydra-Matic, and 702 had Powerglide attachments. A total of 379,705 Chieftain eights were built. Of these, 68,565 had synchromesh; 293,343 had Hydra-Matic and 17,797 had Powerglide attachments. Production lines started cranking out 1953 Pontiacs on November 17 of the previous year and they were introduced to the public December 6, 1952. Model year output came to 418,619 units. The calendar year counted production of 414,011 cars. This maintained Pontiac's rank as the fifth largest American automaker another season. After the devastating fire August 12 at the Hydra-Matic transmission plant in Livonia, Mich., cars were made for a time at the Pontiac, Mich., factory, with Chevrolet Powerglide transmissions installed. Following the untimely death of Arnold Lenz, Robert Critchfield became general manager of Pontiac Motor Division. Plans to install V-8s in 1953 Pontiacs were set back by Lenz's fatal accident and flathead straight eights continued to be used. However, the 1953 Pontiac chassis is designed to accommodate the 1955-style V-8.

1953 Superior-Pontiac ambulance. JAG

1953 Superior-Pontiac funeral car. JAG

1953 Superior-Pontiac funeral car. JAG

1953 Superior-Pontiac funeral car. JAG

Notes on model nomenclature: Body style suffix 'SD' indicates Super Deluxe trim. The term Catalina was Pontiac's nomenclature for pillarless hardtop styling. Body style 2562, the Special station wagon, came standard with three seats. Body style 2562F was the Special station wagon with two seats, the second of the folding type. Body style 2537SD, T Body Style numbers were embossed on the firewall data plate and preceded by the prefix '53' to designate the model year.

1954 PONTIAC

1954 Pontiac Chieftain Deluxe four-door sedan, eight-cylinder.

CHIEFTAIN LINE - (SIX) SERIES 25 (EIGHT) SERIES 27 - In 1954 the Chieftains represented Pontiac's least costly line of A-body models on a 122-in. wheelbase and had styling changes common to all Pontiacs. Included were a grille with an oval centerpiece; new hood ornament and nameplate; and thinner "Silver Streaks." Chieftain Specials had straight upper beltline moldings; small stainless steel gravel guards; four "Silver Streaks" on the deck lid; and short front fender spears. Chieftain Deluxes had broad, full-length "sweepspears" that blended into the gravel guards; the gravel guards had rear fender extensions and the upper beltline trim "dipped" down. There were also four deck lid streaks. The Chieftain Custom series included the `Super Deluxe' Catalina Coupe, which was outwardly distinguished by decorative edge plates on the roof pillars. Custom Catalina hardtops also have special plated interior roof bows. Interior trims ranged from two-tone pattern cloth-and-elascofab combinations on standard models to all-leather options on Catalinas, convertibles and Deluxe station wagons. A new B-O-P assembly plant in Arlington, Texas, began operations this year.

1954 Pontiac Chieftain Deluxe four-door sedan . JAG

PONTIAC I.D. NUMBERS: VIN located on tag on left front door post. Matching engine serial number located on raised pad on front left side of cylinder block. Serial numbers took the form ( )-[ ]X{ }-1001 to ( )-[ ]X{ }-ending number. First symbol ( ) indicated the assembly plant: P=Pontiac, Mich.; C=California (South Gate); L=Linden, N.J.; W=Wilmington, Del.; K=Kansas City, Kan.; A=Atlanta, Ga.; F=Framingham, Mass.; T=Arlington, Texas. Second symbol [ ] indicated engine type: 6=inline six-cylinder; 8=inline eight-cylinder. Third symbol indicated model year: Z=1954. Fourth symbol { } is a letter indicating type of transmission: S=synchromesh; H=Hydra-Matic or (Star Chief only) C=conventional (synchromesh); A=automatic (Hydra-Matic). Remaining symbols are the sequential unit production number for each car line at each assembly plant. Beginning number at each plant is 1001. Ending numbers for 1954 were: [SERIES 25 SIX with synchromesh] (Mich.) 12,141; (Calif.) 1799; (N.J.) 2429; (Dela.) 2233; (Kan.) 2622; (Ga.) 1866 and (Mass.) 2033; (Texas) 1399. [SERIES 25 SIX with/Hydra-Matic] (Mich.) 2858; (Calif.) 1076; (N.J.) 1090; (Del.) 1096; (Kan.) 1117; (Ga.) 1067; (Mass.) 1053.; (Texas) 1023. [SERIES 27 EIGHT with synchromesh] (Mich.) 16612; (Calif.) 2351; (N.J.) 3471; (Del.) 3032; (Kan.) 3890; (Ga.) 3265; (Mass.) 3146; (Texas) 2043. [SERIES 27 EIGHT with Hydra-Matic] (Mich.) 60,891; (Calif.) 8698; (N.J.) 16,002; (Del.) 10,002; (Kan.) 12,490; (Ga.) 7477; (Mass.) 7854; (Texas) 4330. [SERIES 28 with synchromesh] (Mich.) 1371; (Calif.) 1015; (N.J.) 1046; (Del.) 1049; (Kan.) 1036; (Ga.) 1010; (Mass.) 1035; (Texas)

1008. [SERIES 28 with Hydra-Matic] (Mich.) 60,543; (Calif.) 8165; (N.J.) 13,680; (Del.) 8629; (Kan.) 12,117; (Ga.) 8076; (Mass.) 6382; (Texas) 4925. Fisher Body/style number on plate under hood on left of firewall can be helpful for identification of model and ordering parts. A prefix to the main number indicates model year, 54=1954. The first two symbols in the main number indicate series 25, 27, or 28 Star Chief. The next two symbols indicate the body style. Some numbers have an alphabetical suffix indicating trim level, such as D=Deluxe and SD=Super Deluxe. These numbers appear in body/style number column of charts below adjacent to corresponding body style listings.

CHIEFTAIN SIX

Model Number	Body/Style Number	Body Type & Seating	Factory Price	Shipping Weight	Prod. Total
CHIEFTAIN SIX SPECIAL/DELUXE					
6Z	2569W(D)	4-dr Sed-6P	2027/2131	3391/3406	NA
6Z	2511W(D)	2-dr Sed-6P	1968/2072	3331/3351	NA
6Z	2537D	2-dr Del Cat HT-6P	2316	3421	NA
6Z	2562DF	4-dr Del Sta Wag-6P	2504	3646	NA
6Z	2562(F)	4-dr Spl Sta Wag-8/6P	2364/2419	3691/3601	NA
CHIEFTAIN CUSTOM SIX					
6Z	2537SD	2-dr Cus Cat HT-6P	2582	3421	NA

NOTE 1: See Historical Footnotes for series production total.

NOTE 2: Data above slash for standard/below slash for Deluxe.

1954 Pontiac Star Chief Custom Catalina two-door hardtop. OCW

CHIEFTAIN EIGHT

Model Number	Body/Style Number	Body Type & Seating	Factory Price	Shipping Weight	Prod. Total
CHIEFTAIN EIGHT SPECIAL/DELUXE					
8Z	2569W(D)	4-dr Sed-6P	2102/2206	3451/3466	NA
8Z	2511W(D)	2-dr Sed-6P	2043/2148	3396/3416	NA
8Z	2537D	2-dr Del Cat HT-6P	2392	3491	NA
8Z	2562DF	4-dr Del Sta Wag-6P	2579	3716	NA
8Z	2562(F)	4-dr Spl Sta Wag-8/6P	2439/2494	3771/3676	NA
CHIEFTAIN CUSTOM EIGHT					
8Z	2537SD	2-dr Cus Cat HT-6P	2458	3491	NA

NOTE 1: See Historical Footnotes for series production total.

NOTE 2: Data above slash for standard/below slash for Deluxe.

NOTE 3: (D) indicates model is available in Special and Deluxe sub-series.

NOTE 4: (F) indicates folding second seat in station wagons.

1954 Pontiac Custom Star Chief four-door sedan, eight-cylinder.

1954 Pontiac Chieftain Deluxe Catalina two-door hardtop with wire wheel hubcaps. JAG

STAR CHIEF LINE - (EIGHT) SERIES 28 - A brand new long wheelbase Star Chief line was created by adding an 11-inch frame extension towards the rear of the GM A-body platform and fitting longer rear sheet metal. Two `28' sub-series, Deluxe and Custom, were provided. Both came only with eight-cylinder power. All Star Chiefs had five "Silver Streaks" on the deck lid, special visored taillight doors with rear fender extensions, longer `sweepspears' and three small stylized stars on rear fender fins. Deluxe trims were regular equipment, but the "Super Deluxe" Custom Sedan and Custom Catalina were further distinguished by extra-rich cloth-and-leather upholstery inside and distinctive roof trim outside. The Star Chief Custom Catalina hardtops also have special plated interior roof bows.

STAR CHIEF DELUXE

Model Number	Body/Style Number	Body Type & Seating	Factory Price	Shipping Weight	Prod. Total
8Z	2869WD	4-dr Sed-6P	2301	3536	NA
8Z	2867DTX	2-dr Conv-6P	2630	3776	NA

STAR CHIEF CUSTOM

8Z	2869WSD	4-dr Sed-6P	2394	3526	NA
8Z	2837SD	2-dr Cus Cat HT-6P	2557	3551	NA

ENGINES

(SIX) Six-cylinder. L-head. Cast iron block. Displacement: 239.2 cu. in. Bore & Stroke: 3-9/16 x 4 in. Compression Ratio: (synchromesh) 7.0:1; (Hydra-Matic) 7.7:1. Brake hp: (synchromesh) 115 @ 3800 rpm; (Hydra-Matic) 118 @ 3800 rpm. Four main bearings. Solid valve lifters. Carburetor: Carter WCD-2010-S two-barrel.

(EIGHT) Eight-cylinder. L-head. Cast iron block. Displacement: 268.4 cu. in. Bore & Stroke: 3-3/8 x 3-3/4 in. Compression Ratios: (synchromesh) 6.8:1; (Hydra-Matic) 7.7:1. Brake hp: (synchromesh) 122 @ 3800 rpm; (Hydra-Matic) 127 @ 3800 rpm. Five main bearings. Solid valve lifters. Carburetors: (synchromesh) Carter WCD 719SA used in early production; WCD 720SA used on most; (Hydra-Matic) Carter WCD 2122S.

CHASSIS FEATURES: Wheelbase: (Chieftains) 122 in.; (Star Chiefs) 124 in. Overall Length: (Chieftain passenger cars) 202-11/16 in.; (Chieftain station wagons) 205.3 in.; (Star Chiefs) 213.7 in. Front tread: (All) 58.5 in. Rear tread: (All) 59.05 in. Tires: (passenger cars) 7.10 x 15 four-ply; (station wagons) 7.10 x 15 six-ply; (optional passenger cars only) 7.60 x 15 four-ply.

1954 Pontiac Star Chief Custom Catalina two-door hardtop (rear view). OCW

OPTIONS: Power steering ($134). Wood grain Di-Noc exterior trim ($80 all station wagons). Venti-heat underseat heater and defroster. Chieftain 7-tube radio. Directional signals. Autronic Eye. Back-up lamps. Non-glare rearview mirror. Rear fender panels (skirts came with steel underscore on Deluxes). Exhaust deflector. No-Mar fuel guard door trim. Deluxe steering wheel (standard on Deluxes). Illuminated hood ornament. Windshield sun visor. Traffic light viewer. Latex foam seat cushions. Windshield washers. Outside rearview mirror. Visor vanity mirror. Glovebox lamp. Trunk lamp. Underhood lamp. Lighted ashtray. Hand brake signal. Grille guard. Wing guards. E-Z-Eye glass. Dual fog lamps. Rear seat speaker. Electric antenna. Safety spot lamp. Chrome trim rings. Safti-jack. Oil bath air cleaner. (Dealer installed options): Seat covers. Hand spot lamp. Venti-shades. Fold-away umbrella. Draft deflectors; Rear window wiper. Tissue dispenser. Magna Tray. Fuel door lock. Illuminated compass. Color tipon. Road reflector flares. Thermaster refrigerator. Thermaster bottle. Auto-Home Remington electric shaver. Continental tire extension. Simulated wire wheel discs. Power brakes ($36). Air-conditioning. Electric window lifts. Padded dashboard. Door edge guards. Door handle guards. Arctic windshield wipers. Dash panel courtesy lamps. Wide brake pedals. Reduced ratio power steering. Grille bug screen. Comfort-Control 300-position manual seat. Remote control outside mirrors. Deluxe steering wheel for Special station wagons. A three-speed synchromesh gearbox with column-mounted gearshift was standard on all models. Dual-Range four-speed Hydra-Matic drive was available at $178 extra. Rear axle ratios: (six) 4.1:1; (eight) 3.9:1; (Star Chief with Hydra-Matic) 3.23:1 (six/mountain) 4.3:1, (eight/mountain) 4.1:1; (Hydra-Matic) 3.08:1. The high-compression Hydra-Matic cylinder head was available, as an option, on cars with synchromesh.

1954 Pontiac Star Chief Deluxe convertible (rear view). JAG

HISTORICAL FOOTNOTES: Production began December 1, 1953. The 1954 models were introduced December 18, 1953. Calendar year production was 370,887. Model year production was 287,744. The only model year production breakouts available are: [CHIEFTAIN] A total of 22,670 Chieftain sixes were built. Of these 19,666 had synchromesh and 3004 had Hydra-Matic attachments. A total of 149,986 Chieftain eights were built. Of these, 29,906 had synchromesh and 120,080, had Hydra-Matic attachments. [STAR CHIEF] A total of 115,088 Star Chiefs were built. Of these, 571 had synchromesh and 114,517 had Hydra-Matic attachments. The new Buick-Olds-Pontiac (BOP) assembly plant in Arlington, Texas, opened on June 3, 1953. A Catalina hardtop built on June 18, 1954, was the company's five millionth automobile produced. The sedan delivery was not cataloged this year although rumors persist that four were built in early production.

1954 Meteor-Pontiac funeral car. JAG

1955 PONTIAC

1955 Pontiac Chieftain '860' Colony station wagon, V-8.

CHIEFTAIN LINE - (V-8) - SERIES 27 - Completely new bodies and chassis were featured on all 1955 Pontiacs. Changes from 1954 included a massive, divided bumper grille; revised body moldings; split "Silver Streak" bands; twin streaks atop rear fenders; swept style front wheel cutouts; and wraparound windshields. Chieftains were divided into three sub-series. One was a unique station wagon. This Custom Safari had two-door hardtop styling and Star Chief trim and appointments on the smaller Series 27 chassis. The two-door Custom Safari was announced January 31, 1955. It is one of a few Pontiacs recognized as Milestone Cars. These Safaris feature two-door hardtop styling with slanting tailgates, width-wise grooved roofs, Pontiac rear fenders and luxury interior appointments. Except for this offering, which was really considered a Star Chief, Chieftains featured constant width slanting vertical slash moldings. Chieftain 860s had small hubcaps; painted taillight housings; and no upper beltline moldings. Chieftain 870s had full wheel discs; chrome taillight rings; and upper beltline trim.

PONTIAC I.D. NUMBERS: VIN located on left front door hinge pillar. Matching engine serial number on pad on front of right-hand cylinder bank. Serial numbers took the form ( )-[ ]55{ }-1001 to ( )-[ ]55{ }-ending number. The first symbol ( ) was a letter indicating assembly plant: P=Pontiac, Mich.; T=Arlington, Texas; A=Atlanta, Ga.; F=Framingham, Mass; K=Kansas City, Kan.; L=Linden, N.J.; C=South Gate, Calif.; W=Wilmington, Del. The second symbol [ ] indicated series: 7=Series 27; 8=Series 28. The third and fourth symbols indicated model year: 55=1955. The fifth symbol indicated transmission: S=synchromesh; H=Hydra-Matic. The following symbols were the sequential unit production number starting at 1001 for each series at each assembly plant. Ending numbers for 1955 were: [SERIES 27 with synchromesh] (Mich.) 26879; (Texas) 3331; (Ga.) 6802; (Mass.) 4714; (Kan.) 5868; (N.J.) 6536; (Calif.) 4572; (Del.) 5564. [SERIES 27 with Hydra-Matic] (Mich.) 12,6714; (Texas) 14,339; (Ga.) 26,027; (Mass.) 15,847; (Kan.) 30,873; (N.J.) 33,154; (Calif.) 31,707; (Del.) 24,851. [SERIES 28 with synchromesh] (Mich.) 1696; (Texas) 1026; (Ga.) 1018; (Mass.) 1085; (Kan.) 1061; (N.J.) 1134; (Calif.) 1061; (Del.) 1075. [SERIES 28 with Hydra-Matic] (Mich.) 85,247; (Texas) 10,511; (Ga.) 17,315; (Mass.) 10,484; (Kan.) 20,584; (N.J.) 24,173; (Calif.) 20,372; (Del.) 17,278. Fisher Body/style number on plate under hood on left of firewall can be helpful for identification of model and ordering parts. A prefix to the main number indicates model year, 55=1955. The first two symbols in the main number indicate series 27 or 28 Star Chief. The next two symbols indicate the body style. Some numbers have an alphabetical suffix indicating trim level, such as D=Deluxe and SD=Super Deluxe. These numbers appear in body/style number column of charts below adjacent to corresponding body style listings.

1955 Pontiac Chieftain 870 two-door sedan. OCW

CHIEFTAIN 860 (SPECIAL)

Model Number	Body/Style Number	Body Type & Seating	Factory Price	Shipping Weight	Prod. Total
860-27	2519	4-dr Sed-6P	2164	3621	65,155
860-27	2511	2-dr Sed-6P	2105	3586	58,654
860-27	2562	4-dr Sed-6P	2518	3736	6091
860-27	2563F	2-dr Sta Wag-6P	2434	3736	8618

CHIEFTAIN 870 (Deluxe)

Model Number	Body/Style Number	Body Type & Seating	Factory Price	Shipping Weight	Prod. Total
870-27	2519D	4-dr Sed-6P	2268	3621	91,187
870-27	2511D	2-dr Sed-6P	2209	3586	28,950
870-27	2537D	2-dr Del Cat HT-6P	2335	3631	72,608
870-27	2563DF	4-dr Wagon-6P	2603	3786	19,439

STAR CHIEF CUSTOM (SERIES 27)

Model Number	Body/Style Number	Body Type & Seating	Factory Price	Shipping Weight	Prod. Total
27	2764DF	2-dr Safari-6P	2962	3746	3760

NOTE 1: 354,466 Chieftain 860s and 870s were built.

NOTE 2: 57,730 had synchromesh and 296,736 had Hydra-Matic.

NOTE 3: The two-door Star Chief Custom Safari is included in these totals.

NOTE 4: Two Series 27 chassis were converted into hearses or ambulances.

1955 Pontiac Star Chief two-door convertible, V-8.

STAR CHIEF LINE - (V-8) - SERIES 28 - Completely new A-body styling with an 11-inch rear frame extension characterized the 1955 Star Chiefs. All models featured tapered slanting vertical slash moldings, which were also used on the Series 27 two-door Star Chief Custom Safari. Star Chiefs, including the Safari, also had three stylized star emblems on front fenders and doors. The Catalina coupe and the convertible had wide fluted lower rear fender extensions. The Custom four-door sedan had stainless steel moldings encircling the side windows. Full wheel discs were regular equipment on all Star Chiefs.

1955 Pontiac Chieftain 870 four-door sedan. OCW

STAR CHIEF (SERIES 28)

Model Number	Body/Style Number	Body Type & Seating	Factory Price	Shipping Weight	Prod. Total
28	2819D	4-dr Sed-6P	2362	3666	44,800
28	2867DTX	2-dr Conv-6P	2691	3901	19,762

STAR CHIEF CUSTOM (SERIES 28)

Model Number	Body/Style Number	Body Type & Seating	Factory Price	Shipping Weight	Prod. Total
28	2819SD	4-dr Sed-6P	2455	3666	35,153
28	2837SD	2-dr Cat HT-6P	2499	3676	99,929

NOTE 1: 199,624 Series 28 Star Chiefs were built.

NOTE 2: 1156 had synchromesh and 198,468 had Hydra-Matic.

NOTE 3: This does not include two-door Star Chief Custom Safari production.

NOTE 4: 280 Series 28 chassis were converted into hearses or ambulances.

1955 Pontiac Star Chief Custom Safari. OCW

1955 Pontiac Star Chief Custom Safari (rear view). OCW

BASE ENGINE: V-8: Overhead valves. Cast iron block. Displacement: 287.2 cu. in. Bore & Stroke: 3-3/4 x 3-1/4 in. Compression Ratio: (synchromesh) 7.4:1; (Hydra-Matic) 8.0:1. Brake hp: (synchromesh) 173 @ 4400 rpm; (Hydra-Matic) 180 @ 4600 rpm. Five main bearings. Hydraulic valve lifters. Carburetors: Carter WGD models 2182S, 2182SA, 2182SB, 2207S, or 2207SB two-barrel. Also, Rochester 2GC two-barrel.

1955 Pontiac Star Chief Custom Catalina two-door hardtop. OCW

CHASSIS FEATURES: Wheelbase: (Series 27) 122 in.; (Series 28) 124 in. Overall Length: (Series 27 passenger cars) 203.2 in.; (Series 27 station wagons) 202.9 in.; (Series 28) 210.2 in. Front tread: (All) 58.66 in. Rear tread: (All) 59.05 in. Tires: (passenger cars) 7.10 x 15; (station wagons 7.60 x 15, tubeless type. The use of 7.60 x 15 tires was recommended for Star Chiefs).

1955 Pontiac Star Chief four-door sedan. JAG

1955 Pontiac Star Chief Super Deluxe convertible. JAG

OPTIONS: Power steering ($108). Power brakes ($36). Fender skirts ($11). Power windows ($97). Four-way power seat ($40). Venti-heat underseat heater and defroster. Chieftain seven-tube radio. Directional signals. Autronic Eye. Back-up lamps. Non-glare rearview mirror. Exhaust deflector. No-Mar fuel guard door trim. Deluxe steering wheel (standard on Deluxes). Illuminated hood ornament. Windshield sun visor. Traffic light viewer. Latex foam seat cushions. Windshield washers. Outside rearview mirror. Visor vanity mirror. Glovebox lamp. Trunk lamp. Underhood lamp. Lighted ashtray. Handbrake signal. Grille guard. Wing guards. E-Z-Eye glass. Dual fog lamps. Rear seat speaker. Electric antenna. Safety spot lamp. Chrome trim rings. Safti-jack. Oil bath air cleaner. (Dealer installed options): Seat covers. Hand spot lamp. Venti-shades. Fold-away umbrella. Draft deflectors; Rear window wiper. Tissue dispenser. Magna Tray. Fuel door lock. Illuminated compass. Color tipon. Road reflector flares. Thermaster refrigerator. Thermaster bottle. Auto-Home Remington electric shaver. Continental tire extension. Simulated wire wheel discs. Power brakes ($36). Air-conditioning. Electric window lifts. Padded dashboard. Door edge guards. Door handle guards. Arctic windshield wipers. Dash panel courtesy lamps. Wide brake pedals. Reduced ratio power steering. Grille bug screen. Comfort-Control 300-position manual seat. Remote control outside mirrors. Deluxe steering wheel for Special station wagons. A three-speed synchromesh gearbox with column-mounted gearshift was standard on all models. Dual-Range four-speed Hydra-Matic drive was available at $178 extra. Available after March 1, 1955, for $35 was an optional engine "power-pack." It consisted of a Rochester 4GC four-barrel carburetor providing a boost of 20 hp over standard V-8s or a maximum of 200 hp on Hydra-Matic equipped cars. Carter WCFB model 2268S and 2283S four-barrel carburetors were also used on some 1955 Pontiacs as optional equipment. A variety of rear axle gear ratios was available.

1955 Pontiac "Memphian" ambulance from the Memphis Coach Co. JAG

HISTORICAL FOOTNOTES: Production of 1955 Pontiacs started October 4, 1954. They were introduced to the public 15 days later, with the Star Chief Custom two-door Safari bowing the following January 31. Calendar year production of 581,860 cars made Pontiac America's sixth ranked manufacturer. Hydra-Matic transmission was in 90.6 percent of these cars. Model year production was 554,090 units. The new engine introduced in 1955 was Pontiac's *first* overhead valve V-8, although it was the *second* V-8 for the company, as the first had been used in 1932 models. An all-time monthly production record was recorded in December 1955. Chieftain station wagons for 1955 utilized Chevrolet station wagon rear fender styling. Styles number 2562 and 2562DF had distinctive rear ventipanes. The two-door Chieftain station wagon, style number 2563F, was sometimes called the Colony wagon.

1956 PONTIAC

1956 Pontiac Chieftain 870 four-door station wagon, V-8.

CHIEFTAIN LINE - (V-8) - SERIES 27 - New Pontiac styling for 1956 featured combination bumper grilles with enclosed circular parking lights and round, bomb-type bumper guards. All models had reversed vertically slanting slash accent moldings and "sweepspear" body rub trim. On Chieftains the slash accents were of constant width. There were reflectorized oval embossments on rear fenders with gull-wing and circle medallions on the deck lid. Special level Chieftain 860s lacked upper belt moldings, wore small hubcaps and had plain taillight rings. Deluxe level Chieftain 870 models (except station wagons), had visored taillight rings, full wheel discs and upper beltline trim. The two-door Custom Safari was continued as a Star Chief on the Chieftain chassis, now with the base four-barrel Star Chief engine. An 860 Catalina Coupe was new as were 860 and 870 four-door hardtops, the latter pair designated as Catalina Sedans. In some factory literature Chieftain 870s are called Super Chiefs.

PONTIAC I.D. NUMBERS: VIN located on left front door hinge pillar. Matching engine serial number on pad on front of right-hand cylinder bank. Serial numbers took the form ( )-[ ]56{ }-1001 to ( )-[ ]56{ }-ending number. The first symbol ( ) was a letter indicating assembly plant: P=Pontiac, Mich.; T=Arlington, Texas; A=Atlanta, Ga.; F=Framingham, Mass; K=Kansas City, Kan.; L=Linden, N.J.; C=South Gate, Calif.; W=Wilmington, Del. The second symbol [ ] indicated series: 7=Series 27; 8=Series 28. The third and fourth symbols indicated model year: 56=1956. The fifth symbol indicated transmission: S=synchromesh; H=Hydra-Matic. The following symbols were the sequential unit production number starting at 1001 for each series at each assembly plant. Ending numbers for 1956 were: [SERIES 27 with synchromesh] (Mich.) 12,447; (Texas) 2383; (Ga.) 3633; (Mass.) 3050; (Kan.) 3526; (N.J.) 3089; (Calif.) 3117; (Del.) 3139. [SERIES 27 with Hydra-Matic] (Mich.) 97,877; (Texas) 14,815; (Ga.) 22,073; (Mass.) 13,307; (Kan.) 27,978; (N.J.) 26,487; (Calif.) 33,138; (Del.) 26,575. [SERIES 28 with synchromesh] (Mich.) 1259; (Texas) 1016; (Ga.) 1013; (Mass.) 1038; (Kan.) 1022; (N.J.) 1052; (Calif.) 1014; (Del.) 1026. [SERIES 28 with Hydra-Matic] (Mich.) 47,697; (Texas) 8896; (Ga.) 11,452; (Mass.) 6999; (Kan.) 13,124; (N.J.) 13,766; (Calif.) 15,590; (Del.) 13,092. Fisher Body/style number on plate under hood on left of firewall can be helpful for identification of model and ordering parts. A prefix to the main number indicates model year, 56=1956. The first two symbols in the main number indicate series 27 or 28 Star Chief. The next two symbols indicate the body style. Some numbers have an alphabetical suffix indicating trim level, such as D=Deluxe and SD=Super Deluxe. These numbers appear in body/style number column of charts below adjacent to corresponding body style listings.

1956 Pontiac Star Chief Safari two-door station wagon. OCW

CHIEFTAIN 860 (SPECIAL)

Model Number	Body/Style Number	Body Type & Seating	Factory Price	Shipping Weight	Prod. Total
860-27	2719	4-dr Sed-6P	2294	3617	41,987
860-27	2739	4-dr Cat HT-6P	2439	3682	35,201
860-27	2711	2-dr Sed-6P	2236	3557	41,908
860-27	2737	2-dr Cat HT-6P	2366	3617	46,335
860-27	2763	2-dr Sta Wag-6P	2564	3717	6099
860-27	2762FC	4-dr Sta Wag-6P	2648	3812	12,702

CHIEFTAIN 870 (Deluxe)

Model Number	Body/Style Number	Body Type & Seating	Factory Price	Shipping Weight	Prod. Total
870-27	2719D	4-dr Sed-6P	2409	3617	22,082
870-27	2739D	4-dr Cat HT-6P	2530	3682	25,372
870-27	2737D	2-dr Cat HT-6P	2476	3617	24,744
870-27	2763DF	4-dr Sta Wag-6P	2744	3762	21,674

STAR CHIEF CUSTOM (SERIES 27)

Model Number	Body/Style Number	Body Type & Seating	Factory Price	Shipping Weight	Prod. Total
27	2764DF	2-dr Sta Wag-6P	3124	3762	4042

NOTE 1: 184,232 Chieftain 860s were built.

NOTE 2: 24,117 Chieftain 860s had synchromesh and 160,115 had Hydra-Matic.

NOTE 3: 93,872 Chieftain 870s (or Super Chiefs) were built.

NOTE 4: 3289 Chieftain 870s had synchromesh and 90,583 had Hydra-Matic.

NOTE 5: 10 Custom Safaris had synchromesh and 4,032 had Hydra-Matic.

1956 Pontiac 860 two-door sedan. JAG

STAR CHIEF LINE - (V-8) - SERIES 28 - All Star Chiefs were distinguished by tapered diagonal accent slash moldings on front doors. Catalinas and convertibles had wide fluted lower rear fender extensions. The Custom Catalina sedan had stainless steel window surround moldings and all Custom Star Chiefs used hooded taillight rings.

1956 Pontiac Custom Star Chief Catalina four-door hardtop, V-8.

STAR CHIEF (SERIES 28)

Model Number	Body/Style Number	Body Type & Seating	Factory Price	Shipping Weight	Prod. Total
28	2819D	4-dr Sed-6P	2523	3697	18,346
28	2867DTX	2-dr Conv-6P	2853	3917	13,510

STAR CHIEF CUSTOM (SERIES 28)

Model Number	Body/Style Number	Body Type & Seating	Factory Price	Shipping Weight	Prod. Total
28	2839SD	4-dr Cat HT-6P	2731	3767	48,035
28	2837SD	2-dr Cat HT-6P	2661	3687	43,392

NOTE 1: 123,584 Series 28 Star Chiefs were built.

NOTE 2: 440 had synchromesh and 123,144 had Hydra-Matic.

NOTE 3: Does not include two-door Star Chief Custom Safari.

NOTE 4: 301 vehicles converted into professional vehicles.

CHIEFTAIN ENGINES: V-8: Overhead valves. Cast iron block. Displacement: 316.6 cu. in. Bore & Stroke: 3.94 x 3.25 in. Compression Ratio: (synchromesh) 7.9:1; (Hydra-Matic) 8.9:1. Brake hp: (synchromesh) 192 @ 4400 rpm; (Hydra-Matic) 205 @ 4800 rpm. Five main bearings. Hydraulic valve lifters. Carburetor: (synchromesh) Rochester 2GC two-barrel with black tag number 8696; (Hydra-Matic) Rochester 2GC two-barrel with brass tag number 8695. The two-door Custom Safari came standard with a Star Chief four-barrel V-8.

STAR CHIEF ENGINES: V-8: Overhead valve. Cast iron block. Displacement: 316.6 cu. in. Bore & Stroke: 3.94 x 3.25 in. Compression ratio: (synchromesh) 7.9:1. (Hydra-Matic) 8.9:1. Brake hp: (synchromesh) 216 @ 4800 rpm; (Hydra-Matic) 227 @ 4800 rpm. Five main bearings. Hydraulic valve lifters. Carburetors: (synchromesh) Rochester 4GC four-barrel with black tag number 7900; (Hydra-Matic) Rochester 4GC four-barrel with brass tag number 8697. Some cars were also equipped with Carter WCFB model 2364S four-barrels.

CHASSIS FEATURES: Wheelbase: (Series 27) 122 in.; (Series 28) 124 in. Overall Length: (Series 27 passenger cars) 205.6 in.; (Series 27 Chieftain station wagons) 206 in.; (Series 27 Safari) 206.7 in.; (Series 28) 212.6 in. Front tread: (All) 58.66 in. Rear tread: (All) 59.05 in. Tires: (Passenger cars) 7.10 x 15; (station wagons) 7.60 x 15, tubeless.

CONVENIENCE OPTIONS: Power brakes ($38). Power windows ($97). Power steering ($108). Six-Way power seat ($93). Radios ($90 or $118). Seat belts ($11 per passenger). Air-conditioning ($431). Hydra-Matic attachments were now considered "standard," but cost extra. The D-56 Dual-Range type ($188) was used in Chieftains in both the 860 and 870 sub-series. A new Strato-Flight Hydra-Matic ($205) was employed in two-door Star Chief Custom Safaris and all Series 28 models. A three-speed synchromesh gearbox with column-mounted shift was the base price transmission. In March 1956, an "extra hp" V-8 was released. It also displaced 317 cu. in., but came with 10.0:1 compression heads, dual four-barrel Rochester carburetors (part no. 7009820) and additional high-performance components. The output of this engine was rated 285 hp @ 5100 rpm. Pontiac experts have estimated that 200 cars were equipped with this motor. Standard rear axle gear ratios were as follows: (synchromesh) 3.64:1; (Hydra-Matic) 3.23:1. Additional ratios were also available. Dual exhausts were optional on all Pontiacs except the Chieftain 860 three-seat station wagon (not available) and cars with "extra hp" V-8s (standard). Four-barrel carburetion was optional for Chieftain 860 and 870 models.

1956 Pontiac Star Chief four-door sedan . JAG

HISTORICAL FOOTNOTES: Production of 1956 models started October 3, 1955. They were introduced October 21, 1955. Calendar year output was 332,268 cars. Model year output was 405,730 cars. Pontiac remained the sixth largest American automaker. On August 3, 1956, the six millionth Pontiac was built. Semon "Bunkie" Knudsen took over as Pontiac general manager on July 1, 1956. The 1956 Star Chief two-door Custom Safari is recognized as a "Milestone Car" by the Milestone Car Society. The 227 hp 1956 Star Chief four-door sedan was good for 0-to-60 mph in 11.4 seconds and an 18.1 second quarter-mile.

1957 PONTIAC

1957 Pontiac Chieftain two-door sedan, V-8.

CHIEFTAIN LINE - (V-8) - SERIES 27 - Pontiac introduced new "Star Flight" styling. General features were missile-shaped side trim; flatter tailfins; extended rear fenders with V-shaped tips; lower hoods; a more massive bumper grille; longer horizontal taillights; and 14-inch wheels. The budget-priced line was now called the Chieftain. The Super Chief name totally replaced the old Chieftain 870 designation for cars on the small wheelbase with Deluxe trim. The two-door Star Chief Custom Safari remained on the Series 27 platform and again had a four-barrel V-8 as base engine. Chieftains had small hubcaps; three stars on rear fenders; and Chieftain front fender scripts. Super Chiefs had full wheel discs; upper belt moldings; three stars on rear fenders; and Super Chief front fender scripts. The distinctive Custom Safari had Star Chief trims and a companion four-door Custom Safari Transcontinental station wagon was announced in late December 1956.

PONTIAC I.D. NUMBERS: VIN located on left front door hinge pillar. Matching engine serial number on pad on front of right-hand cylinder bank. Serial numbers took the form ( )-[ ]57{ }-1001 to ( )-[ ]57{ }-ending number. The first symbol ( ) was a letter indicating assembly plant: P=Pontiac, Mich.; T=Arlington, Texas; A=Atlanta, Ga.; F=Framingham, Mass; K=Kansas City, Kan.; L=Linden, N.J.; C=South Gate, Calif.; W=Wilmington, Del. The second symbol [ ] indicated series: 7=Series 27; 8=Series 28. The third and fourth symbols indicated model year: 57=1957. The fifth symbol indicated transmission: S=synchromesh; H=Hydra-Matic. The following symbols were the sequential unit production number starting at 1001 for each series at each assembly plant. Ending numbers for 1957 were: [SERIES 27 with synchromesh] (Mich.) 7722; (Texas) 1656; (Ga.) 2041; (Mass.) 2040; (Kan.) 2301; (N.J.) 2223; (Calif.) 1765; (Del.) 1970. [SERIES 27 with Hydra-Matic] (Mich.) 94,357; (Texas) 10,608; (Ga.) 18,541; (Mass.) 11,045; (Kan.) 24,194; (N.J.) 21,243; (Calif.) 22,055; (Del.) 22,332. [SERIES 28 with synchromesh] (Mich.) 1212; (Texas) 1004; (Ga.) 1005; (Mass.) 1010; (Kan.) 1019; (N.J.) 1028; (Calif.) 1016; (Del.) 1015. [SERIES 28 with Hydra-Matic] (Mich.) 45,497; (Texas) 6679; (Ga.) 9462; (Mass.) 5007; (Kan.) 11,022; (N.J.) 11,067; (Calif.) 11,387; (Del.) 10,558. Fisher Body/style number on plate under hood on left of firewall can be very helpful for identification of model and ordering parts. A prefix to the main number indicates model year, 57=1957. The first two symbols in the main number indicate series 27 or 28 Star Chief. The next two symbols indicate the body style. Some numbers have an alphabetical suffix indicating trim level, such as D=Deluxe and SD=Super Deluxe. These numbers appear in Body/style number column of charts below adjacent to corresponding body style listings.

1957 Pontiac Chieftain four-door sedan. JAG

CHIEFTAIN

Model Number	Body/Style Number	Body Type & Seating	Factory Price	Shipping Weight	Prod. Total
27	2719	4-dr Sed-6P	2527	3670	35,671
27	2739	4-dr Cat HT-6P	2614	3745	40,074
27	2711	2-dr Sed-6P	2463	3625	21,343
27	2737	2-dr Cat HT-6P	2529	3665	51,017
27	2762FC	4-dr Sta Wag-9P	2898	3945	11,536
27	2763F	2-dr Sta Wag-6P	2841	3800	2,934

SUPER CHIEF

27	2719D	4-dr Sed-6P	2664	3695	15,153
27	2739D	4-dr Cat HT-6P	2793	3750	19,758
27	2737D	2-dr Cat HT-6P	2735	3680	15,494
27	2762DF	4-dr Sta Wag-6P	3021	3875	14,095

STAR CHIEF CUSTOM (SERIES 27)

27	2764DF	2-dr Sta Wag-6P	3636	3955	1292
27	2762SDF	4-dr Sta Wag-6P	3481	3860	1894

NOTE 1: All Pontiac station wagons used Safari name starting in 1957.

NOTE 2: 162,575 Chieftains were built.

NOTE 3: 12,867 Chieftains had synchromesh and 149,708 had Hydra-Matic.

NOTE 4: 64,692 Super Chiefs were built.

NOTE 5: 1063 had Super Chiefs had synchromesh and 63,629 had Hydra-Matic.

NOTE 6: 3186 Star Chief Custom Safaris were built.

NOTE 7: Four Custom Safaris had synchromesh and 3182 had Hydra-Matic.

NOTE 8: 192 Super Chiefs were used for hearse and ambulance conversions.

1957 Pontiac Super Chief Catalina two-door hardtop, V-8.

STAR CHIEF LINE - (V-8) - SERIES 28 - Star Chiefs were identified by suitable front fender scripts, four stars on rear fenders, chrome semi-cylindrical trim at the back of missile-shaped inserts and full wheel discs. The Custom (Super Deluxe) sedan was reinstated and distinguished by off-shoulder interior styling patterns. A unique, limited-edition Custom Bonneville Convertible was announced in early December 1956 and released on January 11, 1957. This car was in the Custom Star Chief sub-series. Released only one-to-a-dealer, Bonneville availability was limited to 630 production examples and two prototypes. The pre-production prototypes had four bucket seats and small trim differences. A fuel-injected V-8 was used in all of these cars.

STAR CHIEF (SERIES 28)

Model Number	Body/Style Number	Body Type & Seating	Factory Price	Shipping Weight	Prod. Total
28	2819D	4-dr Sed-6P	2839	3740	3774
28	2867DTX	2-dr Conv-6P	3105	3970	12,789

STAR CHIEF CUSTOM (SERIES 28)

28	2819SD	4-dr Sed-6P	2896	3755	8874
28	2839SD	4-dr Cat HT Sed-6P	2975	3820	44,283
28	2837SD	2-dr Cat HT-6P	2901	3750	32,862
28	2867SDX	2-dr Bonn Conv-6P	5782	4285	630

NOTE 1: 103,588 Series 28 Star Chiefs were built.

NOTE 2: 309 Star Chiefs had synchromesh and 103,279 had Hydra-Matic.

NOTE 3: Totals do not include Series 27 two- or four-door Custom Safaris.

NOTE 4: 376 Star Chief chassis were built for professional car conversions.

1957 Pontiac Star Chief Custom Bonneville two-door convertible, V-8.

ENGINES

(CHIEFTAIN) V-8; Overhead valves. Cast iron block. Displacement: 347 cu. in. Bore & Stroke: 3.94 x 3.56 in. Compression Ratio: (synchromesh) 8.5:1; (Hydra-Matic) 10.0:1. Brake hp: (synchromesh) 227 @ 4600 rpm; (Hydra-Matic) 252 @ 4600 rpm. Five main bearings. Hydraulic valve lifters. Carburetor: Rochester 2GC two-barrel.

(CUSTOM SAFARI/SUPER CHIEF/STAR CHIEF) V-8: Overhead valves. Cast iron block. Displacement: 347 cu. in. Bore & Stroke: 3.94 x 3.56 in. Compression Ratio: (synchromesh) 8.5:1; (Hydra-Matic) 10.0:1. Brake hp: (synchromesh) 244 @ 4800 rpm: (Hydra-Matic) 270 @ 4800 rpm. Five main bearings. Hydraulic valve lifters. Carburetor: (Early production) Rochester 4GC four-barrel; (Late production) A Carter AFB four-barrel was used in mixed production with the Rochester 4GC type.

(BONNEVILLE) V-8: Overhead valves. Cast iron block. Displacement: 347 cu. in. Bore & Stroke: 3.94 x 3.56 in. Compression Ratio: 10.25:1. Brake hp: (estimated) 315 @ 4800 rpm. Five main bearings. Hydraulic valve lifters. Induction: Rochester mechanical fuel-injection.

(NASCAR/TRI-POWER) In December 1956 three different triple two-barrel engines were released. The first was an option for the standard Hydra-Matic V-8. The others were options for the "extra hp" (NASCAR-certified) V-8 with either synchromesh or Hydra-Matic attachment. Specifications were as follows: (1) Standard V-8. 347 cid. 10.0:1 compression. 290 hp @ 5000 rpm. Hydraulic valve lifters. 3 x 2V Rochester carburetors. Single-breaker ignition with Hydra-Matic only. (2) (Extra-Horsepower V-8/synchromesh) 347 cid. 10.0:1 compression. 317 hp @ 5200 rpm. Hydraulic valve lifters. 3 x 2V Rochester carburetors. Dual-breaker ignition. (3) (Extra-Horsepower V-8/Hydra-Matic) 347 cid. 10.0:1 compression. 317 hp @ 5200 rpm. Hydraulic valve lifters. 3 x 2V Rochester carburetors. Single-breaker ignition.

CHASSIS FEATURES: Wheelbase: (Series 27) 122 in.; (Series 28) 124 in. Overall Length: (Series 27 passenger cars) 206.8 in.; (Series 27 station wagons) 207.7 in.; (Series 28) 213.8 in. Front tread: 59.0 in. Rear tread: 59.4 in. Tires: (Chieftain with synchromesh) 7.50 x 14; (station wagons and Bonneville) 8.50 x 14; (others) 8.00 x 14.

OPTIONS: Power steering ($108). Power brakes ($39). Eight-way power seat ($97). Six-way manual seat ($41). Power windows ($102). Radios ($99 and $125). Heater and defroster ($91). Air conditioning ($431). Tinted glass ($34). Lamp group ($23.10). Mirror group ($12.35). Power Sweep Contour electric wiper/washer ($25.25). Deluxe steering wheel and padded dash ($31.70). Electric clock ($10.50). Whitewalls ($58.70). Deluxe carpet floor mat ($11). Cowl vent chrome trim and Custom wheel discs ($21.80). Deluxe basic group ($255.50). Hydra-Matic attachments were again considered "standard," but cost extra. Strato-Flight Hydra-Matic ($231) was used in all lines. A three-speed synchromesh gearbox with column-shift was the base price transmission. Four-barrel carburetion was optional in Chieftains. Dual exhausts were $24 extra. Rear axle ratios: (synchromesh) 3.42:1; (Hydra-Matic) 3.08:1. In December 1956, a 3.23:1 axle was made standard for Hydra-Matic equipped cars and the 3.08:1 axle was made a Plains ratio option for all cars except Safari models.

HISTORIC FOOTNOTES: Production of 1957 models started October 17, 1956. They were introduced November 19, 1956. Model year output was 334,041 cars. Calendar year output was 343,298 cars. Pontiac held a 5.4 percent share of the U.S. market and was ranked the sixth largest automaker. First news of the Bonneville convertible was released December 2, 1956, the same day the Tri-Power carburetor options were announced. The four-door Custom Star Chief Safari Transcontinental wagon and the Bonneville convertible were both introduced on January 11, 1957. E.M. "Pete" Estes became the chief engineer of Pontiac this year. The 1957 Pontiac Super Chief two-door sedan with the 290 hp V-8 was capable of doing 0-to-60 mph in 8.5 seconds and the quarter-mile in 16.8 seconds. The 1957 Star Chief two-door Custom Safari is a Milestone Car.

1957 Pontiac Chieftain Catalina two-door hardtop. RK

1957 Pontiac Chieftain Catalina two-door hardtop . OCW

1957 Pontiac Super Chief Catalina four-door hardtop. OCW

1957 Pontiac Super Chief Safari four-door station wagon. OCW

1957 Pontiac Star Chief Custom Catalina two-door hardtop. OCW

1957 Pontiac Star Chief Custom Safari. OCW

1957 Pontiac Star Chief Custom Safari . OCW

1957 Pontiac Star Chief four-door sedan. OCW

1957 Pontiac Star Chief convertible. RK

1957 Pontiac Star Chief convertible . OCW

1958 PONTIAC

1958 Pontiac Chieftain two-door sedan, V-8.

CHIEFTAIN LINE - (V-8) - SERIES 25 AND SERIES 27 - The 1958 Pontiacs featured all new styling and chassis engineering that was hailed as a bold advance over the past. General appearance characteristics included honeycomb grilles, a longer, lower silhouette, quad headlamps and tail lamps, recessed floors and concave rear fender panels. Chieftains could be identified by the script model nameplates at the front of concave insert panels on the rear doors or fenders and three stars on the rear fenders. Small hubcaps were standard on all Chieftains, but many were sold with optional full wheel discs. Tail-lamps without trim rings were seen on Chieftains, except the convertible. The ragtop was in a separate series sharing a unique ribbed rear deck lid with the Bonneville convertible. Princess pattern Lustrex upholstery with Morrokide imitation leather trim was seen inside Chieftains, except the convertible, which had special Seville-finish Morrokide seats in "off shoulder" combination patterns.

PONTIAC I.D. NUMBERS: VIN located on left front door hinge pillar. Matching engine serial number on pad on front of right-hand cylinder bank. Serial numbers took the form ( )-[ ]58{ }-1001 to ( )-[ ]58{ }-ending number. The first symbol ( ) was a letter indicating assembly plant: P=Pontiac, Mich.; T=Arlington, Texas; A=Atlanta, Ga.; F=Framingham, Mass.; K=Kansas City, Kan.; L=Linden, N.J.; C=South Gate, Calif.; W=Wilmington, Del. The second symbol [ ] indicated series: 7=Series 27; 8=Series 28; 5=Series 25 Bonneville. The third and fourth symbols indicated model year: 58=1958. The fifth symbol indicated transmission: S=synchromesh; H=Hydra-Matic. The following symbols were the sequential unit production number starting at 1001 for each series at each assembly plant. Ending numbers for 1957 were: [SERIES 27 with synchromesh] (Mich.) 4036; (Texas) 1429; (Ga.) 1508; (Mass.) 1296; (Kan.) 2003; (N.J.) 1568; (Calif.) 1592; (Del.) 1427. [SERIES 27 with Hydra-Matic] (Mich.) 43,381; (Texas) 7317; (Ga.) 11,942; (Mass.) 6113; (Kan.) 17,504; (N.J.) 14,411; (Calif.) 12585; (Del.) 12,574. [SERIES 28 with synchromesh] (Mich.) 1159; (Texas) 1006; (Ga.) 1008; (Mass.) 1011; (Kan.) 1016; (N.J.) 1026; (Calif.) 1018; (Del.) 1015. [SERIES 28 with Hydra-Matic] (Mich.) 25986; (Texas) 5695; (Ga.) 8672; (Mass.) 4130; (Kan.) 10785; (N.J.) 8446; (Calif.) 8168; (Del.) 8157. [BONNEVILLE SERIES 25 with synchromesh] (Ga.) 1003; (Calif.) 1021; (Mass.) 1005; (Kan.) 1023; (N.J.) 1020; (Mich.) 1163; (Texas) 1016; (Del.) 1015. [BONNEVILLE SERIES 25 with Hydra-Matic] (Ga.) 2543; (Calif.) 3324; (Mass.) 1969; (Kan.) 2640; (N.J.) 3180; (Mich.) 9141; (Texas) 1677; (Del.) 2858. Fisher Body/style number on plate under hood on left of firewall can be helpful for identification of model and ordering parts. A prefix to the main number indicates model year, 58=1958. The first two symbols in the main number indicate series 27 or 28 Star Chief or 25 Bonneville. The next two symbols indicate the body style. Some numbers have an alphabetical suffix indicating trim level, such as D=Deluxe and SD=Super Deluxe. These numbers appear in Body/style number column of charts below adjacent to corresponding body style listings.

1958 Pontiac Chieftain Catalina two-door hardtop. OCW

CHIEFTAIN (SERIES 27)

Model Number	Body/Style Number	Body Type & Seating	Factory Price	Shipping Weight	Prod. Total
27	2749	4-dr Sed-6P	2638	3815	44,999
27	2739	4-dr Cat HT-6P	2792	3900	17,946
27	2741	2-dr Sed-6P	2573	3755	17,394
27	2731	2-dr Cat HT-6P	2707	3765	26,003
27	2793	4-dr Sta Wag-6P	3019	4140	9701
27	2794	2-dr Sta Wag-9P	3088	4185	5417

CHIEFTAIN (SERIES 25)

Model Number	Body/Style Number	Body Type & Seating	Factory Price	Shipping Weight	Prod. Total
25	2567	2-dr Conv-5P	3019	3965	7359

1958 Pontiac Chieftain convertible. OCW

SUPER CHIEF LINE - (V-8) - SERIES 28 - In 1958 the Super Chief nameplate was used to designate three cars on the long wheelbase (Star Chief) chassis with two-barrel (Chieftain) V-8s as base engines. Identification features included full wheel discs, taillamps with chrome rings and rear fender coves decorated with Super Chief script and four stars. Deluxe steering wheels were used. The four-door sedan was upholstered in a blend of Palisades pattern Lustrex with Plaza pattern bolsters. Catalina buyers could choose either all-Morrokide or Morrokide and Lustrex trims at the same price.

SUPER CHIEF (SERIES 28 Deluxe)

Model Number	Body/Style Number	Body Type & Seating	Factory Price	Shipping Weight	Prod. Total
28	2849D	4-dr Sed-6P	2834	3865	12,006
28	2839D	4-dr Cat HT-6P	2961	3925	7886
28	2831D	2-dr Cat HT-6P	2880	3805	7236

1958 Pontiac Star Chief Catalina four-door hardtop, V-8.

STAR CHIEF LINE - (V-8) - SERIES 27 AND SERIES 28 - Pontiac's "something really special" cars were four Super Deluxe level Star Chiefs. A distinctive four-door Custom Safari station wagon was on the shorter Chieftain platform, while other models had the 124-in. wheelbase shared with Super Chiefs. Identification features included Star Chief front fenders script plates, four stars within the concave insert panels, tail lamp trim rings and funnel-shaped decorative scoops at the front of the insert panels. These scoops were embellished with golden rectangular 'V' badges and triple wind-split moldings. Chrome wheel discs were regular equipment outside, while a Deluxe steering wheel and electric clock were found inside. Upholstery trims were tridimensional Prado pattern Lustrex in the Catalina sedan, with all-leather optional at no extra cost on both Catalinas. A roof rack, horizontal tailgate moldings, and distinct Safari gate scripts were featured on the Custom Safari and all Star Chiefs boasted "stardust" carpeting. Jewel-tone Lucite acrylic lacquer paint finish was standard and exclusive on Star Chiefs and Bonnevilles.

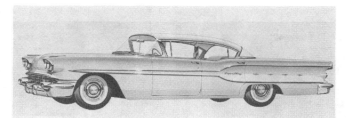

1958 Pontiac Super Chief four-door sedan. OCW

1958 Pontiac Super Chief Catalina two-door hardtop. OCW

1958 Pontiac Super Chief Catalina two-door hardtop. OCW

1958 Pontiac Super Chief Catalina four-door hardtop. OCW

1958 Pontiac Super Chief Catalina four-door hardtop. OCW

1958 Pontiac Star Chief Custom Safari four-door station wagon. OCW

1958 Pontiac Star Chief Catalina two-door hardtop. OCW

1958 Pontiac Chieftain four-door station wagon. OCW

1958 Pontiac Bonneville Custom convertible with fuel injection. OCW

1958 Pontiac Bonneville Custom convertible with Tri-Power. JAG

1958 Barnette-Pontiac hearse-ambulance with Tri-Power. JAG

71

STAR CHIEF (SERIES 28 SUPER DELUXE)

Model Number	Body/Style Number	Body Type & Seating	Factory Price	Shipping Weight	Prod. Total
28	2849SD	4-dr Cus Sed-6P	3071	3915	10,547
28	2839SD	4-dr Cat HT-6P	3210	3965	21,455
28	2831SD	2-dr Cat HT-6P	3122	3850	13,888

STAR CHIEF CUSTOM SAFARI

Model Number	Body/Style Number	Body Type & Seating	Factory Price	Shipping Weight	Prod. Total
27	2793SD	4-dr Cus Sta Wag-6P	3350	4180	2905

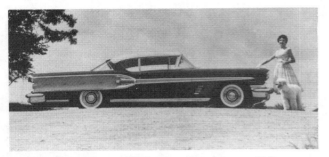

1958 Pontiac Bonneville Custom Sport coupe, V-8.

BONNEVILLE LINE - (V-8) - SERIES 25 - Bonneville became a line name instead of a single model designation in 1958. A convertible and sport coupe were offered. Base powerplants in Bonnevilles were the Star Chief V-8s and both cars were on the Chieftain wheelbase, but with the same longer, ribbed rear deck lid used on the Series 25 Chieftain convertible. This made the bodies slightly longer than Series 27 types. Identification features included Bonneville front fender scripts, Bonneville block letters on hoods and decks, four bright metal chevrons on the lower front fender sides, four stars on the rear fender panels and rocket-shaped, ribbed semi-cylindrical moldings at the front of the concave inserts. Standard equipment included Deluxe steering wheel, chrome wheel discs, and special upholstery.

1958 Pontiac Bonneville Custom Sport coupe, V-8. OCW

BONNEVILLE (SERIES 25 SUPER DELUXE)

Model Number	Body/Style Number	Body Type & Seating	Factory Price	Shipping Weight	Prod. Total
25	2547SD	Cus Spt Cpe-5P	3481	3825	9144
25	2567SD	Cus Conv-5P	3586	4040	3096

ENGINES

(CHIEFTAIN/SUPER CHIEF) Base V-8s: Overhead valves. Cast iron block. Displacement: 370 cu. in. Bore & Stroke: 4.06 x 3.56 in. Compression Ratio: (synchromesh) 8.6:1; (Hydra-Matic) 10.0:1. Brake hp: (synchromesh) 240 @ 4500 rpm ; (Hydra-Matic) 270 @ 4600 rpm. Five main bearings. Hydraulic valve lifters. Carburetor: (early) Rochester 2GC two-barrel; (late) same with air bypass idle.

(STAR CHIEF/BONNEVILLE) Base V-8s: Overhead valves. Cast iron block. Displacement: 370 cu. in. Bore & Stroke: 4.06 x 3.56 in. Compression Ratio: (synchromesh) 8.6:1; (Hydra-Matic) 10.0:1. Brake hp: (synchromesh) 255 @ 4500 rpm; (Hydra-Matic) 285 @ 4600 rpm. Five main bearings. Hydraulic valve lifters. Carburetor: (Regular production) Carter AFB four-barrel; (Special) 500 cars were built with Rochester 4GC four-barrel carburetors late in the year. These were available only in four sales zones and were likely 'PM' optioned cars assembled for NASCAR certification.

CHASSIS FEATURES: Wheelbase: (Series 25 and 27) 122 in.; (Series 28) 124 in. Overall Length: (Series 25) 211.7 in.; (Series 27) 210.5 in.; (Series 28) 124 in. Front tread: 58.8 in. Rear tread: 59.4 in. Tires: (coupes and sedans) 8.00 x 14; (station wagons and all w/air-conditioning) 8.50 x 14.

1958 Pontiac Chieftain four-door sedan. OCW

OPTIONS: Power steering ($108). Power brakes ($38). Power windows ($108). Power seat ($77). Deluxe radio ($102). Deluxe Electromatic radio ($161). Power antenna ($30). Rear seat speaker ($13.75, $18.90 and $21 on Safari/Bonneville, Star Chief and Chieftain/Super Chief respectively.) Heater and defroster ($96). Dual exhaust ($31). White sidewall tires 8.00 x 14, four-ply ($65). Two-tone paint in standard colors ($27). E-Z Eye Glass ($38). Electric clock ($20). Windshield washer ($14). Electric contour wipers ($14). Oil filter ($10). Padded dash ($19). Foam seat ($13). Deluxe steering wheel ($14). Outside rearview mirror ($7). Wheel discs ($18). Brake-on light ($6). Air-conditioning ($430). Air suspension ($175). Bonneville bucket seats ($84). Transmission and axle options: A three-speed synchromesh gearbox with column mounted gear shift was the base price transmission. Four-speed Strato-Flight Hydra-Matic was $231.34 extra. In late production a Borg-Warner heavy-duty police gearbox was optional. At least one car, built for racing at Daytona Beach, left the factory with a floor mounted four-speed manual transmission. Transmission attachment date was now recorded by series. A total of 19,599 cars were built in Series 25. Of these, 210 had synchromesh and 19,389 had Hydra-Matic attachments. A total of 124,685 cars were built in Series 27. Of these, 6943 had synchromesh and 117,742 had Hydra-Matic attachments. A total of 73,019 cars were built in Series 28. Of these, 258 had synchromesh and 72,761 had Hydra-Matic attachments. The difference between output of individual models and total series production was 321 cars, which indicates the approximate number of Pontiac chassis delivered for professional car conversions this year. Of these, 320 were Series 27 chassis and one was a Series 28 chassis. Rear axle options included Safe-T-Track differential and the following gear ratios: (Hydra-Matic) 3.23:1; (optional Hydra-Matic) 3.08:1; (synchromesh) 3.42:1; (optional synchromesh) 3.64:1; (dealer installed) 3.90:1 and 4.10:1. Powerplant options: The four-barrel V-8 could be installed as an option in Chieftains and Super Chiefs. Tri-Power carburetion on standard blocks was $84 for these lines and $93.50 on Star Chiefs and Bonnevilles. This "standard" Tri-Power setup used three two-barrel Rochester carburetors, 10.5:1 cylinder heads, high-lift camshaft and gave 300 hp @ 4600 rpm. Rochester fuel-injection was a $500 option on any 1958 Pontiac and this package included 10.5:1 cylinder heads and gave 310 hp @ 4800 rpm. Pontiac experts believe that 200 Bonnevilles carried this option. In March 1958, two NASCAR-certified "extra hp" (Tempest 395-A) V-8s were released. The 'PK' option was $254 on Chieftains or Super Chiefs and $233 on Star Chiefs or Bonnevilles. It included a four-barrel carburetor, 10.5:1 cylinder heads, higher-lift camshaft, low-restriction dual exhausts and other special components good for 315 hp @ 5000 rpm. The 'PM' option was $331 on lower-priced lines and $320 on upper lines and included the special features with Tri-Power induction for 330 hp @ 5200 rpm. Both displaced 370 cu. in.

1958 Pontiac Chieftain four-door sedan. OCW

HISTORICAL FOOTNOTES: Model year production was 217,303 units for a 5.1 percent share of market. Calendar year output was 219,823 cars. To celebrate General Motors' 50th anniversary, a special "Golden Jubilee" trim and paint scheme was announced in November. This color was coded `Z' with DuPont stock number 2865L. Special

"Golden Jubilee" ornamentation was applied to a limited number of cars, all of which are believed to have been Star Chief Custom four-door sedans. The number made is not known. Cars with optional fuel-injection had fuel-injection call-out on the front fenders. Cars with Tri-Power engines had a different type of front fender call-out. A Tri-Power Bonneville convertible was selected as the Official Pace Car for the Indianapolis 500 Mile Race in May 1958. The 1958 Bonneville hardtop with the 300 hp engine was road tested by a magazine. Zero-to-60 mph took 7.6 seconds and the quarter-mile took 16 seconds.

1959 PONTIAC

CATALINA SERIES - (V-8) - SERIES 21 - Major styling changes for 1959 Pontiacs included lower, longer bodies with more interior room; new twin grille theme; twin-fin rear fenders; 'V' contour hoods; increased glass area; and flat, rear over-hanging roofs on four-door Vista hardtops. The old Chieftain line was renamed, adopting the term Catalina as a new series name. Identification features included Catalina script on rear fins; plain deck lids; and bodysides trimmed by clean "Sweepspear" moldings with undecorated projectile flares. Standard equipment included directional signals; electric wipers; dual sun visors; dome lamps; cigarette lighter; dual headlamps; front and rear ashtrays; coat hooks; instrument panel Snak Bar; dual horns; tubeless tires; bumper jack; and wheel lug wrench.

PONTIAC I.D. NUMBERS: VIN located on left front door hinge pillar. Matching engine serial number on pad on front of right-hand cylinder bank. Assembly plant codes: P=Pontiac, Mich.; T=Arlington, Texas; A=Atlanta, Ga.; F=Framingham, Mass.; K=Kansas City, Kan.; L=Linden, N.J.; C=South Gate, Calif.; W=Wilmington, Del. [CATALINA] Serial numbers took the following form - 159WI001 and up. The first character (1) indicating Series 21; the second and third characters (59) indicating model year; the fourth character (W) indicating factory. Serial numbers at each factory began with 1001 and transmission type was no longer indicated. [STAR CHIEF] Serial numbers took the same general form as Catalina I.D. numbers, but with a '4' as the first character to designate Series 24. [BONNEVILLE CUSTOM] Serial numbers for Bonneville passenger cars began with an '8' and for Custom Safaris with a "7' representing the series the cars were in.

CATALINA

Model Number	Body/Style Number	Body Type & Seating	Factory Price	Shipping Weight	Prod. Total
21	2119	4-dr Sed-6P	2704	3955	72,377
21	2139	4-dr Vista HT-6P	2844	4005	45,012
21	2111	2-dr Spt Sed-6P	2633	3870	26,102
21	2137	2-dr HT-6P	2768	3900	38,309
21	2167	2-dr Conv-5P	3080	3970	14,515
21	2135	4-dr Sta Wag-6P	3101	4345	21,162
21	2145	4-dr Sta Wag-9P	3209	4405	14,084

NOTE 1: 231,561 Catalinas were built.

NOTE 2: 9939 Catalinas had synchromesh and 221,622 had Hydra-Matic.

1959 Pontiac Star Chief two-door sedan, V-8.

CUSTOM STAR CHIEF SERIES (V-8) - SERIES 24 - The Super Chief disappeared and 1959 Custom Star Chiefs were large-sized Pontiacs utilizing the base Catalina engines. There were Star Chief emblems on the fins, four stylized stars on the projectile flares, "sweepspear" body side moldings and a narrow deck lid ornament to aid with identification. Regular equipment included all standard Catalina features, plus two-speed electric wipers, Deluxe steering wheel, electric clock, Deluxe chrome wheel covers and loop-pile Lurex-flexed carpeting.

CUSTOM STAR CHIEF

Model Number	Body/Style Number	Body Type & Seating	Factory Price	Shipping Weight	Prod. Total
24	2419	4-dr Sed-6P	3005	4005	27,872
24	2439	4-dr Vista HT-6P	3138	4035	30,689
24	2411	2-dr Spt Sed-6P	2934	3930	10,254

NOTE 1: 68,815 Custom Star Chiefs were built.

NOTE 2: 333 Custom Star Chiefs had synchromesh and 68,482 had Hydra-Matic.

1959 Pontiac Bonneville two-door convertible, V-8.

BONNEVILLE CUSTOM LINE - (V-8) - SERIES 27 AND SERIES 28 - The Bonneville Customs were the prestige offering. They were big, powerful Pontiacs with high level trim and appointments and four-barrel V-8s. Bonnevilles were set apart by golden scripts on the right-hand grille, rear fins and deck lid; four groups of short, horizontal louvers on the projectile-shaped rear fender flares; and crest medallions on the deck lid and doors. Regular equipment included all Star Chief features, plus padded dashboard, inside door safety reflectors, rear seat foam cushions, dash courtesy lights and padded assist rails for passengers.

1959 Pontiac Star Chief four-door sedan. OCW

Model Number	Body/Style Number	Body Type & Seating	Factory Price	Shipping Weight	Prod. Total
27	2735	4-dr Sta Wag-6P	3532	4370	4673

BONNEVILLE CUSTOM (SERIES 28)

Model Number	Body/Style Number	Body Type & Seating	Factory Price	Shipping Weight	Prod. Total
28	2839	4-dr Vista HT-6P	3333	4085	38,696
28	2837	2-dr HT-6P	3257	3985	27,769
28	2867	2-dr Conv-6P	3478	4070	11,426

NOTE 1: 4673 Bonneville Custom Safari station wagons (Series 27) were built.

NOTE 2: 16 Custom Safaris had synchromesh and 4657 had Hydra-Matic.

NOTE 3: 78,271 Bonnevilles (Series 28) were built.

NOTE 4: 673 Bonneville Customs (Series 28) w/synchromesh and 77,596 w/Hydra-Matic.

NOTE 5: 380 (124-in. wheelbase cars) used for hearse/ambulance conversions.

BASE ENGINES

(CATALINA/CUSTOM STAR CHIEF) V-8s: Overhead valves. Cast iron block. Displacement: 389 cu. in. Bore & Stroke: 4.06 x 3.75 in. Compression Ratio: (synchromesh) 8.6:1; (Hydra-Matic) 10.0:1. Brake hp: (synchromesh) 245 @ 4200 rpm; (Hydra-Matic) 280 @ 4400 rpm. Five main bearings. Hydraulic valve lifters. Carburetor: (synchromesh) Rochester model no. 7015910 two-barrel; (Hydra-Matic) Rochester model no. 7015909 two-barrel.

1959 Pontiac Catalina four-door Vista hardtop. OCW

1959 Pontiac Catalina convertible. OCW

1959 Pontiac Catalina two-door hardtop. OCW

1959 Pontiac Catalina two-door hardtop (rear view). OCW

1959 Pontiac Bonneville four-door Vista hardtop. OCW

1959 Pontiac Bonneville two-door hardtop. JAG

1959 Pontiac Bonneville two-door hardtop (rear view). JAG

(BONNEVILLE CUSTOM) V-8: Overhead valves. Cast iron block. Displacement: 389 cu. in. Bore & Stroke: 4.06 x 3.75 in. Compression Ratio: (synchromesh) 8.6:1; (Hydra-Matic) 10.0:1. Brake hp: (synchromesh) 260 @ 4200 rpm; (Hydra-Matic) 300 @ 4600 rpm. Five main bearings. Hydraulic valve lifters. Carburetor: (synchromesh) Carter AFB-2820S (no. 532301) four-barrel; (Hydra-Matic) Carter AFB-2820S (no. 532302) four-barrel.

CHASSIS FEATURES: Wheelbase: (Series 21 and 27) 122 in.; (Series 24 and 28) 124 in. Overall Length: (Catalina passenger cars) 213.7 in.; (Star Chief and Bonneville passenger cars) 220.7 in.; (All station wagons) 214.3 in. Front tread: 63.7 in. Rear tread: 64 in. Pontiac promoted "Wide Track Drive" for the first time this year. Tires: (passenger cars) 8.00 x 14; (Station wagons and all w/air conditioning) 8.50 x 14.

1959 Pontiac Bonneville four-door station wagon. OCW

OPTIONS: Push-button radio ($74). Wonder Bar radio ($100). Sportable radio ($104). Electric antenna ($20). Rear seat speaker ($11). Fresh air heater and defroster ($74). Air-conditioning ($355). Tinted glass ($35). Back-up lights ($9). Windshield washers ($11). Deluxe steering wheel in Catalina ($12). Parking brake signal ($4). Padded dash ($16). Two-speed power brakes ($35). Power windows (four-door) $85; (two-door) $48. Power tailgate window ($27). Six-way power seat ($81). Ever-Level air ride ($155). Oil filter ($8). Heavy-duty air cleaner ($6). Clear plastic seat covers ($30). Whitewall 8.00 x 14 tires ($34). Whitewall 8.50 x 14 tires ($37). Two-tone paint ($11). Front foam seat cushion ($9). Bonneville convertible bucket seats ($84). Catalina decor trim ($45). Lamp group ($23). Safety group ($34). Mirror group ($10). Custom wheel covers ($26). Full wheel discs on Catalina ($14). Outside rearview mirror ($5). Tilt mirror ($4). Undercoating ($15). Antifreeze ($7). Tissue dispenser ($6). Safety belts ($12). A three-speed manual gearbox with column-mounted gearshift was standard on all models. Four-speed Super Hydra-Matic (Strato-Flight) transmission was $180 extra. Rear axle ratios were approximately the same as 1958. Safe-T-Track non-slip differential was $42 extra. A number of optional V-8s were offered, all on the 389 cid block. The Tempest 420E option was available as a super-economy offering, for no extra charge, in any Pontiac. It had an especially fuel efficient camshaft, model no. 7015958 Rochester two-barrel carburetor, and 8.6:1 compression ratio for 215 hp @ 3600 rpm. The four-barrel Bonneville V-8 was available in Catalinas and Star Chiefs at $20 extra. Tri-

Power on the standard Hydra-Matic block (10.0:1 compression ratio) was $73 for Bonnevilles and $81 for other series. This engine produced 315 hp @ 4600 rpm. Extra hp options included four-barrel and Tri-Power induction on the special heavy-duty NASCAR-certified block, both with 10.5:1 compression ratio. Brake hp ratings were 330 and 345, respectively, with both peaking at 4800 rpm. Dual exhausts, normally a $26 option, were standard with these engines.

HISTORICAL FOOTNOTES: Production start-up took place September 11, 1958. Introductions were made one month later. Model year output was 383,320 units for a 6.9 percent market share. Calendar year production included 388,856 cars for fourth place in the industry. One or two El Camino type car-based pickup trucks were built from the 1959 Catalina chassis as prototypes. One of these vehicles was used as a "yard car" at the Pontiac factory in Pontiac, Mich., for many years. Reports of a second "El Catalina" in the West have surfaced from time to time. Pontiac introduced its famous eight-lug aluminum wheels on August 27, 1959, though it's likely that they were intended for 1960 sale. *Motor Trend* magazine selected the 1959 Pontiac as its "Car of the Year." Pontiacs were victorious in many 1959 stock car races, including the Daytona 500 and Darlington 500, with drivers such as Fireball Roberts behind the wheel. The hot "Wide-Tracks" also captured the National Hot Rod Association's "Top Eliminator" title and earned the checkered flag at Pikes Peak. The 280 hp 1959 Catalina two-door hardtop (or Sport Coupe) was tested at 8.8 seconds for 0-to-60 mph and 16.9 seconds for the quarter-mile. Catalina was no longer a body style designation. Vista was now Pontiac's nomenclature for pillarless hardtop styling. The Sport Coupe was a two-door hardtop. The Sport Sedan was the two-door pillared sedan. Nine-passenger station wagons now used a rear-facing third seat of fold-away design. Station wagons were still called Safaris and all Safaris had four-door bodies. Tail lamps used on all station wagons and Catalinas were short horizontal-oval types without trim rings. Tail lamps used on Custom Star Chiefs and Bonneville Customs were long horizontal types with dual trim rings. The 1959 Bonneville Custom was picked as "Best Buy in the $2,000-$3,000 Class" by *Car Life* magazine.

1960 PONTIAC

1960 Pontiac Catalina four-door Safari, V-8.

CATALINA SERIES - (V-8) - SERIES 21 - Pontiac's major styling changes for 1960 included undivided-horizontal bar grilles, straight full-length side trim moldings and a new deck lid which was nearly flush with the tops of the fenders. Catalinas had plain beltline moldings, Catalina front fender scripts, and Pontiac block letters on the belt latch panel. Standard features included turn signals, oil filter, five tubeless tires and courtesy lamps on convertibles.

PONTIAC I.D. NUMBERS: The VIN is located on a plate attached to left front door post. First symbol identifies series: 21=Catalina; 23=Ventura; 24=Star Chief; 27=Bonneville Safari; 28=Bonneville. Second and third symbols indicate model year: 60=1960. Fourth symbol identifies assembly plant: P=Pontiac, Mich.; S=South Gate, Calif.; L=Linden, N.J.; W=Wilmington, Del.; K=Kansas City, Kan.; D=Doraville, Ga.; A=Arlington, Texas; E=Euclid, Ohio. Remaining symbols are the unit's sequential production number starting with 1001 at each factory. Body/style number plate on left side of cowl below hood indicates manufacturer and various codes. Body/style number prefixed by model year code (60=1960). First two symbols in main body/style number are the series code, last two symbols are the body style code. These four numbers appear in second column of charts below. Trim, paint and some accessory codes may also be shown on the body/style number plate. Pontiac engines are stamped with a production code and motor serial number matching the VIN. Production code on pad on front of right-hand cylinder bank has an alpha-numerical stamping identifying the engine. All 1960 V-8s were 389 cid. Engine codes included: A1 (283 hp); A2 (215 hp); B1 (303 hp); B2 (281 hp); C1 (318 hp/Tri-Power); C4 (318 hp/Tri-Power); E3 (215 hp); F1 (330 hp); F4 (330 hp); M1 (345 hp/Tri-Power); M4 (345 hp/Tri-Power).

1960 Pontiac Catalina Safari four-door station wagon. OCW

CATALINA

Model Number	Body/Style Number	Body Type & Seating	Factory Price	Shipping Weight	Prod. Total
21	2119	4-dr Sed-6P	2702	3935	72,650
21	2139	4-dr Vista HT-6P	2842	3990	32,710
21	2111	2-dr Spt Sed-6P	2631	3850	25,504
21	2137	2-dr HT-6P	2766	3835	27,496
21	2167	2-dr Conv-6P	3078	3940	17,172
21	2145	4-dr Sta Wag-9P	3207	4365	14,149
21	2135	4-dr Sta Wag-6P	3099	4310	21,253

NOTE 1: 210,934 Catalinas were built.

NOTE 2: 10,831 Catalinas had synchromesh and 200,101 had Hydra-Matic.

NOTE 3: Some "AmbleWagons" on the standard Safari chassis may have been sold.

1960 Pontiac Catalina convertible. OCW

VENTURA SERIES - (V-8) - SERIES 23 - The Ventura was a Custom trim level Pontiac on the short wheelbase. Identifying cars in this series were plain belt moldings, Ventura front fender scripts and the model name, in block letters, on the trunk latch panel. Venturas had all Catalina features plus custom steering wheel, electric clock, Deluxe wheel discs, full carpeting, triple-tone Morrokide seats, right-hand ash trays and special decor moldings.

VENTURA

Model Number	Body/Style Number	Body Type & Seating	Factory Price	Shipping Weight	Prod. Total
23	2339	4-dr Vista HT-6P	3047	3990	28,700
23	2337	2-dr HT-6P	2971	3865	27,577

1960 Pontiac Star Chief two-door sedan, V-8.

NOTE 1: 56,277 Ventura were built.

NOTE 2: 2381 Venturas had synchromesh and 53,896 had Hydra-Matic.

STAR CHIEF SERIES - (V-8) SERIES 24 - Built off the long wheelbase with the Catalina two-barrel V-8 for base power, Star Chiefs had the same regular equipment as Venturas, plus dual-speed wipers. Distinguishing touches included Star Chief front fender scripts and four stylized stars at the rear of the lower beltline moldings.

STAR CHIEF

Model Number	Body/Style Number	Body Type & Seating	Factory Price	Shipping Weight	Prod. Total
24	2419	4-dr Sed-6P	3003	3995	23,038
24	2439	4-dr Vista HT-6P	3136	4040	14,856
24	2411	2-dr Spt Sed-6P	2932	3910	5797

NOTE 1: 43,691 Star Chiefs were built.

NOTE 2: 166 Star Chiefs had synchromesh and 43,525 had Hydra-Matic.

1960 Pontiac Bonneville two-door hardtop Sport coupe, V-8.

BONNEVILLE LINE - (V-8) SERIES 27 AND SERIES 28 - Pontiac's top line could be told by distinctive front fender scripts, Bonneville lettering on the deck latch panel, beltline moldings ending in three dashes of chrome at the rear and a V-shaped crest on the lower front fenders. Bonnevilles incorporated rear foam seat cushions, padded dashboards with walnut inserts, courtesy lamps, and four-barrel V-8s in addition to everything found in lower-priced Pontiacs. All-Morrokide seats were standard and genuine cowhide leather was available as an option.

BONNEVILLE CUSTOM (SERIES 27)

Model Number	Body/Style Number	Body Type & Seating	Factory Price	Shipping Weight	Prod. Total
27	2735	4-dr Sta Wag-6p	3532	4370	5163

BONNEVILLE (SERIES 28)

28	2839	4-dr Vista HT-6P	3333	4085	39,037
28	2837	2-dr HT-6P	3257	3985	24,015
28	2867	2-dr Conv-5P	3478	4070	17,062

NOTE 1: 5163 Bonneville Custom Safaris were built.

NOTE 2: 12 Safaris had synchromesh and 5151 had Hydra-Matic.

NOTE 3: 80,651 Series 28 Bonnevilles were built.

NOTE 4: 1111 Series 28 Bonnevilles had synchromesh; 79,540 had Hydra-Matic.

NOTE 5: 537 Bonneville chassis were sold to hearse/ambulance makers.

1960 Pontiac Bonneville two-door hardtop . OCW

1960 Pontiac Catalina four-door Vista hardtop. OCW

ENGINES

(CATALINA/VENTURA/STAR CHIEF) V-8: Overhead valves. Cast iron block. Displacement: 389 cu. in. Bore & Stroke: 4.05 x 3.75 in. Compression Ratio: (synchromesh) 8.6:1; (Hydra-Matic) 10.25:1. Brake hp: (synchromesh) 215 @ 3600 rpm; (Hydra-Matic) 283 @ 4400 rpm. Five main bearings. Hydraulic valve lifters. Carburetor: Rochester 2GC two-barrel.

(BONNEVILLE) V-8: Overhead valves. Cast iron block. Displacement: 389 cu. in. Bore & Stroke: 4.06 x 3.75 in. Compression Ratio: (synchromesh) 8.6:1; (Hydra-Matic) 10.25:1. Brake hp: (synchromesh) 281 @ 4400 rpm ; (Hydra-Matic) 303 @ 4600 rpm. Five main bearings. Hydraulic valve lifters. Carburetor: Carter AFB four-barrel.

CHASSIS FEATURES: Wheelbase: (Series 21, 23, and 27) 123 in.; (Series 24 and 28) 124 in. Overall Length: (Catalina, Ventura, and Bonneville Custom Safari) 213.7 in.; (All others) 220.7 in. Front tread: 63.7 in. Rear tread: 64 in. Tires: (Passenger cars) 8.00 x 14; (station wagons and all with air-conditioning) 8.50 x 14.

1960 Pontiac Ventura four-door Vista hardtop. OCW

1960 Pontiac Catalina four-door Vista hardtop . OCW

OPTIONS: Air-conditioning ($430). Electric antenna ($30) Aluminum hubs and drums ($107). E-Z-Eye glass ($43). Circ-L-Aire heater defroster ($43) Direct Aire heater defroster ($94). Sportable radio ($129). Wonder Bar radio ($125). Super Deluxe radio ($89). Rear seat speaker ($14). Luggage carrier ($99). Padded dash ($19). Bucket seats ($100). Safeguard speedometer ($15). Magi-Cruise ($13). Custom wheel discs ($17-$32); Deluxe wheel discs ($16). Windshield washer ($13). Continental spare tire and cover ($258). Underhood utility lamp ($7). Remote control mirror ($12). Power windows ($58 or $106). Power steering ($108). Power brakes ($43). Custom steering wheel ($15). A column-shift three-speed manual transmission was standard. Super Hydra-Matic (Strato-Flight) transmission was $231.34 extra. A four-speed manual floor mounted transmission became available in mid-year, though not as a regular production option (RPO). Most went into professionally-driven NASCAR racers. The unit was basically the same one used by Corvettes and Chevrolets and retailed for $188.30 from Chevrolet. The Pontiac price is probably the same. A variety of rear axle ratios were available. Safe-T-Track differential was $43 extra and optional dual exhausts cost $31. The Tempest 66E option or '425E' two-barrel 215 hp economy engine was optional on all models at no extra cost, but only with Hydra-Matic. The Bonneville four-barrel carburetor

was $23.94 extra in other lines. Tri-Power on the standard (10.5:1 compression) block produced 315 hp on cars with synchromesh and 318 hp on Hydra-Matic equipped units, both @ 4600 rpm. Price for this option was $89/$99/$132/$142 depending on the engine/transmission combination. (Note: High-performance engine prices also varied by series and transmission, with lowest cost on high-trim models with Hydra-Matic). Tri-Power on the Tempest 425 block (NASCAR motor with 10.75:1 compression) gave 348 hp @ 4600 rpm and prices for the option were $316/$326/$359/$369. Four-barrel induction on the Tempest 425 V-8 gave 333 hp @ 4600 rpm and prices were $230/$251/$273/$294.

1960 Pontiac Bonneville convertible. OCW

HISTORICAL FOOTNOTES: Production began August 31, 1959. Introductions were October 1, 1959. Calendar year output was 450,206 (including early 1961 Tempests) for 6.6 percent market share. Model year production was 396,716. Four NASCAR Grand Nationals and three other stock car races were won by Pontiacs. Jim Wangers drove a 1960 Pontiac to the NHRA "Top Eliminator" title. Mickey Thompson installed four Pontiac engines in his Challenger I World Land Speed Record car and drove it 363.67 mph. The 333 hp Catalina two-door hardtop was timed at 7.8 seconds for 0-to-60 mph and 16 seconds for the quarter-mile. Safari remained Pontiac's nomenclature for a station wagon. All 1960 Safaris were four-door types and nine-passenger (three-seat) versions had power tailgate windows and rear-facing folding seats. The term Vista meant four-door pillarless hardtop. The term Sport Sedan meant two-door pillared coupe. Safaris had distinctive single tail lamps and rear decor trim. Starlight two-toning was $40 in regular colors or $52 in special colors. AmbleWagons were low-cost professional cars built off a standard Pontiac station wagon chassis by the Automotive Conversion Corp., Troy, Mich.

1961 PONTIAC

1961 Pontiac Catalina convertible. OCW

CATALINA SERIES - (V-8) - SERIES 23 - Downsizing was seen at Pontiac this year. Thanks to a new perimeter frame design the bodies on standard sized cars were smaller and lighter in weight. A radically new compact named the Tempest was introduced as a Pontiac entry in the growing small car market. Major design differences included a return to the twin grille styling theme, sculptured side panels, taller rooflines and squared-off bodies with small tailfins added. Standard equipment on Catalinas included turn signals, oil filter, cigarette lighter, sun visors, electric windshield wipers and five tubeless blackwall tires.

PONTIAC I.D. NUMBERS: VIN on left front door post. First symbol tells series: 21=Tempest; 23=Catalina; 25=Ventura; 26=Star Chief; 27=Bonneville Safari; 28=Bonneville. Second and third symbols tell year: 61=1961. Fourth symbol tells assembly plant: P=Pontiac, Mich.; S=South Gate, Calif.; L=Linden, N.J.; W=Wilmington, Del.; K=Kansas City, Kan.; D=Doraville, Ga.; A=Arlington, Texas; E=Euclid, Ohio. Fifth through last symbols are the sequential numbers starting at 1001 for each assembly plant. Body/style number plate under hood tells manufacturer, Fisher style number, assembly plant, trim code, paint code, accessory codes. Style number consists of 61 (for 1961) prefix and four symbols that appear in second column of charts below. First two symbols indicate series; second two symbols indicate body type. VIN appears on front of

engine at right-hand cylinder bank along with an alpha-numerical engine production code. Engine production codes included: [195 cid/110 hp four] DA/DS; [195 cid/120 hp four] OSY; [195 cid/155 hp four] XS/YS/XA; [195 cid/140 hp four] OA; [215 cid/155 hp aluminum V-8] YA. [389 cid/215 hp V-8] A2/G4; [389 cid/230 hp V-8] E3/W3/E7/W7/; [389 cid/235 hp V-8] P4/B4/H4 [389 cid/267 hp V-8] S1/S5; [389 cid/287 hp V-8] A1/A5; [389 cid/303 hp V-8] B1/T1/PO/B5/T5/. [389 cid/318 hp H.O. Tri-Power V-8] C4/RC4/CO/RCO/I9/R19; [389 cid/333 hp V-8] F4/FO/RMO/U9; [389 cid/348 hp H.O. Tri-Power V-8] M4/RM4/MO/V9; [389 cid/363 hp Super-Duty Tri-Power V-8] RMP. [421 cid/373 hp Super-Duty V-8] 11-5.

CATALINA

Model Number	Body/Style Number	Body Type & Seating	Factory Price	Shipping Weight	Prod. Total
23	2369	4-dr Sed-6P	2702	3725	38,638
23	2339	4-dr Vista HT-6P	2842	3785	17,589
23	2311	2-dr Spt Sed-6P	2631	3650	9846
23	2337	2-dr HT-6P	2766	3680	14,524
23	2367	2-dr Conv-5P	3078	3805	12,379
23	2345	4-dr Sta Wag-9P	3207	4175	7783
23	2335	4-dr Sta Wag-6P	3099	4135	12,595

NOTE 1: 113,354 Catalinas were built.

NOTE 2: 6337 had synchromesh and 107,017 had Hydra-Matic.

1961 Pontiac Catalina two-door hardtop. OCW

VENTURA SERIES - (V-8) - SERIES 25 - The Ventura continued as a Catalina-sized car with Custom level trim inside and out. Identification included chrome outline moldings for side spears, Ventura script inside the spear on the door and bright metal roof drip moldings. Unlike the Catalinas with horizontal-oval tail lamps and small hubcaps, Venturas carried two round taillamps and full Deluxe wheel discs. Interiors were trimmed in three-tone Jeweltone Morrokide. Standard equipment included custom steering wheel, electric clock and right-hand ashtray, plus all features seen on Catalinas.

VENTURA

Model Number	Body/Style Number	Body Type & Seating	Factory Price	Shipping Weight	Prod. Total
25	2539	4-dr Vista HT-6P	3047	3795	13,912
25	2537	2-dr HT-6P	2971	3685	13,297

NOTE 1: 27,209 Venturas were built.

NOTE 2: 1940 had Synchromesh and 25,269 had Hydra-Matic.

1961 Pontiac Star Chief four-door sedan. OCW

STAR CHIEF SERIES - (V-8) - SERIES 26 - Star Chiefs could be outwardly identified by chrome outline moldings on the concave portion of the side spears which encircled a Star Chief script on the front door, thin horizontal moldings on the convex section of the spear, three chrome stars stacked on the side of the fins and triple tail lights on each side. Standard equipment was comprised of all found in Venturas, plus two-speed wipers. Interiors were furnished in Jacquard woven cloth with metallic highlights accented by Jeweltone Morrokide.

STAR CHIEF

Model Number	Body/Style Number	Body Type & Seating	Factory Price	Shipping Weight	Prod. Total
26	2669	4-dr Sed-6P	3003	3840	16,024
26	2639	4-dr Vista HT-6P	3136	3870	13,557

NOTE 1: 29,581 Star Chief chassis were made.

NOTE 2: 130 had Synchromesh and 29,451 had Hydra-Matic.

1961 Pontiac Bonneville convertible. OCW

BONNEVILLE SERIES - (V-8) - SERIES 28 - Cars in Pontiac's top series were distinguished by golden Bonneville nameplates on the left-hand grille, bright metal moldings on side spears, Bonneville block letters on the convex portion of the spears where front fenders and doors met and triple taillamps set into bright metal housings. Everything included on Star Chiefs was considered standard. Rear foam cushions, padded instrument panels and courtesy lamps were added. Upholstery ranged from nylon and Morrokide combinations on closed cars to all-Morrokide on convertibles, with full genuine leather trims optional.

BONNEVILLE

Model Number	Body/Style Number	Body Type & Seating	Factory Price	Shipping Weight	Prod. Total
28	2839	4-dr Vista HT-6P	3331	3895	30,830
28	2837	2-dr HT-6P	3255	3810	16,906
28	2867	2-dr Conv-5P	3476	3905	18,264

NOTE 1: A total of 66,385 Bonnevilles were built.

NOTE 2: 1480 had synchromesh and 64,905 had Hydra-Matic.

NOTE 3: About 385 Bonneville chassis went to professional car makers.

BONNEVILLE CUSTOM SERIES - (V-8) - SERIES 27 - Comprising a separate series by itself was the Bonneville Custom Safari, which was built off the Catalina platform with Bonneville power and appointments. The majority of trim and equipment was similar to other Bonnevilles, but the four-door station wagon had unique Safari rear fender scripts, vertical taillamps and a circular keyhole ornament on the tailgate.

BONNEVILLE CUSTOM

Model Number	Body/Style Number	Body Type & Seating	Factory Price	Shipping Weight	Prod. Total
27	2735	4-dr Sta Wag-6P	3530	4185	3323

NOTE 1: 3323 Custom Safaris were built.

NOTE 2: 18 had synchromesh and 3305 had Hydra-Matic.

1961 Pontiac Tempest four-door sedan, four-cylinder.

TEMPEST - (4-CYL) - SERIES 21 - In appearance the Tempest was pure Pontiac with twin grilles, sculptured body panels, V-contour hood and bodyside windsplits. It was technically innovative featuring an integral body and frame, flexible "rope" driveshaft, torque tube drive, independent rear suspension, rear-mounted transaxle and a four-cylinder base powerplant created by cutting a 389 cid V-8 in half. Standard equipment included electric wipers, turn signals, dual sun visors and five tubeless blackwall tires. A four-door sedan and Safari station wagon were first to appear, but were joined by a pair of two-door hardtop Sport Coupes later in the year. One of these was a Deluxe model with bucket seats, named the LeMans.

TEMPEST

Model Number	Body/Style Number	Body Type & Seating	Factory Price	Shipping Weight	Prod. Total
21	2119	4-dr Sed-6P	2702	2800	22,557
21	2127	2-dr HT-6P	2113	2785	7432
21	2135	4-dr Sta Wag-6P	2438	2980	7404

TEMPEST (WITH CUSTOM TRIM PACKAGE)

21	2119	4-dr Sed-6P	2884	2800	40,082
21	2127	2-dr LeMans HT-6P	2297	2795	7455
21	2135	4-dr Sta Wag-6P	2611	2980	15,853

NOTE 1: 98,779 Tempest with four-cylinder engines were built.

NOTE 2: 26,737 Tempest fours had synchromesh and 72,042 had Hydra-Matic.

NOTE 3: 2004 Tempests were built with optional (Buick) aluminum V-8s.

NOTE 4: Three Tempest V-8s had synchromesh and 2001 had Hydra-Matic.

1961 Pontiac Tempest LeMans two-door. OCW

BASE ENGINES

(CATALINA/VENTURA/STAR CHIEF) Base V-8s: Overhead valves. Cast iron block. Displacement: 389 cu. in. Bore & Stroke: 4.06 x 3.75 in. Compression Ratio: (synchromesh) 8.6:1; (Hydra-Matic) 10.25:1. Brake hp: 215 @ 3600 rpm; (Hydra-Matic) 267 @ 4200 rpm. Five main bearings. Hydraulic valve lifters. Carburetor: Rochester Number 7019060 two-barrel.

(BONNEVILLE/BONNEVILLE CUSTOM) Base V-8s: Overhead valves. Cast iron block. Displacement: 389 cu. in. Bore & Stroke: 4.06 x 3.75 in. Compression Ratios: (synchromesh) 8.6:1; (Hydra-Matic) 10.25:1. Brake hp: (synchromesh) 235 @ 3600 rpm; (Hydra-Matic) 303 @ 4600 rpm. Five main bearings. Hydraulic valve lifters. Carburetor: Carter AFB3123S four-barrel.

(TEMPEST "INDY FOUR") Inline. Four-cylinder. Overhead valves. Cast iron block. Displacement: 194.5 cu. in. Bore & Stroke: 4.06 x 3.75 in. Compression Ratio: (synchromesh) 8.6:1; (Hydra-Matic) 10.25:1. Brake hp: (synchromesh) 110 @ 3800 rpm; (Hydra-Matic) 120 @ 3800 rpm. Five main bearings. Hydraulic valve lifters. Carburetor: Rochester Number 7019061 two-barrel.

OPTIONAL PONTIAC V-8 ENGINES:

215 cid. Compression ratio: 8.8:1 Carburetion: two-barrel. Brake hp: 155 @ 4600 rpm. (optional in Tempest).

389 cid. Compression ratio: 8.6:1 Carburetion: two-barrel. Brake hp: 230 @ 4000 rpm. (optional in all models with Hydra-Matic).

389 cid. Compression ratio: 8.6:1 Carburetion: four-barrel. Brake hp: 235 @ 3600 rpm. (standard in Bonneville; optional all others with synchromesh).

389 cid. Compression ratio: 10.25:1 Carburetion: two-barrel. Brake hp: 267 @ 4200 rpm. (optional in Catalina and Ventura with Hydra-Matic).

389 cid. Compression ratio: 10.25:1 Carburetion: two-barrel. Brake hp: 283 @ 4400 rpm. (optional in Star Chief with Hydra-Matic).

389 cid. Compression ratio: 10.25:1 Carburetion: two-barrel. Brake hp: 303 @ 4600 rpm. (optional in Bonneville with Hydra-Matic).

389 cid. Compression ratio: 10.25:1 Carburetion: four-barrel. Brake hp: 287 @ 4400 rpm. (optional in Catalina with Hydra-Matic).

389 cid. Compression ratio: 10.75:1 Carburetion: three two-barrels. Brake hp: 318 @ 4600 rpm. (optional in all models with any transmission).

389 cid. Compression ratio: 10.75:1 Carburetion: four-barrel. Brake hp: 333 @ 4800 rpm. (optional in all models with any transmission).

389 cid. Compression ratio: 10.75:1 Carburetion: three two-barrels. Brake hp: 348 @ 4800 rpm. (optional in all models with any transmission).

421 cid. Compression ratio: 11:1 Carburetion: two four-barrels. Brake hp: 405 @ 5600 rpm. (Super-Duty: available only in Catalina two-door; off-road use only).

1961 Pontiac Tempest four-door station wagon. OCW

CHASSIS FEATURES: Wheelbase: (Series 23, 25, and 27) 119 in.; (Series 26 and 28) 123 in.; (Series 21) 112 in. Overall Length: (Series 23 and 25) 210 in.; (Series 27 and Series 23 Safaris) 209.7 in.; (Series 26 and 28) 217 in.; (Tempest) 189.3 in. Front tread: (Pontiac) 62.5 in.; (Tempest) 56.8 in. Rear tread: (Pontiac) 62.5 in.; (Tempest) 56.8 in. Tires: (Pontiac) 8.00 x 14; (Pontiac Safaris) 8.50 x 14; (Tempests) 6.00 x 15.

OPTIONS

[PONTIAC] Air-conditioning ($430). Electric antenna ($30). Guide-Matic headlamp control ($43). Power brakes ($43). Six-way power seat ($97). Power windows ($104). Safeguard speedometer ($19). Magic-Cruise ($16) Aluminum hubs and drums ($107). Bucket seats ($116). Heavy-duty springs ($19) E-Z Eye glass ($43). Luggage carrier ($99) Power tailgate ($32) and more. A three-speed manual transmission was standard. Four-speed Super Hydra-Matic was $231.34 extra. A four-speed manual gearbox with floor shift was $306.66 extra on full-sized cars. Rear axle ratios: (synchromesh) 3.23:1; (Hydra-Matic) 2.87:1. Other ratios were available. Safe-T-Track differential was $43 extra. The four-barrel induction system was $24 extra on all cars except Bonnevilles. Tri-Power induction was priced $110 to $168 depending upon model and transmission. The four-barrel Tempest '425A' high-performance engine was priced $230 to $293 depending upon model and transmission. The Tri-Power Tempest '425A' high-performance engine was priced $338 to $396 depending upon model and transmission.

1961 Pontiac Bonneville two-door hardtop. OCW

[TEMPEST] Basic group ($167-$172); Power tailgate window ($54). Deluxe wheel discs ($16) Windshield washer ($13) Power steering ($75). Bumper guards ($16). Back-up lights ($11-$12). Cool-Pack air-conditioner ($318). Interior decor group ($70-$75). Lower exterior decor group ($13). Upper exterior decor group ($40). Protection group ($40-$42). A three-speed manual transmission was standard. A two-speed Tempes-Torque automatic transmission with dashboard-mounted "spoon" lever control was $172 extra. Engine options included a high-output one-barrel edition of the four with 140 hp @ 4400 rpm; a four-barrel edition of the four with 155 hp @ 4800 rpm and a 215 cid/155 hp Buick V-8 with 8.8:1 compression, two-barrel carburetor, and 155 hp @ 4600 rpm ($216 extra).

HISTORICAL FOOTNOTES: Production start-up: September 1, 1960. Introduction: October 6, 1960. Model year assemblies were 340,635. Calendar year output was 360,336 Pontiacs and Tempests. Pontiac had a 6.3 percent market share. The term Vista means four-door hardtop. The term Sport Sedan means two-door pillared coupe. The term Safari means station wagon. Bucket seats available only in body style 2867. Pontiac took 21 of 52 NASCAR Grand Nationals. Bunkie Knudsen was the general manager of Pontiac Motor Division. Two road tests were done on Pontiacs with the 348 hp V-8. The first featured a Ventura hardtop that went 0-to-60 mph in 8.2 seconds and did the quarter-mile in 15.5 seconds. The second featured a Catalina S/S drag racing car based on the two-door hardtop. It went from 0-to-60 mph in 4.6 seconds and did the quarter-mile in 13.7 seconds.

1962 PONTIAC

1962 Pontiac Catalina convertible with eight-lug wheels. OCW

CATALINA SERIES - (V-8) - SERIES 23 - Standard Pontiacs grew about an inch-and-a-half for 1962. Styling revisions included a V-shaped twin grille, full-length side sculpturing and new rear end styling with curved tail lamps. Vista sedans no longer sported the "flat-top" look and Sport Coupes had multi-plane roofs with a "convertible-like" appearance. Ventura trim became an add-on package for two Catalinas. Regular equipment on Catalinas included turn signals, oil filter, cigarette lighter, sun visors, heater and defroster, windshield wiper and five tubeless tires. Nine-passenger Catalina Safaris had power tailgate windows. Outwardly the cars came with small hubcaps, unaccented side spears and Catalina front fender scripts.

1962 Pontiac Catalina four-door Vista hardtop, V-8.

PONTIAC I.D. NUMBERS: VIN on left front door post. First symbol tells series: 21=Tempest; 23=Catalina; 26=Star Chief; 27=Bonneville Safari; 28=Bonneville; 29=Grand Prix. Second and third symbols tell year: 62=1962. Fourth symbol tells assembly plant: P=Pontiac, Mich.; S=South Gate, Calif.; L=Linden, N.J.; W=Wilmington, Del.; K=Kansas City, Kan.; D=Doraville, Ga.; A=Arlington, Texas. The remaining symbols in VIN are the sequential production number beginning at 1001 for each

factory. Body/style number plate under hood tells manufacturer, Fisher style number, assembly plant, trim code, paint code, accessory codes. Style number consists of 62 (for 1962) prefix and four symbols that appear in second column of charts below. First two symbols indicate series; second two symbols indicate body type. VIN appears on front of engine at right-hand cylinder bank along with an alpha-numerical engine production code. Engine production codes included: [195 cid/110 hp four] 89Z/85Z; [195 cid/115 hp four] 79Y; [195 cid/120 hp four] 86Z; [195 cid/140 hp four] 76Y; [195 cid/166 hp four] 77Y/87Z; [215 cid/185 hp aluminum V-8] 91Z/97Z. [389 cid/215 hp V-8] 01A/03B. [389 cid/230 hp V-8] 20L/21L/40R/41R. [389 cid/235 hp V-8] 02B. [389 cid/267 hp V-8] 15H/17H. [389 cid/283 hp V-8] 35M/37M. [389 cid/303 hp V-8] 16J/16K/18K/39N/36P/38P. [389 cid/318 hp H.O. Tri-Power V-8] 10B/27J/49N. [389 cid/333 hp V-8] O8B/25/47NJ. [389 cid/348 hp H.O. Tri-Power V-8] 11B/28J/50N. [421 cid/405 hp Super-Duty V-8].

CATALINA

Model Number	Body/Style Number	Body Type & Seating	Factory Price	Shipping Weight	Prod. Total
23	2389	4-dr Sed-6P	2796	3765	68,124
23	2389	4-dr Vista HT-6P	2936	3825	29,251
23	2311	2-dr Sed-6P	2725	3705	14,263
23	2347	2-dr HT-6P	2860	3730	46,024
23	2367	2-dr Conv-5P	3172	3855	16,877
23	2345	4-dr Sta Wag-9P	3301	4220	10,716
23	2335	4-dr Sta Wag-6P	3193	4180	19,399

NOTE 1: 204,654 Catalinas were built.

NOTE 2: 13,104 had synchromesh and 191,550 had Hydra-Matic.

1962 Pontiac Star Chief four-door sedan. OCW

STAR CHIEF SERIES - (V-8) - SERIES 26 - Star Chiefs were distinguished by full-length body rub moldings and three slanting stars on the rear fins. Standard equipment included all Catalina features, plus custom steering wheel; electric clock; Deluxe wheel discs; right-hand ashtray and decor molding; dual speed wipers; and special upholstery. Interior trims included Pyramid Pattern cloth and Morrokide combinations or all-Morrokide.

STAR CHIEF

Model Number	Body/Style Number	Body Type & Seating	Factory Price	Shipping Weight	Prod. Total
26	2669	4-dr Sed-6P	3097	3875	27,760
26	2639	4-dr Vista HT-6P	3230	3925	13,882

NOTE 1: A total of 41,642 Star Chiefs were built.

NOTE 2: 196 had synchromesh and 41,446 had Hydra-Matic.

BONNEVILLE SERIES - (V-8) - SERIES 28 - Trim on Bonneville included chrome side spear moldings with ribbed bands in the concave portion, elongated V-shaped rear fender medallions, ribbed trim moldings on the deck lid latch panel, Bonneville block letters on the front fenders and deck lid latch panel and series identification on the left-hand radiator grille. Standard equipment included all items found on Star Chiefs plus rear foam cushions, padded dashes and courtesy lamps. Upholstery was of fine woven Morrokide or optional all-leather. High-wing bucket seats were optional in convertibles.

1962 Pontiac Bonneville two-door hardtop. OCW

1962 Pontiac Bonneville convertible. OCW

1962 Pontiac Bonneville two-door hardtop (rear view). OCW

BONNEVILLE

Model Number	Body/Style Number	Body Type & Seating	Factory Price	Shipping Weight	Prod. Total
28	2839	4-dr Vista HT-6P	3425	4005	44,015
28	2847	2-dr HT-6P	3349	3900	31,629
28	2867	2-dr Conv-5P	3570	4005	21,582

NOTE 1: 97,772 Series 28 Bonnevilles were built.

NOTE 2: 1874 Series 28 Bonnevilles had synchromesh; 95,848 had Hydra-Matic.

NOTE 3: 496 Series 28 chassis were provided to professional car builders.

BONNEVILLE CUSTOM SERIES - (V-8) - SERIES 27 - The Custom Safari again formed a separate series. It was the heaviest and most expensive Pontiac. Pleated Morrokide upholstery in two-tones was featured, as well as a concealed luggage locker.

BONNEVILLE CUSTOM

Model Number	Body/Style Number	Body Type & Seating	Factory Price	Shipping Weight	Prod. Total
27	2735	4-dr Sta Wag-6P	3624	4255	4527

NOTE 1: 4527 Series 27 Bonneville Custom station wagons were built.

NOTE 2: 35 had synchromesh and 4492 had Hydra-Matic.

1962 Pontiac Grand Prix two-door hardtop with eight-lug wheels. OCW

GRAND PRIX SERIES - (V-8) SERIES 29 - The new Grand Prix replaced the Ventura model, although Ventura-Catalinas were still available as a trim option. The "GP" was identified by clean side styling with a checkered flag badge in the concave section of side spears, rocker panel molding, an anodized grille insert and nose piece and special rear end styling. The from-the-factory equipment list included all Bonneville features (except courtesy lamps), plus solid color Morrokide upholstery, bucket seats and center console with tachometer.

GRAND PRIX

Model Number	Body/Style Number	Body Type & Seating	Factory Price	Shipping Weight	Prod. Total
29	2947	2-dr HT-5P	3490	3835	30,195

NOTE 1: 30,195 GPs were built.

NOTE 2: 3939 had Synchromesh and 26,556 had Hydra-Matic.

1962 Pontiac Tempest Safari four-door station wagon. OCW

TEMPEST - (4-CYL) - SERIES 21 - Styling changes for Tempests included a new wider-spaced split grille theme with a third grille section (incorporating a V-shaped emblem) placed in the center and the addition of bolt-in bright metal fins at the rear. There were five basic models, but two were called Customs and could be optioned with the LeMans trim package. Standard equipment included heater and defroster, electric wipers, turn signals, left-hand visors and five tubeless blackwall tires. Those delivered in Custom trim level had twin sun visors, cigarette lighters, Deluxe steering wheel, custom upholstery and special exterior trim. The Custom Convertible sported courtesy lamps.

TEMPEST

Model Number	Body/Style Number	Body Type & Seating	Factory Price	Shipping Weight	Prod. Total
21	2119	4-dr Sed-6P	2240	2815	16,057 (21,373)
21	2127	2-dr Cpe-6P	2186	2785	15,473
21	2117	2-dr HT-6P	2294	2800	12,319
21	2167	2-dr Conv-5P	2564	2955	5076
21	2135	4-dr Sta Wag-6P	2511	2995	6504 (11,170)

TEMPEST CUSTOM (LEMANS OPTION)

Model Number	Body/Style Number	Body Type & Seating	Factory Price	Shipping Weight	Prod. Total
21	2117	2-dr HT-6P	2418	N/A	39,662
21	2167	2-dr Conv-5P	2742	N/A	15,599

NOTE 1: 141,535 Tempest fours were built.

NOTE 2: 28,867 Tempest fours had synchromesh; 112,668 had Tempes-Torque.

NOTE 3: 1658 Tempest V-8s were built.

NOTE 4: 86 Tempest V-8s had synchromesh and 1572 had Tempes-Torque automatic.

NOTE 5: Figures in parenthesis are production of Tempests with Deluxe package.

NOTE 6: Sport Coupe and convertible came Custom-only; no Deluxe option.

BASE ENGINES

(CATALINA) V-8. Overhead valves. Cast iron block. Displacement: 389 cu. in. Bore & Stroke: 4.06 x 3.75 in. Compression Ratio: (synchromesh) 8.6:1; (Hydra-Matic) 10.25:1. Brake hp: (synchromesh) 215 @ 3600 rpm; (Hydra-Matic) 267 @ 4200 rpm. Five main bearings. Hydraulic lifters. Carburetor: Rochester two-barrel.

(STAR CHIEF) V-8s for Star Chiefs were the same as listed for Catalinas, except the Star Chief Hydra-Matic engine had a slightly higher output of 283 hp @ 4400 rpm due to the use of a different Rochester two-barrel carburetor.

(BONNEVILLE/GRAND PRIX) V-8. Overhead valves. Cast iron block. Displacement: 389 cu. in. Bore & Stroke: 4.06 x 3.75 in. Compression Ratio: (synchromesh) 8.6:1; (Hydra-Matic) 10.25:1. Brake hp: (synchromesh) 235 @ 3600 rpm; (Hydra-Matic) 303 @ 4600 rpm. Five main bearings. Hydraulic valve lifters. Carburetor: Carter AFB four-barrel.

(TEMPEST "INDY FOUR") Inline. Four-cylinder. Overhead valves. Cast iron block. Displacement: 194.5 cu. in. Bore & Stroke: 4.06 x 3.75 in. Compression Ratio: (synchromesh) 8.6:1; (Tempes-Torque) 10.25:1. Brake hp: (synchromesh) 110 @ 3800 rpm; (Tempes-Torque) 120 @ 3800 rpm. Carburetor: Rochester one-barrel.

OPTIONAL V-8 ENGINES:

215 cid. Compression ratio: 10.25:1. Carburetion: four-barrel. Brake hp: 190 @ 4800 rpm. (optional in Tempest).

389 cid. Compression ratio: 8.6:1. Carburetion: two-barrel. Brake hp: 215 @ 3600 rpm. (standard in Catalina and Star Chief with synchromesh).

389 cid. Compression ratio: 8.6:1. Carburetion: four-barrel. Brake hp: 235 @ 3600 rpm. (standard on Bonneville with manual, optional all others).

389 cid. Compression ratio: 8.6:1. Carburetion: two-barrel. Brake hp: 230 @ 4000 rpm. (optional all models with automatic).

389 cid. Compression ratio: 10.25:1. Carburetion: two-barrel. Brake hp: 267 @ 4200 rpm. (optional on Catalina with automatic).

389 cid. Compression ratio: 10.25:1. Carburetion: two-barrel. Brake hp: 283 @ 4400 rpm. (optional on Star Chief with automatic).

389 cid. Compression ratio: 10.25:1. Carburetion: four-barrel. Brake hp: 305 @ 4600 rpm. (standard on Bonneville & Grand Prix with automatic, optional on Catalina & Star Chief with automatic).

389 cid. Compression ratio: 10.75:1. Carburetion: three two-barrels. Brake hp: 318 @ 4600. (optional all models with any transmission).

389 cid. Compression ratio: 10.75:1. Carburetion: four-barrel. Brake hp: 333 @ 4800. (optional all models, any transmission).

389 cid. Compression ratio: 10.75. Carburetion: three two-barrels. Brake hp: 348 @ 4800. (optional all models, any transmission).

389 cid. Compression ratio: 10.75:1. Carburetion: four-barrel. Brake hp: 385 @ 5200 rpm. (Super Duty-optional on Catalina two-door only).

421 cid. Compression ratio: 11.0:1. Carburetion: two four-barrels. Brake hp: 405 at 5600 rpm. (Super-Duty, optional on Catalina two-door only).

CHASSIS FEATURES: Wheelbase: (Series 23 Safari and Series 27) 119 in.; (Series 23 and 29) 120 in.; (Series 26 and 28) 123 in.; (Series 21) 112 in. Overall Length: (Series 23 and Safari and Series 27) 212.3 in.; (Series 23 and 29) 211.6 in.; (Series 26 and 28) 218.6 in. Front tread: (Pontiac) 62.5 in.; (Tempest) 56.8 in. Rear tread: (Pontiac) 62.5 in.; (Tempest) 56.8 in. Tires: (Pontiac) 8.00 x 14; (Tempest) 6.00 x 15.

1962 Pontiac Tempest convertible. OCW

OPTIONS

[PONTIAC] Guidematic headlamp control ($43). Bucket seats for body style 2867 ($116). Console for Body Style 2867 w/bucket seats ($161). Padded dash ($16). Power bench seat ($97). Power bucket seat ($28). Power brakes ($43). Power steering ($108). Magi-Cruise ($16). Ventura trim for Body Styles 2339 and 2347 ($118.) Aluminum hubs and drums ($108-$122). Two-speed wipers ($5). Windshield washers ($13). Power tailgate window ($31). Power windows ($18). Split-back Safari seat ($116). A three-speed manual transmission was standard. Super Hydra-Matic was $231.34 extra. Four-speed synchromesh with floor shift was $231.34 extra. Dual exhausts were standard with the Trophy `425A' V-8s and $30.88 extra on others. Safe-T-Track differential was $42 extra. Four-barrel carburetion was standard on Bonneville and Grand Prix and $24 extra on others. Tri-Power induction was $116-$174 extra depending on model and transmission. The four-barrel '425A' V-8 was $199-$294 extra depending on model and transmission. The Tri-Power `425A' V-8 was $312-$401 extra depending on model and transmission. Approximately 1514 cars were built with 421 cid Super-Duty V-8s. This motor represented a stroked version of the Trophy V-8 block with two four-barrel carburetors. Such engines developed 405 hp @ 5600 rpm and cost $2250 extra. Seven rear axle gear ratios were provided, the 3.64:1 and 3.90:1 on special order only.

[TEMPEST] Air-conditioner ($319). Back-up lights ($11-$13). Bumper guards ($16). Electric clock ($16). Tinted windshield ($20). Padded dash ($4). Remote control mirror ($12). Power steering ($75). Power tailgate window ($54). Manual radio ($54). Push-button radio ($62). Upper decor group ($19-$34). Lower decor group ($34). Interior decor group ($70-$75). Exterior decor group combo ($54-$67). Code 088 LeMans option group: (Custom Convertible) $178; (Custom Sports Coupe) $124. A three-speed manual transmission was standard. Two-speed Tempes-Torque automatic or four-speed synchromesh were $172.80 extra. Four-barrel carburetion on the "Indy Four" (166 hp @ 4800 rpm) was $38.74 extra. The two-barrel aluminum Buick V-8 (185 hp @ 4800 rpm) was $261.36 extra. A 3.55:1 rear axle was standard and 3.31:1 was optional.

1962 Superior-Pontiac limousine. JAG

HISTORICAL FOOTNOTES: Production started August 15, 1961. Introductions took place September 21, 1961. The model year saw 521,933 assemblies. In the calendar year, 547,350 cars were made, putting Pontiac in third place in vehicle production in the U.S. Pontiacs took 14 of 18 United States Auto Club stock car races and 22 of 53 NASCAR events. Joe Weatherly won the driving championship in a Pontiac. Bunkie Knudsen moved to Chevrolet and E.M. "Pete" Estes took over as the new general manager of Pontiac Motor Division. Jim Wanger's 1962 Catalina Super-Duty hardtop was tested in a car buff magazine. The 405 hp "Poncho" went from 0-to-60 mph in 5.4 seconds and did the quarter-mile in 13.9 at 107 mph. A Catalina with a special 370 hp "Royal Bobcat" package from Royal Pontiac (Royal Oak, Mich.) ran 0-to-60 mph in 6.5 seconds and did the quarter-mile in 14.5. Carol Cox took the NHRA Winternationals with a 13.06 quarter-mile performance in a Catalina S/SA drag car. Vista means four-door hardtop. Safari means station wagon. Body styles 2117 and 2167 came only as Tempest Custom or Tempest Custom with LeMans option. Bucket seats, center console and floor mounted gearshift control were standard on Body Style 2947.

1963 PONTIAC

1963 Pontiac Catalina four-door sedan, V-8.

CATALINA - (V-8) - SERIES 23 - Styling and luxury were emphasized by Pontiac in 1963 and GM banned factory competition efforts. Styling was totally new with clean, square lines, angled roofs, upward curving tail lamps, recessed split grilles and non-panoramic windshields. Catalinas wore small hubcaps, plain full-length body moldings and Catalina front fender scripts. Turn signals, oil filters, cigarette lighter, sun visors, heater and defroster, electric wipers and five tubeless tires were standard equipment. Safaris had oversize 8.50 x 14 tires and the nine-passenger job had a power tailgate window.

PONTIAC I.D. NUMBERS: VIN on left front door post. First symbol tells series: 21=Tempest; 22=LeMans; 23=Catalina; 26=Star Chief; 28=Bonneville; 29=Grand Prix. Second and third symbols tell year: 63=1963. Fourth symbol tells assembly plant: P=Pontiac, Mich.; S=South Gate, Calif.; L=Linden, N.J.; W=Wilmington, Del.; K=Kansas City, Kan.; D=Doraville, Ga.; A=Arlington, Texas. Following symbols are sequential production number starting with 1001 at each assembly plant. Body/style number plate under hood tells manufacturer, Fisher style number, assembly plant, trim code, paint code, accessory codes. Style number consists of 63 (for 1963) prefix and four symbols that appear in second column of charts below. First two symbols indicate series; second two sym-

bols indicate body type. VIN appears on front of engine at right-hand cylinder bank along with an alpha-numerical engine production code. Engine production codes included: [195 cid/115 hp four] 89Z/85Z/79Y. [195 cid/120 hp four] 86Z/83Z. [195 cid/140 hp four] 76Y. [195 cid/166 hp four] 77Y/84Z/87Z. [326 cid/260 hp V-8] 68X/71X/60O/69O. [326 cid/280 hp V-8] 70X/59O. [389 cid/215 hp V-8] 01A/03B. [389 cid/230 hp V-8] 20L/21L/40R/41R. [389 cid/235 hp V-8] 02B/04B. [389 cid/267 hp V-8] 15H/17H. [389 cid/283 hp V-8] 35M/37M. [389 cid/303 hp V-8] 06B/16K/18K/36P/38P. [389 cid/313 hp H.O. Tri-Power V-8] 07B/48N/26G. [421 cid/320 hp V-8] 22B/43N/34J. [421 cid/353 hp V-8] 08B/47Q/25G. [421 cid/370 hp H.O. Tri-Power V-8] 11B/28G/50Q. [421 cid/405 hp Super-Duty V-8] 12-5. [421 cid/420 hp Super-Duty V-8] 13-5.

CATALINA

Model Number	Body/Style Number	Body Type & Seating	Factory Price	Shipping Weight	Prod. Total
23	2311	2-dr Sed-6P	2725	3685	14,091
23	2369	4-dr Sed-6P	2795	3755	79,961
23	2347	2-dr HT-6P	2859	3725	60,795
23	2339	4-dr Vista HT-6P	2935	3815	31,256
23	2367	2-dr Conv-5P	3300	3835	18,249
23	2335	4-dr Sta Wag-6P	3171	4175	18,446
23	2345	4-dr Sta Wag-9P	3193	4230	11,751

NOTE 1: 234,549 Catalinas were built.
NOTE 2: 16,811 had synchromesh and 217,738 had Hydra-Matic.

1963 Pontiac Catalina four-door station wagon. OCW

STAR CHIEF - (V-8) - SERIES 26 - Star Chiefs had full-length body moldings, Deluxe wheel discs, star emblems on the rear roof pillar and Star Chief front fender scripts. Rocker panel moldings were also seen. Standard equipment included all Catalina features plus, custom steering wheel, electric clock, dual-speed wipers and special upholstery.

STAR CHIEF

Model Number	Body/Style Number	Body Type & Seating	Factory Price	Shipping Weight	Prod. Total
26	2669	4-dr Sed-6P	3096	3885	28,309
26	2639	4-dr Vista HT-6P	3229	3915	12,448

NOTE 1: 40,757 Star Chiefs were built.
NOTE 2: 175 had synchromesh and 40,582 had Hydra-Matic.

BONNEVILLE - (V-8) - SERIES 28 - Bonnevilles came with all Star Chief features, plus rear foam cushions, padded instrument panels and courtesy lamps. They were outwardly identified by broad, ribbed moldings on the front fenders and doors, rear fin badges, left-hand grille nameplates, rocker panel moldings and block-lettered horizontal decor panels on the deck lid latch panel that carried the Bonneville name.

1963 Pontiac Bonneville two-door convertible, V-8.

BONNEVILLE

Model Number	Body/Style Number	Body Type & Seating	Factory Price	Shipping Weight	Prod. Total
28	2847	2-dr HT-6P	3348	3895	30,995
28	2839	4-dr Vista HT-6P	3423	3985	49,929
28	2867	2-dr Conv-5P	3568	3970	23,459
28	2835	4-dr Safari-6P	3623	4245	5,156

1963 Pontiac Bonneville two-door hardtop with eight-lug wheels. OCW

NOTE 1: 110,316 Bonnevilles were built.

NOTE 2: 1819 had synchromesh and 108,497 had Hydra-Matic attachments.

NOTE 3: 777 Bonneville chassis were provided for professional car builders.

1963 Pontiac Grand Prix two-door hardtop.

GRAND PRIX - (V-8) - SERIES 29 - The GP was restyled from bumper to bumper. It had a clean look with no side trim, a grille emphasizing negative space with bright accents and enclosed parking lamps, grilled-over tail lamps mounted on the deck lid and a concave rear window treatment. Standard equipment included the full list of Bonneville items, plus special solid color Morrokide upholstery, woodgrained steering wheel and dash trim, bucket type front seats and a center console with a vacuum gage. The Grand Prix badges were now mounted on the sides of the rear fenders and rocker panel moldings were employed.

GRAND PRIX

Model Number	Body/Style Number	Body Type & Seating	Factory Price	Shipping Weight	Prod. Total
29	2957	2-dr HT-5P	3490	3915	72,959

NOTE 1: 72,959 GPs were built.

NOTE 2: 5157 had synchromesh and 67,802 had Hydra-Matic.

TEMPEST - (4-CYL) - SERIES 21 - The term "senior compact" was often used to describe the new Tempests. They had the same wheelbase and technical features as earlier Tempests, but they were two inches wider and five inches longer. Design changes included a slight "coke bottle" shape, more angular rooflines, creased side panels, longer trunks, split grille styling, wider wheel openings and dual vertically-stacked tail lamps. Standard equipment included heater and defroster, electric wipers, turn signals, left-hand sun visors and five black tubeless tires. Oversize 6.50 x 15 tires were uses on V-8 equipped Tempests and Safaris.

TEMPEST

Model Number	Body/Style Number	Body Type & Seating	Factory Price	Shipping Weight	Prod. Total
21	2127	2-dr Coupe-6P	2188	2810	13,307
21	2117	2-dr HT-6P	2294	2820	(13,157)
21	2119	4-dr Sed-6P	2241	2815	12,808
					(15,413)
21	2167	2-dr Cus Conv-5P	2554	2955	5012
21	2135	4-dr Sta Wag-6P	2512	2995	4203
					(5932)

NOTE 1: 69,831 Series 21 Tempests were built.

NOTE 2: 16,657 had synchromesh and 53,174 had Tempes-Torque.

NOTE 3: Figures in parenthesis are Tempests with optional Deluxe trim.

NOTE 4: Production of body style 2117 is not broken out separately.

TEMPEST LEMANS - (V-8) - SERIES 22 - The LeMans nameplate was listed as a separate series. Standard equipment on LeMans included dual sun visors, Deluxe steering wheel, custom interior, bucket seats, console and power convertible top. Identification features included model badges on front fenders, partially blacked-out grilles, horizontal taillights and a horizontal decor panel on the deck latch panel.

TEMPEST LEMANS

Model Number	Body/Style Number	Body Type & Seating	Factory Price	Shipping Weight	Prod. Total
22	2217	2-dr HT-6P	2418	2865	45,701
22	2267	2-dr Cus Conv-5P	2742	3035	15,957

NOTE 1: 61,659 LeMans were built.

NOTE 2: 18,034 had synchromesh and 43,625 had Tempes-Torque.

NOTE 3: 23,227 Sport Coupes and 8744 convertibles were four-cylinder.

NOTE 4: All other LeMans were V-8 powered.

1963 Pontiac Tempest LeMans Custom convertible. OCW

1963 Pontiac Tempest LeMans two-door hardtop. OCW

BASE ENGINES

(CATALINA) V-8: Overhead valves. Cast iron block. Displacement: 389 cu. in. Bore & Stroke: 4.06 x 3.75 in. Compression Ratio: 8.6:1 (synchromesh); (Hydra-Matic) 10.25:1. Brake hp: (Synchromesh) 215 @ 3600 rpm; (Hydra-Matic) 267 @ 4200 rpm. Five main bearings. Hydraulic lifters. Carburetor: Rochester two-barrel (synchromesh) model 7023066; (Hydra-Matic) 7023066.

(STAR CHIEF) V-8s on Star Chiefs had the same specifications as listed for Catalinas except the Star Chief Hydra-Matic engine had a more powerful 283 hp rating.

(BONNEVILLE/GRAND PRIX) V-8: Overhead valves. Cast iron block. Displacement: 389 cu. in. Bore & Stroke: 4.06 x 3.75 in. Compression Ratio: (synchromesh) 8.6:1; (Hydra-Matic) 10.25:1. Brake hp: (synchromesh) 235 @ 3600 rpm; (Hydra-Matic) 303 @ 4600 rpm. Five main bearings. Hydraulic valve lifters. Carburetor: Carter AFB four-barrel.

(TEMPEST/LEMANS "INDY FOUR") Inline. Four-cylinder. Overhead valves. Cast iron block. Displacement 194.5 cu. in. Bore & Stroke: 4.06 x 3.75 in. Compression Ratio: (synchromesh) 8.6:1; (automatic) 10.25:1. Brake hp: (synchromesh) 115 @ 4000 rpm; (automatic) 120 @ 3800 rpm. Five main bearings. Hydraulic valve lifters. Carburetor: Rochester one-barrel.

OPTIONAL V-8 ENGINES

(TEMPEST)

326 cid. Compression ratio: 10.25:1. Carburetion: two-barrel. Brake hp: 260 at 4800 rpm. (optional Tempest and LeMans).

(PONTIAC)

389 cid. Compression ratio: 8.6:1. Carburetion: two-barrel. Brake hp: 215 @ 3600 rpm. (standard on Star Chief and Catalina with manual transmission).

389 cid. Compression ratio: 8.6:1. Carburetion: four-barrel. Brake hp: 235 @ 3600 rpm. (standard Bonneville with manual; optional all others).

389 cid. Compression ratio: 8.6:1. Carburetion: two-barrel. Brake hp: 230 @ 4000 rpm. (optional all models with automatic).

389 cid. Compression ratio: 10.25:1. Carburetion: two-barrel. Brake hp: 267 @ 4200 rpm. (standard on Catalina with automatic).

389 cid. Compression ratio: 10.25:1. Carburetion: two-barrel. Brake hp: 283 @ 4400 rpm. (standard on Star Chief with automatic).

389 cid. Compression ratio: 10.25:1. Carburetion: three two-barrels. Brake hp: 313 @ 4600 rpm. (optional all models).

421 cid H.O. Compression ratio: 10.75:1. Carburetion: four-barrel. Brake hp: 353 @ 5000 rpm. (optional all "B-body" models with any transmission).

421 cid H.O. Compression ratio: 10.75:1. Carburetion: three two-barrels. Brake hp: 370 @ 5200 rpm. (optional on all "B-body" models with any transmission).

421 cid. Compression ratio: 12.0:1. Carburetion: four-barrel. Brake hp: 390 @ 5800 rpm. (Super Duty-optional in Catalina two-door only).

421 cid. Compression ratio: 12.0:1. Carburetion: two four-barrels. Brake hp: 405 @ 5600 rpm. (Super Duty-optional in Catalina two-door only).

421 cid. Compression ratio: 13.0:1. Carburetion: two four-barrels. Brake hp: 410 @ 5600 rpm. (Super Duty-optional in Catalina two-door only).

1963 Pontiac Catalina convertible. OCW

CHASSIS FEATURES: Wheelbase: (All Pontiac Safaris) 119 in.; (Series 23 and 29) 120 in.; (Series 26 and 28) 123 in.; (Tempests) 112 in. Overall Length: (All Pontiac Safaris) 212.8 in.; (Series 23 and 29) 211.9 in.; (Series 26 and 28) 218.9 in.; (All Tempests) 194.3 in. Front tread: (Pontiac) 64 in.; (Tempest) 57.3 in. Rear tread: (Pontiac) 64 in.; (Tempest) 58 in. Standard tires: (Pontiac) 8.00 x 14; (Tempest) 6.00 x 15.

OPTIONS

[PONTIAC] Air-conditioning ($430). Console including tachometer ($161). Instrument gage cluster ($21-$59). Luggage carrier ($94). Remote control mirror ($12). Power brakes ($57). Power seat ($96). Power tilt left-hand bucket seat ($71). Tachometer ($54). Cordova top ($86). Ventura trim on body styles 2339, 2347 and 2369 ($118). Sports wheelcovers ($30-46). Aluminum hubs and drums ($122-$138). A three-speed manual transmission was standard. A heavy-duty three-speed manual gearbox was $48 extra on Catalinas and Bonnevilles. A four-speed manual gearbox with floor shift was $231 extra. Super Hydra-Matic was also $231 extra. Dual exhausts were standard with '425A' V-8s and $31 extra on others. Safe-T-Track differential was $43 more. Four-barrel carburetion was standard on Bonneville and Grand Prix and $35 extra on others. Tri-Power induction was $126 on Catalinas and Star Chiefs and $116 on Grand Prix and Bonnevilles. This engine, with 10.25:1 compression, now gave 313 hp @ 4600 rpm. The `421' engines, with 10.75:1 compression heads, were now called H.O. motors. The four-barrel edition was priced $291-$343 extra depending upon model and transmission. It produced 353 hp @ 5000 rpm. The Tri-Power 421 H.O. engine was priced $404-$445 extra depending on model and transmission. It produced 370 hp @ 5200 rpm. A variety of axle ratios were available.

1963 Superior-Pontiac nine-passenger Embassy limousine. JAG

[TEMPEST] Air-conditioner ($319). LeMans console shift ($48). Padded dash ($16). Power convertible top ($54). Power tilt left bucket seat ($67). Power steering ($75). Power tailgate window ($54). Push-button radio ($62). Bucket seats ($134). Custom steering wheel ($6-$9). Deluxe steering wheel with ring ($4). Tachometer ($54). Cordova top ($75). Two-speed wipers and washer ($17). A three-speed manual transmission was standard. Two-speed Tempes-Torque automatic was $173 extra. A four-speed manual gearbox with floor shift was priced $189. Four-barrel carburetion on the "Indy Four" was $39 extra. A new V-8 was available at $167 over base price. Based on a standard Pontiac V-8 with bore size reduced, this engine displaced 326 cu. in. (5.3 liters). Bore & Stroke measured 3.72 x 3.75 in. With a two-barrel carburetor and 10.25:1 compression it produced 260 hp @ 4800 rpm. A heavy-duty clutch was available for the one-barrel and four-barrel versions of the "Indy Four" at prices of $27 and $66, respectively. Standard axle ratio for Tempests was 3.55:1 and optional was 3.31:1.

1963 Superior-Pontiac combination car. JAG

HISTORICAL FOOTNOTES: Production began September 4, 1962. Introductions were on October 4, 1962. Model year output was 590,071 for an 8.9 percent share of market. Calendar year output was 625,268, making Pontiac the third largest auto producer. Pontiac had four NASCAR wins and startled the drag racing world with the release of "Swiss Cheese" Catalina factory lightweight racing cars. The name came from the fact that their frames were drilled to decrease the weight. The 370 hp 1963 Grand Prix was good for 0-to-60 mph in 6.6 seconds and did the quarter-mile in 15.1 seconds. Vista means four-door hardtop. Safari means station wagon. Sports Sedan was sometimes used to identify two-door pillared coupes. Body style 2957 had a distinctive roofline not shared with other lines. Bucket seats now available for Catalina coupes and convertibles with the Ventura option, plus Bonnevilles including the Custom Safari station wagon. The following "Super-Duty 421" vehicles were built in 1963: 13 Catalina and Grand Prix four-barrels; 59 Catalinas and Grand Prix with two four-barrel carburetors; five unspecified models (believed to be Catalinas with aluminum front ends) with dual four-barrel induction; and 11 Tempests with the dual-quad engine.

1964 PONTIAC

1964 Pontiac Catalina 2+2 two-door hardtop, V-8.

CATALINA - (V-8) - SERIES 23 - Full-size Pontiacs were face-lifted for 1964. They looked shorter, but were about an inch longer overall. Trim identification features seen on Catalinas included three-quarter length side moldings running from the front wheel opening back, Catalina front fender scripts and series medallions on the rear fender. Standard equipment was about the same as a year earlier. Full wheel discs and rocker moldings were options seen on many Catalinas. The Catalina 2

+ 2 option package was available on style numbers 2347 and 2367 at approximately $291. The Ventura trim package was available as an interior decor option for Catalina style numbers 2339, 2347 and 2367 at approximately $118.

PONTIAC I.D. NUMBERS: VIN on left front door post. First symbol tells engine type: 6=six-cylinder; 8=V-8. Second symbol indicates series: 0=Tempest; 1=Tempest Custom; 2=LeMans; 3=Catalina; 6=Star Chief; 8=Bonneville; 9=Grand Prix. Third symbol tells year: 64=1964. Fourth symbol tells assembly plant: P=Pontiac, Mich.; S=South Gate, Calif.; L=Linden, N.J.; K=Kansas City, Kan., GMAD plant; D=Doraville, Ga.; A=Arlington, Texas; F=Fremont, Ohio; B=Baltimore, Md.; M=Kansas City, Kan. Chevrolet assembly plant. Following symbols are sequential production number starting with 1001 at each assembly plant. Body/style number plate under hood tells manufacturer, Fisher style number, assembly plant, trim code, paint code, accessory codes. Style number consists of 64 (for 1964) prefix and four symbols that appear in second column of charts below. First two symbols indicate series; second two symbols indicate body type. VIN appears on front of engine at right-hand cylinder bank along with an alpha-numerical engine production code. Engine production codes included: [215 cid/140 hp six] 80Z/81Z/85Z/83Y/88Y/89Y. [326 cid/250 hp V-8] 92X/96O. [326 cid/280 hp V-8] 94X/97O. [389 cid/215 hp V-8] O1A/O2B/O3B. [389 cid/230 hp V-8] O4L/O5L/O8R/O9R. [389 cid/239 hp V-8] O3B/O4B. [389 cid/235 hp] 22B. [389 cid/240 hp V-8] 13H. [389 cid/257 hp V-8] 19M. [389 cid/267 hp V-8] 11H/12H. [389 cid/276 hp V-8] 30P. [389 cid/283 hp V-8] 10A/17M/18M. [389 cid/303 hp V-8] 25K/26K/27P/28P. [389 cid/306 hp V-8] 23B/29N/ [389 cid/330 hp H.O. Tri-Power V-8] 32B/33G/34N. [421 cid/320 hp V-8] 35B/38S/43N. [421 cid/350 hp H.O. Tri-Power V-8] 44B/47S/49N. [421 cid/370 hp H.O. Tri-Power V-8] 45B/46G/50Q. [389 cid/325 hp four-barrel GTO V-8] 78X with synchromesh; 79J with Hydra-Matic. [389 cid/348 hp GTO Tri-Power V-8] 76X with synchromesh; 77J with Hydra-Matic. (Note: Some marque experts claim a few GTOs were built with factory-installed and/or dealer-installed 421 V-8s.)

1964 Pontiac Catalina 2+2 convertible. JAG

CATALINA

Model Number	Body/Style Number	Body Type & Seating	Factory Price	Shipping Weight	Prod. Total
23	2369	4-dr Sed-6P	2806	3770	84,457
23	2339	4-dr HT-6P	2945	3835	33,849
23	2311	2-dr Sed-6P	2735	3695	12,480
23	2347	2-dr HT-6P	2869	3750	74,793
23	2367	2-dr Conv-5P	3181	3825	18,693
23	2345	4-dr Sta Wag-9P	3311	4235	13,140
23	2335	4-dr Sta Wag-6P	3203	4190	20,356

NOTE 1: 257,768 Catalinas were built.

NOTE 2: 15,194 had synchromesh and 242,574 had Hydra-Matic.

NOTE 3: 7998 cars had the 2 + 2 option package.

1964 Pontiac Catalina four-door sedan. JAG

STAR CHIEF - (V-8) - SERIES 26 - Star Chiefs had Deluxe steering wheels and wheelcovers as standard equipment, as well at two-speed wipers and electric clocks. Trim features included Catalina-like side spears, front fender model scripts, and three stylized stars stacked on rear fenders.

STAR CHIEF

Model Number	Body/Style Number	Body Type & Seating	Factory Price	Shipping Weight	Prod. Total
26	2669	4-dr Sed-6P	3107	3885	26,453
26	2639	4-dr HT-6P	3239	3945	11,200

NOTE 1: 37,653 Star Chiefs were built.

NOTE 2: 132 had synchromesh and 37,521 had Hydra-Matic.

1964 Pontiac Bonneville two-door convertible, V-8.

BONNEVILLE - (V-8) - SERIES 28 - Bonnevilles had no bodyside moldings. Identifiers included V-shaped front fender badges, ribbed lower body beauty moldings (on rocker panels) with front and rear fender extensions and Bonneville block lettering on the rear fender sides. Courtesy lamps, padded dashboards and rear foam seat cushions were standard, plus all items found on the Star Chief equipment list. A Bonneville Brougham trim package was available for style number 2839 and included special interior trim and roof pillar nameplates.

BONNEVILLE

Model Number	Body/Style Number	Body Type & Seating	Factory Price	Shipping Weight	Prod. Total
28	2839	4-dr HT-6P	3433	3995	57,630
28	2847	2-dr HT-6P	3358	3920	34,769
28	2867	2-dr Conv-5P	3578	3985	22,016
28	2835	4-dr Sta Wag-6P	3633	4275	5844

NOTE 1: 115,060 Bonnevilles (123-in. wheelbase) were built.

NOTE 2: 1470 cars (123-in. wheelbase) had synchromesh and 113,590 had Hydra-Matic.

NOTE 3: 5844 Bonneville (119-in. wheelbase) were built.

NOTE 4: 42 cars (119-in. wheelbase) had synchromesh and 5802 had Hydra-Matic.

NOTE 5: 645 Bonneville (123-in. wheelbase) chassis provided for conversions.

1964 Pontiac Grand Prix two-door hardtop. OCW

GRAND PRIX - (V-8) - SERIES 29 - The Grand Prix was identified by model lettering and badges behind the front wheel cutout, rectangular front parking lamps, more deeply recessed grilles and GP lettering on the left-hand grille. Concave rear window treatments, grilled-over taillamps and wood-grained trim for dashboards and steering wheels were seen. Standard equipment included dual exhausts, bucket seats, center console and front foam seat cushions.

GRAND PRIX

Model Number	Body/Style Number	Body Type & Seating	Factory Price	Shipping Weight	Prod. Total
29	2957	2-dr HT-5P	3499	3930	63,810

NOTE 1: 63,810 Grand Prix were built.

NOTE 2: 3124 had synchromesh and 60,686 had Hydra-Matic.

TEMPEST - (6-CYL) - SERIES 20 - Tempests were enlarged again and had separate frame construction with conventional drive train engineering. A six-cylinder engine, assembled by Pontiac Motor Division from Chevrolet-produced components, was the base powerplant. There were three lines. Identifying Series 20 base Tempests were small hubcaps, the absence of upper belt line moldings and triple windsplits behind front wheel openings. Cars with optional V-8 power were dressed with front fender badges.

TEMPEST

Model Number	Body/Style Number	Body Type & Seating	Factory Price	Shipping Weight	Prod. Total
20	2069	4-dr Sed-6P	2313	2970	15,516 (3911)
20	2027	2-dr HT-6P	2259	2930	17,169 (4596)
20	2035	4-dr Sta Wag-6P	2605	3245	4597 (2237)

NOTE 1: No brackets=Tempest six production; brackets=Tempest V-8 production.

1964 Pontiac Tempest Custom convertible. OCW

TEMPEST CUSTOM - (6 CYL) - SERIES 21 - Tempest Customs had the same general styling features as base Tempests, but could be easily identified by the bright upper beltline moldings accenting the "Coke bottle" shape. There were also Tempest Custom nameplates on the rear fenders. Extra standard equipment included carpeting, Deluxe steering wheel and courtesy lamps on convertibles.

TEMPEST CUSTOM

Model Number	Body/Style Number	Body Type & Seating	Factory Price	Shipping Weight	Prod. Total
21	2169	4-dr Sed-6P	2399	2990	15,851 (14,097)
21	2167	2-dr Conv-5P	2641	3075	4465 (3,522)
21	2127	2-dr HT-6P	2345	2955	12,598 (13,235)
21	2135	4-dr Sta Wag-6P	2691	3260	4254 (6442)

NOTE 1: No brackets=Tempest six production; brackets=Tempest V-8 production.

TEMPEST LEMANS - (6-CYL) - SERIES 22 - LeMans series Tempests had distinct styling touches such as LeMans nameplates on the rear fendersides, ribbed decor plates for the deck lid latch panel, model badges on the deck lid, simulated slanting louvers ahead of rear wheel cutouts and LeMans script plates for the dashboard. Bucket seats were standard on all models. The famous Grand Turismo Omologato (GTO) option package was released for LeMans models this year. The idea behind this package was to circumvent a corporate high-performance ban by providing the 389 cid V-8 as an option in the most luxurious Pontiac intermediate. GTOs featured special appearance items in place of some regular LeMans styling touches.

1964 Pontiac Tempest LeMans two-door coupe. OCW

1964 Pontiac Tempest LeMans two-door hardtop. OCW

TEMPEST LEMANS

Model Number	Body/Style Number	Body Type & Seating	Factory Price	Shipping Weight	Prod. Total
22	2227	2-dr Cpe-5P	2491	2975	11,136 (20,181)
22	2237	2-dr HT-5P	2556	2995	7409 (23,901)
22	2267	2-dr Conv-5P	2796	3125	5786 (11,773)

NOTE 1: No brackets=Tempest six production; brackets=Tempest V-8 production.

TEMPEST LEMANS (WITH GTO OPTION)

Model Number	Body/Style Number	Body Type & Seating	Factory Price	Shipping Weight	Prod. Total
22	2227	2-dr Cpe-5P	2852	3106	7384
22	2237	2-dr HT-5P	2963	3126	18,422
22	2267	2-dr Conv-5P	3081	3360	6644

1964 Pontiac Tempest LeMans two-door coupe (with GTO option), V-8.

BASE ENGINES

(CATALINA) V-8. Overhead valves. Cast iron block. Displacement: 389 cu. in. Bore & Stroke: 4 x 3.75 in. Compression Ratio: (synchromesh) 8.6:1; (Hydra-Matic) 10.5:1. Brake hp: (synchromesh) 235 @ 4000 rpm; (Hydra-Matic) 267 @ 4200 rpm. Five main bearings. Hydraulic valve lifters. Carburetor: Rochester two-barrel model 7023066.

(STAR CHIEF) V-8. Overhead valves. Cast iron block. Displacement: 389 cu. in. Bore & Stroke: 4 x 3.75 in. Compression Ratio: (synchromesh) 8.6:1; (Hydra-Matic) 10.5:1. Brake hp: (synchromesh) 235 @ 4000 rpm; (Hydra-Matic) 283 @ 4400 rpm. Five main bearings. Hydraulic valve lifters. Carburetor: Rochester two-barrel model 7023066.

(BONNEVILLE) V-8. Overhead valves. Cast iron block. Displacement: 389 cu. in. Bore & Stroke: 4.06 x 3.75 in. Compression Ratio: (synchromesh) 8.6:1; (Hydra-Matic) 10.25:1. Brake hp: (synchromesh) 255 @ 4000 rpm; (Hydra-Matic) 306 @ 4600 rpm. Five main bearings. Hydraulic valve lifters. Carburetor: Carter AFB model 3647S four-barrel.

(GRAND PRIX) Base V-8s for Grand Prix were the same used on Bonnevilles. Horsepower ratings were slightly lower in the case of the Hydra-Matic attachments (303 hp), since a type HM 61-10 ("Slim Jim") transmission was used.

(TEMPEST) Six-cylinder. Inline. Overhead valves. Cast iron block. Displacement: 215 cu. in. Bore & Stroke: 3.75 x 3.25 in. Compression Ratio: 8.6:1. Brake hp: 140 @ 4200 rpm. Seven main bearings. Hydraulic valve lifters. Carburetor: Rochester one-barrel.

1964 Pontiac Tempest LeMans two-door convertible (with GTO option), V-8.

OPTIONAL V-8 ENGINES

[TEMPEST]

326 cid. Basically the same as 1963, except two-barrel engine was now 250 hp @ 4600 rpm and a four-barrel 326 was added. It had 280 hp @ 4800 rpm. (both engines optional in Tempest and LeMans).

389 cid. Compression ratio: 10.75:1. Carburetion: four-barrel. Brake hp: 325 @ 4800 rpm. (standard on GTO only).

389 cid. Compression ratio: 10.75:1. Carburetion: three two-barrels. hp: 348 @ 4900 rpm. (optional on GTO only).

1964 Pontiac Catalina four-door hardtop. JAG

1964 Pontiac Bonneville two-door hardtop. OCW

1964 Pontiac Tempest LeMans convertible. JAG

[PONTIAC]

389 cid. Compression ratio: 8.6:1. Carburetion: two-barrel. Brake hp: 230 @ 4000 rpm. (optional all models with automatic).

389 cid. Compression ratio: 8.6:1. Carburetion: two-barrel. Brake hp: 235 @ 4000 rpm. (standard on Catalina and Star Chief with synchromesh).

389 cid. Compression ratio: 8.6:1. Carburetion: four-barrel. Brake hp: 255 @ 4000 rpm. (standard on Bonneville with synchromesh, optional on all other models).

389 cid. Compression ratio: 10.5:1. Carburetion: four-barrel. Brake hp: 306 @ 4800 rpm. (optional on all B-body models).

389 cid. Compression ratio: 10.5:1. Carburetion: two-barrel. Brake hp: 267 @ 4200 rpm. (standard on Catalina with synchromesh).

389 cid. Compression ratio: 10.5:1. Carburetion: four-barrel. Brake hp: 303 @ 4600 rpm. (standard on Bonneville and Grand Prix with automatic).

389 cid. Compression ratio: 10.75:1. Carburetion: three two-barrels. Brake hp: 330 @ 4600 rpm. (optional on all B-body models).

421 cid. Compression ratio: 10.5:1. Carburetion: four-barrel. Brake hp: 320 @ 4400 rpm. (optional in all B-body models).

421 cid. Compression ratio: 10.75:1. Carburetion: three two-barrels. Brake hp: 370 @ 5200 rpm. (optional in all B-body models).

421 cid. Compression ratio: 10.75:1. Carburetion: three two-barrels. Brake hp: 350 @ 4600 rpm. (optional all B-body models).

1964 Pontiac Bonneville Safari four-door six-passenger station wagon. OCW

1964 Superior-Pontiac airport limousine. JAG

CHASSIS FEATURES: Wheelbase: (All Pontiac Safaris) 119 in.; (Series 23 and 29 passenger cars) 120 in.; (Series 26 and 28 passenger cars) 123 in.; (All Tempests) 115 in. Overall Length: (All Pontiac Safaris) 213.8 in.; (Series 23 and 29 passenger cars) 213 in.; (Series 26 and 28 passenger cars) 220 in.; (All Tempests) 203 in. Front track: (Pontiac) 62.5 in. (Tempest) 58 in. Rear track: (Pontiac) 64 in.; (Tempest) 58 in. Standard tires: (Pontiac) 8.00 x 14; (Tempest) 6.50 x 14.

OPTIONS

[PONTIAC] Air-conditioning ($430). Console including tachometer ($161). Instrument gage cluster ($21-$59). Luggage carrier ($94). Remote control mirror ($12). Power brakes ($57). Power seat ($96). Power tilt left-hand bucket seat ($71). Tachometer ($54). Cordova top ($86). Ventura trim on body styles 2339, 2347 and 2369 ($118). Sports wheelcovers ($30-$46). Aluminum hubs and drums ($122-$138). Three-speed manual transmission was standard. Hydra-Matic

was optional. A four-speed manual transmission with floor shift was optional. The four-barrel V-8 was optional in Catalinas and Star Chiefs. The economy version of the 389 cid V-8 was a no cost option giving 230 hp @ 4000 rpm with Hydra-Matic only. Tri-Power on the 389 V-8 was available with 10.75:1 compression heads in two forms. The first gave 330 hp @ 4600 rpm; the second gave 348 hp @ 4900 rpm. Tri-Power 421 cid V-8s, also with 10.75:1 heads, came in two variations. The first gave 350 hp @ 4600 rpm; the second gave 370 hp @ 3800 rpm.

[TEMPEST] Air-conditioner ($319). LeMans console shift ($48). Padded dash ($16). Power Convertible top ($54). Power tilt left bucket seat ($67). Power steering ($75). Power tailgate window ($54). Push-button radio ($62). Bucket seats ($134). Custom steering wheel ($6-$9). Deluxe steering wheel with ring ($4). Tachometer ($54). Cordova top ($75). Two-speed wipers and washer ($17). Three-speed manual transmission was standard. Automatic transmission was optional. A four-speed manual transmission was optional. A 326 cubic V-8 was optional in Tempest, Tempest Custom, and Tempest LeMans lines for cars without the GTO option. With synchromesh and 8.6:1 heads this motor gave 250 hp @ 4600 rpm. With Hydra-Matic and 10.5:1 heads this motor gave 280 hp @ 4800 rpm. The 389 cid V-8 was available exclusively in the GTO. It came with 10.75:1 compression and two different induction setups. The standard version had four-barrel carburetion and gave 325 hp @ 4,800 rpm. Tri-Power was optional on the same block and produced 348 hp @ 4900 rpm. The GTO could also be ordered with a heavy-duty three-speed manual gearbox or a Muncie close-ratio four-speed manual box with Hurst linkage. GTO option package included 389 cid high-performance V-8; special GTO nameplates for the grille, fenders, deck lid, and glovebox door; simulated engine-turned aluminum dash panel inserts; and dual simulated air scoops on the hood. Many special GTO accessories were available.

HISTORICAL FOOTNOTES: Production started September 3, 1963. Pontiac introductions were held October 3, 1963. Model year output of 715,261 cars was good for a 9.1 percent share of market. Calendar year output of 693,634 vehicles maintained Pontiac Motor Division's third rank in the industry. The Catalina 2+2 and GTO options were introduced for performance buyers this season. Victor Borge and the Smothers Brothers were among famous people who helped promote Pontiac sales. Pete Estes remained general manager of the division. At least three high-performance Pontiacs were road tested by contemporary magazines. The 325 hp GTO convertible went 0-to-60 mph in 7.7 seconds and did the quarter-mile in 15.8 seconds at 93 mph. Its top speed was 115 mph. The 348 hp GTO hardtop went 0-to-60 mph in 6.6 seconds and did the quarter-mile in 14.8 seconds. The 1964 Catalina 2+2 with the 370 hp Tri-Power "421" did 0-to-60 mph in 7.2 seconds and covered the quarter-mile in 16.1 seconds. The term Sport Coupe was now commonly used to identify the pillarless two-door hardtop body. The term Vista was phased out and Safari nomenclature was still used to identify station wagons.

1965 PONTIAC

1965 Pontiac Catalina 2 + 2 two-door hardtop, V-8.

CATALINA - (V-8) - SERIES 252 - Styling changes for full-size 1965 Pontiacs included larger bodies; twin air-slot grilles; vertically stacked barrel-shaped headlamps visored by cut-back front fenders; V-shaped hoods with a prominent center bulge; curved side glass; and symmetrical Venturi contours with fin-shaped creases along the lower bodysides. Catalinas had thin moldings along the lower body crease, V-shaped front fender badges and Catalina rear fender scripts. Coupes and convertibles with the optional 2 + 2 Sports package were trimmed with "421" engine badges on front fenders, 2 + 2 numbering on rear fenders and deck lid, and simulated louvers behind the front wheel cut-outs. Catalinas with the Ventura package also had special trims. Standard equipment for all Catalinas included turn signals; oil filter; cigarette lighter; front foam seat cushions; sun visors; heater and defroster; electric windshield wipers; front seat belt; and five tubeless blackwall tires. Safaris came standard with oversized 8.55 x 14 tires. The nine-passenger Safari had a power tailgate window.

PONTIAC I.D. NUMBERS: VIN on left front door post. First symbol indicates GM division: 2=Pontiac. Second and third symbols indicate series: 33=Tempest; 35=Tempest Custom; 37=LeMans; 52=Catalina; 56=Star Chief; 62=Bonneville; 66=Grand Prix. Fourth and fifth symbols indicate body style and appear as last two symbols in body/style number column of charts below. Sixth symbol indicates model year: 5=1965. Seventh symbol tells assembly plant: P=Pontiac, Mich.; C=South Gate, Calif.; E=Linden, N.J.; X=Kansas City, Kan.; D=Doraville, Ga.; R=Arlington, Texas; Z=Fremont, Calif.; B=Baltimore, Md.; K=Kansas City, Mo.; U=Lordstown, Ohio. Following symbols are sequential production numbers starting with 100001 at each assembly plant. Body/style number plate under hood tells manufacturer, Fisher style number, assembly plant, trim code, paint code, accessory codes. Style number consists of 65 (for 1965) prefix and four symbols that appear in second column of charts below. First two symbols indicate series; second two symbols indicate body type. VIN appears on front of engine at right-hand cylinder bank along with an alpha-numerical engine production codes included:[215 cid/125 hp six] ZD/ZE. [215 cid/140 hp six ZK/ZL/ZM/ZN/ZR/ZS. [326 cid/250 hp V-8] WP/YN60. [326 cid/285 hp V-8] WR/YP. [389 cid/256 hp V-8] WA/WB/YA/YB. [389 cid/260 hp V-8] XA/XB. [389 cid/276 hp V-8] WDB/O4B. [389 cid/290 hp] WC/YC/YD. [389 cid/293 hp V-8] XC. [389 cid/325 hp V-8] YE/YF. [389 cid/333 hp V-8] WE. [389 cid/338 hp Tri-Power V-8] WF/YG. [421 cid/338 hp V-8] WG/YH. [421 cid/356 hp Tri-Power V-8] YJ/WH. [421 cid/376 hp Tri-Power V-8] WJ/YK. [389 cid/335 hp four-barrel GTO V-8] WT with synchromesh; YS with Hydra-Matic. [389 cid/360 hp GTO Tri-Power V-8] WS with synchromesh; YR with Hydra-Matic.

1965 Pontiac Catalina four-door sedan. OCW

CATALINA (SERIES 252)

Model Number	Body/Style Number	Body Type & Seating	Factory Price	Shipping Weight	Prod. Total
252	25269	4-dr Sed-6P	2748	3772	78,853
252	25239	4-dr HT-6P	2885	3843	34,814
252	25211	2-dr Sed-6P	2678	3702	9526
252	25237	2-dr HT-6P	2809	3748	92,009
252	25267	2-dr Conv-6P	3103	3795	18,347
252	25245	4-dr Sta Wag-9P	3241	4244	15,110
252	25235	4-dr Sta Wag-6P	3136	4211	22,399

NOTE 1: 271,058 Catalinas were built.

NOTE 2: 14,817 had synchromesh and 256,241 had Hydra-Matic.

NOTE 3: Figures include 11,521 cars with W51 Catalina 2 + 2 option.

NOTE 4: 5316 Catalina 2 + 2 had synchromesh and 6205 had Hydra-Matic.

NOTE 5: No body style breakouts are available for the 2 + 2 option.

NOTE 6: No record of the number of Ventura options sold.

1965 Pontiac Star Chief four-door sedan. OCW

STAR CHIEF - (V-8) - SERIES 256 - External decorations on Star Chief included stylized stars on the rear roof pillar, Star Chief script on the rear fender and wider chrome moldings along the fin-shaped body crease. All features found in Catalinas were standard equipment and extras included Deluxe wheel discs and steering wheels, electric clock, dual-speed wipers and special upholstery.

STAR CHIEF (SERIES 256)

Model Number	Body/Style Number	Body Type & Seating	Factory Price	Shipping Weight	Prod. Total
256	25669	4-dr Sed-6P	3042	3858	22,183
256	25639	4-dr HT-6p	3171	3917	9132

NOTE 1: 31,315 Star Chiefs were built.

NOTE 2: 97 had synchromesh and 31,214 had Hydra-Matic.

1965 Pontiac Bonneville two-door convertible, V-8.

BONNEVILLE - (V-8) - SERIES 262 - Bonneville identification features included Bonneville lettering on the left-hand side of the hood and on the rear fenders, elongated V-shaped badges behind front wheel cut-outs, and wide stainless steel accent panels along the lower body under the fin-shaped crease. Standard equipment was everything found on Star Chief plus padded instrument panel, front and rear arm-rests, padded assist grip, courtesy lamps, and cloth and vinyl uphol-stery combinations. An undetermined number of four-door hardtops had the Brougham option package that included Ponchartrain cloth and Morrokide upholstery, a cordova top and "Brougham by Fisher" roof pillar badges. Bonneville passenger cars wore fender skirts.

1965 Pontiac Bonneville Brougham four-door hardtop. JAG

BONNEVILLE (SERIES 262)

Model Number	Body/Style Number	Body Type & Seating	Factory Price	Shipping Weight	Prod. Total
262	26239	4-dr HT-6P	3362	3993	62,480
262	26237	2-dr HT-6P	3288	3909	44,030
262	26267	2-dr Conv-6P	3520	3935	21,050
262	26235	4-dr Sta Wag-6P	3557	4282	6460

NOTE 1: 134,663 Bonnevilles and Bonneville station wagons were built.

NOTE 2: 1449 had synchromesh and 133,214 had Hydra-Matic.

NOTE 3: 643 Bonnevilles chassis were provided for conversions.

1965 Pontiac Grand Prix two-door hardtop sport coupe, V-8.

GRAND PRIX - (V-8) - SERIES 266 - The Grand Prix hardtop sports coupe was the most distinctive of all 1965 full-sized Pontiacs. For special identification it had an air slot grille with a unique, vertically divided, aluminized insert that incorporated rectangular parking lamps. The fin-shaped crease along the lower body was trimmed with a wide stainless steel molding. The letters 'GP' appeared on the left-hand lip of the hood and Grand Prix lettering was placed on the front fenders behind the wheel opening. A badge for further identification was placed on the sides of the rear fenders. As on Bonneville passenger cars, the Grand Prix wore fender skirts. Standard equipment included all features found on Bonneville, plus monotone Morrokide upholstery. Buyers had a choice of special front bench seats or bucket seats with a console and tachometer. A glovebox lamp was also included.

GRAND PRIX (SERIES 266)

Model Number	Body/Style Number	Body Type & Seating	Factory Price	Shipping Weight	Prod. Total
266	26657	2-dr HT Cpe-5P	3426	4282	57,881

NOTE 1: 57,881 Grand Prix were built.

NOTE 2: 1973 had synchromesh and 55,908 had Hydra-Matic attachments.

TEMPEST - (6-CYL) - SERIES 233 - Design refinements characterized the three Tempest lines for 1965 and included vertically stacked head-lamps, larger wheel openings, crisper side body sculpturing and more deeply recessed grilles. Base models in the 233 Series were identified by the absence of upper beltline moldings and plainer interior trims. Vinyl rubber floor mats were used. Standard equipment included heater and defroster, electric wipers, seat belts, turn signals and five black tubeless tires. Safari station wagons came with 7.35 x 14 over-sized tires as regular equipment.

TEMPEST (SERIES 233)

Model Number	Body/Style Number	Body Type & Seating	Factory Price	Shipping Weight	Prod. Total
233	23369	4-dr Sed-6P	2263	2963	15,705
233	23327	2-dr Cpe-6P	2211	2943	18,198
233	23335	4-dr Sta Wag-6P	2549	3237	5622

NOTE 1: 39,525 Tempests were built.

NOTE 2: 9255 had synchromesh and 30,270 had automatic attach-ments.

TEMPEST CUSTOM - (6-CYL) - SERIES 235 - Tempest Custom mod-els had bright upper beltline moldings to accent the Venturi shaped body styling. Standard extras included carpeting and Deluxe steering wheel. The Custom convertible had courtesy lamps.

TEMPEST CUSTOM (SERIES 235)

Model Number	Body/Style Number	Body Type & Seating	Factory Price	Shipping Weight	Prod. Total
235	23569	4-dr Sed-6P	2496	3021	25,242
235	23527	2-dr Cpe-6P	2295	2965	18,367
235	23537	2-dr HT-6P	2359	2983	21,906
235	23567	2-dr Conv-6P	2584	3064	8346
235	23535	4-dr Sta Wag-6P	2633	3250	10,792

NOTE 1: 84,653 Tempest Customs were built.

NOTE 2: 10,630 had synchromesh and 74,023 had automatic attachments.

1965 Pontiac Tempest LeMans two-door. JAG

1965 Pontiac Tempest LeMans two-door hardtop (with GTO option). OCW

TEMPEST LEMANS - (6-CYL) - SERIES 237 - Special identifying features seen on the Tempest LeMans models included grilled-over tail lamps, LeMans front fender nameplates, LeMans lettering on the sides of rear fenders and simulated louvers behind front wheel cutouts (two-door models only). All features found on Tempest Customs were considered standard equipment, as well as vinyl interior trim, custom foam front seat cushions, front bucket seats on two-door styles and power-operated folding tops on LeMans convertibles. Cars equipped with GTO equipment had standard V-8 power. The GTO was not yet a separate series, although special identification features on GTOs replaced some items regularly seen on LeMans Tempests. This included GTO lettering for the left-hand grille, rear fender sides and deck lid; a single hood scoop and elongated V-shaped badges behind the front wheel openings.

TEMPEST LEMANS (SERIES 237)

Model Number	Body/Style Number	Body Type & Seating	Factory Price	Shipping Weight	Prod. Total
237	23769	4-dr Sed-6P	2496	3021	14,227
237	23727	2-dr Cpe-5P	2437	2996	18,881
237	23737	2-dr HT-5P	2501	3014	60,548
237	23767	2-dr Conv-5P	2736	3107	13,897

1965 Pontiac Tempest LeMans two-door convertible (with GTO option), V-8.

TEMPEST LEMANS (SERIES 237 WITH GTO OPTION)

237	23727	2-dr Cpe-5P	2787	3478	8319
237	23737	2-dr HT-5P	2855	3478	55,722
237	23767	2-dr Conv-5P	3093	3700	11,311

NOTE 1: 182,905 LeMans Tempests were built including cars with the GTO option.

NOTE 2: 75,756 had synchromesh attachments and 107,149 had automatic.

NOTE 3: 75,352 GTOs are included in these totals.

NOTE 4: 56,378 had synchromesh and 18,974 had automatic.

NOTE 5: Four-speed gearboxes were in 18.8 percent of all 1965 Tempests.

1965 Pontiac Catalina convertible. JAG

1965 Pontiac Catalina 2+2 two-door convertible. OCW

BASE ENGINES

(CATALINA) V-8: Overhead valves. Cast iron block. Displacement: 389 cu. in. Bore & Stroke: 4.06 x 3.75 in. Compression Ratio: (synchromesh) 8.6:1; (Hydra-Matic) 10.5:1. Brake hp: (synchromesh) 256 @ 4600 rpm; (Hydra-Matic) 290 @ 4600 rpm. Five main bearings. Hydraulic valve lifters. Carburetor: Rochester two-barrel.

1965 Pontiac Bonneville Safari four-door station wagon. JAG

(BONNEVILLE/GRAND PRIX) V-8: Overhead valves. Cast iron block. Displacement: 389 cu. in. Bore & Stroke: 4.06 x 3.75 in. Compression Ratio: (synchromesh) 8.6:1; (Hydra-Matic) 10.5:1. Brake hp: (synchromesh) 333 @ 5000 rpm; (Hydra-Matic) 325 @ 4800 rpm. Five main bearings. Hydraulic valve lifters. Carburetor: Carter AFB four-barrel.

(TEMPEST/TEMPEST CUSTOM) Inline six. Overhead valves. Cast iron block. Displacement: 215 cu. in. Bore & Stroke: 3.75 x 3.25 in. Compression Ratio: 8.6:1. Brake hp: 140 @ 4200 rpm. Seven main bearings. Hydraulic valve lifters. Carburetor: Rochester one-barrel.

1965 Pontiac Bonneville two-door hardtop. OCW

CHASSIS FEATURES: Wheelbase: (All Pontiac Safaris) 121 in.; (Series 252 and 266 passenger cars) 121 in.; (Series 256 and 262 passenger cars) 124 in.; (All Tempests) 115 in. Overall Length: (All Pontiac Safaris) 217.9 in.; (Series 252 and 266 passenger cars) 214.6 in.; (Series 256 and 262 passenger cars) 221.7 in.; (Tempest Safaris) 204.4 in.; (Tempest passenger cars) 206.2 in. Front tread: (Pontiacs) 62.5 in.; (Tempests) 58 in. Rear tread: (Pontiacs) 64 in. (Tempests) 58 in. Standard tires: (Pontiacs) 8.25 x 14; (Tempest) 6.95 x 14; (GTO) 7.75 x 14.

OPTIONS

[PONTIAC] Bonneville Brougham option for style number 26239 ($161). Front bucket seats or Bonneville style numbers 26237 and 26267 ($116). Console ($108). Remote control deck lid ($11). Electro Cruise and fuel warning ($96). Tinted glass ($43). Tinted windshield ($29). Instrument gauge cluster ($21-38). Safari luggage carrier ($86). Glareproof tilt mirror ($4). Remote control rearview mirror ($12). Power brakes ($43). Power door locks ($46-$70). Six-way power seat ($97). Power windows ($106). Power tilt bucket seats L.H.

($71). AM/FM manual radio ($151). Push-button AM radio ($89). Split-back Safari seat ($38). Front bucket seats for Catalina two-door hardtop and convertible with special trims ($204). Super-Lift shock absorbers ($40). Sports option 2 + 2 package for style number 25237 ($419). Sports option 2 + 2 package for style number 25267 ($397). Tachometer, except on cars with four-speed and console ($54). Cordova top ($97-$108). Safari cordova top ($135). Ventura trim package for style numbers 25237, 25239, and 25269 ($118). Wire wheel discs ($20-$71). Aluminum hubs and drums ($120-$138). A three-speed manual transmission was standard. Turbo-Hydramatic transmission and four-speed manual transmission were $231 extra. A heavy-duty clutch was $9 extra on Catalinas with certain engines. Safe-T-Track differential was $43 extra. Dual exhausts were $31 extra, but standard on Grand Prix. The four-barrel V-8 with heavy-duty clutch was $44 extra for Catalinas and Star Chiefs. A Tri-Power 389 cid V-8 with 10.75:1 compression and 338 hp @ 4800 rpm was $134-$174 extra depending on model and transmission. A four-barrel 421 cid V-8 with 10.5:1 compression and 338 hp @ 4600 rpm was $108-$174 extra depending on model and was standard in cars with the 2 + 2 Sports Option. A Tri-Power 421 cid V-8 with 10.75:1 compression and 356 hp @ 4800 rpm was $241-$307 extra depending upon model. The Tri-Power H.O. V-8 of 421 cid with 10.75:1 compression was $344-$410 extra depending on model. It produced 376 hp @ 5500 rpm. A two-barrel premium fuel version of the 389 cid V-8 was $21 extra in Catalinas and Star Chiefs with three-speed manual transmission. Transistor ignition was $75 extra on air-conditioned cars and $65 extra on others. A transistorized regulator was $11 extra. Various rear axle ratios were available.

1965 Superior-Pontiac Embassy nine-passenger limousine. JAG

[TEMPEST] Air-conditioner ($346). Carpets ($19). Electric clock ($19). Remote control deck lid ($11). GTO option for style numbers 23727, 23737, and 23767 ($296). Handling & ride package ($16). Parking brake signal ($3). Safari luggage carrier ($65). Panel cluster and tachometer rally gauge ($86). AM/FM push-button radio ($137). Safeguard speedometer ($16). Super-Life shock absorbers ($40). Custom sports steering wheel ($39-$43). Tilt steering with power assist only ($43). Power steering ($97). Power brakes ($43). Cordova tops ($72-$86). Wire wheel discs ($54-$71). Custom wheel discs ($20-$37). Rally wheels ($36-53). Two-speed wipers and washers ($17) and much more. A three-speed manual transmission was standard. A four-speed manual transmission was $188 extra. Two different two-speed automatic gearboxes were available. With six-cylinder power the first automatic was $188 extra; with V-8s the second was $199 extra. Transistor ignition was priced the same as on full-sized cars. Dual exhausts were standard with the GTO option and $31 extra on other cars. Safe-T-Grip differential was $38 extra. A two-barrel 326 cid V-8 with 9.2 compression and 250 hp @ 4600 rpm was $108 extra on all Tempests. With four-barrel induction and 10.5:1 compression heads, this engine produced 285 hp @ 5500 rpm and was $173 extra on all Tempests. A four-barrel 389 cid V-8 with 335 hp @ 5000 rpm was standard with the GTO option. A Tri-Power 389 cid V-8 with 10.75:1 compression and 360 hp @ 5200 rpm was $116 extra in GTOs only. A variety of rear axle ratios were available.

1965 Superior-Pontiac ambulance. JAG

HISTORICAL FOOTNOTES: Production started August 24, 1964.

Introductions were done on September 24, 1964. The one-millionth Tempest was built late in the year. Calendar year output was 860,652. Model year output was 802,000. On April 13, 1965, the 10 millionth Pontiac was made. It was a gold Catalina. The 335 hp GTO convertible went 0-to-60 mph in 7.2 seconds and did the quarter-mile in 16.1 seconds. The 1965 Catalina 2 + 2 hardtop with the 338 hp "421" did 0-to-60 mph in 7.4 seconds and the quarter-mile in 15.8 seconds. The 1965 Catalina 2+2 hardtop with the 376 hp "421" was even faster. It could do 0-to-60 mph in 7.2 seconds and the quarter-miles took 15.5. Pontiac fans could get a GTO record and poster for 25-cents, which is a collector's item today. Pete Estes moved to Chevrolet and John Z. DeLorean became the general manager of Pontiac Motor Division. The term Safari was used to denote station wagons. In the Tempest series a Sport Coupe was a pillared two-door sedan.

1966 PONTIAC

1966 Pontiac Catalina Vista Sedan four-door hardtop, V-8.

CATALINA - (V-8) - SERIES 252 - Styling changes for full-sized 1966 Pontiacs were subtle ones. New plastic grilles were adopted and head-lamp extension caps gave a more integrated frontal appearance. Catalinas now had thin full-length horizontal belt moldings, instead of body crease trim. An identifying script was placed on the front fenders behind the wheel openings. A rear fender badge was also seen. Standard equipment was the same as the previous year. Cars with the Ventura option had special upholstery and fender lettering.

PONTIAC I.D. NUMBERS: VIN on left front door post. First symbol indicates GM division: 2=Pontiac. Second and third symbols indicate series: 33=Tempest; 35=Tempest Custom; 37=LeMans; 52=Catalina; 56=Star Chief; 62=Bonneville; 66=Grand Prix. Fourth and fifth symbols indicate body style and appear as last two symbols in Body/style number column of charts below. Sixth symbol indicates model year: 6=1966. Seventh symbol tells assembly plant: P=Pontiac, Mich.; C=South Gate, Calif.; E=Linden, N.J.; X=Kansas City, Kan.; D=Doraville, Ga.; R=Arlington, Texas; Z=Fremont, Calif.; B=Baltimore, Md.; K=Kansas City, Mo.; U=Lordstown, Ohio. Following symbols are sequential production number starting with 100001 at each assembly plant. Body/style number plate under hood tells manufacturer, Fisher style number, assembly plant, trim code, paint code, accessory codes. Style number consists of 66 (for 1966) prefix and four symbols that appear in second column of charts below. First two symbols indicate series; second two symbols indicate body type. VIN appears on front of engine at right-hand cylinder bank along with an alpha-numerical engine production code. Engine production codes included:[230 cid/155 hp ohc six] ZF/ZG; [230 cid/165 hp ohc six] ZK/ZS/ZN/ZM. [230 cid/207 hp ohc six] ZD/ZE. [326 cid/250 hp V-8] WP/WX/YN/XF. [326 cid/285 hp V-8] WR/YP/XG. [389 cid/256 hp V-8] WA/WB/YA. [389 cid/260 hp V-8] XA/XB. [389 cid/290 hp V-8] WC/YC/YD/YU/YV. [389 cid/293 hp V-8] XC. [389 cid/325 hp V-8] YE/YF/YL/YW/YX. [389 cid/333 hp V-8] WE. [421 cid/338 hp V-8] WK/YZ/YT/WG/YH. [421 cid/356 hp Tri-Power V-8] YJ/YM/WH. [421 cid/376 hp Tri-Power V-8] WJ/YK. [389 cid/335 hp four-barrel GTO V-8] WT/WW with synchromesh; YS/XE with Hydra-Matic. [389 cid/360 hp GTO Tri-Power V-8] WS/WV with synchromesh; XS/YR with Hydra-Matic.

CATALINA (SERIES 252)

Model Number	Body/Style Number	Body Type & Seating	Factory Price	Shipping Weight	Prod. Total
252	25269	4-dr Sed-6P	2831	3785	80,483
252	25239	4-dr HT-6P	2968	3910	38,005
252	25211	2-dr Sed-6P	2762	3715	7925
252	25237	2-dr HT-6P	2893	3835	79,013
252	25267	2-dr Conv-6P	3219	3860	14,837
252	25245	4-dr Sta Wag-9P	3338	4315	12,965
252	25235	4-dr Sta Wag-6P	3217	4250	21,082

NOTE 1: 247,927 Catalinas were built.

NOTE 2: 5003 Catalinas had synchromesh and 242,924 had Hydra-Matic.

CATALINA 2+2 - (V-8) - SERIES 254 - The Catalina 2+2 models were in a separate series for 1966. They could be easily identified by appearance items such as a twin lens taillamp treatment, 2+2 badges on the deck lid and rear fenders, vertical air slots behind the doors and "Pontiac 421" front fender emblems. Standard equipment included a four-barrel 421 cid V-8 with 338 hp, low-restriction exhausts, chromed air cleaner and valve covers and three-speed Hurst linkage transmission. Heavy-duty suspension, carpeting, bucket seats, Sports Custom steering wheel and non-glare inside rearview mirror were standard. Available axle ratios included 3.08, 3.23, and 3.42.

1966 Pontiac Catalina 2+2 two-door hardtop. OCW

CATALINA 2+2 (SERIES 254)

Model Number	Body/Style Number	Body Type & Seating	Factory Price	Shipping Weight	Prod. Total
254	25437	2-dr HT-5P	3298	4005	N/A
254	25467	2-dr Conv-5P	3602	4030	N/A

NOTE 1: 6383 Catalina 2+2s were built.

NOTE 2: 2208 Catalina 2+2s had synchromesh and 4175 had Hydra-Matic.

NOTE 3: Body style breakouts were not recorded for this series.

STAR CHIEF EXECUTIVE - (V-8) - SERIES 256 - For identification, models in the 256 Series had "Executive" lettering behind front wheel openings. They wore thin horizontal body rub moldings, stylized rear fender stars and Jeweltone monochromatic Morrokide upholstery. Star Chief Executives incorporated all Catalina equipment, plus deluxe wheel discs and steering wheel, electric clock and dual-speed wipers.

1966 Pontiac Star Chief Executive four-door sedan. OCW

STAR CHIEF EXECUTIVE (SERIES 256)

Model Number	Body/Style Number	Body Type & Seating	Factory Price	Shipping Weight	Prod. Total
256	25669	4-dr Sed-6P	3114	3920	24,489
256	25639	4-dr HT-6P	3244	3980	10,583
256	25637	2-dr HT-6P	3170	3920	10,140

NOTE 1: 45,212 Star Chief Executives were built.

NOTE 2: 134 Star Chief Executives had synchromesh and 45,078 had Hydra-Matic.

BONNEVILLE - (V-8) - SERIES 262 - Bonnevilles could easily be distinguished by their broad accent panels below the lower body crease, Bonneville block lettering on the left-hand grille and behind the front wheel openings and by their standard fender skirts. Regular equipment on closed cars included cloth upholstery, padded dashboards and front rear armrests. The convertible had deeply piped Morrokide covered seats. The Brougham option package added tufted Plaza pattern cloth upholstery and model identification badges for the rear roof pillars, but cordova tops were optional, even on Broughams.

1966 Pontiac Bonneville two-door convertible, V-8.

BONNEVILLE (SERIES 262)

Model Number	Body/Style Number	Body Type & Seating	Factory Price	Shipping Weight	Prod. Total
262	26239	4-dr HT-6P	3428	4070	68,646
262	26237	2-dr HT-6P	3354	4020	42,004
262	26267	2-dr Conv-6P	3586	4015	16,229
262	26245	4-dr Sta Wag-9P	3747	4390	8452

NOTE 1: 135,954 Bonnevilles were built.

NOTE 2: 729 Bonnevilles had synchromesh and 35,840 had Hydra-Matic.

NOTE 3: 553 Bonneville chassis were provided for conversions.

1966 Pontiac Grand Prix two-door hardtop coupe, V-8.

GRAND PRIX (V-8) - SERIES 266 - Grand Prix were distinguished by wire mesh grilles enclosing rectangular parking lamps GP identification on front fenders and elongated V-shaped emblems on the ribbed lower beauty panels. A monochromatic interior of deeply piped Morrokide was featured. Standard equipment was the same as in 1965, except Strato Bucket seats were new. Fender skirts were seen again.

GRAND PRIX (SERIES 266)

Model Number	Body/Style Number	Body Type & Seating	Factory Price	Shipping Weight	Prod. Total
266	26657	2-dr HT-5P	3492	4015	36,757

NOTE 1: 36,757 Grand Prix were built.

NOTE 2: 917 Grand Prix had synchromesh and 35,840 had Hydra-Matic.

STANDARD TEMPEST - (6-CYL) - SERIES 233 - Tempests were completely restyled with smoother bodies, rounder contours, wider wheel openings, recessed split grilles and stacked headlamps. Each of four series now had completely distinctive ornamentation. An undetermined number of cars in each series were built with a sporty-looking Sprint option package. The really big news was under the hood, where a unique overhead camshaft six-cylinder engine was now employed as the base power plant for all models, except GTOs. Standard Tempest trim appointments included, windsplit moldings behind front wheel openings, Tempest rear fender scripts and nylon-faced fabric upholstery with Jeweltone Morrokide accents.

STANDARD TEMPEST (SERIES 233)

Model Number	Body/Style Number	Body Type & Seating	Factory Price	Shipping Weight	Prod. Total
233	23369	4-dr Sed-6P	2331	3075	17,392
233	233307	2-dr Cpe-6P	2278	3040	22,266
233	23335	4-dr Sta Wag-6P	2624	3340	4095

NOTE 1: 43,753 standard Tempests were built.

NOTE 2: 10,610 had standard Tempests synchromesh and 33,143 had automatic.

TEMPEST CUSTOM - (6-CYL) - SERIES 235 - Tempest Custom trimmings included thin moldings accenting the smooth new "Coke bottle" shape and Tempest Custom script/badge identification on the rear fenders. Deluxe steering wheels and carpets were extra standard features. Convertibles sported courtesy lamps and Morrokide trims.

1966 Pontiac Tempest Custom two-door Sprint Coupe, OHC six-cylinder.

TEMPEST CUSTOM (SERIES 235)

Model Number	Body/Style Number	Body Type & Seating	Factory Price	Shipping Weight	Prod. Total
235	23569	4-dr Sed-6P	2415	3100	23,988
235	23539	4-dr HT-6P	2547	3195	10,996
235	23507	2-dr Cpe-6P	2362	3060	17,182
235	23517	2-dr HT-6P	2426	3075	31,322
235	23567	2-dr Conv-6P	2655	3170	5557
235	23535	4-dr Sta Wag-6p	2709	3355	7614

NOTE 1: 96,659 Tempest Customs were built.

NOTE 2: 13,566 Tempest Customs had synchromesh and 83,093 had automatic.

1966 Pontiac Tempest Custom four-door hardtop. OCW

TEMPEST LEMANS - (6-CYL) - SERIES 237 - LeMans models had special trim features that set them apart. They included simulated louvers on the forward edge of front fenders, elongated V-shaped emblems behind front wheel openings and LeMans lettering on the rear fender sides. A new "shadow box" roofline was seen on the two-door hardtop coupe. Standard equipment included Morrokide-and-cloth trim combinations in four-door hardtops and all-Morrokide in others. Convertibles, hardtops, and Sport Coupes (two-door sedans) came with the choice of bucket or notch back front seats with folding armrest. All LeMans had carpeting; front foam seat cushions; lamps for ashtray; cigarette lighter and glovebox; and a power top on convertibles.

TEMPEST LEMANS (SERIES 237)

Model Number	Body/Style Number	Body Type & Seating	Factory Price	Shipping Weight	Prod. Total
237	23739	4-dr HT-6P	2701	3195	13,897
237	23707	2-dr Cpe-6p	2505	3090	16,654
237	23717	2-dr HT-6P	2568	3125	78,109
237	23767	2-dr Conv-6P	2806	3220	13,080

NOTE 1: 121,740 LeMans were built.

NOTE 2: 22,862 LeMans had synchromesh and 98,878 had automatic attachments.

1966 Pontiac Tempest GTO two-door hardtop. OCW

TEMPEST GTO - (V-8) - SERIES 242 - GTO line was now a separate series with distinctive trim on the new Tempest sheet metal. A wire mesh grille insert without horizontal divider bars was used. The grille incorporated rectangular parking lamps and a GTO nameplate on the left-hand side. A single scoop appeared on the hood, elongated V-shaped badges were mounted behind the front wheel openings, GTO lettering appeared on the deck lid and rear fenders, the upper beltline contour was pin striped and horizontal twin-slot tail lamps were used. Standard equipment included all LeMans items, plus a special 389 cid four-barrel V-8; walnut grain dash panel inserts; dual exhausts; heavy-duty shock absorbers, springs and stabilizer bar; and 7.75 x 14 redline or whitewall tires.

TEMPEST GTO (SERIES 242)

Model Number	Body/Style Number	Body Type & Seating	Factory Price	Shipping Weight	Prod. Total
242	24207	2-dr Cpe-5	2783	3445	10,363
242	24217	2-dr HT-5P	2847	3465	73,785
242	24267	2-dr Conv-5P	3082	3555	12,798

BASE ENGINES

(CATALINA/STAR CHIEF EXECUTIVE) V-8: Overhead valves. Cast iron block. Displacement: 389 cu. in. Bore & Stroke: 4.06 x 3.75 in. Compression Ratio: (synchromesh) 8.6:1; (Hydra-Matic) 10.5:1. Brake hp: (synchromesh) 256 @ 4600 rpm; (Hydra-Matic) 290 @ 4600 rpm. Five main bearings. Hydraulic valve lifters. Carburetor: Rochester two-barrel model 7026066. **(CATALINA 2 + 2)** V-8. Overhead valves. Cast iron block. Displacement: 421 cu. in. Bore & Stroke: 4.094 x 4.00 in. Compression Ratio: 10.5:1. Brake hp: 338 @ 4600 rpm. Five main bearings. Hydraulic valve lifters. Carburetor: Carter AFB model 4033S.

(BONNEVILLE) V-8: Overhead valves. Cast iron block. Displacement: 389 cu. in. Bore & Stroke: 4.06 x 3.75 in. Compression Ratio: (synchromesh) 8.6:1; (Hydra-Matic) 10.5:1. Brake hp: (synchromesh) 333 @ 5000 rpm; (Hydra-Matic) 325 @ 4800 rpm. Five main bearings. Hydraulic valve lifters. Carburetor: Carter AFB four-barrel model 4033S.

(GRAND PRIX) V-8: Overhead valves. Cast iron block. Displacement: 389 cu. in. Bore & Stroke: 4.06 x 3.75 in. Compression Ratio: (synchromesh) 8.6:1; (Hydra-Matic) 10.5:1. Brake hp: (synchromesh) 333 @ 4600 rpm; (Hydra-Matic) 325 @ 4800 rpm. Five main bearings. Hydraulic valve lifters. Carburetor: Carter AFB four-barrel model 4033S.

(TEMPEST/TEMPEST CUSTOM) OHC-Six: Overhead valves. Cast iron block. Displacement: 230 cu. in. Bore & Stroke: 3.87 x 3.25 in. Compression Ratio: 9.0:1. Brake hp: 165 @ 4700 rpm. Seven main bearings. Hydraulic lifters. Carburetor: Rochester one-barrel.

(GTO) V-8: Overhead valves. Cast iron block. Displacement: 389 cu. in. Bore & Stroke: 4.06 x 3.75 in. Compression Ratio: 10.75:1. Brake hp: 335 @ 5000 rpm. Five main bearings. Hydraulic valve lifters. Carburetor: Carter AFB four-barrel model 4033S.

CHASSIS FEATURES: Wheelbase: (Pontiac Safaris) 121 in.; (series 252 and 266, passenger cars) 121 in.; (series 256 and 262 passenger cars) 124 in.; (Tempests) 115 in. Overall Length: (Pontiac Safaris) 218.1 in.; (series 252 and 266 passenger cars) 214.8 in.; (series 256 and 262 passenger cars) 221.8 in.; (2 + 2) 214.8 in.; (Tempest Safari) 203.6 in.; (Tempest and GTO passenger cars) 206.4 in. Front tread: (Pontiacs) 63 in.; (Tempests) 58 in. Rear tread: (Pontiacs) 64 in.; (Tempests) 58 in. Standard tires: (Pontiac) 8.25 x 14; (Tempest convertible and hardtop) 7.35 x 14; (other Tempests) 6.95 x 14. Oversized tires for all Safaris are noted above.

OPTIONS

[PONTIAC] Options were about the same availability and price as 1965, with following variations noted: Whitewall tires ($29). Bucket seats ($105). Tilt steering wheel ($43); Power steering ($97). Air-conditioning ($30). Power brakes ($43). Super Hydra-Matic transmission ($230). Heavy-duty suspension ($16). Manual AM radio ($89).

1966 Pontiac Tempest two-door coupe. JAG

1966 Pontiac Tempest LeMans two-door coupe. OCW

1966 Pontiac Tempest Custom two-door hardtop. JAG

1966 Pontiac Tempest GTO convertible. OCW

1966 Pontiac Tempest Custom convertible. JAG

1966 Superior-Pontiac Embassy limousine. JAG

1966 Pontiac Tempest LeMans four-door hardtop. JAG

1966 Superior-Pontiac combination car. JAG

1966 Pontiac Tempest LeMans convertible. OCW

1966 Superior-Pontiac funeral car. JAG

[TEMPEST] Power steering ($95). Air-conditioning ($343). Sprint option package ($127). Standard whitewalls ($41). Ride and Handling package ($16). Rally wheel rims ($40). Custom steering wheel ($29). Safe-T-Track ($37). The 338 hp version of the 389 cid V-8 with 10.75:1 compression and Tri-Power was dropped. Tempest and GTO V-8 options were the same as in 1965. The new overhead camshaft six-cylinder Tempest engine was the only significantly changed power train option. This engine came in two forms. Specifications for the base 165 hp version are given above under standard Tempest engines. An optional choice was the "Sprint" version with 10.5:1 compression, four-barrel Rochester carburetor and 207 hp @ 5200 rpm.

HISTORICAL FOOTNOTES: Production began September 13, 1965, and model introductions took place October 7, 1965. Model year output was 831,331 units. Calendar year production was 866,385 units. The big news of the year was introduction of the overhead cam six. Also, Pontiac earned an over 10 percent share of market for the first time ever. In magazine road tests, the 335 hp GTO coupe was found to go 0-to-60 mph in 6.8 seconds and down the quarter-mile in 15.4 seconds. The 360 hp GTO convertible had the same 0-to-60 mph time and did the quarter-mile in 15.5 seconds at 93 mph. The 207 hp Tempest Sprint could go 0-to-60 mph in 8.2 seconds and do the quarter-mile in 16.7 seconds at 82 mph. The term Safari and station wagon were synonymous. Style number 26657 had distinct roofline styling. The Brougham option was available for Bonneville four-door hardtops. The term Vista was sometimes used to describe full-sized four-door hardtops. The Ventura option was available for Catalina hardtops, convertibles, and Vistas. The term Sport Coupe was used to describe two-door Tempest pillared sedans, not hardtops. In this edition, we have changed the description of these models to "Cpe" to avoid confusion. Two-door Tempests with the Sprint option had horizontal racing stripes between the wheel openings.

1967 PONTIAC

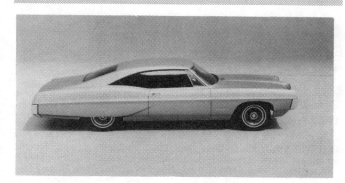

1967 Pontiac Catalina two-door hardtop (with Ventura option), V-8.

CATALINA - (V-8) - SERIES 252 - Integral bumper-grilles, "wasp waist" body styling, angular wedge-shaped front fender tips and recessed windshield wipers characterized full-sized Pontiacs for 1967. A crisp horizontal beltline crease and flare sculpturing between the doors and rear wheel openings were other new design traits. All standard GM safety features were found in Catalinas, plus woodgrain trimmed dashboards and nylon blend carpeting. Small hubcaps were regular equipment and there were Pontiac letters on the left-hand grille and the word Catalina on the sides of fenders. Taillamps were mainly horizontal with a single long lens that curved downwards at each side. Cars with Ventura or 2+2 options were trimmed differently.

PONTIAC I.D. NUMBERS: VIN on left front door post. First symbol indicates GM division: 2=Pontiac. Second and third symbols indicate series: 23=Firebird; 33=Tempest; 35=Tempest Custom; 37=LeMans; 39=Tempest Safari; 42=GTO; 52=Catalina; 56=Star Chief; 62=Bonneville; 66=Grand Prix. Fourth and fifth symbols indicate body style and appear as last two symbols in body/style number column of charts below. Sixth symbol indicates model year: 7=1967. Seventh symbol tells assembly plant: P=Pontiac, Mich.; C=South Gate, Calif.; E=Linden, N.J.; X=Kansas City, Kan.; R=Arlington, Texas; Z=Fremont, Calif.; B=Baltimore, Md.; K=Kansas City, Mo.; U=Framingham, Mass.; V=Lordstown, Ohio. Following symbols are sequential production number starting with 100001 at each assembly plant. Body/style number plate under hood tells manufacturer, Fisher style number, assembly plant, trim code, paint code, accessory codes. Style number consists of 67 (for 1967) prefix and four symbols that appear in second column of charts below. First two symbols indicate series; second two symbols indicate body type. VIN appears on front of engine at right-hand cylinder bank along with an alpha-numerical

engine production code. Engine production codes included: [230 cid/155 hp ohc six] ZF/ZG; [230 cid/165 hp ohc six] ZK/ZS/ZN/ZM. [230 cid/215 hp ohc six] ZD/ZE/ZR/ZL. [326 cid/250 hp V-8] WP/WX/YN/XF/WH/WC/YJ/XL. [326 cid/285 hp V-8] WK/WO/WR/YM/YP/XG/XO/XR. [400 cid/260 hp V-8] YB. [400 cid/265 hp V-8] WA/YA/YB/WB. [400 cid/290 hp V-8] YC/YD. [400 cid/293 hp V-8] XC. [400 cid/325 hp V-8] YE/YF/YT/WI/WQ/WZ/WU/XN. [400 cid/333 hp V-8] WE/WD/XZ/XY/XH. [400 cid/350 hp] XZ/XY/XJ. [428 cid/360 hp V-8] WG/WK/XD/Y2/YH/YY/YZ/YT. [428 cid/376 hp V-8] WJ/WL/XK/YK. [400 cid/255 hp two-barrel GTO V-8; automatic only] XL/XM. [400 cid/335 hp four-barrel special GTO V-8] WT/WW with synchromesh; YS with Turbo Hydramatic. [400 cid/360 hp GTO special V-8] WS/WV with synchromesh; XP/XS/YR/YZ with Hydra-Matic.

1967 Pontiac Catalina 2+2 two-door hardtop with eight-lug wheels. OCW

CATALINA (SERIES 252)

Model Number	Body/Style Number	Body Type & Seating	Factory Price	Shipping Weight	Prod. Total
252	25269	4-dr Sed-6P	2866	3825	80,551
252	25239	4-dr HT-6	3020	3960	37,256
252	25211	2-dr Sed-6P	2807	3735	5633
252	25287	2-dr HT Cpe-6P	2951	3860	77,932
252	25267	2-dr Conv-6P	3276	3910	10,033
252	25245	4-dr Sta Wag-9P	3374	4340	11,040
252	25235	4-dr Sta Wag-6P	3252	4275	18,305

NOTE 1: 211,405 Catalinas were built.

NOTE 2: 3653 had synchromesh and 207,752 had Turbo-Hydramatic.

NOTE 3: 1768 Catalinas had 2+2 option with no body style breakout available.

EXECUTIVE - (V-8) - SERIES 256 - The Star Chief name was dropped. Executives had the same equipment as Catalinas, plus electric clocks, deluxe wheelcovers, deluxe steering wheels, decor moldings and special ornamentation. Trim features included V-shaped deck lid emblems and Executive front fender side lettering. Only wagons with external woodgrained paneling were called Safaris and the Executive Safari was born.

1967 Pontiac Executive nine-passenger station wagon. OCW

EXECUTIVE (SERIES 256)

Model Number	Body/Style Number	Body Type & Seating	Factory Price	Shipping Weight	Prod. Total
256	25669	4-dr Sed-6P	3165	3955	19,861
256	25639	4-dr HT-6P	3296	4020	8699
256	25687	2-dr HT Cpe-6P	3227	3925	6931
256	25645	4-dr Sta Wag-9P	3722	4370	5593
256	25635	4-dr Sta Wag-6P	3600	4290	5903

NOTE 1: 35,491 Executive passenger cars were built.

NOTE 2: 84 Executive passenger cars had synchromesh; 35,407 Turbo-Hydramatic.

NOTE 3: 11,496 Executive station wagons were also built.

NOTE 4: 38 Executive wagons had synchromesh and 11,458 had Turbo-Hydramatic.

1967 Pontiac Bonneville two-door hardtop. JAG

BONNEVILLE - (V-8) - SERIES 262 - As usual, the word Bonneville appeared on the left-hand grille on cars in Pontiac's luxury class series. Similar lettering was on the rear fender below the beltline crease. Tail-lamps were of the same overall shape as on Catalinas and Executives, but three individual lenses were seen. Fender skirts were featured along with rocker panel and rear panel accent moldings. Standard equipment included all items found on Executives plus notch back front seats with center armrests, burl style dashboard trim and a four-barrel V-8. Station wagons had rear folding seats, courtesy lamps, power tailgate windows and load area carpeting.

BONNEVILLE (SERIES 262)

Model Number	Body/Style Number	Body Type & Seating	Factory Price	Shipping Weight	Prod. Total
262	26239	4-dr HT-6P	3517	4110	56,307
262	26287	2-dr HT Cpe-6P	3227	3925	31,016
262	26267	2-dr Conv-6P	3680	4010	8902
262	26245	4-dr Sta Wag-9P	3819	4415	6771

NOTE 1: 96,708 Bonneville passenger cars were built.

NOTE 2: 278 Bonneville passenger cars had synchromesh; 96,430 Turbo-Hydramatic

NOTE 3: 6771 Bonneville station wagons were built.

NOTE 4: 29 Bonneville wagons had synchromesh and 6742 had Turbo-Hydramatic.

NOTE 5: 483 Bonneville chassis sold to professional car converters.

1967 Pontiac Grand Prix two-door convertible, V-8.

GRAND PRIX - (V-8) - SERIES 266 - The Grand Prix was set apart this year by distinct styling touches and a new convertible body style. For identification there were GP letters on the left-hand grille, Grand Prix rear fender lettering, hide-away headlights, front parking lamps hidden behind slits in the fender and straight horizontal twin-slot tail-lamps. Fender skirts and lower body accent moldings were seen as well. Grand Prix featured all standard GM safety equipment, plus a 350 hp V-8, front Strato Bucket seats and a console. The hardtop coupe did not have vent windows. Convertibles had GP initials leaded into the vent window glass.

GRAND PRIX (SERIES 266)

Model Number	Body/Style Number	Body Type & Seating	Factory Price	Shipping Weight	Prod. Total
266	26657	2-dr HT Cpe-5P	3549	4005	37,125
266	26667	2-dr Conv-5P	3813	4040	5856

NOTE 1: A total of 42,981 Grand Prix were built.

NOTE 2: 760 Grand Prix had synchromesh and 42,221 had Turbo-Hydramatic.

TEMPEST - (6-CYL) - SERIES 233 - All Tempests were mildly face-lifted with grille and rear panel treatments varying by series. The base models had new molded plastic grille bars arranged vertically, in groups of four, with wide spaces between them. Three block-shaped taillamp lenses set into rectangular frames were seen. The Tempest name appeared behind the front wheel opening and the rear fender had three horizontal slits on the side that housed side markers. All GM safety features were standard, plus vinyl floor mats, cigar lighters, armrests, heater and defroster, five blackwall tubeless tires and standard type steering wheel.

STANDARD TEMPEST (SERIES 233)

Model Number	Body/Style Number	Body Type & Seating	Factory Price	Shipping Weight	Prod. Total
233	23369	4-dr Sed-6P	2388	3140	13,136
233	23307	2-dr Cpe-6P	2341	3110	17,978
233	23335	4-dr Sta Wag-6P	2666	3370	3495

NOTE 1: A total of 34,609 standard Tempests were built.

NOTE 2: 7154 standard Tempests had synchromesh; 27,455 had automatic.

1967 Pontiac Tempest station wagon. OCW

TEMPEST CUSTOM - (6-CYL) - SERIES 235 - Standard equipment on Tempest Custom models included special interior trim, carpeting, Deluxe steering wheel and courtesy lamps on convertibles. There were no horizontal slits on the rear fender sides and the nameplate behind the front wheel opening carried Tempest Custom lettering. Upper belt-line and wheel opening decor moldings were used.

TEMPEST CUSTOM (SERIES 235)

Model Number	Body/Style Number	Body Type & Seating	Factory Price	Shipping Weight	Prod. Total
235	23569	4-dr Sed-6P	2482	3145	17,445
235	23539	4-dr HT-6P	2608	3240	5493
235	23507	2-dr Cpe-6P	2434	3130	12,469
235	23517	2-dr HT Cpe-6P	2494	3140	30,512
235	23567	2-dr Conv-6P	2723	3240	4082
235	23535	4-dr Sta Wag-6P	2760	3370	5324

NOTE 1: A total of 75,325 Tempest Customs were built.

NOTE 2: 8302 Tempest Customs had synchromesh and 67,023 had automatic.

1967 Pontiac Tempest four-door hardtop. OCW

1967 Pontiac Tempest LeMans two-door hardtop. OCW

TEMPEST LEMANS - (6-CYL) - SERIES 237 and 239 - When the name LeMans appeared on the back fenders Tempest buyers got carpeting, front foam seat cushions and lamps for the ashtray, cigar lighter, and glovebox as standard equipment. Buyers of two-door models in this line found three vertical air slots on rear fenders and had a choice of bucket or notch back bench seats with armrests. The four-door hardtop came with cloth-and-Morrokide trim and short slanting chrome slashes on the rear roof pillar. Other styles had all-Morrokide upholstery. A special station wagon with woodgrained exterior paneling was called the Series 239 Tempest Safari and was generally finished in LeMans level-trim appointments.

TEMPEST LEMANS (SERIES 237)

Model Number	Body/Style Number	Body Type & Seating	Factory Price	Shipping Weight	Prod. Total
237	23739	4-dr HT-6P	2771	3265	8424
237	23707	2-dr Cpe-5P	2586	3155	10,693
237	23717	2-dr HT Cpe-5P	2648	3155	75,965
237	23767	2-dr Conv-5P	2881	3250	9820

TEMPEST SAFARI (SERIES 239)

Model Number	Body/Style Number	Body Type & Seating	Factory Price	Shipping Weight	Prod. Total
239	23935	4-dr Sta Wag-6P	2936	3390	4511

NOTE 1: 104,902 LeMans passenger cars were built.

NOTE 2: 14,770 LeMans passenger cars had synchromesh and 90,132 had automatic.

NOTE 3: 4511 Tempest Safari wagons were built.

NOTE 4: 129 Tempest Safari wagons had synchromesh and 4382 had automatic.

1967 Pontiac GTO two-door hardtop, V-8.

TEMPEST GTO - (V-8) - SERIES 242 - On GTOs the trim along the center grille divider now went from one side of the car to the other, with a dip around the center divider. V-shaped fender badges behind the front wheel opening were eliminated. Like the Grand Prix, the GTO had twin pin stripes along the upper beltline region. Bodyside accent moldings were slightly revised. Rectangular front grille parking lamps were still used in front and the taillights now took the form of four thin rectangles at each side. All LeMans features were standard, plus walnut grain dash inserts, heavy-duty shocks, springs and stabilizer bars, redline or whitewall tires, dual exhausts and a 335 hp four-barrel 400 cid V-8.

TEMPEST GTO (SERIES 242)

Model Number	Body/Style Number	Body Type & Seating	Factory Price	Shipping Weight	Prod. Total
242	24207	2-dr Cpe-5P	2871	3425	7029
242	24217	2-dr HT Cpe-5P	2935	3430	65,176
242	24267	2-dr Conv-5P	3165	3515	9517

NOTE 1: 81,722 GTOs were built.

NOTE 2: 39,128 GTOs had synchromesh and 42,594 had automatic.

FIREBIRD - (6-CYL) - SERIES 223 - The first Firebird was made at Lordstown, Ohio, in early January 1967. The new car line was officially released February 23, 1967. External features included sculptured body styling, twin grilles of a bumper-integral design, front vent windows, and three vertical air slots on the leading edge of rear body panels. Bucket seats were standard. Two body styles were offered and came with any of the Tempest or GTO powertrains. However, the two body styles were marketed in five "model-options" created by adding regular production options (RPOs) in specific combinations. Production records were not kept according to the RPO packages, but by the number of sixes and V-8s built with standard or deluxe appointments. The model-option such as Sprint, HO, and 400 are described in the optional equipment section below.

1967 Pontiac Firebird two-door convertible, V-8.

FIREBIRD (SERIES 223)

Model Number	Body/Style Number	Body Type & Seating	Factory Price	Shipping Weight	Prod. Total
223	22337	2-dr HT Cpe-5P	2666	2955	67,032
223	22367	2-dr Conv-5P	2903	3247	15,528

Note 1: Prices/weights for base Firebird with 165 hp ohc six and synchromesh.

PRODUCTION NOTES:

Standard ohc six Firebirds (synchromesh)	5258		
(automatic)	5597	(Total)	10,855
Standard V-8 Firebirds (synchromesh)	8,224		
(automatic)	15,301	(Total)	23,525
Deluxe ohc six Firebirds (synchromesh)	2,963		
(automatic)	3846	(Total)	6809
Deluxe V-8 Firebirds (synchromesh)	11,526		
(automatic)	29,845	(Total)	41,371
Totals	27,971	54,589	82,560

BASE ENGINES

(CATALINA/EXECUTIVE) Base V-8: Overhead valves. Cast iron block. Displacement: 400 cu. in. Bore & Stroke: 4.125 x 3.746 in. Compression Ratio: (synchromesh) 8.6:1; (Turbo-Hydramatic) 10.5:1. Brake hp: (synchromesh) 265 @ 4600 rpm; (Turbo-Hydramatic) 290 @ 4600 rpm. Five main bearings. Hydraulic valve lifters. Carburetor: Rochester model 7027066 two-barrel.

1967 Pontiac Catalina Ventura two-door hardtop with eight-lug wheels. OCW

1967 Pontiac Catalina four-door station wagon. JAG

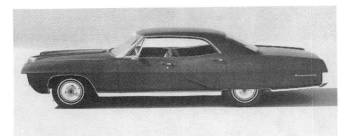

1967 Pontiac Bonneville four-door hardtop. OCW

1967 Pontiac Bonneville two-door convertible. OCW

1967 Pontiac Tempest Safari station wagon . JAG

1967 Pontiac Tempest coupe. OCW

1967 Pontiac Tempest Safari station wagon. JAG

1967 Pontiac Tempest LeMans convertible. JAG

1967 Pontiac Tempest GTO convertible. OCW

98

1967 Pontiac Bonneville Brougham four-door hardtop with eight-lug wheels. OCW

(BONNEVILLE) Base V-8s: Overhead valves. Cast iron block. Displacement: 400 cu. in. Bore & Stroke: 4.125 x 3.746 in. Compression Ratio: (synchromesh) 8.6:1; (Turbo-Hydramatic) 10.5:1. Brake hp: (synchromesh) 333 @ 5000 rpm; (Turbo-Hydramatic) 325 @ 4800 rpm. Five main bearings. Hydraulic valve lifters. Carburetor: Carter AFB model 4243S four-barrel.

(GRAND PRIX) Base V-8: Same general specifications as on Bonneville Turbo-Hydramatic V-8, except that a high lift camshaft giving 350 hp @ 5000 rpm was used on the Grand Prix.

(TEMPEST/TEMPEST CUSTOM/FIREBIRD) OHC-Six: Overhead valves. Cast iron block. Displacement: 230 cu. in. Bore & Stroke: 3.87 x 3.25 in. Compression Ratio: 9.0:1. Brake hp: 165 @ 4700 rpm. Seven main bearings. Hydraulic lifters. Carburetor: Rochester one-barrel. **(GTO)** Base V-8: Overhead valves. Cast iron block. Displacement: 400 cu. in. Bore & Stroke: 4.125 x 3.746 in. Compression Ratio: 10.75:1. Brake hp: 335 @ 5000 rpm. Five main bearings. Hydraulic valve lifters. Carburetor: Rochester model 7027263 Quadra-Jet four-barrel. (Note: The two-barrel V-8 was a delete-option, not the base engine.)

CHASSIS FEATURES: Wheelbase: (Pontiac station wagons) 121 in.; (Series 252 and 266 passenger cars) 121 in.; (Series 256 and 262 passenger cars) 124 in.; (Tempests) 115 in.; (Firebirds) 108 in. Overall Length: (Pontiac station wagons) 218.4 in.; (Series 252 and 266 passenger cars) 215.6 in.; (Series 256 and 262 passenger cars) 222.6 in.; (Tempest station wagons) 203.4 in.; (Tempest and GTO passenger cars) 206.6 in.; (Firebirds) 188.4 in. Front tread: (Pontiac) 63 in.; (Tempest) 58 in.; (Firebird) 60 in. Rear tread: (Pontiac) 64 in.; (Tempest) 59 in.; (Firebird) 60 in. Standard tires: (two-door and four-door Catalina sedans) 8.25 x 14; (other full-size Pontiacs) 8.55 x 14; (Tempest) 7.75 x 14; (Firebird) E70 x 14; (GTO) F70 x 14.

OPTIONS

[PONTIAC] Custom air conditioner ($421). Air injector exhaust control ($44). Console ($105). Cruise control ($63). Front disc brakes ($105). Rear window defogger ($21). Headrests ($42-$52). Capacitor ignition ($104-$115). Cornering lamps ($34). Low-fuel lamp ($6). Custom gauge panel cluster ($21-$36). Power antenna ($29). Power steering ($95-$105). AM/FM stereo ($239). Safeguard speedometer ($16). Reclining right-hand seat ($84). Super-Lift shock absorbers ($40). Front shoulder belts ($23-$26). Fender skirts ($26). Ride & handling package ($9). Strato Bucket seats on Bonneville coupe and convertible only ($114). Cordo top ($105-$132). Turbo-Hydramatic ($226). Four-speed manual transmission ($226). Three-speed manual transmission with floor shift ($42). Ventura Custom option with bench seats ($134). Ventura Custom convertible option with bucket seats ($206). Ventura Custom hardtop option with bucket seats ($248). Aluminum hubs and drums ($118-$135). Rally II wheels ($65-$73). 2+2 Sport Option ($389-$410). (Note: The 2+2 Sport Option included deluxe wheel discs and steering wheel, decor moldings, bucket seats, four-barrel 428 cid V-8, three-speed manual floor shift, dual exhausts and heavy-duty stabilizer bar. Lower 2+2 price applies to Catalina convertible; higher price to hardtop coupe.) The 265 hp base Catalina V-8 was a no-cost economy option in other full-sized lines. Base Bonneville V-8s were $35-$44 extra in Catalinas or Executives with prices depending upon model and transmission. The 428 cid V-8 with 10.5:1 compression and four-barrel carburetor was optional in all full-sized Pontiacs at $79-$114 extra, with prices depending upon model, transmission and use of air injector exhaust control. A 428 cid HO (high-output) V-8 was available in all full-sized Pontiacs for $119-$263 extra, with prices depending on model, transmission and use of air injector exhaust control.

[TEMPEST/FIREBIRD] Dual-stage air cleaner ($9). Custom air conditioner ($343). Carpeting ($19). GTO console ($68). Cruise control ($53). Remote control deck lid ($13). GTO tailpipe extensions ($21). Head rests ($42). Station wagon luggage carrier ($63). Remote control outside mirror ($7). Rally gauge cluster ($84). Power antenna ($29). AM/FM radio ($134). Reclining right-hand bucket seat ($84). Stereo tape player ($128). Tilt steering ($42). Three-speed manual transmis-

sion w/floor shift ($42). Three-speed manual transmission w/full-synchromesh ($84). Four-speed manual transmission ($184). Automatic transmission with base OHC-6 ($226). Automatic transmission with 326 cid V-8 ($195). Turbo-Hydramatic in GTO only ($226). Wire wheel discs ($53-$70). Rally I wheels ($40-$57). Rally II wheels ($56-$72). Integral hubs and drums ($83-$100). Sprint package ($106-$127). (Sprint package includes heavy-duty stabilizer shaft, ohc six with four-barrel carburetor, three-speed manual transmission with floor shift, sport type shocks, front fender emblems, wheel opening moldings on Tempests and Tempest Customs and Sprint side stripes on coupes and convertibles). The 326 cid V-8 with 9.2:1 compression, two-barrel carburetion and 250 hp @ 4600 rpm was $95 extra in Tempests. The Sprint OHC-6 with 10.5:1 compression, four-barrel carburetion and 207 hp @ 5200 rpm. was $58 extra in Tempests. The 326 cid V-8 with 10.5:1 compression, four-barrel carburetion and 285 hp @ 5000 rpm was $159 extra in Tempests, except station wagons. (Note: Above options not available in GTOs).

1967 Pontiac Tempest GTO two-door hardtop. OCW

[GTO] The 255 hp 400 cid V-8 with 8.6:1 compression and 255 hp @ 4400 rpm was a no cost GTO economy option. A second option in this series was the RAM AIR 400 cid V-8 with the same specifications as base GTO engines. It also gave 360 hp, but at a higher peak of 5400 rpm.

1967 Pontiac Firebird coupe. OCW

[FIREBIRD "MODEL-OPTION" PACKAGES]

FIREBIRD SPRINT: Sprint models featured a 215 hp ohc six with four-barrel carburetion. A floor-mounted three speed manual gearbox and heavy-duty suspension was standard. Body still moldings with "3.8 Liter Overhead Cam" emblems were seen. Bodyside racing stripes were an option. The Firebird Sprint convertible was priced $3019 and the Firebird Sprint coupe was $2782. The additional weight over respective base models was 55 pounds.

FIREBIRD 326: Firebird 326s featured a 250 hp version of the base Tempest V-8 with two-barrel carburetion. The Firebird 326 convertible was priced $2998 and weighed 3415 pounds. The Firebird 326 coupe was priced $2761 and weighed 3123 pounds.

FIREBIRD 326-HO: Firebird 326-HOs used a 285 hp version of the base Tempest V-8 with 10.5:1 compression and four-barrel carburetion. Three-speed manual transmission with column shift, dual exhausts, HO side stripes, heavy-duty battery and F70 x 14 wide oval tires were standard. The Firebird 326-HO convertible was priced $3062 and the Firebird 326-HO coupe was priced $2825.

FIREBIRD 400: Firebird 400s used a 325 hp version of the GTO V-8 with four-barrel carburetion. Standard equipment included dual scoop hood, chrome engine parts, three-speed heavy-duty floor shift and sport type suspension. The letters `400' appeared on the right-hand side of the deck lid. The Firebird 400 convertible was priced $3177 and the Firebird 400 coupe was priced $2777. Options included a RAM AIR induction setup that gave 325 hp at a higher rpm peak and cost over $600 extra.

HISTORICAL FOOTNOTES: Pontiacs were introduced in the fall of 1966 and the Firebird debuted February 23, 1967. Calendar year production was 857,171 units. This was the only year that a Grand Prix convertible was ever offered. Interesting conversions of 1967 Pontiacs include the George Barris-built "Monkeemobile" GTO phaeton (made for the TV show) and the "Fitchbird," a performance-oriented package for Firebirds marketed by race car builder/driver John Fitch. New features included 400 cid and 428 cid V-8s and the so-called "His-And-Her" transmission that allowed conventional shifting of the automatic gear selector. In magazine road tests, the 1967 Firebird Sprint hardtop with 215 hp did 0-to-60 mph in 10 seconds and the quarter-mile in 17.5 seconds. With the 325 hp Firebird 400 option, the numbers went down to 6.4 and 14.3, respectively. The Firebird 400 hardtop with the 325 hp motor was clocked by a second test driver at 14.7 seconds and 98 mph in the quarter-mile. A total of 7724 Catalina 2+2s with the standard 428 cid/360 hp V-8 were built. Another 1405 full-size Pontiacs had the 428 HO/376 hp engine. The term Safari was used only for station wagons with woodgrained trim. The term Sports Coupe was used to describe Tempest and GTO two-door pillared coupes (See Cpe in charts). The Bonneville Brougham package, available for four-door sedans and hardtops only, was $273 extra and included front foam seat cushions, power windows and Strato Bench seats.

1968 PONTIAC

1968 Pontiac Catalina four-door sedan. JAG

CATALINA - (V-8) - SERIES 252 - New styling features for full-sized 1968 Pontiacs included peripheral front bumpers, pointed noses, split grilles new interiors, revised instrument panels and redesigned tail lamps. Standard equipment for Catalinas included General Motors safety features; cigar lighter, glovebox and ashtray lamps, woodgrained dash trim, carpeting, concealed two-speed wipers and a two-barrel V-8. Convertibles and station wagons had Morrokide seats and the nine-passenger wagon had a power tailgate window. Code 554 Ventura Custom trim option available on style numbers 25287 and 25267 with bucket seats ($178-$219) and all other Catalinas, except two-door sedan, with bench seats ($105). Ventura Custom option includes special interior trim and Ventura fender lettering. Catalina lettering appeared on the front fender tip, except cars with the Ventura package carried the Ventura name instead.

PONTIAC I.D. NUMBERS: VIN on left front door post. First symbol indicates GM division: 2=Pontiac. Second and third symbols indicate series: 23=Firebird; 33=Tempest; 35=Tempest Custom; 37=LeMans; 39=Tempest Safari; 42=GTO; 52=Catalina; 56=Star Chief; 62=Bonneville; 66=Grand Prix. Fourth and fifth symbols indicate body style and appear as last two symbols in Body/Style Number column of charts below. Sixth symbol indicates model year: 8=1968. Seventh symbol tells assembly plant: L=Van Nuys, Calif.; 1=Oshawa, Ontario, Canada; P=Pontiac, Mich.; C=South Gate, Calif.; E=Linden, N.J.; X=Kansas City, Kan.; R=Arlington, Texas; Z=Fremont, Calif.; B=Baltimore, Md.; K=Kansas City, Mo.; G=Framingham, Mass.; V=Lordstown, Ohio. Following symbols are sequential production number starting with 100001 at each assembly plant. Body/style number plate under hood tells manufacturer, Fisher style number, assembly plant, trim code, paint code, accessory codes. Style number consists of 68 (for 1968) prefix and four symbols that appear in second column of charts below. First two symbols indicate series; second two symbols indicate body type. VIN appears on front of engine at right-hand cylinder bank along with an alpha-numerical engine production code. Engine production codes included: [230 cid/175 hp ohc six] ZK/ZN. [230 cid/215 hp ohc six] ZD/ZE/ZO. [350 cid/265 hp V-8] WP/YN/WD/WC/YJ. [350 cid/320 hp V-8] WR/YM/YP/WK. [400 cid/265 hp V-8] XM/YA. [400 cid/290 hp] WA/WB/YC. [400 cid/330 hp V-8] WZ/YT; [400 cid/335 hp] WQ/WI/YW/XN. [400 cid/340 hp] WE/YE. [400 cid/350 hp] XZ/XH. [428 cid/375 hp V-8] WG/YH. [428 cid/390 hp] WJ/YK. [400 cid/265 hp two-barrel GTO V-8; automatic only] XM. [400 cid/335 hp four-barrel special GTO V-8] WT/WW with synchromesh; YS with Turbo-Hydramatic. [400 cid/350 hp GTO special V-8] WT manual transmission only. [400 cid/360 hp special GTO V-8] WS/XS with synchromesh; YZ/XP Hydra-Matic.

1968 Pontiac Catalina "Enforcer" police car. JAG

CATALINA (SERIES 252)

Model Number	Body/Style Number	Body Type & Seating	Factory Price	Shipping Weight	Prod. Total
252	25269	4-dr HT-6P	3004	3888	94,441
252	25239	4-dr HT-6P	3158	4012	41,727
252	25211	2-dr Sed-6p	2945	3839	5247
252	25287	2-dr HT-6P	3089	3943	92,217
252	25267	2-dr Conv-6P	3391	3980	7339
252	25245	4-dr Sta Wag-9P	3537	4408	13,363
252	25235	4-dr Sta Wag-6P	3390	4327	21,848

NOTE 1: 240,971 Catalina passenger cars were built.

NOTE 2: 2257 had Catalina passenger cars had synchromesh; 238,714 automatic.

NOTE 3: 35,211 Catalina station wagons were built.

NOTE 4: 289 Catalina station wagons had synchromesh and 34,922 had automatic.

1968 Pontiac Executive four-door hardtop sedan, V-8.

EXECUTIVE - (V-8) - SERIES 256 - Executives had all Catalina equipment, plus Deluxe steering wheel, decor moldings, Deluxe wheel discs and map, courtesy and trunk lamps. Executive lettering appeared behind front wheel openings.

EXECUTIVE (SERIES 256)

Model Number	Body/Style Number	Body Type & Seating	Factory Price	Shipping Weight	Prod. Total
256	25669	4-dr Sed-6P	3309	4022	18,869
256	25639	4-dr HT-6P	3439	4077	7848
256	25687	2-dr HT-6P	3371	3975	5880
256	25645	4-dr Sta Wag-6P	3890	4453	5843
256	25635	4-dr Sta Wag-6P	3744	4378	6195

NOTE 1: 32,597 Executive passenger cars were built.

NOTE 2: 47 Executive passenger cars had synchromesh; 32,550 had automatic.

NOTE 3: 12,038 Executive station wagons were built.

NOTE 4: 23 Executive station wagons had synchromesh and 12,015 had automatic.

BONNEVILLE - (V-8) - SERIES 262 - Bonnevilles had all Executive features, plus fender skirts, carpeted lower door trim, elm burl vinyl dash trim and a 340 hp V-8. Convertibles had leather and Morrokide interiors. Wagons had notch back front seats with folding armrest, folding third

seat, courtesy lamps, power tailgate window and carpeted load area. The Bonneville name, in block letters, appeared behind the front wheel opening and on the deck lid latch panel. Bonneville taillights were of the same shape used a year earlier, but were now of a single design, the lens being longer than used on Catalinas and Executives. The code 511 Bonneville Brougham trim option was available on style numbers 26239 and 26287 ($273) and 26267 ($316). It includes front foam cushions, spare tire cover, power windows and Strato bench seat.

BONNEVILLE (SERIES 262)

Model Number	Body/Style Number	Body Type & Seating	Factory Price	Shipping Weight	Prod. Total
262	26239	4-dr HT-6P	3660	4171	57,055
262	26287	2-dr HT-6P	3592	4054	29,598
262	26267	2-dr Conv-6P	3800	4090	7358
262	26245	4-dr Sta Wag-6P	3987	4485	6926
262	26269	4-dr Sed-6P	3530	4122	3499

NOTE 1: 98,005 Bonneville passenger cars were built.

NOTE 2: 208 Bonneville passenger cars had synchromesh; 97,797 had automatic.

NOTE 3: 6926 Bonneville station wagons were built.

NOTE 4: Nine Bonneville station wagons had synchromesh; 6917 had automatic.

NOTE 5: 495 Bonnevilles were provided for conversions.

1968 Pontiac Grand Prix two-door hardtop coupe, V-8.

GRAND PRIX - (V-8) - SERIES 266 - Only the Grand Prix coupe was back for 1968. Standard were all General Motors safety features, plus deluxe wheel discs, fender skirts, dual exhausts, padded bucket seats with contoured backs and armrests, center console and a 400 cid/350 hp four-barrel V-8 with three-speed manual attachment. New styling included a peripheral bumper, extra-long horizontal taillamps integrated into bumper, downswept rear deck, redesigned dash panel and hidden headlights. A `GP' badge appeared on the left-hand grille and right-hand corner of the deck lid with engine displacement badges on rocker panel moldings.

1968 Pontiac Grand Prix two-door hardtop coupe, V-8.

GRAND PRIX (SERIES 266)

Model Number	Body/Style Number	Body Type & Seating	Factory Price	Shipping Weight	Prod. Total
266	26657	2-dr HT Cpe-6P	3697	4075	31,711

NOTE 1: 31,711 Grand Prix were built.

NOTE 2: 306 Grand Prix had synchromesh and 31,405 had automatic.

TEMPEST - (6-CYL) - SERIES 233 - Tempests now had long hood/short deck styling. Two- and four-door models were built with different wheelbases. A peripheral bumper grille was used and taillights were placed in the bumper. Regular equipment on standard Tempests included GM safety features, heater and defroster, door armrests and an overhead cam six-cylinder engine. Cars with the base engine had ohc six lettering on rocker panels. Tempest Sprint package available at prices of $106-$126 depending on series and body style. Tempest Sprint package includes four-barrel ohc six, heavy-duty stabilizer shaft, three-speed manual transmission, sport type shocks, ohc six rocker panel molding emblems and (on some models) wheel opening moldings and Sprint side stripes.

TEMPEST (SERIES 233)

Model Number	Body/Style Number	Body Type & Seating	Factory Price	Shipping Weight	Prod. Total
233	23369	4-dr Sed-6P	2509	3307	11,590
233	23327	2-dr Cpe-6p	2461	3242	19,991

NOTE 1: 31,581 standard Tempests were built.

NOTE 2: 5876 had synchromesh and 25,705 had automatic.

TEMPEST CUSTOM - (6-CYL) - SERIES 235 - Tempest Customs had all features found on series 233 models, plus special interior and exterior trim, carpeting, Deluxe steering wheel, armrests with ashtrays, cigarette lighter, ignition buzzer alarm, front and rear bodyside marker lights and dual horns. Station wagons and convertibles had all-Morrokide seats and carpeting, with panel courtesy lamps on convertibles. Tempest lettering along with custom badges appeared at tips of front fenders.

TEMPEST CUSTOM (SERIES 235)

Model Number	Body/Style Number	Body Type & Seating	Factory Price	Shipping Weight	Prod. Total
235	23569	4-dr Sed-6P	2602	3297	17,304
235	23539	4-dr HT-6P	2728	3382	6147
235	23527	2-dr Cpe-6P	2554	3252	10,634
235	23537	2-dr HT Cpe-6P	2614	3277	40,574
235	23567	2-dr Conv-6P	2839	3337	3518
235	23535	4-dr Sta Wag-6P	2906	3667	8253

NOTE 1: 75,325 Custom Tempests were built.

NOTE 2: 8302 had synchromesh and 67,023 had automatic.

1968 Pontiac LeMans four-door hardtop sedan, six-cylinder.

TEMPEST LEMANS - (6-CYL) - SERIES 237 AND SERIES 239 - Standard in LeMans were all GM safety features, plus disappearing wipers, dual horns and Morrokide interior. Two-door models came with a choice of bucket or notch back armrest seats. The four-door hardtop had cloth and Morrokide upholstery and a choice of notch back or bench seats. Deluxe steering wheel, carpeting, cigar lighter, armrests and ashtrays, ignition alarm, panel courtesy lamps, ashtray and glovebox lamps were also featured. The LeMans convertible had a power top and special courtesy lights. The series 239 Safari was generally appointed in LeMans level trim with woodgrained interior and exterior paneling. The word LeMans was on the rear fender of each LeMans. The word Safari was on front of wood-trimmed station wagons.

TEMPEST LEMANS (SERIES 237)

Model Number	Body/Style Number	Body Type & Seating	Factory Price	Shipping Weight	Prod. Total
237	23739	4-dr HT-6P	2916	3407	9002
237	23727	2-dr Cpe-6P	2724	3287	8439
237	23737	2-dr HT Cpe-6P	2786	3302	110,036
237	23767	2-dr Conv-6P	3015	3377	8820

1968 Pontiac LeMans four-door hardtop (rear view). OCW

TEMPEST SAFARI (SERIES 239)

Model Number	Body/Style Number	Body Type & Seating	Factory Price	Shipping Weight	Prod. Total
239	23935	4-dr Sta Wag-6P	3017	3677	4414

NOTE 1: 136,297 LeMans cars were built.

NOTE 2: 12,233 LeMans cars had synchromesh and 124,074 had automatic.

NOTE 3: 4414 LeMans Safari station wagons were built.

NOTE 4: 122 LeMans Safaris had synchromesh and 4292 had automatic.

GTO - (V-8) - SERIES 242 - Standard in GTOs were all GM safety features, dual exhausts, three-speed manual transmission with Hurst shifter, sports type springs and shock absorbers, fastback redline tires, bucket or notch back armrest seats, cigar lighter, carpeting, ignition alarm, disappearing wipers, panel courtesy, ashtray and glovebox lamps, deluxe steering wheel and 350 hp 400 cid four-barrel V-8 (or two-barrel 400 cid regular fuel V-8). GTOs had hidden headlights; a steel-reinforced "Endura" rubber front bumper; twin scoop hoods; GTO lettering on left-hand grille and right-hand deck lid; V-shaped badge behind front wheel opening; V-shaped nose emblems; and distinct taillamps.

GTO (SERIES 242)

Model Number	Body/Style Number	Body Type & Seating	Factory Price	Shipping Weight	Prod. Total
242	24237	2-dr HT Cpe-5P	3101	3506	77,704
242	24267	2-dr Conv-5P	2996	3346	9980

NOTE 1: 87,684 GTOs were built.

NOTE 2: 36,299 had synchromesh and 51,385 had automatic.

1968 Pontiac Firebird 350 HO hardtop coupe, V-8.

FIREBIRD - (6-CYL) - SERIES 223 - Base Firebird equipment included the standard GM safety features, front bucket seats, vinyl upholstery, simulated burl woodgrain dashboard, outside mirror, side marker lights, E70 x 14 black sidewall wide-oval tires with Space Saver spare and 175 hp overhead cam six-cylinder engine. Styling was nearly identical to 1967-1/2 Firebirds except that vent windows were replaced with one-piece side door glass. Technical changes included bias-mounted rear shock absorbers and multi-leaf rear springs.

BASE FIREBIRD (SERIES 233)

Model Number	Body/Style Number	Body Type & Seating	Factory Price	Shipping Weight	Prod. Total
223	22337	2-dr HT Cpe-5P	2781	3061	90,152
223	22367	2-dr Conv-5P	2996	3346	16,960

FIREBIRD PRODUCTION NOTES

Model No.	Engine/Trim	Synchro.	Auto.	Total
Model 223	Standard ohc six	7528	8441	15,969
Model 224	Standard V-8	16,632	39,250	55,882
Model 225	Deluxe ohc six	1216	1309	2525
Model 226	Deluxe V-8	7534	25,202	32,736
		32,910	74,202	107,112

BASE ENGINES

(CATALINA/EXECUTIVE) V-8. Overhead valves. Cast iron block. Displacement: 400 cu. in. Bore & Stroke: 4.13 x 3.75 in. Compression Ratio: (synchromesh) 8.6:1; (Turbo-Hydramatic) 10.5:1. Brake hp: (synchromesh) 265 @ 4600 rpm; (Turbo-Hydramatic) 290 hp @ 4600 rpm. Five main bearings. Hydraulic valve lifters. Carburetor: Rochester two-barrel. (Note: the 290 hp V-8 was considered standard for 1968 Catalinas).

(BONNEVILLE) Turbo-Hydramatic was considered standard on Bonnevilles and came attached to a 400 cid V-8 with 10.5:1 compression, a Rochester four-barrel carburetor and 340 hp @ 4800 rpm. Bonnevilles with synchromesh utilized the same 8.6:1 compression V-8 used in other lines.

(TEMPEST/TEMPEST CUSTOM/LEMANS/FIREBIRD) Base OHC-Six. Overhead valves. Cast iron block. Displacement: 250 cu. in. Bore & Stroke: 3.88 x 3.53 in. Compression Ratio: 9.0:1. Brake hp: 175 @ 4800 rpm. Seven main bearings. Hydraulic valve lifters. Carburetor: Rochester one-barrel.

1968 Pontiac GTO convertible. OCW

(GTO/GRAND PRIX) Base V-8: Overhead valves. Cast iron block. Displacement: 400 cu. in. Bore & Stroke: 4.12 x 3.75 in. Compression Ratio: 10.75:1. Brake hp: 350 @ 5000 rpm. Five main bearings. Hydraulic valve lifters. Carburetor: Rochester four-barrel.

HIGH PERFORMANCE ENGINES

400 cid. Compression ratio: 10.75:1. Carburetion: four-barrel. Brake hp: 330 @ 4800 rpm (standard in Firebird Formula 400).

400 cid. Compression ratio: 10.5:1. Carburetion: four-barrel. Brake hp: 340 @ 4800 rpm (standard in Bonneville, optional in other B-body models).

400 cid. Compression ratio: 10.5:1. Carburetion: four-barrel. Brake hp: 350 @ 5000 rpm (standard in Grand Prix).

400 cid. Compression ratio: 10.75:1. Carburetion: four-barrel. Brake hp: 350 @ 5000 rpm (standard in GTO).

400 cid. Compression ratio: 10.75:1. Carburetion: four-barrel. Brake hp: 335 @ 5000 rpm (optional in Firebird Formula 400).

400 cid. Compression ratio: 10.75:1. Carburetion: four-barrel. Brake hp: 360 @ 5100 rpm (optional in GTO).

400 cid. Compression ratio: 10.75:1. Carburetion: four-barrel. Brake hp: 366 @ 5400 rpm (optional in GTO).

428 cid. Compression ratio: 10.5:1. Carburetion: four-barrel. Brake hp: 375 @ 4800 rpm (optional in Catalina, Executive, Bonneville and Grand Prix).

428 cid. Compression ratio: 10.75:1. Carburetion: four barrel. Brake hp: 390 @ 5200 rpm (optional in Catalina, Executive, Bonneville and Grand Prix).

CHASSIS FEATURES: Wheelbase: (Series 252, 266, and all Pontiac station wagons) 21 in.; (Series 256 and 262) 124 in.; (Tempest two-door) 112 in.; (Tempest four-door) 116 in.; (Firebird) 108 in. Overall Length: (All Pontiac station wagons) 217.8 in.; (Series 252 and 266) 216.5 in.; (Series 256 and 262) 223.5 in.; (Tempest station wagons) 211 in.; (Tempest two-door) 200.7 in.; (Tempest four-door) 204.7 in.; (Firebird) 188.8 in. Front tread: (Pontiac) 63 in.; (Tempest and Firebird) 60 in. Rear tread: (Pontiac) 64 in.; (Tempest and Firebird) 60 in.

OPTIONS

[PONTIAC] Custom air-conditioner ($421). Auxiliary gauge panel ($21-$37). Console ($105). Remote-control deck lid ($14). Rear window defogger ($21). Door guards ($6-$10). Electric clock ($16). Head restraints ($42-$53). Custom gear shift knob ($4). Underhood utility

1968 Pontiac Catalina two-door hardtop. OCW

1968 Pontiac Bonneville nine-passenger station wagon. JAG

1968 Pontiac Bonneville four-door sedan. OCW

1968 Pontiac Bonneville convertible. OCW

1968 Pontiac Bonneville four-door hardtop. OCW

1968 Pontiac Firebird coupe. OCW

1968 Pontiac Firebird convertible. OCW

1968 Pontiac Firebird HO convertible. JAG

1968 Pontiac GTO two-door hardtop. OCW

lamp ($7). Visor vanity mirror ($2-$4). Power brakes ($42). Power antenna ($30). Left power bucket seat ($69). Power steering ($105-$116). Power windows ($104). Power vent windows ($53). AM/FM Stereo ($239). Split back station wagon second seat ($37). Hood-mounted tachometer ($63). Strato bucket seats ($114). Wire wheel discs ($53-$74). Heavy-duty 15-inch wheels ($11). Aluminum hubs and drums ($126-$147). Rally II wheels ($63-$84). Transmission options included Turbo-Hydramatic ($237), Four-speed manual ($226), Close-ratio three-speed manual with floorshift ($42), and close-ratio four-speed manual ($226). The 265 hp two-barrel 400 cid V-8 was $9 extra on Catalinas and Executives with three-speed manual transmission. The 350 hp four-barrel 400 cid V-8 was $35-$44 extra on the same models. The 375 hp four-barrel 428 cid V-8 was $79-$114 extra on all Pontiacs with price depending on transmission. The 390 hp four-barrel 428 cid V-8 was $199-$263 extra on all Pontiacs with price depending on model and transmission. Dual exhausts were $31 extra. Safe-T-Track differential was $42 extra. A variety of axle ratios were available.

1968 Pontiac Tempest Custom station wagon. JAG

[TEMPEST/GTO/FIREBIRD] Custom air conditioner ($360). Custom carpets ($19). Console ($51-$68). Cruise control ($53). Front disc brakes ($63). Auxiliary gauge cluster ($32). Rally gauge cluster ($51). Rally gauge cluster with tachometer ($84). Tinted windows ($35). Tinted windshield ($26). Right reclining bucket seat head restraint ($84). Dual horns ($4). Station wagon luggage carrier ($63). Four-way power seat ($70). Power brakes ($42). Power steering ($69). Left four-way power bucket seat ($70). AM/FM radio ($134). Rally stripes on GTO ($11). Rally stripes for Firebirds except 350 HO ($15). Safe-guard speedometer ($16). Super-Lift shocks for Tempest/GTO ($42). Adjustable front and rear shocks for Firebird ($42). Hood-mounted tachometer ($63). Cordova top ($84-$95). Wire wheel discs ($53-$74). Rally I wheels ($40-$61). Rally II wheels. Transmission options included two-speed automatic ($195), four-speed manual ($184), and heavy-duty three-speed manual with floor shift ($84). The 265 hp two-barrel regular fuel 350 cid V-8 was $106 extra. The 320 hp four-barrel HO 350 cid V-8 was $170 extra. Dual exhausts were $31 extra. Safe-T-Track differential was $42 extra. GTO transmission options included Turbo-Hydramatic ($237) and close-ratio four-speed manual with floor shift ($184). The 366 hp four-barrel HO 400 cid V-8 was $631.12 extra. Dual exhausts were standard. Heavy-duty Safe-T-Track differential was $63 extra. Firebird transmission options included all offered for Tempests and GTOs. Firebird engine options are listed in Firebird RPO packages section below.

FIREBIRD RPO PACKAGES

FIREBIRD SPRINT PACKAGE: Included three-speed manual transmission with floor shift, ohc six Sprint emblems, body sill moldings and four F70 x 14 tires. Engine: 250 cid ohc six with 10.5:1 compression, Rochester four-barrel carburetor and 215 hp @ 5200 rpm. Price: $116 over base model cost.

FIREBIRD 350 PACKAGE: Included three-speed manual transmission with column shift and F70 x 14 tires. Engine: 350 cid (3.88 x 3.75 bore & stroke) V-8 with 9.2:1 compression, Rochester two-barrel carburetor and 265 hp @ 4600 rpm. Price: $106 over base model cost.

FIREBIRD 350-HO PACKAGE: Included three-speed manual transmission with column shift, dual exhausts, HO side stripes, heavy-duty battery and four F70 x 14 tires. Engine: 350 cid V-8 with 10.5:1 compression, Rochester four-barrel carburetor and 320 hp @ 5100 rpm. Price: $181 over base model cost.

FIREBIRD 400 PACKAGE: Included three-speed manual transmission with floor shift, chrome air cleaner, chrome rocker covers, chrome oil cap, sports type springs and shock absorbers, heavy-duty battery, dual exhausts, hood emblem and dual scoop hood, F70 x 14 red stripe or whitewall tires and "Power Flex" variable pitch cooling fan. Engine: 400 cid V-8 with 10.75:1 compression, Rochester four-barrel carburetor and 330 hp @ 4800 rpm. Price: $351-$435 depending on transmission. Lower price applies to cars with Turbo-Hydramatic four-speed manual transmissions.

FIREBIRD RAM AIR 400 PACKAGE: Same inclusions as above, except for addition of de-clutching fan and twin functional hood scoops. Engine: 400 cid V-8 with 10.75:1 compression, Rochester four-barrel carburetor and 335 hp @ 5000 rpm. Price: $616 over base model cost.

HISTORICAL FOOTNOTES: Production started August 21, 1967. The model introductions were September 21, 1967. Model year output was 910,977 cars. Calendar year output was 943,253 cars. The GTO Endura nose was a popular new option. This was the first year for two wheelbases in the Tempest series, with four-doors on the longer chassis. The 1968 Firebird 400 with the 335 hp option was capable of 0-to-60 mph in 7.6 seconds and the quarter-mile in 15.4 seconds. The 360 hp GTO hardtop did 0-to-60 mph in 6.6 seconds and the quarter-mile took 15.5 seconds. There were 6252 standard 428 V-8 engines installed and 453 full-size 428 HO Pontiacs were built.

1969 PONTIAC

CATALINA - (V-8) - SERIES 252 - New styling features for full-sized 1969 Pontiacs included split bumpers, revised rooflines and ventless windows. Wheelbases increased one inch. Catalinas had all GM safety features, carpeting, peripheral front bumpers with Endura rubber center inserts, "pulse" windshield wipers with concealed blades, front foam seat cushions, upper level ventilation systems and a choice of low-compression (regular fuel) two-barrel V-8s or a 290 hp 400 cid V-8. Station wagons had woodgrained dashboards and new two-way tailgates with power rear windows on nine-passenger styles. The Ventura trim package was offered for closed cars only.

PONTIAC I.D. NUMBERS: VIN on left top of instrument panel, visible through windshield. First symbol indicates GM division: 2=Pontiac. Second and third symbols indicate series: 23=Firebird; 33=Tempest; 35=Tempest Custom; 37=Tempest Safari; 39=LeMans; 42=GTO; 52=Catalina; 56=Star Chief; 62=Bonneville; 76=Grand Prix. Fourth and fifth symbols indicate body style and appear as last two symbols in body/style number column of charts below. Sixth symbol indicates model year: 9=1969. Seventh symbol tells assembly plant: A=Atlanta, Ga.; L=Van Nuys, Calif.; 1=Oshawa, Ontario, Canada; P=Pontiac, Mich.; C=South Gate, Calif.; E=Linden, N.J.; X=Kansas City, Kan.; R=Arlington, Texas; Z=Fremont, Calif.; B=Baltimore, Md.; K=Kansas City, Mo.; G=Framingham, Mass.; V=Lordstown, Ohio. Following symbols are sequential production number starting with 100001 at each assembly plant. Body/style number plate under hood tells manufacturer, Fisher style number, assembly plant, trim code, paint code, accessory codes. Style number consists of 69 (for 1969) prefix and four symbols that appear in second column of charts below. First two symbols indicate series; second two symbols indicate body type. VIN appears on front of engine at right-hand cylinder bank along with an alpha-numerical engine production code. Engine production codes included: [250 cid/175 hp six] ZC/ZF/ZK/ZN. [250 cid/215 hp six] ZL/ZE. [250 cid/230 hp six] ZH/ZD. [350 cid/265 hp V-8] WU/YU/XS/XR/YN/WP/WM YE XB/WC XL YJ. [350 CID/325 HP v-8] WN/XG/[350 cid/330 hp V-8] WV/XU. [400 cid/265 hp V-8] XM/XX/YA/YB/YF. [400 cid/290 hp] WD/WE/YD/WA/WB. [400 cid/330 hp] WZ/YT. [400 cid/335 hp] WQ/YW. [400 cid/345 hp] WH/XN. [400 cid/350 hp] WX/XH/Wt. [400 cid/350 hp] WT/YS. [400 cid/366 hp] WS/WW/YZ. [428 cid/340 hp] WG; [428 cid/360 hp] WG/YH/XJ/YL/XE. [428 cid/370 hp] XK/WF/XF. [428 cid/390 hp] WJ/YK/WL/XG.

1969 Pontiac Catalina two-door hardtop. OCW

CATALINA (SERIES 252)

Model Number	Body/Style Number	Body Type & Seating	Factory Price	Shipping Weight	Prod. Total
252	25269	4-dr Sed-6P	3090	3945	48,590
252	25239	4-dr HT-6P	3244	4005	38,819
252	25237	2-dr HT-6P	3174	2935	84,006
252	25267	2-dr Conv-6P	3476	2985	5436
252	25246	4-dr Sta Wag-9P	3664	4520	13,393
252	25236	4-dr Sta Wag-6P	3519	4455	20,352

NOTE 1: 212,851 Catalina passenger cars were built.

NOTE 2: 837 Catalina passenger cars had synchromesh and 212,014 had automatic.

NOTE 3: 33,745 Catalina station wagons were built.

NOTE 4: 170 Catalina station wagons had synchromesh and 33,575 had automatic.

1969 Pontiac Executive Safari station wagon. OCW

EXECUTIVE - (V-8) - SERIES 256 - Standard equipment on Executive included everything found on Catalinas, plus deluxe wheelcovers, three-spoke padded vinyl steering wheel, simulated elm burl dash trim, rear foam seat cushions, electric clock and Morrokide upholstery. Executive Safaris also had woodgrained exterior paneling with simulated teakwood molding trim, vinyl floor mats and a concealed cargo locker.

1969 Pontiac Executive two-door hardtop. JAG

EXECUTIVE (SERIES 256)

Model Number	Body/Style Number	Body Type & Seating	Factory Price	Shipping Weight	Prod. Total
256	25669	4-dr Sed-6P	3394	4045	14,831
256	25639	4-dr HT-6P	3525	4065	6522
256	25637	2-dr HT-6P	3456	2970	4492
256	25646	4-dr Sta Wag-9P	4017	4545	6805
256	25636	4-dr Sta Wag-6P	3872	4475	6411

NOTE 1: 25,845 Executive passenger cars were built.

NOTE 2: 25 Executive passenger cars had synchromesh and 25,820 had automatic.

NOTE 3: 13,216 Executive station wagons were built.

NOTE 4: 14 Executive station wagons had synchromesh and 13,202 had automatic.

1969 Pontiac Bonneville two-door convertible, V-8.

1969 Pontiac Bonneville two-door convertible (rear view). OCW

BONNEVILLE - (V-8) - SERIES 262 - Bonnevilles had all features found on Executives, plus a die-cast grille, choice of several Bonneville Custom interiors, extra-thick foam seat padding, front center fold-down armrest, fender skirts, carpeted lower door panels and a 360 hp four-barrel V-8. The convertible had all-Morrokide upholstery with leather accents. Station wagons featured a notchback front seat with folding armrest, a folding third seat and courtesy lamps. Bonneville lettering appeared on the left-hand grille, the rocker panel moldings and the center edge of the deck lid. The Brougham option was again available, but for coupes and convertibles only.

BONNEVILLE (SERIES 262)

Model Number	Body/Style Number	Body Type & Seating	Factory Price	Shipping Weight	Prod. Total
262	26269	4-dr Sed-6P	3626	4180	4859
262	26239	4-dr HT-6P	3756	4180	40,817
262	26237	2-dr HT-6P	3688	4080	27,773
262	26267	2-dr Conv-6P	3896	4130	5438
262	26246	4-dr Sta Wag-9P	4104	4600	7428

NOTE 1: 89,334 Bonneville passenger cars were built.

NOTE 2: 44 Bonneville passenger cars had synchromesh and 89,290 had automatic.

NOTE 3: 7428 Bonneville station wagons were built.

NOTE 4: Seven Bonneville wagons had synchromesh and 7421 had automatic.

NOTE 5: 447 Bonneville chassis were provided for conversions.

1969 Pontiac Grand Prix 'J' hardtop coupe, V-8.

GRAND PRIX - (V-8) - SERIES 276 - An all-new Grand Prix on an exclusive 118 in. platform was a popular offering this year. Styling highlights were a V-shaped grille, square headlamp surrounds, an aircraft inspired interior and the longest hood of any production car in history. Standard equipment included dual exhaust, Strato Bucket seats, padded integral console with floor shift, hidden radio antenna, carpeted lower door panels, upper level ventilation system and "pulse" type recessed windshield wipers. An 'SJ' option package was available. A 350 hp V-8 was standard.

GRAND PRIX (SERIES 276)

Model Number	Body/Style Number	Body Type & Seating	Factory Price	Shipping Weight	Prod. Total
276	27657	2-dr HT Coupe-5P	3866	3715	112,486

NOTE 1: 112,486 Grand Prix were built.

NOTE 2: 1014 Grand Prix had synchromesh and 111,472 had automatic.

NOTE 3: Approximately 676 cars above had four-speed manual transmission.

TEMPEST - (6-CYL) - SERIES 233 - Tempests were mildly face-lifted with new grille and taillight treatments. Two-door hardtops and convertibles now had ventless side window styling. Standard equipment on base models included all GM safety features, carpets, Morrokide accented upholstery trims and the ohc six. A Tempest script was placed on the leading edge of front fenders.

TEMPEST (SERIES 233)

Model Number	Body/Style Number	Body Type & Seating	Factory Price	Shipping Weight	Prod. Total
233	23369	4-dr Sed-6P	2557	3250	9741
233	23327	2-dr Cpe-6P	2510	3180	17,181

NOTE 1: 26,922 standard Tempest were built.

NOTE 2: 4450 had synchromesh and 22,472 had automatic.

TEMPEST CUSTOM - (6-CYL) - SERIES 235 - This was now called the Custom 'S' series and front fender scripts carried this designation. Standard equipment included all Tempest features, plus all-Morrokide upholstery, concealed windshield wipers, dual horns, ignition buzzer and panel courtesy lamps on convertibles. Cars with six-cylinder engines had ohc six badges on the body sill moldings. Small hubcaps were a regular feature.

TEMPEST CUSTOM 'S' (SERIES 235)

Model Number	Body/Style Number	Body Type & Seating	Factory Price	Shipping Weight	Prod. Total
235	23569	4-dr Sed-6P	2651	3235	16,532
235	23539	4-dr HT-6P	2777	3315	3918
235	23527	2-dr Cpe-6P	2603	3210	7912
235	23537	2-dr HT-6P	2663	3220	46,886
235	23567	2-dr Conv-6P	2888	3265	2379
235	23535	4-dr Sta Wag-6P	2956	5696	6963

NOTE 1: 84,590 Tempest Custom 'S' models were built.

NOTE 2: 4045 Tempest 'S' had synchromesh and 80,545 had automatic.

TEMPEST LEMANS - (6-CYL) - SERIES 237 AND 239 - LeMans models incorporated all Custom 'S' equipment, plus a 3.23:1 rear axle, deluxe three-spoke steering wheel, "pulse" wipers, lamp packages and several seating arrangement choices. Two-door models were available with bucket or notchback seats; four-door hardtop buyers had a choice of bench or notchback seats with center armrests. LeMans convertibles had power tops and Safaris had woodgrained exterior paneling and concealed headlamps. The Sprint option was available for all six-cylinder Tempests, except station wagons. LeMans block lettering appeared on the front fender tips and there were bright metal window and wheel opening moldings. Wood-trimmed station wagons had Safari fender scripts. The Safari was not a LeMans, but was close to it in overall level of trim.

TEMPEST LEMANS (SERIES 237)

Model Number	Body/Style Number	Body Type & Seating	Factory Price	Shipping Weight	Prod. Total
237	23769	4-dr HT-6P	2965	3360	6475
237	23727	2-dr Cpe-6P	2773	3225	5033
237	23737	2-dr HT-6P	2835	3245	82,817
237	23767	2-dr Conv-6P	3064	3290	5676

TEMPEST SAFARI (SERIES 239)

Model Number	Body/Style Number	Body Type & Seating	Factory Price	Shipping Weight	Prod. Total
239	23936	4-dr Sta Wag-6P	3198	3690	4115

NOTE 1: 100,001 LeMans passenger cars were built.

NOTE 2: 6303 LeMans passenger cars had synchromesh and 93,698 had automatic.

NOTE 3: 4115 Tempest Safaris were built.

NOTE 4: 86 Tempest Safaris had synchromesh and 4029 had automatic.

1969 Pontiac GTO two-door hardtop coupe, V-8.

GTO - (V-8) - SERIES 242 - GTOs were based on LeMans with additional standard equipment features including a 400 cid/350 hp V-8, dual exhausts, 3.55:1 rear axle ratio, heavy-duty clutch, three-speed gearbox with floor shifter, Power-Flex cooling fan, sports type springs and shock absorbers, redline wide-oval tires, carpeting, Deluxe steering wheel and choice of bucket or notchback seats. A cross-hatched grille insert with horizontal divider bars appeared and hidden headlights were standard. GTO lettering was seen, on the left-hand grille, right-hand side of deck lid and behind the front wheel openings. Taillamps were no longer completely surrounded by bumpers and carried lenses with bright metal trim moldings. Side marker lights were of a distinctive rectangular shape, instead of the triangular type used on other Tempests. A special high-performance "The Judge" option was released December 19, 1968. It included one of two available RAM AIR V-8s as standard equipment as well as many other muscle car features. Though more expensive than base GTOs, a "The Judge" was the least expensive of several cars now on the market with comparable equipment.

GTO (SERIES 242)

Model Number	Body/Style Number	Body Type & Seating	Factory Price	Shipping Weight	Prod. Total
242	24237	2-dr HT-5P	2831	3080	58,126
242	24267	2-dr Conv-5P	3382	3553	7328
242	2437	2-dr Judge HT-5P	3161	NA	6725
242	24267	2-dr Judge Conv-5P	4212	NA	108

NOTE 1: 72,287 GTOs and 'The Judge' optioned GTOs were built.

NOTE 2: 31,433 GTOs and Judges had synchromesh and 40,854 had automatic.

NOTE 3: 8491 GTOs and Judges (including 362 convertibles) had RAM AIR III V-8s.

NOTE 4: RAM AIR III engines were coded `YZ' or `WS'.'

NOTE 5: 759 GTOs and Judges (including 59 convertibles) had RAM AIR IV V-8s.

NOTE 6: RAM AIR IV engines were coded `XP' (automatic) or `WW' (synchromesh).

FIREBIRD - (6-CYL) - SERIES 223 - Firebirds were restyled late in 1968 to incorporate revisions similar to those planned for the Chevrolet Camaro. Design changes included flatter wheel openings, front fender windsplits, new rooflines and a creased lower beltline. The gas filler was moved behind the rear license plate and a boxier split bumper grille was used. Headlamps were set into square body-colored Endura bezels. The high-performance Trans Am was introduced March 8, 1969. This was the most highly refined "model-option" to come from Pontiac up to this point in time. Because of slow sales and late introductions of next-year-models, 1969 Firebirds left in stock were carried over and sold through the following fall. Standard equipment for base Firebirds included vinyl bucket seats, grained dashboards, carpeting, outside mirrors, side marker lamps and E70 x 14 tires. "Model-options" included Firebird Sprint, Firebird 350 and 350 HO, Firebird 400 and 400 HO and Firebird RAM AIR 400, in addition to the midyear Trans Am.

1969 Pontiac Firebird Trans Am two-door hardtop, V-8.

FIREBIRD (SERIES 223)

Model Number	Body/Style Number	Body Type & Seating	Factory Price	Shipping Weight	Prod. Total
223	22337	2-dr HT-5P	2831	3080	75,362
223	22367	2-dr Conv-5P	3045	3330	11,649

TRANS AM

Model Number	Body/Style Number	Body Type & Seating	Factory Price	Shipping Weight	Prod. Total
223	22337	2-dr HT-5P	3556	N/A	689
223	22367	2-dr Conv-5P	3770	N/A	8

NOTE 1: 87,709 Firebirds and Trans Ams were built.

NOTE 2: 20,840 Firebirds and Trans Ams had synchromesh; 66,868 had automatic.

1969 Pontiac Executive four-door sedan. JAG

1969 Pontiac Bonneville Brougham four-door hardtop. OCW

1969 Pontiac GTO "The Judge" two-door hardtop. OCW

1969 Pontiac GTO convertible. OCW

1969 Pontiac GTO convertible (rear view). OCW

1969 Pontiac GTO "The Judge" convertible. OCW

1969 Pontiac Firebird coupe. JAG

1969 Pontiac Firebird convertible. OCW

1969 Pontiac Firebird Trans Am convertible. JAG

1969 Pontiac Firebird Trans Am convertible (rear view). JAG

NOTE 3: 114 Trans Ams had the L-74 RAM AIR III V-8 and Turbo-Hydramatic.

NOTE 4: 520 Trans Ams had the L-74 RAM AIR V-8 and synchro-mesh.

NOTE 5: All eight Trans Am convertibles were L-74s; four had manual gearboxes.

NOTE 6: Nine Trans Ams had the L-67 RAM AIR IV engine and Turbo-Hydramatic.

NOTE 7: 46 Trans Ams had the L-67 RAM AIR IV engine and synchro-mesh.

1969 Pontiac Firebird Trans Am coupe (rear view). JAG

BASE ENGINES

(CATALINA/EXECUTIVE) V-8. Overhead valves. Cast iron block. Displacement: 400 cu. in. Bore & Stroke: 4.13 x 3.75 in. Compression Ratio: 10.5:1. Brake hp: 290 @ 4600 rpm. Five main bearings. Hydraulic valve lifters. Carburetor: Rochester two-barrel. (Note: The 265 hp regular fuel V-8 was a no-cost option on cars with three-speed manual transmission only).

1969 Pontiac Executive four-door hardtop. JAG

(BONNEVILLE) V-8. Overhead valves. Cast iron block. Displacement: 400 cu. in. Bore & Stroke: 4.13 x 3.75 in. Compression Ratio: 10.5:1. Brake hp: 360 @ 4600 rpm. Five main bearings. Hydraulic valve lifters. Carburetor: Rochester four-barrel.

(TEMPEST/CUSTOM/FIREBIRD) OHC six. Overhead valves. Cast iron block. Displacement: 250 cu. in. Bore & Stroke: 3.88 x 3.53 in. Compression Ratio: 9.0:1. Brake hp: 175 @ 4800 rpm. Seven main bearings. Hydraulic valve lifters. Carburetor: Rochester one-barrel.

(GTO) V-8. Overhead valves. Cast iron block. Displacement: 400 cu. in. Bore & Stroke: 4.13 x 3.75 in. Compression Ratio: 10.75:1. Brake hp: 350 @ 5000 rpm. Five main bearings. Hydraulic valve lifters. Carburetor: Rochester four-barrel.

CHASSIS FEATURES: Wheelbase: (Series 252 and all Pontiac station wagons) 122 in.; (Series 256 and 262) 125 in.; (Series 276) 118 in.; (Tempest two-door) 112 in.; (Tempest four-door) 116 in.; (Firebird) 108 in. Overall Length: (All Pontiac station wagons) 220.5 in.; (Series 252) 217.5 in.; (Series 256 and 262) 223.5 in.; (Series 276) 210.2 in.; (All Tempest station wagons) 211 in.; (Tempest two-door) 201.5 in.; (Tempest four-door) 205.5 in.; (Firebird) 191.1 in. Front tread: (Pontiac) 63 in.; (Others) 60 in. Rear tread: (Pontiac) 64 in.; (Others) 60 in.

OPTIONS

[PONTIAC/TEMPEST] Heavy-duty aluminum front brake drums ($72). Load floor carpeting ($53). Console ($56). Cruise control ($58). GTO type exhaust extensions ($21). Instant air heater ($16). Luggage carrier for station wagons ($63-$84). Power rear antenna ($32). Power disc front brakes ($64-$74). Power door locks ($45-$68). Wonder Touch steering ($100-$105). GTO Rally Stripes ($14). GTO retractable headlight covers ($53). Custom Sport steering wheel ($34-$50). Tilt wheel with power steering ($45). Hood mounted tachometer ($63). Cordova top ($100-$142). Rally II wheels ($64-$84). Arctic wiper blades ($6). Station wagon rear window deflector ($26).

Recessed wipers on base Tempest ($19). Leather GP trim ($199). Three-speed manual transmissions were provided at base prices, including a heavy-duty type in Grand Prix. Turbo-Hydramatic $227 extra. Grand Prix buyers had two other options, close or wide-ratio four-speed manual gearboxes, both at $185. The regular fuel V-8 was a no charge option in any line. The Bonneville four-barrel was $38 extra on lower lines. The 375 hp four-barrel 428 cid V-8 was $67-$105 extra on all Pontiacs (except Catalina and Executive station wagons) with price depending on series and transmission. The 390 hp four-barrel 428 cid HO V-8 was $150-$255 extra with the same qualifications. Dual exhaust and Safe-T-Track differential were priced as in 1968. (GTO) Transmission options included Turbo-Hydramatic/Turbo-Hydramatic/Hydramatic ($227) and wide or close-ratio four-speed manual ($185). The 366 hp and 370 hp RAM AIR V-8s were available with the price of RAM AIR IV set at $558. Dual exhausts were standard. Heavy-duty Safe-T-Track was again $63.

[FIREBIRD] Custom air conditioner ($376). Heavy-duty battery ($4). Brake pedal trim package ($5). Electric clock ($16). Console ($54.) Cruise control ($58). Remote control deck lid ($15). Rally gage cluster with tachometer ($84). Rally gauge cluster with clock ($47). Tinted windows ($33). Tinted windshield ($22). Custom stick-shift knob ($5). Leather and Morrokide trim ($199). Remote control outside mirror ($11). Power brakes ($42). Power steering ($105). Left power bucket seat ($74). Power convertible top ($53). Power windows ($105). Wire wheel discs ($53-$74). Rally II wheels ($63-$84). Turnpike cruise option package ($177). Transmission options included two-speed automatic ($174-$185); Turbo-Hydramatic ($195-$227); Three-speed manual with floor shift ($42). Heavy-duty three-speed manual with floor shift ($84) and wide or close-ratio four-speed manual ($185 each). The Sprint option package (Code 342) was $111-$132 and included the 215 hp ohc six, which was not offered separately. The 265 hp two-barrel regular fuel 350 cid V-8 was $11 extra. The 330 hp four-barrel 350 cid HO V-8 was $175 extra. Dual exhausts and Safe-T-Track were priced as in 1968. (FIREBIRD) Transmission options included all offered for Tempests and GTOs. Engine options are listed in Firebird RPO packages section below.

FIREBIRD RPO PACKAGES

FIREBIRD SPRINT PACKAGE: Included three-speed manual transmission with floor shift, ohc six emblems and four F70 x 14 tires (no Sprint stripes). Engine: 250 cid ohc six with 10.5:1 compression, Rochester four-barrel carburetor and 230 hp @ 5400 rpm. Price: $121 over base model cost.

FIREBIRD 350 PACKAGE: Option code 343. Engine code L-30. Included three-speed manual transmission with column shift and F70 x 14 tires. Engine: 350 cid V-8 with 9.2:1 compression, Rochester two-barrel carburetor and 265 hp @ 4600 rpm. Price: $111 over base model cost.

FIREBIRD 350-HO PACKAGE: Option code 344. Engine code L-76. Included three-speed manual transmission with column shift, dual exhausts and heavy-duty battery. Engine: 350 cid V-8 with 10.5:1 compression, Rochester four-barrel carburetor and 325 hp @ 5100 rpm. Price $186 over base model cost.

FIREBIRD 400 PACKAGE: Option code 345. Engine code W-S6. Included chrome engine parts, dual exhausts, heavy-duty battery, three-speed manual transmission with floor shift, F70 x 14 red stripe or whitewall tires and variable pitch cooling fan. Engine: 400 cid V-8 with 10.75:1 compression, Rochester four-barrel carburetor and 330 hp @ 4800 rpm. Special hood is used with non-functional scoops. Ride and handling package required. Price: $275-$358 over base model cost depending on transmission.

FIREBIRD RAM AIR 400 PACKAGE: Option code 348. Engine code L-74. Same inclusions as above, except for addition of de-clutching fan and twin functional hood scoops with operating mechanism. Engine: Same as 1968. Price: $351-$435 over base model cost depending on transmission attachment.

FIREBIRD RAM AIR IV PACKAGE: Option code 347. Engine code L-67. Same equipment inclusions as above, plus special hood scoop emblems. Engine: 400 cid V-8 with special camshaft and valve train, 10.75:1 compression, Rochester four-barrel carburetor and 345 hp @ 5400 rpm. Price: $832 over base model cost. Specific transmissions required.

TRANS AM PACKAGE: Code 322 UPC WS-4. Engine code L-74. Included heavy-duty three-speed manual gearbox with floor shifter: 3.55:1 axle; fiberglass-belted tires; heavy-duty shocks and springs; one-inch stabilizer bar; power front disc brakes; variable ratio power steering; engine air exhaust louvers; rear deck air foil; black textured grille; full-length body stripes; white and blue finish; leather covered steering wheel and special identification decals. Base engine specifications: See 1968 Firebird RAM AIR 400 package listing optional engine package. Price for standard Trans Am: $725 over base model cost.

HISTORICAL FOOTNOTES: Production began August 26, 1968. Introductions took place a month later, except for the Trans Am. It was introduced on March 8, 1969. Calendar year assemblies came to 772,104 cars for a 10.3 percent share of market. This was to be Pontiac's last year as America's third-ranking automaker. The 370 hp GTO

Judge hardtop could do 0-to-60 mph in 6.2 seconds and the quarter-mile in 14.5 seconds. Bonneville Brougham trim group (Code 522) available for convertible ($316) and coupe ($273). Grand Prix 'SJ' option ($316). Rally Group option ($153-$195). Turnpike Cruise package included tilt steering and four-way bench or bucket seat ($177-$208). Ventura package available on all Catalinas except convertible ($105). A short stroke 303 cid tunnel-port V-8 Trans Am engine was used in a small number of Firebirds used exclusively for SCCA Trans Am racing. There were 26,049 full-size Pontiacs with the standard 428 cid engine (360 hp). Also, there were 1820 full-size Pontiacs with the 428 HO engine (390 hp).

1970 PONTIAC

1970 Pontiac Catalina two-door hardtop. OCW

NOTE 1: 193,986 Catalina passenger cars were built.

NOTE 2: 579 Catalina passenger cars had synchromesh; 193,407 had automatic.

NOTE 3: 29,394 Catalina station wagons were built.

NOTE 4: 113 Catalina station wagons had synchromesh and 29,281 had automatic.

EXECUTIVE (V-8) - SERIES 256 - Executives featured all Catalina equipment plus Deluxe wheelcovers, walnut-grained dash and door trim, Morrokide or cloth and Morrokide interiors, rear seat armrests, electric clock and convenience lights. Executive lettering appeared behind the front wheel openings. Station wagons in this line included such extras as woodgrained exterior paneling and full carpeting. The balance of regular trim and equipment features were similar to that seen on Catalinas.

1970 Pontiac Catalina four-door sedan. OCW

CATALINA - (V-8) - SERIES 252 - Radiator grilles inspired by Grand Prix, taillights set into bumpers, hoods with wider and flatter center bulges, hidden radio antennas and wrapover front fender tips characterized 1970 Pontiacs. Catalinas had plain body sill moldings, Catalina or Ventura lettering behind front wheel openings, untrimmed taillights, the word "Pontiac" centered on edge of rear deck, horizontal blade grilles and no fender skirts. Standard in Catalinas were carpeting, upper level ventilation, Endura side moldings, walnut-grained vinyl inserts, padded dashboards and fiberglass blackwall tires. Station wagons had Morrokide upholstery with power tailgate windows included on nine-passenger styles. The Ventura Custom option was available on all Catalinas except convertibles at $105 extra.

PONTIAC I.D. NUMBERS: VIN on top of dash at left, viewable through windshield. First symbols tell GM division: 2=Pontiac. Second and third symbols tell series: 23=Firebird; 24=Espirit; 26=Formula 400; 28=Trans Am; 33=Tempest/T-37; 35=LeMans; 37=LeMans Sport; 42=GTO; 52=Catalina; 56=Executive; 62=Bonneville; 76=Grand Prix. Fourth and fifth symbols indicate body style and appear as last two digits of body/style number in charts below. Sixth symbol indicates model year: 0=1970. Seventh symbol indicates assembly plant: A=Atlanta, Ga.; B=Baltimore, Md.; C=South Gate, Calif.; E=Linden, N.J.; G=Framingham, Mass.; L=Van Nuys, Calif.; N=Norwood, Ohio; P=Pontiac, Mich.; R=Arlington, Texas; X=Kansas City, Kan.; Z=Fremont, Calif.; 1=Oshawa, Ontario, Canada; 2=St. Therese, Quebec, Canada. Remaining symbols are sequential unit production number at factory, starting with 100001. Fisher Body plate on cowl tells style number: (model year prefix 70, plus number in second column of charts below), body number, trim code, paint code and other data. Six-cylinder engine code stamped on distributor mounting on right side of block. V-8 engine code on front of block below right cylinder head. Engine production codes for 1970 were: [250 cid/155 hp six] CG/RF/ZB/ZG. [350 cid/255 hp V-8] WU/YU/W7/X7. [400-cid/265 hp V-8] XX/YB. [400-cid/290 hp V-8] WE/YD. [400-cid/330 hp V-8] WT/YS/XV/XZ. [400-cid/345 hp V-8] WS/YZ. [400-cid/350 hp V-8] WT/WX/YS/YH. [400-cid/366 hp V-8] WS/YZ. [400-cid/370 hp V-8] WW/WH/XP/XN. [455-cid/360 hp V-8] YH. [455-cid/370 hp V-8] WA/WG/YC/YA/XF.

CATALINA (SERIES 252)

Model Number	Body/Style Number	Body Type & Seating	Factory Price	Shipping Weight	Prod. Total
252	25269	4-dr Sed-6P	3164	3997	84,795
252	25239	4-dr HT-6P	3319	4042	35,155
252	25237	2-dr HT-6P	3249	3952	70,350
252	25267	2-dr Conv-6P	3604	4027	3686
252	25246	4-dr Sta Wag-9P	3791	4607	12,450
252	25236	4-dr Sta Wag-6P	3646	4517	16,944

1970 Pontiac Executive four-door sedan. OCW

EXECUTIVE (SERIES 256)

Model Number	Body/Style Number	Body Type & Seating	Factory Price	Shipping Weight	Prod. Total
256	25669	4-dr Sed-6	3538	4087	13,061
256	25639	4-dr HT-6	3669	4132	5376
256	25637	2-dr HT-6	3600	4042	3499
256	25646	4-dr Sta Wag-9	4160	4632	5629
256	25636	4-dr Sta Wag-6	4015	4552	4861

NOTE 1: 21,936 Executive passenger cars were built.

NOTE 2: Six Executive passenger cars had synchromesh and 21,930 had automatic.

NOTE 3: 10,490 Executive station wagons were built.

NOTE 4: Eight Executive wagons had synchromesh and 10,482 had automatic .

BONNEVILLE - (V-8) - SERIES 262 - Die-cast cross-hatched grille inserts and horn ports, creased body still moldings with rear fender extensions, Bonneville front fender lettering, decorative taillight accents and right-hand deck lid edge nameplates characterized Series 262 models outwardly. Standard equipment included all items found on

Executives, plus extra-heavy padded bench seats, special interior trims, illuminated wiper and headlamp switches, fold down front seat armrests, rear armrests with ashtrays, and larger tires. Bonneville station wagons did not have standard exterior paneling, but notch back front seats, folding third seats, courtesy lamps and load area carpeting were included at base price. Brougham trim was optionally available on hardtops and convertibles. The Bonneville Brougham package was available on style numbers 26237 and 26239 and included front foam cushions, power windows, visor vanity mirror, remote control mirror, electric clock, remote control deck lid and heavy-duty air cleaner.

1970 Pontiac Bonneville convertible. OCW

1970 Pontiac Bonneville convertible (rear view). OCW

BONNEVILLE (SERIES 262)

Model Number	Body/Style Number	Body Type & Seating	Factory Price	Shipping Weight	Prod. Total
262	26269	4-dr Sed-6P	3770	4181	3802
262	26239	4-dr HT-6P	3900	4226	44,241
262	26237	2-dr HT-6P	3832	4111	23,418
262	26267	2-dr Conv-6P	4040	4161	3537
262	26246	4-dr Sta Wag-9P	4247	4686	7033

NOTE 1: 75,348 Bonneville passenger cars were built.

NOTE 2: 28 Bonneville passenger cars had synchromesh and 75,320 had automatic.

NOTE 3: 7033 Bonneville station wagons were built.

NOTE 4: Six Bonneville wagons used synchromesh and 7027 had automatic.

1970 Pontiac Grand Prix 'SJ' hardtop coupe, V-8.

GRAND PRIX - (V-8) - SERIES 276 - A minimum of styling changes, such as taillamp revisions and recessed door handles, appeared on 1970 Grand Prix. Series script replaced chrome slash moldings on the rear roof pillar. Standard equipment included dual exhaust, aircraft inspired interiors, front Strato Bucket seats, integral console with floor shift, carpeted lower door panels and trim panels, chrome body decor moldings and special upholstery trims. The 'SJ' option was available again at $223-$244 extra and included 'SJ' badges, lamp group, larger tires and the 455-cubic-inch V-8.

GRAND PRIX (SERIES 276)

Model Number	Body/Style Number	Body Type & Seating	Factory Price	Shipping Weight	Prod. Total
276	27657	2-dr HT Cpe-5P	3985	3784	65,750

NOTE 1: A total of 65,750 Grand Prix were built.

NOTE 2: 500 Grand Prix had synchromesh and 65,250 had automatic.

NOTE 3: Of the cars with synchromesh, 329 had four-speed manual gearboxes.

TEMPEST - (6-CYL) - SERIES 233 - Tempests were given new Firebird-look bumper grilles, wraparound front parking and taillights, crease sculptured side styling and body color nose panels. Standard equipment included front door armrests; panel, ashtray and cigar lighter lamps; 37-amp Delcotrons; dome lamps; automatic interior lamp switches; in-the-windshield hidden antennas; wraparound side reflex markers; cloth and Morrokide interiors; fiberglass belted black-wall tires; and side guard door beams. Tempest lettering was carried behind front wheel openings. In February 1970, the cut-price Tempest T-37 hardtop coupe was introduced. This move was followed by the appearance of a pair of economy type high-performance cars, the GT-37 coupe and GT-37 hardtop coupe.

TEMPEST (SERIES 233)

Model Number	Body/Style Number	Body Type & Seating	Factory Price	Shipping Weight	Prod. Total
233	23369	4-dr Sed-6P	2670	3295	9187
233	23337	2-dr HT-6P	2750	3360	
233	23327	2-dr Cpe-6P	2623	3225	11,977

1970 Pontiac Tempest GT-37 two-door sedan. OCW

1970 Pontiac Tempest GT-37 two-door sedan (rear view). OCW

TEMPEST (MIDYEAR ADDITIONS TO SERIES 233)

T-37	23337	2-dr HT Cpe-6P	2683	3250	20,883
GT-37	23337	2-dr HT Cpe-6P	2920	3360	
GT-37	23327	2-dr Cpe-6P	2907	3300	

NOTE 1: 42,047 Series 233 Tempests were built.

NOTE 2: 5148 had synchromesh and 36,899 had automatic.

NOTE 3: Totals for similar body styles listed above are combined.

NOTE 4: 1419 GT-37 coupes and hardtops (combined) were built.

LEMANS - (6-CYL) - SERIES 235 - LeMans nameplates were now attached to the mid-priced Tempests, which were formerly called Custom models. Added extras included loop pile carpets, Morrokide seats and sides, day/night rearview mirrors and rear armrests with ashtrays. Styling included body decor moldings, LeMans rear fender lettering, four short horizontal chrome slashes behind front wheel openings and LeMans block letters on the right-hand edge of the deck lid.

LEMANS (SERIES 235)

Model Number	Body/Style Number	Body Type & Seating	Factory Price	Shipping Weight	Prod. Total
235	23569	4-dr Sed-6P	2782	3315	15,255
235	23539	4-dr HT-6P	2921	3385	3872
235	23527	2-dr Cpe-6P	2735	3240	5656
235	23537	2-dr HT-6P	2795	3265	52,304
235	23535	4-dr Sta Wag-6P	3092	3585	7165

NOTE 1: 84,252 LeMans were made.

NOTE 2: 2315 LeMans had synchromesh and 81,937 had automatic.

LEMANS SPORT - (6-CYL) - SERIES 237 - The "high rung" Tempest line was now identified as the LeMans Sport series and had a "Sport" script below the rear fender model lettering. Standard equipment included all LeMans features plus glove compartment and ashtray lamps, front foam cushions, knit and expanded Morrokide trim and padded woodgrained dashboards. Four-door hardtops had notch back seats; hardtop coupes and convertibles had bucket seats or notch back bench seats. The LeMans Sport Safari had exterior wood trim.

LEMANS SPORT (SERIES 237)

Model Number	Body/Style Number	Body Type & Seating	Factory Price	Shipping Weight	Prod. Total
237	23739	4-dr HT-6P	3083	3405	3657
237	23727	2-dr Cpe-6P	2891	3265	1673
237	23737	2-dr HT-6P	2953	3290	58,356
237	23767	2-dr Conv-6P	3182	3330	4670
237	23736	4-dr Sta Wag-6P	3328	3775	3872

NOTE 1: 72,179 LeMans Sports were built.

NOTE 2: 3413 LeMans Sports had synchromesh and 68,766 had automatic.

GTO - (V-8) - SERIES 242 - The GTOs utilized Tempest sheet metal combined with a standard Endura rubber nose. Twin oval cavities housed recessed grilles with GTO letters on the left-hand insert. There was also GTO lettering behind the front wheel openings and flared, crease-sculptured fenders. Standard equipment included bucket seats; vinyl trimmed padded dashboard; twin air scoops; heavy-duty clutch; sports type springs and shock absorbers; carpeting; glovebox, ashtray and panel courtesy lamps; dual exhausts; Deluxe steering wheel; three-speed manual floor shift; and G78 x 14 blackwall fiberglass tires. A Code 332-WT1 "The Judge" option was again available at $337 over base model price. It included the 400-cid RAM AIR V-8; Rally II wheels less trim rings; G70 x 14 fiberglass blackwall tires; rear deck air foil; side stripes; Judge stripes and decals; black textured grilles; and T-handle shifters (on cars with manual gearboxes).

1970 Pontiac GTO two-door hardtop coupe, V-8.

GTO (SERIES 242)

Model Number	Body/Style Number	Body Type & Seating	Factory Price	Shipping Weight	Prod. Total
242	24237	2-dr HT-5P	3267	3641	32,737
242	24267	2-dr Conv-5P	3492	3691	3615

GTO (SERIES 242 with WT-1 "THE JUDGE" OPTION)

Model Number	Body/Style Number	Body Type & Seating	Factory Price	Shipping Weight	Prod. Total
242	24237	2-dr HT-5P	3604	N/A	3629
242	24267	2-dr Conv-5P	3829	N/A	168

NOTE 1: 40,149 GTOs and Judges were built in 1970.

NOTE 2: 16,033 GTOs and Judges had synchromesh and 24,116 had automatic.

NOTE 3: 366 hp RAM AIR V-8s in 4356 GTO/Judge hardtops and 288 convertibles.

NOTE 4: 370 hp RAM AIR IV V-8s in 767 GTO/Judge hardtops and 37 convertibles.

BASE FIREBIRD - (6-CYL) - SERIES 223 - Standard equipment on base Firebirds included a 250 cid/155 hp six, E78 -14 black fiberglass tires, front and rear bucket type seats, vinyl upholstery, woodgrained dashboard, carpeting, outside rearview mirror, manual front disc brakes, six-inch wheel rims and door storage pockets. Styling changes included Endura rubber front ends with dual recessed grilles, single headlights, split side marker lamps, enlarged wheel openings, flush door handles and smooth, clean, curvy body panels. Firebird lettering and engine badges appeared behind front wheel cutouts.

BASE FIREBIRD (SERIES 223)

Model Number	Body/Style Number	Body Type & Seating	Factory Price	Shipping Weight	Prod. Total
223	22387	2-dr HT-4P	2875	3140	18,874

NOTE 1: 18,874 base Firebirds were built.

NOTE 2: 2899 base Firebirds had synchromesh and 15,975 had automatic.

NOTE 3: 3134 Firebirds were built with six-cylinder power.

FIREBIRD ESPRIT - (V-8) - SERIES 224 - The Esprit was outwardly identified by model script on the rear roof pillar, bright roof rail and wheel opening moldings, V-8 displacement badges under front fender Firebird lettering, and bird emblems above the grille. Standard equipment included all found on base models, plus knit vinyl upholstery, vinyl-covered Deluxe steering wheel, dual body-color outside sport mirrors, concealed windshield wipers and antenna, trunk floor mats, wheel trim rings, custom trim, decor moldings and a 350-cid two-barrel V-8 with 8.8:1 compression and 255 hp @ 4600 rpm. A three-speed manual gearbox with floor-mounted shift lever was regular equipment.

FIREBIRD ESPRIT (SERIES 224)

Model Number	Body/Style Number	Body Type & Seating	Factory Price	Shipping Weight	Prod. Total
224	22487	2-dr HT-4P	3241	3435	18,961

NOTE 1: A total of 18,961 Firebird Esprits were built.

NOTE 2: 2104 had synchromesh and 16,857 had automatic.

1970 Pontiac Firebird Formula 400 two-door hardtop, V-8.

FIREBIRD FORMULA 400 - (V-8) - SERIES 226 - Standard equipment on Formula 400s included all GM safety features, 1-1/8 inch front and 5/8-inch rear stabilizer bars, high-rate springs, wind-up rear axle controls, F70 x 14 bias-belted blackwall tires, seven-inch wheel rims, manual front disc brakes and rear drums, carpets, vinyl interiors, front and rear bucket type seats, dual outside sport mirrors, concealed wipers and antennas and deluxe steering wheel. Power came from a 400-cid four-barrel V-8 with 10.25:1 compression and 265 hp @ 4600 rpm, which was linked to a three-speed Hurst floor shift. External distinctions included extra-long twin hood scoops and Formula 400 nameplates.

1970 Pontiac Firebird Formula 400 coupe (rear view). OCW

1970 Pontiac Executive four-door station wagon. OCW

1970 Pontiac Executive four-door station wagon (rear view). OCW

1970 Pontiac Tempest LeMans four-door hardtop. OCW

1970 Pontiac Tempest LeMans four-door hardtop (rear view). OCW

1970 Pontiac GTO convertible. OCW

1970 Pontiac GTO convertible (rear view). OCW

1970 Pontiac GTO "The Judge" two-door hardtop. JAG

1970 Pontiac GTO "The Judge" two-door hardtop (rear view). JAG

1970 Pontiac Firebird Trans Am coupe. JAG

1970 Pontiac Tempest LeMans four-door hardtop. OCW

FIREBIRD FORMULA 400 (SERIES 226)

Model Number	Body/Style Number	Body Type & Seating	Factory Price	Shipping Weight	Prod. Total
226	22687	2-dr HT-4P	3370	3470	7708

NOTE 1: 7708 Firebird Formula 400s were built.

NOTE 2: 2777 had synchromesh and 4931 had automatic.

1970 Pontiac Firebird Trans Am coupe (rear view). JAG

TRANS AM - (V-8) - SERIES 228 - Trans Am had all GM safety features, plus front air dams; front and rear spoilers; shaker hood; side air extractors; rear end spoilers; aerodynamically styled outside mirrors with left-hand remote control type; front and rear stabilizers; heavy-duty shock absorbers and springs; engine-turned dash inserts; Rally gauge cluster; concealed wipers; bucket seats; carpets; vinyl upholstery; power brakes and steering; 11-inch wide 15-inch diameter Rally rims; and F60-15 white letter tires. Standard V-8 in the Trans Am was a 335 hp RAM AIR engine. The factory called this the RAM AIR HO. The 400-cid four-barrel V-8 was coded as the L74 engine. It had 10.5:1 compression heads and developed peak power at 5000 rpm. The base transmission was a wide-ratio four-speed manual gearbox with Hurst floor shift. Trans Ams had white or blue finish with contrasting racing stripes.

TRANS AM (SERIES 228)

Model Number	Body/Style Number	Body Type & Seating	Factory Price	Shipping Weight	Prod. Total
228	22887	2-dr HT-5P	4305	3550	3196

NOTE 1: 3196 Trans Ams were built.

NOTE 2: 1769 had synchromesh and 1398 had automatic.

NOTE 3: 3108 Trans Ams were L74s (1339 with automatic; 1769 with manual).

NOTE 4: 88 Trans Ams were LS1s (59 with automatic; 29 with manual).

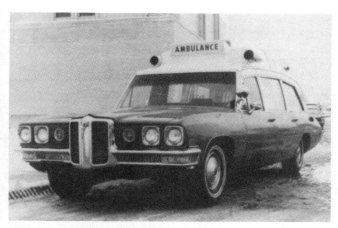

1970 Superior-Pontiac ambulance. JAG

BASE ENGINES

(CATALINA/EXECUTIVE) V-8. (Convertible and station wagon) 400-cid V-8 with two-barrel carburetor, 10.0:1 compression and 290 hp @ 4600 rpm. (Other styles) 350-cid V-8 with two-barrel carburetor, 8.8:1 compression and 255 hp @ 4600 rpm.

(BONNEVILLE) Base V-8s: (Station wagon) 455-cid V-8 with four-barrel carburetor, 10.75:1 compression and 370 hp @ 4600 rpm. (Other styles) 455-cid V-8 with four-barrel carburetor, 10.0:1 compression and 360 hp @ 4300 rpm. This engine had overhead valves, cast iron block, 4.15 x 4.21-in. bore & stroke, five main bearings and hydraulic valve lifters.

(GRAND PRIX) V-8. A 400-cid V-8 with four-barrel carburetor, 10.25:1 compression and 350 hp @ 5000 rpm was standard in Grand Prix. A 455-cid V-8 with four-barrel carburetor, 10.25:1 compression and 370 hp @ 4600 rpm was base V-8 on 'SJ' optioned cars.

(TEMPEST/LEMANS/FIREBIRD) Base six-cylinder: A Chevrolet manufactured 250-cid Six with 8.5:1 compression and 135 hp @ 4600 rpm was standard in all Tempests, but not GTOs. This engine had overhead valves, cast iron block, 3.88 x 3.53-in. bore & stroke, seven main bearings, hydraulic valve lifters and a Rochester Model M or Model MV one-barrel carburetor.

(GTO) V-8. The standard engine in GTOs was the 400-cid four-barrel V-8 with 10.25:1 compression and 350 hp @ 5000 rpm.

CHASSIS FEATURES: Wheelbase: (series 252 and all Pontiac station wagons) 122 in.; (series 256 and 262) 125 in.; (series 276) 118 in.; (Tempest two-door) 112 in.; (Tempest four-door) 116 in.; (Firebird) 108 in. Overall Length: (all Pontiac station wagons) 220.9 in.; (series 252) 217.9 in.; (series 256 and 262) 223.9 in.; (series 276) 210.2 in.; (Tempest station wagons) 210.6 in.; (Tempest two-door) 202.5 in.; (Tempest four-door) 206.5 in.; (GTO) 202.9 in.; (Firebird) 191.6 in. Front tread: (Pontiac) 63 in. (others) 60 in. Rear tread: (Pontiac) 64 in.; (others) 60 in.

OPTIONS

[PONTIAC/GRAND PRIX/TEMPEST] Tempest air conditioning ($376). Pontiac air conditioning ($422). Automatic level control ($79). Auxiliary panel gauges ($21-$79). Cruise control ($63). Rear window defroster ($53). Driver-controlled GTO exhausts ($63). Tinted windshield ($22-$30). Tempest Instant Air ($16). Luggage carrier for station wagons ($63-$84). Left remote-control outside mirror ($11). Tempest wheelhouse moldings ($16). Power brakes ($42-$64). Remote-control deck lid ($15). Power front bucket seat for Tempest and Grand Prix ($73). AM/FM stereo ($239). Rally gauge cluster with tachometer for Tempest and Grand Prix ($84). Safeguard speedometer ($16). Catalina passenger car fender skirts ($37). Grand Prix leather trim ($199). Rally II wheel rims for passenger cars and Tempest station wagons ($63-$84). Base Tempest recessed wipers ($19). Bonneville Brougham trim ($378). Grand Prix 'SJ' group ($223-$244). GTO Judge package ($337). Turnpike Cruise package ($177-$208). Three-speed manual transmissions were provided at base prices, including a heavy-duty type in Grand Prix. Turbo-Hydramatic was $227 extra. Grand Prix had two other options, close- or wide-ratio four-speed manual gearboxes, both at $227 extra. The 400-cid two-barrel regular fuel V-8 (265 hp) was $53 extra in Catalinas with Turbo-Hydramatic. The four-barrel Bonneville V-8 was $47 more in Catalina station wagons, Catalina convertibles or Executives and $100 extra in other Catalinas. The two-barrel premium fuel 400-cid V-8 was $53 extra in Catalina coupes and hardtops. The 455-cid four-barrel V-8 with 10.0:1 compression and 360 hp @ 4300 rpm was $150-$169 extra in Catalinas and Executives with price depending upon transmission. The 455-cid four-barrel high-performance V-8 with 10.25:1 compression and 370 hp @ 4600 rpm was $200-$253 extra in Catalina and Executives, $95 extra in Bonnevilles and $58 extra in Grand Prix without decor packages. (TEMPEST) Transmission options included two-speed automatic on cars with six-cylinder power ($164-$174); Turbo-Hydramatic on V-8s ($227); three-speed manual with heavy-duty floor shift ($84) and wide-ratio four-speed manual ($185). The 255 hp regular fuel 350-cid V-8 with 8.8:1 compression was $111 extra. The 265 hp regular fuel two-barrel 400-cid V-8 with 8.8:1 compression was $53-$163 extra in Tempests, with price depending upon model and transmission. The 400-cid four-barrel V-8 with 10.0:1 compression and 330 hp @ 4800 rpm was $210 extra. Dual exhausts were $31 extra and Safe-T-Track differential was $42-$63 extra. (GTO) Transmission options included Turbo-Hydramatic ($227) and wide- or close-ratio four-speed manual gearboxes ($185). The 366 hp HO V-8 was $169 extra on cars without "The Judge" options. The 370 hp RAM AIR IV engine was $390 extra with "The Judge" and $558 extra on other GTOs. In midyear the 360 hp 455-cid V-8 was added as a third GTO power option. Dual exhausts were standard. Heavy-duty Safe-T-Track was again $63.

[FIREBIRD] Air conditioning ($376). Electric clock ($16). Rally gauge cluster ($47). Rally gauge cluster with tachometer ($95). Cruise control ($58). Rear window defogger ($26). Electric rear window defroster ($53). Tinted glass, all windows ($33). Tinted windshield ($26). Dual horns ($4). Convenience lamps ($12). Dual outside mirrors in body color with left-hand remote-controlled ($26). Decor moldings ($47). Wonder Touch power brakes ($42). Power door locks ($45). Power door and seat back locks ($68). Variable ratio power steering ($105). Stereo tape player ($105). AM/FM push-button radio ($134). AM/FM stereo ($239). Cordova top ($74-$90). Deluxe steering wheel ($16). Formula steering wheel ($42-$58). Tilt steering wheel ($45). Wire wheel discs ($53-$74). Rally II rims ($63-$84). Transmission options

included all offered for Tempests and GTOs. The 350-cid two-barrel V-8 was $111 extra in base Firebirds. The two-barrel regular fuel 400-cid V-8 was $53 extra in Esprits. The L74 RAM AIR V-8 was $169 extra in Formula Firebirds. A mountain ratio performance axle was $17 extra. Safe-T-Track differential was $42 extra.

1970 Superior-Pontiac limousine and funeral car. JAG

HISTORICAL FOOTNOTES: Pontiacs were introduced September 18, 1970, and the all-new second-generation Firebird bowed February 26, 1971. Calendar year output was 422,212 units for sixth place in the sales rankings. The totals were pulled down by a painful UAW strike. James McDonald became the new general manager of Pontiac Motor Division, replacing John Z. DeLorean, who moved to Chevrolet. The 1970 GTO with the 400-cid/366-hp V-8 was capable of 0-to-60 mph in six seconds flat. It did the quarter-mile in 14.6 seconds. The 455-cid/360-hp GTO hardtop registered 6.6 seconds 0-to-60 and a 14.8 second quarter-mile. The Firebird 400 with 330 hp did 0-to-60 mph in 6.4 seconds and covered the quarter-mile in 14.9 seconds. The W55 Turnpike Cruise option included cruise control, tilt steering wheel, and power seats.

1971 PONTIAC

1971 Pontiac Catalina two-door hardtop, V-8.

CATALINA - (V-8) - SERIES 252 - Full-size Pontiacs had all-new styling with "fuselage" bodies, more massive V-shaped split radiator grilles, and dual headlamps set high into the hood line with horizontal grilles below. Standard equipment on Catalinas included integral molded foam front seat cushion and solid foam back, loop-pile carpeting, cloth and Morrokide upholstery on hardtops and sedans and all-Morrokide on convertibles, woodgrained dash accents, Deluxe steering wheel, center flow ventilation, glovebox lamp, dual-action parallel sweep concealed wipers, bright rocker panel moldings, hood rear edge moldings, hub caps, roof drip moldings on hardtops, blackwall tires, power front disc brakes and rear drums. Convertibles had rear quarter interior courtesy lamps. Catalina Safaris had all-Morrokide upholstery, ashtray lamps, vinyl cargo covering, right-hand outside mirror, power tailgate window, disappearing tailgate and L78-15 tires. Nine-passenger styles had forward facing third seats and split back second seats.

PONTIAC I.D. NUMBERS: VIN on top of dash at left, viewable through windshield. First symbol tells GM division: 2=Pontiac. Second and third symbols tell series: 13=Ventura II; 23=Firebird; 24=Esprit; 26=Formula 400; 28=Trans Am; 33=Tempest/T-37; 35=LeMans; 37=LeMans Sport; 42=GTO; 52=Catalina; 58=Catalina Brougham; 62=Bonneville; 68=Grand Ville; 76=Grand Prix. Fourth and fifth symbols indicate body style and appear as last two digits of body/style number in charts below. Sixth symbol indicates model year: 1=1971. Seventh symbol indicates assembly plant: A=Atlanta, Ga.; B=Baltimore, Md.; C=South Gate, Calif.; D=Doraville, Ga.; E=Linden, N.J.; L=Van Nuys, Calif.; N=Norwood, Ohio; P=Pontiac, Mich.; R=Arlington, Texas; X=Kansas City, Kan.; Z=Fremont, Calif.; 1=Oshawa, Ontario, Canada; 2=St. Therese, Quebec, Canada. Remaining symbols are sequential unit production number at factory, starting with 100001. Fisher Body plate on cowl tells style number: (Model year prefix 71, plus number in second column of charts below), body num-

ber, trim code, paint code and other data. Six-cylinder engine code stamped on distributor mounting on right side of block. V-8 engine code on front of block below right cylinder head. Engine production codes for 1971 were: [250-cid/155 hp six] ZB/CAA/ZG/CAB. [307-cid/200 hp V-8] CCA/CCC. [350-cid/250 hp V-8] WR/WU/XU/XR/WN/WP/YN/YP. [400-cid/265 hp V-8] WS/WX/XX/YX. [400-cid/300 hp V-8] WT/WK/YS. [455-cid/280 hp V-8] WG/YG. [455-cid/325 hp V-8] WJ/YC/WL/WC/YE/YA.

1971 Pontiac Catalina two-door hardtop. OCW

1971 Pontiac Catalina two-door hardtop (rear view). OCW

CATALINA (SERIES 252)

Model Number	Body/Style Number	Body Type & Seating	Factory Price	Shipping Weight	Prod. Total
252	25269	4-dr Sed-6P	3421/3770	4033/4077	59,355
252	25239	4-dr HT-6P	3590/3939	4063/4170	22,333
252	25257	2-dr HT-6P	3521/3870	3998/4042	46,257
252	25267	2-dr Conv-6P	3807/4156	4065/4161	2036
252	25235	4-dr Sta Wag-6P	3892/4315	4735/4815	10,322
252	25245	4-dr Sta Wag-9P	4039/4462	4820/4905	9283

NOTE 1: Automatic transmission became standard equipment in March 1971.

NOTE 2: Data above slash applied in fall 1970/below slash, after March.

NOTE 3: 129,983 Catalina passenger cars were built.

NOTE 4: 144 Catalina passenger cars had synchromesh and 129,893 had automatic.

NOTE 5: 19,616 Catalina station wagons were built.

NOTE 6: 30 Catalina station wagons had synchromesh and 19,586 had automatic.

CATALINA BROUGHAM - (V-8) - SERIES 258 - Cars in this entirely new series had the same basic equipment as Catalinas, plus special luxury upholstery, electric clock, Castillian leather appearance instrument panel inserts, ashtray lamps, wheel opening moldings, Deluxe wheelcovers, bright roof drip moldings and rear foam-padded seats on four-door sedans. A Brougham script was placed on the rear roof pillar.

CATALINA BROUGHAM (SERIES 258)

Model Number	Body/Style Number	Body Type & Seating	Factory Price	Shipping Weight	Prod. Total
258	25869	4-dr Sed-6P	3629/4000	4098/4149	6069
258	25839	4-dr HT-6P	3783/4154	4128/4179	9001
258	25857	2-dr HT-6P	3713/4084	4068/4119	8823

NOTE 1: Automatic transmission became standard equipment in March 1971.

NOTE 2: Data above slash applied in fall 1970/below slash, after March.

NOTE 3: 23,892 Catalina Broughams were built.

NOTE 4: Six Catalina Broughams had synchromesh and 23,886 had automatic.

1971 Pontiac Bonneville four-door hardtop. OCW

BONNEVILLE AND GRAND SAFARI - (V-8) - SERIES 262 - Bonnevilles were no longer top line Pontiacs, as a new Grand Ville series was placed even higher and had more standard features. Station wagons in Series 262 used a nameplate that was a mixture of both lines. They were called Grand Safaris. The wagons, however, used the Bonneville engines and series code. Identifying features of Bonnevilles include model nameplates on the left-hand grille and behind the front wheelwells and slanting vertical slashes on the body sill moldings. Bonnevilles had the same basic equipment as Catalinas, plus ashtray, panel courtesy and trunk lamps, pedal trim plates; custom cushion steering wheel; electric clock; wheel well moldings; bright roof drip moldings; H78-15 tires and power steering. The four-door sedan also had foam rear seat padding and side window reveal moldings. Grand Safaris had the same equipment as Catalina station wagons plus fold-down front seat center armrests, carpeted load area, dash panel courtesy lamps, pedal trim plates, electric clocks, custom cushion steering wheels, side window reveal moldings, wheel opening moldings, roof drip moldings, power steering and Deluxe wheelcovers. There were Grand Safari nameplates on the left-hand grille and behind the front wheel cutouts. Woodgrained exterior paneling was optional.

1971 Pontiac Grand Safari station wagon. OCW

BONNEVILLE AND GRAND SAFARI (SERIES 262)

Model Number	Body/Style Number	Body Type & Seating	Factory Price	Shipping Weight	Prod. Total
262	26269	4-dr Sed-6P	3968/4210	4188/4213	6513
262	26239	4-dr HT-6P	4098/4340	4248/4273	16,393
262	26257	2-dr HT-6P	4030/4272	4163/4188	8778
262	26235	4-dr Sta Wag-6P	4401/4643	4843/4855	3613
262	26245	4-dr Sta Wag-9P	4548/4790	4913/4970	5972

NOTE 1: Automatic transmission became standard equipment in March 1971.

NOTE 2: Data above slash applied in fall 1970/below slash, after March.

NOTE 3: 31,879 Bonnevilles were built.

NOTE 4: Four had synchromesh and 31,875 had automatic.

NOTE 5: All Grand Safaris had automatic.

GRAND VILLE - (V-8) - SERIES 268 - Standard equipment on cars in Series 268 was the same as on Bonnevilles, plus Carpathian Elm burl vinyl instrument panel trim, rear door dome lamp switches, roof rail assist grips, formal roofline, belt reveal moldings and four-barrel V-8 power. The convertible and the hardtop coupe had notch back bench seats and the former model also featured two rear quarter interior lamps. Several appearance distinctions such as cross-hatched grille inserts and dual stacked horizontal taillights were shared with Bonnevilles. Grand Villes, however, did not have slash louvers on body sill moldings and used "Grand Ville" lettering on the left-hand grille and behind front fender cutouts.

1971 Pontiac Grand Ville four-door hardtop. OCW

GRAND VILLE (SERIES 268)

Model Number	Body/Style Number	Body Type & Seating	Factory Price	Shipping Weight	Prod. Total
268	26849	4-dr HT-6P	4324/4566	4278/4303	30,524
268	26847	2-dr HT-6P	4255/4497	4198/4223	14,017
268	26867	2-dr Conv-6P	4464/4706	4240/4266	1784

NOTE 1: Automatic transmission became standard equipment in March 1971.

NOTE 2: Data above slash applied in fall 1970/below slash, after March.

NOTE 3: 46,330 Grand Villes were built.

NOTE 4: Two had synchromesh and 46,328 had automatic.

NOTE 5: 194 Grand Ville chassis were supplied to professional car makers.

1971 Pontiac Grand Prix two-door hardtop, V-8.

GRAND PRIX - (V-8) - SERIES 276 - Grand Prix now had single headlamps (still in square housings), a bumper running across the grille and an attractive looking semi-boattail rear end. Model script plates decorated the left-hand front panel, the roof pillars and the right-hand edge of the deck lid. Buyers had a choice of notch back bench or bucket seats at the same price. Standard equipment included right-hand front door armrest ashtray; carpeted lower door panels; safety armrests with ashtrays; loop-pile carpets; foam seat padding; pedal trim plates; custom cushion steering wheel; Castillian leather appearance dash trim; upper level ventilation; courtesy and glovebox lamps; concealed wipers; wheel opening, roof drip, belt reveal and hood rear edge moldings; Deluxe wheelcovers; power flex cooling fan; power steering; power brakes (with front discs); seven-inch wide safety wheel rims; G78-14 blackwall tires and center console on cars with bucket seats. The 'SJ' option package was priced $195 extra. This option (code 324) included 455-cid four-barrel V-8, Rally gauge cluster, luggage lamp, body color outside mirrors (left-hand remote control), vinyl pin stripes, 'SJ' emblems and Delco X battery. A limited-edition Hurst SSJ Grand Prix was marketed.

GRAND PRIX (SERIES 276)

Model	Body/Style	Body Type	Factory Price	Shipping Weight	Prod. Total
276	27657	2-dr HT-5P	4314/4557	3838/3863	58,325

NOTE 1: Automatic transmission became standard equipment in March 1971.

NOTE 2: Data above slash applied in fall 1970/below slash, after March.

NOTE 3: 58,325 Grand Prix were built.

NOTE 4: 116 had synchromesh and 58,208 had automatic.

LEMANS T-37 - (6 CYL) - SERIES 233 - Revisions to Pontiac intermediates included new model names, new series designations, redesigned grilles and reworked GTO nose and hood. Pontiac T-37 lettering was seen behind the front wheelwells of the lowest priced models. Standard equipment included cloth and Morrokide bench seats, vinyl floor covering, Deluxe steering wheel, upper level ventilation in hardtops, black grained instrument panel, door operated dome lamp switches, conventional roof drip moldings, windshield and rear window reveal moldings, dual-action parallel sweep wipers, front disc brakes and E78-14 black wall tires. Pillared coupes and sedans also had chrome edged ventiplanes. The GT-37 was available again and was advertised as "The GTO For Kids Under 30." This option (code 334) was offered in just two hardtop versions. It included vinyl accent stripes, Rally II wheels (less trim rings), G70-14 tires (white-lettered), dual exhausts with chrome extensions, heavy-duty three-speed manual transmission with floor shift, body-colored outside mirrors (left-hand remote control), hood locking pins, and GT-37 nameplates. It was designed to provide buyers with a low-cost high-performance option.

1971 Pontiac GT-37 two-door hardtop. OCW

1971 Pontiac GT-37 two-door hardtop (rear view). OCW

T-37 (SERIES 233)

Model Number	Body/Style Number	Body Type & Seating	Factory Price	Shipping Weight	Prod. Total
233	23327	2-dr Sed-6P	2747/2868	3189/3445	7184
233	23369	4-dr Sed-6P	2795/2916	3219/3475	8336
233	23337	2-dr HT-6P	2807/2928	3194/3450	29,466

NOTE 1: Data above slash for six/below slash for V-8.

NOTE 2: 44,986 T-37s were built.

NOTE 3: 5525 T-37s had synchromesh and 39,461 had automatic.

NOTE 4: A combined total of 5802 GT-37s built as 1971 and 1971-1/2 models.

LEMANS (6-CYL) - SERIES 235 - LeMans models had the word "Pontiac" on the left-hand grille and carried vertical slash louvers behind the wheelwells and LeMans lettering behind the rear fender crease lines. Extra features on LeMans included richer upholstery, loop-pile carpets, safety rear armrests with integral ashtrays, woodgrained dash, concealed wipers, rocker panel moldings, hood rear edge moldings, side window reveals on coupes and vent windows on four-door styles. Station wagons had two-way tailgates and power front disc brakes.

LEMANS (SERIES 235)

Model Number	Body/Style Number	Body Type & Seating	Factory Price	Shipping Weight	Prod. Total
235	23527	2-dr Sed-6P	2877/2998	3199/3455	2734
235	23569	4-dr Sed-6P	2025/3046	3229/3485	11,979
235	23539	4-dr HT-6P	3064/3185	3314/3570	3186
235	23537	2-dr HT-6P	2938/3059	3199/3455	40,966
235	23536	4-dr Sta Wag-6P	3353/3474	3765/3995	6311
235	23546	4-dr Sta Wag-9P	3465/3586	3825/4045	4363

NOTE 1: Data above slash for six/below slash for V-8.

NOTE 2: 69,179 LeMans were built.

NOTE 3: 1231 LeMans had synchromesh and 67,948 had automatic.

LEMANS SPORT - (6-CYL) - SERIES 237 - Standard equipment in LeMans Sport models included all items found in LeMans models plus dual horns, pedal trim plates, ashtray and glovebox lamps, courtesy lamps on convertibles, carpeted lower door panels, custom cushion steering wheel and wheelwell moldings. Buyers of two-door hardtops and convertibles had a choice of knit vinyl bucket seats or notch bench seats and the four-door hardtop used knit vinyl bench seats. LeMans Sport model nameplates were seen on the sides of rear fenders. GTO type Endura rubber noses were a $74 styling option for all LeMans Sport models including station wagons. This front end was also marketed as part of the code 602 LeMans Sport Endura styling option including GTO hood, GTO Endura bumper, and GTO headlamp assembly.

LEMANS SPORT (SERIES 237)

Model Number	Body/Style Number	Body Type & Seating	Factory Price	Shipping Weight	Prod. Total
237	23739	4-dr Spt HT-6P	3255/3376	3314/3570	2451
237	23737	2-dr Spt HT-6P	3125/3246	3199/3455	34,625
237	23767	2-dr Spt Conv-6P	3359/3480	3289/3545	3865

NOTE 1: Data above slash for six/below slash for V-8.

NOTE 2: 40,941 LeMans Sports were built.

NOTE 3: 1229 had synchromesh and 39,712 had automatic.

GTO - (V-8) - SERIES 242 - A new Endura nose piece identified the 1971 GTO. It had larger twin grille cavities, round parking lamps and integral body colored bumpers. Other characteristics included twin air slots at the front of the hood and GTO lettering on left-hand grille, front fendersides and right-hand edge of the deck lid. Standard equipment included all items found on LeMans models plus engine-turned aluminum dash inserts, dual exhausts with extensions through valance panel, power-flex cooling fan, heavy-duty stabilizer bars, shock absorbers and springs and G70-14 blackwall tires. For $395 extra "The Judge" option was available. This option (code 332) included 455-cid four-barrel HO V-8, Rally II wheels (less trim rings), hood air inlet system, T-handle gear shift control (with manual transmission), rear deck lid air foil, specific side stripes, "The Judge" decals, RAM AIR decals, and black-textured grille.

1971 Pontiac GTO convertible. OCW

GTO (SERIES 242)

Model Number	Body/Style Number	Body Type & Seating	Factory Price	Shipping Weight	Prod. Total
242	24237	2-dr HT-5P	3446	3619	9497
242	24267	2-dr Conv-5P	3676	3664	661

1971 Pontiac GTO "The Judge" with 455 HO V-8. OCW

1971 Pontiac GTO "The Judge" with 455 HO V-8 (rear view). OCW

GTO (WITH "THE JUDGE" OPTION)

Model Number	Body/Style Number	Body Type & Seating	Factory Price	Shipping Weight	Prod. Total
242	24237	2-dr HT-5P	3840	N/A	357
242	24267	2-dr Conv-5P	4070	N/A	17

NOTE 1: A total of 10,532 GTOs were built.

NOTE 2: 2287 had synchromesh and 7945 had automatic.

BASE FIREBIRD - (6-CYL) - SERIES 223 - Styling changes for 1971 Firebirds were of the minor variety. High-back seats were used, new wheelcovers appeared and all models, except Trans Ams, had simulated louvers behind the front wheel cutouts. Standard equipment on the basic Firebird included vinyl bucket seats, woodgrained dash, deluxe steering wheel, Endura front bumper, bright grille moldings, standard hubcaps, narrow rocker panel moldings, front disc brakes and E78-14 tires. Base engine was the 145 hp 250-cid Six.

BASE FIREBIRD (SERIES 223)

Model Number	Body/Style Number	Body Type & Seating	Factory Price	Shipping Weight	Prod. Total
223	22387	2-dr HT-4P	3047	3164	23,021

NOTE 1: 23,022 base Firebirds were built.

NOTE 2: 2778 base Firebirds had synchromesh and 20,244 had automatic.

NOTE 3: 2975 base Firebirds were built with six-cylinder powerplants.

FIREBIRD ESPRIT - (V-8) - SERIES 224 - Esprits included custom trim features with knit vinyl upholstery, custom cushion steering wheel, trunk mat, bright roof drip moldings, wheel opening moldings, concealed wipers, twin body-colored outside mirrors, wheel trim rings and dual horns as standard extras. Power was supplied by the two-barrel 350-cid V-8 with 8.0:1 compression and 250 hp @ 4400 rpm. A floor-mounted three-speed manual transmission was the standard gearbox.

FIREBIRD ESPRIT (SERIES 224)

Model Number	Body/Style Number	Body Type & Seating	Factory Price	Shipping Weight	Prod. Total
224	22487	2-dr HT-4P	3416	3423	20,185

NOTE 1: 20,185 Firebird Esprits were built.

NOTE 2: 947 Firebird Esprits had synchromesh and 19,238 had automatic.

1971 Pontiac Firebird Formula 400 two-door hardtop. OCW

FIREBIRD FORMULA - (V-8) - SERIES 226 - Standard equipment on Formula Firebirds included vinyl bucket seats, custom cushion steering wheel, flame chestnut woodgrain appearance dash panel, right and left body-colored outside mirrors, (left-hand remote-controlled), Endura rubber front bumper, fiberglass hood with simulated twin air scoops, black-textured grille insert, bright grille moldings, dual horns, front disc brakes, handling package, dual exhausts with chrome extensions and the heavy-duty three-speed manual transmission. Also featured were standard hubcaps, F70-14 blackwall tires and Formula 350 or 400 or 455 identification numbering. Engine choices were the two-barrel 350-cid V-8, the four-barrel 400-cid V-8 or the four-barrel 455-cid V-8.

FIREBIRD FORMULA (SERIES 226)

Model Number	Body/Style Number	Body Type & Seating	Factory Price	Shipping Weight	Prod. Total
226	22687	2-dr HT-4P	3445	3473	7802

NOTE 1: 7802 Formula Firebirds were built.

NOTE 2: 1860 Formula Firebirds had synchromesh and 5942 had automatic.

NOTE 3: Data shown for "Formula 350."

NOTE 4: "Formula 400" was $100 extra; "Formula 455" was $158 extra.

1971 Pontiac Trans Am two-door hardtop sports coupe, V-8

TRANS AM - (V-8) - SERIES 228 - Standard equipment on Trans Ams included vinyl bucket seats, Rally gauges (with clock and tachometer), Endura front bumper, Formula steering wheel, twin body-color outside mirrors (left-hand remote control), special honeycomb wheels, functional front fender air extractors, rear deck lid spoiler, black textured grille insert, bright grille moldings, front and rear wheel opening air spoilers, concealed wipers, Trans Am identification markings, performance dual exhausts with extensions, special air cleaner with rear-facing cold air intake on hood controlled by throttle, power flex cooling fan, power steering, Safe-T-Track differential, handling package, dual horns, power brakes with discs in front and drums at rear and F60-15 white lettered tires. The RPO LS5 455 HO engine with four-barrel carburetion, 8.4:1 compression and 335 hp @ 4800 rpm was standard in all Trans Ams, as was a heavy-duty three-speed manual gearbox with floor shifter.

TRANS AM SERIES 228)

Model Number	Body/Style Number	Body Type & Seating	Factory Price	Shipping Weight	Prod. Total
228	22887	2-dr HT-4	4594	3578	2116

NOTE 1: 2116 Trans Ams were built.

NOTE 2: 885 Trans Ams had synchromesh and 1231 had automatic.

VENTURA II - (6 CYL) - SERIES 213 - The Ventura II line was introduced on March 11, 1970, as an addition to the Pontiac family. It was based on the compact-sized Chevy II Nova with wider taillamp lenses and split, twin-slot type grille. Standard equipment included all required safety features plus heater and defroster, outside rearview mirror, cloth and Morrokide upholstery, foam front seat padding, woodgrained dashboard accents, padded Morrokide door panels with woodgrained trim inserts and E78 x 14 tires. The 250-cid six-cylinder 145 hp engine was base powerplant. The Ventura Sprint option code 322) included three-speed manual transmission with floor shift, wheel trim rings, left-hand remote control color-keyed mirrors, custom carpets, custom sport steering wheel, blacked-out grille, side striping, 14 x 6-inch rims and THR E78-14 whitewall tires.

VENTURA II (SERIES 213)

Model Number	Body/Style Number	Body Type & Seating	Factory Price	Shipping Weight	Prod. Total
213	21327	2-dr Cpe-5P	2458	2934	34,681
213	21369	4-dr Sed-5P	2488	2983	13,803

NOTE 1: 48,484 Ventura IIs were built.

NOTE 2: 8542 Ventura IIs had synchromesh and 39,942 had automatic.

BASE ENGINES

(CATALINA) Base engine for all Catalinas was the 350-cid two-barrel V-8 with 8.0:1 compression and 250 hp @ 4400 rpm.

(CATALINA SAFARI/CATALINA BROUGHAM) Base engine for all Catalina Broughams was the 400-cid two-barrel V-8 with 8.2:1 compression and 265 hp @ 4400 rpm.

(BONNEVILLE/GRAND SAFARI) Base V-8 for cars and station wagons in Series 262 was the 455-cid V-8 with 8.2:1 compression and 280 hp @ 4400 rpm.

(GRAND VILLE) Base engine for Grand Villes was the 455-cid four-barrel V-8 with 8.2:1 compression and 325-hp @ 4400 rpm. This was the only Grand Ville engine.

1971 Pontiac Hurst SSJ Grand Prix coupe with Linda Vaughn. OCW

(GRAND PRIX) Base engine for Grand Prix was the 400-cid four-barrel V-8 with 8.2:1 compression and 300 hp @ 4800 rpm. The 455-cid V-8 used in Grand Villes was standard in the Grand Prix 'SJ' and optional on base Grand Prix.

(T-37/LEMANS/LEMANS SPORT/FIREBIRD/VENTURA II SIX) Base engine for six-cylinder T-37s was the 250-cid Chevrolet-built powerplant with a one-barrel carburetor, 8.5:1 compression and 145 hp @ 4200 rpm.

(T-37/LEMANS/LEMANS SPORT/FIREBIRD V-8) Base engines for eight-cylinder T-37s was the 350-cid V-8 with a two-barrel carburetor, 8.0:1 compression and 250 hp @ 4400 rpm.

(GTO) Base V-8 on GTOs was the four-barrel, 400-cid engine with 8.2:1 compression and 300 hp @ 4800 rpm.

(GTO "THE JUDGE") The 335 hp four-barrel 455-cid HO V-8 was standard on cars with "The Judge" option.

OPTIONAL V-8 ENGINES

350-cid. Compression ratio: 8:1. Carburetion: two-barrel. Brake hp: 250 @ 4400 rpm. (standard in Firebird Esprit and Catalina; optional in LeMans).

400-cid. Compression ratio: 8.2:1. Carburetion: four-barrel. Brake hp: 300 @ 4800 rpm. (standard in GTO).

400-cid. Compression ratio: 8.2:1. Carburetion: four-barrel. Brake hp: 300 @ 4800 rpm. (standard in Grand Prix/Firebird Formula 400; optional in LeMans/Catalina).

455-cid. Compression ratio: 8.2:1. Carburetion: two-barrel. Brake hp: 280 @ 4400 rpm. (standard in Bonneville; optional in Catalina).

455-cid. Compression ratio: 8.2:1. Carburetion: four-barrel. Brake hp: 325 @ 4400 rpm. (standard in Grand Ville; optional in Firebird Formula 455/LeMans/GTO/Catalina/Bonneville).

455-cid. Compression ratio: 8.4:1. Carburetion: four-barrel. Brake hp: 335 @ 4800 rpm. (standard on Trans Am; optional in GTO/LeMans).

CHASSIS FEATURES: Wheelbase: (All Pontiac station wagons) 127 in.; (Series 252 and 258) 123.5 in.; (Series 262 and 268) 126 in.; (Grand Prix) 118 in.; (Ventura) 111 in.; (Others) Same as 1970. Overall Length: (All Pontiac station wagons): 230.2 in.; (Series 252 and 258) 220.2 in.; (Series 262 and 268) 224.2 in.; (Grand Prix) 212.9 in.; (Tempest station wagons) 210.9 in.; (Tempest two-doors) 202.3 in.; (Tempest four-doors) 206.8 in.; (Firebird) 191.6 in.; (Ventura) 194.5 in.

OPTIONS

[PONTIAC/GRAND PRIX]: Automatic air conditioning ($521). Automatic level control ($79). Luggage carrier ($84). Electric clock ($18). Cruise control ($68). All tinted glass ($51). Tinted windshield ($36). Bumper guards ($16). Cornering lights ($37). Grand Prix power bucket seats ($79). 60/40 Bench seat with six-way power adjustments ($79). AM/FM stereo and tape system ($373). Pontiac station wagon and GP cordova tops ($142). Cordova top on other Pontiacs ($119). Grand Prix wire wheel discs ($58). Rally II wheels ($63-$90). Custom Grand Ville trim group ($132-$237). Grand Prix 'SJ' option ($195).

[TEMPEST/FIREBIRD]: Manual air conditioning ($408). T-37 custom carpets ($21). Firebird rear console ($26). Firebird, GTO and LeMans Sport front seat console ($60-$61). Cruise control ($63). All tinted glass ($38). Tinted windshield ($31). Bumper guards ($16). Formula and GTO air inlet hood ($84). Body-colored mirrors with left-hand remote controlled ($26). Firebird power brakes ($47). LeMans front disc brakes ($70). Wonder Touch brakes ($47). Tape player and stereo

cassette ($134). Firebird Rally gauge cluster with tachometer and clock ($95). Firebird Formula rear deck spoiler ($33). Vinyl side stripes for two-door LeMans or GP ($31-$63). Tilt steering wheel with power steering required ($45). Formula steering wheel ($42). Hood-mounted tachometer on LeMans ($63). Firebird cordova top ($74-$90). LeMans cordova top ($100). Firebird and LeMans wire wheel discs ($84). Rally II wheels ($90). Honeycomb styled wheels on T-37 ($63); on other LeMans and Firebirds ($100-$126). LeMans Sport Endura styling option ($74). T-37 hardtop coupe 'GT' option ($237). "The Judge" option ($395). Code 331 Firebird ride & handling package ($205) included honeycomb wheels, F60-15 white-lettered fiberglass tires, Trans Am front and rear stabilizer bars and Trans Am rear springs.

[VENTURA II]: Manual air conditioner ($392). Custom carpets ($21). Front seat console ($59). Rear window defogger ($32). Left-hand remote control mirror ($26). Disc front brakes ($70). Wonder Touch brakes ($47). Power steering ($103). Custom cushion steering wheel ($16). Sun roof ($184). Rally II wheels ($63). Chrome wheel trim rings ($26). Custom bucket seat group ($242). Sprint option package ($233-$254).

[MIXED POWER TRAIN OPTIONS] The 350-cid two-barrel V-8 was $121 extra in base Firebirds, T-37s and LeMans. The 400-cid two-barrel V-8 was $53 extra in Esprits and Catalinas and $174 extra in T-37 and LeMans. The 400-cid four-barrel V-8 was $100 extra in Formulas and Catalinas, $221 extra in all T-37s and LeMans (except standard in GTO) and $47 extra in Catalina Broughams. The 455-cid two-barrel V-8 was $58 extra in Catalina Broughams and $111 extra in Catalinas. The 455-cid four-barrel V-8 was $47 extra in Bonnevilles, $58 extra in GTO and Grand Prix, $105 extra in Catalina Broughams and $158 extra in Catalinas. The 455-cid HO engine was standard in Trans Ams and "The Judge", $137 extra in other GTOs, $237 extra in Formula Firebirds and $358 extra in T-37 and LeMans coupes and convertibles. In most cases, specific transmissions were required with the above powertrain options. Dual exhausts were $41 extra. Safe-T-Track differential was $46 extra. Heavy-duty Safe-T-Track differential was $67 extra. Special order, performance and economy rear axles were each $11 extra. Heavy-duty batteries were $11 extra and Delco X maintenance free batteries were $26 extra. Optional in Ventura was a 307-cid Chevrolet V-8 with two-barrel carburetion, 8.5:1 compression and 200 hp @ 4600 rpm.

HISTORICAL FOOTNOTES: Production of the 1971 models started August 10, 1970, and the Ventura II was added to the line March 11, 1971. Model year production was 586,856 cars. Calendar year output was 728,615 cars for a 7.4 percent market share and number three ranking in the industry. A special Hurst SSJ Grand Prix was marketed this year. These cars were built in conjunction with Hurst Performance Products Co. Pontiac opened a 48,000 square foot emissions and testing laboratory and did a 100,000 square foot assembly plant expansion.

1972 PONTIAC

CATALINA - (V-8) - SERIES 2L - New energy-absorbing bumpers, redesigned radiator styled grilles, and revised taillamp treatments characterized full-size Pontiacs for 1972. Catalinas featured front fender model lettering, horizontal blade grilles and single deck taillamps with chrome outlined quadrants. Standard equipment included solid foam front seat cushions with integral springs, solid foam front seat backs, nylon carpets, center-flow ventilation, front ashtrays, teakwood dash trim, ashtray and glovebox lamps, trunk mat, concealed wipers and windshield radio antennas. Other features included bright roof gutter moldings (on most models), hood rear edge moldings, power steering, power brakes with front discs and G78-15 blackwall tires. Closed body styles were upholstered in cloth and Morrokide. Convertibles featured all-Morrokide trims, twin rear quarter interior lamps and power tops with glass rear windows. Catalina Safaris also had all-Morrokide seats, Deluxe steering wheel, vinyl load floor coverings, L78-15 tires and power tailgate windows on nine-passenger jobs. All full-size Pontiacs had V-8 power and Turbo-Hydramatic transmission.

PONTIAC I.D. NUMBERS: The serial numbering system was changed slightly this year. The first symbol was again the GM divisional code, using a '2' for Pontiacs. The second symbol was alphabetical, using letters to indicate series as follows: (Y) for Ventura; (S) for basic Firebird; (T) for Firebird Esprit; (U) for Formula Firebird; (V) for Trans Am; (D) for LeMans; (G) for Luxury LeMans; (L) for Catalina; (M) for Catalina Brougham; (N) for Bonneville; (P) for Grand Ville and (K) for Grand Prix. The third and fourth symbols indicated the body style. The fifth symbol was a new numerical engine code as follows: VIN on top of dash at left, viewable through windshield. First symbol tells GM division: 2=Pontiac. Second symbol tells series: Y=Ventura II; S=Firebird; T=Esprit; U=Formula 400; V=Trans Am; D=LeMans; G=Luxury LeMans; K=Grand Prix; L=Catalina; M=Catalina Brougham; N=Bonneville; P=Grand Ville. Third and fourth symbols indicate body style

and appear as last two letters of Body/Style Number in charts below. Fifth symbol indicates engine (See chart at beginning of "Engines" section below.) Sixth symbol indicates model year: 2=1972. Seventh symbol indicates assembly plant: A=Atlanta, Ga.; C=South Gate, Calif.; D=Doraville, Ga.; G=Framingham, Mass.; L=Van Nuys, Calif.; N=Norwood, Ohio; P=Pontiac, Mich.; W=Willow Run, Mich.; X=Kansas City, Kan.; Z=Fremont, Calif.; 2=St. Therese, Quebec, Canada. Remaining symbols are sequential unit production number at factory, starting with 100001. Fisher Body plate on cowl tells style number: (model year prefix 72, plus (this year only) 1971 type body/style number codes, body number, trim code, paint code and other data. Six-cylinder engine code stamped on distributor mounting on right side of block. V-8 engine code on front of block below right cylinder head. Engine production codes for 1972 were: [250-cid/110 nhp six] W6/CBJ/Y6/CBG/CBA/CBC [307-cid/130 nhp V-8] CKG/CAY/CKH/CAZ/CTK/CMA. [350-cid/160 nhp V-8] WR/YU/YV/YR. [400-cid/180 nhp V-8] YX/ZX. [400-cid/200 nhp] WS/WK/YS/ZS. [400-cid/250 nhp] YY. [455-cid/190 nhp] YH/ZH. [455-cid/220 nhp] YC/YA. [455-cid/300 nhp] YB/YE. [455-cid/210 nhp] n.a. [455-cid/240 nhp] n.a. [455-cid/200 nhp] U.

1972 Pontiac Catalina two-door hardtop. OCW

CATALINA (2L SERIES)

Model Number	Body/Style Number	Body Type & Seating	Factory Price	Shipping Weight	Prod. Total
2L	2L69	4-dr Sed-6p	3713	4154	83,004
2L	2L39	4-dr HT-6P	3874	4179	28,010
2L	2L57	2-dr HT-6P	3808	4129	60,233
2L	2L67	2-dr Conv-6P	4080	4204	2399
2L	2L35	4-dr Sta Wag-6P	4232	4743	14,536
21	2L45	4-dr Sta-Wag-9P	4372	4818	12,766

CATALINA BROUGHAM - (V-8) - SERIES 2M - Broughams had the same features as L Series Catalinas plus special interior trim, carpeted lower door panels, custom cushion steering wheel, electric clock, Deluxe wheelcovers and door handles with body-color inserts. Chrome signatures were seen on the roof pillar to identify Broughams externally. They used the same horizontal blade grille and single deck taillamps as Catalinas.

CATALINA BROUGHAM (2M SERIES)

Model Number	Body/Style Number	Body Type & Seating	Factory Price	Shipping Weight	Prod. Total
2M	2M69	4-dr Sed-6p	3916	4188	8007
2M	2M39	4-dr HT-6P	4062	4238	8762
2M	2M57	2-dr HT Cpe-6P	3996	4158	10,545

1972 Pontiac Bonneville two-door hardtop. OCW

BONNEVILLE (V-8) - SERIES 2N - Bonnevilles had single deck taillights with chrome outline quadrants like Catalinas, but cross-hatched grille inserts like Grand Villes. Bonneville lettering appeared on the left-hand grille, behind the front wheel openings and between the taillights. The standard equipment list was the same as the Catalina Brougham's, plus dash panel courtesy and trunk lamps, trunk compartment sidewall panels, formal roofline, bright metal window reveal moldings on four-door sedan and H78-15 blackwall tires. Bonneville Grand Safaris had the same equipment as Catalina station wagons, plus bench seats with center armrests, carpeted lower door panels and cargo area, custom cushion steering wheel, electric clock, dash panel courtesy lamps and Deluxe wheelcovers.

BONNEVILLE (2N SERIES)

Model Number	Body/Style Number	Body Type & Seating	Factory Price	Shipping Weight	Prod. Total
2N	2N69	4-dr Sed-6P	4169	4288	9704
2N	2N39	4-dr HT-6P	4293	4388	15,806
2N	2N57	2-dr HT Cpe-6P	4228	4238	10,568
2N	2N35	4-dr Sta Wag-6p	4581	4918	5675
2N	2N45	4-dr Sta Wag-9P	4721	4938	8540

GRAND VILLE - (V-8) - SERIES 2P - Grand Villes featured Bonneville type cross-hatched grilles and distinctive twin-deck slotted taillights. There was model identification lettering on the left-hand grille, behind the front wheel openings and between the taillights. Standard equipment consisted of all items found on Bonnevilles, plus bench seats with folding center armrests (or notchback bench seats with center armrests), lighted front ashtrays and, on convertibles, two rear quarter interior lamps and power operated tops with glass windows.

1972 Pontiac Grand Ville four-door hardtop. OCW

GRAND VILLE (2P SERIES)

Model Number	Body/Style Number	Body Type & Seating	Factory Price	Shipping Weight	Prod. Total
2P	2P49	4-dr HT-6P	4507	4378	41,346
2P	2P47	2-dr HT Cpe-6P	4442	4263	19,852
2P	2P67	2-dr Conv-6P	4640	4333	2213

1972 Pontiac Grand Prix two-door hardtop coupe, V-8.

GRAND PRIX - (V-8) - SERIES 2K - Grand Prix featured high-intensity single headlamps, new cross-hatched grilles, model identification signature scripts and semi-boattail rear deck styling with triple-lens horizontal taillights. Buyers had a choice of bucket or notch back front bench seats. Standard equipment included carpeting; carpeted lower door panels; a console and floor shift (with bucket seats); custom cushion steering wheel; upper level ventilation; electric clock; front ashtrays; teakwood dash trim; ashtray, dash panel and courtesy lamps;

trunk compartment side panels; Deluxe wheelcovers; concealed wipers; windshield antenna; and moldings for roof gutters, windshield, rear window, window sills, hood rear edge, wheel openings and rocker panels. Other regular features included power steering, power brakes with front discs, power-flex cooling fan, dual exhausts and G78-14 blackwall tires. The 'SJ' option package was again available and included a big V-8, body color outside mirrors, vinyl pin stripes, luggage and door courtesy lamps, and a Rally gauge cluster. All Grand Prix had automatic transmission. The code 332 Grand Prix 'SJ' option included the 455-cid four-barrel V-8, body-color outside mirrors (left-hand remote control), vinyl accent stripes, luggage and door courtesy lamps, Delco X battery and Rally gauge cluster.

GRAND PRIX (SERIES 2K)

Model Number	Body/Style Number	Body Type & Seating	Factory Price	Shipping Weight	Prod. Total
2K	2K57	2-dr HT-5P	4472	3898	91,961

BASE LEMANS - (6-CYL) - SERIES 2D - Standard equipment included bench seats with cloth and Morrokide trim; front and rear foam seats; rear ashtrays in armrests (except coupe); loop-pile carpets (except coupe); Deluxe steering wheel; upper level ventilation (hardtop coupe); teakwood dash accents; windshield radio antenna; concealed wipers (except coupe); ventipanes (except hardtop coupe); chrome valance panel; and bright moldings on the roof gutters, windshield, rear window and body sills of most styles. Station wagons had all-Morrokide seats, under floor cargo compartments, vinyl cargo floor coverings, two-way tailgates with built-in steps, power brakes with front discs and power tailgate windows on nine-passenger jobs. Standard tires were H78-14 size on Safaris and F78-14 size on other styles. The WW-4 option was available on LeMans Style Numbers 2027 and 2037 and included a 400-cid four-barrel V-8, four-speed manual transmission with floor shift, heavy-duty Safe-T-Track differential, front power disc brakes, custom carpets (coupe only) and the Ride and Handling package. The WW-5 option was available on LeMans style numbers 2027 and 2037 and included Turbo-Hydramatic or close-ratio four-speed manual transmission, 455-cid four-barrel HO V-8, heavy-duty Safe-T-Track differential, body-color outside mirrors (left-hand remote control), Formula steering wheel, roof drip moldings and carpets (coupe only), Rally gauge cluster with tachometer, Ride & Handling package, RAM AIR hood and unitized ignition system.

BASE LEMANS (20 SERIES)

Model Number	Body/Style Number	Body Type & Seating	Factory Price	Shipping Weight	Prod. Total
2D	2D27	2-dr Cpe-6P	2722/2840	3294/3510	6855
2D	2D36	4-dr Sta Wag-6P	3271/3389	3799/4015	8332
2D	2D37	2-dr HT-6P	2851/2969	3234/3450	80,383
2D	2D46	4-dr Sta Wag-9P	3378/3496	3839/4055	5266
2D	2D69	4-dr Sed-6P	2814/2932	3269/3485	19,463

NOTE 1: Data above slash for six/below slash for V-8.

NOTE 2: A total of 120,299 LeMans were built.

NOTE 3: 9601 LeMans had synchromesh and 110,698 had automatic.

LEMANS SPORT (6-CYL) - SERIES D67 - The LeMans convertible was considered a separate sub-series called the LeMans Sport line. This model carried special "Sport" signature scripts and had standard bucket seats. Many sources list this style with the LeMans series, but the factory broke it out separately in calculating production totals. The code 332 LeMans 'GT' package was available on style numbers 2D37 and 2D67 and included three-speed heavy-duty manual transmission, G70 x 14 white-letter tires, body-color mirrors, Rally II wheels (less trim rings), vinyl tape stripes, dual exhausts with side splitters and 'GT' decals. The code 734 LeMans Sport option was available on style number 2D37 and included bucket seats, custom door and rear quarter trim, custom rear seat and special front fender nameplate.

1972 Pontiac LeMans Sport convertible. OCW

LEMANS SPORT (2D SUB-SERIES)

Model Number	Body/Style Number	Body Type & Seating	Factory Price	Shipping Weight	Prod. Total
2D	2D67	2-dr Spt Conv-5P	3228/3346	3284/3500	3438

NOTE 1: Data above slash for six/below slash for V-8.

NOTE 2: 3438 LeMans Sport "Sport convertibles" were built.

NOTE 3: 317 LeMans Sport "Sport convertibles" with synchromesh; 3121 automatic.

1972 Pontiac Luxury LeMans two-door hardtop, V-8.

LUXURY LEMANS - (V-8) - SERIES 2G - A distinctive grille treatment with twin cavities divided by bright horizontal blades was used on Luxury LeMans models. Twin-ribbed full-length bodyside moldings, fender skirts and roof pillar letter badges were additional external distinctions. The standard equipment list was the same as for LeMans styles, plus all-Morrokide bucket seats in hardtop coupes or notchback bench seats in any body style. Interior trim features included all-Morrokide or cloth and Morrokide upholstery combinations, carpeted lower door panels with reflectors, custom cushion steering wheel, pedal trim plates, front door assist straps, bright armrest accents and ashtray and glovebox lamps.

LUXURY LEMANS (2G SERIES)

Model Number	Body/Style Number	Body Type & Seating	Factory Price	Shipping Weight	Prod. Total
2G	2G37	2-dr HT-5P	3196	3488	8641
2G	2639	4-dr HT-6P	3319	3638	37,615

NOTE 1: 46,256 Luxury LeMans models were built.

NOTE 2: 269 Luxury LeMans had synchromesh and 45,987 had automatic.

1972 Pontiac GTO "The Judge" two-door hardtop. OCW

GTO - (V-8) - SERIES D OPTION - The GTO was no longer a separate series. There was a code 334 GTO option package available for the style number 2D37 LeMans hardtop coupe and the 2D27 LeMans two-door coupe. It included the Code T engine, three-speed heavy-duty manual floor shift transmission, G70-14 blackwall tires, body-color mirrors, Endura styling option, special twin air slot hood, front fender air extractors, firm shock absorbers, front and rear stabilizer bars and GTO identification at a price of $344 over base model cost. The code X and code Y engines were optional. Only 5807 GTOs left the factory and body style break-outs are not available. (Note: These cars are included in the LeMans production totals given above).

BASE FIREBIRD - (6-CYL) - SERIES 2S - The possibility of dropping the Firebird was raised this year and styling changes were minimal. There was a new honeycomb mesh grille insert, new interior trims and redesigned hubcaps and wheelcovers. Standard equipment in the basic

model included front and rear bucket type seats with all-vinyl trim, solid foam seat cushions with integral springs, loop-pile carpets, Deluxe steering wheel, upper-level ventilation, woodgrained dash accents, ashtray light, Endura front bumper, small full-width front air dam, hubcaps, windshield radio antenna, bright moldings on windshield, rear window and grille, thin body sill moldings, front disc brakes, three-speed manual column shift transmission and E78-14 blackwall tires.

BASE FIREBIRD (2S SERIES)

Model Number	Body/Style Number	Body Type & Seating	Factory Price	Shipping Weight	Prod. Total
2S	2S87	2-dr HT-4P	2838/2956	3357/3359	12,000

NOTE 1: Data above slash for six/below slash for V-8.

NOTE 2: 12,001 basic Firebirds were built.

NOTE 3: 1263 Firebirds had synchromesh and 10,738 had automatic.

FIREBIRD ESPRIT - (V-8) - SERIES 2T - The Esprit had model signature script moldings on the roof pillar. Standard equipment was the same as in basic Firebirds, plus custom cloth and Morrokide trim, distinctive door trim panels, perforated headliner, added sound insulation, custom cushion steering wheel, rear armrest ashtrays, trunk mat, dash assist grip, wheel trim rings, body-color mirrors (left-hand remote-controlled), body-color door handle inserts, concealed wipers, bright roof rail trim, window sill moldings, rear hood edge accents, wheel opening moldings and wide rocker panel accent strips. Three-speed manual floor shift transmission was also included.

FIREBIRD ESPRIT (2T SERIES)

Model Number	Body/Style Number	Body Type & Seating	Factory Price	Shipping Weight	Prod. Total
2T	2T87	2-dr HT-4P	3194	3359	11,415

NOTE 1: 11,415 Firebirds Esprits were built.

NOTE 2: 504 Firebird Esprits had synchromesh and 10,911 had automatic.

FIREBIRD FORMULA - (V-8) - SERIES 2U - Formula Firebirds had the same equipment features as Esprits, plus a fiberglass hood with forward-mounted twin air scoops, special Formula identification, 1-1/8 inch front stabilizer bars, firm control shock absorbers, dual exhausts with chrome extensions and F70-14 tires.

FORMULA FIREBIRD (2U SERIES)

Model Number	Body/Style Number	Body Type & Seating	Factory Price	Shipping Weight	Prod. Total
2U	2U87	2-dr HT-4P	3221	3424	5,250

NOTE 1: 5249 Formula Firebirds were built.

NOTE 2: 1082 Formula Firebirds had synchromesh and 4167 had automatic.

FIREBIRD TRANS AM - (V-8) - SERIES 2V - Trans Ams had the same standard features as Firebirds, plus a Formula steering wheel, engine-turned dash trim, Rally gauge cluster with clock and tachometer, front air dam, front and rear wheel opening flares, full-width rear deck spoiler, engine air extractors, shaker hood, 15-inch Rally II rims with trim rings, black-textured grille inserts, fast-rate power steering, power brakes with front discs, 1-1/4 inch stabilizer bars, 7/8 inch rear stabilizer bars, special high-rate rear springs, Safe-T-Track differential, air cleaner with rear-facing cold air induction system, power-flex cooling fan, four-speed close-ratio manual transmission with floor shift (or Turbo-Hydramatic) and F60-15 white lettered tires.

1972 Pontiac Firebird Trans Am coupe. OCW

1972 Pontiac Firebird Trans Am coupe (rear view). OCW

FIREBIRD TRANS AM (2V SERIES)

Model Number	Body/Style Number	Body Type & Seating	Factory Price	Shipping Weight	Prod. Total
2V	2V87	2-dr HT-4P	4256	3564	1286

NOTE 1: 1286 Trans Ams were built.

NOTE 2: 458 Trans Ams had synchromesh and 828 had automatic.

VENTURA II - (6-CYL) - SERIES 2Y - There were virtually no changes in the 1972 Ventura II. Minor alterations included variations in fender lettering, interior trim modifications and a new steering wheel. Standard equipment included bench seats with cloth and Morrokide trim, front seat foam cushions, vinyl covered floor mats, rear ashtrays in armrests, deluxe steering wheel, woodgrained vinyl dash trim, hubcaps, front door vent windows, bright moldings on windshield and rear window, E78-14 blackwall tires and three-speed manual column shift transmission. Two specialty "model-options" were the Ventura 'SD' and the Sprint. The code 332 Ventura (coupe) Sprint option included three-speed manual floor shift transmission, E78 x 14 whitewalls, body-colored mirrors (left-hand remote control), custom sport steering wheel, chrome wheel trim rings, custom carpets, blacked-out grille, side striping, 14 x 16 inch rims and Sprint I decals. The Ventura 'SD' (for 'Sport Deluxe') was a limited-edition package offered only in cars built at Van Nuys, Calif. It was introduced in midyear and a production run of 500 units was predicted.

1972 Pontiac Ventura II two-door sedan (with Sprint option), V-8.

VENTURA II (SERIES 2Y)

Model Number	Body/Style Number	Body Type & Seating	Factory Price	Shipping Weight	Prod. Total
2Y	2Y69	4-dr Sed-5P	2454/2544	2979/3129	21,584
2Y	2Y27	2-dr Cpe-5P	2426/2516	2944/3094	51,203

NOTE 1: Data above slash for six/below slash for V-8.

NOTE 2: 72,787 Ventura IIs were built.

NOTE 3: 6421 Ventura IIs had synchromesh and 26,644 had automatic.

ENGINES

Code*	Type	CID	Carb.	Comp. Ratio	Net H.P. at RPM
D	6-cyl	250	1-V	8.5:1	110 @ 4200
F	V-8	307	2-V	8.5:1	140 @ 4000
M	V-8	350	2-V	8.0:1	160 @ 4400
N	V-8	350	2-V	8.0:1	175 @ 4400**

Code*	Type	CID	Carb.	Comp. Ratio	Net H.P. at RPM
R	V-8	400	2-V	8.2:1	175 @ 4000
P	V-8	400	2-V	8.2:1	200 @ 4000**
S	V-8	400	4-V	8.2:1	200 @ 4000
T	V-8	400	4-V	8.2:1	250 @ 4000**
V	V-8	455	2-V	8.2:1	185 @ 4000
U	V-8	455	2-V	8.2:1	200 @ 4000**
W	V-8	455	4-V	8.2:1	220 @ 3600
Y	V-8	455	4-V	8.2:1	250 @ 3600**
X	V-8	455	4-V	8.4:1	300 @ 4000**

* VIN engine code; not engine production code.

** dual exhaust.

1972 Pontiac Safari station wagon. OCW

(CATALINA) Base V-8 in Catalinas was the code N engine. The base V-8 in Catalina Safaris was the code R engine. code S, V, Y, W, T, and U engines were optional.

(CATALINA BROUGHAM) Base V-8 in Catalina Broughams was the code R engine. Code S/V/Y/W/T/U engines were optional.

(BONNEVILLE) Base V-8 in Bonnevilles was the code V engine. Code T/W/U engines were optional.

(GRAND VILLE) Base V-8 in Grand Ville was the code W engine. The only available option was the code Y engine.

(GRAND PRIX) Base V-8 in Grand Prix was the code S engine. Options were the code T/Y engines, with the latter included in the `SJ' option package as regular equipment.

(LEMANS) Base six-cylinder powerplant in LeMans was the code D engine. Base V-8 was the code M engine. Codes R/S/T/W/Y/X engines were other options.

(LUXURY LEMANS) Base V-8 in Luxury LeMans models was the code M engine. Code R/S/W/Y engines were additional options.

(BASE FIREBIRD) Base six-cylinder powerplant in Firebirds was the code D engine. Base V-8 was the code M engine and the code N engine was optional.

(FIREBIRD ESPRIT) Base V-8 in Firebirds Esprits was the code M engine. Options included code N and code R powerplants.

(FORMULA FIREBIRD) Base V-8 in Formula Firebirds was the code M engine. Options included the code N, T and X powerplants. Depending on engines, cars were identified as Formula 350s, Formula 400s or Formula 455s.

(TRANS AM) The code X engine was the only Trans Am power plant this year.

(VENTURA II) Base six-cylinder powerplant in Ventura IIs was the code D engine. The code F engine was optional, except for cars registered in California, where the code M engine was used as the approved V-8.

CHASSIS FEATURES: Wheelbase: Wheelbases for all lines were the same as 1971. Overall Length: For Venturas, Firebirds, and base LeMans overall lengths were the same as for comparable body styles in 1971. Luxury LeMans models were 202.8 in. long; all Pontiac Safaris were now 228 in. long; Catalinas were 222.4 in. long; Bonneville/Grand Villes were 226.2 in. long and Grand Prix were 213.6 in. long.

OPTIONS: Pontiac automatic air conditioning ($507). Firebird and LeMans air conditioning ($397). Formula or LeMans rear deck spoiler ($32-$46). Pontiac automatic level control ($77). Firebird rear seat console ($26). Ventura and Firebird front seat console ($57). LeMans two-door hardtop and Sport convertible console ($59). Cruise Control ($62-$67). Deck lid remote control ($14). Electric rear window defroster ($62). Base LeMans Endura styling option ($41). All-windows Soft-Ray glass ($39-$49). Soft-Ray windshield ($30-$35). Auxiliary gauge panel for Catalina ($38). Bumper guards ($5-$15). Warning lamps ($21). Auxiliary lamp group ($18). Convenience lamp group ($11). Safari luggage carrier ($62-$82). Front disc brakes ($46-$68). Wonder Touch brakes ($44-$46). Power bench seats ($67-$77-$103). Power left bucket seat ($77). Ventura power steering ($100). Variable ratio power steering for LeMans and Firebirds ($113). AM/FM Stereo and 8-Track ($363). Rally gauge cluster with clock and tachometer ($92). Honeycomb wheels ($62-$123). Rally II wheel rims ($56-$87). Woodgrained Safari exterior paneling ($154). LeMans 'GT' package ($23). Grand Ville Custom trim group ($231). Ventura sun roof ($179). LeMans Sport option ($164). Ventura Sprint option ($190). LeMans WW-4 performance option ($510-$796). LeMans WW5 RAM AIR option ($982-$995). Dual exhausts ($40). Performance or economy ratio rear axles ($10). Safe-T-Track differential was $45 extra and heavy-duty Safe-T-Track was $66 extra. Heavy-duty batteries were $10-$15 extra and a Delco X battery was $26 extra. Functional air inlet hoods for Formulas and specially-equipped LeMans models were $56 extra.

HISTORICAL FOOTNOTES: Production startup date was August 12, 1971. Factory introductions were held September 23, 1971. Model year output was 707,017 cars. Calendar year totals of 702,571 assemblies gave Pontiac Motor Division fifth place. On October 1, 1972, Martin J. Caserio became Pontiac's general manager. The 1972 GTO hardtop with 300 net hp was tested at 7.1 seconds 0-to-60 and 15.4 seconds in the quarter-mile. The 1972 Firebird Esprit did 0-to-60 mph in 9.9 seconds and the quarter-mile in 17.6 seconds. The GTO returned to option status this year and Pontiac made Turbo-Hydramatic and disc brakes standard on all models.

1972 Pontiac Firebird Formula with 455 RAM AIR package. OCW

1973 PONTIAC

CATALINA - (V-8) - SERIES 2L - Catalina front end styling was new and was characterized by full-width grilles having thin horizontal blades. Catalina lettering was seen behind the front wheel openings. Standard equipment was similar to the previous model year with small hubcaps, untrimmed wheel cutouts and thin body sill moldings. Taillamp treatments were simpler than on other lines. The Catalina convertible and Catalina Brougham series were deleted. Base Catalinas came with a 350-cid two-barrel V-8, Turbo-Hydramatic and variable-ratio power steering.

1973 Pontiac Catalina two-door hardtop, V-8.

PONTIAC I.D. NUMBERS: VIN on top of dash at left, viewable through windshield. First symbol tells GM division: 2=Pontiac. Second symbol tells series: Y=Ventura; Z=Ventura Custom; S=Firebird; T=Esprit; U=Formula 400; V=Trans Am; D=LeMans; F=LeMans Sport; G=Luxury LeMans; H=Grand Am; K=Grand Prix; L=Catalina; N=Bonneville; P=Grand Ville. Third and fourth symbols indicate body style and appear as last two digits of Body/Style Number in charts below. Fifth symbol indicates engine (See chart at beginning of "Engines" section below.) Sixth symbol indicates model year: 3=1973. Seventh symbol indicates assembly plant: A=Atlanta, Ga.; C=South Gate, Calif.; D=Doraville, Ga.; G=Framingham, Mass.; L=Van Nuys, Calif.; N=Norwood, Ohio; P=Pontiac, Mich.; Z=Fremont, Calif. Remaining symbols are sequential unit production number at factory, starting with 100001. Fisher Body plate on cowl tells style number: (model year prefix 73, plus new type Body/Style Number codes (i.e. 2L69 for Catalina four-door sedan), body number, trim code, paint code and other data. Six-cylinder engine code stamped on distributor mounting on right side of block. V-8 engine code on front of block below right cylinder head. Engine production codes for 1972 were: [250-cid/100 nhp six] CCC/CCD/CCA/CCB/CDR/CDS/CAW. [350-cid/150 nhp V-8] YL/Y2/YR/Y7/YV/YL/XR/XV/ZR/ZV/XC. [350-cid/175 nhp V-8] WV/ZB/ZD/WD/XC/X2/WF/WA/XF/WC/WL/WN/YW. [400-cid/170 nhp V-8] YP/Y4/YX/Y1/ZX/ZK/YZ. [400-cid/185 nhp V-8] P. [400-cid/200 nhp V-8] S. [400-cid/230 nhp V-8] WK/WS/WP/YS/Y3/YN/YT. [400-cid/250 nhp V-8] X4/X1/X3/XH/W5/Y6/YF/YG/XN/XX/X5/XZ/XK. [455-cid/215 nhp V-8] W. [455-cid/250 nhp V-8] WW/WT/YC/YA/ZC/ZZ/ZE/XE/XA/XJ/XL/XO/XT/X7/XY/XM. [455-cid/310 nhp Super-Duty V-8] ZJ/XD/W8/Y8.

CATALINA (2L SERIES)

Model Number	Body/Style Number	Body Type & Seating	Factory Price	Shipping Weight	Prod. Total
2L	L69	4-dr Sed-6P	3770	4234	100,592
2L	L39	4-dr HT-6P	3938	4270	31,663
2L	L57	2-dr HT-6P	3869	4190	74,394
2L	L45	4-dr Sta Wag-9P	4457	4873	14,654
2L	L35	4-dr Sta Wag-6P	4311	4791	15,762

BONNEVILLE - (V-8) - SERIES 2N - Bonnevilles had a new "eggcrate" mesh grille running from side to side. Double twin-deck taillamps were used along with wide body sill moldings having rear panel extensions. Bonneville lettering appeared on the left side of the grille, behind front wheel openings and between the taillamps. Bonnevilles were now the same as Catalinas, but had higher levels of interior and exterior trim including Deluxe wheelcovers, decor moldings and custom upholstery combinations. Fender skirts were no longer standard equipment, but other features were about the same as in 1972. A special RTS handling package was introduced for the hardtop. This "Bonneville RTS coupe" was priced $4225 and included radial tires and heavy-duty underpinnings at this cost. Bonneville Safaris were moved to the Grand Ville series.

BONNEVILLE (2N SERIES)

Model Number	Body/Style Number	Body Type & Seating	Factory Price	Shipping Weight	Prod. Total
2N	N69	4-dr Sed-6P	4163	4333	15,830
2N	N39	4-dr HT-6P	4292	4369	17,202
2N	N57	2-dr HT-6P	4225	4292	13,866

1973 Pontiac Grand Ville convertible. OCW

GRAND VILLE - (V-8) - SERIES 2P - Grand Ville passenger cars were now the same as other full-size Pontiacs. The new grille on this line was similar to the Bonneville type except that a signature script model badge was placed above the left-hand grille instead of on it. Stacked, horizontally-slit taillamps were an exclusive feature. Full wheel discs, wide body sill moldings, roof pillar nameplates (except convertible) and fender skirts were additional identification aids. Standard equipment was about the same as in 1972. The Bonneville Safaris became Grand Ville Safaris. The big wagons were on a three-inch longer wheelbase than other Pontiacs. Safari features were about the same as those seen on 1972 Bonneville station wagons.

1973 Pontiac Grand Ville four-door hardtop. OCW

GRAND VILLE (2P SERIES)

Model Number	Body/Style Number	Body Type & Seating	Factory Price	Shipping Weight	Prod. Total
2P	P49	4-dr HT-6P	4592	4376	44,092
2P	P47	2-dr HT-6P	4524	4321	23,963
2P	P67	2-dr Conv-6P	4766	4339	4447
2P	P45	4-dr Sta Wag-9P	4821	4925	10,776
2P	P35	4-dr Sta Wag-6P	4674	4823	6894

1973 Pontiac Grand Prix two-door hardtop, V-8.

GRAND PRIX - (V-8) - SERIES 2K - The Grand Prix retained a link to previous styling themes, with several refinements. A new type of wide grille design was used and opera windows were an available styling option. The Grand Prix was on a shorter wheelbase and looked trimmer, even though overall size was increased. V-shaped hood styling was emphasized again. A new feature was African crossfire mahogany accents for the instrument panel. A custom cushion steering wheel and all-Morrokide trims were used. The general level of trim, appointments and standard equipment was the same as in 1972. The `SJ' option was offered again, with production counted separately for the first time. It included firm shock absorbers, thick front stabilizer bar, Rally RTS suspension, and the 250 hp V-8.

123

1973 Pontiac Grand Prix two-door hardtop (rear view). OCW

GRAND PRIX (2K SERIES)

Model Number	Body/Style Number	Body Type & Seating	Factory Price	Shipping Weight	Prod. Total
2K	K57	2-dr HT-5P	4583	4025	133,150
2K	K57	'SJ' HT-5P	4962	4400	20,749

LEMANS - (6-CYL) - SERIES 2D AND SERIES 2AF - Pontiac's A-body intermediate line had highly revised "Buck Rogers" styling this season. Design characteristics included V-shaped hoods, split rectangular grilles, single headlamps mounted in square housings, highly sculptured fenders and "Colonnade" style rooflines. The Colonnade styling provided heavier roof pillars to meet federal rollover standards with large window openings cut deep into the beltline in limousine style. LeMans lettering appeared behind the front wheel opening and thin body sill moldings were used. The LeMans Sport convertible was discontinued and replaced by the Series 2AF LeMans Sport Coupe. This model constituted a separate sub-series and came standard with bucket seats and louvered rear quarter window styling. Station wagons were officially called Safaris again. Available options on the LeMans or LeMans Sport Coupes included the `GT' and `GTO' packages. Base models had a uniform vertical blade grille insert, with flat textured finish on the GTO. The GTO option also included the 400-cid four-barrel V-8, dual air scoop hood, wide oval tires, dual exhausts, floor mounted three-speed manual gearbox, rear sway bars, baby moon hubcaps, 15 x 7 inch wheel rims, specific body striping and suitable model identification trim.

LEMANS (2AD SERIES)

Model Number	Body/Style Number	Body Type & Seating	Factory Price	Shipping Weight	Prod. Total
2AD	D29	4-dr HT-6P	2918/3036	3605/3821	26,554
2AD	D37	2-dr HT-6P	2920/3038	3579/3795	68,230
2AD	D45	4-dr Sta Wag-9P	3429/3547	3993/4209	6127
2AD	D35	4-dr Sta Wag-6P	3296/3414	3956/4172	10,446

LEMANS SPORT (2AF SERIES)

Model Number	Body/Style Number	Body Type & Seating	Factory Price	Shipping Weight	Prod. Total
2AF	F37	2-dr HT-5P	3008/3126	3594/3810	50,999

NOTE 1: Data above slash for six/below slash for V-8.

NOTE 2: 4806 LeMans/LeMans Sport two-door Colonnade hardtops had GTO option.

LUXURY LEMANS - (V-8) - SERIES 2AG - Luxury LeMans models also featured Colonnade styling, but with higher level interior and exterior appointments, plus standard V-8 power. Styling features included wide beauty moldings running the full-width of the body at about mid-wheel height; fender skirts with chrome edge moldings; rear deck beauty panels between the taillights; vertical blade grilles with vertical chrome division moldings; Deluxe wheelcovers; and "Luxury" signatures above the LeMans fender lettering. Luxury LeMans upholstery combinations were patterned after those seen in Grand Villes.

LUXURY LEMANS (2AG SERIES)

Model Number	Body/Style Number	Body Type & Seating	Factory Price	Shipping Weight	Prod. Total
2AG	G29	4-dr HT-6P	3344	3867	9377
2AG	G37	2-dr HT-6P	3274	3799	33,916

GRAND AM - (V-8) - SERIES 2AH - One of the most distinctive cars offered in the sales sweepstakes this model year was the Pontiac Grand Am. This A-body intermediate had an international flavor. Standard equipment included a sloping three-piece nose section of body-color injection-molded urethane plastic; twin sloping vertical-slot triple quadrant grilles; bucket seats with adjustable lumbar support; 14 inch custom cushion steering wheel; African crossfire mahogany dash trim; 10 inch diameter power front disc brakes; Grand Prix style dashboard; full-instrumentation with Rally gauge cluster; variable-ratio power steering; heavy-duty suspension; steel-belted wide-base G70-15 radial tires on 15 x 7 inch wheels; Pliacell shock absorbers; thick front and rear stabilizer bars; specific trim stripes; and special nameplates. Upholstery options included cloth with corduroy insert panels or perforated, leather-like Morrokide. A V-8 engine was also standard.

1973 Pontiac Grand Am Colonnade two-door hardtop, V-8.

1973 Pontiac Grand Am Colonnade two-door hardtop (rear view). OCW

GRAND AM (2AH SERIES)

Model Number	Body/Style Number	Body Type & Seating	Factory Price	Shipping Weight	Prod. Total
2AH	H29	4-dr HT-6P	4353	4018	8691
2AH	H37	2-dr HT-6P	4264	3992	34,445

BASE FIREBIRD - (6-CYL) - SERIES 2F2 - Base Firebirds had a new "eggcrate" grille insert. Styling was not greatly changed from 1972, but the Endura nose had been substantially improved to meet U.S. government crash standards. Standard equipment was basically similar to that offered in 1972 models.

BASE FIREBIRD (SERIES 2FS)

Model Number	Body/Style Number	Body Type & Seating	Factory Price	Shipping Weight	Prod. Total
2FS	S87	2-dr HT-4P	2895/3013	3159/3380	14,096

NOTE 1: Data above slash for six/below slash for V-8.

NOTE 2: 1370 cars were built with six-cylinder power.

FIREBIRD ESPRIT - (V-8) - SERIES 2FT - The Firebird Esprit could be most easily identified by the model signature scripts on the roof pillars. Also considered standard equipment were a custom interior, concealed windshield wipers, twin body-color mirrors (left-hand remote-controlled) and African crossfire mahogany dash and console accent panels.

FIREBIRD ESPRIT (SERIES 2FT)

Model Number	Body/Style Number	Body Type & Seating	Factory Price	Shipping Weight	Prod. Total
2FT	T87	2-dr HT-4P	3249	3309	17,249

FIREBIRD FORMULA - (V-8) - SERIES 2FU - Formula Firebirds could again be identified by the special twin-scoop hoods. Other features included a custom cushion steering wheel, heavy-duty suspension, black textured grille, dual exhausts, and F70-14 tires plus all items include on lower priced lines.

FIREBIRD FORMULA (SERIES 2FU)

Model Number	Body/Style Number	Body Type & Seating	Factory Price	Shipping Weight	Prod. Total
2FU	U87	2-dr HT-4P	3276	3318	10,166

FIREBIRD TRANS AM - (V-8) - SERIES 2FV - The most significant change to Firebird Trans Ams this season was the addition of the "chicken" graphics treatment for the hood. Stylist John Schinella created this modernized rendition of the legendary Indian symbol. Standard equipment included Formula steering wheel, Rally gauge cluster with clock and tachometer, full-width rear deck spoiler, power steering and front disc brakes, Safe-T-Track differential, wheel opening flares, front fender air extractors, dual exhausts with chrome extensions, heavy-duty underpinnings, Rally II wheels with trim rings, dual body-color mirrors (left-hand remote-controlled), F60-15 white-lettered tires and a choice of Turbo-Hydramatic or four-speed manual transmission.

1973 Pontiac Trans Am two-door hardtop coupe, V-8.

1973 Pontiac Grand Am four-door sedan. OCW

ENGINES

Code	Type	CID	Carb.	Comp. Ratio	Net HP at RPM
D	6-cyl	250	1-V	8.25:1	100 @ 3600
F	V-8	307	2-V	8.5:1	130 @ 4000*
M	V-8	350	2-V	7.6:1	150 @ 4000
N	V-8	350	2-V	7.6:1	175 @ 4400**
R	V-8	400	2-V	8.0:1	170 @ 3600
P	V-8	400	2-V	8.0:1	185 @ 4000**
S	V-8	400	4-V	8.0:1	200 @ 4000
T	V-8	400	4-V	8.0:1	250 @ 4400**
W	V-8	455	4-V	8.0:1	215 @ 3600
Y	V-8	455	4-V	8.0:1	250 @ 4000**
X	V-8	455	4-V	8.4:1	310 @ 4000**

* Canada only.

** Dual exhausts.

(CATALINA) The base Catalina V-8 was the code M engine. Codes R/P/S/T/W/Y engines were optional. The code R engine was standard in Catalina Safaris.

(BONNEVILLE) The base Bonneville V-8 was the code R engine. Code P/S/T/W/Y engines were optional.

(GRAND VILLE) The base Grand Ville V-8 was the code W engine. The code Y engine was optional.

(GRAND PRIX) The base Grand Prix V-8 was the code T engine. The code Y/X engines were optional.

(LEMANS/VENTURA) Base six-cylinder powerplant in LeMans models was the code D engine. Base V-8 in LeMans passenger cars was the code R engine. Code P/S/T/W/Y engines were optional in passenger cars. The code R engine was standard in Safari V-8s with code S/W engines as options. The code T engine was standard in cars with the GTO package.

(LUXURY LEMANS) Base V-8 powerplant in Luxury LeMans models was the code M engine. code R/S/Y engines were optional.

(GRAND AM) Base V-8 powerplant in Grand Ams was the code R engine. Code S/Y/X engines were optional.

(BASE FIREBIRD) Standard six-cylinder powerplant in basic Firebirds was the code D engine. Base V-8 was the code M engine. No other options were listed.

(FIREBIRD ESPRIT) Base V-8 powerplant in Esprits was the code M engine. The only option was also a V-8, the code R engine.

(FIREBIRD FORMULA) Base V-8 powerplant in the Formula Firebird series was the code M engine. Code R/Y/X engines were optional V-8s.

(FIREBIRD TRANS AM) Base V-8 powerplant in Trans Ams was the code Y engine. The code X engine was the only powertrain option.

OPTIONAL V-8 ENGINES

350-cid. Compression ratio: 7.6:1. Carburetion: two-barrel. Brake hp: 150 @ 4000 rpm. (standard in Catalina, Luxury LeMans, Firebird Esprit; optional in Ventura/LeMans/Firebird).

350-cid. Compression ratio: 7.6:1. Carburetion: two-barrel. Brake hp: 175 @ 4400 rpm. (optional in Ventura/LeMans/Catalina; standard in Firebird Formula 350).

400-cid. Compression ratio: 8:1. Carburetion: two-barrel. Brake hp: 170 @ 3600 rpm. (standard in Grand Am, Safari, Bonneville; optional in LeMans/Catalina/Firebird Esprit).

400-cid. Compression ratio: 8:1. Carburetion: two-barrel. Brake hp: 185 @ 4000 rpm. (optional in LeMans/Grand Am/Catalina).

400-cid. Compression ratio: 8:1. Carburetion: four-barrel. Brake hp: 200 @ 4000 rpm. (standard in Grand Safari; optional in Catalina/Bonneville).

400-cid. Compression ratio: 8:1. Carburetion: four-barrel. Brake hp: 230 @ 4400 rpm. (standard in GTO, Grand Prix; optional in LeMans/Grand Am/Formula 400/Catalina/Bonneville).

455-cid. Compression ratio: 8:1. Carburetion: four-barrel. Brake hp: 215 @ 3600 rpm. (standard in Grand Ville; optional in Catalina/Bonneville).

455-cid. Compression ratio: 8:1. Carburetion: four-barrel. Brake hp: 250 @ 4000 rpm. (standard in Trans Am; optional in Grand Prix/Grand Ville/Catalina/Bonneville/GTO/LeMans/Formula 455).

455-cid. Compression ratio: 8:1. Carburetion: four-barrel. Brake hp: 290 @ 4000 rpm. (optional in Trans Am/Formula 455).

CHASSIS FEATURES: Wheelbase: (All Pontiac Safaris) 127 in.; (All Pontiac passenger cars) 124 in.; (A-body two-doors) 112 in.; (A-body four-doors) 116 in.; (Grand Prix) 116 in.; (Firebird) 108 in.; (Ventura) 111 in. Overall Length: (All Pontiac Safaris) 228.8 in.; (All Pontiac passenger cars) 224.8 in.; (Grand Am two-door) 208.6 in.; (Grand Am four-door) 212.6 in.; (Grand Prix) 216.6 in.; (Other A-body two-doors) 207.4 in.; (Other A-body four-doors) 211.4 in.; (A-body Safaris) 213.3 in. (Firebird) 192.1 in.; (Ventura) 197.5 in.

FIREBIRD TRANS AM (SERIES 2FV)

Model Number	Body/Style Number	Body Type & Seating	Factory Price	Shipping Weight	Prod. Total
2FV	V87	2-dr HT-4P	4204	3504	4802

VENTURA - (6-CYL) - SERIES 2Y - The name Ventura II was shortened to Ventura and cars in the Y Series had several styling refinements. A "double-decker" twin slot grille was continued in use on cars with base level trim. Standard equipment included Deluxe steering wheel, bench seats with cloth and Morrokide trim, front and rear armrests, high/low ventilation system, rubber floor mats and hubcaps. A Sprint package including custom cushion steering wheel, custom carpeting, body color outside mirrors, custom striping, model identification trim and 14 x 6 inch wheel rims was available on two-door models. There were now a pair of two-door styles available, the notchback coupe and the hatchback coupe, along with a four-door notch back sedan. Cars with the Sprint package wore a Firebird style twin rectangular grille.

VENTURA (SERIES 2Y)

Model Number	Body/Style Number	Body Type & Seating	Factory Price	Shipping Weight	Prod. Total
2Y	Y69	4-dr Sed-5P	2481/2599	3124/3336	21,012
2Y	Y27	2-dr Cpe-5P	2452/2570	3064/3276	49,153
2Y	Y17	2-dr Hatch-5P	2603/2721	3170/3382	26,335

NOTE 1: Data above slash for six/below slash for V-8.

NOTE 2: Totals include base Venturas, Customs and Sprints of same body style.

VENTURA CUSTOM - (6-CYL) - SERIES 2Z - Ventura Customs included a choice of cloth or all-Morrokide upholstery, custom cushion steering wheel, bright metal front seat side panels, glovebox lamp, nylon carpeting, Deluxe wheelcovers, pedal trim plates, body decor moldings and body sill beauty strips. The hatch back coupe include load area carpeting and dome lamp, fold-down rear seat and a Space Saver spare tire. As on base models Ventura block letters were seen behind the front wheel openings, but additional identification was provided by signature scripts reading "Custom" positioned on the rear roof pillars.

VENTURA CUSTOM (SERIES 2Z)

Model Number	Body/Style Number	Body Type & Seating	Factory Price	Shipping Weight	Prod. Total
2Z	Z69	4-dr Sed-5P	2638/2756	3157/3369	(Note 2)
2Z	Z27	2-dr Coupe-5P	2609/2727	3097/3309	(Note 2)
2Z	Z17	2-dr Hatch-5P	2759/2877	3203/3415	(Note 2)

NOTE 1: Data above slash for six/below slash for V-8.

NOTE 2: Ventura Custom totals included in base Ventura chart above.

1973 Pontiac Luxury LeMans coupe. OCW

1973 Pontiac Luxury LeMans coupe (rear view). OCW

1973 Pontiac Luxury LeMans Colonnade four-door notchback hardtop. JAG

1973 Pontiac LeMans Safari station wagon. OCW

1973 Pontiac LeMans two-door hardtop (with GTO option). OCW

1973 Pontiac Ventura two-door hatchback coupe, six-cylinder.

1973 Pontiac Firebird Trans Am coupe (rear view). OCW

1973 Pontiac Ventura four-door sedan. OCW

1973 Superior-Pontiac landaulet funeral car. JAG

126

OPTIONS: Custom Safari option package ($317). GTO LeMans option package ($368). LeMans Ride & Handling package ($188). LeMans GT option ($237). Grand Prix 'SJ' option ($379). Electric sun roof for A-body models ($325), Ventura sun roof ($179). Grand Prix electric sun roof ($325). Ventura vinyl top ($82) Firebird AM/FM stereo ($233); with tape deck ($363). Firebird power windows ($75). LeMans vinyl top ($97). LeMans AM/FM stereo ($233); with tape deck ($363). LeMans power windows ($103). LeMans Rally II wheels ($87). Pontiac six-way power seat ($103). Pontiac power windows ($129). Pontiac AM/FM stereo ($233); with tape deck ($363). Safari 60/40 bench seats ($77). Grand Prix vinyl roof ($116). Grand Prix power windows ($75).

HISTORICAL FOOTNOTES: Model year production was 919,872, the highest ever for Pontiac Motor Division. Calendar year output of 866,598 cars was also recorded for a 9.5 percent market share. On November 27, 1972, a blue Catalina sedan became the 16th millionth Pontiac ever made. The SD-455 Trans Am was capable of 0-to-60 mph in 7.3 seconds and the quarter-mile in 15 seconds. The 250 nhp Grand Am traveled from 0-to-60 mph in 7.9 seconds and made it down the drag strip in 15.7. Production of SD-455 Trans Ams totaled 252 cars, of which 180 had automatic transmission and 72 had manual transmission. Fifty Formula Firebirds also had the SD-455 muscle engine.

1974 PONTIAC

1974 Pontiac Grand Ville four-door hardtop sedan, V-8.

CATALINA - (V-8) - SERIES 2BL - The front and rear of 1974 Catalinas was restyled and some body styles also had new rooflines. A radiator grille was used again. It had a chrome shell with a broad vertical center bar forming two openings. Each was filled with a cross-hatched grille accented by five bright horizontal division bars. Two-piece rectangular parking lamps were set into the front panel below the headlamps and above the bumper. Pontiac lettering appeared on the left front panel. Catalina lettering and engine displacement numbers were placed behind front wheel openings. Twin rectangular tail lights were used at each side in the rear. Hardtop coupes featured Colonnade-type rooflines. All full-sized Pontiacs had the following as standard equipment: woodgrained dash trim; high/low ventilation; windshield radio antenna; front and rear energy-absorbing bumpers; ashtrays; glovebox lamp; inside hood release; nylon carpeting; safety belt warning system; windshield, roof drip, hood rear edge and rear window moldings (except Grand Prix and Safaris); power steering; power brakes with front discs; Turbo-Hydramatic transmission; and V-8 engines. Catalinas also had a two-spoke steering wheel, cloth and Morrokide front bench seat, trunk mat and G78-15 blackwall tires. Catalina Safaris had all-Morrokide upholstery, storage compartments, Glide-Away tailgates, power tailgate windows, right-hand outside mirror, tailgate vertical rub stripes, rear quarter and tailgate window moldings and L78-15 tires. The nine-passenger model came with a split-back second seat and rear-facing third seat.

PONTIAC I.D. NUMBERS: VIN on top of dash at left, viewable through windshield. First symbol tells GM division: 2=Pontiac. Second symbol tells series: Y=Ventura; Z=Ventura Custom; S=Firebird; T=Esprit; U=Formula 400; V=Trans Am; D=LeMans; F=LeMans Sport; G=Luxury LeMans; H=Grand Am; K=Grand Prix; L=Catalina; N=Bonneville; P=Grand Ville. Third and fourth symbols indicate body style and appear as last two digits of body/style number in charts below. Fifth symbol indicates engine (See chart at beginning of "Engines" section below.) Sixth symbol indicates model year: 4=1974. Seventh symbol indicates assembly plant: A=Atlanta, Ga.; C=South Gate, Calif.; D=Doraville, Ga.; G=Framingham, Mass.; L=Van Nuys, Calif.; N=Norwood, Ohio; P=Pontiac, Mich.; W=Willow Run, Mich.; X=Kansas City, Kan.; Z=Fremont, Calif.; 1=Oshawa, Canada. Remaining symbols are sequential unit production number at factory, starting with 100001. Fisher Body plate on cowl tells style number (model year prefix 74, plus "2" for Pontiac and body/style number from charts below), plus body number, trim code, paint code and other data. Six-cylinder engine code

stamped on distributor mounting on right side of block. V-8 engine code on front of block below right cylinder head. Engine production codes for 1972 were: [250-cid/100 nhp six] CCR/CCX/CCW. [350-cid/155 nhp V-8] WA/WB/YA/YB/YC/AA/ZA/ZB. [350-cid/170 nhp V-8] WN/WP/YN/YP/YS/ZP. [400-cid/175 nhp V-8] YH/YJ/AH/ZH/ZJ. [400-cid/200 nhp V-8] WT/YT/AT/ZT/YZ. [455-cid/215 nhp V-8] YY/YU/YX/AU/ZU/ZX/YW/ZW/YR. [455-cid/310 nhp Super-Duty V-8] W8/Y8.

1974 Pontiac Catalina four-door sedan. OCW

CATALINA (SERIES 2BL)

Model Number	Body/Style Number	Body Type & Seating	Factory Price	Shipping Weight	Prod. Total
2BL	L69	4-dr Sed-6P	4190	4294	46,025
2BL	L39	4-dr HT-6P	4347	4352	11,769
2BL	L57	2-dr HT-6	4278	4279	40,657
2BL	L45	4-dr Sta Wag-9P	4834	5037	6486
2BL	L35	4-dr Sta Wag-6P	4692	4973	5662

BONNEVILLE - (V-8) - SERIES 28N - Bonnevilles featured "eggcrate" style grille inserts and one-piece horizontal parking lamps. Bonneville lettering was seen on the left-hand front body panel and behind the front wheel openings, as well as on the rear deck. Taillights were similar to the Catalina type, but accented with a deck latch panel beauty strip. Standard equipment included all items found on Catalinas, plus a choice of cloth and Morrokide or all-Morrokide upholstery, custom cushion steering wheel, electric clock, rear door light switches (on four-doors), dash courtesy lamps, pedal trim plates, trunk mat with side panels, Deluxe wheelcovers, decor moldings at wheelwells, wide body sill moldings with rear extensions, luggage lamp, rubber bumper strips and H78-15 blackwall tires.

BONNEVILLE (SERIES 2BN)

Model Number	Body/Style Number	Body Type & Seating	Factory Price	Shipping Weight	Prod. Total
2BN	N69	4-dr Sed-6P	4510	4384	6770
2BN	N39	4-dr HT-6P	4639	4444	6151
2BN	N57	2-dr HT-6P	4572	4356	7639

1974 Pontiac Grand Ville convertible. OCW

GRAND VILLE AND GRAND SAFARI - (V-8) - SERIES 2BP - Grand Villes

Model Number	Body/Style Number	Body Type & Seating	Factory Price	Shipping Weight	Prod. Total
2BP	P49	4-dr HT-6P	4939	4515	21,714
2BP	P47	2-dr HT-6P	4871	4432	11,631
2BP	P67	2-dr Conv-6P	5113	4476	3000
2BP	P45	4-dr Sta Wag-9P	5256	5112	5255
2BP	P35	4-dr Sta Wag-6P	5109	5011	2894

1974 Pontiac Grand Prix two-door hardtop coupe, V-8.

GRAND PRIX - (V-8) - SERIES 2GK - Grand Prix styling changes included a shorter grille that did not drop below the bumper line, thinner and more rectangular parking lamps, twin vertical taillights and a crease sculptured contour line behind the front wheel opening. Standard equipment was the same as in Bonnevilles, plus carpeted lower door panels, black custom cushion steering wheel, cigar lighter and courtesy lamps, lateral restraint front bucket seats or notchback front bench seat, aircraft style wraparound instrument panel with integrated console (except with bench seats), rear quarter opera window styling, windowsill and wide body sill moldings, floor shift (bucket seats only), dual exhausts and G78-15 tires. Approximately 92 percent of all Grand Prix had bucket seats and the `SJ' option package, which collectors consider a separate model, was available again.

GRAND PRIX (SERIES 2GK)

Model Number	Body/Style Number	Body Type & Seating	Factory Price	Shipping Weight	Prod. Total
GRAND PRIX J					
2GK	K57	2-dr HT-6P	4936	4096	85,976
GRAND PRIX SJ					
2GK	K57	2-dr HT-5P	5321	4300	13,841

LEMANS AND LEMANS SPORT - (6-CYL) - SERIES 2AD/2AF - LeMans models had new front bumpers with rubber-faced protective guards, more angular front fender corner sections, twin rectangular grilles accented by bright horizontal division bars and vertically curved taillights with new rear bumpers. Standard equipment in all A-body cars included woodgrained dash trim; deluxe two-spoke steering wheel; safety belt warning system; high/low ventilation; nylon carpeting; inside hood release; concealed wipers; windshield radio antenna; new energy-absorbing bumpers; hubcaps; manual front disc brakes; windshield, roof drip, body sill, rear and rear quarter window moldings; and F78-14 blackwall tires. Base models had cloth-and-Morrokide front bench seats. The LeMans Sport coupe featured a notchback armrest front seat, woodgrained glovebox trim, and louvered rear quarter window treatment.

LEMANS (SERIES 2AD)

Model Number	Body/Style Number	Body Type & Seating	Factory Price	Shipping Weight	Prod. Total
2AD	D29	4-dr HT-6P	3236/3361	3628/3844	17,266
2AD	D37	2-dr HT-6P	3216/3341	3552/3768	37,061
2AD	D45	4-dr Sta Wag-9P	4186	4371	4743
2AD	D35	4-dr Sta Wag-6P	4052	4333	3004

LEMANS SPORT (SERIES 2AF)

Model Number	Body/Style Number	Body Type & Seating	Factory Price	Shipping Weight	Prod. Total
2AF	F37	2-dr HT-6P	3300/3425	3580/3796	37,955

NOTE 1: Data above slash for six/below; no slash for V-8.

1974 Pontiac LeMans GT two-door hardtop, V-8.

LUXURY LEMANS - (V-8) - SERIES 2AG - Luxury LeMans models had special vertically segmented grille inserts; wide body sill moldings with front and rear extensions; distinctive curved vertical taillamps accented with chrome moldings; a deck latch panel beauty strip; luxury scripts behind the front wheel openings; and fender skirts. Standard equipment included deluxe wheelcovers; custom cushion steering wheel; and V-8 power. The Luxury LeMans hardtop provided buyers with a choice of front bucket seats or a notch back type with armrest. This model also incorporated ashtray and glovebox lamps, cloth-and-Morrokide or all-Morrokide trims; door-pull straps; pedal trim plates; dual horns; decor moldings; and special taillight styling. The Luxury LeMans Safari came with woodgrained dash trim; all-Morrokide seats; under-floor storage compartment; liftgate; textured steel cargo floor; tailgate vertical rub strips; power front disc brakes; and all other base LeMans station wagon features. The nine-passenger versions had a rear-facing third seat, electric tailgate release and swing-out rear quarter ventipanes.

1974 Pontiac Luxury LeMans coupe. OCW

1974 Pontiac Luxury LeMans coupe (rear view). OCW

LUXURY LEMANS (SERIES 2AG)

Model Number	Body/Style Number	Body Type & Seating	Factory Price	Shipping Weight	Prod. Total
2AG	G29	4-dr HT-6P	3759	3904	4513
2AG	G37	2-dr HT-6P	3703	3808	25,882
2AG	G45	4-dr Sta Wag-9P	4459	4401	1178
2AG	G35	4-dr Sta Wag-6P	4326	4363	952

1974 Pontiac Grand Am two-door hardtop. OCW

GRAND AM - (V-8) - SERIES 2AH - Standard equipment for all Grand Ams was based on the Luxury LeMans list, with the following variations: courtesy lamps; custom sport steering wheel; mahogany dash trim; electric clock; turn signal stalk headlight dimmer switch; integrated console with mahogany trim; floor-mounted gear shift lever; lateral-restraint bucket seats with adjustable lumbar support; custom finned wheelcovers; Endura bumper protective strips; power brakes with front discs; Rally gauges with trip odometer; power steering; Turbo-Hydramatic transmission; and radial-tuned suspension with GR70-15 tires. Styling distinctions included a special vertically segmented polyurethane nose panel, exclusive taillight design and specific striping and badge ornamentation.

1974 Pontiac Grand Am four-door Colonnade hardtop. OCW

GRAND AM (SERIES 2AH)

Model Number	Body/Style Number	Body Type & Seating	Factory Price	Shipping Weight	Prod. Total
2AH	H29	4-dr HT-5P	4623	4073	3122
2AH	H37	2-dr HT-5P	4534	3992	13,961

BASE FIREBIRD - (6-CYL) - SERIES - 2FS - New Firebird styling changes included a shovel-nosed Endura front end, a horizontal slotted taillamp treatment, lowered rear fender line and twin horizontal rectangular grille inserts with vertical blades. All Firebird models had ashtray lamps, nylon carpeting, high/low ventilation, Endura styling and windshield radio antenna. The basic Firebird also featured a Deluxe two-spoke steering wheel, single-buckle seat and shoulder belt arrangement, narrow rocker panel moldings and E78-14 tires.

FIREBIRD (SERIES 2FS)

Model Number	Body/Style Number	Body Type & Seating	Factory Price	Shipping Weight	Prod. Total
2FS	S87	2-dr HT-4P	3335/3460	3283/3504	26,372

NOTE 1: Data above slash for six/below slash for V-8.

NOTE 2: 7063 base Firebirds had six-cylinder engines.

FIREBIRD ESPRIT - (V-8) - SERIES 2FT - As usual, a model badge on the rear roof pillar was a trait of Esprit models. Standard extras on this line included custom cushion steering wheel, custom interior package, body-color door handle inserts, concealed wipers with articulated left arm, Deluxe wheelcovers, dual horns, dual outside mirrors (left-hand remote-controlled), roof drip and wheel opening moldings, wide body sill moldings, window sill and rear hood edge moldings, three-speed manual floor shift (with base engine only), safety belt warning system and E78-14 tires.

FIREBIRD ESPRIT (SERIES 2FT)

Model Number	Body/Style Number	Body Type & Seating	Factory Price	Shipping Weight	Prod. Total
2FT	T87	2-dr HT-4	3687	35440	22,583

FORMULA FIREBIRD - (V-8) - SERIES 2FU - In addition to equipment standard in Esprits, Formula Firebirds featured hubcaps, dual-scoop fiberglass hoods, special heavy-duty suspension, black-textured grilles, dual exhausts and F70-14 tires. Available model options included Formula 350, Formula 400, and Formula 455.

FORMULA FIREBIRD (SERIES 2FU)

Model Number	Body/Style Number	Body Type & Seating	Factory Price	Shipping Weight	Prod. Total
2FU	U87	2-dr HT-4P	3659	3548	14,519

1974 Pontiac Trans Am two-door hardtop coupe, V-8.

FIREBIRD TRANS AM - (V-8) - SERIES 2FV - Standard equipment on Trans Am included formula steering wheel, Rally gauges with clock and dash panel tachometer, swirl grain dash trim, full width rear deck lid spoiler, power steering and front disc brakes, limited-slip differential, wheel opening air deflectors (flares), front fender air extractors, dual exhausts with chrome extensions, Rally II wheels with trim rings, special heavy-duty suspension, four-speed manual transmission (or M40 Turbo-Hydramatic), dual outside racing mirrors and F60-15 white-lettered tires.

FIREBIRD TRANS AM (SERIES 2FV)

Model Number	Body/Style Number	Body Type & Seating	Factory Price	Shipping Weight	Prod. Total
2FV	V87	2-dr HT-4P	4446	3655	10,255

VENTURA - (6-CYL) - SERIES 2XY - The Firebird-style grille seen on 1973 Ventura Sprints was now used on all models in this line. There were minimal styling changes otherwise. Standard equipment included Deluxe two-spoke steering wheel, bench front seat with cloth and Morrokide trim, woodgrained door inserts, front and rear armrests, high/low ventilation, rubber floor covering, hubcaps, vent windowless styling, and E78-14 tires. Cars with the Sprint option package (two-doors only) had black-textured grilles. The most interesting option was the GTO package, which was now available exclusively for Ventura coupes.

VENTURA (SERIES 2XY)

Model Number	Body/Style Number	Body Type & Seating	Factory Price	Shipping Weight	Prod. Total
2XY	Y69	4-dr Sed-5P	2921/3046	3169/3398	21,012
2XY	Y27	2-dr Cpe-5P	2892/3017	3184/3376	49,153
2XY	Y17	2-dr Hatch-5P	3018/3134	3257/3486	26,335

VENTURA WITH GTO OPTION

Model Number	Body/Style Number	Body Type & Seating	Factory Price	Shipping Weight	Prod. Total
2XY	Y27	2-dr Cpe-5P	3212	3400	(7058)

NOTE 1: Data above slash for six/below slash for V-8.

NOTE 2: GTO option total (in parenthesis) included in Ventura coupe total.

1974 Pontiac Ventura two-door sedan (with GTO option), V-8.

VENTURA CUSTOM - (6-CYL) - SERIES 2XZ - Ventura Customs had all features found on base models plus a choice of cloth or all-Morrokide trim, custom cushion steering wheel, bright metal front seat side panels, glovebox lamp, nylon carpeting, pedal trim plates, right-hand door jamb switch, deluxe wheelcovers and drip, scalp, and rocker panel moldings. Hatchback coupes also had load floor carpeting, fold-down seats, Space Saver spare tires, cargo area dome lights, and trimmed sidewalls.

VENTURA CUSTOM (SERIES 2XZ)

Model Number	Body/Style Number	Body Type & Seating	Factory Price	Shipping Weight	Prod. Total
2XZ	Z69	4-dr Sed-5P	3080/3205	3208/3398	(Note 2)
2XZ	Z27	2-dr Cpe-5P	3051/3176	3184/3413	(Note 2)
2XZ	Z17	2-dr Hatch-5P	3176/3301	2362/3491	(Note 2)

VENTURA CUSTOM W/GTO OPTION

Model Number	Body/Style Number	Body Type & Seating	Factory Price	Shipping Weight	Prod. Total
2XZ	Z27	2-dr Cpe-5P	3371	3437	(Note 3)

NOTE 1: Data above slash for six/below slash for V-8.

NOTE 2: Ventura/Ventura Custom combined by body style; see Ventura chart.

NOTE 3: Ventura/Ventura Custom GTO production combined; see Ventura chart.

1974 Pontiac Catalina coupe. OCW

ENGINES

Code	Type	CID	Carb.	C. R.	H.P. at rpm
D	6-Cyl	250	1-V	8.2:1	100 @ 3600
M	V-8	350	2-V	7.6:1	155 @ 4000
N	V-8	350	2-V	7.6:1	170 @ 4000 **
J	V-8	350	4-V	7.6:1	185 @ 4000
K	V-8	350	4-V	7.6:1	200 @ 4000 **
R	V-8	400	2-V	7.6:1	175 @ 3600
P	V-8	400	2-V	8.0:1	190 @ 4000
S	V-8	400	4-V	8.0:1	200 @ 4000
T	V-8	400	4-V	8.0:1	225 @ 4000 **
W	V-8	455	4-V	8.0:1	215 @ 3600
Y	V-8	455	4-V	8.0:1	250 @ 4000 **
X	V-8	455	4-V	8.4:1	290 @ 4000

NOTE: Dual exhausts are indicated by symbol (**)

(CATALINA) Base V-8 in Catalina was the code R engine. Code P/S/T/W/Y engines were optional in federally certified cars. Code S and code T engines were not available for cars sold in California.

1974 Pontiac Bonneville coupe (rear view). OCW

(BONNEVILLE) Base V-8 in Bonnevilles was the code R engine. Code P/S/T/W/Y engines were optional in federally certified cars. Code S and code T engines were not available for cars sold in California.

(GRAND VILLE/GRAND SAFARI) Base V-8 in Grand Villes and Grand Safaris was the code W engine. The code Y engine was optional only in passenger cars.

(GRAND PRIX) Base V-8 in Grand Prix was the code T engine. The code Y powerplant was optional and was also part of the 'SJ' option package.

(LEMANS/LEMANS SPORT) Base six-cylinder powerplant for passenger cars in both series was the code D engine. Base V-8 for Safaris and passenger cars was the code M engine. Code J/R/T/Y engines were optional in federally certified passenger cars. Code R/P/S/W engines were optional in federally certified Safaris. Code J and code S engines were not available in any cars sold in California. Code M and code T engines were not available in Safari station wagons sold in California.

(LUXURY LEMANS) Base V-8 in Luxury LeMans passenger cars was the code M engine. Code J/R/T/Y engines were optional in federally certified passenger cars. Base V-8 in Luxury LeMans Safaris (with federal certification) was the code M engine. Base V-8 in Luxury LeMans Safaris sold in California was the code R engine. Additional Safari options included code P/S/T/W engines. The code J engine was not available in passenger cars sold in California. The code S and code T engines were not available in Safaris sold in California.

(GRAND AM) Base V-8 in Grand AM was the code P engine. Code T and code Y engines were optional. The code X Super-Duty 455-cid V-8, which had been listed as optional in 1973, but never issued, was no longer listed in 1974.

(BASE FIREBIRD) The standard six-cylinder powerplant in the basic Firebird was the code D engine. The base V-8 was the code M engine. There were no other options.

(FIREBIRD ESPRIT) Base V-8 in Firebird Esprits was the code M engine. The code R engine was the only option in this line.

(FORMULA FIREBIRD) Base V-8 in Formula Firebirds was the code M engine. Code R/T/Y/X engines were optional. All Firebirds built for sale in California were required to have automatic transmission.

(FIREBIRD TRANS AM) Base V-8 in Trans Am was the code T engine. Code Y and code X engines were optional. The latter power plant (SD-455) was officially called the LS2 option and was installed in 731 cars with Turbo-Hydramatic and 212 cars with synchromesh attachment.

(VENTURA) The base six-cylinder powerplant for Venturas was the code D engine. The base V-8 for Venturas was the code M engine. The code J engine was included in the Ventura GTO option package and was a separate option in federally certified cars, but not in cars built for California sale.

(VENTURA CUSTOM) The base six-cylinder powerplant for Venturas was the code D engine. The base V-8 for Venturas was the code M engine. The code J engine was included in the Ventura GTO option package and was a separate option in federally certified cars, but not in cars built for California sale.

CHASSIS FEATURES: Wheelbase: (B-body passenger cars) 124 in.; (B-body Safaris) 127 in.; (G-Body) 116 in.; (A-body two-doors) 112 in.; (A-body four-doors) 116 in.; (F-Body) 108 in.; (X-Body) 111 in. Overall Length: (B-body passenger cars) 226 in.; (B-body Safaris) 231.3 in.; (G-Body) 217.5 in.; (Grand Am two-door) 210.9 in.; (Grand Am four-door) 214.9 in.; (A-body two-door) 208.8 in.; (A-body Safaris) 216 in.; (A-body four-doors) 212.8 in.; (F-Body) 196 in.; (X-Body) 199.4 in. (Note: GM body nomenclature such as A-body now corresponds to first letter in body/style number).

OPTIONS: Pontiac and Grand Am air conditioning ($488-$522). Ventura air conditioning ($396). Firebird air conditioning ($412). Clock and Rally gauge cluster ($29-$49). Clock tachometer and Rally gauge cluster ($51-$100); with trip odometer on Grand Prix ($51-$90). Firebird rear seat console ($26). Ventura and Firebird front seat console ($58). Cruise control ($69-$70). Rear window defogger ($33-$38). LeMans air scoop hood ($87). LeMans D37 and Trans Am hood decals ($55). Formula Firebird RAM AIR hood ($56). Rear quarter windowless louver styling option on LeMans Sport ($35). Safari remote tailgate release ($14). Grand Prix reclining bucket seats ($112). Ventura bucket seats ($132). Grand Prix notchback seat ($50 credit since bucket seats were standard). Grand Am and Grand Prix accent stripes ($31). LeMans and Grand Prix electric sun roof ($325); manual sun roof ($275). Firebird radial tuned suspension with FR78-14 whitewall tires ($107-$145); same on Formula ($24-$36). Ventura radial tuned suspension ($113-$170); same with Sprint package ($91). Custom finned wheelcovers on LeMans and Firebird ($24-$50). Honeycomb wheels on Grand Prix, Grand Am, and Firebird ($54-$123). Rally II rims ($37-$87). Transmission options included three-speed manual with column shift standard in Ventura and LeMans. Three-speed manual with floor shift in Venturas was $26 extra. Heavy-duty three-speed manual with floor shift was $82 extra in certain LeMans hardtops. Four-speed manual was $197 extra in LeMans; $207 extra in Venturas and Firebirds and a $45 delete option in Grand Ams. M38 Turbo-Hydramatic was $221 extra in base Firebirds and certain LeMans; $206 extra in Venturas and $221 extra in Esprits, Formulas, and Luxury LeMans. M40 Turbo-Hydramatic was standard in Grand Am; a no-charge option in Trans Am; $21 extra in LeMans Safaris and $242 extra in LeMans, Esprit, and Formulas. Full-sized Pontiacs and Grand Prix had standard Turbo-Hydramatic .

1974 Pontiac Catalina four-door hardtop. OCW

OPTION PACKAGES: A code 308 custom trim package was available on style numbers FU87 and FV87 and included pedal trim, custom appointments, door handle decor inserts, Deluxe front bucket and custom rear seats and fitted trunk mat. A code 342 LeMans GT option package was available at $202-$246 and included Rally II wheels less trim rings, G70 x 14 tires, dual exhausts with chrome extensions, specific accent stripes, dual sport mirrors (left-hand remote control), wheel opening moldings and three-speed manual transmission with floor shift. The code 342 Grand Prix 'SJ' option sold for $354-$385 and included the 455-cid four-barrel V-8, body color mirrors (left-hand remote control), custom wheelcovers, accent stripes, Delco X battery, Rally gauge cluster with trip odometer, GR70 x 15 steel-belted tires, special shock absorbers, and heavy-duty stabilizer bars. The code 341 Ventura Sprint option sold for $88-$168 and included specific front end styling, body-color sport mirrors, custom cushion steering wheel, custom carpets, cargo area carpeting, vinyl accent stripes, Rally II wheels less trim rings and a deck lid Sprint decal. The Ventura GTO option package sold for $195 and included a 350-cid four-barrel V-8, front and rear stabilizer bars, radial-tuned suspension, Pliacell shock absorbers, power steering, front and rear drum brakes, E78-14 tires, heavy-duty three-speed manual gearbox, dual exhausts with splitter extensions, 3.08:1 ratio axle; Rally II rims less trim rings, special grille driving lights, rear-facing "shaker" air scoop and computer selected high-rate rear springs. This was the eleventh and last GTO.

HISTORICAL FOOTNOTES: The 1974 Pontiacs were introduced on September 20, 1973. Model year production of 580,748 cars was registered and included LeMans models made in Canada. Calendar year production was 502,083 units. A total of 212 Firebirds were built with LS2 SD-455 engines. This was the last year for a GTO (so far).

1975 PONTIAC

1975 Pontiac Catalina four-door sedan. OCW

CATALINA - (V-8) - SERIES 2BL - Full-sized Pontiacs were redesigned for 1975, with most models featuring new roofline treatments. Catalinas had a distinctive radiator grille with a wide vertical center divider and chrome accent moldings forming three stacked rectangles on either side. Triple-stacked taillights were also used, which were shorter than those seen on other lines. The two-door notchback hardtop had an exclusive roofline featuring wide rear quarter windows, thin C-pillars, and a large backlight. Standard equipment was about the same as on 1974 Catalinas, except that a new efficiency system and radial-tuned suspension became regular features.

PONTIAC I.D. NUMBERS: VIN on top of dash at left, viewable through windshield. First symbol tells GM division: 2=Pontiac. Second symbol tells series: X=Astre; B=Ventura SJ; S=Firebird; T=Esprit; U=Formula 400; V=Trans Am; D=LeMans; F=LeMans Sport; G=Luxury LeMans; H=Grand Am; K=Grand Prix; L=Catalina; P=Bonneville Grand Safari; R=Grand Ville Brougham. Third and fourth symbols indicate body style and appear as last two digits of body/style number in charts below. Fifth symbol indicates engine. (See chart at beginning of "Engines" section below.) Sixth symbol indicates model year: 5=1975. Seventh symbol indicates assembly plant: A=Atlanta, Ga.; C=South Gate, Calif.; G=Framingham, Mass.; L=Van Nuys, Calif.; N=Norwood, Ohio; P=Pontiac, Mich.; T=Tarrytown, N.Y.; U=Lordstown, Ohio; W=Willow Run, Mich.; X=Kansas City, Kan.; 1=Oshawa, Canada. Remaining symbols are sequential unit production numbers at factory, starting with 100001. Fisher Body plate on cowl tells style number: (model year prefix 75, plus division code and body/style number code (i.e. 2L69 for Catalina four-door sedan), body number, trim code, paint code and other data. Six-cylinder engine code stamped on distributor mounting on right side of block. V-8 engine code on front of block below right cylinder head. Engine production codes for 1975 were: [140-cid/78 nhp four-cylinder] BB/BC. [140-cid/87 hp four-cylinder] AM/AS/AR/AT/CAM/CAW/CBB/CBD/CAR/CAU. [140-cid/80 nhp four-cylinder] CAS/CAT. [250-cid/105 nhp six-cylinder] JU/JT/JL. [260-cid/110 nhp V-8] QA/QD/QE/QJ/TE/TJ. [350-cid/145 hp V-8] RI/RS. [350-cid/155 hp V-8] YA/YB. [350-cid/165 hp V-8] RW/RX. [350-cid/175 hp V-8] WN/YN/ZP/RN/RO. [400-cid/170 nhp V-8] YH. [400-cid/185 nhp V-8] YT/YM/YS/WT/ZT. [455-cid/200 nhp V-8] YW/YU/ZW/ZU/WX.

1975 Pontiac Grand Safari four-door station wagon, V-8.

CATALINA (SERIES 2BL)

Model Number	Body/Style Number	Body Type & Seating	Factory Price	Shipping Weight	Prod. Total
2BL	L69	4-dr Sed-6P	4612	4347	40,398
2BL	L57	2-dr HT-6P	4700	4334	40,657
2BL	L45	4-dr Sta Wag-9P	5295	5000	4992
2BL	L35	4-dr Sta Wag-6P	5149	4933	3964

1975 Pontiac Bonneville four-door notchback hardtop. JAG

BONNEVILLE - (V-8) - SERIES 2BP - The N Series was dropped and Bonnevilles moved to the P Series (formerly Grand Ville) with Grand Safaris included. A radiator grille with criss-crossed dividers and "egg-crate" inserts was seen. Headlamps were mounted in rectangular housings with square parking lamps on the outside wrapping around the corners of the fenders. New rear quarter window treatments were employed. Taillights were wider than the Catalina type and wrapped around the corners of the rear fenders. Standard equipment was about the same as on 1975 Bonnevilles with the addition of the high-efficiency ignition system and radial-tuned suspension.

BONNEVILLE (SERIES 2BP)

Model Number	Body/Style Number	Body Type & Seating	Factory Price	Shipping Weight	Prod. Total
2BP	P49	4-dr HT-6P	5153	4503	12,641
2BP	P47	2-dr HT-6P	5085	4370	7854
2BP	P45	4-dr Sta Wag-9P	5580	5090	4752
2BP	P35	4-dr Sta Wag-6P	5433	5035	2568

GRAND VILLE BROUGHAM - (V-8) - SERIES 2BR - Grand Ville Broughams were essentially Bonnevilles with a slightly higher level of interior and exterior appointments. Identifying features included wide body sill accent moldings with rear extensions, fender skirts and Grand Ville Brougham signature scripts behind the front wheelhousings.

GRAND VILLE BROUGHAM (SERIES 2BR)

Model Number	Body/Style Number	Body Type & Seating	Factory Price	Shipping Weight	Prod. Total
2BR	R49	4-dr HT-6P	5896	4558	15,686
2BR	R47	2-dr HT-6P	5729	4404	7447
2BR	R67	2-dr Conv-6P	5858	5035	4519

1975 Pontiac Grand Ville Brougham convertible. JAG

131

1975 Pontiac Grand Prix two-door hardtop coupe, V-8.

GRAND PRIX - (V-8) - SERIES 2GK - Styling refinements were seen in the grille, taillight design, and decorative trim of the 1975 Grand Prix. Both the grille and taillights were segmented to produce a more vertical look. The sports-oriented 'SJ' package returned and a new luxury-image 'U' option group was introduced. Modern collectors consider these to be separate models. So did Pontiac, and individual production totals are available for all three types of Grand Prix. Standard equipment was a near match for that featured the year before, except for ignition and suspension systems, which received the same improvements seen on full-size lines. The style number K57 coupe was available with the 'U' package including distinctive two-tone paint finish, Deluxe wheelcovers, outside mirrors, custom interior trim, and Cordova top. Every Grand Prix now had speedometers calibrated in kilometers and headlight dimmer switches built into the turn signal stalk.

GRAND PRIX (SERIES 2GK)

Model Number	Body/Style Number	Body Type & Seating	Factory Price	Shipping Weight	Prod. Total
GRAND PRIX J					
2GK	K57	2-dr HT-5P	5296	4032	64,581
GRAND PRIX SJ					
2GK	K57	2-dr HT-5P	5573	N/A	7146
GRAND PRIX LJ					
2GK	K57	2-dr HT-5P	5995	N/A	14,855

LEMANS/LEMANS SPORT - (6-CYL) - SERIES 2AD/2AF - The 1975 base LeMans and LeMans Sport series were basically unchanged from the previous year except for a new "eggcrate" grille insert and some minor trim variations. An available styling option on two-door hardtop coupes was a louvered rear quarter window treatment, which was also standard on Series 2AF LeMans Sport sport coupes.

LEMANS (SERIES 2AD)

Model Number	Body/Style Number	Body Type & Seating	Factory Price	Shipping Weight	Prod. Total
2AD	D29	4-dr HT-6P	3612/3742	3729/3948	15,065
2AD	D37	2-dr HT-6P	3590/3720	3656/3875	20,636
2AD	D45	4-dr Sta Wag-9P	4688	4500	2393
2AD	D35	4-dr Sta Wag-6P	4555	4401	3898

LEMANS SPORT (SERIES 2AF)

Model Number	Body/Style Number	Body Type & Seating	Factory Price	Shipping Weight	Prod. Total
2AF	F37	2-dr HT-5P	3708/3838	3688/3907	23,817

NOTE 1: Data above slash for six/below slash or no slash for V-8.

1975 Pontiac Grand Am four-door Colonnade hardtop, V-8.

GRAND AM - (V-8) - SERIES 2AH - The Grand Am continued to feature a unique vertically segmented polyurethane nose and louvered rear quarter windows on coupes. Little was changed except for some pin striping and grille insert details. The standard equipment list was about the same as in 1974 with the addition of the high-efficiency ignition system. At the end of the 1975 run this nameplate was temporarily dropped.

1975 Pontiac Grand Am two-door hardtop. OCW

GRAND AM (SERIES 2AHO)

Model Number	Body/Style Number	Body Type & Seating	Factory Price	Shipping Weight	Prod. Total
2AH	H29	4-dr HT-5P	4976	4055	1893
2AH	H37	2-dr HT-5P	4887	4008	8786

1975 Pontiac Grand LeMans coupe. OCW

GRAND LEMANS - (V-8) - SERIES 2AG - The Luxury LeMans became the Grand LeMans this year. There was a distinctive grille design with six groupings of vertical blades arranged three on each side of the center divider. Stand-up hood ornaments appeared and fender skirts were used as standard equipment on all models, except Grand LeMans Safaris.

GRAND LEMANS (SERIES 2AG)

Model Number	Body/Style Number	Body Type & Seating	Factory Price	Shipping Weight	Prod. Total
2AG	G29	4-dr HT-6P	4157/4287	3786/3905	4906
2AG	G37	2-dr HT-6P	4101/4231	3723/3942	19,310
2AG	G45	4-dr Sta Wag-9P	4882	4500	1501
2AG	G35	4-dr Sta Wag-6P	4749	4462	1393

NOTE 1: Data above slash for six/below slash or no slash for V-8.

1975 Pontiac Formula Firebird two-door hardtop coupe, V-8.

FIREBIRDS - (6-CYL) - SERIES 2FS (BASE)/2FT/(ESPRIT)/2FU/(FORMULA)/2FV/(TRANS AM) - Firebirds continued to look much the same as in 1974, except for a new roofline with a wraparound backlight. High-Efficiency ignition and radial-tuned suspension systems were added to the equipment list. As usual, base models had conventional wipers and minimal trim. Esprits had concealed wipers, decor

moldings, door handle inserts and roof pillar signature scripts. Formulas featured heavy-duty chassis components and a distinctive twin scoop hood. The Trans Am had flares, spoilers, extractors, shaker hood scoop and Firebird decals. There were some changes in a technical sense. The base powerplant in Esprit was now the Chevy-built six. At the beginning of the year, the biggest engine for Trans Am was the 400-cid version. At midyear, the code Y engine (455-cid) was reinstated, but only with single exhausts and a catalytic converter. Due to the decrease in brute horsepower, the M38 Turbo-Hydramatic was the only automatic transmission used. In addition, all Firebirds certified for sale in California were required to use this transmission.

1975 Pontiac Firebird 350 coupe. OCW

FIREBIRDS (MODEL CODE INDICATES SERIES)

Model Number	Body/Style Number	Body Type & Seating	Factory Price	Shipping Weight	Prod. Total
FIREBIRD					
2FS	S87	2-dr HT-4P	3713/3843	3386/3610	22,293
ESPRIT					
2FT	T87	2-dr HT-4P	3958/4088	3431/3655	20,826
FORMULA					
2FU	U87	2-dr HT-4P	4349	3631	13,670
TRANS AM					
2FV	V87	2-dr HT-4P	4740	3716	27,274

NOTE 1: Data above slash for six/below slash or no slash for V-8.

NOTE 2: 8314 Firebirds were six-cylinders.

NOTE 3: 26,417 Trans Am had the 400-cid four-barrel (L78) engine.

NOTE 4: 20,277 L78 Trans Ams had Turbo-automatic and 6140 had synchromesh.

NOTE 5: 857 Trans Ams were built with the 455-cid four-barrel (L75) engine.

NOTE 6: All L75 Trans Ams had synchromesh .

VENTURA - (6-CYL) - SERIES 2XE (VENTURA S)/SERIES 2XY (VENTURA)/SERIES 2XZ (VENTURA CUSTOM)/SERIES 2XB (VENTURA SJ) - Venturas were completely restyled. The new 1975 frontal treatment featured distinctive grille ports with integral parking lights and an energy-absorbing front bumper. Rooflines were made somewhat slimmer with lower beltlines and more glass area than before. The Ventura was the basic model at the beginning of the year, with features about the same as 1974 base models. The GM efficiency system was made standard equipment, but on Venturas did not include radial tires. The next-step-up line was the Custom series with such things as custom interior trim, body decor moldings and custom cushion steering wheel. Equipment variations over base models were again about the same as in 1974. A Ventura `SJ' series was new. Features included custom finned wheelcovers, custom steering wheel, Grand Prix style instrument cluster, extra acoustical insulation, cigar lighter, rocker panel moldings and decor trim for wheel openings, rear end, roof and side windows. Interior trims were similar to the Grand AM type and Ventura `SJ' lettering appeared behind the front wheelhousings. In the middle of the model run a Ventura with less equipment than the base model was introduced as the Ventura S.'

VENTURA S (SERIES 2XE)

Model Number	Body/Style Number	Body Type & Seating	Factory Price	Shipping Weight	Prod. Total
2XE	E27	2-dr Cpe-5P	3162/3292	3276/3443	(Note 2)

VENTURA (SERIES 2XY)

2XY	Y69	4-dr Sed-5P	3304/3434	3335/3502	20,619
2XY	Y27	2-dr Coupe-5P	3293/3423	3299/3466	28,473
2XY	Y17	2-dr Hatch-5P	3432/3562	3383/3550	8841

1975 Pontiac Ventura two-door hatchback coupe, V-8.

VENTURA CUSTOM (SERIES 2XZ)

2XZ	Z69	4-dr Sed-5P	3464/3594	3378/3545	(Note 3)
2XZ	Z27	2-dr Cpe-5P	3449/3579	3338/3505	(Note 3)
2XZ	Z17	2-dr Hatch-5P	3593/3565	3398/3565	(Note 3)

1975 Pontiac Ventura three-door hatchback (rear view). OCW

VENTURA SJ (SERIES 2XB)

2XB	B69	4-dr Sed-5P	3846/3976	3370/3537	1449
2XB	B27	2-dr Cpe-5P	3829/3959	3340/3507	2571
2XB	B17	2-dr Hatch-5P	3961/4091	3400/3567	1622

NOTE 1: Data above slash for six/below slash for V-8.

NOTE 2: Ventura `S' production included with base Ventura totals.

NOTE 3: Ventura Custom production included with base Ventura/Ventura S totals.

NOTE 4: Approximately 63 percent of all Venturas were built with V-8s.

ASTRE - (4-CYL) - SERIES 2HC (ASTRE `S')/SERIES 2HV (BASE ASTRE)/SERIES 2HX (ASTRE `SJ') - Pontiac's entry in the 1975 subcompact wars was the Astre. It was initially offered in hatchback coupe and Safari body styles, both of which came with base or `SJ' trim. The Astre `S' economy series was introduced at midyear and included the two original body styles, plus an exclusive notchback coupe. Standard equipment included all GM safety, anti-theft, convenience and emissions control features, three-speed manual floor shift transmission, manual steering, manual brakes with front discs, heater and defroster, front bucket seats, carpeting and A78-13 bias ply tires. The `SJ' models came standard with special upholstery, custom carpets, custom steering wheel, woodgrain dash inserts, Rally gauge cluster with tachometer and clock, Rally II wheels and four-speed manual transmission. Also available was an Astre `GT' option package that added the two-jet induction system, front and rear stabilizer bars, Rally wheels, body-color sport mirrors and radial-tuned suspension. A limited number of Astre-based panel delivery trucks were built in the U.S. for the Canadian market.

ASTRE S (SERIES 2HC)

Model Number	Body/Style Number	Body Type & Seating	Factory Price	Shipping Weight	Prod. Total
2HC	C11	2-dr Cpe-4P	2841	2416	8339
2HC	C77	2-dr Hatch-4P	2954	2487	40,809
2HC	C15	2-dr Sta Wag-4P	3071	2539	15,322

1975 Pontiac Astre three-door hatchback. OCW

BASE ASTRE (SERIES 2HV)

2HV	V77	2-dr Hatch-4P	3079	2499	(Note 2)
2HV	V15	2-dr Sta Wag-4P	3175	2545	(Note 2)
2HV	N/A	2-dr Panel-2P	N/A	N/A	131

1975 Pontiac Astre GT three-door hatchback. OCW

ASTRE 'SJ' (SERIES 2HX)

| 2HX | X77 | 2-dr Hatch-4P | 3610 | 2558 | (Note 3) |
| 2HX | X15 | 2-dr Sta Wag-4P | 3686 | 2602 | (Note 3) |

NOTE 1: Astre output was broken out by body styles, but not by series.

NOTE 2: Base Astre production included with totals for same Astre 'S' model.

NOTE 3: Astre 'SJ' output included with totals for same Astre 'S' model.

ENGINES

Code	Type	CID	Carb.	Comp. Ratio	Net H.P. at rpm
A	4-cyl	140	1-V	8.0:1	78 @ 4200 (C)
B	4-cyl	140	2-V	8.0:1	87 @ 4400 (C)
D	6-cyl	250	1-V	8.25:1	105 @ 3800 (C)
E	V-8	350	2-V	8.0:1	145 @ 3200 (B)
H	V-8	350	4-V	8.0:1	165 @ 3800 (B)
F	V-8	260	2-V	8.0:1	110 @ 3400 (O)
M	V-8	350	2-V	7.6:1	155 @ 4000
J	V-8	350	4-V	7.6:1	175 @ 4400
R	V-8	400	2-V	7.6:1	170 @ 4000
S	V-8	400	4-V	7.6:1	185 @ 3600
Y	V-8	455	4-V	7.6:1	200 @ 3500

Letters after the horsepower rating for engines in the chart below indicate manufacture by Chevrolet (C); Buick (B), or Oldsmobile (O) divisions. Catalytic converters were required on all engines and dual exhausts were not available.

(CATALINA) Base V-8 for federally certified Catalinas was the code R engine. Base V-8 for California Catalinas and federally certified Catalina Safaris was the code S engine. Base V-8 in California Safaris was the code Y engine, which was also optional in federally certified passenger cars.

(BONNEVILLE) Bonneville engine offerings were the same used in Catalinas.

GRAND VILLE BROUGHAM ENGINES

Base V-8 for Grand Ville Broughams was the code S engine. The code Y engine was optional. Both V-8s were available in cars certified for federal and California sale.

(GRAND PRIX) Base V-8 in Grand Prix was the code S engine. The code R engine was optional in federally certified cars only and the code Y engine was optional in all and was also part of the 'SJ' package.

(LEMANS/LEMANS SPORT/GRAND LEMANS) Base six-cylinder powerplant for passenger cars in both series was the code D engine. The code M engine was the base V-8 for federally certified passenger cars. The code J engine was the base V-8 for California cars and the code S engine was optional in all passenger cars. The code R engine was base powerplant for federally certified Safaris. The code S engine was base V-8 for California Safaris and optional in others.

(GRAND AM) Base V-8 in federally certified Grand Ams was the code R engine. The code S engine was base V-8 in cars built for California sale. The code Y engine was optional in all Grand Ams.

(FIREBIRD) Base Firebirds and Esprits had the same engine offerings. For these models the code D six-cylinder powerplant was standard equipment. The code M engine was the base V-8 in cars certified for non-California sale. The code J engine was the base V-8 for California cars and optional in all others. This was also the base engine in Formulas. The code S engine was optional in Formulas and standard in Trans Ams. The code Y engine was released as a midyear option for Trans Ams.

(VENTURA) Base six-cylinder powerplant for all Venturas was the code D engine. Base V-8 for all Venturas was the code F engine. The code H and J engines were optional in all Ventura series.

(ASTRE) Standard four-cylinder engine on coupes was the code A power plant. The code B engine was standard in 'SJ' and optional in other series.

CHASSIS FEATURES: Wheelbase: (B-body Safari) 127 in.; (B-body passenger car) 123.4 in.; (Grand Prix) 116 in.; (A-body two-door) 112 in.; (A-body four-door) 116 in.; (Ventura) 111.1 in.; (Firebird) 108.1 in.; (Astre) 97 in. Overall Length: (B-body Safari) 231.3 in.; (B-body passenger car) 226 in.; (Grand Prix) 212.7 in.; (Grand AM four-door) 215 in.; (Grand Am two-door) 211 in.; (A-body Safaris) 215.4 in.; (LeMans four-door) 212 in.; (LeMans two-door) 208 in.; (Firebird) 196 in.; (Ventura) 199.6 in.; (Astre) 175.4 in.

OPTIONS: Astre vinyl roof ($79). Astre air conditioning ($398). Astre Safari luggage rack ($50). Astre AM/FM stereo ($213). Code B engine ($50). Ventura vinyl top ($87). Ventura tape deck ($215). Ventura, LeMans and Firebird AM/FM stereo ($233). LeMans and Firebird vinyl top ($99). LeMans Safari luggage rack ($68). LeMans and Grand Prix power seats ($70). LeMans and Pontiac AM/FM stereo with tape ($363). Firebird tape deck ($130). Pontiac six-way power seat ($117). Pontiac 60/40 seats ($81). Pontiac Safari luggage rack ($89). Grand Prix vinyl top ($119). Grand Prix power windows ($91). Grand Prix sun roof ($350). Grand Prix custom trim ($120). Ventura and LeMans power brakes ($47); with front discs ($70).

HISTORICAL FOOTNOTES: The 1974 Pontiacs appeared in showrooms on September 27, 1974. Calendar year output was 523,469 cars. A new sales promotion tool was a program of price rebates on compact models. Road testers found the 1975 Trans Am with the 185 nhp V-8 capable of 0-to-60 mph in 9.8 seconds and the quarter-mile in 16.8 seconds.

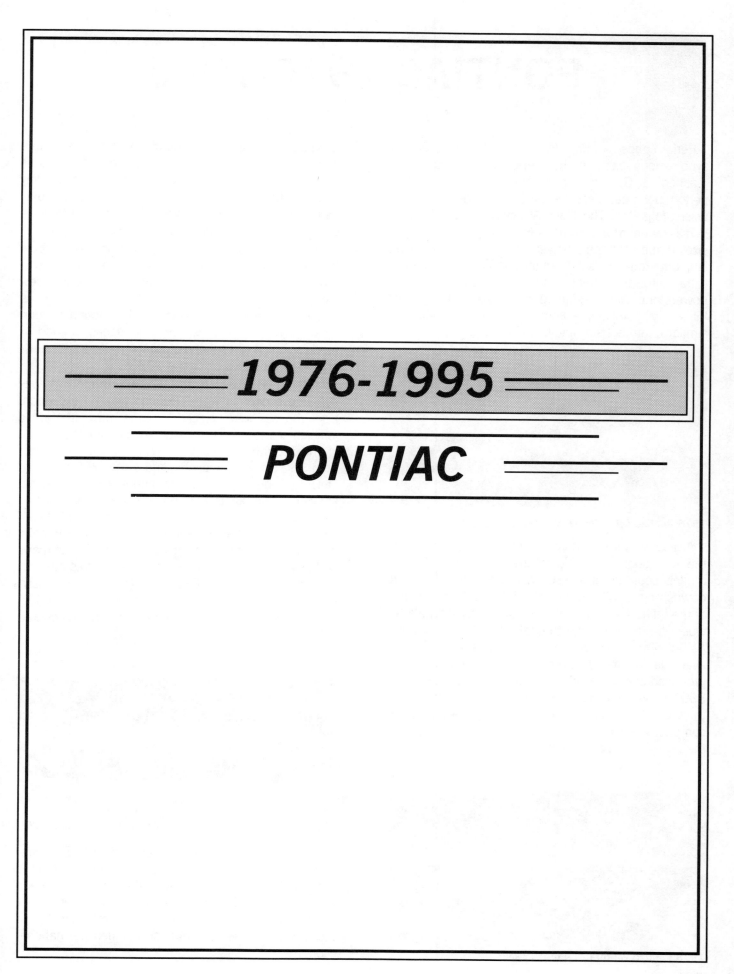

1976-1995

PONTIAC

PONTIAC 1976-1995

Performance and Pontiac almost seemed synonymous back in the 1960s. As the company reached its Golden Anniversary year in 1976, that performance had become somewhat subdued. But, it wasn't forgotten. The Trans Am still carried a 400 cid V-8 as standard and could hold a big 455 V-8. Engine sizes diminished the next year, to a maximum of 403 cid, but Pontiac usually managed to put something extra into its Firebird lineup. Already, though, powerplants were beginning the shrinkage that would hit every domestic automaker. Bodies would get similar treatment starting in 1977.

1976 Pontiac Astre Formal Window coupe. (P)

A new Sunbird subcompact arrived in 1976 to join the less sporty Astre. That pair and several other models could get a five-speed gearbox. In addition to downsizing of full-size models, 1977 brought the end of the inline six as a Pontiac engine; only V-type sixes would be used through the next decade and beyond. As in other GM divisions, the variety of engines available (built by more than one manufacturer) produced considerable confusion in the late 1970s. A 350 cid V-8, for instance, might come from any of three GM factories. At mid-year 1977 a new Phoenix compact arrived, ready to take over Ventura's spot as the only compact with a four-cylinder engine.

1978 Pontiac Ventura LJ four-door sedan.

Collectors, though, would be far more interested in a limited production model that appeared at the same time: the Can Am edition of the LeMans coupe. Only 1377 of those were built. Pontiac's new "Iron Duke" four would find its way under plenty of GM hoods - even some on cars outside the GM fold.

Grand Am returned in 1978, sporting a soft rubber front-end panel. Pontiac's mid-size cars were downsized, as sales hit record levels. Next year, a new "crossflow" cylinder head went into four-cylinder powerplants and Trans Ams had the option of four-wheel power disc brakes. For added looks, Grand Prix models could get a set of real wire wheels--a choice not offered on Pontiacs since the 1930s.

As the 1980s began, the whole auto industry was suffering economic woes. Pontiac was no exception. High hopes were placed on the new front-drive "efficiency sized" Phoenix, which was Pontiac's version of the soon-to-be-notorious X-car. No engines larger than 350 cid were available and a new 265 cid (4.3-liter) V-8 highlighted the continuing trend toward smaller powerplants. Fours and V-6s soon would become the norm, through V-8s remained available in a number of models. Diesel power went under Pontiac hoods as an option for the first time in 1980. Not many enthusiasts are likely to seek those examples out, but an electronic-control (E/C) 301 cid (4.9-liter) V-8, used by performance models, may prove more tempting. More desirable yet: the turbocharged 301 V-8 offered in Trans Am.

1979 Pontiac Firebird Trans Am Silver Anniversary coupe. (P)

The popular Grand Prix was restyled for 1981. Later that year came another Chevrolet clone, the little T1000, based on Chevette. Sales may have been weak, but that didn't keep Pontiac (or other companies) from jacking up prices mightily during these years, as serious inflation plagued the national economy.

1980 Pontiac Phoenix LJ hatchback sedan. (JG)

Firebird's aging design needed attention, so wind-tunnel testing helped to produce an aero-restyled 'bird for 1982. It was still a rear-drive car, but with a more contemporary look. Front-wheel-drive was the trend, though, and Pontiac concurred by offering new J2000 and 6000 models. The latter featured a wedge profile that soon would become standard in "sporty" sedans. The Catalina nameplate was retired, but Bonneville returned in G-body form, kin to Grand Prix. Bowing in another way to the changing automotive scene, the "Iron Duke" four added fuel injection.

1982 Pontiac Firebird Trans Am coupe. (OCW)

"World class" was the way Pontiac described the 6000 STE performance-oriented sedan introduced for 1983 with a standard V-6 engine. Most domestic automakers seemed eager to emulate the European sedans, in styling as well as performance and handling. Firebirds adopted a five-speed manual gearbox and a convertible arrived bearing the 2000 badge. Not since 1975 had Pontiac offered a ragtop. Parisienne was the name given to a new full-size, rear-drive sedan/wagon. Even with the rise of four and V-6 power, Pontiacs had more V-8s this year than in 1982.

After several years in retirement, the Sunbird name returned in 1984 on the former 2000 series, which added a turbocharger option. Even more significant was the arrival of the two-seater Fiero, wearing a plastic body over a "space frame/chassis." Fiero sold briskly at first, but sagged somewhat later, never quite meeting the company's hopes. Total sales rose impressively this year, after four depressed seasons. At

the corporate level, Pontiac joined Chevrolet and GM of Canada to become the new C-P-C group.

Pontiac's stated goal was to develop cars that were performance-oriented" and "fun to drive," appealing to entry-level, younger buyers. Joining Fiero in 1985 was the "driver-oriented" Grand Am. It was created to attract the "new values" motorist (to use two more automotive buzzwords of the mid-1980s). Furthering that goal in 1986 was a new Grand Am SE and Sunbird GT. Later, a Fiero GT fastback bowed. Collectors in search of a memorable model could instead turn to Grand Prix, especially to the limited-production Grand Prix 2+2. Since only 200 were built and sold only in the South, they're likely to remain among the rarest modern-day Pontiacs.

Collectors tend to think in terms of Trans Am and Grand Prix models. A sensible choice, since that pair has been popular all along and likely to remain so. A turbo V-8 Trans Am or one with cross-flow fuel injection might be a bit more mechanically troublesome than a high-output carbureted edition, but is still worth hanging onto. Tucked here and there among the other Pontiac models, though, are a few with slightly less obvious attractions, but smaller price tags. If you can't snag a '77 Can Am, '86 Grand Prix 2+2 or full-performance Trans Am, there's always an S/E or Formula Firebird or an ordinary LeMans with a good selection of appearance options.

The 6000 line accounted for 23.3 percent of Pontiac's sales in 1986. One in every five of the 6000s sold was the up-level STE with electronic anti-lock brakes. A resurgence in the muscle car market helped sales of the Pontiac Firebird Trans Am as half the Firebirds built through June 1986 were TAs.

1984 Pontiac Fiero MS4 coupe. (P)

Continuing in 1987 to emphasize its youthful performance car image, improvements were made to the 2.5-liter L-4 engine (Grand Am, Fiero, and 6000) to increase horsepower and torque. Also introduced was the 210-hp tuned-port fuel-injected 5.7-liter V-8 (similar to the Corvette powerplant) made available in the Trans Am as an option. GM's new assembly plant in Fairfax, Kan., produced the revised-for-1987 front-drive Grand Prix based on the W platform. GM permanently closed its Norwood, Ohio, plant so

beginning in 1987 all Firebird (and sister car Camaro) production was done at the Van Nuys, Calif., plant. Introduced in June 1987 as a 1988 model, the entry-level LeMans, a South Korean import, replaced the now defunct 1000.

1985 Parisienne Brougham sedan. (AA)

Because the front-drive Bonneville did not sell to expectations the previous year, the new-for-1988 Bonneville SSE model--and the SE version--received GM's new 3800 3.8-liter V-6 as standard equipment. Also not selling to expectations was the Fiero, which attracted only 27,304 buyers in 1988 even though a new five-speed transmission and Formula option package were introduced to perk up sales. The low sales caused 1988 to be the final year for Fiero. Based on total sales of 740,928 units in 1988, Pontiac regained the number three domestic sales slot that it lost 15 years prior, finishing behind Chevrolet and Ford. Pontiac's emphasis on youthful performance car image was definitely working as the median age of Pontiac buyers decreased from 46 years old in 1981 to 38 in 1988.

Nineteen eighty-nine marked the 20th Anniversary of the Trans Am and Pontiac observed the occasion by producing 1,500 units with special exterior graphics and a potent 250-hp 3.8-liter turbocharged engine under the hood. A turbo would also find its way under the hood of 2,000 McLaren Turbo Grand Prix rated at 205 hp. After a delay in its initial 1988 target date, all-wheel drive made its GM automobile debut in the Pontiac 6000 STE AWD version. Built in Oklahoma City, the modular AWD unit used in the 6000 STE was designed to fit most GM front-drive platforms. Pontiac dropped its rear-drive B-body Safari wagon.

Aside from the addition of a four-door Grand Prix, which was an immediate sales booster, the big Pontiac news for 1990--and beyond--was the launch of the all purpose van (APV) called the Trans Sport. The composite-bodied minivan found 40,750 buyers in its first year, and continues through 1995 to be Pontiac's

flagship in the increasingly popular light truck market. The 1991 Firebird, a warm-over of the previous year's Firebird, was launched in the spring of 1990 with refined front and rear fascias and speculation rampant as to what would be the next generation replacement for the aging F-car platform (Firebird/Camaro). Since that time, the Firebird has undergone major refinements to its body panels, drivetrain, suspension, and interior ergonomics, but it remains in 1995 among the dwindling ranks of rear drive musclecars. The AWD innovation was reduced to option status on the 6000 S/E (which replaced the STE for 1990), and in 1992 the 6000 was dropped from the Pontiac lineup after a paltry 708 units were sold. The LeMans followed suit in 1993 after sales totaled 7,700 units, little more than half from the previous year.

1995 Pontiac Sunfire GT coupe. PMD

As we wind down on the 20th century, the Pontiac lineup consists of some long familiar names: Bonneville, Firebird, Grand Am, Grand Prix, Trans Sport, and one new-for-1995 model, that being the Sunfire--a replacement for the long-standing Sunbird. Aerodynamic improvements to decrease coefficient of drag numbers, safety improvements such as anti-lock brakes and air bags as standard equipment, smaller yet more powerful and fuel efficient engines, and the use of space-age materials that are lighter yet stronger are some of the continuing refinements that have been incorporated into these Pontiacs during the first half of this decade. And one needs only to look at Pontiac's concept cars currently being displayed at auto shows around the country to see that the "excitement" that Pontiac has emphasized so often as its production standard will continue well into the 21st century.

1976 PONTIAC

A sporty new subcompact (Sunbird) entered Pontiac's 1976 lineup, while major changes hit the personal-luxury Grand Prix. Many models had smaller engines than before, including a 260 cid V-8 under LeMans hoods and a 350 for the new Grand Prix. A new five-speed manual transmission (overdrive fifth gear), intended to boost gas mileage, was offered as an option on Astre and Sunbird, and on the LeMans Sport Coupe and the Ventura with 260 V-8. Also to improve economy, cars with air conditioning got a lower idle speed when the unit was not operating. Most models got lower axle ratios (especially the 2.41:1 final drive ratio). All Pontiacs now had a catalytic converter (except Astre/Sunbird with the single-barrel 140 four), which had been introduced a year earlier. A Radial Tuned Suspension (RTS) was standard on LeMans, Firebird, Grand Prix and full-size models; optional on Astre, Sunbird and Ventura. Most Pontiacs could also get a new Rally RTS handling package that included a rear stabilizer bar. Bumpers and brakes were revised this year to meet new federal standards. Firebirds used a urethane foam bumper system, Astres a leaf spring and rubber-block energy absorbers, other models had a hydraulic energy absorber.

I.D. DATA: The 13-symbol Vehicle Identification Number (VIN) was located on the upper left surface of the instrument panel, visible through the windshield. The first digit is '2', indicating Pontiac division. The second symbol is a letter indicating series: 'C' = Astre; 'M' = Sunbird; 'Y' = Ventura; 'Z' = Ventura SJ; 'D' = LeMans; 'F' = LeMans Sport Coupe; 'G' = Grand LeMans; 'S' = Firebird; 'T' = Firebird Esprit; 'U' = Firebird Formula; 'W' = Firebird Trans Am; 'L' = Catalina; 'P' = Bonneville; 'R' = Bonneville Brougham; 'J' = Grand Prix; 'K' = Grand Prix SJ. Next come two digits that denote body type: '11' = two-door pillar coupe; '17' = two-door hatchback coupe; '27' = two-door thin-pillar coupe; '37' = two-door HT coupe; '47' = two-door HT coupe; '57' = two-door HT coupe; '77' = two-door hatchback coupe; '87' = two-door HT coupe; '29' = four-door HT sedan; '49' = four-door HT sedan; '69' = four-door thin-pillar four-window sedan; '15' = two-door station wagon; '35' = four-door two-seat wagon; '45' = four-door three-seat wagon. The fifth symbol is a letter indicating engine code: 'A' = L4-140 one-barrel; 'B' = L4-140 two-barrel; 'C' = V-6-231 two-barrel; 'D' = L6-250 one-barrel; 'F' = V-8-260 two-barrel; 'H' or 'M' = V-8-350 two-barrel; 'E' or 'J' = V-8-350 four-barrel 'R' = V-8-400 two-barrel; 'S' = V-8-400 four-barrel 'W' = V-8-455 four-barrel. The sixth symbol denotes model year ('6' = 1976). Next is a plant code: 'A' = Lakewood, Ga.; 'C' = South Gate, Calif.; 'G' = Framingham, Mass.; 'L' = Van Nuys, Calif.; 'N' = Norwood, Ohio; 'P' = Pontiac, Mich.; 'T' = Tarrytown, N.Y.; 'U' = Lordstown, Ohio; 'W' = Willow Run, Mich.; 'X' = Fairfax, Kan.; '1' = Oshawa, Ontario; '2' = Ste. Therese, Quebec. The final six digits are the sequential serial number, which began with 100,001.

1976 Pontiac Astre coupe. (P)

ASTRE -- SERIES 2H -- FOUR -- Pontiac's subcompact came in two-door coupe or hatchback form, or as a Safari two-door station wagon. Round headlamps sat in squarish recessed housings. A recessed two-section crosshatch (eggcrate) grille held rather large, inset parking/signal lights. On the body-color grille divider (a Pontiac "trademark") was the typical v-shaped emblem. Below the bumper was a wide air intake slot. Two new interior trim packages were available. The luxury version included doeskin seats, luxury door trim, upgraded sound insulation and thick, cut-pile carpeting. Standard equipment included a 140 cid (2.3-liter) four-cylinder engine with one-barrel carburetor, three-speed manual gearbox (floor shift), front bucket seats, heater/defroster, A78 x 13 blackwall tires, inside hood release, and window and roof drip moldings. A new five-speed manual gearbox became optional. Astre's GT option was offered on both hatchback and wagon, included a two-barrel version of the 140 four, four-speed gearbox, BR78 x 13 SBR tires, and rally gauge cluster.

ASTRE (FOUR)

Model Number	Body/Style Number	Body Type & Seating	Factory Price	Shipping Weight	Prod. Total
2H	C11	2-dr. Cpe-4P	3064	2439	18,143
2H	C77	2-dr. Hatch Cpe-4P	3179	2505	19,116
2H	C15	2-dr. Safari Wag-4P	3306	2545	13,125

SUNBIRD -- SERIES 2H -- FOUR -- New for 1976, the sporty subcompact Sunbird rode a 97 inch wheelbase. Base engine was a 140 cid (2.3-liter) four, with new 231 cid (3.8-liter) V-6 from Buick optional. Sunbird's standard interior included bucket seats in cloth and Morrokide. Both rectangular quad headlamps and the twin crosshatch grille inserts were recessed between the customary Pontiac divider with v-shaped emblem. Standard equipment included a three-speed floorshift manual transmission, heater/defroster, front bucket seats, carpeting, custom wheel covers, window and roof drip moldings, wheel opening moldings, and A78 x 13 blackwall tires. A luxury appointment group was optional. So was a new five-speed manual transmission.

SUNBIRD (FOUR/V-6)

Model Number	Body/Style Number	Body Type & Seating	Factory Price	Shipping Weight	Prod. Total
2H	M27	2-dr. Cpe-4P	3431/3607	2653/--	52,031

1976 Pontiac Ventura SJ Cordova Landau coupe. (P)

VENTURA -- SERIES 2X -- SIX/V-8 -- Compact in size, Ventura came in base and SJ trim, in three body styles: two-door coupe or hatchback, and four-door sedan. Ventura rode a 111 inch wheelbase and carried a standard 250 cid inline six-cylinder engine. Two V-8s were optional: 260 or 350 cu. in. displacement. A new five-speed manual gearbox became optional on models with the 260 cid V-8 engine. Options included cruise control and a landau coupe roof. An appearance group including special body striping and black window frames was offered on two-door models. Single round headlamps were mounted in squarish housings. On each side of a peaked divider bar were crosshatch grille inserts arranged in three rows (with two horizontal divider bars). Park/signal lamps stood behind bars at the outer ends of the grille. Ventura's standard equipment included the 250 cid six with three-speed manual (floor lever) transmission, heater/defroster, E78 x 14 blackwall tires, windshield and back window moldings, and carpeting. Hatchbacks and sedans also had roof drip moldings. Hatchbacks included a fold-down back seat. Ventura SJ added custom finned wheel covers, dual horns, courtesy lamps, rocker panel and wheel opening moldings, window moldings, and full-width front seats.

Model Number	Body/Style Number	Body Type & Seating	Factory Price	Shipping Weight	Prod. Total
VENTURA (SIX/V-8)					
2X	Y27	2-dr. Cpe-5P	3326/3416	3234/3393	28,473
2X	Y17	2-dr. Hatch Cpe-5P	3503/3593	3348/3507	6428
2X	Y69	4-dr. Sed-5P	3361/3451	3271/3430	27,773
VENTURA SJ (SIX/V-8)					
2X	Z27	2-dr. Cpe-5P	3612/3702	3290/3449	4815
2X	Z17	2-dr. Hatch Cpe-5P	3775/3865	3380/3539	1823
2X	Z69	4-dr. Sed-5P	3637/3727	3326/3485	4804

FIREBIRD -- SERIES 2F -- SIX/V-8 -- Four models made up the famed Firebird lineup: base, Esprit, and performance-minded Formula and Trans Am. Each featured body-colored urethane bumpers at both ends this year. Base powerplant was the 250 cid inline six, but Trans Am could go as high as a 455 cid V-8. New options this year included a canopy top, new appearance package (Formula only), and fuel economy indicator. Trans Am came in five body colors: Cameo White, Firethorn Red, Sterling Silver, Carousel Red, and Goldenrod Yellow. Firebird's typical twin-section grille with mesh pattern sat in a sloping front panel. Single square headlamps were recessed. Park/signal lamps stood at the ends of a wide opening below the

bumper strip. Standard Firebird/Esprit equipment included the 250 cid six with three-speed manual gearbox, dual horns, FR78 x 15 blackwall SBR tires, power steering, and radial-tuned suspension. Esprit included sport mirrors (driver's side remote-controlled) and deluxe wheel covers. Formula had a 350 cid two-barrel V-8, either four-speed manual or Turbo-Hydramatic, the sport mirrors, and a full-length console. Trans Am included an air dam, rear decklid spoiler, shaker hood, Rally II wheels with trim rings, rally gauges, GR70 x 15 tires, and the 400 cid four-barrel V-8.

1976 Pontiac Firebird Trans Am Special Edition. (P)

Model Number	Body/Style Number	Body Type & Seating	Factory Price	Shipping Weight	Prod. Total
FIREBIRD (SIX/V-8)					
2F	S87	2-dr. HT Cpe-4P	3906/4046	3383/3563	21,209
FIREBIRD ESPRIT (SIX/V-8)					
2F	T87	2-dr. HT Cpe-4P	4162/4302	3431/3611	22,252
FIREBIRD FORMULA (V-8)					
2F	U87	2-dr. HT Cpe-4P	4566	3625	20,613
FIREBIRD TRANS AM (V-8)					
F	W87	2-dr. HT Cpe-4P	4987	3640	46,701

LEMANS -- SERIES 2A -- SIX/V-8 -- Quad rectangular headlamps gave LeMans a new front-end appearance. Base and Grand LeMans came in two-door hardtop coupe and four-door hardtop sedan form, while the LeMans Sport Coupe was (obviously) coupe only. Two-door models had a formal-look rear quarter window, while the Sport Coupe's window was louvered. Park/signal lamps were at outer ends of a single bumper slot, next to the bumper guards. The LeMans grille consisted of thin vertical bars, arranged in sections per side of the peaked divider bar (which displayed a Pontiac emblem). Two four-door (two-seat) wagons were available: LeMans Safari and Grand LeMans Safari. Both could also have an optional rear-facing third seat. Grand LeMans had a wide variety of interior possibilities: standard notchback full-width seat (cloth and vinyl); optional 60/40 seating (cloth, vinyl, or velour); and bucket seats (perforated vinyl, corduroy, velour, or leather). LeMans standard equipment included the 250 cid six with three-speed manual shift, rocker panel moldings, FR78 x 15 SBR tires, radial-tuned suspension, and dual horns. Wagons had a 400 cid two-barrel V-8, Turbo-Hydramatic, power brakes, and HR78 x 15 tires. Grand LeMans models had either a five-speed manual gearbox or Turbo-Hydramatic, along with deluxe wheel covers and an electric clock. Both Grand LeMans and the Sport Coupe had wheel opening moldings, and either full-width seating or bucket seats. A new five-speed manual transmission was available on the LeMans Sport Coupe.

1976 Pontiac Grand LeMans coupe. (P)

Model Number	Body/Style Number	Body Type & Seating	Factory Price	Shipping Weight	Prod. Total
LEMANS (SIX/V-8)					
2A	D37	2-dr. HT Cpe-6P	3768/3908	3651/3826	21,130
2A	D29	4-dr. HT Sed-6P	3813/3953	3760/3935	22,199
LEMANS SAFARI (V-8)					
2A	D35	4-dr. 2S Wag-6P	4687	4336	Note 1
2A	D45	4-dr. 3S Wag-9P	4820	4374	Note 1
LEMANS SPORT COUPE (SIX/V-8)					
2A	F37	2-dr. HT Cpe-6P	3916/4056	3668/3843	15,582
GRAND LEMANS (SIX/V-8)					
2A	G37	2-dr. HT Cpe-6P	4330/4470	3747/3922	14,757
2A	G29	4-dr. HT Sed-6P	4433/4573	3860/4035	8411
GRAND LEMANS SAFARI (V-8)					
2A	G35	4-dr. 2S Wag-6P	4928	4389	Note 1
2A	G45	4-dr. 3S Wag-9P	5061	4427	Note 1

Note 1: A total of 8249 two-seat and 5901 three-seat LeMans Safari wagons were produced (base and Grand).

1976 Pontiac Grand Prix LJ 50th Anniversary T-top coupe. (P)

GRAND PRIX -- SERIES 2G -- V-8 -- Front-end appearance of Pontiac's personal-luxury coupe was the same as Bonneville (above), with the same sharp hood creases that came to a point at the front, and the same new wrapover-fin grille. New base engine was the 350 cid (5.7-liter) V-8. Grand Prix got a new full-width front seat with fold-down center armrest. Standard Grand Prix equipment included the 350 cid V-8 with two-barrel carburetor, Turbo-Hydramatic, power brakes and steering, GR78 x 15 blackwall SBR tires, radial-tuned suspension, clock, heater/defroster, full-width seats with center armrest, window and hold moldings, rocker panel and wheel opening moldings, and roof drip moldings. Grand Prix SJ added the 400 cid four-barrel V-8, bucket seats (with console), special wheel covers, and courtesy lights. A limited-edition Golden Anniversary model featured special paint and striping, removable roof panels, and a commemorative stand-up hood ornament. An LJ luxury appointments group included velour bucket seats, thick cut-pile carpeting, and two-tone body color.

Model Number	Body/Style Number	Body Type & Seating	Factory Price	Shipping Weight	Prod. Total
GRAND PRIX (V-8)					
2G	J57	2-dr. HT Cpe-5P	4798	4048	110,814
GRAND PRIX SJ (V-8)					
2G	K57	2-dr. HT Cpe-5P	5223	4052	88,232
GRAND PRIX LJ (V-8)					
2G	N/A	2-dr. HT Cpe-5P	N/A	N/A	29,045

Note: LJ was actually a $625 option package for Grand Prix.

CATALINA -- SERIES 2B -- V-8 -- Pontiac's lowest-priced full-size model was similar in appearance to Bonneville (below), but had five thick horizontal bars across its grille. A Custom option, however, gave it the same new front-end look as Bonneville. Standard equipment

included a 400 cid two-barrel V-8, Turbo-Hydramatic, power brakes and steering, HR78 x 15 blackwall SBR tires, radial-tuned suspension, and heater/defroster.

Model Number	Body/Style Number	Body Type & Seating	Factory Price	Shipping Weight	Prod. Total
CATALINA (V-8)					
2B	L57	2-dr. HT Cpe-6P	4844	4256	15,262
2B	L69	4-dr. Sed-6P	4767	4276	47,235
CATALINA SAFARI (V-8)					
2B	L35	4-dr. 2S Wag-6P	5324	4944	4735
2B	L45	4-dr. 3S Wag-9P	5473	5000	5513

1976 Pontiac Bonneville Brougham sedan. (P)

BONNEVILLE -- SERIES 2B -- V-8 -- Base and Brougham models were available in the top full-size field. Bonneville Brougham was the newest model, offered in two-door hardtop coupe or four-door hardtop sedan form. All models (including Grand Safari wagon) featured a new front-end look with quad rectangular headlamps. A new wrapover "waterfall" grille looked like a set of many "fins" on each side of the divider bar, which held Pontiac's emblem. Headlamps were separated from the fender-tip wraparound park/signal lights. Wraparound taillamps had upper and lower sections. Four-door wagons came with two seats, but a forward facing third seat was available. Standard equipment for the base Bonneville was similar to Catalina, but included a four-barrel 400 cid V-8, driver's remote mirror, accent paint stripes, power windows, and electric clock. Wagons came with a 455 cid V-8 engine and LR78 x 15 tires.

Model Number	Body/Style Number	Body Type & Seating	Factory Price	Shipping Weight	Prod. Total
BONNEVILLE (V-8)					
2B	P47	2-dr. HT Cpe-6P	5246	4308	9189
2B	P49	4-dr. HT Sed-6P	5312	4460	14,942
BONNEVILLE BROUGHAM (V-8)					
2B	R47	2-dr. HT Cpe-6P	5734	4341	10,466
2B	R49	4-dr. HT Sed-6P	5906	4514	20,236
GRAND SAFARI (V-8)					
2B	P35	4-dr. 2S Wag-6P	5746	5035	3462
2B	P45	4-dr. 3S Wag-9P	5895	5091	6176

1976 Pontiac Grand LeMans Safari station wagon. (CP)

FACTORY PRICE AND WEIGHT NOTE: For Ventura, LeMans, and Firebird, prices and weights to left of slash are for six-cylinder, to right for V-8 engine.

ENGINE DATA

BASE FOUR (Astre, Sunbird): Inline. Overhead cam. Four-cylinder. Aluminum block and cast iron head. Displacement: 140 cu. in. (2.3 liters). Bore & stroke: 3.50 x 3.63 in. Compression ratio: 7.9:1. Brake horsepower: 70 @ 4400 rpm. Torque: 107 lb.-ft. @ 2400 rpm. Five main bearings. Hydraulic valve lifters. Carburetor: one-barrel Rochester. VIN Code: A. OPTIONAL FOUR (Astre, Sunbird): Same as 140 cid four above, except Horsepower: 84 @ 4400 rpm. Torque: 113 lb.-ft. @ 3200 rpm. Carburetor: two-barrel Holley 366829. VIN Code: B. OPTIONAL V-6 (Sunbird): 90-degree, overhead-valve V-6. Cast iron block and head. Displacement: 231 cu. in. (3.8 liters). Bore & stroke: 3.80 x 3.40 in. Compression ratio: 8.0:1. Brake horsepower: 105 @ 3400 rpm. Torque: 185 lb.-ft. @ 2000 rpm. Four main bearings. Hydraulic valve lifters. Carburetor: two-barrel Rochester. VIN Code: C.

BASE SIX (Ventura, Firebird, LeMans): Inline. Overhead valve. Six-cylinder. Cast iron block and head. Displacement: 250 cu. in. (4.1 liters). Bore & stroke: 3.87 x 3.53 in. Compression ratio: 8.3:1. Brake horsepower: 110 @ 3600 rpm. Torque: 185 lb.-ft. @ 1200 rpm. Seven main bearings. Hydraulic valve lifters. Carburetor: one-barrel Rochester. VIN Code: D. OPTIONAL V-8 (Ventura, LeMans): 90-degree, overhead valve V-8. Cast iron block and head. Displacement: 260 cu. in. (4.3 liters). Bore & stroke: 3.50 x 3.39 in. Compression ratio: 7.5:1. Brake horsepower: 110 @ 3400 rpm. Torque: 205 lb.-ft. @ 1600 rpm. Five main bearings. Hydraulic valve lifters. Carburetor: two-barrel Rochester. VIN Code: F.

1976 Pontiac Formula Firebird coupe. (P)

BASE V-8 (Grand Prix, Firebird Formula); OPTIONAL (Firebird, LeMans): 90-degree, overhead valve V-8. Cast iron block and head. Displacement: 350 cu. in. (5.7 liters). Bore & stroke: 3.88 x 3.75 in. Compression ratio: 7.6:1. Brake horsepower: 160 @ 4000 rpm. Torque: 280 lb.-ft. @ 2000 rpm. Five main bearings. Hydraulic valve lifters. Carburetor: two-barrel Rochester. VIN Code: H or M. OPTIONAL V-8 (Ventura): 90-degree, overhead valve V-8. Cast iron block and head. Displacement: 350 cu. in. (5.7 liters). Bore & stroke: 3.80 x 3.85 in. Compression ratio: 8.0:1. Brake horsepower: 140 @ 3200 rpm. Torque: 280 lb.-ft. @ 1600 rpm. Five main bearings. Hydraulic valve lifters. Carburetor: two-barrel Rochester. OPTIONAL V-8 (Ventura): Same as 350 cid V-8 above, with Rochester four-barrel carburetor. Horsepower: 155 @ 3400 rpm. Torque: 280 lb.-ft. @ 1800 rpm. BASE V-8 (Catalina, Bonneville, LeMans Safari wagon); OPTIONAL (LeMans, Grand Prix): 90-degree, overhead valve V-8. Cast iron block and head. Displacement: 400 cu. in. (6.6 liters). Bore & stroke: 4.12 x 3.75 in. Compression ratio: 7.6:1. Brake horsepower: 170 @ 4000 rpm. Torque: 310 lb.-ft. @ 1600 rpm. Five main bearings. Hydraulic valve lifters. Carburetor: two-barrel Rochester. VIN Code: R. BASE V-8 (Trans Am, Bonneville Brougham, Grand Prix SJ); OPTIONAL (LeMans, Firebird, Grand Prix, Catalina, Bonneville): Same as 400 cid V-8 above, except Horsepower: 185 @ 3600 rpm. Torque: 310 lb.-ft. @ 1600 rpm. Carburetor: four-barrel Rochester. VIN Code: S. BASE V-8 (Catalina and Grand Safari wagons); OPTIONAL V-8 (LeMans, Firebird, Grand Prix, Catalina, Bonneville): 90-degree, overhead valve V-8. Cast iron block and head. Displacement: 455 cu. in. (7.5 liters). Bore & stroke: 4.15 x 4.21 in. Compression ratio: 7.6:1. Brake horsepower: 200 @ 3500 rpm. Torque: 330 lb.-ft. @ 2000 rpm. Five main bearings. Hydraulic valve lifters. Carburetor: four-barrel Rochester. VIN Code: W.

CHASSIS DATA: Wheelbase: (Astre/Sunbird) 97.0 in.; (Ventura) 111.1 in.; (Firebird) 108.1 in.; (LeMans two-door) 112.0 in.; (LeMans four-door) 116.0 in.; (Grand Prix) 116.0 in.; (Catalina cpe/sed) 123.4 in.; (Catalina wag) 127.0 in.; (Bonneville) 123.4 in. Overall Length: (Astre) 177.6 in.; (Sunbird) 177.8 in.; (Ventura) 199.6 in.; (Firebird) 196.8 in.; (LeMans two-door) 208.0 in.; (LeMans four-door) 212.0 in.; (LeMans wag) 215.4 in.; (G.P.) 212.7 in.; (Catalina cpe/sed, Bonneville) 226.0 in.; (Catalina wag) 231.3 in. Height: (Astre hatch) 50.0 in.; (Astre notch/wag) 51.8 in.; (Sunbird) 49.8 in.; (Ventura two-door) 52.3 in.; (Ventura four-door) 53.2 in.; (Firebird) 49.1 in.; (LeMans two-door) 52.7 in.; (LeMans four-door) 53.5 in.; (LeMans wag) 55.3 in.; (Esprit/Formula) 49.4 in.; (Trans Am) 49.6 in.; (G.P.) 52.6 in.; (Catalina cpe) 53.5 in.; (Catalina sed, Bonneville) 54.2 in.; (Catalina wag) 57.8 in. Width: (Astre/

1976 Pontiac Astre three-door hatchback (rear view). OCW

1976 Pontiac Sunbird coupe. OCW

1976 Pontiac Firebird Trans Am coupe. JAG

1976 Pontiac Firebird Esprit coupe. OCW

1976 Pontiac Ventura SJ four-door sedan. OCW

1976 Pontiac Firebird Esprit coupe (rear view). JAG

1976 Pontiac Grand LeMans four-door sedan. JAG

1976 Pontiac Grand Prix SJ coupe. JAG

1976 Pontiac LeMans Sport Coupe two-door hardtop. JAG

1976 Pontiac Bonneville Brougham two-door sedan. JAG

Sunbird) 65.4 in.; (Ventura) 72.4 in.; (Firebird) 73.0 in.; (LeMans) 77.4 in.; (G.P.) 77.8 in.; (Catalina cpe/sed, Bonneville) 79.6 in.; (Catalina wag) 79.4 in. Front Tread: (Astre/Sunbird) 55.2 in.; (Ventura) 61.8 in.; (Firebird) 60.9 in.; (Firebird Formula) 61.3 in.; (Trans Am) 61.2 in.; (Firebird) 61.6 in.; (G.P.) 61.6 in.; (Catalina/Bonneville) 63.9 in. Rear Tread: (Astre/Sunbird) 54.1 in.; (Ventura) 59.6 in.; (Firebird) 60.0 in.; (Firebird Formula) 60.4 in.; (LeMans) 61.1 in.; (Trans Am) 60.3 in.; (G.P.) 61.1 in.; (Catalina/Bonneville) 64.0 in. Standard Tires: (Astre) A78 x 13; (Sunbird) A78 x 13 exc. V-6, B78 x 13; (Ventura) E78 x 14; (Firebird) FR78 x 15; (Firebird Formula) N/A; (Trans Am) GR70 x 15; (LeMans) FR78 x 15 exc. wagon, HR78 x 15; (G.P.) GR78 x 15; (Catalina) HR78 x 15 exc. wagon, LR78 x 15; (Bonneville) HR78 x 15.

TECHNICAL: Transmission: Three-speed manual transmission standard on Astre, Sunbird, Ventura, LeMans, and Firebird six (floor lever except Ventura/LeMans). Optional four-speed manual shift on Astre/Sunbird four-cylinder. Optional four-speed on Astre/Sunbird six. Four-speed manual shift on Firebird V-8. Three-speed Turbo-Hydramatic standard on Grand Prix, Catalina, and Bonneville; optional on others. Astre/Sunbird automatic available. Standard final drive ratio: (Astre) 2.92:1 w/three-speed, 2.93:1 w/four-speed, 2.92:1 w/auto.; (Sunbird) 2.92:1 w/three-speed, 2.93:1 w/four-speed, 2.92:1 w/auto., 3.42:1 w/87 hp four, 2.56:1 w/V-6; (Ventura six) 2.73:1 w/three-speed, 2.73:1 or 3.08:1 w/auto.; (Ventura V-8) 2.56:1; (Firebird six) 2.73:1; (Firebird V-8) 2.41:1; (LeMans) 2.73:1 w/three-speed, 2.73:1 or 3.08:1 w/auto.; (LeMans V-8-260) 3.08:1 w/three-speed, 2.73:1 w/auto.; (LeMans V-8-350/400) 2.41:1; (LeMans V-8-400 wagon) 2.41:1; (Trans Am) 3.08:1 w/four-speed, 2.56:1; (Catalina) 2.41:1 exc. wagon, 2.56:1; (Bonneville) 2.56:1. Steering: Recirculating ball. Front Suspension: (Astre) coil springs and control arms; (Firebird/LeMans) coil springs w/lower trailing links and anti-sway bar; (others) coil springs and anti-sway bar. Rear Suspension: (Astre/Sunbird) rigid axle with coil springs, lower trailing radius arms and upper torque arms; (Ventura/Firebird) semi-elliptic leaf springs with anti-sway bar; (LeMans/Bonneville/Grand Prix) rigid axle with coil springs, lower trailing radius arms, upper torque arms and anti-sway bar; Brakes: Front disc, rear drum. Ignition: Electronic. Body construction: (Astre/Sunbird) unit; (Ventura) unit w/front frame section; (Firebird) unit w/separate partial frame; (others) separate body and frame. Fuel tank: (Astre) 16 gal.; (Sunbird) 18.5 gal.; (Ventura) 20.5 gal.; (Firebird) 20.2 gal.; (LeMans) 21.8 gal.; (Grand Prix) 25 gal.; (Catalina) 25.8 gal. exc. wagon, 22 gal.; (Bonneville) 25.8 gal.

DRIVETRAIN OPTIONS: Engines: 140 cid two-barrel four: Astre/Sunbird ($56). 231 cid V-6: Sunbird ($176). 260 cid two-barrel V-8: Ventura/LeMans ($90). 350 cid two-barrel V-8: Ventura/LeMans/Firebird ($140). 350 cid four-barrel V-8: Ventura/LeMans/Firebird ($195); Firebird Formula ($55); Grand Prix ($55). 400 cid two-barrel V-8: LeMans ($203); Grand Prix ($63). 400 cid four-barrel V-8: LeMans/Firebird ($258); LeMans wagon ($55); Firebird Formula ($118); Catalina/Bonneville ($73); Grand Prix ($118). 455 cid V-8: LeMans ($321); LeMans wagon ($118); Catalina/Bonneville ($137); Bonneville brougham ($64); Grand Prix ($181); Grand Prix SJ ($63). Performance pkg. (455 V-8): Trans Am ($125). Transmission/Differential: Three-speed floor shift: Ventura ($29). Four-speed manual transmission: Astre/Sunbird ($60). Close-ratio four-speed: Firebird ($242). Five-speed manual transmission: Astre/Sunbird ($244); Ventura ($262); LeMans spt cpe ($262); Firebird ($262); Formula/Trans Am (NC). Turbo-Hydramatic: Astre ($244); Ventura/LeMans ($262); Grand LeMans (NC). M40 Turbo-Hydramatic: LeMans ($286); Grand LeMans ($24); LeMans wagon (NC). Safe-T-Track differential: Astre/Sunbird ($48); Ventura/LeMans/Firebird ($51); Catalina/Bonneville ($55); Grand Prix Suspension: Radial-tuned suspension: Astre ($130-$162). Rally RTS handling pkg.: Astre ($12); Sunbird ($24); Ventura ($40); LeMans ($57-$101); Grand Prix ($66-$89). Firm ride pkg.: Ventura/LeMans ($10); Catalina/Bonneville ($10). Super lift shock absorbers: LeMans ($46); Catalina/Bonneville ($47); Grand Prix ($46). Automatic level control: Catalina/Bonneville ($46-$93). Other: H.D. radiator: Astre/Sunbird ($28); Ventura ($18). Super-cooling radiator: LeMans/Firebird/Grand Prix ($27-$49); Catalina/Bonneville ($27-$50). H.D. battery ($15-$17). H.D. alternator: LeMans/Firebird ($42); Catalina/Bonneville ($43); Grand Prix ($42). Engine block heater ($11-$12). Medium trailer group: LeMans ($97-$119); Catalina/Bonneville ($98-$121); Grand Prix ($97-$119). Heavy trailer group ($109-$165). California emissions ($50).

OPTION PACKAGES: Astre GT pkg.: hatch/Safari ($426-$465). Astre luxury appointment group: hatch/Safari ($104). Astre custom exterior ($59-$88). Sunbird luxury appointment group ($139). Sunbird luxury trim group ($126). Ventura special appearance group: two-door ($70-$92). LeMans custom trim group: sedan ($88). Firebird custom trim group ($81). Firebird Formula appearance pkg. ($100). Catalina custom group ($201-$228). Grand Prix LJ luxury appointments group ($336-$680). Grand Prix SJ golden anniversary pkg. ($550).

MAJOR CONVENIENCE/APPEARANCE OPTIONS: Air conditioning ($424-$512). Automatic air conditioning: LeMans ($513); Grand Prix ($542); Catalina/Bonneville ($549). Cruise control ($73); N/A on Sunbird/Astre. Power seat: LeMans/Catalina/Bonneville/G.P. ($124-$126). Power windows ($99-$159); N/A on Sunbird/Astre. Cornering lamps: Catalina/Bonneville/Grand Prix ($41). Power sun roof: LeMans/Grand Prix ($370). Removable sun roof: Sunbird ($149). Landau top: LeMans ($109-$119); Catalina/Bonneville ($125-$150). Rear-facing third seat: Safari ($149). Woodgrain siding: Safari wagons ($154-$156).

HISTORICAL FOOTNOTES: Introduced: September 25, 1975. Model year production: 748,842. Calendar year production (U.S.): 784,630. Calendar year sales by U.S. dealers: 753,093. Model year sales by U.S. dealers: 700,931. This was Pontiac's Golden Anniversary year, marking the 50th anniversary of the introduction of the Oakland. Production rose for the model year, and sales jumped even more. Only the subcompact Astre found fewer customers in 1976 than the prior year.

1977 PONTIAC

This year brought a switch from the old inline six to V-6 powerplants as base engines, as well as downsizing of full-size models. This move, it was claimed, would produce a "new generation of full-size cars." In keeping with the coming reduction of engine displacements, the 455 cid V-8 was dropped. Three different 350 V-8s were used, from three different manufacturers. Highlight of the season may have been the introduction of the Can Am Limited Edition LeMans, which appeared at the Greater Los Angeles Auto Show in January 1977. A new Formula package, based on the sporty Firebird model, was offered this year on Astre and Sunbird models. Two all-new Pontiac engines were available: the "Iron Duke" 151 cid (2.5-liter) four, and a 301 cid (5.0-liter) V-8. Both had the same bore and stroke dimensions: 4.00 x 3.00 in. The four produced 90 hp @ 4400 rpm; the V-8, 135 hp @ 3800 rpm. Weighing just 452 pounds, the 301 was said to be one of the lightest domestic V-8 engines on the market.

I.D. DATA: Pontiac's 13-symbol Vehicle Identification Number (VIN) was located on the upper left surface of the instrument panel, visible through the windshield. The first digit is '2', indicating Pontiac division. The second symbol is a letter indicating series: 'C' = Astre; 'M' = Sunbird; 'X' = Phoenix; 'Y' = Ventura; 'Z' = Ventura SJ; 'D' = LeMans; 'F' = LeMans Sport Coupe; 'G' = Grand Prix; 'S' = Firebird; 'T' = Firebird Esprit; 'U' = Firebird Formula; 'W' = Firebird Trans Am; 'L' = Catalina; 'N' = Bonneville; 'Q' = Bonneville Brougham; 'J' = Grand Prix; 'K' = Grand Prix LJ; 'H' = Grand Prix SJ. Next come two digits that denote body type: '07' = 2-dr. hatchback coupe; '11' = 2-dr. pillar coupe; '17' = 2-dr. hatchback coupe; '27' = 2-dr. sport coupe; '37' = 2-dr. HT coupe; '57' = 2-dr. HT coupe; '77' = 2-dr. hatchback coupe; '87' = 2-dr. HT coupe; '29' = 4-dr. HT sedan; '69' = 4-dr. thin-pillar four-window sedan; '15' = 2-dr. station wagon; '35' = 4-dr. two-seat wagon. The fifth symbol is a letter indicating engine code: 'B' = L4-140 two-barrel; 'V' = L4-151 two-barrel; 'C' = V-6-231 two-barrel; 'Y' = V-8-301 two-barrel; 'U' = V-8-305 four-barrel; 'P' = V-8-350 four-barrel (L76); 'R' = V-8-350 four-barrel (L34); 'L' = V-8-350 four-barrel (LM1); 'Z' = V-8-400 four-barrel; 'K' = V-8-403 four-barrel. The sixth symbol denotes model year ('7' = 1977). Next is a plant code: 'A' = Lakewood, Ga.; 'L' = Van Nuys, Calif.; 'N' = Norwood, Ohio; 'P' = Pontiac, Mich.; 'T' = Tarrytown, N.Y.; 'U' = Lordstown, Ohio; 'W' = Willow Run, Mich.; 'X' = Fairfax, Kan.; '1' = Oshawa, Ontario; '2' = Ste. Therese, Quebec. The final six digits are the sequential serial number, starting with 100,001 (except Astre/Sunbird, 500,001).

1977 Pontiac Astre Safari station wagon. (P)

ASTRE -- SERIES 2H -- FOUR -- Once again, the subcompact Astre came in coupe, hatchback coupe, and two-door Safari wagon form. This year it had a fresh front-end look with new grille, as well as revised interior trim. Astre's front end held single round headlamps in round recessed housings. On each side of the body-color v-shaped center panel (with Pontiac v-shaped emblem) were four holes in a single row, that formed the grille. The outer "holes" were actually the park/sig-

143

nal lights, while the others contained a set of thin vertical strips. New Astre options included 13 inch cast aluminum wheels. A luxury trim group included luxury seating, custom door trim with map pockets, rear ashtrays and other extras, available in hatchback and Safari models. Base engine for the coupe was the 140 cid (2.3-liter) four, but hatchback and Safari models carried the new "Iron Duke" 151 cid (2.5-liter) four and standard four-speed manual. A five-speed gearbox was optional, along with three-speed Turbo-Hydramatic.

ASTRE (FOUR)

Model Number	Body/Style Number	Body Type & Seating	Factory Price	Shipping Weight	Prod. Total
2H	C11	2-dr. Cpe-4P	3304	2480	10,327
2H	C77	2-dr. Hatch Cpe-4P	3429	2573	12,120
2H	C15	2-dr. Safari Wag-4P	3594	2608	10,341

1977 Pontiac Formula Sunbird coupe. (P)

SUNBIRD -- SERIES 2H -- FOUR/V-6 -- Like most other Pontiacs this year, Sunbird had a new grille and front end appearance. Quad rectangular headlamps stood alongside a recessed grille that consisted of roundish elements, similar to Firebird's. Base engine was the new 151 cid (2.5-liter) four, with 231 cid (3.8-liter) V-6 available. Also optional: cast aluminum wheels. A new Sunbird Sport-Hatch (hatchback) version appeared, with special paint and striping, to join the original two-door coupe.

SUNBIRD (FOUR/V-6)

Model Number	Body/Style Number	Body Type & Seating	Factory Price	Shipping Weight	Prod. Total
2H	M27	2-dr. Cpe-4P	3659/3779	2662/--	41,708
2H	M07	2-dr. Hatch Cpe-4P	3784/3904	2693/--	13,690

1977 Pontiac Ventura SJ coupe. (P)

VENTURA -- SERIES 2X -- FOUR/V-6/V-8 -- Ventura featured a new grille design, as well as a posher interior with Grand Prix-style dash. Base and SJ models came in coupe, hatchback, and sedan models. Base engine was the 231 cid (3.8-liter) V-6, with a 301 or 350 cid V-8 available. Three-speed column shift was standard; four-speed manual optional with V-8 power; a five-speed with the available four-cylinder engine. Ventura's grille had a wide body-color center panel (with customary Pontiac emblem) to split the twin sections. Each section contained six rectangular holes (two rows), each of which had an internal vertical-theme pattern. Single round rectangular headlamps met two-section marker lenses on the fender sides. Front bumpers held two small slots. Parking/signal lamps were behind the outer grille section.

VENTURA (V-6/V-8)

Model Number	Body/Style Number	Body Type & Seating	Factory Price	Shipping Weight	Prod. Total
2X	Y27	2-dr. Cpe-5P	3596/3661	3127/3212	26,675
2X	Y17	2-dr. Hatch Cpe-5P	3791/3856	3249/3334	4015
2X	Y69	4-dr. Sed-5P	3650/3715	3167/3252	27,089

VENTURA SJ (V-6/V-8)

Model Number	Body/Style Number	Body Type & Seating	Factory Price	Shipping Weight	Prod. Total
2X	Z27	2-dr. Cpe-5P	3945/4010	3206/3291	3418
2X	Z17	2-dr. Hatch Cpe-5P	4124/4189	3293/3378	1100
2X	Z69	4-dr. Sed-5P	3972/4037	3236/3321	4339

PHOENIX -- SERIES 2X -- FOUR/V-6/V-8 -- Phoenix was a late arrival to the Pontiac lineup; see 1978 listing for data.

PHOENIX (V-6/V-8)

Model Number	Body/Style Number	Body Type & Seating	Factory Price	Shipping Weight	Prod. Total
2X	X27	2-dr. Cpe	4075/4075	3227/3339	10,489
2X	X69	4-dr. Sed	4122/4122	3275/3387	13,639

Ventura/Phoenix Engine Note: A four-cylinder engine was available for $120 credit.

1977 Pontiac Formula Firebird coupe. (P)

FIREBIRD -- SERIES 2F -- V-6/V-8 -- New front-end styling for the Firebird coupe featured quad rectangular headlamps and an "aggressive" grille. Four models were offered: base, Esprit, and performance Formula and Trans Am. Formula's new hood held simulated air scoops; at its rear was a spoiler. Wheelbase was 108 in., and engine choices ranged from a 231 cid (3.8-liter) V-6 to the 403 cid (6.6-liter) V-8. Firebird's new grille was deeply recessed, directly in line with the quad rectangular headlamps. Its simple pattern consisted of a series of roundish (hexagonal) holes, resembling fencing more than a customary grille. A "Pontiac" nameplate went on the driver's side of the grille. Crossbar-trimmed amber park/signal lamps were also recessed, but into the outer ends of twin air intake slots below the bumper strip. The center front panel protruded forward to a slight point and contained the usual Pontiac emblem, but its sides were more sharply angled than the prior version. Esprit could have a new blue Sky Bird appearance package, with blue velour seating, two-tone blue body, and blue cast aluminum wheels. Firebird Formula came with a new 301 cid (5.0-liter) two-barrel V-8. Its body displayed blacked-out trim, dual hood scoops, and large "Formula" graphics on the lower door. Trans Am had a new shaker hood and came with a standard 400 or 403 cid V-8, but also available was an optional "T/A 6.6" powerplant.

Model Number	Body/Style Number	Body Type & Seating	Factory Price	Shipping Weight	Prod. Total
FIREBIRD (V-6/V-8)					
2F	S87	2-dr. HT Cpe-4P	4269/4334	3264/3349	30,642
FIREBIRD ESPRIT (V-6/V-8)					
2F	T87	2-dr. HT Cpe-4P	4550/4615	3312/3397	34,548
FIREBIRD FORMULA (V-8)					
2F	U87	2-dr. HT Cpe-4P	4976	3411	21,801
FIREBIRD TRANS AM (V-8)					
2F	W87	2-dr. HT Cpe-4P	5456	3526	68,745

1977 Pontiac LeMans Sport Coupe. (CP)

LEMANS -- SERIES 2A -- V-6/V-8 -- The mid-size LeMans had a new front end appearance and revised engine selection. Base engine was the 231 cid (3.8-liter) V-6, except for Safari wagons that had a standard 350 cid (5.7-liter) V-8. The 6.6-liter V-8 was available on all models. New LeMans options included 15 inch cast aluminum wheels, wire wheel covers, and new-styled deluxe wheel covers. Grand LeMans could get a new AM/FM radio with digital clock. A LeMans GT option (for Sport Coupe) included distinctive two-tone paint, bold striping, Rally RTS handling package, and body-color Rally II wheels. Base LeMans models had quad rectangular headlamps alongside a grille made up only of heavy vertical bars, forming six sections on each side of a protruding center divider. That divider formed a point that carried forward from the prominent hood creases, and contained the triangular Pontiac emblem at the tip. Headlamp frames continued outward to surround wraparound single-section marker lenses. Park/signal lights were at the outer ends of twin bumper slots. Grand LeMans had a similar front-end look, but its grille sections included a horizontal divider, forming a 5 x 2 pattern of square holes on each side. Each of those 20 holes contained a smaller square. One of the more notable Pontiacs of the decade was the Can Am, a performance version of the LeMans Sport Coupe. Only 1377 were produced. Can Am included the performance T/A 400 cid (6.6-liter) V-8 (403 V-8 in California) along with body-colored Rally II wheels, a blacked-out grille assembly, and GR70 x 15 SBR tires. Can Am was promoted as a "fun car" along with Trans Am, offered only in Cameo White body color. Equipment included Turbo-Hydramatic, power brakes, variable-ratio power steering, front and rear stabilizer bars, body-color Rally II wheels, front/rear protective rubber bumper strips, and body-color dual sport mirrors (driver's side remote-controlled). A Grand Prix instrument panel assembly included a rally gauge cluster and clock. A Rally RTS handling package was standard. Appearance features included tri-tone colored accent tape striping on hood, front fenders, doors, and sport mirrors; black lower bodyside with accent stripe; black rocker panel moldings; full-width rear deck spoiler with tri-tone accent stripe (front and rear); tri-tone "CAN AM" identification on front end, front fender, and rear deck; blacked-out windshield, backlight, door window and belt moldings; and unique "CAN AM" interior identification. The Trans Am-style "shaker" hood scoop had tri-tone "T/A 6.6" identification and accent stripes. Early Can Am models also included a selection of options: Saf-T-Track rear axle, white-letter GR70 x 15 tires, custom sport steering wheels, Soft Ray tinted glass, dual horns, front/rear floor mats, and custom color-keyed seatbelts. Other available options included air conditioning, radio, and choice of white, black, or firethorn interior trim color (or firethorn/white) in notchback, full-width, or bucket seats.

1977 Pontiac Grand LeMans coupe. (P)

Model Number	Body/Style Number	Body Type & Seating	Factory Price	Shipping Weight	Prod. Total
LEMANS (V-6/V-8)					
2A	D37	2-dr. HT Cpe-6P	4045/4110	3550/3635	16,038
2A	D29	4-dt. HT Sed-6P	4093/4158	3638/3723	23,060

Model	Body	Body Type	Factory	Shipping	Prod.
LEMANS SAFARI (V-8)					
2A	D35	4-dr. 2S Wag-6P	4877	4135	10,081
LEMANS SPORT COUPE (V-6/V-8)					
2A	F37	2-dr. HT Cpe-6P	4204/4269	3558/3643	12,277
LEMANS CAN AM (V-8)					
2A	N/A	2-dr. HT Cpe-6P	N/A	N/A	1377
GRAND LEMANS (V-6/V-8)					
2A	G37	2-dr. HT Cpe-6P	4602/4667	3587/3672	7581
2A	G29	4-dr. HT Sed-6P	4730/4795	3740/3825	5584
GRAND LEMANS SAFARI (V-8)					
2A	G35	4-dr. 2S Wag-6P	5132	4179	5393

1977 Pontiac Grand Prix SJ coupe. (P)

GRAND PRIX -- SERIES 2G -- V-8 -- Three personal-luxury models were offered this year: base, sporty SJ, and luxury LJ. Base and LJ models had a standard 350 cid (5.7-liter) V-8, while SJ came with a 6.6-liter V-8 (optional in the others). New Grand Prix options included CB radios and a digital AM/FM stereo information center and clock. This year's grille was no longer a wrapover style: only five vertical sections of bold elements on each side of the divider. The grille pattern repeated in two sections below the bumper. Quad rectangular headlamps were now separated by clear park/signal lights, forming three separate units on each side. Narrow amber vertical marker lenses stood to the rear of front fender tips. Both hood and decklid showed sharp creases. Standard equipment included power brakes and steering, GR78 x 15 blackwall steel-belted radial tires, three-speed automatic transmission, heater/defroster, wheel opening and rocker panel moldings, window and roof drip moldings, and a clock. LJ added velour seat upholstery, a remote-controlled driver's mirror, and deluxe wheel covers. SJ had a 6.6-liter V-8 engine, GR70 x 15 tires, Rally II wheels with trim rings, accent striping, bucket seats with console, Rally RTS handling package, and rally gauges.

1977 Pontiac Grand Prix T-top coupe. JAG

145

Model Number	Body/Style Number	Body Type & Seating	Factory Price	Shipping Weight	Prod. Total
GRAND PRIX (V-8)					
2G	J57	2-dr. HT Cpe-6P	5108	3804	168,247
GRAND PRIX LJ (V-8)					
2G	K57	2-dr. HT Cpe-6P	5471	3815	66,741
GRAND PRIX SJ (V-8)					
2G	H57	2-dr. HT Cpe-6P	5742	3976	53,442

1977 Pontiac Catalina sedan. (P)

CATALINA -- SERIES 2B -- V-8 -- Though reduced in outside dimensions, and weighing considerably less than before, both Catalina and Bonneville offered more head and rear leg room. The new design featured less door glass curvature, as well as a higher roofline. Full-size models rode a 116 inch wheelbase. Front ends held quad rectangular headlamps. Mechanical features included a Freedom battery and engine/air conditioning electrical diagnostic connector. Catalinas had a new brushed-knit cloth interior. Catalina's horizontal-theme grille had a slightly v-shaped center vertical segment (with Pontiac v emblem). It was part of a bold frame containing three horizontal bars (upper, lower and center), which stood ahead of a set of horizontal ribs, forming four sections in all (two on each side). Parking/signal lights were below the bumper rub strip, while two-section marker lenses wrapped around the front fender, following the line of the quad rectangular headlamps. Two horizontal slots were in the bumper, just inside the bumper guards. Base engine was a 231 cid (3.8-liter) V-6; optional, either a 350 cid or 403 cid V-8. Safari (and Grand Safari) wagons had a new three-way tailgate, two lockable storage areas, standard 350 cid V-8, and available rear-facing third seat. All full-size coupes and sedans could have a CB radio option. Standard equipment included automatic transmission, power brakes and steering, FR78 x 15 blackwall glass-belted radial tires, heater/defroster, and moldings at roof drip, window, wheel openings, and rocker panels.

1977 Pontiac Catalina four-door sedan (rear view). OCW

Model Number	Body/Style Number	Body Type & Seating	Factory Price	Shipping Weight	Prod. Total
CATALINA (V-6/V-8)					
2B	L37	2-dr. HT Cpe-6P	5052/5118	3473/3570	14,752
2B	L69	4-dr. Sed-6P	5049/5115	3501/3598	46,926
CATALINA SAFARI (V-8)					
2B	L35	4-dr. 2S Wag-6P	5491	4024	13,058

1977 Pontiac Bonneville coupe. (P)

1977 Pontiac Bonneville coupe (rear view). OCW

BONNEVILLE -- SERIES 2B -- V-8 -- Offered in coupe and sedan form, the new Bonneville had a flush eggcrate-style grille pattern on each side of the central v segment (with Pontiac emblem). Left and right grille segments formed a 4 x 4 pattern, with each segment containing internal crosshatching (a pattern within a pattern). The grille pattern repeated in two bumper slots, just inside the bumper guards. Framing for the quad rectangular headlamps continued outward to enclose four-section marker lenses. Park/signal lights were in the bumper. Interior choices were Lombardy velour cloth or Morrokide. Base engine was the 350 cid (5.7-liter) four-barrel V-8, with 6.6-liter V-8 available. Brougham included a luxury interior package, and could have Valencia striped cloth trim. Standard Bonneville equipment was similar to Catalina's, but included rear fender skirts, deluxe wheel covers, and luxury steering wheel. Brougham added a Cordova top, driver's remote mirror, 60/40 seat with center armrest, power windows, and custom interior trim. Wagons had HR78 x 15 tires and a three-way tailgate with power back window.

Model Number	Body/Style Number	Body Type & Seating	Factory Price	Shipping Weight	Prod. Total
BONNEVILLE (V-8)					
2B	N37	2-dr. HT Cpe-6P	5410	3579	37,817
2B	N69	4-dr. Sed-6P	5456	3616	13,697
BONNEVILLE BROUGHAM (V-8)					
2B	Q37	2-dr. HT Cpe-6P	5896	3617	15,901
2B	Q69	4-dr. Sed-6P	5991	3680	47,465
GRAND SAFARI (V-8)					
2B	N35	4-dr. 2S Wag-6P	5771	4066	18,304

1977 Pontiac Bonneville Grand Safari station wagon. (CP)

1977 Pontiac Astre coupe. OCW

1977 Pontiac Astre Formula coupe. OCW

1977 Pontiac Sunbird coupe. OCW

1977 Pontiac Ventura three-door hatchback. OCW

1977 Pontiac Firebird Trans Am coupe. OCW

1977 Pontiac LeMans Can Am Sport Coupe. OCW

1977 Pontiac LeMans GT Sport Coupe. OCW

1977 Pontiac Grand LeMans Safari station wagon. OCW

1977 Pontiac Ventura SJ four-door sedan. JAG

1977 Pontiac Bonneville Brougham coupe (rear view). OCW

Note 1: A third seat was available in all LeMans and Catalina/Bonneville Safari wagon models.

FACTORY PRICE AND WEIGHT NOTE: Prices and weights to left of slash are for V-6, to right for V-8 engine except Sunbird, four and V-6.

ENGINE DATA

BASE FOUR (Astre coupe); OPTIONAL (Sunbird):Inline. Overhead cam. Four-cylinder. Aluminum block. Displacement: 140 cu. in. (2.3 liters). Bore & stroke: 3.50 x 3.63 in. Compression ratio: 8.0:1. Brake horsepower: 84 @ 4400 rpm. Torque: 117 lb.-ft. @ 2400 rpm. Five main bearings. Hydraulic valve lifters. Carburetor: two-barrel VIN Code: B. BASE FOUR (Astre hatch/wagon, Sunbird);OPTIONAL (Astre coupe, Ventura): Inline. Overhead valve. Four-cylinder. Cast iron block and head. Displacement: 151 cu. in. (2.5 liters). Bore & stroke: 4.00 x 3.00 in. Compression ratio: 8.3:1. Brake horsepower: 90 @ 4400 rpm. Torque: 128 lb.-ft. @ 2400 rpm. Five main bearings. Hydraulic valve lifters. Carburetor: two-barrel Holley 5210C. VIN Code: V.

BASE V-6 (Ventura, Firebird, LeMans, Catalina); OPTIONAL (Sunbird): 90-degree, overhead-valve V-6. Cast iron block and head. Displacement: 231 cu. in. (3.8 liters). Bore & stroke: 3.80 x 3.40 in. Compression ratio: 8.0:1. Brake horsepower: 105 @ 3200 rpm. Torque: 185 lb.-ft. @ 2000 rpm. Four main bearings. Hydraulic valve lifters. Carburetor: two-barrel Rochester 2GC. VIN Code: C.

BASE V-8 (Firebird Formula, Bonneville, Grand Prix);OPTIONAL (Ventura, Firebird, LeMans, Catalina): 90-degree, overhead valve V-8. Cast iron block and head. Displacement: 301 cu. in. (5.0 liters). Bore & stroke: 4.00 x 3.00 in. Compression ratio: 8.2:1. Brake horsepower: 135 @ 3800 rpm. Torque: 235-245 lb.-ft. @ 2000 rpm. (full-size, 250 @ 1600). Five main bearings. Hydraulic valve lifters. Carburetor: two-barrel VIN Code: Y. OPTIONAL V-8 (Ventura, Firebird):90-degree, overhead valve V-8. Cast iron block and head. Displacement: 305 cu. in. (5.0 liters). Bore & stroke: 3.74 x 3.48 in. Compression ratio: 8.5:1. Brake horsepower: 145 @ 3800 rpm. Torque: 245 lb.-ft. @ 2400 rpm. Five main bearings. Hydraulic valve lifters. Carburetor: two-barrel Rochester 2GC. VIN Code: U. OPTIONAL V-8 (Firebird, LeMans, Catalina, Bonneville, Grand Prix): 90-degree, overhead valve V-8. Cast iron block and head. Displacement: 350 cu. in. (5.7 liters). Bore & stroke: 3.88 x 3.75 in. Compression ratio: 7.6:1. Brake horsepower: 170 @ 4000 rpm. Torque: 280 lb.-ft. @ 1800 rpm. Five main bearings. Hydraulic valve lifters. Carburetor: four-barrel Rochester M4MC. VIN Code: P. ALTERNATE V-8 (Firebird, LeMans, Catalina, Bonneville, Grand Prix): 90-degree, overhead valve V-8. Cast iron block and head. Displacement: 350 cu. in. (5.7 liters). Bore & stroke: 4.00 x 3.48 in. Compression ratio: 8.5:1. Brake horsepower: 170 @ 3800 rpm. Torque: 270 lb.-ft. @ 2400 rpm. Five main bearings. Hydraulic valve lifters. Carburetor: four-barrel Rochester M4MC. Chevrolet-built. VIN Code: L. ALTERNATE V-8 (Firebird, LeMans, Catalina, Bonneville, Grand Prix): 90-degree, overhead valve V-8. Cast iron block and head. Displacement: 350 cu. in. (5.7 liters). Bore & stroke: 4.06 x 3.38 in. Compression ratio: 8.0:1. Brake horsepower: 170 @ 3800 rpm. Torque: 275 lb.-ft. @ 2000 rpm. Five main bearings. Hydraulic valve lifters. Carburetor: four-barrel Rochester M4MC. Oldsmobile-built. VIN Code: R. BASE V-8 (Grand Prix SJ);OPTIONAL (Firebird, LeMans, Catalina, Bonneville, Grand Prix): 90-degree, overhead valve V-8. Cast iron block and head. Displacement: 400 cu. in. (6.6 liters). Bore & stroke: 4.12 x 3.75 in. Compression ratio: 7.6:1. Brake horsepower: 180 @ 3600 rpm. Torque: 325 lb.-ft. @ 1600 rpm. Five main bearings. Hydraulic valve lifters. Carburetor: four-barrel Rochester M4MC. VIN Code: Z. BASE V-8 (Firebird Trans Am): Same as 400 cid V-8 above, except Compression ratio: 8.0:1. Horsepower: 200 @ 3600 rpm. Torque: 325 lb.-ft. @ 2400 rpm. ALTERNATE V-8 (Firebird, LeMans, Catalina, Bonneville, Grand Prix): 90-degree, overhead valve V-8. Cast iron block and head. Displacement: 403 cu. in. (6.6 liters). Bore & stroke: 4.35 x 3.38 in. Compression ratio: 8.0:1. Brake horsepower: 185 @ 3600 rpm. Torque: 320 lb.-ft. @ 2200 rpm. Five main bearings. Hydraulic valve lifters. Carburetor: four-barrel Rochester M4MC. VIN Code: K.

CHASSIS DATA: Wheelbase: (Astre/Sunbird) 97.0 in.; (Ventura) 111.1 in.; (Firebird) 108.1 in.; (LeMans 2-dr.) 112.0 in.; (LeMans 4-dr.) 116.0 in.; (Grand Prix) 116.0 in.; (Catalina/Bonneville) 115.9 in. Overall Length: (Astre) 177.6 in.; (Sunbird) 177.8 in.; (Ventura) 199.6 in.; (Firebird) 196.8 in.; (LeMans 2-dr.) 208.0 in.; (LeMans 4-dr.) 212.0 in.; (LeMans wag) 215.4 in.; (G.P.) 212.7 in.; (Catalina/Bonneville) 213.8 in.; (Catalina wag) 214.7 in. Height: (Astre hatch) 50.0 in.; (Astre notch/wag) 51.8 in.; (Sunbird) 49.8 in.; (Ventura 2-dr.) 52.3 in.; (Ventura 4-dr.) 53.2 in.; (Firebird) 49.1 in.; (Esprit/Formula) 49.4 in.; (Trans Am) 49.6 in.; (LeMans 2-dr.) 52.7 in.; (LeMans 4-dr.) 53.5 in.; (LeMans wag) 55.3 in.; (G.P.) 52.9 in.; (Catalina/Bonneville sed) 53.2 in.; (Catalina wag) 57.3 in. Width: (Astre/Sunbird) 65.4 in.; (Ventura) 72.4 in.; (Firebird) 73.0 in.; (LeMans) 77.4 in.; (G.P.) 77.8 in.; (Catalina/Bonneville) 75.4 in. Front Tread: (Astre/Sunbird) 55.2 in.; (Ventura) 61.2 in.; (Ventura SJ) 61.8 in.; (Firebird) 60.9 in.; (Firebird Formula) 61.3 in.; (Trans Am) 61.2 in.; (LeMans) 61.6 in.; (G.P.) 61.6 in.; (Catalina/Bonneville) 61.7 in. Rear Tread: (Astre/Sunbird) 54.1 in.; (Ventura) 59.0 in.; (Firebird) 60.0 in.; (Firebird Formula) 60.4 in.; (Trans Am) 60.3 in.; (LeMans) 61.1 in.; (G.P.) 61.1 in.; (Catalina/Bonneville) 60.7 in. Standard Tires: (Astre) A78 x 13 exc. wagon, BR78 x 13; (Sunbird)

A78 x 13; (Ventura) E78 x 14; (Firebird) FR78 x 15; (Trans Am) GR70 x 15; (LeMans) FR78 x 15 exc. wagon, HR78 x 15; (Grand Prix) N/A; (Grand Prix SJ) GR70 x 15; (Catalina) FR78 x 15 exc. wagon, HR78 x 15; (Bonneville) FR78 x 15.

TECHNICAL: Transmission: Three-speed manual transmission standard on Ventura, LeMans, and Firebird. Four-speed manual standard on Astre/Sunbird and Firebird Formula; optional on Firebird and Ventura V-8. Five-speed manual optional on Astre/Sunbird and Ventura four-cylinder. Three-speed Turbo-Hydramatic standard on other models, optional on all. Standard final drive ratio: (Astre cpe) 3.42:1; (Astre hatch/wag) 2.73:1; (Sunbird) 2.73:1 w/four, 2.56:1 w/V-6; (Ventura) 3.42:1 w/four, 3.08:1 w/V-6, 3.23:1 w/V-8; (Firebird) 3.08:1 w/four, 3.23:1 w/V-8-301, 2.41:1 w/V-8-350; (Trans Am) 3.23:1 or 3.42:1; (LeMans) 3.08:1 w/V-6, 2.56:1 w/V-8-301, 2.41:1 w/V-8-350/400, 2.56:1 w/V-8-403; (Grand Prix) 2.56:1 w/V-8-301, 2.41:1 w/V-8-350/400/403; (Catalina) 2.73:1 w/V-6; (Bonneville) 2.41:1; (Safari) 2.56:1. Steering: Recirculating ball. Front Suspension: (Astre) coil springs and control arms; (Firebird/LeMans) coil springs w/lower trailing links and anti-sway bar; (others) coil springs and anti-sway bar. Rear Suspension: (Astre/Sunbird) rigid axle with coil springs, lower trailing radius arms and upper torque arms; (Ventura/Firebird) semi-elliptic leaf springs with anti-sway bar; (LeMans/Bonneville/Grand Prix) rigid axle with coil springs, lower trailing radius arms, upper torque arms and anti-sway bar. Brakes: Front disc, rear drum. Ignition: Electronic. Body construction: (Astre/Sunbird) unit; (Ventura) unit w/front frame section; (Firebird) unit w/separate partial frame; (others) separate body and frame. Fuel Tank: (Astre) 16 gal.; (Sunbird) 18.5 gal.; (Ventura) 20.5 gal.; (Firebird) 20.2 gal.; (LeMans) 21.8 gal. exc. wagon, 22 gal.; (Grand Prix) 25 gal.; (Catalina/Bonneville) 20 gal. exc. wagon, 22.5 gal.

DRIVETRAIN OPTIONS: Engines: 140 cid two-barrel four: Astre ($20); Ventura cpe/sed ($120 credit). 231 cid V-6: Sunbird ($120). 301 cid V-8: Ventura/Firebird/LeMans ($65); Catalina ($66). 305 cid two-barrel V-8: Ventura ($65). 350 cid four-barrel V-8: Ventura/LeMans/Firebird ($155); LeMans Safari ($90); Firebird Formula ($90); Grand Prix ($90). 400 cid four-barrel V-8: LeMans/Firebird ($220); LeMans wagon ($155); Firebird Formula ($155-$205); Trans Am ($50); Catalina ($223); Bonneville ($157); Grand Prix ($155). 403 cid four-barrel V-8: LeMans ($220); LeMans wagon ($155); Firebird Formula ($155); Catalina ($223); Bonneville ($157); Grand Prix ($155). Transmission/Differential: M15 three-speed manual transmission: LeMans ($282). Three-speed floor shift: Ventura ($31). Four-speed manual floor shift transmission: Ventura w/V-8-301 ($257). Four-speed manual transmission: Firebird ($257). Five-speed manual transmission: Astre/Sunbird ($248); Ventura four ($282). Turbo-Hydramatic: Astre/Sunbird/Ventura/Firebird ($248); LeMans (N/A). Safe-T-Track differential: Astre/Sunbird ($50); Ventura/LeMans/Firebird ($54); Catalina/Bonneville/G.P. ($58). Brakes/Steering: Power brakes: Astre/Sunbird ($58); Ventura/LeMans/Firebird ($61). Power steering: Astre/Sunbird ($129); Ventura/LeMans ($146). Suspension: Rally RTS handling pkg.: Astre ($55-$215); Sunbird ($44-$215); Ventura ($44); Firebird ($46-$116); LeMans ($36-$158); Catalina ($130-$156); Bonneville ($93-$111); Grand Prix ($34-$102). Firm ride pkg. ($11) except Astre/Sunbird. Superlift shock absorbers: LeMans/G.P. ($49); Catalina/Bonneville ($50). Automatic level control: Catalina/Bonneville ($52-$102). Other: H.D. radiator: Astre/Sunbird ($30); Ventura ($27-$55). Super-cooling radiator ($27-$55) except Astre/Sunbird. H.D. battery ($16-$18). Maintenance-free battery ($31). H.D. alternator: LeMans/Firebird ($45); Catalina/Bonneville ($46); Grand Prix ($45). Engine block heater ($12-$13). Class I trailer group: LeMans/G.P. ($109-$133); Bonneville/Catalina ($110-$135). Medium trailer group: LeMans/G.P. ($127-$151); Catalina/Bonneville ($128-$153). Heavy trailer group: Bonneville/Catalina ($139-$199). California emissions ($70). High-altitude option ($22).

OPTION PACKAGES: Astre Formula appearance group ($447-$558). Astre special appearance pkg. w/Formula ($34). Astre luxury appointment group: hatch/Safari ($147). Astre custom exterior ($63-$94). Astre custom interior ($141-$183). Sunbird Formula appearance group ($436-$543). Sunbird special appearance group ($82). Sunbird luxury appointment group ($147). Sunbird luxury trim group ($144). LeMans GT: spt cpe ($446-$463). LeMans custom trim group: sedan/wag ($92-$208). Firebird "Skybird" appearance pkg.: Esprit ($325-$342). Trans Am special edition ($556-$1143). Firebird custom trim group ($27-$118). Firebird Formula appearance pkg. ($127). Catalina special appearance group ($140). Bonneville special appearance group ($135). Safari custom trim group ($167-$286).

MAJOR CONVENIENCE/APPEARANCE OPTIONS: Air conditioning ($442-$540). Automatic air conditioning: LeMans/Grand Prix ($539-$552); Catalina/Bonneville ($579). Cruise control ($80-$84); N/A on Sunbird/Astre. Power seat: LeMans/Catalina/Bonneville/G.P. ($137-$139). Power windows ($108-$151); N/A on Sunbird/Astre. Cornering lamps: Catalina/Bonneville/Grand Prix ($44). Power glass sun roof: LeMans/Grand Prix ($625); Catalina/Bonneville ($898). Power steel sun roof: LeMans/Grand Prix ($394); Catalina/Bonneville ($735). Glass sun roof: Firebird ($587). Padded landau top: Grand Prix/LeMans ($180). Cordova vinyl top: Sunbird ($83-$144); Ventura ($93); LeMans ($111); Grand Prix ($121); Catalina/Bonneville ($135-$140). Canopy top: Firebird ($105). Landau vinyl top: Sunbird

($144); Ventura ($162); LeMans ($111); Grand Prix ($121). Canopy vinyl top: LeMans ($151); Catalina/Bonneville ($107-$112). Formal landau vinyl top: Catalina/Bonneville ($277-$282). Rear spoiler: Astre/Sunbird ($45); Firebird ($51).

HISTORICAL FOOTNOTES: Introduced: September 30, 1976. Model year production: 911,050. Calendar year production (U.S.): 875,958. Calendar year sales by U.S. dealers: 808,467. Model year sales by U.S. dealers: 811,904. Sales rose considerably for the 1977 model year, paving the way for another increase the next time around. The downsized full-size models sold better than their bigger predecessors. A.C. Mair was Pontiac's General Manager at this time.

1978 PONTIAC

Both Astre and Ventura faded away. Following the downsizing of full-size models for 1977, the mid-size LeMans, Grand LeMans and personal-luxury Grand Prix received similar treatment this year. Returning this season was the Grand Am nameplate.

I.D. DATA: Pontiac's 13-symbol Vehicle Identification Number (VIN) was located on the upper left surface of the instrument panel, visible through the windshield. The first digit is '2', indicating Pontiac division. The second symbol is a letter indicating series: 'E' = Sunbird; 'M' = Sunbird; 'Y' = Phoenix; 'Z' = Phoenix LJ; 'D' = LeMans; 'F' = Grand LeMans; 'G' = Grand Am; 'S' = Firebird; 'T' = Firebird Esprit; 'U' = Firebird Formula; 'W' = Firebird Trans Am; 'L' = Catalina; 'N' = Bonneville; 'Q' = Bonneville Brougham; 'J' = Grand Prix; 'K' = Grand Prix LJ; 'H' = Grand Prix SJ. Next come two digits that denote body type: '07' = 2-dr. hatchback coupe; '17' = 2-dr. hatchback coupe; '27' = 2-dr. coupe; '37' = 2-dr. coupe; '87' = 2-dr. HT coupe; '19' = 4-dr. six-window sedan; '69' = 4-dr. four-window sedan; '15' = 2-dr. station wagon; '35' = 4-dr. two-seat wagon. The fifth symbol is a letter indicating engine code: 'V' = L4-151 two-barrel; 'A' = V-6-231 two-barrel; 'Y' = V-8-301 two-barrel; 'W' = V-8-301 four-barrel; 'U' = V-8-305 four-barrel; 'X' = V-8-350 four-barrel; 'R' = V-8-350 four-barrel (L34); 'L' = V-8-350 four-barrel (LM1); 'Z' = V-8-400 four-barrel The sixth symbol denotes model year ('8' = 1978). Next is a plant code: 'A' = Lakewood, Ga.; 'B' = Baltimore; 'L' = Van Nuys, Calif.; 'N' = Norwood, Ohio; 'P' = Pontiac, Mich.; 'T' = Tarrytown, N.Y.; 'U' = Lordstown, Ohio; 'W' = Willow Run, Mich.; 'X' = Fairfax, Kan.; '1' = Oshawa, Ontario; '2' = Ste. Therese, Quebec. The final six digits are the sequential serial number.

1978 Pontiac Sunbird coupe. (JAG)

SUNBIRD -- SERIES 2H -- FOUR/V-6 -- Basic appearance of Pontiac's remaining subcompact was similar to 1977 with staggered, recessed quad rectangular headlamps at the ends of each front-end opening. This year's narrow grilles consisted of all vertical bars on each side of the tapered, body-color divider (with Pontiac emblem). 'Sunbird' script was on the cowl, below the bodyside molding. Bright taillamps frames had two horizontal separator ribs. Backup lights sat at inner ends and amber lenses in the center of each unit. Base engine was the 151 cid (2.5-liter) four with four-speed manual. Equipment includes A78 x 13 tires (B78 x 13 on wagons), heater/defroster, and bucket seats. Sport coupe and hatchback models included bright grille and drip moldings and custom wheel covers.

SUNBIRD (FOUR/V-6)

Model Number	Body/Style Number	Body Type & Seating	Factory Price	Shipping Weight	Prod. Total
2H	E27	2-dr. Cpe-4P	3540/3710	2662/ --	20,413
2H	M07	2-dr. Hatch Cpe-4P	3912/4082	2694/ --	25,380
2H	M27	2-dr. Spt Cpe-4P	3773/3943	2662/ --	32,572
2H	M15	2-dr. Sta Wag-4P	3741/3911	2610/ --	8424

1978 Pontiac Formula Sunbird Sport three-door hatchback.

1978 Pontiac Sunbird Formula three-door hatchback (rear view). OCW

PHOENIX -- SERIES 2X -- FOUR/V-6/V-8 -- Ventura was gone, but the compact Phoenix came in two-door coupe, four-door sedan, and hatchback coupe form. A wide center divider at the front held 'Pontiac' lettering below a Pontiac emblem. Grille framing extended to the single recessed rectangular headlamps and tall clear/marker side markers. The grille consisted of four vertical dividers, forming five sections on each side, with subdued vertical bars in each portion. A large Phoenix emblem was low on the cowl. Flush-mount taillamps in bright frames had two divider ribs. Backup lights were in the center of each lens set. Base engine was the 231 cid (3.8-liter) V-6 with three-speed manual shift. Equipment included E78 x 14 blackwall tires, hubcaps, lighter, heater/defroster, and an instrument cluster similar to Grand Prix. LJ added a stand-up hood ornament, wheel opening, and rocker panel moldings, and deluxe wheel covers.

Model Number	Body/Style Number	Body Type & Seating	Factory Price	Shipping Weight	Prod. Total

1978 Pontiac Phoenix LJ coupe. (CP)

PHOENIX (V-6/V-8)

2X	Y27	2-dr. Cpe-6P	3872/4022	3119/3215	26,143
2X	Y69	4-dr. Sed-6P	3947/4097	3169/3265	32,529
2X	Y17	2-dr. Hatch-6P	4068/4218	3202/3298	3252

PHOENIX LJ (V-6/V-8)

2X	Z27	2-dr. Cpe-6P	4357/4507	3228/3324	6210
2X	Z69	4-dr. Sed-6P	4432/4582	3277/3373	8393

Note 1: A four-cylinder engine was available for $170 credit.

1978 Pontiac Firebird Trans Am coupe.

FIREBIRD -- SERIES 2F -- V-6/V-8 -- Appearance of the sporty Firebird was similar to 1977, with rectangular quad headlamps and a dark grille. Wide three-row taillamps had backup lights at the inner ends, close to the license plate. Taillamp ribs filled most of the back panel. Base engine was the 231 cid (3.8-liter) V-6 with three-speed shift. Formula had a 305 cid (5.0-liter) V-8, while Trans Am carried a 400 cid four-barrel V-8. Equipment included Endura bumpers, hubcaps, dual horns, FR78 x 15 SBR tires, bucket seats, and heater/defroster. Esprit added wheel covers, sport mirrors, bright hood and wheel opening moldings, and custom pedal trim. Trans Am included a front air dam, black grille, rear spoiler, sport mirrors, rear wheel air deflectors, Rally II wheels, "shaker" hood and air cleaner, and rally instrument panel with tachometer. Formula and Trans Am had power brakes. Automatic transmission was standard on Formula and Trans Am, but Formula could have a four-speed manual at no extra cost.

1978 Pontiac Firebird Trans Am Gold Special Edition T-top. (CP)

Model Number	Body/Style Number	Body Type & Seating	Factory Price	Shipping Weight	Prod. Total
FIREBIRD (V-6/V-8)					
2F	S87	2-dr. HT Cpe-4P	4545/4695	3254/3377	32,672
FIREBIRD ESPRIT (V-6/V-8)					
2F	T87	2-dr. HT Cpe-4P	4842/4992	3285/3408	36,926
FIREBIRD FORMULA (V-8)					
2F	U87	2-dr. HT Cpe-4P	5448	3452	24,346
FIREBIRD TRANS AM (V-8)					
2F	W87	2-dr. HT Cpe-4P	5799	3511	93,341

1978 Pontiac LeMans Safari station wagon. (CP)

LEMANS -- SERIES 2A -- V-6/V-8 -- The downsized mid-size Pontiacs were 8-17 inches shorter and 530 to 925 pounds lighter than before, boosting fuel economy without loss of interior space. LeMans and Grand LeMans came in two-door coupe and four-door sedan body styles, along with a four-door Safari wagon. Body features included soft, body-colored front/rear bumpers on coupes and sedans. Single rectangular headlamps were used. The headlamp dimmer was now column-mounted. An AM/FM stereo radio with cassette player was available. Options included power vent rear windows (for sedans). Base engine was the 231 cid (3.8-liter) V-6; optional, a 305 cid (5.0-liter) V-8. A wide body-color divider with emblem separated the grille into the customary twin sections. Each 3 x 3 crosshatch grille section stood over subdued vertical bars. Wraparound amber side marker lenses were split into three sections. Two small air slots were below the bumper strip. Wraparound taillamps had two horizontal dividers and stretched full-width to the recessed license plate. Standard equipment included a three-speed manual floor shift, wheel opening moldings, P185/75R14 FBR blackwall tires, hubcaps, and a heater/defroster. Grand LeMans added a hood ornament and moldings, lower bodyside moldings, and black rocker panel moldings.

1978 Pontiac Grand LeMans coupe.

Model Number	Body/Style Number	Body Type & Seating	Factory Price	Shipping Weight	Prod. Total
LEMANS (V-6/V-8)					
2A	D27	2-dr. HT Cpe-6P	4405/4555	3038/3159	20,581
2A	D19	4-dr. HT Sed-6P	4480/4630	3047/3168	22,728
LEMANS SAFARI (V-6/V-8)					
2A	D35	4-dr. 2S Wag-6P	4937/5086	3225/3372	15,714
GRAND LEMANS (V-6/V-8)					
2A	F27	2-dr. HT Cpe-6P	4777/4927	3070/3190	18,433
2A	F19	4-dr. HT Sed-6P	4881/5031	3098/3218	21,252
GRAND LEMANS SAFARI (V-6/V-8)					
2A	F35	4-dr. 2S Wag-6P	5265/5415	3242/3389	11,125

GRAND AM -- SERIES 2A -- V-8 -- A single series, coupe and sedan, made up the Grand Am lineup, which featured a soft front-end panel and two-tone paint. Standard equipment included 205/70R14 steel-belted radial tires and Rally RTS suspension. Base engine was the 301 cid (4.9-liter) V-8; optional, a four-barrel version of the same power-plant. Four body-color vertical strips separated each grille section in the sloping front panel into five segments. The protruding body-color center divider held a Pontiac emblem. Recessed single rectangular headlamps stood above clear park/signal lamps, with the same frame-work wrapping to clear/amber side marker lenses. "Grand Am" name-plates went on the forward end of front fenders. At the rear were horizontally ribbed wraparound taillamps. Grand Am standard equipment was similar to LeMans but included an automatic transmission (with four-speed manual optional), power brakes/steering, two-tone paint, and P205/70R14 blackwall SBR tires.

Model Number	Body/Style Number	Body Type & Seating	Factory Price	Shipping Weight	Prod. Total
GRAND AM (V-8)					
2A	G27	2-dr. Cpe-6P	5464	3209	7767
2A	G19	4-dr. Sed-6P	5568	3239	2841

GRAND PRIX -- SERIES 2G -- V-6/V-8 -- Three Grand Prix models were offered again this year: base, sporty SJ, and luxury LJ. All three now rode a 108 in. wheelbase, measuring 201.2 in. in length (nearly 17 in. shorter than their predecessors). Weights were cut by 600 to 750 pounds. The base Grand Prix had a notchback front seat with either vinyl or cloth upholstery. Grand Prix LJ came with a loose-pillow

style cloth notchback front seat. Optional on SJ and LJ: leather upholstery in Viscount design. Base engine was the 231 cid (3.8-liter) V-6, but LJ had a 301 cid (4.9-liter) two-barrel V-8 and LJ a four-barrel 301. Equipment also included a three-speed manual gearbox, wide rocker panel moldings, wheel opening moldings, clock, and P195/75R14 SBR blackwall tires. SJ added P205/70R14 tires, a 301 cid four-barrel V-8, power brakes and steering, automatic transmission, and vinyl front bucket seats. LJ had wide rocker panel moldings with extensions, a two-barrel 301 V-8, automatic, power brakes/steering, body-color mirrors, and deluxe wheel covers. The new-size Grand Prix displayed a rather tall grille in a bright, heavy frame with four vertical bars on each side of the bright center bar, which held no emblem. A tall hood ornament had 'GP' letters at the base. Clear park/signal lamps stood between each pair of quad headlamps, as in 1977. "Grand Prix" script went above the left headlamp. All told, the grille (and the whole front end) showed a more upright, squared-off look than before. Hood creases were far less prominent, meeting the grille ends rather than coming to a point at the center. Large squarish taillamps contained five horizontal divider ribs. The license plate was mounted in the decklid.

1978 Pontiac Grand Prix SJ coupe.

Model Number	Body/Style Number	Body Type & Seating	Factory Price	Shipping Weight	Prod. Total
GRAND PRIX (V-6/V-8)					
2G	J37	2-dr. Cpe-6P	4800/5030	3101/3224	127,253
GRAND PRIX LJ (V-8)					
2G	K37	2-dr. Cpe-6P	5815	3216	65,122
GRAND PRIX SJ (V-8)					
2G	H37	2-dr. Cpe-6P	6088	3229	36,069

CATALINA -- SERIES 2B -- V-6/V-8 -- Styling of both full-size models was similar to 1977, when the pair was downsized. Catalina's revised grille consisted of five horizontal strips over subdued vertical strips. Small clear park/signal lamps were in the bumper. Alongside the quad rectangular headlamps were two-section amber wraparound marker lenses. The bright grille divider held no emblem. "Catalina" lettering went on the cowl, "Pontiac" over the driver's side headlamps. Wraparound taillamps had three horizontal ribs, with backup lights at the inner ends. The recessed license plate was on a level with the taillamps. Catalina's base engine was the Buick-built 231 cid (3.8-liter) V-6, with 301, 350, and 400/403 cid V-8 available. Equipment included automatic transmission, power brakes/steering, FR78 x 15 radial tires, front/rear bumper strips, and heater/defroster.

Model Number	Body/Style Number	Body Type & Seating	Factory Price	Shipping Weight	Prod. Total
CATALINA (V-6/V-8)					
2B	L37	2-dr. Cpe-6P	5375/5525	3438/3559	9224
2B	L69	4-dr. Sed-6P	5410/5560	3470/3591	39,707
CATALINA SAFARI (V-8)					
2B	L35	4-dr. 2S Wag-6P	5924	3976	12,819

BONNEVILLE -- SERIES 2B -- V-8 -- Like Catalina, the full-size Bonneville was similar to 1977, but had a revised grille. This one had four vertical divider bars on each side of the bright center divider (with emblem), instead of the former eggcrate design. Wraparound marker lenses were in the same frames as headlamps, extending to four-section amber side marker lenses. "Pontiac" lettering went over the left headlamp again. The hood ornament was an octagon within an octagon. As before, small clear park/signal lamps were bumper-mounted. The grille pattern repeated in twin narrow bumper slots. "Bonneville" lettering went on the lower cowl. Wraparound taillamps were new. Standard equipment was similar to Catalina, but a two-barrel 301 V-8 was standard, along with fender skirts and wheel covers. Brougham added a 60/40 front seat, clock, and power windows.

1978 Pontiac Bonneville Brougham sedan.

Model Number	Body/Style Number	Body Type & Seating	Factory Price	Shipping Weight	Prod. Total
BONNEVILLE (V-8)					
2B	N37	2-dr. Cpe-6P	5831	3581	22,510
2B	N69	4-dr. Sed-6P	5931	3637	48,647
BONNEVILLE BROUGHAM (V-8)					
2B	Q37	2-dr. Cpe-6P	6577	3611	36,192
2B	Q69	4-dr. Sed-6P	6677	3667	17,948
GRAND SAFARI (V-8)					
2B	N35	4-dr. 2S Wag-6P	6227	4002	13,847

FACTORY PRICE AND WEIGHT NOTE: Prices and weights to left of slash are for V-6, to right for V-8 engine except Sunbird, four and V-6.

ENGINE DATA

BASE FOUR (Sunbird); OPTIONAL (Phoenix): Inline. Overhead valve. Four-cylinder. Cast iron block and head. Displacement: 151 cu. in. (2.3 liters). Bore & stroke: 4.00 x 3.00 in. Compression ratio: 8.3:1. Brake horsepower: 85 @ 4400 rpm. Torque: 123 lb.-ft. @ 2800 rpm. Five main bearings. Hydraulic valve lifters. Carburetor: two-barrel Holley 5210C. VIN Code: V.

BASE V-6 (Phoenix, Firebird, LeMans, Catalina, Grand Prix); OPTIONAL (Sunbird): 90-degree, overhead-valve V-6. Cast iron block and head. Displacement: 231 cu. in. (3.8 liters). Bore & stroke: 3.80 x 3.40 in. Compression ratio: 8.0:1. Brake horsepower: 105 @ 3200-3400 rpm. Torque: 185 lb.-ft. @ 2000 rpm. Four main bearings. Hydraulic valve lifters. Carburetor: two-barrel Rochester 2GC. VIN Code: A.

BASE V-8 (Grand Am, Bonneville, Grand Prix LJ); OPTIONAL (Grand Prix, Catalina): 90-degree, overhead valve V-8. Cast iron block and head. Displacement: 301 cu. in. (5.0 liters). Bore & stroke: 4.00 x 3.00 in. Compression ratio: 8.2:1. Brake horsepower: 140 @ 3600 rpm. Torque: 235 lb.-ft. @ 2000 rpm. Five main bearings. Hydraulic valve lifters. Carburetor: two-barrel Rochester M2MC. VIN Code: Y. BASE V-8 (Grand Prix SJ); OPTIONAL (Grand Am, Grand Prix): Same as 301 cid V-8 above, with four-barrel carburetor (Rochester M4MC); Horsepower: 150 @ 4000 rpm. Torque: 239 lb.-ft. @ 2000 rpm. VIN Code: W. BASE V-8 (Firebird Formula); OPTIONAL (Phoenix, Firebird, LeMans, Grand Prix SJ/LJ): 90-degree, overhead valve V-8. Cast iron block and head. Displacement: 305 cu. in. (5.0 liters). Bore & stroke: 3.74 x 3.48 in. Compression ratio: 8.4:1. Brake horsepower: 145 @ 3800 rpm. Torque: 245 lb.-ft. @ 2400 rpm. Five main bearings. Hydraulic valve lifters. Carburetor: two-barrel Rochester 2GC. VIN Code: U. OPTIONAL V-8 (Firebird, Catalina, Bonneville): 90-degree, overhead valve V-8. Cast iron block and head. Displacement: 350 cu. in. (5.7 liters). Bore & stroke: 3.80 x 3.85 in. Compression ratio: 8.0:1. Brake horsepower: 155 @ 3400 rpm. Torque: 280 lb.-ft. @ 1800 rpm. Five main bearings. Hydraulic valve lifters. Carburetor: four-barrel Rochester M4MC. Buick-built. VIN Code: X. ALTERNATE V-8 (Firebird, Catalina, Bonneville): 90-degree, overhead valve V-8. Cast iron block and head. Displacement: 350 cu. in. (5.7 liters). Bore & stroke: 4.00 x 3.48 in. Compression ratio: 8.2:1. Brake horsepower: 170 @ 3800 rpm. Torque: 270 lb.-ft. @ 2400 rpm. Five main bearings. Hydraulic valve lifters. Carburetor: four-barrel Rochester M4MC. Chevrolet-built. VIN Code: L. ALTERNATE V-8 (Firebird, Catalina, Bonneville): 90-degree, overhead valve V-8. Cast iron block and head. Displacement: 350 cu. in. (5.7 liters). Bore & stroke: 4.06 x 3.38 in. Compression ratio: 7.9:1. Brake horsepower: 170 @ 3800 rpm. Torque: 275 lb.-ft. @ 2000 rpm. Five main bearings. Hydraulic valve lifters. Carburetor: four-barrel Rochester M4MC. Oldsmobile-built. VIN Code: R. BASE V-8 (Trans Am); OPTIONAL (Firebird Formula, Catalina, Bonneville): 90-degree, overhead valve V-8. Cast iron block and head. Displacement: 400 cu. in. (6.6 liters). Bore & stroke: 4.12 x 3.75 in. Compression ratio: 7.7:1. Brake horsepower: 180 @ 3600 rpm. Torque: 325 lb.-ft. @ 1600 rpm. Five main bearings. Hydraulic valve lifters. Carburetor: four-barrel Rochester M4MC. VIN Code: Z. OPTIONAL T/A V-8 (Firebird Formula/Trans Am): Same as 400 cid V-8 above, except Compression ratio: 8.1:1. Horsepower: 220 @ 4000 rpm. Torque: 320 lb.-ft. @ 2800 rpm.

1978 Pontiac Sunbird Sport three-door hatchback. OCW

1978 Pontiac Grand LeMans Safari station wagon. OCW

1978 Pontiac Phoenix LJ landau coupe (rear view). OCW

1978 Pontiac Grand Am two-door hardtop. OCW

1978 Pontiac Phoenix LJ four-door sedan. OCW

1978 Pontiac Grand Am four-door sedan. OCW

1978 Pontiac Firebird Esprit "Red Bird" coupe. OCW

1978 Pontiac Grand Prix two-door hardtop (rear view). OCW

1978 Pontiac Grand LeMans four-door sedan. OCW

1978 Pontiac Catalina coupe. OCW

NOTE: A 403 cid V-8 was used in California models.

CHASSIS DATA: Wheelbase: (Sunbird) 97.0 in.; (Phoenix) 111.1 in.; (Firebird) 108.1 in.; (LeMans) 108.1 in.; (Grand Prix) 108.1 in.; (Catalina/Bonneville) 115.9 in. Overall Length: (Sunbird) 177.8 in.; (Sunbird hatch) 178.3 in.; (Sunbird wag) 177.6 in.; (Phoenix) 203.4 in.; (Firebird) 196.8 in.; (LeMans cpe) 199.2 in.; (LeMans sed) 198.5 in.; (LeMans wag) 197.8 in.; (G.P.) 201.2 in.; (Catalina/Bonneville) 214.3 in.; (Safari wag) 215.1 in. Height: (Sunbird) 49.6 in.; (Sunbird hatch) 49.9 in.; (Sunbird wag) 51.8 in.; (Phoenix) 52.3 in.; (Firebird) 49.3 in.; (Formula/Trans Am) 49.5 in.; (LeMans cpe) 53.5 in.; (LeMans sed) 54.4 in.; (LeMans wag) 54.8 in.; (G.P.) 53.3 in.; (Catalina/Bonneville cpe) 53.9 in.; (Catalina/Bonneville sed) 54.5 in.; (Safari wag) 57.3 in. Width: (Sunbird) 65.4 in.; (Phoenix) 73.2 in.; (Firebird) 73.4 in.; (LeMans) 72.4 in.; (LeMans wag) 72.6 in.; (G.P.) 72.8 in.; (Catalina/Bonneville) 78.0 in.; (Safari wag) 80.0 in. Front Tread: (Sunbird) 55.2 in. exc. hatch, 54.7 in.; (Phoenix) 61.8 in.; (Firebird) 60.9 in.; (Firebird Formula) 61.3 in.; (Trans Am) 61.2 in.; (LeMans) 58.5 in.; (G.P.) 58.5 in.; (Catalina/Bonneville) 61.7 in.; (Safari) 62.1 in. Rear Tread: (Sunbird) 54.1 in. exc. hatch, 53.6 in.; (Phoenix) 59.6 in.; (Firebird) 60.0 in.; (Firebird Formula) 60.4 in.; (Trans Am) 60.3 in.; (LeMans) 57.8 in.; (G.P.) 57.8 in.; (Catalina/Bonneville) 60.7 in.; (Safari) 64.1 in. Standard Tires: (Sunbird) A78 x 13 exc. wagon, B78 x 13; (Phoenix) E78 x 14; (Firebird) FR78 x 15; (Trans Am) GR70 x 15; (LeMans) P185/75R14; (Grand Am) P205/70R14; (Grand Prix) P195/75R14; (Catalina/Bonneville) FR78 x 15.

TECHNICAL: Transmission: Three-speed manual transmission standard on Phoenix, LeMans, Firebird, and base Grand Prix (floor lever standard on Firebird/LeMans, optional on Phoenix). Four-speed manual standard on Sunbird, optional on Firebird, Phoenix, and Grand Am. Five-speed manual optional on Sunbird. Three-speed Turbo-Hydramatic standard on other models, optional on all. Steering: Recirculating ball. Front Suspension: (Firebird/LeMans) coil springs w/lower trailing links and anti-sway bar; (others) coil springs and anti-sway bar. Rear Suspension: (Sunbird) rigid axle with coil springs, lower trailing radius arms and upper torque arms; (Phoenix) semi-elliptic leaf springs; (Firebird) semi-elliptic leaf springs with anti-sway bar; (LeMans/Bonneville/Grand Prix) rigid axle with coil springs, lower trailing radius arms, upper torque arms and anti-sway bar. Brakes: Front disc, rear drum. Ignition: Electronic. Body construction: (Sunbird) unit; (Firebird) unit w/separate partial frame; (others) separate body and frame. Fuel tank: (Sunbird) 18.5 gal. exc. wagon, 16 gal.; (Phoenix) 21 gal.; (Firebird) 21 gal.; (LeMans) 17.5 gal. exc. wagon, 18.3 gal.; (Grand Am) 15 gal.; (Grand Prix) 15 gal.; (Catalina/Bonneville) 21 gal. exc. wagon, 22 gal.

DRIVETRAIN OPTIONS: Engines: 140 cid two-barrel four: Phoenix ($170 credit). 231 cid V-6: Sunbird ($170). 301 cid, two-barrel V-8: Catalina/Grand Prix ($150). 301 cid, four-barrel V-8: Grand Prix ($200); Grand Prix LJ ($50); Grand Am ($50). 305 cid, two-barrel V-8: Phoenix/Firebird/LeMans/G.P. ($150). 350 cid, four-barrel V-8: Phoenix/Firebird/Catalina ($265); LeMans Safari ($265); Firebird Formula ($115); Bonneville ($115). 400 cid, four-barrel V-8: Firebird ($205). Catalina ($330); Bonneville ($180). T/A 400 cid, four-barrel V-8: Formula ($280); Trans Am ($75). 403 cid, four-barrel V-8: Firebird Formula ($205); Catalina ($330); Bonneville ($180). Transmission/Differential: Three-speed floor shift: Phoenix ($33). Four-speed manual floor shift transmission: Phoenix w/V-8-305 ($125); Firebird/LeMans ($125); Formula ($182 credit). Five-speed manual transmission: Sunbird ($175). Turbo-Hydramatic: Sunbird ($270); Phoenix/Firebird/LeMans/Grand Prix ($307); Formula/Trans Am (NC). Saf-T-Track differential: Sunbird ($56); LeMans/Firebird/G.P. ($60); Catalina/Bonneville ($64). Brakes/Steering: Power brakes (N/A); Phoenix/LeMans/Firebird/G.P. ($76). Power steering: Sunbird ($134); Phoenix/LeMans/G.P. ($152). Suspension: Rally RTS handling pkg.: Sunbird ($2-$230); Phoenix ($172-$217); LeMans ($42-$179); Catalina ($140-$169); Bonneville ($102-$120); Grand Prix ($67-$120). Firm ride pkg. ($12) except Sunbird. Superlift shock absorbers: LeMans/G.P. ($52); Catalina/Bonneville ($53). Automatic level control: LeMans/G.P./Catalina/Bonneville ($63-$116). Other: H.D. radiator: Sunbird ($32); Phoenix ($31-$56). Supercooling radiator ($31-$57) except Sunbird/Phoenix. H.D. battery ($17-$20). H.D. alternator: Sunbird/Phoenix/Firebird ($31); Catalina/Bonneville ($18-$49). Engine block heater ($13-$14). Class I trailer group: Bonneville/Catalina ($117-$143). Medium trailer group: LeMans/G.P. ($116-$141). Heavy trailer group: Bonneville/Catalina ($117-$178). California emissions ($75-$100). High-altitude option ($33).

OPTION PACKAGES: Sunbird Formula group ($448-$621). Sunbird appearance group: cpe ($87). Phoenix cpe/sed appearance pkg. ($73). Firebird "Skybird" appearance pkg.: Esprit ($426-$461). Trans Am special edition ($1259). Firebird custom trim group ($35-$154). Firebird Formula appearance pkg. ($137). Firebird Trans Am special performance pkg. ($249-$324). LeMans Safari security pkg. ($35-$40). LeMans exterior paint appearance ($159). LeMans custom exterior (40-$75). LeMans custom trim group ($134-$247). Full-size exterior paint pkg. ($159). Safari custom trim group ($205-$370). Grand Prix exterior appearance ($119-$165).

MAJOR CONVENIENCE/APPEARANCE OPTIONS: Air conditioning ($470-$581). Automatic air conditioning: LeMans/Grand Prix ($584); Catalina/Bonneville ($626). Cruise control ($90-$95); N/A on Sunbird. Power seat: LeMans/Catalina/Bonneville/G.P. ($151). Power windows ($118-$190); N/A on Sunbird. Cornering lamps: Catalina/Bonneville/Grand Prix ($47). Power glass sunroof: LeMans/Grand Prix ($699); Catalina/Bonneville ($895). Power steel sunroof: LeMans/Grand Prix ($499); Catalina/Bonneville ($695). Glass sunroof: Sunbird ($172). Hatch roof: Firebird/Grand Prix ($625). Full vinyl cordova top: Phoenix ($97); LeMans ($116); Grand Prix ($121); Catalina/Bonneville ($142). Padded landau top: Grand Prix/LeMans ($239); Catalina/Bonneville ($294). Landau cordova top: Sunbird ($153); Phoenix ($179). Canopy top: Firebird ($111). Rear-facing third seat: Safari ($175).

HISTORICAL FOOTNOTES: Introduced: October 6, 1977. Model year production: 900,380. Calendar year production (U.S.): 867,008. Calendar year sales by U.S. dealers: 896,980. Model year sales by U.S. dealers: 871,391. Model year sales set a new record in 1978, beating the 1968 total. Contributing to the rise were strong sales of Trans Am and the shrunken mid-size models, but Sunbird also showed an increase.

1979 PONTIAC

This was not a year of startling change, except for some shifts in engine availability. No surprise there, as the late 1970s were years of considerable revision (and confusion) in powerplant choices. California models had their own engine possibilities, as did cars sold for high altitude operation. Full-size models got a new front and rear appearance as well as new interior trim, and Firebird received a dramatically different look. Wire wheels became optional on Grand Prix. Formula and Trans Am Firebirds could get four-wheel power disc brakes.

I.D. DATA: Pontiac's 13-symbol Vehicle Identification Number (VIN) was located on the upper left surface of the instrument panel, visible through the windshield. The first digit is '2', indicating Pontiac division. The second symbol is a letter indicating series: 'E' = Sunbird; 'M' = Sunbird Sport; 'Y' = Phoenix; 'Z' = Phoenix LJ; 'D' = LeMans; 'F' = Grand LeMans; 'G' = Grand Am; 'S' = Firebird; 'T' = Firebird Esprit; 'U' = Firebird Formula; 'W' = Firebird Trans Am; 'L' = Catalina; 'N' = Bonneville; 'Q' = Bonneville Brougham; 'J' = Grand Prix; 'K' = Grand Prix LJ; 'H' = Grand Prix SJ. Next come two digits that denote body type: '07' = 2-dr. hatchback coupe; '17' = 2-dr. hatchback coupe; '27' = 2-dr. coupe; '37' = 2-dr. coupe; '87' = 2-dr. HT coupe; '19' = 4-dr. six-window sedan; '69' = 4-dr. four-window sedan; '15' = 2-dr. station wagon; '35' = 4-dr. two-seat wagon. The fifth symbol is a letter indicating engine code: 'V' = L4-151 two-barrel; 'A' = V-6-231 two-barrel; 'Y' = V-8-301 two-barrel; 'W' = V-8-301 four-barrel; 'G' = V-8-305 two-barrel; 'H' = V-8-305 four-barrel; 'X' = V-8-350 four-barrel (L37); 'R' = V-8-350 four-barrel (L34); 'L' = V-8-350 four-barrel (LM1); 'Z' = V-8-400 four-barrel; 'K' = V-8-403 four-barrel The sixth symbol denotes model year ('9' = 1979). Next is a plant code: 'A' = Lakewood, Ga.; 'B' = Baltimore; 'L' = Van Nuys, Calif.; 'N' = Norwood, Ohio; 'P' = Pontiac, Mich.; 'T' = Tarrytown, N.Y.; 'U' = Lordstown, Ohio; 'W' = Willow Run, Mich.; 'X' = Fairfax, Kan.; '1' = Oshawa, Ontario; '2' = Ste. Therese, Quebec. The final six digits are the sequential serial number.

1979 Pontiac Sunbird Astre Safari station wagon. (JG)

SUNBIRD -- SERIES 2H -- FOUR/V-6 -- Appearance of the subcompact Pontiac was similar to 1978, but the small twin grilles now contained horizontal strips (formerly vertical). Equipment was similar to 1978, with standard 151 cid (2.5-liter) four and optional 231 cid V-6 or 305 cid V-8. A four-speed manual gearbox was standard. Tires were A78 x 13 except B78 x 13 with V-6 engines. Sport Coupe and Sport Hatch models added custom wheel covers, rocker panel and wheel opening moldings, and custom vinyl bucket seats.

1979 Pontiac Sunbird Formula three-door hatchback. OCW

1979 Pontiac Sunbird Formula three-door hatchback.

SUNBIRD (FOUR/V-6)

Model Number	Body/Style Number	Body Type & Seating	Factory Price	Shipping Weight	Prod. Total
2H	E27	2-dr. Cpe-4P	3781/3981	2593/--	40,560
2H	M07	2-dr. Hatch Cpe-4P	4064/4264	2642/--	24,221
2H	M27	2-dr. Spt Cpe-4P	3964/4164	2593/--	30,087
2H	M15	2-dr. Sta Wag-4P	4138/4338	2651/--	2902

PHOENIX -- SERIES 2X -- V-6/V-8 -- Each side of this year's Phoenix grille contained five side-by-side sections, with subdued vertical bars in each one and clear park/signal lamps in outer ends. Otherwise, appearance was similar to 1978. The compact Phoenix came in five models: base coupe, hatchback and sedan, and LJ coupe and sedan. New two-tone paint was offered in four color combinations. Base engine was the 231 cid (3.8-liter) V-6, with 305 cid two-barrel V-8 optional. A 350 cid V-8 was offered for California and high-altitude models. The four-cylinder credit option was no longer available. Phoenix could get a light-duty trailer-towing package that handled units up to one ton.

Model Number	Body/Style Number	Body Type & Seating	Factory Price	Shipping Weight	Prod. Total
PHOENIX (V-6/V-8)					
2X	Y27	2-dr. Cpe-6P	4089/4284	3127/3345	9233
2X	Y69	4-dr. Sed-6P	4189/4384	3177/3395	10,565
2X	Y17	2-dr. Hatch-6P	4239/4434	3210/3428	923

1979 Pontiac Phoenix LJ coupe. (CP)

1979 Pontiac Phoenix LJ sedan. (P)

PHOENIX LJ (V-6/V-8)

2X	Z27	2-dr. Cpe-6P	4589/4784	3236/3454	1826
2X	Z69	4-dr. Sed-6P	4689/4884	3285/3503	2353

1979 Pontiac Firebird Formula coupe. OCW

FIREBIRD -- SERIES 2F -- V-6/V-8 -- Front ends of the new Firebirds were far different from predecessors. Quad rectangular headlamps now stood in separate recessed housings, in a sharply sloped center panel that had a peak and an emblem--but no grille. Instead, horizontally ribbed lower grilles went into twin slots below the bumper area, with clear park/signal lamps at outer ends. At the rear was a full-width horizontally ribbed panel. Base Firebird equipment included Buick's 231 cid (3.8-liter) V-6, three-speed manual shift, power steering, and FR78 x 15 steel-belted radials. Esprit added wheel covers, sport mirrors (driver's remote), and extra body moldings. Formula had a 301 cid V-8, automatic transmission, power brakes, black-accented grille, non-functional twin hood scoop, Rally II wheels with trim rings, console, and P225/70R15 blackwall SBR tires. Trans Am had a 403 cid four-barrel V-8, four-speed manual transmission, power brakes, air dam, rear spoiler, "shaker" hood, and chrome side-splitter tailpipe extensions.

1979 Pontiac Firebird Formula coupe. (JG)

Model Number	Body/Style Number	Body Type & Seating	Factory Price	Shipping Weight	Prod. Total
FIREBIRD (V-6/V-8)					
2F	S87	2-dr. HT Cpe-4P	4825/5020	3257/3330	38,642
FIREBIRD ESPRIT (V-6/V-8)					
2F	T87	2-dr. HT Cpe-4P	5193/5388	3287/3360	30,853

1979 Pontiac Firebird Trans Am T-top coupe. (P)

FIREBIRD FORMULA (V-8)

2F	U87	2-dr. HT Cpe-4P	6018	3460	24,851

FIREBIRD TRANS AM (V-8)

2F	W87	2-dr. HT Cpe-4P	6299	3551	117,108

FIREBIRD TRANS AM LIMITED EDITION (V-8)

2F	X87	2-dr. HT Cpe-4P	10620	3551	N/A

1979 Pontiac LeMans coupe. (JG)

LEMANS -- SERIES 2A -- V-6/V-8 -- Styling of the mid-size LeMans was similar to before, but the grille contained more holes, now displaying a 6 x 4 pattern. Amber side marker lenses now were split into four sections rather than three. Base engine was the 231 cid (3.8-liter) V-6, with three-speed manual shift. Equipment included body-color bumpers with rub strips, P185/75R14 glass-belted radial tires, hubcaps, and wheel opening moldings. Grand LeMans added a hood ornament and windsplit molding, lower bodyside moldings, brushed aluminum center pillar, and door panel pull straps. Engine options included a 301 cid V-8 (two- or four-barrel carb), and 305 cid four-barrel V-8. Safari wagons had a 5.0-liter V-8 as standard, and could also have a 350 V-8.

1979 Pontiac Grand LeMans sedan. (P)

1979 Pontiac Grand LeMans Safari station wagon. (JG)

Model Number	Body/Style Number	Body Type & Seating	Factory Price	Shipping Weight	Prod. Total
LEMANS (V-6/V-8)					
2A	D27	2-dr. Cpe-6P	4608/4803	3036/3115	14,197
2A	D19	4-dr. Sed-6P	4708/4903	3042/3121	26,958
LEMANS SAFARI (V-6/V-8)					
2A	D35	4-dr. 2S Wag-6P	5216/5411	3200/3328	27,517
GRAND LEMANS (V-6/V-8)					
2A	F27	2-dr. Cpe-6P	4868/5063	3058/3137	13,020
2A	F19	4-dr. Sed-6P	4993/5188	3087/3166	28,577
GRAND LEMANS SAFARI (V-6/V-8)					
2A	F35	4-dr. 2S Wag-6P	5560/5755	3234/3362	20,783

GRAND AM -- SERIES 2A -- V-8 -- Except for amber park/signal and marker lenses, appearance of the Grand Am changed little this year. Equipment was similar to LeMans, but with power steering, two-tone body color, blackout taillamps, P205/70R14 steel-belted radials, and Rally RTS handling package.

1979 Pontiac Grand Am coupe. (P)

GRAND AM (V-6/V-8)

Model Number	Body/Style Number	Body Type & Seating	Factory Price	Shipping Weight	Prod. Total
2A	G27	2-dr. Cpe-6P	5084/5279	3080/3159	4021
2A	G19	4-dr. Sed-6P	5209/5404	3084/3163	1865

1979 Pontiac Grand Prix LJ coupe. (P)

155

1979 Pontiac Grand Prix SJ coupe. (JG)

GRAND PRIX -- SERIES 2G -- V-6/V-8 -- Horizontal and vertical bars now made up the Grand Prix grille, forming a 3 x 7 pattern of wide holes on each side of a narrow (for Pontiac) center divider. Amber park/signal lenses went between each pair of rectangular quad headlamps.

Model Number	Body/Style Number	Body Type & Seating	Factory Price	Shipping Weight	Prod. Total
GRAND PRIX (V-6/V-8)					
2G	J37	2-dr. Cpe-6P	5113/5308	3126/3205	124,815
GRAND PRIX LJ (V-8)					
2G	K37	2-dr. Cpe-5P	6192	3285	61,175
GRAND PRIX SJ (V-8)					
2G	H37	2-dr. Cpe-5P	6438	3349	24,060

1979 Pontiac Catalina coupe. (P)

CATALINA -- SERIES 2B -- V-6/V-8 -- Both Catalina and Bonneville gained a front/rear restyle this year. Coupe and sedan models were offered again, along with a Catalina Safari wagon. Changes included a new grille, park/signal lamps, taillamps, and side marker lamps. Wagons kept their former taillamp design. Though similar to before, the new front end held a horizontal-themed grille made up of four rows (formerly six). Amber wraparound front marker lenses were split into four sections instead of two. As before, small clear park/signal lamps were bumper-mounted. Rectangular quad headlamps continued. Base engine was the 231 cid (3.8-liter) V-6. A 350 cid four-barrel V-8 was available for high-altitude models. Safari wagons carried a 301 cid (4.9-liter) two-barrel V-8 (350 four-barrel in California); and a 403 V-8 was available in high-altitude regions. Both light- and heavy-duty trailering packages were optional. New "Cloud Dillon" cloth seat trim was used. Full-size options included wire wheel covers, power windows and door locks, power six-way 60/40 split front seats, air conditioning, AM/FM stereo, a padded Landau Cordova top, and cushion tilt steering wheel.

Model Number	Body/Style Number	Body Type & Seating	Factory Price	Shipping Weight	Prod. Total
CATALINA (V-6/V-8)					
2B	L37	2-dr. Cpe-6P	5690/5885	3476/3593	5410
2B	L69	4-dr. Sed-6P	5746/5941	3508/3625	28,121
CATALINA SAFARI (V-8)					
2B	L35	4-dr. 2S Wag-6P	6273	3997	13,353

1979 Pontiac Bonneville Brougham sedan. (P)

BONNEVILLE -- SERIES 2B -- V-8 -- Like Catalina, Bonneville and Bonneville Brougham got a design change including new grille, park/signal lamps, taillamps and side markers. All models had new deluxe wheel covers. For the first time, coupes could have optional cloth bucket seats with a console. Bonneville's base engine was a 301 cid (4.9-liter) two-barrel V-8; or 350 four-barrel for California/high-altitude models. Grand Safari got a name change to, simply, Bonneville Safari. A third seat was available again. This year's seat trim was Chamonix cloth (Dante cloth on Brougham, which used a new pillow-style design). Bonneville's grille elements were whole vertical rectangles, not just single vertical bars as in 1978. Five of them appeared on each side of the center divider. Instead of four-section amber side marker lenses, this year's were two-section.

Model Number	Body/Style Number	Body Type & Seating	Factory Price	Shipping Weight	Prod. Total
BONNEVILLE (V-8)					
2B	N37	2-dr. Cpe-6P	6205	3616	34,127
2B	N69	4-dr. Sed-6P	6330	3672	71,906
BONNEVILLE BROUGHAM (V-8)					
2B	Q37	2-dr. Cpe-6P	6960	3659	39,094
2B	Q69	4-dr. Sed-6P	7149	3726	17,364
BONNEVILLE SAFARI (V-8)					
2B	N35	4-dr. 2S Wag-6P	6632	4022	16,925

FACTORY PRICE AND WEIGHT NOTE: Prices and weights to left of slash are for V-6, to right for V-8 engine except Sunbird, four and V-6.

ENGINE DATA

BASE FOUR (Sunbird): Inline. Overhead valve. Four-cylinder. Cast iron block and head. Displacement: 151 cu. in. (2.5 liters). Bore & stroke: 4.00 x 3.00 in. Compression ratio: 8.2:1. Brake horsepower: 85 @ 4400 rpm. Torque: 123 lb.-ft. @ 2800 rpm. Five main bearings. Hydraulic valve lifters. Carburetor: two-barrel Rochester 2SE. VIN Code: V.

BASE V-6 (Phoenix, Firebird, LeMans, Catalina, Grand Prix); OPTIONAL (Sunbird): 90-degree, overhead-valve V-6. Cast iron block and head. Displacement: 231 cu. in. (3.8 liters). Bore & stroke: 3.80 x 3.40 in. Compression ratio: 8.0:1. Brake horsepower: 105 @ 3200-3400 rpm. Torque: 185 lb.-ft. @ 2000 rpm. Four main bearings. Hydraulic valve lifters. Carburetor: two-barrel Rochester M2ME. Buick-built. VIN Code: A.

BASE V-8 (Bonneville, Grand Prix LJ, Safari); OPTIONAL (Firebird, LeMans, Grand Prix, Catalina): 90-degree, overhead valve V-8. Cast iron block and head. Displacement: 301 cu. in. (5.0 liters). Bore & stroke: 4.06 x 3.04 in. Compression ratio: 8.1:1. Brake horsepower: 140 @ 3600 rpm. Torque: 235 lb.-ft. @ 2000 rpm. Five main bearings. Hydraulic valve lifters. Carburetor: two-barrel Rochester M2MC. VIN Code: Y. BASE V-8 (Firebird Formula, Grand Prix SJ); OPTIONAL (Firebird, Trans Am, LeMans, Grand Am, Bonneville, Catalina, Grand Prix): Same as 301 cid V-8 above, with four-barrel carburetor (Rochester M4MC). Horsepower: 150 @ 4000 rpm. Torque: 240 lb.-ft. @ 2000 rpm. VIN Code: W. OPTIONAL V-8 (Sunbird, Phoenix): 90-degree, overhead valve V-8. Cast iron block and head. Displacement: 305 cu. in. (5.0 liters). Bore & stroke: 3.74 x 3.48 in. Compression ratio: 8.4:1. Brake horsepower: 145 @ 3800 rpm. Torque: 245 lb.-ft. @ 2400 rpm. Five main bearings. Hydraulic valve lifters. Carburetor: two-barrel Rochester 2GC. VIN Code: U. ALTERNATE V-8 (Sunbird, Phoenix, Firebird): Same as 305 cid V-8 above, except Horsepower: 133 @ 4000 rpm. Torque: 244 lb.-ft. @ 2000 rpm. OPTIONAL V-8 (LeMans): Same as 305 cid V-8 above, but with four-barrel carburetor. Horsepower: 150 @ 4000 rpm. Torque: 225 lb.-ft. @ 2400 rpm. VIN Code: H. OPTIONAL V-8 (Phoenix, Firebird, Catalina, Bonneville, LeMans Safari): 90-degree, overhead valve V-8. Cast iron block and head. Displacement: 350 cu. in. (5.7 liters). Bore & stroke: 4.00 x 3.48 in. Compression ratio: 8.2:1. Brake horsepower: 160 @ 3800

rpm. Torque: 260 lb.-ft. @ 2400 rpm. Five main bearings. Hydraulic valve lifters. Carburetor: four-barrel Rochester M4MC. Chevrolet-built. VIN Code: L. ALTERNATE V-8 (Phoenix, Firebird, Catalina, Bonneville, LeMans, Safari): Same as 350 cid V-8 above, except Bore & stroke: 3.80 x 3.85 in. Compression ratio: 8.0:1. Brake horsepower: 155 @ 3400 rpm. Torque: 280 lb.-ft. @ 1800 rpm. Buick-built. VIN Code: X. ALTERNATE V-8 (Phoenix, Firebird, Catalina, Bonneville, LeMans, Safari): Same as 350 cid V-8 above, except Bore & stroke: 4.06 x 3.38 in. Compression ratio: 7.9:1. Brake horsepower: 160 @ 3600 rpm. Torque: 270 lb.-ft. @ 2000 rpm. Oldsmobile-built. VIN Code: R. OPTIONAL V-8 (Firebird Formula, Trans Am): 90-degree, overhead valve V-8. Cast iron block and head. Displacement: 400 cu. in. (6.6 liters). Bore & stroke: 4.12 x 3.75 in. Compression ratio: 8.1:1. Brake horsepower: 220 @ 4000 rpm. Torque: 320 lb.-ft. @ 2800 rpm. Five main bearings. Hydraulic valve lifters. Carburetor: four-barrel Rochester M4MC. VIN Code: Z. BASE V-8 (Trans Am); OPTIONAL (Firebird Formula): 90-degree, overhead valve V-8. Cast iron block and head. Displacement: 403 cu. in. (6.6 liters). Bore & stroke: 4.35 x 3.38 in. Compression ratio: 7.9:1. Brake horsepower: 185 @ 3600 rpm. Torque: 320 lb.-ft. @ 2000 rpm. Five main bearings. Hydraulic valve lifters. Carburetor: four-barrel Rochester M4MC. Oldsmobile-built. VIN Code: K.

1979 Pontiac Phoenix LJ four-door sedan. OCW

CHASSIS DATA: Wheelbase: (Sunbird) 97.0 in.; (Phoenix) 111.1 in.; (Firebird) 108.2 in.; (LeMans) 108.1 in.; (Grand Prix) 108.1 in.; (Catalina/Bonneville) 116.0 in. Overall Length: (Sunbird) 179.2 in.; (Sunbird wag) 178.0 in.; (Phoenix) 203.4 in.; (Firebird) 196.8 in.; (LeMans) 198.5 in.; (LeMans wag) 197.8 in.; (G.P.) 201.2 in.; (Catalina/Bonneville) 214.3 in.; (Safari wag) 215.1 in. Height: (Sunbird) 49.6 in.; (Sunbird wag) 51.8 in.; (Phoenix cpe) 52.3 in.; (Phoenix sed) 53.2 in.; (Firebird) 49.3 in.; (LeMans cpe) 53.5 in.; (LeMans sed) 54.4 in.; (LeMans wag) 54.8 in.; (G.P.) 53.3 in.; (Catalina/Bonneville cpe) 53.9 in.; (Catalina/Bonneville sed) 54.5 in.; (Safari wag) 57.3 in. Width: (Sunbird) 65.4 in.; (Phoenix) 72.4 in.; (Firebird) 73.0 in.; (LeMans) 72.4 in.; (LeMans wag) 72.7 in.; (G.P.) 72.7 in.; (Catalina/Bonneville) 76.4 in.; (Safari wag) 79.9 in. Front Tread: (Sunbird) 55.3 in.; (Phoenix) 61.9 in.; (Firebird) 61.3 in.; (LeMans) 58.5 in.; (G.P.) 58.5 in.; (Catalina/Bonneville) 61.7 in.; (Safari) 62.0 in. Rear Tread: (Sunbird) 54.1 in.; (Phoenix) 59.6 in.; (Firebird) 60.0 in.; (LeMans) 57.8 in.; (G.P.) 57.8 in.; (Catalina/Bonneville) 60.7 in.; (Safari) 64.1 in. Standard Tires: (Sunbird) A78 x 13; (Phoenix) E78 x 14; (Firebird) FR78 x 15; (Firebird Formula/Trans Am) P225/70R15; (LeMans) P185/75R14; (Grand Am) P205/70R14; (Grand Prix) P195/75R14; (Catalina/Bonneville) FR78 x 15.

1979 Pontiac Firebird coupe. OCW

1979 Pontiac Firebird Trans Am coupe. OCW

TECHNICAL: Transmission: Three-speed manual transmission standard on Phoenix, LeMans, Firebird, and base Grand Prix. Four-speed manual standard on Sunbird, optional on Firebird, Phoenix and LeMans. Five-speed manual optional on Sunbird. Three-speed Turbo-Hydramatic standard on other models, optional on all. Standard final drive ratio: (Sunbird) 2.73:1 w/four and four-speed, 2.93:1 w/V-6 and four-speed; (Phoenix) 3.08:1 w/four-speed, 2.56:1 w/V-6 and auto., 2.41:1 w/V-8 and auto.; (Firebird V-6) 3.08:1 w/three-speed; (Firebird V-8-302) 2.41:1, 3.08:1, or 2.73:1; (Firebird V8-350) 3.08:1; (Firebird V-8-400) 3.23:1; (Firebird V-8-403) 2.41:1; (LeMans V-6) 2.73:1 w/three-speed, 2.93:1 w/four-speed, 2.41:1 or 3.23:1 w/auto.; (LeMans V-8) 2.14:1, 2.29:1, or 2.73:1; (Grand Prix) 2.93:1 w/V-6, 2.14:1 or 2.29:1 w/V-8; (Catalina/Bonneville) 2.73:1 w/V-6, 2.29:1 or 2.56:1 w/V-8-301, 2.41:1 w/V-8-350; (Safari) 2.56:1 or 2.73:1. Steering: Recirculating ball. Front Suspension: (Sunbird) coil springs and control arms; (Firebird/LeMans) coil springs w/lower trailing links and anti-sway bar; (others) coil springs and anti-sway bar. Rear Suspension: (Sunbird) rigid axle with coil springs, lower trailing radius arms and upper torque arms; (Phoenix) rigid axle w/semi-elliptic leaf springs; (Firebird) semi-elliptic leaf springs with anti-sway bar; (LeMans/Bonneville/Grand Prix) rigid axle with coil springs, lower trailing radius arms and upper torque arms. Brakes: Front disc, rear drum; four-wheel disc brakes available on Firebird Formula and Trans Am. Ignition: Electronic. Body construction: (Sunbird) unit; (Firebird) unit w/separate partial frame; (others) separate body and frame. Fuel tank: (Sunbird) 18.5 gal. exc. wagon, 16 gal.; (Phoenix) 21 gal.; (Firebird) 21 gal.; (LeMans) 18.1 gal. exc. wagon, 18.2 gal.; (Grand Prix) 18.1 gal.; (Catalina/Bonneville) 21 gal.

1979 Pontiac Firebird Trans Am coupe (rear view). OCW

DRIVETRAIN OPTIONS: Engines: 231 cid V-6: Sunbird ($200); Grand Prix LJ ($195 credit). 301 cid, two-barrel V-8: Firebird/LeMans/Catalina/Grand Prix ($195). 301 cid, four-barrel V-8: Firebird ($280); Firebird Formula ($85); Trans Am ($165 credit); LeMans/Grand Prix/Catalina ($255); Grand Prix LJ ($60); Bonneville ($60). 305 cid, two-barrel V-8: Sunbird ($395); Phoenix/Firebird ($195). 305 cid, four-barrel V-8: LeMans/Grand Prix ($255); Grand Prix LJ ($60). 350 cid, four-barrel V-8: Phoenix/Firebird/Catalina ($320); LeMans Safari ($320); Firebird Formula ($125); Bonneville ($125). T/A 400 cid, four-barrel V-8: Formula ($340); Trans Am ($90). 403 cid, four-barrel V-8: Firebird Formula ($250); Safari ($195). Transmission/Differential: Four-speed manual floor shift transmission: Phoenix w/V-8-305 ($135); Firebird/LeMans/G.P. ($135); Grand Prix LJ/SJ ($200 credit).

157

Five-speed manual transmission: Sunbird ($175). Turbo-Hydramatic: Sunbird ($295); Phoenix/Firebird/LeMans/Grand Prix ($335); Trans Am (NC). Limited-slip differential: Sunbird ($59); LeMans/Firebird/G.P. ($63); Catalina/Bonneville ($67). Brakes/Steering: Power brakes: Sunbird ($71); Phoenix/LeMans/Firebird/G.P. ($76). Power four-wheel disc brakes: Firebird Formula/Trans Am ($150). Power steering: Sunbird ($146); Phoenix/LeMans/G.P. ($163). Suspension: Rally RTS handling pkg.: Sunbird ($38-$120); Phoenix ($182-$230); LeMans ($44-$189); Catalina ($150-$180); Bonneville ($109-$128); Grand Prix ($72-$128). Firm ride pkg. ($13) except Sunbird. Superlift shock absorbers: LeMans/G.P. ($54); Catalina/Bonneville ($55). Automatic level control: LeMans/G.P./Catalina/Bonneville ($66-$121). Other: H.D. radiator: Sunbird ($33); Phoenix ($32-$59). H.D. cooling: Sunbird ($26-$59). Super-cooling radiator ($32-$60) except Sunbird/ Phoenix. H.D. battery ($18-$21). H.D. alternator: Sunbird/Phoenix/ Firebird/LeMans/G.P. ($32). Catalina/Bonneville ($23-$55). Engine block heater ($14-$15). Light trailer group: Bonneville/Catalina ($122-$150). Medium trailer group: LeMans/G.P. ($121-$148). Heavy trailer group: Bonneville/Catalina ($122-$187). California emissions ($83-$150). High-altitude option ($35).

OPTION PACKAGES: Sunbird Formula group ($415-$591). Sunbird sport hatch graphics pkg. ($73). Sunbird appearance group: cpe ($91). Phoenix custom exterior ($91-$97). Phoenix exterior appearance pkg. ($166). Phoenix appearance pkg. ($76). Firebird "Red Bird" appearance pkg.: Esprit ($449-$491). Trans Am special edition ($674); w/hatch roof ($1329). Firebird Formula appearance pkg. ($92). Firebird Trans Am special performance pkg. ($250-$434). LeMans Safari security pkg. ($37-$42). LeMans luxury group ($148-$348). LeMans exterior paint appearance ($166). LeMans custom exterior ($46-$98). LeMans custom trim group ($145-$259). Full-size exterior paint pkg. ($166). Grand Prix exterior appearance ($124-$172). Grand Prix appearance pkg. ($197-$264).

MAJOR CONVENIENCE/APPEARANCE OPTIONS: Air conditioning ($496-$605). Automatic air conditioning: LeMans/Grand Prix ($653); Catalina/Bonneville ($688). Cruise control ($103-$108); N/A on Sunbird. Power seat: LeMans/Catalina/Bonneville/G.P. ($163-$166). Power windows ($126-$205); N/A on Sunbird. Cornering lamps: Catalina/Bonneville/Grand Prix ($49). Power glass sun roof: LeMans/ Grand Prix ($729); Catalina/Bonneville ($925). Power steel sun roof: LeMans/Grand Prix ($529); Catalina/Bonneville ($725). Removable glass sun roof: Sunbird ($180). Hatch roof: Firebird/Grand Prix ($655). Full vinyl cordova top: Phoenix ($99); LeMans ($116); Catalina/Bonneville ($145). Padded landau top: Grand Prix/LeMans ($239); Catalina/Bonneville ($298). Landau top: Sunbird ($156); Phoenix ($190). Canopy top: Firebird ($116). Rear-facing third seat: Safari ($183). Wire wheels: Grand Prix ($425-$499).

HISTORICAL FOOTNOTES: Introduced: September 28, 1978. Model year production: 907,412. Calendar year production (U.S.): 713,475. Calendar year sales by U.S. dealers: 781,042. Model year sales by U.S. dealers: 828,603 (including 42,852 early 1980 front-drive Phoenix models). At the end of 1979, Robert C. Stempel (later to become head of General Motors) was named Pontiac's general manager. Sales slipped a bit for the model year, with only Sunbird and LeMans showing a slight increase. Sunbird's "Iron Duke" four-cylinder engine switched to a cross-flow cylinder head, and would soon become the standard powerplant for many GM models, especially transverse-mounted in the new front-drive X-cars. An alternate version was supplied for rear-drive installations.

1980 PONTIAC

A new front-wheel-drive Phoenix, close kin to the Chevrolet Citation X-car and powered by a four or V-6, was the major news of the year. The 400/403 cid V-8s were out. Biggest powerplant was now the 350 cid V-8, and that only on a few models (used more on California Pontiacs, actually). Two new V-8 powerplants appeared: a 265 cid (4.3-liter) two-barrel, and diesel 350 cid (5.7-liter), which came from Oldsmobile. An electronic-control (E/C) 301 cid (4.9-liter) V-8 went under performance-model hoods. Also on the engine front, a turbocharged 301 V-8 became available on Trans Am; and Chevrolet's V-6-229 served as an equivalent to the Buick 231 V-6. As for appearance, full-size models gained a major restyle.

I.D. DATA: Pontiac's 13-symbol Vehicle Identification Number (VIN) was located on the upper left surface of the instrument panel, visible through the windshield. The first digit is '2', indicating Pontiac division. The second symbol is a letter indicating series: 'E' = Sunbird; 'M' = Sunbird Sport; 'Y' = Phoenix; 'Z' = Phoenix LJ; 'D' = LeMans; 'F' = Grand LeMans; 'G' = Grand Am; 'S' = Firebird; 'T' = Firebird Esprit; 'V' = Firebird Formula; 'W' = Firebird Trans Am; 'L' = Catalina; 'N' = Bonneville; 'R' = Bonneville Brougham; 'J' = Grand Prix; 'K' = Grand Prix LJ; 'H' = Grand Prix SJ. Next come two digits that denote body type: '07' = 2-dr. hatchback coupe; '27' = 2-dr. coupe; '37' = 2-dr. coupe;

'87' = 2-dr. plain-back coupe; '19' = 4-dr. six-window sedan; '68' = 4-dr. six-window hatchback; '69' = 4-dr. four-window sedan; '35' = 4-dr. two-seat wagon. The fifth symbol is a letter indicating engine code: 'V' or '5' = L4-151 two-barrel; '7' = V-6-173 two-barrel; 'A' = V-6-231 two-barrel; 'S' = V-8-265 two-barrel; 'W' = V-8-301 four-barrel; 'T' = Turbo V-8-301 four-barrel; 'H' = V-8-305 four-barrel; 'R' = V-8-350 four-barrel; 'N' = diesel V-8-350. The sixth symbol denotes model year ('A' = 1980). Next is a plant code: 'B' = Baltimore; 'L' = Van Nuys, Calif.; 'N' = Norwood, Ohio; 'P' = Pontiac, Mich.; 'T' = Tarrytown, N.Y.; '7' = Lordstown, Ohio; 'X' = Fairfax, Kan.; '6' = Oklahoma City; '1' = Oshawa, Ontario; '2' = Ste. Therese, Quebec. The final six digits are the sequential serial number.

1980 Pontiac Sunbird Sport hatchback coupe. (AA)

SUNBIRD -- SERIES 2H -- FOUR/V-6 -- Only coupe, sport coupe, and sport hatch models were available, as the Safari wagon was dropped. Sunbird had a new eggcrate-pattern grille, and new park/signal lamps. New seating came in five colors. Standard bucket seats now had smooth headrests. Luxury interior trim was now Ramrod striped velour. Options included new sport accent striping. Base engine was the cross-flow 151 cid (2.5-liter) four, with four-speed manual gearbox. Optional: a 231 cid (3.8-liter) V-6 and automatic transmission. The formerly optional 305 cid V-8 had been dropped in mid-1979. The optional five-speed gearbox dropped out this year. An additional hatchback model (E07) was added later in the season.

SUNBIRD (FOUR/V-6)

Model Number	Body/Style Number	Body Type & Seating	Factory Price	Shipping Weight	Prod. Total
2H	E27	2-dr. Cpe-4P	4371/4596	2603/ --	105,847
2H	M07	2-dr. Hatch Cpe-4P	4731/4956	2657/ --	52,952
2H	M27	2-dr. Spt Cpe-4P	4620/4845	2609/ --	29,180
2H	E07	2-dr. Hatch-4P	4808/5033	2651/ --	Note 1

Note 1: Production included in hatchback coupe figure above.

1980 Pontiac Phoenix SJ coupe. (AA)

PHOENIX -- SERIES 2X -- FOUR/V-6 -- The new front-wheel-drive compact debuted in April 1979, and entered its first full model year with minimal change. A two-door coupe and five-door (actually four-door) hatchback sedan were offered. Base drivetrain was Pontiac's 151 cid (2.5-liter) four, transverse mounted, with four-speed manual overdrive transaxle and floor lever. Optional: Chevrolet's 173 cid (2.8-liter) V-6 and automatic shift. Front suspension used MacPherson struts; at the rear was a trailing axle with coil springs and track bar. Each of the twin grille sections consisted of large (3 x 3 pattern) holes over tight crosshatching. Clear vertical parking/signal lamps stood between the grille and single rectangular headlamps. Horizontal taillamps each had two horizontal and two vertical trim strips, with backup lights toward the center, next to the license plate. Body-colored bumpers had bright strips. Standard equipment included P185/80R13 glass-belted radial

blackwall tires, hubcaps with Pontiac crest, and AM radio. Phoenix LJ added a stand-up hood ornament, bright wide rocker panel moldings, wheel covers, accent striping, and sport mirrors. An SJ option package included black grilles and headlamp bezels, Phoenix bird emblem on center pillar, vinyl bucket seats, P205 tires on Rally wheels, Rally RTS suspension, and accent color on lower body and bumpers. New stripe colors were made available for the full year, and base seating carried a different fabric. The sporty SJ option had new two-tone color combinations. A brushed aluminum B-pillar appliqué for the hatchback sedan was first available alone, later only as part of a custom exterior group. Accent paint stripes were first standard, then became optional.

Model Number	Body/Style Number	Body Type & Seating	Factory Price	Shipping Weight	Prod. Total
PHOENIX (FOUR/V-6)					
2X	Y37	2-dr. Cpe-5P	5067/5292	2496/2535	49,485
2X	Y68	5-dr. Hatch-5P	5251/5476	2539/2578	72,875
PHOENIX LJ (FOUR/V-6)					
2X	Z37	2-dr. Cpe-5P	5520/5745	2531/2570	23,674
2X	Z68	5-dr. Hatch-5P	5704/5929	2591/2630	32,257

1980 Pontiac Firebird Esprit "Yellow Bird" T-top coupe. (CP)

FIREBIRD -- SERIES 2F -- V-6/V-8 -- Appearance changes were minimal, but Firebird got a sharply altered engine selection this year. Base engine for base and Esprit models remained the 231 cid (3.8-liter) V-6; optional, the new 265 cid (4.3-liter) V-8 and the 301 cid (4.9-liter) four-barrel. Trans Ams now carried the E/C 301 cid four-barrel V-8, which was optional on Formula models. Both Trans Am and Formula could also get a new turbocharged 301 four-barrel. As in other models, California cars had a modified selection, including a 305 cid V-8 standard in Trans Am and Formula. Base and Esprit Firebirds still had standard three-speed manual shift, while Formula and Trans Am carried automatics. All California Firebirds were automatic-equipped. Dual exhausts came in a lighter weight design this year. Turbo models included a unique hood with special bird decal. Turbo graphics went on the hood and decklid spoiler. Another bird decal was available for non-turbo Trans Ams. A new "Yellow Bird" option package with gold accent striping replaced the former Redbird. Trans Am could again get a black-painted Special Edition package, either with or without a hatch roof. New Trans Am graphics colors included bronze/burgundy and a revised red/gold combination. New seating came in five colors. Dark blue was a new interior color. New optional electronic-tuning stereo radios came with a four-speaker system. Tungsten halogen headlamps remained available.

1980 Pontiac Firebird Formula coupe. (CP)

1980 Pontiac Firebird Turbo Trans Am Indianapolis 500 Pace Car. (IMSC)

Model Number	Body/Style Number	Body Type & Seating	Factory Price	Shipping Weight	Prod. Total
FIREBIRD (V-6/V-8)					
2F	S87	2-dr. HT Cpe-4P	5604/5784	3269/3342	29,811
FIREBIRD ESPRIT (V-6/V-8)					
2F	T87	2-dr. HT Cpe-4P	5967/6147	3304/3377	17,277
FIREBIRD FORMULA (V-8)					
2F	V87	2-dr. HT Cpe-4P	6955	3410	9356
FIREBIRD TRANS AM (V-8)					
2F	W87	2-dr. HT Cpe-4P	7179	3429	50,896

1980 Pontiac Grand LeMans sedan. (P)

1980 Pontiac Grand Am coupe (rear view). OCW

LEMANS -- SERIES 2A -- V-6/V-8 -- Design changes for LeMans and Grand LeMans included new grilles, park/signal lamps, front side marker lamps, and taillamps (for coupe/sedan). Two new interior colors were available: blue and maroon. LeMans door panels had new simulated welt and stitch lines centered between bright mylar moldings. Grand LeMans door panels had wide mylar moldings. All models had standard power brakes. Safari wagons could have a double two-tone paint treatment at no extra cost, instead of the standard simulated woodgraining. That woodgrain came in a new red elm pattern this year. New options included electronic-tuning stereo radios and extended-range speakers. Each grille section consisted of horizontal bars, with

159

clear park/signal lamps behind the outer ends. The wide center panel held a Pontiac emblem above "Pontiac" block lettering. Wraparound clear/amber marker lenses had four horizontal trim ribs. Single rectangular headlamps were used. Base coupe/sedan engine was now Chevrolet's 229 cid (3.8-liter) V-6 with three-speed manual gearbox, whereas other Pontiacs used Buick's 231 V-6. Options included the new 265 cid (4.3-liter) V-8 and Turbo-Hydramatic, as well as a 301 cid (4.9-liter) four-barrel V-8. California models could have a 305 V-8.

Model Number	Body/Style Number	Body Type & Seating	Factory Price	Shipping Weight	Prod. Total
LEMANS (V-6/V-8)					
2A	D27	2-dr. Cpe-6P	5274/5454	3024/3104	9110
2A	D19	4-dr. Sed-6P	5377/5557	3040/3120	20,485
LEMANS SAFARI (V-6/V-8)					
2A	D35	4-dr. 2S Wag-6P	5861/6041	3232/3359	12,912

1980 Pontiac Grand Am coupe. (AA)

GRAND AM -- SERIES 2A -- V-8 -- Grand Am now came in coupe form only, carrying the 301 cid E/C engine (as in Trans Am) with automatic transmission. California Grand Ams had a 305 V-8 instead. In addition to a new soft-fascia front end, Grand Am added ample standard equipment in an attempt to attain a performance image. The list included bucket seats (with console), sport mirrors, Rally IV wheels, and custom sport steering wheel. A new silver upper body accent stripe was standard, and Rally RTS suspension had larger front/rear stabilizer bars. All Grand Am bodies had a new Ontario Gray lower accent color. Each of the twin grille sections was divided into three sections, with thin body-color separators between, and each held horizontal strips. A wide peaked center divider held a Pontiac v-shaped emblem that extended from the hood crease. Front bumpers held two air slots. Single rectangular headlamps stood directly above clear park/signal lamps.

Model Number	Body/Style Number	Body Type & Seating	Factory Price	Shipping Weight	Prod. Total
GRAND AM (V-8)					
2A	G27	2-dr. Cpe-6P	7299	3299	1647

1980 Pontiac Grand Prix SJ coupe. OCW

GRAND PRIX -- SERIES 2G -- V-6/V-8 -- Three Grand Prix models were offered again: base, luxury LJ, and sporty SJ. Standard engine was again the 231 cid (3.8-liter) V-6, except for SJ, which carried the new 301 cid (4.9-liter) E/C four-barrel V-8. Base and LJ models could have the new 265

cid (4.3-liter) V-8. California SJ models had a 305 V-8 with four-barrel, which was also optional on base/LJ. Manual gearboxes were no longer available. Every Grand Prix had automatic transmission as well as power brakes and steering. Appearance changes included a new grille and grille bumper inserts, with a larger look than before. The all-bright grille contained vertical bars on each side of a fairly narrow bright divider. Between each pair of rectangular headlamps were clear park/signal lamps. Taillamp housings, lenses and bezels were new this year. 'GP' lettering was sonic-welded to the center of each lens. Grand Prix LJ and SJ had new tapered wheel opening moldings, and revised multiple accent striping. The optional double two-tone paint treatment also was revised. Inside were new cloth door trim panels. Base models had a pull strap above dual bright/black moldings; SJ/LJ models offered a drop handle. New cloth seats went into base models, whereas LJ had the same seating as base models with luxury trim option. Newly optional: electronic-tuning stereo radios and extended-range speakers. Halogen headlamps also were offered.

1980 Pontiac Grand Prix SJ coupe. (AA)

Model Number	Body/Style Number	Body Type & Seating	Factory Price	Shipping Weight	Prod. Total
GRAND PRIX (V-6/V-8)					
2G	J37	2-dr. Cpe-6P	6219/6399	3139/3263	72,659
GRAND PRIX LJ (V-6/V-8)					
2G	K37	2-dr. Cpe-6P	6598/6778	3279/3406	34,968
GRAND PRIX SJ (V-8)					
2G	H37	2-dr. Cpe-6P	7296	3291	7087

1980 Pontiac Catalina. (AA)

CATALINA/BONNEVILLE -- SERIES 2B -- V-6/V-8 -- Full-size Pontiacs (Catalina, Bonneville, and Bonneville Brougham) all featured new front-end sheet metal as part of their first significant restyle since the 1977 debut in downsized form. Weights were cut about 100 pounds, aerodynamics improved, engine sizes reduced. The new design displayed a lower profile and more aero-look front, with new roof, sail panels, doors, and quarter panels. Lengthening both the front and rear overhang produced a longer overall look, even though dimensions did not change much. The hood was lowered and decklid raised. Air dams and baffles were added to the body. Coupes had a more formal roofline, while four-door sedans had a restyled upper window area. A compact spare added luggage space. Decklids and taillamp housings were new this year. Catalina used narrow taillamps, while Bonneville's were full-width wraparound with two horizontal trim strips. For a change, Catalina and Bonneville shared similar front-end appearance. Both had a bold, all-bright vertical-themed grille (with pattern extended below the bumper). It consisted of four vertical bars on each side of the bright divider, which held a Pontiac emblem. The flush bumper design included plastic inner fender skirts. Tungsten-halogen headlamps,

1980 Pontiac Sunbird coupe. OCW

1980 Pontiac Phoenix five-door hatchback. OCW

1980 Pontiac Phoenix five-door hatchback (rear view). OCW

1980 Pontiac Phoenix SJ five-door hatchback. OCW

1980 Pontiac Phoenix SJ five-door hatchback (rear view). OCW

1980 Pontiac Phoenix LJ coupe. OCW

1980 Pontiac Phoenix LJ coupe (rear view). OCW

1980 Pontiac Grand LeMans Safari station wagon. OCW

1980 Pontiac Grand LeMans Safari station wagon (rear view). OCW

161

which first appeared in mid-year 1979, continued as an option. Headlamp bezels wrapped around the front fenders. Cornering lamps had body-colored bezels and were mounted higher on the fender this year, rather than in the lower bodyside molding. New park/signal lamps were set between the headlamps (similar to the 1979 Grand Prix arrangement). Front side markers had new amber lenses and two horizontal ribs. Coupes and sedans had new two-tone paint treatments and accent striping. Safari wagons again carried simulated woodgrain side paneling, but in a "planked" red elm design. Bonneville Safaris could order ordinary two-tone paint instead of the woodgrain. Bonnevilles had new full-length bodyside moldings as well as a new B-pillar appliqué. New landau padded roofs also were offered. Catalina upholstery was Dover II knit cloth, whereas Bonnevilles had new Patrician striped velour cloth. Brougham seating was Prima cloth knit, which had a longer nap than the former Dante cloth. New Embassy leather was optional on Broughams. To improve ride and durability, the front suspension held new ball joints and a rebushed front stabilizer bar. Wheel covers now had openings for improved brake/bearing cooling. New tire sizes took higher pressures. A new side frame jack was included. New options included electronic-tuning signal-seeking digital AM/FM stereo radios, extended-range speakers, and power outside mirrors. Base engine this year for both Catalina and Bonneville was the 231 cid (3.8-liter) V-6. Bonneville Brougham carried the new 265 cid (4.3-liter) V-8, which was optional on other models. Wagons had a 301 cid (4.9-liter) four-barrel V-8. The Oldsmobile-built diesel was available for Bonneville Brougham and Safari wagons only.

1980 Pontiac Bonneville Brougham four-door sedan. (AA)

1980 Pontiac Bonneville Brougham four-door sedan (rear view). OCW

Model Number	Body/Style Number	Body Type & Seating	Factory Price	Shipping Weight	Prod. Total
CATALINA (V-6/V-8)					
2B	L37	2-dr. Cpe-6P	6341/6521	3394/3503	3319
2B	L69	4-dr. Sed-6P	6397/6577	3419/3528	10,408
CATALINA SAFARI (V-8)					
2B	L35	4-dr. 2S Wag-6P	7044	3929	2931
BONNEVILLE (V-6/V-8)					
2B	N37	2-dr. Cpe-6P	6667/6847	3431/3540	16,771
2B	N69	4-dr. Sed-6P	6792/6972	3478/3587	26,112
BONNEVILLE BROUGHAM (V-8)					
2B	R37	2-dr. Cpe-6P	7696	3571	12,374
2B	R69	4-dr. Sed-6P	7885	3639	21,249
BONNEVILLE SAFARI (V-8)					
2B	N35	4-dr. 2S Wag-6P	7625	3949	5309

FACTORY PRICE AND WEIGHT NOTE: Prices and weights to left of slash are for V-6, to right for V-8 engine except Sunbird/Phoenix, four and V-6.

ENGINE DATA

BASE FOUR (Sunbird, Phoenix): Inline. Overhead valve. Four-cylinder. Cast iron block and head. Displacement: 151 cu. in. (2.5 liters). Bore & stroke: 4.00 x 3.00 in. Compression ratio: 8.2:1. Brake horsepower: 86 @ 4000 rpm (Phoenix, 90 @ 4000). Torque: 128 lb.-ft. @ 2400 rpm (Phoenix, 134 @ 2400). Five main bearings. Hydraulic valve lifters. Carburetor: two-barrel Rochester 2SE. VIN Code: V or 5. OPTIONAL V-6 (Phoenix): 60-degree, overhead valve six-cylinder. Cast iron block and aluminum head. Displacement: 173 cu. in. (2.8 liters). Bore & stroke: 3.50 x 3.00 in. Compression ratio: 8.5:1. Brake horsepower: 115 @ 4800 rpm. Torque: 150 lb.-ft. @ 2000 rpm. Four main bearings. Hydraulic valve lifters. Carburetor: two-barrel Rochester 2SE. VIN Code: 7.

BASE V-6 (LeMans): 90-degree, overhead-valve V-6. Cast iron block and head. Displacement: 229 cu. in. (3.8 liters). Bore & stroke: 3.38 x 3.48 in. Compression ratio: 8.6:1. Brake horsepower: 115 @ 4000 rpm. Torque: 175 lb.-ft. @ 2000 rpm. Four main bearings. Hydraulic valve lifters. Carburetor: two-barrel Rochester M2ME. Chevrolet-built. VIN Code: K. BASE V-6 (Firebird, Grand Prix, Catalina, Bonneville); OPTIONAL (Sunbird): 90-degree, overhead-valve V-6. Cast iron block and head. Displacement: 231 cu. in. (3.8 liters). Bore & stroke: 3.80 x 3.40 in. Compression ratio: 8.0:1. Brake horsepower: 110 @ 3800 rpm (Sunbird, 115 @ 3800). Torque: 190 lb.-ft. @ 1600 rpm (Sunbird, 188 @ 2000). Four main bearings. Hydraulic valve lifters. Carburetor: two-barrel Rochester M2ME. Buick-built. VIN Code: A. OPTIONAL V-8 (Firebird, LeMans, Grand Prix, Catalina, Bonneville): 90-degree, overhead valve V-8. Cast iron block and head. Displacement: 265 cu. in. (4.3 liters). Bore & stroke: 3.75 x 3.00 in. Compression ratio: 8.3:1. Brake horsepower: 120 @ 3600 rpm. Torque: 210 lb.-ft. @ 1600 rpm. Five main bearings. Hydraulic valve lifters. Carburetor: two-barrel. VIN Code: S.

BASE V-8 (Firebird Formula/Trans Am); OPTIONAL (Firebird, LeMans, Grand Prix, Catalina, Bonneville): 90-degree, overhead valve V-8. Cast iron block and head. Displacement: 301 cu. in. (5.0 liters). Bore & stroke: 4.06 x 3.04 in. Compression ratio: 8.1:1. Brake horsepower: 140 @ 4000 rpm. Torque: 240 lb.-ft. @ 1800 rpm. Five main bearings. Hydraulic valve lifters. Carburetor: four-barrel Rochester. VIN Code: W. OPTIONAL E/C V-8 (Firebird Formula, Trans Am, Grand Am, Grand Prix SJ): Same as 301 cid V-8 above, except Horsepower: 155 @ 4400 rpm. Torque: 240 lb.-ft. @ 2200 rpm.

TURBOCHARGED V-8 (Firebird Formula, Trans Am): Same as 301 cid V-8 above, with turbocharger. Compression ratio: 7.6:1. Horsepower: 210 @ 4000 rpm. Torque: 345 lb.-ft. @ 2000 rpm. VIN Code: T. **NOTE**: A 305 cid four-barrel V-8 was available in California Pontiacs (Firebird, LeMans, Grand Am, Grand Prix): Displacement: 305 cu. in. (5.0 liters). Bore & stroke: 3.74 x 3.48 in. Compression ratio: 8.4:1. Brake horsepower: 150 @ 3800 rpm. Torque: 230 lb.-ft. @ 2400 rpm. Five main bearings. Hydraulic valve lifters. VIN Code: H. OPTIONAL V-8 (Safari and California full-size models): 90-degree, overhead valve V-8. Cast iron block and head. Displacement: 350 cu. in. (5.7 liters). Bore & stroke: 4.06 x 3.39 in. Compression ratio: 8.0:1. Brake horsepower: 160 @ 3600 rpm. Torque: 270 lb.-ft. @ 2000 rpm. Five main bearings. Hydraulic valve lifters. Carburetor: four-barrel Rochester E4MC. Oldsmobile-built. VIN Code: R.

DIESEL V-8 (Catalina, Bonneville, Safari): 90-degree, overhead valve V-8. Cast iron block and head. Displacement: 350 cu. in. (5.7 liters). Bore & stroke: 4.06 x 3.39 in. Compression ratio: 22.5:1. Brake horsepower: 105 @ 3200 rpm. Torque: 205 lb.-ft. @ 1600 rpm. Five main bearings. Hydraulic valve lifters. Fuel injection. Oldsmobile-built. VIN Code: N.

CHASSIS DATA: Wheelbase: (Sunbird) 97.0 in.; (Phoenix) 104.9 in.; (Firebird) 108.2 in.; (LeMans) 108.1 in.; (Grand Prix) 108.1 in.; (Catalina/Bonneville) 116.0 in. Overall Length: (Sunbird) 179.2 in.; (Phoenix cpe) 182.1 in.; (Phoenix hatch) 179.3 in.; (Firebird) 196.8 in.; (LeMans) 198.6 in.; (LeMans wag) 197.8 in.; (G.P.) 201.4 in.; (Catalina/Bonneville) 214.0 in.; (Safari wag) 216.7 in. Height: (Sunbird) 49.6 in.; (Sunbird hatch) 49.9 in.; (Phoenix cpe) 53.5 in.; (Phoenix sed) 53.4 in.; (Firebird) 49.3 in.; (LeMans cpe) 53.5 in.; (LeMans sed) 54.4 in.; (LeMans wag) 54.8 in.; (G.P.) 53.3 in.; (Catalina/Bonneville cpe) 54.7 in.; (Catalina/Bonneville sed) 55.2 in.; (Safari wag) 57.1 in. Width: (Sunbird) 65.4 in.; (Phoenix) 69.1 in.; (Firebird) 73.0 in.; (LeMans) 72.4 in.; (LeMans wag) 72.6 in.; (G.P.) 72.7 in.; (Catalina/Bonneville) 76.4 in.; (Safari wag) 79.9 in. Front Tread: (Sunbird) 55.3 in.; (Phoenix) 58.7 in.; (LeMans) 58.5 in.; (G.P.) 58.5 in.; (Catalina/Bonneville) 61.7 in.; (Safari) 62.1 in. Rear Tread: (Sunbird) 54.1 in.; (Phoenix) 57.0 in.; (Firebird) 60.0 in.; (LeMans) 57.8 in. exc. wagon, 58.0 in.; (G.P.) 57.8 in.; (Catalina/Bonneville) 60.7 in.; (Safari) 64.1 in. Standard Tires: (Sunbird) A78 x 13 exc. V-6, B78 x 13; (Phoenix) P185/80R13 GBR; (Firebird) P205/75R15 SBR; (Firebird Formula/Trans Am) P225/70R15 SBR; (LeMans) P185/75R14 GBR exc. wagon, P195/75R14 GBR; (Grand Am) P205/70R14 SBR; (Grand Prix) P195/75R14 GBR; (Catalina/Bonneville) P205/75R15 SBR; (Safari) P225/75R15.

TECHNICAL: Transmission: Three-speed manual transmission standard on base Firebird and LeMans. Four-speed manual standard on Sunbird and Phoenix. Three-speed Turbo-Hydramatic standard on other models, optional on all. Standard final drive ratio: (Sunbird) 2.73:1 or 2.93:1 w/four, 2.93:1 w/V-6 and four-speed, 2.56:1 w/V-6 and auto.; (Phoenix) 2.71:1 w/four-speed, 2.53:1 w/four and auto., 2.84:1 w/V-6 and auto.; (Firebird V-6) 3.08:1 w/three-speed, 2.56:1 w/auto.; (Firebird V-8) 2.41:1; (Firebird Trans Am/Formula) 2.41:1 except 3.08:1 w/turbo or E/C V-8; (LeMans V-6) 2.73:1 w/three-speed, 2.41:1 w/auto.; (LeMans V-8) 2.29:1 or 2.14:1; (LeMans Safari) 2.73:1 w/V-6, 2.41:1 w/V-8-265, 2.29:1 w/V-8-301; (Grand Am) 2.93:1; (Grand Prix) 2.41:1 w/V-6, 2.29:1 w/V-8-265, 2.14:1 w/V-8-301; (Grand Prix SJ) 2.93:1; (Catalina/Bonneville) 3.23:1 w/V-6, 2.56:1 w/V-8-265, 2.41:1 w/V-8-301 or diesel; (Safari) 2.56:1 w/V-8-301, 2.73:1 w/V-8-350 or diesel; (others) recirculating ball. Steering: (Phoenix) rack and pinion; (others) recirculating ball. Front Suspension: (Sunbird) coil springs and control arms; (Phoenix) MacPherson struts w/lower control arms and anti-sway bar; (Firebird/LeMans) coil springs w/lower trailing links and anti-sway bar; (others) coil springs and anti-sway bar. Rear Suspension: (Sunbird) rigid axle with coil springs, lower trailing radius arms and upper torque arms; (Phoenix) single-beam trailing axle w/track bar and coil springs; (Firebird) semi-elliptic leaf springs with anti-sway bar; (LeMans/Bonneville/Grand Prix) rigid axle with coil springs, lower trailing radius arms and upper torque arms. Brakes: Front disc, rear drum. Ignition: Electronic. Body construction: (Sunbird/Phoenix) unit; (Firebird) unit w/separate partial frame; (others) separate body and frame. Fuel tank: (Sunbird) 18.5 gal.; (Phoenix) 14 gal.; (Firebird) 21 gal.; (LeMans) 18.1 gal. exc. wagon, 18.2 gal.; (Grand Prix) 18.1 gal.; (Catalina/Bonneville) 25 gal.; (Safari) 22 gal.

DRIVETRAIN OPTIONS: Engines: 173 cid V-6: Phoenix ($225). 231 cid V-6: Sunbird ($225). 265 cid, two-barrel V-8: Firebird ($150); LeMans/Grand Prix/Catalina/Bonneville ($180). 301 cid, four-barrel V-8: Firebird ($325); Trans Am ($180 credit); LeMans/Grand Prix/Catalina/Bonneville ($295); Bonneville Brougham ($115). E/C 301 cid, four-barrel V-8: Firebird Formula ($150). Turbo 301 cid V-8: Firebird Formula ($530); Trans Am ($350). 305 cid, four-barrel V-8: LeMans/Grand Prix ($295); Firebird ($295); Grand Prix SJ ($150 credit); Grand Am ($150 credit). 350 cid, four-barrel V-8: Catalina/Bonneville ($425); Bonneville Brougham ($245); Safari ($130). Diesel 350 cid V-8: Bonneville Brougham ($915); Safari ($860). Transmission/Differential: Turbo-Hydramatic: Sunbird ($320); Phoenix ($337); Firebird/LeMans ($358). Limited-slip differential: Sunbird ($64); LeMans/Firebird/G.P. ($68); Catalina/Bonneville ($73). Brakes/Steering: Power brakes: Sunbird/Phoenix ($76); Firebird ($81). Power four-wheel disc brakes: Firebird Formula/Trans Am ($162). Power steering: Sunbird ($158); Phoenix/G.P. ($164); LeMans ($174). Suspension: Rally RTS handling pkg.: Sunbird ($44-$227); Phoenix ($52-$219); LeMans ($142-$228); Grand Am ($64); Catalina/Bonneville ($45); Grand Prix ($143-$157). Firm ride pkg. ($14) except Sunbird. Superlift shock absorbers: Phoenix ($55); Catalina/Bonneville ($60). Automatic level control: Catalina/Bonneville ($72-$132). Other: H.D. radiator: Sunbird ($36); Phoenix ($35-$60). H.D. cooling: Sunbird ($28-$64). Supercooling radiator: Firebird ($35-$64); Catalina/Bonneville ($35-$65). H.D. battery ($19-$23) exc. diesel ($46). H.D. alternator: Sunbird ($10-$34); Phoenix ($10-$43); Firebird ($15-$51); LeMans/G.P./Catalina/Bonneville ($15-$51). Engine block heater ($16). Light trailer group: Phoenix ($35-$74). Medium trailer group: LeMans/G.P. ($132-$161). Catalina/Bonneville ($133-$163). California emissions ($250) exc. diesel ($83).

OPTION PACKAGES: Sunbird Formula group ($496-$674). Sunbird sport hatch graphics pkg. ($55). Phoenix custom exterior ($79-$123). Phoenix luxury trim pkg. ($209-$324). Phoenix SJ option ($460-$502). Firebird "Yellow Bird" appearance pkg.: Esprit ($505-$550). Trans Am Special Edition ($748) w/hatch roof ($1443). Firebird Formula appearance pkg. ($100). Firebird Formula/Trans Am special performance pkg. ($281-$481). LeMans Safari security pkg. ($40-$45). LeMans luxury trim group ($161-$271). LeMans two-paint appearance ($180). LeMans custom exterior ($51-$107). LeMans custom trim group ($131-$305). Full-size exterior appearance pkg. ($180). Grand Prix two-tone paint appearance ($134-$186); double two-tone ($213-$288). Full-size custom trim group. ($181-$435).

MAJOR CONVENIENCE/APPEARANCE OPTIONS: Air conditioning ($531-$647). Automatic air conditioning: LeMans/Grand Prix ($700); Catalina/Bonneville ($738). Cruise control ($105-$118); N/A on Sunbird. Power seat ($165-$179); N/A on Sunbird. Power windows ($132-$221); N/A on Sunbird. Cornering lamps: Catalina/Bonneville/Grand Prix ($53). Power glass sun roof: LeMans/Grand Prix ($773); Catalina/Bonneville ($981). Power steel sun roof: LeMans/Grand Prix ($561); Catalina/Bonneville ($770). Removable glass sun roof: Sunbird ($193); Phoenix ($240). Hatch roof: Firebird/Grand Prix ($695). Full vinyl cordova top: LeMans ($124); Catalina/Bonneville ($155). Padded landau top: Phoenix ($179); Grand Prix/LeMans ($239); Catalina/Bonneville ($248). Landau top: Sunbird ($165). Rear-facing third seat: Safari ($199). Wire wheels: Grand Prix ($460-$540).

HISTORICAL FOOTNOTES: Introduced: October 11, 1979, except Phoenix, April 19, 1979. Model year production: 770,821. Calendar year production (U.S.): 556,413. Calendar year sales by U.S. dealers: 614,897. Model year sales by U.S. dealers: 638,656 (not including

42,852 early 1980 front-drive Phoenix models counted in 1979 total). Production fell considerably for the 1980 model year. Unlike many models facing their final year in the lineup, Sunbird had a strong sales year. This was a bad time throughout the industry. Still, sagged sales caused Pontiac to slip back into fourth place among the GM divisions, after ranking No. 3 for three years. Even if Pontiac couldn't sell impressive numbers of cars, it supplied plenty of engines to the other GM divisions. William E. Hoglund became general manager, after a brief turn by Robert Stempel. A white limited-edition Turbo Trans Am served as the Indianapolis 500 Pace Car.

1981 PONTIAC

1981 Pontiac T-1000 five-door hatchback sedan. (P)

Whopping price increases greeted Pontiac customers as the 1981 model year began. Highlights included a notable change in Grand Prix appearance and a new formal look for LeMans sedans. Pontiac also adopted a Chevette clone, dubbed T1000. All models now included a lightweight Freedom II battery, and all gas engines had a Computer Command Control (CCC) system to control the air/fuel mixture. Optional cruise control, available on all models, added a "resume" feature that allowed return to former speed setting by touching the switch. All except T1000 and Firebird could have new puncture-sealing tires.

1981 Pontiac T-1000 five-door hatchback sedan (rear view). OCW

I.D. DATA: Pontiac had a new 17-symbol Vehicle Identification Number (VIN) this year, located on the upper left surface of the instrument panel, visible through the windshield. The first three symbols ('1G2') indicate Pontiac division. Symbol four is restraint system ('A' = manual seatbelts). Symbol five is car line/series: 'M' = T1000; 'Y' = Phoenix; 'Z' = Phoenix LJ; 'D' = LeMans; 'F' = Grand LeMans; 'S' = Firebird; 'T' = Firebird Esprit; 'V' = Firebird Formula; 'W' = Firebird Trans Am; 'X' = Firebird Trans Am Turbo Special Edition; 'J' = Grand Prix; 'K' = Grand Prix LJ; 'P' = Grand Prix Brougham; 'L' = Catalina; 'N' = Bonneville; 'R' = Bonneville Brougham. In sixth and seventh position are two digits that denote body type: '07' = two-door hatchback coupe; '27' = two-door coupe; '37' = two-door hardtop coupe; '87' = two-door hardtop coupe; '19' = four-door six-window sedan; '68' = five-door hatchback sedan; '69' = four-door four-window sedan; '35' = four-door station wagon. Symbol eight is a letter indicating engine code: '5' = L4-151 two-barrel; 'X' = V-6-173 two-barrel; 'A' = V-6-231 two-barrel; 'S' = V-8-265 two-barrel; 'W' = V-8-301 four-barrel; 'T' = Turbo V-8-301

163

four-barrel; 'H' = V-8-305 four-barrel; 'Y' = V-8-307 four-barrel; 'N' = diesel V-8-350. Next is a check digit. The tenth symbol denotes model year ('B' = 1981). Symbol eleven is a plant code: 'B' = Baltimore; 'L' = Van Nuys, Calif.; 'N' = Norwood, Ohio; 'P' = Pontiac, Mich.; 'T' = Tarrytown, N.Y.; '7' = Lordstown, Ohio; 'X' = Fairfax, Kan.; '6' = Oklahoma City; '1' = Oshawa, Ontario; '2' = Ste. Therese, Quebec. The final six digits are the sequential serial number.

T1000 -- SERIES 2T -- FOUR -- Pontiac finally offered an equivalent to Chevrolet's subcompact rear-drive Chevette, with the same 1.6-liter four-cylinder engine. It debuted at the Chicago Auto Show in February 1981, as a mid-year addition. See 1982 listing for details.

T1000 (FOUR)

Model Number	Body/Style Number	Body Type & Seating	Factory Price	Shipping Weight	Prod. Total
2T	M08	3-dr. Hatch-4P	5358	2058	26,415
2T	M68	5-dr. Hatch-4P	5504	2122	43,779

1981 Pontiac Phoenix SJ coupe. (P)

PHOENIX -- SERIES 2X -- V-6/V-8 -- Base and LJ models made up the Phoenix lineup, in two-door coupe or five-door hatchback body styles. Base engine was the 151 cid (2.5-liter) four with four-speed manual transaxle. An SJ option package included black body trim and solid color paint. SJ versions could also get an appearance package with two-tone paint, striping, and bold SJ Phoenix door graphics. Newly optional for the SJ coupe: a decklid spoiler and front air dam. This year's grille was dominated by vertical bars. A new multi-function turn signal lever controlled a pulse windshield wiper. New optional wide bodyside moldings came in all colors. Automatic transmissions could get a floor lever. Phoenix standard equipment included P185/80R13 fiberglass-belted tires, argent hubcaps with Pontiac crest, compact spare tire, body-color bumpers with bright strips, front bench seat, and AM radio. Hatchbacks had bright rocker panel and wheel opening moldings. LJ added a stand-up hood ornament and windsplit molding, bright wide rocker panel moldings, wheel covers, notchback front seat with center armrest, dual horns, and bright window moldings.

Model Number	Body/Style Number	Body Type & Seating	Factory Price	Shipping Weight	Prod. Total
PHOENIX (FOUR/V-6)					
2X	Y37	2-dr. Cpe-5P	6307/6432	2450/2555	31,829
2X	Y68	5-dr. Hatch-5P	6498/6623	2497/2552	62,693
PHOENIX LJ (FOUR/V-6)					
2X	Z37	2-dr. Cpe-5P	6778/6903	2492/2547	11,975
2X	Z68	5-dr. Hatch-5P	6969/7094	2552/2607	21,372

1981 Pontiac Firebird Formula coupe. (P)

FIREBIRD -- SERIES 2F -- V-6/V-8 -- Appearance was the same as 1980, but Firebird's engine selection was modified a bit this year. Formula now carried a standard 265 cid (4.3-liter) V-8, which was optional on the base and Esprit. Trans Am again had a 301 cid (4.9-liter) four-barrel V-8 with Electronic Spark Control. Both Trans Am and Formula could have a turbocharged 301 V-8. The turbo was now available in California. As in 1980, a four-speed manual gearbox was available for Formula and Trans Am with the four-barrel 305 cid (5.0-liter) V-8. Standard power brakes now included a low-drag front caliper. A new two-color bird decal for the hood, and reflective bird decal for Trans Am's gas filler door, became available. Base Firebird standard equipment included the 231 cid (3.8-liter) V-6 and three-speed manual shift (floor lever with console), power brakes/steering, P205/75R15 SBR blackwall tires, blackout grille with argent accents, hubcaps with Pontiac crest, and rosewood-grain instrument panel appliqué. Esprit added an automatic transmission, wheel covers, wheel opening moldings, wide rocker panel moldings, and body-color sport mirrors (left remote). Formula had a 265 cid (4.3-liter) two-barrel V-8 and automatic, P225/70R15 tires, (simulated) twin hood air scoop, body-color mirrors, rear deck spoiler, and Rally II wheels with trim rings. Trans Am included the 301 V-8 and automatic, P225/70R15 tires, black-accent grille and headlamp bezels, wheel-opening air deflectors, side-split tailpipe extensions, engine-turned dash trim plate, rally gauges (with tachometer), Shaker hood, and Rally II wheels.

1981 Pontiac "Bandit" Trans Am T-top coupe. (CP)

Model Number	Body/Style Number	Body Type & Seating	Factory Price	Shipping Weight	Prod. Total
FIREBIRD (V-6/V-8)					
2F	S87	2-dr. HT Cpe-4P	6901/6951	3275/3350	20,541
FIREBIRD ESPRIT (V-6/V-8)					
2F	T87	2-dr. HT Cpe-4P	7645/7695	3312/3387	10,938
FIREBIRD FORMULA (V-6/V-8)					
2F	V87	2-dr. HT Cpe-4P	7854/7904	3397/3472	5927
FIREBIRD TRANS AM (V-8)					
2F	W87	2-dr. HT Cpe-4P	8322	3419	33,493
2F	X87	2-dr. Turbo SE-4P	12257	N/A	Note 1

Note 1: Production included in basic Trans Am total.

LEMANS -- SERIES 2A -- V-6/V-8 -- LeMans displayed a lower and more horizontal front-end look that included a revised front fascia panel and grille. The twin eggcrate-style grilles (4 x 3 pattern), on each side of a tapered center panel with Pontiac emblem, contained new park/signal lamps at their outer ends. Rectangular quad headlamps were new, and wraparound marker lenses had two horizontal trim ribs. Wide wraparound taillamps had one horizontal trim strip and a series of vertical strips, forming squares, with backup lenses at the center adjoining the license plate. Sedans added a new formal roof. A fully padded vinyl top was optional. Base engine was the 231 cid (3.8-liter) V-6 with three-speed manual shift (automatic in station wagons, and in California). Automatic transmissions had a torque converter clutch. New standard equipment included power steering, a compact spare tire, and side-lift frame jack. Custom finned wheel covers were a new option.

Standard equipment included P185/75R14 fiberglass-belted blackwall tires, power brakes and steering, wheel opening moldings, body-color bumpers with bright rub strips, and hubcaps with Pontiac crest. Coupes had black/bright pillar moldings. Grand LeMans added a hood ornament and windsplit molding, window and lower bodyside moldings, black rocker panel moldings, and folding front center armrest.

1981 Pontiac LeMans coupe. (CP)

Model Number	Body/Style Number	Body Type & Seating	Factory Price	Shipping Weight	Prod. Total
LEMANS (V-6/V-8)					
2A	D27	2-dr. Cpe-6P	6689/6739	3035/3151	2578
2A	D69	4-dr. Sed-6P	6797/6847	3052/3168	22,186
2A	D69/Y83	4-dr. LJ Sed-6P	7100/ --	N/A	Note 2

Note 2: Production included in basic sedan total.

Model Number	Body/Style Number	Body Type & Seating	Factory Price	Shipping Weight	Prod. Total
LEMANS SAFARI (V-6/V-8)					
2A	D35	4-dr. 2S Wag-6P	7316/7366	3240/3386	13,358
GRAND LEMANS (V-6/V-8)					
2A	F27	2-dr. Cpe-6P	6976/7026	3063/3179	1819
2A	F69	4-dr. Sed-6P	7153/7203	3108/3224	25,241
GRAND LEMANS SAFARI (V-6/V-8)					
2A	F35	4-dr. 2S Wag-6P	7726/7776	3279/3425	16,683

1981 Pontiac Grand Prix Brougham coupe. (P)

GRAND PRIX -- SERIES 2G -- V-6/V-8 -- All new body sheet metal found its way onto Pontiac's personal-luxury coupe. Grand Prix's new aerodynamic wedge profile featured a low front end and raised deck, improving drag coefficient by some 20 percent. Base and LJ models were offered, along with a new top-rung Brougham instead of the former SJ. Though similar in shape to the 1980 version, the new grille was wider, since parking/signal lamps were no longer between the rectangular headlamps. The pattern of the horizontal-strip grille extended below the bumper strip, into two large slots. Small parking/signal lamps were mounted in the bumper strip. Base engine was the 231 cid (3.8-liter) V-6 with automatic transmission and lock-up torque converter clutch. Optional: a 265 cid (4.3-liter) V-8 or 350 cid diesel. New tires used higher pressure to cut rolling resistance. Standard equipment included power brakes/steering, P195/75R14 blackwall tires, bright-accented bumper strips, stand-up hood ornament, hubcaps with crest, rocker panel and wheel opening moldings, and notchback seat with center armrest. LJ included wide rocker panel moldings (with extensions), dual body-color sport mirrors (driver's remote), and

wide wheel opening moldings. Brougham added a long list of equipment, including opera lamps, padded landau vinyl roof with formal back window, new finned wheel covers, power windows, and 60/40 front seat.

Model Number	Body/Style Number	Body Type & Seating	Factory Price	Shipping Weight	Prod. Total
GRAND PRIX (V-6/V-8)					
2G	J37	2-dr. HT Cpe-6P	7424/7474	3166/3287	74,786
GRAND PRIX LJ (V-6/V-8)					
2G	K37	2-dr. HT Cpe-6P	7803/7853	3195/3316	46,842
GRAND PRIX BROUGHAM (V-6/V-8)					
2G	P37	2-dr. HT Cpe-6P	8936/8986	3231/3342	26,083

1981 Pontiac Catalina sedan. (CP)

CATALINA/BONNEVILLE -- SERIES 2B -- V-6/V-8 -- Pontiac's full-size lineup again included Catalina, Bonneville, and Bonneville Brougham. Front-end appearance was similar to 1980, but the new grille had a tight crosshatch pattern repeated in twin bumper slots. Park/signal lamps were between the headlamps. Bonneville also had new taillamps, and the Catalina sedan added new side window moldings. Base engine was the 231 cid (3.8-liter) V-6, hooked to automatic transmission with locking torque converter clutch. Models with the optional 307 cid (5.0-liter) V-8 required the new four-speed automatic transmission with overdrive top gear. Wagons had the 307 V-8 and four-speed automatic as standard. All full-size models could also have a 350 cid (5.7-liter) diesel V-8. Full-size standard equipment included power brakes and steering, P205/75R15 blackwalls, stand-up hood ornament and windsplit molding, bumper rub strips, rocker panel moldings, and rear bumper guards. Catalina coupes/sedans had vinyl seat upholstery. Bonneville added fender skirts, deluxe wheel covers, notchback front seat, and hood edge molding. Bonneville Brougham included 60/40 notchback front seating, a remote driver's mirror, clock, and power windows. Safari wagons had P225/75R15 tires, three-way tailgate, power tailgate window, driver's remote (passenger manual) outside mirrors, and simulated woodgrain paneling or (on Bonneville) two-tone paint.

1981 Pontiac Bonneville Brougham coupe. (P)

165

1981 Pontiac Bonneville Brougham four-door sedan. OCW

Model Number	Body/Style Number	Body Type & Seating	Factory Price	Shipping Weight	Prod. Total
CATALINA (V-6/V-8)					
2B	L37	2-dr. Cpe-6P	7367/7417	3421/3540	1074
2B	L69	4-dr. Sed-6P	7471/7521	3429/3548	6456
CATALINA SAFARI (V-8)					
2B	L35	4-dr. 2S Wag-6P	8666	3924	2912
BONNEVILLE (V-6/V-8)					
2B	N37	2-dr. Cpe-6P	7649/7699	3443/3562	14,317
2B	N69	4-dr. Sed-6P	7776/7826	3461/3580	32,056
BONNEVILLE BROUGHAM (V-6/V-8)					
2B	R37	2-dr. Cpe-6P	8580/8630	3443/3562	14,317
2B	R69	4-dr. Sed-6P	8768/8818	3461/3580	23,395
BONNEVILLE SAFARI (V-8)					
2B	N35	4-dr. 2S Wag-6P	9205	3949	6855

FACTORY PRICE AND WEIGHT NOTE: Prices and weights to left of slash are for V-6, to right for V-8 engine except Phoenix, four and V-6.

1981 Pontiac Grand LeMans Safari station wagon. OCW

ENGINE DATA

BASE FOUR (T1000): Inline. Overhead cam. Four-cylinder. Cast iron block and head. Displacement: 97 cu. in. (1.6 liters). Bore & stroke: 3.23 x 2.98 in. Compression ratio: 8.6:1. Brake horsepower: 70 @ 5200 rpm. Torque: 82 lb.-ft. @ 2400 rpm. Five main bearings. Hydraulic valve lifters. Carburetor: two-barrel Holley 5210C. VIN Code: 9. BASE FOUR (Phoenix): Inline. Overhead valve. Four-cylinder. Cast iron block and head. Displacement: 151 cu. in. (2.5 liters). Bore & stroke: 4.00 x 3.00 in. Compression ratio: 8.2:1. Brake horsepower: 84 @ 4000 rpm. Torque: 125 lb.-ft. @ 2400 rpm. Five main bearings. Hydraulic valve lifters. Carburetor: two-barrel Rochester 2SE. VIN Code: 5. OPTIONAL V-6 (Phoenix): 60-degree, overhead valve six-cylinder. Cast iron block and aluminum head. Displacement: 173 cu. in. (2.8 liters). Bore & stroke: 3.50 x 3.00 in. Compression ratio: 8.5:1. Brake horsepower: 110 @ 4800 rpm. Torque: 145 lb.-ft. @ 2400 rpm. Four main bearings. Hydraulic valve lifters. Carburetor: two-barrel Rochester. Chevrolet-built. VIN Code: X.

BASE V-6 (Firebird, LeMans, Grand Prix, Catalina, Bonneville): 90-degree, overhead-valve V-6. Cast iron block and head. Displacement: 231 cu. in. (3.8 liters). Bore & stroke: 3.80 x 3.40 in. Compression ratio: 8.0:1. Brake horsepower: 110 @ 3800 rpm. Torque: 190 lb.-ft. @ 1600 rpm. Four main bearings. Hydraulic valve lifters. Carburetor: two-barrel Rochester M2ME. Buick-built. VIN Code: A.

1981 Pontiac Grand LeMans four-door sedan. OCW

BASE V-8 (Firebird Formula); OPTIONAL (Firebird, LeMans, Grand Prix, Catalina, Bonneville): 90-degree, overhead valve V-8. Cast iron block and head. Displacement: 265 cu. in. (4.3 liters). Bore & stroke: 3.75 x 3.00 in. Compression ratio: 8.3:1. Brake horsepower: 120 @ 4000 rpm. Torque: 205 lb.-ft. @ 2000 rpm. Five main bearings. Hydraulic valve lifters. Carburetor: two-barrel Rochester E2ME. VIN Code: S. BASE V-8 (Safari); OPTIONAL (Firebird, Catalina, Bonneville, LeMans Safari): 90-degree, overhead valve V-8. Cast iron block and head. Displacement: 301 cu. in. (5.0 liters). Bore & stroke: 4.00 x 3.00 in. Compression ratio: 8.1:1. Brake horsepower: 135 @ 3600 rpm. Torque: 235 lb.-ft. @ 1600 rpm. Five main bearings. Hydraulic valve lifters. Carburetor: four-barrel Rochester E4ME. VIN Code: W. BASE V-8 (Firebird Trans Am); OPTIONAL (Firebird): Same as 301 cid V-8 above, except Horsepower: 150 @ 4000 rpm. Torque: 245 lb.-ft. @ 2000 rpm.

TURBOCHARGED V-8 (Firebird Formula, Trans Am): Same as 301 cid V-8 above, with turbocharger. Compression ratio: 7.5:1. Horsepower: 200 @ 4000 rpm. Torque: 340 lb.-ft. @ 2000 rpm. VIN Code: T. OPTIONAL V-8 (Firebird Formula/Trans Am): 90-degree, overhead valve V-8. Cast iron block and head. Displacement: 305 cu. in. (5.0 liters). Bore & stroke: 3.74 x 3.48 in. Compression ratio: 8.4:1. Brake horsepower: 145 @ 3800 rpm. Torque: 240 lb.-ft. @ 2400 rpm. Five main bearings. Hydraulic valve lifters. Carburetor: four-barrel Rochester E4ME. Chevrolet-built. VIN Code: H. BASE V-8 (Safari); OPTIONAL (Catalina, Bonneville): 90-degree, overhead valve V-8. Cast iron block and head. Displacement: 307 cu. in. (5.0 liters). Bore & stroke: 3.80 x 3.38 in. Compression ratio: 8.0:1. Brake horsepower: 145 @ 3800 rpm. Torque: 240 lb.-ft. @ 2400 rpm. Five main bearings. Hydraulic valve lifters. Carburetor: four-barrel Rochester E4ME. Oldsmobile-built. VIN Code: Y. DIESEL V-8 (Grand Prix, Catalina, Bonneville, Safari): 90-degree, overhead valve V-8. Cast iron block and head. Displacement: 350 cu. in. (5.7 liters). Bore & stroke: 4.06 x 3.39 in. Compression ratio: 22.5:1. Brake horsepower: 105 @ 3200 rpm. Torque: 205 lb.-ft. @ 1600 rpm. Five main bearings. Hydraulic valve lifters. Fuel injection. Oldsmobile-built. VIN Code: N.

CHASSIS DATA: Wheelbase: (Phoenix) 104.9 in.; (Firebird) 108.2 in.; (LeMans) 108.1 in.; (Grand Prix) 108.1 in.; (Catalina/Bonneville) 116.0 in. Overall Length: (Phoenix cpe) 182.1 in.; (Phoenix hatch) 179.3 in.; (Firebird) 196.1 in.; (LeMans) 198.6 in.; (LeMans wag) 197.8 in.; (G.P.) 201.4 in.; (Catalina/Bonneville) 214.0 in.; (Safari wag) 216.7 in. Height: (Phoenix cpe) 53.5 in.; (Phoenix sed) 53.4 in.; (Firebird) 49.3 in.; (LeMans) 53.5 in.; (LeMans wag) 54.4 in.; (G.P.) 54.7 in.; (Catalina/Bonneville cpe) 56.0 in.; (Catalina/Bonneville sed) 56.7 in.; (Safari wag) 57.1 in. Width: (Phoenix) 69.1 in.; (Firebird) 73.0 in.; (LeMans) 72.4 in.; (LeMans wag) 71.9 in.; (G.P.) 72.7 in.; (Catalina/Bonneville) 75.4 in.; (Safari wag) 75.8 in. Front Tread: (Phoenix) 58.7 in.; (Firebird) 61.3 in.; (LeMans) 58.5 in.; (G.P.) 58.5 in.; (Catalina/Bonneville) 61.7 in.; (Safari) 62.1 in. Rear Tread: (Phoenix) 57.0 in.; (Firebird) 60.0 in.; (LeMans) 57.8 in. exc. wagon, 58.0 in.; (G.P.) 57.8 in.; (Catalina/Bonneville) 60.7 in.; (Safari) 64.1 in. Standard Tires: (Phoenix) P185/80R13 GBR; (Firebird) P205/75R15 SBR; (Firebird Formula/Trans Am) P225/70R15 SBR; (LeMans) P185/75R14 GBR exc. wagon, P195/75R14 GBR; (Grand Prix) P195/75R14 SBR; (Catalina/Bonneville) P205/75R15 SBR; (Safari) P225/75R15 SBR.

TECHNICAL: Transmission: Three-speed manual transmission standard on base Firebird and LeMans. Four-speed manual standard on T1000 and Phoenix. Three-speed Turbo-Hydramatic standard on other models, optional on all. Four-speed overdrive automatic available on

full-size models (standard on Safari). Standard final drive ratio: (Phoenix) 2.69:1 w/four-speed, 2.53:1 w/four and auto., 2.84:1 w/V-6 and auto. 2.96:1 or 3.33:1 w/H.O. V-6; (Firebird V-6) 3.08:1 w/three-speed, 2.56:1 w/auto.; (Firebird V-8-265) 2.41:1; (Firebird V-8-301) 2.56:1 w/auto.; (Firebird Trans Am/Formula) 2.41:1 w/V-8-265, 2.56:1 w/V-8-301, 3.08:1 w/turbo or 305 V-8; (LeMans V-6) 2.73:1 w/three-speed, 2.41:1 w/auto.; (LeMans V-8) 2.29:1; (LeMans Safari) 2.73:1 w/V-6, 2.41:1 w/V-8-265, 2.29:1 w/V-8-301; (Grand Prix) 2.41:1 w/V-6, 2.29:1 w/V-8-265, 2.14:1 w/V-8-301; (Catalina/Bonneville) 2.73:1 w/V-6, 2.41:1 w/V-8 exc. 3.08:1 w/V-8-301 and four-speed auto.; (Safari) 3.08:1 w/V-8-301, 2.73:1 w/diesel. Steering: (Phoenix) rack and pinion; (others) recirculating ball. Front Suspension: (Phoenix) MacPherson struts w/lower control arms and anti-sway bar; (Firebird/LeMans) coil springs w/lower trailing links and anti-sway bar; (others) coil springs and anti-sway bar. Rear Suspension: (Phoenix) single-beam trailing axle w/track bar and coil springs; (Firebird) semi-elliptic leaf springs with anti-sway bar; (LeMans/Bonneville/Grand Prix) rigid axle with coil springs, lower trailing radius arms and upper torque arms. Brakes: Front disc, rear drum. Ignition: Electronic. Body construction: (Phoenix) unit; (Firebird) unit w/separate partial frame; (others) separate body and frame. Fuel Tank: (Phoenix) 14 gal.; (Firebird) 21 gal.; (LeMans) 18.1 gal. exc. wagon, 18.2 gal.; (Grand Prix) 18.1 gal.; (Catalina/Bonneville) 25 gal.; (Safari) 22 gal.

NOTE: Dimensions and technical details for T1000, added at mid-year, not available; see 1982 listing for data.

DRIVETRAIN OPTIONS: Engines: 173 cid V-6: Phoenix ($125). 265 cid, two-barrel V-8: Firebird/LeMans/Grand Prix/Catalina/Bonneville ($50). 301 cid, four-barrel V-8: Safari ($50). E/C 301 cid, four-barrel V-8: Firebird ($215). Turbo 301 cid V-8: Firebird Formula ($652); Trans Am ($437). 305 cid, four-barrel V-8: Firebird Formula ($75); Trans Am ($140 credit). 307 cid, four-barrel V-8: Catalina/Bonneville ($50). Diesel 350 cid V-8: Grand Prix/Catalina/Bonneville Brougham ($695). Transmission/Differential: Turbo-Hydramatic: Phoenix/Firebird/LeMans ($349). Overdrive automatic transmission: Catalina/Bonneville cpe/sed ($153). Limited-slip differential: Firebird/LeMans/G.P./Catalina/Bonneville ($67). Brakes/Steering: Power brakes: Phoenix ($79). Power four-wheel disc brakes: Firebird ($158). Power steering: Phoenix ($168). Suspension: Rally RTS handling pkg.: Phoenix ($173-$245) except w/SJ option ($1-$73); Catalina/Bonneville ($44). Rally handling suspension: LeMans ($202-$241). Superlift shock absorbers: Phoenix/Catalina/Bonneville ($57). H.D. springs: Phoenix/LeMans/G.P./Catalina/Bonneville ($14-$15). Automatic level control: Catalina/Bonneville ($85-$142). Others: H.D. radiator: Phoenix ($38-$63). H.D. cooling: LeMans ($34); Catalina/Bonneville ($34-$63). Super-cooling radiator: Firebird ($34-$63); Catalina/Bonneville ($34-$63). H.D. battery ($22) exc. diesel ($44). H.D. alternator: Phoenix ($10-$43); Firebird ($51); LeMans/G.P./Catalina/Bonneville ($15-$51). Engine block heater ($16). Light trailer group: Phoenix ($120-$135); LeMans/Catalina/Bonneville ($129-$158); G.P. ($139-$158). Medium trailer group: Catalina/Bonneville ($129-$158). California emissions ($46) exc. diesel ($182).

1981 Pontiac Grand Prix LJ coupe. OCW

1981 Pontiac Grand Prix LJ coupe (rear view). OCW

OPTION PACKAGES: Phoenix custom exterior ($85-$130). Phoenix appearance pkg. ($187). Phoenix SJ appearance pkg. ($118). Phoenix luxury trim pkg. ($223-$344). Phoenix SJ option ($404-$449). Trans Am Special Edition ($735); w/hatch roof ($1430). Firebird Formula appearance pkg. ($200). Firebird Formula/Trans Am special performance pkg. ($350-$546). Firebird custom trim ($45-$164). LeMans Safari security pkg. ($40). LeMans luxury trim group ($160-$270). LeMans appearance pkg. ($180). LeMans custom exterior ($44-$100). LeMans custom trim group ($130-$303). Grand Prix appearance ($184). Full-size appearance pkg. ($177). Full-size custom trim group ($176-$398).

MAJOR CONVENIENCE/APPEARANCE OPTIONS: Air conditioning ($560-$625). Automatic air conditioning: LeMans/Grand Prix ($677); Catalina/Bonneville ($708); Safari ($83). Cruise control ($132-$135). Power seat ($173). Power windows ($140-$211). Cornering lamps: Catalina/Bonneville/Grand Prix ($51-$52). Power glass sun roof: LeMans/Grand Prix ($773); Catalina/Bonneville ($981). Power steel sun roof: LeMans/Grand Prix ($561); Catalina/Bonneville ($704). Hatch roof: Firebird/Grand Prix ($663-$695). Full vinyl cordova top: LeMans ($115); Catalina/Bonneville ($142). Padded landau cordova top: Phoenix ($178); LeMans ($192); Grand Prix/Bonneville ($222). Rear-facing third seat: Safari ($194).

HISTORICAL FOOTNOTES: Introduced: September 25, 1980. Model year production: 600,543. Calendar year production (U.S.): 519,292. Calendar year sales by U.S. dealers: 552,384. Model year sales by U.S. dealers: 601,218 (including 34,424 early 1982 J2000 models). Production fell for the model year, for the second year in a row. Sales slipped too, but not by as much. Firebird dropped sharply, though part of that loss may have been due to expectations of a fully restyled version for 1982. Only Grand Prix showed a sales rise. Pontiac's CAFE figure for 1981 was just over 23 mpg (with 22 the required standard). William E. Hoglund was the division's new general manager. In addition to sales of Pontiac's "Iron Duke" four-cylinder engine to other GM divisions, it even found its way under AMC hoods. Early in the year, Pontiac abandoned production of V-8 powerplants, after building them since 1955.

1982 PONTIAC

A new, aerodynamically restyled Firebird was 1982's foremost news from Pontiac. Also new this year: front-wheel-drive J2000 and 6000 models. The old Catalina and Bonneville were gone, but a revised Bonneville G entered the lineup.

I.D. DATA: Pontiac's 17-symbol Vehicle Identification Number (VIN) was on the upper left surface of the instrument panel, visible through the windshield. The first three symbols ('1G2') indicate Pontiac division. Symbol four is restraint system ('A' = manual seatbelts). Symbol five is car line/series: 'L' = T1000; 'B' = J2000; 'E' = J2000 S; 'C' = J2000 LE; 'D' = J2000 SE; 'Y' = Phoenix; 'Z' = Phoenix LJ; 'T' = Phoenix SJ; 'F' = 6000; 'G' = 6000 LE; 'S' = Firebird; 'X' = Firebird S/E; 'W' = Firebird Trans Am; 'J' = Grand Prix; 'K' = Grand Prix LJ; 'P' = Grand Prix Brougham; 'N' = Bonneville G; 'R' = Bonneville G Brougham. In sixth and seventh position are two digits that denote body type: '08' = three-door hatchback coupe; '27' = two-door coupe; '37' = two-door coupe; '77' = three-door hatchback; '87' = two-door coupe; '19' = four-door six-window sedan; '68' = five-door hatchback sedan; '69' = four-door four-window sedan; '35' = four-door station wagon. Symbol eight is a letter indicating engine code: 'C' = L4-97 two-barrel; 'O' = L4-109; 'G' = L4-112 two-barrel; 'R' or '2' = L4-151 FI; 'X' or '1' = V-6-173 two-barrel; 'Z' = H.O. V-6-173 two-barrel; 'A' = V-6-231 two-barrel; '4' = V-6-252 four-barrel; 'T' = diesel V-6-262; 'H' = V-8-305 four-barrel; '7' = V-8-305 FI; 'N' = diesel V-8-350. Next is a check digit. The tenth symbol denotes model year ('C' = 1982). Symbol eleven is a plant code: 'A' = Lakewood, Ga.; 'G' = Framingham, Mass.; 'K' = Leeds, Mo.; 'L' = Van Nuys, Calif.; 'N' = Norwood, Ohio; 'P' = Pontiac, Mich.; 'T' = Tarrytown, N.Y.; 'Y' = Wilmington, Del.; '7' = Lordstown, Ohio; '6' = Oklahoma City; '1' = Oshawa, Ontario. The final six digits are the sequential serial number.

T1000 -- SERIES 2T -- FOUR -- Differing little from Chevrolet's Chevette, the T1000 contained the smallest four-cylinder engine ever in a Pontiac: just 98 cid (1.6 liter). A five-speed manual transmission was available this year on the three-door hatchback version of Pontiac's smallest car. A new dark argent grille with widely separated vertical bars (and wide center bar with emblem) highlighted the front end, which had single rectangular headlamps in black bezels. Small park/signal lamps were bumper-mounted. Bumpers held black rubber end caps. Taillamps were wraparound style. Standard reclining bucket seats were upholstered in vinyl, with Pompey cloth optional. T1000's suspension was returned. Standard equipment included the 1.6-liter OHC four-cylinder engine, four-speed manual transmission, front/rear bumper guards and rub strips, AM radio, P155/80R13 glass-belted blackwall tires, wide black/bright bodyside moldings, argent styled steel wheels, wide vinyl-clad black rocker panel moldings, and black-finish window frames. Three-doors had swingout rear quarter windows.

1982 Pontiac T1000 hatchback coupe. (P)

T1000 (FOUR)

Model Number	Body/Style Number	Body Type & Seating	Factory Price	Shipping Weight	Prod. Total
2T	L08	3-dr. Hatch-4P	5752	2034	21,053
2T	L68	5-dr. Hatch-4P	5945	2098	23,416

1982 Pontiac J2000 LE coupe. (JG)

J2000 -- SERIES 2J -- FOUR -- Introduced as an early 1982 model, the five-passenger subcompact J2000's front-drive chassis rode on a 101.2 in. wheelbase. Two-door coupe, three-door hatchback, four-door sedan, and four-door wagon bodies were available in base form. The sporty SE came only as a hatchback, while the luxury LE appeared as a coupe or sedan. Each model had standard reclining front bucket seats. Hatchbacks and wagons had full-folding back seats, while SE had a split folding rear seat. An S model was added later. A sharply sloped front panel formed a tapered body-color center divider with emblem, between twin recessed grilles. Quad rectangular headlamps were used. Park/signal lamps were below the bumper strip. A full-width air slot between the parking lamps displayed an eggcrate pattern similar to that of the upper grilles. Wide wraparound taillamps sat in a full-width panel with horizontal ribbing, with backup lenses in the center of each unit. Small rear lenses could be seen in the bumper area. The rear license plate was bumper-mounted. Base J2000 engine was a transverse-mounted 112 cid (1.8-liter) four with two-barrel carburetor, hooked to a four-speed manual transaxle. The engine's fast-burn combustion chamber had a centrally positioned spark plug with high turbulence, with 9.0:1 compression. The electronic control module had built-in diagnostics. Front suspension was MacPherson struts; in back, a double-crank trailing-twist rear axle. Variable-rate coil springs helped balance the front and rear suspension. Standard equipment included power brakes, locking fuel filler door, body-color bumpers with rub strips, swing-out rear quarter windows (coupe/hatchback), AM radio with digital clock, Rally wheels, P175/80R13 fiberglass-belted tires, and reclining front bucket seats. Hatchbacks and LE had wide bodyside moldings and rocker panel moldings. SE added Viscount trim, a gauge set, and driver's remote mirror.

J2000 (FOUR)

Model Number	Body/Style Number	Body Type & Seating	Factory Price	Shipping Weight	Prod. Total
2J	B27	2-dr. Cpe-5P	6999	2295	15,865
2J	B77	3-dr. Hatch-5P	7275	2353	21,219
2J	B69	4-dr. Sedan-5P	7203	2347	29,920
2J	B35	4-dr. Sta Wag-5P	7448	2418	16,014

Model Number	Body/Style Number	Body Type & Seating	Factory Price	Shipping Weight	Prod. Total
J2000 S (FOUR)					
2J	E27	2-dr. Cpe-5P	6734	N/A	2722
2J	E69	4-dr. Sedan-5P	6902	N/A	2760
2J	E35	4-dr. Sta Wag-5P	7208	N/A	1245
J2000 LE (FOUR)					
2J	C27	2-dr. Cpe-5P	7372	2300	6313
2J	C69	4-dr. Sedan-5P	7548	2352	14,268
J2000 SE (FOUR)					
2J	D77	3-dr. Hatch-5P	7654	2358	8533

Price Note: J2000 prices rose $50-$93 shortly after introduction.

1982 Pontiac Phoenix First Level sedan. (P)

PHOENIX -- SERIES 2X -- FOUR/V-6 -- Fuel injection was added to the base Phoenix 151 cid (2.5-liter) four this year. A new SJ coupe or hatchback carried as standard a high-output 173 cid (2.8-liter) V-6. A lower-powered version of the V-6 was optional in other Phoenix models, as was the three-speed automatic to replace the standard four-speed manual shift. SJ included standard power steering and brakes, cast aluminum wheels, Rally RTS suspension, black grille and moldings, and SJ graphics package. The Phoenix steering gear moved to the engine cradle this year, for better isolation. Styling was similar to 1981.

1982 Pontiac Phoenix SJ coupe. (JG)

Model Number	Body/Style Number	Body Type & Seating	Factory Price	Shipping Weight	Prod. Total
PHOENIX (FOUR/V-6)					
2X	Y37	2-dr. Cpe-5P	6964/7182	2386/2450	12,282
2X	Y68	5-dr. Hatch-5P	7172/7390	2476/2540	24,026
PHOENIX LJ (FOUR/V-6)					
2X	Z37	2-dr. Cpe-5P	7449/7687	2386/2450	4436
2X	Z68	5-dr. Hatch-5P	7658/7876	2476/2540	7161

Price Note: V-6 price includes the required power brakes.

Model Number	Body/Style Number	Body Type & Seating	Factory Price	Shipping Weight	Prod. Total
PHOENIX SJ (V-6)					
2X	T37	2-dr. Cpe-5P	8723	2450	994
2X	T68	5-dr. Hatch-5P	8884	2540	268

1982 Pontiac Firebird SE coupe. OCW

1982 Pontiac Firebird SE coupe. (P)

FIREBIRD -- SERIES 2F -- FOUR/V-6/V-8 -- Instead of the previous four models, the revised Firebird came in three variations: base, luxury S/E, and Trans Am. Each one had its own suspension and tire setup. Base engine was now a fuel-injected 151 cid (2.5-liter) four, hooked to four-speed manual gearbox. S/E carried a standard 173 cid (2.8-liter) two-barrel V-6, also with four-speed, while Trans Am had a 305 cid (5.0-liter) four-barrel V-8 with the four-speed. Trans Am could also step up to a dual throttle-body (crossfire) fuel injection V-8 with fresh-air hood induction. A low nose now held hidden halogen headlamps, electrically controlled. Park/signal lamps sat in squat slots inboard of the headlamps, barely visible with headlamp doors shut. The twin air slots contained horizontal bars. At the rear was a large, contoured, frameless all-glass hatch. Taillamps were in a full-width back panel. Reclining front bucket seats were standard. A new Formula steering wheel had an energy-absorbing hub. A WS6 suspension (optional on S/E and Trans Am) included P215/65R15 SBR tires on seven-inch aluminum wheels, larger stabilizer bars, four-wheel disc brakes, positraction rear axle, and tuned springs/shocks/bushings. Standard Firebird equipment included P195/75R14 glass-belted blackwall tires, hubcaps, black-finished grille, front air dam, power brakes and steering, front stabilizer bar, side window defoggers, and black-finished instrument panel. S/E added full-width black taillamps, body-color bodyside moldings, lower accent paint (with striping), turbo cast aluminum wheels, P205/70R14 steel-belted blackwalls, and rear stabilizer bar. Trans Am included bird decals on hood and sail panel, front fender air extractors, front/rear wheel opening flares, and aero wing decklid spoiler.

Model Number	Body/Style Number	Body Type & Seating	Factory Price	Shipping Weight	Prod. Total
FIREBIRD (FOUR/V-6)					
2F	S87	2-dr. Cpe-4P	7996/8121	N/A	41,683

Engine Note: A 305 cid V-8 cost $170 more than the V-6 on base Firebird.

Model Number	Body/Style Number	Body Type & Seating	Factory Price	Shipping Weight	Prod. Total
FIREBIRD S/E (V-6/V-8)					
2F	X87	2-dr. Cpe-4P	9624/9819	N/A	21,719
FIREBIRD TRANS AM (V-8)					
2F	W87	2-dr. Cpe-4P	9658	N/A	52,960

6000 -- SERIES 2A -- FOUR/V-6 -- Based on the X-car design, the contemporary-styled 6000 carried five passengers and was designed with "internationally competitive" ride/handling characteristics. Base and LE models came in two-door coupe or four-door sedan body styles. Standard powerplant was a fuel-injected 151 cid (2.5-liter) four with three-speed automatic transmission. Vertical bars made up each side of the split grille. Recessed quad headlamps were used, with parking/signal lamps down in the bumper strip. Wraparound taillamps had hor-

izontal trim ribs. Backup lights adjoined the license plate opening. Standard 6000 equipment included automatic transmission, power brakes/steering, black rocker panel moldings, front air dam, black driver's mirror, wheel opening and roof drip moldings, P185/80R13 blackwall GBR tires, hubcaps, AM radio, side window defoggers, and day/night mirror. LE added deluxe wheel covers, lower door edge moldings, a locking gas filler door, overhead assist straps, and black-finished rocker panel area.

1982 Pontiac 6000 LE sedan. (OCW)

1982 Pontiac 6000 LE coupe (rear view). OCW

Model Number	Body/Style Number	Body Type & Seating	Factory Price	Shipping Weight	Prod. Total
6000 (FOUR/V-6)					
2A	F27	2-dr. Cpe-5P	8729/8854	N/A	6505
2A	F19	4-dr. Sed-5P	8890/9015	N/A	17,751
2A	G27	2-dr. LE Cpe-5P	9097/9222	N/A	7025
2A	G19	4-dr. LE Sed-5P	9258/9383	N/A	26,253

1982 Pontiac Grand Prix coupe (Kyle Petty/STP NASCAR stock car).

GRAND PRIX -- SERIES 2G -- V-6 -- Restyled a year before, Grand Prix continued its aero wedge shape with low front end and higher deck. Appearance was similar to before, but with a tight pattern of vertical bars (formerly horizontal) in the twin grilles. The grille pattern repeated in two tall bumper slots. Small park/signal lamps went into the bumper strip, which crossed the grille just below its up/down midpoint. "Grand Prix" script decorated the left grille. Base engine was the 231 cid (3.8-liter) V-6 from Buick, with automatic transmission (which had a lock-up torque converter clutch). A 252 cid (4.1-liter) V-6 cost

169

just $95 more. No gasoline V-8 was available, but a V-8 diesel cost $924. Four trim levels were available, including two new ones for the Brougham. The base Brougham was trimmed as in 1981, including a notchback loose-pillow 60/40 seat. A new Brougham Landau option included opera lamps, a formal back window, padded landau roof, power windows, and Tampico carpeting. Base, LJ, and Brougham models were offered.

Model Number	Body/Style Number	Body Type & Seating	Factory Price	Shipping Weight	Prod. Total
GRAND PRIX (V-6)					
2G	J37	2-dr. HT Cpe-6P	8333	3276	37,672
GRAND PRIX LJ (V-6)					
2G	K37	2-dr. HT Cpe-6P	8788	3276	29,726
GRAND PRIX BROUGHAM (V-6)					
2G	P37	2-dr. HT Cpe-6P	9209	3276	12,969

1982 Pontiac Bonneville G station wagon. (JG)

BONNEVILLE G -- SERIES 2G -- V-6/V-8 -- This new Bonneville, still rear-drive, was smaller and more fuel-efficient than its predecessor, riding a 108.1 in. wheelbase. Base and Brougham trim levels were available on the formal-roof four-door sedan. A single station wagon model also was offered. Base engine was a 231 cid (3.8-liter) V-6 with three-speed automatic transmission. Optional: either a 252 cid (4.1-liter) V-6, or the 350 diesel V-8. A relatively narrow center divider (with emblem) separated the twin grilles, each made up of vertical bars. Quad rectangular headlamps stood directly above wide park/signal lamps. Two-row wraparound taillamps had a checkerboard look. Standard Bonneville equipment included power brakes and steering, P195/75R14 blackwall GBR tires, body-color bumpers, front bumper guards, wide rocker panels (with extensions), roof drip moldings, a stand-up hood ornament (with windsplit), wheel opening moldings, wheel covers, and electric clock. Brougham added opera lamps, simulated teak instrument panel trim, and 60/40 front seat with fold-down armrest,

Model Number	Body/Style Number	Body Type & Seating	Factory Price	Shipping Weight	Prod. Total
BONNEVILLE G (V-6/V-8)					
2G	N69	4-dr. Sed-6P	8527/8622	3203/ --	44,378
2G	N35	4-dr. Sta Wag-6P	8414/8789	3380/ --	16,100
BONNEVILLE G BROUGHAM (V-6/V-8)					
2G	R69	4-dr. Sed-6P	8985/9080	3213/ --	20,035

FACTORY PRICE AND WEIGHT NOTE: Prices and weights to left of slash are for V-6, to right for V-8 engine except Phoenix/Firebird/6000, four and V-6.

ENGINE DATA

BASE FOUR (T1000): Inline. Overhead cam. Four-cylinder. Cast iron block and head. Displacement: 97 cu. in. (1.6 liters). Bore & stroke: 3.23 x 2.98 in. Compression ratio: 9.2:1. Brake horsepower: 62 @ 5200 rpm. Torque: 82 lb.-ft. @ 2400 rpm. Five main bearings. Hydraulic valve lifters. Carburetor: two-barrel Holley 6510C. VIN Code: C. BASE FOUR (J2000): Inline. Overhead valve. Four-cylinder. Cast iron block and head. Displacement: 112 cu. in. (1.8 liters). Bore & stroke: 3.50 x 2.91 in. Compression ratio: 9.0:1. Brake horsepower: 88 @ 5100 rpm. Torque: 100 lb.-ft. @ 2800 rpm. Five main bearings. Hydraulic valve lifters. Carburetor: two-barrel Rochester E2SE. VIN Code: G. OPTIONAL FOUR (J2000): Inline. Overhead cam. Four-cylinder. Cast iron block and aluminum head. Displacement: 109 cu. in. (1.8 liters). Bore & stroke: 3.34 x 3.13 in. Compression ratio: 9.0:1. Brake horsepower: 82 @ 5200 rpm. Torque: 96 lb.-ft. @ 2800 rpm. Five main bearings. Hydraulic valve lifters. Carburetor: two-barrel

Rochester. VIN Code: O. BASE FOUR (Phoenix, Firebird, 6000): Inline. Overhead valve. Four-cylinder. Cast iron block and head. Displacement: 151 cu. in. (2.5 liters). Bore & stroke: 4.00 x 3.00 in. Compression ratio: 8.2:1. Brake horsepower: 90 @ 4000 rpm. Torque: 134 lb.-ft. @ 2400 rpm. Five main bearings. Hydraulic valve lifters. Throttle-body fuel injection. VIN Code: R or 2. OPTIONAL V-6 (Phoenix, Firebird, 6000): 60-degree, overhead valve six-cylinder. Cast iron block and aluminum head. Displacement: 173 cu. in. (2.8 liters). Bore & stroke: 3.50 x 3.00 in. Compression ratio: 8.5:1. Brake horsepower: 112 @ 4800 rpm (Firebird, 105 @ 4800). Torque: 145 lb.-ft. @ 2400 rpm (Firebird, 142 @ 2400). Four main bearings. Hydraulic valve lifters. Carburetor: two-barrel Rochester E2SE. VIN Code: X or 1. OPTIONAL V-6 (Phoenix SJ): High-output version of 173 cid V-6 above. Compression ratio: 8.9:1. Horsepower: 130 @ 5400 rpm. Torque: 145 lb.-ft. @ 2400 rpm. VIN Code: Z.

BASE V-6 (Grand Prix, Bonneville): 90-degree, overhead-valve V-6. Cast iron block and head. Displacement: 231 cu. in. (3.8 liters). Bore & stroke: 3.80 x 3.40 in. Compression ratio: 8.0:1. Brake horsepower: 110 @ 3800 rpm. Torque: 190 lb.-ft. @ 1600 rpm. Four main bearings. Hydraulic valve lifters. Carburetor: two-barrel Rochester E2ME. Buick-built. VIN Code: A. OPTIONAL V-6 (Grand Prix): 90-degree, overhead-valve V-6. Cast iron block and head. Displacement: 252 cu. in. (4.1 liters). Bore & stroke: 3.96 x 3.40 in. Compression ratio: 8.0:1. Brake horsepower: 125 @ 4000 rpm. Torque: 205 lb.-ft. @ 2000 rpm. Four main bearings. Hydraulic valve lifters. Carburetor: two-barrel Buick-built. VIN Code: 4.

DIESEL V-6 (6000, Bonneville): 90-degree, overhead valve V-6. Cast iron block and head. Displacement: 262 cu. in. (4.3 liters). Bore & stroke: 4.06 x 3.38 in. Compression ratio: 21.6:1. Brake horsepower: 85 @ 3600 rpm. Torque: 165 lb.-ft. @ 1600 rpm. Four main bearings. Hydraulic valve lifters. Fuel injection. VIN Code: T.

BASE V-8 (Firebird Trans Am); OPTIONAL (Firebird): 90-degree, overhead valve V-8. Cast iron block and head. Displacement: 305 cu. in. (5.0 liters). Bore & stroke: 3.74 x 3.48 in. Compression ratio: 8.6:1. Brake horsepower: 145 @ 4000 rpm. Torque: 240 lb.-ft. @ 2000 rpm. Four main bearings. Hydraulic valve lifters. Carburetor: four-barrel Rochester E4ME. Chevrolet-built. VIN Code: H. OPTIONAL V-8 (Trans Am): Same as 305 cid V-8 above, with throttle-body fuel injection. Compression ratio: 9.5:1. Horsepower: 165 @ 4200 rpm. Torque: 240 lb.-ft. @ 2400 rpm. VIN Code: 7.

DIESEL V-8 (Grand Prix/Bonneville): 90-degree, overhead valve V-8. Cast iron block and head. Displacement: 350 cu. in. (5.7 liters). Bore & stroke: 4.06 x 3.39 in. Compression ratio: 21.6:1. Brake horsepower: 105 @ 3200 rpm. Torque: 205 lb.-ft. @ 1600 rpm. Five main bearings. Hydraulic valve lifters. Fuel injection. Oldsmobile-built. VIN Code: N.

1982 Pontiac Firebird coupe. OCW

CHASSIS DATA: Wheelbase: (T1000 three-door) 94.3 in.; (T1000 five-door) 97.3 in.; (J2000) 101.2 in.; (Phoenix) 104.9 in.; (Firebird) 101.0 in.; (6000) 104.8 in.; (Grand Prix) 108.1 in.; (Bonneville) 108.1 in. Overall Length: (T1000 three-door) 161.9 in.; (T1000 five-door) 164.9 in.; (J2000 cpe) 169.4 in.; (J2000 sed) 171.4 in.; (J2000 wag) 175.3 in.; (Phoenix cpe) 182.1 in.; (Phoenix hatch) 179.3 in.; (Firebird) 189.8 in.; (6000) 188.7 in.; (G.P.) 201.9 in.; (Bonneville) 198.6 in.; (Bonneville wag) 197.8 in. Height: (T1000) 52.9 in.; (J2000 cpe) 51.3 in.; (J2000 sed/wag) 53.3 in.; (Phoenix cpe) 53.5 in.; (Phoenix sed) 53.4 in.; (Firebird) 49.8 in.; (6000) 53.3 in.; (G.P.) 54.7 in.; (Bonneville) 55.8 in.; (Bonneville wag) 56.1 in. Width: (T1000) 61.8 in.; (J2000) 64.9 in.; (Phoenix cpe) 69.1 in.; (Phoenix sed) 69.6 in.; (Firebird) 72.0 in.; (6000) 67.7 in.; (G.P.) 72.1 in.; (Bonneville) 71.3 in.; (Bonneville wag) 72.6 in. Front Tread: (T1000) 51.2 in.; (J2000) 55.4 in.; (Phoenix) 58.7 in.; (Firebird) 60.7 in.; (6000) 58.7 in.; (G.P.) 58.5 in.; (Bonneville) 58.5 in. Rear Tread: (T1000) 51.2 in.; (J2000) 55.1 in.; (Phoenix) 57.0 in.; (Firebird) 60.6 in.; (6000) 56.9 in.; (G.P.) 57.8 in.; (Bonneville) 57.8 in.; (Bonneville wag) 58.0 in. Standard Tires: (T1000) P155/80R13 GBR BSW; (J2000) P175/80R13 GBR BSW; (Phoenix) P185/80R13 GBR BSW; (Firebird) P195/75R14 GBR BSW; (Firebird S/E, Trans Am) P205/70R14 SBR BSW; (6000) P185/80R13 GBR BSW; (Grand Prix) P195/75R14 SBR BSW; (Bonneville) P195/75R14 GBR BSW.

TECHNICAL: Transmission: Four-speed manual standard on T1000, J2000, Phoenix, and Firebird (base and S/E). Three-speed Turbo-Hydramatic standard on other models, optional on all. Standard final drive ratio: (T1000) 3.36:1; (J2000) 3.19:1 w/109 four, 3.32:1 w/112 four; (Phoenix) 3.32:1 except 3.65:1 w/H.O. V-6; (Firebird) 3.23:1 w/V-6, 3.23:1 w/V-8; (6000) 2.39:1 w/four, 2.53:1 w/V-6; (Grand Prix) 2.41:1 w/V-6, 2.29:1 w/V-8; (Bonneville) 2.73:1 w/V-6, 2.41:1 w/V-8. Steering: (T1000/J2000/Phoenix/6000) rack and pinion; (others) recirculating ball. Front Suspension: (J2000/Phoenix) MacPherson struts w/lower control arms and anti-sway bar; (Firebird) modified MacPherson struts w/coil springs between lower control arm and X-member; (6000) MacPherson struts w/coil springs; (others) coil springs and anti-sway bar. Rear Suspension: (T1000) rigid axle w/longitudinal trailing radium arms, transverse bar, coil springs and anti-sway bar; (J2000) rigid axle w/coil springs; (Phoenix) single-beam trailing axle w/track bar and coil springs; (Firebird) torque arm/track bar w/coil springs, and anti-sway bar on S/E and Trans Am; (6000) trailing arm and beam w/coil springs and anti-sway bar; (Bonneville/Grand Prix) rigid axle with coil springs, lower trailing radius arms and upper torque arms. Brakes: Front disc, rear drum. Ignition: Electronic. Body construction: (T1000/J2000/Phoenix/Firebird/6000) unit; (others) separate body and frame. Fuel Tank: (T1000) 12.5 gal.; (J2000) 14 gal.; (Phoenix) 14 gal.; (Firebird) 16 gal.; (6000) 15.7 gal.; (Grand Prix) 18.2 gal.; (Bonneville) 20.6 gal.

1982 Pontiac Firebird Trans Am coupe. (OCW)

DRIVETRAIN OPTIONS: Engines: 151 cid four: Firebird S/E ($125 credit). 173 cid V-6: Phoenix/Firebird/6000 ($125). 252 cid, four-barrel V-6: Grand Prix, Bonneville ($95). Diesel 262 cid V-6: 6000 ($824). 305 cid, four-barrel V-8: Firebird ($295); Firebird S/E ($170-$195). Dual EFI engine pkg.: Trans Am ($899). Diesel 350 cid V-8: Grand Prix/Bonneville ($924). Transmission/Differential: Five-speed manual transmission: T1000 ($196). Turbo-Hydramatic: T1000 ($380); J2000 ($370); Phoenix/Firebird ($396); Trans Am ($72). Limited-slip differential: Firebird/Bonneville ($76). Brakes/Steering: Power brakes: T1000/Phoenix ($93). Power four-wheel disc brakes: Firebird ($255) but no charge (NC) w/performance pkg. Power steering: T1000 ($190); J2000 ($180); Phoenix ($195). Suspension: Electronic suspension: 6000 ($165). Rally RTS handling pkg.: J2000 ($46); Phoenix V-6 ($317) except SJ ($88). Superlift shock absorbers: Phoenix/6000/Bonneville ($64). H.D. springs: Phoenix/6000/G.P./Bonneville ($16). Other: H.D. radiator: T1000 ($40-$70); J2000 ($37-$67); Phoenix ($72); Firebird ($40). H.D. cooling: 6000/G.P./Bonneville ($40). H.D. battery ($22-$25) exc. diesel ($50). H.D. alternator: J2000 ($25); Phoenix ($16-$51); Firebird ($15-$51); G.P./Bonneville ($51). Engine block heater ($17-$18). California emissions ($65) exc. diesel ($205).

OPTION PACKAGES: J2000 custom exterior group ($79). J2000 hatchback custom trim group ($195). Phoenix two-tone appearance pkg. ($148-$176). Phoenix luxury trim pkg. ($208-$356). Firebird Trans Am Recaro option ($2486-$2968). Firebird S/E and Trans Am special performance pkg. ($387-$417). Firebird custom exterior ($73-$134). Firebird luxury trim ($299-$844). Grand Prix Brougham Landau pkg. ($810). Grand Prix appearance ($205). Bonneville two-tone paint appearance ($205). Bonneville wagon custom trim group ($211). Lamp groups: ($37-$45) except Bonneville ($21-$51).

MAJOR CONVENIENCE/APPEARANCE OPTIONS: Air conditioning ($595-$675). Cruise control ($145-$165); N/A on 1000. Power seat ($183-$197); N/A on 1000. Power windows ($152-$235); N/A on 1000. Cornering lamps: Bonneville/G.P. ($58). Power glass sun roof: Grand Prix ($875). Removable glass sun roof: J2000/Phoenix/6000 ($261-$275). Hatch roof: Firebird/Grand Prix ($790-$826). Full vinyl cordova top: Bonneville ($140). Padded landau cordova top: Phoenix ($195); Bonneville/G.P. ($220). Woodgrain paneling: Bonneville wagon ($288).

HISTORICAL FOOTNOTES: Introduced: September 24, 1981, except J2000, May 1981; T1000/Phoenix, December 12, 1981; and Firebird/6000, January 14, 1982. Model year production: 547,271. Calendar year production (U.S.): 411,324. Calendar year sales by U.S. dealers: 483,149. Model year sales by U.S. dealers: 461,845 (not including 34,424 early 1982 J2000 models counted in 1981 total). Production fell again for the model year. Sales slipped even further. Several Pontiacs (6000 and some Phoenix models) reached EPA estimates of 40 mpg (highway), while T1000 managed 42, and the new J2000 series 43 on the highway. The new Firebird design had received extensive wind tunnel testing.

1983 PONTIAC

Introduced this year was a "world class" performance-oriented 6000 STE sedan. Firebirds added a five-speed manual gearbox, and the 2000 series of J-bodied subcompacts got a fuel-injected standard engine and five-speed manual shift. On a minor note, the 'T' disappeared from T1000 and 'J' from 2000 models. Far more noteworthy was the arrival of a 2000 (Sunbird) convertible, the first ragtop Pontiac since 1975. Returning this year was a full-size sedan and wagon, under the Parisienne name.

I.D. DATA: Pontiac's 17-symbol Vehicle Identification Number (VIN) was on the upper left surface of the instrument panel, visible through the windshield. The first three symbols ('1G2') indicate Pontiac division. Symbol four is restraint system ('A' = manual seatbelts). Symbol five is car line/series: 'L' = 1000; 'B' = 2000; 'C' = 2000 LE; 'D' = 2000 SE; 'Y' = Phoenix; 'Z' = Phoenix LJ; 'T' = Phoenix SJ; 'F' = 6000; 'G' = 6000 LE; 'H' = 6000 STE; 'S' = Firebird; 'X' = Firebird S/E; 'W' = Firebird Trans Am; 'J' = Grand Prix; 'K' = Grand Prix LJ; 'P' = Grand Prix Brougham; 'N' = Bonneville; 'R' = Bonneville Brougham; 'L' = Parisienne; 'T' = Parisienne Brougham. In sixth and seventh position are two digits that denote body type: '08' = three-door hatchback coupe; '27' = two-door coupe; '37' = two-door coupe; '77' = three-door hatchback; '87' = two-door coupe; '19' = four-door six-window sedan; '68' = five-door hatchback sedan; '69' = four-door four-window sedan; '35' = four-door station wagon. Symbol eight is a letter indicating engine code: 'C' = L4-98 two-barrel; 'O' = L4-109 FI; 'P' = L4-122 FI; 'R' or '2' = L4-151 FI; 'X' or '1' = V-6-173 two-barrel; 'Z' = H.O. V-6-173 two-barrel; 'A' = V-6-231 two-barrel; 'T' = diesel V-6-262; 'H' = V-8-305 four-barrel; '7' = V-8-305 FI; 'N' = diesel V-8-350. Next is a check digit. The tenth symbol denotes model year ('D' = 1983). Symbol eleven is a plant code: 'A' = Lakewood, Ga.; 'B' = Baltimore; 'G' = Framingham, Mass.; 'L' = Van Nuys, Calif.; 'N' = Norwood, Ohio; 'T' = Tarrytown, N.Y.; 'Y' = Wilmington, Del.; '7' = Lordstown, Ohio; '1' = Oshawa, Ontario; '2' = St. Therese, Quebec. The final six digits are the sequential serial number.

1983 Pontiac 1000 hatchback coupe. (P)

1000 -- SERIES 2T -- FOUR -- Body changes included more use of black accents, intended to give a sporty international feel to Pontiac's smallest model. Powertrain was again the overhead-cam 1.6-liter four with four-speed manual transmission. The standard AM radio could be deleted (for credit). Standard equipment also included reclining front bucket seats. Joining this year's option list: sport striping, a custom trim group, and black luggage rack. A diesel was announced, but failed to materialize.

1000 (FOUR)

Model Number	Body/Style Number	Body Type & Seating	Factory Price	Shipping Weight	Prod. Total
2T	L08	3-dr. Hatch-4P	5582	2081	13,171
2T	L68	5-dr. Hatch-4P	5785	2130	12,806

1983 Pontiac 2000 sedan. (P)

1983 Pontiac 2000 LE four-door sedan (rear view). OCW

2000 -- SERIES 2J -- FOUR -- Base powertrain for the 2000 series was now a fuel-injected, overhead-cam 1.8-liter four, hooked to five-speed manual transaxle. Coupe, sedan, hatchback, and station wagon bodies were offered. Appearance was similar to 1982, with the twin grilles now consisting of several horizontal bars. Recessed quad head-lamps stood alongside the small grille inserts. At the center of the front-end panel was a wide, tapered divider with emblem. Small park/signal lamps were below the bumper strip. Standard equipment included power brakes, bumper rub strips, console, side window defog-ger, fully reclining bucket seats, red instrument lighting, woodgrain dash, wide bodyside moldings, and P175/80R13 glass-belted radial tires on Rally wheels. LE's revised equipment list added an AM radio, bright rocker panel and wheel opening moldings, and cushion steering wheel. SE rode P195/70R13 tires on finned turbo cast aluminum wheels and included a rear spoiler, power steering, two-tone paint, and handling package. The new convertible had power windows, fog lamps, and tinted glass. Lear Siegler adjustable front bucket seats were now available for the LE sedan or SE hatchback.

1983 Pontiac 2000 Sunbird convertible. (P)

Model Number	Body/Style Number	Body Type & Seating	Factory Price	Shipping Weight	Prod. Total
2000 (FOUR)					
2J	B27	2-dr. Cpe-5P	6499	2353	22,063
2J	B77	3-dr. Hatch-5P	6809	2413	7331
2J	B69	4-dr. Sedan-5P	6621	2412	24,833
2J	B35	4-dr. Sta Wag-5P	6926	2487	10,214
2000 LE (FOUR)					
2J	C27	2-dr. Cpe-5P	7020	2385	2690
2J	C69	4-dr. Sedan-5P	7194	2436	6957
2J	C35	4-dr. Sta Wag-5P	7497	2517	1780
2J	N/A	2-dr. Conv.-5P	N/A	N/A	626
2000 SE (FOUR)					
2J	D77	3-dr. Hatch-5P	8393	2470	1835

1983 Pontiac Phoenix SJ coupe. (P)

PHOENIX -- SERIES 2X -- FOUR/V-6 -- Restyling was intended to give Phoenix more of a "Pontiac" look. This year's grille consisted of all hori-zontal bars. Otherwise, appearance was similar to 1982. A two-door coupe and five-door hatchback sedan came in base, LJ, or sporty SJ trim. A fuel-injected 151 cid (2.5-liter) four with four-speed manual transaxle was standard, with 173 cid (2.8-liter) V-6 and automatic optional. SJ included a high-output 2.8 V-6 and a performance han-dling package with Goodyear Eagle GT SBR tires on six-inch cast alu-minum turbo wheels. A different package with 13-inch wheels was available for other models. Standard equipment included an AM radio, vinyl front bench seat, P185/80R13 glass-belted radials on Rally wheels, and color-keyed bumpers with black/bright rub strips. LJ added a notchback front seat, narrow rocker panel moldings, black bodyside moldings, and charcoal wheel opening moldings. SJ included power brakes and steering, tachometer, handling suspension, wide black rocker panel moldings, bucket front seats, and P195/70R14 SBR tires on sport aluminum wheels.

1983 Pontiac Phoenix LJ hatchback sedan. OCW

Model Number	Body/Style Number	Body Type & Seating	Factory Price	Shipping Weight	Prod. Total
PHOENIX (FOUR/V-6)					
2X	Y37	2-dr. Cpe-5P	6942/7192	2485/2549	7205
2X	Y68	5-dr. Hatch-5P	7087/7337	2542/2606	13,377

1983 Pontiac Phoenix LJ hatchback sedan (rear view). OCW

PHOENIX LJ (FOUR/V-6)

| 2X | Z37 | 2-dr. Cpe-5P | 7489/7739 | 2526/2590 | 2251 |
| 2X | Z68 | 5-dr. Hatch-5P | 7698/7948 | 2574/2638 | 3635 |

PHOENIX SJ (V-6)

| 2X | T37 | 2-dr. Cpe-5P | 8861 | 2581 | 853 |
| 2X | T68 | 5-dr. Hatch-5P | 8948 | 2642 | 172 |

1983 Pontiac Firebird Trans Am coupe. (P)

FIREBIRD -- SERIES 2F -- FOUR/V-6/V-8 -- Major changes to Firebird were in the powertrain, as styling was similar to the 1982 redesign. Both four- and five-speed manual gearboxes were available this year, along with a four-speed automatic. S/E got a high-output version of the 173 cid (2.8-liter) V-6, along with the five-speed. Base models again carried a standard fuel-injected 151 cid (2.5-liter) four with four-speed manual shift. S/E had new cloth seats and a split-folding back seat (also available in the custom trim package). New Lear Siegler articulated front bucket seats became optional. Trans Am again carried a standard 5.0-liter V-8, but with the new five-speed and a 3.73:1 axle ratio. Standard equipment included power brakes/steering, reclining front bucket seats, and P195/75R14 glass-belted radial tires. S/E added P205/70R14 SBR tires on turbo cast aluminum wheels, a handling suspension, five-speed gearbox, sport mirrors, color-keyed bodyside moldings, and lower accent paint with striping. Trans Am had a rear spoiler and wheel opening flares.

Model Number	Body/Style Number	Body Type & Seating	Factory Price	Shipping Weight	Prod. Total

1983 Pontiac Firebird Trans Am coupe (rear view). OCW

1983 Pontiac Firebird coupe. OCW

FIREBIRD (FOUR/V-6)

| 2F | S87 | 2-dr. Cpe-4P | 8399/8549 | 2866/2948 | 32,020 |

Engine Note: A 305 cid V-8 cost $200-$225 more than the V-6 on base Firebird.

FIREBIRD S/E (V-6/V-8)

| 2F | X87 | 2-dr. Cpe-4P | 10322/10397 | 2965/3145 | 10,934 |

FIREBIRD TRANS AM (V-8)

| 2F | W87 | 2-dr. Cpe-4P | 10396 | 3107 | 31,930 |

1983 Pontiac 6000 coupe. (P)

1983 Pontiac 6000 coupe (rear view). OCW

6000 -- SERIES 2A -- FOUR/V-6 -- The new 6000 STE was created to appeal to buyers who craved Euro-style ride and handling. Offered in a choice of five subtle two-tone combinations, its distinctive body featured six front lights (including center fog lamps), wide bodyside moldings, and wrap-around neutral-density dual-lens taillamps. The inline lighting trio left little room for a grille on each side of the divider: just narrow black horizontal strips. Small park/signal lamps were in the bumper strip. A Driver Information Center displayed warnings and reminders for service. Orthopedic designed front bucket seats were fully adjustable. An electronic-tuning seek/scan stereo radio with graphic equalizer and clock was standard. Also standard: automatic air conditioning and power mirrors, windows, and door

173

locks. Powertrain consisted of a high-output 173 cid (2.8-liter) V-6 hooked to three-speed automatic transaxle. Hitting the ground were Goodyear Eagle GT steel-belted radial tires on 14 inch aluminum wheels. Electronic ride control, with an on-board air compressor adjusting pressure to the shock absorbers, was standard. The compressor could also be used to inflate a tire. Turning to the regular 6000 series, a coupe and sedan were offered in base and LE trim, each with a standard fuel-injected 151 cid (2.5-liter) four and three-speed automatic. Options included a 2.8-liter gas V-6 and 4.3 diesel V-6. Joining the option list was a Y99 high-performance rally suspension package. LE models had a 45/45 seat, with recliner optional. Base/LE twin grilles again consisted of vertical bars. Standard 6000 equipment included an AM radio, rear stabilizer bar, power brakes/steering, black mirrors, black front air dam, black rocker panel moldings, vinyl notchback front seats, and P185/80R13 glass-belted tires on Rally wheels. LE added a black pillar appliqué, quartz digital clock, and map pockets. 6000 STE rode P195/70R14 tires and had power windows, speed control, tinted glass, air conditioning, AM/FM stereo with cassette player and equalizer, two-tone paint, fog lamps, and much more on its basic equipment list.

1983 Pontiac 6000 STE sedan. (P)

Model Number	Body/Style Number	Body Type & Seating	Factory Price	Shipping Weight	Prod. Total
6000 (FOUR/V-6)					
2A	F27	2-dr. Cpe-5P	8399/8549	2693/2741	3524
2A	F19	4-dr. Sed-5P	8569/8719	2736/2779	20,267
2A	G27	2-dr. LE Cpe-5P	8837/8987	2711/2754	4278
2A	G19	4-dr. LE Sed-5P	8984/9134	2750/2793	33,676
6000 STE (V-6)					
2A	H19	4-dr. Sed-5P	13572	2823	6719

1983 Pontiac Grand Prix Brougham coupe. (P)

1983 Pontiac 6000 STE four-door sedan (rear view). OCW

GRAND PRIX -- SERIES 2G -- V-6/V-8 -- Pontiac's personal-luxury coupes were said to get a more modern look this year, but little change was evident beyond a slightly revised grille pattern. Base engine was again the Buick-built 231 cid (3.8-liter) V-6, with three-speed automatic. This year a V-8 option returned: a four-barrel 5.0-liter edition. The 350 cid diesel V-8 also was available. Standard equipment included power steering and brakes.

Model Number	Body/Style Number	Body Type & Seating	Factory Price	Shipping Weight	Prod. Total
GRAND PRIX (V-6/V-8)					
2G	J37	2-dr. Cpe-6P	8698/8923	N/A	41,511
GRAND PRIX LJ (V-6/V-8)					
2G	K37	2-dr. Cpe-6P	9166/9391	N/A	33,785
GRAND PRIX BROUGHAM (V-6/V-8)					
2G	P37	2-dr. Cpe-6P	9781/10006	N/A	10,502

BONNEVILLE -- SERIES 2G -- V-6/V-8 -- Mid-size sedans had the same engine selections as Grand Prix, and looked similar to 1982. Standard equipment included Buick's 231 cid (3.8-liter) V-6 with automatic transmission, power brakes/steering, wide rocker panel moldings with extensions, wheel opening moldings, P195/75R14 tires, bumper guards and rub strips, electric clock, and day/night mirror. Brougham added cloth 60/40 notchback seating, opera lamps, and a bright pillar appliqué.

1983 Pontiac Bonneville Brougham sedan. (P)

Model Number	Body/Style Number	Body Type & Seating	Factory Price	Shipping Weight	Prod. Total
BONNEVILLE (V-6/V-8)					
2G	N69	4-dr. Sed-6P	8899/9124	3214/3290	47,003
2G	N35	4-dr. Sta Wag-6P	9112/9337	3275/3351	17,551
BONNEVILLE BROUGHAM (V-6/V-8)					
2G	R69	4-dr. Sed-6P	9399/9624	3210/3286	19,335

PARISIENNE -- SERIES 2B -- V-6/V-8 -- The full-size, rear-wheel-drive Parisienne had a conventional front end appearance with quad rectangular headlamps and vertical-bar twin grilles. Two sedans and a station wagon were offered. Standard equipment included the 3.8-liter V-6 engine and three-speed automatic, power brakes/steering, P205/75R15 SBR blackwall tires, narrow bright rocker panel and wheel opening moldings, color-keyed bodyside moldings, cloth 50/50 seating, bumper rub strips, and deluxe wheel covers. Brougham added luxury cloth 60/40 seating (with passenger recliner). Wagons rode P225/75R15 tires and had the 5.0-liter V-8 engine and four-speed overdrive automatic.

Model Number	Body/Style Number	Body Type & Seating	Factory Price	Shipping Weight	Prod. Total
PARISIENNE (V-6/V-8)					
2B	L69	4-dr. Sed-6P	9609/9889	N/A	9279
2B	L35	4-dr. Sta Wag-6P	-- /9927	N/A	3027
PARISIENNE BROUGHAM (V-6/V-8)					
2B	T69	4-dr. Sed-6P	9879/10159	N/A	5139

FACTORY PRICE AND WEIGHT NOTE: Prices and weights to left of slash are for V-6, to right for V-8 engine except Phoenix/Firebird/6000, four and V-6.

1983 Pontiac 1000 hatchback sedan. OCW

1983 Pontiac 1000 hatchback sedan (rear view). OCW

1983 Pontiac 2000 SE three-door hatchback. OCW

1983 Pontiac 2000 coupe. OCW

1983 Pontiac 2000 station wagon. OCW

1983 Pontiac SJ Phoenix coupe with Performance and Handling Package. OCW

1983 Pontiac SJ Phoenix coupe with Performance and Handling Package (rear view). OCW

1983 Pontiac Firebird Trans Am T-top coupe. OCW

1983 Pontiac Firebird Trans Am T-top coupe (rear view). OCW

1983 Pontiac 6000 LE four-door sedan. OCW

ENGINE DATA

BASE FOUR (1000): Inline. Overhead cam. Four-cylinder. Cast iron block and head. Displacement: 98 cu. in. (1.6 liters). Bore & stroke: 3.23 x 2.98 in. Compression ratio: 9.0:1. Brake horsepower: 65 @ 5200 rpm. Torque: 80 lb.-ft. @ 3200 rpm. Five main bearings. Hydraulic valve lifters. Carburetor: two-barrel VIN Code: C. **BASE FOUR (2000):** Inline. Overhead cam. Four-cylinder. Cast iron block and aluminum head. Displacement: 109 cu. in. (1.8 liters). Bore & stroke: 3.34 x 3.13 in. Compression ratio: 9.0:1. Brake horsepower: 84 @ 5200 rpm. Torque: 102 lb.-ft. @ 2800 rpm. Five main bearings. Hydraulic valve lifters. Electronic fuel injection. VIN Code: O. **OPTIONAL FOUR (2000):** Inline. Overhead valve. Four-cylinder. Cast iron block and head. Displacement: 122 cu. in. (2.0 liters). Bore & stroke: 3.50 x 3.15 in. Compression ratio: 9.3:1. Brake horsepower: 88 @ 4600 rpm. Torque: 110 lb.-ft. @ 2400 rpm. Five main bearings. Hydraulic valve lifters. Electronic fuel injection. VIN Code: P. **BASE FOUR (Phoenix, Firebird, 6000):** Inline. Overhead valve. Four-cylinder. Cast iron block and head. Displacement: 151 cu. in. (2.5 liters). Bore & stroke: 4.00 x 3.00 in. Compression ratio: 8.2:1. Brake horsepower: 90-94 @ 4000 rpm. Torque: 132-135 lb.-ft. @ 2800 rpm. Five main bearings. Hydraulic valve lifters. Throttle-body fuel injection. VIN Code: R or 2. **OPTIONAL V-6 (Phoenix, Firebird, 6000):** 60-degree, overhead valve six-cylinder. Cast iron block and head. Displacement: 173 cu. in. (2.8 liters). Bore & stroke: 3.50 x 3.00 in. Compression ratio: 8.5:1. Brake horsepower: 112 @ 4800 rpm (Firebird, 107 @ 4800). Torque: 145 lb.-ft. @ 2400 rpm (Firebird, 145 @ 2100). Four main bearings. Hydraulic valve lifters. Carburetor: two-barrel Rochester E2SE. VIN Code: X or 1.

1983 Pontiac Firebird SE coupe. OCW

BASE V-6 (Phoenix SJ, Firebird S/E, 6000 STE): High-output version of 173 cid V-6 above. Compression ratio: 8.9:1. Horsepower: 130-135 @ 5400 rpm. (Firebird, 125 hp) Torque: 145 lb.-ft. @ 2400 rpm. VIN Code: Z. **BASE V-6 (Grand Prix, Bonneville, Parisienne):** 90-degree, overhead-valve V-6. Cast iron block and head. Displacement: 231 cu. in. (3.8 liters). Bore & stroke: 3.80 x 3.40 in. Compression ratio: 8.0:1. Brake horsepower: 110 @ 3800 rpm. Torque: 190 lb.-ft. @ 1600 rpm. Four main bearings. Hydraulic valve lifters. Carburetor: two-barrel Rochester E2ME. Buick-built. VIN Code: A.

DIESEL V-6 (6000): 90-degree, overhead valve V-6. Cast iron block and head. Displacement: 260 cu. in. (4.3 liters). Bore & stroke: 4.06 x 3.38 in. Compression ratio: 21.6:1. Brake horsepower: 85 @ 3600 rpm. Torque: 165 lb.-ft. @ 1600 rpm. Four main bearings. Hydraulic valve lifters. Fuel injection. VIN Code: T.

BASE V-8 (Firebird Trans Am); OPTIONAL (Firebird, Grand Prix, Bonneville): 90-degree, overhead valve V-8. Cast iron block and head. Displacement: 305 cu. in. (5.0 liters). Bore & stroke: 3.74 x 3.48 in. Compression ratio: 8.6:1. Brake horsepower: 150 @ 4000 rpm. Torque: 240 lb.-ft. @ 2400 rpm. Five main bearings. Hydraulic valve lifters. Carburetor: four-barrel Rochester E4ME. Chevrolet-built. VIN Code: H. **OPTIONAL V-8 (Trans Am):** Same as 305 cid V-8 above, with crossfire fuel injection. Compression ratio: 9.5:1. Horsepower: 175 @ 4200 rpm. Torque: 250 lb.-ft. @ 2800 rpm. VIN Code: 7.

DIESEL V-8 (Grand Prix, Bonneville, Parisienne): 90-degree, overhead valve V-8. Cast iron block and head. Displacement: 350 cu. in. (5.7 liters). Bore & stroke: 4.06 x 3.39 in. Compression ratio: 21.6:1. Brake horsepower: 105 @ 3200 rpm. Torque: 200 lb.-ft. @ 1600 rpm. Five main bearings. Hydraulic valve lifters. Fuel injection. Oldsmobile-built. VIN Code: N.

CHASSIS DATA: Wheelbase: (1000 three-door) 94.3 in.; (1000 five-door) 97.3 in.; (2000) 101.2 in.; (Phoenix) 104.9 in.; (Firebird) 101.0 in.; (6000) 104.8 in.; (Grand Prix) 108.1 in.; (Bonneville)

108.1 in. Overall Length: (1000 three-door) 161.9 in.; (1000 five-door) 164.9 in.; (2000 cpe) 173.6 in.; (2000 sed/wag) 175.9 in.; (Phoenix cpe) 182.1 in.; (Phoenix hatch) 183.1 in.; (Firebird) 189.8 in.; (6000) 188.7 in.; (G.P.) 201.9 in.; (Bonneville) 198.6 in.; (Bonneville wag) 197.8 in. Height: (1000) 52.9 in.; (2000 cpe) 53.5 in.; (2000 sed/wag) 54.8 in.; (2000 hatch) 51.9 in.; (Phoenix cpe) 53.5 in.; (Phoenix sed) 53.4 in.; (Firebird) 49.8 in.; (6000) 54.8 in.; (G.P.) 54.7 in.; (Bonneville) 55.8 in.; (Bonneville wag) 56.1 in. Width: (1000) 61.8 in.; (2000) 68.6 in.; (Phoenix) 69.1 in.; (Phoenix sed) 69.6 in.; (Firebird) 72.0 in.; (6000) 68.2 in.; (G.P.) 72.1 in.; (Bonneville) 71.3 in.; (Bonneville wag) 72.6 in. Front Tread: (1000) 51.2 in.; (2000) 55.5 in.; (Phoenix) 58.7 in.; (Firebird) 60.7 in.; (6000) 58.7 in.; (G.P.) 58.5 in.; (Bonneville) 58.5 in. Rear Tread: (1000) 51.2 in.; (2000) 55.1 in.; (Phoenix) 57.0 in.; (Firebird) 61.6 in.; (6000) 57.0 in.; (G.P.) 57.8 in.; (Bonneville) 57.8 in. Standard Tires: (1000) P155/80R13 GBR BSW; (2000) P175/80R13 GBR BSW; (2000 SE) P195/70R13; (Phoenix) P185/80R13 GBR BSW; (Phoenix SJ) P195/70R14 SBR; (Firebird) P195/75R14 GBR BSW; (Firebird S/E, Trans Am) P205/70R14 SBR BSW; (6000) P185/80R13 GBR BSW; (6000 STE) P195/70R14 SBR; (Grand Prix) P195/75R14 SBR BSW; (Bonneville) P195/75R14 GBR BSW.

TECHNICAL: Transmission: Four-speed manual standard on 1000, Phoenix, and base Firebird. Five-speed manual standard on 2000 and Firebird S/E. Three-speed Turbo-Hydramatic standard on other models, optional on all. Standard final drive ratio: (1000) 3.36:1 exc. 3.62:1 w/five-speed; (2000) 3.83:1 w/five-speed, 3.91:1 w/four-speed, 3.18:1 w/auto.; (Phoenix) 3.32:1 except 3.06:1 w/H.O. V-6; (Firebird) 3.42:1 w/four-speed, 3.73:1 w/V-6 and five-speed, 3.23:1 w/V-8 and five-speed, 3.08:1 w/three-speed auto., 3.23:1 or 2.93:1 w/four-speed auto.; (6000) 2.39:1 except 3.33:1 w/H.O. V-6; (Grand Prix/Bonneville) 2.73:1 w/V-6, 2.73:1 w/V-8. Steering: (1000/2000/Phoenix/6000) rack and pinion; (others) recirculating ball. Front Suspension: (2000/Phoenix/6000) MacPherson struts w/lower control arms and anti-sway bar; (Firebird) modified MacPherson struts w/coil springs between lower control arm and X-member; (others) coil springs and anti-sway bar. Rear Suspension: (1000) four-link rigid axle w/torque tube and Panhard rod; (2000) beam axle w/coil springs and trailing arms; (Phoenix) single-beam trailing axle w/track bar and coil springs; (Firebird) torque arm/track bar w/coil springs and anti-sway bar; (6000) trailing arms and beam axle w/coil springs and integral anti-sway bar; (Bonneville/Grand Prix) four-link rigid axle with coil springs, lower trailing radius arms and upper torque arms. Brakes: Front disc, rear drum. Ignition: Electronic. Body construction: (1000/2000/Phoenix/Firebird/6000) unit; (others) separate body and frame. Fuel Tank: (1000) 12.5 gal.; (2000) 14 gal.; (Phoenix) 14.6 gal.; (Firebird) 16 gal.; (6000) 15.7 gal.; (Grand Prix/Bonneville) 17.5 gal.

DRIVETRAIN OPTIONS: Engines: 2.0-liter four: 2000 ($50 credit). 151 cid four: Firebird S/E ($300 credit). 173 cid V-6: Phoenix/Firebird/6000 ($150). Diesel 262 cid V-6: 6000 ($599). 305 cid, four-barrel V-8: Firebird ($350-$375); Firebird S/E ($50-$75); Grand Prix/Bonneville ($225). Crossfire EFI 305 cid V-8: Trans Am ($858). Diesel 350 cid V-8: Grand Prix/Bonneville ($799). Transmission/Differential: Four-speed manual transmission: 2000 ($75 credit). Five-speed manual transmission: 1000 ($75); Firebird ($125). Three-speed automatic transmission: 1000 ($395); 2000 ($320); Phoenix/Firebird ($425); Firebird S/E ($195). Four-speed automatic transmission: Firebird ($525); S/E and Trans Am ($295). Limited-slip differential: Firebird/G.P./Bonneville ($95). Brakes/Steering: Power brakes: 1000 ($95); Phoenix ($100). Power four-wheel disc brakes: Firebird ($274) but no charge (NC) with performance pkg. Power steering: 1000/2000 ($199); Phoenix ($210). Suspension: Electronic suspension: 6000 ($165). Rally handling pkg.: 2000 ($48); Phoenix/6000/Firebird/G.P. ($50). Superlift shock absorbers: 6000/G.P./Bonneville ($64). H.D. springs: Phoenix/6000/G.P./Bonneville ($16). Other: H.D. radiator: 1000/2000 ($40-$70). H.D. cooling ($40-$70). H.D. battery ($25) exc. diesel ($50). H.D. alternator ($25-$51). Engine block heater ($18). California emissions ($75) exc. diesel ($215).

OPTION PACKAGES: 1000 custom trim ($151). 2000 custom exterior group ($56-$86). 2000 custom trim group ($249-$299). 2000 security pkg. ($19). Phoenix upper exterior group ($98-$108); lower ($56). Firebird Trans Am Recaro option ($3160-$3610). Firebird S/E and Trans Am special performance pkg. ($408). Firebird custom exterior ($51-$112). 6000 rally pkg. ($618). 6000 custom exterior ($56). Grand Prix Brougham Landau pkg. ($549). Bonneville wagon custom trim group ($376). Lamp groups ($34-$46) except Bonneville ($22-$52) and 6000 LE ($88).

MAJOR CONVENIENCE/APPEARANCE OPTIONS: Air conditioning ($625-$725). Cruise control ($170). Power seat ($210-$420); N/A on 1000. Power windows ($180-$255); N/A on 1000. Cornering lamps: Bonneville/G.P. ($68). Power glass sun roof: Grand Prix ($895). Removable glass sun roof: 2000/Phoenix/6000 ($295). Hatch roof: Firebird/Grand Prix ($825-$861). Full vinyl cordova top: Bonneville ($155). Padded top: Phoenix ($215); Bonneville/G.P. ($240). Louvered rear sunshields: 2000 ($199); Firebird ($210). Two-tone paint: 2000 ($101); Phoenix ($105-$135); G.P./Bonneville ($205). Lear Siegler bucket seats: 2000 ($400); Firebird ($400-$1294). Woodgrain paneling: Bonneville wagon ($283).

HISTORICAL FOOTNOTES: Introduced: September 23, 1982, except Firebird, November 18, 1982. Model year production: 462,279. Calendar year production (U.S.): 414,842. Calendar year sales by U.S. dealers: 553,135. Model year sales by U.S. dealers: 513,239. Production fell for the fourth year in-a-row. The 6000 series posted a notable sales gain, partly due to the new 6000 STE. Pontiac was trying to boost its performance image at this time, with the debut of a high-output V-8 for Trans Am as well as the Euro-styled 6000 STE. Big (relatively) V-8s may have been popular with many buyers, but they didn't help Pontiac to meet CAFE fuel economy standards. Nevertheless, over one-fourth of engines in 1983 were V-8s, as opposed to less than 16 percent a year earlier.

1984 PONTIAC

Series 2000 got a name change, adding the Sunbird label. Totally new this year was the two-seater plastic-bodied Fiero. In addition, Pontiac offered a turbocharged engine for the 2000 Sunbird, a high-tech 6000 STE, and a high-output carbureted V-8 for Trans Am.

I.D. DATA: Pontiac's 17-symbol Vehicle Identification Number (VIN) was on the upper left surface of the instrument panel, visible through the windshield. The first three symbols ('1G2') indicate Pontiac division. Symbol four is restraint system ('A' = manual seatbelts). Symbol five is car line/series: 'E' = Fiero; 'M' = Fiero Sport; 'F' = Fiero SE; 'L' = T1000; 'B' = 2000 Sunbird; 'C' = 2000 Sunbird LE; 'D' = 2000 Sunbird SE; 'Y' = Phoenix; 'Z' = Phoenix LE; 'T' = Phoenix SJ; 'F' = 6000; 'G' = 6000 LE; 'H' = 6000 STE; 'S' = Firebird; 'X' = Firebird S/E; 'W' = Firebird Trans Am; 'J' = Grand Prix; 'K' = Grand Prix LE; 'P' = Grand Prix Brougham; 'N' = Bonneville; 'R' = Bonneville Brougham; 'S' = Bonneville LE; 'L' = Parisienne; 'T' = Parisienne Brougham. In sixth and seventh position are two digits that denote body type: '08' = three-door hatchback coupe; '27' = two-door coupe; '37' = two-door coupe; '77' = three-door hatchback; '87' = two-door coupe; '19' = four-door six-window sedan; '68' = five-door hatchback sedan; '69' = four-door four-window sedan; '35' = four-door station wagon. Symbol eight is an engine code: 'C' = L4-98 two-barrel; '0' = L4-109 FI; 'J' = turbo L4-109 FI; 'R' or '2' = L4-122 FI; 'X' or '1' = L4-151 FI; 'Z' = H.O. V-6-173 two-barrel; 'A' = V-6-231 two-barrel; 'T' = diesel V-6-262; 'H' = V-8-305 four-barrel; 'G' = H.O. V-8-305; 'N' = diesel V-8-350. Next is a check digit. The tenth symbol denotes model year ('E' = 1984). Symbol eleven is a plant code: 'B' = Baltimore; 'L' = Van Nuys, Calif.; 'N' = Norwood, Ohio; 'P' = Pontiac, Mich.; 'T' = Tarrytown, N.Y.; 'X' = Fairfax, Kan.; 'Y' = Wilmington, Del.; '7' = Lordstown, Ohio; '1' = Oshawa, Ontario; '2' = St. Therese, Quebec. The final six digits are the sequential serial number.

1984 Pontiac Fiero Indy Pace Car Replica. (P)

FIERO -- SERIES 2P -- FOUR -- Displaying little trim apart from a tiny shield emblem ahead of the front hood, Fiero was described as a "revolutionary two-seat, mid-engine sports car," the first such model built in America. The sleek (if somewhat stubby) wedge shape with compact front area offered a drag coefficient of 0.377. Glass surfaces were nearly flush with the body. Headlamps were hidden. Flush-mounted at the rear were black, full-width, neutral-density reflex taillamps. If trim was absent, black accents were not. "Enduraflex" body panel skins were corrosion-resistant. SMC panels went on horizontal portions (hood, roof, decklid, upper rear quarter panel). Reinforced reaction injection molded (RRIM) urethane panels with higher resistance to dents were used in vulnerable spots, including front fenders and doors.

Fiero used a space frame of high-strength steel, described as similar to a racing car's roll cage. Rear-wheel drive, Fiero rode a 93.4 in. wheelbase and carried a 92 hp, 151 cid (2.5-liter) four-cylinder engine. Three models were available: coupe with four-speed transmission, 2.42:1 axle ratio and 13 inch tires; sport coupe with 4.10:1 axle ratio; and an SE with special WS6 performance handling package and standard rear deck luggage rack. Inside the cockpit was a free-standing instrument cluster with electric speedometer, trip odometer, gas gauge, voltmeter, and temperature gauge. Lights warned of door or engine compartment lid ajar, upshift indicator, seatbelts not affixed, oil pressure, and need to check engine. A column-mounted lever controlled turn signals, dimmer, wiper/washer, and (optional) cruise control. Fiero standard equipment included a four-speed manual transmission, P185/80R13 blackwall SBR tires, retractable halogen headlamps, driver's remote mirror, bodyside moldings, rub strips, full-length console, tachometer, map pocket, reclining bucket seats, and four-spoke steering wheel. SE had P215/80R13 tires and a padded Formula steering wheel.

1984 Pontiac Fiero coupe (rear view). OCW

FIERO (FOUR)

Model Number	Body/Style Number	Body Type & Seating	Factory Price	Shipping Weight	Prod. Total
2P	E37	2-dr Cpe-2P	7999	2458	7099
2P	M37	2-dr Spt Cpe-2P	8499	2458	62,070
2P	F37	2-dr SE Cpe-2P	9599	2458	67,671

1000 -- SERIES 2T -- FOUR -- As before, the Chevette clone came in three- and five-door hatchback form. A new sport package included a black spoiler, sport striping, black sport mirrors, special handling components, and formula steering wheel. Base 1000 engine was the 98 cid (1.6-liter) overhead-cam four, with four-speed manual gearbox. Five-speed manual shift was optional, as was three-speed automatic. Standard equipment included an AM radio, front air dam, clock, mini console, black/bright grille, argent styled steel Rally wheels, reclining front bucket seats, black rocker panel moldings, black bumper guards and rub strips, and locking glovebox.

1000 (FOUR)

Model Number	Body/Style Number	Body Type & Seating	Factory Price	Shipping Weight	Prod. Total
2T	L08	3-dr Hatch-4P	5621	2081	19,628
2T	L68	5-dr Hatch-4P	5824	2130	17,118

1984 Pontiac 1000 hatchback sedan. (P)

1984 Pontiac 2000 Sunbird convertible. (P)

2000 SUNBIRD -- SERIES 2J -- FOUR -- Biggest news for Sunbird was a turbocharged 1.8-liter overhead-cam engine, standard on S/E and optional in base and LE models (except wagons). Pontiac claimed the turbo could hit 60 mph in 9 seconds with standard four-speed manual gearbox. Along with the turbo four came a WS6 performance handling package, P205/60R14 Goodyear Eagle GT steel-belted radial tires on new turbo wheels, tachometer, boost gauge, and power steering. Introduced in 1983, the LE convertible included a power top, five-speed manual transmission, dual sport mirrors (driver's remote), power windows, special moldings, AM radio, tinted glass, power brakes and steering, and rear-seat entrance lamps. Styling was similar to 1983, but lower air slots were narrower, without the former eggcrate pattern. Clear fog lamps replaced the usual small inset grilles on S/E and LE, giving them the look of 6000 STE. Standard equipment included a five-speed gearbox, Rally wheels, reclining front bucket seats, power brakes, P175/80R13 glass-belted tires, bumper rub strips, digital clock, console, and side window defoggers. LE added an AM radio, Formula three-spoke steering wheel, cloth bucket seats, bright rocker panel moldings, and fog lamps. SE included a tachometer, power steering, leather-wrapped steering wheel, turbo cast aluminum wheels, two-tone paint, black rocker panel moldings, P205/60R14 tires, and handling package. Convertibles had power steering, tachometer, power windows, power top, tinted glass, bright rocker moldings, and sport mirrors (driver's remote).

1984 Pontiac 2000 Sunbird three-door hatchback. OCW

Model Number	Body/Style Number	Body Type & Seating	Factory Price	Shipping Weight	Prod. Total
2000 SUNBIRD (FOUR)					
2J	B27	2-dr Cpe-5P	6675	2353	53,070
2J	B77	3-dr Hatch-5P	6995	2413	12,245
2J	B69	4-dr Sedan-5P	6799	2412	59,312
2J	B35	4-dr Sta Wag-5P	7115	2487	15,143
2000 SUNBIRD LE (FOUR)					
2J	C27	2-dr Cpe-5P	7333	2385	5189
2J	C69	4-dr Sedan-5P	7499	2436	11,183
2J	C35	4-dr Sta Wag-5P	7819	2517	2011
2J	N/A	2-dr Conv.-4P	11749	2449	5458
2000 SUNBIRD SE (FOUR)					
2J	D27	2-dr Cpe-5P	9019	N/A	2141
2J	D77	3-dr Hatch-5P	9489	N/A	2165
2J	D69	4-dr Sedan-5P	9185	N/A	1373

1984 Pontiac Phoenix hatchback sedan. (P)

1984 Pontiac Phoenix hatchback sedan (rear view). OCW

PHOENIX -- SERIES 2X -- FOUR/V-6 -- For its final season, the X-bodied Phoenix compact came in the same body styles and trim levels and changed little. Base engine was Pontiac's own 151 cid (2.5-liter) four with fuel injection, hooked to four-speed manual transaxle. Optional: a high-output 173 cid (2.8-liter) V-6, along with the Y99 handling suspension. Standard equipment included an AM radio, vinyl bench seating, P185/80R13 tires, color-keyed bumpers, and halogen headlamps. LE added cloth notchback seating, a three-spoke Formula steering wheel, custom wheel covers, narrow rocker panel moldings, wide black vinyl bodyside moldings, and charcoal wheel opening moldings. SE included power brakes and steering, a leather-wrapped steering wheel, tachometer, P195/70R14 tires on sport aluminum wheels, wide black rocker panel moldings, graphics, and cloth reclining front bucket seats.

Model Number	Body/Style Number	Body Type & Seating	Factory Price	Shipping Weight	Prod. Total
PHOENIX (FOUR/V-6)					
2X	Y37	2-dr Cpe-5P	7090/7440	2485/2549	7461
2X	Y68	5-dr Hatch-5P	7165/7515	2542/2606	11,545
PHOENIX LE (FOUR/V-6)					
2X	Z37	2-dr Cpe-5P	7683/8033	2526/2590	1357
2X	Z68	5-dr Hatch-5P	7816/8166	2574/2638	1783

Price Note: Phoenix V-6 prices include $100 for the required power brakes.

Model Number	Body/Style Number	Body Type & Seating	Factory Price	Shipping Weight	Prod. Total
PHOENIX SJ (V-6)					
2X	T37	2-dr Cpe-5P	9071	2581	701

1984 Pontiac Firebird Trans Am T-top coupe. OCW

1984 Pontiac Firebird Trans Am T-top coupe. (P)

FIREBIRD -- SERIES 2F -- FOUR/V-6/V-8 -- Trans Am got a performance boost with a high-output four-barrel version of the 305 cid (5.0-liter) V-8. That powerplant, first offered as an option late in the 1983 model year, replaced the former crossfire fuel-injected V-8. It was rated 190 hp @ 4800 rpm, and produced 240 lb.-ft. of torque. This year's Trans Am came with a standard five-speed manual gearbox and 3.73:1 axle ratio, ready to deliver 0-60 mph times in the 7.2 second neighborhood (and quarter miles claimed in the low 15s). Four-cylinder engines in the base Firebird also got a boost with a swirl port combustion chamber, 9.0:1 compression ratio, and cooler spark plugs. Firebird S/E again came with a standard 173 cid (2.8-liter) high-output V-6. New S/E features included a color-coordinated, leather-wrapped steering wheel, shift lever, and parking brake handle. As before, Firebird could have the four-cylinder engine or 305 V-8 instead of its standard V-6. Trans Am could get an optional aero package, in 15 color combinations, including new front/rear fascia, bigger air dam, door and rocker panel extensions, and wide lower body graphics. Also available: a Recaro package with gold strobe graphics and gold deep-dish turbo wheels. Appearance was similar to 1983. Base Firebird equipment included a 151 cid (2.5-liter) four with four-speed manual shift, power brakes/steering, P195/75R14 tires on Rally sport wheels, tinted lift-back glass, and vinyl reclining front bucket seats. S/E included front and rear stabilizer bars, the high-output 2.8-liter V-6, five-speed gearbox, handling suspension, tachometer, leather map pocket, cloth seat upholstery, lower accent paint (with striping), sport mirrors, color-keyed bodyside moldings, and P205/70R14 tires on turbo cast aluminum wheels. Trans Am included the 305 V-8 with five-speed, black aero turbo cast aluminum wheels, rear wheel opening flares, rear spoiler, and front fender air extractors.

Model Number	Body/Style Number	Body Type & Seating	Factory Price	Shipping Weight	Prod. Total
FIREBIRD (FOUR/V-6)					
2F	S87	2-dr Cpe-4P	8349/8724	2866/2948	62,621

Engine Note: A 305 cid V-8 cost $300 more than the V-6 on base Firebird.

Model Number	Body/Style Number	Body Type & Seating	Factory Price	Shipping Weight	Prod. Total
FIREBIRD S/E (V-6/V-8)					
2F	X87	2-dr Cpe-4P	10649/10849	2965/3145	10,309
FIREBIRD TRANS AM (V-8)					
2F	W87	2-dr Cpe-4P	10699	3107	55,374

1984 Pontiac 6000 LE station wagon. (P)

6000 -- SERIES 2A -- FOUR/V-6 -- Aero restyling highlighted this year's mid-size 6000 series, headed by the performance-oriented 6000 STE, which added an electronic instrument panel with digital speedometer and analog tachometer. A new bar-chart display showed fuel level, temperature, and voltage. STE also included a programmable Driver's Information Center that monitored car systems. Electronics also controlled the ride, and the stereo radio (which had a five-band graphic equalizer). No other Pontiac offered this radio. At the suspension, an air compressor automatically provided pressure to the shocks to maintain optimum height and increase the spring rate as the car's load changed. As before, 6000 STE had a minimal option list: just a choice of six two-tone colors, suede leather interior, and removable sun roof. A high-output 173 cid (2.8-liter) V-6 rated 130 hp provided the power to a three-speed automatic transaxle. Four-wheel disc brakes were new this year. A station wagon joined the basic 6000 coupe/sedan lineup. Base engine was a 151 cid (2.5-liter) four with fuel injection, hooked to three-speed automatic transaxle. Optional again: a 173 cid (2.8-liter) V-6 or diesel V-6. Wider wraparound taillamps now reached to the backup lenses alongside the license plate. Grille inserts now had a pattern made up of both vertical and horizontal bars. Standard 6000 equipment included power brakes and steering, AM radio, black rocker panel moldings, black bumper rub strips, mini bumper guards, vinyl notchback front seating, P185/75R14 tires on Rally wheels, bodyside moldings with black vinyl insert, and wheel opening moldings. LE added a black pillar appliqué, cloth upholstery, locking fuel filler door, and map pockets. 6000 STE included the high-output V-6, power windows, AM/FM stereo radio with cassette, black wide bodyside and rocker panel moldings, two-tone paint, air conditioning, four-wheel power disc brakes, tinted glass, electronic ride control, and reclining 45/45 front seating with cloth upholstery and dual six-way adjustment with lumbar support. 6000 STE tires were P195/70R14 blackwalls.

1984 Pontiac 6000 LE station wagon (rear view). OCW

Model Number	Body/Style Number	Body Type & Seating	Factory Price	Shipping Weight	Prod. Total
6000 (FOUR/V-6)					
2A	F27	2-dr Cpe-5P	8699/8949	2693/2741	4171
2A	F19	4-dr Sed-5P	8873/9123	2736/2779	35,202
2A	F35	4-dr Sta Wag-5P	9221/9471	2911/ --	8423
2A	G27	2-dr LE Cpe-5P	9142/9392	2711/2754	4731
2A	G19	4-dr LE Sed-5P	9292/9542	2750/2793	41,218
2A	G35	4-dr LE Wag-5P	9612/9862	2919/ --	9211
6000 STE (V-6)					
2A	H19	4-dr Sed-5P	14437	2823	19,236

GRAND PRIX -- SERIES 2G -- V-6/V-8 -- The rear-drive, six-passenger personal-luxury Pontiac again came in three models: base, LE, and Brougham. Appearance was similar to 1983, with many vertical bars in the side-by-side twin grilles. Standard equipment included the 231 cid (3.8-liter) V-6, three-speed automatic, power brakes/steering, P195/75R14 SBR tires, cushioned steering wheel, formal rear quarter windows, narrow rocker panel moldings, wheel opening moldings, chrome lower bumpers, black bumper guards, clock, and woodgrain dash. LE added wide rocker panel moldings with extensions, a four-spoke sport steering wheel, color-keyed sport mirrors, and wide windowsill and hood edge moldings. Brougham included power windows, 55/45 seating, and teakwood grain instrument panel.

1984 Pontiac Grand Prix coupe. (P)

Model Number	Body/Style Number	Body Type & Seating	Factory Price	Shipping Weight	Prod. Total
GRAND PRIX (V-6/V-8)					
2G	J37	2-dr Cpe-6P	9145/9520	N/A	36,893
GRAND PRIX LE (V-6/V-8)					
2G	K37	2-dr Cpe-6P	9624/9999	3207	31,037
GRAND PRIX BROUGHAM (V-6/V-8)					
2G	P37	2-dr Cpe-6P	10299/10674	3217	9514

1984 Pontiac Bonneville LJ sedan. (P)

BONNEVILLE -- SERIES 2G -- V-6/V-8 -- The station wagon was dropped from the Bonneville line this year, but an LE model joined the base and Brougham four-door sedans. Base engine was the 231 cid (3.8-liter) V-6 with three-speed automatic; optional, a 305 cid (5.0-liter) gas V-8 or 350 diesel, with either three- or four-speed automatic. Appearance was similar to 1983. Standard equipment included the 231 cid V-6, three-speed automatic, power brakes/steering, wide rocker panel moldings with extensions, P195/75R14 tires, clock, bumper guards and rub strips, and wheel opening moldings. Brougham added 55/45 cloth seating, opera lamps, and padded vinyl Cordova top.

1984 Pontiac Bonneville LE four-door sedan. OCW

Model Number	Body/Style Number	Body Type & Seating	Factory Price	Shipping Weight	Prod. Total
BONNEVILLE (V-6/V-8)					
2G	N69	4-dr Sed-6P	9131/9506	3214/3290	40,908
2G	S69	4-dr LE Sed-6P	9358/9733	3275/3351	17,451
BONNEVILLE BROUGHAM (V-6/V-8)					
2G	R69	4-dr Sed-6P	9835/10210	3210/3286	15,030

1984 Pontiac Parisienne four-door sedan. (P)

1984 Pontiac Parisienne four-door sedan (rear view). OCW

PARISIENNE -- SERIES 2B -- V-6/V-8 -- Pontiac's full-size rear-drive sedan held six passengers in the traditional style. Also available: a four-door station wagon and Brougham sedan. All models rode a 116-in. wheelbase. Appearance was similar to 1983. Each of the twin grilles contained six vertical bars, with added vertical bars within each segment. Large park/signal lamps were in the bumper, with quad rectangular headlamps above. Wraparound amber side markers extended outward from the headlamp framework. Buick's 231 cid (3.8-liter) V-6 was the base powerplant, with three-speed automatic transmission. Wagons carried the 305 cid (5.0-liter) V-8 and four-speed overdrive automatic; that combination was optional on sedans. All models could also get the Oldsmobile 350 V-8 diesel. Standard equipment included power brakes/steering, cloth 50/50 seating, narrow bright rocker panel moldings, color-keyed bodyside moldings, two-tone paint, bumper rub strips, quartz clock, P205/75R15 tires, and bright wheel opening moldings. Brougham had cloth 55/45 seating with passenger recliner.

Model Number	Body/Style Number	Body Type & Seating	Factory Price	Shipping Weight	Prod. Total
PARISIENNE (V-6/V-8)					
2B	L69	4-dr Sed-6P	9881/10431	N/A	18,713
2B	L35	4-dr Sta Wag-6P	--/10394	3948	16,599
PARISIENNE BROUGHAM (V-6/V-8)					
2B	T69	4-dr Sed-6P	10281/10831	N/A	25,212

FACTORY PRICE AND WEIGHT NOTE: Prices and weights to left of slash are for V-6, to right for V-8 engine except Phoenix/Firebird/6000, four and V-6.

ENGINE DATA

BASE FOUR (1000): Inline. Overhead cam. Four-cylinder. Cast iron block and head. Displacement: 98 cu. in. (1.6 liters). Bore & stroke: 3.23 x 2.98 in. Compression ratio: 9.0:1. Brake horsepower: 65 @ 5200 rpm. Torque: 80 lb.-ft. @ 3200 rpm. Five main bearings. Hydraulic valve lifters. Carburetor: two-barrel VIN Code: C. **BASE FOUR (2000):** Inline. Overhead cam. Four-cylinder. Cast iron block and aluminum head. Displacement: 109 cu. in. (1.8 liters). Bore & stroke: 3.34 x 3.13 in. Compression ratio: 9.0:1. Brake horsepower: 84 @ 5200 rpm. Torque: 102 lb.-ft. @ 2800 rpm. Five main bearings. Hydraulic valve lifters. Electronic fuel injection. VIN Code: O. **OPTIONAL TURBO FOUR (2000):** Same as 109 cid four above, with port fuel injection and turbocharger. Compression ratio: 8.0:1. Horsepower: 150 @ 5600 rpm. Torque: 150 lb.-ft. @ 2800 rpm. VIN Code: J. **OPTIONAL FOUR (2000):** Inline. Overhead cam. Four-cylinder. Cast iron block and head. Displacement: 122 cu. in. (2.0 liters). Bore & stroke: 3.50 x 3.15 in. Compression ratio: 9.3:1. Brake horsepower: 88 @ 4800 rpm. Torque: 110 lb.-ft. @ 2400 rpm. Five main bearings. Hydraulic valve lifters. Electronic fuel injection. VIN Code: P. **BASE FOUR (Fiero, Phoenix, Firebird, 6000):** Inline. Overhead valve. Four-cylinder. Cast iron block and head. Displacement: 151 cu. in. (2.5 liters). Bore & stroke: 4.00 x 3.00 in. Compression ratio: 9.0:1. Brake horsepower: 92 @ 4000-4400 rpm. Torque: 132-134 lb.-ft. @ 2800 rpm. Five main bearings. Hydraulic valve lifters. Throttle-body fuel injection. VIN Code: R or 2. **OPTIONAL V-6 (Phoenix, Firebird, 6000):** 60-degree, overhead valve six-cylinder. Cast iron block and aluminum head. Displacement: 173 cu. in. (2.8 liters). Bore & stroke: 3.50 x 3.00 in. Compression ratio: 8.5:1. Brake horsepower: 112 @ 4800 rpm (Firebird, 107 @ 4800). Torque: 145 lb.-ft. @ 2100 rpm. Four main bearings. Hydraulic valve lifters. Carburetor: two-barrel Rochester E2SE. VIN Code: X or 1.

BASE V-6 (Phoenix SJ, Firebird S/E, 6000 STE): High-output version of 173 cid V-6 above. Compression ratio: 8.9:1. Horsepower: 130 @ 5400 rpm (Firebird, 125 hp). Torque: 145 lb.-ft. @ 2400 rpm. VIN Code: Z. **BASE V-6** (Grand Prix, Bonneville, Parisienne): 90-degree, overhead-valve V-6. Cast iron block and head. Displacement: 231 cu. in. (3.8 liters). Bore & stroke: 3.80 x 3.40 in. Compression ratio: 8.0:1. Brake horsepower: 110 @ 3800 rpm. Torque: 190 lb.-ft. @ 1600 rpm. Four main bearings. Hydraulic valve lifters. Carburetor: two-barrel Rochester E2ME. Buick-built. VIN Code: A.

DIESEL V-6 (6000): 90-degree, overhead valve V-6. Cast iron block and head. Displacement: 260 cu. in. (4.3 liters). Bore & stroke: 4.06 x 3.38 in. Compression ratio: 21.6:1. Brake horsepower: 85 @ 3600 rpm. Torque: 165 lb.-ft. @ 1600 rpm. Four main bearings. Hydraulic valve lifters. Fuel injection. VIN Code: T.

BASE V-8 (Firebird Trans Am); OPTIONAL (Firebird, Grand Prix, Bonneville): 90-degree, overhead valve V-8. Cast iron block and head. Displacement: 305 cu. in. (5.0 liters). Bore & stroke: 3.74 x 3.48 in. Compression ratio: 8.6:1. Brake horsepower: 150 @ 4000 rpm. Torque: 240 lb.-ft. @ 2400 rpm. Five main bearings. Hydraulic valve lifters. Carburetor: four-barrel Rochester E4ME. Chevrolet-built. VIN Code: H. OPTIONAL V-8 (Trans Am): High-output version of 305 cid V-8. Compression ratio: 9.5:1. Horsepower: 190 @ 4800 rpm. Torque: 240 lb.-ft. @ 3200 rpm.

DIESEL V-8 (Grand Prix, Bonneville, Parisienne): 90-degree, overhead valve V-8. Cast iron block and head. Displacement: 350 cu. in. (5.7 liters). Bore & stroke: 4.06 x 3.39 in. Compression ratio: 22.5:1. Brake horsepower: 105 @ 3200 rpm. Torque: 200 lb.-ft. @ 1600 rpm. Five main bearings. Hydraulic valve lifters. Fuel injection. Oldsmobile-built. VIN Code: N.

1984 Pontiac Fiero coupe. OCW

CHASSIS DATA: Wheelbase: (Fiero) 93.4 in.; (1000 three-door) 94.3 in.; (1000 five-door) 97.3 in.; (2000) 101.2 in.; (Phoenix) 104.9 in.; (Firebird) 101.0 in.; (6000) 104.9 in.; (Grand Prix) 108.1 in.; (Bonneville) 108.1 in.; (Parisienne) 115.9 in. Overall Length: (Fiero) 160.7 in.; (1000 three-door) 161.9 in.; (1000 five-door) 164.7 in.; (2000) 173.7 in.; (2000 wag) 175.8 in.; (Phoenix) 183.0 in.; (Firebird) 189.9 in.; (6000) 188.1 in.; (6000 wag) 191.2 in.; (G.P.) 201.9 in.; (Bonneville) 198.5 in.; (Parisienne) 212.0 in.; (Parisienne wag) 215.0 in. Height: (Fiero) 46.9 in.; (1000) 52.8 in.; (2000 cpe) 51.9 in.; (2000 conv.) 52.7 in.; (2000 sed) 53.8 in.; (2000 wag) 54.1 in.; (Phoenix) 53.7 in.; (Firebird) 49.7 in.; (6000) 53.3-53.8 in.; (G.P.) 54.7 in.; (Bonneville) 55.8 in.; (Parisienne) 56.4 in.; (Parisienne wag) 58.1 in. Width: (Fiero) 68.9 in.; (1000) 61.8 in.; (2000 cpe/conv.) 65.9 in.; (2000 hatch) 66.6 in.; (2000 sed/wag) 66.2 in.; (Phoenix cpe) 69.0-69.1 in.; (Firebird) 72.0 in.; (6000) 72.0 in.; (G.P.) 72.3 in.; (Bonneville) 71.6 in.; (Parisienne) 75.2 in. exc. wagon, 79.3 in. Front Tread: (Fiero) 57.8 in.; (1000) 51.2 in.; (2000) 55.4 in.; (Phoenix) 58.7 in.; (Firebird) 60.7 in.; (6000) 58.7 in.; (G.P.) 58.5 in.; (Bonneville) 58.5 in.; (Parisienne) 61.7 in.; (Parisienne wag) 62.2 in. Rear Tread: (Fiero) 58.7 in.; (1000) 51.2 in.; (2000) 55.2 in.; (Phoenix) 57.0 in.; (Firebird) 61.6 in.; (6000) 57.0 in.; (G.P.) 57.8 in.; (Bonneville) 57.8 in.; (Parisienne) 60.7 in.; (Parisienne wag) 64.1 in. Standard Tires: (Fiero) P185/80R13; (1000) P155/80R13; (2000) P175/80R13 GBR BSW; (2000 SE/conv.) P195/70R13 SBR; (Phoenix) P185/80R13 GBR; (Phoenix SE) P195/70R14; (Firebird) P195/75R14; (Firebird Trans Am) P205/70R14 SBR BSW; (6000) P185/75R14 SBR; (6000 STE) P195/70R14 SBR; (Grand Prix) P195/75R14 SBR; (Bonneville) P195/75R14 SBR; (Parisienne sed) P205/75R15 SBR; (Parisienne wag) P225/75R15 SBR.

TECHNICAL: Transmission: Four-speed manual standard on Fiero, 1000, Phoenix, and base Firebird. Five-speed manual standard on 2000 and Firebird S/E, optional on 1000. Three-speed Turbo-Hydramatic standard on other models, optional on all. Four-speed overdrive automatic available on Firebird, 6000, Grand Prix, Bonneville, and Parisienne. Standard final drive ratio: (Fiero) 4.10:1 w/four-speed, 3.18:1 w/auto.; (1000) 3.36:1; (2000) 2.55:1 w/five-speed, 2.96:1 or 3.32:1 w/auto.; (Phoenix four) 3.33:1 or 3.43:1 w/auto.; (Phoenix V-6) 2.69:1 w/four-speed, 2.84:1 w/auto.; (Phoenix H.O. V-6) 2.96:1 w/four-speed, 3.33:1 w/auto.; (Firebird) 3.42:1 w/four-speed, 3.73:1 w/four and five-speed or auto.; 3.42:1 or 3.23:1 w/V-6, 3.73:1 w/H.O. V-6, 3.73:1 or 3.23:1 w/V-8; (Firebird H.O. V-8) 3.23:1 w/five-speed, 3.42:1 w/auto.; (6000) 2.39:1 w/four, 2.84:1 or 3.06:1 w/V-6,

3.33:1 w/H.O. V-6; (Grand Prix/Bonneville) 2.41:1 w/V-6, 2.29:1 or 2.73:1 w/V-8; (Parisienne) 2.73:1. Steering: (Fiero/1000/2000/Phoenix/6000) rack and pinion; (others) recirculating ball. Front Suspension: (2000/Phoenix/6000) MacPherson struts w/lower control arms and anti-sway bar; (Firebird) modified MacPherson struts w/coil springs between lower control arm and X-member; (others) coil springs and anti-sway bar. Rear Suspension: (Fiero) MacPherson struts w/lower control arms; (1000) four-link rigid axle w/torque tube and Panhard rod; (2000) beam axle w/coil springs and trailing arms; (Phoenix) single-beam trailing axle w/track bar and coil springs; (Firebird) torque arm/track bar w/coil springs and anti-sway bar; (6000) trailing arms and beam axle w/coil springs and integral anti-sway bar; (Bonneville/Grand Prix/Parisienne) four-link rigid axle with coil springs, lower trailing radius arms and upper torque arms. Brakes: Front disc, rear drum except 6000 STE, four-wheel disc. Ignition: Electronic. Body construction: (Fiero/1000/2000/Phoenix/6000) unit; (others) separate body and frame. Fuel Tank: (Fiero) 10.2 gal.; (1000) 12.5 gal.; (2000) 13.6 gal.; (Phoenix) 14.6 gal.; (Firebird) 15.9 gal.; (6000) 15.7 gal.; (Grand Prix/Bonneville) 18.1 gal.; (Parisienne sed) 25 gal.; (Parisienne wag) 22 gal.

DRIVETRAIN OPTIONS: Engines: Turbo 1.8-liter four: 2000 ($1309-$1546). 2.0-liter four: 2000 ($50 credit). 151 cid four: Firebird S/E ($350 credit). 173 cid V-6: Phoenix/Firebird/6000 ($250). H.O. 173 cid V-6: Phoenix ($400). Diesel 262 cid V-6: 6000 ($575). 305 cid, four-barrel V-8: Firebird S/E ($550); Firebird S/E ($220); Grand Prix/Bonneville/Parisienne ($375). H.O. 305 cid V-8: Trans Am ($530). Diesel 350 cid V-8: Grand Prix/Bonneville/Parisienne ($801). Transmission/Differential: Four-speed manual transmission: 2000 ($75 credit). Five-speed manual transmission: 1000 ($75); Firebird ($125). Three-speed automatic transmission: 1000 ($395); 2000 ($320-$395); Phoenix/Firebird ($425). Four-speed automatic transmission: Firebird ($525); S/E and Trans Am ($295); 6000/Grand Prix/Bonneville/Parisienne ($175). Limited-slip differential: Firebird/G.P./Bonneville/Parisienne ($95). Brakes/Steering: Power brakes: 1000 ($95); Phoenix ($100). Power four-wheel disc brakes: Firebird ($179) but no charge (NC) with performance pkg. Power steering: 1000/2000 ($204); Phoenix ($215). Suspension: Electronic suspension: 6000 ($165). Rally tuned suspension: 2000 ($48); Phoenix/6000/Firebird/G.P. ($50). Rally tuned suspension: 2000 ($48); Phoenix/6000/Firebird/G.P. ($49). Superlift shock absorbers: 6000/G.P./Bonneville/Parisienne ($64). H.D. springs: Bonneville ($16). Other: H.D. cooling ($40-$70). H.D. battery ($25-$26) exc. diesel ($52). H.D. alternator ($25-$51). Engine block heater ($18-$19). California emissions ($99).

OPTION PACKAGES: Fiero special performance pkg. ($459). 1000 sport/handling pkg. ($464). 1000 custom trim ($167). 2000 custom exterior group ($86). 2000 custom trim group ($308-$358). 2000 security pkg. ($19). Phoenix upper exterior group ($98-$108); lower ($56). Firebird Trans Am Recaro option ($3061-$3160). Firebird S/E and Trans Am special performance pkg. ($134-$408). Firebird aero exterior appearance pkg. ($199). Firebird black appearance pkg. ($123-$152). Firebird custom exterior ($51-$112). 6000 rally pkg. ($341-$449). 6000 custom exterior ($56). 6000 wagon security pkg. ($44). Grand Prix Brougham Landau pkg. ($469). Lamp groups ($30-$47) except 6000 LE ($79-$88).

1984 Pontiac 6000 STE four-door sedan. OCW

MAJOR CONVENIENCE/APPEARANCE OPTIONS: Air conditioning ($630-$730). Cruise control ($175). Power seat ($210-$430); N/A on 1000/Fiero. Power windows ($185-$260); N/A on 1000. Cornering lamps: Bonneville/G.P. ($68); Parisienne ($55). Power glass sun roof: 2000 ($300); Grand Prix ($895). Removable glass sun roof: Fiero/2000/Phoenix/6000 ($300). Hatch roof: Firebird/Grand Prix ($825-$861). Full vinyl cordova top: Bonneville ($160). Padded cordova landau top: Phoenix ($220); G.P. ($245). Sport landau top: 6000 ($735-$773). Padded top: Bonneville ($245); Parisienne ($185). Louvered rear sunshields: 2000 ($199); Firebird ($210). Two-tone paint: 2000 ($101-$151); Phoenix ($105-$135); Firebird ($205-$291); G.P./Bonneville ($205). Lear Siegler bucket seats: 2000 ($400). Firebird ($400-$759); leather ($945-$1304). Third seat: 6000 wagon ($215). Woodgrain paneling: 6000/LE wagon ($250-$325); Parisienne wagon ($387).

181

HISTORICAL FOOTNOTES: Introduced: September 22, 1983. Model year production: 827,576. Calendar year production (U.S.): 491,370. Calendar year sales by U.S. dealers: 704,684. Model year sales by U.S. dealers: 707,007. After four bad years, Pontiac enjoyed a gigantic surge in production for model year 1984. Sales, too, rose markedly. Sunbird and 6000 sales showed the greatest gains, along with the big Parisienne. The new Fiero delivered a claimed 12.5 second time to 60 mph with the standard four-speed manual gearbox, as well as EPA mileage estimates of 27 (city) and 47 (highway). With 4.10:1 axle, acceleration time dropped by one second. Pontiac became part of the new GM C-P-C group, and J. Michael Losh took over as the division's general manager.

1985 PONTIAC

Grand Am was the big name for 1985: a new "driver-oriented" sports coupe. It joined a set of recently introduced models intended to expand Pontiac's performance image beyond the long-lived Trans Am. That list included the plastic-bodied Fiero, turbo-powered Sunbird, and European-influenced 6000 STE.

I.D. DATA: Pontiac's 17-symbol Vehicle Identification Number (VIN) was on the upper left surface of the instrument panel, visible through the windshield. The first three symbols ('1G2') indicate Pontiac division. Symbol four is restraint system ('A' = manual seatbelts). Symbol five is car line/series: 'E' = Fiero; 'M' = Fiero Sport; 'F' = Fiero SE; 'G' = Fiero GT; 'L' = T1000; 'B' = Sunbird; 'C' = Sunbird LE; 'D' = Sunbird SE; 'E' = Grand Am; 'V' = Grand Am LE; 'F' = 6000; 'G' = 6000 LE; 'H' = 6000 STE; 'S' = Firebird; 'X' = Firebird SE; 'W' = Firebird Trans Am; 'J' = Grand Prix; 'K' = Grand Prix LE; 'P' = Grand Prix Brougham; 'N' = Bonneville; 'R' = Bonneville Brougham; 'S' = Bonneville LE; 'L' = Parisienne; 'T' = Parisienne Brougham. In sixth and seventh position are two digits that denote body type: '08' = three-door hatchback coupe; '27' = two-door coupe; '37' = two-door coupe; '77' = three-door hatchback; '87' = two-door coupe; '67' = two-door conv. coupe; '19' = four-door six-window sedan; '68' = 5-dr. hatchback sedan; '69' = 4-dr. four-window sedan; '35' = 4-dr. station wagon. Symbol eight is an engine code: 'C' = L4-98 two-barrel; 'O' = L4-109 FI; 'J' = turbo L4-109 FI; 'P' = L4-122 FI; 'U' or '2' = L4-151 FI; 'X' or '5' = V-6-173 two-barrel; '5', '9' or 'W' = V-6-173 FI; 'L' = V-6-181 FI; 'A' = V-6-231 two-barrel; '7' = V-6-262 FI; 'T' = diesel V-6-262; 'H' = V-8-305 four-barrel; 'G' = H.O. V-8-305; 'F' = V-8-305 FI; 'N' = diesel V-8-350. Next is a check digit. The tenth symbol denotes model year ('F' = 1985). Symbol eleven is a plant code: 'A' = Lakewood, Ga.; 'L' = Van Nuys, Calif.; 'N' = Norwood, Ohio; 'P' = Pontiac, Mich.; 'T' = Tarrytown, N.Y.; 'X' = Fairfax, Kan.; 'M' = Lansing, Mich.; '7' = Lordstown, Ohio; '1' = Oshawa, Ontario; '2' = St. Therese, Quebec. The final six digits are the sequential serial number.

1985 Pontiac Fiero GT coupe. (P)

FIERO -- SERIES 2P -- FOUR -- A new GT model joined the original trio this year, carrying a 173 cid (2.8-liter) V-6 engine with multi-port fuel injection. The new V-6 was optional in sport and SE coupes. The GT's appearance stemmed from the 1984 Fiero Indianapolis 500 Pace Car, including new "Enduraflex" front/rear fascia, rocker panel extensions, and (optional) decklid spoiler. A WS6 performance suspension and P215/60R14 Eagle GT tires (on turbo wheels) were available. The standard 151 cid (2.5- liter) four came with a new Isuzu five-speed manual gearbox. V-6 models had a four-speed. Either one could get three-speed automatic. Otherwise, appearance was similar to 1984.

FIERO (FOUR)

Model Number	Body/Style Number	Body Type & Seating	Factory Price	Shipping Weight	Prod. Total
2P	E37	2-dr. Cpe-2P	8495	2454	5280
2P	M37	2-dr. Spt Cpe-2P	8995	2500	23,823
2P	F37	2-dr. SE Cpe-2P	9995	2525	24,734
2P	G37	2-dr. GT Cpe-2P	11795	N/A	22,534

1985 Pontiac 1000 hatchback sedan. (P)

1000 -- SERIES 2T -- FOUR -- At the entry-level end of the Pontiac scale, both three- and five-door models could now have the optional five-speed manual gearbox. Base engine remained the 1.6-liter overhead-cam four, with four-speed manual. Seven new body colors were available, and four new interior colors. Appearance was similar to 1984.

1000 (FOUR)

Model Number	Body/Style Number	Body Type & Seating	Factory Price	Shipping Weight	Prod. Total
2T	L08	3-dr. Hatch-4P	5445	2081	8647
2T	L68	5-dr. Hatch-4P	5695	2130	8216

1985 Pontiac Sunbird LE Turbo convertible. (P)

SUNBIRD -- SERIES 2J -- FOUR -- Turbo power was available under Sunbird hoods in the form of a 150 hp version of the 1.8-liter OHC four-cylinder engine. That powerplant had multi-port fuel injection, and delivered 150 lb.-ft. of torque. The turbo option was available on both base and LE models (but not the wagon). It included P205/60R14 SBR tires on turbo wheels, WS6 suspension, tachometer and turbo boost gauge, power steering, new hood louvers, and special turbo identification. Other models had a non-turbo edition of the 1.8 engine. Two-door notchback and hatchback coupes were offered, along with a sedan, four-door station wagon, and convertible. Appearance changed little from 1984. Standard equipment included a non-turbo 1.8-liter four, five-speed manual transmission, reclining front bucket seats, remote hatch/trunk release, and console. LE added an AM radio and wheel trim rings. Convertibles had power steering, power windows, and tinted glass. Sunbird SE included the turbocharged engine and four-speed manual transaxle, as well as power steering and sport mirrors.

1985 Pontiac Sunbird SE three-door hatchback. OCW

Model Number	Body/Style Number	Body Type & Seating	Factory Price	Shipping Weight	Prod. Total
SUNBIRD (FOUR)					
2J	B27	2-dr. Cpe-5P	6875	2353	39,721
2J	B77	3-dr. Hatch-5P	7215	2413	5235
2J	B69	4-dr. Sedan-5P	6995	2412	44,553
2J	B35	4-dr. Sta Wag-5P	7335	2487	7371
SUNBIRD LE (FOUR)					
2J	C27	2-dr. Cpe-5P	7555	2385	3424
2J	C69	4-dr. Sedan-5P	7725	2436	6287
2J	C35	4-dr. Sta Wag-5P	8055	2517	1036
2J	C67	2-dr. Conv.-4P	12035	N/A	2114
SUNBIRD SE (FOUR)					
2J	D27	2-dr. Cpe-5P	9295	2360	965
2J	D77	3-dr. Hatch-5P	9765	2435	535
2J	D69	4-dr. Sedan-5P	9455	2416	658

1985 Pontiac Grand Am LE coupe. (P)

1985 Pontiac Grand Am LE coupe (rear view). OCW

GRAND AM -- SERIES 2N -- FOUR/V-6 -- Ranked as a "sports specialty coupe," Grand Am (like many other mid-1980s domestic models) was targeted at youthful, upscale buyers who demanded good handling and performance, and might otherwise turn to imports. The five-passenger coupe came in base and LE trim. Standard engine was the fuel-injected "Tech IV" 151 cid (2.5-liter) four, with five-speed manual gearbox. A 125 hp, 181 cid (3.0-liter) V-6 with multi-port fuel injection and automatic transmission also was available. So was a Y99 rally suspension package to enhance the basic model's handling characteristics. Grand Am sported sculptured lines with smooth body curves, with Pontiac's traditional (yet modern) split grille up front. A tapered hood sloped back to a flush-fit, steeply raked windshield. Inside were reclining front bucket seats, a console, instrument panel pods close to the steering wheel, and analog speedometer and gas gauge. Full analog gauges and electronic instruments were both optional. So was a six-function Driver Information Center. Optional hi-tech turbo cast aluminum wheels and 215/60R14 Goodyear Eagle GT tires were said to give the car an "aggressive wide track stance."

Model Number	Body/Style Number	Body Type & Seating	Factory Price	Shipping Weight	Prod. Total
GRAND AM (FOUR/V-6)					
2N	E27	2-dr. Cpe-5P	7995/8480	2419/ --	40,273
GRAND AM LE (FOUR/V-6)					
2N	V27	2-dr. Cpe-5P	8485/8970	2447/ --	42,269

1985 Pontiac Firebird Trans Am T-top coupe. (P)

FIREBIRD -- SERIES 2F -- FOUR/V-6/V-8 -- According to Firebird's chief designer, John Schinella, the famed coupe became "more of a thoroughbred in 1985" with a "more aggressive" image and dramatic restyling. Also new was a V-8 powerplant with tuned-port fuel injection, intended to deliver a 0-60 MPH time in the 8.1 second neighborhood. Optional in Trans Am, the 205 hp V-8 produced 270 lb.-ft. of torque. Engine choices also included the base 151 cid (2.5-liter) four, fuel-injected 173 cid (2.8-liter) V-6, standard 5.0-liter V-8, and 190 hp high-output V-8. Firebird's standard ride/handling package now included all of the components of the former Y99 option (except tires). An improved Y99 package included 15 inch wheels. Basic appearance was similar to 1984. But Trans Am displayed new aero-tuned rocker and quarter panel extensions, a new hood with twin louvers near the front, and built-in fog lamps where the big air slots otherwise would be. Diamond spoke wheels were a new option this year.

Model Number	Body/Style Number	Body Type & Seating	Factory Price	Shipping Weight	Prod. Total
FIREBIRD (FOUR/V-6)					
2F	S87	2-dr. Cpe-4P	8763/9013	2866/2948	46,644

Engine Note: A 305 cid V-8 cost $300 more than the V-6 on base Firebird.

FIREBIRD SE (V-6/V-8)					
2F	X87	2-dr. Cpe-4P	11063/11263	2965/3145	5208
FIREBIRD TRANS AM (V-8)					
2F	W87	2-dr. Cpe-4P	11113	3107	44,028

1985 Pontiac 6000 STE four-door sedan. (AA)

6000 -- SERIES 2A -- FOUR/V-6 -- A new 173 cid (2.8-liter) V-6 engine with multi-port fuel injection was available in the 6000 series, and standard in the performance-minded 6000 STE. Base engine was a 151 cid (2.5-liter) "Tech IV" four; optional, a carbureted 2.8 V-6 or 4.3-liter diesel V-6. STE got a front/rear restyle, as well as a few body changes evident from the side. A new front fascia included a wide bumper rub strip. At the rear were full-width, neutral-density taillamps. Wider bodyside moldings were used. Standard again was an electronic instrument panel with Driver Information Center, but color was added to the cluster. In addition to coupe and sedan bodies, the 6000 again offered a station wagon with woodgrain side paneling (and optional rear-facing third seat). Grille shape was similar to 1984, but with a wider center divider bar and horizontal bars in each insert. 6000 STE again had a long standard equipment list, which included power four-wheel disc brakes, power windows, rally-tuned electronic ride control, AM/FM stereo with cassette, 45/45 cloth upholstery with six-way adjustment and lumbar support, speed control, fog lamps, dual exhausts, electronic air conditioning, and two-tone paint.

1985 Pontiac 6000 STE four-door sedan (rear view). OCW

Model Number	Body/Style Number	Body Type & Seating	Factory Price	Shipping Weight	Prod. Total
6000 (FOUR/V-6)					
2A	F27	2-dr. Cpe-5P	8899/9159	2698/2741	4493
2A	F19	4-dr. Sed-5P	9079/9339	2736/2779	54,424
2A	F35	4-dr. Sta Wag-5P	9435/9695	2815/ --	8491
2A	G27	2-dr. LE Cpe-5P	9385/9645	2711/2754	3777
2A	G19	4-dr. LE Sed-5P	9539/9799	2750/2793	54,284
2A	G35	4-dr. LE Wag-5P	9869/10129	2832/ --	8025
6000 STE (V-6)					
2A	H19	4-dr. Sed-5P	14829	2823	22,728

1985 Pontiac Grand Prix Brougham coupe. OCW

GRAND PRIX -- SERIES 2G -- V-6/V-8 -- A new vertical-bar grille was evident at Grand Prix's front end, and new taillamps at the rear. Nine new paint colors were available, making an even dozen. A Delco 2000 AM radio was standard. Base engine remained the 231 cid (3.8-liter) V-6 with three-speed automatic. Optional: the 5.0-liter V-8 with either three- or four-speed automatic. Standard equipment included formal rear quarter windows, power steering/brakes, narrow rocker panel moldings, wheel opening moldings, chrome lower bumpers, mini black bumper guards, bright-accented bumper rub strips, clock, and P195/75R14 steel-belted radials. LE added wide rocker panel moldings with extensions, color-keyed sport mirrors, and wide windowsill and hood edge moldings. Brougham added 55/45 notchback seating, power windows, and door courtesy lights.

1985 Pontiac Grand Prix Brougham coupe. (AA)

184

Model Number	Body/Style Number	Body Type & Seating	Factory Price	Shipping Weight	Prod. Total
GRAND PRIX (V-6/V-8)					
2G	J37	2-dr. Cpe-6P	9569/9959	3148/ --	30,365
GRAND PRIX LE (V-6/V-8)					
2G	K37	2-dr. Cpe-6P	10049/10439	3168/ --	21,195
GRAND PRIX BROUGHAM (V-6/V-8)					
2G	P37	2-dr. Cpe-6P	10749/11139	3186/ --	8223

1985 Pontiac Bonneville Brougham sedan. (P)

BONNEVILLE -- SERIES 2G -- V-6/V-8 -- Three trim levels made up the Bonneville line: base, LE, and elegant Brougham. All had a standard 231 cid (3.8-liter) V-6 with three-speed automatic. And all could get an optional 5.0-liter V-8 with either three- or four-speed automatic. A dozen body colors were available, including nine new ones. An electronic-tuning sound system was available for the first time. Standard equipment included power brakes and steering, bumper guards and rub strips, wide rocker panel moldings with extensions, wheel opening moldings, cloth notchback seating, clock, and P195/75R14 steel-belted radial blackwall tires. LE added belt reveal moldings, a pillar appliqué, and sport steering wheel. Brougham included 55/45 notchback seats with cloth upholstery, lower door courtesy lights, and opera lamps.

Model Number	Body/Style Number	Body Type & Seating	Factory Price	Shipping Weight	Prod. Total
BONNEVILLE (V-6/V-8)					
2G	N69	4-dr. Sed-6P	9549/9939	3214/3290	34,466
2G	S69	4-dr. LE Sed-6P	9789/10179	3275/3351	10,503
BONNEVILLE BROUGHAM (V-6/V-8)					
2G	R69	4-dr. Sed-6P	10280/10669	3210/3286	8425

1985 Pontiac Parisienne sedan. (JG)

PARISIENNE -- SERIES 2B -- V-6/V-8 -- Rear-drive was very much alive at Pontiac in the form of the last remaining full-size models, which displayed a fresh look this year. Though similar overall to the 1984 edition, this year's sedan quarter panels, deck lid, and taillamps came from the 1981 Bonneville rather than Chevrolet Caprice (as had been the case). The new look included a revised bumper and rub strips, and fender skirts with moldings. Extra-wide lower bodyside moldings and color-keyed bodyside moldings were new. A new wind-split hood molding became standard. Broughams included opera lamps. The four-door sedan came in base and Brougham trim. The Safari wagon carried eight passengers. A new notchback seat was standard, with "loose pillow" style; 45/55 seating available. A fuel-injected 262 cid (4.3-liter) V-6 was now the base powerplant, with three-speed automatic. Wagons had a standard 5.0-liter V-8 (optional on sedan), and both could get the 350 cid diesel for the last time.

1985 Pontiac Parisienne Brougham four-door sedan. OCW

Model Number	Body/Style Number	Body Type & Seating	Factory Price	Shipping Weight	Prod. Total
PARISIENNE (V-6/V-8)					
2B	L69	4-dr. Sed-6P	10395/10635	3350/ --	25,638
2B	L35	4-dr. Sta Wag-8P	-- /10495	3944	17,638
PARISIENNE BROUGHAM (V-6/V-8)					
2B	T69	4-dr. Sed-6P	11125/11365	3378/ --	38,831

FACTORY PRICE AND WEIGHT NOTE: Prices and weights to left of slash are for V-6, to right for V-8 engine except Firebird/Grand Am/6000, four and V-6.

1985 Pontiac Parisienne Brougham four-door sedan (rear view). OCW

ENGINE DATA

BASE FOUR (1000): Inline. Overhead cam. Four-cylinder. Cast iron block and head. Displacement: 98 cu. in. (1.6 liters). Bore & stroke: 3.23 x 2.98 in. Compression ratio: 9.0:1. Brake horsepower: 65 @ 5200 rpm. Torque: 80 lb.-ft. @ 3200 rpm. Five main bearings. Hydraulic valve lifters. Carburetor: two-barrel. VIN Code: C. BASE FOUR (Sunbird): Inline. Overhead cam. Four-cylinder. Cast iron block and aluminum head. Displacement: 109 cu. in. (1.8 liters). Bore & stroke: 3.34 x 3.13 in. Compression ratio: 9.0:1. Brake horsepower: 82 @ 5200 rpm. Torque: 102 lb.-ft. @ 2800 rpm. Five main bearings. Hydraulic valve lifters. Electronic fuel injection. VIN Code: 0. OPTIONAL TURBO FOUR (Sunbird): Same as 109 cid four above, with port fuel injection and turbocharger. Compression ratio: 8.0:1. Horsepower: 150 @ 5600 rpm. Torque: 150 lb.-ft. @ 2800 rpm. VIN Code: J. OPTIONAL FOUR (Sunbird): Inline. Overhead valve. Four-cylinder. Cast iron block and head. Displacement: 122 cu. in. (2.0 liters). Bore & stroke: 3.50 x 3.15 in. Compression ratio: 9.3:1. Brake horsepower: 88 @ 4800 rpm. Torque: 110 lb.-ft. @ 2400 rpm. Five main bearings. Hydraulic valve lifters. Electronic fuel injection. VIN Code: P. BASE FOUR (Fiero, Grand Am, Firebird, 6000): Inline. Overhead valve. Four-cylinder. Cast iron block and head. Displacement: 151 cu. in. (2.5 liters). Bore & stroke: 4.00 x 3.00 in. Compression ratio: 9.0:1. Brake horsepower: 92 @ 4400 rpm (Firebird, 88 @ 4400). Torque: 132-134 lb.-ft. @ 2800 rpm. Five main bearings. Hydraulic valve lifters. Throttle-body fuel injection. VIN Code: U or 2. OPTIONAL V-6 (6000): 60-degree, overhead valve six-cylinder. Cast iron block and aluminum head. Displacement: 173 cu. in. (2.8 liters). Bore & stroke: 3.50 x 3.00 in. Compression ratio: 8.5:1. Brake horsepower: 112 @ 4800 rpm. Torque: 145 lb.-ft. @ 2100 rpm. Four main bearings. Hydraulic valve lifters. Carburetor: two-barrel. VIN Code: X.

BASE V-6 (Firebird SE, 6000 STE); OPTIONAL (Fiero, Firebird): Fuel-injected version of 173 cid V-6 above. Compression ratio: 8.9:1. Horsepower: 130 @ 4800 rpm (Firebird, 135 @ 5100). Torque: 160-165 lb.-ft. @ 3600 rpm. VIN Code: 5, 9 or W. OPTIONAL V-6 (Grand

Am): 90-degree, overhead-valve V-6. Cast iron block and head. Displacement: 181 cu. in. (3.0 liters). Bore & stroke: 3.80 x 2.70 in. Compression ratio: 9.0:1. Brake horsepower: 125 @ 4900 rpm. Torque: 154 lb.-ft. @ 2400 rpm. Four main bearings. Hydraulic valve lifters. Fuel injection. VIN Code: L. BASE V-6 (Grand Prix, Bonneville): 90-degree, overhead-valve V-6. Cast iron block and head. Displacement: 231 cu. in. (3.8 liters). Bore & stroke: 3.80 x 3.40 in. Compression ratio: 8.0:1. Brake horsepower: 110 @ 3800 rpm. Torque: 190 lb.-ft. @ 1600 rpm. Four main bearings. Hydraulic valve lifters. Carburetor: two-barrel Rochester E2ME. Buick-built. VIN Code: A. BASE V-6 (Parisienne): 90-degree, overhead-valve V-6. Cast iron block and head. Displacement: 262 cu. in. (4.3 liters). Bore & stroke: 4.00 x 3.48 in. Compression ratio: N/A. Brake horsepower: 130 @ 3600 rpm. Torque: 210 lb.-ft. @ 2000 rpm. Four main bearings. Hydraulic valve lifters. Throttle-body fuel injection. VIN Code: 7.

DIESEL V-6 (6000): 90-degree, overhead valve V-6. Cast iron block and head. Displacement: 260 cu. in. (4.3 liters). Bore & stroke: 4.06 x 3.38 in. Compression ratio: 21.6:1. Brake horsepower: 85 @ 3600 rpm. Torque: 165 lb.-ft. @ 1600 rpm. Four main bearings. Hydraulic valve lifters. Fuel injection. VIN Code: T.

BASE V-8 (Firebird Trans Am); OPTIONAL (Firebird, Grand Prix, Bonneville, Parisienne): 90-degree, overhead valve V-8. Cast iron block and head. Displacement: 305 cu. in. (5.0 liters). Bore & stroke: 3.74 x 3.48 in. Compression ratio: 9.5:1. Brake horsepower: 165 @ 4200 rpm. Torque: 250 lb.-ft. @ 2400 rpm. Five main bearings. Hydraulic valve lifters. Carburetor: four-barrel. Chevrolet-built. VIN Code: H. OPTIONAL V-8 (Trans Am): High-output version of 305 cid V-8. Compression ratio: 9.5:1. Horsepower: 190 @ 4800 rpm. Torque: 240 lb.-ft. @ 3200 rpm. VIN Code: G. OPTIONAL V-8 (Trans Am): Fuel-injected version of 305 cid V-8. Horsepower: 205 @ 4400 rpm. Torque: 275 lb.-ft. @ 3200 rpm. VIN Code: F.

DIESEL V-8 (Parisienne): 90-degree, overhead valve V-8. Cast iron block and head. Displacement: 350 cu. in. (5.7 liters). Bore & stroke: 4.06 x 3.39 in. Compression ratio: 22.5:1. Brake horsepower: 105 @ 3200 rpm. Torque: 200 lb.-ft. @ 1600 rpm. Five main bearings. Hydraulic valve lifters. Fuel injection. Oldsmobile-built. VIN Code: N.

CHASSIS DATA: Wheelbase: (Fiero) 93.4 in.; (1000 three-door) 94.3 in.; (1000 five-door) 97.3 in.; (Sunbird) 101.2 in.; (Grand Am) 103.4 in.; (Firebird) 101.0 in.; (6000) 104.8 in.; (Grand Prix) 108.1 in.; (Bonneville) 108.1 in.; (Parisienne) 116.0 in. Overall Length: (Fiero) 160.7 in.; (1000 three-door) 161.9 in.; (1000 five-door) 164.9 in.; (Sunbird) 175.4 in.; (Sunbird wag) 176.5 in.; (Grand Am) 177.5 in.; (Firebird) 189.9 in.; (6000) 188.8 in.; (6000 wag) 191.2 in.; (G.P.) 201.9 in.; (Bonneville) 200.2 in.; (Parisienne) 212.4 in.; (Parisienne wag) 215.1 in. Height: (Fiero) 46.9 in.; (1000) 52.8-52.9 in.; (Sunbird cpe) 51.9 in.; (Sunbird conv.) 52.7 in.; (Sunbird sed) 53.8 in.; (Sunbird wag) 54.1 in.; (Grand Am) 52.5 in.; (Firebird) 49.7 in.; (6000) 53.3-53.8 in.; (G.P.) 54.7 in.; (Bonneville) 55.8 in.; (Parisienne sed) 56.4 in.; (Parisienne wag) 58.1 in. Width: (Fiero) 68.9 in.; (1000) 61.8 in.; (Sunbird cpe/conv.) 65.9 in.; (Sunbird hatch) 66.6 in.; (Sunbird sed/wag) 66.2 in.; (Grand Am) 67.3 in.; (Firebird) 72.4 in.; (6000) 67.7-67.8 in.; (G.P.) 72.3 in.; (Bonneville) 71.6 in.; (Parisienne) 76.4 in. exc. wagon, 79.3 in. Front Tread: (Fiero) 57.8 in.; (1000) 51.2 in.; (Sunbird) 55.4 in.; (Grand Am) 55.6 in.; (Firebird) 60.7 in.; (6000) 58.7 in.; (G.P.) 58.5 in.; (Bonneville) 58.5 in.; (Parisienne) 61.8 in.; (Parisienne wag) 62.2 in. Rear Tread: (Fiero) 58.7 in.; (1000) 51.2 in.; (Sunbird) 55.2 in.; (Grand Am) 55.1 in.; (Firebird) 61.6 in.; (6000) 56.9 in.; (G.P.) 57.8 in.; (Bonneville) 57.8 in.; (Parisienne) 60.8 in.; (Parisienne wag) 64.1 in. Standard Tires: (Fiero) P185/80R13; (1000) P155/80R13 GBR BSW; (Sunbird) P175/80R13 GBR BSW; (Grand Am) P185/80R13 SBR BSW; (Firebird) P195/75R14 SBR BSW; (Firebird SE) P205/70R14 SBR BSW; (6000) P185/75R14 SBR; (6000 STE) P195/70R14 SBR; (Grand Prix) P195/75R14 SBR; (Bonneville) P195/75R14 SBR; (Parisienne sed) P205/75R15 SBR; (Parisienne wag) P225/75R15 SBR.

TECHNICAL: Transmission: Four-speed manual standard on Fiero, 1000, and base Firebird. Five-speed manual standard on Sunbird, Firebird, and Grand Am, optional on 1000. Three-speed Turbo-Hydramatic standard on other models. Four-speed overdrive automatic available on Firebird, 6000, Grand Prix, Bonneville, and Parisienne. Standard final drive ratio: (Fiero) N/A; (1000) 3.36:1; (Sunbird) 2.55:1 w/five-speed, 2.96:1 or 3.32:1 w/four-speed, 3.33:1 or 3.43:1 w/auto.; (Grand Am) 2.48:1 w/five-speed, 2.84:1 w/auto.; (Firebird) 3.42:1 w/four-speed, 3.73:1 w/four- and five-speed or auto., 3.42:1 w/V-6, 3.27:1 w/V-8; (Trans Am) 3.27:1 except 3.70:1 w/ H.O. V-8 and 3.27:1 w/FI V-8; (6000) 2.39:1 w/four, 2.84:1 or 3.06:1 w/V-6; (6000 STE) 3.18:1; (Grand Prix/Bonneville) 2.41:1; (Parisienne) 2.56:1; (Parisienne wagon) 2.73:1. Steering: (Fiero/1000/Sunbird/Phoenix/6000) rack and pinion; (others) recirculating ball. Front Suspension: (Sunbird/Phoenix/6000) MacPherson struts w/ lower control arms and anti-sway bar; (Grand Am) MacPherson struts w/anti-sway bar; (Firebird) modified MacPherson struts w/coil springs between lower control arm and X-member; (others) coil springs and anti-sway bar. Rear Suspension: (Fiero) MacPherson struts w/ lower control arms; (1000) four-link rigid axle w/torque tube and Panhard rod; (Sunbird) beam axle w/coil springs and trailing arms; (Grand Am) semi-independent beam axle w/trailing arms and coil springs;

(Firebird) torque arm/track bar w/coil springs and anti-sway bar; (6000) trailing arms and beam axle w/coil springs and integral anti-sway bar; (Bonneville/Grand Prix/Parisienne) four-link rigid axle with coil springs, lower trailing radius arms and upper torque arms. Brakes: Front disc, rear drum except 6000 STE, four-wheel disc. Ignition: Electronic. Body construction: (Fiero/1000/Sunbird/Phoenix/Firebird/6000) unit; (others) separate body and frame. Fuel Tank: (Fiero) 10.2 gal.; (1000) 12.2 gal.; (Sunbird) 13.6 gal.; (Grand Am) 13.6 gal.; (Firebird) 15.9 gal.; (6000) 15.7 gal.; (Grand Prix/Bonneville) 18.1 gal.; (Parisienne) 25 gal.; (Parisienne wag) 22 gal.

DRIVETRAIN OPTIONS: Engines: Turbo 1.8-liter four: Sunbird ($1248-$1486); standard on SE. 173 cid, two-barrel V-6: 6000 ($260). 173 cid, FI V-6: Fiero ($595); Firebird ($350); 6000 ($435). 181 cid V-6: Grand Am ($560). Diesel 262 cid V-6: 6000 ($335). 305 cid, four-barrel V-8: Firebird ($650); Firebird SE ($300); Grand Prix/Bonneville ($390); Parisienne ($240). H.O. 305 cid V-8, four-barrel or FI: Trans Am ($695). Diesel 350 cid V-8: Parisienne sed ($341); Parisienne wagon ($101). Transmission/Differential: Four-speed manual transmission: Fiero SE ($50 credit); Sunbird ($75 credit). Five-speed manual transmission: 1000 ($75). Three-speed automatic transmission: Fiero ($425-$475); Fiero GT ($750); 1000 ($395); Sunbird ($350-$425); Grand Am ($425). Four-speed automatic transmission: Firebird ($325); 6000/Grand Prix/Bonneville/Parisienne ($175). Limited-slip differential: Firebird/G.P./Bonneville/Parisienne ($95-$100). Brakes/Steering: Power brakes: 1000 ($94). Power four-wheel disc brakes: Firebird ($179) but no charge (NC) w/performance pkg. Power steering: 1000 ($204); Sunbird ($215). Suspension: Electronic suspension: 6000 ($165). Rally tuned suspension: Firebird ($30); Sunbird/Grand Am/6000/Firebird/G.P. ($50); Parisienne ($49). Superlift shock absorbers: 6000/G.P./Bonneville/Parisienne ($64). H.D. springs: Parisienne ($16). Other: H.D. cooling ($40-$70). H.D. battery ($25-$26) exc. diesel ($52). H.D. alternator ($25-$51). Engine block heater ($18-$19). California emissions ($99).

OPTION PACKAGES: Fiero special performance pkg. ($174-$491). 1000 sport/handling pkg. ($464). 1000 custom trim ($167). Sunbird custom exterior group ($86). Sunbird custom trim group ($308-$358). Sunbird security pkg. ($19). Firebird Trans Am special performance pkg. ($664). Firebird black appearance pkg. ($123-$152). Firebird custom exterior ($51-$112). Firebird luxury interior trim ($349-$359). 6000 sport landau coupe ($665-$703). 6000 rally pkg. ($441-$479). 6000 custom exterior ($56). 6000 wagon security pkg. ($44). Grand Prix Brougham Landau pkg. ($469). Lamp groups ($21-$47) except 6000 LE ($79-$88).

MAJOR CONVENIENCE/APPEARANCE OPTIONS: Air conditioning ($630-$730). Cruise control ($175). Power seat ($215-$488); N/A on 1000/Fiero. Power windows ($185-$260); N/A on 1000. Cornering lamps: Bonneville/G.P. ($68); Parisienne ($55). Power glass sun roof: Parisienne ($1195). Removable glass sun roof: Fiero/Sunbird/Grand Am/6000 ($300-$310). Hatch roof: Firebird/Grand Prix ($825-$875). Full vinyl roof: Bonneville ($160). Padded cordova landau roof: G.P. ($245). Aero wing spoiler: Trans Am ($199). Padded full vinyl roof: Bonneville ($245); Parisienne ($185). Louvered rear sunshields: Sunbird ($199); Firebird ($210). Two-tone paint: Sunbird ($101-$151); Firebird/6000 ($205); G.P./Bonneville ($205-$291); Parisienne sed ($205). Lear Siegler bucket seats: Sunbird ($400); Firebird ($400-$759); leather ($945-$1304). Recaro bucket seats: Firebird ($636-$995). Woodgrain paneling: Parisienne wagon ($345).

HISTORICAL FOOTNOTE: Introduced: October 2, 1984, except Sunbird/Firebird, November 8, 1984; 1000, November 11, 1984; and Fiero, January 10, 1985. Model year production: 735,161. Calendar year production (U.S.): 684,901. Calendar year sales by U.S. dealers: 796,795. Model year sales by U.S. dealers: 785,643. First built only in Canada, the 6000 series expanded production to the Tarrytown, New York, plant for 1985. Sales rose moderately for the model year, with 6000 and Parisienne posting impressive increases. Small cars weren't doing as well. Fiero sales continued relatively good, if beneath expectations. The 6000 was Pontiac's best seller. Well over half of Pontiacs now carried fuel-injected engines.

1986 PONTIAC

"Driver-oriented" models continued to get ample attention with the introduction of a SE variant for Grand Am and a Sunbird GT. All Pontiacs now had the required high-mount center stop lamp. Most appealing to collectors would be the limited-production Grand Prix 2+2 coupe.

I.D. DATA: Pontiac's 17-symbol Vehicle Identification Number (VIN) was on the upper left surface of the instrument panel, visible through the windshield. The first three symbols ('1G2') indicate Pontiac division. Symbol four is restraint system ('A' = manual seatbelts). Symbol five is car line/series: 'E' = Fiero; 'M' = Fiero Sport; 'F' = Fiero SE; 'G' = Fiero GT; 'L' = T1000; 'B' = Sunbird; 'U' = Sunbird GT; 'D' = Sunbird

SE; 'E' = Grand Am; 'V' = Grand Am LE; 'W' = Grand Am SE; 'F' = 6000; 'G' = 6000 LE; 'E' = 6000 SE; 'H' = 6000 STE; 'S' = Firebird; 'X' = Firebird SE; 'W' = Firebird Trans Am; 'J' = Grand Prix; 'K' = Grand Prix LE; 'P' = Grand Prix Brougham; 'N' = Bonneville; 'R' = Bonneville Brougham; 'S' = Bonneville LE; 'L' = Parisienne; 'T' = Parisienne Brougham. In sixth and seventh position are two digits that denote body type: '08' = three-door hatchback coupe; '27' = two-door coupe; '37' = two-door coupe; '77' = three-door hatchback; '87' = two-door coupe; '97' = two-door conv. coupe; '19' = four-door six-window sedan; '68' = five-door hatchback sedan; '69' = four-door four-window sedan; '35' = four-door station wagon. Symbol eight is an engine code: 'C' = L4-98 two-barrel; 'O' = L4-109 FI; 'J' = turbo L4-109 FI; 'R' or 'U' = L4-151 FI; 'X' = V-6-173 two-barrel; 'S', 'W' or '9' = V-6-173 FI; 'L' = V-6-181 FI; 'A' = V-6-231 two-barrel; 'Z' = V-6-262 FI; 'H' = V-8-305 four-barrel; 'G' = H.O. V-8-305; 'F' = V-8-305 FI. Next is a check digit. The tenth symbol denotes model year ('G' = 1986). Symbol eleven is a plant code: 'A' = Lakewood, Ga.; 'L' = Van Nuys, Calif.; 'N' = Norwood, Ohio; 'P' = Pontiac, Mich.; 'T' = Tarrytown, N.Y.; 'X' = Fairfax, Kan.; 'M' = Lansing, Mich.; '7' = Lordstown, Ohio; '1' = Oshawa, Ontario; '2' = St. Therese, Quebec. The final six digits are the sequential serial number.

1986 Pontiac Fiero GT coupe. (P)

FIERO -- SERIES 2P -- FOUR/V-6 -- Three models made up the two-seater coupe line: base, Sport, and SE. A black-accented aero package gave SE its own styling cues. Its standard 151 cid (2.5-liter) fuel-injected "Tech IV" four, with dual-trumpet exhaust, coupled with a five-speed manual transaxle (from Isuzu). Optional again: a 173 cid (2.8-liter) V-6 with multi-port fuel injection. SE came with a standard Rally Tuned suspension, including 14 inch cast aluminum wheels. Four-cylinder SE models had P195/70R14 tires; V-6, P215/60R14. Standard reclining bucket seats wore Pallex cloth. Optional leather/suede/cloth trim replaced the former fleece/suede. Standard tires for base and Sport Coupe models were P185/75R14, with new tri-tech wheel covers (aluminum wheels optional). New sail-panel stereo speakers replaced the former headrest units. Body colors included black, silver, red, white, and gold. Overall appearance was similar to 1985, but the smooth-surfaced front end now held a single center air slot, with separate openings for parking/signal lamps. A fastback GT model was announced for late arrival.

1986 Pontiac Fiero GT coupe (rear view). PMD

FIERO (FOUR/V-6)

Model Number	Body/Style Number	Body Type & Seating	Factory Price	Shipping Weight	Prod. Total
2P	E37	2-dr. Cpe-2P	8949/ --	2480	9143
2P	M37	2-dr. Spt Cpe-2P	9449/ --	2493	24,866
2P	F37	2-dr. SE Cpe-2P	10595/11240	7499	32,305
2P	G97	2-dr. GT Cpe-2P	-- /12875	N/A	17,660

1986 Pontiac 1000 hatchback sedan. (P)

1000 -- SERIES 2T -- FOUR -- For its final year, the subcompact 1000 again came in two body styles: three- and five-door hatchback. Standard engine was again the 1.6-liter OHC four, with four-speed manual shift. A five-speed and automatic were optional. An optional sport handling package included a heavier front stabilizer bar and a rear stabilizer bar, as well as cast aluminum wheels, dual mirrors, and sport body striping. Also optional: a new four-spoke steering wheel. Standard equipment included a Delco AM radio, front mini-console, reclining front seats, and folding full-width back seat.

1000 (FOUR)

Model Number	Body/Style Number	Body Type & Seating	Factory Price	Shipping Weight	Prod. Total
2T	L08	3-dr. Hatch-4P	5749	2059	12,266
2T	L68	5-dr. Hatch-4P	5969	2118	9423

1986 Pontiac Sunbird Turbo GT hatchback coupe. (P)

SUNBIRD -- SERIES 2J -- FOUR -- Most notable of Sunbird's changes was the new GT level, offered on coupe, hatchback, convertible, and sedan bodies. A station wagon remained available at the base level, and the SE lineup included a convertible. Aimed at enthusiasts, the GT included a sloped front fascia with partly hidden quad halogen headlamps, and a rear spoiler. GT equipment included narrow black bodyside moldings and dual sport mirrors. Two-door GT models also had wheel flares, turbo aluminum wheels, and P215/60R14 Eagle GT tires. A turbocharged version of the 1.8-liter engine, rated at 150 hp, delivered a claimed 8.5 second 0-60 mph time. GT also included a performance handling package and power steering. Inside was a back-lit round-dial instrument cluster that included a turbo boost gauge and tachometer, and an electric speedometer. A rally console extension included a thumbwheel mileage/event reminder. The four-spoke rally urethane steering wheel had horn bars on each side of the hub. Leather wrapping was optional. Genor cloth upholstery was standard. Base and SE models were still around, but LE became an option package for base sedans and wagons rather than a model on its own. Sedans and wagons got a blackout taillamp treatment to replace the former bright framing. SE models had a revised taillamp design, wide bodyside moldings, fog lamps (making six front lights in all), and blackout trim on belt moldings, drip rails, and door handles. All models had a backlit instrument cluster, with standard temperature gauge. The base four-cylinder 1.8-liter engine developed 84 hp, but the former 2.0-liter option was no longer available.

1986 Pontiac Sunbird GT hatchback coupe. (P)

Model Number	Body/Style Number	Body Type & Seating	Factory Price	Shipping Weight	Prod. Total
SUNBIRD (FOUR)					
2J	B69	4-dr. Sedan-5P	7495	2336	60,080
2J	B35	4-dr. Sta Wag-5P	7879	2397	7445
SUNBIRD SE (FOUR)					
2J	D27	2-dr. Cpe-5P	7469	2285	37,526
2J	D77	3-dr. Hatch-5P	7829	2330	3822
2J	D67	2-dr. Conv.-4P	12779	2464	1598
SUNBIRD GT (FOUR)					
2J	U27	2-dr. Cpe-5P	9459	2396	18,118
2J	U77	3-dr. Hatch-5P	9819	2419	2442
2J	U69	4-dr. Sedan-5P	9499	2398	2802
2J	U67	2-dr. Conv.-4P	14399	2573	1268

GRAND AM -- SERIES 2N -- FOUR/V-6 -- A sporty four-door joined the original Grand Am coupe, along with a "sophisticated" SE series aimed at enthusiasts. SE, said its design studio head, offered a "boldly aggressive appearance." The approach was similar to that used for the 6000 STE. This edition had an aero ground-effects package that included a low front bumper air dam, side skirts, and deep rear extension, as well as flush composite headlamps and built-in fog lamps. SE also had a unique monochrome paint treatment, with grille, emblems, and cast aluminum wheels color-coordinated to the body. At the rear were neutral-density taillamps. Standard engine was a 181 cid (3.0-liter) V-6 with multi-port fuel injection, hooked to a three-speed automatic. The Y99 rally tuned suspension included thick front/rear stabilizer bars and P215/60R14 Eagle GT tires. SE interiors contained tone-on-tone Pallex seat trim, color-coordinated with the body color. Standard equipment included a four-way (manual-control) driver's bucket seat; leather-wrapped steering wheel, parking brake handle and gearshift knob; header-mount reading lamp; rear roof courtesy lamp; visor vanity mirror; and seek/scan AM/FM stereo. Options included a six-speaker sound system, tilt steering, and cruise control. Appearance of the "ordinary" base and LE Grand Am changed little this year, except for new high-gloss black moldings on LE models. Base engine was the "Tech IV" 151 cid (2.5-liter) four with fuel injection, and five-speed manual transaxle. New Flame Red was one of the dozen available body colors. Turbo cast aluminum wheels were optional again. Base/LE models could also get the 3.0-liter V-6, with three-speed automatic.

1986 Pontiac Grand Am SE sedan. (P)

1986 Pontiac Grand Am SE coupe. PMD

1986 Pontiac Grand Am SE sedan. (P)

Model Number	Body/Style Number	Body Type & Seating	Factory Price	Shipping Weight	Prod. Total
GRAND AM (FOUR/V-6)					
2N	E27	2-dr. Cpe-5P	8549/9624	2423/ --	69,545
2N	E69	4-dr. Sedan-5P	8749/9824	2496/ --	49,166
GRAND AM LE (FOUR/V-6)					
2N	V27	2-dr. Cpe-5P	9079/10154	2458/ --	48,530
2N	V69	4-dr. Sedan-5P	9279/10354	2521/ --	31,790
GRAND AM SE (V-6)					
2N	W27	2-dr. Cpe-5P	11499	2605	15,506
2N	W69	4-dr. Sedan-5P	11749	2683	8957

1986 Pontiac Firebird coupe. (P)

FIREBIRD -- SERIES 2F -- FOUR/V-6/V-8 -- New taillamps and center filler panel gave the base Firebird a modified look, different from the upscale models. New lower body accent paint with sports striping became standard. Also standard: dual sport mirrors and rear spoiler. The optional hood bird graphic decal also changed in appearance. All models had a power pull-down hatch, with electric remote release optional; and all carried 15-inch tires. New options included a programmable, electrically controlled day/night mirror. All base and SE models with V-6 or V-8 now had the optional Rally Tuned suspension with P215/65R15 tires on seven-inch Rally II wheels. New lightweight pistons went into the base "Tech IV" 151 cid (2.5-liter) four, which drove a standard five-speed manual gearbox. SE carried a standard 173 cid (2.8-liter) V-6 with multi-port fuel injection. Both base and SE models could have a 5.0-liter four-barrel V-8 with either five-speed or automatic. Trans Am had a standard 155 hp version of the 5.0-liter V-8, and an option of tuned-port fuel injection that delivered 190 hp. Five-speed manual shift was standard, and four-speed overdrive automatic required with the TPI engine. The standard Y99 Rally Tuned suspension came with P215/60R15 tires on seven-inch cast aluminum

wheels. Trans Am's WS6 suspension package included four-wheel disc brakes, a limited-slip differential, larger front/rear stabilizer bars, and P245/50VR16 Gatorback tires. A new backlit instrument cluster included an electric speedometer, which read up to 140 mph reading when equipped with the TPI V-8.

1986 Pontiac Trans Am T-top coupe. (P)

Model Number	Body/Style Number	Body Type & Seating	Factory Price	Shipping Weight	Prod. Total
FIREBIRD (FOUR/V-6)					
2F	S87	2-dr. Cpe-4P	9279/9629	2789/ --	59,334

Engine Note: A 305 cid V-8 cost $400 more than the V-6 on base Firebird.

FIREBIRD SE (V-6/V-8)					
2F	X87	2-dr. Cpe-4P	11995/12395	2909/ --	2,259
FIREBIRD TRANS AM (V-8)					
2F	W87	2-dr. Cpe-4P	12395	3132	48,870

1986 Pontiac 6000 STE wagon. (P)

1986 Pontiac 6000 SE station wagon (rear view). PMD

6000 -- SERIES 2A -- FOUR/V-6 -- Most notable of the improvements in the 6000 line was standard anti-lock braking, introduced during the model year on 6000 STE as part of its standard four-wheel power disc brake system. Radio controls moved to the steering wheel this year (duplicated on the dash). 6000 STE had a revised grille (lacking the traditional Pontiac split design), along with aerodynamic flush halogen headlamps and fog lamps. Standard STE engine was a 173 cid (2.8-liter) V-6 with multi-port fuel injection, delivering 130 hp. The standard three-speed automatic transmission now connected with a 3.18:1 final drive ratio. An electronic instrument cluster remained standard, with

new vacuum fluorescent unit. A new pod held controls for power windows, door locks and mirrors. As before, 6000 STE had an almost non-existent options list: just a six-way power driver/passenger seat with recliners, sun roof, and suede interior trim. Base and LE models had a standard 151 cid (2.5-liter) four with three-speed automatic. Options included both carbureted and fuel-injected versions of the 2.8 V-6. Four-speed overdrive automatic was available for V-6 models.

Model Number	Body/Style Number	Body Type & Seating	Factory Price	Shipping Weight	Prod. Total
6000 (FOUR/V-6)					
2A	F27	2-dr. Cpe-6P	9549/10159	2668/--	4739
2A	F19	4-dr. Sed-6P	9729/10339	2713/--	81,531
2A	F35	4-dr. Sta Wag-6P	10095/10705	2849/--	10,094
2A	G27	2-dr. LE Cpe-6P	10049/10659	2687/--	4803
2A	G19	4-dr. LE Sed-6P	10195/10805	2731/--	67,697
2A	G35	4-dr. LE Wag-6P	10579/11189	2867/--	7556
2A	E19	4-dr. SE Sed-6P	--/11179	N/A	7348
2A	E35	4-dr. SE Wag-6P	--/11825	N/A	1308
6000 STE (V-6)					
2A	H19	4-dr. Sed-5P	15949	3039	26,299

1986 Pontiac Grand Prix 2+2 Aerodynamic Coupe. (P)

GRAND PRIX -- SERIES 2G -- V-6/V-8 -- As before, three series were available on the rear-drive personal-luxury coupe: base, LE, and Brougham. Standard engine was Buick's 231 cid (3.8-liter) V-6, with three-speed automatic. A 5.0-liter V-8 with four-speed overdrive automatic was optional. Taillamps and bezels were slightly revised. Three-section taillamps had a 'GP' octagon in the center lens. Though similar to 1985, this year's grille had fewer vertical bars. Interiors had a notch-back seat with center armrest. A new optional visor vanity mirror came with dual-intensity lamps. Only 200 examples of the 2+2 coupe were built, all of them sold by dealers in southeastern states. The 2+2 was a street version of the NASCAR racer, driven by Richard Petty in the 1986-87 season. Under the hood was a 165 hp version of the 305 cid V-8, producing 245 lb.-ft. of torque. Selling price was $18,214, but dealers quickly marked up the few units available to around $22,000. Claimed quarter-mile time was 17.6 seconds, with a speed of 80 mph. The 2+2 had a gray body with twin-shade red striping on the lower panels. A 'Pontiac 2+2' nameplate in red/gray on black went on the left of the black honeycomb grille. 'Pontiac 2+2' lettering also went on the door, and 'Pontiac Grand Prix' identification on the deck. The 2+2 option was RPO code Y97.

1986 Pontiac Grand Prix 2+2 Aerodynamic Coupe (rear view). PMD

Model Number	Body/Style Number	Body Type & Seating	Factory Price	Shipping Weight	Prod. Total
GRAND PRIX (V-6/V-8)					
2G	J37	2-dr. Cpe-6P	10259/10974	3161/--	21,668
2G	N/A	2-dr. 2+2 Cpe-5P	--/18214	N/A	200
GRAND PRIX LE (V-6/V-8)					
2G	K37	2-dr. Cpe-6P	10795/11510	3178/--	13,918
GRAND PRIX BROUGHAM (V-6/V-8)					
2G	P37	2-dr. Cpe-6P	11579/12294	3201/--	4798

1986 Pontiac Bonneville Brougham sedan. (P)

BONNEVILLE -- SERIES 2G -- V-6/V-8 -- Appearance was similar to 1985. The six-passenger mid-size sedan came in base, LE, and Brougham trim, in a dozen body colors. Base engine was the 231 cid (3.8-liter) V-6 with three-speed automatic. Optional: a 5.0-liter V-8 with four-speed overdrive automatic. Standard equipment included power brakes and steering, AM radio, notchback front seat with fold-down center armrest, and custom wheel covers. LE added a four-spoke sport steering wheel, pillar appliqué, and belt reveal moldings. Brougham added a 55/45 front seat, cushion steering wheel, and door courtesy lamps.

Model Number	Body/Style Number	Body Type & Seating	Factory Price	Shipping Weight	Prod. Total
BONNEVILLE (V-6/V-8)					
2G	N69	4-dr. Sed-6P	10249/10964	3143/--	27,801
2G	S69	4-dr. LE Sed-6P	10529/11244	3152/--	7179
BONNEVILLE BROUGHAM (V-6/V-8)					
2G	R69	4-dr. Sed-6P	11079/11794	3172/--	5941

1986 Pontiac Parisienne Brougham sedan. (P)

PARISIENNE -- SERIES 2B -- V-6/V-8 -- Once again, the full-size rear-drive Pontiacs came in base or Brougham trim as a four-door sedan, or as an eight-passenger station wagon. New fine-textured velour cloth trim went into Brougham sedans. Turbo-finned cast aluminum wheels were optional on sedans. Optional instruments now included a voltmeter instead of a fuel economy gauge. Base engine was a 4.3-liter fuel-injected V-6, with three-speed automatic. Wagons carried a 5.0-liter V-8 and four-speed automatic.

Model Number	Body/Style Number	Body Type & Seating	Factory Price	Shipping Weight	Prod. Total
PARISIENNE (V-6/V-8)					
2B	L69	4-dr. Sed-6P	11169/11734	3427/--	27,078
2B	L35	4-dr. Sta Wag-8P	--/11779	--/3985	14,464
PARISIENNE BROUGHAM (V-6/V-8)					
2B	T69	4-dr. Sed-6P	11949/12514	3456/--	43,540

FACTORY PRICE AND WEIGHT NOTE: Prices and weights to left of slash are for V-6, to right for V-8 engine except Fiero/Firebird/Grand Am/6000, four and V-6. Most prices of optional V-6 (or V-8) include an extra $175 for the cost of the required four-speed overdrive automatic transmission.

1986 Pontiac 6000 STE four-door sedan. PMD

ENGINE DATA

BASE FOUR (1000): Inline. Overhead cam. Four-cylinder. Cast iron block and head. Displacement: 98 cu. in. (1.6 liters). Bore & stroke: 3.23 x 2.98 in. Compression ratio: 9.0:1. Brake horsepower: 65 @ 5200 rpm. Torque: 80 lb.-ft. @ 3200 rpm. Five main bearings. Hydraulic valve lifters. Carburetor: two-barrel VIN Code: C. BASE FOUR (Sunbird): Inline. Overhead cam. Four-cylinder. Cast iron block and aluminum head. Displacement: 109 cu. in. (1.8 liters). Bore & stroke: 3.34 x 3.13 in. Compression ratio: 8.8:1. Brake horsepower: 84 @ 5200 rpm. Torque: 98 lb.-ft. @ 2800 rpm. Five main bearings. Hydraulic valve lifters. Electronic fuel injection. VIN Code: O. OPTIONAL TURBO FOUR (Sunbird): Same as 109 cid four above, with multi-port fuel injection and turbocharger. Compression ratio: 8.0:1. Horsepower: 150 @ 5600 rpm. Torque: 150 lb.-ft. @ 2800 rpm. VIN Code: J. BASE FOUR (Fiero, Grand Am, Firebird, 6000): Inline. Over-head valve. Four-cylinder. Cast iron block and head. Displacement: 151 cu. in. (2.5 liters). Bore & stroke: 4.00 x 3.00 in. Compression ratio: 9.0:1. Brake horsepower: 92 @ 4400 rpm. (Firebird, 88 @ 4400). Torque: 132-134 lb.-ft. @ 2800 rpm. Five main bearings. Hydraulic valve lifters. Throttle-body fuel injection. VIN Code: R or U. OPTIONAL V-6 (6000): 60-degree, overhead valve six-cylinder. Cast iron block and aluminum head. Displacement: 173 cu. in. (2.8 liters). Bore & stroke: 3.50 x 3.00 in. Compression ratio: 8.5:1. Brake horse-power: 112 @ 4800 rpm. Torque: 145 lb.-ft. @ 2100 rpm. Four main bearings. Hydraulic valve lifters. Carburetor: two-barrel VIN Code: X.

BASE V-6 (Firebird SE, 6000 STE); OPTIONAL (Fiero, Firebird): Fuel-injected version of 173 cid V-6 above. Compression ratio: 8.9:1. Horsepower: 125 @ 4800 rpm. (Fiero, 140 @ 5200; Firebird, 135 @ 5100) Torque: 155-175 lb.-ft. @ 3600 rpm. VIN Code: S, W, or 9. BASE V-6 (Grand Am SE); OPTIONAL (Grand Am): 90-degree, over-head-valve V-6. Cast iron block and head. Displacement: 181 cu. in. (3.0 liters). Bore & stroke: 3.80 x 2.70 in. Compression ratio: 9.0:1. Brake horsepower: 125 @ 4900 rpm. Torque: 150 lb.-ft. @ 2400 rpm. Four main bearings. Hydraulic valve lifters. Multi-port fuel injection. VIN Code: L. BASE V-6 (Grand Prix, Bonneville): 90-degree, over-head-valve V-6. Cast iron block and head. Displacement: 231 cu. in. (3.8 liters). Bore & stroke: 3.80 x 3.40 in. Compression ratio: 8.0:1. Brake horsepower: 110 @ 3800 rpm. Torque: 190 lb.-ft. @ 1600 rpm. Four main bearings. Hydraulic valve lifters. Carburetor: two-barrel Buick-built. VIN Code: A. BASE V-6 (Parisienne): 90-degree, overhead-valve V-6. Cast iron block and head. Displacement: 262 cu. in. (4.3 liters). Bore & stroke: 4.00 x 3.48 in. Compression ratio: N/A. Brake horsepower: 130 @ 3600 rpm. Torque: 210 lb.-ft. @ 2000 rpm. Four main bearings. Hydraulic valve lifters. Throttle-body fuel injection. VIN Code: Z.

BASE V-8 (Firebird Trans Am, Parisienne wagon); OPTIONAL (Firebird, Grand Prix, Bonneville, Parisienne): 90-degree, overhead valve V-8. Cast iron block and head. Displacement: 305 cu. in. (5.0 liters). Bore & stroke: 3.74 x 3.48 in. Compression ratio: 9.5:1. Brake horsepower: 150 @ 4200 rpm. (Trans Am, 155 @ 4000; Parisienne, 165 @ 4200). Torque: 235-245 lb.-ft. @ 2000-2400 rpm. Five main bearings. Hydraulic valve lifters. Carburetor: four-barrel Chevrolet-built. VIN Code: H. OPTIONAL V-8 (Trans Am): High-output version of 305 cid V-8. Compression ratio: 9.5:1. Horsepower: 190 @ 4800 rpm. Torque: 240 lb.-ft. @ 3200 rpm. VIN Code: G. OPTIONAL V-8 (Trans Am): Fuel-injected version of 305 cid V-8. Horsepower: 205 @ 4000 rpm. Torque: 270 lb.-ft. @ 3200 rpm. VIN Code: F.

CHASSIS DATA: Wheelbase: (Fiero) 93.4 in.; (1000 three-door) 94.3 in.; (1000 five-door) 97.3 in.; (Sunbird) 101.2 in.; (Grand Am) 103.4 in.; (Firebird) 101.0 in.; (6000) 104.9 in.; (Grand Prix) 108.1 in.; (Bonneville) 108.1 in.; (Parisienne) 116.0 in. Overall Length: (Fiero) 160.7 in.; (1000 three-door) 161.9 in.; (1000 five-door) 164.9 in.; (Sunbird) 175.4 in.; (Sunbird wag) 176.5 in.; (Grand Am) 177.5 in.; (Firebird) 188.1 in.; (6000) 188.8 in.; (6000 wag) 193.2 in.; (G.P.) 201.9 in.; (Bonneville) 200.2 in.; (Parisienne) 212.3 in.; (Parisienne wag) 215.1 in. Height: (Fiero) 46.9 in.; (1000) 52.8-52.9 in.; (Sunbird cpe) 51.9 in.; (Sunbird conv.) 52.7 in.; (Sunbird sed) 53.8 in.; (Sunbird wag) 54.1 in.; (Grand Am) 52.5 in.; (Firebird) 50.0 in.; (6000 cpe) 53.3 in.; (6000 sed) 53.7 in.; (6000 wag) 54.1 in.; (G.P.) 54.7 in.; (Bonneville) 55.8 in.; (Parisienne sed) 56.6 in.; (Parisienne wag) 57.4 in. Width: (Fiero) 68.9 in.; (1000) 61.8 in.; (Sunbird cpe/conv.) 65.9 in.; (Sunbird hatch) 66.6 in.; (Sunbird sed/wag) 66.2 in.; (Grand Am) 66.5 in.; (Firebird) 72.4 in.; (6000) 72.3 in.; (Bonneville) 71.6 in.; (Parisienne) 75.3 in. exc. wagon, 79.3 in. Front Tread: (Fiero) 57.8 in.; (1000) 51.2 in.; (Sunbird) 55.4 in.; (Grand Am) 55.5 in.; (Firebird) 60.7 in.; (6000) 58.7 in.; (G.P.) 58.5 in.; (Bonneville) 58.5 in.; (Parisienne) 61.8 in.; (Parisienne wag) 62.2 in. Rear Tread: (Fiero) 58.7 in.; (1000) 51.2 in.; (Sunbird) 55.2 in.; (Grand Am) 55.2 in.; (Firebird) 61.6 in.; (6000) 57.0 in.; (G.P.) 57.8 in.; (Bonneville) 57.8 in.; (Parisienne) 60.7 in.; (Parisienne wag) 64.1 in. Standard Tires: (Fiero) P185/75R14 SBR BSW; (Fiero SE) P195/70R14; (1000) P155/80R13 GBR BSW; (Sunbird) P175/80R13 SBR BSW; (Grand Am) P185/80R13 SBR BSW; (Firebird) P215/65R15 SBR BSW; (6000) P185/75R14 SBR; (6000 STE) P195/70R14 SBR; (Grand Prix) P195/75R14 SBR; (Bonneville) P195/75R14 SBR; (Parisienne sed) P205/75R15 SBR; (Parisienne wag) P225/75R15 SBR.

TECHNICAL: Transmission: Four-speed manual standard on Fiero V-6 and 1000. Five-speed manual standard on Fiero four, Sunbird, Firebird and Grand Am; optional on 1000. Three-speed Turbo-Hydramatic standard on other models. Four-speed overdrive automatic available on Firebird, 6000, Grand Prix, and Bonneville; standard on Parisienne. Standard final drive ratio: (Fiero) 2.48:1 w/five-speed, 3.18:1 w/auto.; (Fiero V-6) 2.96:1 w/five-speed, 3.06:1 w/auto.; (1000) 3.36:1; (Sunbird) 2.55:1 w/five-speed, 3.43:1 w/auto.; (Sunbird turbo) 2.96:1 w/four-speed, 3.33:1 w/auto.; (Grand Am) 2.48:1 w/five-speed, 2.84:1 w/auto.; (Firebird) 3.73:1 or 3.70:1 w/four, 3.42:1 w/V-6, 2.77:1 w/V-8; (Trans Am) 3.27:1 except 3.70:1 w/H.O. V-8; (6000) 2.39:1 w/four, 2.84:1 or 3.06:1 w/V-6; (6000 STE) 3.18:1; (Grand Prix/Bonneville) 2.41:1; (Parisienne) 2.56:1; (Parisienne wagon) 2.73:1. Steering/Suspension/Brakes/Body: same as 1985, except anti-lock braking on 6000 STE. Fuel Tank: (Fiero) 10.2 gal.; (1000) 12.2 gal.; (Sunbird) 13.6 gal.; (Grand Am) 13.6 gal.; (Firebird) 15.5 gal.; (6000) 15.7 gal.; (Grand Prix/Bonneville) 18.1 gal.; (Parisienne sed) 25 gal.; (Parisienne wag) 22 gal.

DRIVETRAIN OPTIONS: Engines: Turbo 1.8-liter four: Sunbird ($1511) except SE conv. ($1296); standard on GT. 173 cid, two-barrel V-6: 6000 ($435). 173 cid, FI V-6: Fiero ($645); Firebird ($350); 6000 ($560). 181 cid V-6: Grand Am ($610). 262 cid V-6: Grand Prix ($150). 305 cid, four-barrel V-8: Firebird ($750); Firebird SE ($400); Grand Prix/Bonneville ($540); Parisienne ($390). H.O. 305 cid V-8, four-barrel or FI: Trans Am ($695). Transmission/Differential: Four-speed manual transmission: Fiero SE ($50 credit); Sunbird ($75 credit). Five-speed manual transmission: 1000 ($75); Sunbird ($75). Three-speed automatic transmission: Fiero ($465); Fiero GT ($515); 1000 ($425); Sunbird ($390-$465); Grand Am ($465). Four-speed automatic transmission: Firebird ($465); 6000/Grand Prix/Bonneville/Parisienne ($175). Limited-slip differential: Firebird/G.P./Bonneville/Parisienne ($75). Brakes/Steering: Power brakes: 1000 ($100). Power four-wheel disc brakes: Firebird ($179) but no charge (NC) w/performance pkg. Power steering: 1000/Sunbird ($215). Suspension: Rally tuned suspension: Fiero/Sunbird/Grand Am/6000/G.P./Parisienne ($50). Superlift shock absorbers: 6000/G.P./Bonneville/Parisienne ($64). H.D. springs: Parisienne ($16). Other: H.D. cooling ($40-$70). H.D. battery ($26). H.D. alternator ($25-$51). Engine block heater ($18-$19). California emissions ($99).

1986 Pontiac Grand Am four-door sedan. PMD

OPTION PACKAGES: 1000 sport/handling pkg. ($358). 1000 custom trim ($151). Sunbird custom exterior group ($86). Sunbird custom trim group ($244-$493). Sunbird security pkg. ($19). Firebird Trans Am special performance pkg. ($664). Firebird luxury interior trim ($349-$359). 6000 custom exterior ($56). Grand Prix Brougham Landau pkg. ($469). Lamp groups ($21-$47).

MAJOR CONVENIENCE/APPEARANCE OPTIONS: Air conditioning ($645-$750). Cruise control ($175); N/A on 1000. Power seat ($215-$225); N/A on 1000/Fiero. Dual eight-way power seats: 6000 STE ($508). Power windows ($195-$285); N/A on 1000. Cornering lamps: Bonneville/G.P. ($68); Parisienne ($55). Power glass sun roof: Parisienne ($1230). Removable glass sun roof: Fiero/Sunbird/Grand Am/6000 ($310). Hatch roof: Firebird/Grand Prix ($850-$886). Full vinyl roof: Bonneville ($160). Padded vinyl roof: G.P. ($245-$322). Padded full vinyl roof: Bonneville ($245); Parisienne ($185). Rear spoiler: Fiero ($269); Firebird SE ($70). Louvered rear sunshields: Sunbird ($199); Firebird ($210); Trans Am ($95). Two-tone paint: Sunbird ($101-$151); Grand Am ($101); Firebird/6000 ($205); G.P./Bonneville ($205); Parisienne sed ($205). Recaro bucket seats: Firebird ($636-$995).

HISTORICAL FOOTNOTES: Introduced: October 3, 1985, except Grand Am, August 28, 1985, and Fiero, January 3, 1986. Model year production: 952,943. Calendar year production (U.S.): 775,247. Calendar year sales by U.S. dealers: 841,441. Model year sales by U.S. dealers: 840,137. Pontiac's anti-lock braking (ABS), like that of other GM divisions, came from the Teves organization in West Germany. The division's market share rose by one percent in model year 1986, as a result of moderately increased sales. Even with V-6 power available, Fiero sales continued below the anticipated level, and fell this year (though over 71,000 did find customers). Grand Am, on the other hand, wasn't so far from doubling its 1985 sales total. Pontiac's version of the N-body design attracted considerably more buyers than the equivalents from Buick and Oldsmobile. Firebird sales slipped a bit, but the Trans Am remained popular. Grand Prix and Bonneville declined rather sharply. Poor sales of the subcompact 1000 prompted its discontinuance for 1987, when a new front-drive Bonneville would appear. Pontiac was also planning to introduce a Korean import under the LeMans name for 1987.

1987 PONTIAC

PONTIAC I.D. NUMBERS: Vehicle identification number (VIN) is located on top left-hand surface of instrument panel visible through the windshield. The VIN has 17 symbols. The first symbol indicates the country of manufacture (U.S.) The second symbol indicates the manufacturer (General Motors). The third symbol indicates the make/division (2=Pontiac). The fourth, fifth and sixth symbols are the same as the body style (model) number. The eighth symbol indicates the engine. The ninth symbol is a check digit. The 10th symbol indicates model-year. The 11th symbol indicates the assembly plant. The last six symbols are the consecutive unit number at the factory.

1987 Pontiac Fiero GT coupe. PMD

FIERO -- SERIES 2P -- FOUR/V-6 -- The Fiero was Pontiac's distinctive P-body two-passenger, mid-engined sports car. A lineup of sporty Fieros drove into 1987 with a full range of fun-to-drive model offerings: Coupe, Sport Coupe, SE Coupe, and GT Coupe. Each had distinctive styling and performance features that appealed to every taste and budget. New for the base Coupe and Sport Coupe were exciting new front and rear fascias that gave each model a cleaner, more aerodynamic look. All except the GT also had a new front license plate carrier. New SE colors were offered, too. The standard 2.5-liter EFI four had increased air flow and power for 1987 due to enlargements of both the TBI system and the intake manifold. It featured an updated Direct Ignition System. This system replaced the ignition distributor with a solid state, multiple-coiled, computer-controlled spark plug firing system for improved efficiency and reduced engine maintenance. The Fiero Coupe and Sport Coupe came equipped with 14-in. Tri-Tech wheel covers.

14-in. Hi-Tech Turbo wheels were optional on the Sport Coupe. The interiors of the base Coupe and Sport Coupe carried a four-spoke steering wheel, full-length console, cloth-appointed bucket seats and trim, and clean instrumentation. The Fiero SE was aimed at driving enthusiasts. It had unique styling with an optional rear deck lid spoiler. Inside was complete instrumentation in backlit gauges, a full-length console, a four-spoke sport steering wheel, and Pallex cloth trim on Euro-style bucket seats. GT colors available at the start of the year were again Black and Silver, plus a new Medium Red Metallic. Other colors were added later. The Fiero GT, which was introduced in mid-1986, returned in 1987. It included the Gertag/GM gearbox and a 2.8-liter 135-hp V-6 good for eight second 0-60 mph times. With optional automatic transmission the same acceleration took nine seconds. The GT had fastback styling, exclusive use of the WS6 performance suspension, and 15-in. diamond-spoke aluminum wheels with different size tires front and rear. It also had dual twin-trumpet exhausts, and an optional wing spoiler. Inside was a backlit instrument cluster with tachometer, trip odometer, temperature and fuel gauges, a leather-wrapped three-spoke steering wheel, and Euro-style bucket seats.

FIERO -- SERIES 2P -- I-4/V-6

Model Number	Body/Style Number	Body Type & Seating	Factory Price	Shipping Weight	Prod. Total
2P	E37	2-dr Cpe-2P	8299	2546	Note 1
2P	M37	2-dr Spt Cpe-2P	9989	2546	Note 1
2P	F37	2-dr SE Cpe-2P	11239	2567	Note 1
2P	G37	2-dr GT Cpe-2P	13489	2708	Note 1

NOTE 1: Fiero series production totaled 44,432.

1000 -- SERIES 2T -- FOUR -- The 1000 was Pontiac's version of Chevy's Chevette. Both were derived from the four-cylinder Opel T-body sub-compact (Opel was a GM-owned German automaker). A split grille with vertical segmentation characterized the Pontiac edition. It bowed in mid-1981 as the T-1000 and had not been expected back in 1987. However, it did return for one last year. This sub-compact was an economical entry-level model good for little more than around-town use. It came in three-door and five-door body styles, both with simple and boxy styling. In its 1987 *Product Highlights and Changes* folder issued February 19, 1987, Pontiac Motor Division listed no revisions for 1000s. They did not even get new paint colors. Standard equipment included front and rear bumper guards, front and rear bumper rub strips, chrome-plated steel bumpers, all-vinyl seats, cigar lighter, cut-pile carpets, AM radio with clock, front mini console, inside hood release, reclining front bucket seats, sport steering wheel, Delco Freedom II battery, anti-corrosion treatment, and fluidic windshield washer/wiper system. The standard interior featured a folding full-width rear seat.

1000 -- SERIES 2T -- I-4

Model Number	Body/Style Number	Body Type & Seating	Factory Price	Shipping Weight	Prod. Total
2T	L08	3-dr Hatch-4P	5959	2114	Note 1
2T	L68	5-dr Hatch 4P	6099	2173	Note 1

NOTE 1: 1000 series production totaled 5628.

SUNBIRD -- SERIES 2J -- -FOUR -- The J-body Sunbirds were much-improved spinoffs of the Chevrolet Vega/Pontiac Astre sub-compact cars. Base Sunbird models were carried over from 1986 without changes, except for a new manual transmission shift knob and several new interior trims and exterior finishes. New body colors for 1987 Sunbirds included Light Sapphire Metallic; Dark Sapphire Metallic; Medium Rosewood Metallic; and Dark Rosewood Metallic. Standard equipment included a front air dam, dual rectangular headlights, front and rear bumpers, cigar lighter, cut-pile carpeting, a front floor console, an inside hood release, reclining bucket seats, side window defogers, Delco Freedom II battery, extensive anti-corrosion protection, and a fluidic windshield washer system. When cloth trim was ordered, a new low-back front bucket seat with separate head rest was included for added comfort. The level 1 cloth trim option was of a luxurious new "Ripple cloth" design. An LE (Luxury Edition) option was available for the two-door Sedan and Safari Wagon. It included the GT-style six-lamp front fascia, custom trim, high-tech taillights, a deluxe console, and LE identification. Specific new front and rear fascias were added to the SE (Sport Edition) model, which also carried black exterior moldings. The SE front included new semi-hidden headlights. The Sunbird GT had a standard turbocharged engine, new color-keyed fender flares (except Sedan), and a color-keyed spoiler and mirrors with monochromatic finish. The Gertag/GM five-speed, revised axle half shafts, and WS6 performance suspension were standard on GTs. The latter included 28-mm front/21-mm rear stabilizer bars, high-rate springs and rear bushings, 14.0:1 ratio power steering, and P215/60R14 tires. New body side striping could be ordered for solid color GTs, while those with optional two-tone paint treatments included specific body striping as standard equipment. New to the options list was an Easy-Entry passenger seat, an Ultima cloth articulating seat, and new 13-in. aluminum Sport Tech wheels (replacing Turbo Torque wheels). The old Safari name was added to wagons.

191

1987 Pontiac Sunbird SE coupe. PMD

Model Number	Body/Style Number	Body Type & Seating	Factory Price	Shipping Weight	Prod. Total
SUNBIRD -- SERIES 2J -- I-4					
2J	B69	4-dr Sed-5P	7999	2404	Note 1
2J	B35	4-dr Safari-5P	8529	2466	Note 1
SUNBIRD SE -- SERIES 2J -- I-4/I-4 Turbo					
2J	D27	2-dr Cpe-5P	7979	2353	Note 1
2J	D77	3-dr Hatch-5P	8499	2466	Note 1
2J	D87	2-dr Conv-5P	13799	2532	Note 1
SUNBIRD GT -- SERIES 2J -- I-4/I-4 Turbo					
2J	U27	2-dr Cpe-5P	10299	2353	Note 1
2J	U69	4-dr Sed-5P	10349	2404	Note 1
2J	U77	3-dr Hatch-5P	10699	2399	Note 1
2J	U67	2-dr Conv-5P	15569	2532	Note 1

NOTE 1: Sunbird series production totaled 87,286.

GRAND AM -- SERIES 2N -- Pontiac's Grand Am was an upscale N-body front-wheel-drive compact. New features for 1987 included a backlit analog gauge cluster, passive seat belts, redesigned manual shifter knob, raised rear speakers, and nine new paint colors: Light Sapphire Metallic, Medium Sapphire Metallic, Medium Garnet Metallic, Light Rosewood Metallic, Medium Rosewood Metallic, Light Copper Metallic, Medium Copper Metallic, Beige, and Black Metallic. New 14-in. wheels with Tri-Port wheel covers and 195/70R14 tires were a new option for base and LE models. A split-folding rear seat was new for LEs and SEs and was standard in SEs. Other new options included an Ultima cloth articulating seat, new leather trim for LE and SE, and a 2.0-liter Turbo engine at midyear. Composite lamps were now standard on LEs. A new console with integral armrest was optional in base models and standard in others. The 2.5-liter engine utilized a new tuned intake manifold with high-flow cylinder head. Last, but not least, came new four-spoke urethane- and leather-clad steering wheels. Standard equipment included an acoustic insulation package, automatic front safety belts (after January 1987), front and rear soft fascia bumpers, center high-mounted stop light, compact spare tire, Delco Freedom II battery, dual front radio speakers, dual horn, anti-corrosion protection, fluidic windshield washers, flush windshield and backlight, glove compartment, GM Computer Command Control system, headlights-on warning, heater vent system with ducted rear-seat heat, inside hood release, low-noise engine cooling fan, multi-function control lever, U63 Delco AM radio, rear seat integral headrests, reclining front bucket seats, soft ray tinted glass, and wide body side moldings. LEs also had deluxe cloth interior, deluxe color-keyed safety belts, deluxe exterior ornamentation, deluxe Thaxton carpeting, dual sport side-view mirrors and two-tone paint. The SE also included composite headlights, cruise control, deluxe integral fog lamps, remote fuel filler, power door locks, a UM7 Delco AM/FM stereo, rally gauges and tachometer, rear seat center armrest, specific monotone paint treatment with color-keyed grille, emblems and aluminum wheels, rally-tuned suspension, tilt steering, and visor vanity mirror.

Model Number	Body/Style Number	Body Type & Seating	Factory Price	Shipping Weight	Prod. Total
GRAND AM -- SERIES 2N -- I-4/V-6					
2N	E27	2-dr Cpe-5P	9299	2492	Note 1
2N	E69	4-dr Sed-5P	9499	2565	Note 1
GRAND AM LE -- SERIES 2N -- I-4/V-6					
2N	V27	2-dr Cpe-5P	9999	2528	Note 1
2N	V69	4-dr Sed-5P	10199	2590	Note 1
GRAND AM SE -- SERIES 2N -- I-4/V-6					
2N	W27	2-dr Cpe-5P	12659	2608	Note 1
2N	W69	4-dr Sed-5P	12899	2686	Note 1

NOTE 1: Grand Am series production totaled 226,507.

FIREBIRD -- SERIES 2F -- V-6/V-8 -- The sporty F-body Firebird had few changes for 1987. The dropping of the SE Coupe was the big one. A new Formula option was offered. A body-color aero spoiler with a high-mounted stop light embedded in it was one change. Base Firebirds also had a new seat with adjustable headrest and Ripple cloth upholstery. New options included body-color body side moldings, molded door panel trim (except GTA), and availability of the Y99 performance suspension on base models. A 5.7-liter multi-port fuel injected V-8 performance engine was optional in cars with the Formula package and standard in the GTA, which was itself a new Trans Am option. A four-way manual adjustable seat was now standard in Trans Ams. Base Firebirds featured a full-length console with instrument panel, side window defoggers, front air dam, GM Computer Command Control system, hatch "pull-down" feature, rectangular-shaped concealed quartz halogen headlights, U63 Delco AM radio, cloth reclining front bucket seats, folding rear seat, three-spoke Formula steering wheel, lockable storage compartment, and "wet-arm" (fluidic) windshield wipers. Formulas added a body-color aero rear deck lid spoiler, analog instrumentation, domed hood, 16 x 8-in. Hi-Tech aluminum wheels, and special performance suspension. Trans Ams added an aero body skirting package, hood and front fender air extractors, hood air louvers, fog lamps, soft ray tinted glass, and a rally-tuned suspension. GTAs added articulating front bucket seats, a limited-slip rear axle, special aero package, special performance suspension, leather-wrapped steering wheel, and lightweight 16 x 8-in. diamond-spoke gold-colored wheels.

Model Number	Body/Style Number	Body Type & Seating	Factory Price	Shipping Weight	Prod. Total
FIREBIRD -- SERIES 2F -- V-6					
2F	S87	2-dr Cpe-5P	10359	3105	Note 1
FIREBIRD -- SERIES 2F -- V-8					
2F	S87	2-dr Cpe-5P	13259	3274	Note 1

NOTE 1: Firebird series production totaled 80,439.

NOTE 2: The Formula, Trans Am, and GTA packages were optional equipment.

1987 Pontiac 6000 STE four-door sedan. PMD

6000 -- SERIES 2A -- I-4/V-6 -- There were no styling changes for the 1987 model year. New for the base model was a tethered gas cap, a lightweight scissors jack, composite headlights, a revised instrument panel appliqué, 14-in. cast aluminum wheels, restyled taillight lenses and bezels, a bright grille, and an improved Delco maintenance-free battery. Also the 6000 Station Wagon used the Safari name, as did other Pontiac wagons. The LE was dropped as a model and became an interior trim option for the base 6000. It included wide body side moldings, two-tone lower paint accents, new door map pockets, and London/Empress cloth interior trim. The LE model's B-pillar appliqués became a delete-option. New for 6000 SEs was a standard aero package and rear deck lid spoiler, door map pockets, new taillight lenses with black bezels, a new black grille, and newly optional leather seat inserts. Changes in STE models included a new body-color lower air dam, new body-color taillight bezels, a "wet-arm" wiper system, new door map pockets, and button type front floor mat retainers. Also the black rocker panel moldings used previously were deleted. Standard equipment on base 6000s included acoustical insulation, black door window frames, carpeted lower door panels, center high-mounted stop light, compact spare tire, composite headlights, cut-pile carpeting, Delco Freedom II battery, extensive anti-corrosion protection, fluidic windshield wiper/washer system, black front air dam, front and rear door lamp switches, glove compartment with lock, GM Computer Command Control system, inside hood release, warm red instrument panel lighting, multi-function control lever, Delco U63 AM radio, radio noise suppression equipment, side window defoggers, and soft fascia front and rear bumpers. Cars with the LE option also had color-keyed safety belts, door map pockets, dual horns, locking fuel filler door, lower two-tone paint accents, map pockets on front seat backs, and four-spoke sport steering wheel. Added on SE models were front bucket seats and a console, a dual outlet sport exhaust system, rally gauges with tachometer, and a leather-wrapped SE steering wheel. The top-of-the-

line 6000 STE also had an accessory kit with flares, a raincoat, and first aid supplies, controlled-cycle wipers, deluxe carpeted floor mats, a driver information center, electronically operated side view mirrors, electronic ride control system, GM Computer Control system, locking fuel filler door, power door locks, Delco "touch control" AM/FM stereo with cassette, rear seat with fold-down center armrest, specific STE leather-wrapped steering wheel with integral radio controls, tilt steering wheel, visor vanity mirror, and a windshield sun shade with pockets.

Model Number	Body/Style Number	Body Type & Seating	Factory Price	Shipping Weight	Prod. Total
6000 -- SERIES 2A -- I-4/V-6					
2A	F27	2-dr Cpe-5P	10,499	2792	Note 1
2A	F19	4-dr Sed-5P	10,499	2755	Note 1
2A	F35	4-dr Safari-5P	10,899	2925	Note 1
6000 LE -- SERIES 2A -- I-4/V-6					
2A	G19	4-dr Sed-5P	11,099	2824	Note 1
2A	G35	4-dr Safari-5P	11,499	2977	Note 1
6000 SE -- SERIES 2A -- I-4/V-6					
2A	E19	4-dr Sed-5P	12,389	2986	Note 1
2A	E35	4-dr Safari-5P	13,049	3162	Note 1
6000 STE -- SERIES 2A -- I-4/V-6					
2A	H19	4-dr Sed-5P	18,099	3101	Note 1

NOTE 1: 6000 series production totaled 138,518.

1987 Pontiac Grand Prix 2+2 Aerodynamic Coupe. PMD

GRAND PRIX -- SERIES 2G -- V-6/V-8 -- Pontiac's rear-drive intermediate luxury coupe was fading in popularity by 1987. It offered comfortable, reliable motoring combined with mediocre fuel economy. Three trim levels were offered: Grand Prix, Grand Prix LE, and Grand Prix Brougham. There was also a limited-edition 2+2 model with a fastback rear window treatment designed to enhance aerodynamics and homologate the special "big window" body for NASCAR Grand National stock car racing. Every Grand Prix featured mini bumper guards front and rear, carpeted lower door areas, center high-mounted stop light, front and rear lower chrome bumpers, compact spare tire, custom wheel covers, Delco Freedom II battery, dome light, dual horns, dual rectangular headlights, electronic clock, engine coolant recovery system, extensive anti-corrosion protection, formal roof line with formal rear quarter windows, front stabilizer bar, glove compartment with lock and key, GM Computer Command Control system, inside hood release, multi-function control lever, power steering, and windsplit hood ornament. Grand Prix LEs also featured color-keyed safety belts, dual sport side view mirrors, 55/45 notchback front seat in Pallex cloth with fold-down center armrest, four-spoke sport steering wheel, and wide rocker panel moldings. The Grand Prix Brougham added door courtesy lamps, power windows, Majestic cloth seat trim (instead of Pallex cloth), and luxury cushion steering wheel. The 2+2 was designed for fans of luxury sport driving. It included performance-oriented power and handling features. Styling changes began up front with a rounded front fascia incorporating a four-sectioned honeycomb grille-work. The upper sections blended smoothly into the molded fascia panel, while the lower sections were mounted in the body-colored bumper. A deep front air dam added to the sporty character. Like the front fascia, it was made of reaction injection molded (RIM) urethane. Further back, the aerodynamic flavor of the fastback model continued with a sweeping, permanently fixed rear window. A fiberglass panel covered the area between the rear seat and the aft portion of the window. This panel was finished in matte black to reduce glare on the window. Access to the luggage compartment was possible through an abbreviated fiberglass rear deck lid. A four-inch high spoiler, molded into the deck lid, enhanced the smooth air flow over the vehicle and also served as a housing for the center high-mounted stop light. The 2+2 came with a high-performance drivetrain. Its specifically tuned suspension featured four gas-filled shocks, 77 N-mm front and 24 N-mm rear coil springs, 29mm front and 16mm

rear stabilizer bars, 15x7 -in. Rally II wheels, and Goodyear Eagle GT tires. Complimenting the performance suspension of the 2+2 was a firm 12.7:1 steering ratio. Interior features included a leather-wrapped three-spoke tilt steering wheel, cloth-covered front bucket seats, a center console, rally cluster instrumentation (with tach, odometer, and digital clock), and AM/FM stereo with seek-and-scan, and a cassette deck. Air conditioning, cruise control, full tinted glass, dual sport mirrors, power windows, and power locks were also standard in 2+2s. They were finished in a Silver primary exterior color with Gray interior.

Model Number	Body/Style Number	Body Type & Seating	Factory Price	Shipping Weight	Prod. Total
GRAND PRIX -- SERIES 2G -- V-6/V-8					
2G	J37	2-dr Cpe-5P	11,069	3231	Note 1
GRAND PRIX LE-- SERIES 2G -- V-6/V-8					
2G	K37	2-dr Cpe-5P	11,799	3263	Note 1
GRAND PRIX BROUGHAM -- SERIES 2G -- V-6/V-8					
2G	P37	2-dr Cpe-5P	12,519	3265	Note 1
GRAND PRIX 2+2-- SERIES 2G -- V-6/V-8					
2G	RPOY97	2-dr Aero Cpe-5P	17,800	3530	Note 1/2

NOTE 1: Grand Prix series production totaled 16,542.

NOTE 2: Only 200 Grand Prix 2+2s are believed to have been built.

BONNEVILLE -- SERIES 2H -- V-6 -- The Bonneville badge went on an all-new front-wheel-drive Sedan in 1987. Pontiac described it as a "state-of-the-art" Sports Sedan. It was in the full-size car class, and was constructed with a great deal of attention paid to detail to give it a high-quality image. Aggressive, aerodynamic looks characterized this contemporary new entry. All models were powered by a transversely-mounted V-6 with a sequential fuel injection (SFI) system. This engine was teamed with a four-speed automatic transaxle. Power rack-and-pinion steering, power disc brakes, and a fully-independent MacPherson strut suspension system provided precise road feel. Styling cues started with a fluid shape featuring a bold and aggressively tapered nose that swept to reveal a narrow horizontal grille opening proudly showcasing the Pontiac crest. The roof line was designed to give generous head room, while a gently curved rear window swept into the carefully sculptured rear deck. The rear view of the Bonneville was dominated by a boldly ribbed taillight design, with lamps that wrapped neatly around each body corner for maximum visibility. The cumulative design effect was one of smoothness combined with an aggressive road stance. "We wanted to create a more youthful, sophisticated sedan." said John Schinella, chief designer of Pontiac Design Studio 2. "Smooth, graceful surfaces, rounded front and rear curves, and more contemporary proportions have helped to achieve a more integral design for the all-new Bonneville." The interior featured round gauges, backlit dials and pointers, an electric speedometer, fuel, and engine temperature gauges, and a function monitoring system with graphic telltales. A rich wood-look treatment on the instrument panel blended with the four-spoke steering wheel for total driver appeal. Seating was carefully tailored and sculpted to provide excellent support and long distance comfort. Door map pockets were a standard feature, along with tinted glass, and air conditioning. There were two models (base Bonneville and Bonneville LE), plus an RPOY80 Bonneville SE option package. Standard on the base model was acoustical insulation, Aero Torque wheel covers, a front center armrest seat, automatic front safety belts (effective November 1986), carpets, center high-mounted stop light, cluster warning lamps, compact spare tire, complete instrumentation, Delco Freedom II battery, dual horns, extensive corrosion protection, flow-through ventilation, GM Computer Command Control system, inside hood release, dome lamp, glovebox lamp, trunk lamp, lower door panel carpeting, multi-function control lever, power rack-and-pinion steering, UL6 Delco AM radio with clock, and fluidic windshield wipers. LE models added a rear seat with pull-down center armrest, deluxe carpets, deluxe trunk trim, dual side view sport mirrors, power windows with door pod switches, right- and left-hand manual front seat recliners, a 45/55 split bench front seat with armrest, and wide body side moldings. The Bonneville SE also featured complete rally instrumentation with tachometer, controlled-cycle windshield wipers, a driver information center, gas pressure struts, special springs, a leather-wrapped steering wheel, a rally-tuned suspension, tilt steering wheel, 15 x 6-in. Tri-Port cast aluminum wheels, and Eagle GT steel-belted radial tires.

BONNEVILLE -- SERIES H -- V-6

Model Number	Body/Style Number	Body Type & Seating	Factory Price	Shipping Weight	Prod. Total
2H	HX5	4-dr Spt Sed-5P	13,399	3316	Note 1
2H	HZ5	4-dr LE Spt Sed-5P	14,866	3316	Note 1
2H	HZ5/Y80	4-dr SE Spt Sed-5P	15,806	3324	Note 1

NOTE 1: Bonneville series production totaled 111,419.

SAFARI -- SERIES 2L -- V-8 -- Although the Safari name was used on 1987 Sunbird and 6000 wagons, the separate Safari series still offered Pontiac's massive (for 1987) full-sized Station Wagon. It used the traditional front engine, rear-wheel-drive layout that dated back many years. This model was the only remaining "Parisienne" model, but that model name was no longer used. Standard Safari features included tinted glass, air conditioning, AM/FM stereo radio, dual sport mirrors, whitewall tires, and a 5.0-liter V-8 coupled to a four-speed automatic transmission. For towing purposes, the Safari was available with a seven-wire trailer light cable, plus an optional heavy-duty cooling system. Additional standard fare included soft ray tinted glass, Power Master front disc/rear drum power brakes, white-accented bumper rub strips front and rear, carpeting on the floor and load floor, carpeted lower door panels, center high-mounted stop light, extensive anti-corrosion protection, GM Computer Command Control system, inside hood release, remote-control driver's mirror, power steering, notchback front seat with center armrest, rear-facing third seat with Hartford vinyl trim, load-carrying rear springs, front stabilizer bar, three-spoke steering wheel, tailgate window control, and custom wheel covers.

SAFARI -- SERIES 2L -- V-8

Model Number	Body/Style Number	Body Type & Seating	Factory Price	Shipping Weight	Prod. Total
2L	BL8	4-dr Sta Wag-8P	13,959	4109	Note 1

NOTE 1: Safari series production totaled 11,935.

FIERO ENGINES

[BASE] Inline. Overhead valves. Four-cylinder. Cast iron block and head. Displacement:151 cu. in. (2.5L Tech IV). Bore x stroke: 4.00 x 3.00 in. Compression ratio: 9.0:1. Brake horsepower: 98 @ 4800 rpm. Torque: 132-134 lb.-ft. @ 2800 rpm. Five main bearings. Hydraulic valve lifters. Fuel system: EFI/TBI. RPO Code: LR8. Standard with five-speed manual in base, Sport Coupe, and SE. Available with three-speed automatic in same models. [VIN code U]. [OPTIONAL] V-block. Overhead valves. Six-cylinder. Cast iron block and aluminum head. Displacement:173 cu. in. (2.8L). Bore x stroke: 3.50 x 2.99 in. Compression ratio: 8.9:1. Brake horsepower: 135 @ 4500 rpm. Torque: 160-165 lb.-ft. @ 3600 rpm. Fuel system: EFI/MFI. RPO Code: L44. Standard with five-speed manual in GT (optional in SE). Available with three-speed automatic in SE and GT. [VIN code W].

PONTIAC 1000 ENGINES

[BASE] Inline. OHC. Four-cylinder. Cast iron block and head. Displacement:98 cu. in. (1.6L). Bore x stroke: 3.23 x 2.98 in. Compression ratio: 9.0:1. Brake horsepower: 65 @ 5200 rpm. Torque: 80 lb.-ft. @ 3200 rpm. Five main bearings. Hydraulic valve lifters. Fuel system: 2V carburetor. RPO Code: L17. Standard with four-speed manual. Optional with five-speed manual or three-speed automatic. [VIN code C].

SUNBIRD ENGINES

[BASE] Inline. OHC. Four-cylinder. Cast iron block and aluminum head. Displacement:121 cu. in. (2.0L). Bore x stroke: 3.39 x 3.39 in. Brake horsepower: 96 @ 4800 rpm. Fuel system: EFI/TBI. RPO Code: LT2. Standard with five-speed manual in base, Safari, and SE (optional in GT). Available with three-speed automatic in all. [VIN code K]. [OPTIONAL] Inline. OHC. Four-cylinder. Turbocharged. Cast iron block and aluminum head. Displacement:121 cu. in. (2.0L). Bore x stroke: 3.39 x 3.39 in. Brake horsepower: 165 @ 5600 rpm. Fuel system: EFI/MFI. RPO Code: LT3. Standard with five-speed manual in GT (optional in SE). Available with three-speed automatic in SE and GT. [VIN code M].

GRAND AM ENGINES

[BASE] Inline. Overhead valves. Four-cylinder. Cast iron block and head. Displacement:151 cu. in. (2.5L Tech IV). Bore x stroke: 4.00 x 3.00 in. Compression ratio: 9.0:1. Brake horsepower: 98 @ 4800 rpm. Torque: 132-134 lb.-ft. @ 2800 rpm. Five main bearings. Hydraulic valve lifters. Fuel system: EFI/TBI. RPO Code: L68. Standard with five-speed manual in base and LE (credit option in SE). Available with three-speed automatic, except in SE. [VIN code R]. [OPTIONAL] V-block. Overhead valves. Six-cylinder. Cast iron block and aluminum head. Displacement:181 cu. in. (3.0L). Bore x stroke: 3.80 x 2.70 in. Brake horsepower: 125 @ 4900 rpm. Fuel system: EFI/MFI. RPO Code: LN7. Standard with three-speed automatic in SE (optional in base and LE). [VIN code L].

FIREBIRD ENGINES

[BASE V-6] V-block. Overhead valves. Six-cylinder. Cast iron block and aluminum head. Displacement:173 cu. in. (2.8L). Bore x stroke: 3.50 x 2.99 in. 135 @ 5100 rpm. Fuel system: EFI/MFI. RPO Code: LB8. Standard with five-speed manual in base Firebird. Available with four-speed automatic in base Firebird. [VIN code W]. [BASE V-8] V-block. Overhead valves. Eight-cylinder. Cast iron block and head. Displacement: 305 cu. in. (5.0L). Bore x stroke: 3.74 x 3.48 in. Brake horsepower: 155 @ 4200 rpm. Fuel system: four-barrel carburetor. RPO Code: LG4. Produced in U.S. or Canada. Standard with five-speed

manual in base Firebird V-8, Formula, and Trans Am. Available with four-speed automatic in same models. [VIN code E]. [OPTIONAL V-8] V-block. Overhead valves. Eight-cylinder. Cast iron block and head. Displacement: 305 cu. in. (5.0L). Bore x stroke: 3.74 x 3.48 in. Brake horsepower: 165 @ 4400 rpm. Fuel system: four-barrel carburetor. RPO Code: LB9. Produced in U.S. or Canada. Available with five-speed manual in Formula, and Trans Am (delete-option in GTA). Available with four-speed automatic in same applications. [VIN code F]. [GTA V-8] V-block. Overhead valves. Eight-cylinder. Cast iron block and head. Displacement: 350 cu. in. (5.7L). Bore x stroke: 3.74 x 3.48 in. Brake horsepower: 210 @ 4000 rpm. Torque: 315 lb.-ft. @ 3200 rpm. Fuel system: four-barrel carburetor. RPO Code: B2L. Standard with four-speed automatic in GTA (optional in Formula and Trans Am). Includes low-profile air induction system with aluminum plenum and individual aluminum tuned runners, an extruded dual fuel rail assembly with computer controlled fuel injectors, and a special low-restriction exhaust system. [VIN code 8].

6000 ENGINES

[BASE] Inline. Overhead valves. Four-cylinder. Cast iron block and head. Displacement: 151 cu. in. (2.5L Tech IV). Bore x stroke: 4.00 x 3.00 in. Compression ratio: 9.0:1. Brake horsepower: 98 @ 4800 rpm. Torque: 132-134 lb.-ft. @ 2800 rpm. Five main bearings. Hydraulic valve lifters. Fuel system: EFI/TBI. RPO Code: LR8. Standard with three-speed automatic in base 6000, base Safari, 6000 LE, and Safari LE. [VIN code U]. [STANDARD V-6] V-block. Overhead valves. Six-cylinder. Cast iron block and aluminum head. Displacement: 173 cu. in. (2.8L). Bore x stroke: 3.50 x 2.99 in. Brake horsepower: 125 @ 4800 rpm. Fuel system: EFI/MFI. RPO Code: LB6. Standard V-6 (with three-speed automatic) in all 6000 models except STE. Standard in STE with four-speed automatic (and optional in all other models). Also available as a delete-option, with five-speed manual transmission, in SE and STE models. [VIN code 9].

GRAND PRIX ENGINES

[STANDARD] V-block. Overhead valves. Six-cylinder. Cast iron block. Displacement: 231 cu. in. (3.8L). Bore x stroke: 3.80 x 3.40 in. Brake horsepower: 110 @ 3800 rpm. Fuel system: two-barrel carburetor. RPO Code: LD5. Standard V-6 (with three-speed automatic) in all Grand Prix models except 2+2. [VIN code A]. [OPTIONAL] V-block. Overhead valves. Six-cylinder. Cast iron block. Displacement: 263 cu. in. (4.3L). Bore x stroke: 4.00 x 3.48 in. Brake horsepower: 140 @ 4200. Fuel system: EFI/TBI. RPO Code: LB4. Optional V-6 (with three-speed automatic) in all Grand Prix models except 2+2. Also available in same models with optional four-speed automatic. [VIN code Z]. [STANDARD V-8] V-block. Overhead valves. Eight-cylinder. Cast iron block. Displacement: 305 cu. in. (5.0L). Bore x stroke: 3.74 x 3.48 in. Brake horsepower: 150 @ 4000 rpm. Fuel system: four-barrel carburetor. RPO Code: LG4. Produced in U.S. and Canada. Standard V-8 in all Grand Prix including 2+2. [VIN code H].

1987 Pontiac Bonneville LE four-door sedan. PMD

BONNEVILLE ENGINE

[STANDARD] V-block. Overhead valves. Six-cylinder. Cast iron block. Displacement: 231 cu. in. (3.8L). Bore x stroke: 3.80 x 3.40 in. Brake horsepower: 150 @ 4400 rpm. Fuel system: EFI/SFI. RPO Code: LG3. Standard V-6 in all Bonneville models. [VIN code 3].

SAFARI ENGINE

[STANDARD V-8] V-block. Overhead valves. Eight-cylinder. Cast iron block. Displacement: 307 cu. in. (5.0L). Bore x stroke: 3.80 x 3.85 in. Brake horsepower: 140 @ 3200 rpm. Fuel system: four-barrel carburetor. RPO Code: LV2. Produced in U.S. and Canada. Standard V-8 in all Safaris. [VIN code Y].

FIERO CHASSIS: Wheelbase: 93.4 in. (all). Overall length: 162.7 in. (Coupe, Sport Coupe); 165.1 in. (SE, GT). Width: 69 in. (all) Height: 46.9 in. (all). Front tread: 57.8 in. Rear tread: 57.8 in. Standard tires: P185/75R15 BSW (Coupe, Sport Coupe); P195/70R14 BSW (SE); P205/60R14 front and P215/60R14 rear (GT).

PONTIAC 1000 CHASSIS: Wheelbase: 94.3 in. (all). Overall length: 161.9 in. (three-door); 164.9 in. (five-door). Width: 61.8 in. (all) Height: 52.8 in. (all). Front tread: 51.2 in. Rear tread: 51.2 in. Standard tires: P155/80R13 BSW (all).

SUNBIRD CHASSIS: Wheelbase: 101.2 in. (all). Overall length: 173.7 in. (Coupe/Hatchback/Convertible); 175.7 (Sedan); 175.9 (Wagon). Width: 66.0 in. (Coupe/Convertible); 66.3 in. (Others) Height: 51.9 in. (Coupe/Hatchback/Convertible); 53.8 in. (sedan); 54.1 in. (Safari Wagon). Front tread: 54.4 in. Rear tread: 54.1 in. Standard tires: P175/80R13 BSW (all except Turbo). Standard tires: P215/60R14 (Turbo).

GRAND AM CHASSIS: Wheelbase: 103.4 in. (Coupe/Sedan). Overall length: 177.5 (all). Width: 66.9 in. (Coupe); 67.5 in. (Sedan). Height: 52.5 (Coupe/Sedan). Front tread: 55.6 in. Rear tread: 55.1 in. Standard tires: P185/80R13 BSW (Base/LE). Standard tires: P215/60R14 (SE).

FIREBIRD CHASSIS: Wheelbase: 101.0 in. (All). Overall length: 188.0 (Base/Formula); 191.6 in. (Trans Am/GTA). Width: 72.0 in. (all). Height: 49.7 in. (all). Front tread: 60.7 in. Rear tread: 61.6 in. Standard tires: P215/65R15 BSW (Base/Formula/GTA). Standard tires: P215/65R15 RWL (Trans Am).

6000 CHASSIS: Wheelbase: 104.9 in. (all). Overall length: 188.8 in. (Coupe/Sedan); 193.2 in. (Safari). Width: 72 in. (all). Height: 53.3 in. (Coupe); 53.7 in. (Sedan); 54.1 in. (Safari). Front tread: 58.7 in. Rear tread: 57.0 in. Standard tires: 185/75R14 (All except STE). Standard tires: 195/70R14 (STE).

GRAND PRIX CHASSIS: Wheelbase: 108.1 in. (all). Overall length: 201.9 in. (all). Width: 72.3 in. (all). Height: 54.7 in. (all). Front tread: 55.4 in. Rear tread: 55.1 in. Standard tires: 195/75R14 (All except 2+2). Standard tires: 215/65R15 Goodyear Eagle GT (2+2).

1987 Pontiac Bonneville SE four-door sedan. PMD

BONNEVILLE CHASSIS: Wheelbase: 110.8 in. (all). Overall length: 198.7 in. (all). Width: 72.1 in. (all). Height: 55.5 in. (all). Front tread: 58.7 in. Rear tread: 57.0 in. Standard tires: 205/75R14 (All except SE). Standard tires: 215/65R15 Goodyear Eagle GT (SE).

SAFARI CHASSIS: Wheelbase: 116.0 in. (all). Overall length: 215.1 in. (all). Width: 79.3 in. (all). Height: 57.4 in. (all). Front tread: 62.1 in. Rear tread: 64.1 in. Tires: P225/75R15 WSW steel-belted radials.

FIERO TECHNICAL: Chassis: Mid-engine/rear drive. Base transmission: Three-speed automatic. Optional transmission (with V-6): Gertag-designed GM-developed five-speed automatic. Axle ratio: 3.18:1 (manual) or 2.84 (automatic). Steering: Rack-and-pinion. Front suspension: Independent control arms with coil springs. Rear suspension: Independent control arms with coil springs. Front brakes: Disc. Rear brakes: disc. Fuel tank: 12 gal.

PONTIAC 1000 TECHNICAL: Chassis: Front engine/front drive. Base transmission: Four-speed manual. Optional transmission: Three-speed automatic or five-speed manual. Front suspension: Independent control arms with coil springs. Rear suspension: Live axle with links and coil springs. Front brakes: Vented disc. Rear brakes: drum. Fuel tank: 12.2 gal.

SUNBIRD TECHNICAL: Chassis: Front engine/front drive. Base transmission: Five-speed manual with overdrive. Optional transmission: Three-speed automatic. Front suspension: MacPherson struts with coil springs. Rear suspension: Beam axle with coil springs. Front brakes: Power-assisted vented discs. Rear brakes: Power-assisted drums. Fuel tank: 13.6 gal.

GRAND AM TECHNICAL: Chassis: Front engine/front drive. Base transmission: Five-speed manual with overdrive. Optional transmission: Three-speed automatic. Axle ratio: 3.35:1 (with 2.5L engine and manual). Axle ratio: 3.61:1 (with Turbo engine and manual). Axle

ratio: 2.84:1 (with 3.0L engine or 2.5L engine with automatic). Axle ratio: 3.18:1 (with Turbo engine and automatic). Front suspension: MacPherson struts with coil springs. Rear suspension: Beam axle with coil springs. Front brakes: Power-assisted vented discs. Rear brakes: Power-assisted drums. Fuel tank: 13.6 gal.

FIREBIRD TECHNICAL: Chassis: Front engine/rear drive. Base transmission: Five-speed manual with overdrive. Optional transmission: Four-speed automatic. Axle ratio: 3.42:1 (with V-6). Axle ratio: 3.23:1 (with 5.0L 4V V-8 and five-speed manual). Axle ratio: 2.73:1 (with 5.0L 4V V-8 and four-speed automatic). Axle ratio: 3.08:1 (with 5.0L TPI V-8 and five-speed manual). Axle ratio: 2.77:1 (with 5.7L V-8). Axle ratio: 3.45:1 (with 5.0L TPI V-8 and five-speed manual). Front suspension: MacPherson struts with coil springs. Rear suspension: Live axle with coil springs. Front brakes: Power-assisted vented discs. Rear brakes: Power-assisted drums (rear disc brakes standard on GTA). Fuel tank: 15.5 (V-6/TPI V-8s). Fuel tank: 16.2 gal. (4V V-8).

6000 TECHNICAL: Chassis: Front engine/front drive. Base transmission: Three-speed automatic with overdrive. Optional transmissions: Four-speed automatic and five-speed manual. Axle ratio: 2.39:1 (with 2.5L). Axle ratio: 3.33:1 (with 2.8L V-6 and four-speed automatic). Axle ratio: 3.18:1 (performance ratio with 2.8L V-6 and three-speed automatic). Axle ratio: 3.61:1 (with 2.8L V-6 and five-speed manual). Front suspension: MacPherson struts with coil springs. Rear suspension: Beam axle with coil springs. Front brakes: Power-assisted vented discs. Rear brakes: Power-assisted drums (ABS vented discs on STE). Fuel tank: 15.7 gal.

GRAND PRIX TECHNICAL: Chassis: Front engine/rear drive. Base transmission (except 2+2): Three-speed automatic with overdrive. Base transmission (2+2): Turbo-Hydramatic THM 200-4R four-speed overdrive automatic. Optional transmission (except 2+2): Four-speed automatic. Axle ratio: 2.41:1 (standard with 3.8L V-6 and three-speed automatic; with 4.3L V-6 and four-speed automatic; and with 5.0L V-8 and four-speed automatic, except in 2+2). Axle ratio: 2.29:1 (standard with 4.3L V-6 and three-speed automatic). Axle ratio: 3.08:1 (standard in Grand Prix 2+2 with 5.0L V-8; optional in other models with 3.8L V-6 and three-speed automatic; optional in other models with 4.3L V-6 and four-speed automatic; and optional in other models with 5.0L V-8 and four-speed automatic). Axle ratio: 2.73:1 (optional with 4.3L V-6 and three-speed manual). Front suspension: MacPherson struts with coil springs. Rear suspension: Beam axle with coil springs. Front brakes: Power-assisted vented discs. Rear brakes: Power-assisted drums. Fuel tank: 13.6 gal.

1987 Pontiac Bonneville SE four-door sedan (rear view). PMD

BONNEVILLE TECHNICAL: Chassis: Front engine/front drive. Base transmission: Four-speed automatic. Axle ratio: 2.73:1 (standard with 3.8L V-6 in Base Bonneville and Bonneville SE). Axle ratio: 2.97:1 (standard with 3.8L V-6 in Bonneville SE). Front suspension: MacPherson struts with coil springs. Rear suspension: MacPherson struts with coil springs. Front brakes: Power-assisted vented discs. Rear brakes: Power-assisted drums. Fuel tank: 18.0 gal.

SAFARI TECHNICAL: Chassis: Front engine/rear drive. Base transmission: Four-speed automatic. Axle ratio: 2.73:1 (standard). Axle ratio: 3.08:1 (optional). Front suspension: Control arms with coil springs. Rear suspension: Live axle, links and coil springs. Front brakes: Power-assisted vented discs. Rear brakes: Power-assisted drums. Fuel tank: 22.0 gal.

FIERO OPTIONS: W61 Fiero Coupe option group #1 ($1317). W61 Fiero Sport Coupe option group #1 ($1217). W61 Fiero SE Coupe option group #1 ($1127). W61 Fiero GT Coupe option group #1 ($1181). W63 Fiero Sport Coupe option group #2 ($1581). W63 Fiero SE Coupe option group #2 ($1613). WS1 Performance value package ($259). MM5 five-speed manual transmission (no charge). MX1 three-speed automatic transmission ($490). C60 air conditioning

($775). UA1 heavy-duty battery ($26). V08 heavy-duty cooling system, except with Coupe or GT or L44 engine ($40 with A/C or $70 w/o A/C). C49 electric rear window defogger ($145). NB2 California emissions ($99). Engine block heater, except base Coupe ($18). A01 tinted glass with A/C in Coupe or Sport Coupe ($120); in SE or GT (no charge). V56 luggage rack, except with base Coupe or optional deck lid spoiler ($115). B34 carpeted front floor mats ($24). U63 AM radio equipment in Coupe ($122). UM7 seek-and-scan stereo radio equipment ($217-$317). UM8 seek-and-scan stereo radio equipment with cassette ($339-$439). UX1 seek-and-scan stereo radio equipment with cassette, graphic equalizer and more ($160-$489). UT4 seek-and-scan stereo radio equipment with cassette, graphic equalizer, touch control and more ($200-$529). UQ6 speaker system ($150). UL5 AM radio delete ($58 credit). UL5 AM/FM radio delete ($373 credit). AR9 suede leather and Pallex cloth trim for SE and GT ($375). D80 rear deck lid spoiler ($269). AD3 glass sun roof ($375). N78 14-in. High Tech turbo aluminum wheels with locks for Sport Coupe or SE only ($241). Plus, various tire and wheel options.

PONTIAC 1000 OPTIONS: W61 option group #1 ($835). W63 option group #2 ($988). MM5 five-speed manual transmission ($75). MX1 three-speed automatic transmission ($450). C60 air conditioning ($675). V10 cold climate group ($44). C49 electric rear window defogger ($145). NB2 California emissions ($99). A01 tinted glass ($105). B37 Carpeted front and rear floor mats ($33). N41 power steering, with automatic transmission required ($225). U69 AM/FM radio ($92). U58 AM/FM radio with three speakers ($119). UL5 AM radio delete ($56 credit). AR9 Oxen vinyl trim bucket seats (standard) or Genor cloth trim bucket seats ($30). D88 mid-body accent stripes ($60). AD3 removable glass sun roof ($350). White sidewall tires ($61 extra). P06 wheel trim rings ($39).

SUNBIRD OPTIONS: W61 Sunbird Sedan & Safari Wagon option group #1 ($433). W63 Sunbird Sedan & Safari Wagon option group #2 ($1531). W67 Sunbird Sedan & Safari option group #3 ($1895-$1945). W61 Sunbird SE, except Convertible, option group #1 ($383). W63 Sunbird SE, except Convertible, option group #2 ($1481). W67 Sunbird SE, except Convertible, option group #3 ($1644). W61 Sunbird SE Convertible, option group #1 ($972). W63 Sunbird SE Convertible, option group #2 ($1135). Turbo engine as SE option ($1312-$1527). WS1 Performance value package for SE Convertible ($278). MX1 three-speed automatic transmission ($415). C60 air conditioning ($675). D06 armrest front seat ($58). D06 custom console ($45). D07 custom trim ($45 charge to $45 credit, depending on model). DM1 Turbo decal (no charge). C49 electric rear window defogger ($145). NB2 California emissions ($99). K05 engine block heater ($18). U14 rally gauge cluster with tachometer ($127). U21 rally gauge cluster with tachometer ($49). A01 tinted glass with A/C in Coupe or Sport Coupe ($105). V56 rear deck luggage carrier ($115). Roof luggage carrier for Safari ($115). B34 carpeted front floor mats ($24). Two-tone paint ($101-$151)). U63 AM radio equipment (122). UM7 seek-and-scan stereo radio equipment ($217-$317). UM8 seek-and-scan stereo radio equipment with cassette ($339-$439). UT4 seek-and-scan stereo radio equipment with cassette, graphic equalizer, "touch control" and more ($529-$629). UL5 AM radio delete ($58 credit). D42 cargo area security screen for Hatchback only ($69). AR9 Ripple cloth bucket seats for Sunbird/Sunbird SE ($75). AH13 manual seat adjuster ($35). D80 deck lid spoiler ($70). D98 accent striping ($61). D88 sport stripes for Sunbird GT ($55). AD3 removable glass sun roof, except Convertible. Rally tuned suspension $50. Optional tires (($64-$388) depending upon model. B20 custom trim groups ($168-$643). Y91 LE Custom group ($443-$493). PX1 13-in. Sport Tech aluminum wheels and locks ($215). N78 14-in. Hi-Tech Turbo wheels.

1987 Pontiac Grand Am LE four-door sedan. PMD

GRAND AM OPTIONS: W61 Grand Am Coupe option group #1 ($1128). W63 Grand Am Coupe option group #2 ($1304). W67 Grand Am Coupe option group #3 ($1609). W61 Grand Am Sedan option group #1 ($1128). W63 Grand Am Sedan option group #2 ($1304). W67 Grand Am Sedan option group #3 ($1734). W61 Grand Am LE Coupe option group #1 ($1575). W63 Grand Am LE Coupe option group #2 ($1853). W61 Grand Am LE Sedan option group #1 ($1211). W63 Grand Am LE Sedan option group #2 ($1978). W61 Grand Am SE Coupe option group #1 ($906). W63 Grand Am SE Coupe option group #2 ($1210). W61 Grand Am SE

Sedan option group #1 ($981). W63 Grand Am SE Sedan option group #2 ($1210). WS1 base/LE performance value package #1 ($319). WS3 base/LE performance value package #2 ($728). L68 engine in SE with MM5 transmission ($660 credit). LN7 engine in base/LE models, requires MX1 transmission ($660). MM5 five-speed manual transmission in SE ($490 credit). MX1 three-speed automatic transmission in Grand Am/Grand Am LE ($490). C60 air conditioning ($675). C49 electric rear window defogger ($145). Y80 driver enthusiast package ($799). NB2 California emissions ($99). K05 engine block heater ($18). U14 rally gauge cluster with tachometer and trip odometer ($127). V56 rear deck luggage carrier ($115). B34 carpeted front floor mats, base model ($33). B53 carpeted front floor mats, LE/SE models ($33). UM7 seek-and-scan stereo radio equipment ($217). UM8 seek-and-scan stereo radio equipment with cassette ($132-$339). UX1 seek-and-scan ETR radio with graphic equalizer and cassette ($282-$489). UT4 seek-and-scan stereo radio equipment with cassette, graphic equalizer, "touch control" and more ($322-$529). UL5 AM radio delete ($56 credit). AR9 custom seats with Pallex cloth and leather trim in LE/SE ($150). AQ9 articulating seat, except base model ($450). AD3 removable sun roof ($350). Y99 rally-tuned suspension ($59). Optional tires (($68-$318) depending upon model. N78 14-in. Hi-Tech Turbo wheels.

1987 Pontiac Trans Am GTA coupe. PMD

FIREBIRD OPTIONS: W61 Firebird Coupe option group #1 ($1273). W63 Firebird Coupe option group #2 ($1792). W61 Firebird Formula option group #1 ($1273). W63 Firebird Formula option group #2 ($1842). W61 Firebird Trans Am Coupe option group #1 ($1697). W63 Firebird Trans Am Coupe option group #2 ($1949). W61 Firebird GTA Coupe option group #1 ($1701). W63 Firebird GTA Coupe option group #2 ($1958). WS1 base Firebird performance value package #1 ($265). WS3 base Firebird performance value package #2 ($709). WS1 Trans Am performance value package #1 ($839). W66 Formula option for base Firebird, includes LG4 5.0L V-8, QDZ tires, N96 Hi-Tech Turbo wheels, WS6 performance package, U21 gauge cluster, rear aero wing spoiler, and Formula exterior ornamentation ($1070). Y84 GTA option for Trans Am consists of B2L 5.7L V-8, QDZ tires, PW7 gold diamond spoke wheels, WS6 performance package, KC4 oil cooler, J65 four-wheel disc brakes, G80 limited-slip axle, articulating seats with custom trim, DD9 power paddle type mirrors, NP5 leather appointment group, B34 front and rear mats, and GTA exterior ornamentation ($2700). G4 5.0L V-8 ($400). LB9 5.0L TPI V-8, except in GTA ($745). LB9 5.0L TPI V-8 in GTA ($300 credit). B2L 5.7L V-8 in Formula or Trans Am, requires MXO automatic transmission, KC4 oil cooler, WS6 performance package, J65 four-wheel disc brakes, and G80 limited-slip axle ($1045). MXO four-speed automatic transmission ($490). MM5 five-speed manual transmission in GTA ($490 credit). C60 air conditioning ($825). G80 limited-slip axle ($100). UA1 heavy-duty battery ($26). DX Trans Am hood decal ($95). C49 electric rear window defogger ($145). NB2 California emissions ($99). KC4 engine oil cooler ($110). U21 rally gauge cluster with tachometer, trip odometer in base Firebird ($150). U52 electronic instrument cluster ($275). CC1 locking hatch roof ($920). B34 front and rear floor mats ($35). Dual remote-control power sport mirrors ($91). WX1 two-tone accent paint delete base Firebird and Formula ($150 credit). J65 four-wheel power disc brakes ($179). UM7 seek-and-scan stereo radio equipment ($217). UM6 seek-and-scan stereo radio equipment with cassette ($339). UX1 seek-and-scan ETR radio with graphic equalizer and cassette ($489). UT4 seek-and-scan stereo radio equipment with cassette, graphic equalizer, "touch control" and more ($529). UQ7 subwoofer speaker system ($150). UL5 AM radio delete ($56 credit). U75 power antenna ($70). D42 cargo area security screen ($69). AH3 four-way manual seat adjuster ($35). B20 custom interior with reclining bucket seats and Pallex cloth trim ($319-$349). B20 custom interior with reclining bucket seats and Pallex cloth and leather trim ($619-$649). B20 custom interior with articulating bucket seats and Pallex cloth trim ($619-$649). Y99 rally-tuned suspension ($59). WS6 special performance package including QDZ tires and performance suspension components on Trans Am ($385). Optional tires ($68-$318) depending upon model. [Note: QDZ tires are P245/50VR 16.] N24 15-in. Hi-Tech color-coordinated turbo wheels with locks ($215). N90 15-in. diamond-spoke color-coordinated wheels with lock ($215).

6000 OPTIONS [Except STE]: W61 6000 Coupe option group #1 ($1274). W63 6000 Coupe option group #2 ($1700). W67 6000 Coupe option group #3 ($1907). W61 6000 Sedan option group #1 ($1274). W63 6000 Sedan option group #2 ($1750). W67 6000 Sedan option group #3 ($2032). W61 6000 Safari option group #1 ($1274). W63 6000 Safari option group #2 ($1781). W67 6000 Safari option group #3 ($2013). W61 6000 LE Sedan option group #1 ($1522). W63 6000 LE Sedan option group #2 ($1999). W67 6000 LE Sedan option group #3 ($2032). W61 6000 LE Safari option group #1 ($1513). W63 6000 LE Safari option group #2 ($1980). W67 6000 LE Safari option group #3 ($2294). W61 6000 SE Sedan option group #1 ($1461). W63 6000 SE Sedan option group #2 ($1949). W67 6000 SE Sedan option group #3 ($2137). W61 6000 SE Safari option group #1 ($1452). W63 6000 SE Safari option group #2 ($1930). W67 6000 SE Safari option group #3 ($2118). WS1 performance value package #1 ($260). WS3 performance value package #2 ($549). LB6 2.8L V-6 in 6000/6000LE ($610). MXO four-speed automatic transmission ($175). MM5 five-speed manual transmission, 6000STE only ($440 credit). C60 air conditioning ($775). BC5 carpeted sidewalls and tailgate in Safari. V10 cold weather group ($18-$44). CS1 Safari rear window deflector ($40). C49 electric rear window defogger ($145). NB2 California emissions ($99). U21 rally gauge cluster with tachometer ($100). U52 electronic instrument cluster with tachometer ($150-$250). AQ1 tinted glass ($120). V56 deck lid luggage carrier ($115). V55 roof top luggage carrier ($115). B34 carpeted front and rear floor mats ($35). UM7 seek-and-scan stereo radio equipment ($217). UM8 seek-and-scan stereo radio equipment with cassette ($339). UX1 AM/FM ETR stereo with cassette and more ($489). UL5 AM radio delete ($56 credit). U75 rear-mounted power radio antenna ($70). WV4 bicycle roof carrier ($70). WV3 roof carrier ski racks on Safari SE ($70). AQ4 Safari third seat with swing-out windows ($215). AT6 reclining passenger seat ($45). A76 reclining driver and passenger seats ($90). B20 custom trim ($125). A65 notchback center arm rear seat with Ripple cloth trim ($30). AM6 45/55 split bench seat with center armrest and Ripple cloth or Sierra vinyl trim in 6000 or Empress/London cloth trim in LE ($133). AS7 45/55 split bench seat ($83). AR9 bucket seats with leather trim ($320). D90 upper band accent stripes ($40). AD3 glass sun roof ($350-$365). CF5 power glass sun roof ($918). Y99 rally tuned suspension on 6000 and 6000 LE ($50).Various tire options ($68-$130). WW9 Sport Landau top, 6000 coupe, includes Landau top, D55 sport mirrors, vinyl accent stripes, and N91 wire wheel covers. N78 aluminum sport wheels with locks ($215). N91 simulated wire wheel covers ($214). C25 rear window wiper/washer ($125). Simulated wood-grain side trim.

6000 STE OPTIONS: AG9 power seat locks delete option ($538 credit). AG3 memory control seat ($150). NB2 California emissions ($99). AS7 45/55 split bench seat with suede, Pallex cloth, and leather trim ($545). CF5 power glass sun roof ($895).

GRAND PRIX OPTIONS: W61 Grand Prix Coupe option group #1 ($1313). W63 Grand Prix Coupe option group #2 ($1867). W61 Grand Prix LE option group #1 ($1844). W63 Grand Prix LE option group #2 ($2117). W61 Grand Prix Brougham option group #1 ($1874). W63 Grand Prix Brougham option group #2 ($2078). WS1 Grand Prix performance value package #1 ($703). WS3 Grand Prix LE performance value package #2 ($500). LB4 4.3L V-6 ($200). LG4 5.0L four-barrel V-8 ($590). MXO four-speed automatic transmission ($175). C60 air conditioning ($775). G80 limited-slip axle ($100). V10 Cold weather group ($18-$44). V08 heavy-duty cooling system ($66-$96). C49 electric rear window defogger ($145). NB2 California emissions ($99). U14 rally cluster with trip odometer ($71). U21 rally gauge cluster with tachometer ($153). AO1 tinted glass ($120). CC1 hatch roof with removable glass panels and rear courtesy lamps, not available with sun roof ($906). B34 carpeted front and rear floor mats ($35). B53 carpeted front and rear floor mats ($35). BX2 wide rocker panel molding for base Grand Prix without two-tone paint ($86). B84 two-tone paint with custom upper accent stripes on base or LE Grand Prix ($205). W71 sport two-tone paint treatment on base Grand Prix ($291); on Grand Prix LE ($205). UK4 AM/FM stereo ($178). UK5 AM/FM stereo with cassette ($300). UX1 AM/FM ETR stereo with cassette and more ($450). UL5 AM radio delete ($56 credit). U75 rear mounted power radio antenna ($70). AM6 55/45 notchback seat with center armrest in base Grand Prix with Ripple cloth trim ($133). AR9 bucket seats with recliners and console with Ripple cloth trim in base Grand Prix ($292). AR9 bucket seats with recliners and console with Pallex cloth trim in Grand Prix LE ($89). AR9 bucket seats with recliners and console with Pallex cloth and leather trim in Grand Prix LE ($389). AT6 reclining passenger seat in Grand Prix without bucket seats ($60). D90 painted upper body accent stripes ($65). CF5 power glass sun roof including manual sliding sun shade ($925). Y99 rally-tuned suspension ($50). Tire options ($68-$156). AB6 padded formal landau roof including rear window insert and exterior opera lamps ($337). C04 padded landau roof, not available with two-tone paint W70 ($260). PB7 14-in. Argent Silver Rally II wheels with trim rings ($125). PD8 14-in. turbo-finned aluminum wheels with locking package ($246). N91 wire wheel covers with locking package ($214).

BONNEVILLE OPTIONS: W61 Bonneville Sedan option group #1 ($457). W63 Bonneville Sedan option group #2 ($837). W67 Bonneville Sedan option group #3 ($1369). W61 Bonneville LE option group #1 ($790). W63 Bonneville LE option group #2 ($1066). W67 Bonneville LE Sedan option group #3 ($1593). W61 Bonneville SE option group #1 ($580). W63 Bonneville SE option group #2 ($856). W67 Bonneville SE Sedan option group #3 ($1333). WS1 Bonneville performance value package #1 ($215). WS3 Bonneville LE performance value package #2 ($356). Y80 Bonneville SE option group, includes QYZ tires, PG5 aluminum wheels, CD4 pulse wipers, NP5 leather-wrapped steering wheel, C75 lamp package with fog lamps, UW1 driver information center, AS7 split seat, D55 console, Y99 suspension, sporty exhausts, black door lock cylinders, and gray window sill moldings on Bonneville LE ($940). V08 heavy-duty cooling system ($66). C49 electric rear window defogger ($145). UW1 driver information center in LE, requires U21 rally gauges ($125). G67 electronic ride control, except on SE or teamed with Y99 rally suspension ($170). NB2 California emissions ($99). K05 engine block heater ($44). B34 carpeted front and rear floor mats ($35). B53 carpeted front and rear floor mats ($35). U21 gauges in Bonneville and Bonneville SE ($100). Y56 luggage carrier ($115). DD8 automatic tilt rear view mirror ($80). D64 two-tone paint ($105). UM7 ETR AM/FM stereo ($178). UM6 AM/FM stereo with cassette and clock ($300). UX1 AM/FM ETR stereo with cassette and more ($450). UT4 AM/FM ETR stereo with "everything" ($775 in Base and LE; $685 in SE). UTO Bose sound system ($1248 in SE; $1298 in Base and LE). UL5 AM radio delete ($56 credit). US7 power radio antenna ($70). AT6 reclining passenger seat in base Bonneville, requires 45/55 seat ($70). A78 reclining seats, requires 45/55 seat, in base Bonneville ($140). A80 reclining power seats ($150). AM6 55/45 notch back seat with center armrest in base Bonneville with cloth trim ($133). AM6 55/45 notchback seat with center armrest in Bonneville LE with Majestic cloth and leather trim ($379). AS7 45/55 seat with console and cloth trim in Bonneville LE ($110). AS7 45/55 seat with console and Majestic cloth and leather trim in Bonneville LE ($489); in Bonneville SE ($379). CF5 power glass sun roof including courtesy and dual reading lamps ($1254-$1284). Y99 rally-tuned suspension ($50). Tire options ($76-$206). N91 wire wheel covers with locking package ($199). PD6 14-in. diamond-spoke aluminum wheels with locking package ($215). PG5 15-in. Tri-Port aluminum wheels with locking package ($246). U89 trailering wiring harness ($30).

SAFARI OPTIONS: W61 option group #1 ($882). W63 option group #2 ($1309). G80 limited-slip axle ($100). Y08 cooling system ($40-$66). C49 electric rear window defogger ($145). NB2 California emissions system ($99). K05 engine block heater ($44). U14 rally gauges ($99). V55 roof rack with air deflector ($155). B34 carpeted front and rear floor mats ($35). UM6 ETR AM/FM stereo with cassette, etc. ($122). UX1 AM/FM ETR stereo with cassette, graphic equalizer, clock, etc. ($272). UL5 AM/FM stereo delete ($273 credit). U75 power antenna ($70). A65 notch back seat with Hartford or Palex cloth trim (no charge). AM6 55/45 split notchback seat with Hartford or Pallex cloth trim ($133). AT6 reclining passenger seat with 55/45 seats only ($70). G66 Superlift shock absorbers ($64). U94 trailer wiring package ($30). YD1 trailering package with or without engine block heater ($40-$66). N91 wire wheel covers with locking package ($214). BX3 simulated wood-grain siding with door edge moldings and wood-tone body side molding ($345).

Note: Full option package contents, descriptions and applications information can often be determined by consulting factory literature. The data above is edited for size and clarity. This information provided only as a guide to help collectors appraise the relative value of cars with numerous options. Option prices originally charged by individual dealers may have varied.

HISTORICAL FOOTNOTE: J. Michael Losh was general manager of Pontiac Motor Division in 1987. E.M. Schlesinger was general sales and service manager. William J. O'Neil was director of public relations. Pontiac sales and market share dropped in the model-year. The model-year sales totals were 715,536 units. This total included the following sub-totals by car-line: [6000] 7,582; [1988 LeMans imported] 26,948; [Sunbird] 81,930; [Fiero] 47,156; [Firebird] 77,565; [Grand Am] 216,065; [6000] 133,881; [Bonneville] 95,324; [Grand Prix] 17,088; and "Parisienne" Safari] 11,927. This gave Pontiac 6.8 percent of the U.S. car market, down from 7.5 percent a year earlier. Production of Firebirds was cut-back to one factory this year. The F-cars were made only in the Van Nuys, California, assembly plant. The Norwood, Ohio, factory was permanently closed in August 1987. Dow Chemical Co. teamed with Pontiac to build a special Grand Am "idea" car featuring Dow advanced materials. Under its hood was a 3-liter turbocharged four with Dow magnesium engine block that produced 313 hp @ 5500 rpm and 326 lb.-ft. of torque @ 4500 rpm. It also had Dow brake fluid and coolant, plus special Dow plastics and foam materials incorporated in its interior and exterior design. Pontiac participated in motorsports with the Entech Camel Lights Fiero racing car. It featured a carbon fiber/aluminum body on a chassis with honeycomb, bonded monocoque construction. The suspension was of double wishbone pushrod design in front, and lower wishbone/top rockers design at the rear. Under the engine cover was a 182-cid Super-Duty four-cylinder Pontiac engine. A company named Corporate Concepts Limited, from Capac, Mich., marketed a 1987 MERA Fiero

Conversion that gave the Fiero the look of a Lamborghini or Ferrari. It came with a 135-hp version of the Fiero's V-6. More excitement was generated by a futuristic-looking concept vehicle called the Trans Sport, which was the prototype for what would become a production APV minivan. In January 1987, *Car and Driver* named the Bonneville SE one of the 10 best cars of the year. On the vehicle service front, Pontiac dealers introduced new GM-CAMS technology to enhance service department diagnostics. On August 18, 1987, a plane crash in Detroit took the lives of 14 General Motors employees bound for the GM Desert Proving Ground at Mesa, Ariz. They included four members of the Chevrolet-Pontiac-Canada (CPC) Engineering Dept., Lewis E. Dresch, 45, Patrick A. Gleason, 49, John Matthews, 38, and Jay T. Strausbaugh, 29.

1988 PONTIAC

PONTIAC I.D. NUMBERS: Vehicle identification number (VIN) is located on top left-hand surface of instrument panel visible through the windshield. The VIN has 17 symbols. The first symbol indicates the country of manufacture (U.S.) The second symbol indicates the manufacturer (G=General Motors). The third symbol indicates the make/division (2=Pontiac). The fourth, fifth, and sixth symbols are the same as the body style (model) number. The eighth symbol indicates the engine. The ninth symbol is a check digit. The 10th symbol indicates model-year. The 11th symbol indicates the assembly plant. The last six symbols are the consecutive unit number at the factory.

FIERO -- SERIES 2P -- FOUR/V-6 -- Pontiac's distinctive P-body two-passenger, mid-engined sports car remained in the lineup with Coupe and GT Coupe models for 1988. Each had distinctive styling and performance features. In addition, a new Formula option package was released for the Coupe. The Formula group included the spirited 2.8-liter MFI V-6 engine, GM Muncie/Gertag five-speed transaxle, WS6 suspension with special front and rear shocks, special springs, 15-in. black diamond-spoke wheels, and Goodyear Eagle GT+4 tires (P205/60R15 front/P215/60R15 rear), a 28mm front stabilizer bar, special bushings, and special front/rear control arms. A rear spoiler and Formula graphics completed the package. Standard in base Coupes, the famous Tech IV engine had a new secondary force balancer system to smooth and quiet engine operation, plus a redesigned crankshaft with a gear drive for the balancers located in the pan. The in-the-pan oil pump and filter were also redesigned. Also new were completely redesigned independent front and rear suspension systems, a revised four-wheel disc brake system, standard High-Tech Turbo cast wheels, radial spare tires, a standard AM/FM stereo sound system, an interior upgrade to Pallex cloth trim, a new Camel interior color, and a new midyear Bright Yellow exterior color. New standard features for GTs included Eagle GT+4 tires, Metrix cloth trim, and monochromatic exterior colors. New GT model options were black or gold diamond-spoke cast aluminum wheels, an inflatable lumbar support seat, and "soft" leather seat trim. Every Fiero Coupe featured black-finished air deflectors, body side moldings, door handles and lock cylinders, reclining bucket seats, center high-mounted stop lamp, clearcoat paint, color-keyed safety belts, compact spare radial tire, Delco Freedom II battery, dome lamp, dual map lights, Enduraflex body panels, extensive anti-corrosion protection, full-length console, GM Computer Command Control system, halogen headlights with a retracting feature, hobnail carpeting, locking fuel filler door, map pocket on instrument panel, front/rear side marker lights, "mill and drill" construction, left-hand remote-controlled sport mirror, right-hand manual sport mirror, multi-function control lever, UM7 Delco AM/FM ETR radio, radio noise suppression kit, side window defoggers, soft fascia system front/rear, space-frame body construction, four-spoke rally steering wheel, sun visors, independent front and rear suspension, five-speed manual transmission, Hi-Tech turbo aluminum wheels, and 2.8-liter Tech IV engine with EFI. The Formula added or substituted the 2.8-liter V-6 engine with EFI, a rear deck spoiler, special front/rear shock absorbers, special springs, a 23mm rear stabilizer bar, WS6 performance suspension, P205/60R15 (front) and P215/60R15 (rear) Goodyear Eagle GT+4 tires, a tuned dual-port exhaust system, and 15-in. diamond-spoke black-finished aluminum wheels. The GT added or substituted an aero package with special aerodynamic front and rear fascias, body side skirts, controlled-cycle windshield wipers, an instrumentation package with console-mounted lamp group, deluxe luggage compartment trim, sun visor map pockets, a monochromatic exterior color scheme, power windows, UM6 Delco AM/FM ETR radio, remote deck lid release, Soft Ray tinted glass, deluxe three-spoke leather-wrapped tilt steering wheel, and choice of gold-finished diamond-spoke aluminum wheels in addition to black-finished.

FIERO -- SERIES 2P -- I-4/V-6

Model Number	Body/Style Number	Body Type & Seating	Factory Price	Shipping Weight	Prod. Total
2P	PE1	2-dr Cpe-2P	8999	2597	Note 1
2P	PE1	2-dr Formula-2P	10999	2602	Note 1
2P	PG7	2-dr GT Cpe-2P	13999	2790	Note 1

NOTE 1: Fiero series production totaled 26,401.

LEMANS -- SERIES 2T -- FOUR -- A Korean-built (by Daewoo Motor Co. Ltd.) car using a classic Pontiac nameplate replaced the Pontiac 1000 as the company's entry-level offering. Four versions were offered: Aerocoupe Value Leader, LE Aerocoupe, LE Sedan, and SE Sedan. Standard equipment for the Value Leader model started with a 1.6-liter EFI four, power front disc/rear drum brakes, electric rear window defogger, extensive anti-corrosion protection, folding rear seat, full-size spare tire, adjustable headrest, integral roof luggage rack mounting provisions, rear compartment light, ashtray light, glovebox light, two-tone lower body side paint accent, luggage compartment security cover, left-hand remote-control mirror, one-key locking system, rack-and-pinion steering, reclining front bucket seats, side window defogger, soft headliner, MacPherson front strut suspension with stabilizer bar, semi-independent trailing arm/torsion bar rear suspension with coil springs, P175/70R13 steel-belted radial tires, four-speed manual transmission, trip odometer, twill cloth upholstery, two-tone paint, custom wheel covers, and wide body side moldings. Every Aerocoupe LE and LE Sedan added or substituted front and rear assist handles, full analog instrumentation, dual remote-control sport mirrors, UM7 Delco AM/FM ETR stereo, Soft Ray tinted glass, swing-out rear windows (Aerocoupe only), tachometer, five-speed manual transmission, and visor vanity mirror. The SE Sedan added or substituted fog lamps, Mosaik/Turin cloth upholstery, specific SE up-level bucket seats, special seat height adjusters, a split-folding rear seat, and a tilt steering wheel.

1988 Pontiac LeMans Aerocoupe hatchback. PMD

LEMANS -- SERIES 2T -- I-4

Model Number	Body/Style Number	Body Type & Seating	Factory Price	Shipping Weight	Prod. Total
2T	TX2	3-dr V/L Cpe-4P	5995	2019	Note 1
2T	TN2	3-dr Cpe-4P	7325	2058	Note 1
2T	TN5	4-dr LE Sed-4P	7925	2121	Note 1
2T	TR5	4-dr SE Sed-4P	8399	2150	Note 1

NOTE 1: LeMans series production totaled 64,037.

1988 Pontiac Sunbird GT convertible. PMD

SUNBIRD -- SERIES 2J --FOUR -- The J-body Sunbirds were even more improved spinoffs of the Chevrolet Vega/Pontiac Astre this year. There were six models (including a new Coupe) in three series: Base, SE, and GT Turbo. Both base Sunbirds and SEs came with a 2.0-liter EFI engine and standard five-speed manual gearbox. Interiors were upgraded with monotone Pallex cloth upholstery and a Delco ETR AM/FM stereo as standard features. Two new colors Medium Red Metallic and Camel Metallic were introduced. Also new were Goodyear P185/80R13 standard tires on

base and SE models, and Goodyear P215/60R14 Eagle GT+4s on the Wagon with rally-tuned suspension. Other 1988 changes included wide body side moldings as standard equipment on base models, and color-keyed seat belts as standard equipment on GTs. Standard base-model equipment included the new OHC four-cylinder motor, black-finished door window frames, wipers and wide body side moldings, power front disc/rear drum brakes, reclining front bucket seats, center high-mounted stop light, clearcoat paint, compact spare, cut-pile carpeting, Delco Freedom II battery, front door lamp switches, dual rectangular headlights, extensive anti-corrosion protection, fluidic wipers, front air dam, front floor console, front-wheel-drive, GM Computer Command Control system, inside hood release, day/night rear view mirror, rack-and-pinion steering, UM7 Delco ETR AM/FM stereo, side window defoggers, MacPherson strut front suspension, five-speed manual transmission, warm red instrument panel lighting, and five-port wheel covers. The Sunbird SE added or substituted new Coupe styling with wraparound front parking lights and partially hidden halogen headlights. The Sunbird GT added or substituted a turbocharged four-cylinder engine, a special hood with simulated air louvers, higher-rate springs and bushings, sport side view mirrors, power steering, special instrumentation with a turbo boost gauge, special performance suspension with 28mm front and 21mm rear stabilizer bars, a tachometer and trip odometer, P215/60R14 steel-belted BSW tires, 14-in. Turbo cast Hi-Tech aluminum wheels, and wheel flares.

Model Number	Body/Style Number	Body Type & Seating	Factory Price	Shipping Weight	Prod. Total
SUNBIRD -- SERIES 2J -- I-4					
2J	JB5	4-dr Sed-5P	8499	2367	Note 1
SUNBIRD SE -- SERIES 2J -- I-4/I-4					
2J	JD5	4-dr Sed-5P	8799	2427	Note 1
2J	JD1	2-dr Cpe-5P	8599	2394	Note 1
2J	JD8	4-dr Sta Wag-5P	9399	2427	Note 1
SUNBIRD GT TURBO -- SERIES 2J -- I-4/I-4 Turbo					
2J	JU1	2-dr Cpe-5P	10899	2412	Note 1
2J	JU3	2-dr Conv-5P	16199	2577	Note 1

NOTE 1: Sunbird series production totaled 93,689.

1988 Pontiac Grand Am SE coupe. PMD

GRAND AM -- SERIES 2N -- This upscale N-body front-drive compact was one of Pontiac's largest selling cars and a top performing vehicle. Introduced for 1988 was a 2.3-liter DOHC 16-valve four-cylinder engine that was available in all models. Standard equipment for base and LE editions was an improved 2.5-liter balance shaft four-cylinder engine with automatic transaxle. A 2.0-liter MFI Turbo four-cylinder engine was standard in SE models. Also new-for-1988 were body-color grilles for all models, standard split-back folding seat on SEs, new glovebox lock and cup holders, improved lighting for the heat/vent/air conditioning (HVAC) control panel, a revised trim plate design for the instrument panel cluster and console, Pallex cloth interior trim for base models (Metrix cloth became standard in LE and SE models), a standard AM/FM stereo system in all models, dual outside sport mirrors on all models, a new Camel interior trim color, and two new exterior colors (Camel Metallic and Maroon Metallic). Standard equipment included: 2.5-liter Tech IV engine with EFI, acoustic insulation package, black-finish door handles and lock cylinders, power front disc/rear drum brakes, reclining front bucket seats, front/rear soft bumper fascias, automatic front safety belts, center high-mounted stop lamp, compact spare tire, complete analog instrumentation, floor-mounted console, Delco Freedom II battery, dual front radio speakers, dual horn, anti-corrosion protection, front-wheel-drive, glove compartment, GM Computer Command Control system, headlights on warning, heater vent system with ducted rear-seat heat, inside hood release, low-noise engine cooling fan, dual sport side view mirrors, multi-function control lever, Pallex

cloth upholstery, power rack-and-pinion steering, UM7 Delco AM/FM ETR stereo radio, rear-seat integral headrests, side window defogger, soft ray tinted glass, MacPherson strut front suspension, five-speed manual transmission, custom wheel covers, and wide body side moldings. Grand Am LEs added or substituted composite headlights, deluxe color-keyed safety belts, deluxe exterior ornamentation, front console with armrest, Metrix cloth upholstery, two-tone paint, and custom color-keyed wheel covers. The Grand Am SE added or substituted a 2.0-liter four-cylinder Turbo engine with MFI, cruise control, deluxe Thaxton carpets, deluxe integral fog lamps, remote fuel filler, leather appointment group with four-spoke rally steering wheel and shift knob and brake release handle, power door locks, rally gauges and tachometer, rear seat center armrest, specific monotone paint treatment with color-keyed grille, emblems and aluminum wheels, rally-tuned suspension with 28mm front/21mm rear stabilizer bars, tilt steering, P215/60R14 Eagle GT+4 tires, and specific SE cast aluminum wheels.

Model Number	Body/Style Number	Body Type & Seating	Factory Price	Shipping Weight	Prod. Total
GRAND AM -- SERIES 2N -- I-4/V-6					
2N	NE1	2-dr Cpe-5P	9869	2493	Note 1
2N	NE5	4-dr Sed-5P	10069	2565	Note 1
GRAND AM LE-- SERIES 2N -- I-4/V-6					
2N	NV1	2-dr Cpe-5P	10569	2519	Note 1
2N	NV5	4-dr Sed-5P	10769	2591	Note 1
GRAND AM SE-- SERIES 2N -- I-4/V-6					
2N	NW1	2-dr Cpe-5P	12869	2713	Note 1
2N	NW5	4-dr Sed-5P	13099	2781	Note 1

NOTE 1: Grand Am series production totaled 235,371.

FIREBIRD -- SERIES 2F -- V-6/V-8 -- The sporty F-body Firebird had 17 major changes and engineering highlights for 1988. Base models shared an improved Tuned Port Induction (TPI) system on V-8 engines, which also had new serpentine accessory belt drives. Base models now came with standard 15 x 7 in. deep-dish Hi-Tech Turbo or diamond spoke aluminum wheels, a redesigned four-spoke steering wheel, an AM/FM stereo with seek-and-scan and clock, Pallex cloth interior trim, new Camel colored interior, monotone paint treatments, and a choice of two new exterior colors (Silver Blue Metallic or Orange Metallic). Formulas had new 16 x 8 in. Hi-Tech Turbo cast aluminum wheels and a new 5.0-liter throttle-body-injection (TBI) V-8 engine, that was also standard in the Trans Am. All TPI 5.0-liter and 5.7-liter engines now came with full-gauge analog clusters, and a 140-mph speedometer. New features for GTA models included a remote deck lid release, power antenna, right-hand visor vanity mirror, power windows, power door locks, body side moldings, air conditioning, tinted glass, lamp group, Pass Key theft deterrent system, controlled-cycle wipers, rear window defogger, cruise control, tilt steering, AM/FM stereo with cassette and graphic equalizer, steering wheel-mounted radio controls, integral rear seat headrests, and Metrix cloth interior trim (optional for Trans Am). In addition, leather-trimmed articulating front bucket seats were a new GTA model option. Base Firebirds featured a 2.8-liter MFI V-6, center high-mounted stop lamp, complete analog instrumentation, full-length console with instrument panel, side window defoggers, front air dam, GM Computer Command Control system, hatch "pull-down" feature, rectangular-shaped concealed quartz halogen headlights, monochromatic paint, UM7 Delco ETR AM/FM stereo, cloth reclining front bucket seats, folding rear seat, four-spoke steering wheel, lockable storage compartment, P215/65R15 BSW tires, five-speed manual transmission, "wet-arm" windshield wipers, and 15 x 7-in. Hi-Tech Turbo or diamond-spoke cast aluminum wheels. Formulas added or substituted a 5.0-liter EFI V-8, body-color aero rear deck lid spoiler, domed hood, Formula graphics, 16 x 8-in. Hi-Tech aluminum wheels, WS6 special performance suspension, and two-tone paint and striping. Trans Ams added or substituted aero package, hood and front fender air extractors, hood air louvers, fog lamps, soft ray tinted glass, and Y99 rally-tuned suspension. GTAs added the 5.7-liter TPI V-8, four-wheel disc brakes, air conditioning, cruise control, dual power mirrors, power articulating front bucket seats, power deck lid release, power door locks, power windows, Delco UT4 ETR "touch control" AM/FM stereo with cassette and anti-theft feature, special performance suspension, leather-wrapped steering wheel, steering wheel radio controls, P245/50VR16 Goodyear Eagle tires, four-speed automatic transmission, and 16 x 8-in. gold-colored lightweight diamond-spoke aluminum wheels.

Model Number	Body/Style Number	Body Type & Seating	Factory Price	Shipping Weight	Prod. Total
FIREBIRD -- SERIES 2F -- V-6					
2F	FS2	2-dr Cpe-5P	10999	3102	Note 1
FIREBIRD -- SERIES 2F -- V-8					
2F	FS2	2-dr Cpe-5P	11399	-	Note 1

1988 Pontiac Firebird Trans Am GTA coupe. PMD

Model Number	Body/Style Number	Body Type & Seating	Factory Price	Shipping Weight	Prod. Total
FIREBIRD FORMULA -- SERIES 2F -- V-8					
2F	FS2	2-dr Cpe-5P	11999	3296	Note 1
FIREBIRD TRANS AM -- SERIES 2F -- V-8					
2F	FW2	2-dr Cpe-5P	13999	3355	Note 1
FIREBIRD TRANS AM GTA -- SERIES 2F -- V-8					
2F	FW2	2-dr Cpe-5P	19299	3406	Note 1

NOTE 1: Firebird series production totaled 62,455.

1988 Pontiac 6000 STE four-door sedan. PMD

6000 -- SERIES 2A -- I-4/V-6 -- The 6000 and 6000 LE were aimed at the family car marketplace. They combined a smooth, comfortable ride with pleasant looks, lots of space, and economy of operation. Both trim levels were available in four-door Sedans or Safari Station Wagons. Standard powertrain for both was a 2.5-liter four-cylinder EFI engine with three-speed automatic transaxle. A 2.8-liiter MFI V-6 was optional. Interiors of the entry-level 6000 Sedan and Safari received a new standard Pallex seat fabric for up-level comfort. The 6000 LE received redesigned contour seats covered with London/Empress fabric. Standard on both levels and models was an AM/FM stereo sound system, tinted glass, color-keyed wheel covers (available in four colors) and P185/75R14 tires. Six new metallic colors were offered: Light Blue, Dark Blue, Camel, Dark Brown, Medium Maroon, and Medium Rosewood. The 6000 S/E Sedan and Safari were aimed at driving enthusiasts who wanted better road handling in a 6000-type car. They both had unique aero styling, a 2.8-liter V-6, a five-speed manual transaxle, and road-hugging P195/70R14 Goodyear Eagle GT+4 all-season tires mounted on color-keyed Turbo Torque cast aluminum wheels. A four-speed automatic transmission was optional. The S/E interior featured Metrix cloth over reclining seats, a leather-wrapped steering wheel, a center shift console, and a fully backlit instrument cluster. The 6000 STE featured a 2.8-liter aluminum head V-6 with direct-fire ignition, serpentine drive belts, and standard four-speed automatic transaxle (five-speed manual optional). Also included were two-tone paint treatments, body-colored lower front air dam, composite headlights, integral fog lights, and specific taillight bezels. Anti-lock brakes were included on the STE, plus new 15-in. aluminum wheels and P195/70R15 Goodyear Eagle GT+4 tires. The suspension was completely re-tuned, as well. At midyear, the STE interior added contoured front seats with power-adjustable lumbar and headrest operation, a redesigned rear seat with integral cup holders, and larger headrests. A Delco-Loc radio anti-theft system was integrated into the steering

wheel hub-mounted radio controls. A warning sticker aimed at deterring theft of the system was included in the car owner's manual and could be affixed to its windows. Also, a new Metrix cloth seat trim with color-keyed seat belts was standard in STEs and an upgraded Ventura cloth and leather interior was made available during the year. A new plateau in the 6000 model offering was the 6000 STE-AWD. This was an STE model with full-time all-wheel-drive system that improved directional control, traction, and handling under most driving conditions. It was introduced late in the model-year. Exclusive to Pontiac, it was the first application of all-wheel-drive to a General Motors passenger car. It also marked the first mass-production usage of a high-torque, transverse-mounted 3.1-liter V-6 engine and automatic transmission combination in a full-time all-wheel-drive vehicle. Standard equipment on base 6000s included 2.5-liter Tech IV engine, acoustical insulation, black door window frames, carpeted lower door panels, center high-mounted stop lamp, compact spare tire, composite headlights, cut-pile carpeting, Delco Freedom II battery, extensive anti-corrosion protection, fluidic windshield wiper/washer system with dual nozzles, black front air dam, front-wheel-drive, glove compartment with lock, GM Computer Command Control system, inside hood release, warm red instrument panel lighting, MacPherson strut front suspension, multi-function control lever, Delco UM7 AM/FM stereo, radio noise suppression equipment, side window defoggers, soft fascia front and rear bumpers, trailing arm and beam rear suspension with integral stabilizer bar, three-speed automatic transmission, and Tri-Port wheel covers. Cars with the LE option also right- and left-hand door map pockets, dual horns, locking fuel filler door, lower two-tone paint accents, map pockets on front seat backs, and four-spoke Sport steering wheel. Added or substituted on SE models were a 2.8-liter V-6, front bucket seats and a console, a dual outlet sport exhaust system, electronic ride control (Safari S/E only), dual sport side view mirrors, rally gauges with tachometer, specific springs and bushings, 28mm front/22mm rear stabilizer bars, a leather-wrapped SE steering wheel, rally-tuned suspension, Goodyear Eagle GT+4 P195/70R14 tires, and Sport aluminum wheels with locks. The top-of-the-line 6000 STE added or substituted: a road kit with flares, a raincoat, and first aid supplies, four-wheel anti-lock disc brakes, controlled-cycle wipers, deluxe carpeted floor mats, a driver information center, electrically operated side view mirrors, electronic ride control system, GM protection plan, lighted visor vanity mirror, locking fuel filler door, lower accent two-toning, map pockets on seat backs, power door locks, Delco UT4 "touch control" AM/FM stereo with cassette, rear seat with fold down center armrest, specific STE leather-wrapped steering wheel with integral radio controls, tilt steering wheel, four-speed automatic transmission, specific STE wheels, and a windshield sun shade with pockets.

Model Number	Body/Style Number	Body Type & Seating	Factory Price	Shipping Weight	Prod. Total
6000 -- SERIES 2A -- I-4/V-6					
2A	AF5	4-dr Sed-5P	11199	2755	Note 1
2A	AF8	4-dr Safari-5P	11639	2925	Note 1
6000 LE -- SERIES 2A -- I-4/V-6					
2A	AG5	4-dr Sed-5P	11839	2824	Note 1
2A	AG8	4-dr Safari-5P	12299	2977	Note 1
6000 SE -- SERIES 2A -- I-4/V-6					
2A	AE5	4-dr Sed-5P	12739	2986	Note 1
2A	AE8	4-dr Safari-5P	13699	3162	Note 1
6000 STE -- SERIES 2A -- I-4/V-6					
2A	AH5	4-dr Sed-5P	18699	3101	Note 1

NOTE 1: 6000 series production totaled 90,934.

1988 Pontiac Grand Prix SE coupe. PMD

1988 Pontiac Grand Prix SE coupe (rear view). PMD

GRAND PRIX -- SERIES 2G -- V-6/V-8 -- A totally new aerodynamically styled, front-wheel-drive Grand Prix bowed in 1988. It came in three trim levels: Grand Prix, Grand Prix LE, and Grand Prix SE. The exterior of this new Grand Prix featured a Pontiac-style split grille, wraparound taillights, soft fascia bumpers, and an aggressive-looking stance. The sleek body had a drag coefficient of .299 and was one of the world's most wind-cheating production cars of the year. It had an aggressively tapered nose and a low hood line promoting smooth air flow towards the flush-mounted 62-degree windshield. Side windows were also flush and the door handles were recessed into the body "B" pillars. It also had flush-fitting composite halogen headlights and hidden windshield wipers. The Grand Prix featured a MacPherson strut front suspension with tapered top coil springs that permitted the lowering of the hood line. A totally new tri-link rear suspension was employed. Suspension components were "lubed-for-life" and all strut cartridges were designed for easier servicing. Excellent braking performance was provided by a four-wheel disc system using composite material rotors. The front rotors were of vented design with twin-piston calipers. Solid rotors and single-bore calipers were found at the rear. Select Grand Prix models were available in five exterior colors: Metallic Silver, Metallic Camel, Metallic Medium Gray, Metallic Medium Red, and White. The Grand Prix and Grand Prix LE were also offered in Metallic Black, Light Metallic Blue, and Medium Metallic Blue, as well as a non-metallic Red. Interiors came in Blue, Camel, and Medium Gray on all models. Standard equipment included a 2.8-liter MFI V-6, acoustical insulation, four-wheel power disc brakes, composite halogen headlights, dual horns, dual sport mirrors (left-hand remote), glovebox with combination lock, ashtray light, glovebox light, dome light, rack-and-pinion steering, UM7 Delco ETR AM/FM stereo, remote fuel filler door release, notchback front bench seat with armrest and Ripple cloth trim, side window defoggers, four-wheel independent suspension, P195/75R14 steel-belted radial tires, four-speed automatic transmission, wet-arm windshield wipers, and custom wheel covers. The Grand Prix LE added or substituted analog instrumentation with a tach, coolant temperature, oil pressure and voltmeter gauges, door map pockets, luggage compartment light, underhood light, instrument panel courtesy light, power windows with illuminated switches, rear folding armrest with pass through to luggage compartment, and 60/40 split reclining seats in Pallex cloth trim. The Grand Prix SE added or substituted cruise control, dual exhausts, fog lamps, an overhead console with storage and lights, articulating power bucket seats and rear-passenger bucket seat, rally-tuned suspension, tilt steering wheel, P215/65R15 Goodyear Eagle GT+4 tires, five-speed manual transmission, and color-keyed 15-in. aluminum sport wheels.

1988 Pontiac Grand Prix LE coupe. PMD

Model Number	Body/Style Number	Body Type & Seating	Factory Price	Shipping Weight	Prod. Total
GRAND PRIX -- SERIES 2W -- V-6/V-8					
2G	WJ1	2-dr Cpe-5P	12539	3038	Note 1
GRAND PRIX LE-- SERIES 2W -- V-6/V-8					
2G	WK1	2-dr Cpe-5P	13239	3056	Note 1
GRAND PRIX SE -- SERIES 2W -- V-6/V-8					
2G	WP1	2-dr Cpe-5P	15249	3113	Note 1

NOTE 1: Grand Prix series production totaled 86,357.

1988 Pontiac Bonneville SE four-door sedan. PMD

BONNEVILLE -- SERIES 2H -- V-6 -- The aerodynamic Bonneville front-wheel-drive Sports Sedan returned in 1988. The LE became the base model. The SE was now the middle model. On top was a new SSE. All Bonnevilles had new dual sport mirrors (left-hand remote-controlled), wood-grained interior trim plates, standard AM/FM stereo, and two new exterior colors called Caramel Metallic and Medium Brown Metallic. New LE features included new wheels, color-accented exterior trim, and a passenger visor mirror. SEs now had variable-ratio power steering, a new "3800" V-6, a new seat, and some new standard "options." The SSE was a Euro-style luxury touring car with a high price sticker and a page and a quarter-long list of added standard equipment from tuned dual exhaust outlets to automatic headlight sentinel control. Standard on the LE model was a 3.8-liter V-6 engine with sequential fuel-injection (SFI), acoustical insulation, air conditioning, front seat with center armrest, body-frame integral construction, carpets, center high-mounted stop lamp, cluster warning lights, compact spare tire, complete instrumentation, Delco Freedom II battery, dual horns, extensive corrosion protection, flow-through ventilation, GM Computer Command Control system, independent front/rear suspension, inside hood release, dome lamp, glovebox lamp, trunk lamp, lower door map pockets (except with UW4 speaker system), lower door panel carpeting, dual sport side view mirrors, power rack-and-pinion steering, UM7 Delco ETR AM/FM radio, automatic front safety belts, rear seat safety shoulder belts, systems monitor feature, four-speed automatic transmission, passenger visor vanity mirror, Aero Torque wheel covers, wide body side moldings, and dual fluidic concealed windshield wipers. SE models added or substituted a 3.3-liter SFI 3800 V-6 engine, rear seat pull-down armrest, complete rally instrumentation with tachometer, controlled-cycle wipers, cruise control, driver information center, gas pressurized struts, front/rear door interior courtesy lamps, power windows with door pod switches, right- and left-hand manual front seat recliners, a 45/55 split bench front seat, special springs, leather-wrapped steering wheel, rally-tuned suspension, tilt steering, P215/65R15 Eagle GT steel-belted radial tires, and 15 x 6-in. Tri-Port cast aluminum wheels. The Bonneville SSE also added or substituted aero extentions on doors and rocker panels, automatic air conditioning, front disc/rear drum anti-lock brakes, console with power seat controls, duplicate steering wheel radio controls, electronic compass, electronic ride control, flash-to-pass headlight control, GM protection plan, headlight washers, key-activated power door locks, heated blue-tint power mirrors, UT4 Delco ETR "touch control" AM/FM stereo with cassette and Delco-Loc, rear seat armrest with storage compartment, 45/55 10-way power adjustable front seats, six-speaker sound system, special purpose suspension, P215/60R16 BSW Goodyear Eagle GT+4 tires, and Aero-Cast 16 x 7-in. aluminum wheels.

BONNEVILLE -- SERIES H -- V-6

Model Number	Body/Style Number	Body Type & Seating	Factory Price	Shipping Weight	Prod. Total
2H	HX5	4-dr LE Spt Sed-5P	14099	3275	Note 1
2H	HZ5	4-dr SE Spt Sed-5P	16299	3341	Note 1
2H	HZ5/Y80	4-dr SSE Spt Sed-5P	21879	3481	Note 1

201

NOTE 1: Bonneville series production totaled 108,563.

SAFARI -- SERIES 2L -- V-8 -- Pontiac's 1988 Safari was a traditional full-size Station Wagon offering luxury, passenger roominess, comfort, generous cargo capacity, and power to handle large loads. Safari's superior eight-passenger carrying capacity is enhanced with a comprehensive list of standard equipment including a rear-facing third seat, air conditioning, stereo radio, dual sport mirrors, tinted glass, and whitewall radial tires. The standard powertrain was unchanged, but new axle ratios were specified for better performance. An electronic spark control system was added for better fuel economy. It was EPA-rated for 17 mpg city/24 mpg highway. The interior of the Safari received some improvements such as new sun visors with center support, new accelerator and brake pedals, and new power seat controls mounted on door pods. Also new were five exterior colors (Light Blue Metallic, Dark Blue Metallic, Camel Metallic, Dark Brown Metallic, and Medium Red Metallic), and a pair of new interior trim colors (Dark Blue and Camel). Standard on all big Safaris was a 5.0-liter four-barrel V-8, air conditioning with Soft Ray tinted glass, Powermaster front disc/rear drum brakes, white-accented front/rear bumper rub strips, carpeting throughout, center high-mounted stop lamp, GM Computer Command Control system, inside hood release, dual sport mirrors (left-hand remote-controlled), power steering, UM7 Delco ETR AM/FM stereo, notchback front seat with center armrest, rear-facing third seat with Hartford vinyl trim, load-carrying springs, front stabilizer bar, three-spoke steering wheel, full-coil suspension, tailgate window control, P225/75R15 steel-belted radial whitewall tires, four-speed automatic transmission, and custom wheel covers.

SAFARI -- SERIES 2L -- V-8

Model Number	Body/Style Number	Body Type & Seating	Factory Price	Shipping Weight	Prod. Total
2L	BL8	4-dr Sta Wag-8P	14519	4109	Note 1

NOTE 1: Safari series production totaled 6397.

FIERO ENGINES

[BASE] Inline. OHV. Four-cylinder. Cast iron block and head. Aluminum intake manifold. Displacement: 151 cu. in.. (2.5L Tech IV). Bore x stroke: 4.00 x 3.00 in. Compression ratio: 9.0:1. Brake horsepower: 98 @ 4800 rpm. Torque: 135 lb.-ft. @ 3200 rpm. Five main bearings. Hydraulic valve lifters. Fuel system: EFI/TBI. RPO Code: LR8. Standard with five-speed manual in base Fiero. Produced in U.S., Canada, or Mexico. [VIN code U]. [OPTIONAL] V-block. OHV. Six-cylinder. Cast iron block and head. Aluminum intake manifold. Displacement: 173 cu. in. (2.8L). Bore x stroke: 3.50 x 2.99 in. Compression ratio: 8.5:1. Brake horsepower: 135 @ 4500 rpm. Torque: 165 lb.-ft. @ 3600 rpm. Fuel system: MPFI. RPO Code: L44. Standard in Formula Fiero and Fiero GT. [VIN code W, S, or 9].

1988 Pontiac LeMans GSE three-door hatchback. PMD

1988 Pontiac LeMans GSE three-door hatchback (rear view). PMD

LEMANS ENGINE

[BASE] Inline. OHV. Four-cylinder. Cast iron block. Aluminum head and intake manifold. Displacement: 98 cu. in. (1.6L). Bore x stroke: 3.11 x 3.21 in. Compression ratio: 8.6:1. Brake horsepower: 74 @ 5600 rpm. Torque: 90 lb.-ft. @ 2800 rpm. Fuel system: EFI/TBI. RPO Code: L73. Standard with four-speed manual. Produced in the Republic of South Korea. [VIN code 6].

SUNBIRD ENGINES

[BASE] Inline. OHC. Four-cylinder. Cast iron block. Aluminum head and intake manifold. Displacement: 121 cu. in.. (2.0L). Bore x stroke: 3.39 x 3.39 in. Compression ratio: 8.8:1. Brake horsepower: 96 @ 4800 rpm. Torque: 118 lb.-ft. @ 3600 rpm. Fuel system: EFI/TBI. RPO Code: LT2. Standard in Sunbird Sedan, Sunbird SE Wagon, Sunbird SE Coupe, and Sunbird SE Sedan. Produced in Brazil or Australia. [VIN code K]. [OPTIONAL] Inline. OHC. Four-cylinder. Turbocharged (Garrett T2.5 turbocharger). Cast iron block. Aluminum head and intake manifold. Displacement: 121 cu. in. (2.0L). Bore x stroke: 3.39 x 3.39 in. Compression ratio: 8.0:1. Brake horsepower: 175 @ 5600 rpm. Torque: 175 lb.-ft. @ 4000 rpm. Fuel system: MPFI with Turbo. RPO Code: LT3. Standard in Sunbird Turbo GT (optional in Sunbird SE Coupe and Sunbird SE Sedan). [VIN code M].

GRAND AM ENGINES

[STANDARD GRAND AM & GRAND AM LE] Inline. OHV. Cast iron block and head. Aluminum intake manifold. Displacement: 151 cu. in.. (2.5L Tech IV). Bore x stroke: 4.00 x 3.00 in. Compression ratio: 9.0:1. Brake horsepower: 98 @ 4800 rpm. Torque: 135 lb.-ft. @ 3200 rpm. Five main bearings. Hydraulic valve lifters. Fuel system: EFI/TBI. RPO Code:L68. Standard in base Grand Am and Grand AM LE. [VIN code U]. [STANDARD GRAND AM SE] Inline. OHC. Turbocharged (Garret T2.5 turbocharger). Cast iron block. Aluminum head and intake manifold. Displacement: 2.0-liter Turbo. Bore x stroke: 3.39 x 3.39 in. Compression ratio: 8.0:1. Brake horsepower: 165 @ 5600 rpm. Torque: 175 lb.-ft. @ 4000 rpm. Fuel system: MPFI. RPO Code: LT3. Standard in Grand Am SE, optional in Grand Am LE. Produced in Brazil or Australia. [OPTIONAL] Inline. DOHC. 16-Valve. Four-cylinder. Cast iron block. Aluminum head and intake manifold. Displacement: 140 cu. in. (2.3L). Quad 4 16-valve. Bore x stroke: 3.62 x 3.35 in. Compression ratio: 9.5:1. Brake horsepower: 150 @ 5200 rpm. Torque: 160 lb.-ft. @ 4400 rpm. Fuel system: MPFI. RPO Code: LD2. Optional in Grand Am, Grand Am LE, and Grand Am SE. [VIN code D].

FIREBIRD ENGINES

[Base V-6] V-block. OHV. Six-cylinder. Cast iron block and head. Aluminum intake manifold. Displacement: 173 cu. in. (2.8L). Bore x stroke: 3.50 x 2.99 in. Compression ratio: 8.5:1. Brake horsepower: 135 @ 4900 rpm. Torque: 160 lb.-ft. @ 3900 rpm. Fuel system: EFI/TBI. RPO Code: LB8. Standard in base Firebird. Produced in U.S., Canada, or Mexico. [VIN code W, S, or 9]. [BASE V-8] V-block. OHV. Eight-cylinder. Cast iron block and head. Aluminum intake manifold. Displacement: 305 cu. in. (5.0L). Bore x stroke: 3.74 x 3.48 in. Brake horsepower: 170 @ 4000 rpm. Torque: 255 lb.-ft. @ 2400 rpm. Compression ratio: 9.3:1. Fuel system: EFI/TBI. RPO Code: L03. Produced in U.S. or Canada. Standard Formula, and Trans Am. Available in base Firebird. [VIN code E or F]. [OPTIONAL V-8] V-block. OHV. Eight-cylinder. Cast iron block and head. Aluminum intake manifold. Displacement: 305 cu. in. (5.0L). Bore x stroke: 3.74 x 3.48 in. Brake horsepower: 190 @ 4000 rpm (automatic) or 215 @ 4400 rpm (manual). Torque: 295 lb.-ft. @ 2800 rpm (automatic) or 285 lb.-ft. @ 3200 rpm (manual). Compression ratio: 9.3:1. Fuel system: TPI. RPO Code: LB9. Available with five-speed manual in Formula, and Trans Am (delete option in GTA). Available with four-speed automatic in same applications. [VIN code E or F]. [GTA V-8] V-block. OHV. Eight-cylinder. Cast iron block and head. Aluminum intake manifold. Displacement: 350 cu. in. (5.7L). Bore x stroke: 4.00 x 3.48 in. Brake horsepower: 225 @ 4400 rpm. Torque: 330 lb.-ft. @ 3200 rpm. Compression ratio: 9.3:1. Fuel system: EFI/TPI. RPO Code: B2L. Standard with four-speed automatic in GTA (optional in Formula and Trans Am). Includes low-profile air induction system with aluminum plenum and individual aluminum tuned runners, an extruded dual fuel rail assembly with computer controlled fuel injectors, and a special low-restriction single exhaust system. [VIN code 8].

6000 ENGINES

[BASE] Inline. OHV. Four-cylinder. Cast iron block and head. Aluminum intake manifold. Displacement: 151 cu. in.. (2.5L Tech IV). Bore x stroke: 4.00 x 3.00 in. Compression ratio: 9.0:1. Brake horsepower: 98 @ 4800 rpm. Torque: 135 lb.-ft. @ 3200 rpm. Five main bearings. Hydraulic valve lifters. Fuel system: EFI/TBI. RPO Code: LR8. Standard in 6000 and 6000 LE. [VIN code U]. [OPTIONAL] V-block. OHV. Six-cylinder. Cast iron block. Aluminum head and intake manifold. Displacement: 173 cu. in. (2.8L). Bore x stroke: 3.50 x 2.99 in. Compression ratio: 8.8:1. Brake horsepower: 125 @ 4500 rpm. Torque: 160 lb.-ft. @ 3600 rpm. Fuel system: MPFI. RPO Code: LB6. Standard in 6000 SE /STE Sedan and Safari; optional in base 6000 and 6000 LE Sedan and Safari. Produced in U.S., Canada, or Mexico.

[VIN code W, S, or 9]. [STANDARD STE-AWD] V-block. OHV. Six-cylinder. Cast iron block. Aluminum head and intake manifold. Displacement: 189 cu. in.. (3.1L). Bore x stroke: 3.50 x 3.30 in. Compression ratio: 8.8:1. Brake horsepower: 135 @ 4800 rpm. Torque: 180 lb.-ft. @ 3600 rpm. Fuel system: MPFI. RPO Code: LHO. Standard in 6000 STE All-Wheel-Drive model. [VIN code T].

GRAND PRIX ENGINES

[STANDARD] V-block. OHV. Six-cylinder. Cast iron block and aluminum head. Displacement: 173 cu. in. (2.8L). Bore x stroke: 3.50 x 2.99 in. Compression ratio: 8.8:1. Brake horsepower: 130 @ 4800 rpm. Torque: 160 lb.-ft. @ 3600 rpm. Fuel system: MPFI. RPO Code: LB6. Standard in Grand Prix. Produced in U.S., Canada, or Mexico. [VIN code W, S, or 9].

BONNEVILLE ENGINE

[STANDARD LE] V-block. OHV. Six-cylinder. Cast iron block and head. Aluminum intake manifold. Displacement: 231 cu. in. (3.8L). Bore x stroke: 3.80 x 3.40 in. Compression ratio: 8.5:1. Brake horsepower: 150 @ 4400 rpm. Torque: 200 lb.-ft. @ 2000 rpm. Fuel system: SFI. RPO Code: LG3. Standard in Bonneville LE model. [VIN code W, S, or 9]. [STANDARD SE/SSE] V-block. OHV. "3800" six-cylinder. Cast iron block and head. Aluminum intake manifold. Displacement: 231 cu. in. (3.8L). Bore x stroke: 3.80 x 3.40 in. Compression ratio: 8.5:1. Brake horsepower: 165 @ 5200 rpm. Torque: 210 lb.-ft. @ 2000 rpm. Fuel system: SFI. RPO Code: LN3. Standard in Bonneville SE/SSE model. [VIN code W, S, or 9].

SAFARI ENGINE

[STANDARD V-8] V-block. OHV. Eight-cylinder. Cast iron block. Displacement: 307 cu. in. (5.0L). Bore x stroke: 3.80 x 3.39 in. Compression ratio: 8.0.1. Brake horsepower: 140 @ 3200 rpm. Torque: 255 lb.-ft. @ 2000 rpm. Fuel system: Four-barrel carburetor. RPO Code: LV2. Standard V-8 in all Safaris. [VIN code Y].

FIERO CHASSIS: Wheelbase: 93.4 in. (all). Overall length: 162.7 in. (Coupe, Sport Coupe); 165.1 in. (SE, GT). Width: 69 in. (all) Height: 46.9 in. (all). Front tread: 57.8 in. Rear tread: 57.8 in. Standard tires: P185/75R15 BSW (Coupe); P205/60R14 front and P215/60R14 rear (Formula/GT).

PONTIAC LEMANS CHASSIS: Wheelbase: 99.21 in. (all). Overall length: 163.70 in. (three-door); 171.89 in. (four-door). Height: 54.72 in. (all). Standard tires: P175/70R13 BSW (all).

SUNBIRD CHASSIS: Wheelbase: 101.2 in. (all). Overall length: 178.2 in. (Coupe and Convertible); 181.7 (Sedan); 175.9 (Wagon). Width: 65.0 in. (Coupe/Sedan/Convertible); 66.3 in. (Wagon) Height: 50.4.in. (Coupe); 53.8 in. (Sedan); 52.6 in. (Convertible); 54.1 in. (Safari Wagon). Front tread: 55.6 in. (Coupe and Sedan); 55.4 in. (Wagon and Convertible). Rear tread: 55.2 in. (All). Standard tires: P185/80R13 BSW (except Convertible and GTs). Standard tires: P215/60R14 (Convertible). Standard tires: P215/60R14 (GT). Optional tires with Y99 rally-tuned suspension on Sunbird SE wagon only: P215/60R14 Goodyear Eagle GT+4. Optional tires with WS6 special performance suspension: P215/60R14 Goodyear Eagle GT+4.

GRAND AM CHASSIS: Wheelbase: 103.4 in. (Coupe/Sedan). Overall length: 177.5 in. (Coupe/Sedan). Width: 66.5 in. (Coupe/Sedan). Height: 52.5 in. (Coupe/Sedan). Front tread: 55.6 in. Rear tread: 55.1 in. Standard tires: P185/80R13 BSW (Base/LE). Standard tires: P215/60R14 (SE).

FIREBIRD CHASSIS: Wheelbase: 101.0 in. (All). Overall length: 188.1 in. (Base/Formula); 191.6 in. (Trans Am/GTA). Width: 72.4 in. (Coupe). Height: 50.0 in. (Coupe). Front tread: 60.7 in. Rear tread: 61.6 in. Standard tires: P215/65R16 BSW (Base). Standard tires (Formula/Trans Am/GTA): P245/50VR16 RWL.

6000 CHASSIS: Wheelbase: 104.9 in. (all). Overall length: 188.8 in. (Sedan); 193.2 in. (Safari). Width: 72 in. (All). Height: 53.7 in. (Sedan); 54.1 in. (Wagon). Front tread: 58.7 in. Rear tread: 57.0 in. Standard tires: 185/75R14 (All except STE). Standard tires: 195/70R14 (STE).

GRAND PRIX CHASSIS: Wheelbase: 107.6 in. (all). Overall length: 194.1 in. (All). Width: 71.0 in. (All). Height: 53.3 in. (All). Front tread: 59.5 in. Rear tread: 58.0 in. Standard tires: 195/75R14 (base and LE). Standard tires: 215/65R15 Goodyear Eagle GT (SE).

BONNEVILLE CHASSIS: Wheelbase: 110.8 in. (all). Overall length: 198.7 in. (All). Width: 72.1 in. (All). Height: 55.5 in. (All). Front tread: 58.7 in. Rear tread: 57.0 in. Standard tires: 205/75R14 BSW (LE). Standard tires: 215/65R15 Goodyear Eagle GT (SE). Standard tires: P215/60R16 BSW (SSE).

SAFARI CHASSIS: Wheelbase: 116.0 in. (all). Overall length: 215.1 in. (All). Width: 79.3 in. (All). Height: 57.4 in. (All). Front tread: 60.3 in. Rear tread: 59.8 in. Tires: P225/75R15.

FIERO TECHNICAL: Chassis: Mid-engine/rear drive. Base transmission: Three-speed automatic. Optional transmission (with V-6): Gertag-designed GM-developed five-speed manual. Axle ratio: 3.35:1 (2.5L with manual). Axle ratio: 2.84:1 (2.5L with automatic). Axle ratio:

3.61:1 (2.8L with manual). Axle ratio: 3.33:1 (2.8L with automatic). Steering: Rack-and-pinion. Front suspension: Independent control arms with coil springs. Rear suspension: Independent control arms with coil springs. Front brakes: Disc. Rear brakes: disc. Fuel tank: 12 gal.

LEMANS TECHNICAL: Chassis: Front engine/front drive. Base transmission: Four-speed automatic. Optional transmission: Three-speed automatic or five-speed manual. Axle ratio: 3.43:1 with automatic. Axle ratio: 3.74:1 with manual. Front suspension: Hydraulic cartridge shocks. Rear suspension: Coil springs. Front brakes: Vented disc. Rear brakes: drum.

SUNBIRD TECHNICAL: Chassis: Front engine/front drive. Base transmission: Five-speed manual with overdrive. Optional transmission: Three-speed automatic. Axle ratio: 3.45:1 (with 2.0L engine and manual). Axle ratio: 3.18:1 (with 2.0L engine and automatic). Axle ratio: 3.61:1 with Turbo engine and manual). Axle ratio: 3.18:1 with Turbo engine and automatic). Front suspension: MacPherson struts with coil springs. Rear suspension: Beam axle with coil springs. Front brakes: Power-assisted vented discs. Rear brakes: Power-assisted drums. Fuel tank: 13.6 gal.

1988 Pontiac Grand Am LE four-door sedan. PMD

GRAND AM TECHNICAL: Chassis: Front engine/front drive. Base transmission: Five-speed manual with overdrive. Optional transmission: Three-speed automatic. Axle ratio: 3.35:1 (with 2.5L engine and manual). Axle ratio: 3.61:1 (with 2.0L engine and manual or 2.3L engine and manual). Axle ratio: 2.84:1 (with 2.3L and automatic or 2.5L and automatic). Axle ratio: 3.18:1 with 2.0L and automatic). Front suspension: MacPherson struts with coil springs. Rear suspension: Beam axle with coil springs. Front brakes: Power-assisted vented discs. Rear brakes: Power-assisted drums. Fuel tank: 13.6 gal.

FIREBIRD TECHNICAL: Chassis: Front engine/rear drive. Base transmission: Five-speed manual with overdrive. Optional transmission: Four-speed automatic. Axle ratio: 3.08:1 (with 5.0L TBI and manual). Axle ratio: 2.73:1 (with 5.0L TBI and four-speed automatic). Axle ratio: 3.45:1 (with 5.0L TPI and five-speed manual). Axle ratio: 3.23:1 (with 5.0L TPI and four-speed automatic). Axle ratio: 3.27:1 (with 5.7L and four-speed automatic and with 5.0L TPI and four-speed automatic in GTA/Trans Am only). Front suspension: MacPherson struts with coil springs. Rear suspension: Live axle with coil springs. Front brakes: Power-assisted vented discs. Rear brakes: Power-assisted drums (rear disc brakes standard on GTA). Fuel tank: 15.5.

6000 TECHNICAL: Chassis: Front engine/front drive. Base transmission: Three-speed automatic with overdrive. Optional transmissions: Four-speed automatic and five-speed manual. Axle ratio: 2.84:1 (with three-speed automatic). Axle ratio: 3.33:1 (with four-speed automatic). Axle ratio: 3.61:1 (with five-speed manual). Front suspension: MacPherson struts with coil springs. Rear suspension: Beam axle with coil springs. Front brakes: Power-assisted vented discs. Rear brakes: Power-assisted drums (ABS vented discs on STE). Fuel tank: 15.7 gal.

GRAND PRIX TECHNICAL: Chassis: Front engine/front drive. Standard drivetrain: 2.8L V-6 with five-speed manual transaxle. Optional drivetrain: 2.8L V-6 with four-speed automatic transaxle. Axle ratio: 3.61:1 (manual); 3.33:1 (automatic). Front suspension: MacPherson struts with tapered top coil springs. Rear suspension: Tri-link independent suspension. Four-wheel power disc brakes. Fuel tank: 16.0 gal.

BONNEVILLE TECHNICAL: Chassis: Front engine/front drive. Base transmission: Four-speed automatic. Axle ratio: 2.73:1 (standard with 3.8L V-6 in Base Bonneville and Bonneville SE). Axle ratio: 2.97:1 (standard with 3.8L V-6 in Bonneville SE/SSE). Front suspension: MacPherson struts with coil springs. Rear suspension: MacPherson struts with coil springs. Front brakes: Power-assisted vented discs. Rear brakes: Power-assisted drums. Anti-lock brake system standard with SSE. Fuel tank: 18.0 gal.

SAFARI TECHNICAL: Chassis: Front engine/rear drive. Base transmission: Four-speed automatic. Axle ratio: 2.93:1 (standard). Axle ratio: 3.23:1 (optional). Front suspension: Control arms with coil springs. Rear suspension: Live axle, links and coil springs. Front brakes: Power-assisted vented discs. Rear brakes: Power-assisted drums. Fuel tank: 22.0 gal.

1988 Pontiac Fiero Formula coupe. PMD

FIERO OPTIONS: Air conditioning with Soft Ray tinted glass. Electric rear window defogger. Deck lid luggage carrier. Front floor carpets. Power door locks. Power windows. UM6 Delco ETR AM/FM stereo. UX1 Delco ETR AM stereo/FM stereo radio. Inflatable driver's side lumbar-support bucket seat. Reclining bucket seat with Ventura cloth and leather trim. Rear deck lid spoiler (not available with deck lid luggage carrier). Subwoofer speaker system, requires stereo and air conditioning. Removable sun roof. P195/70R14 Eagle GT+4 steel-belted radial tires. Three-speed automatic transmission. Gold- or black-finished diamond-spoke aluminum wheels (gold on GT only). Base Coupe and Formula option group #1 with tilt steering, comfort-cycle wipers, and tinted glass. Base Coupe and Formula option group #2 with air conditioning, tinted glass, tilt steering, controlled-cycle wipers, lamp group, passenger visor vanity mirror, and cruise control. Base Coupe and Formula option group #3 with air conditioning, tinted glass, tilt steering, controlled-cycle wipers, lamp group, passenger visor vanity mirror, cruise control, power door locks, and power windows. GT Coupe option group #1 adds tinted glass, passenger visor vanity mirror, cruise control, power door locks, and power sport windows to regular standard features for GT model.

LEMANS OPTIONS: Air conditioning, requires power steering. Front and rear carpeted floor mats. Power steering. UM6 Delco DIN size AM/FM stereo cassette. UM7 Delco ETR DIN-size AM/FM stereo. Black-finished roof luggage rack. Sun roof. Three-speed automatic transmission.

SUNBIRD OPTIONS: Air conditioning with Soft Ray tinted glass. Custom interior trim. Electric rear window defogger. Rally gauge cluster with trip odometer. Deck lid luggage carrier. Roof luggage carrier. Front /rear carpeted floor mats. Power door locks. Power windows, requires power door locks. UM6 Delco ETR AM/FM stereo. UX1 Delco ETR AM stereo/FM stereo radio. Articulating bucket seats with lumbar and backwing bolsters, requires custom trim. Sun roof with removable glass. Three-speed automatic transmission. 14-in. Hi-Tech Turbo cast aluminum wheels with locking package. 13-in. Sport Tech cast aluminum wheels, except GT. Base and SE option group #1 with tinted glass, power steering, and sport mirrors. Base and SE option package #2 with tinted glass, power steering, sport mirrors, color-keyed seat belts, tilt steering, controlled-cycle wipers, and four-spoke steering wheel. Base and SE option package #3 with tinted glass, power steering, sport mirrors, color-keyed seat belts, air conditioning, tilt steering, controlled-cycle wipers, four-spoke steering wheel, lamp group, cruise control, and front seat armrest. Sunbird GT Coupe option group #1 including tinted glass, air conditioning, tilt steering, and controlled cycle wipers, plus GT standard extras. Sunbird GT Convertible option group #1 including air conditioning, tilt steering, and controlled cycle wipers, plus GT Convertible standard extras. Sunbird GT Coupe option group #2 including tinted glass, air conditioning, tilt steering, controlled cycle wipers, lamp group, cruise control, front seat armrest, remote deck lid release, and visor vanity mirror plus GT Coupe standard extras. Sunbird GT Coupe option group #3 including tinted glass, air conditioning, tilt steering, controlled cycle wipers, lamp group, cruise control, front seat armrest, remote deck lid release, visor vanity mirror, power windows, power door locks, and leather-wrapped steering wheel, plus GT Coupe standard extras. Sunbird GT Convertible option group #3 including air conditioning, tilt steering, controlled cycle wipers, lamp group, cruise control, front seat armrest, remote deck lid release, and leather-wrapped steering wheel, plus GT Convertible standard extras.

GRAND AM OPTIONS: Air conditioning. Electric rear window defogger. 2.0-liter four-cylinder turbo engine with MFI. 2.3-liter Quad 4 engine. Gauge package. Deck lid luggage carrier. Pontiac performance sound system, requires power windows. UM6 Delco ETR AM/FM stereo. UX1 Delco ETR AM/FM stereo. Articulating bucket seats with inflatable lumbar and backwing bolsters. Removable sun roof with air deflector. Three-speed automatic transmission. Tri-Port wheels, requires P195/70R14 tires. Hi-Tech Turbo aluminum wheels with locking package. Base Grand Am option group #1 includes air conditioning, tilt steering, and custom console. Base Grand Am option group #2 includes air conditioning, tilt steering, custom console, lamp group, controlled-cycle wipers, and cruise control. Base Grand Am option group #3 includes air conditioning, tilt steering, custom console, lamp group, controlled-cycle wipers, cruise control, power windows, and power door locks. Grand Am LE option group #1 includes air conditioning, tilt steering, lamp group, controlled-cycle wipers, and cruise control, plus standard LE extras. Grand Am LE option group #2 includes air conditioning, tilt steering, lamp group, controlled-cycle wipers, cruise control, remote gas filler, visor vanity mirror, remote deck lid release, and split-folding rear seat, plus standard LE extras. Grand Am LE option group #3 includes air conditioning, tilt steering, lamp group, controlled-cycle wipers, cruise control, remote gas filler, visor vanity mirror, remote deck lid release, split-folding rear seat, power windows, power door locks, fog lamps including header and front courtesy lamps, and power driver's seat, plus standard LE extras. Grand AM SE option package #1 includes tilt steering, lamp group, and power windows, plus standard SE extras. Grand AM SE option package #2 includes tilt steering, lamp group, power windows, power driver's seat, lighted visor vanity mirror, and power sport mirrors, plus standard SE extras.

1988 Pontiac Firebird Formula coupe. PMD

FIREBIRD OPTIONS: Air conditioning with Soft Ray tinted glass. Limited-slip axle. Four-wheel disc brakes. Electric rear window defogger. 5.0-liter EFI V-8. 5.0-liter TPI high-output V-8. 5.7-liter TPI high-output V-8. Gauge package, requires electronic air conditioning controls. Hatch roof with removable glass panels. Luxury trim group. Power antenna. Power door locks. Power windows. UM6 Delco ETR AM/FM stereo. UX1 Delco ETR AM stereo/FM stereo. Subwoofer six-speaker system. Articulating bucket seats with inflatable lumbar and backwing bolsters. Leather seat trim. Four-speed automatic transmission. Deep-dish Hi-Tech 15-in. Turbo cast aluminum wheels with locking package (no-charge option). 15-in. diamond-spoke cast aluminum wheels. 16-in. diamond-spoke cast aluminum wheels. 16-in Hi-Tech Turbo cast aluminum wheels, available with WS6 suspension only. Base Firebird option group #1 includes air conditioning with Soft Ray tinted glass, tilt steering, custom-colored safety belts, body side moldings, controlled-cycle windshield wipers, and passenger visor vanity mirror. Base Firebird option group #2 includes air conditioning with Soft Ray tinted glass, tilt steering, custom-colored safety belts, body side moldings, controlled-cycle windshield wipers, passenger visor vanity mirror, lamp group, cruise control, remote deck lid release, and four-way manual driver's seat adjuster. Base Firebird option group #3 includes air conditioning with Soft Ray tinted glass, tilt steering, custom-colored safety belts, body side moldings, controlled-cycle windshield wipers, passenger visor vanity mirror, lamp group, cruise control, remote deck lid release, four-way manual driver's seat adjuster, power windows, and power door locks. Firebird Formula option group #1 includes air conditioning with Soft Ray tinted glass, tilt steering, custom-colored safety belts, body side moldings, controlled-cycle windshield wipers, and passenger visor vanity mirror. Firebird Formula option group #2 includes air conditioning with Soft Ray tinted glass, tilt steering, custom-colored safety belts, body side moldings, controlled-cycle windshield wipers, passenger visor vanity mirror, lamp group, cruise control, remote deck lid release, and four-way manual driver's seat adjuster. Firebird Formula option group #3 includes air conditioning with Soft Ray tinted glass, tilt steering, custom-colored safety belts, body side moldings, controlled-cycle windshield wipers, passenger visor vanity mirror, lamp group, cruise control, remote deck lid release, four-way manual driver's seat adjuster, power windows, and power door locks. Firebird Trans Am

option group #1 includes air conditioning with Soft Ray tinted glass, tilt steering, custom-colored safety belts, body side moldings, controlled-cycle windshield wipers, passenger visor vanity mirror, lamp group, cruise control, remote deck lid release, and standard Trans Am extras. Firebird Trans Am option group #3 includes air conditioning with Soft Ray tinted glass, tilt steering, custom-colored safety belts, body side moldings, controlled-cycle windshield wipers, passenger visor vanity mirror, lamp group, cruise control, remote deck lid release, power windows, power door locks, leather appointments group, and power sport mirrors, plus standard Trans Am extras.

6000 OPTIONS: Air conditioning with Soft Ray tinted glass. Sport mirrors. 2.8-liter V-6 with MFI. Analog instrument cluster with tachometer. Electronic instrument cluster with tachometer. UM6 Delco ETR AM/FM stereo. UX1 Delco ETR AM stereo/FM stereo. Simulated woodgrain Safari paneling. Paint stripes. Power glass sun roof, includes reading lamps, not available on Safari. Four-speed automatic transmission with overdrive. Five-speed manual transmission. Aluminum sport wheels with locking package. Simulated wire wheel covers with locking package. Base 6000 option group #1 includes air conditioning with Soft Ray tinted glass, sport mirrors, and tilt steering. Base 6000 option group #2 includes air conditioning with Soft Ray tinted glass, sport mirrors, tilt steering, custom-exterior group, sport steering wheel, cruise control, lamp group, and concealed-cycle wipers. Base 6000 option group #3 includes air conditioning with Soft Ray tinted glass, sport mirrors, tilt steering, custom exterior group, sport steering wheel, cruise control, lamp group, concealed-cycle wipers, power door locks, deck lid release, visor vanity mirror, and power windows. 6000 LE option group #1 includes air conditioning with Soft Ray tinted glass, sport mirrors, tilt steering, cruise control, lamp group, and concealed-cycle wipers, plus standard LE extras. 6000 LE option group #2 includes air conditioning with Soft Ray tinted glass, sport mirrors, tilt steering, cruise control, lamp group, concealed-cycle wipers, power door locks, deck lid release, visor vanity mirror, and power window, plus standard LE extras. 6000 LE option group #3 includes air conditioning with Soft Ray tinted glass, sport mirrors, tilt steering, cruise control, lamp group, concealed-cycle wipers, power door locks, deck lid release, power windows, illuminated visor vanity mirror, and mirror with dual reading lamps. plus standard LE extras. 6000 S/E option group #1 includes air conditioning with Soft Ray tinted glass, tilt steering, cruise control, lamp group, and controlled-cycle wipers, plus standard S/E extras. 6000 S/E option group #2 includes air conditioning with Soft Ray tinted glass, tilt steering, cruise control, lamp group, and controlled-cycle wipers, power door locks, deck lid release, visor vanity mirror and power windows, plus standard S/E extras. 6000 S/E option group #3 includes air conditioning with Soft Ray tinted glass, tilt steering, cruise control, lamp group, and controlled-cycle wipers, power door locks, deck lid release, visor vanity mirror, power windows, power driver's seat, and mirror with reading lamp, plus standard S/E extras.

GRAND PRIX OPTIONS: Electronic control air conditioning. Electric rear window defogger. Front and rear carpeted floor mats. Mechanical analog gauges with tachometer and trip odometer. Lower accent two-tone paint. UM6 Delco stereo. UX1 Delco stereo. High-performance sound system with six speakers and power amplifier. Power antenna. Power door locks. Power windows. 40/60 split seat with folding armrest. Reclining bucket seats with console. P195/70R15 Goodyear Eagle GT+4 BSW radial tires, requires 15-in. wheels. P215/65R15 Goodyear Eagle GT+4 BSW tires teamed with Y99 rally-tuned suspension. Four-speed automatic transaxle. Five-speed manual transaxle. 15-in. styled sport wheels. 15-in. aluminum wheels (color-keyed on S/E) with locking packages. Base Grand Prix option group #1 includes air conditioning with electronic control, tilt steering, lamp group, and right-hand vanity mirror. Base Grand Prix option group #2 includes air conditioning with electronic control, tilt steering, lamp group, right-hand vanity mirror, cruise control, and controlled-cycle wipers. Base Grand Prix option group #3 includes air conditioning with electronic control, tilt steering, lamp group, right-hand vanity mirror, cruise control, controlled-cycle wipers, power windows with illuminated switches, power door locks with illuminated switches, and remote deck lid release. Grand Prix LE option group #1 includes air conditioning with electronic control, tilt steering, right-hand vanity mirror, cruise control, controlled-cycle wipers, and power door locks with illuminated switches, plus standard LE extras. Grand Prix LE option group #2 includes air conditioning with electronic control, tilt steering, cruise control, controlled-cycle wipers, power door locks with illuminated switches, deck lid release, power driver's seat, and illuminated passenger visor vanity mirror, plus standard LE extras. Grand Prix LE option group #3 includes air conditioning with electronic control, tilt steering, cruise control, controlled-cycle wipers, power door locks with illuminated switches, deck lid release, power driver's seat, illuminated passenger visor vanity mirror, rear view mirror with dual reading lamps, leather appointment group, security lighting including illuminated entry and time-delay headlight shut-off, and power mirrors, plus standard LE extras. Grand Prix SE option group #1 includes right-hand visor vanity mirror, power door locks with illuminated switches, deck lid release, and power driver's seat, plus standard SE extras. Grand Prix SE option group #2 includes power door locks with illuminated switches, deck lid release, power driver's seat, illuminated passenger visor vanity mirror, and power mirrors, and console extension with electronic compass, trip computer, and service reminder, plus standard SE extras.

1988 Pontiac Bonneville SSE four-door sedan. PMD

BONNEVILLE OPTIONS: Power antenna. Electric rear window defogger. Gauge package including driver information center (included with 45/45 seat option). Leather seat trim. Two-tone paint. Power door locks, Power windows. UM6 Delco radio equipment. UT4 Delco radio equipment. 45/55 split front seat. 45/45 split front seat. Power sun roof. Theft-deterrent system. 14-in. diamond-spoke aluminum wheels with locking package. Bonneville LE option group #1 includes controlled-cycle windshield wipers, tilt steering, and lamp group. Bonneville LE option group #2 includes controlled-cycle windshield wipers, tilt steering, cruise control, and lamp group. Bonneville LE option group #3 includes controlled-cycle windshield wipers, tilt steering, cruise control, lamp group, power windows, power door locks, power driver's seat, deck lid release and illuminated passenger visor vanity mirror. Bonneville LE option group #4 includes controlled-cycle windshield wipers, tilt steering, cruise control, lamp group, power door locks, power windows, power driver's seat, deck lid release, illuminated passenger visor vanity mirror, leather-wrapped steering wheel, lighted entry system, electric fuel door lock, power sport mirrors, and power passenger seat. Bonneville SE option group #1 includes lamp group, and power door locks, plus all standard SE extras. Bonneville SE option group #2 includes lamp group, and power door locks, power driver's seat, deck lid release, illuminated passenger visor vanity mirror, and fog lamps, plus all standard SE extras. Bonneville SE option group #3 includes lamp group, and power door locks, power driver's seat, deck lid release, illuminated passenger visor vanity mirror, fog lamps, lighted entry system, electric fuel door lock, power sport mirrors, power passenger seat, and twilight sentinel, plus all standard SE extras.

SAFARI OPTIONS: Power antenna. Heavy-duty cooling. Electric rear window defogger. Front and rear floor mats. Gauge package including coolant temperature and voltmeter gauges. Luggage carrier including rear air deflector. Power door locks, including power tailgate lock. Power windows. UM6 Delco radio equipment. UX1 Delco radio equipment. 55/45 split front seat with passenger recliner. Superlift shock absorbers. Simulated wood-grain exterior body siding. Trailer wiring harness. Simulated wire wheel covers with locking package. Safari full-size Station Wagon option group #1, includes tilt steering, lamp group, cruise control, and controlled-cycle windshield wipers. Safari full-size Station Wagon option group #2, includes tilt steering, lamp group, cruise control, controlled-cycle windshield wipers, power door locks, power windows, power driver's seat with 55/45 split seat only, carpeted sidewalls and tailgate, cornering lamps, dual remote-control OSRV mirrors, front and rear bumper guards, illuminated passenger visor vanity mirror, and halogen headlights.

HISTORICAL FOOTNOTES: Michael J. Losh continued as Pontiac Motor Division's general manager in 1988, with E.M Schlesinger heading up sales and service responsibilities. Bill O'Neill once again handled public relations. John Sawruk was official Pontiac Historian. The new 6000 STE (GM's first all-wheel-drive car) was predicted to be the hot "image" product of the year. It reflected an effort to make Pontiac A-body cars distinctive from those of other GM divisions. Unfortunately, its introduction was delayed, making it impossible to hit even its low-volume production target of approximately 3000 units. It was, however, the new LeMans sourced from Daewoo, of Korea, that increased the company's model-year unit sales volume. The total was 740,928 cars sold, an increase of more than 25,000. This broke down as follows: [1000] 366; [Daewoo LeMans] 54,671; [Sunbird] 77,864; [Fiero] 27,304; [Firebird] 59,459; [Grand Am] 221,438; [6000] 103,003; [Bonneville] 109,862; {RWD Grand Prix] 2,850; [FWD Grand Prix] 76,723; [Full-size Safari] 7,388. Pontiac regained the number three slot in the U.S. auto sales charts, a position it had last held 15 years earlier in 1973. The front-wheel-drive Bonneville--which had been somewhat of a sales disappointment in 1987--had a more respectable showing this season, although it was the new front-wheel-drive Grand

Prix--introduced at midyear--that became a first-year success story. The top-selling Grand Am also gained from 1987. All 1988 Firebirds were built in Van Nuys, California. All 1988 Parisienne-style Safaris were built in Lakewood, Georgia. All front-wheel-drive Grand Prixs were built at the Fairfax plant near Kansas City. All Grand Ams were made in Lansing, Michigan. All Bonnevilles were built at Willow Run, Michigan. Pontiac 6000s were built at Tarrytown, New York, and Oklahoma City, Oklahoma. Sunbirds were manufactured at Lordstown, Ohio. Additional U.S. market cars were sourced from Canadian factories.

1989 PONTIAC

PONTIAC I.D. NUMBERS: Vehicle identification number (VIN) is located on top left-hand surface of instrument panel visible through the windshield. The VIN has 17 symbols. The first symbol indicates the country of manufacture (U.S.) The second symbol indicates the manufacturer (G=General Motors). The third symbol indicates the make/division (2=Pontiac). The fourth, fifth and sixth symbols are the same as the body style (model) number. The eighth symbol indicates the engine. The ninth symbol is a check digit. The 10th symbol indicates model-year. The 11th symbol indicates the assembly plant. The last six symbols are the consecutive unit number at the factory.

LEMANS -- SERIES 2T -- FOUR -- For 1989, the LeMans continued the sporty, fun-to-drive character of Pontiac's smallest performer initially introduced in June of 1987. Featuring distinctive European styling and engineering by GM's Adam Opel subsidiary in West Germany, and assembly by Daewoo Motor Co. in South Korea, all LeMans models offered high quality in an affordably priced compact that returned the best fuel economy figures in the Pontiac lineup. All five LeMans models featured fuel-injected engines, front-wheel-drive, power-assisted front disc brakes, rack-and-pinion steering, and a clean, wind-cheating aero design. Front suspension was by MacPherson struts with anti-roll bar. Rear suspension was by semi-independent torsion beam and coil springs, with trailing arms, and an anti-roll bar. The LeMans Value Leader Aerocoupe featured a 1.6-liter 74-hp EFI engine, four-speed manual transaxle, fully reclining seats, and a fold-down rear seat back. The next-step-up LeMans SE was offered in Aerocoupe and Sedan models. Both had the base engine, but with a five-speed manual transaxle. The brakes were 8.9-in. solid discs up front. The suspension used 20mm front and 18mm rear anti-roll bars. Also standard was tinted glass, and a Delco AM/FM radio with clock. Swing-out rear windows were featured on the Aerocoupe, while the Sedan had roll-down rear door glass. The Aerocoupe also came with interior door map pockets, and a tachometer. A three-speed automatic transmission, power steering, and air conditioning were available. The LeMans SE offered a 2.0-liter OHC engine, five-speed manual transaxle, larger tires and wheels, tilt steering, tachometer, black air dam, and integral fog lamps. It had larger 10-in. vented disc brakes. The front seats had height adjusters, while the 60/40 split rear seat had fold-down seat backs. On the top of the LeMans lineup was the GSE. It added or substituted body-color cast alloy wheels, semi-metallic brake pads, even larger 10.1-in. front disc brakes, a sport suspension, and 18.3:1 power steering. The GSE also had an exterior aero fascia, rocker extensions, a body-color rear deck lid spoiler, and integrated fog lights. Found at the rear were unique GSE turn signal lenses. A three-spoke steering wheel, and full instrumentation (with tach) were also included.

1989 Pontiac LeMans GSE three-door hatchback. PMD

LEMANS -- SERIES 2T -- I-4

Model Number	Body/Style Number	Body Type & Seating	Factory Price	Shipping Weight	Prod. Total
2T	TX2	3-dr V/L Cpe-4P	6399	2136	Note 1
2T	TN2	3-dr Cpe-4P	7699	2180	Note 1
2T	TS2	3-dr Cpe-4P	9149	2302	Note 1
2T	TN5	4-dr LE Sed-4P	7999	2235	Note 1
2T	TR5	4-dr SE Sed-4P	9429	2357	Note 1

NOTE 1: LeMans series production totaled 44,641.

1989 Pontiac Sunbird LE coupe. PMD

SUNBIRD -- SERIES 2J --FOUR -- The 1989 Pontiac was an aggressively styled, sporty, affordable American car designed to compete head-on with small domestic and imported Sedan and Sport Coupes. Five models were offered and new features across the line included deflected-disc front struts for improved handling, a redesigned instrument panel, a Grand Prix type steering wheel, a Delco Advanced Radio Concept (ARC) sound system, a redesigned console and parking brake lever, and three-point rear seat and shoulder belts. A compact digital disc player was a new option. All models also featured plastisol protection against nicks for lower body paint and clearcoat finishes. The most affordable Sunbird models were the LE Sport Coupe and LE Sport Sedan. Both had a completely restyled front end including new lower hood and fender profiles, fascia, grille, front and side marker lamps, and composite headlights for a sleeker, sportier look and better aerodynamics. A large protective side molding wrapped around the LE Sport Coupe. Sunbird LE models used 22mm front stabilizer bars and the suspension was refined for improved handling without ride degradation. The middle line was the SE. It included only a Sport Coupe. Its standard features included a front with partially hidden headlights, and rally instrumentation. The top-of-the-line Sunbird GT Coupe and Convertible featured a turbocharged four-cylinder engine, a special performance suspension (with 28mm front/19mm rear stabilizer bars), higher-rate springs, fatter tires, and a quicker 14:1 steering ratio. GT styling emphasized sportiness with wheel flares, aero-style covers over the partly hidden headlights, and standard fog lamps. Two-tone paint with a unique body stripe was available in Black over Silver, Black over Red, and Black over Bright Blue. Also included was rally instrumentation.

Model Number	Body/Style Number	Body Type & Seating	Factory Price	Shipping Weight	Prod. Total
SUNBIRD LE -- SERIES 2J -- I-4					
2J	JB5	4-dr Sed-5P	8949	2433	Note 1
2J	JB1	2-dr Cpe-5P	8849	2418	Note 1
SUNBIRD SE -- SERIES 2J -- I-4/I-4					
2J	JD1	2-dr Cpe-5P	9099	2376	Note 1
SUNBIRD GT TURBO -- SERIES 2J -- I-4/I-4 Turbo					
2J	JU1	2-dr Cpe-5P	11399	2422	Note 1
2J	JU3	2-dr Conv-5P	16899	2577	Note 1

NOTE 1: Sunbird series production totaled 139,644.

GRAND AM -- SERIES 2N -- The fifth N-body Grand Am front-drive compact was the best-selling Pontiac. It had new looks to complement its already popular performance and roadability. Models offered were the LE Coupe, LE Sedan, SE Coupe, and SE Sedan. A new front treatment featured a new hood, fenders, grille, and fascia cover that gave a more swept-back, aerodynamic profile. At the rear, both trim levels had

new fascias, end panels, bumpers, and taillights. The license plate opening was relocated to the rear fascia. Side marker lights and parking lights were modified for 1989, and a new one-piece side molding was seen. Paint-work featured a two-layer base coat/clearcoat system. Ride and comfort in all models was improved by new deflected-disc valving in the MacPherson strut front suspension. To ensure long life even beyond GM's six-year/100,000-mile warranty against rust-through, the Grand Am hood and fenders were made of steel galvanized on both sides. Inside the 1989 Grand Am were a sporty, redesigned steering wheel and revised instrument panel graphics, including a new higher-reading speedometer. On Coupes, the passenger seat slid forward to allow easier rear entrance and a mechanical "memory" returned the seat to its original position. All Grand Ams were equipped with new three-point rear seat belts and shoulder harness. An all-new compact digital disc player and a choice of radios was available for all models, along with an optional performance sound system. The Grand Am LE offered distinctive exterior styling at an affordable price. Its new rear end treatment featured amber turn signals and back-up lights between the taillights. The SE models were easy to spot with their monochromatic exteriors. Standard features included composite headlights, integrated front fog lights, a rally tuned suspension (RTS) with 28mm front and 21mm rear anti-roll bars, P215.60R14 tires on newly designed body-color aluminum wheels, revised "clean-look" neutral density taillights incorporating back-up lights, wheel opening flares, new and larger body aero skirting, leather-covered sport steering wheel, shift lever and parking brake, rally instrumentation (including tachometer), cruise control, and split seat back seats. As a prelude to 1990, Pontiac announced plans to build just 200 special Grand Am SEs equipped with a 2.3-liter Twin Cam 16-valve High Output four-cylinder engine linked to a manual transaxle. Pontiac suggested that these cars, scheduled to be built late in the model-year, would enable the division to gain experience with the car in the marketplace prior to its scheduled production in 1990.

1989 Pontiac Grand Am SE coupe. PMD

Model Number	Body/Style Number	Body Type & Seating	Factory Price	Shipping Weight	Prod. Total
GRAND AM LE SERIES 2N -- I-4/V-6					
2N	NE1	2-dr Cpe-5P	10469	2508	Note 1
2N	NE5	4-dr Sed-5P	10669	2592	Note 1
GRAND AM SE-- SERIES 2N -- I-4/V-6					
2N	NW1	2-dr Cpe-5P	13599	2739	Note 1
2N	NW5	4-dr Sed-5P	13799	2826	Note 1

NOTE 1: Grand Am series production totaled 246,418.

FIREBIRD -- SERIES 2F -- V-6/V-8 -- For 1989 Pontiac's premium performer, the Firebird, continued its more than two-decade heritage of high-powered excitement. From performance machine enthusiasts to sporty car buyers looking for trademark styling, the Firebird offered a complete range of power and price. Again there were four regular models: Firebird, Formula, Trans Am, and Trans Am GTA. There was also a special limited-edition 25th Anniversary "Indy Pace Car" version of the GTA with a high-output V-6 pirated from the Buick GNX. All Firebirds came with V-8s, and the base model also came with a V-6 for entry-level sports car buyers. Multec fuel injectors were added to 1989 engines for more reliability and less susceptibility to fuel fouling. The self-adjusting rear disc brakes were completely revised with a new caliper and rotor design. Pass Key anti-theft protection, previously standard only on the GTA, became standard on all Firebirds. An electronically coded resistor embedded in the ignition key activated a control module in the ignition lock, which determined when the anti-theft vehicle start-up system should be activated. GM noted that the system had been successful in reducing Corvette thefts by 40 percent and said that it should be helpful in holding down Firebird owners' insurance premiums. Door glass seals were improved for better sealing and less wind noise. The entire Firebird line also got clearcoat paint over the base color for a long-lasting high gloss finish. New in the color lineup was Bright Blue Metallic. Standard equipment across the entire 1989 Firebird lineup included three-point lap and shoulder belts for rear seat occupants. Available options now offered across the F-car line included removable T-tops, a variety of radios, and an all-new compact digital disc player with the Delco II theft deterrent system that rendered the unit inoperative if power was interrupted. The lowest-priced Firebird was the base model with a standard 2.8-liter V-6 and five-speed manual transmission. For 1989, V-6s received the FE1 suspension package with 30mm front/18mm rear anti-roll bars. Added standard equipment for V-8 models included a Trans Am-style F41 suspension and air conditioning. The base Firebird carried the same exterior striping package as the Formula. The Formula Firebird was aimed at buyers interested in high-performance "street machines" and was designed to provide maximum "oomph" for a minimum price. This package provided the Trans Am engine, which had a 10-hp boost in power due to the use of a new dual catalytic converter low-back-pressure exhaust system. Pontiac claimed this equated to a two- to three-second cut in 0-to-60 mph acceleration times. Also standard on Formulas was the WS6 suspension and tire package, air conditioning, and a revised exterior graphics package with narrower body side stripes. The Trans Am had a standard 5.0-liter TBI 170-hp V-8 engine, five-speed manual transmission, and limited-slip differential. Also included were F41 underpinnings with 34mm front/23mm rear anti-roll bars and recalibrated springs and shocks, Firestone Firehawk GTX tires, 15 x 7-in. cast aluminum wheels, and air conditioning. Described as the "ultimate Firebird" (even though it wasn't in 1989) was the Trans Am GTA. It had a 5.7-liter 235-hp TPI V-8 borrowed from the Corvette, plus five-speed manual transmission, limited-slip differential, WS6 performance suspension with 36mm front/24mm rear anti-roll bars, deflected-disc gas-filled shocks and struts, 16-in. lightweight cross-laced aluminum wheels, Z-rated Goodyear tires, cloth articulating bucket seats, air conditioning, cruise control, power windows, power door locks, power antenna, AM/FM cassette radio with graphic equalizer, and redundant radio controls on the steering wheel hub. Also included on the GTA notchback were 45/55 split folding rear seats with integral headrests. Leather bucket seats with increased thigh support and inflatable lumbar and side bolsters were optional. To commemorate the 20th anniversary of the first Firebird Trans Am, a special series of 1500 20th Anniversary Trans Ams was produced. These cars, the level of the GTA model, were really the "ultimate" Trans Am of this year. Power was provided by a 3.8-liter turbocharged V-6 that developed 250 hp. It was coupled to a four-speed automatic transmission and limited-slip rear axle. All 20th Anniversary Trans Ams were painted White and had Camel colored interiors. Externally, the GTA emblem on the nose was changed to a special "20th Anniversary" insignia. A similar cloisonné emblem could be found on the sail panels. "Turbo Trans Am" emblems on the front fenders replaced the standard GTA script in the same location. Also included with this model was a larger, baffled, competition-type 18-gal. fuel tank, four-wheel power disc brakes, 16-in. gold-finished lightweight diamond-spoke aluminum wheels, stainless steel exhaust splitters, analog gauges with turbo boost gauge, unique contoured rear seats and packaged-in-the-car Official Pace Car decals that could be installed by Pontiac dealers at the request of the buyer.

1989 Pontiac Firebird Formula coupe. PMD

Model Number	Body/Style Number	Body Type & Seating	Factory Price	Shipping Weight	Prod. Total
FIREBIRD -- SERIES 2F -- V-6					
2F	FS2	2-dr Cpe-5P	11999	3083	Note 1
FIREBIRD -- SERIES 2F -- V-8					
2F	FS2	2-dr Cpe-5P	12399	3300	Note 1
FIREBIRD FORMULA -- SERIES 2F -- V-8					
2F	FS2	2-dr Cpe-5P	13949	3318	Note 1
FIREBIRD TRANS AM -- SERIES 2F -- V-8					
2F	FW2	2-dr Cpe-5P	15999	3337	Note 1
FIREBIRD TRANS AM GTA -- SERIES 2F -- V-8					
2F	FW2	2-dr Cpe-5P	20399	3486	Note 1

NOTE 1: Firebird series production totaled 64,406.

Model Number	Body/Style Number	Body Type & Seating	Factory Price	Shipping Weight	Prod. Total
6000 LE -- SERIES 2A -- I-4					
2A	AF5	4-dr Sed-5P	11969	2676	Note 1
6000 LE -- SERIES 2A -- I-4/V-6					
2A	AF5	4-dr Sed-5P	12579	2760	Note 1
2A	AF8	4-dr Safari-5P	13769	2897	Note 1
6000 SE -- SERIES 2A -- I-4/V-6					
2A	AJ5	4-dr Sed-5P	15399	2762	Note 1
2A	AJ8	4-dr Safari-5P	16699	2899	Note 1
6000 STE -- SERIES 2A -- I-4/V-6					
2A	AH5	4-dr Sed-5P	22,599	3381	Note 1

NOTE 1: 6000 series production totaled 100,586.

6000 -- SERIES 2A -- I-4/V-6 -- The Pontiac 6000 line for 1989 provided a complete selection of mid-size cars that catered to a variety of driving needs from the fully-equipped STE AWD badge car to solid transportation in the 6000 Sedan and Safari wagon. Five models were offered in all. The 6000 Sedans had a new appearance with the roof line, upper rear quarter, and trunk lid all restyled. There was a revised taillight treatment and a new rounded backlight (rear window). All 6000 LE and S/E models had a six-light front appearance including integrated fog lamps. All 6000s had a two-stage base coat/clearcoat paint system. Three-point rear seat and shoulder belts were standard on all models. Base models were the LE Sedan and Wagon. The 2.5-liter engine was now standard equipment, along with a three-speed automatic transaxle (four-speed automatic in wagons), a suspension with 22mm front/20mm rear anti-roll bars, and P185/75R14 tires. The 6000 S/E also came as a four-door Sedan or Safari. Both had a standard 2.8-liter V-6, four-speed automatic transaxle, radial tuned suspension, larger tires, aluminum sport wheels, and front disc/rear drum brakes. Electronic ride control was included for S/E wagons. The S/E exteriors were enhanced by body-color front grilles and body side moldings. Also standard was cruise control, controlled cycle wipers, power windows, power door locks, AM/FM stereo cassette radio, and a leather-wrapped four-spoke tilt steering wheel. The 6000 STE was replaced by the 6000 STE AWD model, which came only as a four-door Sedan. It was GM's first all-wheel-drive production car. The AWD system provided improved driving safety and security, increased mobility in low-traction conditions, and improved overall handling and performance. The difference could be seen in the AWD's improved acceleration, traction, and high-speed stability. No driver action was required to activate the automatic all-wheel-drive system. An electro-mechanical center differential locking system was provided for extreme conditions and could be activated by a console-mounted switch. Activating the switch ensured drive power to at least one wheel on the front and rear of the vehicle. A planetary center differential provided a 60 percent front/40 percent rear drive torque split. The STE AWD was the first mass-produced car to be powered by a high-torque, transverse V-6 and automatic transaxle. It had fully independent front and rear suspensions with electronic ride control. At the front, new outer steering links were used, along with a new (27mm) anti-roll bar. At the rear a thick (22mm) anti-roll bar was used in combination with a composite transverse leaf spring. Four-wheel-disc anti-lock brakes were standard, as was quicker-ratio steering The P195/70R15 Goodyear Eagle GT+4 tires were mounted on specific cast aluminum wheels with gold ports. The STE AWD was available only in two monochromatic paint schemes: Medium Red Metallic, and Dark Blue Metallic. The model also had body-color bumpers, aero moldings, a new deck lid spoiler, body color mirrors, and new fog lamps. Inside the standard radio/cassette with graphic equalizer features controls in the center of the new four-spoke leather-wrapped tilt steering wheel. A power driver's seat with lumbar support, power windows, power door locks, and cruise control were standard. An on-board inflator system was mounted in the trunk.

1989 Pontiac 6000 STE four-door sedan with all-wheel drive (AWD). PMD

1989 Pontiac Grand Prix SE coupe. PMD

GRAND PRIX -- SERIES 2G -- V-6/V-8 -- Entering its first full year of production, the highly-touted Pontiac Grand Prix sported a combination of eye-catching good looks, driver-oriented interior features, and multi-level performance that begs to be taken on the road. Standard engine was a 130-hp V-6. Late in the year, a larger 3.1-liter engine was due. Standard equipment included three-point rear seat belts, air conditioning, and a radio with seek up/seek down function. The base model was the Grand Prix Electronic air conditioning and front/rear floor mats were added to its standard equipment list, along with a number of new options. The Grand Prix LE offered a higher level of standard equipment and interior trim Standard equipment included electronic-controlled air conditioning, SE instrumentation, and power windows with an express-down feature. There was also a 60/40 front seat with a folding center armrest. Standard tires were size P195/75R14 all-season radials. The Grand Prix SE was a quick, stylish, driver-friendly Coupe that came standard with the Y99 rally tuned suspension, and a choice of a 2.8-liter four-/five-speed manual or 3.1-liter V-6 four-speed automatic drivetrain. Both included SE-specific dual exhausts. On the exterior, the SE had the belt moldings and hood rear edge molding changed from chrome to black. There was a distinctive front fascia with integral fog lights, an exclusive taillight treatment, body side moldings, and aero body extensions. The SE interior had articulated power bucket seats with adjustable thigh support and electrically adjusted head restraints. In the rear, bucket seats were divided by a large pass-through to the carpeted trunk. Electronic air conditioning, power windows (with driver's express-down feature), power mirrors, and cruise control were installed on all Grand Prix SEs, along with a leather-wrapped tilting sport steering wheel, an LCD speedometer and fuel gauge, and analog gauges including a tachometer. In the spring of 1989, Pontiac announced an exciting limited edition production run of 2000 Turbo Grand Prix. These cars were powered by a McLaren-developed 3.1-liter turbocharged V-6 producing over 200 hp. A special Garrett turbocharger added the real muscle and was designed to effectively eliminate turbo lag while maximizing torque. A specific four-speed automatic transmission backed up the powerhouse engine. Specific struts, springs and standard antilock brakes were featured, too. "Rounding" out the contents were P245/50ZR16 Goodyear Eagle GT+4 tires, and 16 x 8-in. gold cross-lace alloy wheels. All SE options were standard on the Turbo, except a power sun roof and leather interior. Also included was a camel-colored interior, heads-up display (HUD) instrumentation, specific front and rear fascias, deep aerodynamic body side skirting, functional hood louvers, special "fat tire" fenders, new Bright Red or Metallic Black finish, and specific gold-colored cloisonné emblems. One 1989 Turbo Grand Prix was selected as the Official Pace Car for the Daytona 500 stock car race on February 19, 1989.

1989 Pontiac Grand Prix coupe with Sport Appearance Package. PMD

Model Number	Body/Style Number	Body Type & Seating	Factory Price	Shipping Weight	Prod. Total
GRAND PRIX -- SERIES 2W -- V-6/V-8					
2G	WJ1	2-dr Cpe-5P	13899	3167	Note 1
GRAND PRIX LE-- SERIES 2W -- V-6/V-8					
2G	WK1	2-dr Cpe-5P	14949	3188	Note 1
GRAND PRIX SE -- SERIES 2W -- V-6/V-8					
2G	WP1	2-dr Cpe-5P	15999	3217	Note 1

NOTE 1: Grand Prix series production totaled 136,747.

1989 Pontiac Bonneville SSE four-door sedan. PMD

BONNEVILLE -- SERIES 2H -- V-6 -- The Pontiac Bonneville offered performance in a full-size touring sedan. There were three models with the luxurious Bonneville LE at the bottom, and the sporty Bonneville SE above it. The top-of-the-line Bonneville SSE was a European-inspired high-performance "luxo" sedan. Bonneville for 1989 featured evolutionary, rather than revolutionary changes. All Bonnevilles were again powered by the 3.8-liter "3800" V-6 engine. This was a 90-degree V-6 with multi-port sequential fuel injection. It developed 165 hp and 210 lb.-ft. of torque. The 3800, equipped with a balance shaft to eliminate the primary engine shaking force normally found on 90-degree V-6s, was teamed with a four-speed (three plus overdrive) automatic transaxle. Antilock brakes (ABS) were available on all Bonnevilles, and continued as standard equipment on the SSE. The ABS contributed greatly to vehicle maneuverability, enabling the car to stop in a controlled straight line under all surface conditions. Additional detail improvements throughout the line served to enhance driving comfort and utility. A new Grand Prix-style steering wheel with hub-mounted radio and climate controls, in conjunction with automatic air conditioning, was available on LE and SE models and standard on SSE models. The lineup included three sound systems, a base UM7 four-speaker system, an optional six-speaker system, and a Delco "Enhanced Audio" system with eight speakers, which was standard on SSEs. Storage space throughout the car was increased and the trunk utility was improved by raising the rear speakers. A cargo security net was standard in the trunks of SE/SSE models and optional in LEs. Glovebox capacity was increased 50 percent. An additional front seat storage armrest was added for the Level II 55/45 seats. Also, map pockets in the doors were redesigned to improve overall customer conve-

nience. The Bonneville LE emphasized aerodynamic styling, plus good ride and handling. Its changes for 1989 included a new 2.84:1 final drive ratio for improved part throttle response and grade load driveability. The LE came with standard P205/75R14 tires on 14 x 6-in. wheels. A urethane Grand Prix style steering wheel was standard, along with redesigned instruments, a new 115 mph speedometer, and front and rear floor mats. The Bonneville SE added or substituted a Y99 suspension with P215/65R15 Eagle GT+4 tires, and 15 x 6-in. Tri-Port cast aluminum wheels as standard content. The SE also had a leather-wrapped steering wheel, standard 45/55 seats with storage provisions, and full analog instrumentation with a tachometer and 115 mph speedometer. A prestigious full-size touring sedan with European flair and style, the Bonneville SSE boasted head-turning aerodynamic styling. It also combined outstanding handling with excellent ride quality and comfort. Pontiac said that it rivaled some of the world's finest touring sedans in features and quality. The SSE was equipped with its own unique suspension that included ABS brakes, variable-ratio power steering, firmer springs, larger 32mm front anti-roll bar, electronic load leveling and Goodyear P215/60R16 Eagle GT+4 all-season tires. Its standard wheels were 16 x 7-in. body-colored alloys. At mid-year, 16 x 7-in. gold cross-lace wheels were made optional. Inside, the SSE created the finest ergonomic environment possible in an American production car. The deeply-hooded SSE-specific instrument panel featured large, legible full-analog gauges including an electronic compass and driver information center. Standard interior features included redundant radio and heat/vent/AC (HVAC) controls in the steering wheel hub. The new center console between the 45/45 bucket seats contained a storage bin, two accessory power plugs for operating multiple appliances, and power seat control switches. The improved Bonneville SSE sound system utilized a subwoofer, two 6 x 6-in. dual voice coil speakers, and two titanium tweeters in the package shelf, plus two 6 x 9-in. speakers with dual titanium tweeters in the front doors.

Model Number	Body/Style Number	Body Type & Seating	Factory Price	Shipping Weight	Prod. Total
BONNEVILLE LE -- SERIES H -- V-6					
2H	HX5	4-dr Spt Sed-5P	14829	3275	Note 1
BONNEVILLE SE -- SERIES H -- V-6					
2H	HZ5	4-dr Spt Sed-5P	17199	3327	Note 1
BONNEVILLE SSE -- SERIES H -- V-6					
2H	HZ5/Y80	4-dr Spt Sed-5P	22899	3481	Note 1

NOTE 1: Bonneville series production totaled 108,653.

SAFARI -- SERIES 2L -- V-8 -- Pontiac's 1989 Safari remained a traditional full-size Station Wagon based on what had once been the Parisienne. Standard on all big Safaris was a 5.0-liter four-barrel V-8, air conditioning with Soft Ray tinted glass, Powermaster front disc/rear drum brakes, white-accented front/rear bumper rub strips, carpeting throughout, center high-mounted stop lamp, GM Computer Command Control system, inside hood release, dual sport mirrors (left-hand remote-controlled), power steering, UM7 Delco ETR AM/FM stereo, notchback front seat with center armrest, rear-facing third seat with Hartford vinyl trim, load-carrying springs, front stabilizer bar, three-spoke steering wheel, full-coil suspension, tailgate window control, P225/75R15 steel-belted radial whitewall tires, four-speed automatic transmission, and custom wheel covers.

Model Number	Body/Style Number	Body Type & Seating	Factory Price	Shipping Weight	Prod. Total
SAFARI -- SERIES 2L -- V-8					
2L	BL8	4-dr Sta Wag-8P	15659	4109	Note 1

NOTE 1: Safari series production totaled 5146.

LEMANS ENGINE

[STANDARD VL/LE] Inline. OHV. Four-cylinder. Cast iron block. Aluminum head and intake manifold. Displacement: 97.5 cu. in. (1.6L). Bore x stroke: 3.11 x 3.21 in. Compression ratio: 8.6:1. Brake horsepower: 74 @ 5600 rpm. Torque: 90 lb.-ft. @ 2800 rpm. Fuel system: EFI/TBI. RPO Code: L73. Standard with four-speed manual Value Leader and LeMans LE. [VIN code 6]. [STANDARD SE/GSE] Inline. OHC. Four-cylinder. Cast iron block. Aluminum head and intake manifold. Displacement: 121 cu. in. (2.0L). Bore x stroke: 3.39 x 3.39 in. Compression ratio: 8.8:1. Brake horsepower: 95 @ 4800 rpm. Torque: 118 lb.-ft. @ 3600 rpm. Fuel system: EFI/TBI. RPO Code: LT2. Standard with five-speed manual n LeMans SE and GSE models. [VIN code K].

SUNBIRD ENGINES

[STANDARD LE/SE] Inline. OHC. Four-cylinder. Cast iron block. Aluminum head and intake manifold. Displacement: 121 cu. in. (2.0L). Bore x stroke: 3.39 x 3.39 in. Compression ratio: 8.8:1. Brake horsepower: 96 @ 4800 rpm. Torque: 118 lb.-ft. @ 3600 rpm. Fuel system: EFI/TBI. RPO Code: LT2. Standard in Sunbird LE and Sunbird SE models. [VIN code K]. [STANDARD GT] Inline. OHC. Four-cylinder. Turbocharged (Garrett T2.5 turbocharger). Cast iron block. Aluminum head

and intake manifold. Displacement: 121 cu. in. (2.0L). Bore x stroke: 3.39 x 3.39 in. Compression ratio: 8.0:1. Brake horsepower: 165 @ 5600 rpm. Torque: 175 lb.-ft. @ 4000 rpm. Fuel system: MPFI with Turbo. RPO Code: LT3. Standard in Sunbird Turbo GT (optional in Sunbird SE Sport Coupe and Sunbird SE Sport Sedan). [VIN code M].

GRAND AM ENGINES

[STANDARD LE] Inline. OHV. Cast iron block and head. Aluminum intake manifold. Displacement: 151 cu. in. (2.5L Tech IV). Bore & stroke: 4.00 x 3.00 in. Compression ratio: 9.0:1. Brake horsepower: 110 @ 5200 rpm. Torque: 135 lb.-ft. @ 3200 rpm. Five main bearings. Hydraulic valve lifters. Fuel system: EFI. RPO Code: L68. Standard in Grand AM LE. [VIN code U/R]. [STANDARD SE] Inline. OHC. Turbocharged (Garret T2.5 turbocharger). Cast iron block. Aluminum head and intake manifold. Displacement: 2.0-liter Turbo. Bore x stroke: 3.39 x 3.39 in. Compression ratio: 8.0:1. Brake horsepower: 165 @ 5600 rpm. Torque: 175 lb.-ft. @ 4000 rpm. Fuel system: MPFI. RPO Code: LT3. Standard in Grand Am SE, not available in Grand Am LE. [VIN code M]. [OPTIONAL LE/SE] Inline. DOHC. 16-Valve. Four-cylinder. Cast iron block. Aluminum head and intake manifold. Displacement: 140 cu. in. (2.3L MFI). Quad 4 16-valve. Bore x stroke: 3.62 x 3.35 in. Compression ratio: 9.5:1. Brake horsepower: 150 @ 5200 rpm. Torque: 160 lb.-ft. @ 4400 rpm. Fuel system: MPFI. RPO Code: LD2. Optional in Grand Am LE, and delete-option in Grand Am SE. [VIN code D]. [OPTIONAL SE] Inline. DOHC. Quad IV HO. 16-Valve. Four-cylinder. Cast iron block. Aluminum head and intake manifold. Displacement: 140 cu. in. (2.3L MFI High Output). Quad 4 16-valve. Bore x stroke: 3.62 x 3.35 in. Compression ratio: 10.0:1. Brake horsepower: 180 @ 6200 rpm. Torque: 155 lb.-ft. @ 5200 rpm. Fuel system: MPFI. RPO Code: LD2. Optional in SE. [VIN code A].

1989 Pontiac Firebird coupe with Sport Appearance Package. PMD

FIREBIRD ENGINES

[FIREBIRD Base V-6] V-block. OHV. Six-cylinder. Cast iron block and head. Aluminum intake manifold. Displacement: 173 cu. in. (2.8L). Bore x stroke: 3.50 x 2.99 in. Compression ratio: 8.5:1. Brake horsepower: 135 @ 4900 rpm. Torque: 160 lb.-ft. @ 3900 rpm. Fuel system: EFI/TBI. RPO Code: LB8. Standard in base Firebird. Produced in U.S., Canada, or Mexico. [VIN code W, S, or 9]. [FIREBIRD BASE V-8] V-block. OHV. Eight-cylinder. Cast iron block and head. Aluminum intake manifold. Displacement: 305 cu. in. (5.0L). Bore x stroke: 3.74 x 3.48 in. Brake horsepower: 170 @ 4000 rpm. Torque: 255 lb.-ft. @ 2400 rpm. Compression ratio: 9.3:1. Fuel system: EFI/TBI. RPO Code: L03. Produced in U.S. or Canada. Standard Formula, and Trans Am. Available in base Firebird. [VIN code E or F]. [OPTIONAL V-8] V-block. OHV. Eight-cylinder. Cast iron block and head. Aluminum intake manifold. Displacement: 305 cu. in. (5.0L). Bore x stroke: 3.74 x 3.48 in. Brake horsepower: 190 @ 4000 rpm (automatic) or 225 @ 4400 rpm (manual/dual exhausts). Torque: 295 lb.-ft. @ 2800 rpm (automatic) or 285 lb.-ft. @ 3200 rpm (manual). Compression ratio: 9.3:1. Fuel system: TPI. RPO Code: LB9. Available with five-speed manual in Formula, and Trans Am (delete option in GTA). Available with four-speed automatic in same applications. [VIN code E or F]. [GTA V-8] V-block. OHV. Eight-cylinder. Cast iron block and head. Aluminum intake manifold. Displacement: 350 cu. in. (5.7L). Bore x stroke: 4.00 x 3.48 in. Brake horsepower: 235 @ 4400 rpm. Torque: 330 lb.-ft. @ 3200 rpm. Compression ratio: 9.3:1. Fuel system: EFI/TPI. RPO Code: B2L. Standard with four-speed automatic in GTA (optional in Formula and Trans Am). Includes low-profile air induction system with aluminum plenum and individual aluminum tuned runners, an extruded dual fuel rail assembly with computer controlled fuel injectors, and a special low-restriction single exhaust system. [VIN code 8]. [STANDARD INDY PACE CAR TURBO V-6] V-block. Garrett T3 turbocharger. OHV. Six-cylinder. Cast iron block and head. Aluminum intake manifold. Displacement: 231 cu. in. (3.8L). Bore x stroke: 3.80 x 3.40 in. Brake horsepower: 250 @ 4400 rpm. Torque: 340 lb.-ft. @ 2800 rpm. Compression ratio: 8.0:1. Fuel system: EFI/SFI. RPO Code: LG3. Standard in 20th Anniversary Trans Am Indy Pace Car. [VIN code W, S, or 9].

6000 ENGINES

[BASE] Inline. OHV. Four-cylinder. Cast iron block and head. Aluminum intake manifold. Displacement: 151 cu. in.. (2.5L Tech IV). Bore & stroke: 4.00 x 3.00 in. Compression ratio: 9.0:1. Brake horsepower: 98 @ 4800 rpm. Torque: 135 lb.-ft. @ 3200 rpm. Five main bearings. Hydraulic valve lifters. Fuel system: EFI/TBI. RPO Code: LR8. Standard in 6000 LE. [VIN code U]. [OPTIONAL] V-block. OHV. Six-cylinder. Cast iron block. Aluminum head and intake manifold. Displacement: 173 cu. in. (2.8L). Bore x stroke: 3.50 x 2.99 in. Compression ratio: 8.91. Brake horsepower: 130 @ 4500 rpm. Torque: 17 lb.-ft. @ 3600 rpm. Fuel system: EFI. RPO Code: LB6. Standard in 6000 S/E. [VIN code W, S or 9]. [STANDARD STE-AWD] V-block. OHV. Six-cylinder. Cast iron block. Aluminum head and intake manifold. Displacement: 191 cu. in. (3.1L). Bore x stroke: 3.50 x 3.31in. Brake horsepower: 135 @ 4800 rpm. Torque: 180 lb.-ft. @ 3600 rpm. Fuel system: EFI. RPO Code: LHO. Standard in 6000 STE AWD. [VIN code T].

GRAND PRIX ENGINES

[STANDARD] V-block. OHV. Six-cylinder. Cast iron block and aluminum head. Displacement: 173 cu. in. (2.8L). Bore x stroke: 3.50 x 2.99 in. Compression ratio: 8.9:1. Brake horsepower: 130 @ 4500 rpm. Torque: 170 lb.-ft. @ 3600 rpm. Fuel system: EFI/MPI. RPO Code: LB6. Standard in Grand Prix. Produced in U.S., Canada, or Mexico. [VIN code W, S, or 9]. [OPTIONAL] V-block. OHV. Six-cylinder. Cast iron block and aluminum head. Displacement: 191 cu. in. (3.1L). Bore x stroke: 3.50 x 3.31 in. Compression ratio: 8.8:1. Brake horsepower: 140 @ 4500 rpm. Torque: 185 lb.-ft. @ 3600 rpm. Fuel system: EFI/MPI. RPO Code: LHO. Standard in Grand Prix with four-speed automatic transaxles after midyear. Not available with three-speed automatic. [VIN code T]. [OPTIONAL] V-block. OHV. Six-cylinder. Turbo. Cast iron block and aluminum head. Displacement: 191 cu. in. (3.1L). Bore x stroke: 3.50 x 3.31 in. Compression ratio: 8.65:1. Brake horsepower: 205 @ 4800 rpm. Torque: 220 lb.-ft. @ 3200 rpm. Fuel system: EFI/MPI. RPO Code: LHO with LG5 American Sun Roof Corp. (ASC)/McLaren Turbo conversion. [VIN code T].

BONNEVILLE ENGINE

[STANDARD LE/SE/SSE] V-block. OHV. "3800" six-cylinder. Cast iron block and head. Aluminum intake manifold. Displacement: 231 cu. in. (3.8L). Bore x stroke: 3.80 x 3.40 in. Compression ratio: 8.5:1. Brake horsepower: 165 @ 5200 rpm. Torque: 210 lb.-ft. @ 2000 rpm. Fuel system: SFI. RPO Code: LN3. Standard in Bonneville LE/SE/SSE model. [VIN code W, S, or 9].

SAFARI ENGINE

[STANDARD V-8] V-block. OHV. Eight-cylinder. Cast iron block. 307 cu. in. (5.0L). Bore x stroke: 3.80 x 3.39 in. Compression ratio: 8.0:1. Brake horsepower: 140 @ 3200 rpm. Torque: 255 lb.-ft. @ 2000 rpm. Fuel system: Four-barrel carburetor. RPO Code: LV2. Standard V-8 in all Safaris. [VIN code Y].

LEMANS CHASSIS: Wheelbase: 99.2 in. (all). Overall length: 163.70 in. (three-door); 172.4 in. (four-door). Height:0 53.5 in. (Aerocoupe); 53.7 in. (Sedan). Standard tires: P175/70R13 BSW (all).

SUNBIRD CHASSIS: Wheelbase: 101.2 in. (all). Overall length: 178.2 in. (Coupe and Convertible). 181.7 in. (Sedan). Width: 65.0 in. (Sedan/Convertible). 66.0 in. (Coupe/Convertible). Height: 50.4.in. (Coupe); 53.8 in. (Sedan); 51.9 in. (Convertible). Front tread: 55.6 in. (all). Rear tread: 55.2 in. (all). Standard tires: P185/80R13 BSW (LE). Standard tires: P195/70R14 (SE). Standard tires: P215/60R14 Eagle GT+4 (GT). Optional tires with WS6 special performance suspension: P215/60R14 Goodyear Eagle GT+4.

GRAND AM CHASSIS: Wheelbase: 103.4 in. (Coupe/Sedan). Overall length: 180.1 in. (all). Width: 66.5 in. (all). Height: 52.5 in. (all). Front tread: 55.6 in. Rear tread: 55.2 in. Standard tires: P185/80R13 BSW (LE). Standard tires: P215/60R14 (SE).

FIREBIRD CHASSIS: Wheelbase: 101.0 in. (all). Overall length: 188.1 in. (Base/Formula); 191.6 in. (Trans Am/GTA). Width: 72.4 in. (all). Height: 50.0 in. (all). Front tread: 60.7 in. Rear tread: 61.6 in. Tires: P215/65R15 Firestone Firehawk FX (Level I). Standard tires: P215/65R15 Firestone Firehawk GTX (Level II). Tire: P245/50ZR16 Goodyear Eagle ZR50 "Gatorback."

6000 CHASSIS: Wheelbase: 104.9 in. (all). Overall length: 188.8 in. (Sedan); 193.2 in. (Safari). Width: 72.0 in. (all). Height: 53.7 in. (Sedan); 54.1 in. (Wagon). Front tread: 58.7 in. Rear tread: 57.0 in. Standard tires: 185/75R14 (LE). Standard tires: 195/70R14 Goodyear Eagle GT+4 (S/E and STE FWD).

GRAND PRIX CHASSIS: Wheelbase: 107.5 in. (all). Overall length: 193.9) in. (all). Width: 70.9 in. (all). Height: 53.3 in. (all). Front tread: 59.5 in. Rear tread: 58.0 in. Standard tires: 195/75R14 (base and LE). Standard tires: 215/60R15 Goodyear Eagle GT (SE). Standard tires: P245/50ZR16 (ASC/McLaren Turbo).

BONNEVILLE CHASSIS: Wheelbase: 110.8 in. (all). Overall length: 198.7 in. (all). Width: 72.1 in. (all). Height: 55.5 in. (all). Front tread: 60.3 in. Rear tread: 59.8 in. Standard tires: 205/75R14 BSW (LE). Standard tires: 215/65R15 Goodyear Eagle GT+4 (SE). Standard tires: P215/60R16 BSW (SSE).

SAFARI CHASSIS: Wheelbase: 116.0 in. (all). Overall length: 215.1 in. (all). Width: 79.3 in. (all). Height: 57.4 in. (all). Front tread: 60.3 in. Rear tread: 59.8 in. Tires: P225/75R15.

LEMANS TECHNICAL: Chassis: Front engine/front drive. Base transmission: Four-speed manual. Optional transmission: Three-speed automatic or five-speed manual. Axle ratio: 3.43:1 with 1.6L and automatic. Axle ratio: 3.18:1 with 2.0L and three-speed automatic. Axle ratio: 3.72:1 with 1.6L and four-speed manual or either engine and five-speed manual. Front suspension: deflected disc, MacPherson struts and (20mm with 1.6L/22mm with 2.0L) stabilizer bars. Rear suspension: Coil springs, semi-independent torsion beam, trailing arms, and 18mm anti-roll bar. Steering: Rack-and-pinion 24.5:1 ratio (18.3:1 power-assisted on GTE). Turns lock-to-lock: 3.5 (power); 4.57 (manual). Turning circle: 32.8 ft.. Front brakes: 9.25-in. solid discs (1.6L) or 10.1-in. vented disc (2.0L) power-assisted. Rear brakes: 7.9 x 1.8 -in. drum (both engines) power-assisted.

1989 Pontiac Sunbird GT convertible. PMD

SUNBIRD TECHNICAL: Chassis: Front engine/front drive. Base transmission: Five-speed manual. Optional transmission: Three-speed automatic. Axle ratio: 3.45:1 with base engine and five-speed manual. Axle ratio: 3.18:1 with 2.0L TBI engine and three-speed automatic. Axle ratio: 3.61:1 with 1.6L with 2.0L Turbo and five-speed manual. Front suspension: deflected disc, MacPherson struts and (22mm with 2.0L TBI/28mm with 2.0L Turbo) stabilizer bars. Rear suspension: Coil springs, semi-independent torsion beam, trailing arms (and 18mm anti-roll bar with 2.0L Turbo). Steering: Rack-and-pinion 16.0:1 ratio. Turns lock-to-lock: 2.88. Turning circle: 34.3 ft. Front brakes: 9.72-in. vented disc power-assisted. Rear brakes: 7.87 x 1.77-in. drum power-assisted.

GRAND AM TECHNICAL: Chassis: Front engine/front drive. Base transmission: Five-speed manual with overdrive. Optional transmission: Three-speed automatic. Axle ratio: 3.35:1 (with 2.5L engine and manual). Axle ratio: 3.61:1 (with 2.0L engine and manual or 2.3L engine and manual). Axle ratio: 2.84:1 (with 2.3L and automatic or 2.5L and automatic). Axle ratio: 3.18:1 (with 2.0L and automatic). Stall torque ratio: 2.48:1 (with automatic). Front suspension: MacPherson struts with coil springs and 24mm anti-roll bar (28mm anti-roll bar with WS6 suspension). Rear suspension: Trailing crank arm with twist arm, coil springs, and 21mm anti-roll bar. Steering: Power-assisted rack-and-pinion, 16.1:1 ratio, 2.88 turns lock-to-lock, and 35.4-ft. (left); 37.8-ft. (right) turning circle. Front brakes: Power-assisted 9.72-in. vented discs. Rear brakes: Power-assisted 7.87-in. drums. Fuel tank: 13.6 gal.

FIREBIRD TECHNICAL: Chassis: Front engine/rear drive. Base transmission: Five-speed manual. Optional transmission: Four-speed automatic. Front suspension: Fully independent with modified MacPherson strut, and low-friction ball bearing upper strut mount and 30mm (Level I) or 34mm (Level II), or 36mm (Level III) anti-roll bar. Rear suspension: Live axle with coil springs, longitudinal lower control arm and torque arm, transverse track bar, and 18mm (Level I) or 23mm (Level II) or 24mm (Level II) anti-roll bar. Steering: Power recirculating ball; 14.1:1 ratio (Level I), or 12.7:1 quick ratio with sport effort valving (Levels II and III). Turns lock-to-lock: 2.72 (Level I), 2.47 (Level II), or 2.26 (Level II). Turning circle: 37.1 ft. (Level I) or 32.6 ft. (Levels II and III). Brakes: Power vented 10.5-in. front disc/9.5-in. rear drum on Coupes and Formula with 5.0L EFI; power four-wheel vented disc 10.5-in. front/11.7-in. rear with 5.7L or 5.0L with TPI and five-speed on GTA or Formula-assisted vented discs. Rear brakes: Power-assisted 7.87-in. drums. Fuel tank: 13.6 gal.

6000 TECHNICAL: Chassis: Front engine/front drive. Base transmission: Three-speed automatic with overdrive. Optional transmissions: Four-speed automatic with 2.5L or 2.8L engines. Axle ratio: 2.84:1 (with three-speed automatic and 2.5L or 2.8L engines). Axle ratio: 3.33:1 (with four-speed automatic with 2.8L engine). Axle ratio: 3.42:1 (with four-speed automatic and 3.1L engine). Front suspension: MacPherson struts with 22mm

(LE), 28mm (S/E), or 27mm (STE AWD). Rear suspension: Independent, transverse composite leaf spring and 22mm anti-roll bar (STE AWD); or trailing arms and track bar, Panhard rod, coil springs, and 22mm anti-roll bar (S/E), 20mm anti-roll bar standard. Steering: Power-assisted rack-and-pinion with 17.5:1 ratio, 3.05 turns lock-to-lock and 36.96-ft. turning circle. Front brakes: Power assisted vented discs 9.72-in. (standard); 10.24-in. (medium-/heavy-duty), 10.2-in. (STE). Rear brakes: Power assisted 8.86-in. drum (standard); 8.86-in. drum (medium-/heavy-duty), 10.3-in solid discs (STE). Fuel tank: 15.7-gal.

GRAND PRIX TECHNICAL: Chassis: Front engine/front drive. Standard drivetrain: 2.8L V-6 with five-speed manual transaxle or (midyear) 3.1L V-6 with four-speed automatic transaxle. Optional drivetrain: 3.1L ASC/McLaren Turbo V-6 with four-speed automatic transaxle. Axle ratio: 3.41:1 (2.8L with manual); 3.33:1 (2.3L, 3.1L with automatic, and 3.1L ASC/McLaren Turbo). Front suspension: MacPherson struts with tapered top coil springs, lower A arm and 28mm anti-roll bar (30mm anti-roll bar with Y99 suspension). Rear suspension: Tri-link independent suspension with 12mm anti-roll bar (transverse fiberglass leaf spring and 12mm anti-roll bar with Y99 option). Steering: Power-assisted rack-and-pinion with 14.0:1 ratio, 2.25 turns lock-to-lock, and 39.7-ft. turning circle (interim) or 15.7:1 ratio, 2.89 turns lock-to-lock, and 37.4-ft. turning circle. Four-wheel power disc brakes. Front brakes: 10.5-in. composite vented discs. Rear brakes: 10.1-in. composite solid discs. Fuel tank: 16.0 gal.

BONNEVILLE TECHNICAL: Chassis: Front engine/front drive. Base transmission: Four-speed automatic. Axle ratio: 2.73:1 (standard with 3.8L V-6 in Base Bonneville and Bonneville SE). Axle ratio: 2.97:1 (standard with 3.8L V-6 in Bonneville SE/SSE). Front suspension: MacPherson struts with 20N-mm coil springs and 30mm anti-roll bar (LE). Front suspension: MacPherson struts with 28N-mm coil springs and 32mm anti-roll bar (SE). Front suspension: MacPherson struts with 24N-mm coil springs and 32mm anti-roll bar (SSE). Rear suspension: MacPherson struts with variable rate (48-65 N-mm) coil springs and 14mm anti-roll bar (LE). Rear suspension: MacPherson struts with variable rate (55-75 N-mm) coil springs and 18mm anti-roll bar (SE). Rear suspension: MacPherson struts with 47 N-mm coil springs and 18mm anti-roll bar (SSE). Steering: Power-assisted rack-and-pinion with 18.0:1 constant ratio, 2.97 turns lock-to-lock, and 12.1-ft. left/11.9-ft. right turning circle (LE/SE). Steering: Power-assisted rack-and-pinion with 15.3-19.0:1 variable ratio, 2.79 turns lock-to-lock, and 11.7-ft. left/12.4-ft. right turning circle (SSE). Front brakes: Power-assisted 10.1-in. vented discs. Rear brakes: Power-assisted 8.9-in. drums. Anti-lock brake system standard with SSE. Fuel tank: 18.0 gal.

SAFARI TECHNICAL: Chassis: Front engine/rear drive. Base transmission: Four-speed automatic. Axle ratio: 3.31:1 (SSE interim). Axle ratio: 2.97:1 (SE). Axle ratio: 2.84:1 (LE). Front suspension: Control arms with coil springs. Rear suspension: Live axle, links and coil springs. Front brakes: Power-assisted vented discs. Rear brakes: Power-assisted drums. Fuel tank: 22.0 gal.

LEMANS OPTIONS: C60 air conditioning, requires power steering and not available in Value Leader Aerocoupe ($660). N40 power steering, requires air conditioning in Aerocoupe or SE Sedan ($214). UM7 Delco ETR stereo in Value Leader Aerocoupe ($307). UM6 Delco ETR AM/FM with cassette and more in Value Leader Aerocoupe ($429). UM6 Delco ETR AM/FM with cassette and more in LE/SE/GSE ($122). V54 painted roof luggage rack ($95). AD3 removable sun roof ($350). MX1 three-speed automatic transmission ($420).

SUNBIRD OPTIONS: 1SA Sunbird option group #1 ($383-$1013 based on trim level and body style). 1SB Sunbird option group ($680-$1286 based on trim level and body style). 1SC Sunbird option group #3 ($1624-$1711 based on trim level and body style). R6A value package ($442-$445 based on trim level). R6B value package ($366 all). LT2 2.0-liter TBI engine as delete-option in GT ($768 credit). LT3 Turbo engine, mandatory extras, and specific options, except in GT ($1169-$1434). MX1 three-speed automatic transmission ($440). C60 air conditioning ($695). C49 electric rear window defogger ($150). NB2 California emissions package ($100). U39 really cluster gauges and trip odometer in LE ($49). TR9 lamp group ($44 in Sedan/$38 in Coupe). V56 deck lid luggage carrier ($115). D84 custom two-tone paint for LE ($101). D86 deluxe two-tone paint ($101). AU3 power door locks ($155 Coupe/$205 Sedan). A31 power windows, requires power door locks ($220 Coupe/$295 Sedan/no charge Convertible). UM7 Delco radio equipment (standard/no charge). UM6 Delco radio equipment ($152 additional). U1C Delco radio equipment ($244-$396). AK1 color-keyed seat belts for LE/SE only ($26). B20 custom interior with Metrix cloth in GT Coupe only ($335). B20 custom interior with Metrix cloth in GT Convertible only ($142). N36 rally steering wheel in LE/SE only ($26). AD3 removable glass sun roof ($350). Various tire options ($68-$276 extra). PX1 13-in. Sport Tech aluminum wheels with locking package ($265). N78 14-in Hi-Tech Turbo aluminum wheels with locking package ($265).

1989 Pontiac Grand Am LE four-door sedan. PMD

GRAND AM OPTIONS: 1SA Grand Am option group #1 ($876-$1011 based on trim level and body style). 1SB Grand Am option group ($1139-$1350 based on trim level and body style). 1SC Grand Am option group #3 ($1350 all). 1SD Grand Am option group #4 ($2072-$2197 based on trim level and body style). R6A value package ($416). R6B value package ($216). LD 2.3-liter MPI engine ($600 in LE; $108 delete-option in SE). MX1 three-speed automatic transmission ($515). C60 air conditioning ($695). C49 electric rear window defogger ($150). T96 fog lamps for LE only ($97). NB2 California emissions package ($100). UB3 rally cluster gauges and trip odometer in LE ($127). V56 deck lid luggage carrier ($115). D84 custom two-tone paint for LE ($101). D84 custom two-tone paint ($101). AU3 power door locks ($155 Coupe/$205 Sedan). A31 power windows, requires custom console in LE ($220 Coupe/$295 Sedan). UM6 Delco radio equipment ($122). UX1 Delco radio equipment ($150-$272). U1D Delco radio equipment ($423-$545). UW4 performance sound system ($125). AR9 custom reclining bucket seats with Pallex cloth trim (no charge). A09 articulating bucket seats ($245-$450). B20 custom interior with Metrix cloth in LE only ($119-$269 depending on value option package). AD3 removable glass sun roof ($350). Various tire options ($68-$278 extra). N78 14-in. Hi-Tech Turbo aluminum wheels with locking package ($265).

1989 Pontiac Trans Am coupe 20th Anniversary/Indianapolis 500 Pace Car. PMD

1989 Pontiac Trans Am coupe 20th Anniversary/Indianapolis 500 Pace Car (rear view). PMD

FIREBIRD OPTIONS: 1SA Firebird option group #1 ($311). 1SB Firebird option group #2 ($187). 1SA Formula option group #1 ($701). 1SB Formula option group #2 ($517). 1SA Trans Am option group #1 ($701). 1SB Trans Am option group #2 ($552). R6A Trans Am value package ($1089). R6A Trans Am GTA value package ($1020). LO3 5.0-liter TBI V-8 engine in base Firebird ($400). LB9 5.0L MPI V-8 in Formula and Trans Am ($745). LB9 5.0L MPI V-8 in Trans Am GTA ($300 credit). B2L 5.7L MPI V-8 in Formula and Trans Am ($1045). MM5 five-speed manual transmission in Trans Am GTA with LB9 ($490 credit). MXO four-speed automatic transmission, except in GTA ($515). C60 air conditioning ($795). G80 limited-slip axle ($100). C49 electric rear window defogger ($150). N10 dual converter exhaust ($155). KC4 engine oil cooler ($110). NB2 California emissions ($100). CC1 Hatch roof ($920). TR9 lamp group ($34). D66 deluxe two-tone paint ($150). WX1 lower accent two-tone paint delete on Formulas ($150 credit). J65 power brakes ($179). AU3 power door locks ($155). DG7 power remote sport mirrors ($91). A31 power windows ($250). UM6 Delco radio equipment ($132). UX1 Delco radio equipment ($282). UT4 Delco radio equipment ($315-$447). UA1 Delco radio equipment ($79 in GTA) ($526). U75 power antenna ($70). D42 cargo area security screen ($69). AR9 custom reclining bucket seats with Pallex cloth trim (no charge). B20 luxury interior with Metrix cloth trim in Trans Am ($293). AQ9 articulating bucket seats with Ventura leather trim in GTA ($450). QLC high-performance WS6 performance suspension ($385). N24 15-in. charcoal deep-dish Hi-Tech Turbo aluminum wheels with locking package on Formula or GTA (no charge). PEO 16-in. deep-dish Hi-Tech Turbo aluminum wheels with locking package on Formula (no charge). PW7 16-in. color-coordinated diamond-spoke aluminum wheels in silver or gold with locking package on Trans Am or GTA only (no charge).

6000 OPTIONS: 1SA option package #1 for 6000 LE Sedan ($975). 1SB option package #2 for 6000 LE Sedan ($1160). 1SC option package #3 for 6000 LE Sedan ($2076). 1SA option package #1 for 6000 LE Wagon ($975). 1SB option package #2 for 6000 LE Wagon ($1715). 1SC option package #3 for 6000 LE Wagon ($2066). 1SA option package #1 for 6000 S/E Sedan ($1118). 1SA option package #2 for 6000 S/E Wagon ($1068). R6A value option package for 6000 LE Sedan ($395). R6B value option package for 6000 LE Sedan ($180). R6B value option package for 6000 LE Sedan ($385). LB6 2.8-liter MFI V-6 in LE Sedan ($610). MXO four-speed automatic transmission ($200). C60 air conditioning ($795). C49 electric rear window defogger ($150). D86 two-tone paint ($115). AU3 power door locks ($205). A31 power windows ($310). UM6 Delco ETR AM/FM stereo ($122). U1A Delco ETR AM stereo/FM stereo ($519-$554). AM6 45/55 split bench seat ($133). B20 custom interior with 45/55 split seat in Empress/London style ($360-$493). Various tire options (no charge to $68). N78 Sport aluminum wheels with locking package ($265). BX3 wood-grain exterior siding for Wagon ($295).

GRAND PRIX OPTIONS: 1SA Grand Prix option package #1 ($183). 1SB Grand Prix option package #2 ($423). 1SC Grand Prix option package #3 ($858). 1SA Grand Prix LE option package #1 ($520). 1SB Grand Prix LE option package #2 ($863). 1SC Grand Prix LE option package #3 ($1139). 1SA Grand Prix SE option package #1 ($455). 1SB Grand Prix SE option package #2 ($898). R6A Grand Prix value option package ($408). R6A Grand Prix LE value option package. ($425). LG5 ASC/McLaren Turbo conversion ($4888). MXO four-speed automatic in Grand Prix SE ($640). MM5 five-speed manual transmission in Grand Prix and LE ($615 credit). JL9 anti-lock power brakes ($925). C49 electric rear window defogger ($150). DK4 electronic information center ($4275). NB2 California emissions system ($100). UB3 gauge cluster ($85). V56 deck lid luggage carrier ($115). D84 two-tone paint ($105). AU3 power door locks ($155). CF5 power sun roof ($650-$675). A31 power windows ($230). UM6 Delco radio equipment ($132). UX1 Delco radio equipment ($325-$447). UW4 speakers ($125). U75 power antenna ($70). AM6 40/60 split bench seat with Ripple cloth trim in base Grand Prix ($133). AR9 bucket seats with front console and Ripple cloth trim in base Grand Prix with/without value option package ($60-$193). AR9 bucket seats with front console and Pallex cloth trim in Grand Prix LE ($110). AC9 bucket seats with front console and Ventura leather trim in Grand Prix LE ($450). Various tire options ($48-$72). QGW rally tuned suspension package ($184-$232). PF1 15-in. styled steel wheels, except SE ($145). PH3 15-in. aluminum sport wheels with locking package ($120-$265). NWO 16-in. aluminum sport wheels, with/without value option package ($155-$300). 13P 16-in. bright-faced aluminum sport wheels with locking package for Grand Prix SE (no charge).

BONNEVILLE OPTIONS: 1SA Bonneville LE option package #1 ($259). 1SB Bonneville LE option package #2 ($444). 1SC Bonneville LE option package #3 ($1365). 1SA Bonneville SE option package #1 ($284). 1SB Bonneville SE option package #2 ($695). 1SC Bonneville SE option package #3 ($1183). R6A Bonneville LE value option package ($474). R6A Bonneville SE value option package. ($327). C49 electric rear window defogger ($150). NB2 California emissions system ($100). UB3 gauge cluster ($100). V56 deck lid luggage carrier ($115). D84 two-tone paint ($105). JM4 power anti-lock brakes ($925). AU3 power door locks ($205). A31 power windows ($365). UM6 Delco radio equipment ($122). UT4 radio equipment package ($550-$722). U1A compact disc player ($754-$876). UW6 six-speaker performance sound system ($100). US7 power antenna ($70). A78 custom interior in LE ($70). A65 notchback seat with custom trim

in LE ($133). AS7 custom interior trim with split bench seat and console ($235). B20 custom interior with 45/55 split seat in Empress/London cloth trim ($120-$618) depending on value package options or individual option). CF5 power glass sun roof ($1284). Various tire options ($48-$164). QNS Y99 rally tuned suspension package ($116-$164). PF7 15-in. diamond-spoke wheels with locking package on LE ($296). AL7 45/55 articulating split bench seat with Ventura leather trim on SSE ($679). UA6 anti-theft deterrent system ($15).

SAFARI OPTIONS: 1SA option package #1 ($412). 1SB option package #2 ($1474). V08 heavy-duty cooling system ($40). C49 electric rear window defogger ($150). NB2 California emissions system ($100). U39 instrument cluster with gauges and trip odometer ($71). V55 roof top luggage carrier with rear air deflector ($155). AU3 power door locks, includes tailgate lock ($255). A31 power windows ($295) UM7 AM/FM ETR stereo system ($122). UX1 Delco sound system ($272). U75 power antenna ($70). AM6 55/45 split bench seat with Pallex cloth trim ($133). AT6 reclining passenger seat with AM6 only ($45). G66 Superlift shock absorbers ($64). N94 simulated wire wheel covers with locking package ($230). BX3 simulated exterior wood-grain siding, includes door edge moldings and wood-toned body side moldings ($345).

Note: Full option package contents, descriptions and applications information can often be determined by consulting factory literature. The data above is edited for size and clarity. This information provided only as a guide to help collectors appraise the relative value of cars with numerous options. Prices for items included as part of a value option package are usually much less than individual prices. Option prices charged by individual dealers may also vary.

1989 Pontiac Turbo Grand Prix coupe. PMD

HISTORICAL FOOTNOTE: Pontiac's new HUD instrumentation was available only as standard equipment on Turbo Grand Prix. This HUD optically projected key instrument displays to a focal point near the front of the vehicle. It could be viewed through the lower windshield, allowing the driver to view the data while keeping his or her eyes on the road. Vehicle speed, turn signal indicators, the high beam indicator, low fuel warning and "check gauges" warning that monitors low oil pressure and high coolant temperatures are the features of the HUD system displays. Pontiac Motor Division had an active motorsports program in 1989. After finishing third in the Winston Cup manufacturers championship in 1988 (only five points behind the winner) Pontiac was looking forward to the 1989 NASCAR/Winston Cup season with great anticipation. Those returning to drive Pontiac Grand Prix included Rusty Wallace (No. 27 Kodiak/Mobil One/AC Delco Pontiac), Richard Petty (No. 43 STP/Prestone/Goody's Pontiac), Michael Waltrip (No. 30 Country Time/All-Pro/Post Pontiac), and Morgan Shepherd (No. 75 Valvoline Pontiac). In addition, Kyle Petty (No. 42 Peak/Uniden Pontiac), Greg Sacks (No. 88 Crisco/AC Spark Plug Pontiac), Hut Stricklin (No. 57 Heinz Pontiac), and Dale Jarrett (No. 29 Hardee's/Coke Pontiac) were among other "Poncho" pilots. Other Pontiac drivers were Ernie Irvan (No. 2), Ken Bouchard (No. 10), Jim Sauter (No. 31), Joe Ruttman (No. 45), Mickey Gibbs (No. 48), Jimmy Means (No. 52), Derrike Cope (No. 68), J.D. McDuffie (No. 70), and Jimmy Horton (No. 80). In all, 17 teams were using Pontiacs in 1989 NASCAR competition.

1990 PONTIAC

PONTIAC I.D. NUMBERS: Vehicle identification number (VIN) is located on top left-hand surface of instrument panel visible through the windshield. The VIN has 17 symbols. The first symbol indicates the country of manufacture (U.S.). The second symbol indicates the manufacturer (G=General Motors). The third symbol indicates the make/division (2=Pontiac). The fourth, fifth, and sixth symbols are the same as the body style (model) number. The eighth symbol indicates the engine. The ninth symbol is a check digit. The 10th symbol indicates model-year. The 11th symbol indicates the assembly plant. The last six symbols are the consecutive unit number at the factory.

1990 Pontiac LeMans GSE three-door hatchback. PMD

LEMANS -- SERIES 2T -- FOUR -- The 1990 LeMans was Pontiac's lowest-priced car, but had no shortage of Pontiac style or performance relative to other cars in the entry-level subcompact class. It again combined European styling, German engineering and Asian craftsmanship in a highly affordable, economical, and fun package. The LeMans featured the highest fuel economy of the entire Pontiac line (31 mpg city/40 mpg highway) and the long list of standard features made every LeMans model competitive with other imports. There were four 1990 models: Aerocoupe "Value Leader," LE Aerocoupe, LE Sedan, and GSE Aerocoupe. There were several product changes for 1990. The first was a ride and handling improvement package with new spring and shock insulators and a re-tuned suspension for with larger stabilizer bar for 1.6-liter models. It gave improved performance and a quieter cabin. The second change was a brake feel improvement package on all 1.6-liter cars. It included a larger master cylinder and recalibrated front suspension struts. Third came quicker steering on the GSE model. A two-point motorized passive restraint system was added to all LeMans for added front seat comfort, convenience, and safety. All models also had revised door panels. A redesigned standard stereo radio and optional cassette with knob controls were featured on all models except the Value Leader Aerocoupe. Every LeMans was equipped with roof rail moldings that accepted an optional luggage rack kit for greater cargo carrying capability. Also continued from 1990-1/2 was a new cam belt tensioner for 1.6-liter engines. Standard equipment in the Value Leader Aerocoupe included a 1.6-liter TBI engine, four-speed manual transmission, P175/70R13 tires, and 9.5-in. solid front disc brakes. The LeMans LE Sedan and Aerocoupe added or substituted a five-speed manual gearbox and AM/FM stereo with clock. Externally, the LE Sedan had black side mirrors and wide black moldings with bright accents. Light Flame Red Metallic finish was no longer available on the LE Sedan. On the Aerocoupe, lower accent two-tone paint in a new Silver color was standard. In addition, a new-for-1990 color was Medium Smoke Gray Metallic. It was available only on Aerocoupes. Externally, the LE Aerocoupe had swing-out rear quarter windows. Internally, the LE Sedan had reclining front and folding rear seats, roll-down rear windows, tinted glass, and child safety rear door lock. The LeMans GSE Aerocoupe added or substituted a 2.0-liter TBI engine, P185/60R14 tires, 10.1-in. vented front disc brakes, rack-and-pinion steering, a Sport suspension featuring 22mm front/18mm rear stabilizer bars, slot alloy wheels, and power steering. Externally, it had aero fascias and rocker extensions, body-color outside rear view mirrors, a deck lid spoiler, narrower body side moldings and fog lamps. Interior appointments included rally instrumentation, tinted glass, swing-out rear quarter windows, height-adjustable reclining sport seats, specific GSE interior trim, 60/40 split fold down rear seats, a luggage compartment security cover, and an AM/FM stereo. The LeMans was designed after the Opel Kadett. Both the car and the standard engine were built in Korea by Daewoo Motor Co., as part of a joint venture between GM and the Daewoo group.

LEMANS -- SERIES 2T -- I-4

Model Number	Body/Style Number	Body Type & Seating	Factory Price	Shipping Weight	Prod. Total
2T	TX2	3-dr V/L Cpe-4P	7254	2136	Note 1
2T	TN2	3-dr Cpe-4P	8554	2180	Note 1
2T	TS2	3-dr Cpe-4P	10764	2302	Note 1
2T	TN5	4-dr LE Sed-4P	8904	2235	Note 1

NOTE 1: LeMans series production totaled 39,081.

SUNBIRD -- SERIES 2J --FOUR -- The 1990 Pontiac Sunbird offered buyers sporty, expressive styling and performance in an affordably priced, American-built car. Sunbird models appealed to a wide range of car enthusiasts from buyers of economy Sports Sedans to Convertible lovers, to those seeking all-out performance. All Sunbirds were equipped with new low-tension passive restraint systems, with color-keyed seat belts in all models. Improved acoustics helped make the interior pleasanter. The drive axle splines were now free-floating. They had a smoother finish, which allowed them to slide smoothly in their housings to minimize shudder on acceleration. The interior lighting sys-

tem gained a new 45-second delay-off feature for added convenience. A new color option was Bright Torch Red. All Sunbirds had clearcoat finish. Three additional changes highlighted the year: An LE Convertible replaced the GT Convertible; dramatic new styling updates characterized the SE and GT models; and Pontiac offered Sunbird buyers new tire choices and wheel designs. The LE Convertible replaced the Sunbird GT Convertible, making ownership of a Pontiac ragtop more affordable. The LE Convertible featured hydraulic top action and a snap-on boot to cover the top when lowered. The was a Convertible Sport package that included a turbo engine, fatter tires, Hi-tech Turbo wheels, WS6 suspension, GT-type steering, rally instrumentation, and an engine block heater. The LE Convertible also came with power windows, power door locks, tinted glass, power steering, and black sport mirrors as standard equipment. The SE offered buyers the aggressive look of the GT at a lower cost. It had a GT-style front end treatment, larger 14-in. road wheels and P185/75R14 tires, plus standard gauges (trip, fuel, voltage, oil pressure, and temperature), and the same normally aspirated four-cylinder engine used in the LE. The top Sunbird model was the GT. It had an all-new front hood, fenders, fascia, and semi-hidden headlights. Also new was an aero package, replacing 1989's wheel flares with new fenders, a new front fascia with air dam, new rear fascia, and side rocker extensions. The side aero panels included an integral body side molding for protection against parking lot dents. In the exterior lighting department, fog lights were standard on the GT. The 14-in. cast aluminum wheels were also of a new design. The WS6 suspension was standard. Power came from a turbocharged four-cylinder engine coupled to a GM Muncie/Gertag five-speed manual transmission. Rally instrumentation was standard equipment, along with tinted glass, power steering, black dual sport mirrors, an AM/FM stereo cassette, and full instrumentation (including a tach) as standard equipment. During the model-year, a new "Value Leader" version of the Sunbird was introduced. It offered the Coupe and the Sedan with less standard equipment.

Model Number	Body/Style Number	Body Type & Seating	Factory Price	Shipping Weight	Prod. Total
SUNBIRD VALUE LEADER -- SERIES 2J -- I-4					
2J	JB5	4-dr Sed-5P	7958	2398	Note 1
2J	JB1	2-dr Cpe-5P	7858	2376	Note 1
SUNBIRD LE -- SERIES 2J -- I-4					
2J	JB5	4-dr Sed-5P	8899	2500	Note 1
2J	JB1	2-dr Cpe-5P	8799	2478	Note 1
2J	JB3	2-dr Conv-5P	13924	2431	Note 1
SUNBIRD SE -- SERIES 2J -- I-4/I-4					
2J	JD1	2-dr Cpe-5P	9204	2568	Note 1
SUNBIRD GT TURBO -- SERIES 2J -- I-4/I-4 Turbo					
2J	JU1	2-dr Cpe-5P	11724	2674	Note 1

NOTE 1: Sunbird series production totaled 143,932.

GRAND AM -- SERIES 2N -- The 1990 Grand Am delivered Pontiac performance in an agile, front-wheel-drive compact package with a contemporary design. Thanks to its universal appeal to a broad range of buyers, the Grand Am was Pontiac's top-selling line. General Motors produced the one millionth Grand Am in June 1989. The Grand Am lineup consisted of a Coupe and a Sedan and both came in LE and SE trim levels. Changes for 1990 included a new standard 2.3-liter HO engine with double overhead cams (DOHC) with more power on SE models, reduced noise levels (with all engines), a new drive axle design, bigger wheels and tires, new optional "express-down" power windows, and delayed interior lighting on all cars. Vanity mirrors on both sides were standard on all models. Slate Gray replaced Gray as an interior option. Standard in both LE models was a 2.5-liter Tech IV engine, five-speed manual transmission, AM/FM radio, a new up-level console, Tri-Lace wheel covers, an interior lighting package, and P185/75R14 tires. The LE Coupe also added bucket seats. A new Sport Option package was available for LEs. It featured a monotone paint theme in White, Slate Gray, or Bright Red. Fog lamps and P195/70R14 tires on Hi-tech Turbo aluminum wheels were also included in the sport package. Beechwood was available as an interior color only with the LE sport option. Expressive styling and high-performance were offered in the Grand Am SE. A 2.3-liter High Output version of the Quad-4 16-valve DOHC engine was standard. It was teamed with a five-speed Gertag manual transmission. An engine oil cooler was standard in this high (10.1:1) compression powerplant. Other standard equipment included a WS6 suspension, monotone paint treatment, aerodynamic front, side and rear body skirting, black-finished window frames and mirrors, neutral density taillights, AM/FM stereo cassette radio, air conditioning, controlled cycle wipers, fog lamps, cruise control, remote deck lid release, power door locks, power windows with express-down, split folding rear seats, four-spoke rally steering wheel, leather shift knob, leather parking brake handle, rally instrument panel, deluxe cloth upholstery, and P205/55R16 Eagle GT+4 tires on color-coordinated 16 x 6-in. aluminum wheels (or machine-faced aluminum wheels).

Model Number	Body/Style Number	Body Type & Seating	Factory Price	Shipping Weight	Prod. Total
GRAND AM LE SERIES 2N -- I-4/V-6					
2N	NE1	2-dr Cpe-5P	10544	2566	Note 1
2N	NE5	4-dr Sed-5P	10744	2623	Note 1
GRAND AM SE-- SERIES 2N -- I-4/V-6					
2N	NW1	2-dr Cpe-5P	14894	2767	Note 1
2N	NW5	4-dr Sed-5P	15194	2842	Note 1

NOTE 1: Grand Am series production totaled 197,020.

FIREBIRD -- SERIES 2F -- V-6/V-8 -- For 1990, Firebirds had a larger, more powerful base V-6. All TPI V-8s (standard in Trans Ams) had a speed density metering system. All Firebirds also had an inflatable air bag restraint system, a new self-adjusting parking brake, dual body-color sport mirrors, and new instrument panel switches for the rear defogger, rear hatch release, and fog lamps. Brilliant Red Metallic was a new color replacing Flame Red. Base Firebirds had new seat and armrest trim, plus a different rear spoiler design. Standard features included a five-speed manual gearbox, FE1 suspension, P215/65R15 tires, front disc/rear drum brakes, and AM/FM stereo with clock. Hi-tech aluminum wheels (15 x 7 in.) were standard. The Formula model had more of a performance image. Its equipment list added an aero style rear deck lid spoiler, air conditioning, tinted glass, WS6 sport suspension, P245/50ZR16 tires, and a TBI V-8 engine. The Formula's 6-in. deep-dish Hi-tech wheels had machined-finished faces and silver metallic ports. The Trans Am had a more powerful V-8, an F41 handling suspension, limited-slip differential, P215/65R15 Firehawk GTX tires, and 15-in. deep-dish Hi-tech turbo aluminum wheels with machined faces and charcoal metallic ports, plus a leather appointment group. The luxury version of the Trans Am was the GTA. Its standard features included a 5.7-liter TPI V-8, dual catalytic convertor exhaust system, four-speed automatic transmission, four-wheel disc brakes, P245/50ZR-16 Goodyear performance tires, and 16 x 8 in. gold crosslace aluminum wheels. Also standard were a leather-wrapped steering wheel, articulating custom bucket seats with inflatable lumbar and lateral supports, rear defogger, cargo screen, full-featured Delco ETR AM/FM stereo cassette with equalizer, power antenna, power side view mirrors, power windows, and power door locks.

1990 Pontiac Firebird Trans Am GTA coupe. PMD

Model Number	Body/Style Number	Body Type & Seating	Factory Price	Shipping Weight	Prod. Total
FIREBIRD -- SERIES 2F -- V-6					
2F	FS2	2-dr Cpe-5P	11320	3106	Note 1
FIREBIRD -- SERIES 2F -- V-8					
2F	FS2	2-dr Cpe-5P	11670	3266	Note 1
FIREBIRD FORMULA -- SERIES 2F -- V-8					
2F	FS2	2-dr Cpe-5P	14610	3338	Note 1
FIREBIRD TRANS AM -- SERIES 2F -- V-8					
2F	FW2	2-dr Cpe-5P	16510	3338	Note 1
FIREBIRD TRANS AM GTA -- SERIES 2F -- V-8					
2F	FW2	2-dr Cpe-5P	23320	3554	Note 1

NOTE 1: Firebird series production totaled 46,760 (includes 1991 model vehicles introduced early in the 1990 model year).

6000 -- SERIES 2A -- I-4/V-6 -- New features for 1990 Pontiac 6000s included passive restraint belts in all models, use of the 3.1-liter V-6, and an all-wheel-drive option for the S/E (replacing the previous 6000 STE all-wheel-drive model). All models had composite headlights and fog lamps, a front air dam, dual outside rear view mirrors, black door, roof, and reveal moldings, and tinted glass. Standard equipment on the lowest-priced 6000 LE Sedan also included a 2.5-liter EFI four-cylinder engine, three-speed automatic transmission, front-wheel-drive, P185/75R14 tires, and an AM/FM stereo with clock. Highly contoured front seats with Pallex cloth trim were standard. A newly available color was Maple Red. Air conditioning and a rear defogger were standard on the LE Station Wagon, which also had swing-out rear quarter windows and a rear-facing third seat. The 3.1-liter engine was standard in Wagons with a four-speed automatic transmission. The 6000 S/E Sedan and Station Wagon also had the 3.1-liter V-6, plus electronic ride control, P195/70R15 Goodyear Eagle GT+4 tires, power windows, cruise control, power door locks, and AM/FM cassette stereo with seek-and-scan feature and a clock. The S/E models also included 15-in. cast aluminum wheels, trailing arm and beam rear suspension, a dual outlet exhaust system, a Level II suspension system, body color aero moldings, a remote deck lid release, a six-way power driver's seat, power rear view mirror, and reading lamps. The S/E wagon also had a roof top luggage rack, power tailgate release, split folding second seat, and rear window wiper. The 6000 S/E AWD option on the S/E Sedan had a full-time all-wheel-drive system that required no special driver actions to take advantage of its outstanding grip under all conditions. The all-wheel-drive feature included ABS anti-lock disc brakes at all four wheels, the 3.1-liter V-6 with three-speed automatic transmission, fully independent rear suspension, specific aluminum wheels with locks, quicker-ratio power steering, and dual outlet exhausts. This model-option came only in Medium Red Metallic or Dark Blue Metallic, both with gold accents and emblems, special badges, a unique rear spoiler, and specific fog lights. Also included were power windows, power door locks, cruise control, controlled-cycle wipers, air conditioning, an AM/FM stereo cassette radio, and front seat back map pockets.

1990 Pontiac 6000 SE four-door sedan with all-wheel drive (AWD). PMD

Model Number	Body/Style Number	Body Type & Seating	Factory Price	Shipping Weight	Prod. Total
6000 LE -- SERIES 2A -- I-4					
2A	AF5	4-dr Sed-5P	12149	2837	Note 1
6000 LE -- SERIES 2A -- V-6					
2A	AF5	4-dr Sed-5P	12809	2886	Note 1
2A	AF8	4-dr Safari-5P	15309	3156	Note 1
6000 S/E -- SERIES 2A -- I-4/V-6					
2A	AJ5	4-dr Sed-5P	16909	3015	Note 1
2A	AJ8	4-dr Safari-5P	18509	3201	Note 1

NOTE 1: 6000 series production totaled 66,398.

GRAND PRIX -- SERIES 2G -- V-6/V-8 -- The Grand Prix was again Pontiac's personal sports machine. It came in five models from the responsive Grand Prix LE all the way up to a powerful Turbo Grand Prix Coupe. General features included eye-catching styling, a driver-oriented cockpit, and a complete performance spectrum. Changes in the 1990 Grand Prix lineup included the addition of a four-door Sedan, a redesigned analog gauge cluster with new pod switches, a 2.3-liter 16-valve engine option (the 2.8-liter V-6 was dropped), and new Pallex/Metrix cloth upholstery replacing the previous Ripple/Pallex cloth interior choices. New paint colors included Bright Red and Slate Gray Metallic throughout the line, plus Black Metallic, Medium Blue Metallic, and Bright Red for the SE. Camel Metallic, Medium Gray Metallic, and Red finishes were dropped. On interiors, Slate Gray replaced

Medium Gray. Standard equipment on the LE Coupe and Sedan included a 2.3-liter 16-valve dohc "Quad Four" engine, three-speed automatic transmission, P195/75R14 (sedan) or P205/65R15 (Coupe) tires, air conditioning, 60/40 reclining front seats, and an AM/FM stereo with clock. A five-speed manual gearbox was offered only for Coupes with the optional 3.1-liter MFI V-6. Both models with this engine could also be optioned with a four-speed automatic transmission. Other standard features included styled wheel covers on Sedans and styled steel wheels on Coupes and standard Pallex cloth seat trim in both body types. The Grand Prix SE Coupe added or substituted the following standard features: The 3.1-liter V-6, five-speed manual transmission, P215/60R16 tires, power windows, power reclining front seats with articulated thigh, lumbar, lateral and head support, cruise control, an AM/FM stereo with graphic equalizer, clock, and steering wheel controls, and a six-speaker sound system with amplifier. Also included on the SE were a Y99 rally-tuned suspension, split dual exhausts, 16 x 6 cast aluminum wheels with white, bright red, or medium blue machined faces, exterior aero body skirting, fog lamps, specific front and rear fascias, and a monochromatic color scheme. The SE was also appointed in richer Metrix cloth upholstery. The Grand Prix Special Touring Edition (STE) Sedan added even more standard equipment including power reclining bucket front seats with lumbar and articulated thigh supports, a keyless entry system, and a Hi-performance eight-speaker sound system. The STE also had a analog instrument cluster, Metrix cloth trim, a specific contoured three-passenger rear seat with luggage pass-through, a leather-wrapped steering wheel, tilt steering, controlled-cycle wipers, a rear window defogger, and an overhead mini-console. Its P215/60R16 Goodyear Eagle GT+4 tires were mounted on specific STE alloy wheel rims. The STE had a distinctive front end with a unique fascia and integral grille. A light bar containing integral fog lights extended across the entire width of the car. At the rear, the STE had another specific fascia and full-width taillights. A monochromatic paint scheme was standard, with optional lower accent paint treatments available at extra-cost. The top-of-the-line Turbo Grand Prix Coupe added a 3.1-liter turbocharged V-6, standard four-speed automatic transmission, ABS brakes, and 245/50ZR16 tires. Also included were gold cross-lace wheels, a monochromatic paint scheme, a unique ground effects package, functional hood louvers, heads-up instrument panel display, and rear bucket seats with integral headrests.

Model Number	Body/Style Number	Body Type & Seating	Factory Price	Shipping Weight	Prod. Total
GRAND PRIX LE -- SERIES 2W -- I-4/V-6					
2G	WJ5	4-dr Sed-5P	14564	3280	Note 1
2G	WJ1	2-dr Cpe-5P	14564	3189	Note 1
GRAND PRIX SE-- SERIES 2W -- V-6					
2G	WPJ1	2-dr Cpe-5P	17684	3284	Note 1
GRAND PRIX STE -- SERIES 2W -- V-6/V-8					
2G	WT5	4-dr Sed-5P	18539	3385	Note 1
GRAND PRIX TURBO 2W -- V-6					
2G	WJ1/LG5	2-dr Cpe-5P	23775	3500	Note 1

NOTE 1: Grand Prix series production totaled 128,067.

1990 Pontiac Bonneville SSE four-door sedan. PMD

BONNEVILLE -- SERIES 2H -- V-6 -- The 1990 Pontiac Bonnevilles continued to blend style and performance. Models offered were the capable and well-equipped LE, the sportier SE, and the Euro-style look of the Bonneville SSE. Six changes were highlighted: A redesigned front body/frame structure; new wheels and tire combinations; a new grille, taillights, and deck lid lock cover for LE/SE models and new grille for the SSE; seat-mounted safety belts; new express-down power windows; and new remote keyless entry system. All Bonnevilles were

powered by a 3.8-liter SFI V-6 coupled with a four-speed automatic transmission. Features of the Bonneville LE included an F41 suspension, P205/75R14 tires; 14-in. wheel covers; a 2.84:1 rear axle, manual air conditioning, AM/FM stereo with clock; and 45/55 reclining split seat with armrest. The Bonneville SE added or substituted P215/60R Eagle GT+4 tires, 16-in. six-spoke wheels, a 2.97:1 final drive ratio, a cassette stereo, a 45/55 reclining split seat with storage armrest, a rear window defogger, power windows with express-down feature, and power door locks. Also included on the SE was a rear deck lid spoiler, Metrix cloth upholstery, a re-tuned suspension, and variable-ratio power steering. The formerly optional fog lamps, interior lamp group, and rear deck lid release were standard for 1990. The Bonneville SSE added or substituted the following over SE features: ABS brakes, FE2 suspension with electronic-level control and variable-ratio steering, 16-in. Aerolite wheels, a 3.33:1 final drive ratio, automatic air conditioning with temperature indicator light, steering wheel controls for radio/heat/vent and A/C functions, AM/FM stereo with cassette and graphic equalizer, 45/55 bucket seats with console, remote keyless entry system, and theft deterrent system. The SSE had a European-like monochromatic color scheme with wide body-color moldings with gold protective inserts. The door frame, B-pillar, wheel opening, windshield, and side window moldings had high-gloss black finish to distinguish them from the SE (gray moldings) and LE (bright moldings). A standard rear deck lid spoiler emphasized the sporty nature of this Touring Sedan. The door handles were a unique combination of body color and black. A new outside rear view mirror and a new grille enhanced the exterior. The wheels were done in body color, too. Headlight washers and fog lights were included. The interior featured specific gauges, a driver information center, a leather-wrapped steering wheel, and eight radio speakers. Also included on the SSE were an electric fuel filler door release, electric deck lid release, heated and blue-tinted OSRV mirrors, a rear window defogger, and deluxe trunk trim with a deck lid inner liner. The trunk was fitted with a security net, a rear cargo compartment closeout, a trunk-mounted tire inflator, and roadside emergency kit.

Model Number	Body/Style Number	Body Type & Seating	Factory Price	Shipping Weight	Prod. Total
BONNEVILLE LE -- SERIES H -- V-6					
2H	HX5	4-dr Spt Sed-5P	15774	3309	Note 1
BONNEVILLE SE -- SERIES H -- V-6					
2H	HZ5	4-dr Spt Sed-5P	19144	3392	Note 1
BONNEVILLE SSE -- SERIES H -- V-6					
2H	HZ5/Y80	4-dr Spt Sed-5P	23994	3567	Note 1

NOTE 1: Bonneville series production totaled 85,844.

TRANS SPORT -- SERIES 2U -- V-6 -- The Pontiac Trans Sport was introduced in 1990. This MPV (Multi-Purpose-Vehicle) was a van in body style, but had a car-like front-wheel-drive chassis and drivetrain. It was based on an exciting "concept vehicle" that Pontiac built and exhibited in 1986. The Trans Sport featured a space frame substructure attached to a sturdy ladder frame. Body panels were made of reinforced composite materials. There were two models called the (entry-level) Transport and Trans Sport SE. Both were powered by a electronically fuel-injected 3.1-liter V-6 developing 120 hp and coupled to a three-speed automatic transmission. The entry-level Transport was equipped with 2+3 seating with front buckets and a mid-mounted bench. The interior was trimmed in Pallex cloth. The less expensive model had its own lower body treatment. The fascias and aero moldings were done in a contrasting color, which was either Silver Metallic or Medium Gray Metallic, depending on body color. The rear portion of the roof colud be ordered in gloss black (standard) or body color (a delete-option). Also standard were an AM/FM radio with clock and P205/70R-14 tires on 14-in. wheels. The Trans Sport SE featured 2+2+2 modular seating with Metrix cloth trim and specific SE seats. A monocromatic exterior was standard, and the roof had the gloss black treatment that accentuated its deep-tinted glass areas. Front air conditioning, a rear air flow distribution system, an AM/FM cassette radio with seek-and-scan and digital clock, a leather-clad steering wheel, 15-in. cast aluminum road wheels, and P195/70R-15 Goodyear Eagle GT+4 tires were also standard, along with automatic load leveling, a built-in tire inflator, lamp group, tilt steering, and cruise control.

Model Number	Body/Style Number	Body Type & Seating	Factory Price	Shipping Weight	Prod. Total
2U	U06	Wagon	15495	3500	Note 1
2U	U06	SE Wagon	18625	3500	Note 1

NOTE 1: Trans Sport series production totaled 40,750.

LEMANS ENGINE

[STANDARD VL/LE] Inline. OHV. Four-cylinder. Cast iron block. Aluminum head and intake manifold. Displacement: 97.5 cu. in. (1.6L).

Bore x stroke: 3.11 x 3.21 in. Compression ratio: 8.6:1. Brake horsepower: 74 @ 5600 rpm. Torque: 90 lb.-ft. @ 2800 rpm. Fuel system: EFI/TBI. RPO Code: L73. Standard with four-speed manual Value Leader and LeMans LE. [VIN code 6]. [STANDARD GSE] Inline. OHC. Four-cylinder. Cast iron block. Aluminum head and intake manifold. Displacement: 121 cu. in. (2.0L). Bore x stroke: 3.39 x 3.39 in. Compression ratio: 8.8:1. Brake horsepower: 96 @ 4800 rpm. Torque: 118 lb.-ft. @ 3600 rpm. Fuel system: EFI/TBI. RPO Code: LT2. Standard with five-speed manual LeMans GSE models. [VIN code K].

1990 Pontiac Sunbird LE convertible. PMD

SUNBIRD ENGINES

[STANDARD LE/SE] Inline. OHC. Four-cylinder. Cast iron block. Aluminum head and intake manifold. Displacement: 121 cu. in. (2.0L). Bore x stroke: 3.39 x 3.39 in. Compression ratio: 8.8:1. Brake horsepower: 96 @ 4800 rpm. Torque: 118 lb.-ft. @ 3600 rpm. Fuel system: EFI/TBI. RPO Code: LT2. Standard in Sunbird LE and Sunbird SE models. [VIN code K]. [STANDARD GT] Inline. OHC. Four-cylinder. Turbocharged (Garrett T2.5 turbocharger). Cast iron block. Aluminum head and intake manifold. Displacement: 121 cu. in. (2.0L). Bore x stroke: 3.39 x 3.39 in. Compression ratio: 8.0:1. Brake horsepower: 165 @ 5600 rpm. Torque: 175 lb.-ft. @ 4000 rpm. Fuel system: MPFI with Turbo. RPO Code: LT3. Standard in Sunbird Turbo GT (optional in Sunbird LE Convertible). [VIN code M]

1990 Pontiac Grand Am SE coupe. PMD

GRAND AM ENGINES

[STANDARD LE] Inline. OHV. Cast iron block and head. Aluminum intake manifold. Displacement: 151 cu. in. (2.5L Tech IV). Bore & stroke: 4.00 x 3.00 in. Compression ratio: 9.0:1. Brake horsepower: 110 @ 5200 rpm. Torque: 135 lb.-ft. @ 3200 rpm. Five main bearings. Hydraulic valve lifters. Fuel system: EFI/TBI. RPO Code: L68. Standard in Grand AM LE. [VIN code U/R]. [STANDARD SE WITH MANUAL] Inline. DOHC. 16-valve. Quad-4 High-Output. Cast iron block. Aluminum head and intake manifold. Displacement: 138 cu. in. (2.3-liter). Bore x stroke: 3.62 x 3.35 in. Compression ratio: 10.0:1. Brake horsepower: 180 @ 6200 rpm. Torque: 160 lb.-ft. @ 5200 rpm. Fuel system: MPFI. RPO Code: LGO. Standard and exclusive in Grand Am SE with five-speed Manual transmission. [VIN code A]. [STANDARD SE WITH AUTOMATIC] Inline. DOHC. 16-valve. Quad-4. Cast iron block. Aluminum head and intake manifold. Displacement: 138 cu. in. (2.3.-liter). Bore x stroke: 3.62 x 3.35 in. Compression ratio: 9.5:1. Brake horsepower: 160 @ 6200 rpm. Torque: 155 lb.-ft. @ 5200 rpm. Fuel system: MPFI. RPO Code: LD2. Standard in SE with automatic; optional in LE with automatic. [VIN code D].

FIREBIRD ENGINES

[FIREBIRD Base V-6] V-block. OHV. Six-cylinder. Cast iron block and head. Aluminum intake manifold. Displacement: 191 cu. in. (3.1L). Bore x stroke: 3.50 x 3.31 in. Compression ratio: 8.75:1. Brake horsepower: 135 @ 4400 rpm. Torque: 180 lb.-ft. @ 3600 rpm. Fuel system: EFI/MFI. RPO Code: LHO. Standard in base Firebird. Produced in U.S., Canada, or Mexico. [VIN code T]. [FIREBIRD BASE V-8] V-block. OHV. Eight-cylinder. Cast iron block and head. Aluminum intake manifold. Displacement: 305 cu. in. (5.0L). Bore x stroke: 3.74 x 3.48 in. Brake horsepower: 170 @ 4400 rpm. Torque: 255 lb.-ft. @ 2400 rpm. Compression ratio: 9.3:1. Fuel system: EFI/TBI. RPO Code: L03. Produced in U.S. or Canada. Standard Formula. Available in base Firebird. [VIN code E or F]. [OPTIONAL V-8] V-block. OHV. Eight-cylinder. Cast iron block and head. Aluminum intake manifold. Displacement: 305 cu. in. (5.0L). Bore x stroke: 3.74 x 3.48 in. Brake horsepower: 200 @ 4400 rpm (Formula with automatic and Trans Am with five-speed manual) or 225 @ 4600 rpm (GTA and Formula with five-speed manual). Torque: 300 lb.-ft. @ 3200 rpm (Formula with automatic and Trans Am with five-speed manual) or 290 lb.-ft. @ 3200 rpm (GTA and Formula with five-speed manual). Compression ratio: 9.3:1. Fuel system: EFI/TPI. RPO Code: LB9. Available with five-speed manual in Formula, and Trans Am (delete option in GTA). [VIN code E or F]. [GTA V-8] V-block. OHV. Eight-cylinder. Cast iron block and head. Aluminum intake manifold. Displacement: 350 cu. in. (5.7L). Bore x stroke: 4.00 x 3.48 in. Brake horsepower: 235 @ 4400 rpm. Torque: 340 lb.-ft. @ 3200 rpm. Compression ratio: 9.3:1. Fuel system: EFI/TPI. RPO Code: B2L. Standard with four-speed automatic in GTA (optional in Formula and Trans Am). Includes low-profile air induction system with aluminum plenum and individual aluminum tuned runners, an extruded dual fuel rail assembly with computer controlled fuel injectors, and a special low-restriction single exhaust system. [VIN code 8]. [BASE] Inline. OHV. Four-cylinder. Cast iron block and head. Aluminum intake manifold. Displacement: 151 cu. in.. (2.5L Tech IV). Bore & stroke: 4.00 x 3.00 in. Compression ratio: 9.0:1. Brake horsepower: 112 @ 5200 rpm. Torque: 135 lb.-ft. @ 3200 rpm. Five main bearings. Hydraulic valve lifters. Fuel system: EFI/TBI. RPO Code: LR8. Standard in 6000 LE. [VIN code U]. [STANDARD LE Wagon; S/E Sedan and Wagon]. V-block. OHV. Six-cylinder. Cast iron block. Aluminum head and intake manifold. Displacement: 191cu. in. (3.1L). Bore x stroke: 3.50 x 3.31 in. Brake horsepower: 135 @ 4400 rpm. Torque: 180 lb.-ft. @ 3600 rpm. Fuel system: EFI/MFI Code: LHO. Standard in 6000 S/E Sedan and Wagon and LE Wagon. [VIN code T].

GRAND PRIX ENGINES

[STANDARD Grand Prix] Inline. DOHC. 16-valve. Quad-4. Cast iron block. Aluminum head and intake manifold. Displacement: 138 cu. in. (2.3.-liter). Bore x stroke: 3.62 x 3.35 in. Compression ratio: 9.5:1. Brake horsepower: 160 @ 6200 rpm. Torque: 155 lb.-ft. @ 5200 rpm. Fuel system: MPFI. RPO Code: LD2. Standard in SE with automatic; optional in LE with automatic. [VIN code D]. [STANDARD GRAND PRIX SE and STE; OPTIONAL GRAND PRIX LE] V-block. OHV. Six-cylinder. Cast iron and aluminum head. 191 cu. in. (3.1L). Bore x stroke: 3.50 x 3.31 in. Compression ratio: 8.75:1. Brake horsepower: 135 @ 4400 rpm. Torque: 180 lb.-ft. @ 3600 rpm. Fuel system: EFI/MPI. RPO Code: LHO. [VIN code T]. [OPTIONAL] V-block. OHV. Six-cylinder. Turbo. Cast iron block and aluminum head. 191 cu. in. (3.1L). Bore x stroke: 3.50 x 3.31 in. Compression ratio: 8.75:1. Brake horsepower: 205 @ 4800 rpm. Torque: 220 lb.-ft. @ 3200 rpm. Fuel system: EFI/MPI. RPO Code: LHO with LG5 American Sun Roof Corp. (ASC)/McLaren Turbo conversion. [VIN code T].

BONNEVILLE ENGINE

[STANDARD LE/SE/SSE] V-block. OHV. "3800" six-cylinder. Cast iron block and head. Aluminum intake manifold. Displacement: 231 cu. in. (3.8L). Bore x stroke: 3.80 x 3.40 in. Compression ratio: 8.5:1. Brake horsepower: 165 @ 5200 rpm. Torque: 210 lb.-ft. @ 2000 rpm. Fuel system: SFI. RPO Code: LN3. Standard in Bonneville LE/SE/SSE model. [VIN code W, S, or 9].

TRANS SPORT ENGINE

[TRANS SPORT] V-block. OHV. Six-cylinder. Cast iron block and head. Aluminum intake manifold. Displacement: 191 cu. in. (3.1L). Bore x stroke: 3.50 x 3.31 in. Compression ratio: 8.5:1. Brake horsepower: 120 @ 4200 rpm. Torque: 175 lb.-ft. @ 2200 rpm. Fuel system: EFI/TBI. RPO Code: LG6. Standard in base Firebird. Produced in U.S., Canada, or Mexico. [VIN code T].

LEMANS CHASSIS: Wheelbase: 99.2 in. (all). Overall length: 163.7 in. (three-door); 172.4 in. (four-door). Height: 53.5 in. (Aerocoupe); 53.7 in. (Sedan). Standard tires: P175/70R13 BSW (all).

SUNBIRD CHASSIS: Wheelbase: 101.2 in. (all). Overall length: 182 in. (Coupe and Convertible). Width: 67.0 in. Coupe/Convertible). Height: 50.4.in. (Coupe); 51.9 in. (Convertible). Front tread: 55.6 in. (all). Rear tread: 55.2 in. (all). Standard tires: P185/75R14 BSW (LE). Standard tires: P185/75R14 (SE). Standard tires: P215/60R14 Eagle GT+4 (GT).

GRAND AM CHASSIS: Wheelbase: 103.4 in. (Coupe/Sedan). Overall length: 180.1 in. (all). Width: 66.5 in. (all). Height: 52.5 in. (all). Front tread: 55.6 in. Rear tread: 55.2 in. Standard tires: P185/80R13 BSW (LE). Standard tires: P215/60R14 (SE).

FIREBIRD CHASSIS: Wheelbase: 101.0 in. (All). Overall length: 188.1 in. (Base/Formula); 191.6 in. (Trans Am/GTA). Width: 72.4 in. (all). Height: 50.0 in. (all). Front tread: 60.7 in. Rear tread: 61.6 in. Standard tires: P215/65R15 (Base Firebird and Trans Am). Tire: P245/50ZR16 Goodyear Eagle ZR50 "Gatorback" (Formula and GTA).

6000 CHASSIS: Wheelbase: 104.9 in. (all). Overall length: 188.8 in. (Sedan); 193.2 in. (Safari). Width: 72.0 in. (all). Height: 53.7 in. (Sedan); 54.1 in. (Wagon). Front tread: 58.7 in. Rear tread: 57.0 in. Standard Tires: 185/75R14 (LE). Standard tires: 195/70R14 Goodyear Eagle GT+4 (S/E).

GRAND PRIX CHASSIS: Wheelbase: 107.5 in. (all). Overall length: 193.9 in. (Coupe). Overall length: 195.0 in. (Sedan). Width: 72 in. (all). Height: 53.3 in. (all). Front tread: 59.5 in. Rear tread: 58.0 in. Standard tires: 195/75R14 (base and LE). Standard tires: 215/60R15 Goodyear Eagle GT (SE/STE). Standard tires: P245/50ZR16 (ASC/McLaren Turbo).

BONNEVILLE CHASSIS: Wheelbase: 110.8 in. (all). Overall length: 198.7 in. (all). Width: 72.1 in. (all). Height: 55.5 in. (all). Front tread: 60.3 in. Rear tread: 59.8 in. Standard tires: 205/75R14 BSW (LE). Standard tires: 215/65R15 Goodyear Eagle GT+4 (SE). Standard tires: P215/60R16 BSW (SSE).

1990 Pontiac Trans Sport SE minivan. PMD

TRANS SPORT CHASSIS: Wheelbase: 109.9 in. (all). Overall length: 194.5 in. (all). Width: 74.2 in. (all). Height: 65.5 in. (all). Standard tires: 205/70R14 BSW (Base). Standard tires: 195/70R15 Goodyear Eagle GT+4 (SE).

LEMANS TECHNICAL: Chassis: Front engine/front drive. Base transmission: Four-speed manual. Optional transmission: Three-speed automatic or five-speed manual. Axle ratio: 3.43:1 with 1.6L and automatic. Axle ratio: 3.18:1 with 2.0L and three-speed automatic. Axle ratio: 3.72:1 with 1.6L and four-speed manual or either engine and five-speed manual. Front suspension: deflected disc, MacPherson struts and 22mm stabilizer bar. Rear suspension: Coil springs, semi-independent torsion beam, trailing arms, and 18mm anti-roll bar. Steering: Rack-and-pinion 24.5:1 ratio (18.3:1 power-assisted on GSE). Turns lock-to-lock: 3.1:1 (GSE); 3.5 (power); 4.57 (manual). Turning circle: 32.8 ft. Front brakes: 9.25-in. solid discs (1.6L) or 10.1-in. vented disc (2.0L) power-assisted. Rear brakes: 7.9 x 1.8 -in. drum (both engines) power-assisted.

SUNBIRD TECHNICAL: Chassis: Front engine/front drive. Base transmission: Five-speed manual. Optional transmission: Three-speed automatic. Axle ratio: 3.45:1 with base engine and five-speed manual. Axle ratio: 3.18:1 with 2.0L TBI engine and three-speed automatic. Axle ratio: 3.61:1 with 2.0L Turbo and five-speed manual. Axle ratio: 3.18:1 with three-speed automatic (2.08:1 optional). Front suspension: deflected disc, MacPherson struts and (22mm with 2.0L TBI/28mm with 2.0L Turbo) stabilizer bars. Rear suspension: Coil springs, semi-independent torsion beam, trailing arms (and 21mm anti-roll bar with 2.0L Turbo). Steering: Rack-and-pinion 16.0:1 ratio (14.0:1 on GT). Turns lock-to-lock: 3.0 (2.5 on GT). Turning circle: 34.3 ft. (all). Front brakes: 9.72-in. vented disc power-assisted. Rear brakes: 7.87 x 1.77-in. drum power-assisted.

GRAND AM TECHNICAL: Chassis: Front engine/front drive. Base transmission: Five-speed manual with overdrive. Optional transmission: Three-speed automatic. Axle ratio: 3.18:1 (with 2.5L engine and automatic SE). Axle ratio: 2.84:1 (with 2.5L engine and automatic LE). Axle ratio: 3.18:1 (with 2.3L engine and automatic SE). Axle ratio: 2.48:1 (with 2.3L engine and manual). Axle ratio: 3.61 (with 2.3L HO and manual). Stall torque ratio: 2.48:1 (with automatic). Front suspension: MacPherson struts with coil springs and 24mm anti-roll bar (28mm anti-roll bar with standard WS6 suspension on SE). Rear suspension: Trailing crank arm with twist arm, coil springs, (and 21mm anti-roll bar on SE). Steering (LE): Power-assisted rack-and-pinion, 16.0:1 ratio, 3.0 turns lock-to-lock, and 35.4-ft. (left); 37.8-ft. (right) turning circle. Steering (SE): Power-assisted rack-and-pinion, 14.0:1 ratio, 2.5 turns lock-to-lock, and 35.4-ft. (left); 37.8-ft. (right) turning circle. Front brakes: Power-assisted 9.7-in. vented discs. Rear brakes: Power-assisted 7.87-in. drums. Fuel tank: 13.6 gal.

FIREBIRD TECHNICAL: Chassis: Front engine/rear drive. Base transmission: Five-speed manual. Optional transmission: Four-speed automatic. Front suspension: Fully independent with modified MacPherson strut, and low-friction ball bearing upper strut mount and 30mm (Level I) or 34mm (Level II), or 36mm (Level III) anti-roll bar. Rear suspension: Live axle with coil springs, longitudinal lower control arm and torque arm, transverse track bar, and 18mm (Level I) or 23mm (Level II) or 24mm (Level II) anti-roll bar. Steering: Power recirculating ball; 14.1:1 ratio (Level I), or 12.7:1 quick ratio with sport effort valving (Levels II and III). Turns lock-to-lock: 2.72 (Level I), 2.47 (Level II), or 2.26 (Level III). Turning circle: 39.1 ft. (Level I) or 32.6 ft. (Levels II and III). Brakes: Power vented 10.5-in. front disc/9.5-in. rear drum on Coupes and Formula with 5.0L EFI; power four-wheel vented disc 10.5-in. front/11.7-in. rear with 5.7L or 5.0L with TPI and five-speed on GTA or Formula-assisted vented discs. Rear brakes: Power-assisted 7.87-in. drums. Fuel tank: 13.6 gal.

6000 TECHNICAL: Chassis: Front engine/front drive. Base transmission: Three-speed automatic with overdrive. Optional transmissions: Four-speed automatic. Axle ratio: 2.84:1 (with three-speed automatic and 2.5L or 3.1L engines). Axle ratio: 3.33:1 (with four-speed automatic and 3.1L engine). Axle ratio: 3.18:1 (with three-speed automatic and 3.1L engine in S/E AWD). Front suspension: MacPherson struts with 22mm (LE), 28mm (S/E), or 27mm (STE AWD). Rear suspension: Independent, transverse composite leaf spring and 22mm anti-roll bar (STE AWD); or trailing arms and track bar, Panhard rod, coil springs, and 22mm anti-roll bar (S/E), 20mm anti-roll bar standard. Steering: Power-assisted rack-and-pinion with 17.5:1 ratio (16.0:1 in S/E AWD), 3.05 turns lock to lock and 36.96-ft. (38.5 with STE AWD) turning circle. Front brakes: Power assisted vented discs 9.72-in. (standard); 10.24-in. (medium-/heavy-duty), 10.2-in (STE). Rear brakes: Power assisted 8.86-in. drum (standard); 8.86-in. drum (medium-/heavy-duty), 10.3-in solid discs (STE). Fuel tank: 15.7-gal.

1990 Pontiac Turbo Grand Prix STE four-door sedan. PMD

1990 Pontiac Turbo Grand Prix STE four-door sedan (rear view). PMD

GRAND PRIX TECHNICAL: Chassis: Front engine/front drive. Standard drivetrain: 2.3L Quad-4 with three-speed automatic transaxle. Optional drivetrain: 3.1L MFI V-6 with five-speed manual transaxle. Optional drivetrain: 3.1L ASC/McLaren Turbo V-6 with four-speed automatic transaxle. Axle ratio: 3.18 (2.3L with three-speed automatic). Axle ratio: 3.33 (3.1L MFI V-6 with four-speed automatic). Axle ratio: 3.61 (3.1L Turbo with five-speed manual). Front suspension: MacPherson struts with tapered top coil springs, lower A arm and 28mm anti-roll bar (30mm anti-roll bar with Y99 suspension). Rear suspension: Tri-link independent suspension with 12mm anti-roll bar (transverse fiberglass leaf spring and 12mm anti-roll bar with Y99 option). Steering: Power-assisted rack-and-pinion with 15.5:1 ratio, 2.89 turns lock-to-lock, and

37.4-ft. turning circle (standard). Steering: Power-assisted rack-and-pinion with 14.0:1 ratio, 2.25 turns lock-to-lock, and 39.7-ft. turning circle (Y99). Steering: Power-assisted rack-and-pinion with 15.7:1 ratio, 2.25 turns lock-to-lock, and 39.7-ft. turning circle (STE with Y99). Four-wheel power disc brakes. Front brakes: 10.5-in. composite vented discs. Rear brakes: 10.1-in. composite solid discs. Fuel tank: 16.0 gal.

BONNEVILLE TECHNICAL: Chassis: Front engine/front drive. Base transmission: Four-speed automatic. Axle ratio: 2.84:1 (standard with 3.8L V-6 in Bonneville LE). Axle ratio: 2.97:1 (standard with 3.8L V-6 in Bonneville SE). Axle ratio: 3.33:1 (standard with 3.8L V-6 in Bonneville SSE). Front suspension: MacPherson struts with 24N-mm coil springs and 30mm anti-roll bar (LE). Front suspension: MacPherson struts with 248N-mm coil springs and 32mm anti-roll bar (SE). Front suspension: MacPherson struts with 24N-mm coil springs and 32mm anti-roll bar (SSE). Rear suspension: MacPherson struts with variable rate (48-65 N-mm) coil springs and 14mm anti-roll bar (LE). Rear suspension: MacPherson struts with constant-rate (47 N-mm) coil springs and 14mm anti-roll bar (LE/SE). Rear suspension: MacPherson struts with 47 N-mm coil springs and 18mm anti-roll bar (SSE). Steering: Power-assisted rack-and-pinion with 18.1:1 constant ratio, 2.97 turns lock-to-lock, and 39.7-ft. left/39.0-ft. right turning circle (LE/SE). Steering: Power-assisted rack-and-pinion with 15.3:1 to 18.0:1 variable ratio, 2.79 turns lock-to-lock, and 38.4-ft. left/40.7-ft. right turning circle (SSE). Front brakes: Power-assisted 10.1-in. vented discs. Rear brakes: Power-assisted 8.9-in. drums. Anti-lock brake system standard with SSE. Fuel tank: 18.0 gal.

TRANS SPORT: Chassis: Front engine/front drive. Transmission: Three-speed automatic. Axle ratio: 3.18:1 (all). Front suspension: MacPherson struts with 24N-mm coil springs and 30mm anti-roll bar (LE). Front suspension: MacPherson strut, stamped lower control arms, 28mm stabilizer bar. Rear suspension: Open-section transverse beam on stamped steel trailing arms, tube shocks, coil springs and 25.4mm stabilizer bar. Steering: Power-assisted rack-and-pinion with 15.7:1 ratio, and 42.5-ft. turning circle. Front brakes: Power-assisted 10.2-in. vented rotors, 182 sq. in. swept area. Rear brakes: Power-assisted 8.86 x 1.77-in. finned composite cast iron drums with 98.5 sq. in. swept area. Fuel tank: 20.0 gal.

LEMANS OPTIONS: MX1 three-speed automatic transmission ($445). C60 air conditioning, requires power steering and not available in Value Leader Aerocoupe ($680). B37 front and rear floor mats ($33). N40 power steering, requires air conditioning in Aerocoupe or SE Sedan ($214). UM7 Delco ETR stereo in Value Leader Aerocoupe ($307). UM6 Delco ETR AM/FM with cassette and more in Value Leader Aerocoupe ($429). UM6 Delco ETR AM/FM with cassette and more in LE/SE/GSE ($122). V54 painted roof luggage rack ($95). AD3 removable sun roof ($350). WDV warranty enhancements for New York ($65).

SUNBIRD OPTIONS: 1SB Sunbird LE Coupe option group #1 ($416). 1SC Sunbird LE Coupe option group #2 ($1462). 1SD Sunbird LE Coupe option group #3 ($1657). 1SB Sunbird LE Sedan option group #1 ($416). 1SC Sunbird LE Sedan option group #2 ($1468). 1SD Sunbird LE Sedan option group #3 ($1863). 1SB Sunbird LE Convertible option group #1 ($1046). 1SC Sunbird LE Convertible option group #2 ($1368). 1SB Sunbird SE Coupe option group #1 ($416). 1SC Sunbird SE Coupe option group #2 ($1413). 1SD Sunbird SE Coupe option group #3 ($1886). 1SB Sunbird GT Coupe option group #1 ($1122). 1SC Sunbird SE Coupe option group #2 ($1367). R6A Sunbird LE value package ($374). R6A Sunbird SE Coupe value package ($469). LT2 2.0-liter engine in GT ($768 credit). LT3 Turbo engine, mandatory extras, and specific options, optional only in LE Convertible ($1023-$1402). MX1 three-speed automatic transmission ($465). C60 air conditioning ($720). K34 cruise control ($195). C49 electric rear window defogger ($160). NB2 California emissions package ($100). D84 custom two-tone paint for LE ($101). AU3 power door locks ($175 Coupe/$215 Sedan). A31 power windows, requires power door locks ($230 Coupe/$295 Sedan/no charge Convertible). UM7 Delco radio equipment (standard/no charge). UM6 Delco radio equipment ($1702 additional). U1C Delco radio equipment ($226-$396). AR9 reclining bucket seats with Pallex cloth trim (no charge). T43 rear deck lid with spoiler for LE Convertible ($70). AD3 removable glass sun roof ($350). QME tire option ($114). PX1 13-in. N78 14-in Hi-tech Turbo aluminum wheels with locking package ($265-$335).

GRAND AM OPTIONS: 1SB Grand Am LE Coupe option group #1 ($910). 1SC Grand Am LE Coupe option group #2 ($1105). 1SD Grand Am LE Coupe option group #3 ($1817). 1SB Grand Am LE Sedan option group #1 ($910). 1SC Grand Am LE Sedan option group #2 ($1105). 1SD Grand Am LE Sedan option group #3 ($1922). 1SB Grand Am SE Coupe and Sedan option group #1 ($321). R6A Grand Am LE Coupe value package ($394). R6B Grand Am LE Coupe value package without 1SD package ($455). R6B Grand Am LE Coupe value package with 1SD package ($40). R6B Grand Am LE Sedan value package ($520). Advertising ($200). LD2 Quad-4 2.3-liter MPI engine ($660 in LE; $108 delete-option in SE). LG0 Quad-4 High-Output engine (standard on SE/Manual). MX1 three-speed automatic transmission ($540). C60 air conditioning ($720). C49 electric rear window defogger ($160). NB2 California emission requirements ($100). UB3 rally cluster gauges and trip odometer in LE ($127). V56

deck lid luggage carrier ($115). D84 custom two-tone paint for LE ($101). AU3 power door locks ($175 Coupe/$215 Sedan). A31 power windows, requires custom console in LE ($240 Coupe/$305 Sedan). W30 Sport Option package includes SE-style front and rear fascias, SE taillamps, SE Aero package less wheel flares, Quad-4 HO engine, dual exhausts, five-speed manual transmission, P195/70R14 black sidewall tires; Hi-tech Turbo wheels, specific FE2 suspension, rally gauges with tach, and interior courtesy lamps for LE Coupe/Sedan ($1164-$1718 depending on specific package). UM6 Delco radio equipment ($140). U1D Delco radio equipment ($405-$545). AR9 custom reclining bucket seats with Pallex cloth trim (no charge). AD3 removable glass sun roof ($350). QMB tire option ($78 extra). N78 14-in Hi-tech Turbo aluminum wheels with locking package ($265).

FIREBIRD OPTIONS: 1SB Firebird option group #1 ($865). 1SB Firebird option group #2 ($1603).1SB Formula/Trans Am option group #1 ($495). 1SC Firebird and Formula option group #2 ($889). 1SC Firebird and Formula option group #2 ($854). R6A Firebird and Formula value package ($820). R6A Trans Am value package ($889). R6A Trans Am GTA value package ($1020). Advertising ($200). LO3 5.0-liter TBI V-8 engine in base Firebird ($350). LB9 5.0L MPI V-8 in Formula and Trans Am ($745). LB9 5.0L MPI V-8 in Trans Am GTA ($300 credit). B2L 5.7L MPI V-8 in Trans Am ($300). B2L 5.7L MPI V-8 in Formula ($1020). MM5 five-speed manual transmission in Trans Am GTA with LB9 ($515 credit). MXO four-speed automatic transmission, except in GTA ($515). C60 air conditioning ($805). G80 limited-slip axle ($100). C49 electric rear window defogger ($160). N10 dual convertor exhaust ($155). KC4 engine oil cooler ($110). NB2 California emissions ($100). CC1 Hatch roof ($920). D66 deluxe two-tone paint ($150). WX1 lower accent two-tone paint delete on Formulas ($150 credit). J65 four-wheel disc power brakes ($179). AU3 power door locks ($175). A31 power windows ($260). UM6 Delco radio equipment ($150). UX1 Delco radio equipment ($300). U1A Delco radio equipment ($226-$526). U75 power antenna ($75). D42 cargo area security screen ($69). AQ9 articulating bucket seats with Ventura leather trim in GTA ($450). QLC high-performance WS6 performance suspension ($385).

6000 OPTIONS: 1SB option package #1 for 6000 LE Sedan ($995). 1SC option package #2 for 6000 LE Sedan ($1190). 1SD option package #3 for 6000 LE Sedan ($2058). 1SB option package #1 for 6000 LE Wagon ($190). 1SC option package #2 for 6000 LE Wagon ($385). 1SD option package #3 for 6000 LE Wagon ($1243). 1SB option package #1 for 6000 S/E Sedan ($343). 1SB option package #1 for 6000 S/E Wagon ($293). R6A value option package for 6000 LE Sedan ($413). R6B value option package for 6000 LE Sedan ($413). R6B value option package for 6000 LE Sedan ($413). LB6 2.8-liter MFI V-6 in LE Sedan ($660). MXO four-speed automatic transmission ($200). C60 air conditioning ($805). C49 electric rear window defogger ($160). D86 two-tone paint ($115). AU3 power door locks ($205). A31 power windows ($310). UM6 Delco ETR AM/FM stereo ($122). U1A Delco ETR AM stereo/FM stereo ($501-$536). AM6 45/55 split bench seat ($133). B20 custom interior with 45/55 split seat in Empress/London cloth ($350-$483). Various tire options (no charge to $68). N78 Sport aluminum wheels with locking package ($265). BX3 wood-grain exterior siding for Wagon ($295).

1990 Pontiac Grand Prix STE four-door sedan. PMD

GRAND PRIX OPTIONS: 1SB Grand Prix LE Coupe option package #1 ($190). 1SC Grand Prix LE Coupe option package #2 ($470). 1SD Grand Prix LE Coupe option package #3 ($1603). 1SE Grand Prix LE Coupe option package #4 ($2162). 1SB Grand Prix LE Sedan option package #1 ($190). 1SC Grand Prix LE Sedan option package #2 ($385). 1SD Grand Prix LE Sedan option package #3 ($1808). 1SE Grand Prix LE Sedan option package #4 ($2487). 1SB Grand Prix SE Coupe option package #1 ($561). LG5 Turbo Coupe Option Package ($888 credit). R6A Grand Prix LE Coupe value option package ($865). R6A Grand Prix LE Sedan value option package ($409). R6B Grand Prix LE Sedan value option package ($464). R6A Grand Prix SE Coupe

value option package ($975). R6A Grand Prix STE Sedan value option package. ($975). LG5 ASC/McLaren Turbo conversion ($5236). MXO four-speed automatic in Grand Prix SE ($200). MXO four-speed automatic in Grand Prix SE ($640). MM5 five-speed manual transmission in Grand Prix LE ($440 credit). JL9 anti-lock power brakes ($925). C49 electric rear window defogger ($160). NB2 California emissions system ($100). D84 two-tone paint ($105). AU3 power door locks ($175-$215). CF5 power sun roof ($650 or $450 with Turbo conversion). A31 power windows ($240-$301). UM6 Delco radio equipment ($140). UX1 Delco radio equipment ($400). U1A stereo sound system ($226-$666 depending on model). AM9 bucket seat with Pallex cloth trim in Grand Prix LE ($110). AN3 Custom Cloth bucket seat in Grand Prix LE ($140). AQ9 articulating Sport bucket seats with front console and Ventura leather trim ($450-$650). AC3 power seat ($270). BYP Sport Appearance package including SE styling elements for LE Coupe ($160-$285). BYP Sport Appearance package including SE styling elements for LE Sedan ($480). Various tire options ($54-$72). PF1 15-in. styled steel wheels, except SE ($145). PH3 15-in. aluminum sport wheels with locking package ($125-$265).

BONNEVILLE OPTIONS: 1SB Bonneville LE option package #1 ($269). 1SC Bonneville LE option package #2 ($464). 1SD Bonneville LE option package #3 ($1716). 1SE Bonneville LE option package #3 ($2414). 1SB Bonneville SE option package #1 ($330). 1SC Bonneville SE option package #2 ($810). R6A Bonneville LE value option package ($940). R6A Bonneville SE value option package. ($465). R6A Bonneville LE value option package ($610). R6A Bonneville SE value option package. ($535). Advertising ($200). C49 electric rear window defogger ($160). NB2 California emissions system ($100). D84 two-tone paint ($105). JM4 power anti-lock brakes ($925). AU3 power door locks ($215). A31 power windows ($375). UM6 Delco radio equipment ($140). UT4 radio equipment package ($580-$655). U1A compact disc player ($666-$1031). US7 power antenna ($75). AS7 custom interior trim with split bench seat and console ($235). B20 custom interior with 45/55 split seat in Metrix cloth trim ($230-$705 depending on value package options or individual option). AG1 six-way power seat in LE ($270). CF5 power glass sun roof ($1230). Various tire options ($70-$164). PF7 15-in. diamond-spoke wheels with locking package on LE ($296). Bonneville SSE R6A value option package ($1080). UA1 AM/FM stereo in Bonneville SSE ($186). CF5 power glass sun roof in SSE ($1230). UA6 theft deterrent system in SSE ($150). WDV warranty enhancements for New York ($65).

TRANS SPORT OPTIONS: 1SB Trans Sport option package #1 ($1195). 1SC Trans Sport option package #2 ($1960). 1SB Trans Sport SE option package #1 ($765). Advertising ($200). C67 air conditioning in Trans Sport ($805). NB2 California emissions system ($100). B2Q black roof delete (no charge). C49 electric rear window defogger ($160). AJ1 glass package in Trans Sport ($245). AB5 power door locks ($255). A31 power windows ($240). UM6 Delco radio equipment ($140). U1A compact disc player ($376-$516). AB3 six-passenger seating package ($525). ZP7 seven-passenger seating package ($675). N78 14-in. aluminum wheels ($265).

Note: Full option package contents, descriptions and applications information can often be determined by consulting factory literature. The data above is edited for size and clarity. This information provided only as a guide to help collectors appraise the relative value of cars with numerous options. Prices for items included as part of a value option package are usually much less than individual prices. Option prices charged by individual dealers may also vary.

HISTORICAL FOOTNOTE: John Middlebrook replaced J. Michael Losh as the general manager of the Pontiac Division, with Losh taking the same post within Oldsmobile Division. Borrowing the construction treatment utilized by the Fiero, which was canceled two years previous, Pontiac unveiled the Trans Port minivan built of composite materials on a space frame substructure. Trans Sport and Grand Prix models were now sold in Europe. Pontiac sales of 636,390 cars and 29,875 minivans for a total of 666,265 vehicles would represent 13-1/2 percent of General Motors' 1990 light vehicle sales (number two behind Chevrolet).

1991 PONTIAC

PONTIAC I.D. NUMBERS: Vehicle identification number (VIN) is located on top left-hand surface of instrument panel visible through the windshield. The VIN has 17 symbols. The first symbol indicates the country of manufacture (U.S.). The second symbol indicates the manufacturer (G=General Motors). The third symbol indicates the make/division (2=Pontiac). The fourth, fifth, and sixth symbols are the same as the body style (model) number. The eighth symbol indicates the engine. The ninth symbol is a check digit. The 10th symbol indicates model-year. The 11th symbol indicates the assembly plant. The last six symbols are the consecutive unit number at the factory.

LEMANS -- SERIES 2T -- FOUR -- The Pontiac LeMans was based on the German Opel Kadett and built in Korea. The 1991 LeMans line consisted of the Aerocoupe and the LE Coupe and the LE Sedan. The GSE was discontinued. All models featured motorized passive seat belts, fully reclining bucket seats, electric rear window defogger, vented front disk brakes, and electronically fuel-injected engine, and front-wheel-drive. The Aerocoupe also had a four-speed manual transmission, P175R/70R13 tires, steel wheels with full wheel covers, and a two-spoke steering wheel. The LE models added or substituted a five-speed manual transmission, gray lower accent paint, and an AM/FM stereo with clock. New for 1991 were body-color and gray accent moldings (replacing black body side moldings), new Chester and Sarah cloth interior trims (replacing Twill cloth), a new manual transmission shift boot (replacing the molded rubber type), a new cam belt tensioner (1.6-liter engine), and a 10-minute rear defroster time-out (replacing five-minute time-out).

LEMANS -- SERIES 2T -- I-4

Model Number	Body/Style Number	Body Type & Seating	Factory Price	Shipping Weight	Prod. Total
2T	TX2	3-dr V/L Cpe-4P	7574	2169	--
2T	TN2	3-dr Cpe-4P	8304	2191	--
2T	TN5	4-dr LE Sed-4P	8754	2246	--

1991 Pontiac Sunbird GT coupe. PMD

SUNBIRD -- SERIES 2J --FOUR -- The 1991 Sunbird was a sporty and expressive front-drive sub-compact. Four Coupes, one Convertible Coupe, and two Sedans were offered in base, LE, SE, and GT car-lines. New features for 1991 included a 3.1-liter V-6 engine, a stainless steel exhaust system, dual exhausts on GT models, new 15-in. specific GT wheels, a quarter-wave tuner for the two-liter engine, a new Medium Camel interior (replacing Beechwood), added acoustical ride insulation, colored visor vanity mirrors, a self-aligning steering wheel, and a new Bright Red exterior color. Standard equipment on the Sunbird Coupe and Sedan included a 2.0-liter MFI engine, five-speed manual transmission, P185/75R14 tires. steel wheels with tri-lace wheel covers, power rack and pinion steering, and AM/FM stereo with clock. The Sunbird LE Coupe and Sedan had the same basic equipment, but a few upgraded interior/exterior trim items. The Sunbird LE Convertible added or substituted P185/75R14 tires, power door locks, power windows, dual sport mirrors, and tinted glass. As compared to LE models, the Sunbird SE Coupe added or substituted P195/70R14 tires, Hi-Tech Turbo wheels, a rear deck lid spoiler, dual sport mirrors, and tinted glass. The top-of-the-line Sunbird GT Coupe featured a 3.1-liter EFI V-6, five-speed manual transmission, P205/55R15 Eagle GT+4 tires, Sport suspension, GT specific 15-in. alloy wheels, a rear deck lid spoiler, dual Sport mirrors, tinted glass, power rack and pinion steering, and AM/FM stereo with clock.

Model Number	Body/Style Number	Body Type & Seating	Factory Price	Shipping Weight	Prod. Total
BASE SUNBIRD -- SERIES 2J -- I-4					
2J	JC5	4-dr Sed-5P	8784	2592	Note 1
2J	JC1	2-dr Cpe-5P	7858	2376	Note 1
SUNBIRD LE -- SERIES 2J -- I-4					
2J	JB5	4-dr Sed-5P	9544	2608	Note 1
2J	JB1	2-dr Cpe-5P	9444	2590	Note 1
2J	JB3	2-dr Conv-5P	14414	2775	Note 1
SUNBIRD SE -- SERIES 2J -- I-4/I-4					
2J	JD1	2-dr Cpe-5P	10694	2617	Note 1
SUNBIRD GT TURBO -- SERIES 2J -- I-4/I-4 Turbo					
2J	JU1	2-dr Cpe-5P	12444	2793	Note 1

NOTE 1: Sunbird series production totaled 118,615.

GRAND AM -- SERIES 2N -- Since its reintroduction as a 1985 model, the Grand Am was Pontiac's most popular nameplate. Its sales topped the one million mark and nearly a quarter-million Grand Ams were sold in 1989 alone. The 1991 Grand Am line continued to offer the same type of appeal with many features and attractive pricing aimed at a broad range of buyers. The line included two body styles that came in six models. The Grand Am, the Grand Am LE, and the Grand Am SE were all offered as a Coupe or as a Sedan. New features for 1991 included larger front brakes and redesigned cables, a shorter manual shift lever, a new Black color (replacing Black Metallic), and redesigned seat recliner handles. LE models also had a new Sport Performance package, and monotone exterior treatment. SEs also came with ABS VI anti-lock brakes. A 3.77:1 first gear ratio was new for Grand Ams with the 2.3-liter HO engine and five-speed manual transmission. Standard equipment on the Grand Am Coupe and Sedan included the 2.5-liter EFI engine, five-speed manual transmission, P185/75R14 tires, 14-in. steel wheels with tri-lace wheel covers, easy-entry bucket seats (Coupes only), and AM/FM stereo with clock. The Grand Am LE had the same basic equipment features with slightly upgraded interior and exterior trim. The SE added or substituted a 2.3-liter HO MFI "Quad Four" engine, ABS IV anti-lock brakes, 16-in. color-keyed aluminum wheels, an instrumentation package, air conditioning, split folding rear seats, cruise control, a tilt steering wheel, power windows (with driver-window "express-down" feature), power door locks, and an AM/FM cassette stereo with clock.

Model Number	Body/Style Number	Body Type & Seating	Factory Price	Shipping Weight	Prod. Total
GRAND AM LE SERIES 2N -- I-4/V-6					
2N	NG1	2-dr Cpe-5P	10174	2566	Note 1
2N	NG5	4-dr Sed-5P	10374	2566	Note 1
GRAND AM LE SERIES 2N -- I-4/V-6					
2N	NE1	2-dr Cpe-5P	11124	2508	Note 1
2N	NE5	4-dr Sed-5P	11324	2592	Note 1
GRAND AM SE-- SERIES 2N -- I-4					
2N	NW1	2-dr Cpe-5P	16344	2739	Note 1
2N	NW5	4-dr Sed-5P	16544	2826	Note 1

NOTE 1: Grand Am series production totaled 147,467.

1991 Pontiac Firebird Formula coupe. PMD

FIREBIRD -- SERIES 2F -- V-6/V-8 -- The new 1991 Firebirds were actually introduced in the spring of 1990. Their most visible change was a new exterior appearance. All models benefited from restyled front and rear fascias. The front fascias, made of body color resilient "Endura" thermoplastic incorporated low-profile turn signals and integral air dams. At the rear, the GTA, Trans Am and Formula were fitted with a redesigned rear deck lid spoiler. New fascias on GTA and Trans Am models incorporated restyled taillights. The Sport Appearance package on the base Firebird included fog lights in the fascia and carried the aero look to the sides with distinctive lateral skirting. The headlights were more compact, without sacrificing light output. Available in 1991 for all 5.0- and 5.7-liter TPI V-8s was a new "Street Legal Performance" (SLP) package of GM high-performance hardware. The SLP kit, available from GM dealers, boosted engine performance without modifications to the powerplants. The kit could be dealer- or owner-installed. All Firebirds were protected by a Pass-Key theft deterrent system. All Firebirds had a driver's side air bag. The standard radio was upgraded to an AM/FM cassette stereo and the GTA included a cassette with five-band graphic equalizer. Acoustics were improved in all models. New colors included Dark Green Metallic and a Bright White. Standard Firebird equipment included a 3.1-liter MFI V-6, four-speed automatic transmission, FE1 suspension, P215/65R15 tires, 15 x 7-in. Hi-Tech aluminum wheels, disc/drum brakes, new front/rear fascias, and an AM/FM stereo with cassette and clock. The Formula added or substituted a 5.0-liter TBI V-8, five-speed manual gearbox, WS6 Sport Suspension, P245/50ZR16

tires, 16 x 8 -in. Hi-Tech Turbo aluminum wheels, limited-slip differential, and air conditioning. The Trans Am added or substituted a 5.0-liter TPI V-8, F41 Rally Tuned suspension, 16 x 8-in. diamond spoke wheels, aero package with side treatment, leather appointment group (including leather-wrapped steering wheel), and four-way manual driver's seat adjuster. Standard equipment for the Trans Am GTA included the 5.7-liter TPI V-8, four-speed automatic transmission, WS6 Sport suspension, P245/50ZR16 tires, 16 x 8-in. diamond spoke wheels, limited-slip differential, disc/drum brakes, Performance Enhancement group (with engine oil cooler, dual converters, and performance axle), new front/rear fascias, an aero package with side treatment, air conditioning, an upgraded sound system, a power antenna, the leather appointment group, a four-way manual driver's seat, power windows and power door locks, cruise control, remote deck lid release, and power outside mirrors.

Model Number	Body/Style Number	Body Type & Seating	Factory Price	Shipping Weight	Prod. Total
FIREBIRD -- SERIES 2F -- V-6					
2F	FS2	2-dr Cpe-5P	12690	3121	Note 1
2F	FS3	2-dr Conv-5P	19159	--	Note 1
FIREBIRD -- SERIES 2F -- V-8					
2F	FS2	2-dr Cpe-5P	13040	3287	Note 1
2F	FS3	2-dr Conv-5P	19509	--	Note 1
FIREBIRD FORMULA -- SERIES 2F -- V-8					
2F	FS2	2-dr Cpe-5P	15530	3370	Note 1
FIREBIRD TRANS AM -- SERIES 2F -- V-8					
2F	FW2	2-dr Cpe-5P	17530	3343	Note 1
2F	FW3	2-dr Conv-5P	22980	--	Note 1
FIREBIRD TRANS AM GTA -- SERIES 2F -- V-8					
2F	FW2	2-dr Cpe-5P	24530	3456	Note 1

NOTE 1: Firebird series production totaled 20,332.

6000 -- SERIES 2A -- I-4/V-6 -- New features for 1991 Pontiac 6000s were few. They consisted primarily of a new Light Camel Metallic exterior color, a new Tan interior color and the dropping of two models, the 600 S/E Wagon and the 6000 S/E All-Wheel-Drive. That left the LE Sedan, LE Wagon, and S/E Sedan in the lineup. All 6000s came with composite headlights, fog lamps, a front air dam, and black door and window moldings. The 6000 S/E carried the full card of standard features, while the LE Sedan allowed buyers to equip their cars to fit their needs. The 6000 LE Wagon provided all the size benefits of a traditional wagon package. Standard features of the LE Sedan included a 2.5-liter EFI four-cylinder engine, three-speed automatic transmission, P185/75R14 tires, 14-in. rims with tri-lace wheel covers, and AM/FM stereo radio with clock. The 6000 LE Wagon added or substituted a 3.1-liter base V-6 with EFI, a four-speed automatic transmission, and air conditioning. In addition to the Wagon's equipment, the 6000 S/E had P195/70R15 Eagle GT+4 tires, 15-in. aluminum sport wheels, power windows, cruise control, power door locks, a custom trim package with bucket seats and gauges, and an AM/FM cassette stereo with clock.

Model Number	Body/Style Number	Body Type & Seating	Factory Price	Shipping Weight	Prod. Total
6000 LE -- SERIES 2A -- I-4					
2A	AF5	4-dr Sed-5P	12999	2843	Note 1
6000 LE -- SERIES 2A -- V-6					
2A	AF5	4-dr Sed-5P	13659	2970	Note 1
2A	AF8	4-dr Safari-5P	16699	3162	Note 1
6000 S/E -- SERIES 2A -- I-4/V-6					
2A	AJ5	4-dr Sed-5P	18399	3370	Note 1

NOTE 1: 6000 series production totaled 19,603.

GRAND PRIX -- SERIES 2G -- V-6/V-8 -- The Grand Prix had some of the most exciting changes in the 1991 Pontiac lineup. There was a revised model range, with the Grand Prix GTP replacing the Grand Prix Turbo Coupe. This car looked like the turbocharged model, but had an all-new 210-hp Twin Dual Cam V-6. A new four-speed electronic automatic transmission could be had only with the new engine. Coupes had a new exterior appearance. There was also a new SE Coupe sport appearance package, plus a new Aero Performance package. New-for-1991 colors included Bright Blue Metallic, Bright White, Black, and Turquoise. Also new was a Generation II head-up display option. Models available included the LE Sedan, SE Coupe and SE, GT Coupe, and STE Sedan. The GTP was considered a model-option. Standard equipment for LEs included the 2.3-liter Quad 4 engine, three-speed automatic transmission, 15-in. sport wheel covers, P205/70R15 touring tires, air conditioning, 45/55 split reclining front seats, and AM/FM stereo with clock. The SE Coupe and Sedan added or substituted upscale interior and exterior trims. The GT Coupe added or substituted a 3.1-liter MFI V-6, Y99 Rally Tuned suspension, 16-in. cast aluminum wheels, P21560R/16 Eagle GT+4 tire, power windows, power door locks, front bucket seats with power articulated supports, power driver's seat, cruise control, AM/FM cassette stereo with equalizer, clock, and steering wheel controls, and a six-speaker sound system. The STE Sedan had most of the GT features, except its 16-in. cast aluminum wheels were different, it added an electronic information center, a remote keyless entry system and eight-speaker sound system, and it had power reclining front articulated bucket seats. Standard features of the GTP optioned Coupe included the 3.4-liter Twin Dual Cam V-6, five-speed manual transmission, Y99 Rally Tuned suspension, Aero Performance package, P225/60R16 Eagle GT+4 tires on 16 x 8-in. aluminum wheels, air conditioning, power windows, power door locks, front articulated bucket seats, power driver's seat, cruise control, AM/FM cassette with equalizer, clock and steering wheel controls, and six-speaker sound system.

1991 Pontiac Grand Prix GTP coupe. PMD

Model Number	Body/Style Number	Body Type & Seating	Factory Price	Shipping Weight	Prod. Total
GRAND PRIX LE -- SERIES 2W -- I-4					
2G	WH5	4-dr Sed-5P	14294	3248	Note 1
GRAND PRIX LE -- SERIES 2W --V-6					
2G	WH5	4-dr Sed-5P	14294	3274	Note 1
GRAND PRIX SE -- SERIES 2W -- I-4					
2G	WJ5	4-dr Sed-5P	15284	3252	Note 1
2G	WJ1	2-dr Cpe-5P	14894	3188	Note 1
GRAND PRIX SE -- SERIES 2W -- V-6					
2G	WJ5	4-dr Sed-5P	15284	3278	Note 1
2G	WJ1	2-dr Cpe-5P	14294	3274	Note 1
GRAND PRIX GT-- SERIES 2W -- V-6					
2G	WP1	2-dr Cpe-5P	19154	3323	Note 1
GRAND PRIX STE -- SERIES 2W -- V-6/V-8					
2G	WT5	4-dr Sed-5P	19994	3400	Note 1

NOTE 1: Grand Prix series production totaled 114,718.

1991 Pontiac Grand Prix STE four-door sedan. PMD

Model Number	Body/Style Number	Body Type & Seating	Factory Price	Shipping Weight	Prod. Total
TRANS SPORT -- SERIES 2U -- V-6					
2U	U06	Wagon	15619	3514	Note 1
2U	U06	SE Wagon	18889	3626	Note 1

NOTE 1: Trans Sport series production totaled 27,181.

LE MANS ENGINE

[STANDARD VL/LE] Inline. OHV. Four-cylinder. Cast iron block. Aluminum head and intake manifold. Displacement: 97.5 cu. in. (1.6L). Bore x stroke: 3.11 x 3.21 in. Compression ratio: 8.6:1. Brake horsepower: 74 @ 5600 rpm. Torque: 90 lb.-ft. @ 2800 rpm. Fuel system: EFI/TBI. RPO Code: L73. Standard with four-speed manual Value Leader and LeMans LE. [VIN code 6].

SUNBIRD ENGINES

[STANDARD BASE/LE/SE] Inline. OHC. Four-cylinder. Cast iron block. Aluminum head and intake manifold. Displacement: 121 cu. in. (2.0L). Bore x stroke: 3.39 x 3.39 in. Compression ratio: 8.8:1. Brake horsepower: 96 @ 4800 rpm. Torque: 118 lb.-ft. @ 3600 rpm. Fuel system: EFI/TBI. RPO Code: LT2. Standard in Sunbird LE and Sunbird SE models. [VIN code K]. [STANDARD GT] V-block. OHV. Six-cylinder. Cast iron block and aluminum head. Displacement 191 cu. in. (3.1L). Bore x stroke: 3.50 x 3.31 in. Compression ratio: 8.9:1. Brake horsepower: 140 @ 4500 rpm. Torque: 180 lb.-ft. @ 3600 rpm. Fuel system: EFI/MPI. RPO Code: [VIN code T].

1991 Pontiac Grand Am LE four-door sedan. PMD

GRAND AM ENGINES

[STANDARD BASE/LE] Inline. OHV. Cast iron block and head. Aluminum intake manifold. Displacement: 151 cu. in. (2.5L Tech IV). Bore & stroke: 4.00 x 3.00 in. Compression ratio: 9.0:1. Brake horsepower: 110 @ 5200 rpm. Torque: 135 lb.-ft. @ 3200 rpm. Five main bearings. Hydraulic valve lifters. Fuel system: EFI. RPO Code:L68. Standard in Grand AM/ LE. [VIN code U/R]. [STANDARD SE WITH AUTOMATIC] Inline. DOHC. 16-valve. Quad-4. Cast iron block. Aluminum head and intake manifold. Displacement: 138 cu. in. (2.3.-liter). Bore & stroke: 3.62 x 3.35 in. Compression ratio: 9.5:1. Brake horsepower: 160 @ 6200 rpm. Torque: 155 lb.-ft. @ 5200 rpm. Fuel system: MPFI. RPO Code: LD2. Standard in SE with automatic; optional in LE with automatic. [VIN code D]. [STANDARD SE] Inline. DOHC. 16-valve.Quad-4 High-Output. Cast iron block. Aluminum head and intake manifold. Displacement: 138 cu. in. (2.3-liter). Bore & stroke: 3.62 x 3.35 in. Compression ratio: 10.0:1. Brake horsepower: 180 @ 6200 rpm. Torque: 160 lb.-ft. @ 5200 rpm. Fuel system: MPFI. RPO Code: LGO. Standard and exclusive in Grand Am SE with five-speed manual transmission. [VIN code A].

FIREBIRD ENGINES

[FIREBIRD BASE V-6] V-block. OHV. Six-cylinder. Cast iron block and head. Aluminum intake manifold. Displacement: 191 cu. in. (3.1L). Bore & stroke: 3.50 x 3.31 in. Compression ratio: 8.5:1. Brake horsepower: 140 @ 4400 rpm. Torque: 180 lb.-ft. @ 3600 rpm. Fuel system: EFI/MFI. RPO Code: LHO. Standard in base Firebird. [VIN code T]. [FIREBIRD BASE V-8] V-block. OHV. Eight-cylinder. Cast iron block and head. Aluminum intake manifold. Displacement: 305 cu. in. (5.0L). Bore & stroke: 3.74 x 3.48 in. Brake horsepower: 170 @ 4400 rpm. Torque: 255 lb.-ft. @ 2400 rpm. Compression ratio: 9.3:1. Fuel system: EFI/TBI. RPO Code: L03. Standard Formula. Available in base Firebird. [VIN code E or F]. [OPTIONAL V-8] V-block. OHV. Eight-cylinder. Cast iron block and head. Aluminum intake manifold. Displacement: 305 cu. in. (5.0L). Bore & stroke: 3.74 x 3.48 in. Brake horsepower: 205 @ 4200 rpm (Formula, Trans Am, and GTA with automatic); 230 hp at 4400 rpm (all others). Torque: 300 lb.-ft. @ 3200 rpm (GTA/Formula with manual; optional Trans Am); Torque: 285 lb.-ft. @ 3200 rpm (GTA, Trans Am, and Formula with five-speed manual). Compression ratio: 9.3:1. Fuel system: EFI/TPI. RPO Code:

1991 Pontiac Bonneville SSE four-door sedan. PMD

BONNEVILLE -- SERIES 2H -- V-6 -- The Bonneville remained Pontiac's full-size Touring Sedan in 1991. Innovations for the year included a new brake-transmission interlock; London/Empress cloth trims for SE model (optional on LE); 15-in. bolt-on wheel covers for LEs, and P215/65R-15 tires for LEs. The LE was the low model, the SE was the middle model, and the SSE was the top-of-the-line. The LE gave buyers a choice of 45/55 bucket seats with a center console, or 45/55 split bench seat with center armrest. Standard equipment included a four-spoke steering wheel, AM/FM stereo radio with clock, manual air conditioning, F41 suspension, and 2.84:1 final drive. The SE model added or substituted power express windows, P21560R-16 tires, 16-in. six-spoke wheels, a 2.97:1 final drive ratio, AM/FM stereo cassette, 45/55 reclining split front seat with armrest, rear window defogger, and power door locks. A full rally instrumentation package including tachometer, voltmeter, engine, and oil temperature gauges and trip odometer was also included at no extra cost. The Bonneville SSE added or substituted the following over SE features: ABS brakes, FE2 suspension with electronic-level control and variable-ratio steering, 16-in. Aerolite wheels (gold cross-lace wheels were a no-cost option), a 3.33:1 final drive ratio, automatic air conditioning with temperature indicator light, steering wheel controls for radio/heat/vent and A/C functions, AM/FM stereo with cassette and graphic equalizer, eight-speaker sound system, 45/55 12-way articulating bucket seats with console, specific instrument package with full gauges, compass and Driver Information Center, remote keyless entry system, and theft deterrent system, rear window defogger, power antenna, remote deck lid release, and express-down power windows. The SSE again sported a distinctive monochromatic paint treatment. The trunk was fitted with a security net, a rear cargo compartment close-out, a trunk-mounted tire inflator, and a roadside emergency kit.

Model Number	Body/Style Number	Body Type & Seating	Factory Price	Shipping Weight	Prod. Total
BONNEVILLE LE -- SERIES H -- V-6					
2H	HX5	4-dr Spt Sed-5P	16834	3323	Note 1
BONNEVILLE SE -- SERIES H -- V-6					
2H	HZ5	4-dr Spt Sed-5P	20464	3376	Note 1
BONNEVILLE SSE -- SERIES H -- V-6					
2H	HY5	4-dr Spt Sed-5P	25264	3551	Note 1

NOTE 1: Bonneville series production totaled 88,355.

TRANS SPORT -- SERIES 2U -- V-6 -- The 1991 Trans Sport came in Trans Sport (base) and Trans Sport SE models. Standard features of the base model included 2+3 seating with a bench-type second seat, AM/FM radio with clock, and P205/70R-14 tires. The Trans Port SE added or substituted 2+2+2 seating, a leather steering wheel, tilt steering, cruise control, deep-tinted glass, power outside rear view mirrors, electronic control front air conditioning, AM/FM cassette stereo. Electronic Ride Control, P205/65R-15 tires, 15-in. wheels (with Medium Red, White, or machine-faced finish), and a package including a lamp group. New features for 1991 included a stainless steel exhaust system, a roof luggage carrier, larger outside rear view mirrors, and a self-aligning steering wheel. The standard tires used on each model were upgraded, and the SE's new standard power mirrors could also be added to the base model at extra cost. The SE also offered a new 2+3+2 seating option. New colors of Bright Red and Medium Blue Metallic were also offered for the monochromatic-finished SE. Base Trans Sport seats were trimmed with Pallex cloth. Uplevel Metrix fabric was found inside the higher-priced SE.

LB9. Available with five-speed manual in Formula, and Trans Am (delete option in GTA). [VIN code E or F]. [GTA V-8] V-block. OHV. Eight-cylinder. Cast iron block and head. Aluminum intake manifold. Displacement: 350 cu. in. (5.7L). Bore & stroke: 4.00 x 3.48 in. Brake horsepower: 240 @ 4400 rpm. Torque: 340 lb.-ft. @ 3200 rpm. Compression ratio: 9.3:1. Fuel system: EFI/TPI. RPO Code: B2L. Standard with four-speed automatic in GTA (optional in Formula and Trans Am). Includes Performance Enhancement group with dual catalytic converter exhausts, engine oil cooler, and performance axle ratio. [VIN code 8].

PONTIAC 6000 ENGINES

[BASE] Inline. OHV. Four-cylinder. Cast iron block and head. Aluminum intake manifold. Displacement: 151 cu. in. (2.5L Tech IV). Bore & stroke: 4.00 x 3.00 in. Compression ratio: 9.0:1. Brake horsepower: 110 @ 5200 rpm. Torque: 135 lb.-ft. @ 3200 rpm. Five main bearings. Hydraulic valve lifters. Fuel system: EFI. RPO Code: LR8. Standard in 6000 LE Sedan. [VIN code U]. [STANDARD LE WAGON; S/E SEDAN]. V-block. OHV. Six-cylinder. Cast iron block. Aluminum head and intake manifold. Displacement: 191 cu. in. (3.1L). Bore & stroke: 3.50 x 3.31 in. Brake horsepower: 140 @ 4400 rpm. Torque: 185 lb.-ft. @ 3200 rpm. Fuel system: EFI/MFI Code: LHO. Standard in 6000 S/E Sedan and LE Wagon. [VIN code T].

GRAND PRIX ENGINES

[STANDARD GRAND PRIX] Inline. DOHC. 16-valve. Quad-4. Cast iron block. Aluminum head and intake manifold. Displacement: 138 cu. in. (2.3.-liter). Bore & stroke: 3.63 x 3.35 in. Compression ratio: 9.5:1. Brake horsepower: 160 @ 6200 rpm. Torque: 155 lb.-ft. @ 5200 rpm. Fuel system: MPFI. RPO Code: LD2. Standard in LE/SE. [VIN code D]. [STANDARD GRAND PRIX STE and GT; OPTIONAL GRAND PRIX LE/SE] V-block. OHV. Six-cylinder. Cast iron block and aluminum head. Displacement: 191 cu. in. (3.1L). Bore & stroke: 3.50 x 3.31 in. Compression ratio: 8.8:1. Brake horsepower: 140 @ 4400 rpm. Torque: 185 lb.-ft. @ 3200 rpm. Fuel system: EFI/MPI. RPO Code: LHO. [VIN code T]. [STANDARD GRAND PRIX GTP; OPTIONAL ALL OTHERS EXCEPT GRAND PRIX LE] V-block. OHV. Six-cylinder. Cast iron block and aluminum head. Displacement: 207 cu. in. (3.4L). Bore & stroke: 3.62 x 3.31 in. Compression ratio: 9.25:1. Brake horsepower: 210 @ 5200 rpm. Torque: 215 lb.-ft. @ 4000 rpm. Fuel system: EFI/MPI. [VIN code X].

BONNEVILLE ENGINE

[STANDARD LE/SE/SSE] V-block. OHV. "3800" six-cylinder. Cast iron block and head. Aluminum intake manifold. Displacement: 231 cu. in. (3.8L). Bore & stroke: 3.80 x 3.40 in. Compression ratio: 8.5:1. Brake horsepower: 165 @ 4800 rpm. Torque: 210 lb.-ft. @ 2000 rpm. Fuel system: SFI. RPO Code: LN3. Standard in Bonneville LE/SE/SSE model. [VIN code W, S, or 9].

TRANS SPORT ENGINE

[TRANS SPORT] V-block. OHV. Six-cylinder. Cast iron block and head. Aluminum intake manifold. Displacement: 191 cu. in. (3.1L). Bore & stroke: 3.50 x 3.31 in. Compression ratio: 8.5:1. Brake horsepower: 120 @ 4200 rpm. Torque: 175 lb.-ft. @ 2200 rpm. Fuel system: EFI/TBI. RPO Code: LG6. Standard in base Firebird.[VIN code T].

LEMANS CHASSIS: Wheelbase: 99.2 in. (all). Overall length: 163.70 in. (three-door); 172.4 in. (four-door). Height: 53.5 in. (Aerocoupe); 53.7 in. (Sedan). Width: 65.5 in. (three-door); 65.7 in. (four-door). Front tread: 55.1 in. (all) Rear tread: 55.4 in. (all). Standard tires: P175/70R13 BSW (all). Fuel tank: 13.2 gal.

SUNBIRD CHASSIS: Wheelbase: 101.2 in. (all). Overall length: 181.3 in. (all). Overall width: 66.3 in. (all). Height: 52.0.in. (Coupe); 53.6 in. Sedan; 52.1 in. (Convertible). Front tread: 55.6 in. (all). Rear tread: 55.2 in. (all). Standard tires: P185/75R14 BSW (all except SE and GT Coupes). Standard tires: P195/70R14 (SE Coupe). Standard tires: P205/55R15 Eagle GT+4 (GT).

GRAND AM CHASSIS: Wheelbase: 103.4 in. (all). Overall length: 180.1 in. (all). Width: 66.5 in. (all). Height: 52.5 in. (all). Front tread: 55.6 in. Rear tread: 55.2 in. Standard tires: P185/75R15 BSW (Base/LE). Standard tires: P205/55R15 (SE).

FIREBIRD CHASSIS: Wheelbase: 101.0 in. (all). Overall length: 195.1 in. (Base/Formula); 195.2 in. (Trans Am/GTA). Width: 72.4 in. (all). Height: 49.7 in. (all). Front tread: 60.7 in. Rear tread: 61.6 in. Standard tires: P215/65R15 (Base Firebird). Standard tires: P215/60R16 (Trans Am). Standard tires: P245/50ZR16 Goodyear Eagle ZR50 "Gatorback" (Formula and GTA).

6000 CHASSIS: Wheelbase: 104.9 in. (all). Overall length: 185.8 in. (Sedan); 193.2 in. (Wagon). Width: 72.0 in. (all). Height: 53.7 in. (Sedan); 54.1 in. (Wagon). Front tread: 58.7 in. (Sedan); 56.7 in. (Wagon). Rear tread: 57.0 in. (both). Standard Tires: 185/75R14 (LE). Standard tires: 195/70R15 Goodyear Eagle GT+4 (S/E).

GRAND PRIX CHASSIS: Wheelbase: 107.5 in. (all). Overall length: 193.9 in. (Coupe). Overall length: 194.8 in. (Sedan). Width: 70.9 in. (all). Height: 52.8 in.(all). Front tread: 59.5 in. Rear tread: 58.0 in. Standard tires: 205/70R15 (LE/SE). Standard tires: 215/60R15 Goodyear Eagle GT+4 (STE/GT). Standard tires: P225/60R16 Eagle GT+4 (GTP).

BONNEVILLE CHASSIS: Wheelbase: 110.8 in. (all). Overall length: 198.7 in. (all). Width: 72.1 in. (all). Height: 54.1 in. (all). Front tread: 60.3 in. Rear tread: 59.8 in. Standard tires: 205/70R14 BSW (LE). Standard tires: 215/65R15 Goodyear Eagle GT+4 (SE). Standard tires: P215/60R16 BSW (SSE).

TRANS SPORT CHASSIS: Wheelbase: 109.8 in. (all). Overall length: 194.5 in. (all). Width: 74.6 in. (all). Height: 65.2 in. (all). Standard tires: 205/70R-14 BSW (Base). Standard tires: P205/65R-15 (SE).

LEMANS TECHNICAL: Chassis: Front engine/front drive. Standard transmission: Four-speed manual (Aerocoupe only). Standard transmission: Five-speed manual (LE only). Optional transmission: Three-speed automatic (LE only). Axle ratio: 3.43:1 with 1.6L and automatic. Axle ratio: 3.72:1 (both manual). Front suspension: deflected disc, MacPherson struts and 22mm stabilizer bar. Rear suspension: Coil springs, semi-independent torsion beam, trailing arms, and 18mm anti-roll bar. Steering: Rack-and-pinion 24.5:1 ratio (18.3:1 power-assisted optional LEs). Turns lock-to-lock: 3.5 (power); 4.57 (manual). Turning circle: 32.8 ft. Front brakes: 9.25-in. vented discs. Rear brakes: 7.9 x 1.8 -in. drums (power-assisted}.

SUNBIRD TECHNICAL: Chassis: Front engine/front drive. Base transmission: Five-speed manual. Optional transmission: Three-speed automatic. Axle ratio: 3.45:1 with 2.0-liter engine and five-speed manual. Axle ratio: 3.18:1 with 2.0L TBI engine and three-speed automatic. Axle ratio: 3.45:1 with 3.1-liter V-6 and five-speed manual. Axle ratio: 2.08:1 with 3.1-liter V-6 and three-speed automatic in Base Sunbird. Axle ratio: 2.53:1 with 3.1-liter V-6 and three-speed automatic in SE and Base Sunbird. Axle ratio: 2.84:1 with 3.1-liter V-6 and three-speed automatic in LE Convertible and SE. Front suspension: deflected disc, MacPherson struts and (22mm with 2.0L TBI/28mm with 3.1L MFI) stabilizer bars. Rear suspension: Coil springs, semi-independent torsion beam, trailing arms (and 21mm anti-roll bar with 3.1L MFI). Steering: Rack-and-pinion 16.0:1 ratio (14.0:1 on GT). Turns lock-to-lock: 3.0 (2.5 on GT). Turning circle: 34.3 ft. (all). Front brakes: 9.72-in. vented disc power-assisted. Rear brakes: 7.87 x 1.77-in. drum power-assisted.

1991 Pontiac Grand Am LE four-door sedan. PMD

GRAND AM TECHNICAL: Chassis: Front engine/front drive. Base transmission: Five-speed manual with overdrive. Optional transmission: Three-speed automatic. Axle ratio: 3.18:1 (with 2.3L and 2.5L engines and automatic SE). Axle ratio: 2.84:1 (with 2.3L and 2.5L engines and automatic LE). Axle ratio: 3.35:1 (with 2.5L engine and manual). Axle ratio: 3.61:1 (with 2.3L HO engine and manual). Stall torque ratio: 2.48:1 (2.3L with automatic). Stall torque ratio: 2.35:1 (2.5L with automatic). Front suspension: MacPherson struts with coil springs and 24mm anti-roll bar (28mm anti-roll bar with Sport Performance and WS6 suspensions). Rear suspension: Trailing crank arm with twist arm, coil springs, (and 21mm anti-roll bar with Sport Performance and WS6 suspensions). Steering (Standard): Power-assisted rack-and-pinion, 16.0:1 ratio, 2.88 turns lock-to-lock, and 35.4-ft. (left); 37.8-ft. (right) turning circle. Steering (Sport Performance and WS6): Power-assisted rack-and-pinion, 14.0:1 ratio, 2.5 turns lock-to-lock, and 35.4-ft. (left); 37.8-ft. (right) turning circle. Front brakes: Power-assisted 10.24-in. vented discs. Rear brakes: Power-assisted 7.87-in. drums. (ABS standard on SE). Fuel tank: 13.6 gal.

FIREBIRD TECHNICAL: Chassis: Front engine/rear drive. Base transmission: Four-speed automatic (Firebird/GTA). Optional transmission: Five-speed manual. (Formula/Trans Am). Front suspension: Modified MacPherson strut with 30mm (FE1), 34mm (F41), or 36mm (WS6) anti-roll bar. Rear suspension: Live axle with coil springs, control arms, torque arm, track bar, and 18mm (FE1) or 23mm (F41 and WS6) anti-roll bar. Steering: Power recirculating ball, 14.0:1 ratio (FE1), or 12.7:1 quick ratio with sport effort valving (F41 and WS6). Turns lock-to-lock: 2.57 (FE1), or 2.14 (F41 and WS6). Turning circle: 38.5 ft. (FE1) or 38.5 ft. (F41 and WS6). Brakes: Power vented 10.5-in. front disc/9.5 x 2.0-in. rear drum. Fuel tank: 15.5 gal.

6000 TECHNICAL: Chassis: Front engine/front drive. Base transmission: Three-speed automatic with overdrive. Optional transmission: Four-speed automatic. Axle ratio: 2.84:1 (with three-speed automatic and 2.5L or 3.1L engines). Axle ratio: 3.33:1 (with four-speed automatic and 3.1L engine). Front suspension: MacPherson struts with 14.5 N-mm coil springs on LE (16 N-mm on S/E; and 23.5 N-mm Fleet models) and 22mm (27mm on S/E and 24mm all Wagons) anti-roll bars. Rear suspension: Trailing arm and open channel, Panhard rod track bar, and 26.9 N-mm coil springs on LE Sedan (32 N-mm on LE Wagon and S/E Sedan (*), and 22mm anti-roll bar on S/E, 20mm anti-roll bar standard. Steering: Power-assisted rack-and-pinion with 17.5:1 ratio, 3.05 turns lock-to-lock and 36.96-ft. turning circle. Front brakes: Power assisted vented discs 9.72-in. (standard); 10.24-in. (medium-/heavy-duty). Rear brakes: Power assisted 8.86-in. drum (all). Fuel tank: 15.7-gal.

(*) Fleet model rear suspension has 40.5 N-mm coil springs for Sedan and 48.3 N-mm for Wagon.

GRAND PRIX TECHNICAL: Chassis: Front engine/front drive. Standard drive train: 2.3L Quad-4 with three-speed automatic transaxle. Optional drive train: 3.1L MFI V-6 with five-speed manual transaxle. Optional drivetrain: 3.4L Twin Dual Cam V-6 with five-speed manual transaxle. Axle ratio: 3.18 (2.3L with three-speed automatic). Axle ratio: 3.33 (3.1L MFI V-6 with four-speed automatic). Axle ratio: 3.67 (3.4L with five-speed manual). Axle ratio: 3.43 (3.4L with four-speed manual). Front suspension: MacPherson struts with tapered top coil springs, lower A arm and 28mm anti-roll bar (34mm anti-roll bar with Y99 suspension). Rear suspension: Tri-link independent suspension with 12mm anti-roll bar (transverse fiberglass leaf spring and 12mm anti-roll bar with 3.1L; 14mm anti-roll bar with 3.4-liter engine.). Steering: Power-assisted rack-and-pinion with 15.7:1 ratio (14.0:1 with Y99 3.4-liter; 15.7:1 with 3.1-liter engine). 2.6 turns lock-to-lock, and 36.77-ft. turning circle (standard). Steering: Power-assisted rack-and-pinion with 15.7:1 ratio, 2.25 turns lock-to-lock, and 39.7-ft. turning circle (STE with Y99). Four-wheel power disc brakes. Front brakes: 10.5-in. x 1.04-in. composite vented discs. Rear brakes: 10.1-in. x 0.5-in. composite solid discs. Fuel tank: 15.5 gal.

BONNEVILLE TECHNICAL: Chassis: Front engine/front drive. Base transmission: Four-speed automatic. Axle ratio: 2.84:1 (standard with 3.8L V-6 in Bonneville LE). Axle ratio: 2.97:1 (standard with 3.8L V-6 in Bonneville SSE.) Axle ratio: 3.33:1 (standard with 3.8L V-6 in Bonneville SSE). Front suspension: MacPherson struts with 20 N-mm coil springs and 28mm anti-roll bar (LE). Front suspension: MacPherson struts with 24.2 N-mm coil springs and 32mm anti-roll bar (SE). Front suspension: MacPherson struts with 24 N-mm coil springs and 32mm anti-roll bar (SSE). Rear suspension: MacPherson struts with variable rate (48-65 N-mm) coil springs and 14mm anti-roll bar (LE). Rear suspension: MacPherson struts with variable-rate (55-65 N-mm) coil springs and 18mm anti-roll bar (SE). Rear suspension: MacPherson struts with 47 N-mm coil springs and 18mm anti-roll bar (SSE). Steering: Power-assisted rack-and-pinion with 18.1:1 constant ratio, 2.97 turns lock-to-lock, and 39.7-ft. left/39.0-ft. right turning circle (LE/SE). Steering: Power-assisted rack-and-pinion with 15.3:1 to 18.0:1 variable ratio, 2.79 turns lock-to-lock, and 38.4-ft. left/40.7-ft. right turning circle (SSE). Front brakes: Power-assisted 10.1-in. vented discs. Rear brakes: Power-assisted 8.9-in. drums. Anti-lock brake system standard with SSE. Fuel tank: 18.0 gal.

TRANS SPORT TECHNICAL: Chassis: Front engine/front drive. Transmission: Three-speed automatic. Axle ratio: 3.18:1 (all). Front suspension: MacPherson struts with 24 N-mm coil springs and 30mm anti-roll bar (LE). Front suspension: MacPherson strut, stamped lower control arms, 28mm stabilizer bar. Rear suspension: Open-section transverse beam on stamped steel trailing arms, tube shocks, coil springs and 25.4mm stabilizer bar. Steering: Power-assisted rack-and-pinion with 15.7:1 ratio, and 38-ft. turning circle. Front brakes: Power-assisted 10.2-in. vented rotors, 182 sq. in. swept area. Rear brakes: Power-assisted 8.86 x 1.58-in. finned composite cast iron drums with 98.5 sq. in. swept area. Fuel tank: 20.0 gal.

LEMANS OPTIONS: R6A value package for Value Leader model ($662). R6A Value package for SE model ($355). MX1 three-speed automatic transmission ($475). C60 air conditioning, requires power steering and not available in Value Leader Aerocoupe ($705). B37 front and rear floor mats ($33). N40 power steering, requires air conditioning in Aerocoupe or SE Sedan ($225). UM7 Delco ETR stereo in Value Leader Aerocoupe ($307). UM6 Delco ETR AM/FM with cassette and more in Value Leader Aerocoupe ($429). UM6 Delco ETR AM/FM with cassette and more in LE/SE/GSE ($122). AD3 removable sun roof ($350). WDV warranty enhancements for New York ($65).

SUNBIRD OPTIONS: 1SB Sunbird LE Coupe and Sedan option group #1 ($158). 1SC Sunbird LE Coupe and Sedan ($914). 1SD Sunbird LE Coupe and Sedan ($1114). 1SB Sunbird LE Convertible ($910). 1SC Sunbird LE Convertible ($804). 1SB Sunbird SE Coupe and Sedan ($910). 1SC option for SE Coupe and Sedan ($1470). 1SB Sunbird GT Coupe ($862-$910). LHO engine, except no cost in GT ($660). MX1 three-speed automatic transmission ($495). C60 air conditioning ($745). DO6 front seat armrest in GT and SE ($58). NB2 California emissions ($100). K34 cruise control ($225). A90 remote deck lid release ($60). AO1 tinted glass ($105). TR9 lamp group

($29). AU3 power door locks ($210-$250). A31 power windows, requires power door locks ($265 SE/GT Coupe/$330 Sedan/no charge Convertible). UM6 Delco radio equipment ($170 additional). U1C Delco radio equipment ($396). U39 rally gauges ($127). AM9 split folding rear seat ($150). T43 rear deck lip spoiler on LE Convertible ($70). N33 tilt steering wheel ($135). AD3 removable glass sun roof ($350). CD4 controlled cycle wipers on LE ($65). B20 white vinyl trim on LE Convertible ($75). D84 Custom two-tone paint on LE ($101). WDV New York warranty enhancements ($65). QME touring tires ($114). N78 14-in. Hi-Tech Turbo aluminum wheels ($275).

GRAND AM OPTIONS: 1SB package on LE Coupe ($810). 1SC package on LE Coupe ($1265). 1SB package on LE Sedan ($850). 1SC package on LE Sedan ($1370). R6A Value option package on SE Coupe and Sedan ($394). LD2 Quad-4 2.3-liter MPI engine in SE models ($660). LD2 Quad-4 2.3-liter MPI engine in GT models ($140 credit). LGO Quad-4 HO engine (standard on SE and LE with manual shift and W32 performance package) ($555). W32 Sport Performance package including monotone paint treatment, Hi-Tech Turbo aluminum wheels, fog lamps, aero body skirting, rally cluster and more ($1271-$1650 depending upon option pairings). UB3 rally gauge cluster ($127). C60 air conditioning ($745). NB2 California emissions ($100). K34 cruise control ($225). A90 remote deck lid release ($60). C49 electric rear window defogger ($170). V56 luggage carrier ($115). AU3 power door locks ($210-$250). AC3 power driver seat in SE ($305). A31 express down power windows in SE and GT Coupe ($275). A31 express down power window in SE or GT Sedan ($340). AM9 split folding rear seat ($150). N33 tilt steering ($145). AD3 removable glass sun roof ($350). CD4 controlled cycle wipers ($65). AR9 Custom cloth reclining seats with Pallex cloth in base and LE and Metrix cloth in SE (no charge). WDV warranty enhancements ($65). UM6 Delco sound system ($140). U1D Delco sound system ($405-$545). QME touring tires with Ride & Handling suspension ($114). N78 14-in. Hi-Tech Turbo aluminum wheels ($275).

1991 Pontiac Firebird Trans Am GTA coupe. PMD

FIREBIRD OPTIONS: 1SB Firebird V-6 option group ($888). 1SB Firebird V-8 option group ($33). 1SB Formula/Trans Am option group ($223). 1SB Firebird V-8 Convertible ($225).1SB Trans Am Convertible option group ($183). 1SC Firebird V-6 option group ($979). 1SC Firebird V-8 option group ($419).1SC Formula option group ($419). 1SC Trans Am option group ($384). R6A Firebird and Formula value package ($820). R6B Value Option package Firebird and Formula ($814). R6A Trans Am value package ($889). R6A Trans AM GTA Value Option package ($1020). LO3 5.0-liter TBI V-8 engine in base Firebird ($350). LB9 5.0L MPI V-8 in Formula and Trans Am ($745). B2L 5.7L MPI V-8 in Trans Am ($300). B2L 5.7L MPI V-8 in Formula ($1045). MM5 five-speed manual transmission in Trans Am GTA with LB9 ($515 credit). MXO four-speed automatic transmission, except in GTA ($530). C60 air conditioning ($830). G80 limited-slip axle ($100). K34 cruise control, except GTA ($225). A90 rear deck lid release in Trans Am ($60). C49 rear window defogger, except GTA ($170). NB2 California emissions ($100). CC1 Hatch roof ($920). DG7 dual Sport mirror, left-hand remote-control, except GTA ($91). R6P Performance Enhancement group with dual converter exhaust, four-wheel disc brake, engine oil cooler and more ($265). AU3 power door locks ($210). A31 power windows ($280). U75 power antenna ($85). UX1 Delco sound system ($150). U1A Delco radio equipment ($226-$376). D42 cargo area security screen ($69). AH3 four-way adjustable power driver seat, except GTA ($35). AR9 Custom Pallex cloth reclining bucket seat, no cost option, but not available on GTA. AQ9 articulating bucket seats with Ventura leather trim in GTA ($450). W68 Sport Appearance package with front and rear Trans Am fascias, fog lamps, and Trans Am aero side moldings for Firebird only ($450). QLC high-performance WS6 performance suspension ($313). WDV New York warranty enhancements ($25).

6000 OPTIONS: 1SB option package #1 for 6000 LE Sedan ($1009). 1SC option package #2 for 6000 LE Sedan ($1024). 1SD option package #3 for 6000 LE Sedan ($1399). 1SB option package #1 for 6000 LE Wagon ($190). 1SC option package #2 for 6000 LE Wagon ($400). 1SD option package #3 for 6000 LE Wagon ($570). 1SB option package #1 for 6000 S/E Sedan ($73). R6A value option package for 6000 LE Sedan ($463). R6B value option package for 6000 LE Sedan ($478). R6B value option package for 6000 LE Sedan ($248). R6B Value Option package for LE wagon ($518). LHO 3.1-

liter MFI V-6 in LE Sedan ($660). MXO four-speed automatic transmission ($200). C60 air conditioning ($830). K34 cruise control ($225). A90 rear deck lid release ($60). C49 electric rear window defogger ($170). D86 two-tone paint ($115). AU3 power door locks ($250-$290). A31 power windows ($345). B34 front and rear carpet mats ($45). AG1 power seat ($305). UM6 Delco ETR AM/FM stereo ($140). UX1 Delco ETR AM stereo/FM stereo ($310). UA1 Delco sound system ($536). A65 three-passenger seating in base LE ($183). B20 custom interior with 45/55 split seat in Metrix cloth ($350-$533). Various tire options (no charge to $68). N78 Sport aluminum wheels with locking package ($275). BX3 wood-grain exterior siding for Wagon ($295).

GRAND PRIX OPTIONS: 1SB Grand Prix LE ($190). 1SC Grand Prix LE ($400). 1SB Grand Prix SE Sedan ($415). 1SC Grand Prix SE Sedan ($533). 1SD Grand Prix SE Sedan ($869). 1SB Grand Prix SE Coupe ($190). 1SC Grand Prix SE Coupe ($415). 1SD Grand Prix SE Coupe ($428). 1SE Grand Prix SE Coupe ($764). 1SB Grand Prix GT Coupe ($411). 1SB Grand Prix STE Sedan ($500). R6A Value Option for Grand Prix SE Coupe ($703). R6B Value Option package for Grand Prix SE Coupe ($733). R6A Value Option Package for Grand Prix SE Sedan ($699). R6B Value Option package for Grand Prix SE Sedan ($399). R6A Value Option package for Grand Prix GT Coupe ($825). R6B Value Option package for Grand Prix GT Coupe ($801). R6A Value Option package for Grand Prix STE Sedan ($801). MXO four-speed automatic in Grand Prix SE ($200). A90 remote deck lid release ($60). C49 electric rear window defogger ($170). NB2 California emissions system ($100). D84 two-tone paint ($105). JL9 power antilock brakes ($925). CF5 power glass sun roof ($670-$695). AUO Remote Keyless Entry system ($135). UB3 rally gauge cluster with tach ($85). UV6 heads-up display, requires Graphite, Gray or Beige interior trim and bucket seats ($250). V56 rear deck lid luggage carrier ($115). B37 front and rear carpet mats ($45). DG7 dual Sport mirrors ($78). DH6 dual illuminated visor vanity mirrors ($86). A31 power windows on Coupe ($275). A31 power windows on Sedan ($340). AU3 power door locks on Coupe ($210). AU3 power door locks on Sedan ($250). B20 Custom interior trim ($324-$328). BYP Sport Appearance package with lower aero ground effects ($595-$680 depending on model and other options). B4U Aero Appearance package ($2795). Y99 rally handling suspension ($50). UM6 Delco radio equipment ($140). UX1 Delco radio equipment ($540-$590). U1A stereo sound system ($226-$816 depending on model). AR9 bucket seat with Pallex cloth trim in Grand Prix LE ($110). AN3 Custom Cloth bucket seat in Grand Prix LE ($140). AC3 power seat ($305). B20 Custom interior trim ($328). PH3 15-in. aluminum sport wheels with locking package ($275). WDV warranty enhancements for New York ($65).

BONNEVILLE OPTIONS: 1SB Bonneville LE option package ($269). 1SC Bonneville LE option package ($629). 1SD Bonneville LE option package ($1039). 1SB Bonneville SE option package ($265). 1SC Bonneville SE option package ($315). 1SB Bonneville SSE option package ($1259). R6A Bonneville LE value option package ($408). R6A Bonneville SSE value option package ($1080). C49 electric rear window defogger ($170). NB2 California emissions system ($100). D84 Custom two-tone paint ($105). JM4 power front disc/rear drum ABS brakes ($925). AU3 power door locks ($250). A31 power windows ($410). AUO remote keyless entry system ($136). Z05 Convenience package ($315). US7 power antenna ($85). UM6 Delco radio equipment ($140). UX1 Delco sound system ($615-$805). U1A compact disc player ($226-$1031). AS7 45/45 split front seat with console and London/Empress cloth trims for LE and SE models ($235). B320 Custom interior trim ($130-$620). AG1 power seat ($305). CF5 power glass sun roof ($1230). PXO 16-in. spoke cast aluminum wheels ($340). PF7 15-in. six-spoke cast aluminum wheels ($306). QPJ touring tires ($76). QGW touring tires ($88). WDV warranty enhancements ($65).

1991 Pontiac Trans Sport SE minivan. PMD

TRANS SPORT OPTIONS: 1SB Trans Sport option package #1 ($1210). 1SC Trans Sport option package #2 ($935). 1SB Trans Sport SE option package #1 ($275). R6A Value Option package for Trans Sport ($348). C67 air conditioning in Trans Sport ($830). V54 luggage rack ($145). NB2 California emissions system ($100). DG7 dual outside mirrors ($48). C49 electric rear window defogger ($170). AJ1 glass package in Trans Sport ($245). AB5 power door locks ($290-$300). A31 power windows ($275). UM6 Delco radio equipment ($140). U1A compact disc player ($376-$516). AB3 six-passenger seating package ($525). ZP7 seven-passenger seating package ($675). Rear air distribution system ($110). N78 14-in. aluminum wheels ($275).

Note: Full option package contents, descriptions and applications information can often be determined by consulting factory literature. The data above is edited for size and clarity. This information provided only as a guide to help collectors appraise the relative value of cars with numerous options. Prices for items included as part of a value option package are usually much less than individual prices. Option prices charged by individual dealers may also vary.

1992 PONTIAC

PONTIAC I.D. NUMBERS: Vehicle identification number (VIN) is located on top left-hand surface of instrument panel visible through the windshield. The VIN has 17 symbols. The first symbol indicates the country of manufacture (U.S.) The second symbol indicates the manufacturer (G=General Motors). The third symbol indicates the make/division (2=Pontiac). The fourth, fifth, and sixth symbols are the same as the body style (model) number. The eighth symbol indicates the engine. The ninth symbol is a check digit. The 10th symbol indicates model-year. The 11th symbol indicates the assembly plant. The last six symbols are the consecutive serial number at the factory.

LEMANS -- SERIES 2T -- FOUR -- The Pontiac LeMans was based on the German Opel Kadett and built in Korea. The 1992 LeMans line consisted of the SE "Value Leader" Aerocoupe, the SE Aerocoupe, and the SE Sedan. New for 1992 was a sport-tuned exhaust system, amber section taillights, revised engine calibration, new Bright Yellow (Aerocoupe) paint, and the SE badge replacing the LE badge. Standard equipment on the LeMans SE "Value Leader" included a 1.6-liter TBI engine, four-speed manual transmission, P175/70R13 blackwall tires, 9.25-in. vented front disc brakes, steel wheels, Custom wheel covers, wide body side moldings, and a Custom two-spoke sport steering wheel. The LeMans SE Aerocoupe added or substituted a five-speed manual transmission, styled steel wheels, a three-spoke steering wheel, and a Delco AM/FM stereo with clock. The LeMans SE Sedan had all the same equipment as the SE "Value Leader" Aerocoupe, plus a five-speed manual transmission and a Delco AM/FM stereo with clock.

LEMANS -- SERIES 2T -- I-4

Model Number	Body/Style Number	Body Type & Seating	Factory Price	Shipping Weight	Prod. Total
2T	TX2	3-dr V/L Cpe-4P	8050	2164	Note 1
2T	TN2	3-dr SE Cpe-4P	8750	2186	Note 1
2T	TN5	4-dr SE Sed-4P	9465	2241	Note 1

NOTE 1: LeMans series production totaled 19,499.

SUNBIRD -- SERIES 2J --FOUR -- Over half the buyers of Sunbirds were under 35 years old. This was the affordable Pontiac model's 10th anniversary. There were three series: LE, SE, and GT. A Convertible came in the SE line. New functional features included the addition of multi-point fuel injection (and 17 hp) to the 2.0-liter engine, standard antilock brakes on all models, the addition of a brake/transmission shift interlock, and a 1.6-gal. larger fuel tank. There were also four exterior updates: new optional 14- and 15-in. SE wheel covers, a monotone appearance for the GT, monotone LE and SE appearances with red stripes, and four new exterior colors. On the interior, the 1992 models had standard automatic door locks, new interior door trim on Coupes and Convertibles, new front seats and seat fabrics on all models, and a new Graphite interior color. Standard equipment on the Sunbird LE Coupe and Sedan included the 2.0-liter MPFI V-6 engine, five-speed manual transmission, antilock brakes, P185/75R14 tires, power rack and pinion steering, a Delco ETR AM/FM stereo with seek-and-scan and clock, a stainless steel exhaust system, an illuminated entry system, and automatic door locks. The Sunbird SE Coupe and Sedan had the same basics, while the Sunbird SE Convertible added a fully automatic electro-hydraulic top, reclining front bucket seats with grid cloth trim, power door locks, power windows, dual sport mirrors, and tinted glass. A new Convertible option was the "Special Appearance Package," which included white accents, white body striping, 15-in. aluminum wheels, and nameplate decals with any one of five exterior colors. A white vinyl trim interior was also available for ragtops. The Sunbird GT added or substituted a 3.1-liter MPFI V-6, P195/65R15 Goodrich T/A touring tires, a dual exhaust system, 15-in. machine-faced aluminum wheels, tinted glass, and a rear deck lid spoiler.

Model Number	Body/Style Number	Body Type & Seating	Factory Price	Shipping Weight	Prod. Total
SUNBIRD LE -- SERIES 2J -- I-4					
2J	JC5	4-dr Sed-5P	9720	2502	Note 1
2J	JC1	2-dr Cpe-5P	9620	2484	Note 1
SUNBIRD SE -- SERIES 2J -- I-4					
2J	JB5	4-dr Sed-5P	10480	2502	Note 1
2J	JB1	2-dr Cpe-5P	10380	2484	Note 1
2J	JB3	2-dr Conv-5P	15345	2694	Note 1
SUNBIRD GT -- SERIES 2J -- V-6					
2J	JD1	2-dr Cpe-5P	12820	2682	Note 1

NOTE 1: Sunbird series production totaled 73,979.

GRAND AM -- SERIES 2N -- Pontiac's most popular car-line was dramatically redesigned for 1992. Available were SE and GT Coupes and Sedans. The dramatic exterior styling stressed aerodynamic enhancements. Each body style had its own distinctive roof design and flush-mounted window glass with door frames that wrapped into the roof for better entry and exit. The rear doors of Sedans were larger and opened 80 degrees from closed position. Sedans also came with fully retracting rear windows. Though on the same wheelbase as 1991, the Grand Ams were longer and had more interior room. All models now featured two-side galvanized steel body panels and stainless steel exhaust systems. Exterior lighting was enhanced with new high-strength headlamp composite material (polycarbonate). Functional changes included new 2.3-liter Quad 4 and 3.3-liter V-6 engines, ABS on all models, a larger fuel tank, electronic variable orifice (EVO) steering, torque-axis engine mountings, new brake/transmission shift interlock, a more rounded aerodynamic body appearance, split grilles, ribbed body side moldings, and engine tuning and cam chain enhancements. Exterior updates included wrap-in lamps all around, standard fog lamps, flush body-color door handles, a rear deck-mounted radio antenna, low lift-over trunks, high-mounted back lights, and all double-galvanized sheet metal. Interior upgrades included a more comfortable rear seating package, new instrument panel, new console, new door panels, twin instrument panel gloveboxes, cup storage provisions, an easy-access fuse panel, a headliner storage console, a new instrument cluster, column-mounted lights/wiper controls, new seat fabrics, revised radio appearances, and standard automatic door locks. Standard equipment on SE models included fog lamps, monotone paint treatments with wide body side moldings, P185/75R14 tires, bolt-on 14-in. wheelcovers, Delco ETR AM/FM stereo with auto-reversing cassette, 2.3-liter Quad OHC four-cylinder engine, five-speed manual transmission, ABS brakes, and power rack-and-pinion steering. The GT added or substituted aero body moldings, dual/dual chrome-tipped exhaust outlets, neutral-density taillights, P205/55R16 tires, specific 16-in cast aluminum wheels, rally gauges with a tachometer, and a 2.3-liter H.O. DOHC 16-valve four-cylinder engine.

1992 Pontiac Grand Am SE four-door sedan. PMD

Model Number	Body/Style Number	Body Type & Seating	Factory Price	Shipping Weight	Prod. Total
GRAND AM SE SERIES 2N -- Quad 4					
2N	NE1	2-dr Cpe-5P	11899	2728	Note 1
2N	NE5	4-dr Sed-5P	11999	2777	Note 1
GRAND AM SE -- SERIES 2N --V-6					
2N	NE1	2-dr Cpe-5P	12359	-	Note 1
2N	NE5	4-dr Sed-5P	12459	-	Note 1
GRAND AM GT -- SERIES 2N --Quad 4					
2N	NW1	2-dr Cpe-5P	13699	2804	Note 1
2N	NW5	4-dr Sed-5P	13799	2846	Note 1

NOTE 1: Grand Am series production totaled 190,025.

1992 Pontiac Firebird Trans Am convertible. PMD

FIREBIRD -- SERIES 2F -- V-6/V-8 -- Pontiac announced the first Firebird Convertible in 21 years in 1991 and only 2000 were built. The open model was continued in 1992. The full line consisted of Firebird, Firebird Formula, Trans Am, and Trans Am GTA models. The Convertible was available as a base Firebird, or as a Trans Am. Other changes for 1992 included structural enhancements and non-asbestos brake pads. New Yellow, Dark Jade Gray Metallic, and Dark Aqua Metallic exterior paint colors were also added. The interiors had revised AM/FM cassette radio graphics, and new knobs and rings, plus a revised Beige interior. Standard features of the base Firebird included a 3.1-liter MPFI V-6, five-speed manual transmission, FE1 suspension, P215/65R15 tires, 15x7-in. Hi-Tech aluminum wheels, disc/drum brakes, and Delco ETR AM/FM stereo with auto-reverse, cassette and clock. The Firebird Formula added or substituted a 5.0-liter EFI V-8, WS6 Sport suspension, P245/50ZR16 tires, 15x7-in. deep-dish High-Tech aluminum wheels, air conditioning, and a leather appointment group with leather-wrapped steering wheel. The Trans Am added or substituted the following over base Firebird features: 5.0-liter TPI V-8, F41 Rally-Tuned suspension, P215/60R16 tires, 16x8-in. diamond-spoke wheels, limited-slip differential, aero package with special side treatment, and air conditioning. The Trans AM GTA added or substituted the following over the Trans Am: 5.7-liter TPI V-8, four-speed automatic transmission, WS6 Sport suspension, P245/50ZR16 tires, dual converters and performance axle, Delco ETR AM/FM stereo with CD and five-band equalizer, power antenna, leather appointment group, four-way manual driver's seat adjuster, power windows and door locks, cruise control, remote deck lid release, rear window defogger, and power outside mirrors. Both Convertibles came with a choice of black or beige cloth tops that stowed away neatly, under a tonneau cover. Both ragtops carried the aero package as standard equipment (including fog lights, brake cooling ducts in the front fascias, and a distinctive body side treatment). The Trans Am Convertible also had functional hood louvers, air extractors, and available leather-clad articulated bucket seats.

Model Number	Body/Style Number	Body Type & Seating	Factory Price	Shipping Weight	Prod. Total
FIREBIRD -- SERIES 2F -- V-6					
2F	FS2	2-dr Cpe-5P	12505	3121	Note 1
2F	FS3	2-dr Conv-5P	19375	3280	Note 1
FIREBIRD -- SERIES 2F -- V-8					
2F	FS2	2-dr Cpe-5P	12874	3281	Note 1
2F	FS3	2-dr Conv-5P	19744	3440	Note 1
FIREBIRD FORMULA -- SERIES 2F -- V-8					
2F	FS2	2-dr Cpe-5P	16205	3370	Note 1
FIREBIRD TRANS AM -- SERIES 2F -- V-8					
2F	FW2	2-dr Cpe-5P	18105	3343	Note 1
2F	FW3	2-dr Conv-5P	23875	3441	Note 1
FIREBIRD TRANS AM GTA -- SERIES 2F -- V-8					
2F	FW2	2-dr Cpe-5P	25880	3456	Note 1

NOTE 1: Firebird series production totaled 25,180.

GRAND PRIX -- SERIES 2G -- V-6/V-8 -- Pontiac's sporty mid-size car line had enhanced styling and performance for 1992. The focus for the year was on strengthening the Grand Prix Sedan lineup, and increasing the status of the LE Sedan. Functional improvements for 1992 were: Standard antilock brakes on the GT, GTP, and STE models; a standard 3.1-liter V-6 for LEs and SEs (replacing a 2.3-liter engine); a second gear start switch available with a 3.4-liter automatic drivetrain; a new 3.4-liter DOHC V-6 available for LE Sedans; new P215/60R16 touring

tires standard on the SE Sedan; and P225/60R15 Eagle GT+4 tires standard on the STE. Exterior changes included a new LE Sedan with an STE-inspired appearance; grid pattern GT taillights for the LE and SE models; new 16-in. five-blade aluminum wheels for the SE Sedan and GT Coupe (and required on the LE Sedan with 3.4-liter V-6); red molding insert stripes for SE Sedans; an optional Sport Appearance package for SE Sedans; and four new body colors (Bright Aqua, Light Gray, Light Beige, and Jade Gray). In addition, three new interior colors (Graphite, Gray, and Beige) were offered. Each of six models had equipment distinctions, with the important standard features as follows. SE Coupe: 3.1-liter MFI V-6, three-speed automatic transmission, 15-in. bolt-on wheel covers, P20570R15 touring tires, air conditioning, 45/55 split reclining front seats (or articulated power bucket seats with thigh, lumbar, and lateral support), and Delco ETR AM/FM stereo with clock. GT Coupe: 3.1-liter MFI V-6, four-speed automatic transmission, Y99 Rally tuned suspension, ABS brakes, 16-in. cast aluminum wheels, P225/60R16 Eagle GT+4 tires, air conditioning, power windows, power door locks, power bucket seats with thigh, lumbar and lateral support, cruise control, and Delco ETR AM/FM stereo cassette with equalizer and steering wheel controls, and six-speaker sound system. GTP Coupe: 3.4-liter Twin Dual Cam V-6, five-speed manual transmission, Y99 Rally Tuned suspension, ABS brakes, aero performance package, P245/50ZR16 tires, air conditioning, power windows, power door locks, power drover's seat, cruise control, Delco ETR AM/FM stereo cassette with equalizer and steering wheel controls, and six-speaker sound system. LE Sedan: 3.1-liter MFI V-6, three-speed automatic transmission, 15-in. bolt-on wheel covers, P205/70R15 touring tires, air conditioning, 45/55 split reclining front seats, and Delco ETR AM/FM stereo with clock. SE Sedan: 3.1-liter MFI V-6, three-speed automatic transmission, 15-in. bolt-on wheel covers (or 16-in. cast aluminum wheels), P215/60R16 touring tires, air conditioning, 45/55 split reclining front seats (or articulated power bucket seats with thigh, lumbar and lateral support), and Delco ETR AM/FM stereo with clock. STE Sedan: 3.1-liter MFI V-6, four-speed automatic transmission, Y99 Rally Tuned suspension, P225/60R16 Eagle GT+4 tires, electronic information center, air conditioning, power windows, power door locks, power driver's seat, cruise control, remote keyless entry system, Delco ETR AM/FM cassette stereo with equalizer and steering wheel controls, and eight-speaker sound system with sub-woofer amplifier.

Model Number	Body/Style Number	Body Type & Seating	Factory Price	Shipping Weight	Prod. Total
GRAND PRIX LE -- SERIES 2W --V-6					
2G	WH5	4-dr Sed-5P	14890	3243	Note 1
GRAND PRIX SE -- SERIES 2W -- V-6					
2G	WJ5	4-dr Sed-5P	16190	3282	Note 1
2G	WJ1	2-dr Cpe-5P	15390	3214	Note 1
GRAND PRIX STE -- SERIES 2W -- V-6					
2G	WT5	4-dr Sed-5P	21635	3434	Note 1
GRAND PRIX GT-- SERIES 2W -- V-6					
2G	WP1	2-dr Cpe-5P	20340	3357	Note 1

NOTE 1: Grand Prix series production totaled 106,583.

BONNEVILLE -- SERIES 2H -- V-6 -- The Bonneville's 35th year was celebrated with some progress in styling and more standard features than ever before. Major changes to the exterior and interior and a new Sport package were the focus of the program for the SE, SSE, and SSEi models. An enhanced 3800 V-6 was standard (supercharged on SSEi), along with new torque-axis engine mounts, an electronic four-speed automatic transmission, dual airbags, anti theft deterrent system, ABS brakes, larger diameter front brakes, retained accessory power, a heated windshield on SSEi models, traction control on SSEi models, a heads-up instrument display on SSEi models, driver-selected transmission controls with the supercharged V-6, a Two-Flow Electronic variable-ratio steering (standard on SE with Sport Appearance package). New exterior features included all-new sheet metal, flush glass, two levels of new body fascias, new headlights, two levels of new taillights, standard round fog lights, three levels of new body side moldings, a low lift-over deck lid design, three types of new aluminum wheels, and two new tire types (depending on the model). Interior changes for 1992 were: new instrument panel, new floor console, new storage console and assist handles in upper-level headliners, three new seating levels, new fabrics on Level 1 trims, new front and rear door trim designs, new rear seat armrests with pass-through to trunk, new steering wheels with redundant radio controls, three levels of new dash clusters, and an eight-speaker sound system standard on SSEi. Major standard equipment varied by model. On SEs, the list included: driver's side airbag, rack-and-pinion power steering, 3.8-liter 3800 series TPI V-6, four-speed electronic automatic transmission, P215/65R15 blackwall touring tires, 15-in. bolt-on wheel covers, manual air conditioning, Delco ETR AM/FM stereo with seek-and-scan and clock, 45/55 reclining split seat with armrest, armrest rear seat with dual cup

holders and pass-through to trunk, express-down power windows, power door locks, black wide body moldings, and Pass-Key II theft deterrent system. On SSEs, the standard features list included: ABS brakes, driver's side airbag, rack-and-pinion variable-ratio power steering, 3.8-liter 3800 series TPI V-6, four-speed electronic automatic transmission, electric leveling system, P215/65R15 blackwall touring tires, 16-in. aerolite color-keyed (or silver) aluminum wheels, manual air conditioning, Delco ETR AM/FM cassette stereo with equalizer, six speakers and steering wheel controls, 45/45 bucket seats with console, armrest rear seat with dual cup holders and pass-through to trunk, driver information center, rear window defogger, express-down power windows, power door locks, Pass Key II theft deterrent system, ribbed monotone moldings appliqué, and monotone ground effects. On SSEis, the standard features list included: ABS brakes, dual front airbags, rack-and-pinion variable-ratio power steering, 3.8-liter 3800 series supercharged TPI V-6, four-speed electronic automatic transmission with selectable controls, electric leveling system, traction-control system, P225/60R16 Eagle GT+4 blackwall touring tires or P225/60ZR16 speed-rated GT+4 performance tires, 16-in. aerolite color-keyed (or silver) aluminum wheels, automatic air conditioning, Delco ETR AM/FM cassette stereo with equalizer, six speakers and steering wheel controls, 45/45 12-way articulating bucket seats with console and recliner controls, armrest rear seat with dual cup holders and pass-through to trunk, driver information center, rear window defogger, Remote Keyless entry system, illuminated entry system with retained accessory power, full-feature anti-theft system, express-down power windows, power door locks, Pass Key II theft deterrent system, ribbed monotone moldings appliqué, and monotone ground effects.

1992 Pontiac SSEi four-door sedan. PMD

Model Number	Body/Style Number	Body Type & Seating	Factory Price	Shipping Weight	Prod. Total
BONNEVILLE SE -- SERIES H -- V-6					
2H	HX5	4-dr Spt Sed-5P	185999	3362	Note 1
BONNEVILLE SSE -- SERIES H -- V-6					
2H	HZ5	4-dr Spt Sed-5P	23999	3507	Note 1
BONNEVILLE SSEi -- SERIES H -- V-6					
2H	HY5	4-dr Spt Sed-5P	28045	3607	Note 1

NOTE 1: Bonneville series production totaled 116,002.

TRANS SPORT -- SERIES 2U -- V-6 -- The 1992 Trans Sport again came in two models. They were renamed SE and GT. Functional changes for 1992 included an antilock braking system, a new optional trailer towing package, a standard 3800 series V-6 engine for the GT (optional on SE), a new rear air conditioning system, an integrated power roof antenna, and an optional Remote Keyless entry system. New for the exterior were steel wheels with 15-in. bolt-on wheel covers, new tire sizes and styles, and four new body colors. Interior updates included a four-way manual seat adjuster, an optional sun roof, rear "saddlebag" storage provisions, and a rear convenience net. Standard equipment on the SE included a 3.1-liter EFI V-6, three-speed automatic transmission, ABS brakes, P205/70R15 tires on 15-in. wheels, 15-in. bolt-on wheel covers, 2+3 seating with a bench seat in the second position, Delco ETR AM/FM radio with clock, and integrated roof antenna. The GT model's features list included the 3.8-liter EFI V-6, four-speed automatic transmission, ABS brakes, electronic ride control, P205/70R15 touring tires, Sport cast aluminum wheels, 2+2+2 seating, a leather steering wheel, tilt steering, cruise control, deep tinted glass, power outside rear view mirrors, electronic control front air conditioning, Delco ETR AM/FM stereo cassette radio, and integrated roof antenna.

Model Number	Body/Style Number	Body Type & Seating	Factory Price	Shipping Weight	Prod. Total
TRANS SPORT -- SERIES 2U -- V-6					
2U	U06	SE Wagon	16225	3599	Note 1
2U	U06	GT Wagon	20935	3678	Note 1

NOTE 1: Trans Sport series production totaled 30,900.

LEMANS ENGINES

[STANDARD ALL] Inline. OHV. Four-cylinder. Cast iron block. Aluminum head and intake manifold. Displacement: 97.5 cu. in. (1.6L). Bore & stroke: 3.11 x 3.21 in. Compression ratio: 8.6:1. Brake horsepower: 74 @ 5600 rpm. Torque: 90 lb.-ft. @ 2800 rpm. Fuel system: EFI/TBI. RPO Code: L73. Standard with four-speed manual LeMans SE "Value Leader" Aerocoupe; standard with five-speed manual transmission in other models. [VIN code 6].

SUNBIRD ENGINES

[STANDARD BASE/LE/SE] Inline. OHC. Four-cylinder. Cast iron block. Aluminum head and intake manifold. Displacement: 121 cu. in. (2.0L). Bore & stroke: 3.38 x 3.38 in. Compression ratio: 9.2:1. Brake horsepower: 111 @ 5200 rpm. Torque: 125 lb.-ft. @ 3600 rpm. Fuel system: EFI/MPFI. Code: LT2. Standard in Sunbird LE and Sunbird SE models. [VIN code K]. [STANDARD GT] V-block. OHV. Six-cylinder. Cast iron block and aluminum head. 191 cu. in. (3.1L). Bore & stroke: 3.50 x 3.31 in. Compression ratio: 8.8:1. Brake horsepower: 140 @ 4200 rpm. Torque: 185 lb.-ft. @ 3600 rpm. Fuel system: EFI/MPFI. [VIN code T].

GRAND AM ENGINES

[STANDARD SE] Inline. Quad-4 OHC. Cast iron block. Aluminum head and intake manifold. Displacement: 138 cu. in. (2.3.-liter). Bore & stroke: 3.63 x 3.35 in. Compression ratio: 9.5:1. Brake horsepower: 120 @ 5200 rpm. Torque: 140 lb.-ft. @ 3200 rpm. Fuel system: MPFI. RPO Code: L40. Standard in SE. [VIN code A]. [OPTIONAL SE] Inline. Quad-4 DOHC. 16-valve. Cast iron block. Aluminum head and intake manifold. Displacement: 138 cu. in. (2.3.-liter). Bore & stroke: 3.63 x 3.35 in. Compression ratio: 9.5:1. Brake horsepower: 160 @ 6200 rpm. Torque: 155 lb.-ft. @ 5200 rpm. Fuel system: MPFI. RPO Code: LD2. Optional in SE. [VIN code D]. [STANDARD GT] Inline. Quad-4 H.O. DOHC. 16-valve. Quad-4 High-Output. Cast iron block. Aluminum head and intake manifold. Displacement: 138 cu. in. (2.3-liter). Bore & stroke: 3.63 x 3.35 in. Compression ratio: 10.0:1. Brake horsepower: 180 @ 6200 rpm. Torque: 160 lb.-ft. @ 5200 rpm. Fuel system: MPFI. RPO Code: LG0. Standard and exclusive in Grand Am SE with five-speed Manual transmission. [VIN code A]. [OPTIONAL SE/GT] V-block. OHV. Six-cylinder. Cast iron block and aluminum head. 204 cu. in. (3.3L). Bore & stroke: 3.70 x 3.16 in. Compression ratio: 9.0:1. Brake horsepower: 160 @ 5200 rpm. Torque: 185 lb.-ft. @ 2000 rpm. Fuel system: MFI. RPO Code LG7. Optional in Grand Am SE and GT. [VIN code N].

FIREBIRD ENGINES

[FIREBIRD BASE V-6] V-block. OHV. Six-cylinder. Cast iron block and head. Aluminum intake manifold. Displacement: 191 cu. in. (3.1L). Bore & stroke: 3.50 x 3.31 in. Compression ratio: 8.8:1. Brake horsepower: 140 @ 4400 rpm. Torque: 185 lb.-ft. @ 3200 rpm. Fuel system: EFI/MFI. RPO Code: LHO. Standard in base Firebird. [VIN code T]. [FIREBIRD BASE V-8] V-block. OHV. Eight-cylinder. Cast iron block and head. Aluminum intake manifold. Displacement: 305 cu. in. (5.0L). Bore & stroke: 3.74 x 3.48 in. Brake horsepower: 170 @ 4000 rpm. Torque: 255 lb.-ft. @ 2400 rpm. Compression ratio: 9.3:1. Fuel system: EFI/TBI. RPO Code: LO3. Standard five. Available in base Firebird. [VIN code E or F]. [OPTIONAL V-8] V-block. OHV. Eight-cylinder. Cast iron block and head. Aluminum intake manifold. Displacement: 305 cu. in. (5.0L). Bore & stroke: 3.74 x 3.48 in. Brake horsepower: 205 @ 4200 rpm. Torque: 285 lb.-ft. @ 3200 rpm. Compression ratio: 9.3:1. Fuel system: EFI/TPI. RPO Code: LB9. Available with five-speed manual in Formula, and Trans Am (delete option in GTA). [VIN code E or F]. [GTA V-8] V-block. OHV. Eight-cylinder. Cast iron block and head. Aluminum intake manifold. Displacement: 350 cu. in. (5.7L). Bore & stroke: 4.00 x 3.48 in. Brake horsepower: 240 @ 4400 rpm. Torque: 340 lb.-ft. @ 3200 rpm. Compression ratio: 9.3:1. Fuel system: EFI/TPI. RPO Code: B2L. Standard with four-speed automatic in GTA (optional in Formula and Trans Am). Includes Performance Enhancement group with dual catalytic converter exhausts, engine oil cooler, and performance axle ratio. [VIN code 8].

GRAND PRIX ENGINES

[STANDARD GRAND PRIX STE and GT; OPTIONAL GRAND PRIX LE/SE] V-block. OHV. Six-cylinder. Cast iron block and aluminum head. 191 cu. in. (3.1L). Bore & stroke: 3.50 x 3.31 in. Compression ratio: 8.8:1. Brake horsepower: 140 @ 4400 rpm. Torque: 185 lb.-ft. @ 3200 rpm. Fuel system: EFI/MPI. RPO Code: LHO. [VIN code T]. [STANDARD GRAND PRIX GTP; OPTIONAL ALL OTHERS EXCEPT GRAND PRIX LE] V-block. OHV. Six-cylinder. Cast iron block and aluminum head. 207 cu. in. (3.4L). Bore & stroke: 3.62 x 3.31 in. Compression ratio: 9.25:1. Brake horsepower: 210 @ 5200 rpm. Torque: 215 lb.-ft. @ 4000 rpm. Fuel system: EFI/MPI. [VIN code X].

BONNEVILLE ENGINES

[STANDARD SE/SSE] V-block. OHV. "3800" six-cylinder. Cast iron block and head. Aluminum intake manifold. Displacement: 231 cu. in. (3.8L). Bore & stroke: 3.80 x 3.40 in. Compression ratio: 8.5:1. Brake horsepower: 170 @ 4800 rpm. Torque: 220 lb.-ft. @ 3200 rpm. Fuel system: SFI. RPO Code: L27. Standard in Bonneville SE/SSE models. [VIN code C]. [STANDARD SSEi] V-block. OHV. "3800" supercharged six-cylinder. Cast iron block and head. Aluminum intake manifold. Displacement: 231 cu. in. (3.8L). Bore & stroke: 3.80 x 3.40 in. Compression ratio: 8.5:1. Brake horsepower: 205 @ 4400 rpm. Torque: 260 lb.-ft. @ 2800 rpm. Fuel system: SFI and supercharged. RPO Code: L67. Standard and exclusive in Bonneville SSEi model. [VIN code 1].

1992 Pontiac Trans Sport GT minivan. PMD

TRANS SPORT ENGINES

[STANDARD SE] V-block. OHV. Six-cylinder. Cast iron block and head. Aluminum intake manifold. Displacement: 191 cu. in. (3.1L). Bore & stroke: 3.50 x 3.31 in. Compression ratio: 8.5:1. Brake horsepower: 120 @ 4400 rpm. Torque: 175 lb.-ft. @ 2200 rpm. Fuel system: EFI/TBI. RPO Code: LG6. Standard in base Firebird.[VIN code T]. [STANDARD GT] V-block. OHV. "3800" six-cylinder. Cast iron block and head. Aluminum intake manifold. Displacement: 231 cu. in. (3.8L). Bore & stroke: 3.80 x 3.40 in. Compression ratio: 8.5:1. Brake horsepower: 165 @ 4300 rpm. Torque: 220 lb.-ft. @ 3200 rpm. Fuel system: SFI. RPO Code: L27. Standard in Transport GT. [VIN code C].

PONTIAC LEMANS CHASSIS: Wheelbase: 99.2 in. (all). Overall length: 163.70 in. (three-door); 172.4 in. (four-door). Height: 53.5 in. (Aerocoupe); 53.7 in. (Sedan). Width: 65.5 in. (three-door); 65.7 in. (four-door). Front track: 55.1 in. (all) Rear track: 55.4 in. (all). Standard tires: P175/70R13 BSW (all). Fuel tank: 13.2 gal.

SUNBIRD CHASSIS: Wheelbase: 101.3 in. (all). Overall length: 180.7 in. (all). Overall width: 66.3 in. (all). Height: 52.0.in. (Coupe). Front tread: 55.6 in. (all). Rear tread: 55.2 in. (all). Standard tires: P185/75R14 BSW (all except SE and GT Coupes). Standard tires: P195/65R15 Goodrich T/A touring tires. (GT Coupe).

GRAND AM CHASSIS: Wheelbase: 103.4 in. (all). Overall length: 186.9 in. (all). Width: 68.6 in. (all). Height: 53.1 in. (all). Standard tires: P185/75R14 BSW (SE). Standard tires: P205/55R16 (GT).

FIREBIRD CHASSIS: Wheelbase: 101.0 in. (all). Overall length: 195.1 in. (Base/Formula); 195.2 in. (Trans Am/GTA). Width: 72.4 in. (all). Height: 49.7 in. (all). Front tread: 60.7 in. Rear tread: 61.6 in. Standard tires: P215/65R15 (Base Firebird). Standard tires: P215/60R16 (Trans Am). Standard tires: P245/50ZR16 Goodyear Eagle ZR50 "Gatorback" (Formula and GTA).

GRAND PRIX CHASSIS: Wheelbase: 107.5 in. (all). Overall length: 194.8 in. (Coupe). Overall length: 194.8 in. (Sedan). Width: 71.9 in. (all). Height: 53.3 in. (all). Standard tires: See model description.

BONNEVILLE CHASSIS: Wheelbase: 110.8 in. (all). Overall length: 200.6 in. (all). Width: 73.6 in. (all). Height: 55.5 in. (all). Standard tires: See model descriptions.

TRANS SPORT CHASSIS: Wheelbase: 109.8 in. (all). Overall length: 194.5 in. (all). Width: 74.6 in. (all). Height: 65.7 in. (all). Standard tires: 205/70R15 BSW (SE). Standard tires: P205/70R15 touring tires (GT).

LEMANS TECHNICAL: Chassis: Front engine/front drive. Standard transmission: Four-speed manual (SE Aerocoupe "Value Leader" only). Standard transmission: Five-speed manual (Other Models). Standard (except "Value Leader") three-speed automatic transmission. Axle ratio: 3.43:1 with 1.6L and automatic. Axle ratio: 3.72:1 (both manual). Front suspension: deflected disc, MacPherson struts and 22mm stabi-

lizer bar. Rear suspension: Coil springs, semi-independent torsion beam, trailing arms, and 18mm anti-roll bar. Steering: Rack-and-pinion 24.5:1 ratio (18.3:1 power-assisted optional, except "Value Leader"). Turns lock-to-lock: 3.5 (power); 4.57 (manual). Turning circle: 32.8 ft. Front brakes: 9.25-in. vented discs. Rear brakes: 7.9 x 1.8-in. drums (power-assisted}.

SUNBIRD TECHNICAL: Chassis: Front engine/front drive. Base transmission: Five-speed manual. Optional transmission: Three-speed automatic. Axle ratio: 3.45:1 with five-speed manual. Axle ratio: 3.18:1 with three-speed automatic. Front suspension [Level I]: Deflected disc, MacPherson struts and (22mm with 2.0L TBI/28mm with 3.1L MFI) stabilizer bars. Front suspension [Level II]: Deflected disc, MacPherson struts and 28mm stabilizer bars. Rear suspension: Coil springs, semi-independent torsion beam, trailing arms and 21mm anti-roll bar. Steering: Rack-and-pinion 16.0:1 ratio (14.0:1 on cars with base 14-in. tires). Turns lock-to-lock: 3.0 (2.5 on GT). Turning circle: 34.3 ft. (all). Front brakes: 10.5-in. vented disc power-assisted. Rear brakes: 7.87 x 1.77-in. drum power-assisted.

GRAND AM TECHNICAL: Chassis: Front engine/front drive. Base transmission: Five-speed manual with overdrive (M32 or MV5). Optional transmission: Three-speed automatic (MD9). Axle ratio: 3.58:1 (with M32 five-speed). Axle ratio: 2.84:1 (with MD9 automatic). Axle ratio: 3.94:1 (with MV5 five-speed manual). Level I suspension: [Front] Deflected disc; MacPherson struts with coil springs and 26mm anti-roll bar; [Rear] Coil springs; semi-independent torsion beam, trailing arms. Level II suspension: [Front] Deflected disc; MacPherson struts with coil springs and 28mm anti-roll bar; [Rear] Coil springs; semi-independent torsion beam, trailing arms. Level III suspension: [Front] Deflected disc; MacPherson struts, 18mm. direct-acting anti-roll bar. [Rear] Coil springs; semi-independent torsion beam, trailing arms and defected disc, gas-charged shocks. Steering (Level I): Power-assisted rack-and-pinion, 16.0:1 ratio, 2.98 turns lock-to-lock, and 34.1-ft. turning circle. Steering (Level II): Power-assisted rack-and-pinion, 14.0:1 ratio, 2.5 turns lock-to-lock, and 36.4-ft. turning circle. Front brakes: 259.5mm diameter vented discs. Rear brakes: 2.00mm diameter drums. Fuel tank: 15.2 gal.

FIREBIRD TECHNICAL: Chassis: Front engine/rear drive. Base transmission: Four-speed automatic (Firebird/GTA). Optional transmission: Five-speed manual. (Formula/Trans Am). Front suspension: Modified MacPherson strut with 30mm (FE1), 34mm (F41), or 36mm (WS6) anti-roll bar. Rear suspension: Live axle with coil springs, control arms, torque arm, track bar, coil springs and 18mm (FE1), 23mm (F41) or 33mm (WS6) anti-roll bar. Steering: Power recirculating ball; 14.1:1 ratio (FE1), or 12.7:1 quick ratio with sport effort valving (F41 and WS6). Turns lock-to-lock: 2.57 (FE1), or 2.14 (F41 and WS6). Turning circle: 38.5 ft. (all). Brakes: Power vented 10.5-in. front disc/9.5 x 2.0-in. rear drum (10.5-in. rear vented discs on GTA and optional others). Fuel tank: 15.5 gal.

GRAND PRIX TECHNICAL: Chassis: Front engine/front drive. Standard drivetrain SE and LE Sedan: 3.1L MFI V-6 with three-speed automatic. Standard drivetrain GT Coupe and STE Sedan: 3.1L MFI V-6 with five-speed manual transaxle. Optional drivetrain GTP Coupe: 3.4L Twin Dual Cam V-6 with five-speed manual transaxle. Final Drive Ratios: [five-speed manual] 2.84:1; [M13 four-speed manual] 2.40:1; [ME9 four-speed manual] 2.33:1; [three-speed manual] 2.84:1. Front suspension: MacPherson struts with tapered top coil springs, lower A arm, and 28mm anti-roll bar (34mm anti-roll bar with Y99 suspension). Rear suspension: Tri-link independent suspension, transverse fiberglass leaf spring, and 10mm anti-roll bar (12mm anti-roll bar with Y99). Steering: Power-assisted rack-and-pinion with 15.7:1 ratio (14.0:1 with 3.4-liter V-6); 2.6 turns lock-to-lock (2.26 with GT/STE), and 36.7-ft. (39-ft. GT/STE) turning circle. Front brakes: 10.51-in. vented discs, power-assisted. Rear brakes: 10.1-in. solid discs, power-assisted. Fuel tank: 16.5 gal.

BONNEVILLE TECHNICAL: Chassis: Front engine/front drive. Base transmission: Four-speed automatic. Axle ratio: 2.84:1 (standard all). Front suspension: Deflected-disc, MacPherson struts with 32mm stabilizer bar (F41/FE2 and FE1). Rear suspension: Coil springs, semi-independent torsion beam, trailing arms, and 21mm stabilizer bar (F41/FE2) or 17mm stabilizer bar (FE1). Steering (SE): Power-assisted rack-and-pinion 16.54:1 ratio, 2.79 turns lock-to-lock, and 39.4-ft. (left)/40-ft. (right) turning circle. Steering (W21/SSE/SSEi): Power-assisted rack-and-pinion 14.93:1 to 18.91:1 variable ratio, 2.86 turns lock-to-lock, and 38.7-ft. (left)/40.3-ft. (right) turning circle. Front brakes: Power-assisted 10.9-in. vented discs. Rear brakes: Power-assisted 8.85-in. drums. Anti-lock brake system standard with SSE. Fuel tank: 18.0 gal.

TRANS SPORT TECHNICAL: Chassis: Front engine/front drive. Transmission: Three-speed automatic. Axle ratio: 3.18:1 (3.1L V-6). Axle ratio: 3.06:1 (3.4L V-6). Front suspension: MacPherson struts with 24 N-mm coil springs and 30mm anti-roll bar (LE). Front suspension: MacPherson strut, stamped lower control arms, 28mm stabilizer bar. Rear suspension: Open-section transverse beam on stamped steel trailing arms, tube shocks, coil springs and 25.4mm stabilizer bar. Steering: Power-assisted rack-and-pinion, and 38-ft. turning circle. Front brakes: Power-assisted 10.2-in. vented rotors, 182 sq. in. swept area. Rear brakes: Power-assisted 8.86 x 1.58-in. finned composite cast iron drums with 98.5 sq. in. swept area. Fuel tank: 20.0 gal.

LEMANS OPTIONS: R6A value package for Value Leader model ($662). R6A Value package for SE model ($355). MX1 three-speed automatic transmission ($475). C60 air conditioning, requires power steering and not available in Value Leader Aerocoupe ($705). B37 front and rear floor mats ($33). N40 power steering, requires air conditioning in Aerocoupe or SE Sedan ($225). UM7 Delco ETR stereo in Value Leader Aerocoupe ($307). UM6 Delco ETR AM/FM with cassette and more in Value Leader Aerocoupe ($429). UM6 Delco ETR AM/FM with cassette and more in LE/SE/GSE ($122). AD3 removable sun roof ($350). WDV warranty enhancements for New York ($25).

SUNBIRD OPTIONS: 1SB Sunbird LE Coupe and Sedan option group #1 ($903). 1SB Sunbird SE Coupe and Sedan option group #1 ($158). 1SC option for SE Coupe and Sedan ($671). TR9 option group for SE Coupe and Sedan ($1135). 1SB Sunbird SE Convertible option group #1 ($955). 1SC option for SE Convertible ($827). 1SB option group for GT Coupe ($955). R6A option group for LE Coupe and Sedan ($258). R6A option group for SE Coupe and Convertible ($258). R6B option group for SE Coupe and Convertible ($790). R6A option group for SE Sedan ($258). R6B option group for SE Sedan ($720). LHO engine, except no cost in GT ($585). MX1 three-speed automatic transmission ($495). W25 Special Appearance package ($316-$599 depending on value option packages it's teamed with). C60 air conditioning ($745). DO6 front seat armrest in GT and SE ($58). NB2 California emissions ($100). K34 cruise control ($225). C49 electric rear window defogger ($170). AO1 tinted glass ($105). TR9 lamp group ($29). D35 Sport mirrors ($53). A31 power windows, requires power door locks ($265 SE/GT Coupe/$230 Sedan/no charge Convertible). UM6 Delco radio equipment ($170 additional). U1C Delco radio equipment ($396).

1992 Pontiac Grand Am GT coupe. PMD

GRAND AM OPTIONS: 1SB package on GT Coupe ($1327). 1SC package on GT Coupe ($1838). 1SB package on GT Sedan ($1327). 1SC package on GT Sedan ($1903). 1SB package on SE Coupe ($565). 1SC package on SE Coupe ($976). 1SB package on SE sedan ($565). 1SC package on SE Sedan ($1041). R6A Value option package on SE Coupe and Sedan ($253). R6B Value option package on SE Coupe and Sedan ($431). LD2 Quad-4 2.3-liter MPI engine in SE models ($410). LD2 Quad-4 2.3-liter MPI engine in GT models ($140 credit). LGO Quad-4 High-Output engine (standard on SE/Manual). LG7 3.3-liter V-6 in SE ($460). MX1 three-speed automatic transmission ($555). C60 air conditioning ($830). C49 electric rear window defogger ($170). K34 cruise control ($225). UB3 rally gauges ($111). NB2 California emission requirements ($100). K34 cruise control ($225). C49 electric rear window defogger ($170). UB3 rally gauges for SE ($111). DG7 dual sport mirrors ($86). AC3 power seat with Sport interior group ($305). AC3 power seat without Sport interior group ($340). NV7 variable effort power steering ($62). A31 express down power windows in SE and GT Coupe ($275). A31 express down power window in SE or GT Sedan ($340). AM9 split folding rear seat ($150). CD4 controlled cycle wipers ($65). B20 Sport interior group, SE and GT ($265). WDV warranty enhancements ($25). UM6 Delco sound system ($140). UW6 full-range speakers ($85). U1A Delco sound system ($460-$600). QMW touring tires with Ride & Handling suspension ($141). QPD touring tires with Ride & Handling suspension ($158). PC1 custom wheel covers ($275). V2C 16-in. custom wheels on GT ($396). PG1 cross-lace wheel covers on SE without value package ($55). UB3 rally gauges with tach ($78-$127). AM9 split folding rear seat ($150). T43 rear deck lid spoiler SE Convertible without value package or W25 Special Appearance package ($70). N33 tilt steering wheel ($145). AD3 glass sun roof SE Coupe and GT ($350). CD4 controlled cycle windshield wipers ($65). B20/11N9 white vinyl trim for LE Coupe, SE Coupe, SE Convertible and GT ($75). D84 two-tone paint on SE ($101). WDV warranty enhancement for New York ($25). QME touring tires without value option package ($141). QPD touring tires with Ride & Handling package ($158). N78 14-in. Hi-Tech Turbo aluminum wheels ($220-$275). PG1 15-in. cross-lace wheel covers ($55). PF7 cast aluminum wheels with locking package ($220-$275).

FIREBIRD OPTIONS: 1SB Firebird V-6 option group ($413). 1SB Firebird V-8 option group ($223).1SB Formula/Trans Am option group ($223). 1SB Firebird V-6 Convertible ($390). 1SB Firebird V-8 Convertible ($225).1SB Trans Am Convertible option group ($225). 1SC Firebird V-6 option group ($804). 1SC Firebird V-8 option group ($484).1SC Formula/Trans Am option group ($484). 1SC Firebird V-6 Convertible ($721). 1SC Firebird V-8 Convertible ($401). 1SC Trans Am Convertible option group ($366). R6A Firebird and Formula value package ($814). R6A Trans Am Convertible value package ($680). LHO 3.1-liter MPFI V-6 engine in base Firebird Coupe and Convertible ($369). LB9 5.0L MPI V-8 in Formula and Trans Am ($745). LB9 5.0L MPI V-8 in Trans Am GTA ($300 credit). B2L 5.7L MPI V-8 in Trans Am ($300). B2L 5.7L MPI V-8 in Formula ($1045). MM5 five-speed manual transmission in Trans Am GTA with LB9 ($530 credit). MXO four-speed automatic transmission, except in GTA ($530). C60 air conditioning ($830). G80 limited-slip axle ($100). K34 cruise control, except GTA ($225). A90 rear deck lid release in Trans Am ($60). C49 rear window defogger, except GTA ($170). NB2 California emissions ($100). CC1 Hatch roof ($914). DG7 dual Sport mirror, left-hand remote-control, except GTA ($91). R6P Performance Enhancement group with dual converter exhaust, four-wheel disc brake, engine oil cooler and more ($444). AU3 power door locks ($210). A31 power windows ($280). U75 power antenna ($75). UM6 Delco radio equipment ($150). U1A Delco radio equipment ($226-$376). D42 cargo area security screen ($69). AH3 four-way adjustable power driver seat, except GTA ($35). AR9 Custom Pallex cloth reclining bucket seat, no cost option, but not available on GTA. AQ9 articulating bucket seats with Ventura leather trim in GTA ($475). AQ9 articulating bucket seats with Ventura leather trim in Trans Am Convertible ($780). QLC high-performance WS6 performance suspension ($313).

6000 OPTIONS: 1SB option package #1 for 6000 LE Sedan ($995). 1SC option package #2 for 6000 LE Sedan ($1190). 1SD option package #3 for 6000 LE Sedan ($2058). 1SB option package #1 for 6000 LE Wagon ($190). 1SC option package #2 for 6000 LE Wagon ($385). 1SD option package #3 for 6000 LE Wagon ($1243). 1SB option package #1 for 6000 S/E Sedan ($343). 1SB option package #1 for 6000 S/E Wagon ($293). R6A value option package for 6000 LE Sedan ($413). R6B value option package for 6000 LE Sedan ($413). R6B value option package for 6000 LE Sedan ($413). LB6 2.8-liter MFI V-6 in LE Sedan ($660). MXO four-speed automatic transmission ($200). C60 air conditioning ($805). C49 electric rear window defogger ($160). D86 two-tone paint ($115). AU3 power door locks ($205). A31 power windows ($310). UM6 Delco ETR AM/FM stereo ($122). U1A Delco ETR AM stereo/FM stereo ($501-$364). AM6 45/55 split bench seat ($133). B20 custom interior with 45/55 split seat in Empress/London cloth ($350-$483). Various tire options (no charge to $68). N78 Aluminum wheels with locking package ($265). BX3 wood-grain exterior siding for Wagon ($295).

GRAND PRIX OPTIONS: 1SB Grand Prix LE ($175). 1SC Grand Prix LE ($540). 1SB Grand Prix SE Sedan ($450). 1SC Grand Prix SE Sedan ($1023). 1SD Grand Prix SE Sedan ($1389). 1SB Grand Prix SE Coupe ($450). 1SC Grand Prix SE Coupe ($718). 1SD Grand Prix SE Coupe ($1084). 1SB Grand Prix GT Coupe ($841). 1SB Grand Prix STE Sedan ($1145). R6A Value Option for Grand Prix LE Sedan ($543). R6B Value Option package for Grand Prix LE Sedan ($488), R6A Value Option Package for Grand Prix SE Coupe ($818). R6B Value Option package for Grand Prix SE Coupe ($753). R6C Value Option package for Grand Prix SE Coupe ($2228). R6A Value Option package for Grand Prix SE Sedan ($584). R6B Value Option package for Grand Prix SE Sedan ($774). R6C Value Option package for Grand Prix SE Sedan ($1457). LQ1 3.4L DOHC 24-valve Twin Dual Cam V-6 ($995). MXO four-speed automatic in Grand Prix SE ($200). MM5 five-speed manual transmission in Grand Prix LE ($200 credit). A90 remote deck lid release ($60). C49 electric rear window defogger ($170). NB2 California emissions system ($100). D84 two-tone paint ($105). JL9 power antilock brakes ($450). AUO Remote Keyless Entry system ($135). CF5 power sun roof ($670-$695). UB3 rally gauge cluster with tach ($85). U68 electric compass with trip computer and service reminder ($285). UV6 heads-up display, requires Graphite, Gray, or Beige interior trim and bucket seats ($250). V56 rear deck lid luggage carrier ($115). B20 Custom interior trim ($45). DG7 dual Sport mirrors ($78). DH6 dual illuminated visor vanity mirrors ($86). KD1 transmission oil cooler ($75). N33 tilt steering wheel ($450). A31 power windows on Coupe ($275). A31 power windows on Sedan ($340). AU3 power door locks on Coupe ($210). AU3 power door locks on Sedan ($250). BYP Sport Appearance package with lower aero ground effects ($385-$690 depending on model and other options). B4U Aero Appearance package ($2080-$2595). Y99 rally handling suspension ($50). NC5 dual split exhausts ($90). WDV warranty enhancements ($25). UM6 Delco radio equipment ($140). UX1 Delco radio equipment ($540-$590). U1A stereo sound system ($766-$816 depending on model). US7 power antenna ($85). AR9 bucket seat with Pallex cloth trim in Grand Prix LE ($110). AN3 Custom Cloth bucket seat in Grand Prix LE ($140). AQ9 articulating Sport bucket seats with front console and Ventura leather trim ($475). AC3 power seat ($305). B20 Custom interior trim ($324-$383). QPE touring tires ($112). QXJ P22560R-16 tires ($150). QLC P245/50ZR16 tires with GTP Coupe ($209). PH3 15-in. aluminum sport wheels with locking package ($275). NWO 16-in. aluminum Sport wheels ($275).

1992 Pontiac Bonneville SE four-door sedan. PMD

BONNEVILLE OPTIONS: 1SB Bonneville SE option package ($383). 1SC Bonneville SE option package ($901). 1SD Bonneville SE option package ($1242). 1SB Bonneville SSE option package ($845). R6A Bonneville SE value option package ($845). R6B Bonneville SE value option package. ($424). R6C Bonneville SE value option package ($200). R6A Bonneville SSE value option package. ($1835). R6A Bonneville SSEi value option package. ($1195). AS7 45/45 bucket seats and console ($220-$315). AL7 leather trim package ($779-$1419 depending on other options). B20 Custom interior trim ($130). AG1 six-way power seat ($305). AUO Remote Keyless Entry system ($135). B57 monotone appearance package ($180). C97 illuminated entry system ($75). CF5 power glass sun roof ($1216-$1326). C49 electric rear window defogger ($170). C50 heated windshield ($250). JM4 power front disc/rear drum antilock braking system ($450). K05 engine block heater ($18). NB2 California emissions system ($100). NW9 Traction Control system ($175). PF5 16-in. five-blade cast aluminum wheels ($340). PF7 15-in. six-spoke cast aluminum wheels ($306). QPJ touring tires ($76). QNX touring tires ($74). R7E premium equipment package ($1345). T2U convenience group ($213). T2Z enhancement group ($206). T43 rear deck lid spoiler ($95). UA6 Theft Deterrent system ($190). UM6 Delco radio equipment ($140). UX1 Delco sound system ($460-$650). U1A compact disc player ($226-$876). US7 power antenna ($85). V92 trailer provisions ($150-$614 depending on other options and Value Packages). WDV warranty enhancements ($25). W21 SE Sport package ($591-$1185 depending on model, options, and Value Packages).

TRANS SPORT OPTIONS: 1SB Trans Sport option package #1 ($1195). 1SC Trans Sport option package #2 ($1960). 1SB Trans Sport SE option package #1 ($765). Advertising ($200). C67 air conditioning in Trans Sport ($805). NB2 California emissions system ($100). B2Q black roof delete (no charge). C49 electric rear window defogger ($160). AJ1 glass package in Trans Sport ($245). AB5 power door locks ($255). A31 power windows ($240). UM6 Delco radio equipment ($140). U1A compact disc player ($376-$516). AB3 six-passenger seating package ($525). ZP7 seven-passenger seating package ($675). N78 14-in. aluminum wheels ($265).

Note: Full option package contents, descriptions and applications information can often be determined by consulting factory literature. The data above is edited for size and clarity. This information provided only as a guide to help collectors appraise the relative value of cars with numerous options. Prices for items included as part of a value option package are usually much less than individual prices. Option prices charged by individual dealers may also vary.

1993 PONTIAC

PONTIAC I.D. NUMBERS: Vehicle identification number (VIN) is located on top left-hand surface of instrument panel visible through the windshield. The VIN has 17 symbols. The first symbol indicates the country of manufacture (U.S.) The second symbol indicates the manufacturer (G=General Motors). The third symbol indicates the make/division (2=Pontiac). The fourth, fifth, and sixth symbols are the same as the body style (model) number. The eighth symbol indicates the engine. The ninth symbol is a check digit. The 10th symbol indicates model-year. The 11th symbol indicates the assembly plant. The last six symbols are the consecutive unit number at the factory.

LEMANS -- SERIES 2T -- FOUR -- The Pontiac LeMans was based on the German Opel Kadett and built in Korea. The 1993 LeMans line consisted of the "Value Leader" Aerocoupe, the SE Aerocoupe, and the SE Sedan. New for 1993 was a revised, less angular front and rear appearance due to new bumper/fascia, new side marker and park/turn lamp, black bodyside molding that replaced 1992's ribbed molding, revised HVAC controls, two new colors: bright turquoise (Aerocoupe

"Value Leader") and light aqua metallic, and contemporary 13-in. custom wheel cover in argent silver (Aerocoupe "Value Leader" and SE Sedan). Standard equipment on the LeMans "Value Leader" included a 1.6-liter TBI engine, four-speed manual transmission, P175/70R13 blackwall tires, 9.25-in. vented front disc brakes, steel wheels, electric rear window defogger, halogen head lamps, and remote sport mirrors. The LeMans SE Aerocoupe added or substituted a five-speed manual transmission, styled steel wheels, a three-spoke steering wheel, and a Delco AM/FM stereo with clock. The LeMans SE Sedan had all the same equipment as the SE "Value Leader" Aerocoupe, plus a five-speed manual transmission and a Delco AM/FM stereo with clock.

LEMANS -- SERIES 2T -- I-4

Model Number	Body/Style Number	Body Type & Seating	Factory Price	Shipping Weight	Prod. Total
2T	TX2	3-dr V/L Cpe-4P	8154	2137	Note 1
2T	TN2	3-dr SE Cpe-4P	9054	2175	Note 1
2T	TN5	4-dr SE Sed-4P	9854	2203	Note 1

NOTE 1: LeMans series production totaled 7,550.

SUNBIRD -- SERIES 2J --FOUR -- An acoustics package was added across-the-line in 1993, making Sunbird quieter. There were again three series comprising the Sunbird lineup: LE, SE, and GT. New features included a Sport Appearance Package (SE Coupe), glass convertible rear window with available defogger (SE Convertible), low oil level sensor on 2.0L engine, three new exterior colors: Bright White, Light Gray Metallic, and Light Teal Metallic, three new interior colors: beige, gray, and arctic white, and a trunk cargo net. Standard equipment on the Sunbird included the MPFI 2.0-liter four-cylinder engine (LE and SE Coupes), five-speed manual transmission, reclining front bucket seats, antilock brakes, P185/75R14 tires, power rack and pinion steering, a Delco ETR AM/FM stereo with seek-and-scan and clock, a stainless steel exhaust system, and automatic door locks. The Sunbird SE Convertible offered Soft-Ray tinted glass, rear quarter courtesy lights, and front seat armrest and storage bin. The Sunbird GT added or substituted a 3.1-liter MPFI V-6 mated to a Getrag five-speed manual transmission featuring a new concentric slave cylinder clutch design, P195/65R15 tires, and a dual exhaust system.

1993 Pontiac Sunbird SE coupe with Sport Appearance Package. PMD

Model Number	Body/Style Number	Body Type & Seating	Factory Price	Shipping Weight	Prod. Total
SUNBIRD LE -- SERIES 2J -- I-4					
2J	JC5	4-dr Sed-5P	9382	2502	Note 1
2J	JC1	2-dr Cpe-5P	9382	2484	Note 1
SUNBIRD SE -- SERIES 2J -- I-4					
2J	JB5	4-dr Sed-5P	10380	2502	Note 1
2J	JB1	2-dr Cpe-5P	10380	2484	Note 1
2J	JB3	2-dr Conv-5P	15403	2694	Note 1
SUNBIRD GT -- SERIES 2J -- V-6					
2J	JD1	2-dr Cpe-5P	12820	2682	Note 1

NOTE 1: Sunbird series production totaled 82,902.

GRAND AM -- SERIES 2N -- Pontiac's sales leader was again available as SE and GT Coupes and Sedans for 1993. The Grand Am's Quad four-cylinder engine received improvements to enhance noise reduction. Functional changes included one new exterior color: gray purple metallic, two new interior colors: beige and new gray, battery rundown protection, axle ratio changes, revised HVAC controls and graphics, and revised base instrument panel appliqué. Standard equipment

included fog lamps, P185/75R14 tires, bolt-on 14-in. wheelcovers, Delco ETR AM/FM stereo with seek-and-scan and clock, 2.3-liter Quad OHC four-cylinder engine, five-speed manual transmission, stainless steel exhaust, ABS brakes, and power rack-and-pinion steering. The GT added or substituted dual/dual chrome-tipped exhaust outlets, neutral-density taillights, P205/55R16 tires, specific 16-in. cast aluminum wheels, rally gauges with a tachometer, and a 2.3-liter H.O. DOHC 16-valve Quad four-cylinder engine.

1993 Pontiac Grand Am GT coupe. PMD

Model Number	Body/Style Number	Body Type & Seating	Factory Price	Shipping Weight	Prod. Total
GRAND AM SE SERIES 2N -- Quad 4					
2N	NE1	2-dr Cpe-5P	12624	2728	Note 1
2N	NE5	4-dr Sed-5P	12524	2777	Note 1
GRAND AM SE -- SERIES 2N --V-6					
2N	NE1	2-dr Cpe-5P	12984	-	Note 1
2N	NE5	4-dr Sed-5P	13084	-	Note 1
GRAND AM GT -- SERIES 2N --Quad 4					
2N	NW1	2-dr Cpe-5P	13924	2804	Note 1
2N	NW5	4-dr Sed-5P	14024	2846	Note 1

NOTE 1: Grand Am series production totaled 224,255.

FIREBIRD -- SERIES 2F -- V-6/V-8 -- Pontiac's fourth generation Firebird arrived in 1993 with 90 percent new content. This radical revision found most every component of the Firebird completely new or extensively updated. The full line consisted of Firebird, Firebird Formula, and Trans Am. Included among the many changes for 1993 were a 68-degree windshield angle, new aluminum wheels and tires, composite body panels resistant to minor impacts and rust, new instrumentation and locking glove box, new front and rear suspension, a new 3.4-liter V-6 (standard on Firebird) and 5.7-liter V-8 (standard on Formula and Trans Am) and a six-speed manual transmission (standard on Formula and Trans Am), advanced four-wheel anti-lock brakes (standard on all Firebird models with four-wheel disc brakes standard on Formula and Trans Am), dual front air bags (standard on all Firebird models), and keyless entry available on all Firebird models (standard on Trans Am). Colors offered in 1993 were: Dark Green Metallic, Yellow, Bright Red, Medium Red Metallic, Bright Blue Metallic, Gray Purple Metallic, Bright White, and Black. Standard features on all Firebird models included front air dam, tinted glass, sport mirrors, aero rear-deck spoiler, side-window defogger, four-spoke steering wheel with adjustable steering column, P215/60R16 steel-belted touring tires, rear-wheel drive, rack-and-pinion steering, and five-speed manual transmission.

1993 Pontiac Firebird Formula coupe. PMD

231

1993 Pontiac Firebird coupe. PMD

Model Number	Body/Style Number	Body Type & Seating	Factory Price	Shipping Weight	Prod. Total
FIREBIRD -- SERIES 2F -- V-6					
2F	FS2	2-dr Cpe-5P	13995	3241	Note 1
FIREBIRD FORMULA -- SERIES 2F -- V-8					
2F	FV2	2-dr Cpe-5P	17995	3381	Note 1
FIREBIRD TRANS AM -- SERIES 2F -- V-8					
2F	FV2	2-dr Cpe-5P	21395	3452	Note 1

NOTE 1: Firebird series production totaled 14,112.

GRAND PRIX -- SERIES 2W -- V-6/V-8 -- Pontiac touted the 1993 Grand Prix lineup as offering sport styling, performance, and safety "for buyers seeking affordable controlled performance and distinctive styling in a mid-sized automobile." New features included an optional "second-gear start" transmission with 3.1-liter V-6 for enhanced starting on slippery roads, a new interior color: Ruby Red, a Sport Appearance Package for the LE Sedan, four-speed electronic automatic transmission available with the 3.1-liter engine, standard automatic door locks, and provisions for installation of a cellular car phone. Each of six models had equipment distinctions, with the important standard features as follows: air conditioning, power door locks, 3.1-liter MFI V-6, fog lamps, rear-seat headrests, rack-and-pinion steering, four-wheel power disc brakes, and stainless steel exhaust system. Features standard to the individual models include: SE Coupe: 3.1-liter MFI V-6, three-speed automatic transmission, 15-in. bolt-on wheel covers, P20570R15 touring tires, 45/55 split reclining front seats, and Delco ETR AM/FM stereo with clock. GT Coupe: 3.1-liter MFI V-6, four-speed automatic transmission, Y99 rally suspension, 16-in. cast aluminum wheels, P225/60R16 Eagle GT+4 tires, rally gauges with tachometer, power windows, power bucket seats with thigh, lumbar and lateral support, cruise control, and Delco ETR AM/FM stereo cassette with equalizer and steering wheel controls. GTP Coupe: 3.4-liter Twin Dual Cam V-6, five-speed manual transmission, Y99 Rally Tuned suspension, aero performance package, P245/50ZR16 tires, power windows, power driver's seat, cruise control, Delco ETR AM/FM stereo cassette with equalizer and steering wheel controls, and six-speaker sound system. LE Sedan: 3.1-liter MFI V-6, three-speed automatic transmission, 15-in. bolt-on wheel covers, P205/70R15 touring tires, 45/55 split reclining front seats, and Delco ETR AM/FM stereo with clock. SE Sedan: 3.1-liter MFI V-6, three-speed automatic transmission, 16-in. cast aluminum wheels, P215/60R16 touring tires, 45/55 split reclining front seats, and Delco ETR AM/FM stereo with clock. STE Sedan: 3.1-liter MFI V-6, four-speed automatic transmission, Y99 Rally Tuned suspension, P225/60R16 Eagle GT+4 tires, rally gauges with tachometer, power windows, power driver's seat, cruise control, remote keyless entry system, Delco ETR AM/FM cassette stereo with equalizer and steering wheel controls.

Model Number	Body/Style Number	Body Type & Seating	Factory Price	Shipping Weight	Prod. Total
GRAND PRIX LE -- SERIES 2W --V-6					
2G	WH5	4-dr Sed-5P	14890	3333	Note 1
GRAND PRIX SE -- SERIES 2W -- V-6					
2G	WJ5	4-dr Sed-5P	16190	3369	Note 1
2G	WJ1	2-dr Cpe-5P	15390	3231	Note 1
GRAND PRIX STE -- SERIES 2W -- V-6					
2G	WT5	4-dr Sed-5P	21635	3506	Note 1
GRAND PRIX GT-- SERIES 2W -- V-6					
2G	WP1	2-dr Cpe-5P	20340	3326	Note 1

NOTE 1: Grand Prix series production totaled 106,083.

BONNEVILLE -- SERIES 2H -- V-6 -- Pontiac's luxury import sedan fighter, the Bonneville, got additional firepower in the SLE package for 1993. The SLE makeover of the standard Bonneville SE joined the Pontiac flagship SSE and SSEi models in attracting import-oriented buyers. The Pontiac hype machine fired this salvo to promote buying American: "The Bonneville SLE is a driver-oriented, sophisticated sports sedan, designed and engineered to perform and handle like import luxury sedans that cost thousands of dollars more." In addition to the SLE package, other new features offered on Bonneville models were: three exterior colors: gray purple metallic, light gray metallic, and bright white; standard monotone appearance on base molding, ABS graphics added to 16-inch five blade cast aluminum wheels; revised turn signal, wiper, and cruise stalk controls; anti-lock brakes standard on all models; two new interior colors: ruby red and medium gray; soft-touch graphite instrument panel trim plate on all bucket seat vehicles; supercharged 3800 Series V-6 engine available on SSE; traction control available with 16-inch tires/wheels; and Performance and Handling Package replaces W21 Sport Appearance Package (Y52). Major standard equipment varied by model. On SEs, the list included: driver's side airbag, rack-and-pinion power steering, 3.8-liter 3800 series TPI V-6, four-speed electronic automatic transmission, P215/65R15 blackwall touring tires, 15-in. bolt-on wheel covers, manual air conditioning, Pass-Key II theft deterrent system, tinted windows, and stainless steel single exhaust. On SSEs, the standard features list included: driver's side airbag, rack-and-pinion variable-ratio power steering, 3.8-liter 3800 series TPI V-6, four-speed electronic automatic transmission, electronic load leveling system, P215/60R16 blackwall Eagle GA touring tires, 16-in. aerolite color-keyed (or silver) aluminum wheels, manual air conditioning, driver information center, Pass Key II theft deterrent system, cruise control, stainless steel split dual exhaust, monotone ground effects package, leather-wrapped steering wheel with radio controls, and convenience net in trunk. On SSEis, the standard features list included: dual front airbags, rack-and-pinion variable-ratio power steering, 3.8-liter 3800 series supercharged TPI V-6, four-speed electronic automatic transmission, electronic load leveling system, traction-control system, P225/60ZR16 Eagle GT+4 blackwall tires, 16-in. aerolite color-keyed (or silver) aluminum wheels, automatic air conditioning, leather-wrapped steering wheel with radio controls, driver information center, Pass-Key II theft-deterrent system, monotone ground effects package, stainless steel split dual exhaust, tinted glass, and remote keyless entry.

1993 Pontiac Bonneville SE four-door sedan with Sport Luxury Edition Package. PMD

Model Number	Body/Style Number	Body Type & Seating	Factory Price	Shipping Weight	Prod. Total
BONNEVILLE SE -- SERIES H -- V-6					
2H	HX5	4-dr Spt Sed-5P	19444	3444	Note 1
BONNEVILLE SSE -- SERIES H -- V-6					
2H	HZ5	4-dr Spt Sed-5P	24844	3587	Note 1
BONNEVILLE SSEi -- SERIES H -- V-6					
2H	HY5	4-dr Spt Sed-5P	29444	3690	Note 1

NOTE 1: Bonneville series production totaled 98,724.

TRANS SPORT -- SERIES 2U -- V-6 -- With the discontinuation of the GT version of the Trans Sport the 1993 Pontiac minivan lineup consisted only of the Trans Sport SE. A new, standard "Quiet Package" was the big news on the improvement front, which greatly reduced outside noise. Also, 1993 Trans Sport SE purchasers could order through available options all the uplevel features found on the previous year's GT version. New features for the SE included a pop-up sunroof (at mid-year), one new interior color: ruby red, lockable underdash storage, larger HVAC controls, redundant radio controls, AM/FM Stereo cassette with graphic equalizer, cargo lamps, leather seating area option, and increased wheel caster. Standard equipment included: 3.1 liter V-6 with electronic fuel injection, three-speed automatic transmission, anti-lock braking system, stainless steel exhaust, integrated roof antenna, tinted glass, P205/70R15 blackwall all-season tires, 15-inch styled bolt-on wheel covers, analog instrumentation with tachometer, and intermittent wipers.

TRANS SPORT -- SERIES 2U -- V-6

Model Number	Body/Style Number	Body Type & Seating	Factory Price	Shipping Weight	Prod. Total
2U	U06	SE Wagon	16689	3598	26,385

LEMANS ENGINES

[STANDARD ALL] Inline. OHV. Four-cylinder. Cast iron block. Aluminum head and intake manifold. Displacement: 97.5 cu. in. (1.6L). Bore & stroke: 3.11 x 3.21 in. Compression ratio: 8.6:1. Brake horsepower: 74 @ 5600 rpm. Torque: 90 lb.-ft. @ 2800 rpm. Fuel system: EFI/TBI. RPO Code: L73. Standard with four-speed manual LeMans "Value Leader" Aerocoupe; standard with five-speed manual transmission in other models. [VIN code 6].

SUNBIRD ENGINES

[STANDARD BASE/LE/SE] Inline. OHC. Four-cylinder. Cast iron block. Aluminum head and intake manifold. Displacement: 121 cu. in. (2.0L). Bore & stroke: 3.38 x 3.38 in. Compression ratio: 9.2:1. Brake horsepower: 110 @ 5200 rpm. Torque: 124 lb.-ft. @ 3600 rpm. Fuel system: MPFI. Code: LE4. Standard in Sunbird LE and Sunbird SE models. [VIN code K]. [STANDARD GT] V-block. OHV. Six-cylinder. Cast iron block and aluminum head. Displacement: 191 cu. in. (3.1L). Bore & stroke: 3.50 x 3.31. Compression ratio: 8.9:1. Brake horsepower: 140 @ 4200 rpm. Torque: 185 lb.-ft. @ 3200 rpm. Fuel system: MPFI. [VIN code T].

GRAND AM ENGINES

[STANDARD SE] Inline. Quad-4 OHC. Cast iron block. Aluminum head and intake manifold. Displacement: 138 cu. in. (2.3.-liter). Bore & stroke: 3.63 x 3.35 in. Compression ratio: 9.5:1. Brake horsepower: 115 @ 5200 rpm. Torque: 140 lb.-ft. @ 3200 rpm. Fuel system: MPFI. RPO Code: L40. Standard in SE. [VIN code A]. [OPTIONAL SE] Inline. Quad-4 DOHC. 16-valve. Cast iron block. Aluminum head and intake manifold. Displacement: 138 cu. in. (2.3.-liter). Bore & stroke: 3.63 x 3.35 in. Compression ratio: 9.5:1. Brake horsepower: 155 @ 6000 rpm. Torque: 150 lb.-ft. @ 4800 rpm. Fuel system: MPFI. RPO Code: LD2. Optional in SE. [VIN code D]. [STANDARD GT] Inline. Quad-4 H.O. DOHC. 16-valve. Quad-4 High-Output. Cast iron block. Aluminum head and intake manifold. Displacement: 138 cu. in. (2.3-liter). Bore & stroke: 3.63 x 3.35 in. Compression ratio: 10.0:1. Brake horsepower: 175 @ 6200 rpm. Torque: 155 lb.-ft. @ 5200 rpm. Fuel system: MPFI. RPO Code: LG0. Standard in Grand Am GT with five-speed manual transmission. [VIN code A]. [OPTIONAL SE/GT] V-block. OHV. Six-cylinder. Cast iron block and aluminum head. 204 cu. in. (3.3L). Bore & stroke: 3.70 x 3.16 in. Compression ratio: 9.0:1. Brake horsepower: 160 @ 5200 rpm. Torque: 185 lb.-ft. @ 2000 rpm. Fuel system: MFI. RPO Code LG7. Optional in Grand Am SE and GT. [VIN code N].

FIREBIRD ENGINES

[FIREBIRD BASE V-6] V-block. OHV. Six-cylinder. Cast iron block and head. Aluminum intake manifold. Displacement: 207 cu. in. (3.4L). Bore & stroke: 3.62 x 3.31. Compression ratio: 9.0:1. Brake horsepower: 160 @ 4600 rpm. Torque: 200 lb.-ft. @ 3200 rpm. Fuel system: EFI. RPO Code: L32. Standard in Firebird. Not available in Formula and Trans Am. [VIN code S]. [FORMULA/TRANS AM BASE V-8] V-block. OHV. Eight-cylinder. Cast iron block and head. Aluminum intake manifold. Displacement: 350 cu. in. (5.7L). Bore & stroke: 4.00 x 3.48. Compression ratio: 10.5:1. Brake horsepower: 270 @ 4800 rpm. Torque: 325 lb.-ft. @ 2400 rpm. Fuel system: PFI. RPO Code: LT1. Standard in Formula and Trans Am. Not available in Firebird. [VIN code P].

1993 Pontiac Grand Prix LE four-door sedan with Sport Appearance Package. PMD

GRAND PRIX ENGINES

[STANDARD GRAND PRIX LE/SE, STE, and GT] V-block. OHV. Six-cylinder. Cast iron block and aluminum head. 191 cu. in. (3.1L). Bore & stroke: 3.50 x 3.31 in. Compression ratio: 8.9:1. Brake horsepower: 140 @ 4200 rpm. Torque: 185 lb.-ft. @ 3200 rpm. Fuel system: MPFI. RPO Code: LHO. [VIN code T or M]. [STANDARD GRAND PRIX GTP; OPTIONAL ALL OTHERS] V-block. OHV. Six-cylinder. Cast iron block and aluminum head. 207 cu. in. (3.4L). Bore & stroke: 3.62 x 3.30 in. Compression ratio: 9.25:1. Brake horsepower: 210 @ 5200 rpm. Torque: 215 lb.-ft. @ 4000 rpm. Fuel system: MPFI. RPO Code: LQ1. [VIN code X or S].

BONNEVILLE ENGINES

[STANDARD SE/SSE] V-block. OHV. "3800" six-cylinder. Cast iron block and head. Aluminum intake manifold. Displacement: 231 cu. in. (3.8L). Bore & stroke: 3.80 x 3.40 in. Compression ratio: 9.0:1. Brake horsepower: 170 @ 4800 rpm. Torque: 225 lb.-ft. @ 3200 rpm. Fuel system: SPFI. RPO Code: L27. Standard in Bonneville SE/SSE models. [VIN code C]. [STANDARD SSEi] V-block. OHV. "3800" supercharged six-cylinder. Cast iron block and head. Aluminum intake manifold. Displacement: 231 cu. in. (3.8L). Bore & stroke: 3.80 x 3.40 in. Compression ratio: 9.0:1. Brake horsepower: 205 @ 4400 rpm. Torque: 260 lb.-ft. @ 2600 rpm. Fuel system: SPFI and supercharged. RPO Code: L67. Standard and exclusive in Bonneville SSEi model. [VIN code 1].

1993 Pontiac Trans Sport SE minivan. PMD

TRANS SPORT ENGINES

[STANDARD SE] V-block. OHV. Six-cylinder. Cast iron block and head. Aluminum intake manifold. Displacement: 191 cu. in. (3.1L). Bore & stroke: 3.50 x 3.31 in. Compression ratio: 8.5:1. Brake horsepower: 120 @ 4400 rpm. Torque: 175 lb.-ft. @ 2200 rpm. Fuel system: EFI/TBFI. RPO Code: LG6. Standard in SE.[VIN code T]. [OPTIONAL SE] V-block. OHV. "3800" six-cylinder. Cast iron block and head. Aluminum intake manifold. Displacement: 231 cu. in. (3.8L). Bore & stroke: 3.80 x 3.40 in. Compression ratio: 9.0:1. Brake horsepower: 170 @ 4800 rpm. Torque: 225 lb.-ft. @ 3200 rpm. Fuel system: SPFI. RPO Code: L27. [VIN code 3 or C].

LEMANS CHASSIS: Wheelbase: 99.2 in. (all). Overall length: 167.90 in. (three-door); 176.9 in. (four-door). Height: 53.5 in. (Aerocoupe); 53.7 in. (Sedan). Width: 65.5 in. (three-door); 65.7 in. (four-door). Front tread: 55.1 in. (all). Rear tread: 55.4 in. (all). Standard tires: P175/70R13 BSW (all). Fuel tank: 13.2 gal.

SUNBIRD CHASSIS: Wheelbase: 101.3 in. (all). Overall length: 180.7 in. (all). Overall width: 66.3 in. (all). Height: 52.0.in. (Coupe and Convertible), 53.6 in. (Sedan). Front tread: 55.6 in. (all). Rear tread: 55.4 in. (all). Standard tires: P185/75R14 BSW (all except SE and GT Coupes). Standard tires: P195/65R15. (GT Coupe).

GRAND AM CHASSIS: Wheelbase: 103.4 in. (all). Overall length: 186.9 in. (all). Width: 68.6 in. (all). Height: 53.2 in. (all). Front tread: 55.9 in. (all). Rear tread: 55.4 in. (all). Standard tires: P185/75R14 BSW (SE). Standard tires: P205/55R16 (GT).

FIREBIRD CHASSIS: Wheelbase: 101.1 in. (all). Overall length: 195.6 in. (Firebird/Formula); 197.0 in. (Trans Am). Width: 74.5 in. (all). Height: 52.0 in. (Firebird/Formula); 51.7 in. (Trans Am). Front tread: 60.7 in. (all). Rear tread: 60.6 in. (all). Standard tires: P215/60R16 (Firebird); P235/55R16 (Formula); P245/50ZR16 (Trans Am).

GRAND PRIX CHASSIS: Wheelbase: 107.5 in. (all). Overall length: 194.8 in. (Coupe); 194.9 in. (Sedan). Width: 71.9 in. (all). Height: 53.3 in. (Coupe); 54.8 in. (Sedan). Standard tires: See model description.

BONNEVILLE CHASSIS: Wheelbase: 110.8 in. (all). Overall length: 199.5 in. (SE); 201.2 in. (SSE/SSEi). Width: 73.6 in. (all). Height: 55.5 in. (all). Standard tires: See model descriptions.

TRANS SPORT CHASSIS: Wheelbase: 109.8 in. Overall length: 194.5 in. Width: 74.6 in. Height: 65.7 in. Standard tires: P205/70R15 BSW.

LEMANS TECHNICAL: Chassis: Front engine/front drive. Standard transmission: Four-speed manual (Aerocoupe "Value Leader" only). Standard transmission: Five-speed manual (Other Models). Optional (except "Value Leader") three-speed automatic transmission. Axle ratio: 3.43:1 with 1.6L and automatic. Axle ratio: 3.72:1 (both manual). Front suspension: deflected disc, MacPherson struts and 22mm stabilizer bar. Rear suspension: Coil springs, semi-independent torsion beam, trailing arms, and 18mm anti-roll bar. Steering: Rack-and-pinion 24.5:1 ratio (18.3:1 power-assisted optional, except "Value Leader"). Turns lock-to-lock: 3.5 (power); 4.57 (manual). Turning circle: 32.8 ft. Front brakes: 9.25-in. vented discs. Rear brakes: 7.9 x 1.8-in. drums (power-assisted).

SUNBIRD TECHNICAL: Chassis: Front engine/front drive. Base transmission: Five-speed manual. Optional transmission: Three-speed automatic. Axle ratio: 3.45:1 with five-speed manual. Axle ratio: 3.18:1 with three-speed automatic. Front suspension [Level I]: Deflected disc, MacPherson struts and (22mm with 2.0L TBI/28mm with 3.1L MFI) stabilizer bars. Front suspension [Level II]: Deflected disc, MacPherson struts and 28mm stabilizer bars. Rear suspension: Coil springs, semi-independent torsion beam, trailing arms and 21mm anti-roll bar. Steering: Rack-and-pinion 16.0:1 ratio (14.0:1 on cars with base 14-in. tires). Turns lock-to-lock: 3.0 (2.5 on base tire). Turning circle: 34.3 ft. (all). Front brakes: 10.25-in. vented disc power-assisted. Rear brakes: 7.87 x 1.77-in. drum power-assisted.

GRAND AM TECHNICAL: Chassis: Front engine/front drive. Base transmission: Five-speed manual with overdrive (M32 or MV5). Optional transmission: Three-speed automatic (MD9). Axle ratio: 3.58:1 (with M32 five-speed manual). Axle ratio: 3:18:1 (with MD9 automatic). Axle ratio: 3.94:1 (with MV5 five-speed manual). Level I suspension: [Front] Deflected disc; MacPherson struts and 26mm anti-roll bar; [Rear] Coil springs; semi-independent torsion beam, trailing arms. Level II suspension: [Front] Deflected disc; MacPherson struts and 28mm anti-roll bar; [Rear] Coil springs; semi-independent torsion beam, trailing arms. Level III suspension: [Front] Deflected disc; MacPherson struts, 18mm direct-acting anti-roll bar. [Rear] Coil springs; semi-independent torsion beam, trailing arms and defected disc, gas-charged shocks. Steering (Level I): Power-assisted rack-and-pinion, 16.0:1 ratio, 2.98 turns lock-to-lock, and 34.1-ft. turning circle. Steering (Level II & III): Power-assisted rack-and-pinion, 14.0:1 ratio, 2.5 turns lock-to-lock, and 36.4-ft. turning circle. Front brakes: 259.5mm diameter vented discs. Rear brakes: 200.0mm diameter drums. Fuel tank: 15.2 gal.

FIREBIRD TECHNICAL: Chassis: Front engine/rear drive. Base transmission: Five-speed manual (Firebird); six-speed manual (Formula/Trans Am). Optional transmission: Four-speed automatic (all). Front suspension: Short/long arm (SLA) design with gas-filled monotube shocks including front stabilizer bar. Rear suspension: Live axle with revised spring mass and rates with gas-filled monotube shocks. Steering: Power assist rack-and-pinion. Turning circle: 37.8 ft. (Formula). Brakes: Advanced Delco-Moraine ABS VI four-wheel anti-lock brakes (all); front disc/rear drum (Firebird); four-wheel disc (Formula and Trans Am). Fuel tank: 15.5 gal.

GRAND PRIX TECHNICAL: Chassis: Front engine/front drive. Standard drivetrain all except GTP Coupe: 3.1L MPFI V-6 with three-speed automatic. Standard drivetrain GT Coupe and optional all others: 3.4L Twin Dual Cam MPFI V-6 with five-speed manual transaxle. Final Drive Ratios: [M27 five-speed manual] 3.67:1; [M13 four-speed electronic automatic--optional on all] 3.43:1; [MD9 three-speed automatic] 2.84:1; [M13 four-speed electronic automatic--standard GT and STE/optional LE and SE] 3.33:1. Front suspension: MacPherson struts with tapered coil springs, lower A arm, and 28mm anti-roll bar (34mm anti-roll bar with Y99 rally suspension). Rear suspension: Tri-link independent suspension, transverse fiberglass leaf spring, and 12mm anti-roll bar (12mm anti-roll bar with Y99 and 3.1-liter V-6/14mm with Y99 and 3.4-liter V-6). Steering: Power-assisted rack-and-pinion with 15.7:1 ratio (14.0:1 with 3.4-liter V-6); 2.6 turns lock-to-lock (2.26 with GT/STE), and 36.7-ft. (39-ft. GT/STE) turning circle. Front brakes: 10.51-in. vented discs, power-assisted. Rear brakes: 10.1-in. solid discs, power-assisted. Fuel tank: 16.5 gal.

BONNEVILLE TECHNICAL: Chassis: Front engine/front drive. Base transmission: Four-speed electronic automatic. Axle ratio: 2.84:1 (3800 V-6); 3.06:1 (supercharged 3800 V-6). Front suspension: Deflected-disc, MacPherson struts with 32mm stabilizer bar (F41/FE2 and FE1). Rear suspension: Coil springs, semi-independent torsion beam, trailing arms, and 21mm stabilizer bar (F41/FE2) or 17mm stabilizer bar (FE1). Steering (SE): Power-assisted rack-and-pinion with 16.54:1 ratio, 2.79 turns lock-to-lock, and 39.4-ft. (left)/40.0-ft. (right) turning circle. Steering (Y52/SSE/SSEi): Power-assisted rack-and-pinion with 14.93:1 to 18.91:1 variable ratio, 2.86 turns lock-to-

lock, and 38.7-ft. (left)/40.3-ft. (right) turning circle. Front brakes: Power-assisted 10.9-in. vented discs. Rear brakes: Power-assisted 8.85-in. drums. Fuel tank: 18.0 gal.

TRANS SPORT TECHNICAL: Chassis: Front engine/front drive. Transmission: (MD9) Three-speed automatic; optional (M13) four-speed automatic. Axle ratio: 3.18:1 (3.1L V-6). Axle ratio: 3.06:1 (3.4L V-6). Front suspension: MacPherson struts, stamped lower control arms, 28mm stabilizer bar. Rear suspension: Open-section transverse beam on stamped steel trailing arms, tube shocks, coil springs and 25.4mm stabilizer bar. Steering: Power-assisted rack-and-pinion with 15.7:1 ratio, and 38-ft. turning circle. Front brakes: 10.2-in. vented rotors, 182 sq. in. swept area. Rear brakes: 8.86 x 1.58-in. finned composite cast iron drums with 98.5 sq. in. swept area. Fuel tank: 20.0 gal.

LEMANS OPTIONS: MX1 three-speed automatic transmission for SE ($475). C60 air conditioning, requires power steering and available in Value Leader Aerocoupe ($705). B37 front and rear floor mats ($33). N40 power steering, requires air conditioning in Aerocoupe or SE Sedan ($225). UM7 Delco ETR stereo in Value Leader Aerocoupe ($307). UM6 Delco ETR AM/FM with cassette and more in Value Leader Aerocoupe ($429). UM6 Delco ETR AM/FM with cassette and more in SE ($122). AD3 removable sun roof ($350). WDV warranty enhancements for New York ($25).

SUNBIRD OPTIONS: 1SB Sunbird LE and SE option group ($903). 1SC Sunbird LE and SE option group ($1352). 1SD Sunbird LE and SE option group ($2238). 1SB Sunbird SE Convertible option group ($1136). 1SC Sunbird SE Convertible option group ($2020). 1SB option group for GT Coupe ($1136). B4U Sport Appearance Package for SE Coupe, requires V-6 ($612). LHO 3.1-liter MPFI V-6, standard in GT Coupe ($585). W25 Special Appearance package ($524-$599 depending on value option packages it's teamed with). C60 air conditioning ($745). DO6 front seat armrest in GT and SE ($58). NB2 California emissions ($100). K34 cruise control ($225). C49 electric rear window defogger ($170). AO1 tinted glass ($105). TR9 lamp group ($29). D35 Sport mirrors ($53). A31 power windows, requires power door locks ($265 SE/GT Coupe/$330 Sedan/no charge Convertible). UN6 Delco radio equipment ($170). U1C Delco radio equipment ($396).

GRAND AM OPTIONS: 1SB package on GT Coupe/Sedan ($1467). 1SC package on GT Coupe ($1892). 1SC package on GT Sedan ($1957). 1SD package on GT Coupe ($2310). 1SD package on GT Sedan ($2375). 1SB package on SE Coupe/Sedan ($975). 1SC package on SE Coupe/Sedan ($1405). 1SD package on SE Coupe ($1892). 1SD package on SE Sedan ($1957). LD2 Quad-4 2.3-liter MPI engine in SE models ($410). LD2 Quad-4 2.3-liter MPI engine in GT models ($140 credit). LGO Quad-4 High-Output engine, standard on GT (no charge). LG7 3.3-liter V-6 in SE ($460/$90 credit in GT). MX1 three-speed automatic transmission ($555). C60 air conditioning ($830). C49 electric rear window defogger ($170). K34 cruise control ($225). UB3 rally gauges ($111). NB2 California emission requirements ($100). DG7 dual sport mirrors ($86). AC3 power seat with Sport interior group ($340). NV7 variable effort power steering ($62). A31 express down power windows in SE and GT Coupe ($275). A31 express down power window in SE or GT Sedan ($340). AM9 split folding rear seat ($150). CD4 controlled cycle wipers ($65). WDV warranty enhancements ($25). UM6 Delco sound system ($140). U1A Delco sound system ($460-$600). PG1 cross-lace wheel covers on SE without value package ($55).

1993 Pontiac Firebird Trans Am coupe. PMD

FIREBIRD OPTIONS: C60 air conditioning included in option groups 1SA, 1SB, 1SC, and 1SD. B35 rear floor mats included in all except optional in Formula 1SA group. B84 bodyside moldings included in all except optional in Formula 1SA group. A31 power windows included in all except Firebird 1SB group and Formula 1SA group. AU3 power door locks included in all except optional in Firebird 1SB group and Formula 1SA group. AH3 driver's side four-way manual seat adjuster included in select models except optional in Formula 1SA group (not available in Formula

1SB or 1SC groups). K34 cruise control included in all except optional in Firebird 1SB group and Formula 1SA group. DG7 dual Sport mirrors included in all except optional in Firebird 1SB group and Formula 1SA group. AUO remote keyless entry included in Firebird 1SD, Formula 1SC, and Trans Am 1SA groups, optional in all others. UX1 cassette with equalizer, steering wheel controls and 10-speaker sound system included in Firebird 1SD, Formula 1SC, and Trans Am 1SA groups, optional in all others.

GRAND PRIX OPTIONS: 1SB Grand Prix LE ($370). 1SC Grand Prix LE ($929). 1SB Grand Prix SE Sedan ($996). 1SC Grand Prix SE Sedan ($1379). 1SD Grand Prix SE Sedan ($1975). 1SB Grand Prix SE Coupe ($931). 1SC Grand Prix SE Coupe ($1314). 1SD Grand Prix SE Coupe ($1910). 1SB Grand Prix GT Coupe ($306). LQ1 3.4L 24-valve Twin Dual Cam V-6 ($995). MXO four-speed automatic ($200). MM5 five-speed manual transmission in Grand Prix GT Coupe ($200 credit)/STE Sedan ($225 credit). A90 remote deck lid release ($60). C49 electric rear window defogger ($170). NB2 California emissions system ($100). AUO Remote Keyless Entry system ($135). CF5 power sun roof ($695). UB3 rally gauge cluster ($250). U68 electric compass with trip computer and service reminder ($285). UV6 head-up display, requires bucket seats ($250). V56 rear deck lid luggage carrier ($115). B20 Custom interior trim ($355). DG7 dual Sport mirrors ($78). N33 tilt steering wheel ($145). A31 power windows ($275). BYP Sport Appearance package with lower aero ground effects ($366-$783 depending on model and other options). B4U Aero Appearance package ($2565-$2595). WDV warranty enhancements ($25). UM6 Delco radio equipment ($140). UX1 Delco radio equipment ($590). U1A stereo sound system ($226-$816 depending on model). US7 power antenna ($85). AN3 bucket seats ($140). B20 Custom interior trim ($110-$416). QPE touring tires ($112). QXJ P225/60R16 tires ($150). QLC P245/50ZR16 tires with GTP Coupe ($209). PH3 15-in. aluminum sport wheels ($275). NWO 16-in. aluminum Sport wheels ($275).

1993 Pontiac SSEi four-door sedan. PMD

BONNEVILLE OPTIONS: 1SB Bonneville SE option package ($383). 1SC Bonneville SE option package ($1041). 1SD Bonneville SE option package ($1467). 1SB Bonneville SSE option package ($1270). B20 Custom interior trim ($265). AUO Remote Keyless Entry system ($135). CF5 power glass sun roof ($1216-$1230). C49 electric rear window defogger ($170). K05 engine block heater ($18). NB2 California emissions system ($100). NW9 Traction Control system ($175). PF5 16-in. five-blade cast aluminum wheels ($340). QNX touring tires ($74). QVF tires ($90). T43 rear deck lid spoiler ($95). UA6 Theft Deterrent system ($190). UM6 Delco radio equipment ($140). UX1 Delco sound system ($375-$650). U1A compact disc player ($226-$876). US7 power antenna ($85). U92 trailer provisions ($150-$689 depending on other options and Value Packages). WDV warranty enhancements ($25). Y52 Performance & Handling package ($739).

TRANS SPORT OPTIONS: 1SB Trans Sport SE option package ($1035). 1SC Trans Sport SE option package ($1883). 1SD Trans Sport SE option package ($2428). C67 air conditioning ($830). NB2 California emissions system ($100). B2Q black roof delete (no charge). C49 electric rear window defogger ($170). AJ1 glass package ($245). AB5 power door locks ($300). D84 custom two-tone paint ($60). NK4 leather-wrapped steering wheel ($60). V54 roof luggage carrier ($145). K05 engine block heater ($18). UM6 Delco radio equipment ($140). U1A compact disc player ($226-$701). AG9 six-way power driver's seat ($270). ZP7 seven-passenger seating package ($870). PH3 aluminum wheels with locks ($275).

Note: Full option package contents, descriptions and applications information can often be determined by consulting factory literature. The data above is edited for size and clarity. This information provided only as a guide to help collectors appraise the relative value of cars with numerous options. Prices for items included as part of a value option package are usually much less than individual prices. Option prices charged by individual dealers may also vary.

PONTIAC I.D. NUMBERS: Vehicle identification number (VIN) is located on top left-hand surface of instrument panel visible through the windshield. The VIN has 17 symbols. The first symbol indicates the country of manufacture (U.S.) The second symbol indicates the manufacturer (G=General Motors). The third symbol indicates the make/division (2=Pontiac). The fourth, fifth, and sixth symbols are the same as the body style (model) number. The eighth symbol indicates the engine. The ninth symbol is a check digit. The 10th symbol indicates model-year. The 11th symbol indicates the assembly plant. The last six symbols are the consecutive unit number at the factory.

SUNBIRD -- SERIES 2J --FOUR -- Pontiac's subcompact offered a streamlined lineup from the previous year's six Sunbird models to 1994's four model offering. Gone were the GT Coupe and SE Sedan, while the SE Convertible became a LE Convertible. New features included the Sport Appearance Package now standard on the SE Coupe, two new exterior colors: Brilliant Blue and Dark Purple, dual outside rearview mirrors and tinted glass now standard on all models, rear deck lid spoiler, controlled-cycle windshield wipers, and 15-inch wheels/tires now standard on the LE Convertible, automatic door unlock/relock, lamp group now standard on all models, and powertrain noise and vibration reductions. Standard features across-the-lineup included: four-wheel anti-lock braking system, stainless steel exhaust system, oil level indicator, side window defogger, grid cloth fabric interior, illuminated entry, rear quarter courtesy lights, Delco ETR AM/FM stereo with seek-and-scan and clock, reclining front bucket seats, black, fixed mast antenna, air dam, bumpers/fascia with integral rub strips, Sport mirrors, fluidic windshield wipers, and front floor console. Individual model standard features included: LE Coupe/Sedan: 2.0-liter OHC four-cylinder MPFI engine with five-speed manual transmission, P185/75R14 blackwall all season tires, and custom 14-inch bolt-on wheel covers. LE Convertible: 2.0-liter OHC four-cylinder MPFI engine with five-speed manual transmission, convertible top with electro-hydraulic operation and glass backlight, two-passenger rear seat, P195/65R15 blackwall touring tires, 15-inch Crosslace wheel covers, and power windows with driver's side "express-down" feature. SE Coupe: 3.1-liter V-6 MPFI engine with five-speed manual transmission, aero extensions, specific front and rear fascia with semi-hidden headlamps, fog lamps, P195/65R15 blackwall touring tires, 15-inch Crosslace wheel covers, odometer, and carpeted front and rear floor mats.

Model Number	Body/Style Number	Body Type & Seating	Factory Price	Shipping Weight	Prod. Total
SUNBIRD LE -- SERIES 2J -- I-4					
2J	JB5	4-dr Sed-5P	9382	2502	Note 1
2J	JB1	2-dr Cpe-5P	9382	2484	Note 1
2J	JB3	2-dr Conv-5P	15524	2661	Note 1
SUNBIRD SE -- SERIES 2J -- I-4					
2J	JL1	2-dr Cpe-5P	12424	2682	Note 1

NOTE 1: Sunbird series production totaled 103,738.

1994 Pontiac Grand Am GT coupe. PMD

GRAND AM -- SERIES 2N -- Pontiac's Grand Am was again the automaker's sales leader and was again available as SE and GT Coupes and Sedans for 1994. Functional changes included four new exterior colors: Dark Green Metallic, Light Gray Metallic, Brilliant Blue Metallic, and Medium Blue Metallic; 16-inch Sport aluminum wheels; rear deck lid spoiler (standard on GT, optional on SE); power sun roof; driver's side airbag, automatic door lock/unlock/relock; leather interior option (gray or beige); theater dimming interior lights; exit lighting; 3.1-liter 3100 SFI V-6 engine option; four-speed automatic transmission; remote keyless entry; and R134A air conditioning refrigerant (replaced

R12 refrigerant). All Grand Am model standard equipment included: four-wheel anti-lock braking system, GM Computer Command Control, fixed mast antenna, bumpers/soft fascia with integral rub strips, tinted glass, fog lamps, Sport mirrors, "wet-arm" windshield wipers, driver's side airbag, power automatic door locks, illuminated entry (new for 1994), Delco ETR AM/FM stereo with seek up/down and clock, grid cloth fabric interior, 45/45 reclining front bucket seats, three-passenger rear seat with integrated headrests, four-spoke Sport steering wheel, and overhead compartment. Standard equipment specific to a series included: SE Coupe and Sedan: 2.3-liter OHC Quad four-cylinder engine with five-speed manual transmission, P185/75R14 blackwall tires, and 14-in. custom bolt-on wheel covers. GT Coupe and Sedan: 2.3-liter Quad 4 DOHC H.O. 16-valve four-cylinder with five-speed manual transmission, aero extensions including front/rear/side skirts, neutral density wraparound taillights, P205/55R16 blackwall Eagle GT+4 tires, 16-in. bright-faced aluminum or white wheels, air conditioning, controlled-cycle windshield wipers, analog instrumentation including tachometer and trip odometer, tilt wheel adjustable steering column, and stainless steel exhaust system with dual-dual chrome-tipped outlets.

Model Number	Body/Style Number	Body Type & Seating	Factory Price	Shipping Weight	Prod. Total
GRAND AM SE SERIES 2N -- Quad 4					
2N	NE1	2-dr Cpe-5P	12514	2736	Note 1
2N	NE5	4-dr Sed-5P	12614	2793	Note 1
GRAND AM GT -- SERIES 2N -- Quad 4					
2N	NW1	2-dr Cpe-5P	15014	2822	Note 1
2N	NW5	4-dr Sed-5P	15114	2882	Note 1

NOTE 1: Grand Am series production totaled 254,919.

FIREBIRD -- SERIES 2F -- V-6/V-8 -- Pontiac's theme for its Firebird 1994 lineup could have been the "return of the ragtop." Each of its series--Firebird, Formula, and Trans Am--had its 1993 coupe-only offering bolstered with the addition of convertible models (the Trans Am convertible was part of its GT series, while the coupe version was offered both as a Trans Am and as a Trans Am GT). New features for the seven-model lineup included: One new exterior color: Dark Aqua Metallic, floodlit interior door switches, visor straps, Delco 2001 Series radio family, compact disc player without equalizer, 5.7-liter SFI V-8, 5.7-liter Mass Air Flow Control System, four-speed electronically controlled automatic transmission, driver-selectable automatic transmission controls, six-speed transmission 3.42:1 axle ratio, six-speed transmission 1-4 gear skip shift feature, traction control (V-8 automatic only), and two-component clearcoat paint. Across-the-lineup standard equipment included: four-wheel anti-lock brakes; stainless steel exhaust system; GM Computer Command Control; low oil level monitor and warning; front air dam; black, fixed mast antenna; one-piece resilient bodycolor bumpers/fascias; tinted glass; rear deck lid spoiler; controlled-cycle windshield wipers; dual airbags; side window defogger; metrix cloth fabric interior; locking glovebox; reclining front bucket seats and folding rear seats; tilt-wheel adjustable steering column; and Pass-Key II theft deterrent system.

Note: SLP Engineering, Inc., of Toms River, N.J., created 250 cars called Firehawk based on the 1994 Pontiac Formula Coupe. These Firehawks were sold through Pontiac dealers with GMAC financing offered to buyers of these road racers. The Firehawk was offered with a six-speed manual transmission or four-speed automatic, in hardtop or T-top version. Beyond the distinctive Firehawk graphics on the car, the other giveaway feature that this car was more than "Formula" was twin hood scoops that the SLP engineers called "functional cold air induction." The air channeled into the engine bay fed a 5.7-liter, 300-hp V-8 with a compression ratio of 10.25:1. This combination produced 0-to-60 mph launch in 4.9 seconds. The Firehawk rode on a 17-in. tire/wheel combination, and M.S.R.P. was $24,244.

1994 Pontiac Firebird convertible. PMD

Model Number	Body/Style Number	Body Type & Seating	Factory Price	Shipping Weight	Prod. Total
FIREBIRD -- SERIES 2F -- V-6					
2F	FS2	2-dr Cpe-5P	13995	3232	Note 1
2F	FV3	2-dr Conv-5P	21179	3346	Note 1
FIREBIRD FORMULA -- SERIES 2F -- V-8					
2F	FV2	2-dr Cpe-5P	17995	3369	Note 1
2F	FV3	2-dr Conv-5P	24279	3485	Note 1
FIREBIRD TRANS AM -- SERIES 2F -- V-8					
2F	FV2	2-dr Cpe-5P	19895	3461	Note 1
FIREBIRD TRANS AM GT -- SERIES 2F -- V-8					
2F	FV2	2-dr Cpe-5P	21395	3478	Note 1
2F	FV3	2-dr Conv-5P	26479	--	Note 1

NOTE 1: Firebird series production totaled 51,523.

GRAND PRIX -- SERIES 2W -- V-6/V-8 -- The Grand Prix lineup for 1994 was reduced from five models the previous year to two models: the SE Coupe and Sedan. The revamped lineup received an increased level of standard equipment as well as many new features. Among the changes were: dual front airbags (standard on SE Coupe and Sedan); a "Special Edition Coupe" package exterior design; three new exterior colors: Brilliant Blue, Dark Teal, and Medium Teal; one new interior color: Teal; a GTP Performance Package for the SE Coupe; a GT Performance Package for the SE Sedan; 15-in. Sport wheel cover design; 16-in. five-spoke aluminum wheels; new instrument panel design; low oil level sensor for the 3.1-liter engine; rotary HVAC and headlamp controls; stalk-mounted windshield wiper and cruise controls; electronic actuated cruise control; Delco 2001 Series radio family; automatic door lock with unlock and relock features; trip computer with outside temperature display; single stroke parking brake; 3.1-liter 3100 SFI V-6 engine; 210-hp 3.4-liter SFI DOHC V-6 engine; R134A air conditioning refrigerant (replaces R12 refrigerant); and Pass-Key II theft deterrent system. Standard equipment found on both the SE Coupe and Sedan included: black, fixed mast antenna; soft fascia type bumpers with integral rub strips; tinted and safety laminated glass; fog lamps; lower aero ground effects; "wet-arm" controlled-cycle windshield wipers; electronic air conditioning; mechanical analog instrumentation; three-passenger rear seat with integrated headrests; tilt-wheel adjustable steering column; power windows with "express-down" feature; four-wheel disc brakes; stainless steel exhaust system; GM Computer Command Control; and 3.1-liter 3100 SFI V-6 with electronically controlled four-speed automatic transmission and second gear start feature.

Model Number	Body/Style Number	Body Type & Seating	Factory Price	Shipping Weight	Prod. Total
GRAND PRIX SE -- SERIES 2W -- V-6					
2W	WJ5	4-dr Sed-5P	16174	3370	Note 1
2W	WJ1	2-dr Cpe-5P	16770	3275	Note 1

NOTE 1: Grand Prix series production totaled 148,405.

BONNEVILLE -- SERIES 2H -- V-6 -- Pontiac dropped the SSEi model for 1994 opting to offer a new Bonneville SSEi Supercharger Package (WA6) as an option on the SSE Sedan (it was not available on the SE Sedan). The revised two model lineup offered many new features for 1994 including: Electronic brake and engine traction control; rear deck lid spoiler available with all exterior colors; standard 15-in. bolt-on wheel covers for SE; standard 16-in. torque-star cast aluminum wheels for SSE; gray ports on optional 16-in. five-blade wheels for SE; black windshield wipers and front license plate bracket on SSE; SLE grille now standard on SE; monotone paint treatment on SSE grille; new (B57) Monotone Appearance Package; high gloss black bodyside appliqué/fascia inserts on Monotone Appearance Package and SLE Package on SE; black windshield/header moldings with SLE Package on SE; dual airbags now standard on SE and SSE; electronic auto calibrating compass; available six-way power adjustable passenger seat; Delco 2001 Series radio family; one new interior color: Medium Blue; Computer Command Ride suspension; and remote trunk release activates without ignition on. Standard equipment found on both the SE and SSE Sedans included: composite polymer bumpers/fascias; fog lamps; tinted glass; manual air conditioning; power door locks; warning lights cluster including security system light; rear-seat pass-through; tilt-wheel adjustable steering column; Pass-Key II theft deterrent system; power windows with "express down" feature; four-wheel anti-lock brakes; brake/transmission shift interlock safety feature; and 3800 Series SFI V-6 engine with electronically controlled four-speed automatic transmission.

Model Number	Body/Style Number	Body Type & Seating	Factory Price	Shipping Weight	Prod. Total
BONNEVILLE SE -- SERIES H -- V-6					
2H	HX5	4-dr Spt Sed-5P	20424	3446	Note 1
BONNEVILLE SSE -- SERIES H -- V-6					
2H	HZ5	4-dr Spt Sed-5P	25884	3587	Note 1

NOTE 1: Bonneville series production totaled 87,926.

TRANS SPORT -- SERIES 2U -- V-6 -- The Trans Sport SE again comprised Pontiac's minivan lineup. Changes for 1994 were many, and included: updated exterior styling; fog lamps; "hidden" liftgate handle; molded-in rear step pad; center high-mounted stop lamp; monotone paint treatment; three new exterior colors: Light Blue Metallic, Medium Blue Metallic, and Bright Aqua Metallic; one new interior color: Blue; optional solar privacy glass; standard driver's side airbag; integral child seat(s); redesigned forward instrument panel; five- and seven-passenger seating; fold-and-stow modular seats; Milliweave cloth fabric; thinner/lighter (32 lbs.) modular seats; automatic power door locks; vinyl door and sidewall trim; traction control; power sliding door; and coin holder in underdash storage. Standard equipment included: 3.1-liter V-6 engine with three speed automatic transmission; four-wheel anti-lock braking system; stainless steel exhaust system; GM Computer Command Control; four-way manual driver's side seat adjuster; face-level HVAC vents; front side window defogger; "wet-arm" controlled-cycle windshield wiper system; integrated roof antenna; composite polymer bumpers with integral rub strips; tinted glass; P205/70R15 blackwall all-season tires; 15-in. bolt-on styled wheel covers; and lower aero molding.

TRANS SPORT -- SERIES 2U -- V-6

Model Number	Body/Style Number	Body Type & Seating	Factory Price	Shipping Weight	Prod. Total
2U	U06	SE Wagon	17369	3576	43,694

SUNBIRD ENGINES

[STANDARD BASE/LE] Inline. OHC. Four-cylinder. Cast iron block. Aluminum head and intake manifold. Displacement: 121 cu. in. (2.0L). Bore & stroke: 3.38 x 3.38 in. Compression ratio: 9.2:1. Brake horsepower: 110 @ 5200 rpm. Torque: 124 lb.-ft. @ 3600 rpm. Fuel system: MPFI. Code: LE4. Standard in Sunbird LE Series models. [VIN code H]. [STANDARD SE] V-block. OHV. Six-cylinder. Cast iron block and aluminum head. Displacement: 191 cu. in. (3.1L). Bore & stroke: 3.51 x 3.31 in. Compression ratio: 8.9:1. Brake horsepower: 140 @ 4200 rpm. Torque: 185 lb.-ft. @ 3600 rpm. Fuel system: MPFI. Standard in Sunbird SE Coupe, optional in LE Series models. [VIN code T or M].

GRAND AM ENGINES

[STANDARD SE] Inline. Quad-4 OHC. Cast iron block. Aluminum head and intake manifold. Displacement: 138 cu. in. (2.3L). Bore & stroke: 3.63 x 3.35 in. Compression ratio: 9.5:1. Brake horsepower: 115 @ 5200 rpm. Torque: 140 lb.-ft. @ 3200 rpm. Fuel system: MPFI. RPO Code: L40. Standard in SE Coupe/Sedan. [VIN code A]. [OPTIONAL GT] Inline. Quad-4 DOHC. 16-valve. Cast iron block. Aluminum head and intake manifold. Displacement: 138 cu. in. (2.3L). Bore & stroke: 3.63 x 3.35 in. Compression ratio: 9.5:1. Brake horsepower: 155 @ 6000 rpm. Torque: 150 lb.-ft. @ 4800 rpm. Fuel system: MPFI. RPO Code: LD2. Optional in GT Coupe/Sedan. [VIN code D]. [STANDARD GT] Inline. Quad-4 H.O. DOHC. 16-valve. Cast iron block. Aluminum head and intake manifold. Displacement: 138 cu. in. (2.3L). Bore & stroke: 3.63 x 3.35 in. Compression ratio: 10.0:1. Brake horsepower: 175 @ 6200 rpm. Torque: 150 lb.-ft. @ 5200 rpm. Fuel system: MPFI. RPO Code: LG0. Standard in Grand Am GT Coupe/Sedan with MV5 five-speed manual transmission. [VIN code A]. [OPTIONAL SE/GT] V-block. OHV. Six-cylinder. Cast iron block and aluminum head. Displacement: 191 cu. in. (3.1L). Bore & stroke: 3.51 x 3.31 in. Compression ratio: 9.5:1. Brake horsepower: 155 @ 5200 rpm. Torque: 185 lb.-ft. @ 4000 rpm. Fuel system: SPFI. RPO Code L82. Optional in Grand Am SE and GT Coupes/Sedans. [VIN code M or T].

1994 Pontiac Firebird 25th Anniversary Trans Am coupe. PMD

FIREBIRD ENGINES

[FIREBIRD BASE V-6] V-block. OHV. Six-cylinder. Cast iron block and heads. Aluminum intake manifold. Displacement: 207 cu. in. (3.4L). Bore & stroke: 3.62 x 3.31 in. Compression ratio: 9.0:1. Brake horsepower: 160 @ 4600 rpm. Torque: 200 lb.-ft. @ 3600 rpm. Fuel system: SPFI. RPO Code: L32. Standard in Firebird. Not available in Formula and Trans Am. [VIN code S or X]. [FORMULA/TRANS AM BASE V-8] V-block. OHV. Eight-cylinder. Cast iron block and heads. Aluminum intake manifold. Displacement: 350 cu. in. (5.7L). Bore & stroke: 4.00 x 3.48 in. Compression ratio: 10.5:1. Brake horsepower: 275 @ 5000 rpm. Torque: 325 lb.-ft. @ 2400 rpm. Fuel system: SPFI. RPO Code: LT1. Standard in Formula and Trans Am. Not available in Firebird. [VIN code P].

GRAND PRIX ENGINES

[STANDARD GRAND PRIX SE] V-block. OHV. Six-cylinder. Cast iron block and cast aluminum heads. 191 cu. in. (3.1L). Bore & stroke: 3.51 x 3.31 in. Compression ratio: 9.5:1. Brake horsepower: 160 @ 5200 rpm. Torque: 185 lb.-ft. @ 4000 rpm. Fuel system: SPFI. RPO Code: L82. [VIN code T or M]. [OPTIONAL GRAND PRIX SE] V-block. DOHC. Six-cylinder. Cast iron block and cast aluminum heads. 207 cu. in. (3.4L). Bore & stroke: 3.62 x 3.30 in. Compression ratio: 9.25:1. Brake horsepower: 210 @ 5000 rpm. Torque: 215 lb.-ft. @ 4000 rpm. Fuel system: SPFI. RPO Code: LQ1. [VIN code X or S].

BONNEVILLE ENGINES

[STANDARD SE/SSE] V-block. OHV. "3800" six-cylinder. Cast iron block and heads. Aluminum intake manifold. Displacement: 231 cu. in. (3.8L). Bore & stroke: 3.80 x 3.40 in. Compression ratio: 9.0:1. Brake horsepower: 170 @ 4800 rpm. Torque: 225 lb.-ft. @ 3200 rpm. Fuel system: SPFI. RPO Code: C. Standard in Bonneville SE/SSE. [VIN code C]. [OPTIONAL SSE] V-block. OHV. "3800" supercharged six-cylinder. Cast iron block and heads. Aluminum intake manifold. Displacement: 231 cu. in. (3.8L). Bore & stroke: 3.80 x 3.40 in. Compression ratio: 9.0:1. Brake horsepower: 225 @ 5000 rpm. Torque: 275 lb.-ft. @ 3200 rpm. Fuel system: SPFI and supercharged. RPO Code: L67. Optional in Bonneville SSE. [VIN code 1].

TRANS SPORT ENGINES

[STANDARD SE] V-block. OHV. Six-cylinder. Cast iron block and heads. Aluminum intake manifold. Displacement: 191 cu. in. (3.1L). Bore & stroke: 3.50 x 3.31 in. Compression ratio: 8.5:1. Brake horsepower: 120 @ 4400 rpm. Torque: 175 lb.-ft. @ 2200 rpm. Fuel system: EFI/TBFI. RPO Code: LG6. Standard in SE. [VIN code T or M]. [OPTIONAL SE] V-block. OHV. "3800" six-cylinder. Cast iron block and heads. Aluminum intake manifold. Displacement: 231 cu. in. (3.8L). Bore & stroke: 3.80 x 3.40 in. Compression ratio: 9.0:1. Brake horsepower: 170 @ 4800 rpm. Torque: 225 lb.-ft. @ 3200 rpm. Fuel system: SPFI. RPO Code: L27. [VIN code 3 or C].

SUNBIRD CHASSIS: Wheelbase: 101.3 in. (all). Overall length: 180.7 in. (all). Overall width: 66.2 in. (all). Height: 52.2 in. (LE/SE Coupe); 52.4 in. (LE Convertible), 53.9 in. (LE Sedan). Front tread: 55.4 in. (all). Rear tread: 55.4 in. (all). Standard tires: See model descriptions.

GRAND AM CHASSIS: Wheelbase: 103.4 in. (all). Overall length: 186.9 in. (all). Width: 67.5 in. (all). Height: 53.2 in. (all). Front tread: 55.9 in. (all). Rear tread: 55.4 in. (all). Standard tires: See model descriptions.

FIREBIRD CHASSIS: Wheelbase: 101.1 in. (all). Overall length: 195.6 in. (Firebird/Formula); 197.0 in. (Trans Am). Width: 74.5 in. (all). Height: 52.0 in. (Firebird/Formula); 51.7 in. (Trans Am). Front tread: 60.7 in. (all). Rear tread: 60.6 in. (all). Standard tires: P215/60R16 (Firebird); P235/55R16 (Formula/Trans Am); P245/50ZR16 (Trans Am GT).

GRAND PRIX CHASSIS: Wheelbase: 107.5 in. (all). Overall length: 194.8 in. (Coupe); 194.9 in. (Sedan). Width: 71.9 in. (all). Height: 52.8 in. (Coupe); 54.4 in. (Sedan). Front tread: 59.5 in. (all). Rear tread: 58.0 in. (all). Standard tires: P215/60/R16 (Coupe). P205/70R15 (Sedan).

BONNEVILLE CHASSIS: Wheelbase: 110.8 in. (all). Overall length: 199.5 in. (SE); 201.2 in. (SSE). Width: 74.5 in. (all). Height: 55.7 in. (all). Front tread: 60.4 in. (SE); 60.8 in. (SSE). Rear tread: 60.3 in. (SE); 60.6 in. (SSE). Standard tires: P215/65R15 (SE); P225/60R16 (SSE).

TRANS SPORT CHASSIS: Wheelbase: 109.8 in. Overall length: 192.2 in. Width: 74.6 in. Height: 65.7 in. Front tread: 59.2 in. Rear tread: 61.4 in. Standard tires: See model description.

SUNBIRD TECHNICAL: Chassis: Front engine/front drive. Base transmission: (MK7) Five-speed manual (2.0-liter L4)/(MG2) five-speed manual (3.1-liter V-6). Optional transmission: (MD9) Three-speed automatic. Axle ratio: 3.45:1 with 2.0-liter L4 and five-speed manual/3.61:1 with 3.1-liter V-6 and five-speed manual. Axle ratio: 3.18:1 with 2.0-liter L4 and three-speed automatic/2.53:1 with 3.1-liter V-6 and three-speed automatic (2.84:1 on LE Convertible). Front suspension [Level I]: Deflected disc, MacPherson struts and (22mm with 14-

inch tires & wheels/28mm with optional tires/wheels) stabilizer bars. Rear suspension [Level I]: Coil springs, semi-independent torsion beam, trailing arms (19mm anti-roll bar with optional tires/wheels. Front suspension [Level II]: Deflected disc, MacPherson struts and 28mm stabilizer bars. Rear suspension: Coil springs, semi-independent torsion beam, trailing arms and 19mm anti-roll bar. Steering: Rack-and-pinion 16.0:1 ratio (14.0:1 on cars with optional tires/wheels). Turns lock-to-lock: 3.0 (2.5 on optional tires/wheels). Turning circle: 35.3 ft. (all). Front brakes: 10.2-in. vented discs. Rear brakes: 7.87 x 1.77-in. drums, power-assisted.

GRAND AM TECHNICAL: Chassis: Front engine/front drive. Base transmission: Five-speed manual with overdrive (M32 or MV5). Optional transmissions: four-speed automatic (M13)/three-speed automatic (MD9). Axle ratio: 3.58:1 (with M32 five-speed manual); 3.94:1 (with MV5 five-speed manual); 3.43:1 (with M13 four-speed automatic and L40 Quad OHC four-cylinder engine); 3.73:1 (with M13 four-speed automatic and LD2 Quad 4 engine); 2:53:1 (with MD9 three-speed automatic). Front suspension (Standard SE): Deflected disc; MacPherson struts, 27 N-mm spring, and 22mm stabilizer bar. Rear Suspension (Standard SE): 23/39 N-mm dual rate springs, semi-independent trailing arms linked with torsion beam, 19.5mm stabilizer bar. Front suspension (Standard GT): Deflected disc; MacPherson struts, 27 N-mm spring, and 24mm stabilizer bar (automatic)/30mm (manual). Rear suspension (Standard GT): 28/47 N-mm dual rate springs, semi-independent trailing arms linked with torsion beam, 19.5mm stabilizer bar. Steering Power-assisted rack-and-pinion, 14.0:1 ratio. Turns lock-to-lock: 2.5. Turning circle: 36.4 ft. Front brakes: 259.5mm diameter vented discs. Rear brakes: 200.0mm diameter drums. Fuel tank: 15.2 gal.

FIREBIRD TECHNICAL: Chassis: Front engine/rear drive. Base transmission: (M49) Five-speed manual (Firebird); (MM6) six-speed manual (Formula/Trans Am). Optional transmission: (MD8) Four-speed automatic (all). Front suspension: (F41 Firebird) Short/long arm (SLA)/coil over monotube gas-charged shocks, tubular stabilizer bar with links, 30mm stabilizer bar. (FE2 Formula/Trans Am) SLA/coil over monotube gas-charged shocks, tubular stabilizer bar with links, 30mm stabilizer bar. Rear suspension: (F41 Firebird) Salisbury axle with torque arm, trailing arm, track bar, coil springs, 17mm stabilizer bar. (FE2 Formula/Trans Am) Salisbury axle with torque arm, trailing arm, track bar, coil springs, 19mm stabilizer bar. Steering: Power, rack-and-pinion with 16.9:1 ratio (Firebird)/14.4:1 (Formula/Trans Am). Turns lock-to-lock: 2.67 (Firebird)/2.28 (Formula/Trans Am). Turning circle: (Firebird) 37.9 ft. (left) 40.6 ft. (right)/(Formula/Trans Am) 37.7 ft. (left) 40.1 ft. (right). Front brakes: (Firebird/Formula/Trans Am) 10.7 in. vented disc. Rear brakes: (Firebird) 9.5 in. power assisted Duo-Servo drum. (Formula/Trans Am) 11.4 in. power assisted vented disc. Fuel tank: 15.5 gal.

1994 Pontiac Grand Prix SE. PMD

GRAND PRIX TECHNICAL: Chassis: Front engine/front drive. Standard drivetrain: (L82) 3.1L SPFI V-6 engine with (M13) four-speed electronic automatic transmission. Final Drive Ratios: 3.43:1 with (M13) four-speed electronic automatic, optional on all. 3.33:1 (M13) four-speed electronic automatic, standard on SE Coupe/Sedan. Front suspension: MacPherson struts with tapered coil springs, lower A arm, and 28mm anti-roll bar (34mm anti-roll bar with Y99 rally suspension). Rear suspension: Tri-link independent suspension, transverse fiberglass leaf spring, and 12mm anti-roll bar (12mm anti-roll bar with Y99 and 3.1-liter V-6/14mm with Y99 and 3.4-liter V-6). Steering: Power-assisted rack-and-pinion with 15.7:1 ratio (14.0:1 with 3.4-liter V-6). Turns lock-to-lock: 2.6 (2.26 with Y99 and 3.4-liter V-6). Turning circle: 36.7-ft. (39-ft. with Y99 and 3.4-liter V-6). Front brakes: 10.51-in. vented discs, power-assisted. Rear brakes: 10.1-in. solid discs, power-assisted. Fuel tank: 16.5 gal.

BONNEVILLE TECHNICAL: Chassis: Front engine/front drive. Base transmission: (M13) four-speed electronic automatic. Axle ratio: 2.84:1 (3800 V-6); 2.97:1 (supercharged 3800 V-6). Front suspension: (SE) Standard FE1: deflected-disc, MacPherson struts, coil spring over strut (22 N-mm), 30mm stabilizer bar. (SSE) Standard FE2: deflected-disc, MacPherson struts, coil spring over strut (26 N-mm), 32mm stabilizer bar. Rear suspension: (SE) Standard FE1: coil springs (variable rate 48-65 N-mm), independent lower A-arm, 17mm stabilizer bar. (SSE) Standard FE2: automatic level control coil springs (47 N-mm), Chapman struts, independent lower A-arm, 22mm stabilizer bar. Optional front suspension: (SE) F41: Performance and Handling, deflected-disc, MacPherson struts, coil spring over strut (26 N-mm), 32mm stabilizer bar. (SSE) FW1: Computer Command Ride, deflected-disc, MacPherson struts, coil spring over strut (26 N-mm), 32mm stabilizer bar. Optional rear suspension: (SE) F41: coil springs (variable rate 55-75 N-mm), Chapman struts, independent lower A-arm, 17mm stabilizer bar. (SSE) FW1: automatic level control coil springs (47 N-mm), Chapman struts, independent lower A-arm, 22mm stabilizer bar. Steering (Standard SE): Power-assisted rack-and-pinion with 16.54:1 ratio, 2.79 turns lock-to-lock, and 39.4-ft. turning circle. (SSE/optional SE): Variable-effort rack-and-pinion with 14.93:1 to 18.91:1 ratio, 2.86 turns lock-to-lock, and 40.5-ft. turning circle. Front brakes: 10.9-in. vented discs (all). Rear brakes: Power-assisted 8.85-in. drums (all). Fuel tank: 18.0 gal.

TRANS SPORT TECHNICAL: Chassis: Front engine/front drive. Transmission: (MD9) Three-speed automatic; optional (M13) four-speed automatic. Axle ratio: 3.06:1 (3.1L V-6); 3.06:1 (3.8L V-6). Front suspension: MacPherson strut with coil springs (27 N-mm), stamped lower control arms and modular iron steering knuckles, 27mm stabilizer bar. Rear suspension: Open-section transverse beam on stamped steel trailing arms, tube shocks, 48-56 N-mm variable rate coil springs (base suspension)/48.3 N-mm coil springs (uplevel suspension, electronic leveling) 25.4mm stabilizer bar. Steering: Rack-and-pinion with integral power unit with 15.7:1 ratio. Turns lock-to-lock: 3.05. Turning circle: 43.1 ft. Front brakes: 10.9 x 1.3-in. single caliper disc. Rear brakes: 8.86 x 1.77-in. leading trailing drum. Fuel tank: 20.0 gal.

SUNBIRD OPTIONS: 1SB Sunbird LE Coupe/Sedan option group ($1234). 1SC Sunbird LE Coupe/Sedan option group ($1974). 1SD Sunbird LE Coupe/Sedan option group ($1969). 1SB Sunbird LE Convertible option group ($1366). 1SB Sunbird SE Coupe option group ($1234). 1SC Sunbird SE Coupe option group ($1904). LHO 3.1-liter MPFI V-6, standard in SE Coupe ($712). W25 Special Appearance package ($316-$330 depending on value option packages). C60 air conditioning ($785). YF5 California emissions ($100). N33 tilt steering wheel ($145). K34 cruise control ($225). C49 electric rear window defogger ($170). A31 power windows ($265 LE/SE Coupe/$330 LE Sedan/no charge Convertible). UN6 Delco radio equipment ($170). U1C Delco radio equipment ($396).

GRAND AM OPTIONS: 1SB package on GT Coupe/Sedan ($535). 1SC package on GT Coupe ($1046). 1SC package on GT Sedan ($1111). 1SB package on SE Coupe/Sedan ($1575). 1SC package on SE Coupe ($2086). 1SD package on SE Sedan ($2151). LD2 Quad-4 2.3-liter MPI engine in SE models ($410). LD2 Quad-4 2.3-liter MPI engine in GT models ($140 credit). LG0 Quad-4 High-Output engine, standard on GT (no charge). L82 3.1-liter V-6 in SE ($410/$140 credit in GT). MX1 three-speed automatic transmission ($555). MX0 four-speed automatic transmission ($755). C60 air conditioning ($830). C49 electric rear window defogger ($170). K34 cruise control ($225). UB3 rally gauges ($111). YF5 California emission requirements ($100). DG7 dual sport mirrors ($86). AC3 power seat with Sport interior group ($340). CF5 power sun roof ($595). A31 express down power windows ($275-$340 depending on value option packages). AM9 split folding rear seat ($150). WDV warranty enhancements ($25). UM6 Delco sound system ($140). UX1 Delco sound system ($375).

FIREBIRD OPTIONS: 1SB Firebird Coupe option package ($1005). 1SC Firebird Coupe option package ($2421). 1SB Formula Coupe option package ($906). 1SC Formula Coupe option package ($1491). 1SB Firebird Convertible option package ($485). 1SB Formula Convertible option package ($485). C60 air conditioning ($895 on Firebird, standard on Formula/Trans Am). AU0 remote keyless entry ($135). MX0 four-speed automatic transmission ($775). B84 body color side moldings ($60). CC1 hatch roof ($895). U1C Delco sound system with CD player ($226). UP3 Delco sound system with CD player and graphic equalizer ($676). K34 cruise control, standard on Trans Am/Trans Am GT ($225). YF5 California emission requirements ($100). AR9 articulating bucket seats with leather ($780). C49 rear window defogger ($170).

GRAND PRIX OPTIONS: 1SB Grand Prix SE Sedan ($717). 1SC Grand Prix SE Sedan ($1912). LQ1 3.4L DOHC V-6 ($1125). A90 remote deck lid release ($60). C49 electric rear window defogger ($170). AU0 Remote Keyless Entry system ($135). CF5 power sun roof ($695). UV8 cellular phone provisions ($35). UV6 head-up display ($250). B20 Custom interior trim ($391-$1103 depending on value option packages). B4S GTP Performance Package for Grand Prix SE Coupe ($1605). B4Q GT Performance package for Grand Prix SE Sedan ($2103-$2198 depending on value option packages). JL9 anti-lock brakes ($450). UN6 Delco radio equipment ($170). UT6 Delco

radio equipment ($225-$400 depending on value option packages). U1C Delco radio equipment ($226-$396 depending on value option package). AC3 six-way power driver's seat ($305). QPE touring tires for Grand Prix SE Sedan ($112). QXJ P225/60R16 tires ($150). PH3 15-in. aluminum Sport wheels for Grand Prix SE Sedan ($275). NWO 16-in. aluminum Sport wheels for Grand Prix SE Sedan ($275).

BONNEVILLE OPTIONS: 1SB Bonneville SE option package ($628). 1SC Bonneville SE option package ($1281). 1SD Bonneville SE option package ($1942). 1SB Bonneville SSE option package ($1440). WA6 SSEi supercharger package, requires P225/60ZR16 tires ($1167). AUO Remote Keyless Entry system ($135). CF5 power glass sun roof ($981-$995). C49 electric rear window defogger ($170). KO5 engine block heater ($18). NW9 Traction Control system ($175). PF5 16-in. five-blade cast aluminum wheels ($340). QNX touring tires ($84). T43 rear deck lid spoiler ($110). UN6 Delco radio equipment ($170). U1C Delco sound system ($396). UP3 Delco sound system with compact disc player ($686). US7 power antenna ($85). Y52 Performance & Handling package ($649).

1994 Pontiac Trans Sport SE minivan. PMD

TRANS SPORT OPTIONS: 1SB Trans Sport SE option package ($1388). 1SC Trans Sport SE option package ($2383). 1SD Trans Sport SE option package ($2933). B2Q black roof delete (no charge). C49 electric rear window defogger ($170). AJ1 glass package ($245). AB5 power door locks ($300). V54 roof luggage carrier ($175). KO5 engine block heater ($18). UM6 Delco radio equipment ($140). U1A Delco sound system with compact disc player ($206-$541). ZP7 seven-passenger seating package ($870). PH3 aluminum wheels with locks ($275). L27 3.8L V-6 with four-speed auto transmission ($819). E58 power sliding door ($295). C54 pop-up sun roof ($300). NW9 traction control ($350).

Note: Full option package contents, descriptions and applications information can often be determined by consulting factory literature. The data above is edited for size and clarity. This information provided only as a guide to help collectors appraise the relative value of cars with numerous options. Prices for items included as part of a value option package are usually much less than individual prices. Option prices charged by individual dealers may also vary.

1995 PONTIAC

PONTIAC I.D. NUMBERS: Vehicle identification number (VIN) is located on top left-hand surface of instrument panel visible through the windshield. The VIN has 17 symbols. The first symbol indicates the country of manufacture (U.S.) The second symbol indicates the manufacturer (G=General Motors). The third symbol indicates the make/division (2=Pontiac). The fourth, fifth, and sixth symbols are the same as the body style (model). The eighth symbol indicates the engine. The ninth symbol is a check digit. The 10th symbol indicates model-year. The 11th symbol indicates the assembly plant. The last six symbols are the consecutive unit number at the factory.

SUNFIRE -- SERIES 2J --FOUR -- For 13 years previous known as the Sunbird, Pontiac's 1995 subcompact encompassed not only a name alteration to Sunfire, but also new styling, new engineering, and new technology--essentially an all-new car. Standard features of the new Sunfire included: 2.2-liter OHV four-cylinder engine for the SE Series (GT Coupe powered by a 2.3-liter DOHC 16-valve Quad 4); aluminized stainless steel exhaust system; dual airbags; tinted glass; anti-lock braking system; coil-over-shock rear suspension; rear HVAC vents; tilt-wheel adjustable steering column; tachometer; 4.9-liter glovebox; and lamps in the trunk and glovebox. Other amenities included a folding rear seat for extra cargo room (including the SE Convertible) and traction control as an option on the GT Coupe.

1995 Pontiac Sunfire four-door sedan. PMD

Model Number	Body/Style Number	Body Type & Seating	Factory Price	Shipping Weight	Prod. Total
SUNFIRE SE-- SERIES 2J -- I-4					
2J	B54	4-dr Sed-5P	11709	2723	Note 1
2J	B14	2-dr Cpe-5P	11559	2679	Note 1
2J	B34	2-dr Conv-5P	--	2835	Note 1
SUNFIRE GT -- SERIES 2J -- I-4					
2J	D14	2-dr Cpe-5P	--	2829	Note 1

NOTE 1: Sunfire series 1995 production estimate unavailable as SE Convertible and GT Coupe were scheduled for mid-model year introduction.

GRAND AM -- SERIES 2N -- The 2.3-liter DOHC Quad 4 engine became standard equipment in Pontiac's best seller, the 1995 Grand Am. Other new features included: Improved rear suspension with spring-on-center design; a balance shaft system added to the Quad 4 engine; variable effort steering (available on the GT); direct drive power steering; stepper motor cruise control; black bodyside insert (available on the GT); one new exterior color: Medium Dark Purple Metallic; (PF7) 15-in. Star cast aluminum wheel; (PG1) 15-in. five-blade wheel cover; (PC1) 14-in. Custom wheel cover; 195/70R14 tires (standard on SE); P205/55R16 Goodyear Eagle RSA tires (standard on GT). Other standard equipment on both the SE and GT lines included: fixed mast antenna; tinted glass; fog lamps; Sport mirrors; "wet-arm" windshield wipers; bumpers/soft fascia with integral rub strips; driver's side airbag; power, automatic door locks with unlock and relock; Delco ETR AM/FM stereo with seek up/down and clock; grid cloth fabric interior; 45/45 reclining front bucket seats; three-passenger rear seat with integrated headrests; Sport, four-spoke steering wheel; four-wheel anti-lock braking system; GM Computer Command Control; and stainless steel exhaust system.

Model Number	Body/Style Number	Body Type & Seating	Factory Price	Shipping Weight	Prod. Total
GRAND AM SE SERIES 2N -- Quad 4					
2N	NE1	2-dr Cpe-5P	13399	2749	Note 1
2N	NE5	4-dr Sed-5P	13499	2806	Note 1
GRAND AM GT -- SERIES 2N -- Quad 4					
2N	NW1	2-dr Cpe-5P	15349	2888	Note 1
2N	NW5	4-dr Sed-5P	15449	2941	Note 1

NOTE 1: Grand Am series 1995 production estimate 260,000.

1995 Pontiac Grand Am GT coupe. PMD

1995 Pontiac Firebird coupe. PMD

FIREBIRD -- SERIES 2F -- V-6/V-8 -- Pontiac's lone rear-wheel drive vehicle was offered in 1995 in coupe and convertible versions in three series: Firebird, Formula, and Trans Am. The Canadian-produced muscle machines had several changes, among them: Traction control with manual and automatic transmission available with V-8 engine; three new exterior colors: Blue Green Chameleon, Medium Dark Purple Metallic, and Bright Silver Metallic; two new leather interior colors: Bright Red (available on all models), and Bright White (available on convertibles only); 16-in. five-spoke aluminum wheels available with V-8 engine; all-weather speed rated P245/50Z16 tires; power antenna; four-spoke Sport steering wheel; and remote compact disc changer (dealer-installed option). Across-the-lineup standard features included: soft fascia-type bumpers; fixed mast, black right rear antenna; tinted glass; Sport mirrors; controlled-cycle windshield wipers; dual front airbags; Metrix cloth fabric interior; locking glovebox; analog instrumentation; Delco ETR AM/FM stereo radio with auto-reverse cassette, clock and Delco theft lock; reclining front bucket seats and folding rear seats; tilt-wheel adjustable steering column; Pass-Key II theft deterrent system; four-wheel anti-lock braking system; brake/transmission shift interlock (with automatic transmission); low oil level monitor and warning; GM Computer Command Control; and stainless steel exhaust system. Features that were standard equipment exclusively to the Firebird/Formula/Trans Am convertibles included: cruise control; electric rear window defogger; power automatic door locks; remote keyless entry; four-way manual front driver seat/two-way manual front passenger seat; and power windows with "express-down" feature.

Model Number	Body/Style Number	Body Type & Seating	Factory Price	Shipping Weight	Prod. Total
FIREBIRD -- SERIES 2F -- V-6					
2F	FS2	2-dr Cpe-5P	15359	3230	Note 1
2F	FV3	2-dr Conv-5P	22439	3346	Note 1
FIREBIRD FORMULA -- SERIES 2F -- V-8					
2F	FV2	2-dr Cpe-5P	19599	3373	Note 1
2F	FV3	2-dr Conv-5P	25629	3489	Note 1
FIREBIRD TRANS AM -- SERIES 2F -- V-8					
2F	FV2	2-dr Cpe-5P	21569	3445	Note 1
2F	FV3	2-dr Conv-5P	27639	3610	Note 1

NOTE 1: Firebird series 1995 production estimate 49,000.

GRAND PRIX -- SERIES 2W -- V-6 -- Offered in 1995 as either an SE Coupe or Sedan, a (B4S) GTP Performance Package for the Coupe or a (B4Q) GT Performance Package for the Sedan as well as a White Appearance Package available on the SE Coupe added depth to the Grand Prix lineup. Changes were minimal from the previous year and included: one new exterior color: Red Orange Metallic; new uplevel 16-in. H-rated Goodyear P225/60R16 RSA tires; engine oil level monitor with 3.4-liter DOHC V-6 engine; brake/transmission shift interlock; five-spoke aluminum wheels (available with SE Coupe); EVO variable-effort power steering on GT and GTP packages; floor console with improved and repositioned dual cupholders and ashtray; new storage armrest with flip-out cupholder and removable coin holder standard on models with split bench seats; and glovebox latch and right-hand HVAC vent now color-keyed to interior. Standard equipment on both the SE Coupe and Sedan included: black, fixed mast antenna; tinted and safety laminated glass; soft fascia-type bumpers with integral rub strips; fog lamps; "wet-arm" controlled-cycle windshield wipers; dual front airbags; electronic push-button air conditioning; power automatic door locks with unlock and relock features; mechanical analog instrumentation including tachometer; Cordae cloth fabric interior; three-passenger rear seat with integrated headrests; tilt-wheel adjustable steering column; power windows with "express-down" feature; four-wheel disc brakes; Pass-Key II theft-deterrent system; GM Computer Command Control; and stainless steel exhaust system.

Model Number	Body/Style Number	Body Type & Seating	Factory Price	Shipping Weight	Prod. Total
GRAND PRIX SE -- SERIES 2W -- V-6					
2W	WJ5	4-dr Sed-5P	17169	3370	Note 1
2W	WJ1	2-dr Cpe-5P	17919	3275	Note 1

NOTE 1: Grand Prix series 1995 production estimate 100,000.

BONNEVILLE -- SERIES 2H -- V-6 -- For 1995, the SE and SSE Sedan versions again comprised the Bonneville lineup. The Sports Luxury Edition (SLE) package was available to upgrade the SE Sedan. An additional option to enhance the SLE package was the supercharged 3800 V-6 engine. For the SSE Sedan buyers could opt for the SSEi Supercharger Package as an upgrade option. New features for the Bonneville in 1995 included: 205 hp 3800 Series II V-6 as standard powerplant on SE and SSE; Computer Command Ride available on SE; standard cruise control/rally gauges with tachometer and lamp group; one new interior color: graphite (cloth or leather); new tachometer redline for 3800 Series II engine (6000 rpm); Cobra-head shifter (with bucket seats); graphite colored soft-touch instrument panel trimplate; color coordinated interior components; graphite steering wheels/columns for all interior trim colors; rear seat child shoulder harness comfort guide; improved automatic HVAC; automatic air conditioning now available on SE; and 16-in. machine-faced Crosslace cast wheels. Standard features found on both the SE and SSE Sedans included: soft fascia-type bumpers with integral rub strips; fog lamps; tinted glass; dual front airbags; front three-point active height adjustable safety belts; manual air conditioning; power door locks; backlit analog instrumentation including tachometer; power windows with "express down" feature; tilt-wheel adjustable steering column; Pass-Key II theft deterrent system; four-wheel anti-lock braking system; and brake/transmission shift interlock.

Model Number	Body/Style Number	Body Type & Seating	Factory Price	Shipping Weight	Prod. Total
BONNEVILLE SE -- SERIES H -- V-6					
2H	HX5	4-dr Spt Sed-5P	21389	3446	Note 1
BONNEVILLE SSE -- SERIES H -- V-6					
2H	HZ5	4-dr Spt Sed-5P	26389	3587	Note 1

NOTE 1: Bonneville series 1995 production estimate 92,000.

1995 Pontiac Trans Sport SE minivan. PMD

TRANS SPORT -- SERIES 2U -- V-6 -- Changes on Pontiac's 1995 minivan offering, the Trans Sport SE, were minimal from the year before. New features included: Traction Control (carried over from a mid-1994 introduction); brake/transmission shift interlock; one new exterior color: Dark Teal Metallic; three-spoke 15-in. aluminum wheel; four-spoke steering wheel (available with duplicate radio controls); Doral cloth fabric interior; and full overhead console available.

Model Number	Body/Style Number	Body Type & Seating	Factory Price	Shipping Weight	Prod. Total
TRANS SPORT -- SERIES 2U -- V-6					
2U	U06	SE Wagon	18429	3540	35,000 (estimated)

SUNFIRE ENGINES

[STANDARD BASE/SE] Inline. OHV. Four-cylinder. Cast iron block. Cast aluminum head. Displacement: 133 cu. in. (2.2L). Bore & stroke: 3.50 x 3.46 in. Compression ratio: 9.0:1. Brake horsepower: 120 @ 5200 rpm. Torque: 130 lb.-ft. @ 4000 rpm. Fuel system: MPFI. RPO Code: LN2. Standard in Sunfire SE Coupe, Convertible, and Sedan.

[STANDARD GT] Inline. DOHC Quad 4. Four-cylinder. Cast iron block. Cast aluminum head. Displacement: 138 cu. in. (2.3L). Bore & stroke: 3.63 x 3.35 in. Compression ratio: 9.5:1. Brake horsepower: 150 @ 6000 rpm. Torque: 145 lb.-ft. @ 4800 rpm. Fuel system: MPFI. RPO Code: LD2. Standard in Sunfire GT Coupe.

GRAND AM ENGINES

[STANDARD SE/GT] Inline. Quad-4 DOHC. Cast iron block. Cast aluminum head. Displacement: 138 cu. in. (2.3L). Bore & stroke: 3.63 x 3.35 in. Compression ratio: 9.5:1. Brake horsepower: 150 @ 6000 rpm. Torque: 145 lb.-ft. @ 4800 rpm. Fuel system: MPFI. RPO Code: LD2. Standard in SE/GT Coupes and Sedans. [OPTIONAL SE/GT] V-block. OHV. Cast iron block. Cast aluminum head. Displacement: 191 cu. in. (3.1L). Bore & stroke: 3.51 x 3.31 in. Compression ratio: 9.5:1. Brake horsepower: 155 @ 5200 rpm. Torque: 185 lb.-ft. @ 4000 rpm. Fuel system: SPFI. RPO Code: L82. Optional in SE/GT Coupes and Sedans.

FIREBIRD ENGINES

[FIREBIRD BASE V-6] V-block. OHV. Six-cylinder. Cast iron block and heads. Aluminum intake manifold. Displacement: 207 cu. in. (3.4L). Bore & stroke: 3.62 x 3.31 in. Compression ratio: 9.0:1. Brake horsepower: 160 @ 4600 rpm. Torque: 200 lb.-ft. @ 3600 rpm. Fuel system: SPFI. RPO Code: L32. Standard in Firebird. Not available in Formula and Trans Am. [FORMULA/TRANS AM BASE V-8] V-block. OHV. Eight-cylinder. Cast iron block and aluminum heads. Aluminum intake manifold. Displacement: 350 cu. in. (5.7L). Bore & stroke: 4.00 x 3.48 in. Compression ratio: 10.5:1. Brake horsepower: 275 @ 5000 rpm. Torque: 325 lb.-ft. @ 2400 rpm. Fuel system: SPFI. RPO Code: LT1. Standard in Formula and Trans Am. Not available in Firebird.

GRAND PRIX ENGINES

[STANDARD GRAND PRIX SE] V-block. OHV. Six-cylinder. Cast iron block and cast aluminum heads. 191 cu. in. (3.1L). Bore & stroke: 3.51 x 3.31 in. Compression ratio: 9.5:1. Brake horsepower: 160 @ 5200 rpm. Torque: 185 lb.-ft. @ 4000 rpm. Fuel system: SPFI. RPO Code: L82. [OPTIONAL GRAND PRIX SE] V-block. DOHC. Six-cylinder. Cast iron block and cast aluminum heads. 207 cu. in. (3.4L). Bore & stroke: 3.62 x 3.30 in. Compression ratio: 9.25:1. Brake horsepower: 210 @ 5000 rpm. Torque: 215 lb.-ft. @ 4000 rpm. Fuel system: SPFI. RPO Code: LQ1.

1995 Pontiac Bonneville SSE four-door sedan with SSEi Supercharger Package. PMD

BONNEVILLE ENGINES

[STANDARD SE/SSE] V-block. OHV. "3800" six-cylinder. Cast iron block and heads. Aluminum intake manifold. Displacement: 231 cu. in. (3.8L). Bore & stroke: 3.80 x 3.40 in. Compression ratio: 9.4:1. Brake horsepower: 205 @ 5200 rpm. Torque: 230 lb.-ft. @ 4000 rpm. Fuel system: SPFI. RPO Code: L36. Standard in Bonneville SE/SSE. [OPTIONAL SE/SSE] V-block. OHV. "3800" supercharged six-cylinder. Cast iron block and heads. Aluminum intake manifold. Displacement: 231 cu. in. (3.8L). Bore & stroke: 3.80 x 3.40 in. Compression ratio: 9.0:1. Brake horsepower: 225 @ 5000 rpm. Torque: 275 lb.-ft. @ 3200 rpm. Fuel system: SPFI and supercharged. RPO Code: L67. Optional in Bonneville SSE, available in SE only through SLE option package.

TRANS SPORT ENGINES

[STANDARD SE] V-block. OHV. Six-cylinder. Cast iron block and heads. Aluminum intake manifold. Displacement: 191 cu. in. (3.1L). Bore & stroke: 3.50 x 3.31 in. Compression ratio: 8.5:1. Brake horsepower: 120 @ 4400 rpm. Torque: 175 lb.-ft. @ 2200 rpm. Fuel system: TBFI. RPO Code: LG6. Standard in SE. [OPTIONAL SE] V-block. OHV. "3800" six-cylinder. Cast iron block and heads. Aluminum intake manifold. Displacement: 231 cu. in. (3.8L). Bore & stroke: 3.80 x 3.40 in. Compression ratio: 9.0:1. Brake horsepower: 170 @ 4800 rpm. Torque: 225 lb.-ft. @ 3200 rpm. Fuel system: SPFI. RPO Code: L27.

1995 Pontiac Sunfire convertible. PMD

SUNFIRE CHASSIS: Wheelbase: 104.1 in. (all). Overall length: 181.9 in. (SE/GT Coupes); 181.7 in. (SE Sedan); 182.4 in. (SE Convertible). Overall width: 67.4 in. (SE/GT Coupes); 67.3 in. (SE Sedan); 68.4 in. (SE Convertible). Height: 53.2 in. (SE/GT Coupes); 54.8 in. (SE Sedan); 53.9 in. (SE Convertible). Front tread: 57.6 in. (all). Rear tread: 56.8 in. (SE/GT Coupes and SE Sedan); 56.7 in. (SE Convertible). Standard tires: P195/70R14 (SE Coupe/Sedan); P195/65R15 (SE Convertible); P205/55R16 (GT Coupe).

GRAND AM CHASSIS: Wheelbase: 103.4 in. (all). Overall length: 186.9 in. (all). Width: 67.5 in. (all). Height: 53.2 in. (all). Front tread: 55.9 in. (all). Rear tread: 55.4 in. (all). Standard tires: See model descriptions.

FIREBIRD CHASSIS: Wheelbase: 101.1 in. (all). Overall length: 195.6 in. (Firebird/Formula); 197.0 in. (Trans Am). Width: 74.5 in. (all). Height: 52.0 in. (Firebird/Formula/Trans Am Coupes); 52.7 in. (Firebird/Formula/Trans Am Convertibles). Front tread: 60.7 in. (all). Rear tread: 60.6 in. (all). Standard tires: P215/60R16 (Firebird); P235/55R16 (Formula); P245/50ZR16 (Trans Am).

GRAND PRIX CHASSIS: Wheelbase: 107.5 in. (all). Overall length: 194.8 in. (Coupe); 194.9 in. (Sedan). Width: 71.9 in. (all). Height: 52.8 in. (Coupe); 54.8 in. (Sedan). Front tread: 59.5 in. (all). Rear tread: 58.0 in. (all). Standard tires: P215/60/R16 (Coupe); P205/70R15 (Sedan).

BONNEVILLE CHASSIS: Wheelbase: 110.8 in. (all). Overall length: 199.5 in. (SE); 201.1 in. (SSE). Width: 74.5 in. (all). Height: 55.7 in. (all). Front tread: 60.4 in. (SE); 60.8 in. (SSE). Rear tread: 60.3 in. (SE); 60.6 in. (SSE). Standard tires: P215/65R15 (SE); P225/60R16 (SSE).

TRANS SPORT CHASSIS: Wheelbase: 109.8 in. Overall length: 192.2 in. Width: 74.6 in. Height: 65.7 in. Front tread: 59.2 in. Rear tread: 61.4 in. Standard tires: P205/70R15.

SUNFIRE TECHNICAL: Chassis: Front engine/front drive. Base transmission: Five-speed manual (MK7). Optional transmissions: five-speed manual (MD9, optional on SE Coupe/Convertible, standard on GT Coupe); four-speed automatic (MN4, all). Axle ratio: 3.58:1 with 2.2-liter L4 and five-speed manual/3.94:1 with 2.3-liter Quad 4 and five-speed manual/3.91:1 with 2.3-liter Quad 4 and four-speed automatic. Front suspension: Dual path deflected disc front struts, 19mm anti-roll bar (20mm on GT Coupe with 16-in. wheels), cross-axis front ball joints. Rear suspension: Tubular rear axle with coil over shock design. Steering: Rack-and-pinion mounted on cradle (SE and GT), 15.7:1 ratio (13.96:1 on GT). Turns lock-to-lock: 2.88 (2.33 on GT). Turning circle: 37.2 ft. (all). Front brakes: 10.2-in. vented discs. Rear brakes: 7.87 x 1.77-in. drums, power assisted. Fuel tank: 15.2 gal.

GRAND AM TECHNICAL: Chassis: Front engine/front drive. Base transmission: Five-speed manual (M32). Optional transmissions: four-speed automatic (M13, optional on SE and GT)/three-speed automatic (MD9, optional on SE only). Axle ratio: 3.94:1 (with M32 five-speed manual); 2.84:1 (with MD9 three-speed automatic and LD2 Quad 4 engine); 3.69:1 (with M13 four-speed automatic and LD2 Quad 4 engine); 2:93:1 (with M13 four-speed automatic and L82 V-6). Front suspension (Standard SE): Deflected disc; MacPherson struts, 27 N-mm spring, and 22mm stabilizer bar. Rear Suspension (Standard SE): 21 N-mm springs, semi-independent trailing arms, spring-on-center linked with torsion beam, 18mm stabilizer bar. Front suspension (Standard GT): Deflected disc; MacPherson struts, 27 N-mm spring, and 24mm stabilizer bar (automatic)/30mm (manual). Rear suspension (Standard GT): 25 N-mm springs, semi-independent trailing arms, spring-on-center linked with torsion beam, 22mm stabilizer bar. Steering: Power-assisted rack-and-pinion, 13.96:1 ratio. Turns lock-to-lock: 2.5. Turning circle: 35.3 ft. Front brakes: 259.5mm diameter vented discs. Rear brakes: 200.0mm diameter drums. Fuel tank: 15.2 gal.

FIREBIRD TECHNICAL: Chassis: Front engine/rear drive. Base transmission: (M49) Five-speed manual (Firebird); (MM6) six-speed manual (Formula/Trans Am). Optional transmission: (MD8) Four-speed automatic (all). Axle ratio: 3.23:1 (with M49 five-speed manual); 3.42:1 (with MM6 six-speed manual); 3.23:1 (with MD8 four-speed automatic and 3.4-liter V-6); 2.73:1 (with MD8 four-speed automatic and 5.7-liter

V-8. Front suspension: (F41 Firebird) Short/long arm (SLA)/coil over monotube gas-charged shocks, tubular stabilizer bar with links, 30mm stabilizer bar. (FE2 Formula/Trans Am) SLA/coil over monotube gas-charged shocks, tubular stabilizer bar with links, 30mm stabilizer bar. Rear suspension: (F41 Firebird) Salisbury axle with torque arm, trailing arm, track bar, coil springs, 17mm stabilizer bar. (FE2 Formula/Trans Am) Salisbury axle with torque arm, trailing arm, track bar, coil springs, 19mm stabilizer bar. Steering: Power, rack-and-pinion with 16.9:1 ratio (Firebird)/14.4:1 (Formula/Trans Am). Turns lock-to-lock: 2.67 (Firebird)/2.28 (Formula/Trans Am). Turning circle: (Firebird) 37.9 ft. (left) 40.6 ft. (right)/(Formula/Trans Am) 37.7 ft. (left) 40.1 ft. (right). Front brakes: (Firebird/Formula/Trans Am) 10.7 in. vented disc. Rear brakes: (Firebird) 9.5 in. power assisted Duo-Servo drum. (Formula/Trans Am) 11.4 in. power assisted vented disc. Fuel tank: 15.5 gal.

GRAND PRIX TECHNICAL: Chassis: Front engine/front drive. Base transmission: (M13) four-speed electronic automatic transmission. Final Drive Ratios: 3.33:1 with (M13) four-speed electronic automatic and 3.1-liter V-6; 3.43:1 with (M13) four-speed electronic automatic and 3.4-liter V-6. Front suspension: MacPherson struts with tapered coil springs, lower A arm, and 28mm anti-roll bar (34mm anti-roll bar with Y99 rally suspension). Rear suspension: Tri-link independent suspension, transverse fiberglass leaf spring, and 12mm anti-roll bar (12mm anti-roll bar with Y99 and 3.1-liter V-6/14mm with Y99 and 3.4-liter V-6). Steering: Power-assisted rack-and-pinion with 15.7:1 ratio (14.0:1 with 3.4-liter V-6). Turns lock-to-lock: 2.6 (2.26 with Y99 and 3.4-liter V-6). Turning circle: 36.7 ft. (39 ft. with Y99 and 3.4-liter V-6). Front brakes: 10.51-in. vented discs, power-assisted. Rear brakes: 10.1-in. solid discs, power-assisted. Fuel tank: 17.1 gal.

BONNEVILLE TECHNICAL: Chassis: Front engine/front drive. Base transmission: (M13) four-speed electronic automatic. Axle ratio: 2.84:1 (3800 V-6); 2.97:1 (supercharged 3800 V-6). Front suspension: (SE) Standard FE1: deflected-disc, MacPherson struts, coil spring over strut (22 N-mm), 30mm stabilizer bar. (SSE) Standard FE2: deflected-disc, MacPherson struts, coil spring over strut (26 N-mm), 32mm stabilizer bar. Rear suspension: (SE) Standard FE1: coil springs (variable rate 48-65 N-mm), independent lower A-arm, 17mm stabilizer bar. (SSE) Standard FE2: automatic level control coil springs (47 N-mm), Chapman struts, independent lower A-arm, 22mm stabilizer bar. Optional front suspension: (SE) Y52: Computer Command Ride, deflected-disc, MacPherson struts, coil spring over strut (26 N-mm), 32mm stabilizer bar. (SSE) FW1: Computer Command Ride, deflected-disc, MacPherson struts, coil spring over strut (26 N-mm), 32mm stabilizer bar. Optional rear suspension: (SE) Y52: automatic level control coil springs (47 N-mm), Chapman struts, independent lower A-arm, 22mm stabilizer bar. (SSE) FW1: automatic level control coil springs (47 N-mm), Chapman struts, independent lower A-arm, 22mm stabilizer bar. Steering (Standard SE): Power-assisted rack-and-pinion with 16.54:1 ratio, 2.79 turns lock-to-lock, and 39-ft. turning circle. (SSE/optional SE): Variable-effort rack-and-pinion with 14.93:1 to 18.91:1 ratio, 2.86 turns lock-to-lock, and 40.5-ft. turning circle. Front brakes: 10.9-in. vented discs (all). Rear brakes: Power-assisted 8.85-in. drums (all). Fuel tank: 18.0 gal.

TRANS SPORT TECHNICAL: Chassis: Front engine/front drive. Transmission: (MD9) Three-speed automatic; optional (M13) four-speed automatic. Axle ratio: 3.06:1 (with either three-speed automatic and 3.1L V-6 or four-speed automatic and 3.8L V-6). Front suspension: MacPherson strut with coil springs (27 N-mm), stamped lower control arms and nodular iron steering knuckles, 27mm stabilizer bar. Rear suspension: Open-section transverse beam on stamped steel trailing arms, tube shocks, 48-56 N-mm variable rate coil springs (base suspension)/48.3 N-mm coil springs (uplevel suspension), electronic leveling, 25.4mm stabilizer bar. Steering: Rack-and-pinion with integral power unit with 15.7:1 ratio. Turns lock-to-lock: 3.05. Turning circle: 43.1 ft. Front brakes: 10.9 x 1.3-in. single caliper disc. Rear brakes: 8.86 x 1.77-in. leading trailing drum. Fuel tank: 20.0 gal.

SUNFIRE OPTIONS: 1SB Sunfire SE Series option group ($1295). 1SC Sunfire SE Series option group ($1665). 1SD Sunfire SE Series option group ($2226 Coupe/$2331 Sedan). C60 air conditioning ($785). YF5 California emissions ($100). N33 tilt steering wheel ($145). K34 cruise control ($225). C49 electric rear window defogger ($170). A31 power windows ($265 SE Coupe/$330 SE Sedan/no charge Convertible). UN6 Delco stereo equipment ($195). UT6 Delco stereo equipment ($230). T43 rear deck lid spoiler ($70). MX1 three-speed automatic transmission ($495). CF5 power sun roof ($556). R6A Convenience Package ($80).

GRAND AM OPTIONS: 1SB package on SE Coupe/Sedan ($1575). 1SC package on SE Coupe ($2021). 1SC package on SE Sedan ($2286). 1SB package on GT Coupe/Sedan ($597). 1SC package on GT Coupe ($1243). 1SC package on GT Sedan ($1308). L82 3.1-liter V-6 ($350). MX1 three-speed automatic transmission ($555, not available on GT). MXO four-speed automatic transmission ($755). C60 air conditioning ($830). C49 electric rear window defogger ($170). K34 cruise control ($225). UB3 rally gauges ($111). YF5 California emission requirements ($100). CF5 power sun roof ($595). A31 express down power windows ($275-$340 depending on value option packages). AM9 split folding rear seat ($150). AX3 remote keyless entry ($135). UM6 Delco sound system ($140). UX1 Delco sound system ($375).

FIREBIRD OPTIONS: 1SB Firebird Coupe option package ($1005). 1SC Firebird Coupe option package ($2614). 1SB Formula Coupe option package ($1076). 1SC Formula Coupe option package ($1684). 1SB Firebird Convertible option package ($508). 1SB Formula Convertible option package ($508). C60 air conditioning ($895 on Firebird, standard on Formula/Trans Am). AU0 remote keyless entry ($135). MX0 four-speed automatic transmission ($775). B84 body color side moldings ($60). CC1 hatch roof ($995). U1C Delco sound system with CD player ($100). UP3 Delco sound system with CD player and graphic equalizer ($100-$573, depending on value option packages). K34 cruise control, ($225, standard on Trans Am). YF5 California emission requirements ($100). AR9 articulating bucket seats with leather ($780). GU5 rear performance axle ($175, not available on Firebird).

GRAND PRIX OPTIONS: 1SB Grand Prix SE Sedan ($742). 1SC Grand Prix SE Sedan ($1937). A90 remote deck lid release ($60). C49 electric rear window defogger ($170). AU0 Remote Keyless Entry system ($135). CF5 power sun roof ($646). UV8 cellular phone provisions ($35). UV6 head-up display ($250). B20 Custom interior trim ($393-$1063 depending on value option packages). B4S GTP Performance Package for Grand Prix SE Coupe ($2256). B4Q GT Performance package for Grand Prix SE Sedan ($1825-$2275 depending on value option packages). JL9 anti-lock brakes ($450). UN6 Delco stereo equipment ($195). UT6 Delco stereo equipment ($150-$325 depending on value option packages). U1C Delco stereo equipment ($125-$295 depending on value option package). AG1 six-way power driver's seat ($305). QPE touring tires for Grand Prix SE Sedan ($112). PH3 15-in. aluminum Sport wheels for Grand Prix SE Sedan ($259). NWO aluminum Sport wheels for Grand Prix SE Sedan ($259).

1995 Pontiac Bonneville SE four-door sedan with Sport Luxury Edition Package. PMD

BONNEVILLE OPTIONS: 1SB Bonneville SE option package ($270). 1SC Bonneville SE option package ($923). 1SD Bonneville SE option package ($1584). 1SB Bonneville SSE option package ($1440). WA6 SSEi supercharger package ($1167, SSE). FW1 Computer Command Ride ($380, SSE). L67 Supercharged 3.8L 3800 V-6 ($1187, SSE). AU0 Remote Keyless Entry system ($135). CF5 power glass sun roof ($981-$995). C49 electric rear window defogger ($170). K05 engine block heater ($18). NW9 Traction Control system ($175). PF5 16-in. five-blade cast aluminum wheels ($340). T2Z enhancement group ($206, SE). T43 rear deck lid spoiler ($110). UN6 Delco stereo equipment ($170). U1C Delco sound system ($295). UP3 Delco sound system with compact disc player ($485). US7 power antenna ($85). Y52 Performance & Handling package ($1199, SE).

TRANS SPORT OPTIONS: 1SB Trans Sport SE option package ($1418). 1SC Trans Sport SE option package ($2513). 1SD Trans Sport SE option package ($3093). 1SE Trans Sport SE option package ($4197). L27 3.8L V-6 with four-speed automatic ($819). ZP7 seven-passenger seating ($705-$870 depending on value option packages). B2Q black roof delete (no charge). C49 electric rear window defogger ($170). AJ1 glass package ($245). AB5 power door locks ($300). V54 roof luggage carrier ($175). K05 engine block heater ($18). UM6 Delco sound system ($140). U1A Delco sound system with compact disc player ($206-$541). PH6 15-in. aluminum wheels ($259). E58 power sliding door ($350). C54 pop-up sun roof ($300). NW9 traction control ($350). AG9 six-way power driver's seat ($270). G67 Auto Level Control ($200).

Note: Full option package contents, descriptions and applications information can often be determined by consulting factory literature. The data above is edited for size and clarity. This information provided only as a guide to help collectors appraise the relative value of cars with numerous options. Prices for items included as part of a value option package are usually much less than individual prices. Option prices charged by individual dealers may also vary.

1907-1931

OAKLAND

OAKLAND 1907-1931

OAKLAND - Pontiac, Michigan - (1907-1931) - The Oakland was the idea of two men: Edward M. Murphy, who was anxious to move his Pontiac Buggy Company into the automotive age, and Alanson P. Brush, who had been responsible for the design of the early Cadillacs. They met around 1906, by which time Brush had set himself up in business as an engineering consultant in Detroit, and Brush showed Murphy his design for a small two-cylinder car that Cadillac had rejected. Its vertical engine rotated counterclockwise, and its planetary transmission was unusual for a lack of braking bands, clutches running in oil being the substitute. Murphy bought this automotive idea, which he decided should carry the name Oakland (as did his horsedrawn vehicles) and during the summer of 1907 organized the Oakland Motor Car Company. The Oakland car was ready by automobile show time in January 1908, though Brush was no longer in Pontiac; having found Frank Briscoe available with funds, he was back in Detroit building his single-cylinder Brush Runabout. Lackluster sales of less than 300 Oaklands in 1908 must have convinced Murphy that Cadillac had been right in rejecting the Brush-designed twin because for 1909 a line of 40 hp fours with sliding gear transmissions was introduced. Tragically, at the age of forty-four, Edward M. Murphy died suddenly in September that year. Five months earlier he had met with another former buggy man named William C. Durant, and Oakland had become part of Durant's General Motors empire. Oakland became a four exclusively in 1910, and sales of 3000 to 5000 cars a year became the norm. "The Car with a Conscience" was an Oakland slogan, and the marque acquitted itself admirably in motor sport, particularly reliability runs and hill climbs, winning no less than 25 of the latter, including Giant's Despair and Dead Horse Hill. Oakland's first six--a big 334-cubic-inch 60 hp car on a 130-inch wheelbase--arrived in 1913, together with self-starter and electric lights, and an eye-catching rounded-V radiator, for all Oaklands. Almost 9000 cars were sold that year. Production increased to nearly 12,000 in 1915, and more than doubled the year following, when the Oakland range included fours, sixes and a new V-8. Wartime exigencies resulted in the V-8's discontinuation for 1918, with company efforts focused on its six, which would be produced without noticeable change into the 1920s. It was during this period that Billy Durant was undergoing his second-and irrevocable departure from General Motors. In its wake, and with the arrival of Alfred P. Sloan, Jr., all divisions of the corporation were given a fresh look. The peering into Oakland affairs revealed a haphazard production schedule (maybe 50 cars built one day, only 10 the next) and a loss of quality (some cars had to be repaired even before leaving the factory). Fred W. Warner, a Durant man, resigned as Oakland's general manager in 1921, and was succeeded by George W. Hannum, who had begun his career at Autocar in 1907 and who had worked in various GM-related companies before arriving in Pontiac. The official statement from General Motors indicated that Oakland would continue its present line "with gradual improvements." The big news for Oakland arrived in 1924: a new L-head engine, four-wheel brakes, centralized controls, automatic spark advance and Duco. Oakland's choice of color in pioneering the new nitro-cellulose lacquer was a shade of blue that allowed the company promotion of the car as the "True Blue Oakland Six." And it could be had for as low as $995. Unfortunately, insofar as being "true blue" as a GM man, George Hannum wasn't. The GM-decreed slot for the Oakland among the corporation cars was between the top-of-the-line Chevrolet and the bread-and-butter Buick. Among other flagrancies, the Oakland was too heavy for its slot, which was not entirely Hannum's fault since the car's chassis was eight years old. He was guilty of occasionally not considering sales demand when shipping Oaklands to dealers, but Chevrolet was guilty of that too. Nonetheless, and in spite of a healthy annual production of over 35,000 cars in both 1923 and 1924, Hannum was eased out of Oakland. By early 1925 his place had been taken by Alfred R. Glancy, a likable Irishman who had joined Oakland the year previous as assistant general manager. Although the concept of the car had first been bruited in the early Twenties by George Hannum, it was Al Glancy who would introduce the Pontiac, a quality six to sell at a four's price, in 1926. It was a runaway success, and undoubtedly an impetus to the later marketing of the Marquette by Buick and the Viking by Oldsmobile. (Cadillac's LaSalle was on the boards, but not on the market at this time.) The Pontiac was

unique in GM history in being the only offspring ever to kill its parent. After its smashing debut, the demise of the Oakland became only a matter of time. The cars for 1927 were called the Greater Oakland Sixes, with All-American Six becoming a designation for the Oakland senior models that summer, and the cars were restyled for 1929. But most of the attention at the Oakland company was diverted to the Pontiac. In 1930 there was an 85 hp V-8 under the hood of the Oakland, but calendar year production was just 24,443 cars. There were over 188,000 Pontiacs built in that same period. In October of 1930 Irving J. Reuter moved into Al Glancy's job at Oakland. Oaklands for 1931 featured a new synchromesh with silent second. Fewer than 9000 cars were produced that year. With the effects of the Great Depression now weighing heavy everywhere, Pontiac sales plummeted, too. But, still, there were nearly seven times more of them built in '31 than the Oakland. At year's end, Irving Reuter announced the demise of the Oakland name. Its V-8 series would be revamped into a Pontiac model. During 1932 the name of the Oakland Motor Car Company was changed to Pontiac Motor Company.

1908 Oakland Model A touring. HAC

EQUIPMENT: Wood frame, oil lamps, generator, brass horn, 10-spoke wheels in front (all)/12-spoke wheels in rear (all), right-hand steering.

Series	Model	Description	Price	Weight	Production
-	A	3P Runabout	1375	1600	Note 1
-	B	5P Touring	1400	1650	Note 1
-	C	4P Tourabout	-	-	Note 1
-	D	Taxicab	1850	1800	Note 1
-	E	Landaulette	-	-	Note 1

NOTE 1: Estimated production for all Oakland models in 1908 was 200-278 cars.

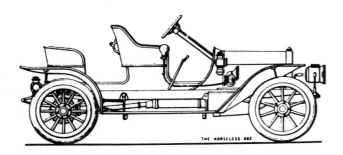

1908 Oakland touring. JAG

ENGINES: Used in 1908 and 1909 production: (Serial number 1-300) KMC engine. Vertical. Two-cylinder. Bore & stroke: 4-1/2 x 5 in. Displacement: 159.1 cu. in. Horsepower: 20. Water-cooled. (Serial number 300-750) GMC engine. Vertical. Two-cylinder. Bore & stroke: 4-1/2 x 5 in. Displacement: 159.1 cu. in. Horsepower: 20. Water-cooled.

TECHNICAL: Planetary transmission with two speeds forward, one reverse. Direct drive on high. Multiple disc clutch. Shaft drive to live rear axle. Tubular front axle (early production only).

CHASSIS: Wheelbase: 96 in. Semi-elliptic front springs 36 x 2 in. Full elliptic rear springs 38 x 2 in. 32-in. wheels (front on two-point ball-bearing; rear on roller bearings). 3-1/2-in. tires.

OPTION: Folding top ($75).

HISTORICAL FOOTNOTE: One of two remaining 1908 Oaklands, a Model B touring, is part of the collection of the Indianapolis Motor Speedway Museum in Speedway, Indiana.

1909 Oakland Model 40G "surrey car" (rear view). JAG

EQUIPMENT: wood frame, spare tire carrier, runningboard-mounted tool boxes, lamps, generator, brass horn, 12-spoke wheels front and rear (all), right-hand steering.

Series (2-cyl.)	Model	Description	Price	Weight	Production
20	20-A	3P Runabout	1250	1700	Note 1
20	20-B	5P Touring	1250	1740	Note 1
20	20-C	4P Touring Roadster	1250	1740	Note 1

Series (4-cyl.)	Model	Description	Price	Weight	Production
40	40-E	3P Runabout	1600	2025	Note 1
40	40-F	5P Touring	1600	2100	Note 1
40	40-G	4P Touring Roadster	1600	2100	Note 1
40	40-H	Toy Tonneau	1600	-	Note 1

NOTE 1: Estimated production for all Oakland models in 1909 was 1,035 cars of which approximately 700 were 40 series and the rest were 20 series.

ENGINES: 40 Series: Four-cylinder. Bore & stroke: 4-1/2 x 5 in. Displacement: 318.1 cu. in. Horsepower: 40. Water-cooled. 20 Series: (used in 1908 and 1909 production: (Serial number 1-300) KMC engine. Vertical. Two-cylinder. Bore & stroke: 4-1/2 x 5 in. Displacement: 159.1 cu. in. Horsepower: 16. Water-cooled. (Serial number 300-750) GMC engine. Vertical. Two-cylinder. Bore & stroke: 4-1/2 x 5 in. Displacement: 159.1 cu. in. Horsepower: 20. Water-cooled.

TECHNICAL: 40 Series: Sliding transmission. Shaft drive. 20 Series: Planetary transmission with two speeds forward, one reverse. Direct drive on high. Multiple disc clutch. Shaft drive to live rear axle.

1909 Oakland Model 40 touring. OCW

1909 Oakland Model F touring. JAG

CHASSIS: 40 Series: Wheelbase: 112 in., 4-in. tires. 20 Series: Wheelbase: 100 in., 3-1/2-in. tires.

OPTIONS: Folding top ($75), storage batteries ($15), tire cover ($3.50), Prestolite tank ($18-$35), Stewart speedometer ($25), windshield ($35), tire chains ($10-$11).

HISTORICAL FOOTNOTE: On April 9, 1909, Oakland joined Buick and Oldsmobile as part of the General Motors Corp. In September 1909, Edward M. Murphy, one of the founders of the Pontiac Buggy Co. and president and general manager of Oakland Motor Car Co., died at age 45.

1910

1910 Oakland Model 24 touring. HAC

EQUIPMENT: Headlamps, taillight, door handles, brass horn, 12-spoke wheels front and rear (all), right-hand steering.

Series (4-cyl.)	Model	Description	Price	Weight	Production
30	24	2P Runabout	1000	1600	Note 1
30	25	5P Touring	1250	1800	Note 1
40	K	5P Touring	1700	2250	Note 1
40	M	2P Roadster	1700	-	Note 1

NOTE 1: Estimated calendar year production for all Oakland models in 1910 was 4,049 cars.

ENGINES: 30 Series: Four-cylinder. Bore & stroke: 4 x 4 in. Displacement: 201.1 cu. in. Horsepower: 30. Water-cooled. 40 Series: Four-cylinder. Bore & stroke: 4-1/2 x 5 in. Displacement: 318.1 cu. in. Horsepower: 40. Water-cooled.

TECHNICAL: 30 Series: Force feed lubrication with pump, jump spark ignition with magneto, bronze and steel multiple disc clutch with cork inserts. 40 Series: Sliding transmission. Shaft drive. Brakes: (all) lined expanding and contracting units on rear wheel drums.

CHASSIS: 30 Series: Wheelbase: 100 in., 3-1/2-in. tires, wheels mounted on ball and roller bearings. 40 Series: Wheelbase: 112 in., 4-in. tires.

OPTIONS: Folding top, full side and front curtains, brass cowl lamps.

HISTORICAL FOOTNOTE: 40 Series Oaklands were assigned serial numbers 3000 to 5000 while 30 Series cars were given serial numbers A-1000 to A-4500.

1911

1911 Oakland Model 24 30-hp runabout. JAG

EQUIPMENT: 30 Series: Pressed steel frame, gas headlights, oil sidelights, right-hand steering. 40 Series: Pressed steel frame, gas headlights, oil sidelights, taillight, horn, robe rail, gas generator, tools, pump, jack, tire repair kit, right-hand steering.

Series (4-cyl.)	Model	Description	Price	Weight	Production
30	24	2P Runabout	1000	-	Note 1

Model 24 Note: A closed-bodied two-passenger coupe body fitted to the Model 24 Runabout chassis was also available. This version of the Model 24 sold for $1,500.

30	25	5P Touring	1150	-	Note 1

Model 25 Note: A Torpedo Touring model of the Model 25 was also available for $1,200.

30	33	5P Touring	1200	-	Note 1
40	K Special	5P Touring	1600	-	Note 1
40	K	5P Touring	1500	-	Note 1
40	M	2P Roadster	1550	-	Note 1

NOTE 1: Estimated calendar year production for all Oakland models in 1911 was 3,386 cars.

1911 Oakland Model M 40-hp roadster. JAG

ENGINES: 30 Series: L-head four-cylinder. Bore & stroke: 4 x 4 in. Displacement: 201.1 cu. in. Horsepower: 30. Water-cooled. 40 Series: L-head four-cylinder. Bore & stroke: 4-1/2 x 5 in. Displacement: 318.1 cu. in. Horsepower: 40. Water-cooled.

TECHNICAL: Both series: Force feed lubrication with pump, jump spark ignition with magneto, selective, sliding-gear transmission working through multiple disc clutch. Brakes: foot or outboard lever-operated expanding and contracting units on rear wheel drums.

CHASSIS: 30 Series: Wheelbase: 100 in. except Model 24 Runabout with 96 in., 3-1/2-in. tires, 37-in. front semi-elliptic springs, 42-in. rear full-elliptic springs. 40 Series: Wheelbase: 112 in., 4-in. tires, 36-in. front semi-elliptic springs, 39-in. rear full-elliptic springs. Both series: Dropped I-beam front axle, strut rods added to rear suspension.

247

1911 Oakland Model 30 five-passenger touring. JAG

OPTIONS: Folding top, speedometer, spare tire carrier.

HISTORICAL FOOTNOTE: George P. Daniels, former president of General Motors Corp., became Oakland's third general manager, and would hold this post through 1914.

1912

1912 Oakland Model 40 sociable roadster. HAC

EQUIPMENT: Inside controls, acetylene tanks (replaced tool boxes mounted on right-hand runningboards at midyear), gas headlights, oil side lights, taillight, horn, tire repair kit, right-hand steering.

Series (4-cyl.)	Model	Description	Price	Weight	Production
-	30	2P Roadster	1200	2400	Note 1
-	30	5P Touring	1250	2600	Note 1
-	40	5P Touring	1450	2900	Note 1
-	40	3P Coupe	1900	3150	Note 1
-	40	3P Roadster	1450	2275	Note 1
-	45	7P Touring	2100	3650	Note 1
-	45	4P Touring	2250	-	Note 1
-	45	Limousine	3000	4150	Note 1

NOTE 1: Estimated model year production for all Oakland models in 1912 was 4,366 cars, while calendar year production was estimated to be 5,838 cars.

ENGINES: Model 30: L-head four-cylinder. Bore & stroke: 4 x 4 in. Displacement: 201.1 cu. in. Horsepower: 30. Water-cooled. Model 40: Four-cylinder. Bore & stroke: 4-1/8 x 4-3/4 in. Displacement: 253.9 cu. in. Horsepower: 40. Water-cooled. Model 45: Four-cylinder. Bore & stroke: 4-1/2 x 5-1/4 in. Displacement: 334 cu. in. Horsepower: 45. Water-cooled.

TECHNICAL: All models: worm and nut steering gear, artillery-type wheels with quick-demountable rims, splash system lubrication, water cooling with centrifugal pump and belt-driven fan, magneto ignition, three-speed, selective, sliding-gear transmission (except Model 30 "Oriole 33" that used transmission utilizing multiple disc clutch carried over from 1911 Model 33), enclosed driveshafts.

CHASSIS: Model 30: Wheelbase: 100 in. for roadster-bodied cars, 106 in. for other coachwork, 3-1/2 in tires, semi-floating rear axle. Model 40: Wheelbase: 112 in., 4 in. tires, semi-floating rear axle. Model 45: Wheelbase: 120 in., 4-1/2 in. tires, full-floating rear axle. All: Drop-forged I-beam front axles, front semi-elliptic springs, rear three-quarter-elliptic springs.

OPTIONS: Folding top, windshield, right side mounted spare tire carrier.

HISTORICAL FOOTNOTE: Oakland automobiles underwent numerous design changes during the 1912 models production run as well as having models drop in and out of sales catalogs depicting that year's offerings. At least 22 distinct automobiles can be found pictured in sales literature promoting 1912 Oaklands. One model that appeared briefly in 1912 was the Model 30 Model "26" that was similar to the Model 30 "Oriole 33," which was basically a carry-over of the 1911 Model 33. Oakland ranked eighth in sales within the industry.

1913

1913 Oakland Model 42 sociable roadster. HAC

EQUIPMENT: Double-drop steel frame on 6-60 and 42 Models, single-drop steel frame on 40 and 35 Models. Model 35s offered both right-hand and left-hand steering. Air or electric self starter systems offered on 6-60 line. Also offered as standard equipment on the Greyhound lineup were electric headlights, side lights, taillamp, Klaxon horn, complete tool kit, tire repair outfit, pump and jack. Aluminum steps used in place of runningboards on 6-60 and 42 Models. All Models: Artillery-spoke wheels with demountable rims.

Series (4-cyl.)	Model	Description	Price	Weight	Production
-	35	3P Roadster	1000	2760	Note 1
-	35	5P Touring	1075	2660	Note 1

Model 35 Note: Both Torpedo-bodied Speedster and Runabout versions based on the Model 35 chassis were also available.

	Model	Description	Price	Weight	Production
-	40	5P Touring	1450	2900	Note 1
-	42	4P Coupe	2500	3700	Note 1
-	42	3P Roadster	1750	-	Note 1
-	42	5P Touring	1750	3600	Note 1
-	45	Limousine	3000	4150	Note 1

Series (6-cyl.)	Model	Description	Price	Weight	Production
Greyhound	6-60	2P Roadster	2550	4235	Note 1
Greyhound	6-60	4P Touring	2550	4160	Note 1
Greyhound	6-60	7P Touring	2550	4235	Note 1

NOTE 1: Calendar year production for Oakland in 1913 was recorded as 7,030 cars.

1913 Oakland touring. JAG

1913 Oakland Model 35 touring. JAG

ENGINES: Model 35: L-head four-cylinder. Bore & stroke: 3-1/2 x 5 in. Displacement: 192.4 cu. in. Horsepower: 30. Water-cooled. Model 40: Four-cylinder. Bore & stroke: 4-1/8 x 4-3/4 in. Displacement: 253.9 cu. in. Horsepower: 40. Water-cooled. Model 42: Four-cylinder. Bore & stroke: 4-1/8 x 4-3/4 in. Displacement: 253.9 cu. in. Horsepower: 40. Water-cooled. Model 45: Four-cylinder. Bore & stroke: 4-1/2 x 5-1/4 in. Displacement: 334 cu. in. Horsepower: 45. Water-cooled. Model 6-60: Six-cylinder. Bore & stroke: 4-1/8 x 4-3/4 in. Displacement: 380.9 cu. in. Horsepower: 60. Water-cooled.

TECHNICAL: Model 35: Spiral timing gears, force-feed lubrication through a camshaft-driven oil pump. Model 42: 4.0:1 final gear ratio, gear-driven engine accessories. Model 6-60: Silent Coventry chain system to drive magneto, water pump, and camshaft. 3.5:1 final gear ratio. Delco system with electric lighting and ignition combined with air self-starter or electric self-starter.

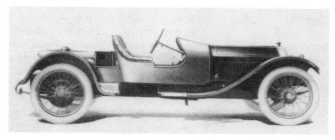

1913 Oakland Model 6-60 roadster. JAG

CHASSIS: Model 35: Wheelbase: 112 in., 3-1/2 in tires, semi-floating rear axle. Model 40: Wheelbase: 114 in., semi-floating rear axle. Model 42: Wheelbase: 116 in., 4 in. tires, full-floating rear axle. Model 45: Wheelbase: 120 in., 4-1/2 in. tires, full-floating rear axle. Model 6-60: Wheelbase: 130 in., 4-1/2 in. tires, underslung rear springs, open shaft drive via a rear parallel torque arm system.

OPTIONS: Folding top, windshield, Delco system on 6-60 optional on Model 42.

HISTORICAL FOOTNOTE: As in the previous year, Oakland sales literature offered many different models, 14 for 1913. The new Model 35 was the sales leader for Oakland in this year.

1914

EQUIPMENT: Model 36: Full runningboards, single-drop channel steel frame, right-hand steering, loop-type handles on "suicide" doors on Cabriolet Coupe as well as fold-down top with detachable side window frames, locking stowage compartment on Roadsters. Model 43: Full runningboards, double-drop channel steel frame, Center Door Sedan also featured loop-type door handles as well as forward door pillar-mounted coach lamps, silk window curtains, interior dome lamp, flip-out windshield glass. Model 6-48: Roadster featured tool box and spare tire carried on rear deck, steering wheel-mounted spark and throttle control, toe board-mounted foot accelerator. Model 6-60: Centrifugal pump on magneto shaft used to circulate coolant.

Series (4-cyl.)	Model	Description	Price	Weight	Production
Light Four	36	2P Cabriolet Coupe	1585	-	Note 1
Light Four	36	3P Roadster	1150	2760	Note 1
Light Four	36	5P Touring	1200	2660	Note 1

Model 36 Notes: A two-passenger roadster-bodied Model 36 was also available in 1914 for $1,100. Also, some sources list the Model 36 three-passenger Roadster as a carry-over Model 35 from 1935.

Series (4-cyl.)	Model	Description	Price	Weight	Production
Big Four	43	4P Coupe	2500	-	Note 1
Big Four	43	4P Sedan	2600	-	Note 1
Big Four	43	5P Touring	1785	-	Note 1

Series (6-cyl.)	Model	Description	Price	Weight	Production
Light Six	6-48	2P Speedster	1785	-	Note 1
Light Six	6-48	Roadster	1785	-	Note 1
Light Six	6-48	5P Touring	1785	3350	Note 1
Big Six	6-60	2P Raceabout	2450	-	Note 1
Big Six	6-60	4P Touring	2450	4235	Note 1
Big Six	6-60	5P Touring	2450	4160	Note 1
Big Six	6-60	7P Touring	2450	4235	Note 1

Model 6-60 Notes: Some sources list the final 950 Model 6-60s built as Model 6-61s. The 6-60/6-61 evolved at midyear 1914 into the Model 6-62, which was available only as a seven-passenger touring for $2,500. Also, some sources list a 6-60 Roadster as part of the Big Six lineup.

NOTE 1: Calendar year production for Oakland in 1914 was recorded as 6,105 cars.

ENGINES: Model 36: Four-cylinder. Bore & stroke: 3-1/2 x 5 in. Displacement: 192.4 cu. in. Horsepower: 35. Water-cooled. Model 43: Four-cylinder. Bore & stroke: 4-1/4 x 5-1/4 in. Displacement: 297.8 cu. in. Horsepower: 48. Water-cooled. Model 6-48: Six-cylinder. Bore & stroke: 3-1/2 x 5 in. Displacement: 288.9 cu. in. Horsepower: 48. Water-cooled. Model 6-60: Six-cylinder. Bore & stroke: 4-1/8 x 4-3/4 in. Displacement: 380.9 cu. in. Horsepower: 60. Water-cooled, four-bearing crankshaft with babbitt bearings.

TECHNICAL: Model 36: Spiral timing gears, force-feed lubrication through a camshaft-driven oil pump. 4.0:1 final gear ratio. Model 43: 4.0:1 final gear ratio (3.5:1 and 3.7:1 optional), gearbox offered three forward speeds and one reverse operated off a cone-type clutch, both enclosed in an extension off the crankcase. Model 6-48: 3.5:1 final gear ratio, same gearbox and clutch system as Model 43, worm and nut steering. Model 6-60: Motor-clutch-transmission formed three-point suspended unit drivetrain.

1914 Oakland Model 36 touring. HAC

CHASSIS: Model 36: Wheelbase: 112 in., 4 in. tires, semi-floating rear axle on roller bearings, semi-elliptic front springs and three-quarter elliptic rear springs. Brakes: 12 in. drum on rear only. Model 43: Wheelbase: 116 in., 4-1/2 in. tires. Model 6-48: Wheelbase: 123-1/2 in., 4 in. tires. Brakes: 14 in. drum on rear only, semi-elliptic front springs and three-quarter elliptic rear springs. Model 6-60: Wheelbase: 130 in., full-floating rear axle, 4-1/2 in. tires. (Midyear 6-62 replacement for Model 6-60 had a longer, 138 in. wheelbase and 5 in. tires.) Brakes: dual set of internal expanding brakes acting on 16 in. drums on rear only.

OPTIONS: Wire wheels for Model 6-48 Roadster and Speedster, spare tire for Model 43 (fifth rim was standard equipment).

HISTORICAL FOOTNOTE: An estimated 100 of the Model 6-62 seven-passenger touring were built. The 7.32-liter (446.6 cu. in.) engine in the 6-62 was the biggest engine ever installed in an Oakland chassis.

1915

1915 Oakland Model 37 touring. HAC

EQUIPMENT: Left-hand steering was now used on all Oakland models. One-man top equipped with storm-proof side curtains, full runningboards, Stewart Speedometer, taillight, headlights with dimmer, shroud light, electric horn. Model 37 Speedster: low-cut side panels, twin bucket seats, folding windshield, tool box and two spare tire on platform behind seats. Model 6-49: Motor-driven tire pump.

1915 Oakland Model 37 roadster. JAG

Series (4-cyl.)	Model	Description	Price	Weight	Production
Light Four	37	2P Speedster	1100	2450	Note 1
Light Four	37	2P Roadster	1150	2530	Note 1
Light Four	37	5P Touring	1200	2660	Note 1
Series (6-cyl.)	Model	Description	Price	Weight	Production
Light Six	6-49	2P Convertible Roadster	1685	-	Note 1
Light Six	6-49	5P Touring	1685	3470	Note 1

Model 6-49 Note: Some sources list a Speedster as being available, but no specifics on this model are available.

NOTE 1: Calendar year production for Oakland in 1915 totaled 11,952 cars.

1915 Oakland Model 6-49 touring. JAG

ENGINES: Model 37: Four-cylinder. Bore & stroke: 3-1/2 x 5 in. Displacement: 192.4 cu. in. Horsepower: 30. Water-cooled. Model 6-49: Six-cylinder. Bore & stroke: 3-1/2 x 5 in. Displacement: 288.9 cu. in. Horsepower: 30. Water-cooled.

TECHNICAL: Model 37: Wedge-connection brake rods that eliminated bearing use, tubular propeller shaft, self-cleaning brake lever rockers. Model 6-49: Delco electrical system featuring low-tension magneto, storage battery and dry cells, three-speed sliding selective gear transmission and leather-faced cone clutch. Both Models: Oakland-Stewart vacuum-gravity fuel feed system.

CHASSIS: Model 37: Wheelbase: 112 in., 4 in. tires (Non-Skid tires mounted on rear), Hotchkiss drive rear axle. Model 6-49: Wheelbase: 123-1/2 in., 4-1/2 in. tires, full-floating rear axle, underslung springs front and rear.

HISTORICAL FOOTNOTE: General Motors President Charles Nash was listed as general manager of Oakland in 1915. Serial numbers for Model 37s ran from 370000 to 373599 while Model 6-49 serial numbers ran from 490000 to 490500. Oakland's first V-8 engine was introduced late in 1915 for use in a 1916 model Oakland.

1916

EQUIPMENT: Single-wire electrical system operated at six volts, one-man folding top. Model 38: Ventilating windshield, ammeter, Stewart speedometer. Model 50: Two folding auxiliary seats.

Series (4-cyl.)	Model	Description	Price	Weight	Production
Light Four	38	Speedster	1050	2440	Note 1
Light Four	38	Roadster	1050	2460	Note 1
Light Four	38	5P Touring	1050	2575	Note 1
Series (6-cyl.)	Model	Description	Price	Weight	Production
Light Six	32	2P Roadster	795	2115	Note 1
Light Six	32	5P Touring	795	2185	Note 1

Model 32 Note: Midyear 1916 the Model 32 became the Model 32-B with no production changes to the car.

Series (8-cyl.)	Model	Description	Price	Weight	Production
-	50	7P Dual Cowl Touring	1585	3515	Note 1

NOTE 1: Calendar year production for Oakland in 1916 totaled 25,675 cars.

ENGINES: Model 38: Four-cylinder. Bore & stroke: 3-1/2 x 5 in. Displacement: 192.4 cu. in. Horsepower: 30. Water-cooled. Model 32: Flathead six-cylinder. Bore & stroke: 2-13/16 x 4-3/4 in. Displacement: 177 cu. in. Horsepower: 30-35. Water-cooled. Model 50: V-8. Bore & stroke: 3-1/2 x 4-1/2 in. Displacement: 346.3 cu. in. Horsepower: 71 @ 2600 rpm. This V-8 engine featured aluminum pistons and a counterbalanced crankshaft.

TECHNICAL: Model 38: More compact unit powerplant due to downsized clutch. Model 32: Three-speed selective-type transmission with cone clutch. Model 50: Three-point unit suspended drive.

CHASSIS: Model 38: Wheelbase: 112 in., 4 in. tires (Non-Skid tires mounted on rear). Model 32: Wheelbase: 110 in., 3-1/2 in. tires (Non-Skid tires mounted on rear). Model 50: Wheelbase: 127 in., 4-1/2 in. tires, overslung half-elliptic front springs and underslung three-quarter rear springs, pressed steel full-floating rear axle. Brakes: 14 in. drum.

HISTORICAL FOOTNOTE: Fred W. Warner was appointed general manager of Oakland in 1916. Serial numbers for Model 38s ran from 380000 to 384001 while Model 32 serial numbers ran from 320000 to 347110. Oakland's first V-8 engined Model 50's serial numbers ran from 500000 to 502000.

1917

EQUIPMENT: Model 34: Dash light to monitor oil flow, driver's side mounted spare tire. Model 50: Unchanged from 1916.

1917 Oakland Model 34 roadster. HAC

Series (6-cyl.)	Model	Description	Price	Weight	Production
Oakland Six	34	2P Roadster	795	2230	Note 1
Oakland Six	34	5P Touring	795	2330	Note 1
Oakland Six	34	Convertible Sedan	1020	2450	Note 1
Oakland Six	34	Convertible Coupe	995	2350	Note 1

Series (8-cyl.)	Model	Description	Price	Weight	Production
Oakland Eight	50	7P Dual Cowl Touring	1585	3515	Note 1

NOTE 1: Calendar year production for Oakland in 1917 totaled 33,171 cars.

ENGINES: Model 34: OHV flathead six-cylinder. Bore & stroke: 2-13/16 x 4-3/4 in. Displacement: 177 cu. in. Horsepower: 41 @ 2500 rpm. Water-cooled. Model 50: V-8. Bore & stroke: 3-1/2 x 4-1/2 in. Displacement: 346.3 cu. in. Horsepower: 71 @ 2600 rpm. This V-8 engine featured aluminum pistons and a counterbalanced crankshaft.

TECHNICAL: Model 34: Circulating splash system engine oiling, cooling via pump mounted on fan shaft operated off fan belt. Model 50: Unchanged from 1916.

CHASSIS: Model 34: Wheelbase: 112 in., 4 in. tires (Non-Skid tires mounted on rear), semi-elliptic rear springs. Model 50: Wheelbase: 127 in., 4-1/2 in. tires, overslung half-elliptic front springs and underslung three-quarter rear springs, pressed steel full-floating rear axle. Brakes: 14 in. drum.

HISTORICAL FOOTNOTE: On Aug. 1, 1917, the Oakland Motor Car Co. became the Oakland Motor Division due to General Motors changing from a holding company to an operating company. Model 34 serial numbers ran from 134 to 3000034.

1918

1918 Oakland Model 34-B roadster. OCW

EQUIPMENT: One-man folding top with detachable side curtains, foot rest for easy operation of accelerator pedal, oil pan-mounted oil gauge, dash instrumentation included amp, oil pressure, and fuel level gauges as well as an odometer and trip odometer, power tire pump.

1918 Oakland Model 34-B Sensible Six roadster (rear view). JAG

Series (6-cyl.)	Model	Description	Price	Weight	Production
Sensible Six	34-B	2P Roadster	1185	2070	Note 1
Sensible Six	34-B	5P Touring	1185	2130	Note 1
Sensible Six	34-B	Sedan	1760	2650	Note 1
Sensible Six	34-B	Coupe	1760	2350	Note 1
Sensible Six	34-B	Roadster Coupe	1210	2175	Note 1
Sensible Six	34-B	5P Touring Sedan	1250	2290	Note 1

5P Touring Sedan Note: Some sources list this model as being replaced midyear 1918 by a "Removable Post Sedan" priced at $1,685. This model was the equivalent of a 1950s four-door hardtop. It did not survive into the 1919 model run.

NOTE 1: Estimated calendar year production for Oakland in 1918 totaled 27,757 cars.

1918 Oakland Model 34-B Sensible Six unit body coupe. JAG

ENGINES: Model 111 Northway OHV six-cylinder. Bore & stroke: 2-13/16 x 4-3/4 in. Displacement: 177 cu. in. Horsepower: 44. Water-cooled.

1918 Oakland Model 34-B Sensible Six touring sedan. JAG

1918 Oakland Model 34-B Sensible Six touring. JAG

TECHNICAL: Jacox irreversible screw-and-double half-nut steering gear, tubular propeller shaft, Northway cone-type clutch in unit with a three-speed selective sliding gear transmission, heating box induction system that utilized exhaust gases to preheat incoming mixture, cup-and-cone ball bearings on wheel spindles, Remy two-unit starting and lighting system, Prestolite three-cell, six-volt battery, bi-plane-type fan in unit with water pump driven by camshaft-activated V-belt, Oakland-Stewart vacuum fuel delivery system. Fuel tank: 13 gal.

1918 Oakland Model 34-B Sensible Six convertible roadster coupe. JAG

CHASSIS: Wheelbase: 112 in., 4 in. tires (Non-Skid tires mounted on rear), 35 in. semi-elliptic front springs and 51 in. underslung semi-elliptic rear springs, Hotchkiss drive and full-floating rear axle. Brakes: 12 in. external contracting and internal expanding brakes with bands faced with wire-woven asbestos. Frame: Channel section pressed steel 4-1/2 in. deep, 2 in. wide, and 1/8 in. thick with five crossmembers; frame width: 40-3/4 in. rear, 28 in. front. Turning circle: 38 ft.

OPTIONS: Wire spoke wheels ($75).

HISTORICAL FOOTNOTE: Due to the material shortages caused by World War I, the Model 34-B was the exclusive Oakland offering from September 1917 to June 1, 1920.

1919

EQUIPMENT: One-man folding top with detachable side curtains, foot rest for easy operation of accelerator pedal, oil pan-mounted oil gauge, dash instrumentation included amp, oil pressure, and fuel level gauges as well as an odometer and trip odometer, power tire pump.

Series (6-cyl.)	Model	Description	Price	Weight	Production
Sensible Six	34-B	2P Roadster	1075	2070	Note 1
Sensible Six	34-B	5P Touring	1075	2130	Note 1
Sensible Six	34-B	Sedan	1650	2650	Note 1
Sensible Six	34-B	Coupe	1650	2350	Note 1

NOTE 1: Estimated calendar year production for Oakland in 1919 totaled 52,124 cars.

ENGINES: Model 111 Northway OHV six-cylinder. Bore & stroke: 2-13/16 x 4-3/4 in. Displacement: 177 cu. in. Horsepower: 44 @ 2600 rpm. Water-cooled.

TECHNICAL: Jacox irreversible screw-and-double half-nut steering gear, tubular propeller shaft, Northway cone-type clutch in unit with a three-speed selective sliding gear transmission, heating box induction system that utilized exhaust gases to preheat incoming mixture, cup-and-cone ball bearings on wheel spindles, Remy two-unit starting and lighting system, Prestolite three-cell, six-volt battery, bi-plane-type fan in unit with water pump driven by camshaft-activated V-belt, Oakland-Stewart vacuum fuel delivery system. Fuel tank: 13 gal.

1919 Oakland Sensible Six sedan. HAC

CHASSIS: Wheelbase: 112 in., 4 in. tires (Non-Skid tires mounted on rear), 35 in. semi-elliptic front springs and 51 in. underslung semi-elliptic rear springs, Hotchkiss drive and full-floating rear axle. Brakes: 12 in. external contracting and internal expanding brakes with bands faced with wire-woven asbestos. Frame: Channel section pressed steel 4-1/2 in. deep, 2 in. wide, and 1/8 in. thick with five crossmembers; frame width: 40-3/4 in. rear, 28 in. front. Turning circle: 38 ft.

OPTIONS: Wire spoke wheels ($75).

HISTORICAL FOOTNOTE: Oakland climbed to rank sixth in industry sales charts.

1920

1920 Oakland Sensible Six touring. HAC

EQUIPMENT: Electric horn, ammeter, power tire pump, speedometer, demountable rims.

Series (6-cyl.)	Model	Description	Price	Weight	Production
Sensible Six	34-C	3P Roadster	1165	2070	Note 1
Sensible Six	34-C	5P Touring	1235	2330	Note 1
Sensible Six	34-C	5P Sedan	1835	2733	Note 1
Sensible Six	34-C	4P Coupe	1835	2550	Note 1

NOTE 1: Oakland production in 1920 is recorded at 35,356 cars.

ENGINES: OHV six-cylinder. Bore & stroke: 2-13/16 x 4-3/4 in. Displacement: 177 cu. in. Horsepower: 44 @ 2600 rpm. Water-cooled.

TECHNICAL: Worm-and-nut design steering gear, cone-type clutch in unit with a three-speed selective sliding gear transmission, heating box induction system that utilized exhaust gases to preheat incoming mixture, positive force-feed engine lubrication via a gear-driven oil pump and drilled crankshaft, three-blade bi-plane-type cooling fan, Oakland-Stewart vacuum fuel delivery system. Fuel tank: 12-1/2 gal.

CHASSIS: Wheelbase: 115 in., 4 in. tires (Non-Skid tires mounted on rear), semi-elliptic springs front and rear, full-floating rear axle, external contracting and internal expanding brakes. Frame: Channel section pressed steel 6-1/2 in. deep.

OPTIONS: Wire spoke wheels ($75).

HISTORICAL FOOTNOTE: George H. Hannum was appointed president and general manager of Oakland in 1920. The 1920 Model 34-C serial numbers ended at 152356-34 (the last 1920 model was built on Jan. 6, 1921).

1921

EQUIPMENT: Electric horn, ammeter, power tire pump, speedometer, demountable rims.

Series (6-cyl.)	Model	Description	Price	Weight	Production
Sensible Six	34-C	3P Roadster	1395	2070	Note 1
Sensible Six	34-C	5P Touring	1395	2421	Note 1
Sensible Six	34-C	5P Sedan	2065	2733	Note 1
Sensible Six	34-C	4P Coupe	2065	2550	Note 1

NOTE 1: Oakland production in 1921 totaled 5,444 cars.

ENGINES: OHV six-cylinder. Bore & stroke: 2-13/16 x 4-3/4 in. Displacement: 177 cu. in. Horsepower: 44 @ 2600 rpm. Water-cooled.

TECHNICAL: Remy two-unit electrical system with thermostatic generator control (provided automatic adjustment of the charging rate for warm or cold weather), worm-and-nut design steering gear, cone-type clutch in unit with a three-speed selective sliding gear transmission, heating box induction system that utilized exhaust gases to preheat incoming mixture, positive force-feed engine lubrication via a gear-driven oil pump and drilled crankshaft, three-blade bi-plane-type cooling fan, Oakland-Stewart vacuum fuel delivery system. Fuel tank: 12-1/2 gal.

CHASSIS: Wheelbase: 115 in., 4 in. tires (Non-Skid tires mounted on rear), semi-elliptic springs front and rear, full-floating rear axle, external contracting and internal expanding brakes. Frame: Channel section pressed steel 6-1/2 in. deep. Final gear ratio: 4.50:1.

OPTIONS: Wire spoke wheels ($75).

HISTORICAL FOOTNOTE: The 1921 Model 34-C serial numbers ran from 152357-34 (built Jan. 7, 1921) to 159700-34 (the last 1921 model was built on July 27, 1921).

1922

EQUIPMENT: Speedometer, ammeter, oil pressure gauge, demountable rims, power tire pump.

Series (6-cyl.)	Model	Description	Price	Weight	Production
Sensible Six	34-D	2P Roadster	-	2495	Note 1
Sensible Six	34-D	5P Touring	1395	2620	Note 1
Sensible Six	34-D	5P Sedan	2065	2733	Note 1
Sensible Six	34-D	4P Coupe	2065	2620	Note 1
Sensible Six	34-D	4P Sports Touring	1265	2565	Note 1

Model 34-D Note: A chassis-only version of the Model 34-D was also available.

NOTE 1: Oakland Model 34-D production in 1922 totaled 7,849 cars.

ENGINES: OHV six-cylinder. Bore & stroke: 2-13/16 x 4-3/4 in. Displacement: 177 cu. in. Horsepower: 44 @ 2600 rpm. Water-cooled.

TECHNICAL: Remy two-unit electrical system with thermostatic generator control (provided automatic adjustment of the charging rate for warm or cold weather), worm-and-nut design steering gear, cone-type clutch in unit with a three-speed selective sliding gear transmission, heating box induction system that utilized exhaust gases to preheat incoming mixture, positive force-feed engine lubrication via a submerged gear pump and drilled crankshaft, Oakland-Stewart vacuum fuel delivery system. Fuel tank: 12-1/2 gal.

1922 Oakland Model 34-C sedan. HAC

CHASSIS: Wheelbase: 115 in., 4 in. tires (Non-Skid tires mounted on rear), 36 in. semi-elliptic front springs and 51 in. semi-elliptic rear springs, full-floating rear axle. Frame: Channel section pressed steel 6-1/2 in. deep.

HISTORICAL FOOTNOTE: The 1922 production of Oaklands had the Model 34-D produced from August 1921 to Dec. 31, 1921. Serial numbers for the Model 34-D ran from 159701-34 to 167550-34. At that point, the Model 34-D was dropped and the Model 6-44 was produced, also as a 1922 Model. Records show that 10,250 1922 Model 6-44s were produced with serial numbers that ran from 1-44 to 10250-44.

1923

1923 Oakland Model 6-54 5-passenger sedan. AA

EQUIPMENT: Drum-type headlights, choke control, steering wheel-mounted wire-operated spark and gas lever control box, speedometer, ammeter, oil pressure gauge, hinged front seats for easier rear seat access, demountable rims (Sports Touring and Sports Roadster both had solid disc rims), power tire pump.

Series (6-cyl.)	Model	Description	Price	Weight	Production
Sensible Six	6-44	2P Roadster	975	2530	Note 1
Sensible Six	6-44	5P Touring	995	2675	Note 1
Sensible Six	6-44	5P Sedan	1545	3060	Note 1
Sensible Six	6-44	5P Coupe	1445	2970	Note 1
Sensible Six	6-44	2P Coupe	1185	2645	Note 1
Sensible Six	6-44	4P Sports Touring	1165	2680	Note 1
Sensible Six	6-44	2P Sports Roadster	-	2610	Note 1

NOTE 1: Oakland Model 6-44 production in 1923 totaled 30,901 cars.

ENGINES: OHV six-cylinder. Bore & stroke: 2-13/16 x 4-3/4 in. Displacement: 177 cu. in. Horsepower: 44 @ 2600 rpm. Water-cooled.

TECHNICAL: Oil dip lubrication for clutch bearing, positive force-feed engine lubrication via a submerged gear pump and drilled crankshaft, Oakland-Stewart vacuum fuel delivery system. Fuel tank: 12 gal.

1923 Oakland Model 6-44 roadster (rear view). JAG

CHASSIS: Wheelbase: 115 in., 4 in. tires (Non-Skid tires mounted on rear), 36 in. semi-elliptic front springs and 51 in. semi-elliptic rear springs, Alemite lubrication system for chassis. Brakes: 12 in. external contracting and internal expanding brakes. Frame: Channel section pressed steel 6-1/2 in. deep. Final gear ratio: 4.66:1.

HISTORICAL FOOTNOTE: The Model 6-44 was produced from January 1922 to June 15, 1923. The first 10,250 Model 6-44s produced were considered early/1922 versions. Model 6-44s with serial numbers that ranged from 10251-44 to 41152-44 were recorded as 1923 models.

1924

1924 Oakland Model 6-54 touring. OCW

EQUIPMENT: Steel disc wheels, rear-mounted spare tire carrier, permanent tops, speedometer, ammeter, oil gauge, windshield cleaner, cowl ventilator, tools and jack, roller shades. Sports Touring and Sports Roadster featured bumpers, motometer with wing cap, windshield wings, dash gasoline gauge, nickeled lamp rims, visor, and rearview mirror.

Series (6-cyl.)	Model	Description	Price	Weight	Production
Oakland Six	6-54A	3P Roadster	995	2420	Note 1
Oakland Six	6-54A	5P Touring	995	2845	Note 1
Oakland Six	6-54A	5P Sedan	1445	2860	Note 1
Oakland Six	6-54A	4P Coupe	1395	2720	Note 1
Oakland Six	6-54A	3P Business Coupe	1195	2620	Note 1
Oakland Six	6-54A	4P Sports Touring	1195	2550	Note 1
Oakland Six	6-54A	3P Sports Roadster	1195	2510	Note 1

NOTE 1: Oakland Model 6-54A model year production (Aug. 23, 1923, to July 29, 1924) totaled 37,080 cars.

ENGINES: L-head six-cylinder. Bore & stroke: 2-13/16 x 4-3/4 in. Displacement: 177 cu. in. Horsepower: 44 @ 2600 rpm. Water-cooled.

TECHNICAL: Automatic spark advance, three-speed selective sliding gear transmission, force-feed lubrication, screw and split-nut steering.

CHASSIS: Wheelbase: 113 in., 4 in. tires (Non-Skid tires mounted on rear), semi-elliptic front and rear springs. Brakes: Four-wheel mechanical brakes.

OPTIONS: Glass enclosures ($60 for Touring model, $40 for Sport Touring model).

HISTORICAL FOOTNOTE: All 1924 Oaklands were finished in a blue shade of Duco Satin Finish proxylin "enamel" paint and were advertised as the "True Blue Oakland Six." Essentially a nitro-cellulose lacquer solution, the air-dried proxylin material cut the time required to paint an Oakland body from 336 hours to 13-1/2 hours.

1925

1925 Oakland Model 6-54 landau sedan. AA

EQUIPMENT: Theft-proof ignition lock, steel disc wheels and balloon cord tires (except Special Sedan equipped with artillery-type wood-spoke wheels and balloon tires), automatic windshield wipers, door locks, permanent tops, rear-mounted spare tire carrier, cowl ventilator, speedometer, ammeter, oil gauge, odometer, tools, tire pump and jack, roller shades. Special Touring and Special Roadster featured front bumper, rear fender guards, motometer with wing cap, windshield wings, nickel-plated head, cowl, and taillamps.

Series (6-cyl.)	Model	Description	Price	Weight	Production
Oakland Six	6-54B	3P Roadster	1095	2420	Note 1
Oakland Six	6-54B	5P Touring	1095	2845	Note 1
Oakland Six	6-54B	5P Sedan	1545	2860	Note 1
Oakland Six	6-54B	4P Coupe	1495	2720	Note 1
Oakland Six	6-54B	3P Landau Coupe	1295	2620	Note 1
Oakland Six	6-54B	5P Landau Sedan	1645	2885	Note 1
Oakland Six	6-54B	4P Special Touring	1195	2550	Note 1
Oakland Six	6-54B	3P Special Roadster	1195	2510	Note 1
Oakland Six	6-54B	5P Special Sedan	1375	-	Note 1
Oakland Six	6-54B	5P Coach	1215	2745	Note 1

NOTE 1: Oakland Model 6-54B model year production (July 17, 1924, to May 29, 1925) totaled 27,423 cars.

ENGINES: L-head six-cylinder. Bore & stroke: 2-7/8 x 4-3/4 in. Displacement: 177 cu. in. Compression ratio: 5.0:1. Horsepower: 44 @ 2600 rpm. Water-cooled.

TECHNICAL: Interchangeable bronze-backed engine bearings, single plate self-ventilated clutch, silent chain cam drive, full pressure engine lubrication system, full automatic spark control, exhaust-heated manifold with provision for winter and summer adjustment, three-speed selective sliding gear transmission, parking brake on transmission, worm and half-nut steering gear, steering knuckles supported by ball thrust bearings.

CHASSIS: Wheelbase: 113 in., 31 x 4.95 balloon cord tires, semi-elliptic front and rear springs, semi-floating rear axle using spiral bevel drive gears. Brakes: 12-3/8 in. external contracting brakes on all four wheels. Final gear ratio: 4.7:1.

HISTORICAL FOOTNOTE: A.R. Glancy was promoted from vice-president and assistant general manager to Oakland's president and general manager in 1925 (ironically, in 1903, Glancy wrote a thesis to prove the automobile had no future). All Oaklands this year had Fisher bodies finished in permanent Duco colors.

1926

1926 Oakland Greater Six landau sedan. JAG

EQUIPMENT: Air cleaner, oil filter, wood-spoke artillery wheels, speedometer, oil pressure gauge, automatic wipers, door locks, window lifts, tools, tire pump and jack. Sport Roadster featured a two-passenger rumbleseat, golf bag compartment, windshield wings, front bumpers, rear fender guards.

Series (6-cyl.)	Model	Description	Price	Weight	Production
Oakland Six	6-54C	2P Roadster	975	2425	Note 1
Oakland Six	6-54C	5P Touring	1025	2500	Note 1
Oakland Six	6-54C	5P Sedan	1195	2765	Note 1
Oakland Six	6-54C	3P Landau Coupe	1125	2615	Note 1
Oakland Six	6-54C	5P Landau Sedan	1295	2885	Note 1
Oakland Six	6-54C	2P Sport Roadster	1175	2550	Note 1
Oakland Six	6-54C	5P Coach	1215	2640	Note 1

NOTE 1: Oakland Model 6-54C model year production (July 2, 1925, to June 17, 1926) totaled 58,827 cars.

1926 Oakland Greater Six roadster. OCW

ENGINES: L-head six-cylinder. Bore & stroke: 2-7/8 x 4-3/4 in. Displacement: 185 cu. in. Compression ratio: 5.0:1. Horsepower: 44 @ 2600 rpm. Water-cooled.

TECHNICAL: Harmonic balancer built into crankshaft, full-pressure oiling system.

CHASSIS: Wheelbase: 113 in., 30 x 5.25 balloon cord tires, semi-elliptic front and rear springs. Brakes: 12-3/8 in. external contracting brakes on all four wheels.

OPTION: Steel disc wheels.

HISTORICAL FOOTNOTE: Under the umbrella of the Oakland Motor Division, production of 1926 Pontiacs began on Dec. 28, 1925, the first year models consisting of a five-passenger coach and a two-passenger coupe. In June of 1926 approval was given to build a new "Daylight Plant" for the assembly of 1,000 Pontiacs and 600 Oaklands per day.

1927

EQUIPMENT: Dimmer pedal to operate Guide Tilt-Ray double filament headlamps, shift lever ball, steering wheel rim. Sport Phaeton and Sport Roadster: plate glass windshield wings, front bumper, rear guards, windshield wiper, rearview mirror, nickeled headlamps.

Series (6-cyl.)	Model	Description	Price	Weight	Production
Greater Oak. Six	6-54D	5P Sedan	1195	2765	Note 1
Greater Oak. Six	6-54D	3P Landau Coupe	1125	2615	Note 1
Greater Oak. Six	6-54D	5P Landau Sedan	1295	2885	Note 1
Greater Oak. Six	6-54D	2P Sport Roadster	1175	2600	Note 1
Greater Oak. Six	6-54D	5P Sport Phaeton	1095	2500	Note 1
Greater Oak. Six	6-54D	5P Coach	1215	2640	Note 1

NOTE 1: Oakland Model 6-54D model year production (June 7, 1926, to May 24, 1927) totaled 44,658 cars.

1927 Oakland Greater Six sport phaeton. AA

ENGINES: L-head six-cylinder. Bore & stroke: 2-7/8 x 4-3/4 in. Displacement: 185 cu. in. Horsepower: 45 @ 2600 rpm. Water-cooled (10-1/2 quart cooling capacity).

TECHNICAL: Harmonic balancer fitted with coil springs, chrome-vanadium steel spring leaves, lightweight undercut transmission gears, rubber joint inserted in driveshaft behind front universal joint to isolate rear end noise, rubber engine-to-chassis mounting.

CHASSIS: Wheelbase: 113 in., 30 x 5.25 balloon cord tires, semi-elliptic front and rear springs. Brakes: 12-3/8 in. external contracting brakes on all four wheels.

HISTORICAL FOOTNOTE: Oakland 1927 Model 6-54D production began with serial number 120801-54 and ended with serial number 167943-54. Between July 29, 1926, and Jan. 9, 1927, a Greater Oakland Six Landau Sedan with a clear viewing panel over the engine compartment was run nonstop on a treadmill as a public display in Detroit. Done to promote the stamina and performance of the Model 6-54D, the car reached 100,000 after six months and was still running strong.

1928

1928 Oakland All-American four-door sedan. AA

EQUIPMENT: Spare tire now standard on all Oakland models, Fisher vision and ventilation windshield, rear view mirror, single stop and backing lamp, dash gasoline gauge, sun visors (closed models only), radiator shell, lamp rims, and hood latches all chrome-plated. Sport Phaeton and Sport Roadster: trunk racks.

Series (6-cyl.)	Model	Description	Price	Weight	Production
Oak. All-Amer. Six	212	5P Sedan	1145	2980	Note 1
Oak. All-Amer. Six	212	5P Sedan (two-door)	1045	2840	Note 1
Oak. All-Amer. Six	212	3P Landau Coupe	1045	2805	Note 1
Oak. All-Amer. Six	212	5P Landau Sedan	1265	-	Note 1
Oak. All-Amer. Six	212	2P Sport Roadster	1075	2730	Note 1
Oak. All-Amer. Six	212	5P Sport Phaeton	1075	2740	Note 1
Oak. All-Amer. Six	212	3P Sport Cabriolet	1145	2825	Note 1

NOTE 1: Oakland first edition/1928 Model 212 model year production (June 22, 1927, to June 25, 1928) totaled 60,121 cars.

1928 Oakland All-American Six roadster. JAG

ENGINES: L-head six-cylinder. Bore & stroke: 3-1/4 x 4-1/4 in. Displacement: 212 cu. in. Horsepower: 60 @ 2800 rpm. Compression ratio: 4.9:1. Water-cooled.
TECHNICAL: General Motors Research (GMR) cylinder head incorporated a convex baffle over pistons to reduce detonation and permit a higher compression ratio, four bearing crankshaft forged with

integral counterweight setup and torsional damper, side engine block-mounted distributor, pioneering use of fuel pump and fuel filter (replaced vacuum tank system).
CHASSIS: Wheelbase: 117 in., 29 x 5.50 tires mounted on 19 in. wood-spoke artillery style wheels. Brakes: External, four-wheel brakes with 12-3/8 in. drums measuring 1-7/8 in. wide. Final gear ratio: 4.41:1.
OPTIONS: All 1928 Oaklands had frames drilled for the installation of optional Delco-Remy-Lovejoy shock absorbers. Sport Roadster: sidemount tire covers, six wheel equipment and wire spoke wheels.
HISTORICAL FOOTNOTE: 1928 would be the final year that Oakland would experience increased sales.

1929

1929 Oakland All-American Six convertible cabriolet. JAG

EQUIPMENT: Horseshoe shaped radiator shell split by a vertical center bar, cadet visor, automatic windshield wiper, rearview mirror.

Series (6-cyl.)	Model	Description	Price	Weight	Product.
Oak. All-Amer. Six	212	5P Sedan	1245	3305	Note 1
Oak. All-Amer. Six	212	5P Sedan (two-door)	1145	3185	Note 1
Oak. All-Amer. Six	212	5P Special Sedan	1320	3305	Note 1
Oak. All-Amer. Six	212	5P Landaulet Sedan	1375	3275	Note 1
Oak. All-Amer. Six	212	5P Brougham Sedan	1195	3285	Note 1
Oak. All-Amer. Six	212	3P Coupe	1145	3090	Note 1
Oak. All-Amer. Six	212	2P Sport Roadster	1145	2920	Note 1
Oak. All-Amer. Six	212	5P Sport Phaeton	1145	2990	Note 1
Oak. All-Amer. Six	212	3P Convertible Cabriolet	1265	3145	Note 1

NOTE 1: Oakland second edition/1929 Model 212 model year production (Sept. 24, 1928, to Oct. 9, 1929) totaled 50,693 cars.

1929 Oakland All-American roadster. OCW

ENGINES: L-head six-cylinder. Bore & stroke: 3-3/8 x 4-1/4 in. Displacement: 228 cu. in. Horsepower: 68 @ 3000 rpm. Water-cooled.

1929 Oakland All-American Six coupe. JAG

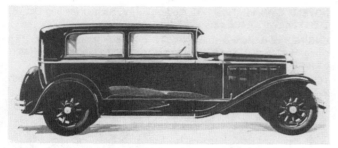

1929 Oakland All-American Six two-door sedan. JAG

TECHNICAL: Four-point rubber engine mountings, frame crossmembers beefed up to accommodate weightier bodies.

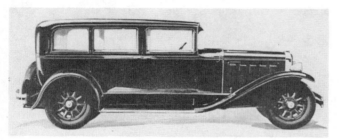

1929 Oakland All-American Six four-door sedan. JAG

CHASSIS: Wheelbase: 117 in. Brakes: Midland Steeldraulic four-wheel brakes. Final gear ratio: From 4.42:1 to 4.73:1.

1929 Oakland All-American Six sport roadster. JAG

OPTIONS: Lovejoy shock absorbers, six wire wheels with wide-faced hubcaps and chrome-plated sidemount clamps, tire cover for rear-mounted spare.

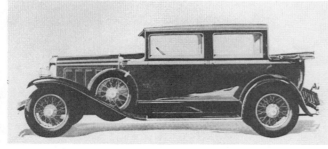

1929 Oakland All-American Six convertible landau sedan. JAG

HISTORICAL FOOTNOTE: On Jan. 24, 1929, Oakland chief engineer Ben Anibal filed U.S. patent number 1897783 for his V-design eight-cylinder engine that would become the 1930-31 Oakland engine. On March 8, 1929, the one-millionth Oakland was built. At the conclusion of 1929, Oakland ranked 21st in industry sales among 33 automakers.

1930

1930 Oakland Model 101 V-8 coupe. JAG

EQUIPMENT: Front and rear bumpers and guards now standard at slightly higher prices, safety indicator lamps atop front fenders, vibrator horn mounted on the front fender tie bar, cadet visor, automatic windshield wiper, nonglare rearview mirror, adjustable driver's seat, natural finish Jaxon wood spoke wheels, Lovejoy hydraulic shock absorbers.

Series (8-cyl.)	Model	Description	Price	Weight	Production
Oakland V-8	101	5P Sedan	995	3205	Note 1
Oakland V-8	101	5P Sedan (two-door)	895	3095	Note 1
Oakland V-8	101	5P Custom Sedan	1045	3210	Note 1
Oakland V-8	101	3P Coupe	895	3010	Note 1
Oakland V-8	101	2P Sport Roadster	895	2770	Note 1
Oakland V-8	101	5P Sport Phaeton	945	2910	Note 1
Oakland V-8	101	3P Sport Coupe	965	3075	Note 1

NOTE 1: Oakland Model 101 model year production (December 1929 to October 1930) totaled 21,943 cars.

1930 Oakland Eight Model 101 roadster. JAC

ENGINES: V-8. Bore & stroke: 3-7/16 x 3-3/8 in. Displacement: 251 cu. in. Horsepower: 85. Compression ratio: 5.0:1. Water-cooled.

TECHNICAL: Three main bearing engine crankshaft of 180 degree, single plane design, horizontally positioned valves operated directly by rocker arms working from a centrally located, chain driven camshaft, four-point engine mountings with rubber insulators at the rear and laminated springs at the front corners, plus a special synchronizer (one end of this device was attached to the frame while the other end passed into the block where it was actuated by revolutions of the camshaft), 9-5/8 in. single plate clutch, three-speed transmission.

257

1930 Oakland Model 101 V-8 phaeton. JAG

CHASSIS: Wheelbase: 117 in., 28 x 5.50 in. tires. Brakes: Self-energizing internal four-wheel brakes. Final gear ratio: 4.42:1 (optional ratios of 3.9:1 and 5.2:1 were available).

OPTIONS: Six wire wheels and chrome-plated sidemount trim rings, front fenders with tire wells.

HISTORICAL FOOTNOTE: On Oct. 15, 1930, Irving J. Reuter moved from the presidency of Olds Motor Works to become general manager of Oakland Motor Division. Oakland car number 273501 was the first V-8 built by the automaker since 1917. Due to the stock market crash of October 1929, Oakland's 1930 industry sales would drop by one-third compared to the previous year.

1931

1931 Oakland Eight Model 301 sedan. JAC

EQUIPMENT: Single bar bumpers.

Series (8-cyl.)	Model	Description	Price	Weight	Production
Oakland V-8	301	5P Sedan	995	3138	Note 1
Oakland V-8	301	5P Sedan (two-door)	895	3173	Note 1
Oakland V-8	301	5P Custom Sedan	1055	3138	Note 1
Oakland V-8	301	3P Coupe	895	3088	Note 1
Oakland V-8	301	3P Sport Coupe	975	3153	Note 1
Oakland V-8	301	3P Convertible Coupe	995	3105	Note 1

NOTE 1: Oakland Model 301 model year production (ending Oct. 8, 1931) totaled 13,408 cars.

ENGINES: V-8. Bore & stroke: 3-7/16 x 3-3/8 in. Displacement: 251 cu. in. Horsepower: 85 @ 3400 rpm. Compression ratio: 5.0:1. Water-cooled.

TECHNICAL: New synchromesh transmission, new chassis frame with 2-1/8 in. thick flange widths and 5-1/2 in. depth of channel.

1931 Oakland Model 301 V-8 custom sedan. JAG

CHASSIS: Wheelbase: 117 in., 28 x 5.50 in. tires mounted on 45-spoke Motor Wheel Corp. wire wheels with semi-drop base rims. Brakes: 13 in. diameter drum brakes. Final gear ratio: 4.55:1 (revised to 3.90:1 after June 1931).

HISTORICAL FOOTNOTE: After dismal sales of the 1931 Model 301 and the lingering effects of the Great Depression, in midyear 1932 the Oakland Motor Division was no more, being absorbed by the Pontiac Motor Company. In fact, as early as the beginning of the year at the New York Auto Show only models with the Pontiac nameplate were shown, some being Oaklands with the names switched.

STYLE NUMBER DESIGNATIONS

The cars of Oakland (1907 to 1931) and Pontiac (1926 to 1995) are listed by the model year and the official factory style number. The style number is located on the firewall identification plate inside the engine compartment. (Cars manufactured prior to 1933 utilize the term job number synonymously with the term style number.)

OAKLAND

1907-25
STANDARD SEDAN...SED
SPECIAL SEDAN...SPESED
LANDAULET SEDAN...LETSED
BROUGHAM SEDAN...BRSED
CUSTOM SEDAN...CUSSED
LANDAU SEDAN...LANSED
SPORT SEDAN...SSED
2-DR SEDAN...COACH
STANDARD COUPE...COUPE
LANDAU COUPE...LCPE
SPORT COUPE...SCPE
CONVERTIBLE COUPE...CCPE
BUSINESS COUPE...BCPE
ROADSTER...ROAD
SPORT ROADSTER...SROAD
PHAETON...PHAE
SPORT PHAETON...SPHAE
RUNABOUT...RUN
SPEEDSTER...SPDTR

1926
STANDARD...6330
LANDAU SEDAN...6360
2-DR SEDAN...6340
LANDAU COUPE...6350
SPORT ROADSTER...SROAD
SPORT PHAETON...SPHAE

1927
STANDARD SEDAN...7060
LANDAU SEDAN...7080
2-DR SEDAN...7070
LANDAU COUPE...7090
SPORT ROADSTER...SROAD
SPORT PHAETON...SPHAE

1928
STANDARD SEDAN...7500
LANDAU SEDAN...7520
2-DR SEDAN...7510
LANDAU COUPE...7530
SPORT COUPE...7540
SPORT ROADSTER...SROAD
SPORT PHAETON...SPHAE

1929
STANDARD SEDAN...8770
SPECIAL SEDAN...8775
LANDAULET SEDAN...8780
BROUGHAM SEDAN...8820
2-DR SEDAN...8790
STANDARD COUPE...8800
CONVERTIBLE COUPE...8810
SPORT ROADSTER...SROAD
SPORT PHAETON...SPHAE

1930
STANDARD SEDAN...30359
CUSTOM SEDAN...30360
2-DR SEDAN...30351
STANDARD COUPE...30357
SPORT COUPE...30358
SPORT ROADSTER...SROAD
SPORT PHAETON...SPHAE

1931
STANDARD SEDAN...31359
CUSTOM SEDAN...31369
2-DR SEDAN...31351
STANDARD COUPE...31357
SPORT COUPE...31358
CONVERTIBLE...31368
SPORT ROADSTER...SROAD
SPORT PHAETON...SPHAE

PONTIAC

1926/SIX-CYLINDER
STANDARD COUPE...6640
DELUXE COUPE...6640D
2-DR SEDAN...6650
LANDAU SEDAN...7160
DELUXE LANDAU SEDAN...7160D
STEWART BODIES
ROADSTER...ROAD
SPORT ROADSTER...SROAD
PHAETON...TOUR

1927/SIX-CYLINDER
STANDARD COUPE...7430
2-DR SEDAN...7440
LANDAU SEDAN...7450

DELUXE LANDAU SEDAN...7450D
SPORT COUPE...7460
STEWART BODIES
ROADSTER...ROAD
SPORT ROADSTER...SROAD
PHAETON...TOUR

1928/SIX-CYLINDER
STANDARD SEDAN...8220
LANDAULET...8230
2-DR SEDAN...8240
STANDARD COUPE...8250
LANDAU COUPE...8260
STEWART BODIES
ROADSTER...ROAD
SPORT ROADSTER...SROAD
PHAETON...TOUR

1929/SIX-CYLINDER
STANDARD SEDAN...8920
LANDAULET SEDAN...8930
2-DR SEDAN...8940
STANDARD COUPE...8950
CONVERTIBLE COUPE (RUMBLESEAT)...8960
STEWART BODIES
ROADSTER...ROAD
SPORT ROADSTER...SROAD
PHAETON...TOUR

1930/SIX-CYLINDER
2-DR SEDAN...30301
STANDARD SEDAN...30302
STANDARD COUPE...30307
SPORT COUPE
(RUMBLESEAT)...30306
CUSTOM SEDAN...30309
STEWART BODIES
ROADSTER...ROAD
SPORT ROADSTER...SROAD
PHAETON...TOUR

1931/SIX-CYLINDER
2-DR SEDAN...31301
STANDARD COUPE...31307
SPORT COUPE (RUMBLESEAT)...31308
STANDARD SEDAN...31309
CONVERTIBLE COUPE (RUMBLESEAT)...31318
CUSTOM SEDAN...31319
STEWART BODIES
ROADSTER...ROAD
SPORT ROADSTER...SROAD
PHAETON...TOUR

1932/SIX-CYLINDER
2-DR SEDAN...32301
SPORT COUPE...32308
4-DR SEDAN...32309
BUSINESS COUPE...32317
CONVERTIBLE COUPE...32318
CUSTOM SEDAN...32319
V-8
2-DR SEDAN...32351
SPORT COUPE...32358
4-DR SEDAN...32359
BUSINESS COUPE...32367
CONVERTIBLE COUPE...32368
CUSTOM SEDAN...32369

1933/EIGHT-CYLINDER
2-DR SEDAN...33301
4-DR SEDAN...33309
STANDARD COUPE...33317
CONVERTIBLE COUPE...33318
SPORT COUPE...33328
TOURING SEDAN...33331
ROADSTER...ROAD

1934/EIGHT-CYLINDER
2-DR STD SEDAN...34301
4-DR STD SEDAN...34309
STANDARD COUPE...34317
CONVERTIBLE COUPE...34318
4-DR TOURING SDN...34319
SPORT COUPE...34328
2-DR TOURING SDN...34331

1935/MASTER SIX-CYLINDER
BUSINESS COUPE...2107A
2-DR SEDAN...2101A
2-DR TOURING SDN...2111A
4-DR SEDAN...2109A
4-DR TOURING SDN...2119A
DELUXE SIX-CYLINDER
BUSINESS COUPE...2107
SPORT COUPE...2157

CONVERTIBLE COUPE...2167
2-DR SEDAN...2101
2-DR TOURING SDN...2111
4-DR SEDAN...2109
4-DR TOURING SDN...2119
EIGHT-CYLINDER
BUSINESS COUPE...2007
OPERA COUPE...2077
SPORT COUPE...2057
CONVERTIBLE COUPE...2067
2-DR SEDAN...2001
2-DR TOURING SDN...2011
4-DR SEDAN...2009
4-DR TOURING SDN...2019

1936/MASTER SIX-CYLINDER
BUSINESS COUPE...2607A
SPORT COUPE...2657A
CONVERTIBLE COUPE...2667A
2-DR SEDAN...2601A
2-DR SEDAN...2601AB
2-DR TOURING SDN...2611A
2-DR TOURING SDN...2611AB
4-DR SEDAN...2609A
4-DR TOURING SDN...2619A
DELUXE SIX-CYLINDER
BUSINESS COUPE...2607
SPORT COUPE...2657
CONVERTIBLE COUPE...2667
2-DR SEDAN...2601
2-DR TOURING SDN...2611
4-DR SEDAN...2609
4-DR TOURING SDN...2619
EIGHT-CYLINDER
BUSINESS COUPE...2807
SPORT COUPE...2857
CONVERTIBLE COUPE...2867
2-DR SEDAN...2801
2-DR TOURING SDN...2811
4-DR SEDAN...2809
4-DR TOURING SDN...2819

1937/SIX-CYLINDER
BUSINESS COUPE...2627B
SPORT COUPE...2627
CONVERTIBLE COUPE...2667
2-DR SEDAN...2601
2-DR TOURING SDN...2611
4-DR SEDAN...2609
4-DR TOURING SDN...2619
4-DR CONV. SEDAN...2649
STATION WAGON...STAWAG
EIGHT-CYLINDER
BUSINESS COUPE...2827B
SPORT COUPE...2827
CONVERTIBLE COUPE...2867
2-DR SEDAN...2801
2-DR TOURING SDN...2811
4-DR SEDAN...2809
4-DR TOURING SDN...2819
4-DR CONV. SEDAN...2849

1938/SIX-CYLINDER
BUSINESS COUPE...2627B
SPORT COUPE...2627
CONVERTIBLE COUPE...2667
2-DR SEDAN...2601
2-DR TOURING SDN...2611
4-DR SEDAN...2609
4-DR TOURING SDN...2619
4-DR CONV. SEDAN...2649
STATION WAGON...STAWAG
EIGHT-CYLINDER
BUSINESS COUPE...2827B
SPORT COUPE...2827
CONVERTIBLE COUPE...2867
2-DR SEDAN...2801
2-DR TOURING SDN...2811
4-DR SEDAN...2809
4-DR TOURING SDN...2819
4-DR CONV. SEDAN...2849

1939/SPECIAL (QUALITY 6)
BUSINESS COUPE...2527B
SPORT COUPE...2527
2-DR TOURING SDN...2511
4-DR TOURING SDN...2519
STATION WAGON...STAWAG
DELUXE 6
BUSINESS COUPE...2627B
SPORT COUPE...2627
CONVERTIBLE COUPE...2667

2-DR TOURING SDN...2611
4-DR TOURING SDN...2619
DELUXE 8
BUSINESS COUPE...2827B
SPORT COUPE...2827
CONVERTIBLE COUPE...2867
2-DR TOURING SDN...2811
2-DR SUNROOF SDN...2811A
4-DR TOURING SDN...2819
4-DR SUNROOF SDN...2819A
1940/SPECIAL 6
BUSINESS COUPE...2527B
SPORT COUPE...2527
2-DR TOURING SDN...2511
4-DR TOURING SDN...2519
STATION WAGON...STAWAG
DELUXE 6
BUSINESS COUPE...2627B
SPORT COUPE...2627
CONVERTIBLE COUPE...2667
2-DR TOURING SDN...2611
4-DR TOURING SDN...2619
DELUXE 8
BUSINESS COUPE...2827B
SPORT COUPE...2827
CONVERTIBLE COUPE...2867
2-DR TOURING SDN...2811
4-DR TOURING SDN...2819
TORPEDO 8
SPORT COUPE...2927C
4-DR TOURING SDN...2919
1941/DELUXE TORPEDO 6
BUSINESS COUPE...2527B
SPORT COUPE...2527
CONVERTIBLE COUPE...2567
2-DR SEDAN...2511
4-DR 4 WINDOW...2569
4-DR 6 WINDOW...2519
STATION WAGON...STAWAG
STREAMLINER 6
COUPE...2627D
4-DR SEDAN...2609D
CUSTOM 6
COUPE...2427
4-DR 6 WINDOW...2419
DELUXE TORPEDO 8
BUSINESS COUPE...2727B
SPORT COUPE...2727
CONVERTIBLE COUPE...2767
2-DR SEDAN...2711
4-DR 4 WINDOW...2769
4-DR 6 WINDOW...2719
STATION WAGON...STAWAG
STREAMLINER 8
COUPE...2827
4-DR SEDAN...2809
SUPER STREAMLINER 8
COUPE...2827D
4-DR SEDAN...2809D
CUSTOM 8
COUPE...2927
4-DR 6 WINDOW...2919
1942/TORPEDO 6
BUSINESS COUPE...2527B
SPORT COUPE...2527
SEDAN COUPE...2507
CONVERTIBLE COUPE...2567
2-DR SEDAN...2511
4-DR 4 WINDOW...2569
4-DR 6 WINDOW...2519
STREAMLINER 6
COUPE...2607
4-DR 6 WINDOW...2609
STATION WAGON...STAWAG
STREAMLINER CHIEFTAIN
COUPE...2607D
4-DR 6 WINDOW...2609D
STATION WAGON...STAWAG
TORPEDO 8
BUSINESS COUPE...2727B
SPORT COUPE...2727
SEDAN COUPE...2707
CONVERTIBLE COUPE...2767
2-DR SEDAN...2711
4-DR 4 WINDOW...2769
4-DR 6 WINDOW...2719
STREAMLINER 8
COUPE...2807
4-DR 6 WINDOW...2809
STATION WAGON...STAWAG
STREAMLINER (CHIEFTAIN)
COUPE...2807D
4-DR 6 WINDOW...2809D
STATION WAGON...STAWAG

1946/TORPEDO 6
BUSINESS COUPE...2527B
SPORT COUPE...2527
SEDAN COUPE...2507
CONVERTIBLE COUPE...2567
2-DR SEDAN...2511
4-DR SEDAN...2519
STREAMLINER 6
SEDAN COUPE...2607
4-DR SEDAN...2609
STATION WAGON SDN...STAWAG
TORPEDO 8
BUSINESS COUPE...2727B
SPORT COUPE...2727
SEDAN COUPE...2707
CONVERTIBLE COUPE...2767
2-DR SEDAN...2711
4-DR SEDAN...2719
STREAMLINER 8
SEDAN COUPE...2807
4-DR SEDAN...2809
STATION WAGON STD...STAWAG
1947/TORPEDO 6
BUSINESS COUPE...2527B
SPORT COUPE...2527
SEDAN COUPE...2507
CONVERTIBLE COUPE...2567
2-DR SEDAN...2511
4-DR SEDAN...2519
STREAMLINER 6
SEDAN COUPE...2607
4-DR SEDAN...2609
STATION WAGON STD...STAWAG
TORPEDO 8
BUSINESS COUPE...2727B
SPORT COUPE...2727
SEDAN COUPE...2707
CONVERTIBLE COUPE...2767
2-DR SEDAN...2711
4-DR SEDAN...2719
STREAMLINER 8
COUPE...2807
4-DR SEDAN...2809
STATION WAGON STD...STAWAG
1948/TORPEDO 6
BUSINESS COUPE...2527B
SPORT COUPE...2527
SEDAN COUPE...2507
SEDAN COUPE...2507D
CONVERTIBLE COUPE...2567
2-DR SEDAN...2511
4-DR SEDAN...2519
4-DR SEDAN...2519D
STREAMLINER 6
COUPE...2607
COUPE...2607D
4-DR SEDAN...2609
4-DR SEDAN...2609D
STATION WAGON STD...STAWAG
STATION WAGON DLX...STAWAG
TORPEDO 8
BUSINESS COUPE...2727B
SPORT COUPE...2727
SEDAN COUPE...2707
SEDAN COUPE...2707D
CONVERTIBLE...2767
2-DR SEDAN...2711
4-DR SEDAN...2719
4-DR SEDAN...2719D
STREAMLINER 8
COUPE...2807
COUPE...2807D
4-DR SEDAN...2809
4-DR SEDAN...2809D
STATION WAGON STD...STAWAG
STATION WAGON DLX...STAWAG
1949/CHIEFTAIN 6 & 8
BUSINESS COUPE...2527B
SEDAN COUPE...2527
SEDAN COUPE DLX...2727D
CONV. COUPE DLX...2567DX
2-DR SEDAN...2511
2-DR SEDAN DLX...2511D
4-DR SEDAN...2569
4-DR SEDAN DLX...2569D
STREAMLINER 6 & 8
SEDAN COUPE...2507
SEDAN COUPE DLX...2507D
4-DR SEDAN...2508
4-DR SEDAN DLX...2508D
STATION WAGON WOOD...2561
STA. WAG. WOOD DLX...2561D
STATION WAGON METAL...2562
STA. WAG. METAL DLX...2562
SEDAN DELIVERY...2571

1950/CHIEFTAIN 6 & 8
BUSINESS COUPE...2527B
SEDAN COUPE...2527
SEDAN COUPE DLX...2527D
CONV. COUPE DLX...2567DTX
CATALINA COUPE DLX...2537D
CATALINA COUPE
SUPER DELUXE...2537SD
2-DR SEDAN...2511
2-DR SEDAN DLX...2511D
4-DR SEDAN...2569
4-DR SEDAN DLX...2569D
STREAMLINER 6 & 8
SEDAN COUPE...2507
SEDAN COUPE DLX...2507D
4-DR SEDAN...2508
4-DR SEDAN DLX...2508D
STATION WAGON...2562
STATION WAGON DLX...2562D
SEDAN DELIVERY...2571
1951/CHIEFTAIN 6 & 8
BUSINESS COUPE...2527B
SEDAN COUPE...2527
SEDAN COUPE DLX...2527D
CONV. COUPE DLX...2567DTX
CATALINA CPE DLX...2537D
CATALINA COUPE
SUPER DELUXE...2537SD
2-DR SEDAN...2511
2-DR SEDAN DLX...2511D
4-DR SEDAN...2569
4-DR SEDAN DLX...2569D
STREAMLINER 6 & 8
SEDAN COUPE...2507
SEDAN COUPE DLX...2507D
STATION WAGON...2562
STATION WAGON DLX...2562D
SEDAN DELIVERY...2571
1952/CHIEFTAIN 6 & 8
CONV. COUPE DLX...2567DTX
CATALINA COUPE DLX...2537D
CATALINA COUPE
SUPER DELUXE...2537SD
2-DR SEDAN...2511
2-DR SEDAN DLX...2511D
4-DR SEDAN...2569
4-DR SEDAN DLX...2569D
STATION WAGON...2562
STATION WAGON DLX...2562
SEDAN DELIVERY...2571
1953/CHIEFTAIN 6 & 8
CONV. COUPE DLX...2567DTX
CATALINA COUPE DLX...2537D
CATALINA CUSTOM...2537SD
2-DR SEDAN...2511W
2-DR SEDAN DLX...2511WD
4-DR SEDAN...2569W
4-DR SEDAN DLX...2569WD
STA. WAGON 2-SEAT...2562F
STA. WAGON 3-SEAT...2562
STA. WAGON DLX...2562DF
SEDAN DELIVERY...2571
1954/CHIEFTAIN 6 & 8
CATALINA CPE DLX...2537D
CATALINA COUPE
SUPER DELUXE...2537SD
2-DR SEDAN...2511W
2-DR SEDAN DLX...2511WD
4-DR SEDAN...2569W
4-DR SEDAN DLX...2569WD
STA. WAGON 3-SEAT...2562
STA. WAGON 2-SEAT...2562F
STA. WAGON DLX...2562DF
STAR CHIEF 8
CONV. COUPE...2867DTX
CATALINA CPE CUST....2837SD
4-DR SEDAN DLX...2869WD
4-DR SEDAN CUST....2869WSD
1955/CHIEFTAIN 25
CATALINA CPE 870...2537D
2-DR SEDAN 860...2511
2-DR SEDAN 870...2511D
4-DR SEDAN 860...2519
4-DR SEDAN 870...2719D
4-DR STA WAGON 860...2562
4-DR STA WAGON 870...2562DF
2-DR STA WAGON 860...2563F
STAR CHIEF 25
CUST. STA. WAGON...2564DF
STAR CHIEF 28
CONV. COUPE...2867DTX
CATALINA COUPE CUST....2837SD
4-DR SEDAN...2819D
4-DR SDN CUST....2819SD

1956/CHIEFTAIN 27
CATALINA CPE 860...2737
CATALINA CPE 870...2737D
CATALINA SDN 860...2739
CATALINA SDN 870...2739D
2-DR SDN 860...2711
4-DR SDN 860...2719
4-DR SDN 870...2719D
4-DR STA WAG 860...2762FC
4-DR STA WAG 870...2762DF
2-DR STA WAG 860...2768
STAR CHIEF 27
CUST STA WAGON...2764DF
STAR CHIEF 28
CONV. COUPE...2867DTX
CATALINA CPE CUST....2837SD
CATALINA SD CUST....2839SD
4-DR SEDAN...2819D

1957/CHIEFTAIN 27
CATALINA COUPE...2737
CATALINA SEDAN...2739
2-DR SEDAN...2711
4-DR SEDAN...2719
4-DR STATION WAGON...2762FC
2-DR STATION WAGON...2763F
SUPER CHIEF 27
CATALINA COUPE...2737D
CATALINA SEDAN...2739D
4-DR SEDAN...2719D
4-DR SAFARI...2762DF
STAR CHIEF 27
4-DR SAFARI CUST....2762SDF
2-DR SAFARI CUST....2764DF
STAR CHIEF 28
CONV. COUPE...2867DTX
CONV. COUPE CUSTOM (BONNEVILLE)...2867SDX
CATALINA CPE CUST....2837SD
CATALINA SEDAN CUST....2839SD
4-DR SEDAN...2819D
4-DR SEDAN...2819SD

1958/BONNEVILLE 25
SPORT COUPE...2547SD
CONV. COUPE...2567SD
CHIEFTAIN 25
CONV. COUPE...2567
CHIEFTAIN 27
CATALINA COUPE...2731
CATALINA SEDAN...2739
2-DR SEDAN...2741
4-DR SEDAN...2749
4-DR SAFARI...2794
STAR CHIEF 27
4-DR SAFARI...2793D
4-DR SAFARI...2793SD
SUPER CHIEF 28
CATALINA COUPE...2831D
CATALINA SEDAN...2839D
4-DR SEDAN...2849D
STAR CHIEF 26
CATALINA COUPE...2831SD
CATALINA SEDAN...2839SD
4-DR SEDAN...2849SD

1959/CATALINA 21
2-DR SPORT SEDAN...2111
4-DR SEDAN...2119
4-DR SAFARI...2135
2-DR SPORT COUPE...2137
4-DR VISTA...2139
4-DR SAFARI...2145
CONV. COUPE...2167
STAR CHIEF 24
TWO DR SPORT SEDAN...2411
4-DR SEDAN...2419
4-DR VISTA...2439
BONNEVILLE 27
4-DR SAFARI...2735
BONNEVILLE 28
2-DR SPORT COUPE...2837
4-DR VISTA...2839
CONV. COUPE...2867

1960/CATALINA 21
2-DR SPORT SDN...2111
4-DR SEDAN...2119
4-DR SAFARI...2135
2-DR SPORT CPE...2137
4-DR VISTA...2139
4-DR SAFARI...2145
CONV. COUPE...2167
VENTURA 23
2-DR SPORT CPE...2337
4-DR VISTA...2339
STAR CHIEF 24
2-DR SPORT SDN...2411
4-DR SEDAN...2419
4-DR VISTA...2439

BONNEVILLE 27
4-DR SAFARI...2735
BONNEVILLE 28
2-DR SPORT CPE...2837
4-DR VISTA...2839
CONV. COUPE...2867

1961/TEMPEST 21
4-DR SEDAN...2119
2-DR CUST. COUPE...2117
2-DR STD COUPE...2127
4-DR SAFARI...2135
CATALINA 23
TWO DR SPORT SDN...2311
4-DR SAFARI 6-PASS...2335
2-DR SPORT COUPE...2337
4-DR VISTA...2339
4-DR SAFARI 9-PASS...2345
CONV. COUPE...2367
4-DR SEDAN...2369
VENTURA 25
2-DR SPORT CPE...2537
4-DR VISTA...2539
STAR CHIEF 26
FOUR DOOR VISTA...2639
4-DR SEDAN...2669
BONNEVILLE 27
4-DR SAFARI 6-PASS...2735
BONNEVILLE 28
2-DR SPORT CPE...2837
4-DR VISTA...2839
CONV. COUPE...2867

1962/TEMPEST 21
2-DR SPORT CPE...2117
4-DR SEDAN...2119
2-DR STD COUPE...2127
4-DR SAFARI...2135
CONV. COUPE...2167
CATALINA 23
2-DR SPORT CPE...2311
4-DR SAFARI 5-PASS...2335
4-DR VISTA...2339
4-DR SAFARI 9-PASS...2345
2-DR SPORT CPE...2347
CONV. COUPE...2367
4-DR SEDAN...2369
STAR CHIEF 26
4-DR VISTA...2639
4-DR SEDAN...2669
BONNEVILLE 27
4-DR SAFARI 6-PASS...2735
BONNEVILLE 28
4-DR VISTA...2839
2-DR SPORT COUPE...2847
CONV. COUPE...2867
GRAND PRIX 29
2-DR SPORT CPE...2947

1963/TEMPEST STANDARD
2-DR CPE (W/POST)...2127
4-DR STA WAGON...2135
4-DR SDN (W/POST)...2119
TEMPEST CUSTOM
2-DR CPE (W/POST)...2117
CONV. COUPE...2167
LEMANS
2-DR CPE (W/POST)...2217
CONV. COUPE...2267
CATALINA
2-DR SPORT SEDAN (W/POST)...2311
2-SEAT STA WAGON...2335
2-DR SPORT COUPE...2347
4-DR HARDTOP...2339
3-SEAT STA WAGON...2345
CONV. COUPE...2367
4-DR SDN (W/POST)...2369
STAR CHIEF
4-DR HARDTOP...2639
4-DR SDN (W/POST)...2669
BONNEVILLE
4-DR STA WAGON...2835
2-DR SPORT COUPE...2847
4-DR HARDTOP...2839
CONV. COUPE...2867
GRAND PRIX
2-DR SPORT COUPE...2957

1964/TEMPEST STANDARD
2-DR CPE (W/POST)...2027
4-DR STA WAGON...2035
4-DR SDN (W/POST)...2069
TEMPEST CUSTOM
2-DR CPE (W/POST)...2127
4-DR STA WAGON...2135
4-DR SDN (W/POST)...2169
CONV. COUPE...2167
LEMANS
2-DR CPE (W/POST)...2227

2-DR HARDTOP CPE...2237
CONV. COUPE...2267
CATALINA
2-DR SPORT SEDAN (W/POST)...2311
2-SEAT STA WAGON...2335
2-DR SPORT COUPE...2347
4-DR HARDTOP...2339
3-SEAT STA WAGON...2345
CONV. COUPE...2367
4-DR. SDN (W/POST)...2369
STAR CHIEF
4-DR HARDTOP...2639
4-DR SDN (W/POST)...2669
BONNEVILLE
4-DR STA WAGON...2835
2-DR SPORT COUPE...2847
4-DR HARDTOP...2839
CONV. COUPE...2867
GRAND PRIX
2-DR SPORT COUPE...2957

1965/TEMPEST
2-DR COUPE...23327
4-DR STA WAGON 2-SEAT...23335
4-DR SEDAN...23369
TEMPEST CUSTOM
2-DR COUPE...23527
2-DR STA WAGON 2-SEAT...23535
2-DR HARDTOP...23537
2-DR CONV....23567
4-DR SEDAN...23569
LEMANS
2-DR COUPE...23727
2-DR HARDTOP...23737
2-DR CONV....23767
4-DR SEDAN...23769
CATALINA
2-DR SEDAN...25211
4-DR STA WAGON 2-SEAT...25235
2-DR HARDTOP...25237
4-DR HARDTOP...25239
4-DR STA WAGON 3-SEAT...25245
2-DR CONV....25267
4-DR SEDAN...25269
STAR CHIEF
4-DR HARDTOP...25639
4-DR SEDAN...25669
BONNEVILLE
4-DR STA WAGON 2-SEAT...26235
2-DR HARDTOP...26237
4-DR HARDTOP...26239
2-DR CONV....26267
GRAND PRIX
2-DR HARDTOP...26657

1966/TEMPEST
2-DR SPORT COUPE...23307
4-DR SEDAN...23369
4-DR STA WAGON 2-SEAT...23335
TEMPEST CUSTOM
2-DR SPORT CPE...23507
4-DR SEDAN...23569
2-DR HARDTOP...23517
4-DR HARDTOP...23539
4-DR STA WAGON 2-SEAT...23535
LEMANS
2-DR SPORT CPE...23707
2-DR HARDTOP...23717
4-DR HARDTOP...23739
2-DR CONV....23767
GTO
2-DR COUPE...24207
2-DR HARDTOP...24217
2-DR CONV....24267
CATALINA
2-DR SEDAN...25211
4-DR STA WAGON 2-SEAT...25235
4-DR STA WAGON 3-SEAT...25245
4-DR HARDTOP...25239
2-DR CONV....25267
4-DR SEDAN...25269
2-DR HARDTOP...25237
2+2
2-DR SPORT CPE...25437
2-DR CONV....25467
STAR CHIEF EXECUTIVE
2-DR HARDTOP...25637
4-DR HARDTOP...25639
4-DR SEDAN...25669
BONNEVILLE
2-DR HARDTOP...26237
4-DR HARDTOP...26239
2-DR CONV....26267
4-DR STA WAGON 3-SEAT...26245
GRAND PRIX
2-DR HARDTOP...26657

1967/FIREBIRD
2-DR HARDTOP...22337
2-DR CONV....22367
TEMPEST
2-DR SPORT CPE...23307
4-DR SEDAN...23369
4-DR STA WAGON 2-SEAT...23335
TEMPEST CUSTOM
2-DR COUPE...23507
4-DR SEDAN...23569
2-DR HARDTOP...23517
4-DR HARDTOP...23539
2-DR CONV....23567
2-DR STA WAGON 2-SEAT...23535
LEMANS
2-DR SPORT CPE...23707
2-DR HARDTOP...23717
4-DR HARDTOP...23739
2-DR CONV....23767
TEMPEST SAFARI
4-DR STA WAGON 2-SEAT...23935
GTO
2-DR SPORT CPE...24207
2-DR HARDTOP...24217
2-DR CONV....24267
CATALINA
2-DR SEDAN...25211
4-DR SEDAN...25269
2-DR HARDTOP...25287
4-DR HARDTOP...25239
2-DR CONV....25267
4-DR STA WAGON 2-SEAT...25235
4-DR STA WAGON 3-SEAT...25245
EXECUTIVE
2-DR HARDTOP...25687
4-DR HARDTOP...25639
4-DR SEDAN...25669
4-DR STA WAGON 2-SEAT...25635
4-DR STA WAGON 3-SEAT...25645
BONNEVILLE
2-DR HARDTOP...26287
4-DR HARDTOP...26239
2-DR CONV....26267
4-DR STA WAGON 3-SEAT...26245
GRAND PRIX
2-DR HARDTOP...26657
2-DR CONV....26667
1968/FIREBIRD
2-DR HARDTOP...22337
2-DR CONV....22367
TEMPEST
2-DR COUPE...23327
4-DR SEDAN...23369
TEMPEST CUSTOM
2-DR COUPE...23257
2-DR STA WAGON 2-SEAT...23535
2-DR HARDTOP...23537
4-DR HARDTOP...23539
2-DR CONV....23567
4-DR SEDAN...23569
LEMANS
2-DR COUPE...23727
2-DR HARDTOP...23737
4-DR HARDTOP...23739
2-DR CONV....23767
TEMPEST SAFARI
4-DR STA WAGON 2-SEAT...23935
GTO
2-DR HARDTOP...24237
2-DR CONV....24267
CATALINA
2-DR SEDAN...25211
4-DR SEDAN...25269
2-DR HARDTOP...25287
4-DR HARDTOP...25239
2-DR CONV....25267
4-DR STA WAGON 2-SEAT...25235
4-DR STA WAGON 3-SEAT...25245
EXECUTIVE
4-DR STA WAGON 2-SEAT...25635
4-DR HARDTOP...25639
4-DR STA WAGON 3-SEAT...25645
4-DR SEDAN...25669
2-DR HARDTOP...25687
BONNEVILLE
4-DR HARDTOP...26239
4-DR STA WAGON 3-SEAT...26245
2-DR CONV....26267
4-DR SEDAN...26269
2-DR HARDTOP...26287
GRAND PRIX
2-DR HARDTOP...26657
1969/FIREBIRD
2-DR HARDTOP...22337

2-DR CONV....22367
TEMPEST
2-DR SPORT CPE...23327
4-DR SEDAN...23369
CUSTOM "S"
2-DR SPORT CPE...23527
4-DR SEDAN...23569
2-DR HARDTOP...23537
4-DR HARDTOP...23539
2-DR CONV....23567
4-DR STA WAGON 2-SEAT...23535
4-DR STA WAGON 3-SEAT...23536
LEMANS SPORT
2-DR SPORT CPE...23727
2-DR HARDTOP...23737
4-DR HARDTOP...23739
2-DR CONV....23767
LEMANS SAFARI
4-DR STA WAGON 2-SEAT...23936
GTO
2-DR HARDTOP...24237
2-DR CONV....24267
CATALINA
4-DR SEDAN...25269
2-DR HARDTOP...25237
4-DR HARDTOP...25239
2-DR CONV....25267
4-DR STA WAGON 2-SEAT...25236
4-DR STA WAGON 3-SEAT...25246
EXECUTIVE
4-DR SEDAN...25669
2-DR HARDTOP...25637
4-DR HARDTOP...25639
4-DR STA WAGON 2-SEAT...25636
4-DR STA WAGON 3-SEAT...25646
BONNEVILLE
4-DR SEDAN...26269
2-DR HARDTOP...26237
4-DR HARDTOP...26239
2-DR CONV....26267
4-DR STA WAGON 3-SEAT...26246
GRAND PRIX
2-DR HARDTOP J...27647
2-DR HARDTOP SJ...27657
1970/FIREBIRD
2-DR HARDTOP...22387
2-DR HDTP ESPRIT...22487
2-DR HARDTOP FORMULA 400...22687
2-DR HARDTOP TRANS AM....22887
TEMPEST
2-DR COUPE...23327
2-DR HARDTOP...23337
4-DR SEDAN...23369
LEMANS
2-DR COUPE...23527
4-DR STA WAGON 2-SEAT...23535
2-DR HARDTOP...23537
4-DR HARDTOP...23539
4-DR SEDAN...23569
LEMANS SPORT
2-DR COUPE...23727
2-DR HARDTOP...23737
4-DR HARDTOP...23739
2-DR CONV....23767
4-DR STA WAGON 2-SEAT...23736
GTO
2-DR HARDTOP...24237
2-DR CONV....24267
CATALINA
4-DR STA WAGON 2-SEAT...25236
2-DR HARDTOP...25237
4-DR HARDTOP...25239
4-DR STA WAGON 3-SEAT...25246
2-DR CONV....25267
4-DR SEDAN...25269
EXECUTIVE
4-DR STA WAGON 2-SEAT...25636
2-DR HARDTOP...25637
4-DR HARDTOP...25639
4-DR STA WAGON 3-SEAT...25646
4-DR SEDAN...25669
BONNEVILLE
2-DR HARDTOP...26237
4-DR HARDTOP...26239
4-DR STA WAGON 3-SEAT...26245
2-DR CONV....26267
4-DR SEDAN...26269
GRAND PRIX
2-DR HARDTOP J...27647
2-DR HARDTOP SJ...27657
1971/VENTURA II
2-DR COUPE...21327
4-DR SEDAN...21369
2-DR COUPE...21427
4-DR SEDAN...21469

FIREBIRD
2-DR HARDTOP...22387
2-DR HDTP ESPRIT...22487
2-DR HDTP FORMULA...22687
2-DR HDTP TRANS AM...22887
T37
2-DR COUPE...23327
2-DR HARDTOP...23337
4-DR SEDAN...23369
LEMANS
2-DR COUPE...23327
4-DR STA WAGON 2-SEAT...23536
2-DR HARDTOP...23537
4-DR HARDTOP...23539
4-DR STA WAGON 3-SEAT...23546
4-DR SEDAN...23569
LEMANS SPORT
2-DR HARDTOP...23737
4-DR HARDTOP...23739
2-DR CONV....23767
GTO
2-DR HARDTOP...24237
2-DR CONV....24267
CATALINA
4-DR STA WAGON 2-SEAT...25235
4-DR HARDTOP...25239
4-DR STA WAGON 3-SEAT...25245
2-DR HARDTOP...25257
2-DR CONV....25267
4-DR SEDAN...25269
CATALINA BROUGHAM
4-DR HARDTOP...25839
2-DR HARDTOP...25857
4-DR SEDAN...25869
BONNEVILLE
4-DR STA WAGON 2-SEAT...26235
4-DR HARDTOP...26239
4-DR STA WAGON 3-SEAT...26245
2-DR HARDTOP...26257
4-DR SEDAN...26269
GRAND VILLE
2-DR HARDTOP...26847
4-DR HARDTOP...26849
2-DR CONV....26867
GRAND PRIX
2-DR HARDTOP J...27647
2-DR HARDTOP SJ...27657
1972/VENTURA II
2-DR SEDAN...21327
4-DR SEDAN...21369
2-DR SEDAN...21427
4-DR SEDAN...21469
FIREBIRD
2-DR HARDTOP...22387
2-DR HDTP ESPRIT...22487
2-DR HDTP FORMULA...22687
2-DR HDTP TRANS AM...22887
LEMANS
2-DR SEDAN...23527
2-DR HARDTOP...23537
4-DR SEDAN...23569
4-DR STA WAGON 2-SEAT...23536
4-DR STA WAGON 3-SEAT...23546
LEMANS SPORT
CONVERTIBLE...23867
LEMANS LUXURY 2-DR HARDTOP...24437
4-DR HARDTOP...24439
CATALINA
2-DR HARDTOP...25257
4-DR HARDTOP...25239
4-DR SEDAN...25269
CONVERTIBLE...25267
4-DR STA WAGON 2-SEAT...25235
4-DR STA WAGON 3-SEAT...25245
CATALINA BROUGHAM
2-DR HARDTOP...25857
4-DR HARDTOP...25839
4-DR SEDAN...25869
BONNEVILLE
2-DR HARDTOP...26257
4-DR HARDTOP...26239
4-DR SEDAN...26269
4-DR STA WAGON 2-SEAT...26235
4-DR STA WAGON 3-SEAT...26245
GRAND VILLE
2-DR HARDTOP...26847
4-DR HARDTOP...26849
CONVERTIBLE...26867
GRAND PRIX
2-DR HARDTOP J...27647
2-DR HARDTOP SJ...27657
1973/VENTURA
2-DR HATCH BACK...2XY17
2-DR NOTCH BK SDN...2XY27
4-DR NOTCH BK SDN...2XY69

2-DR HATCH BACK...2XZ17
2-DR NOTCH BK SDN...2XZ27
4-DR NOTCH BK SDN...2XZ69
FIREBIRD
2-DR HARDTOP...2FS87
2-DR HDTP ESPRIT...2FT87
2-DR HDTP FORMULA...2FU87
2-DR HDTP TRANS AM...2FV87
LEMANS
4-DR NOTCH BACK HDTP 6-WINDOW...2AD29
4-DR STATION WAGON 2-SEAT...2AD35
2-DR NOTCH BACK HDTP...2AD37
4-DR STATION WAGON 3-SEAT...2AD45
LEMANS SPORT
2-DR NOTCH BACK HARDTOP...2AF37
LEMANS LUXURY 4-DR NOTCH BACK HDTP 6-WINDOW...2AG29
2-DR NOTCH BACK HARDTOP...2AH37
GRAND AM
4-DR NOTCH BACK HDTP 6-WINDOW...2AH29
2-DR NOTCH BACK HARDTOP...2AH37
GRAND PRIX
2-DR NOTCH BACK HARDTOP J...2GK57
2-DR NOTCH BACK HARDTOP SJ...2GK57
CATALINA
4-DR STATION WAGON 2-SEAT...2BL35
4-DR NOTCH BACK HDTP 4-WINDOW...2BL39
4-DR STATION WAGON 3-SEAT...2BL45
2-DR NOTCH BK HDTP...2BL57
4-DR NOTCH BACK SDN 4-WINDOW...2BL69
BONNEVILLE
4-DR NOTCH BK HDTP 4-WINDOW...2BN39
2-DR NOTCH BK HDTP...2BN57
4-DR NOTCH BACK SDN 4-WINDOW...2BN69
GRAND VILLE
4-DR STATION WAGON 2-SEAT...2BP35
4-DR STATION WAGON 3-SEAT...2BP45
2-DR NOTCH BK HDTP...2BP47
4-DR NOTCH BK HDTP 4-WINDOW...2BP49
CONVERTIBLE...2BP67
1974/VENTURA
2-DR HATCH BK...2XY17
2-DR NOTCH BK SDN...2XY27
4-DR NOTCH BK SDN...2XY69
VENTURA CUSTOM
2-DR HATCH BK...2XZ17
2-DR NOTCH BK SDN...2XZ27
4-DR NOTCH BK SDN...2XZ69
FIREBIRD
2-DR HARDTOP...2FS87
2-DR HDTP ESPRIT...2FT87
2-DR HDTP FORMULA...2FU87
2-DR HARDTOP TRANS AM...2FV87
LEMANS
4-DR NOTCH BK HDTP...2AD29
4-DR STATION WAGON 2-SEAT...2AD35
2-DR NOTCH BK HDTP...2AD37
4-DR STATION WAGON 3-SEAT...2AD45
LEMANS SPORT
2-DR NOTCH BK HDTP...2AF37
LEMANS LUXURY 4-DR NOTCH BK HDTP...2AG29
4-DR STATION WAGON 2-SEAT...2AG35
2-DR NOTCH BK HDTP...2AG37
4-DR STATION WAGON 3-SEAT...2AG45
GRAND AM
4-DR NOTCH BK HDTP...2AH29
2-DR NOTCH BK HDTP...2AH37
GRAND PRIX
2-DR NOTCH BK HDTP...2GK57
2-DR NOTCH BK HDTP SJ...2GK57
CATALINA
4-DR STATION WAGON 2-SEAT...2BL35
4-DR NOTCH BK HDTP...2BL39
4-DR STATION WAGON 3-SEAT...2BL45
2-DR NOTCH BK HDTP...2BL57
4-DR NOTCH BK SDN...2BL69
BONNEVILLE
4-DR NOTCH BK HDTP...2BN39
2-DR NOTCH BK HDTP...2BN57
4-DR NOTCH BK SDN...2BN69
GRAND VILLE
4-DR STATION WAGON 2-SEAT...2BP35
4-DR STATION WAGON 3-SEAT...2BP45
2-DR NOTCH BK HDTP...2BP47
4-DR NOTCH BK HDTP...2BP49
CONVERTIBLE...2BP67
1975/ASTRE
2-DR STATION WAGON...2HV15
2-DR HATCH BACK...2HV77
ASTRE SJ
2-DR STATION WAGON...2HX15
2-DR HATCH BACK...2HX77
VENTURA
2-DR HATCH BACK...2XY17
2-DR NOTCH BK SDN...2XY27

4-DR NOTCH BK SDN...2XY69
VENTURA SJ
2-DR HATCH BACK...2XB17
2-DR NOTCH BK SDN...2XB27
4-DR NOTCH BK SDN...2XB69
FIREBIRD
2-DR HARDTOP...2FS87
2-DR HDTP ESPRIT...2FT87
2-DR HDTP FORMULA...2FU87
2-DR HDTP TRANS AM...2FW87
LEMANS
4-DR NOTCH BK HDTP...2AD29
4-DR STATION WAGON 2-SEAT...2AD35
2-DR NOTCH BK HDTP...2AD37
4-DR STATION WAGON 3-SEAT...2AD45
LEMANS SPORT
2-DR NOTCH BK HDTP...2AF37
GRAND LEMANS
4-DR NOTCH BK HDTP...2AG29
4-DR STATION WAGON 2-SEAT...2AG35
2-DR NOTCH BK HDTP...3AG37
4-DR STATION WAGON 3-SEAT...2AG45
GRAND AM
4-DR NOTCH BK HDTP...2AH29
2-DR NOTCH BK HDTP...2AH37
GRAND PRIX
2-DR NOTCH BK HDTP...2GK57
2-DR NOTCH BK HDTP SJ...2GK57
CATALINA
4-DR STATION WAGON 2-SEAT...2BL35
4-DR STATION WAGON 3-SEAT...2BL45
2-DR NOTCH BK HDTP...2BL57
4-DR NOTCH BK SEDAN...2BL69
BONNEVILLE
4-DR STATION WAGON 2-SEAT...2BP35
4-DR STATION WAGON 3-SEAT...2BP45
2-DR NOTCH BK HDTP...2BP47
4-DR NOTCH BACK HDTP...2BP49
GRAND VILLE
2-DR NOTCH BK HDTP...2BR47
4-DR NOTCH BK HDTP...2BR49
CONVERTIBLE...2BR67
GRAND VILLE
4-DR STATION WAGON 2-SEAT...2BP35
4-DR STATION WAGON 2-SEAT...2BP45
2-DR NOTCH BK HDTP...2BP47
4-DR NOTCH BK HDTP...2BP49
CONVERTIBLE...2BP67
1976/ASTRE
COUPE...C11
SAFARI...C15
HATCH BACK...C77
LEMANS
SEDAN...D29
SAFARI...D35
COUPE...D37
SPORT COUPE...F37
GRAND LEMANS
SEDAN...G29
SAFARI...G35
COUPE...G37
GRAND PRIX
COUPE...J57
COUPE SJ (LJ OP AVL)...K57
CATALINA
SAFARI...L35
COUPE...L57
SEDAN...L69
SUNBIRD
COUPE...M27
GRAND SAFARI
GRAND SAFARI...P35
BONNEVILLE
COUPE...P47
SEDAN...P49
BONNEVILLE BROUGHAM
COUPE...R47
SEDAN...R49
FIREBIRD
FIREBIRD...S87
ESPRIT...T87
FORMULA...U87
TRANS AM...W87
VENTURA
HATCH BACK...Y17
COUPE...Y27
SEDAN...Y69
VENTURA SJ
HATCH BACK...Z17
COUPE...Z27
SEDAN...Z69
1977/ASTRE
COUPE...C11
SAFARI...C15
HATCH BACK...C77

LEMANS
SEDAN...D29
SAFARI...D35
COUPE...D37
SPORT COUPE...F37
GRAND LEMANS
SEDAN...G29
SAFARI...G35
COUPE...G37
GRAND PRIX
COUPE SJ...H57
COUPE...J37
SEDAN...K57
CATALINA
SAFARI...L35
COUPE...L37
SEDAN...L69
SUNBIRD
COUPE...M27
SPORT HATCH...M07
GRAND SAFARI...N35
BONNEVILLE
COUPE...N37
SEDAN...N69
BONNEVILLE BROUGHAM
COUPE...Q37
SEDAN...Q69
FIREBIRD
FIREBIRD...S87
ESPRIT...T87
FORMULA...U87
TRANS AM...W87
VENTURA
HATCH BACK...Y17
COUPE...Y27
SEDAN...Y69
VENTURA SJ
HATCH BACK...Z17
COUPE...Z27
SEDAN...Z69
PHOENIX
COUPE...X27
SEDAN...X69
1978/LEMANS
COUPE...D27
SEDAN...D19
WAGON...D35
GRAND LEMANS
COUPE...F27
SEDAN...F19
WAGON...F35
GRAND AM
COUPE...G27
SEDAN...G19
GRAND PRIX
COUPE...J37
COUPE LJ...K37
COUPE SJ...K37
CATALINA
COUPE...L37
SEDAN...L69
WAGON...L35
BONNEVILLE
COUPE...N37
SEDAN...N69
GRAND SAFARI
GRAND SAFARI...N35
BONNEVILLE BROUGHAM
COUPE...Q37
SEDAN...Q69
PONTIAC SUNBIRD
COUPE...E27
SPORT COUPE...M27
SPORT HATCH...M07
SPORT SAFARI...M15
PHOENIX
HATCH BACK...Y17
COUPE...Y27
SEDAN...Y69
PHOENIX LJ
COUPE...Z27
SEDAN...Z69
FIREBIRD
FIREBIRD...S87
ESPRIT...T87
FORMULA...U87
TRANS AM...W87
10TH ANNIVERSARY...X87
1979/LEMANS
COUPE...D27
SEDAN...D19
WAGON...D35
GRAND LEMANS
COUPE...F27
SEDAN...F19

WAGON...F35
GRAND AM
COUPE...G27
SEDAN...G19
GRAND PRIX
COUPE...J37
COUPE LJ...K37
COUPE SJ...H37
CATALINA
COUPE...L37
SEDAN...L69
WAGON...L35
BONNEVILLE
COUPE...N37
SEDAN...N69
GRAND SAFARI
GRAND SAFARI...N35
BONNEVILLE BROUGHAM
COUPE...Q37
SEDAN...Q69
PONTIAC SUNBIRD
COUPE...E27
SPORT COUPE...M27
SPORT HATCH...M07
SPORT SAFARI...M15
PHOENIX
HATCH BACK...Y17
COUPE...Y27
SEDAN...Y69
PHOENIX LJ
COUPE...Z27
SEDAN...Z69
FIREBIRD
FIREBIRD...S87
ESPRIT...T87
FORMULA...U87
TRANS AM...W87
ANNIVERSARY...X87
1980/PONTIAC SUNBIRD
COUPE...E27
SPORT COUPE...M27
SPORT HATCH...M07
GRAND PRIX
GRAND PRIX...J37
GRAND PRIX LJ...K37
GRAND PRIX SJ...H37
CATALINA
COUPE...L37
SEDAN...L69
BONNEVILLE
COUPE...N37
SEDAN...N69
SAFARI...N35
BONNEVILLE BROUGHAM
COUPE...R37
SEDAN...R69
PHOENIX
COUPE...Z37
5-DR HATCH BACK...Z68
FIREBIRD
FIREBIRD...S87
ESPRIT...T87
FORMULA...V87
TRANS AM...287
PACE CAR...X87
LEMANS
COUPE...D27
SEDAN...D19
SAFARI...D35
GRAND LEMANS
COUPE...F27
SEDAN...F19
SAFARI...F35
GRAND AM
COUPE...G27
1981/PONTIAC SUNBIRD
COUPE...E27
SPORT COUPE...M27
SPORT HATCH...M07
HATCH...E07
GRAND PRIX
GRAND PRIX...J37
GRAND PRIX LJ...K37
GRAND PRIX BROUGHAM...P37
CATALINA
COUPE...L37
SEDAN...L69
SAFARI...L35
BONNEVILLE
COUPE...N37
SEDAN...N69
SAFARI...N35
BONNEVILLE BROUGHAM
COUPE...R37
SEDAN...R69

PHOENIX
COUPE...Y37
5-DR HATCH...Y68
PHOENIX LJ
COUPE...Z37
5-DR HATCH...Z68
FIREBIRD
FIREBIRD...S87
ESPRIT...T87
FORMULA...V87
TRANS AM...W87
LEMANS
COUPE...D27
SEDAN...D69
SAFARI...D35
GRAND LEMANS
COUPE...F27
SEDAN...F69
SAFARI...F35
1982/FIREBIRD
FIREBIRD...S87
TRANS AM...W87
FIREBIRD SE...X87
PONTIAC 6000
COUPE...F27
SEDAN...F19
PONTIAC 6000 LE
COUPE...G27
SEDAN...G19
GRAND PRIX
GRAND PRIX...J37
GRAND PRIX LJ...K37
GRAND PRIX BROUGHAM...P37
BONNEVILLE MODEL G
SEDAN...N69
WAGON...N35
MODEL G BROUGHAM
SEDAN...R69
T1000
3-DR HATCH COUPE...L08
5-DR HATCH SEDAN...L68
J2000
COUPE...B27
SEDAN...B69
3-DR HATCH BACK...B77
WAGON...B35
J2000 LE
COUPE...C27
SEDAN...C69
J2000 SE
3-DR HATCH BACK...D77
PHOENIX
COUPE...Y37
5-DR HATCH BACK...Y68
PHOENIX LJ
COUPE...Z37
5-DR HATCH BACK...Z68
PHOENIX SJ
COUPE...T37
5-DR HATCH BACK...T68
1983/FIREBIRD
FIREBIRD...S87
TRANS AM...W87
FIREBIRD SE...X87
PONTIAC 6000
COUPE...F27
SEDAN...F19
PONTIAC 6000 LE
COUPE...G27
SEDAN...G19
PONTIAC 6000 STE
SEDAN...H19
GRAND PRIX
GRAND PRIX...J37
GRAND PRIX LJ...K37
GRAND PRIX BROUGHAM...P37
BONNEVILLE MODEL G
SEDAN...N69
WAGON...N35
MODEL G BROUGHAM
SEDAN...R69
PONTIAC 1000
3-DR HATCH COUPE...L08
5-DR HATCH SEDAN...L68
PONTIAC 2000
COUPE...B27
SEDAN...B69
3-DR HATCH BACK...B77
WAGON...B5
PONTIAC 2000 LE
COUPE...C27
SEDAN...C69
WAGON...C35
PONTIAC 2000 SE
3-DR HATCH BACK...D77

PHOENIX
COUPE...Y37
5-DR HATCH BACK...Y68
PHOENIX LJ
COUPE...Z37
5-DR HATCH BACK...Z68
PHOENIX SJ
COUPE...T37
5-DR HATCH BACK...T68
1984/FIREBIRD
FIREBIRD...S87
TRANS AM...W87
FIREBIRD S/E...X87
PONTIAC 6000
COUPE...F27
SEDAN...F19
WAGON...F35
PONTIAC 6000 LE
COUPE...G27
SEDAN...G19
WAGON...F35
PONTIAC 6000 STE
SEDAN...H19
GRAND PRIX
GRAND PRIX...J37
GRAND PRIX LE...K37
GRAND PRIX BROUGHAM...P37
BONNEVILLE
BONNEVILLE...N69
BONNEVILLE LE...S69
BONNEVILLE BROUGHAM...R69
PARISIENNE
SEDAN...L69
WAGON...L35
PARISIENNE BROUGHAM
SEDAN...T69
PHOENIX
COUPE...Y37
4-DR HATCH BACK...Y68
PHOENIX LE
COUPE...Z37
5-DR HATCH BACK...Z68
PHOENIX SE
COUPE...T37
PONTIAC 1000
3-DR HATCH BACK...L08
5-DR HATCH BACK...L68
FIERO
COUPE...E37
SPORT COUPE...M37
SE COUPE...F37
PONTIAC 2000 SUNBIRD
COUPE...B27
SEDAN...B69
3-DR HATCH BACK...B77
WAGON...B35
PONTIAC 2000 SUNBIRD LE
COUPE...D27
SEDAN...D69
3-DR HATCH BACK...D77
2000 SUNBIRD LE CONV.
CONVERTIBLE...C67
1985/FIREBIRD
FIREBIRD...S87
TRANS AM...W87
FIREBIRD S/E...X87
PONTIAC 6000
COUPE...F27
SEDAN...F19
WAGON...F35
PONTIAC 6000 LE
COUPE...G27
SEDAN...G19
WAGON...G35
PONTIAC 6000 STE
SEDAN...H19
GRAND AM
GRAND AM...E27
GRAND LE...V27
GRAND PRIX
GRAND PRIX...J37
GRAND PRIX LE...K37
GRAND PRIX BROUGHAM...P37
BONNEVILLE
BONNEVILLE...N69
BONNEVILLE LE...S69
BONNEVILLE BROUGHAM...R69
PARISIENNE
SEDAN...L69
PARISIENNE BROUGHAM
SEDAN...T69
PHOENIX
COUPE...Y37
4-DR HATCH BACK...Y68

PHOENIX LE
COUPE...Z37
5-DR HATCH BACK...Z68
PHOENIX SE
COUPE...T37
PONTIAC 1000
3-DR HATCH BACK...L08
5-DR HATCH BACK...L68
FIERO
COUPE...E37
SPORT COUPE...M37
SE COUPE...F37
PONTIAC SUNBIRD
COUPE...B27
SEDAN...B69
3-DR HATCH BACK...B77
WAGON...B35
PONTIAC SUNBIRD LE
COUPE...C37
SEDAN...C69
WAGON...C35
PONTIAC SUNBIRD S/E
COUPE...D27
SEDAN...D69
3-DR HATCH BACK...D77
PONTIAC SUNBIRD LE CONV.
CONVERTIBLE...C67

1986/FIREBIRD
FIREBIRD...S87
TRANS AM...W87
FIREBIRD S/E...X87
PONTIAC 6000
COUPE...F27
SEDAN...F19
WAGON...F35
PONTIAC 6000 LE
COUPE...G27
SEDAN...G19
WAGON...G35
PONTIAC 6000 STE
SEDAN...H19
SE SEDAN...E19
SE WAGON...E35
GRAND AM
GRAND AM...E27
SEDAN...E69
GRAND AM LE COUPE...V27
SEDAN...V69
SE COUPE...W27
SE SEDAN...W69
GRAND PRIX
GRAND PRIX...J37
GRAND PRIX LE...K37
GRAND PRIX BROUGHAM...P37
BONNEVILLE
BONNEVILLE...N69
BONNEVILLE LE...S69
BONNEVILLE BROUGHAM...R69
PARISIENNE
SEDAN...L69
WAGON...L35
PARISIENNE BROUGHAM
SEDAN...T69
PONTIAC 1000
3-DR HATCH BACK...L08
5-DR HATCH BACK...L68
FIERO
COUPE...E37
SPORT COUPE...M37
SE COUPE...F37
GT...G97
PONTIAC SUNBIRD
SEDAN...B69
WAGON...B35
PONTIAC SUNBIRD S/E
COUPE...D27
CONVERTIBLE...D67
3-DR HATCH BACK...D77
PONTIAC SUNBIRD GT
COUPE...U27
SEDAN...U69
3-DR HATCH BACK...U77
CONVERTIBLE...U67

1987/FIREBIRD
FIREBIRD...S87
TRANS AM...W87
TRANS AM GTA (OPTION PACKAGE)...W87
PONTIAC 6000
COUPE...F27
SEDAN...F19
WAGON...F35
PONTIAC 6000 LE
SEDAN...G19
WAGON...G35

PONTIAC 6000 STE
SEDAN...H19
SE SEDAN...E19
SE WAGON...E35
GRAND AM
GRAND AM COUPE...E27
SEDAN...E69
GRAND AM LE COUPE...V27
SEDAN...V69
SE COUPE...W27
SE SEDAN...W69
GRAND PRIX
GRAND PRIX...J37
GRAND PRIX LE...K37
GRAND PRIX BROUGHAM...P37
BONNEVILLE
BONNEVILLE...X69
BONNEVILLE LE...Z69
SAFARI
WAGON...L35
PONTIAC 1000
3-DR HATCH BACK...L08
5-DR HATCH BACK...L68
FIERO
COUPE BASIC...E37
SPORT COUPE...M37
SE COUPE...F37
GT...G97
PONTIAC SUNBIRD
SEDAN...B69
WAGON...B35
PONTIAC SUNBIRD S/E
COUPE...D27
CONVERTIBLE...D67
3-DR HATCH BACK...D77
PONTIAC SUNBIRD GT
COUPE...U27
SEDAN...U69
3-DR HATCH BACK...U77
CONVERTIBLE (GT)...U67

1988/FIREBIRD
FIREBIRD...S87
FORMULA (OPTION PACKAGE)...W66
TRANS AM...W87
TRANS AM GTA (OPTION PACKAGE)...Y84
PONTIAC 6000
SEDAN...F19
WAGON...F35
PONTIAC 6000 LE
SEDAN...G19
WAGON...G35
PONTIAC 6000 STE
SEDAN...H19
SE SEDAN...E19
SE WAGON...E35
GRAND AM
GRAND AM COUPE...E27
SEDAN...E69
GRAND AM LE COUPE...V27
SEDAN...V69
SE COUPE...W27
SE SEDAN...W69
GRAND PRIX
GRAND PRIX...J37
GRAND PRIX LE...K37
GRAND PRIX SE...P37
BONNEVILLE
BONNEVILLE LE...X69
BONNEVILLE SE...Z69
BONNEVILLE SSE...Y69
SAFARI
WAGON...L35
FIERO
COUPE BASIC...E37
FORMULA PACKAGE...W66
GT...G97
PONTIAC SUNBIRD
SEDAN...B69
WAGON...D35
PONTIAC SUNBIRD S/E
COUPE...D27
SE WAGON...D35
PONTIAC SUNBIRD GT
COUPE...U37
CONVERTIBLE (GT)...U67
LEMANS
VALUE LEADER...X08
REGULAR AERO...N08
SEDAN...W19
SE SEDAN...R19

1989/FIREBIRD
FIREBIRD...S87
FORMULA (OPTION PACKAGE)...W66
TRANS AM...W87

TRANS AM GTA (OPTION PACKAGE)...Y84
PONTIAC 6000 LE
SEDAN...F69
WAGON...F35
PONTIAC 6000 STE
SEDAN...H69
SE SEDAN...J69
SE WAGON...J35
GRAND AM
LE COUPE...E27
SEDAN LE...E69
SE COUPE...W27
SE SEDAN...W69
GRAND PRIX
COUPE...J37
LE COUPE...K37
SE COUPE...P37
BONNEVILLE
LE SEDAN...X69
SE SEDAN...Z69
SSE SEDAN...Y69
SAFARI
WAGON...L35
SUNBIRD
LE COUPE...B37
LE SEDAN...B69
SE COUPE...D37
GT COUPE...U37
GT CONVERTIBLE...U67
LEMANS
3-DR AEROCOUPE...X08
(VALUE LEADER)
LE AEROCOUPE...N08
LE SEDAN...N19
SE SEDAN...R19
GSE AEROCOUPE...S08

1990/FIREBIRD
FIREBIRD...S87
FORMULA (OPTION PACKAGE)...W66
TRANS AM...W87
TRANS AM GTA (OPTION PACKAGE)...Y84
PONTIAC 6000 LE
SEDAN...F69
WAGON...F35
PONTIAC 6000 STE
SE SEDAN...J69
SE SEDAN AWD...J69
SE WAGON...J35
GRAND AM
LE COUPE...E27
SEDAN LE...E69
SE COUPE...W27
SE SEDAN...W69
GRAND PRIX
COUPE...J37
SE COUPE...P37
4-DR SEDAN...J19
4-DR STE SEDAN...T19
BONNEVILLE
LE SEDAN...X69
SE SEDAN...Z69
SSE SEDAN...Y69
SUNBIRD
LE COUPE...B37
LE SEDAN...B69
SE COUPE...D37
GT COUPE...U37
LE CONVERTIBLE...B67
LEMANS
3-DR AEROCOUPE...X08
(VALUE LEADER)
LE AEROCOUPE...N08
LE SEDAN...N19
GSE AEROCOUPE...S08
TRANS SPORT
FRONT-WHEEL DRIVE...M06

1991/FIREBIRD
HATCH BACK COUPE...S87
TRANS AM HATCH BACK COUPE...W87
PONTIAC 6000
LE SEDAN...F69
LE WAGON...F35
S/E SEDAN...J69
GRAND AM
COUPE...G27
SEDAN...G69
LE COUPE...E27
LE SEDAN...E69
SE COUPE...W27
SE SEDAN...W69
GRAND PRIX
LE SEDAN...H19
SE SEDAN...J19
SE COUPE...J37

GT COUPE...P37
STE SEDAN...T19
BONNEVILLE
LE SEDAN...X69
SE SEDAN...Z69
SSE SEDAN...Y69
SUNBIRD
COUPE...C37
SEDAN...C69
LE COUPE...B37
LE SEDAN...B69
LE CONVERTIBLE...B67
SE COUPE...D37
GT COUPE...U37
LEMANS
3-DR AEROCOUPE...X08
(VALUE LEADER)
LE 3-DR AEROCOUPE...N08
LE SEDAN...N19
TRANS SPORT
TRANS SPORT...M06
1992/FIREBIRD
FIREBIRD CONVERTIBLE...S67
FIREBIRD...S87
FORMULA (W66)...S87
TRANS AM CONVERTIBLE...W67
TRANS AM...W87
TRANS AM GTA (Y84)...W87
GRAND AM
SE COUPE...E37
SE SEDAN...E69
GT COUPE...W37
GT SEDAN...W69
GRAND PRIX
LE SEDAN...H19
SE SEDAN...J19
SE COUPE...J37
GT COUPE...P37
STE SEDAN...T19
BONNEVILLE
SE SEDAN...X69
SSE SEDAN...Z69
SSEI SEDAN...Y69
SUNBIRD
LE COUPE...C37

LE SEDAN...C69
SE COUPE...B37
SE SEDAN...B69
SE CONVERTIBLE...B67
GT COUPE...D37
LEMANS
AEROCOUPE (VALUE LEADER)...X08
SE AEROCOUPE...N08
SE SEDAN...N19
TRANS SPORT
TRANS SPORT SE...M06
TRANS SPORT GT (Y92)...M06
1993/FIREBIRD
FIREBIRD 2-DR COUPE...S87P
FORMULA 2-DR COUPE...V87P
TRANS AM 2-DR COUPE...V87P/Y83
GRAND AM
SE 2-DR COUPE...E37P
SE 4-DR SEDAN...E69P
GRAND PRIX
LE 4-DR SEDAN...H19P
SE 2-DR COUPE...J37N
SE 4-DR SEDAN...J19P
GT 2-DR COUPE...P37N
STE 4-DR SEDAN...T19P
BONNEVILLE
SE 4-DR SEDAN...X69P
SSE 4-DR SEDAN...Z69P
SSEI 4-DR SEDAN...Y69P
SUNBIRD
LE 2-DR COUPE...C37P
LE 4-DR SEDAN...C69P
SE 2-DR COUPE...B37P
SE 4-DR SEDAN...B69P
SE 2-DR CONVERTIBLE...B67P
LEMANS
VALUE LEADER 3-DR AEROCOUPE...X08P
SE 3-DR AEROCOUPE...N08P
SE 4-DR SEDAN...N19P
TRANS SPORT
SE MINIVAN...M06P
1994/FIREBIRD
FIREBIRD 2-DR COUPE...S87R
FORMULA 2-DR COUPE...V87R

TRANS AM 2-DR COUPE...V87R/Y82
GRAND AM
SE 2-DR COUPE...E37R
SE 4-DR SEDAN...E69R
GRAND PRIX
SE 4-DR SEDAN...J19R
SE 2-DR COUPE...J37R
BONNEVILLE
SE 4-DR SEDAN...X69R
SSE 4-DR SEDAN...Z69R
SUNBIRD
LE 2-DR COUPE...B37R
LE 4-DR SEDAN...B69R
SE 2-DR COUPE...L37R
LE 2-DR CONVERTIBLE...B67R
TRANS SPORT
SE MINIVAN...M06R
1995/FIREBIRD
FIREBIRD 2-DR COUPE...S87S
FORMULA 2-DR COUPE...V87S
TRANS AM 2-DR COUPE...V87S
FIREBIRD 2-DR CONVERTIBLE...S67S
FORMULA 2-DR CONVERTIBLE...V67S
TRANS AM 2-DR CONVERTIBLE...V67S
GRAND AM
SE 2-DR COUPE...E37S
SE 4-DR SEDAN...E69S
GT 2-DR COUPE...W37S
GT 4-DR SEDAN...W69S
GRAND PRIX
SE 2-DR COUPE...J37S
SE 4-DR SEDAN...J19S
BONNEVILLE
SE 4-DR SEDAN...X69S
SSE 4-DR SEDAN...Z69S
SUNFIRE
SE 2-DR COUPE...B37S
SE 4-DR SEDAN...B69S
SE 2-DR CONVERTIBLE...B67S
GT 2-DR COUPE...D37S
TRANS SPORT
SE MINIVAN...M06S

A 1937 Pontiac show car was split down the center for auto showgoers to get a close look at how that year's Pontiacs were constructed.

INTERESTING PONTIAC FACTS

By John Sawruk

• Pontiac's first postwar V-8 design was a flathead.

• Pontiac built an experimental car in 1954 with an L-head six-cylinder in the rear mounted transversely.

• The 1955 GMC L'Universelle Show Van had a front-wheel drive Pontiac V-8 powertrain.

• The 1956 Pontiac Club de Mer show car had a brushed metal skin. Guess who the head of Pontiac Advance Design was at that point?

• The 1957 and 1958 Pontiac fuel injection systems used different intake manifolds; 1957 was tubular and 1958 was cast.

• Pontiac used Cadillac bodies during development of the transaxle, which led to the 1961 Tempest.

• The first 1961 Tempest four-cylinder engines were made by putting bob weights in place of piston and rod assemblies in 1958 V-8 engines in Chieftains.

• 1958 big Pontiacs were used to develop the XB-60 "rope-drive" transaxle for the 1961 Tempest.

• Around 1959 Pontiac made 389 cid aluminum cylinder blocks in conjunction with Reynolds Aluminum. They had no liners. In the same period, aluminum heads without seat inserts were made; valve seat wear was a serious problem.

• Drawings of never made Pontiacs originally planned include:

— The elusive 1954 Sedan Delivery, marked "Canceled 9/14/53".

— A 1954 Business Coupe and Sedan Coupe, marked "Canceled 8/17/53".

— A 1954 short wheelbase convertible.

— A 1956 proposal with the transmission mounted under the seat. It had a flat floor and two driveshafts.

• Various 1959 studies with different side trim or models versus what was released for production. These included a Star Chief Safari station wagon and a "Ventura," which was the beginning of the Grand Prix concept.

— A 1961 Star Chief two-door sedan.

— A 1962 Ventura series (not just a Catalina with the Ventura option).

— 1963 Tempests with different front end styling versus what was finally used in production.

— A 1966 Ventura Safari station wagon with woodgrain.

• The name "Ventura" was often used on concept sketches for proposed Pontiacs and Tempests.

• There are reports of a factory prototype 1964 Tempest with a turbine engine.

• There are reports of a factory prototype 1964 Tempest with front-wheel drive.

• Pontiac partially developed a Rochester six-barrel carburetor. It had a 3-2 barrels on a common base.

• The 1966 Tri-Power and 1967 four-barrel intake manifold/carburetor/ air cleaner systems had equivalent power. The restrictive Tri-Power intake manifold was replaced by a 1967 four-barrel design that was related to the early 1960's NASCAR manifold. In addition, the small Tri-Power air cleaners were quite restrictive also versus the large element used with the four-barrel.

• One Pontiac OHC V-8 is currently running in a private owner's car.

• Several different Pontiac OHC V-8s were built.

• There was a plan for cast iron eight-lug wheels for the 1966 Tempest. Brake drum distortion and high unsprung weight killed the program.

• Pontiac built a 1967 Firebird with a ground effects machine in the trunk to increase traction.

• Many Canadian Pontiacs, including the Canadian specific muscle cars, used Chevrolet engines.

• A 1968 GTO Hatchback prototype was built. It was white with blue stripes (ala the 1969 Trans Am).

• The prototype 1969 Trans Am was silver. It has a fiberglass hood with push down and rotate style hood locks.

• Some 1970 GTOs were equipped with an optional vacuum controlled exhaust system called "The Tiger Button". A knob, similar to that used for RAM AIR, changed the exhaust sound. Few were sold before the option was canceled.

• A drawing has been found that indicates the original plan for the 1971 GT-37 was to have it use the 1970 GT-37 stripe, which is the same as the 1969 Judge.

• The major change in 1971 vs. 1970 horsepower ratings didn't come from the change in compression ratio. Instead, it comes from the use of more realistic net hp ratings in 1971 (which included a fan, an air cleaner, exhaust system, etc.) versus the gross hp used in 1970.

• The 1972 "A" duck tail spoiler was never installed in production. Factory pictures exist showing it installed on a LeMans GT and a GTO. Some parts appear to have been sold through GM Parts Division and installed.

• The 1972 GTO was originally going to have a 350 cid four-barrel engine as standard.

• What became the 1973 Grand Am was originally intended to be the GTO.

• One 1973 "A" SD 455 was built. It was in a Grand Am and was an engineering prototype. There were no production 1973 "A" SD 455s.

• No 1973 production "A" cars were produced with functional NASA scoops. However, one prototype, now in private hands, does exist. In addition, some other units may have been sold through GM Parts Division and installed.

• What became the 1973 "A" was intended to be released as a 1972, but was delayed by the long GM strike.

• SD455 Formula Firebirds came from the factory with Trans Am hoods and shakers.

• There was a 1959 proposal for a Pontiac version of the El Camino. One prototype still exists in a private owner's hands. This proposal resurfaced in 1978. A prototype vehicle, using the Grand Am appearance, was built. This vehicle, now updated to 1980 appearance, is in the Pontiac Historical Vehicle Collection. A similar proposal, using LeMans sheet metal, was proposed to be sold by GM Truck and Coach.

• The 1979 Firebird Type K came close to going into production. The build process required that a Firebird be partially built in the plant, transferred to an outside body facility, and then returned to the plant for completion. As a result, the total number of Firebirds able to be built was reduced due to the assembly line interruptions. A financial analysis of the situation showed Pontiac would lose profit from this situation and the project was canceled.

• One of the 1980 Phoenix optional trims combined a basically black interior with saddle colored seat inserts. The trim brochure shows saddle inserts on the door trim panels also, but due to a factory error, some cars were built with all black door panels.

• Many factory photos and Product Description Manuals (an assembly guide) are incorrect versus how the cars were actually made.

• The 1953 and 1954 Pontiacs had provisions to accommodate the V-8 finally introduced in 1955. Some people have reported seeing possible 1953-'54 prototype V-8 cars in Pontiac/Detroit area junkyards.

• The first stamped steel rocker arm (to be used in the 1955 Pontiac and Chevy engines, ultimately) was made at home by a Pontiac Engineer.

- Notes from Pete Estes indicate the 1959 "Wide-Track was primarily viewed as a styling feature, with the handling advantage seen as secondary."

- Pontiac built experimental 1961 Tempests with 316, 347, and 389 cid engines.

- A 1961 Tempest was built with a side-mounted radiator and an engine compartment with seals.

- A 1961 Catalina was built with a 336 cid V-8 for performance and economy testing.

- Automatic overdrive transmissions were tried in large Pontiacs in 1961 and 1969, at least.

- While "Ventura" was used as a generic code name for many Pontiac styling proposals, a document has been found that indicates it was the intended name for what became the 1962 Grand Prix. It also says the car was to use special springs for a one inch lower ride height.

- Vinyl tops for large Pontiac coupe models were announced as being available as of 1-30-62. "Cobra" grain vinyl was used.

- A 35,000 mile chassis lube was intended for the 1962 Tempest.

- The 1963 Tempest 326 cid V-8 was really a 336. In 1964 it became a 326.

- A 421 cid SOHC V-8 "Sports Engine" was seriously developed by Pontiac. A 395 cid was also proposed. 1963 test data on the 421 SOHC showed the four-barrel version produced more power than the Tri-power one.

- An Engineering report dated 5-29-63 is titled "Preliminary Performance and Fuel Economy Comparison - G.T.O. (with periods!) versus 326 HO engine and 326 low compression ratio engine".

- Data was found that indicates an informational description of what became the 1964 GTO was published inside Pontiac on 7-3-63, revised 8-13-63, 8-19-63, and 10-18-63. The 8-13-63 list indicates the GTO crest was to be red, white, and blue. It also shows that the GTO was intended to have a 116 inch wheelbase (with a modified suspension) versus the Tempest 115 inches.

- Pontiac designed and built a front-wheel drive 1964 Tempest with a 326 cid V-8. It used unequal length driveshafts. The engine was mounted longitudinally.

- There was a plan for a six bolt rocker cover for the 1964 Pontiac V-8.

- There was a Hilborn-like fuel injection system designed by Pontiac Engineering for the GTO.

- Pontiac tested a water heated 2-4 barrel ram intake manifold for the 1965 GTO engine.

- A RPD speed-density fuel injection system was tested on a 1965 GTO engine with a modified 3-2 manifold, a ram manifold, and a cross-ram manifold.

- A 265 cid OHC6 was built for possible use in the Catalina and Tempest. It apparently had a longer stroke. One-barrel and four-barrel versions were built.

- 1966 Engineering Bulletin #66-22, dated 10-14-65, indicates the release of a "LeMans Ride Option for GTO". It was to include LeMans V-8 springs, shocks, and stabilizer bar. The purpose was "for the owner who desires a GTO with its looks and performance but with LeMans type ride."

- An engineering drawing dated 8-23-65 shows the cast iron styled wheel/brake for the 1966 Tempest. It shows eight lug nuts. It had 24 cooling fins versus 16 on the aluminum version. This wheel never went into production due to high weight and distortion.

- What became the 1966 230 cid OHC6 was originally to have been 215 cid.

- Pontiac Engineering Bulletin 66-20 indicates that the OHC6 was to have black painted ribs on the cam cover and timing belt cover. Red paint was to be on the "Overhead Cam" letters, the "PMD" letters, and the ribs that framed the PMD letters.

- Pontiac developed a rear mounted transmission, the EX-724, which was used in five experimental independent rear suspension transaxle cars.

- Pontiac designed an independent rear suspension with inboard disc brakes. A number of experimental cars were built.

- Pontiac designed a variable venturi carburetor. The design had no throttle blades. Rochester Products took the work over.

- Pontiac Engineering Bulletin 66-16 indicates that an electrically heated front seat and seat back was to have been a special order option on the 1966 Bonneville Brougham only.

- Pontiac developed (starting around 1967) a X-4 engine. It was an aluminum, two cycle, four-cylinder, air cooled, fuel injected engine.

- As late as 7-15-66, the 1967 Firebird was called the "PF" car. What appears to be the "Banshee" name is hazy on the drawings. What became the Firebird 400 was originally to be the "TT" with a different hood and emblems than finally used. TT stood for "Tourist Trophy". Some data indicates the TT was also to have the four-barrel OHC 6 available.

- The original 1967 Firebird option list shows "D35 - Bullet outside rearview mirror".

- Some 1969 development projects on the Pontiac 303 cid Trans-Am engine included center feed crankshaft oiling and gravity feed camshaft oiling.

- In 1969, Pontiac proposed an aluminum 297 cid V-8. Experimental 250 cid versions were built.

- In 1969, Pontiac built a 230 OHC 6 "Hemi". It had 325 gross hp.

- What became the 1969 Tempest Custom S was originally to be called the "Pontiac TC".

- Around 1969, Pontiac Engineering installed a 318 cid Plymouth V-8 in a Catalina for a performance and economy study.

- The 1970-1/2 Firebird came close to having a production Bendix Fuel Injection System (TBI type).

- In 1981, Pontiac proposed a "Safari" pickup based on the Sunbird. Production would have been in 1985 or 1986. The Norwood plant recently built one on its own.

- The 1982 Firebird was designed to contain the Pontiac manufactured V-8. The Turbo 301 required engine repackaging to make it fit.

- Alcoa made an "all-aluminum" Pontiac. It was a 1942 two-door streamliner and had its engine and other parts made of aluminum.

- In 1943, Pontiac designed a one-quarter-ton 4X4 truck proposed for build by Chevrolet.

- Some non-military work started again at Pontiac Engineering in 1943.

- Work was started on a five-inch Rocket Bomb in 1944. Pontiac also started making a 155mm shell.

- GM Coaches were worked on at Pontiac in 1944.

- There was almost no road testing due to restrictions on manpower and fuel in 1944.

- An experimental Pontiac 6 with a supercharger was built in 1945.

- An experimental Pontiac 6 with an aluminum intake manifold dual carburetor set-up was built in 1945.

- Postwar Pontiac V-8 projects included:
— 269 cid Flathead (8:1 compression ratio) - two designs
— 268 cid OHV
— 272 cid OHV using an Oldsmobile block
— 287 cid that became the 1955 production V-8. It was apparently related to the 268 cid above.

- In 1947, Pontiac demonstrated a car with the 269 cid flathead V-8 to GM management.

- 272 cid OHV V-8 - first Pontiac engines made in 1948.

- A 265 cid OHV Pontiac 6 was designed in 1948.

- 269 cid flathead V-8 work was dropped in May 1949 by Pontiac as not suitable for high compression.

- Pontiac built one 1200 OHV V-6, 251 cid for GM use in late 1949.

- Pontiac 268 cid OHV V-8s were made in 1950.

- A 248 cid OHV 6 was proposed to replace the 239 cid flathead six. It used the GMC Truck 248 cid block and crankshaft.

- A two-barrel, high output 239 cid flathead six was developed. Work stopped in 1950.

- A 239 cid F-head (not flathead) six was designed in 1950.

- There were plans for a longer wheelbase 1950 Pontiac.

- The 1951 Pontiac was originally planned to have a new "A" body to be shared with Chevrolet and Oldsmobile, with considerable interchangeability.

• What became the 1953 Pontiac was originally intended to be the 1952 model.

• Prior to the development of the 1977 151 cid four-cylinder (which started in 1974), four-cylinder proposals using V-8 tooling (like the old 195 cid version) were looked at. Possibly the most unusual was a S-4. This engine used the most forward cylinder on one side, then the two inner cylinders on the other side, and an end cylinder on the same side as the first. A prototype was built using a V-8 block and bob weights. It had unacceptable vibrations, later analyzed mathematically.

• There was a serious production design to use the 1.8 liter, four-cylinder, non-turbo engine in the 1984 Fiero. The intent was to provide even higher levels of fuel economy.

• People have expressed interest in whether or not any high performance items existed for Pontiacs before 1955 before the V-8 engine. They are as follows:

• People did run pre-1955 Pontiacs in NASCAR. However, little else is known about this. (it's suspected they weren't too successful!)

• Special rear springs were offered in 1951 for Taxicabs, Police Cars, and Special Order Export. They were different from the Station Wagon and Sedan Delivery springs.

• In 1950 there was a "City Police" generator. It was used in conjunction with a 19 plate battery and a special voltage regulator . It was specifically not heavy-duty. It was for cars operated at low speeds with heavy electrical loads. It was not intended for use over 60 mph except for short periods.

• In 1954 a heavy-duty Hydra-Matic conversion package was available. It has an external transmission oil cooler, larger annular pistons, a modified engine water pump, and some other parts. It was intended for police cars, taxis, and road mail carriers. it could not be used on air conditioned cars. The cooler mounted on the transmission.

• 1954 air conditioned cars used a six bladed fan, 13 pound radiator cap, special equipment generator and battery, and heavy-duty fuel pump. Non-A/C cars used a seven pound cap. Eventually, special water temperature gauges were used in A/C cars because of this difference.

• It's believed that approximately 100 1971-1/2 GT-37s were built. Evidence of cars built at Fremont, as well as Pontiac, was uncovered. After a lot of searching in various records, no announcement was found that the 1971-1/2 existed although the stripes did find their way into the parts catalog.

• For those that wonder: Yes, the candy apple green color on the 1971 evaporative emissions line clip near the canister is correct!

• 1229 1986-1/2 Grand Prix 2 + 2s were made. Despite original plans, no 1987s were made. There were also four 1986-1/2 prototypes (including a black one and a maroon one). Beware, some people have already made additional ones by buying parts from Pontiac. All production ones were silver fastbacks.

A 1959 Star Chief Catalina Vista four-door hardtop designed as a cutaway traveled the auto show circuit in late 1958-'59 to promote features built-in to the new models offered by Pontiac.

VROOM WITH A VIEW

Known by any number of names including "glass" car, "phantom" car, or "The Transparent Car," whatever it was identified as it was indeed a sight to behold. A Pontiac Deluxe Six four-door sedan appeared at the 1939 World's Fair in New York as part of General Motors' "Highways and Horizons" exhibit. The World's Fair Pontiac featured 1939 Body by Fisher body panels molded of plexiglass. The transparent exterior allowed fairgoers to see the structural and operating parts ordinarily hidden from view. Through the use of chrome and copper-plating, as well as bronze and enamel finishes, the various functioning parts were easily distinguished. All rubber parts were constructed of white rubber. The World's Fair Pontiac was displayed against a mural designed by artist Dean Cornwall that traced the steps in making an automobile body. The car was later updated with 1940 plexiglass body panels and today is owned by well known Indiana car collector Frank Kleptz.

Updated 1940 Pontiac DeLuxe Six four-door sedan plexiglass-bodied display car.

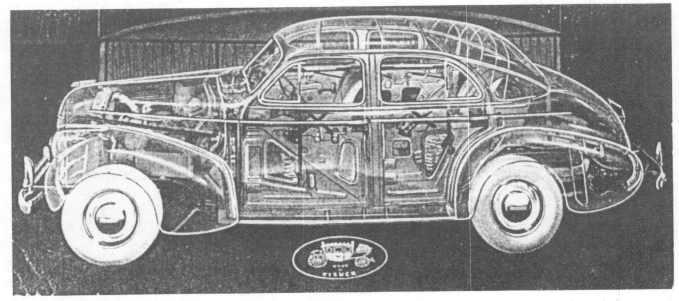

A 1940 Pontiac Torpedo four-door sedan plexiglass-bodied car. Controversy exists whether this car, an artist's rendering, was ever constructed as its history and whereabouts remain a mystery.

The 1963 Pontiac Super-Duty Catalina hardtop from front (above) and rear (below).

PONTIAC LIGHTWEIGHTS

Pontiac was the first automaker to build factory lightweight cars. Ever since its NASCAR engine options were issued in mid-1957, the company found that racing sold cars. By 1960, the "Poncho" performance image had make Pontiacs the third most popular U.S. cars for the first time. Chevy's new-for-1962 409 cid engine was a threat, though. Pontiac's best match was the 1961 Super-Duty389 Catalina (368 hp with Tri-Power), of which maybe 25 were built.

More power and less weight were needed to keep the Pontiacs competitive. So, PMD put its lightest, most powerful car on a diet with a horsepower supplement. Extensive use of aluminum body parts and a special 421 cid/405 hp V-8 created the 3,600 lb. 1962 Super-Duty Catalina.

The new engine featrured four-bolt mains, forged pistons and twin Carter four-barrels on a special manifold linked to either a Borg-Warner T-85 three-speed or T-10 four-speed. Actual horsepower was over 500.

Massive 421 cid/405 hp V-8 created for the Super-Duty Catalina.

PONTIAC CONCEPT CARS

1953 Parisienne. Pontiac's definition called this a town car, but most town cars are four-doors. This is more of a "landau," as far as definitions go. It had a special wraparound rear window as well as front windshield. Original press releases said it had a plexiglass dome fitted over the driver's compartment in the event of bad weather. However, the car still exists and raises doubts about this claim. The Parisienne rode on a standard 122 inch chassis and was powered by Pontiac's straight eight engine. It was updated in 1954 with a new grille and different paint. Joe Bortz obtained the car and had it restored to its original 1953 format. (GM photo)

1954 Bonneville Special. Harley Earl named this dream car design after the famed Bonneville Salt Flats of Utah. For years it was thought that one car was made, but now there are two. Both now survive in the Bortz Collection. The Bonneville Specials were two-seat sports cars on a 100 inch chassis. One was painted a metallic reddish bronze color, the other is green. A transparent plexiglass canopy encloses the entire passenger compartment. Hinged at the center, the canopies raise at each side on springs counter-balanced at the touch of a release catch. The doors are then opened from the inside. The cars have bucket seats, a center console and a modified multi-carbureted straight eight. (GM photo)

1954 Strato Streak. Pontiac called their four-door, four-passenger show car a "sports car." Most people would argue that definition, but the Strato Streak had many far-sighted features. Among them the pillarless four-door (but not hardtop) construction. The doors are hung from the front and from the rear on each side, with strength provided at the center by extra rigidity in the frame. Since the rear doors open into the windstream, they are equipped with special locks to prevent their being opened, except when the car is stopped and in neutral. The front seats swivel 90 degrees for ease of entry and exit. (GM photo)

1954 Firebird I. While not really a Pontiac prototype, the name of this dream car was later given to Pontiac's specialty car of 1967. The original Firebird was a feature attraction at the '54 GM Motorama show. Powered by 379 hp jet aircraft gas turbine engine, the Firebird was one of several experimental gas turbine cars built by GM, Chrysler and Ford, although the GM project was the first American-built gas turbine auto. (GM photo)

1955 'Strato Star.' This six-passenger coupe made its debut at the Jan. 20, 1955 opening of GM's Motorama show in New York City. It featured ultraslim door pillars and lots of glass. For easy access, hinged panels in the roof automatically rose when the doors were opened. Note the unusual parking light pods hanging below the front bumpers. (GM photo)

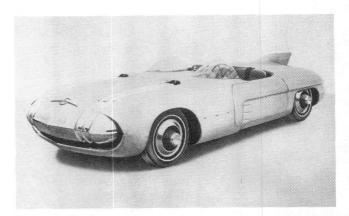

1956 Club de Mer. Power for this sportscar from Pontiac came from a dual-quad carbureted 300 hp V-8 engine. It used the unusual DeDion rear suspension and rear mounted transmission. All in all a very radical car. It was built on a 104 inch chassis. And, instead of fiberglass, the Club de Mer was constructed of aluminum.

1957 Firebird II. As with Firebird I, the Firebird II wasn't a Pontiac project. It was a GM Engineering project to test the gas turbine engine concept. This version was more family-oriented with room for four passengers. For the first time, titanium was used in an automobile body and the car had a special electromagnetically controlled four-speed transmission. It also had self-leveling hydro-pneumatic suspension.

1958 Firebird III. Just as Firebird II was starting to look more like a conventional automobile, along comes Firebird III shooting for the stars. GM and Harley Earl pulled out all the stops. There was a single central control lever, accessible from both seats, which controlled steering, acceleration and braking; a speed-hold device (now known as cruise-control); automatic control systems developed from those in Firebird II; remote door-opening by means of ultrasonic control; air-conditioning which maintains the car's interior at a constant temperature (even when it is standing still); automatic illumination of the lamps; a power unit which, though more powerful (225 hp), was also 25 percent more economical; electroluminescent instrument displays; and an anti-skid braking system. Whew!

1959 Bonneville X-400. The '59 model was the first of several X-400 show cars that Pontiac built for the show circuit. This car featured several styling and engineering features, such as supercharged engine, hidden headlights and special interiors.

1960 X-400. The second X-400 again had the Latham supercharged engine. This car was built on a Bonneville chassis but had Catalina rear quarters. Other styling changes included Lucas headlights, fiberglass top boot, blue dot taillights and leather upholstery in a waffle-pattern. The car was painted a metallic blue. It is now in the Joe Bortz "Blue Suede Shoes" collection.

1961 Tempest Monte Carlo. GM Styling boss, William Mitchell, built the Monte Carlo as a companion car to the Corvair Sebring Spyder. The two cars were taken to sportscar racing tracks across the country to test reaction. The Monte Carlo had a Latham supercharged four-cylinder engine, cut-down windshield, head rests for both driver and passenger, and mag wheels. The car survives in the San Antonio Museum of Transportation.

1962 Grand Prix X-400. There was no production Grand Prix convertible for '62 so the X-400 caused quite a stir on the show circuit. Built as a personal car for Bill Mitchell, the engine of the X-400 was again a Latham supercharged unit based on the 421 cid Super Duty engine. Finished in brilliant red, the car was a standout wherever it went.

1963 Grand Prix X-400. The third of the X-400 show cars had a fiberglass hood with scoops, Lathan supercharged engine with four sidedraft Weber carburetors, brushed aluminum rocker panels, rectangular exhaust ports ahead of the rear wheel, special wheels and fiberglass boot. The vertical headlights proved popular at shows. This car survives in the hands of an Arizona collector who is slowly restoring it.

1963 Maharani. Based on a '63 Bonneville convertible, the Maharani's main feature was the special interior. It was created by gluing peacock feathers into patterns to trim the side panels. The pleated leather seats featured a rainbow pattern. The exterior color was a pearlescent turquoise color.

1964 GM-X. Billed as the "sports car of the next decade," the GM-X had enough instrumentation to keep a jet pilot busy. There were 21 dials, 29 switches, 30 warning lights and four control levers. It was built for display at the '64 New York World's Fair.

1964 Firebird IV. The Firebird IV, on display at the '64 New York World's Fair, had a silver "Fire-Frost" body and an all-silver interior. It was designed for fast cross-country trips on automatic highways. An electronic screen provided the driver with a clear view of road/traffic conditions behind his car. The screen also received television programs when the car was on automatic operation. Additional features included a stereo, game table and refrigerator. A narrow light bar served as the Firebird's single headlight.

1964 Runabout. The third GM dream car built for exhibit at the '64 New York World's Fair was this unusual little "Runabout." The Runabout had a single front wheel which could be turned 180 degrees. This allowed it to be parallel parked in one backward and one sideways movement. A lock-out device limited the wheel's turning span in normal driving. Instead of a steering wheel the Runabout was controlled by two linked hand controls. Included in the Runabout's design were two built-in shopping carts. Both the interior and exterior were finished in blue.

1965 Banshee coupe. One of the styling exercises built on the way to the first production Firebird. This car has Opel GT-like headlights and a Corvette-like kickup on the rear door.

1967 Bonneville Le Grand Conchiche. Basically a two-door limousine, the Le Grand was as impractical as it was poorly timed. Built at the height of the muscle car era, the car would have been more in step with the previous decade. The chauffeur's compartment had bucket seats. There was no top provided for the car.

1969 Fiero. Fiero means "fierce," and this Pontiac show car lived up to its name. The racing influence is shown by the two headrests for driver and passenger. GM had finally started producing dream cars that were more realistic than some of the earlier types. The Fiero was billed as the Firebird of tomorrow. It had a 400 cid HO Pontiac V-8 engine and was designed with aerodynamics in mind.

1969 Cirrus. If you see a vague similarity between the '69 Cirrus and the '64 GM-X, congratulations. You've spotted what Pontiac did to come up with a show car for '69. The engine was the 400 HO Pontiac V-8. (Pontiac photo courtesy of Robert Ackerson)

1971 "Firearri." Bill Mitchell was sports car enthusiast of the first degree. Many of his styling exercises are very sports car-oriented (Monza GT/SS/Stingray/Pontiac Monte Carlo, etc.). This Mitchell-designed car has a Ferrari V-12 racing engine along with its very obvious Ferrari-like snout. Needless to say, the car was not exhibited publicly.

1973 Phantom. Bill Mitchell wanted to leave at General Motors a memory of the cars that he loved. The Phantom was the result. Mitchell styled his Phantom with a long hood, V-type windshield ('30s style), modern headlights, flush windows, and front wheel drive. (Pontiac photo)

1974 Banshee III. This John Schinella-designed show car was built on a '74 Firebird chassis. The side windows were fixed, but a small flip-out window was provided for toll booths. The engine was the Super-Duty 455 cid LS-2. The car was painted a metallic maroon with red leather interior.

196? Scorpian. The Scorpian was the platform that John Z. DeLorean (then general manager of Pontiac Motor Div.) used to build the Banshee XP-833.

NEW GENERATION OF PONTIAC CONCEPT CARS

Pontiac Banshee concept car.

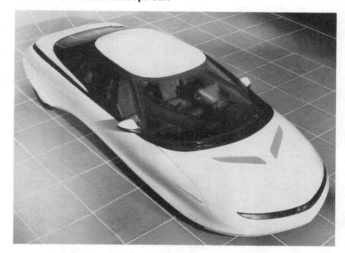

1987 Pontiac Pursuit concept car.

1992 Pontiac Salsa concept car -- convertible module with rear seat folded forward.

1994 Pontiac Sunfire concept car.

OAKLAND/PONTIAC CARS BUILT DATA THROUGH 1972

The following information was compiled from the car building tags in the Past Records Department, together with some data received from the Material Record Department. In one instance the first car built does not carry the first serial number due to various delays of the #1 car in production.

The total cars built include the assembly plants and export.

The serial numbers are for Pontiac production.

In the case of Linden and California the numbers start with 1001 but have the prefix "C" for California and "L" for Linden, instead of "P" for Pontiac (through 1942)

Canadian production is included in totals in cases where our serial numbers were used by them.

YEAR	MAKE	MODEL	NAME	WHEELBASE	CAR SERIAL NUMBERS	STARTED PRODUCTION	FINISHED PRODUCTION	CARS BUILT	TOTAL BUILT
1918 1919	Oak. 6	34-B			30001-34 to 116440	Sept. 1917	6-1-20	86,439	86,439
1920	Oak. 6	34-C			11701-34 to 152356	Jan. 1920	1-6-21	35,356	35,356
1921	Oak. 6	34-C			152357-34 to 159700	Jan. 1921	7-27-21	5,444	5,444
1922	Oak. 6	34-C			159701-34 to 167550	Aug. 1921	Approx. 12-31-21	7,849	49,001
1922	Oak. 6	6-44			1-44 to 41152	Jan. 1922	Approx. 6-15-23	41,152	
1923									
1924	Oak. 6	6-54A			1054 to 37080	Aug. 1923	7-29-24	37,080	37,080
1925	Oak. 6	6-54B			37110-54 to 64523	7-17-24	5-29-25	27,423	27,423
1926	Oak. 6	6-54C	0/6		64601-54 to 120714	7-2-25	6-17-26	58,827	58,827
1927	Oak. 6	6-54D	CO/6	113"	120801-54 to 167943	6-7-26	5-24-27	44,658	44,658
1926	Pont. 6	6-27		110"	P-1 to 202100	12-28-25	10-31-27	204,553	204,553

Start of "Pontiac" Car 1926. Built were 6-27 1st Edition. 1927 Built were 6-27 2nd Edition

YEAR	MAKE	MODEL	NAME	WHEELBASE	CAR SERIAL NUMBERS	STARTED PRODUCTION	FINISHED PRODUCTION	CARS BUILT	TOTAL BUILT
1928	Oak. 6	6-212	AA6	117"	170001-AAS to 226438	6-2-27	6-25-28	60,121	

212 Cu. In. Engine - All American 6, 1st Edition

1928	Pont. 6	6-28		110"	P-204001 to 408894	12-7-27	11-3-28	224,784	284,905
1929	Oak. 6	6-212	AA6	117"	227001-AAS to 272642	9-24-28	10-9-29	50,693	

228 Cu. In. Engine - All American 6, 2nd Edition

1929	Pont. 6	6-29		110"	P-410101 to 590498	12-28-28	10-31-29	200,503	251,196
1930	Oak. V-8	101	V-8	117"	273501 to 295245	11-23-29	9-25-30	21,943	
1930	Pont. 6	6-30		110"	P-591501 to 648004	12-14-29	9-26-30	62,888	84,831
1931	Oak. V-8	301	V-8	117"	296001 to 309415	12-15-30	10-8-31	13,408	

Last Model with "Oakland" Name

1931	Pont. 6	401		112"	P-649001 to 728006	11-9-30	10-9-31	84,708	98,116

Engine with Tapered Valve Guides

1932	Pont. V-8	302	V-8	117"	P8-310001 to 316282	12-22-31	3-22-32	6,281	

Free Wheeling and Ride Control

1932	Pont. 6	402		114"	P6-729001 to 763983	12-8-31	8-23-32	39,059	45,340
1933	Pont. 8	601	Str. 8	115"	P8-770001 to 838455	12-7-32	10-6-33	90,198	90,198

Torque Tube Drive - Built In Trunk - Chevrolet Brakes - Dash Starter Button

YEAR	MAKE	MODEL	NAME	WHEELBASE	CAR SERIAL NUMBERS	STARTED PRODUCTION	FINISHED PRODUCTION	CARS BUILT	TOTAL BUILT
1934	Pont. 8	603	Str. 8	117-1/4"	P8-838501 to 908952	12-21-33	9-11-34	78,859	78,959
Dubonnet Front Susp. - Bendix Brakes - Accel. Pedal Starter Switch									
1935	Pont. 6	701-A	Deluxe 6	112"	P6AA-1001 to 32187	11-28-34	7-31-35	36,032	
Dubonnet Front Susp. on 701A & 605, I-Beam Front Susp. on 7013 - Spare Wheel & Tire in Rear Compartment - Hydraulic Brakes, Dual W/S Wiper. Front door hinged at center pillar.									
1935	Pont. 6	701B	Master 6	112"	P6AB-1001 to 46572	1-2-35	7-31-35	49,302	
1935	Pont. 8	605	Deluxe 8	116-5/8"	P8AA-1001 to 42561	11-30-34	7-31-35	44,134	129,463
1936	Pont. 6	36-26A	Deluxe 6	112"	P6BA-1001 to 41352	9-16-35	8-4-36	44,040	
I-Beam Front Susp.									
1936	Pont. 6	36-26B	Master 6	112"	P6BB-1001 to 91362	913-35	8-4-36	93,475	
Dubonnet Front Susp.									
1936	Pont. 8	36-28	Deluxe 8	116-5/8"	P8BA-1001 to 38371	9-11-35	7-31-36	36,755	176,270
1937	Pont. 8	37-26	Deluxe 6	117"	P6CA-1001 to 154827	9-28-36	8-17-37	179,244	
SLA Front Susp. - Two Prop. Shafts - Direct Acting Rear Shocks									
1937	Pont. 8	37-28	Deluxe 8	122"	P8CA-1001 to 49442	10-8-36	8-20-37	56,945	236,189
1938	Pont. 6	38-26		117"	P6DA-1001 to 60416	9-8-37	7-15-38	77,713	
SLA Front Susp. - Strg. Column Gearshift Spec. Eqpt.									
1938	Pont. 8	38-28	Deluxe 8	122"	P8DA-1001 to 15729	9-15-37	7-15-38	19,426	97,139
1939	Pont. 6	39-25	Quality 6	114-11/16"	P6EA-1001 to 43679	9-19-38	6-20-39	55,736	
SLA Front Susp. - Strg. Column Gearshift Standard. Hypoid Axle - No Plain Back Sedans - Body Splash Apron instead of R/S available on 26 & 28. Spare tire upright in rear compartment on all-(Dual Taillamps, Dual Horns, Ashtray, Cigar Lighter are Std. on 28)									
1939	Pont. 6	39-26	Deluxe 6	120-1/4"	P6EB-1001 to 41263	9-8-38	6-20-39	53,830	
1939	Pont. 8	39-28	Deluxe 8	120-1/4"	P6EA-1001 to 27627	9-14-38	6-20-39	34,774	144,340
1940	Pont. 6	40-25	Spec. 6	116-1/2"	P6HA-1001 to 84545	10-9-39	7-3-40	106-982	
Dual Carb. on 49-29. Built in Radio Speaker Grille in instrument panel. Sealed Beam Head Lamps. Dual Horns & Taillamps on all. Dual Carb. avail. on 49-29. Underseat Heater. Dual Sun Visors, Ashtray.									
1940	Pont. 6	40-26	Deluxe 6	120-1/4"	P6HB-1001 to 44296	8-21-39	7-3-40	58,452	
1940	Pont. 8	40-28	Deluxe 8	120-1/4"	P8HA-1001 to 16817	8-21-39	7-3-40	20,433	
1940	Pont. 8	40-29	Torpedo 8	121-1/2"	P8HB-1001 to 24376	9-15-39	7-3-40	31,224	217,001
1941	Pont. 6	41-24	Custom 6	"C" Body 122"	P6JC-1001 to 6345	8-6-40	7-30-41	8,257	
Dual Carb. Std. on all 8-Cyl. "B" Series also have super streamliner models. "A" & "C" Models still have hump on deck door. "B" Models are plain back. Built in splash apron between bumper & Chassis - All cars less runningboard except in Opt. on "C" Series built in oil cleaner standard-cigar lighter.									
1941	Pont. 6	41-25	Deluxe 6	"A" Body 118-13/16"	P6JA-1001 to 80460	9-9-40	7-30-41	117,976	
1941	Pont. 6	41-26	Streamliner 6	"B" Body 122"	P6JB-1001 to 62545	8-1-40	7-30-41	82,527	
1941	Pont. 8	41-27	Deluxe 8	"A" Body 118-13/16"	P8JA-1001 to 27215	9-10-40	7-30-41	37,823	
1941	Pont. 8	41-28	Streamliner 8	"B" Body 122"	P8JB-1001 to 52428	8-1-40	7-30-41	66,287	
1941	Pont. 8	41-29	Custom 8	"C" Body 122"	P8JC-1001 to 12572	8-6-40	7-30-41	17,191	330,061
1942	Pont. 6	42-25	Torpedo 6	"A" Body 188-13/16"	P6KA-1001 to 25802	8-25-41	2-2-42	29,886	
About same as 1941)"B" Series had Chieftain Model until Dec. 15, 1941, when chrome & stainless were changed to paint on most all parts due to material shortage during World War II. All car production was discontinued in February 1942, for the duration of the war.									
1942	Pont. 6	42-26	Streamliner 6	"B" Body 122"	P6KB-1001 to 11115	8-25-41	2-10-42	*12,742	
1942	Pont. 8	42-27	Torpedo 8	"A" Body 118-13/16"	P8KA-1001 to 13146	8-25-41	2-2-42	14,421	
1942	Pont. 8	42-28	Streamliner 8	"B" Body 122"	P8KB-1001 to 22928	9-25-41	2-2-42	**26,506	83,555

*Includes 2,458 Chieftains

**Includes 11,041 Chieftains

277

Due to World War II production was not resumed until 1946 model.

*Cars built at B O P Assembly Plants have serial numbers starting with 1001 same as at Pontiac Plant except the letter "P" changes to "C" South Gate, California, "L" Linden, New Jersey, "W" Wilmington, Delaware, "K" Kansas City, Kansas, "A" Doraville, Georgia, "F" Framingham, Massachusetts.

YEAR	MAKE	MODEL	NAME	WHEELBASE	*CAR SERIAL NUMBER	STARTED PRODUCTION	FINISHED PROD. PONTIAC PLANT	CARS BUILT	TOTAL BUILT
1946	Pont. 6	46-25	Torpedo 6	118-13/16" "A" Body	P6LA-1001 up	6-10-46	12-30-46	26,636	

First Model after World War II, same general lines as 1942 - Grille redesigned, chrome moldings on "B" fenders.

YEAR	MAKE	MODEL	NAME	WHEELBASE	*CAR SERIAL NUMBER	STARTED PRODUCTION	FINISHED PROD. PONTIAC PLANT	CARS BUILT	TOTAL BUILT
1946	Pont. 8	46-27	Torpedo 8	118-13/16" "A" Body	P8LA-1001 up	6-10-46	12-30-46	18,273	
1946	Pont. 6	46-26	Streamliner 6	122" "B" Body	P6LB-1001 up	9-13-45	12-30-46	43,430	
1946	Pont. 8	46-28	Streamliner 8	122" "B" Body	P8LB-1001 up	9-13-45	12-30-46	49,301	137,640
1947	Pont. 6	47-25	Torpedo 6	118-13/16"	P6MA-1001 up	12-30-46	1-9-48	67,125	

Same general lines as 1946 - no chrome moldings on fenders - Grille has horizontal bars only.

YEAR	MAKE	MODEL	NAME	WHEELBASE	*CAR SERIAL NUMBER	STARTED PRODUCTION	FINISHED PROD. PONTIAC PLANT	CARS BUILT	TOTAL BUILT
1947	Pont. 8	47-27	Torpedo 8	118-13/16"		12-19-46	1-9-48	34,815	
1947	Pont. 6	47-26	Streamliner 6	122"	P6MB-1001 up	12-30-46	1-9-48	42,336	
1947	Pont. 8	47-28	Streamliner 8	122"	P8MB-1001 up	12-26-46	1-9-48	86,324	230,600

YEAR	MAKE	MODEL	NAME	WHEEL BASE	*CAR SERIAL NUMBER PREFIX #1001 Up		STARTED PRODUCTION	FINISHED PROD. PONTIAC PLANT	CARS BUILT		TOTAL BUILT	GRAND TOTAL BUILT
					SMT	HMT			SMT	HMT		
1948	Pont. 6	48-25	Torpedo 6	118-13/16"	P6PA	P6PA	12-29-47	12-22-48	13,937	25,325	49,262	

"A" Body Same General lines as 1947 - No beads on fenders - Deluxe Models with chrome molding on front fenders introduced - Hydra Matic Trans. - Brown Dinoc Interior.

YEAR	MAKE	MODEL	NAME	WHEEL BASE	SMT	HMT	STARTED PRODUCTION	FINISHED PROD. PONTIAC PLANT	SMT	HMT	TOTAL BUILT	GRAND TOTAL BUILT
1948	Pont. 6	48-26	Streamliner 6	122	P6PB	P6PB	1-9-48	12-22-48	13,834	23,858	37,742	
("B" Body Model)												
1948	Pont. 8	48-27	Torpedo 8	118-13/16"	P8PA	P8PA	1-6-48	12-22-48	11,006	24,294	35,360	
("A" Body Model)												
1948	Pont. 8	48-28	Streamliner 8	122	P8PB	P8PB	12-22-47	12-22-48	24,464	98,469	123,115	245,419
("B" Body Model)												
1949	Pont. 6	49-25	Chieftain and Streamliner	120	P6RS	P6RH	1-12-49	11-10-49	40,139	29,515	69,654	

"A" Body New Model - Push Button Starter - Rear Fenders part of body - Metal Sta. Wgn. - Air Ride Tires - Body Air Ducts - Direct Acting Front Shocks - Low Water Pump.

YEAR	MAKE	MODEL	NAME	WHEEL BASE	SMT	HMT	STARTED PRODUCTION	FINISHED PROD. PONTIAC PLANT	SMT	HMT	TOTAL BUILT	GRAND TOTAL BUILT
1949	Pont. 8	49-27	Chieftain and Streamliner	120	P8RS	P8RH	1-12-49	11-10-49	40,716	174,449	235,165	304,819
1950	Pont. 6	50-25	Chieftain and Streamliner	120	P6TS	P6TH	11-10-49	11-17-50	90,412	24,930	115,542	

Catalina Body introduced - 8 Cylinder Bore increased - 1949 Body with revisions - Comb. Fuel and Vacuum Pump made Standard on 6 Cylinder - Dash Type Heater added - Carbon Core ignition wires.

YEAR	MAKE	MODEL	NAME	WHEEL BASE	SMT	HMT	STARTED PRODUCTION	FINISHED PROD. PONTIAC PLANT	SMT	HMT	TOTAL BUILT	GRAND TOTAL BUILT
1950	Pont. 8	50-27	Chieftain and Streamliner	120	P8TS	P8TH	11-19-49	11-17-40	67,699	263,188	330,887	446,429
1951	Pont. 6	51-25	Chieftain and Streamliner	120	P6US	P6UH	11-27-50	11-19-51	43,553	10,195	53,748	

Same General Lines as 1950 - 6 Cylinder timing chain bumper - Rochester Carburetor - Generator from 35 to 40 amps - Speedo. Driven Gear integral with main shaft on HM Trans. - 7-lb. Radiator Cap - Chrome with clear paint - End of Streamliners May 1951.

YEAR	MAKE	MODEL	NAME	WHEEL BASE	SMT	HMT	STARTED PRODUCTION	FINISHED PROD. PONTIAC PLANT	SMT	HMT	TOTAL BUILT	GRAND TOTAL BUILT
1951	Pont. 8	51-27	Chieftain and Streamliner	120	P8US	P8UH	11-27-50	11-19-51	64,424	251,987	316,411	370,159
1952	Pont. 6	52-25	Chieftain	120	P6WS	P6WH	11-2-51	11-7-52	15,582	4,227	19,809	

Same General Lines as 1951 - Deluxe Models trimmed in three colors - Dual Range HMT - High Comp. Heads for HMT - one-piece die-cast hood ornament - Piston Pin Lock Rings - Nylon Speedometer Gears.

YEAR	MAKE	MODEL	NAME	WHEEL BASE	SMT	HMT	STARTED PRODUCTION	FINISHED PROD. PONTIAC PLANT	SMT	HMT	TOTAL BUILT	GRAND TOTAL BUILT
1952	Pont. 8	52-27	Chieftain	120	P8WS	P8WH	11-2-51	11-7-52	32,962	218,602	251,564	271,373

YEAR	MAKE	MODEL	NAME	WHEEL BASE	SMT	HMT	STARTED PRODUCTION	FINISHED PROD. PONTIAC PLANT	CARS BUILT SMT	CARS BUILT HMT	TOTAL BUILT	GRAND TOTAL BUILT
1953	Pont. 6	53-25	Chieftain	122	P6XS	P8XH	11-17-52	11-20-53	33,705	4,507 @702	38,914	
	Pont. 8	53-27	Chieftain	122	P8XS	P8WH	11-17-52	11-20-53	68,565	293,343 @17,797	379,705	418,619

New Model - 6 and 8 Cyl. Dip Stick moved back - 6 Cyl. Fuel Pump moved back - Concentric Gearshifts - Serial # Plates welded - Wraparound back window - one-piece curved W/S - Starter switch integral with Ign. Lock - Power Steering and Autronic Eye Spec. Eqpt.

YEAR	MAKE	MODEL	NAME	WHEEL BASE	SMT	HMT	STARTED PRODUCTION	FINISHED PROD. PONTIAC PLANT	CARS BUILT SMT	CARS BUILT HMT	TOTAL BUILT	GRAND TOTAL BUILT
1954	Pont. 6	54-25	Chieftain	122	P6ZS	P6ZH	12-1-53	9-3-54	19,666	3,004	22,670	
	Pont. 8	54-27	Chieftain	122	P8ZS	P8ZH	12-1-53	9-3-54	29,906	120,000	149,986	
	Pont. 8	54-28	Star Chief	124	P82C	P8ZA	12-1-53	9-3-54	571	114,517	115,888	287,744

Same General Lines as 1953. 124" Wheelbase(11" extended deck; 28 Model introduced. Nickel Chrome reinstated. Power Brakes and Air Conditioner Special Equipment.

@ Cars equipped with Powerglide Transmission due to fire at Detroit Transmission Division.

*Prefix shown is for cars built at Pontiac Plat.- B O P Assembly Plant cars are the same except the letter "P" is changed to: C - South Gate, California, W - Wilmington Delaware, A- Doraville, Georgia, T- Arlington, Texas, L - Lincoln, New Jersey, K - Kansas City, Kansas, F - Framingham, Massachusetts.

YEAR	MAKE	MODEL	NAME	WHEEL BASE	SMT	HMT	STARTED PRODUCTION	FINISHED PROD. PONTIAC PLANT	CARS BUILT SMT	CARS BUILT HMT	TOTAL BUILT	GRAND TOTAL BUILT
1955	Pont. V-6	55-27	Chieftain	122	P755S	P755H	10-4-54	9-16-55	57,730	296,736	54,466	
	Pont. V-8	55-28	Star Chief	124	P855S	P855H			1,156	198,468	199,624	354,090

New Model - V-8 Engine - No Silver Streak on Deck Lid. - No Spring Covers - 12-Volt Electrical System - Wraparound Windshield.

YEAR	MAKE	MODEL	NAME	WHEEL BASE	SMT	HMT	STARTED PRODUCTION	FINISHED PROD. PONTIAC PLANT	CARS BUILT SMT	CARS BUILT HMT	TOTAL BUILT	GRAND TOTAL BUILT
1956	Pont. V-6	56-27	Chieftain	122	P756S	P756H	10-3-55	10-3-56	24,117	160,115	184,232	
	Pont. V-8	56-27	Super Chief	122	P756S	P756H			3,289	90,563	93,872	
	Pont. V-8	56-27	Star Chief / Station Wagon	122	P756S	P755H			10	4,032	4,042	
	Pont. V-8	56-28	Star Chief	124	P856S	P856H			440	123,144	123,554	405,730

Same General Lines as 1955 - New C/C HMT, four-door Catalina Sedan introduced on all three Series. Electric W/S Wiper Spec. Eqpt. - Extra Horsepower Engine.

YEAR	MAKE	MODEL	NAME	WHEEL BASE	SMT	HMT	STARTED PRODUCTION	FINISHED PROD. PONTIAC PLANT	CARS BUILT SMT	CARS BUILT HMT	TOTAL BUILT	GRAND TOTAL BUILT
1957	Pont. V-6	57-27	Chieftain	122	P7575S	P757H	10-17-56	9-13-57	12,267	149,708	162,574	
	Pont. V-8	57-27	Super Chief	122	P757S	P7575H			1,063	63,629	(64,692)	
	Pont. V-8	57-27	Star Chief / Station Wagon	122	P757S	P757H			4	3,182	3,186	
	Pont. V-8	57-27	Star Chief	124	P857S	P857H			309	103,279	103,588	334,041

New Look. Removed Hood Center Grilles - First Fuel Injection - Dual Exhaust Openings in Dumper Spec. Eqpt. - 347 Cu. In. Engine. Last Year for U/S Heater - Last Year for RHD.

YEAR	MAKE	MODEL	NAME	WHEEL BASE	SMT	HMT	STARTED PRODUCTION	FINISHED PROD. PONTIAC PLANT	CARS BUILT SMT	CARS BUILT HMT	TOTAL BUILT	GRAND TOTAL BUILT
1958	Pont. V-6	58-25	Chieftain	122	P558S	P558H	10-14-57	7-31-58	210	19,389	19,599	
	Pont. V-8	58-27	Bonneville / Chieftain / Super Chief / Station Wagon	122	P558S / P758S / P758S	P558H / P758H / P758H			6,943	117,742	124,685	
	Pont. V-8	58-28	Super Chief / Star Chief	124	P858S / P858S	P858H / P858H			258	72,761	73,019	217,303

Rubber Harmonic Balancer Weight. 370 Cu. In. Engine. Four Head Lamps & four Taillamps - suspended Brake & Clutch Pedals - Coil Springs Front & Rear - "X" Frame - Recessed Floor - No Fins. Air Suspension - Special Eqpt. Borg Warner SM Trans. Spec. Eqpt. Locking Differential Spec. Eqpt.

YEAR	MAKE	MODEL	NAME	WHEEL BASE	SMT	HMT	STARTED PRODUCTION	FINISHED PROD. PONTIAC PLANT	CARS BUILT SMT	CARS BUILT HMT	TOTAL BUILT	GRAND TOTAL BUILT
1959	Pont. V-6	59-21	Catalina	122	159P		9-1-58	8-18-59	9,939	221,622	231,561	
	Pont. V-8	59-24	Star Chief	124	459P				333	68,482	68,815	
	Pont. V-8	59-27	Bonneville	122	759P				16	4,657	4,673	
	Pont. V-8	59-28	Bonneville	124	859P				675	77,596	78,271	383,320

389 Cu. In. Engine. Flexible Brake Shoes, Acrylic Lacquer All Jobs. V Tailfins, Fuel Filler Door in Rear - Discontinued Air Suspension. Wide Track Wheels. Overlap W/S Wipers. Heater Floor Ducts. Economy Engine. Flex Coupling Steering Cast for Power Steering.

1960–1961

YEAR	MAKE	MODEL	NAME	WHEEL BASE	CAR SERIAL NUMBER PREFIX #1001 Up SMT	HMT	STARTED PRODUCTION	FINISHED PROD. PONTIAC PLANT	CARS BUILT SMT	HMT	TOTAL BUILT	GRAND TOTAL BUILT
1960	Pont. V-6	60-21	Catalina	122	169P		8-31-59	8-12-60	10,831	200,101	210,934	
	Pont. V-8	60-23	Ventura	122	360P				2,301	53,896	56,277	
	Pont. V-8	60-24	Star Chief	124	440P				166	43,525	43,691	
	Pont. V-8	60-27	Bonneville	122	760P				12	5,151	5,163	
	Pont. V-8	60-28	Bonneville	124	860P				1,111	79,540	80,651	396,716

Ventura Added. Custom 16-1/2" Dia. Strg. Wheel with Hand Grips. Lower Front Floor Tunnel. Wide Track Wheels Continued. Four-Speed SMT Special Order - Perm. Antifreeze Replaced Methanol.

*Prefix shown is for cars built at Pontiac Plant - B O P Assembly Plant cars are the same except the letter "P" is changed. Transmission type not identified after 1958 (S for SMT and H for HMT after the 8).

YEAR	MAKE	MODEL	NAME	WHEEL BASE	SMT	HMT	STARTED PRODUCTION	FINISHED PROD. PONTIAC PLANT	CARS BUILT SMT	HMT	TOTAL BUILT	GRAND TOTAL BUILT
1961	Pont. V-8	61-23	Catalina	119	361P		9-1-60	7-23-61	6,337	107,017	113,354	
		61-25	Ventura	119	561P				1,940	25,269	27,209	
		61-26	Star Chief	123	661P				130	29,451	29,581	
		61-27	Bonneville (Sta.Wgn.)	119	761P				18	3,305	3,323	
		61-28	Bonneville	123	861P				1,480	64,905	66,385	
			PONTIAC TOTAL						9,905	229,947	239,852	
Tempest 195-(L-4)		61-21	Tempest	112	161P				26,737	72,042	*98,779	
**215 (V-8)		62-21	Tempest	112	161P				3	2,001	*2,004	
			TEMPEST TOTAL						26,740	74,043	100,783	340,635

Wide Track Tread reduced 1-1/2" - Ventura Series discontinued at end of model - Small tailfins added.

New Series - Tempest added 4-Cyl. Eng. Std. & Buick Aluminum V-8 Optional, Body & Frame Integral - Trans. mounted to Differential - Completely new bodies - coordinated with Buick, Oldsmobile & Chevrolet.

** Aluminum Engine made by Buick.
* Includes K.D. Export 480 SMT & 240 Automatic.

1962

YEAR	MAKE	MODEL	NAME	WHEEL BASE	SERIAL NUMBER	STARTED PRODUCTION	FINISHED PRODUCTION	CARS BUILT SMT	AUTO.	TOTAL BUILT	GRAND TOTAL
1962	Pont. V-8	62-23	Catalina	120	362P	8-15-61	8-10-62	13,104	191,550	204,654	
		62-26	Star Chief	123	662P			196	41,446	41,642	
		62-27	Bonneville (Sta.Wgn.)	120	762P			35	4,492	4,527	
		62-28	Bonneville	123	862P			1,874	95,848	97,722	
		62-29	Grand Prix	120	962P			3,639	26,556	30,195	
			PONTIAC TOTAL					18,848	359,892	378,740	
Tempest 195-(L4)		62-21	Tempest	112	162P			28,867	112,668	141,335	
**215 (V-8)		62-21	Tempest	112	162P			86	1,572	1,658	
			TEMPEST TOTAL					28,953	114,240	***143,193	521,933

Grand Prix Series added with Bucket Seats Std. & Special Decor treatment.

LeMans Custom Option added. 4-Cyl Engine standard. 8-Cyl. Alum. Engine (Buick) Optional.

** Aluminum Engine made by Buick.
*** Includes K.D. Export 48-L4 Automatic, SMT, 72-V-8 Automatic.

YEAR	MAKE	MODEL	NAME	WHEEL BASE	SERIAL NUMBER	STARTED PRODUCTION	FINISHED PRODUCTION	CARS BUILT SMT	CARS BUILT AUTO.	TOTAL BUILT	GRAND TOTAL
1963	Pont. V-8	63-23	Catalina (Exc. sta. wag.)	120	361P	9-4-62	8-4-63	16,811	217,738	234,549	
			Catalina sta. wag.	119							
		63-26	Star Chief	123	661P			175	40,582	40,757	
		63-28	Bonneville	123	861P			1,819	108,497	*110,316	
		63-29	Grand Prix	120	961P			5,157	67,802	72,959	
							PONTIAC TOTAL	23,962	434,619	458,581	
	Tempest	63-21	Tempest	112	161T	16,657	53,174	69,831			
		63-22	LeMans	112	261T	18,034	43,625	61,659			
							TEMPEST TOTAL	34,691	96,799	*131,490	590,071

Wide Track increased from 61.1 to 64 - Self adjusting Brakes. Two year Coolant Option. Generator changed to Alternator.

Power Brakes added. 326 V-8 Engine introduced. 4-Cyl Engine Std. last year with Trans. Axle.

* 5,156 were Station Wagons (119" Wheelbase).
** 195-(L4) Engine Standard for 81,280 cars. 326 (V-8) Engine Option for 50,210 cars.

YEAR	MAKE	MODEL	NAME	WHEEL BASE	SERIAL NUMBER	STARTED PRODUCTION	FINISHED PRODUCTION	CARS BUILT SMT	CARS BUILT AUTO.	TOTAL BUILT	GRAND TOTAL
1964 Major Face Lift	Pont. V-8	64-23	Catalina (Exc. sta. wag.)	120	834P	9-3-63	8-2-64	15,194	242,574	257,768	
			Catalina Sta. Wgn.	119							
		64-26	Star Chief	123	864P			132	37,521	37,653	
		64-28	Bonneville	123	884P			1,470	113,590	37,653	
			Bonneville Sta.Wgn.	119	42			5,802	5,844		
		64-29	Grand Prix	120	894P			3,124	60,686	63,810	
							PONTIAC TOTAL	19,962	460,173	480,135	
	Tempest	64-20	Tempest	115	04T			15,029	32,997	48,026	
		64-21	Custom	115	14T			11,663	62,801	*74,464	
		64-22	LeMans	115	24T			43,313	69,323	112,636	
							TEMPEST TOTAL	70,005	165,121	*235,126	715,261

Completely new (Still coordinated with Buick, Chevrolet & Oldsmobile.) - Frame separate with conventional rear axle & suspension & trans. Chevy-type 6-Cyl. engine standard exc. W62 GTO Option has 389 (Pont.) engine standard.

* Includes 480 CKD Units for 64-21.
** Engine Breakdown for Tempest -

215 (6-Cyl)		98,778
326 (V-8)		103,898
389 (V-8 GTO)		32,450
Tempest Engine Total		235,126

* Digit 6 or 8 precedes Car Serial Number to denote 6 or 8 cylinder (8 cylinder is an RPO).

YEAR	MAKE	MODEL	NAME	WHEEL BASE	SERIAL NUMBER	STARTED PRODUCTION	FINISHED PRODUCTION	CARS BUILT SMT	CARS BUILT AUTO.	TOTAL BUILT	GRAND TOTAL
1965	Pont. V-8	65-52	Catalina	121	252	8-24-65	8-19-65	14,817	256,241	*271,058	
			Cata. Sta.Wgn.	121							
		65-56	Star Chief	124	256			97	31,218	31,315	
		65-62	Bonneville	124	262			1,449	133,214	134,663	
			Bonn. Sta.Wgn.	121							
		65-66	Grand Prix	121	266			1,973	55,908	57,881	

Pontiac wheelbase increased 1" except Sta.Wgn. up 2". Articulated overlap W/S Wipers standard.

| | | | **PONTIAC TOTAL** | | | | | 18,336 | 476,581 | 494,917 | |

* Includes 11,521 WS1 (2 + 2) Option - 5,316 Manual & 6,205 Automatic.

				WHEEL BASE	SERIAL NUMBER			SMT	AUTO.	TOTAL BUILT	GRAND TOTAL
	Tempest	65-33	Standard	115	233			9,255	30,270	39,525	
		65-35	Custom	115	235			10,630	74,023	84,653	
		65-37	LeMans	115	237			75,756	107,149	**182,905	

Tempest Face Lift with vertical head lamps added. Two-door HT Cpe. & Four-door Sedan added.

| | | | **TEMPEST TOTAL** | | | | | 95,641 | 211,442 | 307,083 | 802,000 |

** Includes W62 GTO Option - 56,378 Manual & 18,974 Automatic = 75,342.
768 KD Export, included in totals, (35 Series = 648, 37 Series = 120)

YEAR	MAKE	MODEL	NAME	WHEEL BASE	SERIAL NUMBER	STARTED PRODUCTION	FINISHED PRODUCTION	SMT	AUTO.	TOTAL BUILT	GRAND TOTAL
1966	Pontiac	66-52	Catalina	121	252	9-13-65	8-3-66	5,003	242,924	247,927	
			Catalina Sta.Wgn.	119							
		66-54	2 + 2	121	254			2,208	4,175	6,383	
		66-56	Star Chief	124	256			134	45,078	45,212	
			Executive								
		66-62	Bonneville	124	262			729	135,225	135,954	
		66-66	Grand Prix	121	266			917	35,840	36,757	

Pontiac has full plastic floating grille. An industry first. Sta.Wgn. with Wood Grain appearance to side added to Executive. Conv. added to Grand Prix.

| | | | **PONTIAC TOTAL** | | | | | 8,991 | 463,242 | 472,233 | |

				WHEEL BASE	SERIAL NUMBER			SMT	AUTO.	TOTAL BUILT	GRAND TOTAL
	Tempest	66-33	Standard	115	233			10,610	33,143	43,753	
		66-35	Custom	115	235			13,566	83,093	*96,659	
		66-37	LeMans	115	237			22,862	98,878	*121,740	
		66-42	GTO	115	242			61,279	35,667	96,946	

Tempest rear tread up 1" to 59". Face lift. Wood appearance on side of Station Wagon added as a body style.

| | | | **TEMPEST TOTAL** | | | | | 108,317 | 250,781 | 359,098 | 831,331 |

* Includes 624 KD Export (35 Series 240, 37 Series 384).
** Body Style Code # and year added to VIN for complete identification.

YEAR	MAKE	MODEL	NAME	WHEEL BASE	SERIAL NUMBER	STARTED PRODUCTION	FINISHED PRODUCTION	CARS BUILT SMT	CARS BUILT AUTO.	TOTAL BUILT	GRAND TOTAL
1967	Pontiac V-8	67-52	Catalina	121	252	8-29-66	7-30-67	3,653	207,752	211,405	

Pontiac first in 1967. Recessed Park W/S Wiper Blades. Star Chief renamed "Executive". Wood Grained Sta. Wgns. added. Grand Prix has concealed head lamps. 389 & 421 Cu. In. Engines increased to 400 & 428 Cu. In. Cornering Lamps introduced.

YEAR	MAKE	MODEL	NAME	WHEEL BASE	SERIAL NUMBER	STARTED PRODUCTION	FINISHED PRODUCTION	CARS BUILT SMT	CARS BUILT AUTO.	TOTAL BUILT	GRAND TOTAL
			Cata. S. Wgn.	121				423	28,922	29,345	
		67-56	Executive	124	256			84	35,407	35,491	
		67-62	Bonneville	124	262			278	96,430	96,708	
		67-66	Grand Prix	121	266			760	42,221	42,981	
		67-56	Executive Sta.Wgn.	121	256			38	11,458	11,496	
		67-56	Bonneville Sta.Wgn.	121	262			29	6,742	6,771	
			PONTIAC TOTAL					5,265	428,932	434,197	
Tempest		67-33	Standard	115	233			7,154	27,455	34,609	

New Safari Wagon with Wood Grain Exterior. GT 400 Engine on GTO. New styling for improved appearance. New Options include Capacitor Discharge System & Cruise Control located in Turn Signal Lever.

YEAR	MAKE	MODEL	NAME	WHEEL BASE	SERIAL NUMBER	STARTED PRODUCTION	FINISHED PRODUCTION	CARS BUILT SMT	CARS BUILT AUTO.	TOTAL BUILT	GRAND TOTAL
		67-35	Custom	115	235			8,302	67,023	75,325	
		67-37	LeMans	115	237			14,770	90,132	104,902	
		67-39	Safari	115	239			129	4,382	4,511	
		67-42	GTO	115	242			39,128	42,594	81,722	
			TEMPEST TOTAL					69,483	231,586	301,069	
1967	Firebird	67-23	Std. 6 Cyl.	108	223			5,258	5,597	10,855	

New Series, 6 Cyl. Standard. 8 Cylinder & Deluxe models merchandised as an R.P.O.

YEAR	MAKE	MODEL	NAME	WHEEL BASE	SERIAL NUMBER	STARTED PRODUCTION	FINISHED PRODUCTION	CARS BUILT SMT	CARS BUILT AUTO.	TOTAL BUILT	GRAND TOTAL
		67-24	Dlx.8 Cyl.	108	223			8,224	15,301	23,525	
		67-25	Dlx.6 Cyl.	108	223			2,963	3,846	6,809	
		67-26	Dlx.6 Cyl.	108	113			11,526	29,845	41,371	
			FIREBIRD TOTAL					27,971	54,589	82,560	817,826
1968	Pontiac V-8	68-52	Catalina	121	252	**8-21-67	**8-5-68	2,257	238,714	240,971	

First year for MVSS. Energy Absorbing Steering Column and Inst. Panel, All Series. Electric Side Marker Lamp. Uniform Shift Quadrant (A.T.) Anti-Theft Features - Ignition Key Buzzer Reminder - Visible V.I. Plate. Concealed Head Lamps Std. on G.P.

YEAR	MAKE	MODEL	NAME	WHEEL BASE	SERIAL NUMBER	STARTED PRODUCTION	FINISHED PRODUCTION	CARS BUILT SMT	CARS BUILT AUTO.	TOTAL BUILT	GRAND TOTAL
			Sta.Wgn.	121				289	34,922	35,211	
		68-56	Executive	124	256			47	32,550	32,597	
		68-62	Bonneville	124	262			208	97,797	98,005	
		68-66	Grand Prix	121	266			306	31,405	31,711	
		68-56	Executive Sta.Wgn.	121	256			23	12,015	12,038	
		68-62	Bonneville Sta.Wgn.	121	262			9	6,917	6,926	
			PONTIAC TOTAL					3,139	454,320	457,459	
Tempest		68-33	Standard	*	233			5,876	25,705	31,581	

Concealed W/S Wipers added on Tempest. Concealed Head Lamp Opt. on GTO. Many added safety features. GTO Industry First, Endura Bumper.

YEAR	MAKE	MODEL	NAME	WHEEL BASE	SERIAL NUMBER	STARTED PRODUCTION	FINISHED PRODUCTION	CARS BUILT SMT	CARS BUILT AUTO.	TOTAL BUILT	GRAND TOTAL
		68-35	Custom	*	235			6,141	80,289	86,430	
		68-37	LeMans	*	237			12,223	124,074	136,297	
		68-39	Safari	*	239			122	4,292	4,414	
		68-42	GTO	112	242			36,299	51,385	87,684	
			TEMPEST TOTAL					60,661	285,745	346,406	

YEAR	MAKE	MODEL	NAME	WHEEL BASE	VEHICLE IDENTIF. NUMBER	STARTED PRODUCTION	FINISHED PRODUCTION	CARS BUILT MANUAL	CARS BUILT AUTO.	TOTAL BUILT	GRAND TOTAL
	Firebird	68-23	Std. 6 Cyl.	108	223			7,528	8,441	15,969	
		68-24	Std. 8 Cyl.	108	224			16,632	39,250	55,882	
		68-25	Dlx.6 Cyl.	108	225			7,534	25,202	32,736	
			FIREBIRD TOTAL					32,910	74,202	107,112	910,977
1969	Pontiac V-8	69-52	Catalina	121	252	8-26-68	7-16-69	837	212,014	212,851	
			Catalina Sta.Wgn.	121				170	33,575	33,745	
		69-56	Executive	124	256			25	25,820	25,845	
		69-62	Bonneville	124	262			44	89,290	89,334	
		69-56	Executive Sta.Wgn.	121	256			14	13,202	13,216	
		69-62	Bonneville Sta.Wgn.	121	262			7	7,421	7,428	
			PONTIAC TOTAL					1,097	381,322	382,419	
	Tempest	69-33	Standard	*	233			4,450	22,472	26,922	
		69-35	Custom	*	235			4,045	80,545	84,590	
		69-37	LeMans	*	237			6,303	93,698	100,001	
		69-39	Safari	*	239			86	4,029	4,115	
		69-42	GTO	112	242			31,433	40,854	72,287	
		69-76	Grand Prix	118	276			1,014	111,472	112,486	
			TEMPEST TOTAL					47,331	353,070	400,401	
	Firebird	69-23	Standard	108	223			20,840	66,868	87,708	
			FIREBIRD TOTAL							87,708	870,528

Front door vent windows eliminated. New Mon-Jet Carb. Auto. Hood adjustment on closing. New Upper Level Ventilation.

* Two-door Coupes Wheelbase 112", Four-door Sedans & Station Wagons 116".
** Assembly Plants (Plant #8 at Pontiac - Started 8-22-67 - Finished 7-26-68)

Percent Pontiac Series Manual Trans. 0.686
Percent Tempest Series Manual Trans. 17.51
Percent Firebird Series Manual Trans. 30.72

Head Restraints Standard on all Series - Split Front Bumper with Endura Center Section - Column Mounted Ignition Lock - Upper Level Ventilation - Dual Hinged Tailgate.

Vent Windows removed on Coupes and Conv. - Dual Hinged Tailgate.

Grand Prix - Industry First, W/S Imbedded Radio Antenna - Wheelbase changed from 121" to 118" to give a personal car look - Recessed inside Door Releases a General Motors exclusive.

Merchandised as Firebird, Firebird Sprint, Firebird 350, and Firebird 400.

* Two-door Coupes Wheelbase 112", Four-door Sedans & Station Wagons 116".

Percent Pontiac Series Manual Trans. 0.286
Percent Tempest Series Manual Trans. 11.820
Percent Firebird Series Manual Trans. 23.760

YEAR	MAKE	MODEL	NAME	WHEEL BASE	VEHICLE IDENTIF. NUMBER	STARTED PRODUCTION	FINISHED PRODUCTION	CARS BUILT MANUAL	CARS BUILT AUTO.	TOTAL BUILT	GRAND TOTAL
1970	Pontiac V-8	70-52	Catalina	121	252	8-11-69	7-16-70	579	193,407	193,986	
W/S imbedded antenna added to all series as standard. Fiberglass Belted Tires Standard on all lines. Headlamp Delay, Rotary I.P. Glovebox Lock on all lines.											
			Catalina Sta.Wgn.	121	113			29,281	29,394		
		70-56	Executive	124	256			6	21,930	21,936	
		70-62	Bonneville	124	262			28	75,320	75,348	
		70-56	Executive Sta.Wgn.	121	256			8	10,482	10,490	
		70-62	Bonneville Sta.Wgn.	121	262			6	7,027	7,033	
			PONTIAC TOTAL					740	337,447	338,187	
1970	Tempest	70-33	Standard	*	233			5,148	36,899	42,047	
Side Markers with Reflectors added to all lines as standard. Electrically Operated Power Door Locks. Silent Rear Window Defroster. Body Colored O/S Rear View Mirror.											
		70-35	Custom	*	235			2,315	81,937	84,252	
		70-37	LeMans	*	237			3,413	68,766	72,179	
		70-42	GTO	112	242			16,033	24,116	40,149	
		70-76	Grand Prix	118	276			500	65,250	65,750	
			TEMPEST TOTAL					27,409	276,968	304,377	
	Firebird	70-23	Firebird	108	223			2,899	15,975	18,874	
Flush Design O/S Door Handles and "Lock and Slam" Type Door Locks added standard. 250 Engine made standard. Merchandised as Models but designed as 223 with Optional Engines.											
		70-24	Esprit	108	224			2,104	16,857	18,961	
		70-26	Formula	108	226			2,777	4,931	7,708	
		70-28	Trans Am	108	228			1,828	1,368	3,196	
			FIREBIRD TOTAL					9,608	39,131	48,739	691,303

* Two-door coupes Wheelbase 112", four-door Sedans & Station Wagons 116".

Percent Pontiac Series Manual Trans. 0.218
Percent Tempest Series Manual Trans. 9.005
Percent Firebird Series Manual Trans. 19.713

YEAR	MAKE	MODEL	NAME	WHEEL BASE	VEHICLE IDENTIF. NUMBER	STARTED PRODUCTION	FINISHED PRODUCTION	CARS BUILT MANUAL	CARS BUILT AUTO.	TOTAL BUILT	GRAND TOTAL
1971	Pontiac	71-52	Catalina	124	252	8-10-70	7-20-71	** 144	129,839	129,983	
Ventura Option replaced by the Catalina Brougham. The Executive Series dropped. Bonneville offered at a new lower price and the Convertible dropped. Grand Ville Series added in three body styles, Catalina & Bonneville Station Wagons now known as Safari and Grand Safari.											
			Safari Sta.Wgn.	127	258			30	19,586	19,616	
		71-58	Catalina Brougham	124				6	23,886	23,892	
		71-62	Bonneville	126	252			** 4	31,875	31,879	
			Grand Safari Sta.Wgn.	127				0	9,585	9,585	
		71-68	Grand Ville	126	268			2	46,328	46,330	
			PONTIAC TOTAL					** 186	261,099	261,285	

285

YEAR	MAKE	MODEL	NAME	WHEEL BASE	VEHICLE IDENTIF. NUMBER	STARTED PRODUCTION	FINISHED PRODUCTION	CARS BUILT MANUAL	CARS BUILT AUTO.	TOTAL BUILT	GRAND TOTAL
	LeMans	71-33	T-37	*	233			5,525	39,461	44,986	

The T-37 carried over from 1970-1/2. LeMans Station Wagon gets dual action tailgate standard. LeMans Sport Wagon dropped. Wood siding available on LeMans Station Wagon.

YEAR	MAKE	MODEL	NAME	WHEEL BASE	VEHICLE IDENTIF. NUMBER	STARTED PRODUCTION	FINISHED PRODUCTION	CARS BUILT MANUAL	CARS BUILT AUTO.	TOTAL BUILT	GRAND TOTAL
		71-35	LeMans	*	235			1,231	67,948	69,179	
		71-37	LeMans Sport	*	237			1,229	39,712	40,941	
		71-42	GTO	112	242			2,587	7,945	10,532	
			LEMANS TOTAL					10,688	213,274	223,962	
1971	Firebird	71-23	Firebird	108	223			2,778	20,244	23,022	

Introduced as a 1970-1/2 carry-over with minor changes. Seat construction revised. Front Fender Extractors added.

YEAR	MAKE	MODEL	NAME	WHEEL BASE	VEHICLE IDENTIF. NUMBER	STARTED PRODUCTION	FINISHED PRODUCTION	CARS BUILT MANUAL	CARS BUILT AUTO.	TOTAL BUILT	GRAND TOTAL
		71-24	Esprit	108	224			947	19,238	20,185	
		71-26	Formula	108	226			1,860	5,942	7,802	
		71-28	Trans Am	108	228			885	1,231	2,116	
			FIREBIRD TOTAL					6,470	46,655	53,125	
	Ventura II	71-21	Ventura II (6 Cyl.)	111	213	2-1-71	7-24-71	6,439	19,365	25,804	

New series introduced in two body styles. Released and built by Chevrolet.

YEAR	MAKE	MODEL	NAME	WHEEL BASE	VEHICLE IDENTIF. NUMBER	STARTED PRODUCTION	FINISHED PRODUCTION	CARS BUILT MANUAL	CARS BUILT AUTO.	TOTAL BUILT	GRAND TOTAL
		71-21	Ventura II (8 Cyl.)	214	2,103				20,577	22,680	
			VENTURA II TOTAL					8,542	39,942	48,484	**586,856
1972	Pontiac	72-52	Catalina	124	252	8-12-71	6-30-72		173,661	173,661	

New Single Position Hood Latch. Rear Bumpers will withstand 2-1/2 mph impact.

YEAR	MAKE	MODEL	NAME	WHEEL BASE	VEHICLE IDENTIF. NUMBER	STARTED PRODUCTION	FINISHED PRODUCTION	CARS BUILT MANUAL	CARS BUILT AUTO.	TOTAL BUILT	GRAND TOTAL
			Safari Sta. Wgn.	127	252				27,306	27,306	
		72-58	Catalina Brougham	124	258				27,316	27,316	
		72-62	Bonneville	126	262				36,084	36,084	
			Grand Safari Sta. Wgn.	127	262				14,541	14,541	
		72-68	Grand Ville	126	268				63,417	63,417	
			PONTIAC TOTAL					9,601	342,325	342,325	
	LeMans	72-35	LeMans	*	235				110,698	120,299	

GTO Std. engine changed to 400 four-barrel. T37 Series canceled. Luxury LeMans offered new with distinctive features.

YEAR	MAKE	MODEL	NAME	WHEEL BASE	VEHICLE IDENTIF. NUMBER	STARTED PRODUCTION	FINISHED PRODUCTION	CARS BUILT MANUAL	CARS BUILT AUTO.	TOTAL BUILT	GRAND TOTAL
		72-67	LeMans Sport	112	238			317	3,121	3,438	
		72-44	LeMans Luxury	*	244			269	45,987	46,256	
		72-76	Grand Prix	116	276				91,961	91,961	
			LEMANS TOTAL					10,187	251,767	261,954	

* Two-door Coupes Wheelbase 112", four-door Sedans & Station Wagons 116".

Percent Pontiac Series Manual Trans. 0.07
Percent LeMans Series Manual Trans. 4.77
Percent Firebird Series M.T. 12.20
Percent Ventura II M.T. 17.61

YEAR	MAKE	MODEL	NAME	VEHICLE IDENTIF. NUMBER	WHEEL BASE	STARTED PRODUCTION	FINISHED PRODUCTION	CARS BUILT MANUAL	CARS BUILT AUTO.	TOTAL BUILT	GRAND TOTAL
1972	Firebird	72-23	Firebird	223	108			1,263	10,738	12,001	
Six month strike at Lordstown Plant curtailed production.											
		72-24	Esprit	224	108			504	10,911	11,415	
		72-26	Formula	226	108			1,082	4,167	5,249	
		72-28	Trans Am	228	108			458	828	1,286	
							FIREBIRD TOTAL	3,307	26,644	29,951	
	Ventura II	72-21	Ventura II	213	111		VENTURA TOTAL	6,421	66,366	72,787	707,017
V-8 offered as option.											

* Two-door Coupes Wheelbase 112", Four-door Sedans & Station Wagons 116"

Percent LeMans Series Manual Trans. 3.88
Percent Firebird Series Manual Trans. 11.00
Percent Ventura II Manual Trans. 9.6

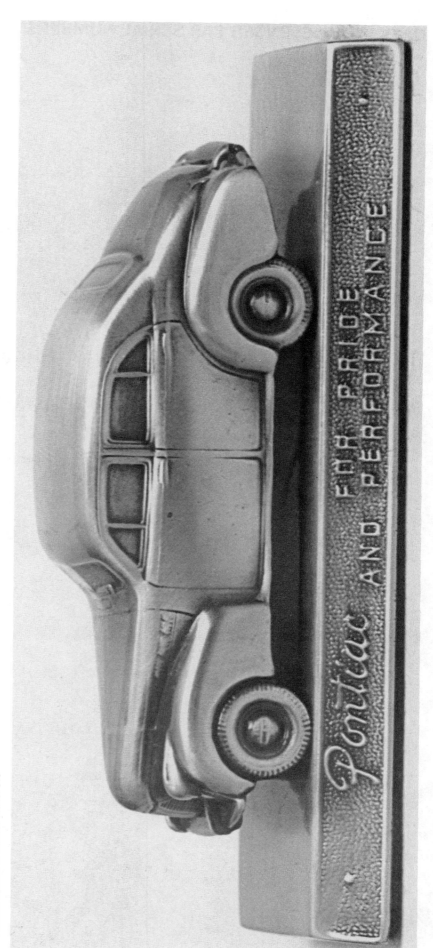

OAKLAND PASSENGER CAR SERIAL NUMBERS 1912-1920

Year	Model	Cyls.	Price	Serial Numbers
1912	30	4	$1200	{7001-8000
				{11001-11500
	40	4	1450	{8001-9000
				{9630-11000
	45	4	2100	9001-9500
1918	35	4	1075	35001-37500
	42	4	1600	40001-43601
	60	6	2400	60001-60951
1914	36	4	1200	360000-364000
	48	6	1785	480000-481150
	62	6	2500	620000-620100
1915	37	4	1200	370000-373599
	49	6	1685	490000-490500

(Number on front heel board)

Year	Model	Cyls.	Price	Serial Numbers
1916	32	6	795	{320000-328000
				{330000-347100
	38	4	1050	380000-384001
1916-17	50	8	1585	500000-502000

(Number on heel board of driver's compartment, or on left rear cross frame member.)

Year	Model	Cyls.	Price	Serial Numbers
1917	34	6	875	134-3000034
1918	34-B	6	----	3000134 up
1919	34-B	6	----	11699934
1920	34-C	6	1165	11700134 to 15235634

(1918 number on heel board; 1919 on heel board and on right rear side member.)

PONTIAC PRODUCTION, DELIVERY, AND REGISTRATION HISTORY THROUGH 1978

Model Year

Year	Total Production	Total Production	Pontiac Sales	Pontiac Registrations	% Tot. Indust.	Position	No. of Dealers
1926	76,742	76,695	61,107	50,269	1.54	12	3,151
1927	127,883	135,159	128,858	114,293	4.36	7	4,385
1928	210,883	203,701	196,096	183,994	5.86	5	4,891
1929	185,764	188,188	160,574	158,273	4.08	5	4,546
1930	58,206	61,782	65,610	68,3289	2.60	4	2,680
1931	80,404	77,635	74,116	73,148	3.83	5	2,333
1932	42,748	42,633	48,671	47,926	4.37	5	2,174
1933	87,885	85,666	86,652	85,348	5.71	5	2,504
1934	76,553	80,191	72,877	72,645	3.85	5	3,179
1935	124,926	175,268	147,075	140,122	5.11	6	3,885
1936	173,137	178,496	178,931	171,669	5.04	6	3,962
1937	236,189	235,322	212,054	212,403	6.10	5	3,953
1938	97,139	95,128	103,314	98,399	5.20	6	3,666
1939	144,312	170,726	164,830	159,836	6.02	6	3,721
1940	217,001	249,303	239,477	235,815	6.90	5	3,881
1941	330,061	282,087	283,601	286,123	7.67	5	3,579
1942*	83,556	15,404	16,685	8,020	7.08	5	2,971
1943	-	-	12,681	-	-	-	2,881
1944	-	-	4,726	-	-	-	3,046
1945	-	5,606	1,330	-	-	-	3,066
1946	137,640	131,538	121,613	113,109	6.23	6	3,106
1947	230,600	222,991	210,911	206,411	6.52	6	3,389
1948	245,419	253,472	243,144	228,939	6.56	5	4,100
1949	304,871	336,466	323,322	321,033	6.64	5	4,231
1950	446,429	469,813	453,047	440,528	6.95	5	4,254
1951	370,159	345,617	340,688	337,821	6.68	5	4,217
1952	271,373	278,140	267,401	266,351	6.41	5	4,178
1953	418,619	415,335	391,002	385,692	6.72	5	4,127
1954	287,774	370,887	365,638	358,167	6.47	6	4,023
1955	554,108	581,860	546,531	530,007	7.39	6	3,978
1956	405,730	332,268	353,623	358,668	6.02	6	3,874
1957	334,041	343,298	322,497	319,719	5.34	6	3,823
1958	217,303	219,823	235,872	229,740	4.94	6	3,716
1959	383,320	388,856	386,879	382,137	6.33	4	3,669
1960	396,488	450,206	409,932	399,646	6.08	5	3,578
1961	340,635	360,336	380,134	372,871	6.37	3	3,519
1962	521,933	547,350	541,627	528,654	7.62	3	3,501

Year	Total Production	Total Production	Pontiac Sales	Pontiac Registrations	% Tot. Indust.	Position	No. of Dealers
1963	590,071	625,268	617,536	606,791	8.03	3	3,500
1964	715,261	693,634	693,716	687,902	8.53	3	3,488
1965	802,000	860,652	827,571	831,448	8.93	3	3,461
1966	831,331	866,385	834,843	830,856	9.22	3	3,435
1967	817,826	857,171	836,937	834,146	9.98	3	3,408
1968	910,977	943,253	893,745	877,382	9.33	3	3,387
1969	870,528	805,941	782,513	795,605	8.42	3	3,376
1970	691,303	463,285	540,191	544,715	6.49	4	3,295
1971	586,853	807,812	710,352	608,097	6.91	3	3,279
1972	706,978	748,756	756,521	712,775	6.79	4	3,297
1973	919,872	904,107	807,418	807,546	7.11	4	3,319
1974	580,748	511,838	497,372	504,081	5.79	5	3,273
1975	532,043	532,953	503,857	478,142	5.79	5	3,238
1976	748,842	818,522	753,093	706,460	7.24	4	3,248
1977	911,050	930,322	808,467	800,230	7.39	4	3,238
1978	900,380	916,818	896,980	857,083	7.83	4	3,242

* Through March 1942

PONTIAC CONVERTIBLE PRODUCTION 1955-1975

1955:	Star Chief	19,762
1956:	Star Chief	13,510
1957:	Star Chief	12,789
	Bonneville	630
		13,419
1958:	Chieftain	7,359
	Bonneville	3,076
		10,435
1959:	Catalina	14,515
	Bonneville	11,426
		25,941
1960:	Catalina	17,172
	Bonneville	17,062
		34,234
1961:	Catalina	12,379
	Bonneville	18,264
		30,643
1962:	Catalina	16,877
	Bonneville	21,582
		38,459
1963:	Tempest DeLuxe	3,634
	LeMans 8	7,213
	LeMans 4	8,744
	Catalina	18,249
	Bonneville	23,459
		61,299
1964:	Tempest Custom	7,987
	LeMans	17,559
	GTO	6,644
	Catalina	18,673
	Bonneville	22,016
		72,879
1965:	Tempest Custom	8,346
	LeMans	13,897
	GTO	11,311
	Catalina	18,347
	Bonneville	21,050
		72,951
1966:	Tempest Custom	5,557
	LeMans	13,080
	GTO	12,798
	Catalina	14,837
	Bonneville	62,571

1967:	Firebird	15,582
	Tempest Custom	4,082
	LeMans	9,820
	GTO	9,517
	Catalina	10,033
	Bonneville	8,902
	Grand Prix	5,856
		63,792
1968:	Firebird	16,960
	LeMans Custom	3,518
	LeMans	8,320
	GTO	9,980
	Catalina	7,339
	Bonneville	7,358
		53,975
1969:	Firebird	11,649
	LeMans Custom	2,379
	LeMans	5,676
	GTO	7,436
	Catalina	5,436
	Bonneville	5,438
		38,014
1970:	LeMans Sport	4,670
	GTO	3,783
	Catalina	3,686
	Bonneville	7,033
		19,172
1971:	LeMans Sport	3,865
	GTO	678
	Catalina	2,036
	Grand Ville	1,789
		8,368
1972:	LeMans	3,438
	Catalina	2,399
	Grand Ville	2,213
		8,050
1973:	Grand Ville	4,447
1974:	Grand Ville	3,000
1975:	Grand Ville Brougham	4,519

GTO PRODUCTION 1964 THROUGH 1974

Year	GTO Hardtops	Judge Convert.	Comb. Totals Hardtops	Convert.	Hardtops	Convert.	Grand Totals
* 1964	25,806	6,644	-	-	25,806	6,644	32,450
* 1965	60,147	11,311	-	-	60,147	11,311	71,458
1966	84,148	12,798	-	-	84,148	12,798	96,946
1967	72,205	9,517	-	-	72,205	9,517	81,722
1968	77,704	9,980	-	-	77,704	9,980	87,684
1969	58,126	7,328	6,725	108	64,851	7,436	72,287
1970	32,737	3,615	3,629	168	36,366	3,783	40,149
1971	9,497	661	357	17	9,854	678	10,532
* 1972	5,807	-	-	-	5,807	-	5,807
* 1973	4,806	-	-	-	4,806	-	4,806
* 1974	7,058	-	-	-	7,058	-	7,058
TOTALS	438,041	61,854	10,711	293	448,752	62,147	510,899

*indicates that GTO was offered as an optional "package" available on the following models:

1964 and 1965:	LeMans coupe and convertible
1972:	LeMans coupe and hardtop coupe only
1973:	LeMans coupe
1974:	Ventura coupe

Source: Pontiac Motor Division, General Motors Corporation

PONTIAC FIREBIRD PRODUCTION THROUGH 1977

Year	Base Firebird	Firebird Esprit	Firebird Formula	Firebird Trans Am	Total Firebird Prod.
1967	2H 67,032	-	-	-	
	2C 15,528	-	-	-	
	Total 82,560	-	-	-	
1968	2H 90,152	-	-	-	82,560
	2C 16,960	-	-	-	
	Total 107,112	-	-	-	
1969	2H 75,362	-	-	-	107,112
	2C 11,649	-	-	-	
	Total 87,011	-	-	697	
1970	37,835	-	7,708	3,196	87,708
1971	23,021	20,185	7,802	2,116	48,739
1972	12,000	11,415	5,250	1,286	53,124
1973	14,096	17,249	10,166	4,802	29,951
1974	26,372	22,583	14,519	10,255	46,313
1975	22,293	20,826	13,670	27,274	73,729
1976	21,209	22,252	13,670	46,701	84,063
1977	30,642	34,548	21,801	68,745	110,775
					155,736

2H=Two-door hardtop
2C=Two-door convertible

TRANS AM PRODUCTION BREAKDOWN BY ENGINE/TRANSMISSION 1969-1976

1969	Automatic	Manual	Total
Ram Air IV 400 4-bbl. (L67)	9	46	55
Ram Air H.O. 400 4-bbl. (L74)	114	520	634
Convertibles with L74	4	4	8
TOTAL	127	570	697
1970			
Ram Air S.D. 400 4-bbl. (LS1)	59	29	88
Ram Air H.O. 400 4-bbl. (L74)	1,339	1,769	3,108
TOTAL	1,398	1,798	3,196
1971			
455 H.O. 4-bbl. (LS5)	1,231	885	2,116
TOTAL	1,231	885	2,116
1972			
455 H.O. 4-bbl. (LS5)	828	458	1,286
TOTAL	828	458	1,286
1973			
455 S.D. 4-bbl. (LS2)	180	72	252
455 4-bbl. (L75)	3,130	1,420	4,550
TOTAL	3,310	1,492	4,802
1974			
455 S.D. 4-bbl. (LS2)	731	212	943
455 4-bbl. (L75)	4,648	-	4,648
400 4-bbl. (L78)	2,914	1,750	4,664
TOTAL	8,293	1,962	10,255
1975			
455 4-bbl. (L75)	-	857	857
400 4-bbl. (L78)	20,277	6,140	26,417
TOTAL	20,277	6,977	27,274
1976			
455 4-bbl. (L75)	-	7,528	7,528
400 4-bbl. (L78)	33,752	5,424	39,176
TOTAL	33,752	12,952	46,704

(643 Limited Edition T-tops were produced in 1976 of which 429 had L75 engines)

CONDITIONS

Excellent

1) EXCELLENT: Restored to current maximum professional standards of quality in every area, or perfect original with components operating and appearing as new. A 95-plus point show car that is not driven.

Fine

2) FINE: Well-restored, or a combination of superior restoration and excellent original. Also, an *extremely* well-maintained original showing very minimal wear.

Very Good

3) VERY GOOD: Completely operable original or "older restoration" showing wear. Also, a good amateur restoration, all presentable and serviceable inside and out. Plus, combinations of well-done restoration and good operable components or a partially restored car with all parts necessary to complete and/or valuable NOS parts.

Good

4) GOOD: A driveable vehicle needing no or only minor work to be functional. Also, a deteriorated restoration or a very poor amateur restoration. All components may need restoration to be "excellent," but the car is mostly useable "as is."

Restorable

5) RESTORABLE: Needs *complete* restoration of body, chassis and interior. May or may not be running, but isn't weathered, wrecked or stripped to the point of being useful only for parts.

Parts Car

6) PARTS CAR: May or may not be running, but is weathered, wrecked and/or stripped to the point of being useful primarily for parts.

PRICING

Pontiac

1926	6	5	4	3	2	1
Model 6-27, 6-cyl.						
2d Cpe	500	1600	2700	5400	9500	13,500
2d Sed	450	1500	2500	5000	8800	12,500
1927						
Model 6-27, 6-cyl.						
2d Spt Rds	650	2050	3400	6800	11,900	17,000
2d Spt Cabr	600	1900	3200	6400	11,200	16,000
2d Cpe	450	1450	2400	4800	8400	12,000
2d DeL Cpe	450	1500	2500	5000	8800	12,500
2d Sed	400	1300	2200	4400	7700	11,000
4d Lan Sed	450	1450	2400	4800	8400	12,000
1928						
Model 6-28, 6-cyl.						
2d Rds	650	2050	3400	6800	11,900	17,000
2d Cabr	600	1900	3200	6400	11,200	16,000
4d Phae	600	1900	3200	6400	11,200	16,000
2d Sed	400	1200	2000	4000	7000	10,000
4d Sed	450	1140	1900	3800	6650	9500
4d Trs	400	1250	2100	4200	7400	10,500
2d Cpe	450	1400	2300	4600	8100	11,500
2d Spt Cpe	450	1500	2500	5000	8800	12,500
4d Lan Sed	500	1550	2600	5200	9100	13,000
1929						
Model 6-29A, 6-cyl.						
2d Rds	750	2400	4000	8000	14,000	20,000
4d Phae	700	2300	3800	7600	13,300	19,000
2d Conv	700	2300	3800	7600	13,300	19,000
2d Cpe	450	1400	2300	4600	8100	11,500
2d Sed	400	1200	2000	4000	7000	10,000
4d Sed	400	1200	2000	4000	7000	10,000
4d Spt Lan Sed	400	1300	2200	4400	7700	11,000

NOTE: Add 5 percent for horizontal louvers on early year cars.

1930	6	5	4	3	2	1
Model 6-30B, 6-cyl.						
2d Spt Rds	750	2400	4000	8000	14,000	20,000
4d Phae	750	2350	3900	7800	13,700	19,500
2d Cpe	400	1300	2200	4400	7700	11,000
2d Spt Cpe	450	1400	2300	4600	8100	11,500
2d Sed	400	1200	2000	4000	7000	10,000
4d Sed	400	1200	2000	4000	7000	10,000
4d Cus Sed	400	1250	2100	4200	7400	10,500
1931						
Model 401, 6-cyl.						
2d Conv	750	2400	4000	8000	14,000	20,000
2P Cpe	450	1400	2300	4600	8100	11,500
2d Spt Cpe	450	1450	2400	4800	8400	12,000
2d Sed	400	1200	2050	4100	7100	10,200
4d Sed	400	1250	2100	4200	7400	10,500
4d Cus Sed	400	1300	2200	4400	7700	11,000
1932						
Model 402, 6-cyl.						
2d Conv	900	2900	4800	9600	16,800	24,000
2d Cpe	450	1500	2500	5000	8800	12,500
2d RS Cpe	500	1550	2600	5200	9100	13,000
2d Sed	400	1250	2100	4200	7400	10,500
4d Cus Sed	400	1300	2200	4400	7700	11,000
Model 302, V-8						
2d Conv	1050	3350	5600	11,200	19,600	28,000
2d Cpe	600	1850	3100	6200	10,900	15,500
2d Spt Cpe	600	1900	3200	6400	11,200	16,000
2d Sed	450	1500	2500	5000	8800	12,500
4d Sed	500	1550	2600	5200	9100	13,000
4d Cus Sed	550	1700	2800	5600	9800	14,000
1933						
Model 601, 8-cyl.						
2d Rds	850	2750	4600	9200	16,100	23,000
2d Conv	800	2500	4200	8400	14,700	21,000
2d Cpe	500	1550	2600	5200	9100	13,000
2d Spt Cpe	550	1700	2800	5600	9800	14,000
2d Sed	450	1400	2300	4600	8100	11,500
2d Trg Sed	450	1400	2350	4700	8200	11,700
4d Sed	450	1450	2400	4800	8400	12,000
1934						
Model 603, 8-cyl.						
2d Conv	750	2400	4000	8000	14,000	20,000
2d Cpe	550	1700	2800	5600	9800	14,000
2d Spt Cpe	550	1750	2900	5800	10,200	14,500
2d Sed	400	1250	2100	4200	7400	10,500
2d Trg Sed	400	1300	2200	4400	7700	11,000
4d Sed	400	1300	2200	4400	7600	10,900
4d Trg Sed	400	1300	2200	4400	7700	11,000
1935						
Master Series 701, 6-cyl.						
2d Cpe	400	1300	2200	4400	7700	11,000
2d Sed	450	1130	1900	3800	6600	9400
2d Trg Sed	450	1140	1900	3800	6650	9500
4d Sed	400	1200	2000	4000	7000	10,000
4d Trg Sed	400	1250	2100	4200	7400	10,500
DeLuxe Series 701, 6-cyl.						
2d Cpe	450	1400	2300	4600	8100	11,500
2d Spt Cpe	450	1450	2400	4800	8400	12,000
2d Cabr	600	1900	3200	6400	11,200	16,000
2d Sed	450	1140	1900	3800	6650	9500
2d Trg Sed	450	1150	1900	3850	6700	9600
4d Sed	450	1160	1950	3900	6800	9700
4d Trg Sed	400	1200	2000	4000	7000	10,000

Series 605, 8-cyl.	6	5	4	3	2	1
2d Cpe	450	1450	2400	4800	8400	12,000
2d Spt Cpe	450	1500	2500	5000	8800	12,500
2d Cabr	750	2400	4000	8000	14,000	20,000
2d Sed	450	1150	1900	3850	6700	9600
2d Trg Sed	400	1200	2000	4000	7000	10,000
4d Sed	400	1300	2200	4400	7700	11,000
4d Trg Sed	450	1400	2300	4600	8100	11,500
1936						
DeLuxe Series Silver Streak, 6-cyl.						
2d Cpe	450	1450	2400	4800	8400	12,000
2d Spt Cpe	500	1550	2600	5200	9100	13,000
2d Cabr	800	2500	4200	8400	14,700	21,000
2d Sed	450	1130	1900	3800	6600	9400
2d Trg Sed	450	1150	1900	3850	6700	9600
4d Sed	450	1160	1950	3900	6800	9700
4d Trg Sed	400	1200	2000	4000	7000	10,000
DeLuxe Series Silver Streak, 8-cyl.						
2d Cpe	500	1550	2600	5200	9100	13,000
2d Spt Cpe	550	1700	2800	5600	9800	14,000
2d Cabr	700	2300	3800	7600	13,300	19,000
2d Sed	400	1200	2000	4000	7000	10,000
2d Trg Sed	400	1200	2050	4100	7100	10,200
4d Sed	400	1200	2000	4000	7100	10,100
4d Trg Sed	400	1250	2050	4100	7200	10,300
1937-1938						
DeLuxe Model 6DA, 6-cyl.						
2d Conv	1000	3250	5400	10,800	18,900	27,000
4d Conv Sed	1050	3350	5600	11,200	19,600	28,000
2d Bus Cpe	450	1450	2400	4800	8400	12,000
2d Spt Cpe	500	1550	2600	5200	9100	13,000
2d Sed	450	1130	1900	3800	6600	9400
2d Trg Sed	450	1140	1900	3800	6650	9500
4d Sed	400	1200	2000	4000	7000	10,000
4d Trg Sed	400	1200	2000	4000	7100	10,100
4d Sta Wag	1050	3350	5600	11,200	19,600	28,000
DeLuxe Model 8DA, 8-cyl.						
2d Conv	1100	3500	5800	11,600	20,300	29,000
4d Conv Sed	1150	3600	6000	12,000	21,000	30,000
2d Bus Cpe	500	1550	2600	5200	9100	13,000
2d Spt Cpe	550	1700	2800	5600	9800	14,000
2d Sed	400	1250	2100	4200	7400	10,500
2d Trg Sed	400	1250	2100	4200	7400	10,600
4d Sed	400	1250	2100	4200	7400	10,600
4d Trg Sed	400	1300	2150	4300	7500	10,700
1939						
Special Series 25, 6-cyl.						
2d Bus Cpe	450	1450	2400	4800	8400	12,000
2d Spt Cpe	500	1550	2600	5200	9100	13,000
2d Trg Sed	400	1300	2200	4400	7700	11,000
4d Trg Sed	400	1300	2200	4400	7700	11,000
4d Sta Wag	1050	3350	5600	11,200	19,600	28,000
DeLuxe Series 26, 6-cyl.						
2d Conv	950	3000	5000	10,000	17,500	25,000
2d Bus Cpe	450	1500	2500	5000	8800	12,500
2d Spt Cpe	500	1600	2700	5400	9500	13,500
2d Sed	400	1300	2200	4400	7700	11,000
4d Sed	400	1350	2200	4400	7800	11,100
DeLuxe Series 28, 8-cyl.						
2d Conv	1000	3250	5400	10,800	18,900	27,000
2d Bus Cpe	500	1550	2600	5200	9100	13,000
2d Spt Cpe	550	1700	2800	5600	9800	14,000
2d Sed	450	1400	2300	4600	8100	11,500
4d Trg Sed	450	1400	2300	4600	8100	11,600
1940						
Special Series 25, 6-cyl., 117" wb						
2d Bus Cpe	450	1450	2400	4800	8400	12,000
2d Spt Cpe	500	1550	2600	5200	9100	13,000
2d Sed	400	1250	2100	4200	7300	10,400
4d Sed	400	1250	2100	4200	7400	10,500
4d Sta Wag	1000	3100	5200	10,400	18,200	26,000
DeLuxe Series 26, 6-cyl., 120" wb						
2d Conv	1000	3100	5200	10,400	18,200	26,000
2d Bus Cpe	450	1500	2500	5000	8800	12,500
2d Spt Cpe	500	1600	2700	5400	9500	13,500
2d Sed	400	1200	2000	4000	7000	10,000
4d Sed	400	1300	2150	4300	7500	10,700
DeLuxe Series 28, 8-cyl., 120" wb						
2d Conv	1000	3250	5400	10,800	18,900	27,000
2d Bus Cpe	500	1550	2600	5200	9100	13,000
2d Spt Cpe	550	1700	2800	5600	9800	14,000
2d Sed	400	1300	2150	4300	7500	10,700
4d Sed	400	1300	2150	4300	7600	10,800
Torpedo Series 29, 8-cyl., 122" wb						
2d Spt Cpe	550	1750	2900	5800	10,200	14,500
4d Sed	500	1600	2700	5400	9500	13,500
1941						
DeLuxe Torpedo, 8-cyl.						
2d Bus Cpe	450	1400	2300	4600	8100	11,500
2d Spt Cpe	450	1450	2400	4800	8400	12,000
2d Conv	1000	3250	5400	10,800	18,900	27,000
2d Sed	400	1250	2100	4200	7300	10,400
4d 4W Sed	400	1250	2100	4200	7400	10,600
4d 6W Sed	400	1250	2100	4200	7400	10,500
Streamliner, 8-cyl.						
2d Sed	450	1500	2500	5000	8800	12,500
4d Sed	450	1450	2400	4800	8400	12,000
Super Streamliner, 8-cyl.						
2d Cpe	500	1550	2600	5200	9100	13,000
4d Sed	450	1500	2500	5000	8800	12,500
Custom, 8-cyl.						
2d Spt Cpe	550	1800	3000	6000	10,500	15,000

	6	5	4	3	2	1
4d Sed	550	1700	2800	5600	9800	14,000
4d Sta Wag	1050	3350	5600	11,200	19,600	28,000
4d DeL Sta Wag	1100	3500	5800	11,600	20,300	29,000

NOTE: Deduct 10 percent for 6-cyl. models.

1942

	6	5	4	3	2	1
Torpedo, 8-cyl.						
2d Conv	800	2500	4200	8400	14,700	21,000
2d Bus Cpe	400	1300	2200	4400	7700	11,000
2d Spt Cpe	450	1400	2300	4600	8100	11,500
2d 5P Cpe	450	1450	2400	4800	8400	12,000
2d Sed	400	1250	2100	4200	7400	10,500
4d Sed	400	1250	2100	4200	7300	10,400
4d Metro Sed	400	1300	2150	4300	7600	10,800
Streamliner, 8-cyl.						
2d Cpe	450	1450	2400	4800	8400	12,000
4d Sed	450	1400	2300	4600	8100	11,500
4d Sta Wag	1000	3100	5200	10,400	18,200	26,000
Chieftain, 8-cyl.						
2d Cpe	450	1500	2500	5000	8800	12,500
4d Sed	450	1400	2350	4700	8200	11,700
4d Sta Wag	1000	3250	5400	10,800	18,900	27,000

NOTE: Deduct 10 percent for 6-cyl. models.

1946

	6	5	4	3	2	1
Torpedo, 8-cyl.						
2d Conv	800	2500	4200	8400	14,700	21,000
2d Bus Cpe	450	1450	2400	4800	8400	12,000
2d Spt Cpe	450	1500	2500	5000	8800	12,500
2d 5P Cpe	500	1500	2550	5100	8900	12,700
2d Sed	450	1400	2300	4600	8100	11,500
4d Sed	450	1400	2300	4600	8100	11,600
Streamliner, 8-Cyl.						
5P Cpe	500	1550	2600	5200	9100	13,000
4d Sed	450	1400	2350	4700	8300	11,800
4d Sta Wag	1000	3250	5400	10,800	18,900	27,000
4d DeL Sta Wag	1050	3350	5600	11,200	19,600	28,000

NOTE: Deduct 5 percent for 6-cyl. models.

1947

	6	5	4	3	2	1
Torpedo, 8-cyl.						
2d Conv	800	2500	4200	8400	14,700	21,000
2d DeL Conv	850	2750	4600	9200	16,100	23,000
2d Bus Cpe	450	1450	2400	4800	8400	12,000
2d Spt Cpe	450	1500	2500	5000	8800	12,500
2d 5P Cpe	500	1500	2550	5100	8900	12,700
2d Sed	450	1400	2300	4600	8100	11,500
4d Sed	450	1400	2300	4600	8100	11,600
Streamliner, 8-cyl.						
2d Cpe	500	1550	2600	5200	9100	13,000
4d Sed	450	1400	2350	4700	8300	11,800
4d Sta Wag	1000	3250	5400	10,800	18,900	27,000
4d DeL Sta Wag	1050	3350	5600	11,200	19,600	28,000

NOTE: Deduct 5 percent for 6-cyl. models.

1948

	6	5	4	3	2	1
Torpedo, 8-cyl.						
2d Bus Cpe	450	1500	2500	5000	8800	12,500
2d Spt Cpe	500	1550	2600	5200	9100	13,000
2d 5P Cpe	500	1600	2650	5300	9200	13,200
2d Sed	450	1400	2300	4600	8100	11,500
4d Sed	400	1300	2200	4400	7700	11,000
DeLuxe Torpedo, 8-cyl.						
2d Conv	850	2650	4400	8800	15,400	22,000
2d Spt Cpe	500	1600	2700	5400	9500	13,500
2d 5P Cpe	550	1700	2800	5600	9800	14,000
4d Sed	500	1500	2550	5100	8900	12,700
DeLuxe Streamliner, 8-cyl.						
2d Cpe	500	1600	2700	5400	9500	13,500
4d Sed	450	1450	2400	4800	8400	12,000
4d Sta Wag	1050	3350	5600	11,200	19,600	28,000

NOTE: Deduct 5 percent for 6-cyl. models.

1949-1950

	6	5	4	3	2	1
Streamliner, 8-cyl.						
2d Cpe Sed	400	1200	2050	4100	7100	10,200
4d Sed	400	1200	2000	4000	7100	10,100
4d Sta Wag	450	1400	2300	4600	8100	11,500
4d Wood Sta Wag ('49 only)	550	1700	2800	5600	9800	14,000
Streamliner DeLuxe, 8-cyl.						
4d Sed	400	1250	2050	4100	7200	10,300
2d Cpe Sed	400	1250	2100	4200	7300	10,400
4d Stl Sta Wag	400	1300	2200	4400	7700	11,000
4d Woodie (1949 only)	600	1900	3200	6400	11,200	16,000
2d Sed Dely	550	1700	2800	5600	9800	14,000
Chieftain, 8-cyl.						
4d Sed	400	1250	2100	4200	7300	10,400
2d Sed	400	1200	2050	4100	7100	10,200
2d Cpe Sed	400	1250	2100	4200	7400	10,600
2d Bus Cpe	400	1250	2100	4200	7400	10,500
Chieftain DeLuxe, 8-cyl.						
4d Sed	400	1250	2100	4200	7400	10,500
2d Sed	400	1250	2050	4100	7200	10,300
2d Bus Cpe (1949 only)	450	1400	2300	4600	8100	11,500
2d HT (1950 only)	600	1850	3100	6200	10,900	15,500
2d Cpe Sed	400	1300	2150	4300	7500	10,700
2d Sup HT (1950 only)	600	1900	3200	6400	11,200	16,000
2d Conv	800	2500	4200	8400	14,700	21,000

NOTE: Deduct 5 percent for 6-cyl. models.

1951-1952

	6	5	4	3	2	1
Streamliner, 8-cyl. (1951 only)						
2d Cpe Sed	400	1250	2050	4100	7200	10,300
4d Sta Wag	450	1400	2300	4600	8100	11,500
Streamliner DeLuxe, 8-cyl. (1951 only)						
2d Cpe Sed	400	1250	2100	4200	7400	10,500
4d Sta Wag	450	1450	2400	4800	8400	12,000
2d Sed Dely	500	1600	2700	5400	9500	13,500
Chieftain, 8-cyl.						
4d Sed	400	1250	2100	4200	7400	10,500
2d Sed	400	1250	2050	4100	7200	10,300
2d Cpe Sed	400	1250	2100	4200	7400	10,600
2d Bus Cpe	400	1250	2100	4200	7400	10,500
Chieftain DeLuxe, 8-cyl.						
4d Sed	400	1250	2100	4200	7400	10,600
2d Sed	400	1250	2100	4200	7400	10,500
2d Cpe Sed	400	1300	2200	4400	7700	11,000
2d HT	600	2000	3300	6600	11,600	16,500
2d HT Sup	650	2100	3500	7000	12,300	17,500
2d Conv	850	2650	4400	8800	15,400	22,000

NOTE: Deduct 5 percent for 6-cyl. models.

1953

	6	5	4	3	2	1
Chieftain, 8-cyl., 122" wb						
4d Sed	400	1250	2100	4200	7400	10,600
2d Sed	400	1250	2100	4200	7400	10,500
4d Paint Sta Wag	450	1400	2300	4600	8100	11,500
4d Woodgrain Sta Wag	450	1450	2400	4800	8400	12,000
2d Sed Dely	600	1850	3100	6200	10,900	15,500
Chieftain DeLuxe, 8-cyl.						
4d Sed	400	1300	2150	4300	7500	10,700
2d Sed	400	1250	2100	4200	7400	10,600
2d HT	600	1900	3200	6400	11,200	16,000
2d Conv	900	2900	4800	9600	16,800	24,000
4d Mtl Sta Wag	400	1300	2200	4400	7700	11,000
4d Sim W Sta Wag	450	1450	2400	4800	8400	12,000
Custom Catalina, 8-cyl.						
2d HT	600	1900	3200	6400	11,200	16,000

NOTE: Deduct 5 percent for 6-cyl. models.

1954

	6	5	4	3	2	1
Chieftain, 8-cyl., 122" wb						
4d Sed	400	1300	2150	4300	7600	10,800
2d Sed	400	1300	2150	4300	7500	10,700
4d Sta Wag	450	1450	2400	4800	8400	12,000
Chieftain DeLuxe, 8-cyl.						
4d Sed	400	1300	2200	4400	7700	11,000
2d Sed	400	1300	2150	4300	7600	10,800
2d HT	600	1900	3200	6400	11,200	16,000
4d Sta Wag	450	1500	2500	5000	8800	12,500
Custom Catalina, 8-cyl.						
2d HT	700	2150	3600	7200	12,600	18,000
Star Chief DeLuxe, 8-cyl.						
4d Sed	450	1450	2400	4800	8400	12,000
2d Conv	950	3000	5000	10,000	17,500	25,000
Custom Star Chief, 8-cyl.						
4d Sed	500	1550	2600	5200	9100	13,000
Custom Catalina						
2d HT	700	2300	3800	7600	13,300	19,000

NOTE: Deduct 5 percent for 6-cyl. models.

1955

	6	5	4	3	2	1
Chieftain 860, V-8						
4d Sed	400	1200	2000	4000	7000	10,000
2d Sed	400	1200	2000	4000	7100	10,100
2d Sta Wag	450	1450	2400	4800	8400	12,000
4d Sta Wag	450	1400	2300	4600	8100	11,500
Chieftain 870, V-8, 122" wb						
4d Sed	400	1250	2100	4200	7400	10,500
2d Sed	400	1250	2100	4200	7400	10,600
2d HT	650	2050	3400	6800	11,900	17,000
4d Sta Wag	450	1450	2400	4800	8400	12,000
Star Chief Custom Safari, 122" wb						
2d Sta Wag	800	2500	4200	8400	14,700	21,000
Star Chief, V-8, 124" wb						
4d Sed	450	1400	2300	4600	8100	11,500
2d Conv	1200	3850	6400	12,800	22,400	32,000
Custom Star Chief, V-8, 124" wb						
4d Sed	450	1500	2500	5000	8800	12,500
Custom Catalina						
2d HT	750	2400	4000	8000	14,000	20,000

1956

	6	5	4	3	2	1
Chieftain 860, V-8, 122" wb						
4d Sed	400	1200	2000	4000	7000	10,000
4d HT	400	1300	2200	4400	7700	11,000
2d Sed	400	1200	2000	4000	7000	10,000
2d HT	600	1900	3200	6400	11,200	16,000
2d Sta Wag	500	1550	2600	5200	9100	13,000
4d Sta Wag	450	1500	2500	5000	8800	12,500
Chieftain 870, V-8, 122" wb						
4d Sed	400	1250	2050	4100	7200	10,300
4d HT	450	1450	2400	4800	8400	12,000
2d HT	700	2150	3600	7200	12,600	18,000
4d Sta Wag	500	1600	2700	5400	9500	13,500
Custom Star Chief Safari, V-8, 122" wb						
2d Sta Wag	850	2650	4400	8800	15,400	22,000
Star Chief, V-8, 124" wb						
4d Sed	400	1300	2200	4400	7700	11,000
2d Conv	1300	4200	7000	14,000	24,500	35,000
Custom Star Chief, V-8, 124" wb						
4d HT	550	1700	2800	5600	9800	14,000
Custom Catalina						
2d HT	800	2500	4200	8400	14,700	21,000

1957

	6	5	4	3	2	1
Chieftain, V-8, 122" wb						
4d Sed	400	1200	2000	4000	7000	10,000
4d HT	400	1300	2200	4400	7700	11,000
2d Sed	400	1300	2150	4300	7500	10,700
2d HT	550	1800	3000	6000	10,500	15,000
4d Sta Wag	450	1400	2300	4600	8100	11,500
2d Sta Wag	450	1450	2400	4800	8400	12,000
Super Chief, V-8, 122" wb						
4d Sed	400	1250	2100	4200	7400	10,500
4d HT	450	1450	2400	4800	8400	12,000
2d HT	650	2050	3400	6800	11,900	17,000
4d Sta Wag	500	1550	2600	5200	9100	13,000
Star Chief Custom Safari, V-8, 122" wb						
4d Sta Wag	750	2400	4000	8000	14,000	20,000
2d Sta Wag	850	2750	4600	9200	16,100	23,000
Star Chief, V-8, 124" wb						
4d Sed	450	1450	2400	4800	8400	12,000
2d Conv	1250	3950	6600	13,200	23,100	33,000
2d Bonneville Conv*	2200	6950	11,600	23,200	40,600	58,000
Custom Star Chief, V-8, 124" wb						
4d Sed	450	1500	2500	5000	8800	12,500
4d HT	550	1700	2800	5600	9800	14,000
2d HT	800	2500	4200	8400	14,700	21,000

*Available on one-to-a-dealer basis.

1958

	6	5	4	3	2	1
Chieftain, V-8, 122" wb						
4d Sed	350	975	1600	3250	5700	8100
4d HT	400	1250	2100	4200	7400	10,500
2d Sed	450	1080	1800	3600	6300	9000
2d HT	550	1800	3000	6000	10,500	15,000
2d Conv	1000	3250	5400	10,800	18,900	27,000
4d 9P Safari	400	1300	2200	4400	7700	11,000
Super-Chief, V-8, 122" wb						
4d Sed	350	1040	1700	3450	6000	8600
4d HT	450	1450	2400	4800	8400	12,000
2d HT	600	1900	3200	6400	11,200	16,000
Star Chief, V-8, 124" wb						
4d Cus Sed	450	1080	1800	3600	6300	9000
4d HT	500	1550	2600	5200	9100	13,000

	6	5	4	3	2	1
2d HT	650	2050	3400	6800	11,900	17,000
4d Cus Safari	550	1700	2800	5600	9800	14,000
Bonneville, V-8, 122" wb						
2d HT	1150	3600	6000	12,000	21,000	30,000
2d Conv	1900	6000	10,000	20,000	35,000	50,000
NOTE: Add 20 percent for fuel-injection Bonneville.						

1959

	6	5	4	3	2	1
Catalina, V-8, 122" wb						
4d Sed	350	975	1600	3200	5600	8000
4d HT	450	1080	1800	3600	6300	9000
2d Sed	350	900	1500	3000	5250	7500
2d HT	550	1700	2800	5600	9800	14,000
2d Conv	850	2650	4400	8800	15,400	22,000
Safari, V-8, 124" wb						
4d 6P Sta Wag	400	1200	2000	4000	7000	10,000
4d 9P Sta Wag	400	1200	2050	4100	7100	10,200
Star Chief, V-8, 124" wb						
4d Sed	450	1080	1800	3600	6300	9000
4d HT	400	1300	2200	4400	7700	11,000
2d Sed	450	1140	1900	3800	6650	9500
Bonneville, V-8, 124" wb						
4d HT	450	1450	2400	4800	8400	12,000
2d HT	650	2050	3400	6800	11,900	17,000
2d Conv	1050	3350	5600	11,200	19,600	28,000
Custom Safari, V-8, 122" wb						
4d Sta Wag	450	1500	2500	5000	8800	12,500

1960

	6	5	4	3	2	1
Catalina, V-8, 122" wb						
4d Sed	350	950	1500	3050	5300	7600
4d HT	450	1080	1800	3600	6300	9000
2d Sed	350	975	1600	3200	5600	8000
2d HT	550	1700	2800	5600	9800	14,000
2d Conv	850	2750	4600	9200	16,100	23,000
Safari, V-8, 122" wb						
4d Sta Wag	400	1300	2200	4400	7700	11,000
4d 6P Sta Wag	450	1400	2300	4600	8100	11,500
Ventura, V-8, 122" wb						
4d HT	400	1200	2000	4000	7000	10,000
2d HT	550	1800	3000	6000	10,500	15,000
Star Chief, V-8, 124" wb						
4d Sed	450	1140	1900	3800	6650	9500
4d HT	400	1300	2200	4400	7700	11,000
2d Sed	400	1200	2000	4000	7000	10,000
Bonneville, V-8, 124" wb						
4d HT	450	1450	2400	4800	8400	12,000
2d HT	700	2150	3600	7200	12,600	18,000
2d Conv	1000	3250	5400	10,800	18,900	27,000
Bonneville Safari, V-8, 122" wb						
4d Sta Wag	500	1550	2600	5200	9100	13,000

1961

	6	5	4	3	2	1
Tempest Compact, 4-cyl.						
4d Sed	350	800	1350	2700	4700	6700
2d Cpe	350	820	1400	2700	4760	6800
2d Cus Cpe	350	840	1400	2800	4900	7000
4d Safari Wag	350	840	1400	2800	4900	7000
NOTE: Add 20 percent for Tempest V-8.						
Catalina, V-8, 119" wb						
4d Sed	350	900	1500	3000	5250	7500
4d HT	350	1020	1700	3400	5950	8500
2d Sed	350	950	1500	3050	5300	7600
2d HT	450	1450	2400	4800	8400	12,000
2d Conv	650	2050	3400	6800	11,900	17,000
4d Safari Wag	400	1200	2000	4000	7000	10,000
Ventura, V-8, 119" wb						
4d HT	450	1140	1900	3800	6650	9500
2d HT	550	1700	2800	5600	9800	14,000
Star Chief, V-8, 123" wb						
4d Sed	350	1020	1700	3400	5950	8500
4d HT	400	1200	2000	4000	7000	10,000
Bonneville, V-8, 123" wb						
4d HT	400	1250	2100	4200	7400	10,500
2d HT	550	1700	2800	5600	9800	14,000
2d Conv	850	2650	4400	8800	15,400	22,000
Bonneville Safari, V-8, 119" wb						
4d Sta Wag	400	1300	2200	4400	7700	11,000

1962

	6	5	4	3	2	1
Tempest Series, 4-cyl., 122" wb						
4d Sed	350	800	1350	2700	4700	6700
2d Cpe	350	820	1400	2700	4760	6800
2d HT	450	1080	1800	3600	6300	9000
2d Conv	450	1450	2400	4800	8400	12,000
4d Safari	350	840	1400	2800	4900	7000
NOTE: Add 20 percent for Tempest V-8.						
Catalina Series, V-8, 120" wb						
4d Sed	350	900	1500	3000	5250	7500
4d HT	350	1020	1700	3400	5950	8500
2d Sed	350	950	1500	3050	5300	7600
2d HT	450	1450	2400	4800	8400	12,000
2d Conv	600	1900	3200	6400	11,200	16,000
4d Sta Wag	450	1140	1900	3800	6650	9500
2d HT (421/405)	1950	6250	10,400	20,800	36,400	52,000
2d Sed (421/405)	1950	6250	10,400	20,800	36,400	52,000
Star Chief Series, V-8, 123" wb						
4d Sed	350	975	1600	3200	5600	8000
4d HT	450	1140	1900	3800	6650	9500
Bonneville Series, V-8, 123" wb, Sta Wag 119" wb						
4d HT	400	1200	2000	4000	7000	10,000
2d HT	550	1700	2800	5600	9800	14,000
2d Conv	750	2400	4000	8000	14,000	20,000
4d Sta Wag	400	1250	2100	4200	7400	10,500
Grand Prix Series, V-8, 120" wb						
2d HT	550	1700	2800	5600	9800	14,000
NOTE: Add 30 percent for 421.						
Add 30 percent for "421" S-D models.						

1963

	6	5	4	3	2	1
Tempest (Compact) Series, 4-cyl., 112" wb						
4d Sed	350	780	1300	2600	4550	6500
2d Cpe	350	840	1400	2800	4900	7000
2d HT	350	1020	1700	3400	5950	8500
2d Conv	450	1450	2400	4800	8400	12,000
4d Sta Wag	350	840	1400	2800	4900	7000
NOTE: Add 20 percent for Tempest V-8.						
LeMans Series, V-8, 112" wb						
2d HT	400	1200	2000	4000	7000	10,000
2d Conv	500	1550	2600	5200	9100	13,000
Catalina Series, V-8, 119" wb						
4d Sed	350	850	1450	2850	4970	7100
4d HT	350	1040	1700	3450	6000	8600
2d Sed	350	950	1500	3050	5300	7600
2d HT	500	1550	2600	5200	9100	13,000
2d Conv	550	1800	3000	6000	10,500	15,000
4d Sta Wag	400	1200	2000	4000	7000	10,000
Catalina Super-Duty						
2d HT (421/405)	1900	6000	10,000	20,000	35,000	50,000
2d HT (421/410)	1950	6250	10,400	20,800	36,400	52,000
2d Sed (421/405)	1900	6000	10,000	20,000	35,000	50,000
2d Sed (421/410)	1900	6000	10,000	20,000	35,000	50,000
NOTE: Add 5 percent for 4-speed.						
Star Chief Series, V-8, 123" wb						
4d Sed	350	900	1500	3000	5250	7500
4d HT	450	1140	1900	3800	6650	9500
Bonneville Series, V-8, 123" wb						
2d HT	550	1700	2800	5600	9800	14,000
4d HT	400	1250	2100	4200	7400	10,500
2d Conv	700	2300	3800	7600	13,300	19,000
4d Sta Wag	400	1250	2100	4200	7400	10,500
Grand Prix Series, V-8, 120" wb						
2d HT	550	1800	3000	6000	10,500	15,000
NOTE: Add 5 percent for Catalina Ventura.						
Add 30 percent for "421" engine option.						

1964

	6	5	4	3	2	1
Tempest Custom 21, V-8, 115" wb						
4d Sed	350	800	1350	2700	4700	6700
2d HT	350	1020	1700	3400	5950	8500
2d Conv	450	1450	2400	4800	8400	12,000
4d Sta Wag	350	840	1400	2800	4900	7000
NOTE: Deduct 10 percent for 6-cyl. where available.						
LeMans Series, V-8, 115" wb						
2d HT	450	1450	2400	4800	8400	12,000
2d Cpe	400	1250	2100	4200	7400	10,500
2d Conv	500	1550	2600	5200	9100	13,000
2d GTO Cpe	600	1900	3200	6400	11,200	16,000
2d GTO Conv	850	2650	4400	8800	15,400	22,000
2d GTO HT	700	2150	3600	7200	12,600	18,000
NOTE: Deduct 20 percent for Tempest 6-cyl.						
Catalina Series, V-8, 120" wb						
4d Sed	350	900	1500	3000	5250	7500
4d HT	350	1020	1700	3400	5950	8500
2d Sed	350	900	1500	3000	5250	7500
2d HT	450	1450	2400	4800	8400	12,000
2d Conv	550	1800	3000	6000	10,500	15,000
4d Sta Wag	450	1080	1800	3600	6300	9000
Star Chief Series, V-8, 123" wb						
4d Sed	350	900	1500	3000	5250	7500
4d HT	450	1140	1900	3800	6650	9500
Bonneville Series, V-8, 123" wb						
4d HT	400	1250	2100	4200	7400	10,500
2d HT	500	1550	2600	5200	9100	13,000
2d Conv	700	2150	3600	7200	12,600	18,000
4d Sta Wag	400	1250	2100	4200	7400	10,500
Grand Prix Series, V-8, 120" wb						
2d HT	550	1700	2800	5600	9800	14,000
NOTES: Add 30 percent for tri power.						
Add 5 percent for Catalina-Ventura option.						
Add 10 percent for 2 plus 2.						

1965

	6	5	4	3	2	1
Tempest Series, V-8, 115" wb						
4d Sed	350	790	1350	2650	4620	6600
2d Spt Cpe	350	850	1450	2850	4970	7100
2d HT	350	1020	1700	3400	5950	8500
2d Conv	400	1200	2000	4000	7000	10,000
4d Sta Wag	350	840	1400	2800	4900	7000
NOTE: Add 20 percent for V-8.						
LeMans Series, V-8, 115" wb						
4d Sed	350	840	1400	2800	4900	7000
2d Cpe	350	1020	1700	3400	5950	8500
2d HT	400	1250	2100	4200	7400	10,500
2d Conv	550	1800	3000	6000	10,500	15,000
2d GTO Conv	900	2900	4800	9600	16,800	24,000
2d GTO HT	750	2400	4000	8000	14,000	20,000
2d GTO Cpe	700	2150	3600	7200	12,600	18,000
NOTE: Deduct 20 percent for 6-cyl. where available.						
Add 5 percent for 4-speed.						
Catalina Series, V-8, 121" wb						
4d Sed	350	820	1400	2700	4760	6800
4d HT	350	975	1600	3200	5600	8000
2d Sed	350	900	1500	3000	5250	7500
2d HT	400	1250	2100	4200	7400	10,500
2d Conv	500	1550	2600	5200	9100	13,000
4d Sta Wag	400	1250	2100	4200	7400	10,500
Star Chief Series, V-8, 123" wb						
4d Sed	350	840	1400	2800	4900	7000
4d HT	350	1020	1700	3400	5950	8500
Bonneville Series, V-8, 123" wb						
4d HT	450	1140	1900	3800	6650	9500
2d HT	450	1450	2400	4800	8400	12,000
2d Conv	650	2050	3400	6800	11,900	17,000
4d 2S Sta Wag	400	1250	2100	4200	7400	10,500
Grand Prix Series, 120" wb						
2d HT	450	1450	2400	4800	8400	12,000
NOTE: Add 30 percent for "421" H.O. Tri-power V-8.						
Add 30 percent for tri power.						
Add 10 percent for 2 plus 2.						
Add 10 percent for Catalina-Ventura option.						
Add 10 percent for Ram Air.						

1966

	6	5	4	3	2	1
Tempest Custom, OHC-6, 115" wb						
4d Sed	350	790	1350	2650	4620	6600
4d HT	350	800	1350	2700	4700	6700
2d HT	450	1120	1875	3750	6500	9300
2d Cpe	350	975	1600	3200	5600	8000
2d Conv	400	1200	2000	4000	7000	10,000
4d Sta Wag	350	780	1300	2600	4550	6500
NOTE: Add 20 percent for V-8.						
Lemans Series, OHC-6, 115" wb						
4d HT	350	830	1400	2950	4830	6900
2d Cpe	350	950	1550	3150	5450	7800
2d HT	400	1200	2000	4000	7000	10,000
2d Conv	450	1400	2300	4600	8100	11,500
NOTE: Add 20 percent for V-8.						
GTO Series, V-8, 115" wb						
2d HT	650	2050	3400	6800	11,900	17,000
2d Cpe	550	1800	3000	6000	10,500	15,000
2d Conv	800	2500	4200	8400	14,700	21,000
NOTE: Add 5 percent for 4-speed.						

	6	5	4	3	2	1
Catalina, V-8, 121" wb						
4d Sed	350	800	1350	2700	4700	6700
4d HT	350	975	1600	3200	5600	8000
2d Sed	350	900	1500	3000	5250	7500
2d HT	450	1400	2300	4600	8100	11,500
2d Conv	600	1900	3200	6400	11,200	16,000
4d Sta Wag	400	1200	2000	4000	7000	10,000
2 Plus 2, V-8, 121" wb						
2d HT	450	1500	2500	5000	8800	12,500
2d Conv	550	1800	3000	6000	10,500	15,000
Executive, V-8, 124" wb						
4d Sed	350	900	1500	3000	5250	7500
4d HT	350	1020	1700	3400	5950	8500
2d HT	450	1400	2300	4600	8100	11,500
Bonneville, V-8, 124" wb						
4d HT	450	1140	1900	3800	6650	9500
2d HT	450	1500	2500	5000	8800	12,500
2d Conv	700	2150	3600	7200	12,600	18,000
4d Sta Wag	400	1200	2000	4000	7000	10,000
Grand Prix, V-8, 121" wb						
2d HT	500	1550	2600	5200	9100	13,000

NOTE: Add 30 percent for 421.
Add 20 percent for Ram Air.
Add 30 percent for tri power.
Add 10 percent for Ventura Custom trim option.

1967

	6	5	4	3	2	1
Tempest, 6-cyl., 115" wb						
4d Sed	350	780	1300	2600	4550	6500
2d Cpe	350	840	1400	2800	4900	7000
4d Sta Wag	350	950	1500	3050	5300	7600

NOTE: Add 20 percent for V-8.

	6	5	4	3	2	1
Tempest Custom, 6-cyl., 115" wb						
2d Cpe	350	850	1450	2850	4970	7100
2d HT	350	1040	1700	3450	6000	8600
2d Conv	400	1200	2000	4000	7000	10,000
4d HT	350	860	1450	2900	5050	7200
4d Sed	350	790	1350	2650	4620	6600
4d Sta Wag	350	840	1400	2800	4900	7000

NOTE: Add 20 percent for V-8.

	6	5	4	3	2	1
Lemans, 6-cyl., 115" wb						
4d HT	350	840	1400	2800	4900	7000
2d Cpe	350	860	1450	2900	5050	7200
2d HT	450	1080	1800	3600	6300	9000
2d Conv	450	1400	2300	4600	8100	11,500

NOTE: Add 20 percent for V-8.

	6	5	4	3	2	1
Tempest Safari, 6-cyl., 115" wb						
4d Sta Wag	350	840	1400	2800	4900	7000

NOTE: Add 20 percent for V-8.

	6	5	4	3	2	1
GTO, V-8, 115" wb						
2d Cpe	500	1550	2600	5200	9100	13,000
2d HT	600	1900	3200	6400	11,200	16,000
2d Conv	700	2300	3800	7600	13,300	19,000
Catalina, V-8, 121" wb						
4d Sed	350	800	1350	2700	4700	6700
4d HT	350	975	1600	3200	5600	8000
2d Sed	350	950	1500	3050	5300	7600
2d HT	400	1250	2100	4200	7400	10,500
2d Conv	450	1450	2400	4800	8400	12,000
2 Plus 2, V-8, 121" Wb						
2d HT	450	1500	2500	5000	8800	12,500
2d Conv	700	2150	3600	7200	12,600	18,000
4d 3S Sta Wag	450	1080	1800	3600	6300	9000
Executive, V-8, 124" wb, Sta Wag 121" wb						
4d Sed	350	840	1400	2800	4900	7000
4d HT	350	1020	1700	3400	5950	8500
2d HT	450	1400	2300	4600	8100	11,500
4d 3S Sta Wag	400	1200	2000	4000	7000	10,000
Bonneville, V-8, 124" wb						
4d HT	450	1080	1800	3600	6300	9000
2d HT	450	1400	2300	4600	8100	11,500
2d Conv	550	1800	3000	6000	10,500	15,000
4d Sta Wag	400	1200	2000	4000	7000	10,000
Grand Prix, V-8, 121" wb						
2d HT	400	1300	2200	4400	7700	11,000
Conv	650	2050	3400	6800	11,900	17,000

NOTE: Add 30 percent for 428.
Add 10 percent for Sprint option.
Add 15 percent for 2 plus 2 option.
Add 10 percent for Ventura Custom trim option.

	6	5	4	3	2	1
Firebird, V-8, 108" wb						
2d Cpe	400	1250	2100	4200	7400	10,500
2d Conv	450	1400	2300	4600	8100	11,500

NOTE: Deduct 25 percent for 6-cyl.
Add 15 percent for 350 HO.
Add 10 percent for 4-speed.
Add 30 percent for the Ram Air 400 Firebird.

1968

	6	5	4	3	2	1
Tempest, 6-cyl., 112" wb						
2d Spt Cpe	350	840	1400	2800	4900	7000
2d Cus "S" Cpe	350	900	1500	3000	5250	7500
2d Cus "S" HT	450	1080	1800	3600	6300	9000
2d Cus "S" Conv	400	1200	2000	4000	7000	10,000
2d LeMans	350	840	1400	2800	4900	7000
2d LeMans Spt Cpe	350	975	1600	3200	5600	8000
2d LeMans Conv	550	1700	2800	5600	9800	14,000

NOTE: Add 20 percent for V-8.

	6	5	4	3	2	1
GTO, V-8, 112" wb						
2d HT	550	1800	3000	6000	10,500	15,000
2d Conv	700	2300	3800	7600	13,300	19,000

NOTE: Add 25 percent for Ram Air I, 40 percent for Ram Air II.

	6	5	4	3	2	1
Catalina, V-8, 122" wb						
4d Sed	350	780	1300	2600	4550	6500
4d HT	350	840	1400	2800	4900	7000
2d Sed	350	950	1550	3100	5400	7700
2d HT	450	1080	1800	3600	6300	9000
2d Conv	400	1300	2200	4400	7700	11,000
4d Sta Wag	450	1080	1800	3600	6300	9000
Executive, V-8, 124" wb, Sta Wag 121" wb						
4d Sed	350	900	1500	3000	5250	7500
4d HT	350	975	1600	3200	5600	8000
2d HT	400	1250	2100	4200	7400	10,500
4d 3S Sta Wag	400	1200	2000	4000	7000	10,000
Bonneville, V-8, 125" wb						
4d Sed	350	950	1550	3100	5400	7700
4d HT	350	1020	1700	3400	5950	8500
2d HT	400	1300	2200	4400	7700	11,000
2d Conv	500	1550	2600	5200	9100	13,000
4d Sta Wag	400	1250	2100	4200	7400	10,500
Grand Prix, V-8, 118" wb						
2d HT	400	1300	2200	4400	7700	11,000

NOTES: Add 10 percent for Sprint option.
Add 30 percent for 428.
Add 25 percent for Ram Air I, 40 percent for Ram Air II.
Add 10 percent for Ventura Custom trim option.

	6	5	4	3	2	1
Firebird, V-8, 108" wb						
2d Cpe	400	1200	2000	4000	7000	10,000
2d Conv	450	1400	2300	4600	8100	11,500

NOTE: Deduct 25 percent for 6-cyl.
Add 10 percent for 350 HO.
Add 10 percent for 4-speed.
Add 25 percent for the Ram Air 400 Firebird.

1969

	6	5	4	3	2	1
Tempest, 6-cyl., 116" wb, 2 dr 112" wb						
4d Sed	200	730	1250	2450	4270	6100
2d Cpe	200	745	1250	2500	4340	6200

NOTE: Add 20 percent for V-8.

	6	5	4	3	2	1
Tempest 'S' Custom, 6-cyl., 116" wb, 2 dr 112" wb						
4d Sed	200	745	1250	2500	4340	6200
4d HT	350	770	1300	2550	4480	6400
2d Cpe	200	750	1275	2500	4400	6300
2d HT	350	975	1600	3200	5600	8000
2d Conv	450	1080	1800	3600	6300	9000
4d Sta Wag	350	780	1300	2600	4550	6500

NOTE: Add 20 percent for V-8.

	6	5	4	3	2	1
Tempest Lemans, 6-cyl., 116" wb, 2 dr 112" wb						
4d HT	350	780	1300	2600	4550	6500
2d Cpe	350	780	1300	2600	4550	6500
2d HT	350	1020	1700	3400	5950	8500
2d Conv	400	1250	2100	4200	7400	10,500

NOTE: Add 20 percent for V-8.

	6	5	4	3	2	1
Tempest Safari, 6-cyl., 116" wb						
4d Sta Wag	350	800	1350	2700	4700	6700

NOTE: Add 20 percent for V-8.

	6	5	4	3	2	1
GTO, V-8, 112" wb						
2d HT	650	2050	3400	6800	11,900	17,000
2d Conv	800	2500	4200	8400	14,700	21,000
Catalina, V-8, 122" wb						
4d Sed	350	780	1300	2600	4550	6500
4d HT	350	800	1350	2700	4700	6700
2d HT	350	1020	1700	3400	5950	8500
2d Conv	400	1250	2100	4200	7400	10,500
4d 3S Sta Wag	350	975	1600	3200	5600	8000
Executive, V-8, 125" wb, Sta Wag 122" wb						
4d Sed	350	790	1350	2650	4620	6600
4d HT	350	820	1400	2700	4760	6800
2d HT	450	1080	1800	3600	6300	9000
4d 3S Sta Wag	350	1000	1650	3300	5750	8200
Bonneville, V-8, 125" wb						
4d Sed	350	790	1350	2650	4620	6600
4d HT	350	840	1400	2800	4900	7000
2d HT	450	1140	1900	3800	6650	9500
2d Conv	450	1400	2300	4600	8100	11,500
4d Sta Wag	350	1020	1700	3400	5950	8500
Grand Prix, V-8, 118" wb						
2d HT	400	1200	2000	4000	7000	10,000

NOTES: Add 10 percent for LeMans Rally E Pkg.
Add 30 percent for 428 cid V-8.
Add 25 percent for Ram Air III.
Add 40 percent for Ram Air IV.
Add 40 percent for GTO Judge option.
Add 25 percent for Ram Air IV.

	6	5	4	3	2	1
Firebird, V-8, 108" wb						
2d Cpe	400	1250	2100	4200	7400	10,500
2d Conv	400	1300	2200	4400	7700	11,000
2d Trans Am Cpe	550	1800	3000	6000	10,500	15,000
2d Trans Am Conv	850	2650	4400	8800	15,400	22,000

NOTE: Deduct 25 percent for 6-cyl.
Add 15 percent for "HO" 400 Firebird.
Add 10 percent for 4-speed.
Add 20 percent for Ram Air IV Firebird.
Add 50 percent for '303' V-8 SCCA race engine.

1970

	6	5	4	3	2	1
Tempest, 6-cyl., 116" wb, 2 dr 112" wb						
4d Sed	200	750	1275	2500	4400	6300
2d HT	350	975	1600	3200	5600	8000
2d Cpe	350	780	1300	2600	4550	6500

NOTE: Add 20 percent for V-8.

	6	5	4	3	2	1
LeMans, 6 cyl., 116" wb, 2 dr 112" wb						
4d Sed	350	770	1300	2550	4480	6400
4d HT	350	840	1400	2800	4900	7000
2d Cpe	350	790	1350	2650	4620	6600
2d HT	350	1020	1700	3400	5950	8500
4d Sta Wag	350	820	1400	2700	4760	6800

NOTE: Add 20 percent for V-8.

	6	5	4	3	2	1
LeMans Sport, 6 cyl., 116" wb, 2 dr 112" wb						
4d HT	350	860	1450	2900	5050	7200
2d Cpe	350	900	1500	3000	5250	7500
2d HT	450	1080	1800	3600	6300	9000
2d Conv	450	1140	1900	3800	6650	9500
4d Sta Wag	350	840	1400	2800	4900	7000

NOTE: Add 20 percent for V-8.

	6	5	4	3	2	1
LeMans GT 37, V-8, 112" wb						
2d Cpe	450	1080	1800	3600	6300	9000
2d HT	400	1250	2100	4200	7400	10,500
GTO, V-8, 112" wb						
2d HT	700	2150	3600	7200	12,600	18,000
2d Conv	850	2650	4400	8800	15,400	22,000
Catalina, V-8, 122" wb						
4d Sed	350	780	1300	2600	4550	6500
4d HT	350	900	1500	3000	5250	7500
2d HT	450	1080	1800	3600	6300	9000
2d Conv	400	1200	2000	4000	7000	10,000
4d 3S Sta Wag	350	975	1600	3200	5600	8000
Executive, V-8, 125" wb, Sta Wag 122" wb						
4d Sed	350	790	1350	2650	4620	6600
4d HT	350	975	1600	3200	5600	8000
2d HT	450	1140	1900	3800	6650	9500
4d 3S Sta Wag	350	1000	1650	3300	5750	8200
Bonneville, V-8, 125" wb, Sta Wag 122" wb						
4d Sed	350	840	1400	2800	4900	7000
4d HT	350	1020	1700	3400	5950	8500
2d HT	400	1200	2000	4000	7000	10,000
2d Conv	450	1400	2300	4600	8100	11,500
4d 3S Sta Wag	350	1020	1700	3400	5950	8500
Grand Prix, V-8, 118" wb						
2d Hurst "SSJ" HT	450	1400	2300	4600	8100	11,500

	6	5	4	3	2	1
2d HT	400	1250	2100	4200	7400	10,500

NOTES: Add 10 percent for V-8 LeMans Rally Pkg.
Add 40 percent for GTO Judge.
Add 40 percent for 455 HO V-8.
Add 10 percent for Grand Prix S.J.
Add 25 percent for Ram Air III.
Add 40 percent for Ram Air IV.

	6	5	4	3	2	1
Firebird, V-8, 108" wb						
2d Firebird	400	1300	2200	4400	7700	11,000
2d Esprit	450	1400	2300	4600	8100	11,500
2d Formula 400	450	1450	2400	4800	8400	12,000
2d Trans Am	550	1800	3000	6000	10,500	15,000

NOTES: Deduct 25 percent for 6-cyl.
Add 10 percent for Trans Am with 4-speed.
Add 25 percent for Ram Air IV Firebird.

1971

	6	5	4	3	2	1
Ventura II, 6 cyl., 111" wb						
2d Cpe	200	720	1200	2400	4200	6000
4d Sed	200	745	1250	2500	4340	6200
Ventura II, V-8, 111" wb						
2d Cpe	350	790	1350	2650	4620	6600
4d Sed	350	820	1400	2700	4760	6800
LeMans T37, 6 cyl., 116" wb, 2 dr 112" wb						
2d Sed	350	780	1300	2600	4550	6500
4d Sed	200	720	1200	2400	4200	6000
2d HT	350	975	1600	3200	5600	8000
LeMans, 6 cyl., 116" wb, 2 dr 112" wb						
2d Sed	200	720	1200	2400	4200	6000
4d Sed	200	730	1250	2450	4270	6100
4d HT	350	770	1300	2550	4480	6400
2d HT	450	1080	1800	3600	6300	9000
4d 3S Sta Wag	200	720	1200	2400	4200	6000
LeMans Sport, 6 cyl., 116" wb, 2 dr 112" wb						
4d HT	200	750	1275	2500	4400	6300
2d HT	450	1140	1900	3800	6650	9500
2d Conv	400	1300	2200	4400	7700	11,000

NOTE: Add 20 percent for V-8.

	6	5	4	3	2	1
LeMans GT 37, V-8, 112" wb						
2d HT	400	1300	2200	4400	7700	11,000
GTO						
2d HT	550	1800	3000	6000	10,500	15,000
2d Conv	850	2750	4600	9200	16,100	23,000

NOTE: Add 40 percent for GTO Judge option.

	6	5	4	3	2	1
Catalina						
4d	350	790	1350	2650	4620	6600
4d HT	350	800	1350	2700	4700	6700
2d HT	350	900	1500	3000	5250	7500
2d Conv	400	1200	2000	4000	7000	10,000
Safari, V-8, 127" wb						
4d 2S Sta Wag	350	800	1350	2700	4700	6700
4d 3S Sta Wag	350	820	1400	2700	4760	6800
Catalina Brougham, V-8, 123" wb						
4d Sed	350	820	1400	2700	4760	6800
4d HT	350	830	1400	2950	4830	6900
2d HT	350	950	1550	3100	5400	7700
Grand Safari, V-8, 127" wb						
4d 2S Sta Wag	200	720	1200	2400	4200	6000
4d 3S Sta Wag	200	730	1250	2450	4270	6100
Bonneville						
4d Sed	350	830	1400	2950	4830	6900
4d HT	350	840	1400	2800	4900	7000
2d HT	350	975	1600	3200	5600	8000
Grandville						
4d HT	350	840	1400	2800	4900	7000
2d HT	350	1000	1650	3300	5750	8200
2d Conv	500	1550	2600	5200	9100	13,000
Grand Prix						
2d HT	450	1080	1800	3600	6300	9000
2d Hurst "SSJ" Cpe	400	1250	2100	4200	7400	10,500
Firebird, V-8, 108" wb						
2d Firebird	450	1400	2300	4600	8100	11,500
2d Esprit	400	1300	2200	4400	7700	11,000
2d Formula	450	1450	2400	4800	8400	12,000
2d Trans Am	550	1800	3000	6000	10,500	15,000

NOTES: Add 25 percent for Formula 455.
Deduct 25 percent for 6-cyl.
Add 40 percent for 455 HO V-8.
Add 10 percent for 4-speed.
(Formula Series -350, 400, 455).

1972

	6	5	4	3	2	1
Ventura, 6 cyl., 111" wb						
4d Sed	200	685	1150	2300	3990	5700
2d Cpe	200	660	1100	2200	3850	5500

NOTE: Add 20 percent for V-8.

	6	5	4	3	2	1
LeMans, 6 cyl., 116" wb, 2 dr 112" wb						
2d Cpe	200	720	1200	2400	4200	6000
4d Sed	200	670	1200	2300	4060	5800
2d HT	450	1140	1900	3800	6650	9500
2d Conv	400	1300	2200	4400	7700	11,000
4d 3S Sta Wag	200	720	1200	2400	4200	6000
GTO						
2d HT	500	1550	2600	5200	9100	13,000
2d Sed	400	1200	2000	4000	7000	10,000
Luxury LeMans, V-8						
4d HT	200	745	1250	2500	4340	6200
2d HT	400	1200	2000	4000	7000	10,000

NOTE: Add 20 percent for V-8.

	6	5	4	3	2	1
Catalina, V-8, 123" wb						
4d Sed	200	660	1100	2200	3850	5500
4d HT	200	685	1150	2300	3990	5700
2d HT	350	900	1500	3000	5250	7500
2d Conv	400	1250	2100	4200	7400	10,500
Catalina Brougham, V-8, 123" wb						
4d Sed	200	670	1150	2250	3920	5600
4d HT	200	720	1200	2400	4200	6000
2d HT	350	975	1600	3200	5600	8000
Bonneville						
4d Sed	200	685	1150	2300	3990	5700
4d HT	350	780	1300	2600	4550	6500
2d HT	350	1020	1700	3400	5950	8500
Grandville						
4d HT	350	780	1300	2600	4550	6500
2d HT	350	1040	1750	3500	6100	8700
2d Conv	450	1450	2400	4800	8400	12,000
Safari, V-8, 127" wb						
4d 2S Sta Wag	200	670	1150	2250	3920	5600
4d 3S Sta Wag	200	685	1150	2300	3990	5700

	6	5	4	3	2	1
Grand Safari, V-8, 127" wb						
4d 2S Sta Wag	200	670	1200	2300	4060	5800
4d 3S Sta Wag	200	700	1200	2350	4130	5900
Grand Prix						
2d Hurst "SSJ" HdTp	450	1140	1900	3800	6650	9500
2d HT	350	1000	1650	3300	5750	8200
Firebird, V-8, 108" wb						
2d Firebird	400	1250	2100	4200	7400	10,500
2d Esprit	400	1200	2000	4000	7000	10,000
2d Formula	400	1300	2200	4400	7700	11,000
2d Trans Am	550	1700	2800	5600	9800	14,000

NOTE: Add 10 percent for Trans Am with 4-speed.
Deduct 25 percent for 6-cyl.
Add 40 percent for 455 HO V-8.

1973

	6	5	4	3	2	1
Ventura						
4d Sed	200	700	1050	2100	3650	5200
2d Cpe	200	675	1000	1950	3400	4900
2d HBk Cpe	200	700	1075	2150	3700	5300
Ventura Custom						
4d Sed	200	700	1075	2150	3700	5300
2d Cpe	200	650	1100	2150	3780	5400
2d HBk Cpe	200	700	1050	2050	3600	5100

NOTE: Deduct 5 percent for 6-cyl.

	6	5	4	3	2	1
LeMans						
4d Sed	200	660	1100	2200	3850	5500
2d HT	350	800	1350	2700	4700	6700
LeMans Spt						
2d Cpe	200	720	1200	2400	4200	6000
Luxury LeMans						
2d Cpe	200	745	1250	2500	4340	6200
4d HT	200	720	1200	2400	4200	6000
LeMans Safari, V-8, 116" wb						
4d 2S Sta Wag	200	660	1100	2200	3850	5500
4d 3S Sta Wag	200	660	1100	2200	3850	5500
Grand AM						
2d HT	450	1080	1800	3600	6300	9000
4d HT	350	780	1300	2600	4550	6500
2d GTO Spt Cpe	450	1080	1800	3600	6300	9000

Deduct 5 percent for 6-cyl.

	6	5	4	3	2	1
Catalina						
4d HT	200	700	1050	2050	3600	5100
2d HT	350	780	1300	2600	4550	6500
Bonneville						
4d Sed	200	700	1050	2100	3650	5200
4d HT	200	660	1100	2200	3850	5500
2d HT	350	830	1400	2950	4830	6900
Safari, V-8, 127" wb						
4d 2S Sta Wag	200	660	1100	2200	3850	5500
4d 3S Sta Wag	200	670	1150	2250	3920	5600
Grand Safari, V-8, 127" wb						
4d 2S Sta Wag	200	685	1150	2300	3990	5700
4d 3S Sta Wag	200	670	1200	2300	4060	5800
Grandville						
4d HT	200	685	1150	2300	3990	5700
2d HT	350	850	1450	2850	4970	7100
2d Conv	450	1450	2400	4800	8400	12,000
Grand Prix						
2d HT	350	900	1500	3000	5250	7500
2d 'SJ' HT	350	950	1550	3100	5400	7700
Firebird, V-8, 108" wb						
2d Cpe	400	1200	2000	4000	7000	10,000
2d Esprit	400	1250	2100	4200	7400	10,500
2d Formula	400	1300	2200	4400	7700	11,000
2d Trans Am	450	1400	2300	4600	8100	11,500

NOTE: Add 50 percent for 455 SD V-8 (Formula & Trans Am only).
Deduct 25 percent for 6-cyl.
Add 10 percent for 4-speed.

1974

	6	5	4	3	2	1
Ventura						
4d Sed	150	650	950	1900	3300	4700
2d Cpe	150	575	900	1750	3100	4400
2d HBk	150	650	975	1950	3350	4800
Ventura Custom						
4d Sed	150	650	975	1950	3350	4800
2d Cpe	150	600	900	1800	3150	4500
2d HBk	200	675	1000	1950	3400	4900
2d GTO	350	780	1300	2600	4550	6500

NOTE: Deduct 4 percent for 6-cyl.

	6	5	4	3	2	1
LeMans						
4d HT	150	550	850	1675	2950	4200
2d HT	200	685	1150	2300	3990	5700
4d Sta Wag	150	600	900	1800	3150	4500
LeMans Sport						
2d Cpe	200	675	1000	2000	3500	5000
Luxury LeMans						
4d HT	150	650	975	1950	3350	4800
2d HT	200	745	1250	2500	4340	6200
4d Safari	200	675	1000	2000	3500	5000

NOTE: Add 10 percent for GT option.

	6	5	4	3	2	1
Grand AM						
2d HT	350	975	1600	3200	5600	8000
4d HT	200	670	1200	2300	4060	5800
Catalina						
4d HT	150	650	975	1950	3350	4800
2d HT	200	720	1200	2400	4200	6000
4d Sed	150	500	800	1600	2800	4000
4d Safari	150	650	975	1950	3350	4800
Bonneville						
4d Sed	150	550	850	1675	2950	4200
4d HT	200	675	1000	2000	3500	5000
2d HT	350	770	1300	2550	4480	6400
Grandville						
4d HT	200	700	1050	2050	3600	5100
2d HT	350	780	1300	2600	4550	6500
2d Conv	400	1300	2200	4400	7700	11,000
Grand Prix						
2d HT	350	840	1400	2800	4900	7000
2d 'SJ' Cpe	350	860	1450	2900	5050	7200
Firebird, V-8, 108" wb						
2d Firebird	350	1020	1700	3400	5950	8500
2d Esprit	450	1080	1800	3600	6300	9000
2d Formula	400	1250	2100	4200	7400	10,500
2d Trans Am	400	1300	2200	4400	7700	11,000

NOTE: Add 40 percent for 455-SD V-8 (Formula & Trans Am only).
Deduct 25 percent for 6-cyl.
Add 10 percent for 4-speed.

1975

	6	5	4	3	2	1
Astre S						
2d Cpe	150	575	875	1700	3000	4300
2d HBk	150	575	900	1750	3100	4400
4d Safari	150	600	900	1800	3150	4500
Astre						
2d HBk	150	575	900	1750	3100	4400
4d Safari	150	600	900	1800	3150	4500
NOTE: Add 10 percent for Astre 'SJ'.						
Ventura						
4d Sed	150	575	900	1750	3100	4400
2d Cpe	150	600	900	1800	3150	4500
2d HBk	150	600	950	1850	3200	4600
NOTES: Deduct 5 percent for Ventura 'S'.						
Add 15 percent for Ventura 'SJ'.						
Add 5 percent for Ventura Custom.						
LeMans						
4d HT	150	600	900	1800	3150	4500
2d HT	200	660	1100	2200	3850	5500
4d Safari	150	600	950	1850	3200	4600
NOTE: Add 10 percent for Grand LeMans.						
LeMans Sport						
2d HT Cpe	200	685	1150	2300	3990	5700
Grand AM						
4d HT	150	600	950	1850	3200	4600
2d HT	200	720	1200	2400	4200	6000
NOTE: Add 5 percent for 4-speed.						
Add 20 percent for 455 HO V-8.						
Catalina						
4d Sed	150	550	850	1650	2900	4100
2d Cpe	150	600	900	1800	3150	4500
4d Safari	150	500	800	1600	2800	4000
Bonneville						
4d HT	150	575	875	1700	3000	4300
2d Cpe	150	600	950	1850	3200	4600
4d Gr. Safari	150	575	900	1750	3100	4400
Grand VIlle Brougham						
4d HT	150	575	900	1750	3100	4400
2d Cpe	150	650	975	1950	3350	4800
2d Conv	500	1550	2600	5200	9100	13,000
NOTE: Add 20 percent for 455 V-8.						
Grand Prix						
2d Cpe	200	660	1100	2200	3850	5500
2d 'LJ' Cpe	200	670	1150	2250	3920	5600
2d 'SJ' Cpe	200	685	1150	2300	3990	5700
NOTE: Add 12 percent for 455 V-8.						
Firebird, V-8, 108" wb						
2d Cpe	350	900	1500	3000	5250	7500
2d Esprit	350	1020	1700	3400	5950	8500
2d Formula	350	1020	1700	3400	5950	8500
Trans Am	450	1140	1900	3800	6650	9500
NOTE: Add 18 percent for 455 HO V-8.						
Deduct 25 percent for 6-cyl.						
Add 10 percent for 4-speed.						
Add $150.00 for Honeycomb wheels.						

1976

	6	5	4	3	2	1
Astre, 4-cyl.						
2d Cpe	125	450	750	1450	2500	3600
2d HBk	150	475	750	1475	2600	3700
4d Sta Wag	150	475	775	1500	2650	3800
Sunbird, 4-cyl.						
2d Cpe	150	650	975	1950	3350	4800
Ventura, V-8						
4d Sed	150	600	950	1850	3200	4600
2d Cpe	150	650	950	1900	3300	4700
2d HBk	150	650	975	1950	3350	4800
Ventura SJ, V-8						
4d Sed	150	650	950	1900	3300	4700
2d Cpe	150	650	975	1950	3350	4800
2d HBk	200	675	1000	1950	3400	4900
LeMans, V-8						
4d Sed	150	650	975	1950	3350	4800
2d Cpe	200	675	1000	1950	3400	4900
4d 2S Safari Wag	150	600	950	1850	3200	4600
4d 3S Safari Wag	150	650	950	1900	3300	4700
LeMans Sport Cpe, V-8						
2d Cpe	200	700	1050	2100	3650	5200
Grand LeMans, V-8						
4d Sed	200	675	1000	1950	3400	4900
2d Cpe	200	675	1000	2000	3500	5000
4d 2S Safari Wag	150	650	975	1950	3350	4800
4d 3S Safari Wag	200	675	1000	1950	3400	4900
Catalina, V-8						
4d Sed	150	650	950	1900	3300	4700
2d Cpe	150	650	975	1950	3350	4800
4d 2S Safari Wag	200	700	1050	2050	3600	5100
4d 3S Safari Wag	150	650	950	1900	3300	4700
Bonneville, V-8						
4d Sed	200	675	1000	1950	3400	4900
2d Cpe	200	675	1000	2000	3500	5000
Bonneville Brougham, V-8						
4d Sed	200	700	1050	2050	3600	5100
2d Cpe	200	700	1075	2150	3700	5300
Grand Safari, V-8						
4d 2S Sta Wag	150	650	975	1950	3350	4800
4d 3S Sta Wag	200	675	1000	1950	3400	4900
Grand Prix, V-8						
2d Cpe	200	660	1100	2200	3850	5500
2d Cpe SJ	200	685	1150	2300	3990	5700
2d Cpe LJ	200	745	1250	2500	4340	6200
NOTE: Add 10 percent for T tops & Anniversary model.						
Firebird, V-8						
2d Cpe	200	745	1250	2500	4340	6200
2d Esprit Cpe	350	780	1300	2600	4550	6500
2d Formula Cpe	350	800	1350	2700	4700	6700
2d Trans Am Cpe	350	830	1400	2950	4830	6900
NOTE: Add 20 percent for 455 HO V-8.						
Deduct 25 percent for 6-cyl.						
Add 10 percent for 4-speed.						
Add $150.00 for Honeycomb wheels.						

1977

	6	5	4	3	2	1
Astre, 4-cyl.						
2d Cpe	100	330	575	1150	1950	2800
2d HBk	100	350	600	1150	2000	2900
4d Sta Wag	100	360	600	1200	2100	3000
Sunbird, 4-cyl.						
2d Cpe	150	500	800	1600	2800	4000
2d HBk	150	550	850	1650	2900	4100

[1977 continued]

	6	5	4	3	2	1
Phoenix, V-8						
4d Sed	150	500	800	1550	2700	3900
2d Cpe	150	500	800	1600	2800	4000
Ventura, V-8						
4d Sed	150	500	800	1550	2700	3900
2d Cpe	150	500	800	1600	2800	4000
2d HBk	150	550	850	1650	2900	4100
Ventura SJ, V-8						
4d Sed	150	500	800	1600	2800	4000
2d Cpe	150	550	850	1650	2900	4100
2d HBk	150	550	850	1675	2950	4200
LeMans, V-8						
4d Sed	150	500	800	1600	2800	4000
2d Cpe	150	550	850	1650	2900	4100
4d 2S Sta Wag	150	500	800	1550	2700	3900
4d 3S Sta Wag	150	500	800	1600	2800	4000
LeMans Sport Cpe, V-8						
NOTE: Add 20 percent for Can Am option.						
2d Cpe	150	575	900	1750	3100	4400
Grand LeMans, V-8						
4d Sed	150	550	850	1650	2900	4100
2d Cpe	150	550	850	1675	2950	4200
4d 2S Sta Wag	150	500	800	1600	2800	4000
4d 3S Sta Wag	150	550	850	1650	2900	4100
Catalina, V-8						
4d Sed	150	500	800	1550	2700	3900
2d Cpe	150	500	800	1600	2800	4000
4d 2S Safari Wag	150	475	775	1500	2650	3800
4d 3S Safari Wag	150	500	800	1550	2700	3900
Bonneville, V-8						
4d Sed	150	550	850	1650	2900	4100
2d Cpe	150	550	850	1675	2950	4200
Bonneville Brougham, V-8						
4d Sed	150	575	875	1700	3000	4300
2d Cpe	150	600	900	1800	3150	4500
Grand Safari						
4d 2S Sta Wag	150	550	850	1675	2950	4200
4d 3S Sta Wag	150	575	875	1700	3000	4300
Grand Prix, V-8						
2d Cpe	150	650	950	1900	3300	4700
2d Cpe LJ	200	675	1000	2000	3500	5000
2d Cpe SJ	200	720	1200	2400	4200	6000
Firebird, V-8						
2d Cpe	200	670	1200	2300	4060	5800
2d Esprit Cpe	200	720	1200	2400	4200	6000
2d Formula Cpe	200	750	1275	2500	4400	6300
2d Trans Am Cpe	350	780	1300	2600	4550	6500
NOTE: Add 10 percent for 4-speed.						

1978

	6	5	4	3	2	1
Sunbird						
2d Cpe	100	350	600	1150	2000	2900
2d Spt Cpe	100	360	600	1200	2100	3000
2d Spt HBk	125	370	650	1250	2200	3100
4d Spt Wag	100	360	600	1200	2100	3000
Phoenix						
4d Sed	100	360	600	1200	2100	3000
2d Cpe	125	400	675	1350	2300	3300
2d HBk	125	370	650	1250	2200	3100
Phoenix LJ						
4d Sed	125	370	650	1250	2200	3100
2d Cpe	125	450	700	1400	2450	3500
LeMans						
4d Sed	150	500	800	1600	2800	4000
2d Cpe	150	550	850	1675	2950	4200
4d 2S Sta Wag	150	500	800	1600	2800	4000
Grand LeMans						
4d Sed	150	550	850	1650	2900	4100
2d Cpe	150	575	875	1700	3000	4300
4d 2S Sta Wag	150	550	850	1650	2900	4100
Grand Am						
4d Sed	150	550	850	1675	2950	4200
2d Cpe	150	600	900	1800	3150	4500
Catalina						
4d Sed	150	500	800	1600	2800	4000
2d Cpe	150	550	850	1650	2900	4100
4d 2S Sta Wag	150	550	850	1675	2950	4200
Bonneville						
4d Sed	150	575	875	1700	3000	4300
2d Cpe	150	600	900	1800	3150	4500
4d 2S Sta Wag	150	600	900	1800	3150	4500
Bonneville Brougham						
4d Sed	150	600	900	1800	3150	4500
2d Cpe	150	650	950	1900	3300	4700
Grand Prix						
2d Cpe	200	675	1000	1950	3400	4900
2d Cpe LJ	200	675	1000	2000	3500	5000
2d Cpe SJ	200	700	1050	2100	3650	5200
Firebird, V-8, 108" wb						
2d Cpe	200	670	1200	2300	4060	5800
2d Esprit Cpe	200	720	1200	2400	4200	6000
2d Formula Cpe	200	750	1275	2500	4400	6300
2d Trans Am Cpe	350	780	1300	2600	4550	6500
NOTE: Add 10 percent for 4-speed.						

1979

	6	5	4	3	2	1
Sunbird						
2d Cpe	100	360	600	1200	2100	3000
2d Spt Cpe	125	370	650	1250	2200	3100
2d HBk	125	370	650	1250	2200	3100
4d Sta Wag	125	380	650	1300	2250	3200
Phoenix						
2d Sed	125	370	650	1250	2200	3100
2d Cpe	125	400	675	1350	2300	3300
2d HBk	125	380	650	1300	2250	3200
Phoenix LJ						
4d Sed	125	380	650	1300	2250	3200
2d Cpe	125	400	700	1375	2400	3400
LeMans						
4d Sed	150	550	850	1650	2900	4100
2d Cpe	150	575	875	1700	3000	4300
4d Sta Wag	150	550	850	1650	2900	4100
Grand LeMans						
4d Sed	150	550	850	1675	2950	4200
2d Cpe	150	600	900	1800	3150	4500
4d Sta Wag	150	550	850	1675	2950	4200
Grand Am						
4d Sed	150	600	900	1800	3150	4500
2d Cpe	150	650	950	1900	3300	4700

	6	5	4	3	2	1
Catalina						
4d Sed	150	550	850	1650	2900	4100
2d Cpe	150	550	850	1675	2950	4200
4d Sta Wag	150	550	850	1650	2900	4100
Bonneville						
4d Sed	150	575	900	1750	3100	4400
2d Cpe	150	600	900	1800	3150	4500
4d Sta Wag	150	575	900	1750	3100	4400
Bonneville Brougham						
4d Sed	150	600	950	1850	3200	4600
2d Cpe	150	650	975	1950	3350	4800
Grand Prix						
2d Cpe	200	675	1000	2000	3500	5000
2d LJ Cpe	200	700	1050	2100	3650	5200
2d SJ Cpe	200	650	1100	2150	3780	5400
Firebird, V-8, 108" wb						
2d Cpe	200	745	1250	2500	4340	6200
2d Esprit Cpe	350	770	1300	2550	4480	6400
2d Formula Cpe	350	790	1350	2650	4620	6600
2d Trans Am Cpe	350	975	1600	3200	5600	8000
NOTE: Add 15 percent for 10th Anniversary Edition. Add 10 percent for 4-speed.						
1980						
Sunbird, V-6						
2d Cpe	125	450	700	1400	2450	3500
2d HBk	125	450	750	1450	2500	3600
2d Spt Cpe	125	450	750	1450	2500	3600
2d Cpe HBk	150	475	750	1475	2600	3700
NOTE: Deduct 10 percent for 4-cyl.						
Phoenix, V-6						
2d Cpe	150	475	750	1475	2600	3700
4d Sed HBk	125	450	750	1450	2500	3600
NOTE: Deduct 10 percent for 4-cyl.						
Phoenix LJ, V-6						
2d Cpe	150	475	775	1500	2650	3800
4d Sed HBk	150	475	750	1475	2600	3700
NOTE: Deduct 10 percent for 4-cyl.						
LeMans, V-8						
4d Sed	150	475	750	1475	2600	3700
2d Cpe	150	500	800	1550	2700	3900
4d Sta Wag	150	475	775	1500	2650	3800
NOTE: Deduct 10 percent for V-6.						
Grand LeMans, V-8						
4d Sed	150	475	775	1500	2650	3800
2d Cpe	150	500	800	1600	2800	4000
4d Sta Wag	150	500	800	1550	2700	3900
NOTE: Deduct 10 percent for V-6.						
Grand Am, V-8						
2d Cpe	150	550	850	1650	2900	4100
Firebird, V-8						
2d Cpe	200	700	1200	2350	4130	5900
2d Cpe Esprit	200	720	1200	2400	4200	6000
2d Cpe Formula	200	730	1250	2450	4270	6100
2d Cpe Trans Am	200	750	1275	2500	4400	6300
NOTE: Deduct 15 percent for V-6.						
Catalina, V-8						
4d Sed	150	475	775	1500	2650	3800
2d Cpe	150	500	800	1550	2700	3900
4d 2S Sta Wag	150	500	800	1550	2700	3900
4d 3S Sta Wag	150	500	800	1600	2800	4000
NOTE: Deduct 10 percent for V-6.						
Bonneville, V-8						
4d Sed	150	500	800	1550	2700	3900
2d Cpe	150	500	800	1600	2800	4000
4d 2S Sta Wag	150	500	800	1600	2800	4000
4d 3S Sta Wag	150	550	850	1650	2900	4100
NOTE: Deduct 10 percent for V-6.						
Bonneville Brougham, V-8						
4d Sed	150	550	850	1650	2900	4100
2d Cpe	150	575	875	1700	3000	4300
NOTE: Deduct 10 percent for V-6.						
Grand Prix, V-8						
2d Cpe	200	650	1100	2150	3780	5400
2d Cpe LJ	200	660	1100	2200	3850	5500
2d Cpe SJ	200	670	1150	2250	3920	5600
NOTE: Deduct 10 percent for V-6.						
1981						
T1000, 4-cyl.						
2d Sed HBk	125	450	700	1400	2450	3500
4d Sed HBk	125	450	750	1450	2500	3600
Phoenix, V-6						
2d Cpe	150	475	750	1475	2600	3700
4d Sed HBk	125	450	750	1450	2500	3600
NOTE: Deduct 10 percent for 4-cyl.						
Phoenix LJ, V-6						
2d Cpe	150	475	775	1500	2650	3800
4d Sed HBk	150	475	750	1475	2600	3700
NOTE: Deduct 10 percent for 4-cyl.						
LeMans, V-8						
4d Sed	150	500	800	1550	2700	3900
4d Sed LJ	150	500	800	1600	2800	4000
2d Cpe	150	500	800	1600	2800	4000
4d Sta Wag	150	500	800	1600	2800	4000
NOTE: Deduct 10 percent for V-6.						
Grand LeMans, V-8						
4d Sed	150	600	950	1850	3200	4600
2d Cpe	150	550	850	1675	2950	4200
4d Sta Wag	150	550	850	1675	2950	4200
NOTE: Deduct 10 percent for V-6.						
Firebird, V-8						
2d Cpe	200	720	1200	2400	4200	6000
2 pe Esprit	200	730	1250	2450	4270	6100
2d Cpe Formula	200	745	1250	2500	4340	6200
2d Cpe Trans Am	350	780	1300	2600	4550	6500
2d Cpe Trans Am SE	350	820	1400	2700	4760	6800
NOTE: Deduct 15 percent for V-6.						
Catalina, V-8						
4d Sed	150	550	850	1675	2950	4200
2d Cpe	150	575	875	1700	3000	4300
4d 2S Sta Wag	150	575	875	1700	3000	4300
4d 3S Sta Wag	150	575	900	1750	3100	4400
NOTE: Deduct 10 percent for V-6.						
Bonneville, V-8						
4d Sed	150	575	875	1700	3000	4300
2d Cpe	150	575	900	1750	3100	4400
4d 2S Sta Wag	150	575	900	1750	3100	4400
4d 3S Sta Wag	150	600	900	1800	3150	4500
NOTE: Deduct 10 percent for V-6.						
Bonneville Brougham, V-8						
4d Sed	150	600	900	1800	3150	4500
2d Cpe	150	600	950	1850	3200	4600
Grand Prix, V-8						
2d Cpe	200	650	1100	2150	3780	5400
2d Cpe LJ	200	660	1100	2200	3850	5500
2d Cpe Brgm	200	670	1150	2250	3920	5600
NOTE: Deduct 10 percent for V-6.						
1982						
T1000, 4-cyl.						
4d Sed HBk	150	475	750	1475	2600	3700
2d Cpe HBk	125	450	750	1450	2500	3600
J2000 S, 4-cyl.						
4d Sed	150	500	800	1550	2700	3900
2d Cpe	150	500	800	1600	2800	4000
4d Sta Wag	150	500	800	1600	2800	4000
J2000, 4-cyl.						
4d Sed	150	500	800	1600	2800	4000
2d Cpe	150	550	850	1650	2900	4100
2d Cpe HBk	150	550	850	1675	2950	4200
4d Sta Wag	150	550	850	1675	2950	4200
J2000 LE, 4-cyl.						
4d Sed	150	550	850	1650	2900	4100
2d Cpe	150	550	850	1675	2950	4200
J2000 SE, 4-cyl.						
2d Cpe HBk	150	575	900	1750	3100	4400
Phoenix, V-6						
4d Sed HBk	150	475	775	1500	2650	3800
2d Cpe	150	500	800	1550	2700	3900
NOTE: Deduct 10 percent for 4-cyl.						
Phoenix LJ, V-6						
4d Sed HBk	150	500	800	1550	2700	3900
2d Cpe	150	500	800	1600	2800	4000
NOTE: Deduct 10 percent for 4-cyl.						
Phoenix SJ, V-6						
4d Sed HBk	150	500	800	1600	2800	4000
2d Cpe	150	550	850	1650	2900	4100
6000, V-6						
4d Sed	150	550	850	1675	2950	4200
2d Cpe	150	575	875	1700	3000	4300
NOTE: Deduct 10 percent for 4-cyl.						
6000 LE, V-6						
4d Sed	150	575	875	1700	3000	4300
2d Cpe	150	575	900	1750	3100	4400
NOTE: Deduct 10 percent for 4-cyl.						
Firebird, V-8						
2d Cpe	200	750	1275	2500	4400	6300
2d Cpe SE	350	790	1350	2650	4620	6600
2d Cpe Trans Am	350	830	1400	2950	4830	6900
NOTE: Deduct 15 percent for V-6.						
Bonneville, V-6						
4d Sed	150	600	900	1800	3150	4500
4d Sta Wag	150	600	900	1800	3150	4500
Bonneville Brougham						
4d Sed	150	650	950	1900	3300	4700
Grand Prix, V-6						
2d Cpe	200	700	1200	2350	4130	5900
2d Cpe LJ	200	730	1250	2450	4270	6100
2d Cpe Brgm	200	745	1250	2500	4340	6200
1983						
1000, 4-cyl.						
4d Sed HBk	150	475	775	1500	2650	3800
2d Cpe	150	475	750	1475	2600	3700
2000, 4-cyl.						
4d Sed	150	500	800	1600	2800	4000
2d Cpe	150	550	850	1650	2900	4100
2d Cpe HBk	150	550	850	1675	2950	4200
4d Sta Wag	150	550	850	1675	2950	4200
2000 LE, 4-cyl.						
4d Sed	150	550	850	1675	2950	4200
2d Cpe	150	575	875	1700	3000	4300
4d Sta Wag	150	575	875	1700	3000	4300
2000 SE, 4-cyl.						
2d Cpe HBk	150	575	900	1750	3100	4400
Sunbird, 4-cyl.						
2d Conv	350	1020	1700	3400	5950	8500
Phoenix, V-6						
4d Sed HBk	150	500	800	1550	2700	3900
2d Cpe	150	500	800	1600	2800	4000
NOTE: Deduct 10 percent for 4-cyl.						
Phoenix LJ, V-6						
4d Sed HBk	150	500	800	1600	2800	4000
2d Cpe	150	550	850	1650	2900	4100
NOTE: Deduct 10 percent for 4-cyl.						
Phoenix SJ, V-6						
4d Sed HBk	150	550	850	1650	2900	4100
2d Cpe	150	550	850	1675	2950	4200
6000, V-6						
4d Sed	150	575	875	1700	3000	4300
2d Cpe	150	575	900	1750	3100	4400
NOTE: Deduct 10 percent for 4-cyl.						
6000 LE, V-6						
4d Sed	150	575	900	1750	3100	4400
2d Cpe	150	600	900	1800	3150	4500
NOTE: Deduct 10 percent for 4-cyl.						
6000 STE, V-6						
4d Sed	150	650	950	1900	3300	4700
Firebird, V-8						
2d Cpe	200	750	1275	2500	4400	6300
2d Cpe SE	350	770	1300	2550	4480	6400
2d Cpe Trans Am	350	790	1350	2650	4620	6600
NOTE: Deduct 15 percent for V-6.						
Bonneville, V-8						
4d Sed	150	650	975	1950	3350	4800
4d Brgm	200	675	1000	1950	3400	4900
4d Sta Wag	200	675	1000	1950	3400	4900
NOTE: Deduct 10 percent for V-6.						
Grand Prix, V-8						
2d Cpe	200	660	1100	2200	3850	5500
2d Cpe LJ	200	685	1150	2300	3990	5700
2d Cpe Brgm	200	670	1200	2300	4060	5800
1984						
1000, 4-cyl.						
4d HBk	150	475	775	1500	2650	3800
2d HBk	150	475	750	1475	2600	3700
Sunbird 2000, 4-cyl.						
4d Sed LE	150	550	850	1650	2900	4100
2d Sed LE	150	500	800	1600	2800	4000

	6	5	4	3	2	1
2d Conv LE	350	1020	1700	3400	5950	8500
4d Sta Wag LE	150	550	850	1675	2950	4200
4d Sed SE	150	550	850	1675	2950	4200
2d Sed SE	150	550	850	1650	2900	4100
2d HBk SE	150	575	875	1700	3000	4300
NOTE: Deduct 5 percent for lesser models.						
Phoenix, 4-cyl.						
2d Sed	150	500	800	1550	2700	3900
4d HBk	150	500	800	1600	2800	4000
2d Sed LE	150	500	800	1600	2800	4000
4d HBk LE	150	550	850	1650	2900	4100
Phoenix, V-6						
2d Sed	150	550	850	1650	2900	4100
4d HBk	150	550	850	1675	2950	4200
2d Sed LE	150	550	850	1675	2950	4200
4d HBk LE	150	575	875	1700	3000	4300
2d Sed SE	150	575	900	1750	3100	4400
6000, 4-cyl.						
4d Sed LE	150	600	900	1800	3150	4500
2d Sed LE	150	600	950	1850	3200	4600
4d Sta Wag LE	150	650	950	1900	3300	4700
NOTE: Deduct 5 percent for lesser models.						
6000, V-6						
4d Sed LE	150	600	950	1850	3200	4600
2d Sed LE	150	650	950	1900	3300	4700
4d Sta Wag LE	150	650	975	1950	3350	4800
4d Sed STE	200	675	1000	1950	3400	4900
NOTE: Deduct 5 percent for lesser models.						
Fiero, 4-cyl.						
2d Cpe	200	670	1200	2300	4060	5800
2d Cpe Spt	200	700	1200	2350	4130	5900
2d Cpe SE	200	720	1200	2400	4200	6000
NOTE: Add 40 percent for Indy Pace Car.						
Firebird, V-6						
2d Cpe	200	730	1250	2450	4270	6100
2d Cpe SE	200	750	1275	2500	4400	6300
Firebird, V-8						
2d Cpe	350	790	1350	2650	4620	6600
2d Cpe SE	350	800	1350	2700	4700	6700
2d Cpe TA	350	820	1400	2700	4760	6800
Bonneville, V-6						
4d Sed	150	600	950	1850	3200	4600
4d Sed LE	150	650	950	1900	3300	4700
4d Sed Brgm	150	650	975	1950	3350	4800
Bonneville, V-8						
4d Sed	150	650	975	1950	3350	4800
4d Sed LE	200	675	1000	1950	3400	4900
4d Sed Brgm	200	675	1000	2000	3500	5000
Grand Prix, V-6						
2d Cpe	200	660	1100	2200	3850	5500
2d Cpe LE	200	685	1150	2300	3990	5700
2d Cpe Brgm	200	700	1200	2350	4130	5900
Grand Prix, V-8						
2d Cpe	200	670	1200	2300	4060	5800
2d Cpe LE	200	720	1200	2400	4200	6000
2d Cpe Brgm	350	770	1300	2550	4480	6400
Parisienne, V-6						
4d Sed	150	600	900	1800	3150	4500
4d Sed Brgm	150	600	950	1850	3200	4600
Parisienne, V-8						
4d Sed	150	650	950	1900	3300	4700
4d Sed Brgm	150	650	975	1950	3350	4800
4d Sta Wag	200	675	1000	1950	3400	4900
1985						
1000, 4-cyl.						
4d Sed	150	475	775	1500	2650	3800
2d Sed	150	475	750	1475	2600	3700
2d HBk	150	500	800	1550	2700	3900
4d Sta Wag	150	500	800	1600	2800	4000
Sunbird, 4-cyl.						
4d Sed	150	550	850	1650	2900	4100
2d Cpe	150	500	800	1600	2800	4000
Conv	350	1020	1700	3400	5950	8500
4d Sta Wag	150	550	850	1675	2950	4200
4d Sed SE	150	550	850	1675	2950	4200
2d Cpe SE	150	550	850	1650	2900	4100
2d HBk SE	150	575	875	1700	3000	4300
NOTE: Add 20 percent for turbo.						
Grand AM, V-6						
2d Cpe	150	600	900	1800	3150	4500
2d Cpe LE	150	600	950	1850	3200	4600
NOTE: Deduct 15 percent for 4-cyl.						
6000, V-6						
4d Sed LE	150	600	950	1850	3200	4600
2d Sed LE	150	650	950	1900	3300	4700
4d Sta Wag LE	150	650	975	1950	3350	4800
4d Sed STE	200	675	1000	1950	3400	4900
NOTE: Deduct 20 percent for 4-cyl. where available. Deduct 5 percent for lesser models.						
Fiero, V-6						
2d Cpe	200	720	1200	2400	4200	6000
2d Cpe Spt	200	730	1250	2450	4270	6100
2d Cpe SE	200	745	1250	2500	4340	6200
2d Cpe GT	200	750	1275	2500	4400	6300
NOTE: Deduct 20 percent for 4-cyl. where available.						
Firebird, V-8						
2d Cpe	350	790	1350	2650	4620	6600
2d Cpe SE	350	800	1350	2700	4700	6700
2d Cpe Trans AM	350	820	1400	2700	4760	6800
NOTE: Deduct 30 percent for V-6 where available.						
Bonneville, V-8						
4d Sed	150	600	950	1850	3200	4600
4d Sed LE	150	650	950	1900	3300	4700
4d Sed Brgm	150	650	975	1950	3350	4800
NOTE: Deduct 25 percent for V-6.						
Grand Prix, V-8						
2d Cpe	200	660	1100	2200	3850	5500
2d Cpe LE	200	685	1150	2300	3990	5700
2d Cpe Brgm	200	700	1200	2350	4130	5900
NOTE: Deduct 25 percent for V-6.						
Parisienne, V-8						
4d Sed	150	650	950	1900	3300	4700
4d Sed Brgm	150	650	975	1950	3350	4800
4d Sta Wag	200	675	1000	1950	3400	4900
NOTE: Deduct 20 percent for V-6 where available. Deduct 30 percent for diesel.						
1986						
Fiero, V-6						
2d Cpe Spt	200	720	1200	2400	4200	6000
2d Cpe SE	200	730	1250	2450	4270	6100
2d Cpe GT	200	750	1275	2500	4400	6300
NOTE: Deduct 20 percent for 4-cyl. where available.						
2d HBk	150	475	775	1500	2650	3800
4d HBk	150	500	800	1550	2700	3900
Sunbird						
2d Cpe	150	500	800	1600	2800	4000
2d HBk	150	550	850	1650	2900	4100
2d Conv	350	1040	1700	3450	6000	8600
4d GT Sed	150	550	850	1650	2900	4100
2d GT Conv	450	1050	1750	3550	6150	8800
Grand Am						
2d Cpe	150	650	950	1900	3300	4700
4d Sed	150	600	950	1850	3200	4600
Firebird						
2d Cpe	350	790	1350	2650	4620	6600
2d SE V-8 Cpe	350	800	1350	2700	4700	6700
Trans Am Cpe	350	830	1400	2950	4830	6900
6000						
2d Cpe	150	650	975	1950	3350	4800
4d Sed	150	650	950	1900	3300	4700
4d Sta Wag	150	650	975	1950	3350	4800
4d STE Sed	200	675	1000	2000	3500	5000
Grand Prix						
2d Cpe	200	685	1150	2300	3990	5700
Bonneville						
4d Sed	150	650	975	1950	3350	4800
Parisienne						
4d Sed	200	675	1000	1950	3400	4900
4d Sta Wag	200	670	1200	2300	4060	5800
4d Brgm Sed	200	675	1000	2000	3500	5000
NOTES: Add 10 percent for deluxe models.						
1986-1/2 Grand Prix 2 plus 2						
2d Aero Cpe	450	1050	1800	3600	6200	8900
Deduct 5 percent for smaller engines.						
1987						
1000, 4-cyl.						
2d HBk	150	475	775	1500	2650	3800
4d HBk	150	500	800	1550	2700	3900
Sunbird, 4-cyl.						
4d Sed	150	500	800	1550	2700	3900
4d Sta Wag	150	500	800	1600	2800	4000
2d SE Cpe	150	550	850	1650	2900	4100
2d SE HBk	150	550	850	1675	2950	4200
2d SE Conv	450	1080	1800	3600	6300	9000
4d GT Turbo Sed	150	575	875	1700	3000	4300
2d GT Turbo Cpe	150	550	850	1675	2950	4200
2d GT Turbo HBk	150	575	875	1700	3000	4300
2d GT Turbo Conv	400	1200	2000	4000	7000	10,000
NOTE: Add 5 percent for Turbo on all models except GT.						
Grand Am, 4-cyl.						
4d Sed	150	650	975	1950	3350	4800
2d Cpe	200	675	1000	1950	3400	4900
4d LE Sed	200	675	1000	1950	3400	4900
2d LE Cpe	200	675	1000	2000	3500	5000
4d SE Sed	200	700	1050	2050	3600	5100
2d SE Cpe	200	700	1050	2100	3650	5200
Grand Am, V-6						
4d Sed	200	675	1000	1950	3400	4900
2d Cpe	200	675	1000	2000	3500	5000
4d LE Sed	200	675	1000	2000	3500	5000
2d LE Cpe	200	700	1050	2050	3600	5100
4d SE Sed	200	700	1075	2150	3700	5300
2d SE Cpe	200	650	1100	2150	3780	5400
6000, 4-cyl.						
4d Sed	200	675	1000	2000	3500	5000
2d Cpe	200	675	1000	1950	3400	4900
4d Sta Wag	200	700	1050	2050	3600	5100
4d LE Sed	200	700	1050	2050	3600	5100
4d LE Sta Wag	200	700	1050	2100	3650	5200
6000, V-6						
4d Sed	200	700	1050	2050	3600	5100
2d Cpe	200	675	1000	2000	3500	5000
4d Sta Wag	200	700	1050	2100	3650	5200
4d LE Sed	200	700	1050	2100	3650	5200
4d LE Sta Wag	200	700	1075	2150	3700	5300
4d SE Sed	200	700	1075	2150	3700	5300
4d SE Sta Wag	200	650	1100	2150	3780	5400
4d STE Sed	200	650	1100	2150	3780	5400
Fiero, V-6						
2d Cpe	200	730	1250	2450	4270	6100
2d Spt Cpe	200	745	1250	2500	4340	6200
2d SE Cpe	200	750	1275	2500	4400	6300
NOTE: Deduct 20 percent for 4-cyl.						
Fiero, V-6						
2d GT Cpe	350	780	1300	2600	4550	6500
Firebird, V-6						
2d Cpe	350	800	1350	2700	4700	6700
Firebird, V-8						
2d Cpe	350	830	1400	2950	4830	6900
2d Cpe Formula	350	840	1400	2800	4900	7000
2d Cpe Trans Am	350	860	1450	2900	5050	7200
2d Cpe GTA	350	880	1500	2950	5180	7400
NOTE: Add 10 percent for 5.7 liter V-8 where available.						
Bonneville, V-6						
4d Sed	200	675	1000	2000	3500	5000
4d LE Sed	200	700	1050	2100	3650	5200
Grand Prix, V-6						
2d Cpe	200	670	1200	2300	4060	5800
2d LE Cpe	200	700	1200	2350	4130	5900
2d Brgm Cpe	200	720	1200	2400	4200	6000
Grand Prix, V-8						
2d Cpe	200	720	1200	2400	4200	6000
2d LE Cpe	200	730	1250	2450	4270	6100
2d Brgm Cpe	200	745	1250	2500	4340	6200
Safari, V-8						
4d Sta Wag	200	700	1050	2100	3650	5200
1988						
LeMans, 4-cyl.						
3d HBk	100	300	500	1000	1750	2500
4d Sed	100	330	575	1150	1950	2800
4d SE Sed	100	360	600	1200	2100	3000
Sunbird, 4-cyl.						
4d Sed	125	400	700	1375	2400	3400
2d SE Cpe	125	450	750	1450	2500	3600
4d SE Sed	150	475	750	1475	2600	3700
4d Sta Wag	150	475	775	1500	2650	3800
2d GT Cpe	200	675	1000	2000	3500	5000

	6	5	4	3	2	1
2d GT Conv	350	1020	1700	3400	5950	8500
Grand Am, 4-cyl.						
2d Cpe	150	600	900	1800	3150	4500
4d Sed	150	600	950	1850	3200	4600
2d LE Cpe	150	650	975	1950	3350	4800
4d Sed LE	200	675	1000	1950	3400	4900
2d SE Turbo Cpe	200	670	1150	2250	3920	5600
4d SE Turbo Sed	200	685	1150	2300	3990	5700
6000, 4-cyl.						
4d Sed	150	500	800	1550	2700	3900
4d Sta Wag	150	500	800	1600	2800	4000
4d LE Sed	150	500	800	1600	2800	4000
4d LE Sta Wag	150	550	850	1675	2950	4200
6000, V-6						
4d Sed	150	550	850	1675	2950	4200
4d Sta Wag	150	600	900	1800	3150	4500
4d Sed LE	200	675	1000	2000	3500	5000
4d LE Sta Wag	200	675	1000	2000	3500	5000
4d SE Sed	200	700	1050	2100	3650	5200
4d SE Sta Wag	200	660	1100	2200	3850	5500
4d STE Sed	350	860	1450	2900	5050	7200
Fiero V-6						
2d Cpe	200	720	1200	2400	4200	6000
2d Formula III Cpe	350	780	1300	2600	4550	6500
2d GT Cpe	350	820	1400	2700	4760	6800
Firebird, V-6						
2d Cpe	200	720	1200	2400	4200	6000
Firebird, V-8						
2d Cpe	350	840	1400	2800	4900	7000
2d Formula Cpe	350	975	1600	3200	5600	8000
2d Cpe Trans Am	450	1080	1800	3600	6300	9000
2d Cpe GTA	400	1300	2200	4400	7700	11,000
Bonneville, V-6						
4d LE Sed	200	720	1200	2400	4200	6000
4d SE Sed	350	900	1500	3000	5250	7500
4d SSE Sed	450	1080	1800	3600	6300	9000
Grand Prix, V-6						
2d Cpe	350	780	1300	2600	4550	6500
2d LE Cpe	350	840	1400	2800	4900	7000
2d SE Cpe	350	975	1600	3200	5600	8000

1989

	6	5	4	3	2	1
LeMans, 4-cyl.						
2d HBk	100	325	550	1100	1900	2700
2d LE HBk	100	350	600	1150	2000	2900
2d GSE HBk	125	400	700	1375	2400	3400
4d LE Sed	125	400	675	1350	2300	3300
4d SE Sed	125	450	700	1400	2450	3500
Sunbird, 4-cyl.						
4d LE Sed	150	600	950	1850	3200	4600
2d LE Cpe	150	600	900	1800	3150	4500
2d SE Cpe	150	650	950	1900	3300	4700
2d GT Turbo Cpe	350	800	1350	2700	4700	6700
2d GT Turbo Conv	450	1140	1900	3800	6650	9500
Grand Am, 4-cyl.						
4d LE Sed	200	670	1150	2250	3920	5600
2d LE Cpe	200	660	1100	2200	3850	5500
4d SE Sed	200	750	1275	2500	4400	6300
2d SE Cpe	200	745	1250	2500	4340	6200
6000, 4-cyl.						
4d Sed LE	200	685	1150	2300	3990	5700
6000, V-6						
4d LE Sed	200	730	1250	2450	4270	6100
4d LE Sta Wag	350	770	1300	2550	4480	6400
4d STE Sed	350	975	1600	3200	5600	8000
Firebird, V-6						
2d Cpe	350	780	1300	2600	4550	6500
Firebird, V-8						
2d Cpe	350	840	1400	2800	4900	7000
2d Formula Cpe	350	900	1500	3000	5250	7500
2d Trans Am Pace Car	550	1800	3000	6000	10,500	15,000
Turbo, V-6						
2d Trans Am Cpe	400	1200	2000	4000	7000	10,000
2d GTA Cpe	400	1300	2200	4400	7700	11,000
Bonneville, V-6						
4d LE Sed	350	820	1400	2700	4760	6800
4d SE Sed	350	950	1550	3150	5450	7800
4d SSE Sed	450	1050	1750	3550	6150	8800
Grand Prix, V-6						
2d Cpe	350	840	1400	2800	4900	7000
2d LE Cpe	350	900	1500	3000	5250	7500
2d SE Cpe	350	975	1600	3200	5600	8000

NOTE: Add 40 percent for McLaren Turbo Cpe.

	6	5	4	3	2	1
Safari, V-8						
4d Sta Wag	350	860	1450	2900	5050	7200

1989-1/2 Firebird Trans Am Pace Car V-6 Turbo

	6	5	4	3	2	1
Cpe	550	1800	3000	6000	10,500	15,000

1990

	6	5	4	3	2	1
LeMans, 4-cyl.						
2d Cpe	100	330	575	1150	1950	2800
2d LE Cpe	125	380	650	1300	2250	3200
2d GSE Cpe	125	450	750	1450	2500	3600
4d LE Sed	125	380	650	1300	2250	3200
Sunbird, 4-cyl.						
2d VL Cpe	150	500	800	1600	2800	4000
4d VL Sed	150	550	850	1650	2900	4100
2d LE Cpe	150	550	850	1675	2950	4200
2d LE Conv	350	900	1500	3000	5250	7500
4d LE Sed	150	575	875	1700	3000	4300
2d SE Cpe	200	675	1000	2000	3500	5000
2d GT Turbo Cpe	200	720	1200	2400	4200	6000
Grand Am, 4-cyl.						
2d LE Cpe	200	685	1150	2300	3990	5700
4d LE Cpe	200	720	1200	2400	4200	6000
2d SE Quad Cpe	350	780	1300	2600	4550	6500
4d SE Quad Sed	350	790	1350	2650	4620	6600
6000, 4-cyl.						
4d LE Sed	150	600	900	1800	3150	4500
6000, V-6						
4d LE Sed	200	675	1000	2000	3500	5000
4d LE Sta Wag	200	660	1100	2200	3850	5500
4d SE Sed	200	660	1100	2200	3850	5500
4d SE Sta Wag	200	720	1200	2400	4200	6000
Firebird, V-6						
2d Cpe	350	780	1300	2600	4550	6500
Firebird, V-8						
2d Cpe	350	900	1500	3000	5250	7500
2d Formula Cpe	350	975	1600	3200	5600	8000
2d Trans Am Cpe	450	1080	1800	3600	6300	9000

	6	5	4	3	2	1
2d GTA Cpe	400	1300	2200	4400	7700	11,000
Bonneville, V-6						
4d LE Sed	350	840	1400	2800	4900	7000
4d SE Sed	350	900	1500	3000	5250	7500
4d SSE Sed	350	1020	1700	3400	5950	8500
Grand Prix, 4-cyl.						
2d LE Cpe	200	720	1200	2400	4200	6000
4d LE Sed	200	730	1250	2450	4270	6100
Grand Prix, V-6						
2d LE Cpe	200	750	1275	2500	4400	6300
4d LE Sed	350	770	1300	2550	4480	6400
2d SE Cpe	350	975	1600	3200	5600	8000
4d STE Sed	350	1020	1700	3400	5950	8500

1991

	6	5	4	3	2	1
LeMans, 4-cyl.						
2d Aero Cpe	125	380	650	1300	2250	3200
2d Aero LE Cpe	150	475	775	1500	2650	3800
4d LE Sed	125	450	700	1400	2450	3500
Sunbird, 4-cyl.						
2d Cpe	150	475	775	1500	2650	3800
4d Sed	150	475	775	1500	2650	3800
2d LE Cpe	150	500	800	1600	2800	4000
4d LE Sed	150	500	800	1600	2800	4000
2d LE Conv	350	975	1600	3200	5600	8000
2d SE Cpe	200	675	1000	2000	3500	5000
Sunbird, V-6						
2d GT Cpe	350	780	1300	2600	4550	6500
Grand Am, 4-cyl.						
2d Cpe	200	675	1000	2000	3500	5000
4d Sed	200	675	1000	2000	3500	5000
2d LE Sed	200	700	1050	2100	3650	5200
4d LE Sed	200	700	1050	2100	3650	5200
2d SE Quad 4 Cpe	200	670	1200	2300	4060	5800
4d SE Quad 4 Sed	200	670	1200	2300	4060	5800
6000, 4-cyl.						
4d LE Sed	150	600	900	1800	3150	4500
6000, V-6						
4d LE Sed	200	675	1000	2000	3500	5000
4d LE Sta Wag	200	660	1100	2200	3850	5500
4d SE Sed	200	650	1100	2150	3780	5400
Firebird, V-6						
2d Cpe	350	780	1300	2600	4550	6500
2d Conv	400	1200	2000	4000	7000	10,000
Firebird, V-8						
2d Cpe	350	900	1500	3000	5250	7500
2d Conv	400	1300	2200	4400	7700	11,000
2d Formula Cpe	350	975	1600	3200	5600	8000
2d Trans Am Cpe	450	1080	1800	3600	6300	9000
2d Trans Am Conv	450	1500	2500	5000	8800	12,500
2d GTA Cpe	400	1300	2200	4400	7700	11,000
Bonneville, V-6						
4d LE Sed	350	780	1300	2600	4550	6500
4d SE Sed	350	900	1500	3000	5250	7500
4d SSE Sed	350	975	1600	3200	5600	8000
Grand Prix, Quad 4						
2d SE Cpe	200	660	1100	2200	3850	5500
4d LE Sed	200	660	1100	2200	3850	5500
4d SE Sed	200	670	1200	2300	4060	5800
Grand Prix, V-6						
4d SE Cpe	200	720	1200	2400	4200	6000
2d GT Cpe	350	770	1300	2550	4480	6400
4d LE Sed	200	720	1200	2400	4200	6000
4d SE Sed	350	770	1300	2550	4480	6400
4d STE Sed	350	840	1400	2800	4900	7000

Oakland

	6	5	4	3	2	1
1907						
Model A, 4-cyl., 96" wb - 100" wb						
All Body Styles	1250	3950	6600	13,200	23,100	33,000
1909						
Model 20, 2-cyl., 112" wb						
All Body Styles	1150	3600	6000	12,000	21,000	30,000
Model 40, 4-cyl., 112" wb						
All Body Styles	1050	3350	5600	11,200	19,600	28,000
1910-1911						
Model 24, 4-cyl., 96" wb						
Rds	850	2650	4400	8800	15,400	22,000
Model 25, 4-cyl., 100" wb						
Tr	750	2400	4000	8000	14,000	20,000
Model 33, 4-cyl., 106" wb						
Tr	900	2900	4800	9600	16,800	24,000
Model K, 4-cyl., 102" wb						
Tr	1000	3100	5200	10,400	18,200	26,000
Model M, 4-cyl., 112" wb						
Rds	1000	3250	5400	10,800	18,900	27,000
NOTE: Model 33 1911 only.						
1912						
Model 30, 4-cyl., 106" wb						
5P Tr	550	1800	3000	6000	10,500	15,000
Rbt	600	1850	3100	6200	10,900	15,500
Model 40, 4-cyl., 112" wb						
5P Tr	550	1800	3000	6000	10,500	15,000
Cpe	400	1300	2200	4400	7700	11,000
Rds	600	1900	3200	6400	11,200	16,000
Model 45, 4-cyl., 120" wb						
7P Tr	800	2500	4200	8400	14,700	21,000
4P Tr	850	2650	4400	8800	15,400	22,000
Limo	750	2400	4000	8000	14,000	20,000
1913						
Greyhound 6-60, 6-cyl., 130" wb						
4P Tr	900	2900	4800	9600	16,800	24,000
7P Tr	850	2750	4600	9200	16,100	23,000
Rbt	700	2300	3800	7600	13,300	19,000
Model 42, 4-cyl., 116" wb						
5P Tr	700	2150	3600	7200	12,600	18,000
3P Rds	650	2050	3400	6800	11,900	17,000
4P Cpe	400	1300	2200	4400	7700	11,000
Model 35, 4-cyl., 112" wb						
5P Tr	600	1900	3200	6400	11,200	16,000
3P Rds	600	1900	3200	6400	11,000	16,000

	6	5	4	3	2	1
Model 40, 4-cyl., 114" wb						
5P Tr	650	2050	3400	6800	11,900	17,000
Model 45, 4-cyl., 120" wb						
7P Limo	550	1800	3000	6000	10,500	15,000
1914						
Model 6-60, 6-cyl., 130" wb						
Rbt	650	2050	3400	6800	11,900	17,000
Rds	800	2500	4200	8400	14,700	21,000
Cl Cpl	600	1900	3200	6400	11,200	16,000
Tr	850	2750	4600	9200	16,100	23,000
Model 6-48, 6-cyl., 130" wb						
Spt	450	1450	2400	4800	8400	12,000
Rds	700	2300	3800	7600	13,300	19,000
Tr	750	2400	4000	8000	14,000	20,000
Model 43, 4-cyl., 116" wb						
5P Tr	600	1900	3200	6400	11,200	16,000
Cpe	400	1200	2000	4000	7000	10,000
Sed	450	1140	1900	3800	6650	9500
Model 36, 4-cyl., 112" wb						
5P Tr	550	1800	3000	6000	10,500	15,000
Cabr	550	1750	2900	5800	10,200	14,500
Model 35, 4-cyl., 112" wb						
Rds	550	1700	2800	5600	9800	14,000
5P Tr	550	1750	2900	5800	10,200	14,500
1915-1916						
Model 37-Model 38, 4-cyl., 112" wb						
Tr	550	1700	2800	5600	9800	14,000
Rds	500	1550	2600	5200	9100	13,000
Spd	450	1500	2500	5000	8800	12,500
Model 49-Model 32, 6-cyl., 110"-123.5" wb						
Tr	600	1900	3200	6400	11,200	16,000
Rds	600	1850	3100	6200	10,900	15,500
Model 50, 8-cyl., 127" wb						
7P Rds	700	2300	3800	7600	13,300	19,000
NOTE: Model 37 and model 49 are 1915 models.						
1917						
Model 34, 6-cyl., 112" wb						
Rds	450	1450	2400	4800	8400	12,000
5P Tr	450	1500	2500	5000	8800	12,500
Cpe	450	1140	1900	3800	6650	9500
Sed	450	1080	1800	3600	6300	9000
Model 50, 8-cyl., 127" wb						
7P Tr	700	2300	3800	7600	13,300	19,000
1918						
Model 34-B, 6-cyl., 112" wb						
5P Tr	450	1450	2400	4800	8400	12,000
Rds	450	1400	2300	4600	8100	11,500
Rds Cpe	450	1140	1900	3800	6650	9500
Tr Sed	450	1080	1800	3600	6300	9000
4P Cpe	350	1020	1700	3400	5950	8500
Sed	350	975	1600	3200	5600	8000
1919						
Model 34-B, 6-cyl., 112" wb						
5P Tr	450	1450	2400	4800	8400	12,000
Rds	450	1400	2300	4600	8100	11,500
Rds Cpe	450	1140	1900	3800	6650	9500
Cpe	350	1020	1700	3400	5950	8500
Sed	350	975	1600	3200	5600	8000
1920						
Model 34-C, 6-cyl., 112" wb						
Tr	450	1450	2400	4800	8400	12,000
Rds	450	1400	2300	4600	8100	11,500
Sed	350	1020	1700	3400	5950	8500
Cpe	450	1080	1800	3600	6300	9000
1921-22						
Model 34-C, 6-cyl., 115" wb						
Tr	500	1550	2600	5200	9100	13,000
Rds	450	1500	2500	5000	8800	12,500
Sed	350	1020	1700	3400	5950	8500

	6	5	4	3	2	1
Cpe	450	1080	1800	3600	6300	9000
1923						
Model 6-44, 6-cyl., 115" wb						
Rds	500	1550	2600	5200	9100	13,000
Tr	500	1600	2700	5400	9500	13,500
Spt Rds	500	1600	2700	5400	9500	13,500
Spt Tr	550	1700	2800	5600	9800	14,000
2P Cpe	350	900	1500	3000	5250	7500
4P Cpe	350	880	1500	2950	5180	7400
Sed	350	780	1300	2600	4550	6500
1924-25						
Model 6-54, 6-cyl., 113" wb						
5P Tr	550	1800	3000	6000	10,500	15,000
Spl Tr	600	1850	3100	6200	10,900	15,500
Rds	550	1750	2900	5800	10,200	14,500
Spl Rds	550	1800	3000	6000	10,500	15,000
4P Cpe	450	1140	1900	3800	6650	9500
Lan Cpe	450	1140	1900	3800	6650	9500
Sed	350	975	1600	3200	5600	8000
Lan Sed	350	1020	1700	3400	5950	8500
2d Sed	350	900	1500	3000	5250	7500
2d Lan Sed	350	975	1600	3200	5600	8000
1926-27						
Greater Six, 6-cyl., 113" wb						
Tr	600	1850	3100	6200	10,900	15,500
Spt Phae	600	1900	3200	6400	11,200	16,000
Rds	550	1800	3000	6000	10,500	15,000
Spt Rds	600	1850	3100	6200	10,900	15,500
Lan Cpe	400	1250	2100	4200	7400	10,500
2d Sed	450	1080	1800	3600	6300	9000
Sed	350	1020	1700	3400	5950	8500
Lan Sed	450	1080	1800	3600	6300	9000
1928						
Model 212, All-American, 6-cyl., 117" wb						
Spt Rds	600	2000	3300	6600	11,600	16,500
Phae	650	2050	3400	6800	11,900	17,000
Lan Cpe	400	1300	2200	4400	7700	11,000
Cabr	550	1800	3000	6000	10,500	15,000
2d Sed	400	1200	2000	4000	7000	10,000
Sed	450	1140	1900	3800	6650	9500
Lan Sed	400	1200	2000	4000	7000	10,000
1929						
Model Aas, 6-cyl., 117" wb						
Spt Rds	900	2900	4800	9600	16,800	24,000
Spt Phae	950	3000	5000	10,000	17,500	25,000
Cpe	400	1300	2200	4400	7700	11,000
Conv	850	2650	4400	8800	15,400	22,000
2d Sed	400	1200	2000	4000	7000	10,000
Brgm	400	1300	2200	4400	7700	11,000
Sed	450	1140	1900	3800	6650	9500
Spl Sed	400	1200	2000	4000	7000	10,000
Lan Sed	400	1250	2100	4200	7400	10,500
1930						
Model 101, V-8, 117" wb						
Spt Rds	900	2900	4800	9600	16,800	24,000
Phae	950	3000	5000	10,000	17,500	25,000
Cpe	550	1700	2800	5600	9800	14,000
Spt Cpe	550	1800	3000	6000	10,500	15,000
2d Sed	400	1300	2200	4400	7700	11,000
Sed	400	1250	2100	4200	7400	10,500
Cus Sed	400	1300	2150	4300	7600	10,800
1931						
Model 301, V-8, 117" Wb						
Cpe	550	1800	3000	6000	10,500	15,000
Spt Cpe	600	1900	3200	6400	11,200	16,000
Conv	950	3000	5000	10,000	17,500	25,000
2d Sed	400	1250	2100	4200	7400	10,500
Sed	400	1300	2150	4300	7600	10,800
Cus Sed	400	1300	2200	4400	7700	11,000